COMMENTARY
ON ISAIAH

2 volumes complete in 1

COMMENTARY ON ISAIAH

2 volumes complete in 1

Joseph Addison Alexander

Introduction by
Merrill F. Unger

Editor's Preface by
John Eadie

kregel PUBLICATIONS
Grand Rapids, MI 49501

Commentary on Isaiah, by Joseph Addison Alexander, © 1992
by Kregel Publications, a division of Kregel, Inc., P.O. Box
2607, Grand Rapids, Michigan 49501. All rights reserved.

Cover Design: Alan G. Hartman

Library of Congress Cataloging-in-Publication Data

Alexander, Joseph Addison, 1809-1860.
   Commentary on Isaiah: translated and explained: an abridg-
ment of the author's critical Commentary on Isaiah / by Joseph
Addison Alexander: foreword by Cyril J. Barber.
     p.   cm.
   [Commentary on Isaiah]
   Reprint. Originally published: New York: C. Scribner, 1867.
    1. Bible. O. T. Isaiah—Commentaries. I. Alexander,
Joseph Addison. 1809-1860. Commentary on Isaiah. II. Bible.
O. T. Isaiah. English. Alexander. 1992. III. Title.
BS1515.3.A54   1992   224'.1077—dc20   92-16125
                                             CIP

ISBN 0-8254-2137-3 (paperback)
ISBN 0-8254-2138-1 (deluxe hardback)

1 2 3 4 5 Printing/Year 96 95 94 93 92

Printed in the United States of America

Contents

Commentary on Isaiah, Volume Two

INTRODUCTION TO THE 1953 EDITION

Joseph Addison Alexander's COMMENTARY ON THE PROPHECIES OF ISAIAH is in a very real sense a classic. More than a century has passed since the two volumes of this famous expository work first appeared in 1846-1847 to enjoy a wide ministry of usefulness in the nineteenth century. Nevertheless, this eminent study of the prince of Old Testament prophets has lost none of its essential usefulness and appeal to careful Bible students of the present day. Reverent and scholarly expositions of the Sacred Text of this sort borrow the glow and catch the perennial appeal of the message of the Book of books they so faithfully expound, and enshrine themselves in the affections of God's people somewhat at least in the same manner God's Word enshrines itself in the hearts of men.

The present reprint is the revised edition of 1875 prepared by the learned Dr. John Eadie of Glasgow, Scotland, who with critical acumen pronounced Alexander's work as "among the best commentaries on Isaiah of any age or language."[1] As a distinguished theologian and Oriental scholar Joseph Addison Alexander had few superiors in his generation in America both in the extent and accuracy of his learning. A remarkable linguist commanding a mastery of both Hebrew and Greek, he was eminently qualified as an expositor of the Sacred Text. He assisted in preparing the first American edition of Donnegan's Greek Lexicon (Boston, 1840) and did much to introduce German theological learning in America.

Alexander's comprehensive knowledge of Hebrew makes his work especially useful to students of the original text. But his linguistic abilities were shielded from being narrowly confined to a circumscribed academic sphere by his unusual talent for simplifying and clarifying truth. This latter gift, which unfortunately every great scholar does not possess, gives his work access to a much wider circle of readers. He was a happy combination of a thorough scholar and a skilful popularizer in whom vast learning was mellowed by true evangelical faith and piety. Works of this type which combine piety and learning and which faithfully set forth the mind and purpose of God as revealed in His Word are not outdated by the passing of the years, but, like God's Word Itself, have a relevancy to every age and generation.

Alexander's work on the Psalter, entitled *Psalms Translated and Explained*, which appeared in three volumes in 1850, offers

---

1 Lippincott's **Pronouncing Biographical Dictionary** (Philadelphia, 1870), Vol. I, p. 88.

an example of his success as a theological writer and expositor. In four years this commentary reached a sale of ten thousand copies. His *Commentary on the Prophecies of Isaiah* met with similar success, and its genuine worth led to its revision and re-edition by John Eadie in 1875, after it had proved its wide usefulness for almost three decades.

With professor Charles Hodge, his eminent colleague on the faculty of Princeton Theological Seminary, he planned a series of popular commentaries on the books of the New Testament. He himself contributed those on Acts (two volumes, 1857), Mark (1858) and Matthew, which appeared posthumously in 1861. Also published after his death were two volumes of his sermons in 1860 and *Notes on New Testament Literature* (two volumes, 1861). In 1869 appeared his biography, entitled *Life of J. A. Alexander* by Henry C. Alexander.

Joseph Addison Alexander represents the finest in the spiritual and scholastic attainments of the Presbyterian Church in America. Belonging to an era of deep faith and sound scholarship, he was one of the great names such as Charles Hodge and William Henry Green, that adorned Princeton Theological Seminary and made it a great bastion of truth and a citadel for the defense of the Gospel in the nineteenth and early twentieth century. He was the illustrious precursor of such later stalwart defenders of the faith as Robert Dick Wilson, J. G. Machen and Benjamin B. Warfield.

Joseph Addison Alexander doubtless owed much of his success as a Biblical expositor to his rich heritage by birth. Born in Philadelphia April 24, 1809, he was the third son of Archibald Alexander, famous in his own right as the Presbyterian clergyman who organized Princeton Theological Seminary in 1812 and who became its first professor. The elder theologian was soon to have the joy of seeing his son follow in his footsteps. In 1826 Joseph Addison graduated from Princeton and became an adjunct professor of Ancient Languages and Literatures there in 1830. After a period of travel and study in Europe in 1833-1834 he became adjunct professor of Oriental and Biblical literature, and continued teaching at his alma mater till his death on January 28, 1860. In 1851 he was transferred to the chair of Church History and to that of New Testament Literature in 1859.

By talents, training and vocation Joseph Addison Alexander was eminently qualified to write a commentary on Isaiah. His genuine scholarship and evangelical warmth are everywhere manifest in his work. These qualities make his treatment of the greatest of the Old Testament prophets widely useful to the diligent student.

MERRILL F. UNGER, TH.D. PH.D.
Professor of Old Testament
Dallas Theological Seminary
April 4, 1953

EDITOR'S PREFACE

DR JOSEPH ADDISON ALEXANDER, the able and learned author of this Commentary, the great work of his life, died at Princeton, New Jersey, on the 20th January 1860, having been born at Philadelphia in April 1809. The unexpected death of one so eminent and useful, produced a profound sensation throughout the American States. "Devout men carried him to his burial, and made great lamentation over him." As the son of an accomplished father, the Rev. Dr Archibald Alexander, Joseph Addison enjoyed the best of intellectual and spiritual training. His scholarship was precociously developed, for, at fourteen years of age, he had read through the Koran in the original Arabic. The other oriental tongues he mastered at a very early period; and he also acquired, in the course of his Academic curriculum, a profound acquaintance with the classical languages, and an intimate familiarity with most of the modern tongues of Europe. On the very day before his death, he enjoyed his usual portion of Scripture in the six languages in which it had been his daily habit to read it. He was, in 1835, chosen by the General Assembly Associate Professor of Oriental and Biblical Literature in the Theological Seminary at Princeton, and he had already been, for some years, Assistant Professor of Ancient Languages in the College of New Jersey. In 1851, he was transferred to the chair of Biblical and Ecclesiastical History, and in 1859 his Professorate received the title of the chair of Hellenistic and New Testament literature. We need not say that Dr Alexander nobly and successfully discharged the duties of his office—infecting the students with his own enthusiasm, and setting before them, in his prelections, a model of clear and manly statement, and of industrious and learned research. He was a preacher, too, of no common stamp, and his sermons published since his death give proof of his clearness, eloquence, and power, in applying as well as in expounding evangelical truth. His expositions of the Psalms, Mark, Acts, and a portion of Matthew (this last labour being interrupted by his death), are specimens of lucid, sound, and popular commentary. His colleague Dr Hodge, in an address to the General Assembly in 1860, justly said of him, "I regard Dr Joseph Addison Alexander as incomparably the greatest man I ever knew, —as incomparably the greatest man our church has ever produced." But his crowning labour, his imperishable monument, is his Commentary on

Isaiah. He had made some progress in revisal for a second edition, and some scores of corrections and improvements made by himself on his own copy have been collected by a scholarly friend and transmitted to us. These have been incorporated in this present edition, which may therefore be said to contain its eminent author's latest emendations.

The republication of this Commentary in the present form will, it is hoped, prove an acceptable present to the Biblical students of this country, for it occupies an independent place among the numerous expositions of the evangelical Prophet, which have appeared in earlier or more recent times in Holland, Germany, England, and America. The two ponderous folios of Vitringa bear upon them the evidence of severe study, prodigious industry, vast learning, and unflinching orthodoxy. Yet they are essentially Dutch in their structure—solid, cumbrous, and prolix; stiff in their arrangement, tedious in their details, and copious to satiety in the miscellaneous references and disquisitions with which they are loaded. The views advanced in them are more bulky than tasteful, the arguments offered more numerous than strong, and while at times there is a spirited appreciation of a splendid symbol or a glowing parallelism, the author was too phlegmatic to be thrilled from sympathy with the prince of Hebrew bards; too much engaged in polemical disquisitions and recondite senses to waste time in expressing his slow and unwieldy emotions. The Commentary of Gesenius occupies a place of no mean dignity. Its faithful adherence to the Masoretic text, its sound grammatical notations, its clear and shrewd analysis of syntactic difficulties, its happy surmises in cases of acknowledged dubiety, and its fulness of archæological lore, have conferred upon it a European celebrity. But these literary virtues are more than counterbalanced by its obtrusive neology, its occasional levity, its low and perverted notions of the theocracy, its melancholy denial of prophetic inspiration and foresight, and its virulent hostility to the leading doctrine of a Messiah. The merits of this masterly Treatise are also lessened by its restless employment of the "higher criticism," for the purpose of impugning the integrity of Isaiah, and of so dismembering the book of his oracles, that the larger portion of them are branded as the anonymous productions of a later age, which sought in vain to disguise its intellectual poverty by a patriotic imitation of the fresher writings of an earlier period. It would be a woful day for Christendom, if the question, as to what are and what are not the genuine remains of the son of Amoz, were to be left for final decision to the morbid subjectivity and capricious mania of German unbelief.

The refined taste and classical acquirements of Bishop Lowth are seen in the many beautiful references and apposite illustrations which adorn to profusion his popular work. But the reckless treatment which he applied to the text in his repeated and superfluous alterations and suggestions without evidence or necessity, mars the utility of the scanty exegesis which is contained in his Commentary. The volume of the late Dr Henderson of Highbury is of great merit and ripe scholarship, and commends itself to us as the result of skilful and sanctified erudition. It often suggests the way to discover the truth, if in any case it fail to reveal it. Yet, with all its perspicuity, its brevity or curtness is a marked defect. On many points, in connection with which acute and sagacious decisions are given, we long for a fuller statement of those philological principles by which the critic has been guided, and a more minute enumeration of those objections to his own views which are often dismissed with a simple allusion to their existence, or are set aside with the bare mention of their age, authorship, and valueless character. Mr Barnes of Philadelphia has compiled three excellent volumes of Notes on Isaiah with no little dexterity and success. But these annotations, from their very nature, do not come into competition with the Commentary of Professor Alexander. We have classed together only the more prominent Works on Isaiah for the sake of a brief comparison, and we deem it unnecessary to place on such a list the productions of Hitzig or Hendewerk, Knobel or Ewald, Drechsler or Umbreit, Jenour or Stock, Noyes or Macculloch.

We do not, however, mean to make this republished Exposition the theme of unqualified or indiscriminate eulogy. No one, indeed, saw its defects more readily than did its author himself, and no one could be more prompt to acknowledge or correct them, for with all his gifts and greatness he had the simplicity and candour of a child. Yet we reckon it among the best Commentaries on Isaiah of any age or in any language.. It embodies in it the fruits of many years of continuous toil and research, and its size gives it the advantage of a gratifying fulness. Professor Alexander possessed consummate scholarship. He discovers intimate acquaintance with the nicer peculiarities of Hebrew philology, in its tenses, particles, and more delicate combinations ; and at the same time possesses no little relish for the æsthetic element—the buds and blossoms of oriental poetry. His unfailing stores of auxiliary erudition are ever at disciplined command, and are applied with eminent judgment. The value of his publication is also enhanced by the excellent synoptical accounts of the labours and opinions of former and contemporary authors, which are to be found under almost every verse. The Work is pervaded also by a sound exegetical spirit ; the spirit of one who had been " baptized into Christ." For his daily study of the Bible was never to him a mere professional occupation.

Interesting views of the nature of prophecy in itself, and in its relations as well to the Jewish Commonwealth as to the Church of the Redeemer, abound in the following pages. The reveries of Teutonic criticism are unsparingly held up to scorn, and the " old paths" are proved to be still the safest and best. The Exposition is free from extraneous matter. It has no digressions ; no learned lumber obstructs the reader's way with its conceited and multifarious curiosities. The principles which the author has laid down for his own guidance in the extreme literalness of his version, are sometimes followed, however, with such rigidness and system as might afford facetious remarkings to any satirical reviewer. This peculiarity, however, some may consider no blemish, but may rather hail it as an improvement. In one word, this Transatlantic Commentary is cautious and reverent in its textual criticism,—in its habitual demeanour towards those " words which the Holy Ghost teacheth." It is no less expert, accurate, and felicitous in its philology, basing it on the acknowledged laws of mind and principles of language. Its hermeneutical canons are always sagacious and in general correct, while the exegesis is distinguished by its harmony and vigour, and relieved by its exalted and luminous conceptions. Nevertheless we are not so sanguine as to anticipate for the author whom we have been honoured to introduce, that his readers will assent to all his hypotheses, or will be converted to his marked and favourite interpretations of those paragraphs and sections, the precise meaning and fulfilment of which are in the present day topics of keen and protracted controversy.

This edition has been printed with great care. The editor has read all the sheets with attention as they passed through the press, and has corrected very many errors, both in the Hebrew and English text of the American original. Alexander's Isaiah has already taken its own place in the front rank of biblical works ; and our belief is that a " Contribution " so distinguished by its learning and piety will be cordially welcomed and speedily naturalised among us. May the inspired classics always engage that admiration which they so justly merit for their originality and truthfulness, their simplicity and pathos, their magnificent imagery and varied music. But, above all, may they attract the living faith of every admirer to those blessed truths and promises which they have been so wisely and graciously employed to reveal to a fallen and dying world, for the old prophetic harp was tuned to the utterance of the noblest thoughts and mysteries, the majesty, unity, and spirituality of Jehovah, the holiness of his law, the infinitude of his love, and the might, triumphs, and wonders of that covenant by which our apostate race is to be reclaimed and glorified.

JOHN EADIE.

GLASGOW, 13 LANSDOWNE CRESCENT,
January 1865.

Preface to the Earlier Prophecies

To prevent misapprehension, and facilitate the use of the following work, some explanation may be needed with respect to its design and execution. The specific end at which it aims is that of making the results of philological and critical research available for purposes of practical utility. In attempting to accomplish this important purpose, it was soon found indispensable to fix upon some definite portion of the reading public, whose capacities, acquirements, and wants might be consulted in determining the form and method of the exposition. Some learned and ingenious works in this department have been rendered to a great extent practically useless, by the want of a determinate fitness for any considerable class of readers, being at once too pedantic for the ignorant, and too elementary for the instructed. In the present case there seemed to be some latitude of choice, and yet but one course on the whole advisable. Works exclusively adapted to the use of profound orientalists and biblical scholars are almost prohibited among ourselves at present, by the paucity of competent writers and congenial readers. Works designed for the immediate use of the unlearned must of necessity be superficial and imperfect, and are proved by experience to be not the most effective means of influencing even those for whom they are expressly written. The obscurer parts of Scripture, or at least of the Old Testament, can be most effectually brought to bear upon the popular mind by employing the intermediate agency of an intelligent and educated ministry. The people may be best taught in such cases through their teachers, by furnishing a solid scientific basis for their popular instructions. Under the influence of these considerations an attempt has here been made to concentrate and economise the labours of the ministry in this field, by affording them a partial succedaneum for many costly books, and enabling them to profit by the latest philological improvements and discoveries, without the inconveniences and even dangers which attend a direct resort to the original authorities.

What has now been said will explain a feature of the plan, which might at first sight seem to be at variance with the ultimate design of the whole work, to wit, the exclusion of the practical element, or rather of its formal exhibition in the shape of homiletical and doctrinal reflections. A work upon Isaiah so constructed as to constitute a series of lectures or expository sermons, instead of doing for the clergy what they need and what they wish, would be attempting to do for them that which they can do far better for themselves, by presenting one of the many forms in which the substance of the book may be employed for the instruction and improvement of their people. The effect of this consideration is enhanced by an impression, which the author's recent labours have distinctly made upon his mind, that much of the fanciful and allegorical interpretation heretofore current has arisen from a failure to discriminate sufficiently between the province of the critical interpreter, and that of the expository lecturer or preacher; the effect of which has been to foist into the Scriptures, as a part of their original and proper sense, a host of applications and accommodations, which have no right there, however admissible and even useful in their proper place. Let the professional interpreter content himself with furnishing the raw material in a sound and merchantable state, without attempting to prescribe the texture, colour, shape, or quantity of the indefinitely varied fabrics into which it is the business of the preacher to transform it. From these considerations it will be perceived that the omission now in question has arisen, not merely from a want of room, and not at all from any disregard to practical utility, but on the contrary, from a desire to promote it in the most effectual manner.

Another point, which may be here explained, is the relation of the following commentary to the authorised English Version of Isaiah. It was at first proposed to make the latter the immediate basis of the exposition, simply calling in the aid of the original to rectify the errors, or clear up the obscurities of the translation. The primary reason for abandoning this method was its tendency to generate an indirect and circuitous method of interpretation. A still higher motive for the change was afforded by its probable effect in promoting thorough biblical learning, and discouraging the sluggish disposition to regard the common version as the ultimate authority, and even to insist upon its errors or fortuitous peculiarities as parts of a divine revelation. The contrary disposition to depreciate the merits of the English Bible, by gratuitous departures from its form or substance, is comparatively rare, and where it does exist is to be corrected, not by wilful ignorance, but by profound and discriminating knowledge of the version and original. The practical conclusion in the present case, has been to make the Hebrew text exclusively the subject of direct interpretation, but at the same time to give the common version all the prominence to which it is entitled by its intrinsic excellence, and by its peculiar interest and value to the English reader. It may be thought that the shortest and easiest method of accomplishing this object would have been that adopted by Maurer, Knobel, and some other writers, who, without giving any continuous version of the text, confine their comments to its difficult expressions. It was found upon experiment, however, that much circumlocution might be spared in many cases by a simple version, or at most by an explanatory paraphrase. A literal translation of the whole text has therefore been incorporated in the present Work, not as a mere appendage or accompaniment, much less as a substitute or rival of the common version, which is too completely in possession of the public ear and memory to be easily displaced even if it were desirable, but simply as a necessary and integral part of the interpretation. The grounds of this arrangement will be stated more fully in the Introduction, of which it may as well be said in this place as in any other, that it makes no pretensions to the character of an exhaustive compilation, but is simply, as its name imports, a preparation for what follows, consisting partly in preliminary statements, partly in general summaries, the particulars of which are scattered through the exposition.

Another question, which presented itself early in the progress of the Work was the question whether it should be a record of the author's individual conclusions merely, or to some extent a history of the interpretation. The only argument in favour of the first plan was the opportunity which it afforded of including all Isaiah in a single volume. As to economy of time and labour, it was soon found that as much of these must be expended on a simple statement of the true sense as would furnish the materials for a synopsis of the different opinions. The latter method was adopted, therefore, not merely for this negative reason, but also for the sake of the additional interest imparted to the Work by this enlargement of the plan, and the valuable antidote to exegetical extravagance and crudity, afforded by a knowledge of earlier opinions and even of exploded errors.

These advantages were reckoned of sufficient value to be purchased even by a sacrifice of space, and it was therefore determined to confine the present publication to the Earlier Prophecies (Chaps. I.–XXXIX.), the rest being reserved to form the subject of another volume. The separation was the more convenient, as the Later Prophecies (Chaps. XL.–LXVI.) are now universally regarded as a continuous and homogeneous composition, requiring in relation to its authenticity a special critical investigation.*

But although it was determined that the Work should be historical as well as exegetical, it was of course impossible to compass the whole range of writers on Isaiah, some of whom were inaccessible, and others wholly destitute of anything original, and therefore without influence upon the progress of opinion. This distinction was particularly made in reference to the older writers, while a more complete exhibition was attempted of the later literature. Some recent writers were at first overlooked through accident or inadvertence, and the omission afterwards continued for the sake of uniformity, or as a simple matter of convenience. Some of these blanks it is proposed to fill in any further prosecution of the author's plan. The citation of authorities becomes less frequent and abundant, for the most part, as the Work advances, and the reader is supposed to have become familiar with the individual peculiarities of different interpreters, as well as

---

* [The original American edition thus described, and published at different times, formed two volumes of unequal size, and that division of volumes, the result of necessity, has therefore not been followed in the present reprint.]

with the way in which they usually group themselves in schools and parties, after which it will be generally found sufficient to refer to acknowledged leaders, or the authors of particular interpretations.   The prominence given to the modern German writers has arisen not from choice but from necessity, because their labours have been so abundant, because their influence is so extensive, and because one prominent design of the whole Work is to combine the valuable processes and products of the new philology with sounder principles of exegesis.   Hence too the constant effort to expound the book with scrupulous adherence to the principles and usages of Hebrew syntax as established by the latest and best writers.   The reference to particular grammars was gradually discontinued and exchanged for explanations in my own words, partly for want of a conventional standard alike familiar to my readers and myself, partly because the latter method was soon found upon experiment to be the most effectual and satisfactory in reference to the object which I had in view.

The appearance of the Work has been delayed by various causes, but above all, by a growing sense of its difficulty and of incapacity to do it justice, together with a natural reluctance to confess how little after all has been accomplished.   To some it will probably be no commendation of the work to say that its author has considered it his duty to record the failure as well as the success of exegetical attempts, and to avoid the presumption of knowing everything as well as the disgrace of knowing nothing.   His deliberate conclusion from the facts with which he has become acquainted in the prosecution of his present task, is that quite as much error has arisen from the effort to know more than is revealed, as from the failure to apply the means of illustration which are really at our disposal.   As advantages arising from delay in this case may be mentioned, some additional maturity of judgment, and the frequent opportunity of re-consideration with the aid of contemporary writers on Isaiah, of whom seven have appeared since this book was projected, besides several auxiliary works of great importance, such as Fürst's Concordance, Nordheimer's Grammar, Hävernick's Introduction, Robinson's Palestine, the later numbers of Gesenius's Thesaurus, and the last edition of his Manual Lexicon.   It is proper to add, that although the plan was formed, and the collection of materials begun more than ten years ago, the Work has been wholly, and some parts of it repeatedly, reduced to writing as it passed through the press.   The advantages thus secured of being able to record the last impressions, and to make use of the latest helps, has this accompanying inconvenience, that changes insensibly took place in the details of the execution, tending to impair its uniformity without affecting its essential character.   To such external blemishes it is of course unnecessary to invite attention by any more particular description or apology.

Since the printing of the volume was completed, the typographical errors have been found to be more numerous than was expected, although for the most part less injurious to the work than discreditable to the author who is justly accountable for this defect, on account of the very imperfect state in which the manuscript was furnished to the printer.   Instead of resorting to the usual apologies of distance from the press, and inexperience in the business, or appealing to the fact that the sheets could be subjected only once to his revision, he prefers to throw himself upon the candour and indulgence of his readers, and especially of those who have experienced the same mortification.

*   *   *   *   *   *

[The lacuna indicated by these asterisks is merely a brief list of Errata, which have of course been corrected in the present reprint.]

The want of uniformity too in the insertion or omission of the Hebrew points is certainly a blemish, but will not, it is hoped, occasion any serious inconvenience, even to the inexperienced reader.   It arose from the accidental combination of two different methods, each of which has its advantages, the one as being more convenient for beginners, the other as favouring the useful habit of deciphering the unpointed text, and rendering typographical correctness more attainable.

PRINCETON, *April* 20. 1846.

PREFACE TO THE EARLIER PROPHECIES

THIS Volume * is a sequel to the one which appeared about a year ago, under the title of The Earlier Prophecies, the two together forming a continuous Commentary on Isaiah. While the same plan has been here retained without alteration, I have aimed at greater uniformity of execution, as well as a more critical selection of materials. The reasons for a separate investigation of these later chapters have been stated in the introduction to the other volume. In addition to the authors there enumerated, I have carefully compared the English Version and remarks of Noyes (second edition, Boston, 1843), and die Cyro-jesaianischen Weissagungen of Beck (Leipzig, 1844) ; the first of which, though elegant and scholar-like, is too closely modelled on Gesenius to afford much new matter, and the other is remarkable chiefly for the boldness of its ultra-rationalistic doctrines, and the juvenile flippancy with which they are expressed. Of both these works occasional citations will be met with in the present volume.

In the exposition of the last seven chapters, too polemical an attitude, perhaps, has been assumed with respect to a distinguished living writer, Dr Henderson, to whose abilities and learning I have elsewhere endeavoured to do justice. The prominence here given to his book has arisen from his happening to be not only the best but the sole representative of certain views among the professed expounders of Isaiah. As to the question in dispute, the ground which I have taken and endeavoured to maintain is the negative position that the truth of these " exceeding great and precious promises " is not suspended on the future restoration of the Jews to Palestine, without denying such a restoration to be possible or promised elsewhere.

In this, as well as in the other Volume, I may possibly have pushed the rule of rigorous translation to an extreme ; but if so, it is an extreme from which recession is much easier and safer than recovery from that of laxity and vagueness. By the course thus taken, I am not without hope that

[* This is the Preface prefixed by the Author to his second volume, which he designated The Later Prophecies of Isaiah.—ED.]

some light may be thrown upon the darker parts of Hebrew Grammar, and especially the doctrine of the tenses, which can never be completely solved except by a laborious induction of particulars.   While I deem it proper to observe that I have read only two sheets of the volume during its progress through the press, I am happy to add, that it has passed through the hands of Mr W. W. Turner, to whom so many other works in this department are indebted for the accuracy of their execution.

I have still kept steadily in view, as my immediate readers, to whose wants the work must be adapted, clergymen and students of theology considered as the actual or future teachers of the church.   Through them I may perhaps indulge the hope of doing something to promote correct opinions and a taste for exegetical pursuits, as means of intellectual and spiritual culture, even though this should prove to be my last as well as first contribution to the stores of sacred learning.

PRINCETON, *March* 20. 1847.

COMMENTARY ON ISAIAH

Volume One

INTRODUCTION

I. *The Earlier Prophecies, Chapters 1—39*

THE English words *prophet, prophesy,* and *prophecy,* have long been appropriated, by established usage, to the prediction of future events. To prophesy, according to the universal acceptation of the term, is to foretell, and a prophet is one who does or can foretell things yet to come. This restricted application of the terms in question has materially influenced the interpretation of the prophetic scriptures by modern and especially by English writers. It is necessary, therefore, to compare the common use of these expressions with the corresponding terms in Greek and Hebrew.

The Greek προφήτης (from πρόφημι) is used in the classics not only to denote specifically a foreteller, but more generally an authoritative speaker in the name of God, in which sense it is applied to the official expounders of the oracles, and to poets as the *prophets of the muses,* i. e. as speaking in their name, at their suggestion, or by their inspiration. This latitude of meaning, in the classical usage of the term, agrees exactly with its application in the Greek of the New Testament, not only to those gifted with the knowledge of futurity, but in a wider sense to inspired teachers or expounders of the will of God in the primitive church. It is evident, therefore, that our *prophet, prophesy,* and *prophecy,* are much more restricted in their import than the Greek words from which they are derived, as employed both by the classical and sacred writers.

It may be said, however, that in this restricted usage we adhere to the primary and proper import of the terms, as the πρό in πρόφημι and προφήτης, no less than the *præ* in *prædico,* must have originally signified *before,* i. e. beforehand. Even this might be plausibly disputed, as the primary sense of πρό would seem to be not temporal but local, the idea of priority in time being given by the best lexicographers as secondary to that of antecedence or priority in place, in which case the particle in composition may have originally signified, not so much the futurity of the things declared, as the authority of the person who declared them. (Compare προεστῶς, προϊστάμενος, *antistes, prætor, præfectus, foreman.*) But even granting that the obvious and common supposition is correct, viz., that the πρό in πρόφημι and its derivatives has primary reference to time, the actual extension of

the terms to other authoritative declarations, and especially to those made
in the name of God, is clear from the usage both of the classics and of the
New Testament. Looking merely to these sources of elucidation, we might
still assert with confidence, that the modern use of the words *prophet* and
prophecy is more restricted than that of the Greek terms from which they
are derived.

But this is a very small part of the evidence on which the affirmation
rests. The prophets, of whom the New Testament chiefly speaks, are not
heathen prophets, nor even the προφῆται of the apostolic churches, but the
prophets of the old dispensation. The terms applied to them must therefore be interpreted, not merely by a reference to etymology, or to classical
usage, or to that of the New Testament itself, but by an appeal to the import
and usage of the Hebrew terms, which the Greek ones are designed to represent. As soon as we resort to this sort of illustration, the doubt which
seemed to overhang the question, when considered as a question of Greek
usage, disappears. We have here no probabilities to balance as to the
primary import of a particle, no extension of the meaning of the whole word
to account for or explain away. The etymology of נָבִיא and the cognate
verbal forms, makes it impossible to look upon foresight or prediction as
their primary and necessary import. The only derivation, which can now
be regarded as philologically tenable, is that which makes the word originally signify the act of pouring forth or uttering, a natural figure in all
languages for speech, and more especially for public, solemn, and continuous
discourse. In actual usage, the Hebrew words are admitted by modern
writers of all schools and creeds to signify specifically one who speaks (or
the act of speaking) for God, not only in his name and by his authority, but
under his influence, in other words, by divine inspiration. The precise
meaning of the noun נָבִיא is clear from Exod. vii. 1, where the Lord says
unto Moses, *See, I have made thee a god to Pharaoh, and Aaron thy brother
shall be thy prophet, i. e.* thy interpreter, thy organ of communication. (See
Gesenius's Thesaurus, s. v. נָבָא). The etymology proposed by Redslob,
which gives נָבִיא the sense of a person sprinkled or baptized with the Spirit
of God, if it can be established, only makes the primary and essential reference to inspiration still more certain than the common one. The few departures from this simple elementary idea, which the lexicons still recognise,
may all be reduced to it more easily and naturally than to any other. For
example, when Abraham is called a prophet (Gen. xx. 7), there is no need
of diluting the sense of the expression into that of a mere friend of God,
which is sufficiently implied in the strict and common sense of an inspired
person. It is equally unnecessary, on the other hand, to give the verb the
sense of *raving* or becoming mad, when applied to Saul (1 Sam. xviii. 10),
since it is there expressly mentioned that *an evil spirit from God had come
upon him*, so that he was really *inspired*, however fearful and mysterious
the nature of the inspiration may have been. A complete induction of particulars would shew, with scarcely the appearance of a doubtful case or an
exception, that the essential idea, running through the whole Hebrew usage
of the verb and noun, is that of *inspiration*. The suggestion of Gesenius,
that the verb is used exclusively in passive or reflexive forms because the
prophet was supposed to be under a controlling influence, is not improbable
in itself, and harmonizes fully with the usage of the words as already stated.

Another obvious deduction from the usage of the language is, that although
נָבִיא, like many other terms of such perpetual occurrence, is employed both
in a wider and a mere restricted sense, the distinction thus made is not that

between inspiration in general and the foresight of the future in particular. There is probably not a single instance in which the word denotes the latter, except as one important function of the power which it properly describes. The gift of prophecy included that of prophetic foresight, but it included more. The prophet was inspired to reveal the will of God, to act as an organ of communication between God and man. The subject of the revelations thus conveyed was not and could not be restricted to the future. It embraced the past and present, and extended to those absolute and universal truths which have no relation to time. This is what we should expect *a priori* in a divine revelation, and it is what we actually find it to contain. That the prophets of the old dispensation were not mere foretellers of things future is apparent from their history as well as from their writings. The historical argument is stated forcibly by Gill when he observes, that Daniel proved himself a prophet by telling Nebuchadnezzar what he had dreamed, as much as by interpreting the dream itself; that it was only by prophetic inspiration that Elijah knew what Gehazi had been doing; and that the woman of Samaria very properly called Christ a prophet, because he told her all things that ever she did. In all these cases, and in multitudes of others, the essential idea is that of inspiration, its frequent reference to things still future being accidental, *i. e.* not included in the uniform and necessary import of the terms.

The restriction of these terms in modern parlance to the prediction of events still future has arisen from the fact that a large proportion of the revelations made in Scripture, and precisely those which are the most surprising and impressive, are of this description. The frequency of such revelations, and the prominence given to them, not in this modern usage merely, but in the word of God itself, admit of easy explanation, It is partly owing to the fact that revelations of the future would be naturally sought with more avidity, and treated with more deference, than any other by mankind in general. It is further owing to the fact that, of all the kinds of revelation, this is the one which affords the most direct and convincing proof of the prophet's inspiration. The knowledge of the present or the past, or of general truths, might be imparted by special inspiration, but it might also be acquired in other ways; and this possibility of course makes the evidence of inspiration thus afforded more complete and irresistible than any other. Hence the function of foretelling what was future, although but a part of the prophetic office, was peculiarly conspicuous and prominent in public view, and apt to be more intimately associated with the office itself in the memory of man.

These considerations seem sufficient to account, not only for the change of meaning which the words have undergone in later usage, but also for the instances, if any such there be, in which the Bible itself employs them to denote exclusively prophetic foresight or the actual prediction of the future. But there is still another reason, more important than either of these, afforded by the fact, that the old dispensation, with all its peculiar institutions, was prospective in its character, a preparation for better things to come. It is not surprising, therefore, that a part of this economy so marked and prominent as prophecy, should have exhibited a special leaning towards futurity.

This naturally leads us from the theoretical idea of a prophet as a person speaking by divine authority and inspiration, to the practical consideration of the end or purpose aimed at in the whole prophetic institution. This was not merely the relief of private doubts, much less the gratification of private curiosity. The gift of prophecy was closely connected with the general design of the old economy. The foundation of the system was the Law, as recorded in the five books of Moses. In that, as an epitome, the rest of the Old Testament is contained, at least as to its seminal principles. The single book of Deuteronomy, and that the very one with which critical caprice in modern times has taken the most liberties, exhibits specimens of every style employed by the sacred writers elsewhere. Still more remarkably is this true of the whole Pentateuch, in reference not merely to its manner but its matter, as comprising virtually all that is developed and applied to the revelations of the latter books. To make this development and application was the business of the prophets. The necessity of such an institution was no after-thought. The law itself provides for it. The promise of a prophet like unto Moses, in the eighteenth of Deuteronomy, according to one of its most plausible interpretations, comprehends the promise of a constant succession of inspired men, so far as this should be required by the circumstances of the people, of which succession Christ himself was to be the greatest.

This promise was abundantly fulfilled. In every emergency requiring such an interposition, we find prophets present and active, and in some important periods of the history of Israel they existed in great numbers. These, though not all inspired writers, were all inspired men, raised up and directed by a special divine influence, to signify and sometimes to execute the will of God in the administration of the theocracy. Joshua is expressly represented as enjoying such an influence, and is always reckoned in the Jewish tradition as a prophet. The judges who succeeded him were all raised up in special emergencies, and were directed and controlled by a special divine influence or inspiration. Samuel was one of the most eminent prophets. After the institution of the monarchy, we read constantly of prophets distinct from the civil rulers. After the schism between Judah and Ephraim, there continued to be prophets even in the kingdom of the ten tribes. They were peculiarly necessary there indeed, because the people of that kingdom were cut off from the sanctuary and its services, as bonds of union with Jehovah. The prophetic ministry continued through the Babylonish exile, and ceased some years after the restoration, in the person of Malachi, whom the Jews unanimously represent as the last of their prophets.

In tracing this succession, it is evident that the history attaches no importance to the unbroken series of incumbents, and describes them as deriving their prophetic character, not from their predecessors, but immediately from God. The cases of Joshua and Elisha are perhaps the only ones in which a prophet is expressly said to have inducted his successor into office: and even if it could be fairly inferred from these that such was the ordinary practice, still the silence of the history implies that the validity of the prophetic ministrations was dependent upon no external rite of transfer and upon no unbroken continuity in the succession. This presumption is the stronger as a perfect series cannot be made out, even by inference and combination, from the recorded history, which usually speaks of the prophets so as to suggest the idea, not so much of an order which could never be interrupted or suspended, as of one which should not wholly cease until its purpose was accomplished, and should never be wanting in any emergency which called for a divine interposition. In this, which is the true sense of the promise, it was signally fulfilled, so that although we may not be able to demonstrate a perpetual succession of inspired representatives or messengers from God, we can safely affirm that he never left himself without witness, or his people without counsel, consolation, or reproof.

With respect to the nature of the inspiration under which these prophets spoke and acted, there can be no doubt that the Bible itself represents it as plenary, or fully adequate to the attainment of its end (2 Tim. iii. 16; 2 Pet. i. 21). Where this end was external action, it was sufficiently secured by the gift of courage, strength, and practical wisdom. Where the instruction of God's people was the object, whether in reference to the past, the present, or the future; whether in word, in writing, or in both; whether for temporary ends, or with a view to perpetual preservation; the prophets are clearly represented as infallible, *i. e.* incapable of erring or deceiving, with respect to the matter of their revelation. How far this object was secured by direct suggestion, by negative control, or by an elevating influence upon the native powers, is a question of no practical importance to those who hold the essential doctrine that the inspiration was in all cases such as to render those who were inspired infallible. Between this supposition and the opposite extreme, which denies inspiration altogether, or resolves it into mere excitement of the imagination, and the sensibilities, like the afflatus of a poet or an orator, there seems to be no definite and safe position. Either the prophets were not inspired at all in any proper sense, or they were so inspired as to be infallible.

As to the mode in which the required impression was made, it seems both vain and needless to attempt any definite description of it. The ultimate effect would be the same in any case, if not upon the prophet, upon those who heard or read his prophecies. So far as anything can be inferred from incidental or explicit statements of the Scripture, the most usual method of communication would appear to have been that of immediate vision, *i. e.* the presentation of the thing to be revealed as if it were an object of sight. Thus Micaiah *saw* Israel scattered on the hills like sheep without a shepherd (1 Kings xxii. 17), and Isaiah *saw* Jehovah sitting on a lofty throne (Isa. vi. 1). That this was the most usual mode of presentation, is probable not only from occasional expressions such as those just quoted, but from the fact, that a very large proportion of the prophetic revelations are precisely such as might be painted and subjected to the sense of sight. The same conclusion is confirmed by the use of the words *seer* and *vision* as essentially equivalent to *prophet* and *prophecy*. There is no need, however, of supposing that this method of communication, even if it were the common one, was used invariably. Some things in the prophecies require us to suppose that they were made known to the prophet just as he made them known to others, *i. e.* by the simple suggestion of appropriate words. But this whole question is rather one of curiosity than use, even in reference to interpretation.

A kindred question, but distinct from this, is that respecting the mental and bodily condition of the prophet, under the influence of inspiration. Whatever we imagine to have been the mode of the communication, whether visual or verbal, in the general or in any given case, it may still be made a question whether the prophet, in receiving such communications, was as fully in possession of his faculties, and in the exercise of self-control, as at any other time; or whether, on the contrary, he was in what the Greeks called ἴκστασις, a state of passive subjection to a higher power, holding his own faculties in temporary but complete abeyance. It is well known that the prophets and diviners of the heathen world, during their seasons of pretended inspiration, exhibited the outward signs of violent excitement often amounting to insanity. That this was not regarded as an accidental circumstance, but as a natural and necessary sign of inspiration, may be gathered from the etymological affinity between the Greek words μάντις and μανία or μαίνομαι. The early Fathers uniformly speak of this maniacal excitement as characteristic of the heathen inspiration, whether real or pretended, and describe the inspiration of the Hebrew prophets as distinguished by the opposite peculiarities of calmness, self-possession, and active intelligence. This is distinctly and repeatedly asserted by Chrysostom, Augustine, and Jerome, who ascribes the contrary opinion to Montanus and his followers. In our own day it has been revived, not only by Gesenius and others, who deny the real inspiration of the prophets, but by Hengstenberg, who stedfastly maintains it. In the first part of his Christology, he undertakes to explain the disregard of chronological relations by the prophets, and their fragmentary manner of exhibiting a subject, from the ecstatic state in which they uttered their predictions. This opinion has not only been attacked and ridiculed by later writers of a very different school, but disavowed by others of the same school, especially by Hävernick, who, in his Introduction to the Old Testament (§ 199) argues at length in favour of the doctrine that the mental condition of the prophets in receiving their divine communications cannot have been a morbid one. The most serious objection to the theory of Hengstenberg, besides its opposition to the common judgment of the church in every age, and its apparent derogation from the dignity of the prophetic character, are, the want of any clear support in Scripture, and the inutility of such a supposition to attain the end at which he aims, and which may just as well be answered by supposing that the peculiarities ascribed to the extraordinary state of inspired writers, were directly produced by something negative or positive in the divine communication itself. If they bring remote events into juxtaposition, the simplest explanation of the fact is, not that they were in a state which rendered them incapable of estimating chronological distinctions, but that these distinctions were withheld from them, or that although acquainted with them they intentionally overlooked them and combined the objects on another mode and on another principle. This view of the matter is entirely sufficient to explain what Peter says (1 Peter i. 12), without resorting to a supposition which, unless absolutely necessary, is to be avoided as of doubtful tendency.

It has been disputed whether the prophets of the old dispensation had any training for their work at all analogous to what we call a professional education. Some have supposed the *sons of the prophets*, frequently mentioned in the books of Kings, to have been young men in a course of preparation for the prophetic ministry. To this it has been objected, that their ministry depended on the gift of inspiration, for which no human training could compensate or prepare them. But although they could not act as prophets without inspiration, they might be prepared for those parts of the work which depended upon culture, such as a correct mode of expression, just as men may now be trained by education for the work of the ministry, although convinced that its success depends entirely on the divine blessing. It is not to be forgotten that the inspiration under which the prophets acted left them in full possession of their faculties, native and acquired, and with all their peculiarities of thought and feeling unimpaired. The whole subject of prophetic education is, however, one of surmise and conjecture, rather than of definite knowledge or of practical utility.

To the government the prophets do not seem to have sustained any definite or fixed relation, as component parts of a political system. The extent and manner of their influence, in this respect, depended on the character of the rulers, the state of affairs, and the nature of the messages which they were commissioned to deliver. As a class, the prophets influenced the government, not by official formal action, but as special messengers from God, by whom he was represented in particular emergencies, and whose authority could neither be disputed nor resisted by any magistrate without abjuring the fundamental principles of the theocracy. Even the apostate kings of Israel acknowledged the divine legation of the prophets of Jehovah.

The opinion that the priestly and prophetic functions were regarded as identical, or commonly united in the same persons under the theocracy, is wholly destitute of scriptural foundation. It is no doubt true that priests might be inspired, and that the High Priest may have been so always *ex officio*. Two of the most eminent prophets (Jeremiah and Ezekiel) were unquestionably priests. But the sacerdotal and prophetic offices, as such, were perfectly distinct, as well in function as in purpose, being instituted to promote the same great end in different ways, the one by maintaining the symbolical and sacramental forms of the theocracy, the other by correcting their abuse, and keeping constantly in view their spiritual import and design, as *shadows of good things to come*.

The relation of the prophets to the people and the manner of their intercourse appear to have been subject to no uniform and no rigid law. From Elijah's hairy dress and John the Baptist's imitation of it, some have hastily inferred that the prophets were commonly distinguished by a peculiar dress and an ascetic mode of life. Whether the same conclusion can be drawn from the sackcloth mentioned in Isaiah xx. 2, is considered doubtful. The truth appears to be, that from the very nature of the prophetic ministry it was exempted from the rules of rigid outward uniformity. Eichhorn has justly mentioned as a characteristic difference between the heathen and the Jewish prophets, that whereas the former tried to enhance their authority by darkness and seclusion and mysterious accompaniments, the latter moved among the people without any such factitious advantages.

With respect to the promulgation and preservation of the prophecies, there have been various opinions and many fanciful conjectures. Some suppose the prophets to have been a kind of demagogues or popular orators, whose speeches, unless previously prepared, were afterwards recorded by themselves or others. Another supposition is that the prophets were inspired writers, and that their prophecies were published only as written compositions. A distinction as to this point has by some been drawn between the earlier and the later prophets. From the death of Moses to the accession of Uzziah, a period of nearly seven hundred years, a large proportion of the prophets are supposed to have performed their functions orally and without leaving any thing on record; whereas after that period they were led to act not only for the present but the future. We have no cause to doubt, however, that we now have in possession all that was *written aforetime for our learning*. And in the case of any prophecy, the question whether it was orally delivered before it was written is comparatively unimportant, as our only concern with it is in its written form. The idea that the prophecies now extant are mere summaries of long discourses, is ingenious and plausible in certain cases, but admits of no historical or certain demonstration.

A question of more moment is that with respect to the way in which the writings were preserved, whether by private circulation as detached composition, or by solemn enrolment and deposit in the sanctuary. The modern critics who dispute the integrity and genuineness of many passages lean to the former supposition, but the latter is unquestionably favoured by the whole drift of Scripture and the current of ancient usage, sacred and profane, with respect to writings which were looked upon as sacred. It may well be doubted whether among the ancient Hebrews there was any extensive circulation of books at all, and it seems to me to be as hard to disprove as to prove the position, that the only literature of the nation was THE BOOK or SCRIPTURE (הַסֵּפֶר), which from the time of Moses was kept open, and in which the writings of the prophets may have been recorded as they were produced. At all events, it seems unreasonable and at variance with the tenor of Scripture to suppose that writings held to be inspired were left to circulate at random and to share the fate of other compositions, without any effort to attest their genuineness or to secure their preservation.

Upon this improbable hypothesis some modern critics have constructed a theory as to the formation of the Hebrew Canon. They suppose that the books now composing the Old Testament were long in circulation as detached compositions, or at most in small collections; but that after the Babylonish exile, measures were taken to secure the national literature from destruction by bringing together the most highly esteemed books then extant, to which others were added from time to time until the period of the Maccabees. In a similar manner they account for the threefold division of the Old Testament, into the Law, Prophets, and Scriptures (כְּתוּבִים, ἁγιό-γραφα), found in all Hebrew manuscripts, and referred to, not only by Philo and Josephus, but in the New Testament (Luke xxiv. 44). This they account for, by supposing that the five books of Moses, because of their superior authority, were first placed together by themselves; that the earlier histories and prophecies were then joined in a second volume; and that a fourth was opened for the reception of books which might be afterwards discovered or composed. The obvious design of this whole theory is to account for the admission of books into the canon, which these critics are unwilling to recognise as ancient, such as Daniel, Esther, Chronicles, and many of the Psalms.

Others attempt to account for the threefold division, as founded on the subjects of the different books. But this supposition is precluded by the fact, that historical books are found in all the three divisions; Genesis in the first: Joshua, Judges, Samuel, and Kings in the second; Chronicles, Ezra, Nehemiah, Ruth, and Esther in the third; to which it may be added, that Daniel is found in the third division, and that Jeremiah's Prophecies are separated from his Lamentations.

The uniform tradition of the Jews is, that the sacred books were finally collected and arranged by Ezra and his contemporaries, under the guidance of divine inspiration, and that the threefold division is coeval with the formation of the canon. As to the principle of the division, some of the Jewish doctors teach that it is founded on the different degrees of inspiration under which the books were written, the highest being that of Moses, and the lowest that of the Hagiographa or Scriptures. This last opinion is not only destitute of evidence or scriptural foundation, but at variance with the tenor of the sacred writings, and of dangerous tendency.

The most satisfactory solution of the fact in question is the one which supposes the law to have been placed first as the foundation of the whole, and the remaining books to have been divided, not with respect to their contents or the degree of inspiration in their writers, but with respect to their official character, the second great division being appropriated to the writings of men who were not only inspired but prophets by profession, who possessed not only the prophetic gift but the prophetic office, while the third place was reserved for those who, although equally inspired, held no such station. Thus the books of Joshua, Judges, Samuel, and Kings, having been composed, according to the ancient tradition, by נְבִיאִים or official prophets, are prefixed to the prophecies properly so called, while the writings of David and Daniel, who were not such, are included in the third division.

The principal difficulty in the way of this hypothesis arises from the fact, that different writings of the same man, viz. Jeremiah, are found both in the second and third division. This single exception to the general rule has been accounted for by some, upon the ground, that the book of Lamentations, although written by a Prophet in the strict sense, is more an expression of personal feeling than the other prophecies ; by others, upon the ground of its liturgical character, which naturally led to its insertion in the same part of the Canon with the Psalms. Another objection to this whole explanation of the threefold division has been drawn from the absence of entire uniformity in the application of the name נָבִיא to the official or professional prophet, and of חֹזֶה (seer) to an inspired person, simply as such. The difficulty here referred to does not lie in the promiscuous use of προφήτης in the New Testament, where David, for example, is expressly called a Prophet. This is sufficiently explained by the want of any Greek equivalent to *seer*. But the same solution is not applicable to the use of both words *seer* and *prophet*, in the Old Testament itself, with reference to one and the same person. (*E. g.* Gad the seer, 1 Chron. xxi. 9 ; Gad the prophet, 2 Sam. xxiv. 11.) How far this rare departure from the usage, ought to weigh against the theory in general, or how far it may be accounted for by special circumstances in the case of Gad, are questions which may be considered doubtful. All that need be affirmed is that this hypothesis respecting the division of the Hebrew Canon, although not susceptible of demonstration, is more satisfactory and probable than any other which has been proposed.

The application of the name כְּתוּבִים, ἁγιόγραφα or *Scriptures*, to the third division only, has been variously explained ; but the simplest and most natural solution is, that the first two divisions having been distinguished by appropriate names, the third was left in possession of that which, if there had been no division, would have been appropriate to the whole. Thus understood, the three parts of the Canon are *the Law, the Prophets,* and *the (other) Scriptures.*

In the second of these great divisions, that of the Prophets properly so called, a prominent place, and for the most part the first place, has been always held, so far as we can trace its history, by a book bearing the name of Isaiah. A Talmudical tradition represents it as having formerly been preceded by Jeremiah and Ezekiel. Some of the modern German writers take advantage of this statement, as a ground for the presumption that the book in its present form was not completed until after those of Jeremiah and Ezekiel. This supposition, the design of which is to facilitate the critical rejection of the later prophecies, is not only an unauthorised inference from a fact extremely dubious at best, but at variance with the simultaneous close of the whole canon, which we have seen to be the only well-sustained hypothesis. The Talmudists themselves explain the fact which they allege, upon the ground that Jeremiah and Ezekiel are for the most part minatory prophets, and that the more consolatory writings of Isaiah were subjoined as a relief and antidote. A far more probable solution is, that the arrangement in question, if it ever prevailed, arose from the intimate connection of the second book of Kings with Jeremiah, and perhaps from a traditional ascription of it to that prophet as its author. The necessity of any explanation seems, however, to be superseded by the doubt which overhangs the fact itself, especially when taken in connection with the uniform position of Isaiah before the other two in the most ancient manuscripts now extant, both of the Hebrew text and of the ancient versions.

The name Isaiah is a compound word denoting the *Salvation of Jehovah*, to which some imagine that the Prophet himself alludes in chap. viii. 18. The abbreviated form (יְשַׁעְיָה) is never applied in Scripture to the Prophet, though the Rabbins employ it in titles and inscriptions. Both forms of the name are applied in the Old Testament to other persons, in all which cases the English Version employs a different orthography, viz. *Jeshaiah* or *Jesaiah*. In the New Testament our Version writes the same *Esaias*, after the example of the Vulgate, varying slightly from the Greek 'Ησαίας, used both in the Septuagint and the New Testament. To the name of the Prophet we find several times added that of his father Amoz (אָמוֹץ), which several of the Greek Fathers have confounded with the name of the prophet Amos (עָמוֹס), though they differ both in the first and last letter. This mistake, occasioned by the Septuagint version, which writes both names alike ('Αμώς), may be considered the more venial, as two of the latest writers on Isaiah in the English language have, in the very act of setting Cyril and Eusebius right, themselves committed a like error by misspelling the name Amos (אָמוֹס). The more ancient mistake may have been facilitated by a knowledge of the Jewish maxim, now recorded in the Talmud, that whenever a prophet's father is named, the father was himself a prophet. The Jews themselves, in this case, are contented with observing the affinity between the names Amoz (אָמוֹץ), and Amaziah (אֲמַצְיָהוּ), upon which they gravely found a positive assertion that these men were brothers, and that Isaiah was therefore of the blood-royal, being cousin-german to the first king mentioned in the opening of his prophecies. This tradition has had great vogue among Jews and Christians, some of whom account for the urbanity and polish of Isaiah's manner as a natural effect of his nobility. It is unfortunately true, however, that the Jewish doctors sometimes invent facts for the purpose of filling up the chasms of history, and this is especially to be suspected where the statement seems to rest on an etymological conceit or any other fanciful analogy. At all events, we have no satisfactory assurance of the truth of this tradition, any more than of that which makes the prophet to have been the father-in-law of king Manasseh. The most probable statement is that made by one of the most learned and judicious of the Rabbins (David Kimchi), that the family and tribe to which Isaiah belonged are now entirely unknown. Of his domestic circumstances we know merely, that his wife and two of his sons are mentioned by himself (chap. vii. 3 ; viii. 3, 4), to which some add a third, as we shall see below.

The only historical account of this Prophet is contained in the book which bears his name, and in the parallel passages of Second Kings, which exhibit unequivocal signs of being from the hand of the same writer. The first sentence of Isaiah's own book, which is now commonly admitted to be genuine, assigns as the period of his ministry the four successive reigns of Uzziah, Jotham, Ahaz, and Hezekiah, one of the most eventful periods in the history of Judah. The two first reigns here mentioned were exceedingly prosperous, although a change for the worse appears to have commenced before the death of Jotham, and continued through the reign of

Ahaz, bringing the state to the very verge of ruin, from which it was not restored to a prosperous condition until long after the accession of Hezekiah'. During this period the kingdom of the ten tribes, which had flourished greatly under Jeroboam II., for many years contemporary with Uzziah, passed through the hands of a succession of usurpers, and was at length overthrown by the Assyrians, in the sixth year of Hezekiah's reign over Judah.

Among the neighbouring powers, with whom Israel was more or less engaged in conflict during these four reigns, the most important were Damascene Syria, Moab, Edom, and the Philistines, who, although resident within the allotted bounds of Judah, still endeavoured to maintain their position as an independent and a hostile nation. But the foreign powers which chiefly influenced the condition of south-western Asia during this period, were the two great empires of Assyria in the east, and Egypt in the south-west. By a rapid succession of important conquests, the former had suddenly acquired a magnitude and strength which it had not possessed for ages, if at all. Egypt had been subdued, at least in part, by Ethiopia ; but this very event, by combining the forces of two great nations, had given unexampled strength to the Ethiopian dynasty in Upper Egypt. The mutual jealousy and emulation between this state and Assyria, naturally tended to make Palestine, which lay between them, a theatre of war, at least at intervals, for many years. It also led the kings of Israel and Judah to take part in the contentions of these two great powers, and to secure themselves by uniting, sometimes with Egypt against Assyria, sometimes with Assyria against Egypt. It was this inconstant policy that hastened the destruction of the kingdom of the ten tribes, and exposed that of Judah to imminent peril. Against this policy the prophets, and especially Isaiah, were commissioned to remonstrate, not only as unworthy in itself, but as implying a distrust of God's protection, and indifference to the fundamental law of the theocracy. The Babylonian monarchy, as Hävernick has clearly proved, began to gather strength before the end of this period, but was less conspicuous, because not yet permanently independent of Assyria.

The two most remarkable conjunctures in the history of Judah during Isaiah's ministry, are, the invasion by the combined force of Syria and Israel, in the reign of Ahaz, followed by the destruction of the kingdom of the ten tribes, and the Assyrian invasion in the fourteenth year of Hezekiah, ending in the miraculous destruction of Sennacherib's army, and his own ignominious flight. The historical interest of this important period is further heightened by the fact that two of the most noted eras in chronology fall within it, viz. the era of Nabonassar, and that computed from the building of Rome.

The length of Isaiah's public ministry is doubtful. The aggregate duration of the four reigns mentioned in the title is above one hundred and twelve years ; but it is not said that he prophesied throughout the whole reign, either of Uzziah or Hezekiah. Some, it is true, have inferred that his ministry was co-extensive with the whole reign of Uzziah, because he is said to have written the history of that prince (2 Chron. xxvi. 22), which he surely might have done without being strictly his contemporary, just as he may have written that of Hezekiah to a certain date (2 Chron. xxxii. 32), and yet have died before him. Neither of these incidental statements can be understood as throwing any light upon the question of chronology. Most writers, both among the Jews and Christians, understand the first verse of the sixth chapter as determining the year of King Uzziah's death

to be the first of Isaiah's public ministry. Some of the Jewish writers who
adopt this supposition, at the same time understand Uzziah's death to
mean his civil death, occasioned by the leprosy with which he was smitten
in the twenty-fifth year of his reign, for his sacrilegious invasion of the
house of God, so that he dwelt in a separate house until his death, There
seems to be no sufficient ground for this explanation of the language, or for
the alleged coincidence of the event with the twenty-fifth year of Uzziah's
reign, any more than for the notion of the oriental Christians, that Isaiah
was deprived of the prophetic office, for his sin in not withstanding Uzziah,
and after twenty-eight years of silence was restored in the year of that
king's death,—a fanciful interpretation of the facts recorded in chap. vi. The
modern writers are agreed in understanding the expression literally, and in
connecting the last year of Uzziah's life with the first year of Isaiah's
ministry. It is by no means certain, as we shall see below, that the sixth
chapter is descriptive of Isaiah's inauguration into office, still less that it
was written before any of the others. But it cannot be denied that the
chronological hypothesis just stated is strongly recommended by the fact of
its removing all objections to the truth of the inscription (chap. i. 1),
founded on the extreme longevity which it would otherwise ascribe to the
prophet, by enabling us at once to deduct half a century. If we reckon
from the last year of Uzziah to the fourteenth of Hezekiah, the last in which
we find any certain historical traces of Isaiah, we obtain, as the minimum
of his prophetic ministry, a period of forty-seven years, and this, supposing
that he entered on it even at the age of thirty, would leave him at his death
less than eighty years old. And even if it be assumed that he survived
Hezekiah, and continued some years under his successor, the length of his
life will after all be far less than that of Jehoiada the High Priest, who died
in the reign of Joash at the age of 130 years. (2 Chron. xxiv. 15.)

The Jews have a positive tradition that he did die in the reign of Manasseh, and as a victim of the bloody persecutions by which that king is said
to have filled Jerusalem with innocent blood from one end to the other
(2 Kings xxi. 16). Some accounts go so far as to give the pretext upon
which the murder was committed, namely, that of discrepance between
Isaiah's teaching and the law of Moses, as well as the precise form of his
martyrdom, by being sawn asunder, some say in the body of a tree, which
had opened to receive him. The substantial part of this tradition is received as true by several of the Fathers, who suppose it to be clearly alluded
to in Heb. xi. 37. It has also found favour among many modern writers,
on the ground of its intrinsic credibility, and the antiquity of the tradition.
Hengstenberg assents to it moreover on the ground that it enables us
more easily to account for the peculiar features of the later prophecies
(chap. xl–xlvi.), by supposing them to have been written in the days of
Manasseh, in the old age of the prophet, and after his retirement from active
life. Hävernick, on the other hand, rejects the tradition, first, on the
general ground that fabulous accounts are especially abundant in the Jewish
martyrology, and then on the special ground, that this assumption leaves
us unable to account for the omission of Manasseh's name in the inscription
of the book, without admitting that the title may have been prefixed to a
partial collection of Isaiah's prophecies, or by the hand of a later writer,
which he holds to be unauthorised and dangerous concessions. To the
suggestion that Manasseh may have been omitted because under him Isaiah
had ceased to appear in public as a prophet and employed himself in writing,
it is answered that if Uzziah is distinctly mentioned simply because Isaiah was

inducted into office at the close of his long reign, he could scarcely have omitted Manasseh, under whom so large a proportion of his prophecies were written, if not publicly delivered.   In weighing the arguments of Hävernick, it must not be overlooked that his hypothesis compels him to regard chap. xxxvii. 38 as later than the times of Isaiah, simply because the event there recorded must have taken place in the reign of Manasseh.   This fact, together with the insufficiency of his objections to the contrary hypothesis, may at least dispose us to abstain from such a positive decision of the question as would cut us off from the assumption of a longer term of public service, however probable on other grounds, and however necessary to the full solution of questions which may afterwards present themselves during the process of interpretation.   With this proviso, we may safely leave the precise chronological question, as the Bible leaves it, undetermined.

From the references, which have been already quoted, to the historical writings of Isaiah, some have inferred that he was an official historiographer, in which capacity the older prophets seem to have acted, as appears from the canonical insertion of such books as those of Joshua, Judges, Samuel, and Kings, among the Prophets.   We have no reason to suppose, however, that Isaiah held any secular office of the kind, distinct from his prophetic ministry.   Nor is it clear in what sense the citation of Isaiah by the Chronicles as a historical authority should be understood.   The reference may be simply to the historical portions of his book, or to the corresponding passages of Second Kings, of which, in strict discharge of his official functions, he may well have been the author.   That the books referred to were more copious histories or annals, of which only summaries or fragments are now extant, is a supposition which, however credible or even plausible it may be in itself, is not susceptible of demonstration   The question as to the identity and fate of these historical writings is of no importance to the exegesis of the book before us.   The books still extant under the name of the *Vision* and *Ascension of Isaiah*, are universally admitted to be spurious and apocryphal.   Our attention will therefore be exclusively confined to the canonical Isaiah.

This book not only forms a part of the Old Testament Canon as far as we can trace it back, but has held its place there without any change of form, size, or contents, of which the least external evidence can be adduced. The allusions to this Prophet, and the imitations of him, in the later books of the Old Testament, are not confined to any one part of the book or any single class of passages.   The apocryphal writers who make mention of it, use no expressions which imply that it was not already long complete in its present form and size.   The same thing seems to be implied in the numerous citations of this book in the New Testament.   Without going here into minute details, a correct idea of the general fact may be conveyed by simply stating, that of the sixty-six chapters of Isaiah, as divided in our modern Bibles, forty-seven are commonly supposed to be directly quoted or distinctly alluded to, and some of them repeatedly.   The same thing may be illustrated clearly on a smaller scale by stating, that in the twenty-one cases where Isaiah is expressly named in the New Testament, the quotations are drawn from the first, sixth, eighth, ninth, tenth, eleventh, twenty-ninth, fortieth, forty-second, fifty-third, sixty-first, and sixty-fifth chapters of the book before us.   These facts, together with the absence of all countervailing evidence, shew clearly that the *Book of the Prophet Isaiah* (Luke iv. 17), known and quoted by our Lord and his apostles, was, as a whole, identical with that which we have under the same name.   We find accordingly a long unbroken series of interpreters, Jewish and Christian, through a course of ages, not only acquiescing in this general statement, but regarding all the passages and parts of which the book consists, as clearly and unquestionably genuine. This appears for the most part, it is true, not as the result of any positive reasoning or investigation, but as a negative assumption, resting on the want of any proof or even ground of suspicion to the contrary. Hence it is that in the older writers on Isaiah, even down to the middle of the eighteenth century, the place now occupied by *criticism*, in the modern sense, is wholly blank. No one of course thought it necessary to defend what had never been attacked, or to demonstrate what had never been disputed.

This neglect of critical investigation and discussion, although easily accounted for, as we have seen, led to a violent reaction towards the opposite extreme, as soon as the first impulse had been given to that kind of learned speculation. The critical processes employed, with paradoxical assurance, on the Greek and Roman classics, by the school of Bentley, were transferred to Scripture, and applied not only to particular expressions, but to whole passages and even books. That this new method would be early carried to excess, was not only to be apprehended as a possible contingency, but confidently looked for as a natural and even unavoidable result. The causes which facilitate inventions and discoveries tend also to exaggerate their value. Of this general truth we have abundant illustration without going beyond the field of biblical learning. The supposed discovery that Buxtorf and the Rabbins had attached too much importance to the masoretic pointing, led Cappellus, Houbigant, and Lowth, to reject it altogether—not only its authority but its assistance—and to make the Hebrew text a nose of wax between the fingers of an arbitrary and capricious criticism. The discovery that sufficient use had never yet been made of the analogy of Arabic in Hebrew lexicography, led Schultens and his school to an extreme which seemed to threaten a transfusion of the spirit of one language into the exhausted vessels of another. In like manner, the idea that the Hebrew text had been too *uncritically* handled, seems at first to have been wholly unaccompanied by any apprehension that the process of correction could be either misapplied or pushed so far as to defeat itself. In all such cases the first movements must be tentative. The primary object is to ascertain what *can* be done. In settling this point, it is necessary to assume provisionally more than is expected to abide the test of final and decisive experiment. The writers who originally undertook to separate the genuine and spurious portions of Isaiah, acted of course on the presumption, that any part might prove unsound, and therefore set no bounds to their avidity for textual reforms and innovations. The natural result was a grotesque disguise and mutilation of the book by means of numberless erasures, transpositions, combinations, and gratuitous assumptions of imaginary authors, two or more of whom were often thought to be identified within the bounds of one connected passage.

Particular examples of this critical mania, as displayed by Koppe, Eichhorn, Bertholdt, and others, will be given hereafter in the exposition. What has been here said in the general will suffice to explain the fact that these extravagant results, and the confusion into which they threw the whole subject of interpretation, soon produced a new reaction. Rosenmüller, De Wette, and especially Gesenius, who may be regarded as the representatives of a more moderate and later school, have no hesitation in expressing their contempt for the empirical and slashing criticism of their predecessors, and, as a proof of their sincerity, assert the integrity and unity of many passages which Eichhorn and his fellows had most wantonly dismembered. This is undoubtedly a retrograde movement in the right direction, and as far as it goes has had a salutary influence, by making the criticism of the Hebrew text something more than idle guess-work or fantastic child's play. At the same time, it is not to be dissembled that the ground assumed by these distinguished writers is itself, to use a favourite expression of their own, *unkritisch* and *unwissenschaftlich, i.e.* neither critical nor scientific. The ground of this charge is that their own mode of critical procedure differs from that which they repudiate and laugh at, only in a degree, *i.e.* in the extent to which it is applied. They expunge, transpose, and imagine less ; but still they do all three, and on precisely the same principles. They mark out no new method, they establish no new standard, but are simply the moderate party of the same school which they represent as *antiquirt* and exploded.

The consciousness of this defect betrays itself occasionally in the *naïveté* with which Gesenius and De Wette appeal to their *critical feeling* as the ultimate ground of their decisions. The real principle of these decisions is identical with that assumed by Eichhorn and his school, to wit, that where there is a colourable pretext or the faintest probability in favour of a change, it is entitled to the preference, always provided that it does not shock the critical *Gefühl* of the performer, a proviso which experience has proved to be sufficient to prevent all inconveniences that might arise from a too rigorous construction of the rule. If, for example, after three-fourths of a sentence or a passage have been sacrificed because they may by possibility be spurious, it is found convenient to retain the fourth, for any exegetical purpose or to prove another point, it is effected without scruple or delay by a response of the *Gefühl* in its favour. In this convenient process, the πρῶτον ψεῦδος of the radical reformers, as the earlier critics may be justly called, if not avowed in theory, is still held fast in practice, viz. the doctrine that the general presumption is against the truth and authenticity of everything traditional or ancient, and in favour of whatever can by any means be substituted for it. The difference between this and the old-fashioned criticism seems to be the same as that between the principle of English jurisprudence, that a person accused is to be reckoned innocent until he is proved guilty, and the rule adopted in the criminal proceedings of some other nations, that he ought to be held guilty till he proves his innocence. A fundamental maxim of this whole school of criticism, upper and lower, first and last, extreme and moderate, is this, that what is possible is probable and may be held as certain, if it suits the convenience of the critic ; in other words, " things must be as they may."

Another proof that this whole system is uncritical, or destitute of any settled principle, distinct from that of the exploded method which it supersedes, is furnished by the absence of consistency and unity in its results. In one important point, these writers, it is true, display a singular agreement. This is their unanimous rejection of the twenty-seven chapters at the end of the collection, as the product of a later age ; a unanimity arising neither from the clearness of the case nor from any real unity of principle among the critics who exhibit it, but simply from the fact, now universally admitted, that these chapters form a continuous unbroken composition, so that in order to be rid of any one part it is requisite to sacrifice the whole. The particular grounds of this rejection are stated and examined in the second part of the Introduction. The comparison about to be made here will be restricted to the remainder of the book, with the exception of the four historical chapters which connect the two divisions (chaps. xxxvi.–xxxix.), and which have usually shared the same fate with the twenty-seven.

The earliest chapters are precisely those respecting which these critics are the least divided. It is commonly agreed among them that the six first are genuine productions of Isaiah, to which it can hardly be considered an exception, that chap. ii. 2–4 is supposed by many to be still more ancient. The only observable dissent from this general judgment seems to be the paradoxical opinion of the Dutch writer Roorda, that chap. ii. 2–4 is the only portion written by Isaiah, and that all the rest of the first five chapters is the work of Micah! Chap. vii. 1–16 is regarded by Gesenius as probably not the composition of Isaiah, who is mentioned in the third person. This opinion is refuted by Hitzig and repudiated by the later writers. Koppe's idea that the twelfth chapter is a hymn of later date, after being rejected by Gesenius, and revived by Ewald, has again been set aside by Umbreit. The genuineness of chap. xiii. and chap. xiv. 1–23 is more unanimously called in question, on account of its resemblance to chaps. xl.–lxvi. which this whole class of critics set aside as spurious. Chaps. xv. and xvi. are ascribed by Koppe and Bertholdt to Jeremiah; by Ewald and Umbreit to an unknown prophet older than Isaiah; by Hitzig, Maurer, and Knobel to Jonah; by Hendewerk to Isaiah himself. Eichhorn rejects the nineteenth chapter; Gesenius calls in question the genuineness of vers. 18–20; Koppe denies that of vers. 18–25; Hitzig regards vers. 16–25 as a fabrication of the Jewish priest Onias; while Rosenmüller, Hendewerk, Ewald, and Umbreit, vindicate the whole as a genuine production of Isaiah. The first ten verses of the twenty-first chapter are rejected on the ground of their resemblance to the thirteenth and fourteenth. Ewald ascribes both to a single author; Hitzig denies that they can be from the same hand. Ewald makes the prophecy in chap. xxi. the earlier; Hitzig proves it to be later. Koppe, Paulus, Eichhorn, and Rosenmüller, look upon it as a *vaticinium ex eventu*; Gesenius, Ewald, and the other later writers as a real prophecy. The twenty-third chapter is ascribed by Movers to Jeremiah; by Eichhorn and Rosenmüller to an unknown writer later than Isaiah; by Gesenius and De Wette to Isaiah himself; by Ewald to a younger contemporary and disciple of the prophet. The continuous prophecy contained in chaps. xxiv.–xxvii. Knobel shews to have been written in Palestine about the beginning of the Babylonish exile; Gesenius in Babylon towards the end of the captivity and by the author of chaps. xl.–lxvi.; Umbreit, at the same time, but by a different author; Gramberg, after the return from exile; Ewald, just before the invasion of Egypt by Cambyses; Vatke, in the period of the Maccabees; Hitzig, in Assyria just before the fall of Nineveh; while Rosenmüller, in the last editions of his Scholia, ascribes it to Isaiah himself. Chaps. xxviii.–xxxiii. are supposed by Koppe to contain many distinct prophecies of different authors, and by Hitzig several successive compositions of one and the same author; while most other writers consider them as forming a continuous whole. This is regarded by Gesenius and Hitzig, notwithstanding the objections of preceding critics, as a genuine production of Isaiah; but Ewald doubts whether it may not be the work of a disciple. Most of the writers of this school join chaps. xxxiv. and xxxv. together, as an unbroken context; but Hitzig no less confidently puts them asunder. Rosenmüller, De Wette, and others, set these chapters down as evidently written by the author of chaps. xl.–lxvi., while Ewald on the other hand maintains that this identity is disproved by a difference of style and diction.

No attempt has here been made to detail the grounds of these conflicting judgments, much less to decide between them. This will be done, so far as it seems necessary, in the exposition, and particularly in the introductions to the several chapters. The object aimed at in the foregoing statements is to shew that no additional security or certainty has been imparted in the criticism of the text by these empirical conjectures, and to confirm the previous assertion that they rest on no determinate intelligible principle or standard of comparison. A further confirmation of the same position is afforded by the tests of genuineness and antiquity, explicitly asserted and applied by the writers of this school. A more correct expression would perhaps be tests of spuriousness and later origin ; for, as we have already seen, the use of a criterion, in the hands of these critics, is seldom to establish or confirm, but almost always to discredit, what has commonly been looked upon as genuine.

One of the surest proofs of spuriousness, according to the theory and practice of this school, is the occurrence of idioms and words belonging to a period of Hebrew composition later than the days of Isaiah. This method of discrimination, however unobjectionable in itself, is nevertheless often so employed as to be altogether violent and arbitrary in its application. This is effected, first, by exaggerating, in the general, the real difference between the older and the later writings, and the practical facility of recognising the peculiar style of either. Conclusions which have properly been drawn, in one case, from a variety of premises, including the assumption of the date as a fact already known, are most unreasonably drawn in others, from a single element or item of the same proof in default of all the rest. This kind of sophistry is more delusive in the case of Hebrew than of Greek or Latin criticism, partly because we have fewer data upon which to form a judgment, partly because peculiar causes kept the written Hebrew more unchanged than other languages within a given period, and tended to obliterate in some degree the usual distinctive marks of earlier or later date. This is particularly true if we assume, as there are some strong grounds for doing, that the whole ancient literature of the Hebrews was contained in the canon of their scriptures, so that later writings were continually formed upon a few exclusive models. But whether this be so or not, the influence exerted by the books of Moses on the style and language of succeeding writers was immeasurably greater than in any other case at all analogous.

Besides this general and theoretical exaggeration of the difference between the older and the later Hebrew, there is also chargeable upon these critics an habitual proneness to lose sight of the distinction between what is really peculiar to the later books, or to the times in which they were composed, and that which after all, on any supposition, must be common to the different periods. That there must be a common stock of this kind is self-evident ; and that it must be very great in comparison with that which is peculiar and distinctive, is as fully established by the facts of this case and the analogy of others like it, as any maxim of comparative philology. And yet some German critics of the modern school, although they do not venture to avow the principle, proceed in practice just as if they held the use of an expression by a later writer to be in itself exclusive of its use by one of a preceding age. And even when they do profess to make the distinction just insisted on, they often make it in an arbitrary manner, or prevent its having any practical effect, by confounding archaisms with neologisms, *i. e.* mistaking for corruptions of a later age forms of expression which have been transmitted from the earliest period in the dialect of common life, but are only occasionally used in writing, and especially in poetry, until the language ceases to be spoken, and the difference of learned and colloquial style is thereby lost. The profounder study of comparative philology in very recent times has shewn the fallacy of many such objections to the antiquity of certain passages, and at the same time shaken the authority of similar criticisms in other cases, not admitting of direct refutation.

The bad effect of these fallacious principles of criticism is often aggravated by a want of consistency and fairness in their application. This is especially apparent in the younger German writers of this school, who often push to a practical extreme the theoretical assumptions of their more discreet or more enlightened teachers. Even where this is unintentionally done, it argues an eagerness to prove a point, or to sustain a foregone conclusion, not very likely to be found connected with a high degree of candour and impartiality. A signal illustration of this critical unfairness is the practice of evading the most certain indications of antiquity by noting them as imitations of a later writer. Where the recent date of the composition is already certain, the existence of such imitations may be certain also; but to assume them in the very process of determining the date, is little short of an absurdity. By setting down whatever can be found in other later books as proof of recent origin, and everything which cannot, as a studied imitation of antiquity, the oldest writings extant may be proved to be a hundred or a thousand years younger than themselves. Indeed, it may be stated as a fatal vice of this whole system, that it either proves too little or too much, that it is either pushed too far or that it ought to be pushed further, that the limit of its application is determined by no principle or rule but the convenience or caprice of the interpreter. *Stat pro ratione voluntas.* The critical process is too generally this, that where the admission of a passage as genuine would lead to consequences undesirable in any point of view, the critic fastens upon every singularity of thought or language as a ground of suspicion, and the most unmeaning trifles by accumulation are converted into arguments; whereas in other cases altogether parallel, except that there is no urgent motive for discrediting the passage, indications equally abundant and conclusive are entirely overlooked. Sometimes the evidence of later date is found exclusively in one part of a long unbroken context, all admitted to be written by the same hand, though the critic fails to see that this admission is destructive of his argument so far as it is founded on diversity of language as a test of age. For if a later writer can be so unlike himself, why not an older writer also ?

This remark, however, is applicable rather to the question of identity than that of age. For a favourite process of the modern critics, and especially of some below the highest rank, is that of proving a negative, by shewing that a passage or a book is not the work of its reputed author, without attempting to shew whose it is. Some of the means employed for the attainment of this end might seem incredible, as serious attempts at argument, but for the formal gravity with which they are employed. Sometimes the demonstration is effected by enumerating forms of expression, which occur nowhere else in the undisputed works of the reputed author, and inferring that he therefore could not have employed them in the case under consideration. The first absurdity of this ratiocination lies in the very principle assumed, which is, in fact, if not in form, that whatever any writer has said once, he must, as a general rule, have said again, if not repeatedly. Now what can be more certain or notorious than the fact that what the greatest writers say most frequently, is that which is least characteristic, while the thoughts and expressions which are most admired, quoted, and remembered, are for the most part ἅπαξ λεγόμενα, things which could only be said once, which would not bear to be repeated, by themselves or others ?   What would be thought of an attempt to prove the Ars Poetica spurious, on the ground that the words *exlex, sesquipedalia, cotis, litura, quincunce,* and the phrases *purpureus pannus, ab ovo, lucidus ordo, callida junctura, norma loquendi, in medias res, incredulus odi, sagax rerum, ad unguem, vivas voces, ore rotundo, decies repetita, laudator temporis acti,* the simile of the mountain and the mouse, and the proverbial saying, *occupet extremum scabies* occur nowhere else in the writings of Horace ? But this case, strong as it is, affords a very insufficient illustration of the theory and practice of the German critics now in question.   Not content with the assumption of a false and arbitrary test of identity, they make the application of it more unreasonable still, by rejecting every proof adduced in opposition to their doctrine, as itself suspicious, or unquestionably spurious.   A parallel case would be that of a critic who, on being reminded that the phrase *ab ovo* is used in the same sense in the third satire, and *ad unguem* in the first, should set the argument aside by referring both these compositions to the times of Juvenal or Persius.   With equal justice the tenth eclogue of Virgil might be taken from him, by first rejecting the Georgics and the last ten books of the Æneid as unquestionably spurious, and then enumerating all the single words, grammatical constructions, and peculiar idioms, to which no perfect counterparts are found in the remainder of his poems.

But besides this linguistical method of discrediting a large part of Isaiah as unquestionably not his composition, there is another process used for the same purpose, which may be entitled the rhetorical argument, consisting in the arbitrary affirmation that the style of certain passages is too prosaic, the metaphors too much confused, the rhythm too harsh, the allusions too obscure, the illustrations too familiar, the expression too inelegant, to be imputed to so great a writer.   This mode of criticism is pregnant with absurdities peculiar to itself.   In the first place may be stated the unreasonable weight which it attaches to rhetorical distinctions in general, not to mention the peculiar stress laid on the technicalities of scholastic rhetoric in particular.   This error is connected with a false hypothesis, to be considered afterwards, as to the light in which the prophets viewed themselves and were regarded by their readers.   If they aspired to be nothing more than orators and poets, then rhetorical considerations would of course be paramount ; but if they believed themselves, and were believed by others, to be inspired revealers of the will of God, it is absurd to imagine that they would or could allow the clear and strong expression of that will to be controlled by mere rhetorical punctilios.

Another flaw in this critical process is its puerile assumption that the prophets, even as mere orators and poets, must be always doing their best; that if ever striking, they must strike at all times ; that if ever tender, they must always melt ; that if they ever soar, they must be always in the clouds ; whereas analogy demonstrates that the greatest writers, both in prose and verse, go up by the mountains and down by the valleys, or in other words, exert their highest faculties at intervals, with long and frequent seasons of repose, while poetasters and declaimers prove the hollowness of their claims by a painful uniformity of tension and a wearisome monotony of failure.

A third defect is one which might with equal justice have been charged against some arguments before recited, namely, the vague and indeterminate character of this criterion, as evinced by the diversity of its results. Not only does one critic censure what another critic of the same school leaves unnoticed ; but the same thing is positively represented by the two as a beauty and a deformity, nay more, as fatal to the genuineness of a passage and as a certain demonstration of it. It may seem invidious and perhaps presumptuous to add, that this unsafe and two-edged instrument could scarcely be entrusted to worse hands than those of some late German critics, who, with all their erudition, ingenuity, and show of philosophical *aesthetics*, are peculiarly deficient in that delicate refinement and acute sensibility of taste, which a less profound but far more classical and liberal training has imparted even to inferior scholars of some other nations, and especially of England. To this unfavourable estimate of German taste and literary judgment there are eminent exceptions, even in the ranks of theological and biblical learning ; but among these it would be impossible to class the writers who are most remarkable for an unhesitating reckless use of the rhetorical criterion now in question. On the contrary, it may be stated as a curious and instructive fact, that the imputation of inelegance, awkwardness, obscurity, and coarseness, has been lavished on Isaiah with peculiar prodigality by those interpreters who seem to be most open to the charge themselves, and who, in the very act of passing judgment on the Prophet or his writings as devoid of taste and genius, often shew most painfully and clearly that their circumscribed professional pursuits, however thorough and successful, have been insufficient to compensate for the want of a more enlarged and humanizing culture.

The revulsion of feeling, necessarily occasioned in the great majority of uncultivated minds, by these rhetorical attacks upon some portions of Isaiah, with a view to prove them spurious, must be greatly aggravated by another argument employed for the same purpose, which may be distinguished from the lexicographical, grammatical, and rhetorical tests already mentioned, as the ethical or moral test. This consists simply in accusing certain passages of being animated by a narrow, selfish, mean, and sometimes even by a fierce, malignant, cruel, vindictive, bloodthirsty spirit wholly foreign from Isaiah's character, and from the temper of the age in which he lived. Without insisting on the arbitrary difference assumed in this objection to exist between certain periods of the sacred history, in point of moral elevation and enlargement, let it be observed how perfectly factitious and imaginary this peculiar tone of the disputed passages must be, when it has failed to strike the most enlightened readers of the Prophet for a course of ages. This is a question wholly different from that of philological or even rhetorical distinctions, which might easily escape the view of any but professional and critical readers, and be first discovered by the searching processes of modern scrutiny. But when the critic passes from the field of orthography and etymology to that of morals, he is stepping out of darkness into sunshine, from the bench to the bar, from the position of a judge to that of an advocate, who, far from being able to decide the controversy by a dictum, has to plead his cause at the tribunal of a multitude of trained minds, and enlightened consciences. The want of familiar and devotional acquaintance with the Scriptures, on the part of many learned German critics, must disable them from estimating the advantage thus enjoyed by Christian readers, whose opinions have been formed upon the Gospel, and who certainly would be the first to mark any real inconsistency between it and the spirit of the ancient prophets. To such spectators, and in such a light, there is something almost ludicrous in the solemnity with which some unbelievers in the inspiration of the Bible utter sanctimonious complaints of an immoral and unhallowed temper in those parts of the Old Testament which they, for reasons afterwards to be considered, are unwilling to acknowledge as authentic, while they pass by, with discreet indulgence, indications far more plausible in other places. If it be said, that these immoral tendencies escape the ordinary reader on account of his foregone conclusion that the whole proceeds from God, and therefore must be right ; the answer is, that a hypothesis, which thus brings all the parts of an extensive varied whole into agreement, bears upon its face the clearest marks of truth, and that the fact alleged affords an incidental proof that the position of the adverse party, which compels him to see everything distorted and at variance with itself, must be a false one.

This last suggestion opens a new view of the whole subject. Thus far the question has been stated and discussed as one of criticism merely, not of hermeneutics or of doctrinal belief, with a view to shew that even on historical and literary grounds, the modern German mode of dealing with the text of Isaiah, and of settling the antiquity and genuineness of its several parts, is wholly untenable, because capricious, arbitrary, inconsistent with itself, and at variance with analogy, good taste, and common sense. The reader must, however, have observed that in exposing the caprices of these critics, I have frequently described them as resorting to these methods only where they had strong reasons for desiring to discredit a particular portion of the book, at least so far as to dispute its antiquity. It will now be proper to explain how such a motive can be supposed to exist, the rather as the neological interpreters of Germany are often praised by their admirers, on the ground that, although they are sceptical, their very scepticism renders them impartial, and gives their testimony greater weight in every case except where the question of inspiration is directly and formally at issue. The practical effect of this superficial estimate has been the practice of adhering servilely to these neologists until they openly deny some fundamental doctrine of religion, then protesting against that specific error, and again walking closely in their footsteps, till another opportunity or palpable necessity for protestation or dissent occurs. Besides the want of harmony and unity in any course of criticism or exegesis thus conducted, it is evident that such a mode of dealing with a system, which is known and acknowledged to be unsound in principle, must lead the writer and the reader into many other dangers than the few which are upon the surface. *Incedis per ignes suppositos cineri doloso.* To avoid these hidden and insidious dangers, it is necessary to compare the different theories of criticism and interpretation, not in their formal differences merely, but in their intimate connection with diversities of fundamental principles and doctrinal belief. In order to effect this, it will be expedient to consider briefly the historical progress of opinion with respect to the principles of exegesis, as we have already traced the change of theory and practice in the treatment of the text. These two important parts of the same great subject will be found to illustrate and complete each other.

Isaiah himself, even leaving out of view the large part of his book which a capricious criticism has called in question, may be said to express everywhere his own belief that he was writing under an extraordinary influence, not merely human but divine. This is at least the *prima facie* view which any unsophisticated reader would derive from a simple perusal of his undisputed writings. However mistaken he might think the prophet, in asserting or assuming his own inspiration, such a reader could scarcely hesitate to grant that he believed it and expected it to be believed by others. In one of the oldest and best of the Jewish Apocrypha (Sirach xxiv. 25), Isaiah is called the great and faithful prophet who foresaw what was to happen till the end of time. Josephus and Philo incidentally bear witness to his universal recognition by their countrymen as one inspired of God.

We have seen already that our Lord and his apostles cite the whole book of Isaiah with more frequency than any other part of the Old Testament. It now becomes a question of historical interest at least, in what capacity and character Isaiah is thus quoted, and with what authority he seems to be invested in the New Testament. The simple fact that he is there so often quoted, when connected with another undisputed fact, to wit, that his writings, even at that early date, held a conspicuous place among the *Sacred Scriptures* (ἱερὰ γράμματα, γραφαὶ ἅγιαι) of the Jews, would of itself create a strong presumption that our Lord and his apostles recognised his inspiration and divine authority. We are not left, however, to infer this incidentally; for it is proved directly by the frequent combination of the title Prophet with the name Isaiah (Mat. iii. 3, iv. 14, viii. 17, xii. 17; Luke iii. 4, iv. 17; John i. 23, xiii. 28; Acts viii. 28–30, xxviii. 25); by the repeated statement that he prophesied or spoke by inspiration (Mark vii. 6; Rom. ix. 29); by the express declaration that some of his predictions were fulfilled in the history of Christ and his contemporaries (Mat. iii. 3, iv. 14, viii. 17; Acts xxiii. 25); and by the still more remarkable statement that Isaiah saw Christ and spake of his glory (John xii. 41). These expressions place it beyond all possibility of doubt that the New Testament describes Isaiah as a Prophet in the strictest and the highest sense inspired of God. This is alleged here, not as a reason for our own belief, but simply as a well-attested fact in the history of the interpretation.

Coming down a little lower, we find all the Christian Fathers taking for granted the divine authority and inspiration of the Prophet, and regulating their interpretation of his book accordingly. But not content with thus acknowledging his right to a place among the sacred books of the Old Testament, they ascribe to him a certain pre-eminence as belonging rather to the new dispensation. Eusebius describes him as the great and wonderful prophet, and even as the greatest of prophets. According to Cyril, he is at once a prophet and apostle; according to Jerome, not so much a prophet as an evangelist. The latter elsewhere represents him as *non solum prophetam sed evangelistam et apostolum*, and his book as *non prophetiam sed evangelium:* As the old Jewish doctrine upon this point is maintained by the rabbinical expounders of the Middle Ages, it may be affirmed that both the Old and New Testaments, according to the Jewish and the Christian tradition, represent Isaiah as inspired.

From the Fathers this doctrine passed without change into the Reformed Church, and from the Talmudists and Rabbins to the modern Jews, so far as they continue to adhere to their religion. Much as the Protestant Church has been divided since the Reformation, as to doctrine in general, as to the interpretation of Scripture in particular, and even with respect to the right method of interpreting Isaiah, all schools and parties, until after the middle of the eighteenth century, held fast to the inspiration of the Prophet as a fundamental principle, to which all theories and all exegetical results must be accommodated. Even the lax Arminian school of Grotius and Le Clerc, however much disposed to soften down the sharp points and asperities of orthodox opinion, upon this as well as other subjects, did not venture to disturb the old foundation. The very faults and errors, with which the stricter theologians charged their exegesis, were occasioned in a great degree by their attempt to reconcile more *liberal* and superficial views of the Prophet's meaning with the indisputable axiom of his inspiration. That a secret sceptical misgiving often gave complexion to their exegesis, is extremely probable ; but it is still true, that they did not venture to depart from the traditional opinion of the whole church in all ages, as to the canonical authority and inspiration of the book before us. They sought by various means to belittle and explain away the natural results of this great principle ; but with the principle itself they either did not wish or did not dare to meddle.

After the middle of the eighteenth century, a memorable change took place in Germany, as to the method of interpreting Isaiah. This change was closely connected with the one already mentioned, in relation to the criticism of the text. As the sceptical criticism of the classics was the model upon which that of the Hebrew text was formed, so a like imitation of the classical methods of interpretation became generally current. The favourite idea now was, that the Hebrew books were to be treated simply and solely as remains of ancient Jewish literature, and placed, if not upon a level with the Greek and Roman books, below them, as the products of a ruder period and a less gifted race. This affectation was soon carried out in its details *ad nauseam*. Instead of prophecies, and psalms, and history, the talk was now of poems, odes, orations, and mythology. The ecclesiastical and popular estimate of the books as sacred went for nothing, or was laughed at, as a relic of an antiquated system. This change, although apparently confined to technicalities, could never have been wrought without a deep defection from the ancient faith, as to the inspiration of the Scriptures. Under the pretext of exchanging barbarism for refinement, and of putting biblical and classical pursuits upon a footing of equality, the essential distinction between *literature* and *Scripture* was in fact abolished, without any visible or overt violence, by simply teaching men to treat them and to talk of them without discrimination.

This momentous change was undesignedly promoted by Lowth's ingenious and successful effort to direct attention to Isaiah's character and value as a poet. Believing justly that the exposition of the prophet's writings had been hindered and perplexed by a failure to appreciate the figurative dress in which his thoughts were clothed, the learned and accomplished prelate undertook to remedy the evil by presenting, in the strongest light and in extreme relief, this single aspect of Isaiah's writings. In attempting this, he was unconsciously led to overcolour and exaggerate the real points of difference between the ordinary prose of history or legislation and the lively elevated prose of prophecy, applying to the latter all the distinctive terms which immemorial usage had appropriated to the strictly metrical productions of the Greek and Roman poets. This error led to several unfortunate results, some of which will be considered in another place. The only one that need be mentioned here is the apparent countenance afforded by Lowth's theories and phraseology to the contemporary efforts of the earlier neologists in Germany to blot out the distinction between poetry and prophecy, between the ideal inspiration of the Muses and the real inspiration of the Holy Ghost. This was the more to be regretted, as there does not seem to be the slightest reason for suspecting that the Bishop had departed in the least from the established doctrine of

his own church and of every other, with respect to the divine authority
and origin of this or of the other sacred books.   That Lowth, by his unwarrantable changes of the text, and his exclusive disproportioned protrusion
of the mere poetical elements in Scripture, gave an impulse to a spirit of
more daring innovation in succeeding writers, is not more certain than the
fact, that this abuse of his hypotheses, or rather this legitimate deduction of
their more remote but unavoidable results, was altogether unforeseen.   In
ably and honestly attempting to correct a real error, and to make good an
injurious defect, in the theory and practice of interpretation, he unwittingly
afforded a new instance of the maxim, that the remedy may possibly be
worse than the disease.

By the German writers, these new notions were soon pushed to an extreme.
Besides the total change of phraseology already mentioned, some went so
far as to set down the most express predictions as mere poetical descriptions of events already past.   From this extreme position, occupied by
Eichhorn and some others, De Wette and Gesenius receded, as they did
from the critical extravagance of multiplying authors and reducing the
ancient prophecies to fragments.   They admitted, not only that many portions of Isaiah had reference to events still future when he wrote, but also
that he was inspired, reserving to themselves the right of putting a convenient sense on that equivocal expression.   Among the later German writers
on Isaiah, there is a marked variety of tone, as to the light in which the
Prophet is to be regarded.   While all, in general terms, acknowledge his
genius and the literary merit of his writings, some, in expounding them,
appear to vacillate between condescension and contempt.   Of this class
Hitzig is perhaps the lowest; Knobel and Hendewerk exhibit the same
peculiarities with less uniformity and in a less degree.   Gesenius treats his
subject with the mingled interest and indifference of an antiquary handling
a curious and valuable relic of the olden time.   Ewald rises higher in his
apparent estimation of his subject, and habitually speaks of Isaiah in terms
of admiration and respect.   Umbreit goes still further in the same direction,
and employs expressions which would seem to identify him fully with the
orthodox believing school of criticism, but for his marked agreement with
neology in one particular, about to be stated.

The successive writers of this modern school, however they may differ as
to minor points among themselves, prove their identity of principle by holding that *there cannot be distinct prophetic foresight of the distant future.*
This doctrine is avowed more explicitly by some (as by Hitzig and Knobel)
than by others (as Gesenius and Ewald ;) but it is really the πρῶτον
ψεῦδος of the whole school, and the only bond of unity between them.
There is also a difference in the application of the general rule to specific
cases.   Where the obvious exposition of a passage would convert it into
a distinct prediction, Gesenius and Hitzig usually try to shew that the
words really relate to something near at hand, and within the reach of
a sagacious human foresight, while Ewald and Umbreit in the same case
choose rather to convert it into a vague anticipation.   But they all agree
in this, that where the prophecy can be explained away in either of these
methods, it must be regarded as a certain proof of later date.   This is the
real ground, on which chaps. xl.–xlvi. are referred to the period of the exile,
when the conquests of Cyrus and the fall of Babylon might be foreseen
without a special revelation.   This is the fundamental doctrine of the
modern neological interpreters, the *foregone conclusion,* to which all exegetical results must yield or be accommodated, and in support of which the

arbitrary processes before described must be employed for the discovery of arguments, philological, historical, rhetorical, and moral, against the genuineness of the passage, which might, just as easily be used in other cases, where they are dispensed with, simply because they are not needed for the purpose of destroying an explicit proof of inspiration.

From this description of the neological interpretation there are two important practical deductions. The first and clearest is, that all conclusions founded, or necessarily depending, on this false assumption, must of course go for nothing with those who do not hold it, and especially with those who are convinced that it is false. Whoever is persuaded, independently of these disputed questions, that there may be such a thing as a prophetic inspiration, including the gift of prescience and prediction, must of course be unaffected by objections to its exercise in certain cases, resting on the general negation of that which he knows to be true. The other inference, less obvious but for that very reason more important, is that the false assumption now in question must exert and does exert an influence extending far beyond the conclusions directly and avowedly drawn from it. He who rejects a given passage of Isaiah, because it contains definite predictions of a future too remote from the times in which he lived, to be the object of ordinary human foresight, will of course be led to justify this condemnation by specific proofs drawn from the diction, style, or idiom of the passage, its historical or archaeological allusions, its rhetorical character, its moral tone, or its religious spirit. On the discovery and presentation of such proofs, the previous assumption, which they are intended to sustain, cannot fail to have a warping influence. The writer cannot but be tempted to give prominence to trifles, to extenuate difficulties, and to violate consistency by making that a proof in one case which he overlooks in others, or positively sets aside as inadmissible or inconclusive. This course of things is not only natural but real ; it may not only be expected *a priori*, but established *ex eventu*, as will be apparent from a multitude of cases in the course of the ensuing exposition. All that need here be added is the general conclusion, that the indirect effects of such a principle are more to be suspected than its immediate and avowed results, and that there cannot be a graver practical error than the one already mentioned of obsequiously following these writers as authoritative guides, except when they explicitly apply their πρῶτον ψεῦδος as a test of truth. The only safe and wise course is to treat them, not as judges, but as witnesses, or advocates, and even special pleaders ; to weigh their *dicta* carefully, and always with a due regard to what is known to be the unsound basis of their criticism and exegesis. That this discretion may be vigilantly exercised, without foregoing the advantages arising from the modern philological improvements, is attested by the actual example of such men as Hengstenberg and Hävernick and others, trained in the modern German school of philology, and fully able to avail themselves of its advantages, while at the same time they repudiate its arbitrary principles in favour of those held by older writers, which may now be considered as more sure than ever; because founded on a broader scientific basis, and because their strength has been attested by resistance to assaults as subtle and as violent as they can ever be expected to encounter. Some of the critical and hermeneutical principles thus established may be here exhibited, as furnishing the basis upon which the following exposition of Isaiah is constructed.

In the first place, it may be propounded, as a settled principle of critical investigation, that the bare suggestion of a way in which the text may have been altered in a given case, and the *ipsissima verba* of the author, either by fraud or accident, confounded with the language of a later writer, only creates a feeble probability in favour of the emendation recommended, so as at the utmost to entitle it to be compared with the received opinion. Even the clearest case of critical conjecture, far from determining the question in dispute, only affords us an additional alternative, and multiplies the objects among which we are to choose. Our hypothesis may possibly be right, but it may possibly be wrong, and between these possibilities mere novelty is surely not sufficient to decide. The last conjecture is not on that account entitled to the preference. There are, no doubt, degrees of probability, susceptible of measurement; but in a vast majority of cases, the conjectural results of the modern criticism are precisely such as no one would think of entertaining unless previously determined to abandon the traditional or prevalent belief. If the common text, or the common opinion of its genuineness, be untenable, these critical conjectures may afford the most satisfactory substitute; but they do not of themselves decide the previous question, upon which their own utility depends. If the last chapters of Isaiah cannot be the work of their reputed author, then it is highly probable that they were written towards the close of the Babylonish exile; but it cannot be inferred from this conditional admission, that they are not genuine, any more than we can argue that a statement is untrue, because *if not true* it is false. The characteristic error of the modern criticism is its habitual rejection of a reading or interpretation, not because another is intrinsically better, but simply because there *is* another to supply its place. In other words, it is assumed that, in a doubtful case, whatever is established and received is likely to be spurious, and whatever is suggested for the first time likely to be genuine, and therefore entitled not only to be put upon a footing of equality with that to which it is opposed, but to take precedence of it, so that every doubt must be allowed to operate against the old opinion and in favour of the new one.

But in the second place, so far is this from being the true principle, that the direct reverse is true. Not only are the chances, or the general presumption, not in favour of a change or innovation, as such; they are against it, and in favour of that which has long been established and received. The very fact of such reception is presumptive proof of genuineness, because it shews how many minds have so received it without scruple or objection, or in spite of both. Such a presumption may indeed be overcome by countervailing evidence; but still the presumption does exist, and is adverse to innovations, simply viewed as such. If it were merely on the ground, that the mind, when perplexed by nearly balanced probabilities, seeks something to destroy the equilibrium, and finds it in the previous existence of the one belief and its reception by a multitude of minds, we might allege the higher claims of that which is established and received, if not as being certainly correct, as having been so thought by others. In this the human mind is naturally prone to rest, until enabled by preponderating evidence to make its own decision, so that even in the most doubtful cases, it is safer and easier to abide by what has long been known and held as true, than to adopt a new suggestion, simply because it cannot be proved false. Here again the fashionable modern criticism differs from that which is beginning even in Germany to supersede it, inasmuch as the former allows all the benefit of doubt to innovation, while the latter gives it to received opinions.

The general principle just stated is peculiarly important and appropriate in the criticism of the Hebrew text, because so far as we can trace its history, it has been marked by a degree of uniformity, arising from a kind of supervision, to which no other ancient writings, even the most sacred, seem to have been subjected, not excepting the books of the New Testament. To call this Jewish scrupulosity and superstition does not in the least impair the strong presumption which it raises in favour of the text as it has been transmitted to us, and against the emendations of conjectural criticism. The wonderful resemblance of the Hebrew manuscripts now extant is admitted upon all hands, and explained as an effect of the masoretic labours in the sixth or seventh century, by means of which one Hebrew text acquired universal circulation. But this explanation needs itself to be explained. The possibility of thus reducing many texts to one has nothing to support it in the analogy of other languages or other writings. The variations of the text of the New Testament afford a memorable instance of the contrary. It is in vain to say that no such means were used to harmonise and reconcile the manuscripts; in other words, that no Greek masora existed. How can its absence be accounted for, except upon the ground, that the Hebrew critics followed ancient usage, and recorded a tradition which had been in existence for a course of ages? These considerations do not go to prove the absolute perfection of the masoretic text; but they unquestionably do create a very strong presumption—stronger by far than in any other like case—against innovation and in favour of tradition. The validity of this conclusion is in fact conceded by the signal unanimity with which the recent German critics, of all classes, set aside the fantastic mode of criticism practised by Cappellus, Houbigant, and Lowth, and assume the correctness of the masoretic text in every case except where they are driven from it by the stress of exegetical necessity. That the principle thus universally adopted in relation to the criticism of letters, words, and phrases, is not extended by these critics to the criticism of larger passages, argues no defect or error in the principle itself, but only a want of consistent uniformity in its application. If it be true, as all now grant, that in relation to the elements of speech, to letters, words, and single phrases, we may safely presume that the existing text is right till it is shewn to be wrong, how can it be, that in relation to whole sentences or larger contexts, the presumption is against the very same tradition until positively proved to be correct? That this is a real inconsistency is not only plain upon the face of it, but rendered more unquestionable by the very natural and easy explanation of which it is susceptible. The criticism of words and letters, though identical in principle with that of entire passages, is not so closely connected with the evidence of inspiration and prophetic foresight, and is therefore less subject to the operation of the fundamental error of the rationalistic system. This is the more remarkable because in certain cases, where the main question happens to turn upon a single word or letter, there we find the same capricious licence exercised, without regard to probability or evidence, as in the ordinary processes of criticism on a larger scale. From these theoretical concessions and these practical self-contradictions of the modern critics, we may safely infer the indisputable truth of the critical principles which they are forced to grant, and from which they depart in practice only when adherence to them would involve the necessity of granting that, the absolute negation of which is the fundamental doctrine of their system.

All this would be true and relevant, if the book in question were an ancient classic, handed down to us in the manner just described. But

Isaiah constitutes a part of a collection claiming to be a divine revelation. It is itself expressly recognised as such in the sacred books of the Christian religion. The authenticity and inspiration of the parts are complicated together, and involved in the general question of the inspiration of the whole. Whatever evidence goes to establish that of the New Testament, adds so much to the weight of Isaiah's authority. Whatever strength the claims of the New Testament derive from miracles, from moral effects, from intrinsic qualities, is shared in some measure by the book before us. The same thing is true of the external and internal evidence that the Old Testament proceeds from God. The internal character of this one book, its agreement with the other parts of Scripture, and with our highest conceptions of God, the place which it has held in the estimation of intelligent and good men through a course of ages, its moral and spiritual influence on those who have received it as the Word of God, so far as this can be determined separately from that of the whole Bible or of the entire Old Testament ; all this invests the book with an authority and dignity which shield it from the petty caprices of a trivial criticism. Those who believe, on these grounds, that the book, as a whole, is inspired of God, not only may, but must be unwilling to give ear to every sceptical or frivolous suggestion as to the genuineness of its parts. Even if there were more ground for misgiving than there is, and fewer positive proofs of authenticity, he whose faith is founded, not on detached expressions or minute agreements, but on the paramount claims of the whole as such to his belief and reverence, would rather take for granted, in a dubious case, that God had providentially pre-served the text intact, than lift the anchor of his faith and go adrift upon the ocean of conjecture, merely because he could not answer every fool according to his folly.

The result of these considerations is, that as the neological interpreters assume the impossibility of inspiration and prophetic foresight, as a principle immoveable by any indications to the contrary, however clear and numerous, so those who hold the inspiration of the Scriptures as a certain truth, should suffer this their general belief to influence their judgment on par-ticular questions, both of criticism and interpretation. The effect should not be that of closing the mind against conviction, where the reasons are sufficient to produce it, but simply that of hindering all concessions to an arbitrary and capricious licence of conjecture, and all gratuitous sacrifices of received opinion to the mere possibility of some new notion. It is certainly not to be expected that believers in the inspiration of the Bible as a whole, should be content to give up any of its parts as readily as if it were an old song, or even a more valuable relic of some heathen writer.

In conformity with what has just been stated as the only valid principle of *criticism*, in the technical or strict sense, the laws of *interpretation* may be well defined to be those of common sense, controlled by a regard to the divine authority and inspiration of the book, considered as a fact already established or received as true. The design of biblical interpretation is not to prove, although it may illustrate, the canonical authority of that which is interpreted. This is a question to be previously settled, by a view of the whole book, or of the whole collection which includes it, in connection with the various grounds on which its claims to such authority are rested. Every competent expounder of Isaiah, whether infidel or Christian, comes before the public with his opinion upon this point formed, and with a fixed deter-mination to regulate his treatment of particulars accordingly. The writer who should feign to be neutral or indifferent in this respect, would find it hard to gain the public ear, and harder still to control the public judgment. While the rationalist therefore avowedly proceeds upon the supposition, that the book before him is and can be nothing more than a human composition, it is not only the right but the duty of the Christian interpreter to treat it as the work both of God and man, a divine revelation and a human composition, the contents of which are never to be dealt with in a manner inconsistent either with the supposition of its inspiration or with that of its real human origin. The latter hypothesis is so essential, that there cannot be a sound interpretation, where there is not a consistent and a constant application of the same rules which control the exposition of all other writings, qualified only by a constant recollection of the well-attested claims of the book expounded to the character of a divine revelation. One important practical result of this assumption is, that seeming contradictions and discrepancies are neither to be passed by, as they might be in an ordinary composition, nor regarded as so many refutations of the doctrine that the writing which contains them is inspired of God, but rather interpreted with due regard to the analogy of Scripture, and with a constant preference, where other things are equal, of those explanations which are most in agreement with the general fact of inspiration upon which the exposition rests. The attempt to explain every passage or expression by itself, and to assume the *prima facie* meaning as in every case the true one, without any reference to other parts of the same book, or to other books of the same collection, is absurd in theory and directly contradicted by the universal usage of mankind in determining the sense of other writings, while it practically tends to put the Christian interpreter in a situation of extreme disadvantage with respect to the neologist, who does not hesitate to press into the service of his own interpretation every argument afforded by analogy. The evil effect of this mistaken notion on the part of Christian writers is not merely that they often fail to vindicate the truth, but that they directly contribute to the triumph of its enemies.

With respect to the prophetic parts of Scripture, and to the writings of Isaiah in particular, a few exegetical maxims may be added to the general principles already stated. These, for the most part, will be negative in form, as being intended to preclude certain fallacies and practical errors, which have greatly hindered the correct interpretation of the book before us. The generic formulas here used will be abundantly exemplified hereafter by specific instances arising in the course of the interpretation.

All prophecies are not predictions, *i. e.* all the writings of the Prophets, and of this one in particular, are not to be regarded as descriptive of future events. The contrary error, which has arisen chiefly from the modern and restricted usage of the word prophet and its cognate terms, has generated some of the most crude extravagances of prophetic exegesis. It has been shewn already, by a historical and philological induction, that the scriptural idea of prophecy is far more extensive, that the prophets were inspired to reveal the truth and will of God, in reference to the past and present, no less than the future. In Isaiah, for example, we find many statements of a general nature, and particularly exhibitions of the general principles which govern the divine administration, especially in reference to the chosen people and their enemies or persecutors.

All predictions, or prophecies in the restricted sense, are not specific and exclusive, *i. e.* limited to one occasion or emergency, but many are descriptive of a sequence of events which has been often realized. The vagueness and indefiniteness which might seem to attach to such predictions, and (by making their fulfilment more uncertain) to detract from their impressiveness and value, are precluded by the fact that, while the whole prediction frequently admits of this extensive application, it includes allusions to particular events, which can hardly be mistaken. Thus in some parts of Isaiah, there are prophetic pictures of the sieges of Jerusalem, which cannot be exclusively applied to any one event of that kind, but the terms and images of which are borrowed partly from one and partly from another through a course of ages. This kind of prophecy, so far from being vague and unimpressive, is the clearest proof of real inspiration, because more than any other beyond the reach of ordinary human foresight. Thus the threatening against Babylon, contained in the thirteenth and fourteenth chapters of Isaiah, if explained as a specific and exclusive prophecy of the Medo-Persian conquest, seems to represent the downfall of the city as more sudden and complete than it appears in history, and on the other hand affords a pretext, though a very insufficient one, for the assertion that it may have been composed so near the time of the events foretold as to bring them within the reach of uninspired but sagacious foresight. No such hypothesis, however, will account for the extraordinary truth of the prediction when regarded as a panorama of the fall of Babylon, not in its first inception merely, but through all its stages till its consummation.

All the predictions of Isaiah, whether general or specific, are not to be literally understood. The ground of this position is the fact, universally admitted, that the prophecies abound in metaphorical expressions. To assert that this figurative character is limited to words and clauses, or at most to single sentences, is wholly arbitrary, and at variance with the acknowledged use of parables, both in the Old and New Testament, in which important doctrines and events are presented under a tropical costume, throughout a passage sometimes of considerable length. These facts are sufficient to sustain the negative position, that the prophecies are not invariably clothed in literal expressions, or in other words are not to be always literally understood.

The prophecies of this book are not to be always understood in a figurative or spiritual sense. The contrary assumption has engendered a vast motley multitude of mystical and anagogical interpretations, sometimes superadded to the obvious sense, and sometimes substituted for it, but in either case obscuring the true import and defeating the design of the prediction. The same application of the laws of common sense and of general analogy, which shews that some predictions must be metaphorical, shews that others must be literal. To assert, without express authority, that prophecy must always and exclusively be one or the other, is as foolish as it would be to assert the same thing of the whole conversation of an individual throughout his lifetime, or of human speech in general. No valid reason can be given for applying this exclusive canon of interpretation to the prophecies, which would not justify its application to the Iliad, the Æneid, the Divina Commedia, or the Paradise Lost, an application fruitful only in absurdities. Isaiah's prophecies are therefore not to be expounded on the general principle, that either a literal or figurative sense must be assumed wherever it is possible. We have already seen the fallacies resulting from the assumption, that whatever is possible is probable or certain. To set aside the obvious and strict sense, wherever it can be done without absurdity, is forbidden by the very nature of the difference between literal and figurative language. That which is regular and normal must at times assert its rights or it becomes anomalous. On the other hand, to claim precedence for the strict and proper sense, in every case, is inconsistent with the fact that symbols, emblems, images, and tropes, are characteristic of prophetic language. In a word, the question between literal and tropical interpretation is not to be determined by the application of invariable formulas. The same remark may be applied to the vexed question with respect to types and double senses. The old extreme of constantly assuming these wherever it is possible, and the later extreme of denying their existence, may be both considered as exploded errors. That words may be naturally used with a primary and secondary reference, is clear from all analogy. That some things in the old dispensation were intended to be types of corresponding objects in the new, is clear from the New Testament. A fantastic *philotypia* is not more likely to engender error than a morbid *typophobia*, except that the first is not merely negative in its effects, and may be exercised *ad libitum*, whereas the other prides itself on never adding to the revelation, but is satisfied with taking from it. Both may exist, and both must be avoided, not by the use of nostrums and universal rules, but by the exercise of sound discretion in specific cases, guided by the obvious canon, founded on experience and analogy, that types and double senses do not constitute the staple even of prophetic language, and are therefore not to be wantonly assumed, in cases where a simpler and more obvious exposition is abundantly sufficient to meet all the requisitions of the text and context.

The question, under which of these descriptions any prophecy must be arranged, *i.e.* the question whether it is strictly a prediction, and if so, whether it is general or particular, literal or figurative, can only be determined by a thorough independent scrutiny of each case by itself, in reference to form and substance, text and context, without regard to arbitrary and exclusive theories, but with a due regard to analogy of Scripture in general, and of other prophecies in particular, especially of such as belong to the same writer, or at least to the same period, and apparently relate to the same subject. This is far from being so attractive or so easy as the sweeping application of a comprehensive canon to all cases, like and unlike; but it seems to be the only process likely to afford a satisfactory result, and one main purpose of the following exposition is to prove its efficacy by a laborious and fair experiment.

In executing this design, it is essential that regard should be paid to the exterior form as well as to the substance of a passage, that rhetorical embellishments should be distinguished from didactic propositions, that prosaic and poetical peculiarities should be distinctly and correctly estimated at their real value. Experience has clearly shewn, that such discrimination does not always accompany the habit of perpetually praising the sublimity and beauty of the author's style, a practice perfectly compatible with very indistinct and even false conceptions of rhetorical propriety. The characteristics of Isaiah, as a writer, appear by some to be regarded as consisting merely in the frequent occurrence of peculiar forms of speech, for which they are continually on the watch, and ever ready to imagine if they cannot find them. The favourite phenomenon of this kind with the latest writers is *paronomasia*, an intentional resemblance in the form or sound of words which are nearly related to each other in a sentence. The frequent occurrence of this figure in Isaiah is beyond a doubt; but the number of the instances has been extravagantly multiplied; in some cases, it would almost seem, for the purpose of detracting from the author's merits; sometimes with an honest but mistaken disposition to enhance it. It is an important observation of Ewald's, that a mere assonance of words is probably fortuitous, except where a similar relation can be traced between the thoughts which they express. The truth in reference to this and many other kindred topics, can be ascertained only in the way proposed above, *i.e.* by a due regard to the matter and the manner of each passage in itself considered. This discriminating process necessarily involves a scrupulous avoidance of two opposite extremes, which have, at different periods, and in some cases simultaneously, done much to pervert and hinder the interpretation of the book before us. The first extreme, particularly prevalent in earlier times, is that of understanding the most highly wrought descriptions, the most vivid imagery, the boldest personifications, as mere prose. This is especially exemplified in the irrational and tasteless manner of expounding apologues and parables by many of the older writers, who insist on giving a specific sense to circumstances which are significant only as parts of one harmonious whole. The other extreme, of which we have already traced the origin, is that of turning elevated prose diversified by bursts of poetry, into a regular poem or series of poems, technically so considered, and subjecting them as such to all the tests and rules of classical poetry, and even to the canons of its versification. To expound Isaiah without any reference to the perpetual recurrence of antitheses and other parallel constructions, would be now a proof of utter incapacity. Far more indulgence would be probably extended to the no less extravagant but much less antiquated error of seeking perfect parallels in every sentence, torturing the plain sense into forced conformity with this imaginary standard, altering the text to suit it, and in short converting a natural and unstudied form, in which the Hebrew mind expressed itself without regard to rules or systems, into a rigorous scholastic scheme of prosody. The recurrence of a certain theme, refrain, or burden at nearly equal intervals—a structure natural and common in the elevated prose of various nations, for example in the sermons of the great French preachers—may be very properly compared to the strophical arrangements of the Greek dramatic style. But when, instead of an illustrative comparison, the passages thus marked are gravely classed as real strophes and antistrophes, and formally distributed among imaginary choruses of Prophets, Jews, and so forth, this pedantic affectation of confounding Hebrew prophecies with Greek plays, becomes chargeable with *wasteful and ridiculous excess.* It can only be regarded as a natural and necessary consequence of this overstrained analogy between things which occasionally coincide in form, that some of the most recent German critics do not hesitate to strike whole verses from the text of Isaiah, on the ground that they cannot be genuine because they make the strophes unequal, and that one of them winds up a comparison between prophetic and dramatic poetry with several pages of imagery, farfetched or fortuitous coincidences, both of thoughts and words, between the writings of Isaiah and the Eumenides of Æschylus. The golden mean between these hurtful and irrational extremes appears to lie in the assiduous observance of the true poetical ingredients of Isaiah's style, both in themselves and in their various combinations, with a rigid abstinence from all scholastic and pedantic theories of Hebrew poetry, and all peculiar forms and methods which have sprung from them or tend to their promotion.

Under this last description may be properly included the fantastic and injurious mode of printing most translations of Isaiah since the days of Lowth, in lines analogous to those of classical and modern verse. This arrangement, into which the good taste of the Bishop was betrayed by a natural but overweening zeal for his supposed discovery of rhythm or measure in the Hebrew prophets, and which the bad taste of succeeding writers bids fair to perpetuate, is open to a number of objections. In the first place, it proceeds upon a false or at least exaggerated supposition, that Isaiah wrote in what we are accustomed to call verse. If the predominance of parallel constructions is a sufficient reason for this mode of printing, then it might be adopted with propriety in many works which all the world regard as prose, in various parts at least of Seneca, Augustine, Larochefoueauld, Pascal, Johnson, and even Macaulay. The extent to which it might be carried is exemplified by Bishop Jebb's ingenious effort to extend Lowth's system to the Greek of the New Testament, in doing which he actually prints long extracts from the Gospels in the form of Lowth's Isaiah. Another proof of the unsoundness of the theory, when carried thus far, is the want of unity among the various practitioners, in Germany and England, with respect to the division and arrangement of the clauses, the regard due to the masoretic accents, and the rhythmical principle on which the whole must after all depend. Between some specimens of this mode of typography there seems to be scarcely any thing in common but the uneven termination of the lines. A third objection to this mode of printing is the fact, which any correct eye and ear may bring to an experimental test, that so far from enhancing the effect of the peculiar construction of Isaiah's sentences, it greatly mars it, and converts a *numerous prose* into the blankest of all blank verse, by exciting expectations which of course cannot be realized, suggesting the idea of a poetical metre in the strict sense, and then thwarting it by consecutions wholly inconsistent with the fundamental principles of prosody, however sonorous or euphonic in themselves. In England and America, this modern fashion seems to be already an established usage, and is even pushed so far as to require quotations from certain parts of Scripture to be printed like poetical extracts in a small type and in lines by themselves, a usage which we may expect to see extended to the rest of the Bible on the principles of Jebb. In Germany, the younger and inferior writers appear still enamoured of this wonderful discovery; but some of their more eminent interpreters, above the common average in taste, exhibit symptoms of reaction. Ewald contents himself with marking the divisions of the sentences and clauses after the manner of bars in music, while De Wette, in his excellent translation of the Bible, prints the whole like prose. This is the more significant because DeWette, in his introduction to the Psalms, had carried out Lowth's system of parallelisms in detail, with greater minuteness and precision than any preceding writer. In the preface to his Bible, he speaks of the arrangement of the Hebrew distichs in distinct lines, as of value only to the Hebrew scholar, while Ewald says expressly that the modern custom violates the ancient usage, and mistakes for poetry the mixed or intermediate prophetic style. Partly for these and other reasons of a kindred nature, founded on what I believe to be the true characteristics of Isaiah's style, partly in order to save room for more important matters than the marking of divisions, which the simplest reader even of a version can distinguish for himself so far as they have any real value, the translation of Isaiah will be found in this work printed as prose, and in the closest union with the exposition. This is the method which has been successfully pursued by several judicious German writers of the present day, especially by Hengstenberg, as well in his Christology as in his Commentary on the Psalms, perhaps as a matter of convenience merely, but it may be also with regard to some of the considerations which have just been stated. With respect to the translation in the present volume, this arrangement is moreover rendered necessary by the relation which it is intended to sustain to the exegetical matter which accompanies it. No attempt has here been made to give a new translation of the book, complete in itself, and suited for continuous perusal. The translation is part and parcel of the commentary, closely incorporated with it, and in some degree inseparable from it. After the study of a passage with the aid here furnished, it may no doubt be again read with advantage in this version, for the sake of which it has been not only printed in a different type, but generally placed at the beginning of the paragraph. This explanation seems to be required, as the whole form and manner of the version have been modified by this design. If meant for separate continuous perusal, it must of course have been so constructed as to be easily intelligible by itself; whereas a version introduced as a text or basis of immediate exposition, admitted of a closer approximation to the idiomatic form of the original, with all its occasional obscurity and harshness, than would probably have been endured by readers of refined taste in an independent version.

To this account of the precise relation which the version of Isaiah in this volume bears to the accompanying exposition, may be added a brief statement of the twofold object which the whole work is intended to accomplish, namely, a correct interpretation and a condensed historical synopsis of opinions with respect to it. The arduous task here undertaken is to aid the reader in determining the sense, not only by my own suggestions, but by those of others. This historical element has been introduced both as a means ·of exegetical improvement, and for its own sake, as an interesting chapter of the history of opinion on a highly important subject. In order to appreciate the particular results of this historical analysis, it will be proper to give some account of the materials employed. A brief and general sketch of the progress of opinion and of gradual changes in the method of interpretation having been previously given in a different connection, it will only be necessary here to add a chronological enumeration of the works which have exerted the most lasting and extensive influence on the interpretation of Isaiah.

The first place in this enumeration is of course due to the Ancient Versions, and among these to the Greek translation commonly called the Septuagint, from the old tradition of its having been produced by seventy-two Jews at Alexandria in the reign of Ptolemy Philadelphus. The additional circumstances, such as the translation of the whole law by each man separately, and their entire agreement afterwards, are not found in the oldest authorities, and are now rejected as mere fables. It is even a matter of dispute among the learned, whether the whole of this translation was executed at once or by degrees, by few or many writers, for the use of the synagogues in Egypt, or as a mere literary enterprise. Against the unity of the translation is the different character of the version in different parts. The Pentateuch is commonly regarded as the best, and Daniel as the worst. The version of Isaiah is intermediate between these. It is important as the record òf an ancient exegetical tradition, and on account of the use made of it in the New Testament. The writer shews a special acquaintance with the usages and products of Egypt, but is ˘grammatically very inexact, and governed in translation by no settled principle. Hence he abounds in needless paraphrases and additions, euphemistic variations, and allusions to opinions and events of later times, although the number of these has been exaggerated by some critics. The Hebrew text used by this translator seems to have been the one now extant, but without the masoretic points. The seeming variations used by Houbigant and Lowth as means of textual correction, are most probably the mere result of ignorance or inadvertence. The extreme opinions formerly maintained in reference to this version have been gradually exchanged for a more moderate and discriminating estimate, acknowledging its use in many cases of difficult interpretation, but denying its paramount authority in any. Besides the frequent citation of the Septuagint, occasional reference will be made to the other old Greek versions of Aquila, Symmachus, and Theodotion, fragments of which have been preserved by early writers. Of these interpreters, Aquila is commonly supposed to have been distinguished by his slavish adherence to the letter of the Hebrew, Symmachus by freedom and a greater regard to the Greek idiom, while Theodotion stood in these respects between them.

Next to these versions stands the Chaldee Paraphrase or Targum of Jonathan Ben Uzziel, the date of which is much disputed, but assigned by a majority of modern critics to the time of Christ, or that immediately preceding. It derives its value partly from its high repute and influence among the Jews, partly from its intrinsic character, as being on the whole a skilful and correct translation into a cognate dialect, although disfigured like the Septuagint by many arbitrary explanations, by additions to the text, and by allusions to the usages and doctrines of the later Jews. Its critical as well as exegetical adherence to the masoretic text is much more close than that of the oldest Greek translator.

The ancient Syriac version, commonly called the Peshito, on account of its simplicity and fidelity, is one of the most valuable extant. Its precise date is unknown, but it appears to have been looked upon as ancient, and occasionally needing explanation, even in the days of Ephrem Syrus. It has been ascribed by different critics to a Jewish and a Christian writer, but the latter supposition is the best sustained, both by external and internal evidence. The opinion of some writers, as to the use made by this translator of the Targum and Septuagint, appears to be regarded now as groundless, or at least exaggerated. This version as a whole, is characterised by great exactness and a close adherence to the original expression, rendered easy by the near affinity of Syriac and Hebrew.

The Vulgate or common Latin version of Isaiah, regarded as authentic in the Church of Rome, was executed by Jerome about the end of the fourth century, and afterwards substituted for the old Latin version, commonly called Itala, in use before, of which only fragments are now extant. This version, notwithstanding many errors and absurd interpretations, is on the whole a valuable record of ancient exegetical tradition, and of the fruit of Jerome's oriental studies. Its influence on modern exegesis, more especially within the Church of Rome, has of course been very extensive.

In these four versions we possess what may be called the exegetical tradition of the Jewish Synagogue, the Latin Church, the Greek Church, and the Syrian Church in all its branches. This, in addition to their mere antiquity, entitles them to a consideration which cannot be claimed by other versions, even though intrinsically more correct. At the same time let it be observed, that in addition to the original defects of these translations, their text is no doubt greatly corrupted, having never been subjected to any such conservative process as the Masora or critical tradition of the Jews. This fact alone shews the folly of attempting to ascribe to either of these versions a traditional authority superior to that of the Hebrew text. From

these direct and primary versions, many mediate or secondary ones were
formed in early times, the exegetical authority of which is naturally far
inferior, although they are occasionally useful in determining the text of
their originals, and even in explaining them, while still more rarely they
exhibit independent and remarkable interpretations of the Hebrew text.
To some of these mediate versions, there will be found occasional references in the present work, especially to the Arabic version of the Septuagint, made at Alexandria, and printed in the third volume of the London
Polyglot.   A still more frequent mention will be made of an immediate
Arabic version by the celebrated Jewish teacher and grammarian of the
tenth century, Saadias Gaon, whose translation of the Pentateuch is found
in the same Polyglot, although his verison of Isaiah was not brought to
light till near the end of the last century.   Both in its merits and defects,
it resembles the more ancient versions, but approaches still more closely to
the exegesis of the rabbins.   The occasional citations of this version are
derived from other writers, and particularly from Gesenius.

Next to the Ancient Versions may be named the Greek and Latin Fathers
who have written on Isaiah.   Besides Origen and others, whose interpretations have been wholly or in a great measure lost, there are still extant
those of Eusebius, Cyril of Alexandria, Chrysostom, Theodoret, and Procopius, on the whole or part of the Septuagint version of Isaiah.   These
are valuable, not so much from any direct aid which they afford in the interpretation of the Hebrew text, as for the light which they throw upon the
prevalent theories of interpretation at a remote period, and especially upon
the allegorical and mystical method of expounding the Old Testament, of
which Origen, if not the inventor, was the most successful champion and
practitioner.   Jerome, the only Latin Father who has written on Isaiah,
while he has some defects and faults in common with the Greek expounders, has the great advantage of direct acquaintance with the Hebrew text,
and with the Jewish method of explaining it.   The good effects of this
superior knowledge, and of his untiring diligence, are greatly neutralised by
haste and inadvertence, by a want of consistency and settled principles, and
by a general defect of judgment.   The only Fathers, of whose expositions
a direct use will be made in the present work, are Chrysostom and Jerome,
and of these only in the earlier chapters.   All further references of the
same kind are derived from other commentaries.

Of the Rabbins, several are carefully compared and often quoted.   These
are Solomon Jarchi, noted for his close adherence to the Targum, and the
Jewish tradition ; Aben Ezra, for his independent rationalistic views and
philological acuteness ; David Kimchi, for his learning and good sense, and
for his frequent reference to older writers.   He often cites, among others,
his brother Moses, and his father, Joseph Kimchi.   The Michlal Jophi of
Solomon Ben Melech, with the additional notes of Jacob Abendana, is
chiefly a selection of the best rabbinical interpretations, particularly those
of David Kimchi.   The opinions of Abarbenel and other rabbins are occasionally cited on the authority of other writers.

Of the Reformers, the two greatest are kept constantly in view throughout the exposition.   Luther's translation will be always valued, not only
for its author's sake, but for its own.   Though often inexact and paraphrastical, it almost always gives the true sense, and often gives it with a vigour
and felicity of phrase never attained in like degree by the more accurate
and learned versions of the present day.   Calvin still towers above all interpreters, in large commanding views of revelation in its whole connection,

with extraordinary insight into the logical relations of a passage, even where its individual expressions were not fully understood. These qualities, together with his fixed belief of fundamental doctrines, his eminent soundness of judgment, and his freedom from all tendency to paradox, pedantic affectation, or fanciful conceit, place him more completely on a level with the very best interpreters of our day, than almost any intervening writer. Of the other Reformers, only occasional citations will be met with, such as Zwingli, Œcolampadius, and Fagius.

As a representative of the old school of orthodox interpreters, we may take the annotated version of Junius and Tremellius, distinguished by learning, ingenuity, and exegetical acumen, but disfigured by unnatural and forced constructions, in which the Hebrew idiom is often sacrificed to some paradoxical novelty. Less frequent reference will be made to other writers of the same school and period, who were not accessible directly, or whose influence on later writers has been less considerable.

The honours due to the original and independent founder of a school may be justly claimed by John Cocceius, whose opinions gave occasion to protracted controversies in the Church of Holland. The description usually given of him, that he finds Christ everywhere in the Old Testament, is hardly expressive of his peculiar character, as set forth in his work upon Isaiah. A more exact description would be, that he finds the Church and the events of Church history throughout the prophecies, not as a mystical or secondary meaning, but as the proper and direct one. Of this system many striking specimens will be presented in the exposition.

The description of Cocceius, which has been already quoted, is commonly accompanied by one of Grotius, as his exegetical opposite, who finds Christ nowhere. Here again the portrait is by no means an exact one, at least as he appears in his brief notes on Isaiah. He probably professes to find Christ predicted there as often as Cocceius does, but with this difference, that Grotius finds him always hidden under types, the lower or immediate sense of which is to be sought as near as may be to the date of the prediction. A comparison between these two eminent writers is enough to shew the incorrectness of the common notion, that the hypothesis of types and double senses is peculiar to the stricter theologians of the old school, and the rejection of them characteristic of the more liberal interpreters. Cocceius seldom resorts to the assumption of a double sense, while Grotius seldom recognises Christ as a subject of prophecy, except where he can institute a typical relation. The grand objection to the exegesis of the latter, as exemplified in this book, is its superficial character and the sceptical tendencies which it betrays. Its shining merits are ingenious combinations, happy conjecture, and abundant illustration from the Greek and Roman classics. The nearest approach to him, in all these qualities, without the least appearance of dependence, imitation, or collusion, is found in John Le Clerc, more commonly called Clericus. The likeness is the more exact, because neither he nor Grotius has done justice to his own capacity and reputation in interpreting Isaiah.

The first complete exposition of Isaiah is the great work of Campegius Vitringa, Professor at Franeker, originally published in 1714. Of the preceding commentaries, every one perhaps may be described as holding up some one side of the subject, while the others are neglected. But in this work are collected all the materials which at that time were accessible, not in an undigested state, but thoroughly incorporated and arranged with a degree of judgment, skill, and taste, not easily surpassed. It is besides distinguished by a candour, dignity, and zeal for truth, without the least admixture of acrimonious bigotry, which have secured for it and for its author the esteem of all succeeding writers who have read it,. of whatever school or party. So complete is Vitringa's exposition even now, that nothing more would be required to supply the public wants but the additional results of more profound and extensive philological investigation during the last century, were it not for two defects which the work, with all its varied and transcendent merit, does exhibit. The first is a want of condensation, a prolixity, which, although not without advantages to readers who have leisure to secure them, is entirely unsuited to the tastes and habits of the present age. The other is too strong a leaning to the mystical and allegorical interpretation of the plainest prophecies, arising from a mistaken deference for the old exegetical canon, that the prophecies must be made to mean as much as possible. To this must be added the erroneous hypothesis, not yet exploded, that every prophecy must be specific, and must have its fulfilment in a certain period of history, to determine which recourse must frequently be had to fanciful or forced interpretation.

Nearly contemporary with Vitringa was the learned German Pietist, John Henry Michaelis, Professor at Halle, who, in conjunction with his brother, published there in 1720 a Hebrew Bible with marginal annotations. Those on the first part of Isaiah are by no means equal to the notes of C. B. Michaelis on the Minor Prophets in the same volume. The former are more meagre, and contain less independent exposition, leaning chiefly upon some preceding writers, and especially Sebastian Schmidt. These notes, however, have considerable value on account of their references to parallel passages, less numerous than those of many other writers, but selected with great care, and with a constant view to the elucidation of the text. Occasionally also an original interpretation here presents itself. The whole work is characterised by orthodox belief and a devout spirit.

Independently of both these works, though some years later, appeared the Exposition of Isaiah by John Gill, a Baptist minister in London. Though designed for the doctrinal and practical improvement of the English reader, it is still distinguished from other books of that class by its erudition in a single province, that of talmudic and rabbinic literature. In this department Gill draws directly from his own resources, which are here extensive, while in other matters he contents himself with gathering and combining, often whimsically, the opinions of preceding writers, and especially of those contained in the Critici Sacri and in Pool's Synopsis. His original suggestions are but few and generally founded on his own peculiar views of the Apocalypse, not as an independent prophecy, but as a key to those of the Old Testament.

Before either of the works last mentioned, and nearly contemporary with Vitringa, appeared a Commentary on Isaiah by Dr William Lowth, prebendary of Winchester, which is usually printed with his other expositions of the Prophets, as a part of Bishop Patrick's Commentary on the Bible. The work on Isaiah has exerted little influence on later writers, the less perhaps because eclipsed by the brilliant success of the Translation, published, more than half a century afterwards, by the author's son, Robert Lowth, successively Bishop of Limerick, St David's, Oxford, and London, universally acknowledged to be one of the most accomplished scholars and elegant writers of his age or nation. The influence of Lowth's Isaiah has already been described, so far as it can be regarded as injurious to the cause of sound interpretation or enlightened criticism. Its good effect has been to raise the estimation of Isaiah as a writer of extraordinary genius, and to introduce a method of expounding him, more in accordance with the principles of taste, than some adopted by preceding writers. Besides this work upon Isaiah, he contributed to this end by his lectures, as Professor of Poetry at Oxford, *de Sacra Poesi Hebræorum*, which have been frequently republished on the Continent, and still exert a salutary influence on the German critics. In his criticism of the Hebrew text, he follows the exploded system of Cappellus, Houbigant, and others, who assumed the masoretic text to be as faulty as it could be without losing its identity, and seem to make it the great object of their criticism to change it as extensively as possible. Many of Lowth's favourite interpretations, being founded upon critical conjecture, are now worthless. The style of his English version, which excited universal admiration when it first appeared, has, in the course of nearly seventy years, become less pleasing to the cultivated ear, partly because a taste has been revived for that antique simplicity which Lowth's contemporaries looked upon as barbarous, and of which a far superior specimen is furnished in the common version. Among Lowth's greatest merits, in the exposition and illustration of Isaiah, must be mentioned his familiarity with classical models, often suggesting admirable parallels, and his just views, arising from a highly cultivated taste, in reference to the structure of the prophecies, and the true import of prophetic imagery.

Almost simultaneous with the first appearance of Lowth's Isaiah was the publication of a German version, with Notes for the Unlearned, by John David Michaelis (a nephew of John Henry before mentioned) Professor at Göttingen, and for many years the acknowledged leader of the German Orientalists. His interpretations in this work are often novel and ingenious, but as often paradoxical and fanciful. His version, although frequently felicitous, is marred by a perpetual affectation of colloquial and modern phraseology, for which he sometimes apologises on the ground that the original expression would not have sounded well in German. He agrees with Lowth in his contempt for the masoretic text, which he is constantly attempting to correct ; but is far below him in refinement of taste and in a just appreciation of the literary merits of his author. With respect to more important matters, he may be said to occupy the turning-point between the old and new school of interpreters. While on the one hand, he retains the customary forms of speech and, at least negatively, recognises the divine authority and inspiration of the Prophet, he carries his affectation of independence and free-thinking, in the details of his interpretation, so far, that the transition appears natural and easy to the avowed unbelief of his pupils and successors. Besides the one already mentioned, occasional reference is made to other works of the same author.

The German edition of Lowth's Isaiah, with additional notes by Koppe, a colleague of Michaelis at Göttingen, deserves attention, as the work in which the extravagant doctrines of the modern criticism with respect to the unity, integrity, and genuineness of the prophecies, were first propounded and applied to the writings of Isaiah. The opposite doctrines were maintained, in all their strictness, by a contemporary Swiss Professor, Köcher, a disciple and adherent of the orthodox Dutch school, in a book expressly written against Lowth.

Passing over the comparatively unimportant works of Vogel, Cube, Hensler, and the annotated Latin versions of Dathe and Doederlein, occasionally cited in the present volume, we may mention as the next important link in the *catena* of interpretation, the famous *Scholia* of the younger

Rosenmüller, for many years Oriental Professor at Leipzig. The part relating to Isaiah appeared first in 1791 ; but the publication and republication of the several parts extend through a period of more than forty years. As a whole, the work is distingnished by a critical acquaintance both with Hebrew and the cognate dialects, and an industrious use of the ancient versions, the rabbinical interpreters, and the later writers, particularly Grotius and Vitringa, whole paragraphs from whom are often copied almost verbatim and without express acknowledgment.   From its comprehensive plan and the resources of the writer, this work may be considered as an adaptation of Vitringa to the circumstances of a later period, including, however, an entire change of exegetical and doctrinal opinions.   Without any of the eager zeal and party-spirit, which occasioned the excesses of Koppe and Eichhorn, Rosenmüller equally repudiates the doctrine of prophetic inspiration in the strict sense, and rejects whatever would imply or involve it. The unsoundness of his principles in this respect has given less offence and alarm to readers of a different school, because accompanied by so much calmness and apparent candour, sometimes amounting to a neutral apathy, no more conducive to correct results than the opposite extreme of partiality and prejudice.   This very spirit of indifference, together with the plan of compilation upon which the Scholia are constructed, added perhaps to an original infirmity of judgment, make the author's own opinions and conclusions the least valuable part of this extensive and laborious work.   In the abridged edition, which appeared not long before his death (1835), many opinions of Gesenius are adopted, some of which Gesenius in the mean time had himself abandoned.   The acknowledgment of Messianic prophecies, which Rosenmüller, in his later writings, seems to make, does not extend to prophecies of Christ, but merely to vague and for the most part groundless expectations of a Messiah by the ancient prophets.

An epoch in the history of the interpretation of Isaiah is commonly supposed to be marked by the appearance of the Philological, Critical, and Historical Commentary of Gesenius (Leipzig, 1821). This distinction is not founded upon any new principle or even method of interpretation which the author introduced, but on his great celebrity, authority, and influence, as a grammarian and lexicographer.   Nothing is more characteristic of the work than the extreme predilection of the writer for the purely philological and archæological portions of his task, and the disproportionate amount of space and labour lavished on them.   The evidence of learning and acuteness thus afforded cannot be questioned, but it is often furnished at the cost of other more important qualities.   The ablest portions of the work have sometimes the appearance of *excursus* or detached disquisitions upon certain questions of antiquities or lexicography.   Even in this chosen field, successful as Gesenius has been, later writers have detected some infirmities and failures. Of these the most important is the needless multiplication of distinct senses and the gratuitous attenuation of the meaning in some words of common occurrence.   The merit of Gesenius consists much more in diligent investigation and perspicuous arrangement than in a masterly application of the principles established and exemplified in the best Greek lexicons.   His proneness to mistake distinct applications of a word and accessory ideas suggested by the context, for different meanings of the word itself, is recognised in the occasional correction of the fault by his American translator (see for example Heb. Lex. p. 148), to whom the public would have been indebted for a much more frequent use of the same method.   If any apology is needed for the frequent deviations, in the following exposition, from

Gesenius's decisions, it is afforded by the rule which he professes to have followed in his own use of the cognate dialects: *ultra lexica sapere.* (Preface to Isaiah, p. vi.) With respect to candour and impartiality, Gesenius occupies the same ground with Rosenmüller, that is to say, he is above suspicion as to any question not connected, more or less directly, with his fundamental error, that there can be no prophetic foresight. Another point of similarity between them is their seeming hesitancy and instability of judgment, as exhibited in frequent changes of opinion upon minor points, without a statement of sufficient reasons. The many variations which may be traced in the writings of Gesenius, from his early Lexicons and Commentary on Isaiah to his great Thesaurus, are no doubt proofs of intellectual progress and untiring diligence ; but it is still true, that in many cases opposite conclusions seem to have been drawn from precisely the same premises. The Commentary on Isaiah never reappeared, but the accompanying version was reprinted with a few notes, in 1829. This translation is a spirited and faithful reproduction of the sense of the original, and for the most part of its characteristic form, but not without unnecessary paraphrases and gratuitous departures from the Hebrew idiom. In these respects, and in simplicity of diction, it has been much improved by De Wette, whose translation of Isaiah (contained in his version of the Bible, Heidelberg, 1839) is avowedly founded upon that of Gesenius. The same relation to the Commentary is sustained by Maurer's notes for students (in the first volume of his *Commentarius Criticus in Vet. Test.* Leipzig, 1835), which exhibits in a clear and compact form the substance of Gesenius, with occasional specimens of independent and ingenious exposition.

A very different position is assumed by Hitzig, whose work upon Isaiah (Heidelberg, 1833) seems intended to refute that of Gesenius wherever a dissent was possible, always excepting the sacred fundamental principle of unbelief in which they are united. This polemical design of Hitzig's work has led to many strained and paradoxical interpretations, but at the same time to a remarkable display of exegetical invention and philological acuteness, both in the application of the principles of Ewald's Grammar where it varies from Gesenius, and in original solutions of grammatical and other problems. In some points Hitzig may be said to have receded to the ground of Eichhorn, as for instance in the wildness of his critical conjectures, not so much in reference to words or letters as. to larger passages, and also in his leaning to the old idea of predictions *ex eventu*, or historical allusions clothed in a prophetical costume. The metaphysical obscurity of Hitzig's style, in certain cases, may be either the result of individual peculiarity, or symptomatic of the general progress in the German mind from common-sense rationalism or deism to the more transcendental forms of unbelief. Another characteristic of this writer is his undisguised contempt. if not for Isaiah in particular, for Judaism and its faith in general. In point of taste, he is remarkable at once for high pretensions and for gross defects.

Hendewerk's commentary on Isaiah, (Königsberg, vol. i. 1838, vol. ii. 1843) though indicative of scholarship and talent, has a less marked and independent character than that of Hitzig, and exhibits in a great degree the faults and merits of a juvenile performance. The author's reading seems to have been limited to modern writers, and the controversial attitude which he is constantly assuming with respect to Hengstenberg or Hitzig, while it makes his exposition less intelligible, unless compared with that of his opponents, also impairs the reader's confidence in his impartiality and candour. His original suggestions are in many cases striking and in some truly valuable, as will appear from the examples cited in the exposition.

A place is due, in this part of the chronological succession, to two works on Isaiah in the English language. The first is by the Rev. Albert Barnes of Philadelphia (3 vols. 8vo, Boston, 1840), well known by previous publications on the Gospels and Epistles, and by a later work on Job. His exposition of Isaiah comprehends a large part of the valuable substance of Vitringa, Rosenmüller, and Gesenius, with occasional reference to the older writers, as contained in Pool's Synopsis and the *Critici Sacri*. The great fault of the work is not its want of matter, but of matter well digested and condensed. Particular and even disproportionate attention has been paid to archaeological illustration, especially as furnished by the modern travellers. Practical observations are admitted, but without sufficient uniformity or any settled method. The author's views of inspiration in general, and of the inspiration of Isaiah in particular, are sound, but not entirely consistent with the deference occasionally paid to neological interpreters, in cases where their judgments are, in fact though not in form, determined by a false assumption, which no one more decidedly rejects than Mr Barnes. The New Translation which accompanies the Commentary, seems to be wholly independent of it, and can hardly be considered an improvement, either on the common version, or on that of Lowth.

Some of the same remarks are applicable to the work of Dr Henderson (London, 1840), in which there are appearances of greater haste and less laborious effort, but at the same time of a more extended reading, and a more independent exegetical judgment. The English author, though familiar with the latest German writers who preceded him, is not deterred by their example or authority from the avowal of his doctrinal belief, or from a proper use of analogy in the interpretation of the prophet. Further description of these two works is rendered unnecessary by the frequency with which they are quoted or referred to in the Commentary.

Ewald's exposition of Isaiah, contained in his collective work upon the Hebrew Prophets (Stuttgart, 1841), derives great authority from his acknowledged eminence in Germany, as a profound philosophical grammarian. His attention has been given almost exclusively to the chronological arrangement of the parts and the translation of the text. The latter has great value, not only as containing the results of Ewald's philological researches, but also on account of its intrinsic qualities, and more especially its faithful exhibition of the form of the original in its simplicity. In this respect it is a great advance on all preceding versions. The Commentary is extremely meagre, and remarkable, like most of Ewald's writings, for the absence of all reference to other modern writers or opinions. The liberties taken with the text, though not very numerous, are sometimes very violent and arbitrary. The sweeping criticism, on which his chronological arrangement rests, will be considered in another place. From the rationalistic school of Rosenmüller and Gesenius, Ewald differs in regarding Isaiah as inspired, which admission really extends, however, only to a kind of vague, poetical, anticipation, wholly exclusive of distinct prophetic foresight of the distant future, in rejecting which, as a thing impossible or not susceptible of proof, he coincides with the preceding writers.

Umbreit's practical Commentary on Isaiah (Hamburg, 1842), is little more than a declamatory paraphrase, composed in what an English reader would regard as very questionable taste. The real value of the work consists in a translation of Isaiah, and occasional notes on different questions of philology and criticism. On such points the author coincides for the most part with Gesenius, while in his general views of prophecy he seems to approach nearer to Ewald, with whom he frequently concurs in making that a vague anticipation which the other writers take as a specific prophecy. At the same time, he differs from this whole class of interpreters, in frequently alluding to the Saviour and the new dispensation as the subjects of prediction, but in what sense it is hard to ascertain, the rather as he practically holds the modern doctrine, that distinct prediction of the distant future is sufficient to disprove the genuineness of a passage.

Knobel's Isaiah (Leipzig, 1843), is exceedingly convenient as a condensed synopsis of the principal interpretations. In the expression of his own views, the author shews his strict adherence to the modern school of criticism and exegesis. His critical decisions, with respect to some portions of the book, are very arbitrary, and the detailed proofs, by which he sustains them, in a high degree extravagant. In rejecting the hypothesis of inspiration, and in asserting the mere human character and origin of the prophecies, he is uncommonly explicit and decided, both in this work and in one which he had previously published upon prophecy in general. On the whole, with the exception of a few good exegetical suggestions, he may be looked upon as having retrograded to the ground of the old neologists from that assumed by Ewald and Umbreit.

It is gratifying to be able to conclude the list of German writers with a few names, belonging to a very different school, and connected with a powerful reaction in favour of old principles, as being perfectly consistent with the valuable fruits of late improvements and discoveries. The way of this important movement, so far as Isaiah is concerned, was opened, not by regular interpreters of this book, but by Hengstenberg in his Christology (1829) followed by Kleinert in his volume on the genuineness of Isaiah's prophecy (1829), and still more recently by Hävernick in his Introduction to the Old Testament (1844). An application of the same essential principles to the direct interpretation of Isaiah has been made by Drechsler, Professor at Erlangen, the first volume of whose Commentary (Erlangen, 1845) reached me too late to allow the present use of any part of it except the Introduction, to which reference is made below. Besides the exegetical works already mentioned, occasional references will be found to others, illustrative of certain passages or certain topics. As most of these are too well known to need description, it will be sufficient here to name, as authorities in natural history and geography, the Hierozoicon of Bochart and the Biblical Researches of Robinson and Smith.

It remains now to speak of the arrangement and divisions of the book. The detailed examination of particular questions under this head will be found in the course of the exposition, and for the most part in the special introduction to the several chapters. All that is here intended is a general statement of the case, preparatory to these more minute discussions. The progress of opinion upon this part of the subject has been closely connected with the succession of exegetical and critical hypotheses already mentioned. The same extremes, reactions, compromises, may be traced substantially in both. The older writers commonly assumed that the book was arranged in chronological order by the author himself. Thus Jerome says expressly, that the prophecies belonging to the four reigns follow one another regularly, without mixture or confusion. J. H. Michaelis regards the first verse of the first, sixth, and seventh chapters, and the twenty-eighth verse of the fourteenth chapter, as the

dividing marks of the four reigns.   This supposition of a strict chronological arrangement, although rather taken for granted than determined by
investigation, is by no means so absurd as some have represented it.   It
rests on immemorial tradition, and the analogy of the other books, the few
exceptions tending rather to confirm the rule.   The principal objections to
it are, that the first chapter is evidently later than the second ; that the
sixth, containing the account of Isaiah's ordination to his office, must be
the first in point of date ; and that the seventeenth chapter relates to the
first years of the reign of Ahaz, whereas chap. xiv. 28 is assigned to the
year in which he died.

These objections, though by no means insurmountable, as will be seen
hereafter, led Vitringa to relinquish the hypothesis of strict chronological
arrangement by the author himself, for that of arrangement by another
hand (perhaps by the *men of Hezekiah* mentioned Prov. xxv. 1), in the
order of subjects, those discourses being placed together whose contents are
most alike.   He accordingly divides Isaiah into five books, after the manner
of the Pentateuch and Psalter, the first (chaps. i.–xii.) containing prophecies
directed against Judah and Israel, the second (chaps. xiii.–xxiii.) against
certain foreign powers, the third (chaps. xxiv.–xxxv.) against the enemies
and unworthy members of the church, the fourth (chaps. xl.–xlviii.) relating
chiefly to the Babylonish exile and deliverance from it, the fifth (chaps.
xlix.–lxvi.) to the person and reign of the Messiah, while chaps. xxxvi.–
xxxix. are distinguished from the rest as being purely historical.   The titles
in chap. i. 1, ii. 1, vii. 1, xiii. 1, xiv 28, &c., he regards as genuine,
except that the names of the four kings were added to the first by the compiler, in order to convert what was at first the title of the first chapter only
into a general description of the whole book.

This ingenious hypothesis still leaves it unexplained why certain series
were separated from each other, for example why chaps. xiii.–xxiii. are interposed between chaps. i.–xii. and chaps. xxiv.–xxxv.   This led Koppe,
whom Gesenius describes as the pioneer of the modern criticism, to reject
that part of Vitringa's theory which supposes the book to have received its
present form in the reign of Hezekiah, while he carries out to an absurd
extreme the general hypothesis of compilation and re-arrangement by a
later hand.   According to Koppe and Augusti, the book, as we now have
it, is in perfect confusion, and its actual arrangement wholly without authority.   To confirm and explain this, Eichhorn and Bertholdt assume the
existence of several distinct collections of Isaiah's writings to each of which
additions were gradually made, until the whole assumed its present form.

The same general view is taken of the matter by Hitzig and Ewald, but
with this distinction, that the former thinks the framework or sub-stratum
of the original collections still remains, and needs only to be freed from
subsequent interpolations, while the latter sticks more closely to the earlier
idea, that the whole is in confusion, partly as he supposes from the loss of
many prophecies no longer extant, and can be even partially restored to its
original condition, only by critically reconstructing it under the guidance of
internal evidence.   Ewald accordingly abandons the traditional arrangement altogether, and exhibits the *disjecta membra* in an order of his own.
The critical value of the diagnosis, which controls this process, may be
estimated from a single principle, assumed if not avowed throughout it,
namely, that passages which treat of the same subject, or resemble one
another strongly in expression, *must* be placed together as component parts
of one continuous composition.   The absurdity of this assumption might

be rendered palpable by simply applying it to any classical or modern author, who has practised a variety of styles, but with a frequent recurrence of the same ideas, for example, Horace, Goethe, Moore, or Byron. The practical value of the method may be best shewn by a comparative statement of its actual results in the hands of two contemporary writers, Ewald and Hendewerk, both of whom have followed this eccentric method in the printing of their Commentaries, to the great annoyance of the reader, even when assisted by an index. Without attending to the larger divisions or *cycles* introduced by either, a simple exhibition of the order in which the first chapters are arranged by these two writers, will be amply sufficient for our present purpose.

Hendewerk's arrangement is as follows :—Chap. vi. ; chaps. i.–v. ; chap. vii. (vers. 1–9) ; chap. xvii. (vers. 1–14) ; chap. vii. (vers 10–25) ; chaps. viii. ix. ; chap. x. (vers. 1–27) ; chap. xiv. (vers. 24–27) ; chap. x. (vers. 28–34) ; chaps. xi. xii ; chap. xiv. (vers. 28–32) ; chaps. xv. xvi. ; chaps. xviii. xix. ; chap. xxi. (vers. 11–17) ; chap. xxiii. ; chaps. xxviii. xxix. ; chap. xx. ; chaps. xxxi. xxxii. ; chap. xxii. ; chap. xxxiii. ; chaps. xxxvi.– xxxix ; chaps. xxiv.–xxvii. ; chaps. xxxiv. xxxv. ; chap. xiii. ; chap. xiv. (vers. 1–23) ; chap. xxi. (vers. 1–10) ; chaps. xl.–lxvi.

Ewald's arrangement is as follows :—Chap. vi. ; chaps. ii.–iv.'; chap. v. (vers. 1–25) ; chap. ix. (vers. 7–20) ; chap. x. (vers. 1–4) ; chap. v. (vers. 26–30) ; chap. xvii. (vers. 1–11) ; chaps. vii. viii. ; chap. ix. (vers. 1–6) ; chap. xiv. (vers. 25–32) ; chaps. xv. xvi. ; chap. xxi. (vers. 11–17) ; chap. xxiii. ; chap. i. ; chap. xxii. ; chaps. xxviii.–xxxii. ; chap. xx. ; chap. x. (vers. 5–34) ; chap. xi. ; chap. xvii. (vers. 12–18) ; chap. xviii. ; chap. xiv. (vers. 24–27) ; chap. xxxiii. ; chap. xxxvii. (vers. 22–35) ; chap. xix. ; chap. xxi. (vers. 1–10) ; chap. xiii. ; chap. xiv. (vers. 1–23) ; chaps. xl.– lxvi. ; chaps. xxxiv. xxxv. ; chap. xxiv. ; chap. xxv. (vers. 6–11) ; chap. xxv. (vers. 1–5) ; chap. xxv. (ver. 12) ; chaps. xxvi. xxvii. ; chap. xii. is rejected as of later origin, but without determining its date. These arrangements, and particularly that of Ewald, may be reckoned not only the latest but the last achievement of the *higher criticism*. " The force of nature can no further go." We need look for no invention beyond this, unless it be that of reading the book backwards, or shuffling the chapters like a pack of cards.

Long before this, Gesenius had recoiled from the extremes to which the higher criticism tended, and attempted to occupy a middle ground, by blending the hypothesis of J. H. Michaelis and Vitringa, or in other words assuming a regard both to chronological order and to the affinity of subjects, at the same time holding fast to the favourite idea of successive additions and distinct compilations. He accordingly assumes four parts or books. The first (chap. i.–xii.) consists of prophecies belonging to the earliest period of Isaiah's ministry, with the exception of a few interpolations. The sixth chapter should stand first, according to the Jewish tradition as recorded by Jarchi and Aben Ezra. The first chapter is somewhat later than the second, third, and fourth. The seventh, though authentic, was probably not written by Isaiah. The eleventh and twelfth may also be spurious, but were early added to the tenth. This book he regards as the original collection, and the first verse as its original title or inscription. The second book (chap. xiii.–xxiii.) consists of prophecies against foreign nations, excepting chap. xxii., which he supposes to have found its way here from having been early joined with chap xxi. A characteristic feature of this book is the use of *burden*, as a title or inscription, which he thinks may be certainly ascribed to the compiler. The third book (chap. xxiv.–xxxv.) contains a series of genuine prophecies belonging to the reign of Hezekiah (chaps. xxviii.–xxxiii.), with two other series of later date, placed by the hand of a compiler at the beginning (chaps. xxiv.–xxvii.) and the end (chaps xxxiv. xxxv.) of this collection, while it was further augmented by a historical appendix (chaps. xxxvi.–xxxix.), in which Isaiah makes a prominent figure. The fourth and last book (chaps. xl.–xlvi.), as Gesenius thinks, was added to the others long after the captivity.

Here, as in other cases previously mentioned, Gesenius differs from his predecessors in the *higher criticism*, only in degree, refusing to go with them in the application of their principles, but holding fast the principles themselves. If, on the one hand, he is right in assuming, upon mere conjecture, several different collections of the writings of Isaiah formed successively, and in rejecting, upon mere internal evidence, the parts which do not suit his purpose or his theory, then it is utterly impossible to give any definite reason for refusing our assent to the more thorough application of the same process by the bolder hand of Ewald. If, on the other hand, Gesenius is correct in drawing back from the legitimate results of such a theory, then it is utterly impossible to find a safe or definite position, without receding further and relinquishing the theory itself. This additional reaction has not failed to take place in the progress of the controversy. It is most distinctly marked and ably justified in Hävernick's Introduction to Isaiah, where the author lays it down, not as a makeshift or a desperate return to old opinions without ground or reason, but as the natural result of philological and critical induction, that the writings of Isaiah, as now extant, form a compact, homogeneous, and well-ordered whole, proceeding, in the main, if not in all its parts, from the hand of the original author. Whoever has been called to work his way through the extravagant and endless theories of the 'higher criticism,' without those early prepossessions in its favour which grow with the growth of almost every German scholar, far from finding this new doctrine strange or arbitrary, must experience a feeling of relief at thus landing from the ocean of conjecture on the *terra firma* of historical tradition, analogical reasoning, and common sense. The advantages of such a ground can be appreciated far more justly after such experience than before it, because then there might be a misgiving lest some one of the many possibilities proposed as substitutes for immemorial tradition might prove true ; but now the reader, having found by actual experiment, not only that these ways do not lead him right, but that they lead him nowhere, falls back with strong assurance, not by any means upon all the minor articles of the ancient creed, which he is still bound and determined to subject to critical investigation, but on the general presumption which exists in all such cases, that the truth of what is obvious to common sense and has been held from the beginning, instead of being the exception is the rule, to which the flaws, that may be really discovered by a microscopic criticism, are mere exceptions.

That Hävernick especially has not been governed by a love of novelty or opposition, is apparent from the fact of his retaining in its substance Gesenius's division and arrangement of the book, while he rejects the gratuitous assumptions held by that eminent interpreter in common with his predecessors. According to Hävernick the whole book consists of five connected but distinguishable *groups*, or series of prophecies. The first group (chaps. i.–xii.) contains Isaiah's earliest prophecies, arranged in two series, easily distinguished by internal marks. The first six chapters have a general character, without certain reference to any particular historical occasion, which accounts for the endless difference of opinion as to the precise date of their composition. The remaining six have reference to particular occasions, which are not left to conjecture but distinctly stated. They embrace the principal events under Ahaz, and illustrate the relation of the prophet to them. The sixth chapter, though descriptive of the prophet's ordination, holds its proper place, as an addendum to the foregoing prophecies, designed to justify their dominant tone of threatening and reproof. The second group (chaps. xiii.–xxiii.) contains a series of prophecies against certain foreign powers, shewing the relation of the heathen world to the theocracy, and followed by a sort of appendix (chaps. xxiv.–xxvii.), summing up the foregoing prophecies and shewing the results of their fulfilment to the end of time. He maintains the genuineness of all the prophecies in this division and the correctness of their actual position. The apparent exception in chap. xxii. he accounts for, by supposing that Judah is there represented as reduced by gross iniquity to the condition of a heathen state. Another explanation, no less natural, and more complete, because it accounts for the remarkable prophecy against an individual in the last part of the chapter, is afforded by the supposition, that Judah is there considered as subject to a foreign and probably a heathen influence, viz. that of Shebna. (See the details under chap. xxii.) Hävernick's third group (chaps. xxviii.–xxxiii.) contains prophecies relating to a particular period of Hezekiah's reign, with a more general prospective sequel (chaps. xxxiv. xxxv.), as in the second. Here again he examines and rejects the various arguments adduced by modern critics to disprove the genuineness of certain parts. The fourth group (chaps. xxxvi.–xxxix.) describes in historical form the influence exerted by the Prophet at a later period of the reign of Hezekiah. Regarding this and the parallel part of Second Kings as collateral derivatives from a historical writing of Isaiah, Hävernick is led by the mention in chap. xxxvii. 38, of an event which happened after the supposed death of Isaiah, to ascribe that verse and the insertion of these chapters to a somewhat later hand. He maintains, however, that so far from being inappropriate, they constitute a necessary link between the third group and the fifth (chap. xl.–lxvi.), in which the whole result of his prophetic ministrations to the end of time is vividly depicted.

The critical and philological arguments of Hävernick, in this part of his work, are eminently learned and ingenious, highly original and yet conservative of ancient and invaluable truth. A reference to them is the more important here because they came into my hands too late to influence the expositions of the present volume, the coincidence between them as to principle, if not in all particular conclusions, being only the more satisfactory and striking upon that account. The same remark applies, in some degree to Drechsler's Introduction, which may be considered as a further movement in the same direction, not occasioned by the other, but the fruit of independent labour in the same field and under the same influence. It is certainly an interesting and instructive fact, that in two such cases, the conviction of the unity, integrity, and uncorrupted genuineness of the book before us, even as to its arrangement and the nexus of the parts, should have been reached without collusion, by a thorough sifting of the very arguments alleged against it by the ablest critics of the past and present generation. Drechsler's idea of Isaiah as a whole differs from Hävernick's, in going further from the modern theory, retaining less of its substratum, the hypothesis of different collections, and ascribing to the book, as we possess it, a more absolute and perfect unity. Drechsler dismisses the whole question with respect to the precise date of particular passages, as equally insoluble and unimportant; directs attention to the fact that throughout the book the only editor, compiler, or arranger, of whom any trace can be discerned, is one who exercised the rights of an author; draws from this and other marks of an internal kind, a confirmation of the old opinion, that the form and the contents of the collection are, so far as we can hope to ascertain, from one and the same hand ; and thenceforth assumes it as a principle or maxim, that whatever may have been the date of any passage as originally uttered, we have no need or authority to trace it further back than its reduction to its present shape by the original author.

With respect to the divisions of the book, his theory may seem at first sight artificial, but is really distinguished by simplicity as well as ingenuity. He sets out by assuming two great *crises* or conjunctures in Isaiah's ministry, about which all his prophecies may be arranged. The first is the invasion in the reign of Ahaz, the second the invasion in the reign of Hezekiah. These he regards as the centre of two great prophetic schemes or systems, forming one harmonious whole, but between themselves distinguished by the prevalence of threatening and reproof in one, of promise and consolation in the other. To each of these great critical events in the history corresponds a central point or focus in the prophecy, from which in both directions we may trace a regular connection in the book, stretching back into the past and forward into the future, in the way of preparation on the one hand and completion on the other. The focus of the first great prophetic scheme he fixes in the seventh chapter, that of the other in the thirty-sixth and thirty-seventh. The sixth is a direct preparation for the seventh ; the fifth for the sixth ; the second, third, and fourth, for the fifth ; the first is a general introduction to the whole. Then on the other side, the promises and threatenings of the seventh chapter are repeated, amplified, and varied, first with respect to Judah and Israel in chaps. viii.–xii., then with respect to foreign powers in chaps. xiii.–xxiii., and lastly in a general summing up and application to all times and places in chaps. xxiv.–xxvii., which closes the first system. The other central prophecy, in chaps. xxxvi. and xxxvii., is likewise introduced by a preparatory series (chaps. xxviii.–xxxv.), all relating to Sennacherib's invasion, and on the other hand carried out, first historically (chaps. xxxvii. xxxix.), then prophetically (chaps. xl.–xlvi.) to the end of time.

However fanciful or German this hypothesis may seem, it cannot be attentively considered without giving rise to this reflection, that a book affording the materials and conditions even for a fanciful device, of which unity and symmetry are essential elements, cannot well be a farrago of discordant parts produced at random and combined by chance. The opposite hypothesis, if once assumed, can be applied with ease to any case, however clear the signs of unity may be, for the details of proof are all involved in the primary assumption ; but it is not quite so easy to maintain the hypothesis of harmony where harmony does not exist. It requires little ingenuity or learning to discover and exaggerate appearances of discord even where there is agreement ; but to create the appearance of agreement in the midst of discord is beyond the reach of any sophistry or eloquence except the most consummate. The truth, however, seems to be, that Drechsler's theory, however fanciful it may appear, especially as stated by himself, is but another exhibition of the truth maintained by Hävernick, to wit, that the book before us is, in form as well as substance, the original and genuine production of Isaiah.

The view which has now been taken of the progress of opinion, with respect to the arrangement and division of the book before us, first its downward progress from a firm traditional belief to the extreme of a lawless and irrational scepticism, and then its upward course by dint of argument to an enlightened and confirmed historical assurance, makes it almost impossible to close without a glance at the ulterior stages which may yet remain of this restorative process. Considering the principle on which it has been thus far carried on, the proved unsoundness of the contrary hypothesis, and the analogy of all like cases, it might plausibly be stated, as the probable result of this return to experience and common sense, that men whose eyes have thus been opened will eventually throw to the moles and to the bats the cherished figment, upon which a large part of their errors has been built, to wit, the groundless assumption, that the sacred writings of the Jews were passed from hand to hand by private circulation and transcription, like the Greek and Roman classics, accidentally collected into volumes, mixed together, mutilated, magnified by forgery or ignorant interpolation, and at last sent down to us, to be the subject of empirical decisions without number or agreement. Or if this be gone already, it may be the next step to discard the notion, not monopolized by any class or school of critics, that the several parts of such a book as that before us were, and must have been, delivered as set speeches or occasional discourses, then reduced to writing one by one, and put together by degrees, or even by a later hand and in a distant age. On this gratuitous assumption rests a large part of the most perplexing difficulties which attend the critical interpretation of Isaiah, and which all would disappear if we could see sufficient reason to conclude, that the book is a continuous production of a single mind, at one great effort, long protracted, it may be, but not entirely suspended, or renewed from time to time upon occasion. The mention of distinct events and dates no more establishes the fact here questioned, than the sweep of Paul's chronology, in his epistle to the churches of Galatia, proves that it was written piecemeal from the time of his conversion. All analogy, both scriptural and general, without some countervailing reason for believing otherwise, would favour the conclusion that a book like that before us was produced by a continuous effort. But besides this negative presumption, we have one distinct example of the very thing proposed, or rather two, for it is matter of record that the prophet Jeremiah twice reduced to writing, by divine command, the prophecies of many years (see Jer. xxxvi. 2, 4, 28, 32), or rather of his whole preceding ministry. If this be possible in one case, it is possible in others. If we have no difficulty in supposing that Jeremiah's constant inspiration was sufficient to ensure the truth of such a record, or that he was specially inspired for the very purpose, we need have none in supposing that Isaiah, in the last years of his ministry, recorded the whole series of his prophecies, and left them upon everlasting record, as we have them now. To us it matters little whether he recalled exactly the precise words uttered upon each occasion, or received by a new revelation such a summary as God was pleased to substitute instead of it. Our concern is not with prophecies now lost, whether written or oral, but with those now extant and recorded *for our learning*. It is these, and only these, that we interpret, it is only these that can command our faith. The supposition now suggested, while it would preclude a thousand petty questions gendered by the neological hypothesis, would also, when combined with the traditional devotion of the Jews to the preservation of their scriptures, furnish a solid ground for the belief, that what Isaiah wrote three thousand years ago we read to-day, without resorting to the needless supposition of a miracle, or shutting out the possibility of minor deviations from the autograph in every extant manuscript. All that we needed we should have, to wit, a rational assurance that the book, as a book, without descending to enumerate its letters, is precisely what it was, in form and substance, when originally written.

If this supposition were assumed as the basis of our exposition, it would materially modify its form, in some respects, by putting an end to the accustomed method of division into prophecies with separate dates, and introducing the same method which is practised with respect to Paul's epistles, or the undivided prophecies, like that of Hosea. The conventional division into verses and chapters (the latter wholly modern and in several instances absurd) might be retained as a convenient mode of reference ; but the exegetical division of the first part of Isaiah would no longer be historical or critical, but merely analytical and logical, as in the present universal mode of dealing with the last twenty-seven chapters of the book. In the exposition of the prophecies from chaps. i. to xl., the usual distinctive plan has been adopted, partly in deference to established custom and the authority of other writers, partly because the ideas just expressed were not assumed *a priori*, as an arbitrary basis of interpretation, but deduced from it *a posteriori*, as its actual result. In the mean time, it will be observed that various opportunities have been embraced, to check and counteract the tendency to needless or excessive subdivision.

The prophecies expounded in the first part of the volume may be considered introductory, in various respects, to the remainder of the book, not only because earlier in date, and relating for the most part to a nearer futurity, but also as affording the only satisfactory data, upon which the exposition of the rest can be founded.

II. *The Later Prophecies, Chapters 40—66*

ONE of the most important functions of the prophetic office was the exposition of the Law, that is to say, of the Mosaic institutions, the peculiar form in which the Church was organized until the advent of Messiah. This inspired exposition was of absolute necessity, in order to prevent or to correct mistakes which were constantly arising, not only from the blindness and perverseness of the people, but from the very nature of the system under which they lived. That system, being temporary and symbolical, was necessarily material, ceremonial, and restrictive in its forms; as nothing purely spiritual could be symbolical or typical of other spiritual things, nor could a catholic or free constitution have secured the necessary segregation of the people from all others for a temporary purpose.

The evils incident to such a state of things were the same that have occurred in many other like cases, and may all be derived from the superior influence of sensible objects on the mass of men, and from the consequent propensity to lose sight of the end in the use of the means, and to confound the sign with the thing signified. The precise form and degree of this perversion no doubt varied with the change of times and circumstances, and a corresponding difference must have existed in the action of the Prophets who were called to exert a corrective influence on these abuses.

In the days of Hezekiah, the national corruption had already passed through several phases, each of which might still be traced in its effects, and none of which had wholly vanished. Sometimes the prevailing tendency had been to make the ceremonial form of the Mosaic worship, and its consequent coincidence in certain points with the religions of surrounding nations, an occasion or a pretext for adopting heathen rites and usages, at first as a mere extension and enlargement of the ritual itself, then more boldly as an arbitrary mixture of heterogeneous elements, and lastly as an open and entire substitution of the false for the true, and of Baal, Ashtoreth, or Moloch, for Jehovah.

At other times the same corruption had assumed a less revolting form, and been contented with perverting the Mosaic institutions while externally and zealously adhering to them. The two points from which this insidious process of perversion set out were the nature and design of the ceremonial law, and the relation of the chosen people to the rest of men. As to the first, it soon became a current and at last a fixed opinion with the mass of irreligious Jews, that the ritual acts of the Mosaic service had an intrinsic efficacy, or a kind of magical effect upon the moral and spiritual state of the worshipper. Against this error the Law itself had partially provided by occasional violations and suspensions of its own most rigorous demands, plainly implying that the rites were not intrinsically efficacious, but significant of something else. As a single instance of this general fact it may be mentioned, that although the sacrifice of life is everywhere throughout the ceremonial law presented as the symbol of atonement, yet in certain cases, where the circumstances of the offerer forbade an animal oblation, he was suffered to present one of a vegetable nature, even where the service was directly and exclusively expiatory; a substitution wholly inconsistent with the doctrine of an intrinsic virtue or a magical effect, but perfectly in harmony with that of a symbolical and typical design, in which the uniformity of the external symbol, although rigidly maintained in general, might be dispensed with in a rare and special case without absurdity or inconvenience.

It might easily be shewn that the same corrective was provided by the Law itself in its occasional departure from its own requisitions as to time and place, and the officiating person; so that no analogy whatever really exists between the Levitical economy, even as expounded by itself, and the ritual systems which in later times have been so confidently built upon it. But the single instance which has been already cited will suffice to illustrate the extent of the perversion which at an early period had taken root among the Jews as to the real nature and design of their ceremonial services. The natural effect of such an error on the spirit and the morals is too obvious in itself, and too explicitly recorded in the sacred history, to require either proof or illustration.

On the other great point, the relation of the Jews to the surrounding nations, their opinions seem to have become at an early period equally erroneous. In this as in the other case, they went wrong by a superficial judgment founded on appearances, by looking simply at the means before them, and neither forwards to their end, nor backwards to their origin. From the indisputable facts of Israel's divine election as the people of Jehovah, their extraordinary preservation as such, and their undisturbed exclusive possession of the written word and the accompanying rites, they had drawn the natural but false conclusion, that this national pre-eminence was founded on intrinsic causes, or at least on some original and perpetual distinction in their favour. This led them to repudiate or forget the fundamental truth of their whole history, to wit, that they were set apart and kept apart, not for the ruin and disgrace, but for the ultimate benefit and honour of the whole world, or rather of the whole Church which was to be gathered from all nations, and of which the ancient Israel was designed to be the symbol and the representative. As it had pleased God to elect a certain portion of mankind to everlasting life through Christ, so it pleased him that until Christ came, this body of elect ones, scattered through all climes and ages, should be represented by a single nation, and that this representative body should be the sole depository of divine truth and a divinely instituted worship; while the ultimate design of this arrangement was kept constantly in view by the free access which in all ages was afforded to the Gentiles who consented to embrace the true religion.

It is difficult indeed to understand how the Jews could reconcile the immemorial reception of proselytes from other nations, with the dogma of national superiority and exclusive hereditary right to the divine favour. The only solution of this singular phenomenon is furnished by continual recurrence to the great representative principle on which the Jewish Church was organized, and which was carried out not only in the separation of the body as a whole from other men, but in the internal constitution of the body itself, and more-especially in the separation of a whole tribe from the rest of Israel, and of a single family in that tribe from the other Levites, and of a single person in that family, in whom was finally concentrated the whole representation of the Body on the one hand, while on the other he was a constituted type of the Head.

If the Jews could have been made to understand or to remember that their national pre-eminence was representative, not original; symbolical, not real; provisional, not perpetual; it could never have betrayed them into hatred or contempt of other nations, but would rather have cherished an enlarged and catholic spirit, as it did in the most enlightened; an effect which may be clearly traced in the writings of Moses, David, and Isaiah. That view of the Mosaic dispensation which regards this Jewish bigotry as its genuine spirit is demonstrably a false one. The true spirit of the old economy was not indeed a latitudinarian indifference to its institutions, or a premature anticipation of a state of things still future. It was scrupulously faithful even to the temporary institutions of the ancient Church; but while it looked upon them as obligatory, it did not look upon them as perpetual. It obeyed the present requisitions of Jehovah, but still looked forward to something better. Hence the failure to account, on any other supposition, for the seeming contradictions of the Old Testament, in reference to the ceremonies of the Law. If worthless, why were they so conscientiously observed by the best and wisest men? If intrinsically valuable, why are they disparaged and almost repudiated by the same men? Simply because they were neither worthless nor intrinsically valuable, but appointed temporary signs of something to be otherwise revealed thereafter; so that it was equally impious and foolish to reject them altogether with the sceptic, and to rest in them for ever with the formalist.

It is no less true, and for exactly the same reason, that the genuine spirit of the old economy was equally adverse to all religious mixture with the heathen or renunciation of the Jewish privileges on one hand, and to all contracted national conceit and hatred of the Gentiles on the other. Yet both these forms of error had become fixed in the Jewish creed and character long before the days of Hezekiah. That they were not universal even then, we have abundant proof in the Old Testament. Even in the worst of times, there is reason to believe that a portion of the people held fast to the true doctrine and the true spirit of the extraordinary system under which they lived. How large this more enlightened party was at any time, and to how small a remnant it was ever reduced, we have not the means of ascertaining ; but we know that it was always in existence, and that it constituted the true Israel, the real Church of the Old Testament.

To this class the corruption of the general body must have been a cause not only of sorrow but of apprehension ; and if express prophetic threatenings had been wanting, they could scarcely fail to anticipate the punishment and even the rejection of their nation. But in this anticipation they were themselves liable to error. Their associations were so intimately blended with the institutions under which they lived, that they must have found it hard to separate the idea of Israel as a church from that of Israel as a nation ; a difficulty similar in kind, however different in degree, from that which we experience in forming a conception of the continued existence of the soul without the body. And as all men, in the latter case, however fully they may be persuaded of the separate existence of the spirit and of its future disembodied state, habitually speak of it in terms strictly applicable only to its present state, so the ancient saints, however strong their faith, were under the necessity of framing their conceptions, as to future things, upon the model of those present ; and the imperceptible extension of this process beyond the limits of necessity, would naturally tend to generate errors not of form merely but of substance. Among these we may readily suppose to have had place the idea, that as Israel had been unfaithful to its trust, and was to be rejected, the Church or People of God must as a body share the same fate ; or in other words, that if the national Israel perished, the spiritual Israel must perish with it, at least so far as to be disorganized and resolved into its elements.

The same confusion of ideas still exists among the uninstructed classes, and to some extent among the more enlightened also, in those countries where the Church has for ages been a national establishment, and scarcely known in any other form ; as, for instance, in Sweden and Norway among Protestants, or Spain and Portugal among the Papists. To the most devout in such communities the downfall of the hierarchical establishment seems perfectly identical with the extinction of the Church ; and nothing but a long course of instruction, and perhaps experience, could enable them to form the idea of a disembodied, unestablished Christian Church. If such mistakes are possible and real even now, we have little reason either to dispute their existence or to wonder at it, under the complicated forms and in the imperfect light of the Mosaic dispensation. It is not only credible but altogether natural, that even true believers, unassisted by a special revelation, should have shunned the extreme of looking upon Israel's pre-eminence among the nations as original and perpetual, only by verging towards the opposite error of supposing that the downfall of the nation would involve the abolition of the Church, and human unbelief defeat the purposes and make void the promises of God.

Here then are several distinct but cognate forms of error, which appear to have gained currency among the Jews before the time of Hezekiah, in relation to the two great distinctive features of their national condition, the ceremonial law and their seclusion from the Gentiles. Upon each of these points there were two shades of opinion entertained by very different classes. The Mosaic ceremonies were with some a pretext for idolatrous observances ; while others rested in them, not as types or symbols, but as efficacious means of expiation. The pre-eminence of Israel was by some regarded as perpetual ; while others apprehended in its termination the extinction of the Church itself. These various forms of error might be variously combined and modified in different cases, and their general result must of course have contributed largely to determine the character of the Church and nation.

It was not, perhaps, until these errors had begun to take a definite and settled form among the people, that the Prophets, who had hitherto confined themselves to oral instruction or historical composition, were directed to utter and record for constant use discourses meant to be corrective or condemnatory of these dangerous perversions. This may at least be regarded as a plausible solution of the fact that prophetic writing in the strict sense became so much more abundant in the later days of the Old Testament history. Of these prophetic writings, still preserved in our canon, there is scarcely any part which has not a perceptible and direct bearing on the state of feeling and opinion which has been described. This is emphatically true of Isaiah's Earlier Prophecies, which, though so various in form, are all adapted to correct the errors in question, or to establish the antagonistic truths. This general design of these predictions might be so used as to throw new light upon their exposition, by connecting it more closely with the prevalent errors of the ancient Church than has been attempted in our Commentary on that portion of the book. Guided even by this vague suggestion, an attentive reader will be able for the most part to determine with respect to each successive section whether it was speedily intended to rebuke idolatry, to rectify the errors of the formalist in reference to the ceremonial system, to bring down the arrogance of a mistaken nationality, or to console the true believer by assuring him that though the carnal Israel should perish, the true Israel must endure for ever.

But although this purpose may be traced, to some extent, in all the prophecies, it is natural to suppose that some part of the canon would be occupied with a direct, extensive, and continuous exhibition of the truth upon a subject so momentous ; and the date of such a prophecy could scarcely be assigned to any other period so naturally as to that which has been specified—the reign of Hezekiah, when all the various forms of error and corruption which had successively prevailed were coexistent, when idolatry, although suppressed by law, was still openly or secretly practised, and in many cases superseded only by a hypocritical formality and ritual religion, attended by an overweening sense of the national pre-eminence of Israel, from which even the most godly seem to have found refuge in despondent fears and sceptical misgivings. At such a time,—when the theocracy had long since reached and passed its zenith, and a series of providential shocks, with intervals of brief repose, had already begun to loosen the foundations of the old economy in preparation for its ultimate removal,—such a discourse as that supposed must have been eminently seasonable, if not absolutely needed, to rebuke sin, correct error, and sustain the hopes of true believers. It was equally important, nay, essential to the great end of the temporary system, that the way for its final abrogation should be gradually prepared, and that in the mean time it should be maintained in constant operation.

If the circumstances of the times which have been stated are enough to make it probable that such a revelation would be given, they will also aid us in determining beforehand, not in detail, but in the general, its form and character. The historical occasion and the end proposed would naturally lead us to expect in such a book the simultaneous or alternate presentation of a few great leading truths, perhaps with accompanying refutation of the adverse errors, and with such reproofs, remonstrances, and exhortations, promises and threatenings, as the condition of the people springing from these errors might require, not only at the date of the prediction, but in later times. In executing this design, the prophet might have been expected to pursue a method more rhetorical than logical, and to enforce his doctrine, not so much by dry didactic statements as by animated argument, combined with earnest exhortation, passionate appeals, poetical apostrophes, impressive repetitions, and illustrations drawn both from the ancient and the later history of Israel. In fine, from what has been already said it follows that the doctrines which would naturally constitute the staple of the prophecy in such a case, are those relating to the true design of Israel's vocation and seclusion from the Gentiles, and of the ceremonial institutions under which he was in honourable bondage. The sins and errors which find their condemnation in the statement of these truths are those of actual idolatry, a ritual formality, a blinded nationality, and a despondent apprehension of the failure of Jehovah's promise. Such might even *a priori* be regarded as the probable structure and complexion of a prophecy or series of prophecies intended to secure the end in question. If the person called to this important service had already been the organ of divine communications upon other subjects, or with more direct reference to other objects, it would be reasonable to expect a marked diversity between these former prophecies and that uttered under a new impulse. Besides the very great and striking difference which must always be perceptible between a series of detached compositions, varying, and possibly remote from one another as to date, and a continuous discourse on one great theme, there would be other unavoidable distinctions springing directly from the new and wide scope of prophetic vision, and from the concentration in one vision of the elements diffused through many others. This diversity would be enhanced, of course, by any striking difference of outward circumstances, such as the advanced age of the writer, his matured experience, his seclusion from the world and from active life, or any other changes which might have the same effect; but even in the absence of these outward causes, the diversity would still be very great and unavoidable.

From these probabilities let us now turn to realities. Precisely such a book as that described is extant, having formed a part of the collection of Isaiah's Prophecies as far back as the history of the canon can be traced, without the slightest vestige of a different tradition among Jews or Christians as to the author. The tone and spirit of these chapters are precisely such as might have been expected from the circumstances under which they are alleged to have been written, and their variations from the earlier chapters such as must have been expected from the change in the circumstances themselves.

A cursory inspection of these Later Prophecies is enough to satisfy the reader that he has before him neither a concatenated argument nor a mass of fragments, but a continuous discourse, in which the same great topics are continually following each other, somewhat modified in form and combination, but essentially the same from the beginning to the end. If required to designate a single theme as that of the whole series, we might safely give the preference to Israel, the Peculiar People, the Church of the Old Testament, its origin, vocation, mission, sins and sufferings, former experience, and final destiny. The doctrine inculcated as to this great subject, may be summarily stated thus. The race of Israel was chosen from among the other nations, and maintained in the possession of peculiar privileges, not for the sake of any original or acquired merit, but by a sovereign act of the divine will; not for their own exclusive benefit and aggrandisement, but for the ultimate salvation of the world. The ceremonies of the Law were of no intrinsic efficacy, and when so regarded and relied on, became hateful in the sight of God. Still more absurd and impious was the practice of analogous ceremonies, not in obedience to Jehovah's will, but in the worship of imaginary deities or idols. The Levitical rites, besides immediate uses of a lower kind, were symbols of God's holiness and man's corruption, the necessity of expiation in general, and of expiation by vicarious suffering in particular. Among them there were also types, prophetic symbols, of the very form in which the great work of atonement was to be accomplished, and of Him by whom it was to be performed. Until this work was finished, and this Saviour come, the promise of both was exclusively entrusted to the chosen people, who were bound to preserve it both in its written and its ritual form. To this momentous trust a large portion of the nation had been unfaithful, some avowedly forsaking it as open idolaters, some practically betraying it as formal hypocrites. For these and other consequent offences, Israel as a nation was to be rejected and deprived of its pre-eminence. But in so doing God would not cast off his people. The promises to Israel, considered as the people of Jehovah, should endure to the body of believers, the *remnant according to the election of grace.* These were in fact from the beginning the true Israel, the true seed of Abraham, the Jews who were Jews *inwardly.* In these the continued existence of the Church should be secured and perpetuated, first within the limits of the outward Israel, and then by the accession of believing Gentiles to the spiritual Israel. When the fulness of time should come for the removal of the temporary and restrictive institutions of the old economy, that change should be so ordered as not only to effect the emancipation of the Church from ceremonial bondage, but at the same time to attest the divine disapprobation of the sins committed by the carnal Israel throughout their history. While these had everything to fear from the approaching change, the spiritual Israel had everything to hope,—not only the continued existence of the Church, but its existence under a more spiritual, free, and glorious dispensation, to be ushered in by the appearance of that Great Deliverer towards whom the ceremonies of the Law all pointed.

From this succinct statement of the Prophet's doctrine, it is easy to account for some peculiarities of form and phraseology; particularly for the constant alternation of encouragement and threatening, and for the twofold sense or rather application of the national name, Israel. This latter usage is explained by Paul, in his Epistle to the Romans (chap. ii. 17–29; ix. 6–9; xi. 1–7), where the very same doctrine is propounded in relation to the ancient Church that we have just obtained by a fair induction from Isaiah's later Prophecies. There is in fact no part of the Old Testament to which the New affords a more decisive key in the shape of an authoritative and inspired interpretation.

Another peculiarity of form highly important in the exposition of these Prophecies, is the frequent introduction of allusions to particular events in the history of Israel, as examples of the general truths so constantly repeated. The events thus cited are not numerous, but of the greatest magnitude, such as the calling of Abraham, the exodus from Egypt, the destruction of Babylon, the return from exile, and the advent of Messiah. These events have sometimes been confounded by interpreters, and even so far misconceived as to put a new and false face on the whole prediction, as we shall have occasion more explicitly to state below. At present, let it be observed that the prophetical discourse is continually varied and relieved by these historical allusions.

The fairest and the most decisive test by which the foregoing views of the design and subject of these Later Prophecies can be tried, is one within the reach of any reader who will take the trouble to apply it, by a careful perusal of the prophecies themselves, even without any other comment than the general suggestions which have been already made. If this should still prove insufficient to establish the correctness of the exegetical hypothesis proposed, that end may still be answered by comparing this hypothesis with others which have more or less prevailed among interpreters.

Let us first compare with the hypothesis just stated, the one assumed wholly or in part by Cocceius and others, who appear disposed to recognise in these Later Prophecies specific periods and events in the history of the Christian Church. Of this abundant illustration will be given in the Commentary on the Prophecies themselves. Meantime, it may be stated in the general, that besides the arbitrary character of such interpretation, and the infinite diversity which it exhibits in the hands of different writers, it creates the necessity of putting the most forced interpretations on the plainest terms, and of denying that Babylon, Israel, &c., were intended to mean Babylon, Israel, &c., in any sense warranted by Hebrew usage. And even in those parts of the Prophecy which do refer to later times and to the new dispensation, these interpreters are under the necessity of violating one of the most strongly marked peculiarities of this whole book, viz., the general view which it exhibits of the new dispensation as a whole, from its inception to its consummation, as contrasted with the more specific mention of particular events before the change, even when future to the Prophet's own times. This mode of exposition, at least in its extreme forms, has received its most effective refutation from the lapse of time. When we find such writers as Cocceius, and less frequently Vitringa, seeking the fulfilment of grand prophecies in petty squabbles of the Dutch Church or Republic, which have long since lost their place in general history, the practical lesson thus imported is of more force than the most ingenious arguments, to shew that such interpretation rests upon a false hypothesis.

A very different fate has been experienced by the ancient and still current doctrine, that the main subject of these Prophecies throughout, is the restoration from the Babylonish exile. While this hypothesis has been assumed as undeniable by many Christian writers, it affords the whole foundation of the modern neological criticism and exegesis. It is worth while, therefore, to examine somewhat closely the pretensions of this theory to general reception.

In the first place, let it be observed how seldom, after all, the book mentions Babylon, the Exile, or the Restoration. This remark is made in reference to those cases only where these subjects are expressly mentioned, *i. e.* either named *totidem verbis*, or described in terms which will apply to nothing else. An exact enumeration of such cases, made for the first time, might surprise one whose previous impressions had been all derived from the sweeping declarations of interpreters and critics. It is true the cases may be vastly multiplied by taking into account all the indirect allusions which these writers are accustomed to assume, *i.e.* by applying to the Exile all the places and particular expressions which admit by possibility of such an application. Having first inferred from the explicit prophecies respecting Babylon, that this is the great subject of the book, it is perfectly easy to apply to this same subject hundreds of phrases in themselves indefinite and wholly dependent for specific meaning upon some hypothesis like that in question.

The necessary tendency of such a method to excess, is illustrated by the gradual advances of the later German writers in the specific explanation of these chapters. Where Rosenmüller and Gesenius were contented to find general poetical descriptions of the Exile and the Restoration, Hitzig detects precise chronological allusions to particular campaigns and battles in the progress of Cyrus; and this again is pushed so far by Hendewerk and Knobel, that they sometimes find more striking and minute coincidences between this Hebrew writer and Herodotus or Xenophon, than any of the old-fashioned orthodox writers ever dreamed of finding between him and the New Testament. To hear these writers talk of the battle of Pasargada, the defeat of Neriglassar, the first and second attack on Babylonia, the taking of Sardis, &c., &c., we might fancy ourselves listening to Eusebius or Cocceius, with a simple substitution of profane for sacred history.

The fallacy of this mode of interpretation lies in the fact that the indefinite expressions thus applied to one event or series of events, might just as naturally be applied to others, if these others were first fixed upon as being the main subject of the whole composition. Thus, all admit that there are frequent allusions in these later chapters to the exodus from Egypt. Now if any interpreter should be intrepid and absurd enough to argue that they must have been composed by Moses, and that the great deliverance then wrought must be the subject of the whole book, whatever difficulties, and however insurmountable, this doctrine might encounter in a different direction, it could find none in adapting what is said of crossing seas and rivers, opening fountains, journeys through the desert, subjugation of enemies, rest in the promised land, &c. &c., to the original exodus, with far less violence than to the restoration from captivity. It is equally true, but in a less degree, that Grotius, who refers some portions of this book to the period of the Maccabees, is perfectly successful, after having once assumed this as the subject, in accommodating to it many of the very same expressions which another class of writers no less confidently claim as clear allusions to the Babylonian exile.

The fallacy of such exegetical reasoning may be further exposed by applying the same process to a distinct but analogous case. In the Epistle to the Romans, Paul is now almost universally regarded as foretelling the restoration of the Jews to the favour of God. Assuming this to be the theme not only of those passages in which it is expressly mentioned, but of the whole Epistle, an interpreter of no great ingenuity might go completely through it, putting upon every general expression a specific sense, in strict agreement with his foregone conclusion. All that relates to justification might be limited to the Jews of some future day; the glorious truth that there is no condemnation to believers in Christ Jesus, made a specific and exclusive promise to converted Jews; and the precious promise that all things shall work together for good to them that love God, made to mean that all events shall be so ordered as to bring about the future restoration of the Jews. The very absurdity of such conclusions makes them better illustrations of the erroneous principles involved in similar interpretations of the more obscure and less familiar parts of Scripture.

Setting aside the cases which admit of one application as well as another, or of this application only because of a foregone conclusion, the truth of which cannot be determined by expressions deriving their specific meaning from itself, let the reader now enumerate the instances in which the reference to Babylon, the Exile, and the Restoration, is not only possible but necessary. He must not be surprised if he discovers as the fruit of his researches, that the Prophet speaks of Babylon less frequently than Egypt; that the ruins, desolations and oppressions, which he mentions in a multitude of places are no more Babylonian than Egyptian or Roman in the text itself, and only made so by the interest or fancy of some writers, the authority of others, and the easy faith of the remainder.

In opposition to these strained conclusions, we have only to propound the obvious supposition that the downfall of Babylon is repeatedly mentioned, like the exodus from Egypt, as a great event in the history of Israel ; but that the subject of the prophecy is neither the Egyptian nor the Babylonian bondage, nor deliverance from either, but the whole condition, character, and destiny of Israel as the chosen people and the Church of the Old Testament.

All the hypotheses which have been mentioned are agreed in assuming the unity of these predictions as the product not only of a single age, but of a single writer. This unity, however, was by no means recognised by those who first applied the principles and methods of the Higher Criticism to Isaiah. The earliest hint of any new discovery is commonly ascribed to Koppe, who, in a note upon his German edition of Bishop Lowth's work, suggests that the fiftieth chapter may have been written by Ezekiel or some other Jew in exile. A similar opinion was expressed about the same time by Döderlein and Eichhorn with respect to the entire latter part of Isaiah. The same hypothesis was then carried out in detail by Justi, and adopted by Bauer, Paulus, Bertholdt, and Augusti ; so that not long after the beginning of this century, it was established as the current doctrine of the German schools.

This revolution of opinion, though ostensibly the pure result of critical analysis, was closely connected with the growing unbelief in inspiration, and the consequent necessity of explaining away whatever appeared either to demonstrate or involve it. It must also be noted as a circumstance of great importance in the history of this controversy, that the young theologians of Germany for fifty years were almost as uniformly taught and as constantly accustomed to assume the certainty of this first principle, as their fathers had been to assume the contrary. This fact will enable us to estimate at something like their real value the pretensions to superior candour and impartiality advanced by the neological interpreters, and more especially by some of recent date, who are in truth as strongly biassed by the prejudice of education as their immediate predecessors by the love of novelty and passion for discovery.

The defenders of the unity of this part of Isaiah were in process of time relieved from much of the irksome task which they had undertaken by the concessions of the adverse party, that the Higher Criticism had been pushed too far, and made to prove too much ; in consequence of which a retrocession became necessary, and in fact took place under the guidance of new leaders, not without an earnest opposition on the part of the original discoverers.

This retreat was effected with great skill and conduct, but with no small sacrifice of logical consistency, by Gesenius in the Introduction to his second volume. Without any appeal to general principles or any attempt to distinguish clearly between what he abandons as " extreme " and what he adopts as rational conclusions, he proceeds, by his favourite method of accumulation and arrangement of particulars, to prove that these twenty-seven chapters are the work of the same author, and that in the main they are still in the same order as at first, the only material exception being a surmise that the last chapters may possibly be older than the first; which seems to have been prompted by a natural reluctance to acknowledge that an ancient composition could remain so long unchanged, not without a misgiving with respect to the influence which this concession might exert hereafter on the criticism of the earlier chapters.

Although Gesenius's argument in favour of the unity of these predictions is entirely successful, a large proportion of his detailed proofs are quite superfluous. It is an error of this German school, and of its imitators elsewhere, that identity of authorship must be established by minute resemblances of diction, phraseology, and syntax, which are therefore raked together and displayed with a profusion far more confounding than convincing to the reader. To the great mass of cultivated minds, conviction in such cases is produced by data not susceptible of exhibition in the form of schedules, catalogues, or tables, but resulting from a general impression of continuity and oneness, which might be just as strong if not a single phrase or combination occurred more than once, and the want of which could never be supplied by any number or servility of verbal repetitions. It is thus that the modern imitators of the classics may be almost infallibly detected, though their diction be but a cento of quotations from their favourite author, renewed and multiplied *usque ad nauseam;* while the original is known wherever he appears, however innocent of copying himself.

This error of the higher or lower criticism, even when enlisted on the right side of a question, it is important to expose ; because many of its boasted triumphs in behalf of error have been gained by the very *petitesse* of its expedients. The readers of Isaiah, in particular, have often been bewildered and unfairly prepossessed against the truth, by the interminable catalogues of Hebrew words and phrases which are crowded into prefaces and introductions as preliminary proofs of a position that can only be established, if at all, by the cumulative weight of a detailed interpretation ; the effect of which is often to expose the absolute futility of arguments, considered one by one and in their proper place, which seem to gain reality and force by insulation from the context, and by being thrown together in crude masses, or forced into unnatural protrusion by the forms of a systematic catalogue.

The minute details which constitute this portion of Gesenius's argument against the fragmentary theory, must be sought in his own work, or in those which have transcribed it. Much more important and conclusive is that part of his argument derived from the unquestionable fact, that certain threads may be traced running through the entire texture of these Later Prophecies, sometimes dropped but never broken, crossing each other, and at times appearing to be hopelessly entangled, but all distinguished, and yet all united in the *dénouement.* The perpetual recurrence and succession of these topics is correctly represented by Gesenius as the strongest proof of unity. In opposition to Augusti, who alleges that some topics are more prominent at first than afterwards, and *vice versa*, Gesenius replies that progress and variety are perfectly consistent with the strictest unity ; that the author's ideal situation is the same throughout ; and that all the topics which become more prominent as he proceeds, had at least been lightly touched before, to which he adds another list of verbal parallels between the parts described as most dissimilar. (See Gesen. Comm., vol. ii. p. 15.)

This reasoning is worthy of particular attention, on account of its remarkable affinity with that by which the defenders of the old opinions have maintained the genuineness of disputed places in the Earlier Prophecies, against objections of Gesenius himself, precisely analogous to those of Augusti which he here refutes. It would greatly contribute to the correct decision of these questions, among men who are accustomed to the weighing of evidence on other subjects, if their attention could be drawn to the facility with which the same degree and kind of proof are admitted or excluded by the Higher Critics, according to the end at which they happen to be aiming. Perhaps one of our most valuable safeguards against German innovations is afforded by our civil institutions, and the lifelong familiarity of our people, either through the press or by personal participation, with the public administration of justice and the practical discrimination between truth and falsehood ; an advantage which never can be replaced by any method or amount of mental cultivation.

If then these twenty-seven chapters are confessedly the work of one man, and indeed a continuous discourse on one great subject, and if a perfectly uniform tradition has attached them to the writings of Isaiah, it remains to be considered whether we have any reason to deny or even to dispute the fact so solemnly attested. All the presumptions are in favour of its truth. For two thousand years, at least, the book was universally regarded as Isaiah's, and no other name has ever been connected with it even by mistake or accident. It is just such a book as the necessities of that age might have been expected to call forth. Its genuineness, therefore, as a writing of Isaiah, is not a fact requiring demonstration by detailed and special proof, but one attested both by its external history and its internal structure, unless positive reasons can be given for rejecting a conclusion which appears not only obvious but unavoidable.

Among the objections to Isaiah as the author of these later chapters, there are two upon which the whole weight of the argument depends, and to which all others may be reckoned supplementary. The first of these has reference to the matter of the prophecies, the second to their form. The latter is entirely posterior in date, and has been growing more and more prominent, as the necessity of something to sustain the first and main objection has been forced upon its advocates by the resistance which it has encountered. This chronological relation of the two main objections is here stated not only as a curious fact of literary history, but also as directly bearing on the issue of the whole dispute, for reasons which will be explained below.

The first and main objection to the doctrine that Isaiah wrote these chapters, although variously stated by the writers who have urged it, is in substance this : that the prophet everywhere alludes to the circumstances and events of the Babylonish exile as those by which he was himself surrounded, and with which he was familiar, from which his conceptions and his images are borrowed, out of which he looks both at the future and the past, and in the midst of which he must as a necessary consequence have lived and written.

This objection involves two assumptions, both which must be true, or it is wholly without force. One of these, viz., that the Babylonish exile is the subject of the whole book, has already been disproved; and there is strictly, therefore, no need of considering the other. But in order that the whole strength of our cause may be disclosed, it will be best to shew that even if the supposition just recited were correct, the other, which is equally essential to the truth of the conclusion, is entirely unfounded. This is the assumption that the local and historical allusions of a prophet must be always those of his own times.

Some of the later German writers try to rest this upon general grounds, by alleging that such is the invariable practice of the Hebrew prophets. But as the book in question, *i. e.* the latter portion of Isaiah, is admitted by these very critics to deserve the highest rank among prophetic writings, and to have exercised a more extensive influence on later writers and opinions than any other, it is unreasonable to appeal to a usage of which the book itself may be considered as a normal standard. It is in fact a begging of the question to deny that such was the prophetic usage, when that denial really involves an allegation that it is not so in the case before us.

Another answer to this argument from usage may be drawn from the analogy of other kinds of composition, in which all grant that a writer may assume a " *Standpunkt* " different from his own, and personate those earlier and later than himself. The classical historians do this when they put their own words into the mouths of ancient heroes and statesmen; the dramatic poets when they carry out this personation in detail; and still more imaginative writers, when they throw themselves into the future, and surround themselves by circumstances not yet in existence. If it be natural for poets thus to speak of an ideal future, why may not prophets of a real one? The only answer is, *because they cannot know it ;* and to this point all the tortuous evasions of the more reserved neologists as surely tend as the positive averments of their bolder brethren. In every form, this argument against the genuineness of the book before us is at bottom a denial of prophetic inspiration as impossible. For if the prophet could foresee the future, his allusions only prove that he did foresee it; and the positive assertion that the prophets never do so, unless it be founded upon this hypothesis, is just as foolish as it would be to assert that historians and poets never do the like. Unless we are prepared to go the same length, we cannot consistently reject these prophecies as spurious, on the ground that they allude to events long posterior to the writer's times, even if these allusions were as numerous and explicit as we have seen them to be few when clear, and in all other cases vague and doubtful.

It has indeed been said, in confirmation of this main objection, that a real foresight would extend to more remote as well as proximate events, whereas in this case what relates to the period of the Exile is minutely accurate, while all beyond is either blank or totally erroneous; in proof of which we are referred to the extravagant descriptions of the times which should succeed the Restoration.

Both parts of this reasoning rest upon a false assumption as to the space which is occupied in this book by the Babylonish Exile. If, as we have seen or shall see, the alleged minute descriptions of that period are imaginary, and if the alleged extravagant descriptions of its close relate to events altogether different, then this auxiliary argument must share the fate of that which it is brought in to sustain. To this same category appertains the special objection founded on the mention of Cyrus by name. That it may readily be solved by an application of the same principle will be shewn in the exposition of the passage where the prophecy occurs. (See below, chap. xlv.)

Another erroneous supposition, which has tended to confirm this first objection to the genuineness of the Later Prophecies is, that they must have been intended solely for the contemporaries of the writer. This hypothesis is closely connected with the denial of divine inspiration. The idea that Isaiah wrote for after ages is of course a "*nichtige Annahme*" to an infidel. The Prophet's work, according to this theory, is more confined than that of the orator or poet. These may be said to labour for posterity; but his views must be limited to those about him. Ewald alone of those who deny a real inspiration (unless Umbreit may be likewise so described) admits a far-reaching purpose in the ancient prophecies. The rest appear to be agreed that nothing could be more absurd than consolation under sorrows which were not to be experienced for ages. Here again may be seen the working of a double error, that of making the exile the great subject of the book, and that of denying that it could have been foreseen so long before-hand. Of all the evils afterwards matured, the germ, if nothing more, existed in Isaiah's time. And even if it did not, their appearance at a later date might well have been predicted. If the book, as we have reason to believe, was intended to secure a succession of the highest ends : the warning and instruction of the Prophet's own contemporaries, the encouragement and consolation of the pious exiles, the reproof and conviction of their unbelieving brethren, the engagement of the Persians and especially of Cyrus in the service of Jehovah, the vindication of God's dealings with the Jews both in wrath and mercy, and a due preparation of the minds of true believers for the advent of Messiah : then such objections as the one last cited must be either unmeaning and impertinent, or simply equivalent to a denial of prophetic inspiration.

To the same head may be referred those objections which have been derived from the alleged appearance of opinions in these chapters which are known to have arisen at a later period. Besides the palpable *petitio principii* involved in such an argument, so far as it assumes that to be late which these prophecies if genuine demonstrate to be ancient, there is here again a confident assumption of a fact as certain which at best is doubtful, and in my opinion utterly unfounded, namely, that the strict observance of the Sabbath and a particular regard to the Levitical priesthood and the sanctuary, all belong to a species of Judaism later than the times of the genuine Isaiah. It is by thus assuming their own paradoxical conclusions as unquestionable facts, that the Higher Critics of the German school have been enabled to construct some of their most successful arguments.

All that need be added in relation to the arguments against the genuineness of these chapters drawn from their matter or contents, is the general observation that their soundness may be brought to the test by inquiring whether they do not either take for granted something as belonging to the prophecy which is not found there by a simple and natural interpretation, or proceed upon some general false principle, such as the denial of prophetic inspiration as impossible. If either of these flaws is fatal to the argument affected by it, how much more must it be vitiated by the coexistence of the two, which is the case in many minor arguments of this class, and emphatically true of that main argument to which they are auxiliary, namely, that Isaiah cannot be the writer of these chapters on account of their minute and constant reference to the Babylonian Exile. The alleged fact and the inference are equally unfounded.

The other main objection to the genuineness of these prophecies is founded not upon their matter but their manner, or in other words, their diction, phraseology, and style, which are said to be entirely unlike those of Isaiah. The minute specifications of this argument, so far as they can lay claim even to a passing notice, are reserved for the exposition of the passages from which they are derived, and where they may be calmly viewed in their original connection, and without the artificial glare produced by an immense accumulation of detached examples, which may blind the reader by their number and variety, without affording him the means of judging for himself how many may at best be dubious, how many inconclusive, and how many more entirely irrelevant. For the same reason no reliance will be placed upon a similar display of minute resemblances between these later chapters and the undisputed writings of Isaiah, although such are furnished in abundance by Kleinert, Hävernick, and others. Of the value of such proofs and the soundness of the inferences drawn from them, a reference may be made to the first part of the Introduction. At the same time it cannot be denied that the counterproofs collected by these writers are of great importance, as establishing the fact of their existence upon both sides of the controversy, and as serving, if no higher purpose, that of cancelling such proofs when urged against the genuineness of the prophecies by writers who to all alleged resemblances reply that " such trifles can prove nothing,'' or that the style has been assimilated by a later hand. For this reason some of the most striking coincidences of expression will be noticed in the exposition, as well as the discrepancies which have been alleged in proof of later origin.

It has been already mentioned that this argument from difference of language is much later in its origin than that derived from the historical allusions. This is a significant and important circumstance. Had the Higher Criticism set out from some palpable diversity of diction as a starting-point, and, after vainly trying to identify the writers upon this ground, been compelled to own a corresponding difference of matter and substantial indications of a later age than that of Isaiah, the critical process, although still inconclusive, would at least have been specious, and the difficulty of defence proportionally greater. But what is the true state of the case? Eichhorn and Bertholdt, though disposed to assume not only a later date but a plurality of authors, could find nothing to sustain this assumption in the language of the book itself. Augusti, who occupied the same ground, went so far as to account for the traditional incorporation of these chapters with Isaiah from their perfect imitation of his style and manner. Rosenmüller dwells altogether on the first objection drawn from the allusions to the Babylonish Exile. Even Gesenius admits that the peculiarities of this class are less numerous than might have been expected, but succeeds in specifying some which had been overlooked. From that time the discovery (for such it may well be termed) of these philological diversities has been in constant and accelerated progress. Even Maurer, who is commonly so sparing of details, adds to the black list several particulars. Hitzig enlarges it still further, but unluckily admits that some of the expressions which he notes are not to be found either in the earlier or later books. Ewald as usual supplies the want of detailed proofs by authoritative affirmations. Umbreit considers the work done already, and declines attempting to refute Hengstenberg and Kleinert as a work of supererogation. But this forbearance is abundantly made good by the zeal of Hendewerk and Knobel, who have carried their citation of neologisms so far, that little now seems left for their successors but to gather the remainder of the book by way of gleanings.

But although the general course of this peculiar criticism has been onward, there have not been wanting certain retrograde movements and obliquities to break the uniformity of progress. Every one of the later writers above mentioned rejects some of the examples cited by his predecessors as irrelevant, and not seldom with expressions of contempt. But still the aggregate has grown, and by a further application of the same means may continue growing, until the materials are exhausted, or the Higher Criticism chooses to recede from this extreme, as it receded five and twenty years ago from that of Eichhorn and Augusti, who would no doubt have looked down upon the notion that these twenty-seven chapters were the work of the same hand, with almost as much contempt as on the old belief that this hand was Isaiah's. It is indeed not a matter of conjecture but of history, that Eichhorn in the last edition of his Introduction finds fault with Gesenius for having abandoned the plurality of authors, and evidently pities him as one who from excess of light had gone back into darkness. By a similar reaction we might look for some concession in favour even of Isaiah as the writer; but although such an expectation need not be discouraged by the fear of any scrupulous regard to logic or consistency among the Higher Critics, it is rendered hopeless for the present by the obvious necessity which it involves of abandoning their fundamental principle, the impossibility of inspiration or prophetic foresight. For to this, as the original, the chief, and I had almost said the only ground of the rejection of these chapters, we are still brought back from every survey of the arguments by which it is defended. The obvious deduction from the sketch which has been given of the progress of discovery in this department is, that the philological objection would have slept for ever, had it not become absolutely necessary to secure the rejection of a book, which, if genuine, carried on its face the clearest proofs of inspiration.

Be it remembered, then, that the rejection of these chapters was not forced upon the critics by a palpable diversity of style and diction, but that such diversities were hunted up, laboriously and gradually brought to light, in order to justify the previous rejection. By parity of reasoning it may be foreseen that whoever cannot be convinced of the reality of inspiration, will consider these detailed proofs of later date conclusive; while the reader who knows better, or at least has no misgivings upon that point, will as certainly pronounce them 'trifles light as air.' If we gain nothing more by this investigation, it is at least satisfactory to know that all depends upon a foregone conclusion, and that as to faith in such things no less than in higher matters, he that hath, receiveth, and from him that hath not, shall be taken even that which he hath.

The objection drawn from other more indefinite diversities of tone and manner, such as a more flowing style and frequent repetitions, is so far from having any force, that the absence of these differences would in the circumstances of the case be well adapted to excite suspicion. In other words, Isaiah writing at a later period of life, and when withdrawn from active labour, with his view directed not to the present or a proximate futurity, but one more distant, and composing not a series of detached discourses, but a continuous unbroken prophecy, not only may, but must have differed from his former self as much as these two parts of the collection differ from each other. This antecedent probability is strengthened by the fact that similar causes have produced a still greater difference in some of the most celebrated writers, ancient and modern, who exhibit vastly more unlikeness to themselves in different parts of their acknowledged writings than the most microscopic criticism has been able to detect between the tone or manner of Isaiah's Earlier and Later Prophecies.

The only other objections to the genuineness of these chapters which appear to deserve notice are those derived from the silence or the testimony of the other books. That these are not likely to do more than confirm the conclusions previously reached on one side or the other, may be gathered from the fact that they are urged with equal confidence on both sides of the question. Thus Gesenius argues that if these later chapters had been known to Jeremiah, he would have appealed to them in self-vindication, as he did to Micah. On the other hand, Hengstenberg alleges that by parity of reasoning, Micah iv. 10 could not have been extant, or the enemies of Jeremiah would have quoted it against him. At the same time, he maintains that there are obvious traces of these chapters in the writings of that prophet. The truth is, that the advocates on both sides first determine which is the older writer, and then explain the appearances of quotation or allusion accordingly. The same is true of similar appearances in Nahum, Zephaniah, and Habakkuk, which Hitzig cites as proofs of imitation on the part of the Pseudo-Isaiah, while Hävernick claims them all as proofs of his priority. It is a very important observation of the last mentioned writer, that the influence of Isaiah on these later prophets is not to be estimated by detached expressions, but by more pervading indications, which he thinks are clearly perceptible throughout the writings both of Jeremiah and Ezekiel.

As samples of the arguments in favour of their genuineness drawn from the same quarter, may be cited, Zech. vii. 4–12, where "the former Prophets," who cried in the name of Jehovah to the people "when Jerusalem was inhabited and in prosperity," must include the writer of these chapters. In reference to all these minor arguments, however, it will be felt by every reader that they have no practical effect, except to corroborate the main ones which have been discussed, and with which they must stand or fall.

Enough has now been said to shew that there is no sufficient reason for rejecting the traditional ascription of these chapters to Isaiah. Let us now turn the tables, and inquire what objections lie against the contrary hypothesis. These objections may be all reduced to this, that the oblivion of the author's name and history is more inexplicable, not to say incredible, than anything about the other doctrine can be to a believer in prophetic inspiration. This is a difficulty which no ingenuity has ever yet been able to surmount. That a writer confessedly of the highest genius, living at one of the most critical junctures in the history of Israel, when the word of God began to be precious and prophetic inspiration rare, should have produced such a series of prophecies as this, with such effects upon the exiles and even upon Cyrus as tradition ascribes to them, and then have left them to the admiration of all future ages, without so much as a trace of his own personality about them, is a phenomenon of literary history compared with which the mystery of Junius is as nothing. It would be so even if we had no remains of the same period to compare with these; but how immensely is the improbability enhanced by the fact that the other prophets of the exile, Jeremiah, Ezekiel, Haggai, Zechariah, are not only well known and easily identified, but minutely accurate in the chronological specifications of their prophecies, a feature absolutely wanting in these chapters, though alleged to be the work of a contemporary writer. It is in vain to say, with Ewald, that the suppression of the author's name and the oblivion of his person may be accounted for by the peculiar circumstances of the times, when the other writings of those times still extant not only fail to prove what is alleged, but prove the very opposite.

Even this, however, though sufficiently incredible, is still not all we are required to believe : for we must also grant that these anonymous though admirable writings were attached to those of a prophet who flourished in the preceding century, and with whose productions they are said to have scarcely any thing in common, nay, that this mysterious combination took place so early as to lie beyond the oldest tradition of the Hebrew Canon, and was so blindly acquiesced in from the first that not the faintest intimation of another author or another origin was ever heard of for two thousand years, when the Higher Criticism first discovered that the prophecies in question were the work of many authors, and then (no less infallibly) that they were really the work of only one, but (still infallibly) that this one could not be Isaiah !

It is in vain that the Germans have endeavoured to evade this fatal obstacle by childish suppositions about big rolls and little rolls, or by citing cases of concealment or oblivion wholly dissimilar and far less wonderful, or by negligently saying that we are not bound to account for the fact, provided we can prove it ; as if the proof were not dependent in a great degree upon the possibility of accounting for it, or as if the only business of the Higher Critics were to tie knots which neither we nor they can untie. The question here at issue only needs to be presented to the common sense of mankind, and especially of those who are accustomed to weigh evidence in real life, to be immediately disposed of by the prompt decision that the modern hypothesis is utterly incredible, and that nothing could make it appear otherwise to any man acquainted with the subject, but an irresistible desire to destroy a signal proof and instance of prophetic inspiration.

To this intrinsic want of credibility now add, as positive considerations, the ancient and uniform tradition of the Jews ; the testimony of the general title, which must be regarded as inclusive of these chapters, in the absence of all countervailing evidence ; the influence exerted by these prophecies, according to Josephus, on Cyrus and the Restoration, implying their antiquity and previous notoriety ; the recognition of the whole book as Isaiah's by the son of Sirach (xlviii. 22–25) ; and the indiscriminate citation of its different parts in the New Testament.

Again, to these external testimonies may be added, as internal proofs, the writer's constant representation of himself as living before some of the events which he describes, and as knowing them by inspiration ; his repeated claim to have predicted Cyrus and the Restoration, long before the first appearance of those events ; the obvious allusions to Jerusalem and Judah as the writer's home, to the temple and the ritual as still subsisting, and to idolatry as practised by the people, which the Higher Critics can evade only by asserting that the Jews did not cease to be idolaters in Babylon ; the historical allusions to the state of the world with which the writer was familiar, precisely similar to those in the genuine Isaiah ; the very structure of the prophecies relating to the exile, clear enough to be distinctly verified, and yet not so minute as a contemporary writer must have made them ; and lastly, the identity of Messiah here described with the Messiah of the undisputed prophecies.

It is perhaps impossible for any writer on this subject to do full justice to the adverse arguments, especially to those of a minor and auxiliary character. This is the less to be regretted, because every fresh discussion of the subject makes it more and more apparent that the question really at issue is not whether either party has established its position by direct proofs, but whether it has furnished the other with sufficient reasons for abandoning its own. If the Higher Critics can find nothing in the arguments alleged against them to make inspiration and prophetic foresight credible, they have certainly done still less to drive us from our position, that Isaiah's having written this book is unspeakably more probable than any other supposition.

Having now traced the history of the *criticism* of these prophecies, it may not be amiss to look at that of their *interpretation*, not through the medium of minute chronological or bibliographical details, but by exhibiting the several theories, or schools of exegesis, which at different times, or at the same time, have exerted an important influence on the interpretation of these chapters.

The first of these proceeds upon the supposition that these Later Prophecies have reference throughout to the New Dispensation and the Christian Church, including its whole history, with more or less distinctness, from the advent of Christ to the end of the world. This is a favourite doctrine of the Fathers who have written on Isaiah, to wit, Cyril, Eusebius, Jerome, and of some modern writers, among whom the most distinguished is Cocceius. The difference between those who maintain it respects chiefly the degree of fulness and consistency with which they carry out their general idea, some admitting much more frequently than others the occasional occurrence of predictions which were verified before the Advent.

This system of prophetic exegesis is founded, to a great extent, on the assumption that the Book of Revelation was designed to be a key to the meaning of the ancient prophecies, and not a series of new predictions, often more enigmatical than any of the others. Because Babylon is there named as a power still existing and still threatened with destruction, it was inferred that the name must be symbolical in Isaiah likewise, or at least that it might be so explained at the interpreter's discretion. This opened an illimitable field of conjecture and invention, each interpreter pursuing his own method of determining the corresponding facts in Church History, without any settled rule to guide or to control him.

The extravagant conclusions often reached in this way, and the general uncertainty imparted to the whole work of interpretation, together with the seeming incorrectness of the principle assumed in regard to the Apocalypse, led many, and particularly those in whom the understanding strongly predominated over the imagination, to reject this theory in favour of its opposite, viz., that the main subject of these chapters must be sought as far as possible before the advent, and as a necessary consequence either in the period of the Babylonian Exile, or in that of the Syrian domination, with the periods of reaction which succeeded them respectively, since it was only these that furnished events of sufficient magnitude to be the subject of such grand predictions.

It is evident at once that both these theories involve some truth, and that their application must evolve the true sense of some passages. The fatal vice of both is their exclusiveness. The unbiassed reader of Isaiah can no more be persuaded that he never speaks of the New Dispensation than that he never speaks of the Old. After both systems had been pushed to an extreme, it was found necessary to devise some method of conciliating and combining them.

The first and rudest means employed for this end, even by some of the most strenuous adherents of the two extreme hypotheses, when forced at times to grant themselves a dispensation from the rigorous enforcement of their own rule, was to assume arbitrarily a change of subject when it appeared necessary, and to make the Prophet skip from Babylon to Rome, and from the Maccabees to Doomsday, as they found convenient. This arbitrary mixture of the theories is often perpetrated by Cocceius, and occasionally even by Vitringa; neither of whom seems to think it necessary to subject the application of the prophecies to any general principle, or to account for it in any other way than by alleging that it suits the text and context.

A more artificial method of combining both hypotheses is that of Grotius, whose interpretation of these prophecies appears to be governed by two maxims; first, that they all relate to subjects and events before the time of Christ; and secondly, that these are often types of something afterwards developed. What renders this kind of interpretation unsatisfactory, is the feeling which it seldom fails to generate, that the text is made to mean too much, or rather too many things; that if one of the senses really belongs to it, the other is superfluous: but, above all, that the nexus of the two is insufficient; and although a gradual or even a repeated execution of a promise or a threatening is conceivable, it seems unreasonable that the interpreter should have the discretionary right of saying that the same passage means one thing in ancient times and an altogether different thing in modern times; that the same words, for example, are directly descriptive of Antiochus Epiphanes and Antichrist, of Judas Maccabaeus and Gustavus Adolphus.

A third mode of reconciling these two theories of interpretation is the one pursued by Lowth, and still more successfully by Hengstenberg. It rests upon the supposition that the nearer and the more remote realization of the same prophetic picture might be presented to the Prophet simultaneously or in immediate succession; so that, for example, the deliverance from Babylon by Cyrus insensibly merges into a greater deliverance from sin and ruin by Christ. The principle assumed in this ingenious doctrine is as just as it is beautiful, and of the highest practical importance in interpretation. The only objection to its general application in the case before us is, that it concedes the constant reference to Babylon throughout this book, and only seeks to reconcile this fundamental fact with the wider application of the Prophecies.

It still remains to be considered, therefore, whether any general hypothesis or scheme can be constructed, which, without giving undue prominence to any of the topics introduced, without restricting general expressions to specific objects, without assuming harsh transitions, needless double senses, or imaginary typical relations, shall do justice to the unity and homogeneousness of the composition, and satisfactorily reconcile the largeness and variety of its design with the particular allusions and predictions, which can only be eliminated from it by a forced and artificial exegesis.

Such a hypothesis is that propounded at the beginning of this second part of the Introduction, and assumed as the basis of the following Exposition. It supposes the main subject of these Prophecies, or rather of this Prophecy, to be the Church or people of God, considered in its members and its Head, in its design, its origin, its progress, its vicissitudes, it consummation, in its various relations to God and to the world, both as a field of battle and a field of labour, an enemy's country to be conquered, and an inheritance to be secured.

Within the limits of this general description it is easy to distinguish, as alternate objects of prophetic vision, the two great phases of the Church on earth, its state of bondage and its state of freedom, its ceremonial and its spiritual aspect ; in a word, what we usually call the Old and New Economy or Dispensation. Both are continually set before us, but with this observable distinction in the mode of presentation, that the first great period is described by individual specific strokes, the second by its outlines as a definite yet undivided whole. To the great turning-point between the two dispensations the prophetic view appears to reach with clear discrimination of the intervening objects, but beyond that to take all in at a single glance. Within the boundaries first mentioned, the eye passes with a varied uniformity from one salient point to another ; but beyond them it contemplates the end and the beginning, not as distinct pictures, but as necessary elements of one. This difference might naturally be expected in a Prophecy belonging to the Old Dispensation, while in one belonging to the New we should as naturally look for the same definiteness and minuteness as the older prophets used in their descriptions of the older times ; and this condition is completely answered by the Book of Revelation.

If this be so, it throws a new light on the more specific Prophecies of this part of Isaiah, such as those relating to the Babylonish Exile, which are then to be regarded, not as the main subject of the Prophecy, but only as prominent figures in the great prophetic picture, some of which were to the Prophet's eye already past, and some still future. In this respect the Prophecy is perfectly in keeping with the History of Israel, in which the Exile and the Restoration stand conspicuously forth as one of the great crititical conjunctures which at distant intervals prepared the way for the removal of the ancient system, and yet secured its continued operation till the time of that removal should arrive. How far the same thing may be said of other periods which occupy a like place in the history of the Jews, such as the period of the Maccabees or Hasmonean Princes, is a question rendered doubtful by the silence of the prophecy itself, and by the absence of any indications which are absolutely unambiguous. The specific reference of certain passages to this important epoch both by Grotius and Vitringa, has no antecedent probability against it ; but we cannot with the same unhesitating confidence assert such an allusion as we can in the case of Babylon and Cyrus, which are mentioned so expressly and repeatedly. It may be that historical discovery, the march of which has been so rapid in our own day, will enable us, or those who shall come after us, to set this question finally at rest. In the mean time, it is safest to content ourselves with carefully distinguishing between the old and new economy, as represented on the Prophet's canvass, without attempting to determine by conjecture what particular events are predicted even in the former, any further than we have the certain guidance of the Prophecy itself.

As to a similar attempt in reference to the New Dispensation, it is wholly inconsistent with the view which we have taken of the structure of these Prophecies, and which regards them, not as particular descriptions of this or that event in later times, but as a general description of the Church in its emancipated state, or of the reign of the Messiah, not at one time or another, but throughout its whole course, so that the faint light of the dawn is blended with the glow of sunset and the blaze of noon. The form under which the Reign of Christ is here presented to and by the Prophet, is that of a glorious emancipation from the bondage and the darkness of the old economy, in representing which he naturally dwells with more minuteness upon that part of the picture which is nearest to himself, while the rest is bathed in a flood of light ; to penetrate beyond which, or to discriminate the objects hid beneath its dazzling veil, formed no part of this Prophet's mission, but was reserved for the prophetic revelations of the New Testament.

It is not, however, merely to the contrast of the two dispensations that the Prophet's eye is here directed. It would indeed have been impossible to bring this contrast clearly into view without a prominent exhibition of the great event by which the transition was effected, and of the great person who effected it. That person is the servant of Jehovah, elsewhere spoken of as his anointed or Messiah, and both here and elsewhere represented as combining the prophetic, regal, and sacerdotal characters suggested by that title. The specific relation which he here sustains to the Israel of God, is that of the Head to a living Body ; so that in many cases what is said of him appears to be true wholly or in part of them, as forming one complex person, an idea perfectly accordant with the doctrines and the images of the New Testament. It appears to have been first clearly stated in the dictum of an ancient writer quoted by Augustine : " De Christo et Corpore ejus Ecclesia tanquam de una persona in Scriptura sæpius mentionem fieri, cui quædam tribuuntur quæ tantum in Caput, quædam quæ tantum in Corpus competunt, quædam vero in utrumque." There is nothing in these Prophecies more striking or peculiar than the sublime position occupied by this colossal figure, standing between the Church of the Old and that of the New Testament, as a mediator, an interpreter, a bond of union, and a common Head.

If this be a correct view of the structure of these prophecies, nothing can be more erroneous or unfriendly to correct interpretation, than the idea, which appears to form the basis of some expositions, that the primary object in the Prophet's view is Israel as a race or nation, and that its spiritual or ecclesiastical relations are entirely adventitious and subordinate. The natural result of this erroneous supposition is a constant disposition to give every thing a national and local sense. This is specially the case with respect to the names so frequently occurring, Zion, Jerusalem, and Judah ; all which, according to this view of the matter, must be understood, wherever it is possible, as meaning nothing more than the hill, the city, and the land, which they originally designate. This error has even been pushed by some to the irrational extreme of making Israel as a race the object of the promises, after their entire separation from the Church, and their reduction for the time being to the same position with the sons of Ishmael and of Esau. That this view should be taken by the modern Jews, in vindication of their own continued unbelief, is not so strange as its adoption by some Christian writers, even in direct opposition to their own interpretation of former prophecies, almost identical in form and substance. The specifications of this general charge will be fully given in the Exposition.

The claim of this mode of interpretation to the praise of strictness and exactness is a false one, if the Israel of prophecy is not the nation as such merely, but the nation as the temporary frame-work of the Church, and if the promises addressed to it, in forms derived from this transitory state, were nevertheless meant to be perpetual, and must be therefore independent of all temporary local restrictions. The true sense of the prophecies in this respect cannot be more strongly or explicitly set forth than in the words of the apostle, when he says that " God hath not cast away his people which he foreknew :" " Israel hath not obtained that which he seeketh for, but the election hath obtained it, and the rest were blinded :" " not as though the word of God hath taken none effect, for they are not all Israel which are of Israel.

One effect of the correct view of this matter is to do away with vagueness and uncertainty or random licence in the explanation of particular predictions.   This requires to be more distinctly stated, as at first view the effect may seem to be directly opposite.   It was a favourite maxim with an old school of interpreters, of whom Vitringa may be taken as the type and representative, that the prophecies should be explained to mean as much as possible, because the word of God must of course be more significant and pregnant than the word of man.   Without disputing the correctness of the reason thus assumed, it may be granted that the rule itself is good or bad, in theory and practice, according to the sense in which it is received and applied.   By the interpreters in question it was practically made to mean, that the dignity of prophecy required the utmost possible particularity of application to specific points of history, and the greatest possible number and variety of such applications.   The sincerity with which the rule was recognised and acted on, in this sense, is apparent from the zeal with which Vitringa seeks minute historical allusions under the most general expressions, and the zest with which he piles up mystical senses, as he calls them, on the top of literal ones, plainly regarding the assumption of so many senses, not as a necessary evil, but as a desirable advantage.

The evils of this method are, however, more apparent when the senses are less numerous, and the whole fulfilment of the prophecy is sought in some one juncture ; because then all other applications are excluded, whereas the more they are diversified the more chance is allowed the reader of discovering the true generic import of the passage.   For example, when Vitringa makes the Edom of the prophecies denote the Roman Empire, and also the Church of Rome, and also the unbelieving Jews, he widens the scope of his interpretation so far as unwittingly to put the reader on the true scent of a comprehensive threatening against the inveterate enemies of God and of his people, among whom those specified are only comprehended, if at all, as individual examples.   But when, on the other hand, he asserts that a particular prophecy received its whole fulfilment in the decline of Protestant theology and piety after the Reformation, he not only puts a meaning on the passage which no one else can see there without his assistance, but excludes all other applications as irrelevant.   In some interpreters belonging to the same school, but inferior to Vitringa both in learning and judgment, this mode of exposition is connected with a false view of prophecy as mere prediction, and as intended solely to illustrate the divine omniscience.

Now, in aiming to make everything specific and precise, this kind of exposition renders all uncertain and indefinite, by leaving the particular events foretold, to the discretion or caprice of the interpreter.   Where the event is expressly described in the prophecy itself, as the conquests of Cyrus are in chaps. xliv. and xlv,, there can be no question ; it is only where a strict sense is to be imposed upon indefinite expressions that this evil fruit appears.   The perfect licence of conjecture thus afforded may be seen by comparing two interpreters of this class, and observing with what confidence the most incompatible opinions are maintained, neither of which would be suggested by the language of the prophecy itself to any other reader.   What is thus dependent upon individual invention, taste, or fancy, must be uncertain, not only till it is discovered, but for ever; since the next interpreter may have a still more felicitous conjecture, or a still more ingenious combination, to supplant the old one. It is thus that, in aiming at an unattainable precision, these interpreters have brought upon themselves the very reproach which they were most solicitous to shun, that of vagueness and uncertainty.

If, instead of this, we let the Prophet say precisely what his words most naturally mean, expounded by the ordinary laws of human language and a due regard to the immediate context and to general usage, without attempting to make that specific which the author has made general, any more than to make general what he has made specific, we shall not only shun the inconveniences described, but facilitate the use and application of these prophecies by modern readers. Christian interpreters, as we have seen, have been so unwilling to renounce their interest, and that of the Church generally, in these ancient promises, encouragements, and warnings, that they have chosen rather to secure them by the cumbrous machinery of allegory, anagoge, and accommodation. But if the same end may be gained without resorting to such means; if, instead of being told to derive consolation from God's promises addressed to the Maccabees or to the Jews in exile, because he will be equally gracious to ourselves, we are permitted to regard a vast porportion of those promises as promises to the Church, and the ancient deliverances of the chosen people as more samples or instalments of their ultimate fulfilment; such a change in the relative position of the parties to these covenant transactions, without any change in the matter of the covenant itself, may perhaps not unreasonably be described as recommending the method of interpretation which alone can make it possible. An exegesis marked by these results is the genuine and only realization of the old idea, in its best sense, that the word of God must mean as much as possible. All this, however, has respect to questions which can only be determined by the slow but sure test of a thorough and detailed interpretation.

Before proceeding to apply this test, it will be necessary to consider briefly the arrangement and division of these Later Prophecies. This is not a question of mere taste, or even of convenience, but one which may materially influence the exposition. Here again a brief historical statement may be useful, and not wholly without interest.

The older writers on Isaiah, being free from the influence of any artificial theory, and taking the book just as they found it, treated these chapters as a continuous discourse, with little regard to the usual divisions of the text, except as mere facilities for reference.

Vitringa's fondness for exact, and even formal method, led him to attempt a systematic distribution of these chapters, similar to that which he had given of the Earlier Prophecies. He accordingly throws them into *conciones* or discourses, and divides these into *sectiones*, often coinciding with the chapters, but sometimes either longer or shorter. These subdivisions he provides with his favourite apparatus of *analysis, anacrisis,* &c., under which heads he appropriates distinct paragraphs to the description of the scope, design, occasion, argument, &c., of each section. The inappropriateness of this method, cumbrous at best, to these latter chapters, is betrayed by the inanity of many of the prefaces, which have the look of frames or cases, without anything to fill them. This is particularly true of the paragraphs professing to exhibit the *occasion* upon which the several sections were composed. Here the author not unfrequently is under the necessity of simply referring to the preceding chapter as affording the occasion of the next; an indirect concession that the separation of the parts, at least in that case, is gratuitous and artificial.

J. H. and J. D. Michaelis, Lowth, Gill, and other writers of the same period, while they wholly discard this embarrassing and wearisome machinery, and content themselves with the common division into chapters, are sometimes chargeable with treating these too much as an original arrangement of the author's matter by himself, and thus converting the whole into a series of detached discourses. The same thing is still more apparent in the popular and useful works of Henry, Scott, and others; where the reader is permitted, if not taught, to look upon the chapters as in some sense independent compositions, and to regard the first verse of each as introducing, and the last as winding up a complete subject. This would be hurtful to correct interpretation, even if the chapters were divided with the most consummate skill, much more when they are sometimes the result of the most superficial inspection.

The Higher Critics of the elder race, such as Eichhorn and his followers, carried out their idea of entire corruption, and the consequent necessity of total revolution, not only by assuming a plurality of writers, but by taking for granted that their compositions had been put together perfectly at random, and could be reduced to order only by the constant practice of inventive ingenuity and critical conjecture. The practical effects of this hypothesis were valuable only as exhibiting its folly, and producing a reaction towards more reasonable views. As a specimen of this school may be mentioned Bertholdt's distribution of the prophecies, in which certain chapters and parts of chapters are picked out and classified as having been written before the invasion of Babylonia by Cyrus, others after the invasion but before the siege of Babylon, others during the siege, others after the catastrophe.

Gesenius holds, in opposition to this theory, as we have seen, the oneness of the author and of his design. With respect to the actual arrangement of the book, he is inclined to regard it as original, but grants it to be possible that some transposition may have taken place, and more particularly that the last chapters, as they now stand, may be older than the first.

Hitzig maintains the strict chronological arrangement of the chapters, with the exception of the forty-seventh, which he looks upon as older, but incorporated with the others by the writer himself, He also maintains, with the utmost confidence, the oneness of the composition, and rejects all suggestions of interpolation and corruption with disdain. This departure from his method in the earlier portion of the book is closely connected with his wish to bring the date of the prophecies as near as possible to that of the fulfilment. For the same reason he assumes the successive composition of the parts with considerable intervals between them, during which he supposes the events of the Persian war to have followed one another and repeatedly changed the posture of affairs, In addition to this chronological arrangement of his own, Hitzig adopts Rückert's threefold division of the book into three nearly equal parts, as indicated by the closing words of chaps. xlviii. and lvii. Ewald adopts the same view of the unity and gradual production of these prophecies, but with a different distribution of the parts. Chaps. xl.–xlviii. he describes as the first attempt, exhibiting the freshest inspiration; chaps. xlix.–lx. as somewhat later, with a pause at the end of chap. lvii. To these he adds two postscripts or appendixes, an earlier one ending chap. lxiii. 6, and a later one extending to the close of the book.

Hendewerk divides the whole into two parallel series, the first ending with the forty-fifth chapter. He rejects Rückert's threefold division, as founded on an accidental repetition. He also rejects Hitzig's theory as to chap. xlvii., but goes still further in determining the precise stages of the composition and tracing in the prophecy the principal events in the history of Cyrus. Knobel divides the whole into three parts, chaps. xl.–xlviii., chaps. xlix.–lxii., chaps. lxiii.–lxvi.

A comparison of these minute arrangements shews that they are founded on imaginary illusions, or prompted by a governing desire to prove that the writer must have been contemporary with the exile, a wish which here predominates over the habitual disposition of these critics to explain away apparent references to history, rather than to introduce them where they do not really exist.

Discarding these imaginary facts, Hävernick goes back to the rational hypothesis of a continuous discourse, either uninterrupted in its composition or unaffected in its structure by the interruptions which are now beyond the reach of critical discovery, and for the same reason wholly unimportant. This is substantially the ground assumed by the old interpreters, and even by Gesenius, but now confirmed by the utter failure of all efforts to establish any more artificial distribution of the text. As to arrangement, Hävernick adopts that of Rückert, which is rather poetical than critical, and founded on the similar close of chaps. xlviii. and lvii., coinciding with the usual division into chapters, so as to throw nine into each of the three portions. As an aid to the memory, and a basis of convenient distribution, this hypothesis may be adopted without injury, but not as implying that the book consists of three independent parts, or that any one of the proposed divisions can be satisfactorily interpreted apart from the others. The greater the pains taken to demonstrate such a structure, the more forced and artificial must the exposition of the book become; and it is therefore best to regard this ingenious idea of Rückert as an æsthetic decoration rather than an exegetical expedient.

After carefully comparing all the methods of division and arrangement which have come to my knowledge, I am clearly of opinion that in this part of Scripture, more perhaps than any other, the evil to be shunned is not so much defect as excess; that the book is not only a continued but a desultory composition; that although there is a sensible progression in the whole from the beginning to the end, it cannot be distinctly traced in every minor part, being often interrupted and obscured by retrocessions and resumptions, which, though governed by a natural association in each case, are not reducible to rule or system. The conventional division into chapters, viewed as a mechanical contrivance for facilitating reference, is indispensable, and cannot be materially changed with any good effect at all proportioned to the inconvenience and confusion, which would necessarily attend such a departure from a usage long established and now universally familiar. The disadvantages attending it, or springing from an injurious use of it by readers and expounders, are the frequent separation of parts which as really cohere together as those that are combined, and the conversion of one great shifting spectacle, in which the scenes are constantly succeeding one another in a varied order, into a series of detached and unconnected pictures, throwing no light on each other even when most skilfully divided, and too often exhibiting a part of one view in absurd juxtaposition with another less akin to it, than that from which it has been violently sundered.

A similar caution is required in relation to the summaries or prefatory notes with which the chapters, in conformity to usage and the prevalent opinion, are provided in the present Work. In order to prevent an aggravation of the evils just described, a distinction must be clearly made between these summaries, and logical analysis so useful in the study of an argumentative context. It is there that such a method is at once most useful and most easy; because the logical nexus, where it really exists, is that which may be most successfully detected and exhibited as well as most tenaciously remembered. But in the case of an entirely different structure, and especially in one where a certain cycle of ideas is repeated often, in an order not prescribed by logic but by poetical association, there is no such facility, but on the other hand a tendency to sameness and monotony which weakens rather than excites the attention, and affords one of the strongest confirmations of the views already taken with respect to the structure of the whole book and the proper mode of treating it.

The most satisfactory and useful method of surveying the whole book with a view to the detailed interpretation of the part is, in my opinion, to obtain a clear view of the few great themes with which the writer's mind was filled, and of the minor topics into which they readily resolve themselves, and then to mark their varied combinations as they alternately present themselves, some more fully and frequently in one part of the book, some exclusively in one part, others with greater uniformity in all. The succession of the prominent figures will be pointed out as we proceed in the interpretation of the several chapters. But in order to afford the reader every preliminary aid before attempting the detailed interpretation, I shall close with a brief synopsis of the whole, presenting at a single glance its prominent contents and the mutual relation of its parts.

The prominent objects here presented to the Prophet's view are these five. 1. The carnal Israel, the Jewish nation, in its proud self-reliance and its gross corruption, whether idolatrous or only hypocritical and formal. 2. The spiritual Israel, the true Church, the remnant according to the election of grace, considered as the object of Jehovah's favour and protection, but at the same time as weak in faith and apprehensive of destruction. 3. The Babylonish Exile and the Restoration from it, as the most important intermediate point between the date of the prediction and the advent of Messiah, and as an earnest or a sample of Jehovah's future dealings with his people both in wrath and mercy. 4. The Advent itself, with the person and character of Him who was to come for the deliverance of his people, not only from eternal ruin, but from temporal bondage, and their introduction into " glorious liberty." 5. The character of this new condition of the Church or of the Christian Dispensation, not considered in its elements but as a whole; not in the way of chronological succession, but at one view; not so much in itself, as in contrast with the temporary system that preceded it.

These are the subjects of the Prophet's whole discourse, and may be described as present to his mind throughout; but the degree in which they are respectively made prominent is different in different parts. The attempts which have been made to shew that they are taken up successively and treated one by one, are unsuccessful, because inconsistent with the frequent repetition and recurrence of the same theme. The order is not that of strict succession, but of alternation. It is still true, however, that the relative prominence of these great themes is far from being constant. As a general fact, it may be said that their relative positions in this respect answer to those which they hold in the enumeration above given. The character of Israel, both as a nation and a church, is chiefly prominent in the beginning, the Exile and the Advent in the middle, the contrast and the change of dispensations at the end. With this general conception of the Prophecy, the reader can have very little difficulty in perceiving the unity of the discourse, and marking its transitions for himself, even without the aid of such an abstract as the following.

The form in which the Prophecy begins has been determined by its intimate connection with the threatening in the thirty-ninth chapter. To assure the Israel of God, or true Church, that the national judgments which had been denounced should not destroy it, is the Prophet's purpose in the fortieth chapter, and is executed by exhibiting Jehovah's power, and willingness, and fixed determination to protect and save his own elect. In the forty-first, his power and omniscience are contrasted with the impotence of idols, and illustrated by an individual example. In the forty-second, the person of the great Deliverer is introduced, the nature of his influence described, the relation of his people to himself defined, and their mission or vocation as enlighteners of the world explained. The forty-third completes this exposition by exhibiting the true design of Israel's election as a people, its entire independence of all merit in themselves, and sole dependence on the sovereign will of God. In the forty-fourth the argument against idolatry is amplified and urged, and the divine sufficiency and faithfulness exemplified by a historical allusion to the exodus from Egypt, and a prophetic one to the deliverance from Babylon, in which last Cyrus is expressly named. The last part of this chapter should have been connected with the first part of the forty-fifth, in which the name of Cyrus is repeated, and his conquests represented as an effect of God's omnipotence, and the prediction as a proof of his omniscience,—both which attributes are then again contrasted with the impotence and senselessness of idols. The same comparison is still continued in the forty-sixth, with special reference to the false gods of Babylon, as utterly unable to deliver either their worshippers or themselves. In the forty-seventh the description is extended to the Babylonian government, as wholly powerless in opposition to Jehovah's interference for the emancipation of his people. The forty-eighth contains the winding up of this great argument from Cyrus and the fall of Babylon, as a conviction and rebuke to the unbelieving Jews themselves. The fact that Babylon is expressly mentioned only in these chapters is a strong confirmation of our previous conclusion that it is not the main subject of the prophecy. By a natural transition he reverts in the forty-ninth to the true Israel, and shews the groundlessness of their misgivings, by disclosing God's design respecting them, and shewing the certainty of its fulfilment notwithstanding all discouraging appearances. The difference in the character and fate of the two Israels is still more exactly defined in the fiftieth chapter. In the fifty-first the true relation of the chosen people both to God and to the Gentiles is illustrated by historical examples, the calling of Abram and the exodus from Egypt, and the same power pledged for the safety of Israel in time to come. In the last part of this chapter and the first of the fifty-second, which cohere in the most intimate manner, the gracious purposes of God are represented as fulfilled already, and described in the most animating terms. This view of the future condition of the Church could not be separated long from that of Him by whom it was to be effected; and accordingly the last part of this chapter, forming one unbroken context with the fifty-third, exhibits him anew, no longer as a teacher, but as the great sacrifice for sin. No sooner is this great work finished than the best days of the Church begin, the loss of national distinction being really a prelude to her glorious emancipation. The promise of this great change in the fifty-fourth chapter, is followed in the fifty-fifth by a gracious invitation to the whole world to partake of it. The fifty-sixth continues the same subject, by predicting the entire abrogation of all local, personal, and national distinctions. Having dwelt so long upon the prospects of the spiritual Israel or true Church, the Prophet, in last part of the fifty-sixth and the first part of the fifty-seventh, looks back at the carnal Israel, as it was in the days of its idolatrous apostasy, and closes with a threatening which insensibly melts into a promise of salvation to the true Israel. The fifty-eighth again presents the carnal Israel, not as idolaters but as hypocrites, and points out the true mean between the rejection of appointed rites and the abuse of them. The fifty-ninth explains Jehovah's dealings with the nation of the Jews, and shews that their rejection was the fruit of their own doings, as the salvation of the saved was that of God's omnipotent compassions. In the sixtieth he turns once more to the true Israel, and begins a series of magnificent descriptions of the new dispensation as a whole, contrasted with the imperfections and restrictions of the old. The prominent figures of the picture in this chapter are, immense increase by the accession of the Gentiles, and internal purity and peace. The prominent figure in the sixty-first is that of the Messiah as the agent in this great work of spiritual emancipation. In the sixty-second it is that of Zion, or the Church herself, in the most intimate union with Jehovah and the full fruition of his favour, But this anticipation is inseparably blended with that of vengeance on the enemies of God, which is accordingly presented in the sublime vision of the sixty-third chapter, followed by an appeal to God's former dealings with his people, as a proof that their rejection was their own fault, and that he will still protect the true believers. These are represented in the sixty-fourth as humbly confessing their own sins and suing for the favour of Jehovah. In the sixty-fifth he solemnly anounces the adoption of the Gentiles and the rejection of the carnal Israel because of their iniquities, among which idolatry is once more rendered prominent. He then contrasts the doom of the apostate Israel with the glorious destiny awaiting the true Israel. And this comparison is still continued in the sixty-sixth chapter, where the Prophet, after ranging through so wide a field of vision, seems at last to fix his own eye and his reader's on the dividing line or turning-point between the old and new economy, and winds up the whole drama with a vivid exhibition of the nations gathered to Jerusalem for worship, while the children of the kingdom, *i. e.* Irsael according to the flesh, are cast forth into outer darkness, " where their worm dieth not and their fire is not quenched." Upon this awful spectacle the curtain falls, and we are left to find relief from its impressions in the merciful disclosures of later and more cheering revelation.

Arrangement of the Commentary. The usual division into chapters is retained, as being universally familiar and in general convenient. The analysis of these divisions, and other preliminary statements and discussions, are prefixed as special introductions to the chapters. The literal translation, sometimes combined with an explanatory paraphrase, is followed by the necessary comments and the statement of the different opinions. In the order of the topics, some regard has been had to their comparative importance, but without attempting to secure a perfect uniformity in this respect, which, if it were attainable, would probably add nothing to the force or clearness of the exposition.

Commentary on Isaiah, Volume One

Chapter 1

THE design of this chapter is to shew the connection between the sins and sufferings of God's people, and the necessity of further judgments, as means of purification and deliverance.

The popular corruption is first exhibited as the effect of alienation from God, and as the cause of national calamities, vers. 2–9. It is then exhibited as coexisting with punctilious exactness in religious duties, and as rendering them worthless, vers. 10–20. It is finally exhibited in twofold contrast, first with a former state of things, and then with one still future, to be brought about by the destruction of the wicked, and especially of wicked rulers, vers. 21–31.

The first part of the chapter describes the sin and then the suffering of the people. The former is characterised as filial ingratitude, stupid inconsideration, habitual transgression, contempt of God, and alienation from him, vers. 2–4. The suffering is first represented by the figure of disease and wounds, and then in literal terms as the effect of an invasion by which the nation was left desolate, and only saved by God's regard for his elect from the total destruction of Sodom and Gomorrah, vers. 5–9.

The second part is connected with the first by the double allusion to Sodom and Gomorrah, with which the one closes and the other opens. In this part the Prophet shews the utter inefficacy of religious rites to counteract the natural effect of their iniquities, and then exhorts them to the use of the true remedy. Under the former head, addressing them as similar in character to Sodom and Gomorrah, he describes their sacrifices as abundant and exact, but not acceptable; their attendance at the temple as punctual, and yet insulting; their bloodless offerings as abhorrent, and their holy days as wearisome and hateful on account of their iniquities; their very prayers as useless, because their hands were stained with blood, vers. 10–15. As a necessary means of restoration to God's favour, he exhorts them to forsake their evil courses and to exercise benevolence and justice, assuring them that God was willing to forgive them and restore the advantages which they had forfeited by sin, but at the same time resolved to punish the impenitent transgressor, vers. 16–20.

The transition from the second to the third part is abrupt, and introduced by a pathetic exclamation. In this part the Prophet compares Israel as it is with what it has been and with what it shall be. In the former comparison, he employs two metaphors, each followed by a literal explanation of its meaning : that of a faithful wife become a harlot, and that of adulterated wine and silver, both expressive of a moral deterioration, with special reference to magistrates and rulers, vers. 21–23. In the other comparison, the coming judgments are presented in the twofold aspect of purification and deliverance to the church, and of destruction to its wicked members. The Prophet sees the leading men of Israel destroyed, first as oppressors, to make room for righteous rulers and thus save the state, then as idolaters consumed by that in which they trusted for protection, vers. 24–31.

This chapter is referred to by Grotius and Cocceius to the reign of Uzziah, by Lowth and De Wette to the reign of Jotham, by Gesenius and Ewald to the reign of Ahaz, by Jarchi and Vitringa to the reign of Hezekiah. This disagreement has arisen from assuming that it must be a prediction in the strict sense, and have reference to one event or series of events exclusively, while in the prophecy itself there are no certain indications of the period referred to. The only points which seem to furnish any data for determining the question, are the invasion mentioned in ver. 7, and the idolatry referred to in vers. 28–31. But the former is almost equally applicable to the Syrian invasion under Ahaz and the Assyrian under Hezekiah. And the idolatry is mentioned in connection with the punctilious regard to the forms of the Mosaic ritual. At the same time, it is evident that the chapter contains one continuous coherent composition. It is probable, therefore, that this prophecy belongs to the class already mentioned (in the Introduction) as exhibiting a sequence of events, or providential scheme, which might be realized in more than one emergency ; not so much a prediction as a prophetic lesson with respect to the effects which certain causes must infallibly produce. Such a discourse would be peculiarly appropriate as an introduction to the prophecies which follow ; and its seeming inconsistencies are all accounted for, by simply supposing that it was written for this purpose about the time of Sennacherib's invasion in the fourteenth year of Hezekiah's reign, and that in it the Prophet takes a general survey of the changes which the church had undergone since the beginning of his public ministry.

1. This is a general title of the whole book or one of its larger divisions (chaps. i.–xxxix or i.–xii), defining its character, author, subject, and date. *The Vision* (supernatural perception, inspiration, revelation, prophecy, here put collectively for *Prophecies*) *of Isaiah, the son of Amoz, which he saw* (perceived, received by inspiration) *concerning Judah* (the kingdom of the two tribes, which adhered to the theocracy after the revolt of Jeroboam) *and Jerusalem* (its capital, the chosen seat of the true religion), *in the days of Uzziah, Jotham, Ahaz, Hezekiah, kings of Judah.*—The Septuagint renders עַל *against ;* but as all the prophecies are not of an unfavourable character, it is better to retain the wider sense *concerning.*—Aben Ezra and Abarbenel regard this as the title of the first chapter only, and to meet the objection that a single prophecy would not have been referred to four successive reigns, instead of *which he saw* read *who saw* (i. e. was a seer) *in the days of Uzziah,* &c. But the tenses of חָזָה are not thus absolutely used, and the same words occur in chap. ii. 1, where the proposed construction is impossible. Vitringa's supposition that the sentence originally consisted of the first clause only, and that the rest was added at a later date to make it applicable as a general title, is entirely gratuitous, and opens the door to endless licence of conjecture. Hendewerk goes further, and calls in question the antiquity and genuineness of the whole verse, but without the least authority. According to ancient and oriental usage, it was probably

prefixed by Isaiah himself to a partial or complete collection of his prophecies. To the objection that חָזוֹן is singular, the answer is, that it is used collectively because it has no plural, and appears as the title of this same book or another in 2 Chron. xxxii. 32. To the objection that the prophecies are not all *concerning Judah and Jerusalem*, the answer is, *a potiori fit denominatio*, to which may be added that the prophecies relating to the ten tribes and to foreign powers owe their place in this collection to their bearing, more or less direct, upon the interests of Judah. To the objection that the first chapter has no other title, we may answer that it needs no other, partly because it is sufficiently distinguished from what follows by the title of the second, partly because it is not so much the first in a series of prophecies as a general preface. With respect to the names *Isaiah* and *Amoz*, and the chronology of this verse, see the Introduction, Part I.

2. The Prophet first describes the moral state of Judah, vers. 2-4, and then the miseries arising from it, vers. 5-9. To the former he invites attention by summoning the universe to hear the Lord's complaint against his people, who are first charged with filial ingratitude. *Hear, O heavens; and give ear, O earth*, as witnesses and judges, and as being less insensible yourselves than men: *for Jehovah speaks*, not man. *Sons I have reared and brought up*, literally made great and made high, *and they*, with emphasis on the pronoun which is otherwise superfluous, *even they have revolted from me*, or rebelled against me, not merely in a general sense by sinning, but in a special sense by violating that peculiar covenant which bound God to his people. It is in reference to this bond, and to the conjugal relation which the Scriptures represent God as sustaining to his church or people, that its constituted members are here called his *children*.—Vitringa and others understand *heaven and earth* as meaning *angels and men*; but although these may be included, it is plain that the direct address is to the frame of nature, as in Deut. xxxii. 1, from which the form of expression is borrowed.—Knobel and all other recent writers exclude the idea of bearing witness altogether, and suppose *heaven and earth* to be called upon to listen, simply because Jehovah is the speaker. But the two ideas are entirely compatible, and the first is recommended by the analogy of Deut. xxx. 19, and by its poetical effect.—Cocceius takes גִּדַּלְתִּי in the sense of *bringing up*, but רוֹמַמְתִּי in that of *exalting* to peculiar privileges, which disturbs the metaphor, and violates the usage of the two verbs, which are elsewhere joined as simple synonymes. (See chap. xxiii. 7; Ezek. xxxi. 4.) Both terms are so chosen as to be applicable, in a lower sense, to children, and in a higher sense, to nations.—The English Bible and many other versions read *Jehovah has spoken*, which seems to refer to a previous revelation, or to indicate a mere repetition of his words, whereas he is himself introduced as speaking. The preterite may be here used to express the present, for the purpose of suggesting that he did not thus speak for the first time. Compare Heb. i. 1.

3. Having tacitly compared the insensible Jews with the inanimate creation, he now explicitly compares them with the brutes, selecting for that purpose two which were especially familiar as domesticated animals, subjected to man's power and dependent on him for subsistence, and at the same time as proverbially stupid, inferiority to which must therefore be peculiarly disgraceful. *The ox knoweth his owner, and the ass his master's crib* or feeding-place. *Israel*, the chosen people, as a whole, without regard to those who had seceded from it, *doth not know, my people doth not consider*, pay attention or take notice. Like the ox and the ass, Israel

had a master, upon whom he was dependent, and to whom he owed obedience ; but, unlike them, he did not recognise and would not serve his rightful sovereign and the author of his mercies.—The Septuagint supplies *me* after *know* and *consider* (με οὐχ ἔγνω . . . . με οὐ συνῆχεν). The Vulgate, followed by Michaelis, Lowth, and others, supplies *me* after the first verb, but leaves the other indefinite. Gesenius, De Wette, and Hendewerk supply *him*, referring to *owner* and *master*. Clericus, Ewald, and Umbreit take the verbs in the absolute and general sense of having knowledge and being considerate, which is justified by usage, but gives less point and precision to the sentence.

4. As the foregoing verses render prominent the false position of Israel with respect to God, considered first as a father and then as a master (comp. Mal. i. 6), so this brings into view their moral state in general, resulting from that alienation, and still represented as inseparable from it. The Prophet speaks again in his own person, and expresses wonder, pity, and indignation at the state to which his people had reduced themselves. *Ah, sinful nation*, literally *nation sinning*, *i. e.* habitually, which is the force here of the active participle, *people heavy with iniquity*, weighed down by guilt as an oppressive burden, *a seed of evil-doers*, *i. e.* the offspring of wicked parents, *sons corrupting themselves*, *i. e.* doing worse than their fathers, in which sense the same verb is used, Judges ii. 19. (Calvin : filii degeneres.) The *evil-doers* are of course not the Patriarchs or Fathers of the nation, but the intervening wicked generations. As the first clause tells us what they were, so the second tells us what they did, by what acts they had merited the character just given. *They have forsaken Jehovah*, a phrase descriptive of iniquity in general, but peculiarly expressive of the breach of covenant obligations. *They have treated with contempt the Holy One of Israel*, a title almost peculiar to Isaiah, and expressing a twofold aggravation of their sin: first, that he was infinitely excellent; and then, that he was theirs, their own peculiar God. *They are alienated back again.* The verb denotes estrangement from God, the adverb retrocession or backsliding into a former state.—By a *seed of evil-doers* most writers understand a race or generation of evil-doers, and by *children corrupting* (their ways or themselves, as Aben Ezra explains it) nothing more than wicked men. Gesenius and Henderson render מַשְׁחִיתִים *corrupt*, Barnes *corrupting others*. The sense of *mischievous, destructive*, is given by Luther, and the vague one of *wicked* by the Vulgate. The other explanation, which supposes an allusion to the parents, takes זֶרַע and בָּנִים in their proper meaning, makes the parallelism of the clauses more complete, and converts a tautology into a climax.— The sense of *blaspheming* given to נִאֵץ by the Vulgate and Luther, and that of *provoking to anger* by the Septuagint, Aben Ezra, Kimchi, and others, are rejected by the modern lexicographers for that of *despising* or treating with contempt. The last two are combined by Junius (contemtim irritaverun) and the old French Version (ils ont irrité par mépris).—The Niphal form נָזֹרוּ is by most writers treated as simply equivalent in meaning to the Kal —' they have departed;' but the usage of the participles active and passive (Ps. lxix. 9) in the sense of *strange* and *estranged*, is in favour of the interpretation given by Aquila and Theodotion, ἀπηλλοτριώθησαν εἰς τὰ ὀπίσω.

5. To the description of their moral state, beginnning and ending with apostasy from God, the Prophet now adds a description of the consequences, vers. 5–9. This he introduces by an expostulation on their mad perseverance in transgression, notwithstanding the extremities to which it had reduced them. *Whereupon, i. e.* on what part of the body, *can ye be stricken,*

smitten, punished, *any more*, that *ye add revolt*, departure or apostasy from
God, *i. e.* revolt more and more? Already *the whole head is sick and the
whole heart faint.*—The same sense is attained, but in a less striking form,
by reading, with Hitzig, *why*, to what purpose, *will ye be smitten any more?
why continue to revolt?* If their object was to make themselves miserable,
it was already accomplished.—Calvin, followed by the English version and
others, gives a different turn to the interrogation: *Why should ye be smitten
any more?* of what use is it? *ye will revolt more and more.* But the
reason thus assigned for their ceasing to be smitten is wholly different from
that given in the last clause and amplified in the following verse, viz. that
they were already faint and covered with wounds. The Vulgate version
(super quo percutiemini?) is retained by Luther, Lowth, Gesenius, and
others. The very same metaphor occurs more than once in classical poetry.
Lowth quotes examples from Euripides and Ovid (vix habet in nobis jam
nova plaga locum).—Hendewerk supposes the people to be asked where
they can be smitten with effect, *i. e.* what kind of punishment will do them
good; but this is forced, and does not suit the context. Ewald repeats
whereupon before the second verb: 'upon what untried transgression building, will ye still revolt? which is needless and unnatural.—Instead of *the
whole head, the whole heart,* Winer and Hitzig render *every head* and *every
heart,* because the nouns have not the article. But see chap. ix. 11; Ps.
cxi. 1; the omission of the article is one of the most familiar licences of
poetry. The context too requires that the words should be applied to the
head and heart of the body mentioned in ver. 6, viz. the body politic.—The
head and heart do not denote different ranks (Hendewerk), or the inward and
outward state of the community (Umbreit), but are mentioned as well-known
and important parts of the body, to which the church or nation had been
likened.—Gesenius explains לָחֳלִי to mean *in sickness,* Ewald (inclined *to
sickness,* Knobel (belonging) *to sickness,* Clericus (given up) *to sickness,*
Rosenmüller (abiit) *in morbum.* The general sense is plain from the parallel
term דַּוָּי, *faint* or languid from disease.

6. The idea suggested at the beginning of ver. 5, that there was no
more room for further strokes, is now carried out with great particularity.
From the sole of the foot and (i. e. even) to the head (a common scriptural
expression for the body in its whole extent) *there is not in it* (the people, or
in him, *i. e.* Judah, considered as a body) *a sound place; (it is) wound
and bruise* (μώλωψ, vibex, the tumour produced by stripes) *and fresh stroke.*
The wounds are then described as not only grievous, but neglected. *They
have not been pressed, and they have not been bound* or bandaged, *and it has
not been mollified with ointment,* all familiar processes of ancient surgery.
—Calvin argues that the figures in this verse and the one preceding cannot
refer to moral corruption, since the Prophet himself afterwards explains
them as descriptive of external sufferings. But he seems to have intended
to keep up before his readers the connection between suffering and sin, and
therefore to have chosen terms suited to excite associations both of pain
and corruption.—The last verb, which is singular and feminine, is supposed
by Junius and J. H. Michaelis to agree with the nouns distributively, as
the others do collectively; "none of them is mollified with ointment."
Ewald and Umbreit connect it with the last noun exclusively. All the
verbs are rendered in the singular by Cocceius and Lowth, all in the plural
by Vitringa and J. D. Michaelis. The most probable solution is that proposed by Knobel, who takes רֻכְּכָה indefinitely, "it has not been softened,"
i. e. no one has softened, like the Latin *ventum est* for "some one came."

This construction, although foreign from our idiom, is not uncommon in Hebrew.—מַכָּה טְרִיָה is not a *running* or *putrefying sore* (Eng. Vers. Barnes), but a recently inflicted stroke.—The singular nouns may be regarded as collectives, or with better effect, as denoting that the body was one wound, &c.—The suffix in בּוֹ cannot refer to גּוּיָה understood (Henderson), which would require בָּהּ.—מְתֹם may be an abstract meaning *soundness* (LXX. ὁλοκληρία), but is more probably a noun of place from תָּמַם.

7. Thus far the sufferings of the people have been represented by strong figures, giving no intimation of their actual form, or of the outward causes which produced them. But now the Prophet brings distinctly into view foreign invasion as the instrument of vengeance, and describes the country as already desolated by it. The absence of verbs in the first clause gives great rapidity and life to the description. *Your land* (including town and country, which are afterwards distinctly mentioned) *a waste!* *Your towns* (including cities and villages of every size) *burnt with fire!* *Your ground* (including its produce), *i. e.* as to your ground, *before you* (in your presence, but beyond your reach (*strangers (are) devouring* it, *and a waste* (it is a waste) *like the overthrow of strangers, i. e.* as foreign foes are wont to waste a country in which they have no interest, and for which they have no pity. (Vulg. sicut in vastitate hostili.)—As זָרִים often includes the idea of strangers to God and the true religion, and as מַהְפֵּכָה in every other instance means the overthrow of Sodom and Gomorrah, Hitzig and Ewald adopt Kimchi's explanation of this clause, as containing an allusion to that event, which is the great historical type of total destruction on account of sin, often referred to elsewhere, and in this very context, two verses below. This exposition, though ingenious, is unnecessary, and against it lies almost the whole weight of exegetical authority.—Sadias explains זָרִים not as a plural but a singular noun derived from זָרַם *to flow* or *overflow*, in which he is followed by Döderlin and Lowth ("as if destroyed by an inundation"). But no such noun occurs elsewhere, and it is most improbable that two nouns, wholly different in meaning yet coincident in form, would be used in this one sentence.

8. The extent of the desolation is expressed by comparing the church or nation to a watch-shed in a field or vineyard, far from other habitations, and forsaken after the ingathering. *And the daughter of Zion, i. e.* the people of Zion or Jerusalem, considered as the capital of Judah, and therefore representing the whole nation, *is left*, not forsaken, but left over or behind as a survivor, *like a booth*, a temporary covert of leaves and branches, *in a vineyard, like a lodge in a melon-field, like a watched city, i. e.* watched by friends and foes, besieged and garrisoned, and therefore insulated, cut off from all communication with the country.—Interpreters, almost without exception, explain *daughter of Zion* to mean the city of Jerusalem, and suppose the extent of desolation to be indicated by the metropolis alone remaining unsubdued. But on this supposition they are forced to explain how a besieged city could be *like* a besieged city, either by saying that Jerusalem only suffered *as if* she were besieged (Ewald); or by taking the כ as a *caph veritatis* expressing not resemblance but identity, "like a besieged city as she is" (Gesen. ad loc. Henderson); or by reading "so is the besieged city" (Gesen. Lex. Man.): or by gratuitously taking עִיר נְצוּרָה in the sense of "turris custodiae" or watch-tower (Tingstad. Hitzig. Gesen. Thes.). If, as is commonly supposed, *daughter of Zion* primarily signifies the people of Zion or Jerusalem, and the city only by a transfer of the figure, it is better to retain the former meaning in a

case where departure from it is not only needless but creates a difficulty in the exposition. According to Hengstenberg (Comm. on Psalm ix. 15), *daughter of Zion* means the *daughter Zion*, as *city of Rome* means the *city Rome*. But even granting this, the church or nation may at least as naturally be called a *daughter*, *i. e.* virgin or young woman, as a city. That Jerusalem is not called the *daughter of Zion* from its local situation on the mountain, is clear from the analogous phrases, *daughter of Tyre, daughter of Babylon*, where no such explanation is admissible.—The meaning *saved, preserved*, which is put upon נְצוּרָה by Koppe, Rosenmüller, Maurer, and Gesenius in his Commentary, seems inappropriate in a description of extreme desolation, but does not materially affect the interpretation of the passage.

9. The idea of a desolation almost total is expressed in other words, and with an intimation that the narrow escape was owing to God's favour for the remnant according to the election of grace, who still existed in the Jewish church. *Except Jehovah of hosts had left unto us* (or caused to remain over, to survive, for us) *a very small remnant, we should have been like Sodom, we should have resembled Gòmorrah, i. e.* we should have been totally and justly destroyed.—By the *very small remnant* Knobel understands the city of Jerusalem, compared with the whole land and all its cities; Clericus the small number of surviving Jews. But that the verse has reference to quality as well as quantity, is evident from Rom. ix. 29, where Paul makes use of it, not as an illustration, but as an argument to shew that mere connection with the church could not save men from the wrath of God. The citation would have been irrelevant if this phrase denoted merely a small number of survivors, and not a minority of true believers in the midst of the prevailing unbelief.—Clericus explains Jehovah of Hosts to mean the God of Battles; but it rather means the Sovereign Ruler of "heaven and earth and all the host of them," *i. e.* all their inhabitants (Gen. ii. 1).—Lowth and Barnes translate כִּמְעַט *soon*, as in Ps. lxxxi. 15; but the usual translation agrees better with the context and with Paul's quotation.

10. Having assigned the corruption of the people as the cause of their calamities, the Prophet now guards against the error of supposing that the sin thus visited was that of neglecting the external duties of religion, which were in fact punctiliously performed, but unavailing because joined with the practice of iniquity, vers. 10–15. This part of the chapter is connected with what goes before by repeating the allusion to Sodom and Gomorrah. Having just said that God's sparing mercy had alone prevented their resembling Sodom and Gomorrah in condition, he now reminds them that they do resemble Sodom and Gomorrah in iniquity. The reference is not to particular vices, but to general character, as Jerusalem, when reproached for her iniquities, "is spiritually called Sodom" (Rev. xi. 8). The comparison is here made by the form of address. *Hear the word of Jehovah, ye judges* (or rulers) *of Sodom ; give ear to the law of our God, ye people of Gomorrah.* Word and law both denote the revelation of God's will as a rule of faith and duty. The particular exhibition of it meant, is that which follows, and to which this verse invites attention like that frequent exhortation of our Saviour, *He that hath ears to hear, let him hear.*—Junius, J. D. Michaelis, and the later Germans, take תּוֹרָה in the general sense of doctrine or instruction, which, though favoured by its etymology, is not sustained by usage. Knobel, with more probability, supposes an allusion to the ritual or sacrificial law ; but there is no need either of enlarging or restrict-

ing the meaning of the term.—The collocation of the word is not intended to suggest that the rulers and the people were as much alike as Sodom and Gomorrah (Calvin), but to produce a rhythmical effect. The sense is that the rulers and people of Judah were as guilty as those of Sodom and Gomorrah.

11. Resuming the form of interrogation and expostulation, he teaches them that God had no need of sacrifices on his own account, and that even those sacrifices which he had required might become offensive to him. *For what* (for what purpose, to what end, of what use) *is the multitude of your sacrifices to me* (*i. e.* offered *to me*, or of what use *to me*) *? saith Jehovah. I am full* (*i. e.* sated, I have had enough, I desire no more) *of burnt-offerings of rams and the fat of fed beasts* (fattened for the altar), *and the blood of bullocks and lambs and he-goats I desire not* (or delight not in). Male animals are mentioned, as the only ones admitted in the עֹלָה or burnt-offering; the fat and blood, as the parts in which the sacrifice essentially consisted, the one being always burnt upon the altar, and the other sprinkled or poured around it. Hendewerk and Henderson suppose an allusion to the excessive multiplication of sacrifices; but this, if alluded to at all, is not the prominent idea, as the context relates wholly to the spirit and conduct of the offerers themselves.—Some German interpreters affect to see an inconsistency between such passages as this and the law requiring sacrifices. But these expressions must of course be interpreted by what follows, and especially by the last clause of ver. 13.—Bochart explains מְרִיאִים as denoting a species of wild ox; but wild beasts were not received in sacrifice, and this word simply suggests the idea of careful preparation and assiduous compliance with the ritual. Aben Ezra restricts it to the larger cattle, Jarchi to the smaller; but it means fed or fattened beasts of either kind.

12. What had just been said of the offerings themselves, is now said of attendance at the temple to present them. *When you come to appear before me, who hath required this at your hand to tread my courts*, not merely to frequent them, but to trample on them, as a gesture of contempt? The courts here meant are the enclosures around Solomon's temple, for the priests, worshippers, and victims. The interrogative form implies negation. Such appearance, such attendance, God had not required, although it was their duty to frequent his courts.—Cocceius takes כִּי in its ordinary sense, without a material change of meaning: 'that ye come, &c., who hath required this at your hands?' Junius makes the first clause a distinct interrogation (quod advenitis, an ut appareatis in conspectu meo?), Ewald sees in the expression *at your hand*, an allusion to the sense of *power*, in which יָד is sometimes used; but the expression, in its proper sense, is natural and common after verbs of giving or demanding.—Hitzig supposes the trampling mentioned to be that of the victims, as if he had said, Who hath required you to profane my courts by the feet of cattle? But the word appears to be applied to the worshippers themselves in a twofold sense, which cannot be expressed by any single word in English. They were bound to *tread* his courts, but not to *trample* them. Vitringa lays the emphasis on *your*: Who hath required it at *your* hands, at the hands of such as you? Umbreit strangely thinks the passive verb emphatic: when you come to *be seen* and not to *see*. The emphasis is really on *this*. Who hath required this, this sort of attendance, at your hands? One manuscript agrees with the Peshito in reading לִרְאוֹת *to see;* but the common reading is no doubt the true one, פְּנֵי being used adverbially for the full form אֶת פְּנֵי or אֶל, which is elsewhere construed with the same passive verb (Exod. xxiii. 17; xxxiv. 23, 24).

13. What he said before of animal sacrifices and of attendance at the temple to present them, is now extended to bloodless offerings, such as incense and the מִנְחָה or meal-offering, as well as to the observance of sacred times, and followed by a brief intimation of the sense in which they were all unacceptable to God, viz. when combined with the practice of iniquity. The interrogative form is here exchanged for that of direct prohibition. *Ye shall not add* (*i. e.* continue) *to bring a vain offering* (that is, a useless one, because hypocritical and impious). *Incense is an abomination to me: (so are) new moon and sabbath, the calling of the convocation* (at those times, or at the annual feasts, which are then distinctly mentioned with the weekly and monthly ones): *I cannot bear iniquity and holy day* (abstinence from labour, religious observance), meaning of course, I cannot bear them together. This last clause is a key to the preceding verses. It was not religious observance in itself, but its combination with iniquity, that God abhorred. Aben Ezra: לֹא. אוכל לסבול און עם עצרת J. H. Michaelis: ferre non possum pravitatem et ferias, quæ vos conjungitis. So Cocceius, J. D. Michaelis, Gesenius, Ewald, Henderson, &c. Other constructions inconsistent with the Masoretic accents, but substantially affording the same sense, as those of Rosenmüller (" as for new moon, sabbath, &c., I cannot bear iniquity," &c.) and Umbreit (" new moon and sabbath, iniquity and holy day, I cannot bear "). Another, varying the sense as well as the construction, is that of Calvin (solennes indictiones non potero—vana res est —nec conventum) copied by Vitringa, and, with some modification, by the English Version, Clericus and Barnes (" it is iniquity—even the solemn closing meeting "), which violates both syntax and accentuation. Clericus and Gesenius give to *vain oblation* the specific sense of *false* or *hypocritical;* J. D. Michaelis, Hitzig, and Ewald, that of *sinful;* Cocceius that of *presumptuous* (temerarium); but all these seem to be included or implied in the old and common version *vain* or worthless. (LXX. μάταιον. Vulg. frustra. Luther, vergeblich.) Cocceius and Ewald construe the second member of the sentence thus : " it (the meal-offering) is abominable incense to me ;" which is very harsh. The modern lexicographers (Gesenius, Winer, Fürst) make convocation or assembly the primary idea of עֲצָרָה; but all agree that it is used in applications to time of religious observance.

14. The very rites ordained by God himself, and once acceptable to him, had, through the sin of those who used them, become irksome and disgusting. *Your new moons* (an emphatic repetition, as if he had said, Yes, your new moons) *and your convocations* (sabbaths and yearly feasts) *my soul hateth* (not a mere periphrasis for *I hate*, but an emphatic phrase denoting cordial hatred, *q. d.* odi ex animo), *they have become a burden on me* (implying that they were not so at first), *I am weary of bearing* (or have wearied myself bearing them).—Lowth's version *months* is too indefinite to represent חדשים, which denotes the beginnings of the lunar months, observed as sacred times under the law of Moses (Num. xxviii. 11 ; x. 10). Köcher supposes they are mentioned here again because they had been peculiarly abused ; but Henderson explains the repetition better as a rhetorical epanalepsis, resuming and continuing the enumeration in another form. Hengstenberg has shewn (Christol. vol. iii. p. 87) that מוֹעֲדִים is applied in Scripture only to the Sabbath, passover, pentecost, day of atonement, and feast of tabernacles. The common version of the second clause (*they are a trouble unto me*) is too vague. The noun should have its specific sense of *burden, loud*, the preposition its proper local sense of *on*, and the verb with לְ its

usual force, as signifying not mere existence but a change of state, in which sense it is thrice used in this very chapter (vers. 21, 22, 31). The last particular is well expressed by the Septuagint (ἐγεννήθητέ μοι) and Vulgate (facta sunt mihi), and the other two by Calvin (superfuerunt mihi loco oneris), Vitringa (incumbunt mihi instar oneris), Lowth (they are a burden upon me), and Gesenius (sie sind mir zur Last) ; but neither of these versions gives the full force of the clause in all its parts. The Septuagint, the Chaldee Paraphrase, and Symmachus take נשא in the sense of *forgiving*, which it has in some connections ; but the common meaning agrees better with the parallel expression, *load* or *burden*.

15. Not only ceremonial observances but even prayer was rendered useless by the sins of those who offered it. *And in your spreading* (when you spread) *your hands* (or stretch them out towards heaven as a gesture of entreaty) *I will hide mine eyes from you* (avert my face, refuse to see or hear, not only in ordinary but) *also when ye multiply prayer* (by fervent importunity in time of danger) *I am not hearing* (or about to hear, the participle bringing the act nearer to the present than the future would do). *Your hands are full of blood* (literally *bloods*, the form commonly used when the reference is to bloodshed or the guilt of murder). Thus the Prophet comes back to the point from which he set out, the iniquity of Israel as the cause of his calamities, but with this difference, that at first he viewed sin in its higher aspect, as committed against God, whereas in this place its injurious effects on men are rendered prominent.—By *multiplying prayer* Henderson understands the βαττολογία or vain repetition condemned by Christ as a customary error of his times ; but this would make the threatening less impressive. The force of גם as here used (*not only this but*, or *nay more*) may be considered as included in the old English, yea, of the common version, for which Lowth and Henderson have substituted *even*. The latter also takes כִּי in the sense of *though*, without effect upon the meaning of the sentence, and suggests that the preterite at the end of the verse denotes habitual action ; but it simply denotes previous action, or that their hands were already full of blood. Under *blood* or murder Calvin supposes all sins of violence and gross injustice to be comprehended ; but although the mention of the highest crime against the person may suggest the others, they can hardly be included in the meaning of the word.—Junius and Clericus translate דָּמִים *murders* (cædibus plenæ) ; but the literal translation is at once more exact and more expressive. It is a strange opinion mentioned by Fabricius (Diss. Phil. Theol. p. 329) that the blood here meant is the blood of the victims hypocritically offered.—For the form פְּרִשְׁכֶם see Nordheimer, §§ 101, 2, a. 476.

16. Having shewn the insufficiency of ceremonial rites and even of more spiritual duties to avert or cure the evils which the people had brought upon themselves by their iniquities, he exhorts them to abandon these and urges reformation, not as the *causa qua* but as a *causa sine qua non* of deliverance and restoration to God's favour. *Wash you* (רַחֲצוּ a word appropriated to ablution of the body as distinguished from all other washings), *purify yourselves* (in a moral or figurative sense, as appears from what follows). *Remove the evil of your doings from before mine eyes* (out of my sight, which could only be done by putting an end to them, an idea literally expressed in the last clause), *cease to do evil*.—Luther, Gesenius, and most of the late writers render רַע as an adjective, *your evil doings;* but it is better to retain the abstract form of the original, with Ewald, Lowth, Vitringa, and the ancient versions.—In some of the older versions מעלליכם is loosely and

variously rendered. Thus the LXX. have *souls*, the Vulgate *thoughts*, Calvin *desires*, Luther *your evil nature*. The meaning of the term may now be looked upon as settled.—Some have understood *from before mine eyes* as an exhortation to reform not only in the sight of man but in the sight of God; and others as implying that their sins had been committed to God's face, that is to say, with presumptuous boldness. But the true meaning seems to be the obvious and simple one expressed above. Knobel imagines that the idea of sin as a pollution had its origin in the ablutions of the law; but it is perfectly familiar and intelligible wherever conscience is at all enlightened.—Aben Ezra explains הִזַּכּוּ as the Hithpael of זָכָה, to which Hitzig and Henderson object that this species is wanting in all other verbs beginning with that letter, and that according to analogy it would be הִזְדַּכּוּ. They explain it therefore as the Niphal of זָכַךְ; but Gesenius (in his Lexicon) objects that this would have the accent on the penult. Compare Nordheimer § 77, 1. c.

17. The negative exhortation is now followed by a positive one. Ceasing to do evil was not enough, or rather was not possible, without beginning to do good. *Learn to do good*, implying that they never yet had known what it was. This general expression is explained by several specifications, shewing how they were to do good. *Seek judgment, i. e.* justice; not in the abstract, but in act; not for yourselves, but for others; be not content with abstinence from wrong, but seek opportunities of doing justice, especially to those who cannot right themselves. *Redress wrong, judge the fatherless, i. e.* act as a judge for his benefit, or more specifically, do him justice; *befriend the widow*, take her part, espouse her cause. Orphans and widows are continually spoken of in Scripture as special objects of divine compassion, and as representing the whole class of helpless innocents.—By *learning* to do good, Musculus and Hitzig understand forming the habit or accustoming one's self; but the phrase appears to have a more emphatic meaning.—Gesenius, Hitzig, Hendewerk, Ewald, and Knobel, take חָמוֹץ in the active sense of an oppressor, or a proud and wicked man, and understand the Prophet as exhorting his readers to conduct or guide such, *i. e.* to reclaim them from their evil courses. The Septuagint, the Vulgate, and the Rabbins, make חָמוֹץ a passive participle, and the exhortation one to rescue the oppressed (ῥύσασθε ἀδικούμενον, subvenite oppresso), in which they are followed by Luther, Calvin, Cocceius, Rosenmüller, Henderson, and Umbreit. Vitringa adopts Bochart's derivation of the word from חָמֵץ to *ferment* (emendate quod corruptum est); but Maurer comes the nearest to the truth in his translation (æquum facite iniquum). The form of the word seems to identify it as the infinitive of חמץ, *i. q.* חמם, to be violent, to do violence, to injure. Thus understood, the phrase forms a link between the general expression *seek justice* and the more specific one *do justice to the orphan*. The common version of the last clause (*plead for the widow*) seems to apply too exclusively to advocates, as distinguished from judges.

18. Having shewn that the cause of their ill-success in seeking God was in themselves, and pointed out the only means by which the evil could be remedied, he now invites them to determine by experiment on which side the fault of their destruction lay, promising pardon and deliverance to the penitent, and threatening total ruin to the disobedient, vers. 18–20.—This verse contains an invitation to discuss the question whether God was willing or unwilling to shew mercy, implying that reason as well as justice was on his side, and asserting his power and his willingness to pardon the most aggravated sins. *Come now* (a common formula of exhortation) *and let us*

reason (argue, or discuss the case) *together* (the form of the verb denoting a reciprocal action), *saith Jehovah, Though your sins be as scarlet, they shall be white as snow; though they be red as crimson, they shall be as wool, i. e.* clean white wool.   Guilt being regarded as a stain, its removal denotes restoration to purity.   The implied conclusion of the *reasoning* is that God's willingness to pardon threw the blame of their destruction on themselves.—Gesenius understands this verse as a threatening that God would *contend* with them in the way of vengeance, and blot out their sins by condign punishment; but this is inconsistent with the reciprocal meaning of the verb.   Umbreit regards the last clause as a threatening that their sins, however deeply coloured or disguised, should be discoloured, *i.e.* brought to light; an explanation inconsistent with the natural and scriptural usage of *white* and *red* to signify innocence and guilt, especially that of murder. J. D. Michaelis and Augusti make the verbs in the last clause interrogative: "Shall they be white as snow?" *i. e.* can I so regard them? implying that God would estimate them rightly and reward them justly.   This, in the absence of the interrogative particle, is gratuitous and arbitrary. Clericus understands the first clause as a proposition to submit to punishment (tum agite, nos castigari patiamur, ait enim Jehova); but although the verb might be a simple passive, this construction arbitrarily supposes two speakers in the verse, and supplies *for* after the first verb, besides making the two clauses inconsistent; for if they were pardoned, why submit to punishment?   According to Kimchi, the word translated *crimson* is a stronger one than that translated *scarlet;* but the two are commonly combined to denote one colour, and are here separated only as poetical equivalents.

19. The unconditional promise is now qualified and yet enlarged.   If obedient, they should not only escape punishment but be highly favoured. *If ye consent* to my terms, *and hear* my commands, implying obedience, *the good of the land,* its choicest products, *ye shall eat,* instead of seeing them devoured by strangers.—Luther and others understand *consent and hear* as a hendiadys for *consent to hear* (wollt ihr mir gehorchen); but this is forbidden by the parallel expression in the next verse, where *refuse and rebel* cannot mean *refuse to rebel,* but each verb has its independent meaning.   LXX. ἐὰν ϑέλητε καὶ εἰσακούσητέ μου.   Vulg. si volueritis et audieritis. So Gesenius, Ewald, &c.

20. This is the converse of the nineteenth verse, a threat corresponding to the promise.   *And if ye refuse* to comply with my conditions, *and rebel,* continue to resist my authority, *by the sword* of the enemy *shall ye be eaten.* This is no human menace, but a sure prediction, *for the mouth of Jehovah speaks,* not man's.   Or the sense may be, *the mouth of Jehovah has spoken* or ordained it.   (Targ. Jon. מימרא דיי גזר כן, the word of Jehovah has so decreed.)—According to Gesenius, תְּאֻכְּלוּ literally means *ye shall be caused to be devoured by the sword,* i. e. I cause the sword to devour you.   But, as Hitzig observes, the passive causative, according to analogy, would mean *ye shall be caused to devour,* and so he renders it (so müsset ihr das Schwerdt verzehren).   But in every other case, where such a metaphor occurs, the sword is not said to be eaten, but to eat.   (See Deut. xxxii. 42; Isa. xxxiv. 6; 2 Sam. ii. 26.)   The truth is that אָכַל is nowhere else a causative at all, but a simple passive, or at most an intensive passive of אָכַל (see Exod. iii. 2; Neh. ii. 3, 13).

21. Here the Prophet seems to pause for a reply, and on receiving no response to the promises and invitations of the foregoing context, bursts

forth into a sudden exclamation at the change which Israel has undergone, which he then describes both in figurative and literal expressions, vers. 21–23. In the verse before us he contrasts her former state, as the chaste bride of Jehovah, with her present pollution, the ancient home of justice with the present haunt of cruelty and violence. *How has she become an harlot* (faithless to her covenant with Jehovah), the faithful city (קִרְיָה πόλις, including the ideas of a city and a state, *urbs et civitas*, the body politic, the church, of which Jerusalem was the centre and metropolis), *full of justice* (*i. e.* once full), *righteousness lodged* (*i. e.* habitually, had its home, resided) *in it, and now murderers*, as the worst class of violent wrong-doers, whose name suggests, though it does not properly include, all others.— Kimchi and Knobel suppose a particular allusion to the introduction of idolatry, a forsaking of Jehovah the true husband for paramours or idols. But although this specific application of the figure occurs elsewhere, and is extended by Hosea into allegory, there seems to be no reason for restricting the expressions here used to idolatry, although it may be included.—The particle at the beginning of the verse is properly interrogative, but like the English *how* is also used to express surprise. · " How has she become ? " *i. e.* how could she possibly become ? how strange that she should become! —For the form מִלְאָתִי see Ges. Heb. Gr. § 93, 2. Ewald, § 406. For the tense of יָלִין Nordh. § 967, 1, *b.*

22. The change, which had just been represented under the figure of adultery, is now expressed by that of adulteration, first of silver, then of wine. *Thy silver* (addressing the unfaithful church or city) *is become dross* (alloy, base metal), *thy wine weakened* (literally *cut, mutilated*) *with water.* Compare the words of Martial, *scelus est jugulare Falernum.* The essential idea seems to be that of impairing strength. The Septuagint applies this text in a literal sense to dishonest arts in the sale of wines and the exchange of money. Οἱ κάπηλοί σου μίσγουσι τὸν οἶνον ὕδατι. But this interpretation, besides its unworthiness and incongruity, is set aside by the Prophet's own explanation of his figures, in the next verse.

23. The same idea is now expressed in literal terms, and with special application to magistrates and rulers. They who were bound officially to suppress disorder and protect the helpless, were themselves greedy of gain, rebellious against God, and tyrannical towards man. *Thy rulers are rebels and fellows of thieves* (not merely like them or belonging to the same class, but accomplices, partakers of their sin), *every one of them loving a bribe* (the participle denoting present and habitual action), *and pursuing rewards* (שלמנים) compensations. LXX. ἀνταπόδομα Symm, ἀμοιβάς). *The fatherless* (as being unable to reward them, or as an object of cupidity to others) *they judge not, and the cause of the widow cometh not unto them*, or before them: they will not hear it ; they will not act as judges for their benefit. They are not simply unjust judges, they are no judges at all, they will not act as such, except when they can profit by it. (J. D. Michaelis : dem Waisen halten sie kein Gericht.) *Rulers and rebels* is a sufficient approximation to the alleged paronomasia in שָׂרַיִךְ סוֹרְרִים, a gratuitous and vain attempt to copy which is made by Gesenius (deine Vorgesetzten sind widersetzlich) and Ewald (deine Herren sind Narren !).—Knobel supposes the rebellion here meant to be that of which Judah was guilty in becoming dependent upon Assyria (comp. chap. xxx. 1). But there is nothing to restrict the aplication of the terms, which simply mean that instead of suppressing rebellion they were rebels themselves.

24. To this description of the general corruption the Prophet now adds

a promise of purgation, which is at the same time a threatening of sorer
judgments, as the appointed means by which the church was to be restored
to her original condition, vers. 24–31.—In this verse, the destruction of
God's enemies is represented as a necessary satisfaction to his justice.
Therefore, because the very fountains of justice have thus become corrupt,
saith the Lord, the word properly so rendered, *Jehovah of Hosts*, the eternal
Sovereign, *the mighty one of Israel*, the almighty God who is the God of
Israel, *Ah*, an interjection expressing both displeasure and concern, *I will
comfort myself*, ease or relieve myself *of my adversaries*, literally, *from them*,
i.e. by ridding myself of them, *and I will avenge myself of mine enemies*, not
foreign foes, of whom there is no mention in the context, but the enemies
of God among the Jews themselves.—Cocceius understands by אביר ישראל
the *champion* or *hero of Israel*, and Knobel the *mightiest in Israel;* but the
first word seems clearly to denote an attribute of God, and the second his
relation to his people. Henderson translates the phrase *Protector of Israel;*
but this idea, though implied, is not expressed.   The latest versions follow
Junius and Tremellius in giving to נְאֻם its proper form as a passive participle, used as a noun, like the Latin *dictum*, and applied exclusively to
divine communications.   Henderson : *Hence the announcement of the Lord.*
So Hitzig, Ewald, Umbreit.

25. The mingled promise and threatening is repeated under one of the
figures used in ver. 22.   The adulterated silver must be purified by the
separation of its impure particles. *And I will turn my hand upon thee, i.e.*
take thee in hand, address myself to thy case, *and will purge out thy dross
like purity* itself, *i.e.* most purely, thoroughly, *and will take away all thine
alloy*, tin, lead, or other base metal found in combination with the precious
ores.—Luther, Junius, and Tremellius render עַל *against*, and make the
first clause wholly minatory in its import.   But although to *turn the hand*
has elsewhere an unfavourable sense (Ps. lxxxi. 15 ; Amos i. 8), it does not
of itself express it, but simply means to take in hand, address one's self to
anything, make it the object of attention.   (J. D. Michaelis: in Arbeit
nehmen.)   It appears to have been used in this place to convey both a promise and a threatening, which run together through this whole context.
Augusti and the later Germans use the ambiguous term *gegen* which has
both a hostile and a local meaning.—The Targum of Jonathan, followed by
Kimchi, Schmidius, J. D. Michaelis, and the latest Germans, makes בֹּר a
noun meaning potash or the vegetable alkali used in the smelting of metals.
Henderson: *as with potash.*   The usual sense of *purity* is retained by
Luther (auf's lauterste), the English Version (purely), Gesenius (rein), and
Barnes (wholly).   The particle is taken in a local sense by the Septuagint
(εἰς καθαρόν), Vulgate (ad purum), Cocceius (ad puritatem), Calvin and
Vitringa (ad liquidum), and the clause is paraphrased, as expressing resto-
ration to a state of purity, by Junius (ut justæ puritati restituam te), and
Augusti (bis es rein wird).   But this is at variance with the usage of the
particle.   The conjectural emendations of Clericus (כבר like a furnace),
Secker, and Lowth (בכר in the furnace) are perfectly gratuitous.

26. Here again the figurative promise is succeeded by a literal one of
restoration to a former state of purity, to be effected not by the conversion
of the wicked rulers, but by filling their places with better men. *And I will
restore*, bring back, cause to return, *thy judges*, rulers, *as at first*, in the
earliest and best days of the commonwealth, *and thy counsellors*, ministers
of state, *as in the beginning, after which it shall be called to thee*, a Hebrew
idiom for *thou shalt be called, i.e.* deservedly, with truth, *City of Righteous-*

ness, a faithful State. There is here a twofold allusion to ver. 21. She who from being a faithful wife had become an adulteress or harlot, should again be what she was ; and justice which once dwelt in her should return to its old home.—It is an ingenious but superfluous conjecture of Vitringa, that Jerusalem was anciently called צֶדֶק as well as שָׁלֵם (Gen. xiv. 18), since the same king bore the name of מַלְכִּי־צֶדֶק (king of righteousness) and מֶלֶךְ שָׁלֵם (king of peace), and a later king (Josh. x. 1) was called אֲדֹנִי־צֶדֶק (lord of righteousness). The meaning of the last clause would then be that the city should again deserve its ancient name, which is substantially its meaning now, even without supposing an allusion so refined and far-fetched.

27. Thus far the promise to God's faithful people and the threatening to his enemies among them had been intermingled, or so expressed as to involve each other. Thus the promise of purification to the silver involved a threatening of destruction to the dross. But now the two elements of the prediction are exhibited distinctly, and first the promise to the church. *Zion, the chosen people, as a whole, here considered as consisting of believers only, shall be redeemed,* delivered from destruction, *in judgment, i. e.* in the exercise of justice upon God's part, *and her converts,* those of her who *return* to God by true repentance, *in righteousness,* here used as an equivalent to justice.—Gesenius and the other modern Germans adopt the explanation given in the Targum, which assumes *in judgment and in righteousness* to mean by the practice of righteousness on the part of the people. Calvin regards the same words as expressive of God's rectitude, which would not suffer the innocent to perish with the guilty. But neither of these interpretations is so natural in this connection as that which understands the verse to mean that the very same events, by which the divine justice was to manifest itself in the destruction of the wicked, should be the occasion and the means of a deliverance to Zion or the true people of God.— The Septuagint, Peshito, and Luther, understand by שביה *her captivity* or *captives* (as if from שבה), Calvin and others *her returning* captives (qui reducentur ad eam) ; but the great majority of writers, old and new, take the word in a spiritual sense, which it frequently has elsewhere. See for example chap. vi. 10.

28. The other element is now brought out, viz. the destruction of the wicked, which was to be simultaneous and coincident with the deliverance promised to God's people in the verse preceding. *And the breaking,* crushing, utter ruin, *of apostates,* revolters, deserters from Jehovah, *and sinners,* is or shall be *together i. e.* at the same time with Zion's redemption, *and the forsakers of Jehovah,* an equivalent expression to apostates in the first clause, *shall cease,* come to an end, be totally destroyed. The terms of this verse are appropriate to all kinds of sin, but seem to be peculiarly descriptive of idolatry, as defection or desertion from the true God to idols, and thus prepare the way for the remainder of the chapter, in which that class of transgressors are made prominent.—Umbreit supplies no verb in the first clause, but reads it as an exclamation ; " Ruin to apostates and sinners all together ! " which is extremely harsh without a preposition before the nouns. Ewald, more grammatically, " Ruin of the evil-doers and sinners altogether ! " But the only natural construction is the common one.—Some writers understand *together* as expressing the simultaneous destruction of the two classes mentioned here, apostates and sinners, or of these considered as one class and the forsakers of Jehovah as another. But the expression is far more emphatic, and agrees far better with the context, if we understand it as connecting this destruction with the deliverance in ver. 27, and as being a

final repetition of the truth stated in so many forms, that the same judgments which destroyed the wicked should redeem the righteous, or in other words, that the purification of the church could be effected only by the excision of her wicked members.—Junius differs from all others in supposing the metaphor of ver. 25 to be here resumed. " And the fragments (שֶׁבֶר) of apostates and of sinners likewise, and of those who forsake Jehovah, shall fail or be utterly destroyed."

29. From the final destruction of idolaters the Prophet now reverts to their present security and confidence in idols, which he tells them shall be put to shame and disappointed. *For they shall be ashamed of the oaks* or *terebinths which ye have desired, and ye shall be confounded for the gardens which ye have chosen* as places of idolatrous worship. Paulus and Hitzig think that nothing more is here predicted than the loss of the fine pleasure-grounds in which the wealthy Jews delighted. But why should this part of their property be specified in threatening them with total destruction ? And why should they be *ashamed* of these favourite possessions and *confounded* on account of them ? As these are terms constantly employed to express the frustration of religious trust, and as groves and gardens are continually spoken of as chosen scenes of idol-worship (see for example chaps. lxv. 3; lxvi. 17; Ezek. vi. 13; Hos. iv. 13), there can be little doubt that the common opinion is the true one, namely, that both this verse and the one preceding have particular allusion to idolatry—Vitringa understands the first clause thus : *they* (the Jews of a future generation) *shall be ashamed of the oaks which ye* (the contemporaries of the Prophet) *have desired*. It is much more natural however to regard it as an instance of *enallage personæ* (Gesen. § 134, 3), or to construe the first verb indefinitely, *they, i. e.* men in general, people, or the like, *shall be ashamed*, &c., which construction is adopted by all the recent German writers (Gesenius : zu Schanden wird man, u. s. w.)—Knobel renders כִּי at the beginning *so that*, which is wholly unnecessary, as the verse gives a reason for the way in which the Prophet had spoken of persons now secure and flourishing, and the proper meaning of the particle is therefore perfectly appropriate.— Lowth renders אֵילִים *ilexes*, Gesenius and the other Germans *Terebinthen*, which is no doubt botanically accurate ; but in English *oak* may be retained as more poetical, and as the tree which, together with the terebinth, composes almost all the groves of Palestine.—The proposition before *oaks* and *gardens* may imply removal *from* them, but is more probably a mere connective of the verb with the object or occasion of the action, like the *of* and *for* in English.

30. The mention of trees and gardens, as places of idolatrous worship, suggests a beautiful comparison, under which the destruction of the idolaters is again set forth. They who chose trees and gardens, in preference to God's appointed place of worship, shall themselves be like trees and gardens, but in the most alarming sense. *For,* in answer to the tacit question why they should be ashamed and confounded for their oaks and gardens, *ye* yourselves *shall be like an oak* or terebinth, *fading,* decaying, in *its leaf* or as to *its leaf, and like a garden which has no water,* a lively emblem, to an oriental reader, of entire desolation.—Some writers understand the prophet to allude to the terebinth when dead, on the ground that it never sheds its leaves when living ; but according to Robinson and Smith (Bib. Res. vol. iii. p. 15), the terebinth or " *butm* is not an evergreen, as is often represented ; its small feathered lancet-shaped leaves fall in the autumn and are renewed in the spring."—Both here and in the foregoing verse,

Knobel supposes there is special allusion to the gardens in the valley of Hinnom, where Ahaz sacrificed to Moloch (2 Chron. xxviii. 3 ; Isa. xxx. 33, compared with chap. xxii. 7), and a prediction of their being wasted by the enemy ; but this, to say the least, is not a necessary exposition of the Prophet's general expressions. — For the construction of נֹבֶלֶת עָלֶהָ, see Gesenius, § 116, 3.

31. This verse contains a closing threat of sudden, total, instantaneous destruction to the Jewish idolaters, to be occasioned by the very things which they preferred to God, and in which they confided. *And the strong,* the mighty man, alluding no doubt to the unjust rulers of the previous context, *shall become tow,* an exceedingly inflammable substance, *and his work,* his idols, often spoken of in Scripture as the work of men's hands, shall become *a spark,* the means and occasion of destruction to their worshippers, *and they shall burn both of them together,* and there *shall be no one quenching* or to quench them. — All the ancient versions treat חֹסֶן as an abstract, meaning *strength*, which agrees well with its form, resembling that of an infinitive or verbal noun.   But even in that case the abstract must be used for a concrete, *i. e. strength* for *strong,* which last is the sense given to the word itself by all the modern writers.   Calvin and others understand, by the *strong one* the idol viewed as a protector or a tutelary god, and by פֹּעֲלוֹ his *maker* and worshipper, an interpretation which agrees in sense with the one given above, but inverts the terms, making the idol to be burnt by the idolater, and not *vice versa.*   But why should the worshipper burn himself with his idol?   A far more coherent and impressive sense is yielded by the other exposition. — Gesenius, Hitzig, and Hendewerk suppose the *work* (פֹּעַל as in Jer. xxli. 13), by which the strong man is consumed, to be his conduct in general, Junius his effort to resist God, Vitringa his contrivances and means of safety.   But the frequent mention of idols as the work of men's hands, and the prominence given to idolatry in the immediately preceding context, seem to justify Ewald, Umbreit, and Knobel, in attributing to פֹּעַל that specific meaning here, and in understanding the whole verse as a prediction that the very gods, in whom the strong men of Jerusalem now trusted, should involve their worshippers and makers with themselves in total, instantaneous, irrecoverable ruin.

Chapters 2, 3 & 4

THESE chapters constitute the second prophecy, the two grand themes of which are the reign of the Messiah and intervening judgments on the Jews for their iniquities.   The first and greatest of these subjects occupies the smallest space, but stands both at the opening and the close of the whole prophecy.   Considered in relation to its subject, it may therefore be conveniently divided into three- unequal parts.   In the first, the Prophet foretells the future exaltation of the church and the accession of the Gentiles, chap. ii. 1–4.   In the second, he sets forth the actual condition of the church and its inevitable consequences, chap. ii. 5–iv. 1.   In the third, he reverts to its pure, safe, and glorious condition under the Messiah, chap. iv. 2–6.   The division of the chapters is peculiarly unfortunate, the last verse of the second and the first of the fourth being both dissevered from their proper context. The notion that these chapters contain a series of detached predictions (Koppe, Eichhorn, Bertholdt) is now universally rejected even by the Germans, who consider the three chapters, if not the fifth (Hitzig), as forming

one broken prophecy.   As the state of things which it describes could
scarcely have existed in the prosperous reigns of Uzziah and Jotham, or in
the pious reign of Hezekiah, it is referred with much probability to the reign
of Ahaz (Gesenius, Ewald, Henderson, &c.), when Judah was dependent
on a foreign power and corrupted by its intercourse with heathenism.   The
particular grounds of this conclusion will appear in the course of the interpretation.

Chapter 2

THIS chapter contains an introductory prediction of the reign of the Messiah, and the first part of a threatening against Judah.

After a title similar to that in chap. i. 1, the Prophet sees the church, at
some distant period, exalted and conspicuous, and the nations resorting to
it for instruction in the true religion, as a consequence of which he sees war
cease and universal peace prevail, vers. 2–4.

These verses are found, with very little variation, in the fourth chapter
of Micah (vers. 1–3), to explain which some suppose, that a motto or quotation has been accidentally transferred from the margin to the text of Isaiah
(Justi, Eichhorn, Bertholdt, Credner); others, that both Prophets quote
from Joel (Vogel, Hitzig, Ewald); others, that both quote from an older
writer now unknown (Koppe, Rosenmüller, Maurer, De Wette, Knobel);
others that Micah quotes from Isaiah (Vitringa, Lowth, Beckhaus, Umbreit); others, that Isaiah quotes from Micah (J. D. Michaelis, Gesenius,
Hendewerk, Henderson).   This diversity of judgment may at least suffice
to shew how vain conjecture is in such a case.   The close connection of
the passage with the context, as it stands in Micah, somewhat favours the
conclusion that Isaiah took the text or theme of his prediction from the
younger though contemporary prophet.   The verbal variations may be best
explained, however, by supposing that they both adopted a traditional prediction current among the people in their day, or that both received the
words directly from the Holy Spirit.   So long as we have reason to regard
both places as authentic and inspired, it matters little what is the literary
history of either.

At the close of this prediction, whether borrowed or original, the Prophet
suddenly reverts to the condition of the church in his own times, so different
from that which had been just foretold, and begins a description of the present guilt and future punishment of Judah, which extends not only through
this chapter but the next, including the first verse of the fourth.   The part
contained in the remainder of this chapter may be subdivided into two unequal portions, one containing a description of the sin, the other a prediction
of the punishment.

The first begins with an exhortation to the Jews themselves to walk in
that light which the Gentiles were so eagerly to seek hereafter, ver. 5.   The
Prophet then explains this exhortation by describing three great evils which
the foreign alliances of Judah had engendered, namely, superstitious practices and occult arts : unbelieving dependence upon foreign wealth and
power ; and idolatry itself, vers. 6–8.

The rest of the chapter has respect to the punishment of these great sins.
This is first described generally as humiliation, such as they deserved who
humbled themselves to idols, and such as tended to the exclusive exaltation
of Jehovah, both by contrast and by the display of his natural and moral

attributes, vers. 9–11. This general threatening is then amplified in a detailed enumeration of exalted objects which would be brought low, ending again with a prediction of Jehovah's exaltation in the same words as before, so as to form a kind of choral or strophical arrangement, vers. 12–17. The destruction or rather the rejection of idols, as contemptible and useless, is then explicitly foretold, as an accompanying circumstance of men's flight from the avenging presence of Jehovah, vers. 18–21. Here again the strophical arrangement reappears in the precisely similar conclusions of the nineteenth and twenty-first verses, so that the twenty-second is as clearly unconnected with this chapter in form, as it is closely connected with the next in sense.

1. This is the title of the second prophecy, chaps. ii.–iv. *The word,* revelation or divine communication, *which Isaiah the son of Amoz saw,* perceived, received by inspiration, *concerning Judah and Jerusalem.* As *word* is here a synonyme of *vision* in chap. i. 1, there is no need of rendering דָּבָר *what, thing,* or *things* (Luth. Cler. Henders.), or חָזָה *prophesied* or *was revealed* (Targ. Lowth, Ges.), in order to avoid the supposed incongruity of seeing a word. For the technical use of *word* and *vision* in the sense of prophecy, see 1 Sam. iii. 1, Jer. xviii. 18.—The Septuagint, which renders עַל *against* in chap. i. 1, renders it here *concerning,* and on this distinction, which is wholly arbitrary, Cyril gravely comments.—Hendewerk's assertion that the titles, in which חזה and חזון occur, are by a later hand, is perfectly gratuitous.

2. The prophecy begins with an abrupt prediction of the exaltation of the church, the confluence of nations to it, and a general pacification as the consequence, vers. 2–4. In this verse the Prophet sees the church permanently placed in a conspicuous position, so as to be a source of attraction to surrounding nations. To express this idea, he makes use of terms which are strictly applicable only to the local habitation of the church under the old economy. Instead of saying, in modern phraseology, that the church, as a society, shall become conspicuous and attract all nations, he represents the mountain upon which the temple stood as being raised and fixed above the other mountains, so as to be visible in all directions. *And it shall be* (happen, come to pass, a prefatory formula of constant use in prophecy) *in the end* (or latter part) *of the days* (*i. e.* hereafter) *the mountain of Jehovah's house* (*i. e.* mount Zion, in the widest sense, including mount Moriah, where the temple stood) *shall be established* (permanently fixed) *in the head of the mountains* (*i. e.* above them), *and exalted from* (away from and by implication *more than* or *higher than*) *the hills* (a poetical equivalent to mountains), *and all the nations shall flow unto it.*—The use of the present tense in rendering this verse (Ges. Hitz. Hdwk.) is inconsistent with the phrase בְּאַחֲרִית הַיָּמִים, which requires the future proper (Ew. Hend.). That phrase, according to the Rabbins, always means the days of the Messiah ; according to Lightfoot, the end of the old dispensation. In itself it is indefinite.—The sense of נָכוֹן here is not *prepared* (Vulg.) but *fixed,* established, rendered permanently visible (LXX. ἔσται ἐμφανές).—It was not to be established *on the top* of the mountains (Vulg. Vitr. De W. Umbr.) but either *at the head* (Hitz. Ew.) or simply *high among* the mountains, which idea is expressed by other words in the parallel clause, and by the same words in 1 Kings xxi. 10, 12. That mount Zion should be taken up and carried by the other hills (J. D. Mich.) is neither the literal nor figurative meaning of the Prophet's words.—The verb in the last clause is always used to signify a confluence of nations.

3. This confluence of nations is described more fully, and its motive stated in their own words, namely, a desire to be instructed in the true religion, of which Jerusalem or Zion, under the old dispensation, was the sole depository. *And many nations shall go* (set out, put themselves in motion) *and shall say* (to one another), *Go ye* (as a formula of exhortation, where the English idiom requires *come*), *and we will ascend* (or *let us ascend*, for which the Hebrew has no other form) *to the mountain of Jehovah* (where his house is, where he dwells), *to the house of the God of Jacob, and he will teach us of his ways* (the ways in which he requires us to walk), *and we will go in his paths* (a synonymous expression). *For out of Zion shall go forth law* (the true religion, as a rule of duty), *and the word of Jehovah* (the true religion, as a revelation) *from Jerusalem.* These last words may be either the words of the Gentiles, telling why they looked to Zion as a source of saving knowledge, or the words of the Prophet, telling why the truth may be thus diffused, namely, because it had been given to the church for this very purpose. Cyril's idea that the clause relates to the taking away of God's word from the Jewish church (καταλέλοιπε τὴν Σιών) is wholly inconsistent with the context.—Compare John iv. 22 ; Luke xxiv. 47.—The common version *many people* conveys to a modern ear the wrong sense of *many persons*, and was only used for want of such a plural form as *peoples*, which, though employed by Lowth and others, has never become current, and was certainly not so when the Bible was translated, as appears from the circumlocution used instead of it in Gen. xxv. 23. The plural form is here essential to the meaning.—*Go* is not here used as the opposite of *come*, but as denoting active motion (Vitrin. movebunt se ; J. D. Mich. werden sich aufmachen).—The word *ascend* is not used in reference to an alleged Jewish notion that the Holy Land was physically higher than all other countries, nor simply to the natural site of Jerusalem, nor even to its moral elevation as the seat of the true religion, but to the new elevation and conspicuous position just ascribed to it.—The subjunctive construction *that he may teach* (Luth. Vitr. Ges. Ew. &c.) is rather paraphrastical and exegetical than simply expressive of the sense of the original, which implies hope as well as purpose.—The preposition *of* before *ways* is not to be omitted as a mere connective, " teach us his ways" (Ges. Hend. Um.) ; nor taken in a local sense, " out of his ways" (Knobel) ; but either partitively, " some of his ways" (Vitr.), or as denoting the subject of instruction, " concerning his ways," which is the usual explanation.—The substitution of *doctrine* or *instruction* for *law* (J. D. Mich. Hitz. Hendew. De W. Ew.) is contrary to usage, and weakens the expression.

4. He who appeared in the preceding verses as the lawgiver and teacher of the nations, is now represented as an arbiter or umpire, ending their disputes by a pacific intervention, as a necessary consequence of which war ceases, the very knowledge of the art is lost, and its implements applied to other uses. This prediction was not fulfilled in the general peace under Augustus, which was only temporary ; nor is it now fulfilled. The event is suspended on a previous condition, viz., the confluence of the nations to the church, which has not yet taken place ; a strong inducement to diffuse the gospel, which, in the mean time, is peaceful in its spirit, tendency, and actual effect, wherever and so far as it exerts its influence without obstruction. *And he shall judge* (or arbitrate) *between the nations, and decide for* (or respecting) *many peoples. And they shall beat their swords into ploughshares, and their spears into pruning-hooks. Nation shall not lift up sword against nation, neither shall they learn war any more.* To the figure in the

last clause Lowth quotes a beautiful parallel in Martial's epigram entitled *Falx ex ense:*

> Pax me certa ducis placidos curavit in usus;
> Agricolae nunc sum, militis ante fui.

The image here represented is reversed by Joel (iii. 10), and by Virgil and Ovid (Æn. vii. 635, Georg. i. 506, Ov. Fast. i. 697).—The question whether אִתִּים means ploughshares (Vulg. Lu. Low.), coulters (Rosen. Hn. Kn.) spades (Dutch Vs.), hoes or mattocks (Ges. Hitz. Ew. Um.), is of no exegetical importance, as the whole idea meant to be expressed is the conversion of martial weapons into implements of husbandry. *Hook* in old English, is a crooked knife, such as a *sickle*, which is not however here meant (LXX. Vulg. Lu.), but knife for pruning vines.—Not *learning war* is something more than not continuing to practise it (Calv.), and signifies their ceasing to know how to practise it. To *judge* is here not to *rule* (Calv. Vitr.), which is too vague, nor to *punish* (Cocc.), which is too specific, but to *arbitrate* or act as umpire (Cler. Ges. &c.), as appears from the effect described, and also from the use of the preposition בֵּין meaning not merely *among*, with reference to the sphere of jurisdiction, but *between*, with reference to contending parties. The parallel verb does not here mean to *rebuke* (Jun. Eng. Vs.) nor to *convince* of the truth in general (Calv. Cocc. Vitr.) or of the evil of war in particular (Hendew.), but is used as a poetical equivalent to שָׁפַט, which is used in this sense with the same preposition, Ezek. xxxiv. 17.—On the use of the present tense in rendering this verse (Ges. De W. Ew.) vide supra ad v. 2.

5. From this distant prospect of the calling of the Gentiles, the Prophet now reverts to his own times and countrymen, and calls upon them not to be behind the nations in the use of their distinguished advantages. If even the heathen were one day to be enlightened, surely they who were already in possession of the light ought to make use of it. *O house of Jacob* (family of Israel, the church or chosen people) *come ye* (literally, *go ye*, as in ver. 3), *and we will go* (or *let us walk*, including himself in the exhortation) *in the light of Jehovah* (in the path of truth and duty upon which the light of revelation shines). To regard these as the words of the Jews themselves (Targ. "they of the house of Jacob shall say," &c.), or of the Gentiles to the Jews (Jarchi), or to another (Sanctius), is forced and arbitrary in a high degree. The *light* is mentioned, not in allusion to the illumination of the court of the women at the feast of tabernacles (Deyling. Obs. Sacr. ii. p. 221), but as a common designation of the Scriptures and of Christ himself. Prov. vi. 23; Ps. cxix. 105; Isa. li. 4; Acts xxvi. 23; 2 Cor. iv. 4.

6. The exhortation in ver. 5 implied that the Jews were not actually walking in God's light, but were alienated from him, a fact which is now explicitly asserted and the reason of it given, viz., illicit intercourse with foreign nations, as evinced by the adoption of their superstitious practices, reliance on their martial and pecuniary aid, and last but worst of all, the worship of their idols. In this verse, the first of these effects is ascribed to intercourse with those eastern countries, which are always represented by the ancients as the cradle of the occult arts and sciences. As if he had said, I thus exhort, O Lord, thy chosen people, *because thou hast forsaken thy people the house of Jacob, because they are replenished from the east and* (full of) *soothsayers like the Philistines, and with the children of strangers they abound.*—The various renderings of כִּי by *therefore* (Eng. Vs.) *verily* (Low.), *surely* (Henders.), *but* (Hendew. Ew.), &c., all arise from miscon-

ception or neglect of the connection, which requires the common meaning *for, because* (Sept. Vulg. Ges. Hitz. Umb. Barnes). Abarbenel supposes the words to be addressed to the ten tribes, " Thou, O house of Jacob, hast forsaken thy people," Judah. Others suppose them to be addressed to Judah, but in this sense, " Thou, O house of Jacob, hast forsaken thy nation," *i. e.* thy national honour, religion, and allegiance (Saad. J. D. Mich. Hitz.). The last is a forced construction, and the other is at variance with the context, while both are inconsistent with the usage of the verb, which is constantly used to denote God's alienation from his people and especially his giving them up to their enemies (Judges vi. 13 ; 2 Kings xxi. 14 ; Jer. vii. 29 ; xxiii. 33).—*Filled* cannot mean *inspired* as in Micah iii. 8 (Vitr.), for even there the idea is suggested by the context.—J. D. Michaelis thinks קֶדֶם here synonymous with קָדִים the east wind, " full of the east wind," *i. e.* of delusion (Job xv. 2), which is wholly arbitrary. All the ancient versions supply *as* before this word, and two of them explain the phrase to mean *as of old* (Sept. ὡς τὸ ἀπʼ ἀρχῆς, Vulg. sicut olim). But all modern writers give it the local sense of *east*, applied somewhat indefinitely to the countries east of Palestine, especially those watered by the Tigris and Euphrates. Some read *they are full of the east, i.e.* of its people or its superstitions (Calv. Ges. Rosen. Hitz. De W. Hn. Um.) ; others *more than the east* (Luth. Dutch Vs.) ; but the true sense is no doubt *from the east* (Cler. ex oriente ; Ewald, vom Morgenlande her), denoting not mere influence or imitation, but an actual influx of diviners from that quarter.—Whether the root of עֹנְנִים be עַיִן an eye (Vitr.), עָנָן a cloud (Rosen.), or עָנַן to cover (Ges.), it clearly denotes the practitioners of occult arts. Henderson treats it as a finite verb (they practise magic) ; the English Version supplies *are ;* but the construction which connects it with the verb of the preceding clause, so that the first says *whence* they are filled, and then *wherewith*, agrees best with the mention of repletion or abundance both before and after. The Philistines are here mentioned rather by way of comparison than as an actual source of the corruption. That the Jews were familiar with their superstitions may be learned from 1 Sam. vi. 2 ; 2 Kings i. 2.—The last verb does not mean *they clap their hands* in applause, derision, or joy (Calv. Vitr. Eng. Vs.—they please themselves), nor *they strike hands* in agreement or alliance (Ges. Ros. De W. Hg. Häver. Hn. Um.), but *they abound,* as in Syriac, and in 1 Kings xx. 10 (J. H. Mich. Cler. Eng. Vers. marg. Ewald). The causative sense *multiply* (Lowth) does not suit the parallelism so exactly. The Septuagint and Targum apply the cause to alliance by marriage with the heathen.— By *children of strangers* we are not to understand the fruits, *i. e.* doctrines and practices of strangers (Vitr.), nor is it merely an expression of contempt, as Lowth and Gesenius seem to intimate by rendering it *strange* or *spurious brood.* It rather means strangers themselves, not strange gods or their children, *i. e.* worshippers (J. D. Mich.), but foreigners considered as descendants of a strange stock, and therefore as aliens from the commonwealth of Israel.—The conjectural emendations of the text by reading קסם for קדם (Brent.), בידי for בילדי (Hitz.), and נטשת יה for נטשתה (Houbigant), are wholly unnecessary.—For the form נְטַשְׁתָּה, see Ges. Heb. Gr. § 44, 2, 2.

7. The second proof of undue intercourse with heathen nations, which the Prophet mentions, is the influx of foreign money, and of foreign troops, with which he represents the land as filled. *And his land* (referring to the singular noun *people* in ver. 6) *is filled with silver and gold, and there is no*

end to his treasures; and his land is filled with horses, and there is no end to his chariots.—The common interpretatien makes this verse descriptive of domestic wealth and luxury. But these would hardly have been placed between the superstitions and the idols, with which Judah had been flooded from abroad. Besides, this interpretation fails to account for gold and silver being here combined with horses and chariots. Hitzig supposes the latter to be mentioned only as articles of luxury; but as such they are never mentioned elsewhere, not even in the case of Absalom and Naaman to which he appeals, both of whom were military chiefs as well as nobles. Even the chariots of the peaceful Solomon were probably designed for martial show. The horses and chariots of the Old Testament are horses and chariots of war. The common riding adimals were mules and asses, the latter of which, as contrasted with the horse, are emblematic of peace (Zech. ix. 9; Math. xxi. 7). But on the supposition that the verse has reference to undue dependence upon foreign powers, the money and the armies of the latter would be naturally named together. Thus understood, this verse affords no proof that the prophecy belongs to the prosperous reign of Uzziah or Jotham, since it merely represents the land as flooded with foreign gold and foreign troops, a description rather applicable to the reign of Ahaz. The form of expression, too, suggests the idea of a recent acquisition, as the strict sense of the verb is not *it is full* (E. V. Ges. Hn.), nor even *it is filled*, but *it was* or *has been filled* (LXX. Vulg. Hg. Ew. Kn.). —There is no need of explaining the words *no end* as expressing an insatiable desire (Calv.), or as the boastful language of the people (Vitr.), since the natural hyperbole employed by the Prophet is one by which no reader can be puzzled or deceived. The intimate connection of this verse with that before it is disturbed by omitting *and* at the beginning (Ges. Hg. Um.), nor is there any need of rendering it *also* (E. V.), *yea* (Hn.), or *so that* (Hk. Ew.), either here or in the middle of the sentence.

8. The third and greatest evil flowing from this intercourse with foreign nations was idolatry itself, which was usually introduced under the cloak of mere political alliances (see *e. g.* 2 Kings xvi. 10). Here as elsewhere the terms used to describe it are contemptuous in a high degree. *And his land is filled with idols* (properly *nonentities*, ' gods which yet are no gods,' Jer. ii. 11; 'for we know that an idol is nothing in the world,' 1 Cor. viii. 4), *to the work of their hands they bow down, to that which their fingers have made*, one of the great absurdities charged by the prophets on idolaters, " as if that could be a god to them which was not only a creature but their own creature" (Matthew Henry).—For *idols* the Septuagint has *abominations* (βδελυγμάτων), but the true sense of the Hebrew term is that expressed by Clericus, *diis nihili*.—For *their hands, their fingers*, the Hebrew has *his hands, his fingers*, an enallage which does not obscure the sense, and is retained in the last clause by Cocceius and Clericus (digiti ipsius). Vitringa has *digiti cujusque*. J. D. Michaelis makes the verb singular (jedet betet). Barnes has *his hands*, but *their fingers*.

9. Here the Prophet passes from the sin to its punishment, or rather simultaneously alludes to both, the verb in the first clause being naturally applicable as well to voluntary humiliation in sin as to compulsory humiliation in punishment, while the verb in the last clause would suggest of course to a Jewish reader the twofold idea of pardoning and lifting up. They who bowed themselves to idols should be bowed down by the mighty hand of God, instead of being raised up from their wilful self-abasement by the pardon of their sins. The relative features denote not only succession in time

but the relation of cause and effect. *And so* (by this means, for this reason) *the mean man* (not in the modern but the old sense of inferior, low in rank) *is bowed down, and the great man is brought low, and do not thou* (O Lord) *forgive them.* This prayer, for such it is, may be understood as expressing, not so much the Prophet's own desire, as the certainty of the event, arising from the righteousness of God. There is no need therefore of departing from the uniform usage of the future with אל as a negative imperative, by rendering it *thou dost not* (Ges. Hg.), *wilt not* (Lu. Vitr. Low. Hn.), *canst not* (J. D. Mich. De W. Hk.) or *mayest not forgive* (Um. Kn.) The strict translation is as old as the Vulgate (ne demittas) and as late as Ewald (vergib ihnen nicht).—Whether אִישׁ and אָדָם, as is commonly supposed, denote a difference in rank or estimation, like the Greek ἀνήρ and ἄνθρωπος, the Latin *vir* and *homo*, and the German *Mann* and *Mensch,* when in antithesis, is a question of no moment, because even if they are synonymous, denoting simply *man and man, this man and that man, one man and another* (Hg. Hk. Kn.), their combination here must be intended to describe men of all sorts, or men in general.—On the relative futures, see Ges. Heb. Gr. § 152, 4, *c.* On the construction with אל, Nordheimer, §§ 996, 1065.

10. Instead of simply predicting that their sinful course should be interrupted by a terrible manifestation of God's presence, the Prophet views him as already come or near at hand, and addressing the people as an individual, or singling out one of their number, exhorts him to take refuge under ground or in the rocks, an advice peculiarly significant in Palestine, a country full of caves, often used, if not originally made, for this very purpose (1 Sam. xiii. 6, xiv. 11 ; Judges vi. 2.) *Go into the rock and hide thee in the dust, from before the terror of Jehovah and from the glory of his majesty.* The nouns in the last clause differ, according to their derivation, very much as *sublimity* and *beauty* do in English, and express in combination the idea of sublime beauty or beautiful sublimity. The tone of this address is not sarcastic (Glassius) but terrific. By the *terror of Jehovah* seems to be intended, not the feeling of fear which he inspires (E. V. *for fear of the Lord*), but some terrible manifestation of his presence. The preposition, therefore, should not be taken in the vague sense of *for, on account of* (Jun. Cocc. E. V. Vitr.), but in its proper local sense of *from* (Lowth, Hn.), *before* (J. D. Mich. Ges. Hk. Ew. Um.), or *from before.*— The force and beauty of the passage are impaired by converting the imperative into a future (Targ.), or the singular imperative into a plural (Sept. Pesh. Hg.).—Lowth, on the authority of the Septuagint, Arabic, and a single manuscript, supplies the words *when he riseth to strike the earth with terror,* from the last clause of the nineteenth and twenty-first verses.

11. As the Prophet, in the preceding verse, views the terror of Jehovah as approaching, so here he views it as already past, and describes the effect which it has wrought. *The eyes of the loftiness of man* (i. e. his haughty looks) *are cast down, and the height* (or pride) *of men is brought low, and Jehovah alone is exalted in that day,* not only in fact, but in the estimation of his creatures, as the passive form here used may intimate.—*Man* and *men,* the same words that occur in ver. 9, are variously rendered here by repeating the same noun (Sept. Pesh. Lu. Calv. Vitr. Hn.) by using two equivalents (Lowth, *men and mortals ;* Ewald, *men and people*) or by an antithesis (Vulg. hominis, virorum).—The verb in the first clause agrees in form with the nearest antecedent, or the whole phrase may be regarded as the subject (Ges. Heb. Gr. § 145, 1), as in Ewald's version of it by a triple compound (Hochmuthsaugen).

12. The general threatening of humiliation is now applied specifically to a variety of lofty objects in which the people might be supposed to delight and trust, vers. 12–16. This enumeration is connected with what goes before, by an explanation of the phrases used at the close of the eleventh verse. I say that day, *for there is a day to Jehovah of Hosts* (*i. e.* an appointed time for the manifestation of his power) *upon* (or against) *every thing high and lofty, and upon every thing exalted, and it comes* (or shall come) *down.* —The common construction, *for the day of Jehovah is* or *shall be* (Sept. Vulg. Calv. E. V. Vitr. Lowth, Bar.), does not account for the use of the conjunction or the preposition, the former of which refers to the last words of the verse preceding, and the latter denotes the relation of possession : there is a day to Jehovah, *i. e. he has a day* (Ewald), *has it appointed* (Cocc. Jun. J. D. Mich.), has it in reserve, or less exactly, *holds a day* (Hitzig) or *holds a judgment-day* (Gesenius).—The specific sense of עַל *against* (Jun. Cler. Vitr. Low. Bar. Hen.), may be considered as included in the wider one of *on.*—The version *every one* (Sept. Jun. E. V.) restricts the phrase too much to persons, which is only a part of the idea conveyed by the expression *every thing* (Lu. Cocc. Vitr. J. D. Mich. Ges. &c.) To refer one clause to persons and the other to things (Calv. Barn.) is wholly arbitrary.—The same objection may be made to the common version of גֵּאֶה by *proud*, instead of its primary and comprehensive sense of *high* (Ewald. Gesen. in Lex.).—The translation of שָׁפֵל as an adjective, implying that the day of Jehovah was against *high and low* (Calv. in Comm. Cocc. J. D. Mich.), is inconsistent with the usage of the word, and not so well suited to the parallel clause, in which lofty things alone are threatened with humiliation.

13. To convey the idea of lofty and imposing objects, the Prophet makes use, not of symbols, but of specimens, selected from among the things of this class most familiar to his readers, beginning with the two noblest species of forest trees. *And on all the cedars of Lebanon* (or the White Mountain, the chain dividing Palestine from Syria), *that are high and lofty, and on all the oaks of Bashan* (now called El Bethenyeh, a mountainous district, east of Jordan, famous of old for its pastures and oak-forests).—Cedars and oaks are supposed by some to be here named, as emblems of *great men* in general (Targ. Jerome, Vitr. Low. Ges.), or of the great men of Syria and Israel distinctively (Grotius) ; but this is not in keeping with the subsequent context, in which some things are mentioned, which cannot be understood as emblems, but only as samples of their several classes. The application of the terms to the oak and cedar wood used in the buildings erected by Uzziah and Jotham, (Knobel) is equally at variance with the context and good taste. That they do not refer to the actual prostration of the forests of Palestine or the neighbouring countries by a tempest (Ros. Ew.), may be inferred from the impossibility of so explaining all the analogous expressions which follow.—On the trees and places mentioned in this verse, see Robinson's Palestine, vol. iii. p. 440, and Appendix, p. 158.

14. The mention of Lebanon and Bashan in ver. 13 now leads to that of mountains in general, as lofty objects in themselves, and therefore helping to complete the general conception of high things, which the Prophet threatens with humiliation. *And upon all the high mountains, and upon all the elevated hills.*—For reasons given under the preceding verse, this cannot be regarded as a threatening against states and governments (Lowth), or against the mountaineers of Palestine (Œcolampadius, Musculus), or against the fortresses erected by Jotham in the highlands of Judah (Knobel), or against the fastnesses to which they had recourse in times of danger (Barnes), but must be explained as an additional specification of the general statement in ver. 12, that *every high thing* should be humbled.

15. To trees and hills he now adds walls and towers, as a third class of objects with which the ideas of loftiness and strength are commonly associated. *And upon every high tower and upon every fenced wall,* literally *cut off, i. e.* rendered inaccessible by being *fortified*.—Lowth and others suppose these to be named as symbols of military strength, while Knobel supposes an allusion to the fortifications built by Jotham and Uzziah, and Hitzig assumes a transition just at this point from emblematical to literal expressions ; all which is more or less at variance with the context.

16. The Prophet now concludes his catalogue of lofty and conspicuous objects by adding, first, as a specific item, maritime vessels of the largest class, and then a general expression, summing up the whole in one descriptive phrase, as things attractive and imposing to the eye. *And upon all ships of Tarshish* (such as were built to navigate the whole length of the Mediterranean sea), *and upon all images* (i. e. visible objects) *of desire,* or rather admiration and delight.—It is a very old opinion, that *Tarshish* means the *sea,* and ships of Tarshish seafaring vessels (Sept. πλοίον Θαλάσσης; Luther, Schiffe im Meer ; Cocceius, naves oceani) as distinguished from mere coast or river craft (Piscator). From the earliest times, however, it has also been explained as the name of a place, either Tarsus in Cilicia (Josephus. Targ. on Chron.) or Cilicia itself (Hartmann), or Carthage (Καρχηδῶν Sept. alibi), or a port in Ethiopia (Hensler), or Africa in general (אפריקא Targ. on Jer. and Kings), or a port in India (Jerome on Jer. x. 9. Arabic Vs. 1 King s chap. x.), or which is now the common opinion, *Tartessus* a Phenician settlement in the south-west of Spain, between the mouths of the Baetis or Guadalquivir, sometimes put for the extreme west (Ps. lxxii. 10). As the principal maritime trade, with which the Hebrews were acquainted, was to this region, *ships of Tarshish* would suggest the idea of the largest class of vessels, justly included in this catalogue of lofty and imposing objects. To suppose a direct allusion either to commercial wealth or naval strength (Lowth) is inconsistent with the context, although these ideas would of course be suggested by association. Most writers understand the last clause, like the first, as a specific addition to the foregoing catalogue, denoting some particular object or class of objects, such as pictures (E. V. Gill's ' pictures of Christ and the Virgin Mary, of angels, saints, &c.'), statues (J. H. Mich. Döderlein. Ros.), lofty images or obelisks (Ewald), palaces (Targ. Jon.), tapestry (Calv.), ships (Sept. πᾶσαν Θέαν πλοίων κάλλους. Henderson, ' all the vessels of delightful appearance '), or their decorated sterns, ' pictæ carinæ' (Vitr. J. D. Mich. Hg.), or their gay flags and streamers (Gesenius in Thesauro). But this indefinite diversity of explanation, as well as the general form of the expression, makes it probable that this clause, notwithstanding the parallelism, was intended as a general expression for such lofty and imposing objects as had just been enumerated,—' cedars, oaks, mountains, hills, towers, walls, ships, and in short, all attractive and majestic objects' (Vulg. omne quod visu pulchrum est. Ges. ad loc. De W. Hk. Um. Bar.). Even Lowth's translation, *every lovely work of art,* is, on this hypothesis, too much restricted. The interpretation which has now been given is confirmed by the use of the analogous prosaic phrase כָּל־כְּלִי חֶמְדָּה, to close and sum up an enumeration of particulars. Knobel, to whom we are indebted for this illustration, cites as examples

2 Chron. xxxii. 27, xxxvi. 10, Nah. ii. 10.—For an argument in favour of regarding Tarshish as the name of Carthage, see Murray's Encyclopædia of Geography, Book I, chap. i. § iv. According to Abulfeda, the Arabic geographer, Tunis was anciently called *Tarsis*.

17. This verse, by repeating the terms of ver. 11, brings us back from details to the general proposition which they were designed to illustrate and enforce, and at the same time has the effect of a strophical arrangement, in which the same burden or chorus recurs at stated intervals. *And* (thus, by this means, or in this way) *shall the loftiness of man be cast down, and the pride of men be brought low, and Jehovah alone exalted in that day.* Or, retaining the form of the first two verbs, which are not passive but neuter, and exchanging the future for the present, the sentence may be thus translated. *So sinks the loftiness of man and bows the pride of men, and Jehovah alone is exalted in that day.* For the syntax of the first clause, vide supra ad ver. 11. Cf. Ewald's Heb. Gr. § 567. Gesenius, § 144.

18. To the humiliation of all lofty things the Prophet now adds the entire disappearance of their idols. *And the idols* (as for the idols) *the whole shall pass away.* The construction *he shall utterly abolish* or *cause to disappear* (Calv. E. V. Bar.) is at variance with the usage of the verb as an intransitive. To make it agree with the plural noun, *the idols shall utterly pass away* (E. V. marg. Low. De W. Hk. Hn.), or the verb itself impersonal, *it is past, gone,* or *all over with the idols* (Aug. Ges. Um.), are unusual and harsh constructions. It is best to take כָּלִיל not as an adverb but a noun meaning *the whole,* and agreeing regularly with the verb (Ros. Maur. Hg. Ew.). The omission of the article or suffix (כֻּלָּם or הַכָּלִיל) may be resolved into the poetical usage of employing indefinite for definite expressions (Ges. Heb. Gr. § ii. 4); but Knobel accounts for it still better by suggesting that the full phrase would have been כָּלִיל הָאֱלִילִים (like כָּלִיל הָעִיר Judges xx. 40), but the second noun is placed absolutely at the beginning of the sentence for the sake of emphasis—"the idols, the whole shall pass away," instead of "the whole of the idols shall pass away."—The brevity of this verse, consisting of a single clause, has commonly been regarded as highly emphatic, and, as Hitzig thinks, sarcastic. But Hendewerk supposes what was once the first clause of this verse to have been accidentally transferred to that before it. The eighteenth verse, in his translation, stands as follows—"Jehovah alone is exalted in that day, and the idols are all gone." This conjecture, though ingenious, is entirely unsupported by external evidence, and certainly not favoured by the analogy of ver. 11, where the same three members are combined as in ver. 17.

19. This verse differs from the tenth only by substituting a direct prediction for a warning or exhortation, and by adding the design of God's terrible appearance. *And they* (the idolaters, or men indefinitely) *shall enter into the caves of the rocks and into the holes of the earth, from before the terror of Jehovah and the glory of his majesty in his arising* (*i. e.* when he arises) *to terrify the earth.* The first word rendered *earth* is the same that was translated *dust* in ver. 10, but even there it signifies the solid surface rather than the crumbling particles which we call dust. The most exact translation would perhaps be *ground.*—God is said to *arise* when he addresses himself to anything, especially after a season of apparent inaction. The transitive meaning of the last verb, though unusual, is here required by the context, and is perhaps the primary and proper one (see Gesen. Thes. s. v.).—The paronomasia in לַעֲרֹץ הָאָרֶץ has been imitated by Calvin,

not in hls version but his notes (ad terram terrendam), and by Gesenius (wenn er sich *erhebt* und die Erde *bebt*).

20. This is an amplification of ver. 18, explaining how the idols were to disappear, viz. by being thrown away in haste, terror, shame, and desperate contempt, by those who had worshipped them and trusted in them, as a means of facilitating their escape from the avenging presence of Jehovah. *In that day shall man cast his idols of silver and his idols of gold* (here named as the most splendid and expensive, in order to make the act of throwing them away still more significant) *which they have made* (an indefinite construction, equivalent in meaning to *which have been made*), *for him to worship, to the moles and to the bats* (a proverbial expression for contemptuous rejection).—This last clause has by some been connected immediately with what precedes, *to bow down to moles and bats, i. e.* to crouch for concealment in their dark and filthy hiding-places (Luzzatto), or to worship images as blind as moles and bats (Jerome), or to worship moles and bats themselves (Sept. Tar. Vulg. ut adoraret talpas et vespertiliones), thus exchanging one form of idolatry for another still more disgusting (Grotius). But as the context relates not to the moral deterioration of idolaters, but to their terror and despair, it is commonly agreed that this clause is to be construed with the verb *shall cast*, and the words immediately preceding to be read as a parenthesis. The idols made for them to worship they shall cast to the moles and bats, not to idolaters still blinder than themselves (Glassius), but to literal moles and bats, or the spots which they frequent, *i. e.* dark and filthy places (Knobel, in die Rumpelkammer).—The word לחפר as it stands in all editions and most manuscripts, is the infinitive of חָפַר, *to dig*, preceded by a preposition and followed by a plural noun meaning *holes* (to dig holes, Kimchi) or *rats* (to the digging of rats, Ges. s. v.). But as five manuscripts make these two words one; as several instances of long words erroneously divided occur elsewhere (1 Chron. xxxiv. 6; Jer. xlvi. 20; Lam. iv. 3); and as the next word is also an unusually long one with the very same particle prefixed; most modern writers are agreed that the true reading is לחפרפרות (Theodotion ἀφαρφερώθ) a plural noun derived, by doubling two radicals, from חָפַר, *to dig*, and here used as the name of an animal, probably the *mole* (Jerome, Hk. Hn. Ew.); for although moles are not found, like bats, in dark recesses, they may be mentioned for that very reason to denote that the idolaters should cast away their idols, not only before setting out, but on the way (Hn. Ew.). More probably, however, moles and bats are put together on account of their defect of sight. On either supposition, it is needless to resort to the rabbinical tradition or the Arabic analogy for other meanings, such as *rats* (Ges. Maur. DeW.) or *sparrows* (Hg.) or *nocturnal birds* (Aben Ezra).—The sense of הָאָדָם is *man* in a collective sense, not distributively *a man* (E. V. Low. Bar.), the article being prefixed to universal terms, in various languages, where we omit it (Ges. Heb. Gr. § 107, 1.)—The phrase *they have made for him* is commonly explained as a sudden enallage or change of number, really meaning *they have made for themselves* (Ges. DeW. Hk. Hn.). Others suppose an abrupt transition from a collective to a distributive construction, *which they have made each one for himself* (E. V. Ros.). Others refer the plural to the artificers or idol-makers (Hg. Kn.). Others cut the knot by making the verb singular (Um.) or by omitting לו (Low. Bar.), as do one or two manuscripts. The simplest construction is to take the verb indefinitely, and to make לו mean not *for himself* (Ewald, die man sich machte) but *for him*, referring to *man*, the subject of the sentence. The

best translation of this clause is given in an old French version (qu'on lui aura faites).—The same version renders a preceding phrase *the idols made of his silver*, and the same construction is adopted by Umbreit (die Götzen seines Silbers). But the suffix really belongs to the governing noun (Hk.), or rather to the whole complex phrase (Ges. Heb. Gr. § 119, 3), and the expression is perfectly equivalent in meaning to *his silver idols* which is given in some versions (Hn. Ew.). The use of the present tense in rendering this verse (Ges. Hg. De W. Hk. Um.) does not agree so well with the expression *in that day* as the old common future form retained by Ewald (vide supra, ad ver. 11).—On the proverbial sense of *giving to the bats*, as applied to the desolated families and houses, see Roberts's Oriental Illustrations.

21. Continuing the sentence, he declares the end for which they should throw away their idols, namely, to save themselves, casting them off as worthless encumbrances in order the more quickly to take refuge in the rocks. *To go into the clefts of the rocks, and into the fissures of the cliffs* (or crags) *from before the terror of Jehovah, and from the glory of his majesty, in his arising to terrify the earth*, or as Lowth more poetically renders, *to strike the earth with terror*.—The translation, *going, in going, when they go* (Vitr. Ges. Hk. Hn.), as if the acts were simultaneous, rests on a forced construction, and leaves out of view the very end for which they are described as throwing away their idols, to express which the infinitive must have its proper meaning (Hg. Bar. Ew. Um. Kn.).—The substitution of *flee* (Hg.) or *creep* (Ges. Hk. De W.) for *go* or *enter* is allowable in paraphrase but not in strict translation.—The English phrases *ragged rocks* (E. V.) and *craggy rocks* (Low. Bar.) depart too much from the form of the original, which is a simple noun, as well as from its etymological import, which is rather height than ruggedness.—The meaning of פְעִיP is not *tops* (Calv. Cocc. E. V.), which is elsewhere forbidden by the context (Judges xv. 8, 11), but *fissures* (Sept. σχισμάς, Vulg. cavernas), answering to *clefts*, as *cliffs* to *rocks* in the other clause. The whole phrase is rendered by a compound word in the German versions of Luther (Felsklüfte), De Wette (Bergklüfte), and Hendewerk (Felsblöcke).—The final recurrence of the same *refrain* which closed the eleventh and seventeenth verses, marks the conclusion of the choral or strophical arrangement at this verse, the next beginning a new context.

22. Having predicted that the people would soon lose their confidence in idols, he now shews the folly of transferring that confidence to human patrons, by a general statement of man's weakness and mortality, explained and amplified in the following chapter. *Cease ye from man* (i.e., cease to trust him or depend upon him), *whose breath is in his nostrils* (i. e. whose life is transient and precarious, with obvious allusion to Gen. ii. 7), *for wherein is he to be accounted of* (or at what rate is he to be valued)? The interrogation forcibly implies that man's protection cannot be relied upon.—The version *is he valued* (De Wette) seems inadequate, the passive participle having very commonly the force not only of the perfect but the future participle in Latin (Ges. Heb. Gr. § 131, 1). The reference of these general expressions to Egypt (Hk. Kn.) or to any other human power in particular, disturbs the relation of this verse, as a general proposition, to the specific threatenings in the following chapter :—Some of the early Jews maliciously applied this verse to Christ, and their Christian opponents, instead of denying such a reference as foreign from the context and gratuitous, admitted it, but took the phrase *to cease from* in the sense of letting

alone or ceasing to molest (as in 2 Chron. xxxv. 21), and instead of בַּמֶּה *in what*, read בָּמָה *a high place* (Origen, Jerome : quia excelsus reputatus est ipse).   This strange and forced construction is retained by some of the earlier interpreters of modern times (Œcolampadius, Lyranus, Forerius, Menochius).   Even Luther's version or rather paraphrase (ihr wisset nicht wie hoch er geachtet ist) seems to presuppose it, but may possibly be founded on a misapplication of the words in their natural and proper sense. In the Septuagint this verse is wholly wanting, and Vitringa supposes the translators to have left it out, as being an unwelcome truth to kings and princes ; but such a motive must have led to a much more extensive expurgation of unpalatable scriptures.   It is found in the other ancient versions, and its genuineness has not been disputed.—To *cease from* is to *let alone ;* in what specific sense must be determined by the context (compare 2 Chron. xxxv. 21 with Prov. xxiii. 4).—On the pleonastic or emphatic form, *cease for yourselves*, see Ges. Heb. Gr. § 131, 3, c.

Chapter 3

THIS chapter continues the threatenings against Judah on account of the prevailing iniquities, with special reference to female pride and luxury.

The Prophet first explains his exhortation at the close of the last chapter, by shewing that God was about to take away the leading men of Judah, and to let it fall into a state of anarchy, vers. 1–7. He then shews that this was the effect of sin, particularly that of wicked rulers, vers. 8–15. He then exposes in detail the pride and luxury of the Jewish women, and threatens them not only with the loss of that in which they now delighted, but with widowhood, captivity, and degradation, ver. 16—iv. 1.

The first part opens with a general prediction of the loss of what they trusted in, beginning with the necessary means of subsistence, ver. 1.   We have then an enumeration of the public men who were about to be removed, including civil, military, and religious functionaries, with the practitioners of certain arts, vers. 2, 3. As the effect of this removal, the government falls into incompetent hands, ver. 4. This is followed by insubordination and confusion, ver. 5. At length, no one is willing to accept public office, the people are wretched, and the commonwealth a ruin, vers. 6, 7.

This ruin is declared to be the consequence of sin, and the people represented as their own destroyers, vers. 8, 9.   God's judgments, it is true, are not indiscriminate.   The innocent shall not perish with the guilty, but the guilty must suffer, vers. 10, 11. Incompetent and faithless rulers must especially be punished, who, instead of being the guardians, are the spoilers of the vineyard ; instead of protectors, the oppressors of the poor, vers. 12–15.

As a principal cause of these prevailing evils, the Prophet now denounces female luxury, and threatens it with condign punishment, privation, and disgrace, vers. 16, 17. This general denunciation is then amplified at great length, in a detailed enumeration of the ornaments which were about to be taken from them, and succeeded by the badges of captivity and mourning, vers. 18–24.   The agency to be employed in this retribution is a disastrous war, by which the men are to be swept off, and the country left desolate, vers. 25, 26. The extent of this calamity is represented by a lively exhibition of the disproportion between the male survivors and the other sex, suggesting at the same time the forlorn condition of the widows of the slain, chap. iv. 1.

1. This verse assigns, as a reason for the exhortation in the one preceding, that God was about to take away from the people every ground
of reliance, natural and moral. Cease ye from man, *i.e.* cease to trust
in any human protection, *for behold* (implying a proximate futurity) *the
Lord* (God considered as a sovereign) *Jehovah of Hosts* (as self-existent
and eternal, and at the same time as the God of revelation and the God
of his people) *is taking away* (or about to take away) *from Jerusalem and
from Judah* (not only from the capital, but from the whole kingdom) *the
stay and the staff* (*i.e.* all kinds of support, and first of all), *the whole stay
of bread, and the whole stay of water* (the natural and necessary means of
subsistence). The terms are applicable either to a general famine produced
by natural causes, or to a scarcity arising from invasion or blockade, such
as actually took place when Judah was overrun by Nebuchadnezzar (2
Kings xxv. 4; Jer. lii. 6; xxxviii. 9; Lam. iv. 4).—Instead of *the whole
stay*, prose usage would require *every stay*, the form adopted by Gesenius
and the later Germans. But the other construction is sustained by the
analogy of *the whole head* and *the whole heart*, chap.'i. 5, and by the impossibility of expressing this idea otherwise without circumlocution, as the
addition of another noun excludes the article.—The old version *stay and
staff* is an approximation to the form of the original, in which a masculine and feminine form of the same noun are combined, by an idiom
common in Arabic, and not unknown in Hebrew (Nah. ii. 13), to denote
universality, or rather *all kinds* of the object named. This form of expression is retained in the Greek versions (Sept. ἰσχύοντα καὶ ἰσχύουσαν.
Aqu. ἔρεισμα καὶ ἐρεισμόν. Symm. στήριγμα καὶ στηριγμόν), and the Jewish-
Spanish (sustentador y sustentadora). Others imitate it merely by combining synonymes alike in form (Calv. vigorem et vim. Vitr. fulcimentum
et fulturam. Hitz. Stütze und Stützpunkt; Ew. Stab und Stütze). Others
simply give the sense by reading *every stay* (Ges.), *all stays of every kind*
(J. D. Mich.), *one stay after another* (Hk.), &c.—The last clause is rejected as a gloss by Gesenius in his commentary, on the ground that its
explanation of the first clause as denoting food and drink is inconsistent
with the subsequent context, which explains it to mean public men. This
objection is withdrawn in the second edition of his German version, but
renewed by Hitzig and Knobel, with the addition of another, viz., that
water is not a stay or staff of life. The last is frivolous, and the other
groundless, as the last clause is not an explanation of the first, but begins
a specification of particulars included in it. The stays of which they were
to be deprived were first the stay of food, ver. 1, and then the stay of government, vers. 2, 3.

2. Next to the necessary means of subsistence, the Prophet enumerates
the great men of the commonwealth, vers. 2, 3. The first clause has reference to military strength, the second to civil and religious dignities. In
the second clause there is an inverse parallelism, the first and fourth terms
denoting civil officers, the second and third religious ones. The omission
of the article before the nouns, though not uncommon in poetry, adds much
to the rapidity and life of the description. *Hero and warrior, judge and
prophet, and diviner and elder.*—That the first is not a generic term including all that follow (the great men, viz. the warriors, &c.) is clear from the
parallelism, the terms being arranged in pairs, as often elsewhere (chaps.
xi. 2; xix. 3, 6–9; xxii. 12, 13; xlii. 19).—The idea here expressed by
גִּבּוֹר is not simply that of personal strength and prowess (Sept. γίγαντα καὶ
ἰσχύοντα), but the higher one of military eminence or heroism (J. D. Mich.

Ges. Hn., &c.).—The literal version of the next phrase, *man of war*, has acquired a different sense in modern English. It may here denote either a warrior of high rank, as synonymous with גִּבּוֹר (Vitr. militia clarum) or one of ordinary rank, as distinguished from it (Cocc. ducem et militem ; Kn. Oberste und Gemeine). Compare 2 Sam. xxiii. 8.—*Judge* may either be taken in its restricted modern sense (Hk.), or in the wider one of magistrate or ruler.—To avoid the supposed incongruity of coupling the prophet and diviner together, some take נָבִיא in the bad sense of a false or an unfaithful prophet (J. D. Mich. Ges. Hg.) ; others take קֹסֵם in the good sense of a scribe (Targ.), a prudent man (E. V.), or a sagacious prognosticator or adviser (Sept. Grot. Bar.) ; while Hendewerk refers both words to the prophet, making the first denote his office as a preacher, and the second as a foreteller ; all which is arbitrary, contrary to usage, and entirely superfluous. The people are threatened with the loss of all their *stays*, good or bad, true or false. *Vera et falsa a Judæis pariter auferentur* (Jerome).— The last word in the verse is not to be taken in its primary and proper sense of *old man* (Vulg. senem), much less in the factitious one of *sage* (Low.) or *wise man* (Bs.), since all the foregoing terms are *titles* denoting rank and office, but in its secondary sense of *elder* (Sept. πρεσβύτερον. Lu. Aeltesten) or hereditary chief, and as such, a magistrate under the patriarchal system. It is here equivalent or parallel to *judge*, the one term denoting the functions of the office, the other the right by which it was held.—The change of the singulars in this verse for plurals (Luth. J. D. Mich.), though it does not affect the sense, weakens its expression.

3. To persons of official rank and influence, the Prophet adds, in order to complete his catalogue, practitioners of those arts upon which the people set most value. As the prophet and diviner stand together in ver. 2, so mechanical and magical arts are put together here. The first clause simply finishes the list of public functionaries which had been begun in the preceding verse. *The chief of fifty, and the favourite, and the counsellor, and the skilful artificer, and the expert enchanter.*—The first title is derived from the decimal arrangement of the people in the wilderness for judicial purposes (Exod. xviii. 25, 26), but is afterwards used only as a military title. Hitzig and Knobel understand it here as denoting an officer of low rank, in opposition to *warrior* in the verse preceding.—The next phrase literally signifies *lifted up in countenance* (Vulg. honorabilem vultu), which is commonly understood as a description of an eminent or honourable person. But as the same words are employed to signify respect of persons or judicial partiality, the phrase may here denote one highly favoured by a sovereign, a royal favourite (2 Kings v. 1 ; Lev. ix. 15 ; Deut. x. 17 ; Job xiii. 10 ; Mal. ii. 9), or respected, reverenced by the people (Lam. iv. 16 ; Deut. xviii. 50). Luther translates it as a plural or collective by *respectable people* (ehrliche Leute).—The *counsellor* here meant is not a private or professional adviser, but a public counsellor or minister of state.—חֲכַם is here used in what seems to be its primary sense of *skilful*, with respect to art (compare σοφός in Passow's Greek Lexicon).—The explanation of חֲרָשִׁים as denoting occult arts (Cler. Ges. Hg. Hn. Ewald, *Hexenmeister*), though countenanced by Chaldee and Syriac analogies, has no Hebrew usage to support it, and the expression of the same idea in the other clause is rather a reason for applying this to the mechanical arts, as is done by the Septuagint (σοφὸν ἀρχιτέκτονα), Luther (weise Werkleute), Vitringa (mechanicarum artium peritum), Knobel, and others. Umbreit seems to apply the term specially to the manufacture of idols, as J. D. Michaelis does to that of

arms (gute Waffenschmiede). Gesenius and Hitzig may have been led to reject this old interpretation by a desire to evade the remarkable coincidence between this prophecy and the fact recorded in 2 Kings xxiv. 14, 16. —The last word in the verse is taken strictly, as denoting a " whisper " or the act of whispering, by Aquila (συνετὸν ψιθυρισμῷ), Cocceius (prudentem susurrorum), and Hitzig (kundigen des Geflüsters) ; but its secondary sense of incantation, with allusion to the mutterings and whisperings which formed a part of magical ceremonies, by Symmachus (ὁμιλίᾳ μυστικῇ), the Vulgate (eloquii mystici), and most modern writers. According to J. D. Michaelis and Gesenius, it specially denotes the charming of serpents. The sense of *eloquent orator* (Lu. Calv. Jun. E. V. Vitr. Low.) seems altogether arbitrary. The analogous phrase נְבוֹן דָּבָר (1 Sam. xvi. 18), to which Rosenmüller refers, is itself of doubtful import, and proves nothing.

4. The natural consequence of the removal of the leading men must be the rise of incompetent successors, persons without capacity, experience, or principle, a change which is here ascribed to God's retributive justice. *And I will give children to be their rulers, and childish things shall govern them.* Some apply this, in a strict sense, to the weak and wicked reign of Ahaz (Ew. Hg. Hk. Kn.), others in a wider sense to the series of weak kings after Isaiah (Gro. Low.) But there is no need of restricting it to kings at all, as שַׂר denotes a ruler in general, and in ver. 3 is applied to rulers of inferior rank. The most probable opinion is that the incompetent rulers are called boys or children not in respect to age but character, " non ratione ætatis sed imprudentiæ et ineptitudinis " (J. H. Mich.). Calvin, Cocceius, Lowth, and Gesenius take תַּעֲלוּלִים as a simple equivalent to נְעָרִים, and J. D. Michaelis translates it *sucklings*. Hitzig makes it qualify the verb instead of agreeing with it as its subject. " They (the children) shall rule over them with arbitrary cruelty." Hendewerk and Knobel give the same meaning to the noun, but retain the usual construction. " And tyranny shall rule over them." Most probably, however, תַּעֲלוּלִים is an abstract term used for the concrete, *puerilities* or *childishness* for *childish persons*, or still more contemptuously, *childish things* (Lu. Ew. Um.) The Targum has *weaklings* (חלשׁיא), the Septuagint ἐμπαῖκται, the Vulgate *effoeminati*, Junius and Tremellius *facinorosi*.

5. As the preceding verse describes bad government, so this describes anarchy, the suspension of all government, and a consequent disorder in the relations of society, betraying itself in mutual violence, and in the disregard of natural and artificial claims to deference. *And the people shall act tyrannically, man against man, and man against his fellow. They shall be insolent, the youth to the old man, and the mean man to the noble.* The passive construction, *the people shall be oppressed* (E. V. Low. Bar.), does not agree so well with the usage of the preposition following as the reflexive one now commonly adopted. The insertion of another verb (*man striving against man*, Bar.) is wholly unnecessary. The second verb is commonly explained to mean the insolence or arrogance of upstarts to their betters (Calv. insolescet. Fr. Vs. se portera arrogamment) ; but the best lexicographers give it the stronger sense of acting ferociously (Cocc. Ges. Winer, Fürst), or, to combine both ideas, with ferocious insolence. (Hitzig, stürmen. Gesenius, losstürmen ; Hendewerk, wüthet ; Henderson, outrage.) —The passive participles in the last clause properly signify *despised* and *honoured*, *i. e.* once despised, once honoured (Cler. qui antea spretus erat) ; or, according to the common idiomatic usage of passive participles, *to be*

despised, to be honoured, not so much with reference to moral character as to rank and position in society. The restriction of the first clause to the rigorous exaction of debts (Clericus) is inconsistent with the context and the parallelism. On contempt of old age, as a sign of barbarism, see Lam. iv, 16 : Deut xxviii. 50. Eight manuscripts and fifteen editions read נגשׂ for נָגַשׂ, but all the ancient versions presuppose the common reading.

6. Having predicted the removal of those qualified to govern, the rise of incompetent successors, and a consequent insubordination and confusion, the Prophet now describes this last as having reached such a height that no one is willing to hold office, or, as Matthew Henry says, " the government goes a-begging.'' This verse, notwithstanding its length, seems to contain only the protasis or conditional clause of the sentence, in which the commonwealth is represented as a ruin, and the task of managing it pressed upon one living in retirement, on the ground that he still possesses decent raiment, a lively picture both of general anarchy and general wretchedness. *When a man shall take hold of his brother* (*i. e.*, one man of another) *in his father's house* (at home in a private station, saying,) *thou hast raiment, a ruler shalt thou be to us, and this ruin* (shall be) *under thy hand* (*i. e.* under thy power, control, and management). It is equally consistent with the syntax and the usage of the words to understand the man as addressing his brother, in the proper sense, or in that of a near kinsman, of or belonging to the house of his (the speaker's) father, *i. e.* one of the same family (Vulg. domesticum patris sui. J. H. Mich., cognatum. Hendew., Einen von den seinen). But the offer would then seem to be simply that of headship or chieftainship over a family or house, whereas a wider meaning is required by the connection. For *raiment*, Henderson reads *an abundant wardrobe*, and explains the phrase as meaning, *thou art rich*, because clothing forms a large part of oriental wealth, and the same explanation is given in substance by Clericus, Hendewerk, Barnes, and Umbreit. But Vitringa, Gesenius, Rosenmüller, Knobel, and others, understand the words more probably as meaning " thou hast still a garment,'' whereas we have none, implying general distress as well as anarchy. Vitringa and Lowth make לְכָה a verb, as it is elsewhere, meaning *go or come*, as a particle of exhortation (vide supra chap. ii. 3), and connect שִׂמְלָה with what precedes, but in different ways. Vitringa's construction is that a man shall lay hold of his brother, *in whose paternal house there is raiment*, saying, *come on* (agedum), &c. Lowth's, that a man shall lay hold of his brother *by the garment*, saying, *come*, &c. All other writers seem to be agreed that לְכָה is an unusual mode of writing לְךָ (see Ges. Heb. Gr. § 35).—The כִּי at the beginning has been variously rendered, *for, because* (Sept. Targ. Vulg. Pesh.), *therefore* (Lowth), *if* (Junius), *then if* (Ros.), *then* (Lu. Ges. Bar. Kn.). Henderson uses the periphrasis *should any one*, &c. Hitzig and Ewald agree with Calvin, Vitringa, Clericus, and the English Bible in rendering it *when*, and regarding the two verses as one continuous sentence.—The word *saying*, in the first clause, is inserted by two manuscripts, and supplied by most versions ancient and modern.—Thirty-five manuscripts and two editions read יָדֶיךָ in the plural.

7. This verse contains the refusal of the invitation given in the one preceding. *In that day he shall lift up* (his voice in reply) *saying*, I will *not be a healer, and in my house there is no bread, and there is no clothing ; ye shall not make me a ruler of the people. In that day* may either mean at once, without deliberation, or continue the narrative without special emphasis. Some supply *hand* after *lift up*, as a gesture of swearing, or

the name of God as in the third commandment, and understand the phrase to mean that *he shall swear* (Saad. Lu. Calv. E. V., J. D. Mich.). But the great majority of writers supply *voice*, some in the specific sense of *answering* (Sept. Vulg. Targ. Pesh. Cler.) or in the simple sense of *uttering* (Cocc. Ges. De W. Ew.), but others with more probability in that of speaking with a loud voice (Vitr. Ros.), or distinctly and with emphasis, *he shall protest* (Hn.) or *openly declare* (Low.). The Vulgate, Luther, and Gesenius, have *I am not a healer*, but if that were the sense, the verb would probably be suppressed. The meaning of the words seem to be either *I cannot*, as a confession of unfitness (Targ. Ros. De. W. Hk. Um.), or *I will not*, as an expression of invincible aversion (Calv. Cocc. Cler. E. V. Low. Hn. Kn.).— The Septuagint and Clericus take חֹבֵשׁ in the sense *of prince* or *perfect*. Cocceius translates it literally *binding*, Ewald *binder*. Saadias makes it mean one who binds his head with a diadem ; Montanus an executioner like the Latin *lictor*. The true sense of *healer* is given by the Vulgate (medicus), Calvin (curator), Luther (Artzt), and most of the later versions. There is no need of reading *for in my house* (Calv. Cler. Hn. Ew. Kn.), as the words do not directly give a reason for refusing, but simply deny the fact alleged in the request. Clericus, Lowth, and Henderson carry out their interpretation of the previous verse by supposing the excuse here given to be that he was not rich enough to clothe and feast the people as oriental chiefs are expected to do. But the whole connection seems to shew that it is a profession of great poverty, which, if true, shews more clearly the condition of the people, and if false, the general aversion to office. The last clause does not simply mean *do not make me*, but *you must not*, or *you shall not make me* a ruler. Gesenius and all the later Germans except Ewald substitute the descriptive present for the future in this verse.

8. The Prophet here explains his use of the word *ruin* in reference to the commonwealth of Israel, by declaring that it had in fact destroyed itself by the offence which its iniquities had given to the holiness of God, here compared to the sensitiveness of the human eye. Do not wonder at its being called a ruin, *for Jerusalem totters and Judah falls* (or Jerusalem is tottering and Judah falling), because their *tongue and their doings* (words and deeds being put for the whole conduct) *are against Jehovah* (strictly *to* or *towards*, but in this connection necessarily implying opposition and hostility), *to resist* (*i. e.* so as to resist, implying both the purpose and effect) *his glorious eyes* (and thereby to offend them). The Peshito seems to take these as the words of the man refusing to govern ; but they are really those of the Prophet explaining his refusal, or rather one of the expressions used in making the offer, as כָּשְׁלָה clearly involves an allusion to מַכְשֵׁלָה one of its derivatives. The כִּי is therefore not to be taken in the sense of *yea* (Um.) or *surely* (Calv.), but in its proper sense of *for, because* (Sept. Vulg. &c.). Here as in chap. i. 16, מַעַלְלֵים is variously rendered *ad inventiones* (Vulg.), *studia* (Calv.), *conata* (Mont.), but the only meaning justified by etymology is that of *actions*. Cocceius, who refers the whole prophecy to the times of the New Testament, understands by their resisting God's glorious eyes, the opposition of the Jews to the Son of God when personally present. *Totter* and *fall* are supposed by some to be in antithesis, contrasting the calamities of Jerusalem with the worse calamities of Judah (Knobel), or the partial downfall of the kingdom under Ahaz, with its total downfall under Zedekiah (Vitringa) ; but they are more probably poetical equivalents, asserting the same fact, that Jerusalem and Judah, though peculiarly the Lord's, were

nevertheless to fall and be destroyed for their iniquities.—The present form is adopted here, not only by the modern writers, but by the Septuagint, Vulgate and Luther. The emendation of the text by changing עֲנֵי to עָנָו (Low.) or עֲנִי (J. D. Mich.), is needless and without authority.—For the orthography of עֲנֵי, see Ewald's Heb. Gr. § 30.

9. As they make no secret of their depravity, and as sin and suffering are inseparably connected, they must bear the blame of their own destruction. *The expression of their countenances testifies against them, and their sin, like Sodom, they disclose, they hide it not. Woe unto their soul, for they have done evil to themselves.*—The first clause is applied to *respect of persons* or judicial partiality, by the Targum (בדינא), Clericus (habita hominum ratio), Hitzig (ihr Ansehn der Person), and Gesenius in his Thesaurus. This construction is favoured by the usage of the phrase הִכִּיר פָּנִים (Deut. i. 17, xvi. 19 ; Prov. xxiv. 23, xxviii. 21) ; but the context seems to shew that the Prophet has reference to general character and not to a specific sin, while the parallel expressions in this verse make it almost certain that the phrase relates to the expression of the countenance. Some explain it accordingly of a particular expression, such as shame (Sept.), impudence (Vulg.), obduracy (Jun.), stedfastness (Lowth), confusion (Ges.), insensibility (Ew.). But the various and even contradictory senses thus put upon the word may serve to shew that it is more correctly understood, as denoting the expression of the countenance generally, by Calvin (probatio), Cocceius (adspectus), Gussetius (quod dant cognoscendum), the English Version (shew), De Wette (Ausdruck), and other recent writers. The sense is not that their looks betray them, but that they make no effort at concealment, as appears from the reference to Sodom. Quod unum habebant in peccatis bonum perdunt, peccandi verecundiam (Seneca).—The expression of the same idea first in a positive and then in a negative form is not uncommon in Scripture, and is a natural if not an English idiom. Madame d'Arblay, in her Memoirs of Dr Burney, speaks of Omiah, the Tahitian brought home by Captain Cook, as " uttering first affirmatively and then negatively all the little sentences that he attempted to pronounce." For examples involving this same verb כִּחֵד, see Josh. vii. 19 ; 1 Sam. iii. 17, 18. The explanation of גָּמְלוּ as meaning *recompence, reward* (Vulg. Cler. E. V. Um.), is rejected by most of the modern writers, who make it correspond very nearly to the English *treat*, in the sense of doing either good or evil. " They have treated themselves ill, or done evil to themselves " (Cocc. sibimet ipsis male faciunt. Ewald: sie thaten sich böses). Hengstenberg maintains (Comm. on Psalm vii. 5) that the verb means properly to *do good*, and is used in a bad sense only by a kind of irony. The phrase *to their soul* may be understood strictly (Calv. E. V. Hg. De W.) or as meaning *to their life* (Cler. Ges.) ; but the singular form of the noun seems to imply that it is used as a periphrasis for the reflexive pronoun *to themselves*. David Kimchi says that his father derived הַכָּרַת from הָכַר to be hard, making the ה radical ; but the derivation from נָכַר is now-universally adopted.

10. The righteous are encouraged by the assurance that the judgments of God shall not be indiscriminate. *Say ye of the righteous that it shall be well, for the fruits of their doings they shall eat.* The object of address seems to be not the prophets or ministers of God, but the people at large or men indefinitely. The concise and elliptical first clause may be variously construed—" Say, it is right (or righteous) that (they should eat) good, that they should eat the fruit of their doings."—" Say, it is right (or God

is righteous), for it is good that they should eat," &c.—" Say•(what is) right," *i.e.* pronounce just judgment. The verb is made to govern צַדִּיק directly by Vitringa (justum prædicate beatum), Lowth (pronounce ye a blessing on the righteous), Gesenius (preiset den Gerechten). The preposition *to* is supplied by the Targum, Peshito, Vulgate (dicite justo), English Version, Barnes, and Henderson. The construction most agreeable to usage is that given by Luther, J. D. Michaelis, De Wette, Hendewerk, Ewald, Umbreit, Knobel—" Say ye of the righteous (or concerning him) that," &c. One manuscript reads יֹאבֵל in the singular, but the plural form agrees with צַדִּיק as a collective.

11. This is the converse of the foregoing proposition, a threatening corresponding to the promise. *Woe unto the wicked*, (it shall be) *ill* (with him), *for the thing done by his hands shall be done to him.*—Calvin and Ewald separate לְרָשָׁע from אוֹי and connect it with רַע " woe (or alas !) to the wicked it is (or shall be) ill," a construction favoured by the Masoretic accents. Kimchi makes רַע agree with רָשָׁע in the sense of an *evil wicked man*, *i.e.* one who is wicked both towards God and man. (See Gill ad loc.) This interpretation is adopted by Luther, Cocceius, Vitringa, Clericus, and J. H. Michaelis. De Wette, Hendewerk, and Knobel give the same construction, but take רַע in the sense of wretched, " woe to the wicked, the unhappy." But רַע seems evidently parallel to טוֹב in ver. 10, and cannot therefore be a mere epithet. Umbreit follows the Vulgate, Clericus, &c., in giving to גְמוּל the sense of *recompence*. Luther and Henderson explain it to mean merit or desert; Calvin, Lowth, and Gesenius, more correctly *work*.

12. The Prophet now recurs to the evil of unworthy and incapable rulers, and expresses, by an exclamation, wonder and concern at the result. *My people! their oppressors are childish, and women rule over them. My people! thy leaders are seducers, and the way of thy paths* (the way where thy path lies) *they swallow up* (cause to disappear, destroy).—עַמִּי is usually construed in the first clause as an absolute nominative ; but by making it (as Umbreit does) an exclamation, the parallelism becomes more exact.— Gesenius and Hitzig explain נֹגְשָׂיו as a *pluralis majestaticus* referring to Ahaz, which is needless and arbitrary. מְעַלֵּל is in the singular because it is used adjectively, the predicate being often in the singular when the subject is plural. (Ges. Heb. Gr. § 144, 6, *c.*) Instead of *thy guides*, Luther reads *thy comforters;* others, *those who call thee happy*, which is one of the meanings of the Hebrew word, and was perhaps designed to be suggested here, but not directly as the primary idea. The paronomasia introduced into the last clause by Cocceius (qui ducunt te seducunt te), the Dutch version (die u leyden verleyden u), and Gesenius (deine Führer verführen dich), is not found in the original.

13. Though human governments might be overthrown, God still remained a sovereign and a judge, and is here represented as appearing, coming forward, or assuming his position, not only as a judge but as an advocate, or rather an accuser, in both which characters he acts at once, implying that he who brings this charge against his people has at the same time power to condemn. *Jehovah standeth up to plead, and is standing to judge the nations.* The first verb properly denotes a reflexive act, viz. that of placing or presenting himself. The participle is used to represent the scene as actually passing. The meaning of רִיב is to plead or conduct a cause for another or one's self.—Some understand the last clause to mean that the judge is still standing, that he has not yet taken his place upon the

judgment-seat. According to Clericus, it represents the case as so clear that the judge decides it standing, without sitting down to hear argument or evidence. But these are needless and unnatural refinements.—Vitringa makes רִיב and דִּין synonymous, which is contrary to usage. *Nations* here, as often elsewhere, means the tribes of Israel. See Gen. xlix. 10 ; Deut. xxxii. 8 ; xxxiii. 3, 19 ; 1 Kings xxii. 28 ; Mich. i. 2. There is no need therefore of reading עַמּוֹ for עַמִּים, as Lowth does.

14. This verse describes the parties more distinctly, and begins the accusation. *Jehovah will enter into judgment* (engage in litigation, both as a party and a judge) *with the elders of his people* (the heads of houses, families and tribes) *and the chiefs thereof* (the hereditary chiefs of Israel, here and elsewhere treated as responsible representatives of the people). *And ye* (even ye) *have consumed the vineyard* (of Jehovah, his church or chosen people), *the spoil of the poor* (that which is taken from him by violence) *is in your houses.*—Hendewerk regards the last clause as the language of the Prophet, giving a reason why God would enter into judgment with them ; but it is commonly regarded as the commencement of the judge's own address, which is continued through the following verse.—The particle with which the second clause begins is not equivalent to *for* (Vulg. Lu.) or *but* (Cocc.), but connects what follows with an antecedent thought not expressed. It may here be rendered *even, and so,* or *so then* (Ges.). Lowth has *as for you,* and the pronoun is certainly emphatic, *you* from whom it could least have been expected, *you* who ought to have prevented it.—Henderson thinks that *vineyard* is here used collectively for *vineyards,* and that literal spoliation of the poor is the particular offence denounced, or one here chosen to represent the rest. But the common opinion is more probable, viz. that the Prophet here uses the same metaphor which forms the basis of his parable in chap v.—The proper meaning of הֶעָנִי is the afflicted from whatever cause ; but it is commonly applied to the poor. Ewald translates rigidly *the sufferer's spoil* (des Dulders Raub.)

15. The Lord's address to the elders of Israel is continued in a tone of indignant expostulation. *What mean ye* (literally *what* is *to you,* equivalent in English to what have you, *i. e.* what right, what reason, what motive, what advantage) *that ye crush my people* (a common figure for severe oppression, Job v. 4, Prov. xxii. 22), *and grind the faces of the poor* (upon the ground, by trampling on their bodies, another strong figure for contemptuous and oppressive violence), *saith the Lord Jehovah of Hosts* (which is added to remind the accused of the sovereign authority, omniscience, and omnipotence of Him by whom the charge is brought against them).—The first verb does not mean merely to weaken (Cocc.), bruise (Calv.), or break (Vitr.), but to break in pieces, to break utterly, to *crush* (Lowth).—By the *faces* of the poor some understand their *persons,* or the poor themselves, and by *grinding* them, reducing, attenuating, by exaction and oppression (Ges. Hg. Hk. Hn.) Others refer the phrase to literal injuries of the face by blows or wounds (Ew. Um.) But the simplest and most natural interpretation is that which applies it to the act of grinding the face upon the ground by trampling on the body, thus giving both the noun and verb their proper meaning, and making the parallelism more exact.—The phrase at the beginning of the verse cannot constitute an independent clause, *what mean ye?* (Barnes), but merely serves to introduce the question.

16, 17. The Prophet here resumes the thread which had been dropped or broken at the close of ver. 12, and recurs to the undue predominance of female influence, but particularly to the prevalent excess of female luxury,

not only as sinful in itself, but as a chief cause of the violence and social
disorder previously mentioned, and therefore to be punished by disease,
widowhood, and shameful exposure. These two verses, like the sixth and
seventh, form one continued sentence, the *and* at the beginning of ver. 17
introducing the apodosis, for which reason, and also on account of its relation to *because* in ver. 16, its full force cannot be expressed by a literal
translation. *And Jehovah said* (in addition to what goes before, as if beginning a new section of the prophecy), *because the daughters of Zion* (the
women of Jerusalem, with special reference to those connected with the
leading men) *are lofty* (in their mien and carriage) *and walk with outstretched neck* (literally, *stretched of neck*, so as to seem taller), *and gazing*
(ogling, leering, looking wantonly) *with their eyes, and with a tripping walk
they walk, and with their feet they make a tinkling* (i. e. with the metallic
rings or bands worn around their ankles), *therefore the Lord will make bald
the crown of the daughters of Zion, and their nakedness Jehovah will uncover*
(i. e. he will reduce them to a state the very opposite of their present pride
and finery).—Jerome speaks of men who understood the *daughters of Zion*
here to mean the souls of men. Eichhorn takes it in the geographical sense
of smaller towns dependent on Jerusalem (Josh. xv. 45, 47, 2 Chron, xviii.
18). But the obvious meaning is preferred by almost all interpreters.—
They are described as stretching out the neck, not by bending forwards, nor
by tossing the head backwards (Hn.), but by holding it high (Sept. ὑψηλῷ
τραχήλῳ), so that the phrase corresponds to *lofty* in the clause preceding.—
Above forty editions and eight manuscripts read מְשַׁקְּרוֹת, *deceiving*, i. e. by
a false expression of the eyes (Cocc. mentientes oculis), or by disguising
them with paint (Lowth), in allusion to the very ancient fashion (2 Kings
ix. 30) oculos circumducto nigrore fucare (Cyprian de Hab. Virg.). This
last sense may be put upon the common reading by deriving it from שָׁקַר i. q.
Chald. סְקַר, to stain or dye, which may be the ground of Luther's version,
with painted faces. It is commonly agreed, however, that it comes from
the same verb in the sense of looking, looking around, with the accessory
idea here suggested by the context of immodest, wanton looks. This idea
is expressed by the Septuagint (ἐν νεύμασιν ὀφθαλμῶν), the Vulgate (vagantes
oculis), Gesenius (frech die Augen werfend), Ewald (schielender Augen),
and Henderson (ogling eyes).—The masculine suffix in רַגְלֵיהֶם is regarded
by Henderson and Knobel as containing an allusion to the unfeminine conduct of these women; but the manner here described is rather childish than
masculine, and this form is probably used as the primary one and originally
common to both genders. (See Ges. Heb. Gr. § 119, 1.)—The baldness
mentioned in the last clause is variously explained as an allusion to the
shaving of the heads of prisoners or captives (Knobel), or as a sign of
mourning (Rosenmüller), or as the effect of disease (Ges. Ew. &c.), and particularly of the disease which bears a name (Lev. xiii. 2) derived from the
verb here used (Jun. Cocc. E. V.). Neither of these ideas is expressed,
though all may be implied, in the terms of the original. For the construction of וְסָפוֹף הָלוֹךְ, see Gesen. Heb. Gr. § 126, 3. For that of נְטוּיוֹת
גָרוֹן *vide supra*, chap. i. 4.

18. Although the prediction in v. 17 implies the loss of all ornaments
whatever, we have now a minute specification of the things to be taken away.
This specification had a double use; it made the judgment threatened more
explicit and significant to those whom it concerned, while to others it gave
some idea of the length to which extravagance in dress was carried. There
is no need (as Ewald well observes) of supposing that all these articles were

ever worn at once, or that the passage was designed to be descriptive of a complete dress. It is rather an enumeration of detached particulars which might or might not be combined in any individual case. As in other cases where a variety of detached particulars are enumerated simply by their names, it is now very difficult to identify some of them. This is the less to be regretted, as the main design of the enumeration was to shew the prevalent extravagance in dress, an effect not wholly dependent on an exact interpretation of the several items. The interest of the passage, in its details, is not exegetical, but archæological, in which light it has been separately and elaborately discussed by learned writers, especially by Schroeder in his Commentarius philologico-criticus de vestitu mulierum Hebræarum ad Jesai. iii. ver. 16–24, cum præfatione Alberti Schultens, Lugd. Bat. 1745. Of later date, but less authority, in Hartmann's Hebräerinn am Putztische und als Braut. Nothing more will be here attempted than to give what is now most commonly regarded as the true meaning of the terms, with a few of the more important variations in the doubtful cases. *In that day* (the time appointed for the judgments just denounced) *the Lord will take away* (literally cause to depart, from the daughters of Zion) *the bravery* (in the old English sense of finery) *of the ankle-bands* (the noun from which the last verb in ver. 16 is derived) *and the cauls* (or caps of net-work) *and the crescents* (or little moons, metallic ornaments of that shape).—Schroeder explains שְׁבִיסִים to mean *little suns*, corresponding to the *little moons* which follow, and derives the word as a diminutive from שֶׁמֶשׁ with a permutation of one labial for another. This explanation is adopted by Winer, Ewald, and Knobel. According to Henderson, the word means *tasselled tresses, i. e.* locks of hair braided and hanging to the feet.

19. *The pendants* (literally drops, *i. e.* ear-rings) *and the bracelets* (for the arm, or according to Ewald, collars for the neck, Halsbände) *and the veils* (the word here used denoting the peculiar oriental veil, composed of two pieces hooked together below the eyes, one of which pieces is thrown back over the head, while the other hides the face). The first word in the verse is rendered by the English Version, *chains*, and in the margin, *sweet-balls*, but more correctly by the Septuagint, κάθεμα or pendant.

20. *The caps* (or other ornamental head-dresses) *and the ankle-chains* (connecting the ankle-bands, so as to regulate the strength of the step) *and the girdles, and the houses* (*i. e.* places or receptacles) *of breadth,* (meaning probably the perfume-boxes or smelling-bottles worn by the oriental women at their girdles) *and the amulets* (the same word used above in ver. 3, in the sense of *incantations*, but which seems like the Latin *fascinum* to have also signified the antidote). The first word of this verse is now commonly explained to mean *turbans*, but as these are distinctly mentioned afterwards, this term may denote an ornamental cap, or perhaps a diadem or circlet of gold or silver. (Ewald, Kronen, Eng. Vs. bonnets.) The next word is explained to mean *bracelets* by the Septuagint (ψέλλια) and Ewald (*Armspangen*), but by the English Version more correctly, though perhaps too vaguely, *ornaments of the leg*. For *girdles, smelling-bottles, and amulets,* the English Version has *head-bands, tablets* (but in the margin, *houses of the soul*), *and ear-rings,* perhaps on account of the superstitious use which was sometimes made of these (Gen. xxxv. 4).

21. *The rings*, strictly signet-rings, but here put for finger-rings, or rings in general, *and the nose-jewels*, a common and very ancient ornament in eastern countries, so that the version, *jewels of the face*, is unnecessary, as well as inconsistent with the derivation from נזם, to perforate.

22. *The holiday dresses, and the mantles and the robes and the purses.*
The first word is from חָלַץ to pull off, and is almost universally explained
to mean clothes that are taken off and laid aside, *i. e.* the best suit, holiday
or gala dresses, although this general expression seems misplaced in an
enumeration of minute details. The English version, *changeable suits of
apparel*, though ambiguous, seems intended to express the same idea. The
next two words, according to their etymology, denote wide and flowing upper
garments. The English version of the last word, *crisping-pins*, supposes it
to relate to the dressing of the hair. The same idea seems to be expressed
by Calvin (acus) and Cocceius (acus discriminales.) The word is now
commonly explained, from the Arabic analogy, to signify bags or purses
probably of metal.

23. *The mirrors and the tunics* (inner garments made of linen), *and the
turbans* (the common oriental head-dress, from צָנַף to wrap) *and the veils.*
—The first word is explained to mean their thin transparent dresses, by
the Septuagint (διαφανῆ λακωνικά), Kimchi, Schroeder, Rosenmüller and
Ewald (der feinen Zeuge) ; but most writers understand it to denote the
small metalic mirrors carried about by oriental women. Instead of *turbans*
(Eng. Vs. hoods) Henderson supposes צְנִיפוֹת to denote *ribands* used for
binding the hair or fastening the tiara. The same writer explains the *veil*
here spoken of to be the large veil covering all the other garments, and
therein differing from the small veil mentioned in ver. 19. The same explanation is given by Knobel (Ueberwürfe) ; but other writers make an
opposite distinction.

24. The threatening is still continued, but with a change of form, the
things to be taken away being now contrasted with those which should succeed them. *And it shall be* or *happen* (equivalent in force to *then*, after all
this) that *instead of perfume* (aromatic odour or the spices which afford it)
*there shall be stench, and instead of a girdle a rope, and instead of braided
work baldness* (or loss of hair by disease or shaving, as a sign of captivity
or mourning), *and instead of a full rope a girding of sackcloth, burning instead of beauty.* The inversion of the terms in this last clause, and its
brevity, add greatly to the strength of the expression.—Several of the ancient
versions render מַק by *dust* (Sept. Arab. Syr.), but it strictly denotes dissolution, putrefaction, and is here used as the opposite of בֹּשֶׂם, viz., stench,
not specifically that of corpses, wounds, or the disease supposed to be referred to in ver. 17 (Ros. Ges. Hg. Hk. Ew.), but stench in general, or perhaps with particular allusion to the squalor of captivity or mourning.—נִקְפָּה is
explained to mean a rent, rent garment, rag or rags, as signs of poverty or
grief, by Calvin (laceratio), Cocceius (lacerum), Lowth (rags), and Knobel
(ein Fetzen). But the meaning *cord* or *rope*, given in the Septuagint (σχοινίῳ
ζώση) and Vulgate (pro zono funiculus), is adopted by Clericus (funis),
Gesenius (einen Strick), and most modern writers.—The Septuagint explains מִקְשֶׁה to mean a *golden* ornament of the head ; Vitringa a *solid* ornament of gold, perhaps from קשה, *hard.* It is now explained, from an Arabic
meaning of the same root, to denote *turned work*, or a shape produced by
turning. (See Gesen. s. v.) The cognate מִקְשָׁה is applied to ornamental
work in wood or metal, but this, perhaps, in derision, to the laborious braid-
ing of the hair, as appears from its being in antithesis to *baldness.*—Ewald
reads פְּתִי גִיל as two words meaning *the fulness or wideness* (from פָּתָה, to
open) *of an ample robe* (from גִּיל to revolve or flow around), contrasted with
a tight girding of sackcloth. Gesenius makes the sense the same, but regards פְּתִיגִיל as a compound word denoting the full robe itself. The Eng-

lish version (stomacher) supposes it to be a particular ornamental part of dress.—The ancient versions take כִּי as a conjunction, and connect the last clause with the next verse, " for instead of beauty, thy men," &c. (Sept. Vulg.), or make it an independent clause, by treating תחת as a verb (Targ. Pesh.) ; but all the modern writers are agreed in making כִּי a noun, from בָּנָה, to burn, like עִי אִי, from עָנָה אָוָה. The *burning* mentioned is supposed to be that of the skin from long exposure, by the French version (au lieu du beau teint le hâle), Clericus (adusta facies), and Lowth (a sun-burnt skin). But most interpreters understand by it a *brand*, here mentioned either as a stigma of captivity, or as a self-inflicted sign of mourning. Hitzig gives the noun the general sense of *wound* or *mark ;* but this is un-authorized, and weakens the expression. Sackcloth is mentioned as the coarsest kind of cloth, and also as that usually worn by mourners. The two nouns מַעֲשֶׂה and מִקְשֶׁה are in opposition, the first denoting artificial adjust-ment, the second its precise form.

25. The prophet now assigns as a reason for the grief predicted in ver. 24, a general slaughter of the male population, the effect of which is again described in ver. 26, and its extent in chap. iv. 1, which belongs more directly to this chapter than the next. In the verse before us, he first ad-dresses Zion or Jerusalem directly, but again, as it were, turns away, and in the next verse speaks of her in the third person. *Thy men by the sword shall fall, and thy strength in war.*—מְתַיִךְ does not mean *thy common people*, as opposed to warriors or soldiers of distinction (Luther : dein Pöbel) ; nor does it simply mean *thy people* or inhabitants (Cocc. homines tui ; Fr. Vs. tes gens ; Lowth, thy people) ; but *thy men, i. e.* thy males (Vulg. viri tui. Ges. deine Männer).—The present form used by Gesenius greatly detracts from the minatory force of the future, which is retained by Hitzig, De Wette, Hendewerk, Ewald, Umbreit. The abstract *strength* is resolved into a concrete by the Septuagint (ἰσχύοντες), Vulgate, Luther, Lowth, and Gesenius ; but it is better to retain the original expression, not in the military sense of forces (Hg. Hn.), but as denoting that which constitutes the *strength* of a community, its male population (Calv. robur tuum ; Fr. Vs. ta force ; Ewald, deine Mannschaft).

26. The effect of this slaughter on the community is here described, first by representing the places of chief concourse as vocal with distress, and then by personifying the state or nation as a desolate widow seated on the ground, a sign both of mourning and of degradation. *And her gates* (those of Zion or Jerusalem) *shall lament and mourn*, and *being emptied* (or *exhausted*) *she shall sit upon the ground.* The gates are said to mourn, by a rhetorical substitution of the place of action for the agent (Hendewerk), or because a place filled with cries seems itself to utter them (Knobel). The meaning of נִקָּתָה (which may be either the preterite or participle passive of נָקָה is taken in its proper sense of *emptied* or *exhausted* by Junius (expurgata), Vitringa (evacuata), and Ewald (ausgeleert). This is ex-plained to mean emptied of her strength, *i. e.* weakened by Hendewerk (entkräftet), emptied of her people, *i. e.* solitary, desolate, by the Vulgate (desolata), the English version (desolate), Gesenius (verödet), Hitzig (ein-sam), &c. The reference of this word to her former condition seems pecu-liar to Clericus (quæ munda erat). She is described not as *lying* (Calv. Cler.), but *sitting* on the ground, as on one of Vespasian's coins a woman is represented, in a sitting posture, leaning against a palm-tree, with the legend, *Judæa Capta.*

Chap. iv. ver. 1. The paucity of males in the community, resulting from this general slaughter, is now expressed by a lively figure representing seven women as earnestly soliciting one man in marriage, and that on the most disadvantageous terms, renouncing the support to which they were by law entitled. *And in that day:* (then, after the judgments just predicted) *seven women* (*i. e.* several, this number being often used indefinitely) *shall lay hold on one man* (earnestly accost him), *saying, We will eat our own bread, and wear our own apparel; only let thy name be called upon us* (an idiomatic phrase meaning let us be called by thy name, let us be recognised as thine), *take thou away our reproach,* the " reproach of widowhood " (Isa. liv. 4), or celibacy, or rather that of childlessness, which they imply, and which was regarded with particular aversion by the Jews before the time of Christ.—This verse appears to have been severed from its natural connection in accordance with an ancient notion that the *one man* was Christ, and the *seven women* souls believing on him. This view of the passage may indeed have been either the cause or the effect of the usual division and arrangement of the text. Some writers think that the Prophet intended to present an accumulation of strange things, in order to shew the changed condition of the people; women forsaking their natural modesty, soliciting marriage, with violent importunity, in undue proportion, and on the most disadvantageous terms. But the more probable opinion is the common one, that he simply meant to set forth by a lively figure, the disproportion between the sexes introduced by a destructive war. Instead of *our own bread, our own clothes,* Cocceius would simply read *our bread, our clothes,* and understand the clause as a promise of domestic diligence. The common interpretation agrees better with the other circumstances and expressions of the verse and context. Luther gives אָסֹף a subjunctive form, *that our reproach may be taken from us.* The English version and Henderson make it an infinitive, *to take away;* Barnes a participle, *taking away;* but the imperative construction, which is given in the margin of the English Bible, and preferred by almost all translators, ancient and modern, agrees best with the absence of a preposition, and adds to the vivacity of the address. To this verse Calvin cites a beautiful parallel from Lucan, which is copied by Grotius, and credited to him by later writers—

> Da tantum nomen inane
> Connubii; liceat tumulo scripsisse CATONIS
> MARCIA.

Chapter 4

BESIDES the first verse, which has been explained already, this chapter contains a prophecy of Christ and of the future condition of the Church The Prophet here recurs to the theme with which the prophecy opened (chap. ii. 1–4), but with this distinction, that instead of dwelling on the influence exerted by the church upon the world, he here exhibits its internal condition under the reign of the Messiah.

He first presents to view the person by whose agency the church is to be brought into a glorious and happy state, and who is here described as a partaker both of the divine and human nature, ver. 2. He then describes the character of those who are predestined to share in the promised exaltation, ver. 3. He then shews the necessity, implied in these promises, of previous purgation from the defilement described in the foregoing chapters, ver. 4. When this purgation is effected, God will manifest his presence gloriously throughout his church, ver. 5.   To these promises of purity and honour he now adds one of protection and security, with which the prophecy concludes, ver. 6.

It is commonly agreed that this prediction has been only partially fulfilled, and that its complete fulfilment is to be expected, not in the literal mount Zion or Jerusalem, but in those various assemblies or societies of true believers, which now possess in common the privileges once exclusively enjoyed by the Holy City and the chosen race of which it was the centre and metropolis.

2. At this point the Prophet passes from the tone of threatening to that of promise.   Having foretold a general destruction, he now intimates that some should escape it, and be rendered glorious and happy by the presence and favour of the Son of God, who is at the same time the Son of man. *In that day* (after this destruction) *shall the Branch* (or Offspring) *of Jehovah be for honour and for glory, and the fruit of the earth for sublimity and beauty, to the escaped of Israel*, literally the *escape* or deliverance of Israel, the abstract being used for the collective concrete, meaning those who should survive these judgments.—יהיה ל may be taken either in the sense of *being for, serving as*, or in that of *becoming*, as in chap. i. 14, 21, 22, 31.— As צֶמַח, in its physical and proper sense, means *growth, vegetation*, or that which grows and vegetates (Gen. xix. 25 ; Ps. lxv. 11 ; Hosea viii. 7 ; Ezek. xvi. 7), it is here explained by Hitzig, Maurer, and Ewald, as synonymous with *fruit of the earth*, but in its lowest sense, that of vegetable products or abundant harvests.   To this interpretation, which is adopted by Gesenius in his Thesaurus, it may be objected, first, that such a subject is wholly incongruous with the predicates applied to it, honourable, glorious, sublime, and beautiful ; secondly, that this explanation of צֶמַח is precluded by the addition of the name Jehovah, a difficulty aggravated by the parallelism, which requires the relation between *branch* and *Jehovah* to be the same as that between *fruit* and *earth*, and as the last phrase means the offspring of the earth. so the first must mean the offspring of Jehovah, an expression which can only be applied to persons.   This last objection applies also to the explanation of the phrase as meaning *spiritual gifts* in opposition to temporal or earthly gifts (Calv. Jun. Schleusner).   It does not lie against that proposed by Grotius, and adopted by J. D. Michaelis, Koppe, and Eichhorn, by Gesenius in his Commentary, and more recently by Knobel, which applies the phrase to the better race of Israelites who were to spring up after the return from exile.   But although the sense thus put upon the word is *personal*, it is not *individual*, as in every other case where צֶמַח is used figuratively elsewhere, but collective.   Another objection to it is, that this better race of Israelites are the very persons here called the *escaped of Israel*, who would then be described as a beauty and a glory to themselves.   Knobel evades this objection by denying that the last words of the verse have any connection with the first clause; but his evasion is an arbitrary one, suggested by the difficulty which attends his doctrine.—The first of these objections applies also to Hendewerk's interpretation of the phrase as meaning the government or administration (das regierende Personale des Staates).—The usage of the Hebrew word in application to an individual will be clear from the following examples.   " Behold the days come, saith the Lord, that I will raise unto David a righteous BRANCH, and a king shall reign and prosper " (Jer. xxiii. 5).   " In those days and at that time will I cause the BRANCH of righteousness to grow up unto David, and he shall execute judgment " (Jer. xxxiii. 15).   "Behold I will bring forth my

servant the BRANCH " (Zech. iii. 8). "Behold the MAN whose name is the BRANCH " (Zech. vi. 12). The Branch is here represented as a man, a king, a righteous judge, a servant of God. Hence it is reasonable to conclude that the same person, whom Jeremiah calls the *branch* (or son) *of David*, is called by Isaiah in the verse before us *the branch* (or son) *of Jehovah*. This view of the passage is strongly recommended by the following considerations. It is free from the difficulties which attend all others. It is the ancient Jewish interpretation found in the Chaldee Paraphrase, which explains the Branch of Jehovah as meaning his Messiah, (משיחא דיי.) The parallel passages already quoted are referred to the Messiah even by Gesenius, who only hesitates to make the same admission here, because he thinks the parallel phrase, *fruit of the earth*, cannot be so applied. But no expression could in fact be more appropriate, whether it be translated *fruit of the land* and referred to his Jewish extraction (Hengstenberg), or *fruit of the earth* and referred to his human nature (Vitr. Hn.). On the latter supposition, which appears more probable, the parallel terms correspond exactly to the two parts of Paul's description (Rom. i. 3, 4), and the two titles used in the New Testament in reference to Christ's two natures, SON OF GOD and SON OF MAN.

3. Having foretold the happiness and honour which the Son of God should one day confer upon his people, the Prophet now explains to whom the promise was intended to apply. In the preceding verse they were described by their condition as survivors of God's desolating judgments. In this they are described by their moral character, and by their eternal destination to this character and that which follows it. *And it shall be*, happen, come to pass, *that the left in Zion and the spared in Jerusalem*, singular forms with a collective application, *shall be called holy*, literally *holy shall be said to him*, i. e. this name shall be used in addressing him, or rather may be used with truth, implying that the persons so called should be what they seem to be *every one written*, enrolled, ordained, *to life in Jerusalem*.—The omission of וְהָיָה (Lu. Ges. De W. Ew. Hn.) is a needless departure from the idiomatic form of the original. The expression may be paraphrased, *and this shall be the consequence*, or *this shall follow*, preparing the mind for an event of moment. As חַיִּים may be either a plural adjective or abstract noun, some understand the phrase to mean *enrolled among the living* (Lu. Calv. Cler. E. V. Low. Bar.), others *enrolled to life* (Jun. Cocc. Vitr. J. H. Mich. J. D. Mich. Ges. Hg. De W. Ew. Um. Hn.). In either case the figure denotes not simply actual life, but destination to it. For the origin and usage of the figure itself, see Exod. xxx. 12 ; Num. i. 18 ; Ezek. xiii. 9 : Phil. iv. 3 ; Rev. iii. 5.

4. This verse contains a previous condition of the promise in ver. 3, which could not be fulfilled until the church was purged from the pollution brought upon it by the sins of those luxurious women and of the people generally, a work which could be effected only by the convincing and avenging influences of the Holy Spirit. The construction is continued from the verse preceding. All this shall come to pass, *if* (provided that, on this condition, which idea may be here expressed by *when*) *the Lord shall have washed away* (the Hebrew word denoting specially the washing of the body, and suggesting the idea of the legal ablutions) *the filth* (a very strong term, transferred from physical to moral defilement) *of the daughters of Zion* (the women before mentioned), *and the blood* (literally *bloods*, i. e. bloodshed or blood-guiltiness) *of Jerusalem* (i. e. of the people in general) *shall purge from its midst by a spirit of judgment and a spirit of burning*, i. e. by the judgment

and burning of the Holy Spirit, with a twofold allusion to the purifying and destroying energy of fire, or rather to its purifying by destroying, purging the whole by the destruction of a part, and thereby manifesting the divine *justice* as an active principle.   The *daughters of Zion* are by some understood to be the other towns of Judah (Rosenmüller, Hengstenberg, Umbreit), the objection to which is not its unpoetical character (Gesenius), but its disagreement both with the immediate connection and with the use of the same terms in chap. iii. 16.   Others understand by daughters the inhabitants in general (Sept. sons and daughters), or the female inhabitants regarded as mothers and as forming the character of their children (Hendewerk).   But it is natural that in closing his prediction the Prophet should recur to those luxurious women, to whose influence much of the disorder and oppression which prevailed may have been owing.   He then makes a transition from particular to general expressions.   The idea does not seem to be, the uncleanness of the women and the blood-guiltiness of the men (Hk. Hn.), or the uncleanness and blood-guiltiness both of men and women (Kn.), but the uncleanness of the women and the blood-guiltiness of the people generally.—יָדִיחַ does not mean to *remove* (Cler. Low. Bs.), nor to *drive out* (Lu. Um.), nor to *extirpate* (Ges. Hg. Hk. Ew.), nor to *expiate* (Calv.), but simply to *wash* or *purge out* (Sept. Vulg. Cocc. E. V. Hn.), the verb being specially applied to the washing of the altar and sacrifices (2 Chron. iv. 6 ; Ezek. xl. 38).   Two of these senses are combined by J. H. Michaelis (lavando ejecerit.—The word *spirit* cannot be regarded as pleonastic or simply emphatic (Hn.) without affording licence to a like interpretation in all other cases.   It is variously explained here as meaning *breath* (Hg. Um.), *word* (Targ. Jon. בְּמֵימְרָא דִין), and *power* or *influence* (Ges. Hengstenberg, Bs., &c.).   But since this is the term used in the New Testament to designate that person of the Godhead, whom the Scriptures uniformly represent as the executor of the divine purposes, and since this sense is perfectly appropriate here, the safest and most satisfactory interpretation is that which understands by it a personal spirit, or as Luther expresses it, the Spirit who shall judge and burn.   Even Ewald adopts the same interpretation upon grounds, as it would seem, entirely philological.   Calvin supposes *spirit of burning of judgment* to be equivalent in meaning to *the burning and judgment of the Spirit.*   He also gives the preposition its primary meaning, as do the Seventy (ἐν πνεύματι), *in* (*i. e.* in the person of) *the Spirit.*   The common explanation is *by* (*i. e.* by means of) or *through* (*i. e.* the intervention of) *the Spirit.*—The translation of בָּעֵר by consumption or extermination (Cocc. Ges. Hg. De W. Hk. Um.) is neither so precise nor so poetical as that by *burning* (Sept. Pesh. Vulg. Lu. Calv. E. V. Low. Bs. Ew.).—J. D. Michaelis translates this clause, *by the righteous zeal of the tribunals and by a destructive wind !*

5. The church is not only to be purified by God's judgments, but glorified by his manifested presence, and in that state of glory kept secure by his protection.   The presence of God is here denoted by the ancient symbol of a fiery cloud, and is promised to the church in its whole extent and to its several assemblies, as distinguished from the one indivisible congregation, and its one exclusive place of meeting, under the old economy.   *And Jehovah will create* (implying the exercise of almighty power and the production of a new effect) *over the whole extent* (literally, *place* or *space*) *of mount Zion* (in its widest and most spiritual sense, as appears from what follows), *and over her assemblies, a cloud by day and smoke* (*i. e.* a cloud of smoke), *and the brightness of a flaming fire by night ; for over all the glory*

(previously promised, there shall be) *a covering* (or shelter).—Most of the modern versions make this the apodosis of a sentence beginning with ver. 4, " When the Lord shall have washed, &c., then will Jehovah create," &c. (Cler. Low. Ges. Bs. Hn .Um. Kn.). But although this is grammatical, and leaves the general sense unchanged, the absence of the וֹ at the beginning of ver. 4, and its insertion here, seems to shew that ver. 4 is itself the apodosis of a sentence beginning with ver. 3, and that a new one begins here (Calv. Cocc. Vitr. J. D. Mich. E. V. Hg. De W. Hk. Ew.). The present tense (Ges. De W. Ew. Um.) is not so well suited to the context as the future (Hg, Hk. &c.). The older writers give מְכוֹן the sense of *dwelling-place ;* but the modern lexicographers explain it to mean *place* in general. כל מכון may be rendered either *whole place* or *every place* without a change of sense (*vide supra* chap. i. 5, iii. 1), The two appearances described in this verse are those presented by a fire at different times, a smoke by day and a flame by night. There is no need therefore of explaining עָשָׁן to mean *vapour* (Knobel), or of connecting it with what follows (Sep. Vitr. Cler. Hitzig. Hengstenberg) in violation of the Masoretic accents.—The meaning of the promise is the same whether מִקְרָאֶיהָ be explained to mean *her assemblies* (Low. Hengst. Ew. Um. Kn.) or *her places of assembly* (Lu. J. D. Mich. Ges. Hn.).; but the former is the sense most agreeable to usage.—Lowth omits כל before מכון on the authority of eight manuscripts, and inserts it before מקראה on the authority of one manuscript and the Septuagint. More than forty manuscripts and nearly fifty editions read מקראיה, and almost all interpreters explain it as a plural.—In the last clause כִּי has its usual meaning and not that of *yea* (Low.), *which* (Hn.), or *so that* (Kn.).—Clericus, J. D. Michaelis, and Lee (Heb. Lex. s. v. חֻפָּה) make כָּבוֹד the subject of the last clause, "over all, glory shall be a defence," which is wholly inconsistent with the Masoretic pointing. Instead of *over* Kocher reads *above, i. e.* superior to all former glory, a construction which is given in the Chaldee Paraphrase, יַתִּיר מִן (more than). Some regard this as the statement of a general fact, " over everything glorious there is protection," *i. e.* men are accustomed to protect what they value highly (Vitr. Ros. Hengst. Ew.) ; but the great majority of writers understand it as a prophecy or promise.—חֻפָּה is construed as a passive verb, *it is* or *shall be covered*, by the Septuagint (σκεπασθήσεται) Gesenius, Maurer, Knobel. But as this is a harsh construction, and as the Pual of חָפָה does not occur elsewhere, it is better, with Ewald, Umbreit, Hengstenberg, and the older writers, to explain it as a noun derived from חָפַף, and agreeing with the verb *is* or *shall be* understood, or as Hitzig and Hendewerk suppose, with the same verb in the first clause of the next verse, " For over all the glory a covering and shelter there shall be." The sense is not affected by this last construction, but such a change in the division of the text can be justified only by necessity.

6. The promise of refuge and protection is repeated or continued under the figure of a shelter from heat and rain, natural emblems for distress and danger. *And there shall be a shelter* (properly a booth or covert of leaves and branches, to serve) *for a shadow by day* (as a protection) *from heat, and for a covert and for a hiding-place from storm and from rain.* —Instead of making סֻכָּה the subject of the sentence (E. V. De W. Hn. Um.), some regard it as the predicate referring to a subject understood. *He, i.e.* God, *shall be a shelter*, &c. (Ges. Bs.). *It*, the cloud or the protection, *shall be a shelter*, &c. (Low. Hg.).—That סֻכָּה means *the* tabernacle or temple, which it never does elsewhere, is a notion peculiar to Clericus.—

זֶרֶם is not a whirlwind (Vulg.) or a hail-storm (J. D. Mich.) but an inundation (Jun. Cler. J. H. Mich.) *i. e.* a flood of rain, a pouring, driving rain
(Luther, Wetter, Gesenius, Ungewitter).

Chapter 5

THIS chapter contains a description of the prevalent iniquities of Judah,
and of the judgments which, in consequence of these, had been or were to
be inflicted on the people. The form of the prophecy is peculiar, consisting of a parable and a commentary on it.

The prophet first delivers his whole message in a parabolic form, vers.
1–7. He then explains and amplifies it at great length, vers. 8–30.

The parable sets forth the peculiar privileges, obligations, guilt, and
doom of Israel, under the figure of a highly favoured vineyard which, instead of good fruit, brings forth only wild grapes, and is therefore given up
to desolation, vers. 1–6. The application is expressly made by the Prophet himself, ver. 7.

In the remainder of the chapter, he enumerates the sins which were
included in the general expressions of ver. 7, and describes their punishment. In doing this, he first gives a catalogue of sins with their appropriate
punishments annexed, vers. 8–24. He then describes the means used to
inflict them, and the final issue, vers. 25–30.

The catalogue of sins and judgments comprehends two series of woes or
denunciations. In the first, each sin is followed by its punishment, vers.
8–17. In the second the sins follow one another in uninterrupted succession, and the punishment is reserved until the close, vers. 18–24.

In the former series, the first woe is uttered against avaricious and ambitious grasping after lands and houses, to be punished by sterility and
desolation, vers. 8–10. The second woe is uttered against drunkenness,
untimely mirth, and disregard of providential warnings, appropriately
punished by captivity, hunger, thirst, and general mortality, vers. 11–14.
To these two woes are added a general declaration of their purpose and
effect, to humble man and exalt God, and a repeated threatening of general
desolation as a punishment of both the sins just mentioned, vers. 15–17.

The sins denounced in the second series of woes are presumptuous and
incredulous defiance of God's judgments, the deliberate confounding of
moral distinctions, undue reliance upon human wisdom, and drunkenness
considered as a vice of judges, and as causing the perversion of justice,
vers. 18–23. To these he adds a general threatening of destruction as a
necessary consequence of their forsaking God, ver. 24.

In declaring the means used to effect this condign retribution, the
Prophet sets before us two distinct stages or degrees of punishment. The
first, which is briefly and figuratively represented as a violent and destructive stroke of God's hand, is described as ineffectual, ver. 25. To complete the work, another is provided in the shape of an invading enemy,
before whom, after a brief fluctuatioh, Israel disappears in total darkness,
vers. 26–30.

In its general design and subject, this prophecy resembles those which
go before it; but it differs remarkably from both in holding up to view exclusively the dark side of the picture, the guilt and doom of the ungodly
Jews, without the cheering contrast of purgation and deliverance to be experienced from the same events by the true Israel, the Church of God.

This omission, which of course must be supplied from other prophecies, is by Hitzig incorrectly represented as a reason for regarding this as the conclusion of the one preceding, to confirm which supposition he appeals to certain verbal coincidences, particularly that between ver. 15 and chap. ii. 9, 17. But these and the more general resemblance of the chapters, can only prove at most what must be true on any hypothesis, to wit, that the prophecies relate to the same subject and belong to the same period. A similar coincidence between ver. 25 and chap. ix. 11, 16,·20, x. 4, has led Ewald to interpolate the whole of that passage (from chap. ix. 5, to chap. x. 4), between the twenty-fifth and the twenty-sixth verses of this chapter ; as if the same form of expression could not be employed by the same author upon different occasions, and as if such a treatment of the text did not open the door to boundless licence of conjecture. With still less semblance of a reason, Hendewerk connects this chapter with the first nine verses of the seventh and the whole of the seventeenth, as making up one prophecy. The old opinion, still retained by Gesenius, Henderson, Umbriet, and Knobel, is that this chapter, if not an independent prophecy, is at least a distinct appendix to the one preceding, with which it is connected, not only in the way already mentioned, but also by the seeming allusion in the first verse to chap. iii. 14, where the Church of God is called his vineyard, a comparison which reappears in other parts of Scripture, and is carried out in several of our Saviour's parables.

This chapter, like the first, is applicable not to one event exclusively, but to a sequence of events which was repeated more than once, although its terms were never fully realised until the closing period of the Jewish history, after the true Messiah was rejected, when one ray of hope was quenched after another,. until all grew dark for ever in the skies of Israel.

1. The parable is given in vers. 1–6, and applied in ver. 7. It is introduced in such a manner as to secure a favourable hearing from those whose conduct it condemns, and in some measure to conceal its drift until the application. The Prophet proposes to sing a song, *i. e.* to utter a rhythmical and figurative narrative, relating to a friend of his, his friend's own song indeed about his vineyard. In the last clause he describes the situation of the vineyard, its favourable exposure and productive soil. *I will sing, if you please* (or let me sing I pray you), *of my friend* (*i. e.* concerning him), *my friend's song of his vineyard* (*i. e.* concerning it). *My friend had a vineyard in a hill of great fertility* (literally *in a horn, a son of fatness,* according to the oriental idiom, which applies the terms of human kindred to relations of every kind).—The common version, *now will I sing*, seems to take נָא as an adverb of time, whereas it is a particle of entreaty, used to soften the expression of a purpose, and to give a tone of mildness and courtesy to the address. *Sing* and *song* are used, as with us, in reference to poetry, without employing actual musical performance.—Calvin's translation (*for my beloved, i. e.* in his name, his person, his behalf) is at variance with the usage of the particle. Grotius (*to my beloved*) is inappropriate, as the friend is not addressed, and this is not, a song of praise. Maurer's (*of my beloved, i. e.* belonging to him, like לְדָוִד, a Psalm *of David*), is a form only used in titles or inscriptions. The ל has doubtless the same sense before this word as before *his vineyard.* Knobel supposes *song of my friend* also to denote a song *respecting* him, because he is not introduced as speaking till ver. 3. But for that very reason it is first called a song concerning him, and then his own song. The cognate words יְדִידִי and דּוֹדִי are referred by some to different subjects ; but their identity is plain from the possession of

the vineyard being ascribed to both.—The Vulgate and Luther give to דוֹד
its usual sense of *uncle*, and Cocceius applies it to the Holy Spirit, which is
altogether arbitrary.   It seems to be joined with יָדִיד to vary the expression
of the same idea, that of *friend*, the unusual terms being used not mystically
but poetically.   The Prophet must be understood as speaking of a human
friend until he explains himself.—Umbreit makes קֶרֶן govern the next
phrase; *on the projection (Vorsprung) of a fat place ;* but the latter is in that
case too indefinite.—Clericus supposes an allusion to a horn of oil, Vitringa
to the curved shape of the Holy Land ; but most interpreters agree that
horn is here used, as in various other languages, for the sharp peak of
a mountain (*e. g.* Schreckhorn and Wetterhorn in Switzerland), or as in
Arabic, for a detached hill.   The preposition does not properly mean *on*
but *in*, implying that the vineyard only occupied a part, and that this
was not the summit, but the acclivity exposed to the sun, which is the
best situation for a vineyard.   (Apertos Bacchus amat colles. Virg. Georg.
2, 112.)

2. Not only was the vineyard favourably situated, but assiduously tilled,
protected from intrusion, and provided with everything that seemed to be
needed to secure an abundant vintage.   *And he digged it up, and gathered
out the stones thereof, and planted it with Sorek*, mentioned elsewhere (Jer.
ii. 21) as the choicest kind of vine, which either gave or owed its name to
the valley of Sorek (Judges xvi. 4), *and built a tower in the midst of it*,
partly for protection from men and beasts, and partly for the pleasure and
convenience of the owner, *and also a wine-vat*, to receive the juice from the
wine-press immediately above ; *he hewed in it, i.e.* in a rock (or *hewed* may
be simply used for *excavated* in the ground, a common situation in hot
countries for the *lacus*, reservoir or wine-vat), *and he waited for it, i. e.* he
allowed it time, *to make*, produce, bear, bring forth, *grapes, and it produced
wild grapes*.—Instead of *he waited for it*, Umbreit reads, *he hoped*, Lowth,
Barnes, and Henderson, *he expected*, and the authorised version, *he looked*,
in the old English sense.   But the first translation, which is that of the
Septuagint (ἔμεινε), is entitled to the preference, because it conveys the full
sense of the Hebrew word without creating any difficulty in the subsequent
application of the figure.—J. D. Michaelis, Eichhorn, and Rosenmüller
take בְּאֻשִׁים in the sense of aconite or nightshade, a plant which does not
grow in Palestine.   Most modern writers approve the version of Jerome,
labrusca, the *labrusca vitis* of Pliny, and *labrusca uva* of Columella, an
acrid and unwholesome grape, contrasted with the good grape by Sedulius
(1, 29) precisely as the two are here contrasted by Isaiah :

> Labruscam placidis quid adhuc præponitis uvis ?

For *he digged it up and gathered out the stones thereof,* the Septuagint has
he hedged it and walled it, both which senses may be reconciled with etymology, although rejected by the modern lexicographers.   The question is
of no exegetical importance, as the words in either case denote appropriate
and necessary acts for the culture or protection of the vineyard.

3. Having described the advantageous situation, soil, and culture of the
vineyard, and its failure to produce good fruit, he submits the case to the
decision of his hearers.   *And now*, not merely in a temporal but a logical
sense, " this being the case," *O inhabitant of Jerusalem and man of Judah*,
the singular form adding greatly to the individuality and life of the expression, *judge I pray you*, pray decide or act as arbiters, *between me and my
vineyard*.—To suppose, with Calvin and others, that the people are here

called upon directly to condemn themselves because their guilt was so apparent, is to mar the beauty of the parable by a premature application of its figures. They are rather called upon to judge between a stranger and his vineyard, simply as such, unaware that they are thereby passing judgment on themselves. The meaning and design of the appeal are perfectly illustrated by that which Christ makes (Mat. xxi. 40) in a parable analagous to this and founded on it. There as here the audience are called upon to judge in a case which they regard as foreign to their own, if not. fictitious, and it is only after their decision that they are made to see its bearing on themselves. So too in Nathan's parable to David (2 Sam xii. 1), it was not till " David's anger was greatly kindled against the man," *i.e.* the stranger of whom he understood the prophet to be speaking, that " Nathan said to David, Thou art the man." A disregard of these analogies impairs both the moral force and the poetical unity and beauty of the apologue. The same thing may be said of the attempt made by the Chaldee Paraphrast, Cocceius, Vitringa, and most recently by Umbreit, to put a specific figurative sense on each part of the parable, the wall, the tower, the hedge, &c., which is not more reasonable here than it would be in explaining Æsop's fables. The parable, as a whole, corresponds to its subject as a whole, but all the particulars included in the one are not separately intended to denote particulars included in the other. A lion may be a striking emblem of a hero ; but it does not follow that the mane, claws, &c., of the beast must all be significant of something in the man. Nay, they cannot even be supposed to be so, without sensibly detracting from the force and beauty of the image as a whole.

4. This verse shows that the parable is not yet complete, and that its application would be premature. Having called upon the Jews to act as umpires, he now submits a specific question for their arbitration. *What to do more* (*i. e.* what more is there to be done) *to my vineyard and I have not* (or in the English idiom, *that I have not*) *done in it* (not only *to* or *for* but *in it*, with reference to the place as well as the object of the action) ? *Why did I wait for it to bear grapes and it bore wild grapes?*—Calvin and Gesenius supply *was* instead of *is*, in the first clause, *what was there to do more, i. e.* what more was there to be done, or was I bound to do ? But though grammatically exceptionable, does not agree so well with the connection between this verse and the next as a question and answer. Still less exact in the English Version (followed by Lowth, Barnes, and Henderson), *what more could have been done?* The question whether God had done all that he could for the Jews, when the Scriptures were still incomplete, and Christ had not yet come, however easy of solution, is a question here irrelevant, because it has relation, not to something in the text, but to something supplied by the interpreter, and that not only without necessity, but in violation of the context ; for the next verse is not an answer to the question what God *could have done*, but what he *shall* or *will do*. The most simple, exact, and satisfactory translation of this first clause is that given by Cocceius (quid faciendum amplius vinæ meæ) and Ewald (was ist noch meinem Weinberge zu thun ?)—In the last clause Calvin understands the owner of the vineyard to express surprise at his own unreasonable expectations. *Why did I expect it* (*i. e.* how could I expect it) *to bear grapes?* This construction not only raises a new difficulty in the application of the words to God, but is inconsistent with the context, the whole drift of which is to shew that the expectation was a reasonable one. The interrogation really belongs to the second number only, the first being merely introductory, or

rather to the whole clause as a complex sentence. "Why, when I waited for it to bear grapes, did it bear wild grapes?" As other examples of the same construction, Knobel refers to chap. xii. 1, 1., 2 ; and to Job ii. 10, iv. 2, iii. 11.

5. He now proceeds to answer his own question, in a tone of pungent irony, almost amounting to a sarcasm. The reply which might naturally have been looked for was a statement of some new care, some neglected precaution, some untried mode of culture ; but instead of this he threatens to destroy the vineyard, as the only expedient remaining. The rhetorical effect of this sudden turn in the discourse is heightened by the very form of the last clause, in which the simple future, as the natural expression of a purpose, is exchanged for the infinitive, denoting the bare action without specification of person, time, or number. *And now* (since you cannot tell) *I will let you know if you please* (or let me tell you) *what I am doing to my vineyard, i. e.* according to the idiomatic use of the participle, *what I am about to do,* suggesting the idea of a proximate futurity), *remove its hedge and it shall become a pasture* (literally, *a consuming,* but with special reference to cattle), *break down its wall, and it shall become a trampling-place* (*i. e.* it shall be overrun and trampled down).—*Remove* and *break* are not imperatives but infinitives, equivalent in meaning to *I will remove and break,* but more concise and rapid in expression. Cocceius and Vitringa suppose an ellipsis of the finite verb after the infinitive, "removing I will remove," "breaking down I will break down." This construction, in its full form, is extremely common ; but against the supposition of its ever being elliptically used, there is this objection, that the repetition is designed to be emphatic, an effect which is entirely destroyed by the omission. Knobel supposes that the thorn hedge and stone wall, which are separately mentioned elsewhere, are here put together to denote a more than ordinary care bestowed on the ideal vineyard. The more common opinion is that both were actually used in the same case with a view to different kinds of depredation.—מִרְמָס is a noun of place formed in the usual manner (Gesen. Heb. Gramm. § 83, 14) from the verb רָמַס, which occurs in chap. i. 12.— On the sense *become* (instead of *be for*) *vide supra,* ch. i. 14, 21, 22, 31.

6. To the threatening of exposure he now adds that of desolation arising from neglect of culture, while the last clause contains a beautiful though almost imperceptible transition from the apologue to the reality. By adding to the other threats, which any human vine-dresser might have reasonably uttered, one which only God could execute, the parable at one stroke is brought to a conclusion, and the mind prepared for the ensuing application. *And I place it* (render it) *a desolation. It shall not be pruned and it shall not be dressed, and there shall come up thorns and briers. And I will lay my commands upon the clouds from raining rain upon it, i. e.* that they rain no rain upon it. The addition of the noun *rain* is emphatic and equivalent to *any rain at all.*—The English version *lay waste* is perhaps too strong for the original expression, which rather signifies the letting it run to waste by mere exposure and neglect.—The older versions take יֵעָדֵר in the sense of *digging* (Sept. Vulgate, Luther, Calvin), but the latest writers prefer that of *dressing,* arranging, putting in order.—Gesenius and Ewald follow Cocceius in referring עָלָה to the vineyard as its subject; *it shall come up thorns and briers,* as the eye is said to *run down water* (Lam. iii. 48), and a land to *flow milk and honey* (Exod. iii. 8). The construction, though undoubtedly good Hebrew, is not so obvious as the old and common one. *To command from* or *away from* is to deter from any act by a command,

in other words to *forbid* or to *command not* to do the thing in question.
In this sense only can the preposition *from* be said to have a negative
meaning.

7. The startling menace at the close of the sixth verse would naturally
prompt the question, Who is this that assumes power over clouds and rain,
and what is the vineyard which he thus denounces? To this tacit question we have here the answer. As if he had said, do not wonder that the
owner of the vineyard should thus speak, *for the vineyard of Jehovah of
Hosts is the House of Israel*, the church, considered as a whole, *and the man
of Judah is the plant of his pleasures*, or his favourite plant. *And he waited
for judgment*, practical justice, as in ch. i. 17, *and behold bloodshed, for
righteousness and behold a cry*, either outcry and disturbance, or more specifically the cry of the oppressed, which last is more agreeable to usage,
and at the same time more poetical and graphic.—The כִּי at the beginning
has been variously rendered *but* (Luther, Gesen. Hendw. Umbr.), *to wit*
(Hitzig), *certainly* (Calvin), &c. But the true connection of the verse with
that before it not only admits but requires the strict sense, *for, because,* as
given in the ancient versions, and retained by Cocceius, Ewald, and Knobel.
—J. D. Michaelis and all the later Germans follow Pagninus and Montanus
in translating נֶטַע *plantation*. But the word is unambiguously used in that
sense nowhere else, and it does not agree well with the singular term *man*.
It is true that *plant* and *man* may be put for a collection of plants and
men, but this should not affect the strict translation of the sentence.—The
paronomasia or designed correspondence in the form and sound of the
parallel expressions in the last clause has been copied by Augusti, Gesenius, Hitzig, Ewald, and Knobel. But as Hendewerk has well observed,
such imitations can even approximate to the form of the original, only by
departing more or less from the strict sense of particular expressions, a
loss which can hardly be considered as made good by the mere assonance
of such combinations as *Gerechtigkeit* and *Schlechtigkeit, Beglückung* and
Bedrückung, Milde and *Unbilde.*

8. Here begins a detailed specification of the sins included in the general
expressions of ver. 7. We have first two woes pronounced against as many
sins, each followed by a threatening of appropriate punishment, and a
general threatening which applies to both, vers. 8–17. The first sin thus
denounced is that of ambitious and avaricious grasping after property, not
merely in opposition to the peculiar institutions of the law, but to the fundamental principles of morals, connected as it always is with a neglect of
charitable duties and a willingness to sacrifice the good of others. The
verse before us may be understood, however, as descriptive rather of the
tendency and aim of this ambitious grasping, than of its actual effects.
Woe to the joiners of house with house, or those making house touch house,
field to field they bring together, literally, cause them to approach, *even to a
failure* (or *defect*) *of place, i. e.* until there is no room left, *and ye*, by a
sudden apostrophe addressing those of whom he had been speaking, *are
made* (or *left*) *to dwell by yourselves in the midst of the land*, owning all
from the centre to the circumference, or simply *within its bounds*, within
it. The translation *earth* is equally agreeable to usage, and expresses still
more strongly the extent of their desires; but *land* is more natural and
preferred by almost all interpreters. Ewald regards הוֹי as a simple exclamation (O die Haus reihen an Haus!) But this translation is inadequate,
as an expression of denunciation is required by the context.

9. The inordinate desire of lands and houses shall be punished with the

loss of them, vers. 9, 10.   And first, he threatens that the valuable houses which they coveted, and gained by fraud or violence, shall one day be left empty, an event implying the death, captivity, or degradation of their owners.   *In my ears Jehovah of Hosts* is saying, as if his voice were still ringing in the Prophet's ears, *of a truth* (literally, *if not*, being part of an old formula of swearing, "may it be so and so if," &c. ; so that the negative form conveys the strongest affirmation, *surely, certainly*) *many houses shall become a desolation, great and good for want of an inhabitant.*—The Septuagint and Vulgate, followed by Luther, Calvin, and J. D. Michaelis, make *in my ears* the words of God himself, as if he had said, "these things are in my ears," or "it (the cry, ver. 7) is in my ears, saith Jehovah of Hosts."   But most modern writers follow the Targum and Peshito in construing this clause according to the analogy of chap. xxii. 14 ("in my ears it was revealed by Jehovah of Hosts," or "Jehovah of Hosts revealed himself.")—The common version, *shall be desolate*, does not convey the whole idea, which is that of *becoming*, being changed into (*vide supra*, ver. 6), and is so rendered in most versions.—The sense usually given to טוֹבִים is the specific one of *fair* or *beautiful* (Henderson, *fine ;* Barnes, *splendid.*) But Cocceius and Vitringa take it more correctly in the general sense of *good*, including the ideas of profit and convenience, as well as that of elegance or beauty.—By most interpreters מֵאֵין in the last clause is regarded as a synonyme or at most as an intensive form of אֵין "wholly without inhabitant."   But the causative meaning, "for the want of," "from the absence of," אֵין being properly a noun, affords a better sense here, as explaining how or why the houses should be desolate, and may be justified by the analogy of Jer. xix. 11 ; (J. D. Michaelis, "because there will be no one to inhabit them.   Clericus, Vitringa, and Hendewerk explain it to mean *so that there shall not be*, but without authority from usage.— Henderson's version of the foregoing words, *the numerous houses, the large and fine ones*, and that of Gesenius, from which it is derived, seem to lay too much stress upon the adjectives.—On the form *if not*, compare chap. xiv. 24 ; Deut. i. 35 ; Ps. cxxxi. 2.

10. As the sin related both to lands and houses, so both are mentioned in denouncing punishment.   The desolation of the houses was in fact to arise from the unproductiveness of the lands.   Ruinous failure of crops, and a near approach to absolute sterility are threatened as a condign punishment of those who added field to field and house to house.   The meaning of this verse depends not on the absolute value of the measures mentioned, but on their proportions.   The last clause threatens that the seed sown, instead of being multiplied, should be reduced nine-tenths ; and a similar idea is no doubt expressed by the analogous terms of the preceding clause. *For ten acres* (literally *yokes*, like the Latin *jugerum* from *jugum*) *of vineyard shall make* (produce) *one bath*, a liquid measure here put for a very small quantity of wine to be yielded by so large a quantity of land, *and the seed of a homer, i. e.* seed to the amount of a homer, or in our idiom, *a homer of seed, shall produce an ephah*, a dry measure equal to the liquid *bath*, and constituting one-tenth of a homer, as we learn from Ezek. xlv. 11–14.   The English Version, followed by Lowth, translates כִּי *yea*, while Clericus and Gesenius omit it altogether.   But the particle is necessary, in its usual sense, to connect this verse with the prediction in ver. 9, of which it gives the ground or reason.

11. The second woe is uttered against drunkenness and heartless dissipation, with its usual accompaniment of inattention to God's providential

dealings, and is connected with captivity, hunger, thirst, general mortality, as its appropriate punishment, vers. 11–14. The description of the sin is contained in vers. 11, 12, and first that of drunkenness, considered not as an occasional excess, but as a daily business, diligently prosecuted with a devotion, such as would ensure success in any laudable or lawful occupation. *Woe to those rising early in the morning to pursue strong drink* (literally, *strong drink they pursue*), *delaying in the twilight* (until) *wine inflames them.* —That נֶשֶׁף does not here mean the morning twilight, but as usual the dusk of evening (Prov. vii. 9), is plain from the preposition *in* prefixed. The idea of *continuing till night* (Vulg. Calv. Eng. Vs.) is rather implied than expressed. The allusion is not so much to the disgracefulness of drinking in the morning (Knobel, Henderson), as to their spending day and night in drinking, rising early and sitting up late. Before *wine* in the last clause the older writers supply *and* (Peshito, J. D. Michaelis), *while* (Calvin, Vitringa), or *so that* (Vulgate, Luther, Cocceius, Lowth, Rosen.) Gesenius avoids this by a paraphrase (" sit late at night by wine inflamed"), and Ewald treats the participles in both clauses as adverbial expressions used to qualify the finite verb (" they who early in the morning run after strong drink, late in the evening are inflamed by wine"). The precise construction of the Hebrew may be thus retained—" those who, rising early in the morning, pursue strong drink ; those whom, delaying in the evening, wine inflames." The same application of מְאַחֲרִים occurs in the parallel passage, Prov. xxiii. 29–32. *Strong drink* differs from *wine* only by including all intoxicating liquors, and is here used simply as a parallel expression.—The waste of time here censured is professed and gloried in by the convivial poets of heathen antiquity. Thus Horace says of himself,

> Est qui nec veteris pocula Massici,
> Nec partem solido demere de die,
> Spernit.

The nocturnal part of the prophetic picture is still more exactly copied by Propertius,

> Sic noctem patera, sic ducam carmine, donec
> Injiciat radios in mea vina dies.

Illustrative parallels from modern poetry are needless though abundant.

12. This verse completes the picture begun in ver. 11, by adding riotous mirth to drunkenness. To express this idea, music is joined with wine as the source of their social enjoyment, but the last clause shews that it is not mere gaiety, nor even the excess of it, that is here intended to be prominently set forth, but the folly and wickedness of merriment at certain times, and under certain circumstances, especially amidst impending judgments. The general idea of music is expressed by naming several instruments belonging to the three great classes of stringed, wind, and pulsatile. The precise form and use of each cannot be ascertained, and is of no importance to the meaning of the sentence. *And the harp and the viol, the tabret* (tambourine or small drum), *and the pipe* (or flute), *and wine* (compose) *their feasts; and the work of Jehovah they will not look at* (or regard), *and the operation of his hands they have not seen*, and do not see.—The Targum supplies a preposition before the first nouns, and makes *feasts* the subject of the sentence : " With harp and viol, tabret and pipe, and wine, are their feasts." The Septuagint and Peshito, " with harp, &c., they drink their wine." The Vulgate supplies the preposition before *feasts*, and makes the other nouns the subject—" Harp and viol, &c., are in your feasts." Gese-

nius gives the same sense, but supposes מִשְׁתֵּיהֶם to be used adverbially as in Arabic. Cocceius, Ewald, Maurer, Hitzig, Hendewerk, and Henderson, make it the nominative after the substantive verb understood. "Harp and viol, tabret and pipe, and wine, are their feasts," in these consist their social entertainments. Umbreit and Knobel separate the last two words from what precedes and read, "there is harp and viol, tabret and pipe, and wine is their drink." The general sense is not at all affected by these questions of construction. According to Ewald (Heb. Gr. § 379), with whom Hitzig and Umbreit agree, מִשְׁתֵּיהֶם is not a plural, but the form which לְה derivatives take, even in the singular, before certain suffixes. The *work of Jehovah* here alluded to is not that of creation (Umbreit), nor the law (Aberbenel), nor the design and use of providential favours (Calvin), but his dealings with the people in the way of judgment. Compare chap. x. 12, xxii. 11, xxviii. 21 ; Hab. i. 5, iii. 2 ; Ps. lxiv. 9, and especially Ps. xxviii. 5, from which the expressions here used seem to be taken.

13. Here again the sin is directly followed by its condign punishment, drunkenness, and disregard of providential warnings by captivity, hunger, thirst, and general mortality, vers. 13, 14. But instead of the language of direct prediction (as in vers. 9, 10), the Prophet here employs that of description. *Therefore* (for the reasons given in the two preceding verses) *my people has gone into exile* (or captivity) *for want of knowledge* (a wilful ignorance of God's providential work and operation), *and their glory* (literally *his*, referring to the singular noun people) *are men of hunger* (*i. e.* famished), *and their multitude dry* (parched) *with thirst.* J. D. Michaelis understands captivity as a figurative term for misery, as in Job xlii. 10 ; Ps. xiv. 7. But the context seems to require the literal interpretation.— Luther, Gesenius, and Hendewerk take גָּלָה as a future, which is not to be assumed without necessity. Most recent writers evade the difficulty by rendering it in the present tense. The only natural construction is the old one (Sept. Vulg. Calvin. Vitr. Barnes), which gives the preterite its proper meaning, and either supposes the future to be here, as often elsewhere, spoken of as if already past (J. H. Michaelis), or understands the verse as referring to judgments which have been already suffered, not at one time merely, but on various occasions, as if he had said "this is the true cause of the captivity, the hunger, and the thirst, to which Israel has so often been subjected." The allusion cannot be to the deportation of the ten tribes, who are never called God's people.—Because *he knoweth not, they know not,* and *I knew not,* are phrases sometimes used where we say *unawares* or *suddenly* (*e. g.* Ps. xxxv. 8 ; Sol. Song vi. 12 ; Job ix. 5), Luther so understands מִבְּלִי־דָעַת here, in which he is followed by J. D. Mich. Ros. Ges. Ewald, Hendew. Henders. Hitzig. Umbreit. But as this phrase is not so used elsewhere, and in Hosea iv. 6, means *for want of knowledge,* as the cause of ruin, this exact and ancient version is correctly retained by Lowth, De Wette, Maurer, and Knobel. By כְּבוֹדוֹ and הֲמוֹנוֹ some understand the same class of persons, viz. the rich and noble (Vitr. Ges. Ewald). Others suppose an antithesis between the *nobility* and the *populace* (Luther, Lowth, Umbreit). Either of these verbal explanations is consistent with the import of the threatening as explained already ; but the most probable interpretation seems to be that of Knobel, who supposes the *multitude* or mass of the inhabitants, without regard to rank, to be called the flower or glory of the country, as Goldsmith calls the peasantry "a nation's pride." For מְתֵי *men,* J. D. Michaelis and Lowth read מֵתֵי *dead,* on the authority of the Septuagint, Targum, Peshito, and Luther. Hitzig and Ewald read מְזֵי or

מְזֵה *exhausted,* after the analogy of Deut. xxxii. 24. But the common reading yields a perfectly good sense, not however that of *nobles in hunger* (Vitr. nobiles fame) but simply that of *hungry men,* or *starvelings,* as Henderson expresses it.

14. As the effect of the preceding judgments, the Prophet now describes a general mortality, under the figure of the grave, as a ravenous monster, gaping to devour the thoughtless revellers. Here, as in ver. 13, he seems to be speaking of events already past. *Therefore* (because famine and captivity have thus prevailed) *the grave has enlarged herself and opened her mouth without measure, and down goes her pomp and her noise and her crowd and he that rejoices in her.*—It is equally correct, although not perhaps so natural, to regard עַל־כֵּן as a correlative of לָכֵן in ver. 13, both relating to the sins described in ver. 12, as the occasion of the strokes in question.—The noun שְׁאוֹל is described by Gesenius from a verb שָׁאַל, which he supposes to have been synonymous with שָׁעַל *to be hollow.* Hence the noun would mean an *excavation* and in particular *a grave,* which same sense is deduced by the older writers from שָׁאַל *to ask* or *crave* (Prov. xxx. 15, 16; Hab. ii. 5). The sense of the term here corresponds almost exactly to the poetical use of *grave* in English, as denoting one great receptacle, to which the graves of individuals may be conceived as inlets. It is thus that we speak of a voice from the grave, without referring to the burial-place of any individual. The German *Hölle* (originally *Höhle,* hollow) and the old English *Hell,* corresponds almost exactly to the Hebrew word; but the idea of a place of torment, which is included in their present meaning, is derived from the peculiar use of ᾅδης (the nearest Greek equivalent) in the book of Revelation, and belongs to the Hebrew word only by implication and in certain connections. It seems to be a needless violation of good taste to introduce the Greek word *Hades* (Lowth), especially if treated as a feminine noun (Barnes). For additional remarks upon the usage of the Hebrew word, see chap. xiv. 9.—As the same phrase here used is applied by Habakkuk (ii. 5) to Nebuchadnezzar, "who enlarged his desire as the grave, and was like death, and could not be satisfied," most of the modern writers take נֶפֶשׁ here in the same sense of *appetite,* either strictly (Ewald) or as a figure for the craving maw of a devouring monster (Gesenius). Grotius takes נַפְשׁוֹ as a reflexive pronoun, for which there is no distinct form in Hebrew, and by the grave's *enlarging itself* understands a poetical description of an extraordinary number of dead bodies.—The English Version, following the Vulgate, connects יָרַד with בָּהּ, which is forbidden by the accents and by the usage of the verb and preposition.—As the suffix in נַפְשָׁה must refer to שְׁאוֹל, the simplest construction is that of Hitzig, who refers the other pronouns to the same antecedent, *her pomp* (*i. e.* the grave's), *her crowd, her noise,* so called because they were to have an end in her, as men doomed to die are called *men of death,* 2 Sam. xix. 29. By עָלֵז בָּהּ he understands the man *exulting over her,* laughing at the grave and setting death at defiance (compare chap. xxviii. 15). This construction is approved by Hendewerk, but rejected by the other recent interpreters for the old one, which refers the pronouns to *Jerusalem* or *Zion* understood.—The words rendered *pomp, crowd,* and *noise,* are as variously explained as those in ver. 13; but all agree that they refer to the voluptuous revellers described in ver. 12.

15. To the description of the punishment the Prophet now adds that of its design and ultimate effect, to wit, the humiliation of man and the exalta-

tion of God, vers. 15, 16. The former is here foretold in terms almost
identical with those of chap. ii. 9. *And man is brought low, and man is
cast down and the eyes of the lofty* (or haughty) *are cast down.*—Most of the
older writers render all the verbs of this verse in the future, but Junius,
Cocceius, and the moderns in the present. The Vav conversive probably
denotes nothing more than the dependence of the first two verbs on those
of the preceding verse, as expressive of a subsequent and consequent event.
If so, the sense, though not the form, of the original is well expressed by
Luther, *so that every man is humbled*, &c. That the verse at least includes
a reference to the future, is clear from the future form of the third verb ;
and that this is not in contrast with the past time of the first clause, may
be inferred from the resumption of the latter form in ver. 16. In a case so
dubious, the present form may be preferred, as really including both the
others, or at least consistent with them.—On the use of אִישׁ and אָדָם, see
chap. ii. 9. Luther, who there supposes an antithesis between the terms,
here translates them both by *every man*. The only difference between the
two interpretations, with respect to the import of the Prophet's declaration,
is that in the one case he distinctly mentions two great classes as the subjects of humiliation, while in the other he confounds them all together. In
either case the sense is that the pride of man shall be brought low. " Let
a man be ever so high, death will bring him low ; ever so mean, death will
bring him lower." (Matthew Henry).

16. The same events which humble man exalt God, not by contrast
merely, but by the positive exhibition of his attributes. *And Jehovah of
Hosts is exalted in judgment* (in the exercise of justice), *and the Mighty, the
Holy One, is sanctified* (shewn to be a Holy God) *in righteousness.*—Most
of the earlier and later writers follow the Vulgate in rendering הָאֵל הַקָּדוֹשׁ
simply *the Holy God*. But the accentuation seems to indicate a more
emphatic sense. The English version follows Calvin, and reads *God who is
holy*. Lowth follows Luther, *God the Holy One*. But as אֵל is itself a significant title, it seems best to regard the two epithets as summing up the
natural and moral perfections of the Deity. So Vitringa (Deus ille fortis,
sanctus ille) and Junius (Deus sanctus fortissimus).—Hitzig gives נקדש a
reflexive meaning (sanctifies himself), which, although admissible, is needless, and not favoured by the parallelism.—*In judgment* and *in righteousness* are used precisely in the same sense, chap. i. 27. With respect to the
tense of the verbs, see the foregoing verse.

17. Having paused, as it were, to shew the ultimate effect of these judgments, he now completes the description of the judgments themselves, by
predicting the conversion of the lands possessed by the ungodly Jews into
a vast pasture-ground, occupied only by the flocks•of wandering shepherds
from the neighbouring deserts. *And lambs shall feed as* (in) *their pasture,
and the wastes of the fat ones shall sojourners* (temporary occupants) *devour*.
The explanation of this verse as a promise, that the *lambs* or righteous
should succeed to the possession of the *fat ones* or wealthy sinners (Targ.
Jar. Kim. Calv. Jun. Cocc. Vitr.) is scarcely consistent with the context,
which contains an unbroken series of threatenings. The modern interpreters, who follow Aben Ezra in making this a threatening likewise, apply
it either figuratively to the subjection of the Holy Land to the Gentiles
(Gill), or the entrance of the poor on the possessions of the rich (Hendewerk), or literally to the desolation of the land itself (J. D. Mich. Lowth,
&c.).—Gesenius refers the last clause to tillage, and supposes it to mean
that strangers shall reap the crops of the forsaken lands ; but the common

interpretation is more natural, which makes both clauses have respect to pasturage.—Most writers make גָּרִים a synonyme of גָּרִים *strangers*; but Cocceius treats it as an adjective agreeing with כְּבָשִׂים, " and strange lambs shall devour," &c. Hitzig construes it still more strictly as a participle, " and devour wandering the wastes," &c. But the verb should then be taken in its usual sense of *sojourning*, residing for a time, in reference either to the shepherds or their sheep.—The Vulgate explains חָרְבוֹת מֵחִים to mean *fat* wastes, *i.e.* deserts become fertile (deserta in ubertatem versa); the French version, deserts where the flocks grew fat; Clericus, still more strangely, the flocks themselves which fed in the desert, and should therefore be devoured by strangers, while the lambs were led as usual to pasture by their Babylonian captors. J. D. Michaelis takes חָרֲבוֹת in the sense of *ruins*, here put for that which grows among them; but the word no doubt means waste fields, as in Jer. xxv. 11, Ezek. xxv. 13. Hitzig supposes מֵחִים to denote fat sheep or rams, as in the only other place where it occurs (Ps. lxvi. 15); but most interpreters regard it as a figure for the rich and prosperous, like דִּשְׁנֵי־אֶרֶץ, Ps. xxii. 30 (compare מִשְׁמַנֵּיהֶם, Ps. lxxviii. 31).—The phrase כִּדְבָרָם has been variously explained to mean *as it was said to them* (Targ.), *juxta ductum suum, i. e. without restraint* (J. H. Mich. Lowth), *according to their order, i.e.* their usual order (Vulg.), *as they are driven* (Aben Ezra, J. D. Mich.). But the modern interpreters take דֶּבֶר here and Micah ii. 12 in the sense of *pasture*.—The conjectural emendation of the text by changing גרים into כרים (Capellus, Bauer) or נדים (Durell, Secker, Lowth, Ewald), is of course superfluous.

18. The series of woes is now resumed and continued without any interruption, vers. 18–23. Even the description of the punishment, instead of being added directly to that of the sin, as in vers. 9 and 13, is postponed until the catalogue of sins is closed, and then subjoined in a general form, ver. 24. This verse contains the third woe, having reference to presumptuous sinners who defy God's judgments. They are here represented not as drawn away by sin (James i. 14), but as laboriously drawing it to them by soliciting temptation, drawing it out by obstinate persistency in evil and contempt of divine threatenings. *Woe to the drawers of iniquity* (those drawing, those who draw it) *with cords of vanity and sin* (a parallel expression to iniquity) *as* (or *as with) a cart-rope, i.e.* a strong rope, implying difficulty and exertion.—The interpretation which supposes *iniquity* and *sin* to mean *calamity* and *punishment* (Menochius, Gesenius, Ewald, Hendewerk, Henderson), although it seems to make the sentence clearer, impairs its strength, and takes the words in an unusual and doubtful sense. Knobel objects that men cannot be said to draw sin with cords of sin. But even this figure is perfectly consistent both with reason and experience. Or *vanity* may be taken in the sense of falsehood or sophistical reasoning by which men persuade themselves to sin (Calv. Vitr. Cler.). The Targum, followed by Jarchi, supposes an antithesis between the beginnings of sin and its later stages, slight cords and cart-ropes. But this confounds the sin itself with the instrument by which they draw it; and the same objection lies against the Syriac and Vulgate versions, which make *drawing out*, or protracting, the primary idea, and also against Houbigant's and Lowth's interpretation, which supposes an allusion to the process of rope-making. Luther's idea, that the verse relates to combination among wicked men, " who bind themselves together" to do mischief, is at variance with the usage of the Hebrew verb.—The true interpretation of the verse, which supposes the act described to be that of laboriously drawing sin to one's

self, perhaps with the accessory idea of drawing it out by perseverance, is substantially given by Kimchi, Vitringa, J. D. Michaelis, Hitzig, Maurer, and Umbreit.—The various readings, בעבות for כעבות (Bib. Soncin., 14 MSS.), כחבלי for בחבלי (1 MS., Sept. Aq. Sym. Theod.), and עולה for עגלה (Olshausen, Observ. Crit., p. 8, Henderson *ad loc.*), are all unnecessary, and inferior to the common text.

19. The degree of their presumption and depravity is now evinced by a citation of their language with respect to God's threatened judgments, an ironical expression of impatience to behold them, and an implied refusal to believe without experience. The sentence is continued from the verse preceding, and further describes the sinners there denounced, as *the ones saying* (those who say), *let him speed, let him hasten his work* (his providential work, as in ver. 12), *that we may see, and let the counsel* (providential plan or purpose) *of the Holy One of Israel* (which, in the mouth of these blasphemers, seems to be a taunting irony) *draw nigh and come, and we will know* (*i. e.* according to the Hebrew idiom and the parallel expression) *that we may know* what it is, or that it is a real purpose, and that he is able to accomplish it. Compare Jer. xvii. 15 ; Amos v. 18, vi. 13 ; Isa. xxx. 10, 11, xxviii. 15 ; 2 Peter iii. 4.—The intransitive construction of the first clause, " let him speed, let his work make haste " (Hitzig, Ewald, Umbreit), may be justified by usage, and makes the clauses more exactly parallel ; but the other is preferred, by almost all interpreters, ancient and modern.—Henderson explains this verse as " the only construction which could be put upon the conduct of the wicked Jews ; " but the reference seems to be to actual expression of the wish in words, and not in action merely.—For the form תָּבוֹאָה. see Gesenius, Heb. Gr. § 48, 3.

20. The fourth woe is against those who subvert moral distinctions and confound good and evil, an idea expressed first in literal terms and then by two obvious and intelligible figures. *Woe unto the* (persons) *saying* (those who say) *to evil good and to good evil,* (who address them by these titles or call them so), *putting darkness for light and light for darkness, putting bitter for sweet and sweet for bitter.* These are here combined, not merely as natural opposites, but also as common figures for truth and falsehood, right and wrong. See chap. ii. 5 ; Prov. ii. 13 ; Eccles. ii. 13 ; James iii. 11. A kindred figure is employed by Juvenal (qui nigrum in candida vertunt, Sat. iii. 3). Gesenius and Hitzig apply this verse particularly to unrighteous judges, who are mentioned in ver. 23 ; but a more general sense is here required by the context.

21. Here, as in the foregoing verse, one sin follows another without any intervening description of punishment. This arrangement may imply a very intimate connection between the sins thus brought into juxtaposition. As presumptuous sin, such as vers. 18, 19 describe, implies a perversion of the moral sense, such as ver. 20 describes, so the latter may be said to presuppose an undue reliance upon human reason, which is elsewhere contrasted with the fear of God (Prov. iii. 7), and is indeed incompatible with it. *Woe unto the wise in their eyes* (*i. e.* their own eyes, which cannot be otherwise expressed in the Hebrew) *and before their own faces* (in their own sight or estimation) *prudent,* intelligent, a synonyme of *wise.* The sin reproved, as Calvin well observes, is not mere frivolous self-conceit, but that delusive estimate of human wisdom (fallax sapientiæ spectrum) which may coexist with modesty of manners and a high degree of real intellectual merit, but which must be abjured, not only on account of its effects, but also as involving the worst form of pride.

22. The sixth woe, like the second, is directed against drunkards, but with special reference to drunken judges, vers. 22, 23. The tone of this verse is sarcastic, from its using terms which commonly express not only strength but courage and heroic spirit, in application to exploits of drunkenness. There may indeed be a particular allusion to a species of foolhardiness and brutal ambition not uncommon in our own times, leading men to shew the vigour of their frames by mad excess, and to seek eminence in this way no less eagerly than superior spirits seek true glory. Of such it may indeed be said, their god is their belly and they glory in their shame. *Woe to the mighty men* or *heroes,* (who are heroes only) *to drink wine, and men of strength to mingle strong drink, i. e.* according to the usual interpretation, to mix wine with spices, thereby making it more stimulating and exciting, a practice spoken of by Pliny and other ancient writers. (See also Sol. Song viii. 2.) Hitzig (with whom Hendewerk agrees on this point) denies that this was an oriental usage, and understands the Prophet as referring to the mixture of wine with water. But see Gesenius's Thesaurus, p. 808. In either case the mixing is here mentioned only as a customary act in the offering or drinking of liquors, just as *making tea* might be mentioned as a common act of modern hospitality, whatever part of the preparatory process the phrase may properly denote.

23. The absence of the interjection shews that this is a continuation of the woe begun in the preceding verse, and thus explains the Prophet's recurrence to a sin which he had denounced already (vers. 11, 12) as productive of general inconsideration, but which he now describes as leading to injustice, and therefore as a vice peculiarly disgraceful in a magistrate. The effect here ascribed to drunkenness is not merely that of incapacitating judges for the discharge of their official functions, but that of tempting them to make a trade of justice, with a view to the indulgence of this appetite. *Justifying* (*i. e.* acquitting, clearing, a forensic term) *the guilty* (not simply the wicked in a general sense, but the wrong-doer in a judicial sense) *for the sake* (literally *as the result*) *of a bribe, and the righteousness of the righteous* (*i. e.* the *right* of the innocent or injured party, or his *character* as such *they will take from him* (*i. e.* they do and will do so still). The transition from the plural to the singular in this clause, and from the participle to the future, are familiar idioms of Hebrew syntax. The pronoun at the end may be understood either collectively or distributively, *from each of them.* (See Ges. Heb. Gr. § 143, 4.)

24. To the series of sins enumerated in the six preceding verses there is now added a general description of their punishment. In the first clause, the Prophet represents the divine visitation, with its sudden, rapid, irresistible effect, by the familiar figure of chaff and dry grass sinking in the flames. In the second clause he passes from simile to metaphor, and speaks of the people as a tree whose root is rotten and its growth above ground pulverised. In the third, he drops both figures, and in literal expressions summarily states the cause of their destruction. *Therefore* (because of the abounding of these sins) *as a tongue of fire* (*i. e.* a flame, so called from its shape and motion, Acts ii. 3 ; 1 Kings xviii. 38) *devours chaff* (or stubble), *and as ignited grass falls away, their root shall be as rottenness, and their blossom as fine dust shall go up* (*i. e.* be taken up and scattered by the wind). *For they have rejected the law of Jehovah of Hosts, and the word* (the revealed will) *of the Holy One of Israel they have treated with contempt.*—Montanus explains יְרֻפֶּה as a transitive verb (glumam

debilitat), and the English Version (followed by Lowth and Augusti) goes still further by giving it the sense of *consuming*, which it never has. Calvin, followed by Vitringa, makes it passive, and renders לֶהָבָה as an ablative (a flamma dissolvitur). Gesenius, in his version, gives the verb its usual intransitive or neuter sense, but supplies a preposition before the noun, or takes it as a noun of place (in der Flamme zusammensinkt). In his Lexicon, however, he adopts the construction first proposed by Cocceius, which supposes the two words to be in regimen, and to mean literally *grass of flame*, i. e. flaming or ignited grass.—J. D. Michaelis endeavours to identify the figures of the first and second clause by reading *ashes* instead of *rottenness;* but such transitions are too common to excite surprise.—The Septuagint renders פֶּרַח ἄνθος, the Vulgate *germen*, and others variously bud, blossom, flower, &c. It seems to be intended to express whatever could here be put in antithesis to *root*, as in the proverbial phrase *root and branch*, denoting the whole tree, above ground and below.—For the true sense of the last verb in this verse, see chap. i. 4. Its use in this connection is a strong proof that it cannot mean *provoke*, although the Seventy so translate it even here.—The collocation of the subject and the object in the first clause is unusual. See Ewald's Heb. Gr. § 555. For the syntax of the infinitive and future in the same clause, see Gesen. § 129, Rem. 2.

25. Having declared in the foregoing verse what should be, he recalls to mind what has already been. As if he had said, God will visit you for these things ; nay, he has done so already, but without reclaiming you or satisfying his own justice, for which purpose further strokes are still required. The previous inflictions here referred to are described as a stroke from Jehovah's outstretched hand, so violent as to shake the mountains, and so destructive as to fill the streets with corpses.—*Therefore* (referring to the last clause of ver. 24) *the anger of Jehovah has burned against his people* (literally *in them*, i. e. in the very midst of them as a consuming fire), *and he stretched forth his hand against them* (literally *him*, referring to the singular noun *people*), *and smote them, and the mountains trembled, and their carcass* (put collectively for corpses) *was like sweeping* (refuse, filth) *in the midst of the streets. In all this* (i. e. even after all this, or notwithstanding all this) *his anger has not turned back* (abandoned its object, or regarded it as already gained), *and still his hand is stretched out* (to inflict new judgments).—The future form given to the verb by Clericus is altogether arbitrary. Most of the later writers follow Luther in translating them as presents. But if this verse is not descriptive of the past, as distinguished from the present and the future, the Hebrew language is incapable of making any such distinction. This natural meaning of the language (which no modern version except Ewald's fully expresses) is confirmed by the last clause, which evidently introduces something posterior to what is here described. It is not necessary to suppose, although it is most probable, that what is here described had actually taken place before the Prophet wrote. In this, as in some other cases, he may be supposed to take his stand between a nearer and a more remote futurity, the former being then of course described as past.—The trembling of the mountains is referred by Hendewerk to the earthquake mentioned Amos i. 1, Zech. xiv. 5. Jarchi explains it of the fall of kings and princes. Junius makes the Prophet say that if such strokes had fallen upon mountains *they would have trembled.*—J. D. Michaelis supposes what is said of the dead bodies to be applicable only to a pestilence. It is most probable, however, that these strong expressions were intended simply to convey the idea of violent com-

motion and a general mortality. There is no need of referring what is said exclusively of evils suffered in the days of Joash and Amaziah (Junius) or in those of Ahaz (Vitringa), since the Prophet evidently means to say that *all preceding judgments* had been insufficient and that more were still required.—The act expressed by שָׂא is not so much that of *turning away* as that of *turning back* or ceasing to pursue. (See Hengstenberg on Ps. ix. 4, 18). Saadias and Kimchi derive כסוחה from כסה to *cut* or *tear*, in which they are followed by Calvin (mutilum), Junius (succisum), and the English version (torn). But all the ancient versions and most modern ones make כ a preposition, and the best lexicographers derive the noun from סוח to sweep.—*In the midst of the streets* may be taken strictly to denote *in the middle* (Calvin: in medio viarum), or more indefinitely *in*, *within*. *Vide supra*, ver. 8.

26. The former stroke having been insufficient, a more effectual one is now impending, in predicting which the prophet does not confine himself to figurative language, but presents the approaching judgment in its proper form, as the invasion and ultimate subjection of the country by a formidable enemy, vers. 26–30. In this verse he describes the approach of these invaders as invited by Jehovah, to express which idea he employs two figures not uncommon in prophecy, that of a signal-pole or flag, and that of a hiss or whistle, in obedience to which the last clause represents the enemy as rapidly advancing. *And he raises a signal to the nations from afar, and hisses* (or whistles) *for him from the ends of the earth; and behold in haste, swift he shall come.*—Here as in ver. 25, the older writers understand the verbs as futures, but the later ones as presents. The verbs in the last clause have Vav prefixed, but its conversive power commonly depends upon a future verb preceding, which is wanting here. These verbs appear to form a link between the past time of ver. 25 and the unambiguous future at the end of this. First, *he smote* them, but without effect. Then, he *raises* a signal and *whistles*. Lastly, the enemy thus summoned *will come* swiftly.—The singular suffix in לו has been variously explained as referring to the king whose subjects had been previously mentioned (Targ. Jon.), or to the army as a whole, which had been just described as Gentiles, heathen (Knob. Hitzig), or to the ruling power under whose banners the other nations fought (Vitr. Hendewerk), or simply to *one* of the nations previously mentioned (Gesen. Umbr.)—The nation meant has been also variously explained to be the Romans (Theodoret: τοὺς Ῥωμαίους διὰ τούτων ἤνιξε), the Babylonians (Clericus), and the Assyrians (Gesen. Ewald, &c.). But this very disagreement, or rather the indefinite expressions which occasion it, shew that the terms of the description were designed to be more comprehensive. The essential idea is that the previous lighter judgments should be followed by another more severe and efficacious, by invasion and subjection. The terms are most emphatically applicable to the Romans.— The hissing or whistling, Hitzig supposes to have reference to some mode of alluring birds (Hos. xi. 11; Zech. x. 8); but the common and more probable opinion is that it alludes to the ancient mode of swarming bees, described at length by Cyril. (See his words as given by Bochart, Hieroz. p. 506).—In the last clause a substantive meaning *haste*, and an adjective meaning *light*, are both used adverbially in the sense of *swiftly*.

27. The enemy, whose approach was just foretold, is now described as not only prompt and rapid, but complete in his equipments, firm and vigorous, ever wakeful, impeded neither by the accidents of the, way nor by defective preparation. *There is no one faint* (or exhausted) *and there is no*

one stumbling (or faultering) *among them* (literally *in him*). *He* (the enemy, considered as an individual) *sleeps not, and he slumbers not, and the girdle of his loins is not opened* (or loosed), *and the latchet* (string or band *of his shoes* (or *sandals*) *is not broken.*—The English Version follows Calvin in translating all the verbs as futures. The Vulgate supplies the present in the first clause, and makes the others future. But as the whole is evidently one description, the translation should be uniform ; and as the pre-terite and future forms are intermingled, both seem to be here used for the present, which is given by Luther and most of the late writers.—The last clause is understood by Henderson and others as denoting that they do not disarm or undress themselves for sleep. But as the last verb alway de-notes violent separation, it is most probable that this whole clause relates to accidental interruptions of the march. The question raised by Hende-werk and Henderson as to the kind of *girdle* here referred to, is of no exe-getical importance, as it is only joined with *shoes* to represent the dress in general.—*In him* may be either put collectively for *in them*, or as J. D. Michaelis supposes, may refer to the *army*; and Hendewerk accordingly has *it slumbers not*, &c.—The distinction made by some between יָנוּם and יִישָׁן (Cocceius: non dormitat, multo minus dormit) is unnecessary here, where the verbs seem to be used as mere poetical equivalents.

28. The description is continued, but with special reference to their wea-pons and their means of conveyance. For the former, bows and arrows are here put ; and for the latter, horses and chariots (see ch. ii. 7). *Whose arrows are sharpened and all his bows bent* (literally trod upon) ; *the hoofs of his horses like flint* (or adamant) *are reckoned, and his wheels like a whirl-wind*, in rapidity and violence of motion.—Gesenius, Henderson, and others, omit the relative at the beginning, and Junius renders it as a conjunction (quia). But it serves to make the connection with the verse preceding much more close and sensible.—As שְׁנוּנִים, like the Latin *acutae*, is a par-ticiple, the common version (sharp) does not fully express its meaning. Indeed, from what is said of the bows immediately afterwards, the pro-minent idea would seem to be not that the arrows were *sharp*, but that they were already *sharpened*, implying present readiness for use.—The bows be-ing *trod upon* has reference to the ancient mode of stringing, or rather of shooting, the bow being large, and made of metal or hard wood. Arrian says expressly, in describing the use of the bow by the Indian infantry " placing it on the ground, and stepping on it with the left foot, so they shoot (οὕτως ἐκτοξεύουσι), drawing the string back to a great distance." (See the original passage in Henderson.)—The passive verb נֶחְשָׁבוּ cannot be accurately ren-dered, *they resemble* (Gesen. Hitzig), nor even *they are to be counted* (Augusti, De Wette), but means *they are counted* (Cocceius, Ewald), the preterite form implying that they had been tried and proved so.—The future form given to this whole verse by Calvin and Junius, and to the last clause by Lowth and Barnes, greatly impairs its unity and force as a description.

29. By a sudden transition, the enemy are here represented as lions, roar-ing, growling, seizing their pray, and carrying it off without resistance ; a lively picture, especially to an oriental reader, of the boldness, fierceness, quickness, and success of the attack here threatened. *He has a roar like the lioness, and he shall roar like the young lions, and shall growl, and seize the prey, and secure it, none delivering* (*i. e.* and none can rescue it).—Coc-ceius, Vitringa, and the modern writers, use the present tense, as in the foregoing verses, to preserve the unity of the description. But there the preterite and future forms are mingled, whereas here the future is alone used,

unless the textual reading וישא be retained, and even then the *Vav* may be regarded as conversive. Besides, this seems to be the turning-point between description and prediction. Having told what the enemy is, he now tells what he will do. It seems best, therefore, to adopt the future form used by the ancient versions, by Calvin, and by Luther, who is fond of the present, and employs it in the two foregoing verses.—Most of the modern writers follow Bochart in explaining לָבִיא to denote the *lioness*, which is the more natural in this case from the mention of the *young lions* immediately afterwards. The image, as Henderson suggests, may be that of a lioness attended by her whelps, or rather by her young ones which are old enough to roar and seek their prey (see Ezek. xix. 2, 3, and Gesenius, s. v.).—The meaning of יַפְלִיט is not "he shall embrace" (Vulgate amplexabitur), nor "he shall gather spoil" (Calvin spolia corradet), nor "he shall let it go" in sport before devouring it (Luzatto); but he shall carry it off safe, place it in safety, or secure it (Ewald: tobt und nimmt den Raub und sichert ihn ohne Retter).

30. The roaring of the lion suggests the roaring of the sea, and thus a beautiful transition is effected from the one figure to the other, in describing the catastrophe of all these judgments. Israel is threatened by a raging sea, and looking landward, sees it growing dark there, until, after a brief fluctuation, the darkness becomes total. *And he* (the enemy) *shall roar against him* (Israel) *in that day like the roaring of a sea. And he shall look to the land, and behold darkness! Anguish and light! It is dark in the clouds thereof* (*i. e.* of the land, the skies above it).—The Vulgate, Peshito, and a great majority of modern writers, disregard the Masoretic accents, and connect חשֶׁךְ with צָר, and אוֹר with חָשַׁךְ. Knobel appears to be the first who observed that this arrangement involves the necessity of vowel-changes also, as we must then read צָר for צַר and וְאוֹר for וָאוֹר. Those who adopt this interpretation, either read *darkness of anguish* (Vulgate, Hitzig, Knobel) or *darkness and anguish* (Eng. Vs.), or *darkness, anguish* (Hendewerk). Vitringa still construes אוֹר separately, "*as for* the light," but the others connect it with חָשַׁךְ directly, "and the light is dark," &c. The only objection to the Masoretic interpretation (which, although retained by Cocceius, Rosenmüller, Gesenius, and Maurer, is not the common one, as Hitzig represents), is the alleged incongruity of making *light* and *anguish* alternate, instead of light and darkness, a rhetorical nicety unworthy of attention where there is at best but a choice of difficulties. Henderson says, indeed, that it is "quite at variance with the spirit of the text, which requires a state of profound darkness, without any relieving glimpses of light." But it is just as easy to affirm that "the spirit of the text" requires the other construction, which is, moreover, recommended by its antiquity, traditional authority, simplicity, poetical beauty, and descriptive truth.—On the authority of the Aldine and Complutensian text of the Septuagint, Lowth supposes an omission in the Hebrew, which he thus supplies, "and these shall look to the heaven upward and down to the earth." But, as Barnes has well observed, "there is no need of supposing the expression defective. The Prophet speaks of the vast multitude that was coming up, as a *sea*. On that side there was no safety. It was natural to speak of the other direction as the *land* or shore, and to say that the people would look there for safety. But, says he, there would be no safety there; all would be darkness." Hitzig supplies the supposed effect by putting אוֹר in antithesis to אֶרֶץ, 'one looks to the earth, and behold the darkness of distress, and to the light (*i. e.* the sun or sky) &c.' But the introduction of the preposition is entirely arbitrary

and extremely forced.—Kimchi and Junius explained עֲרִיפֶיהָ to mean *its ruins*, deriving it from עָרַף to destroy (Hos. x. 2). Clericus, following an Arabic analogy, translates it *in conclavibus*, which seems absurd. The common derivation is from עָרַף to distill (Deut. xxxii. 2; xxxiii. 28), according to which it means the *clouds*, either strictly, or as a description of the heavens generally. Lowth, and several of the later Germans, give the particle a causal sense, *through* or *by reason of its clouds ;* but the proper local sense of *in its clouds* or *skies* is retained by Gesenius, Ewald, and all the early writers. The second verb is taken indefinitely by all the modern Germans except Ewald, who translates it *he looks*, but, as if by way of compensation, gives an indefinite meaning to the suffix in עָלָיו which he renders *over* or *upon* one (über einem). The use of the present tense, in rendering the first clause by Cocceius and the later Germans, is hardly consistent with the phrase *in that day*, and destroys the fine antithesis between the future יִנְהֹם and the preterite חָשַׁךְ describing the expected obscuration as already past. —Clericus appears to be alone in referring נִבַּט to the enemy (solo adspectu terram Israeliticam terrebit !). The sense of the last clause, according to the Masoretic interpretation, is well expressed by Gesenius, " (bald) Angst, (bald) Licht," and more paraphrastically by an old French version, " il re-gardera vers la terre, mais voici il y aura des ténébres, *il y aura affliction avec la lumière,* il y aura des ténébres au ciel audessus d'elle."

Chapter 6

THIS chapter contains a vision and prophecy of awful import. At an early period of his ministry, the Prophet sees the Lord enthroned in the temple and adored by the Seraphim, at whose voice the house is shaken, and the Prophet, smitten with a sense of his own corruption and unworthiness to speak for God or praise him, is relieved by the application of fire from the altar to his lips, and an assurance of forgiveness, after which, in answer to the voice of God inquiring for a messenger, he offers himself and is accepted, but with an assurance that his labours will tend only to aggravate the guilt and condemnation of the people who are threatened with judicial blindness, and, as its necessary consequence, removal from the desolated country ; and the prophecy closes with a promise and a threatening both in one, to wit, that the remnant which survives the threatened judgments shall experience a repetition of the stroke, but that a remnant after all shall continue to exist and to experience God's mercy.

The chapter naturally falls into two parts, the vision, vers. 1–8, and the message or prediction, vers. 9–13. The precise relation between these two parts has been a subject of dispute. The question is, whether the vision is an introduction to the message, or the message an appendage to the vision. Those who take the former view suppose that in order to prepare the Prophet for a discouraging and painful revelation, he was favoured with a new view of the divine majesty and of his own unworthiness, relieved by an assurance of forgiveness, and encouraged by a special designation to the self-denying work which was before him. Those who assume the other ground proceed upon the supposition, that the chapter contains an account of the Prophet's original induction into office, and that the message at the close was added to prepare him for its disappointments, or perhaps to try his faith.

Either of these two views may be maintained without absurdity and without materially affecting the details of the interpretation. The second is not only held by Jewish writers, but by the majority of Christian interpreters in modern times. The objection to it, founded on the place which the chapter holds in the collection, is met by some with the assertion, that the prophecies are placed without regard to chronological order. But as this is a gratuitous assumption, and as the order is at least *prima facie* evidence of date, some of the latest writers (Ewald for example) hold that the date of the composition was long posterior to that of the event, and one writer (Hitzig) goes so far as to assume, that this is the latest of Isaiah's writings, and was intended to exhibit, in the form of an *ex post facto* prophecy, the actual result of his official experience. This extravagant hypothesis needs no refutation, and neither that of Ewald, nor the common one, which makes this the first of Isaiah's writings, should be assumed without necessity, that is, without something in the chapter itself forbidding us to refer it to any other date than the beginning of Isaiah's ministry. But the chapter contains nothing which would not have been appropriate at any period of that ministry, and some of its expressions seem to favour, if they do not require, the hypothesis of previous experience in the office. The idea of so solemn an *inauguration* is affecting and impressive, but seems hardly sufficient to outweigh the presumption arising from the order of the prophecies in favour of the other supposition, which requires no facts to be assumed without authority, and although less striking, is at least as safe.

1. *In the year that king Uzziah died* (B.C. 758), *I saw the Lord sitting on a throne high and lifted up, and his skirts* (the train of his royal robe) *filling the palace,* or taking the last word in its more specific sense, *the temple,* so called as being the palace of the great King. " No man hath seen God at any time " (John i. 18), and God himself hath said, " There shall no man see me and live " (Exod. xxxiv. 20). Yet we read not only that " the pure in heart shall see God " (Mat. v. 8), but that Jacob said, " I have seen God face to face " (Gen. xxxii. 30). It is therefore plain that the phrase " to see God " is employed in different senses, and that although his essence is and must be invisible, he may be seen in the manifestation of his glory or in human form. The first of these senses is given here by the Targum and Grotius, the last by Clericus, with more probability, as the act of sitting on a throne implies a human form, and Ezekiel likewise in prophetic vision saw, " upon the likeness of a throne, an appearance as the likeness of a man above upon it " (Ezek. i. 26). It has been a general opinion in all ages of the Church, that in every such manifestation it was God the Son who thus revealed himself. In John xii. 41, it is said to have been Christ's glory that Isaiah saw and spoke of, while Paul cites vers. 9 and 10 (Acts xxviii. 25, 26) as the language of the Holy Ghost. It seems needless to inquire whether the Prophet saw this sight with his bodily eyes, or in a dream, or in an ecstasy, since the effect upon his own mind must have been the same in either case. It is also a question of no moment whether he beheld the throne erected in the holy place, or in the Holy of Holies, or in heaven, or as Jarchi imagines, reaching from earth to heaven. The scene of the vision is evidently taken from the temple at Jerusalem, but not confined to its exact dimensions and arrangements. It has been disputed whether what is here recorded took place before or after the death of Uzziah. Those who regard this as the first of Isaiah's prophecies are forced to assume that it belongs to the

reign of Uzziah. It is also urged in favour of this opinion, that the time after his death would have been described as the first year of Jotham. The design, however, may have been to fix, not the reign in which he saw the vision, but the nearest remarkable event. Besides, *the first year of Jotham* would have been ambiguous, because his reign is reckoned from two different epochs, the natural death of his father, and his civil death, when smitten with the leprosy, after which he resided in a separate house, and the government was administered by Jotham as prince-regent, who was therefore virtually king before he was such formally, and is accordingly described in the very same context as having reigned sixteen and twenty years (2 Kings xv. 30, 33). It does not follow, however, that by Uzziah's death the Prophet here intends his leprosy, as the Targum and some of the rabbins suppose, but merely that the mention of Uzziah is no proof that the vision was seen before he died.—Abarbenel and Rosenmüller refer the epithets *high* and *lofty* to the Lord, as in chap. lvii. 15, and Calvin understands by the *train* the edging of the cloth which covered the throne. But the common explanation is in either case more natural. The conjunction before אֶרְאֶה is not to be connected with הָיָה understood (Hendewerk), or rendered *also* (English version), but explained as an example of a common Hebrew idiom which prefixes this particle to the apodosis of a sentence, especially when the first clause contains a specification of time. It is here substantially equivalent to *then*, and is so rendered by Junius and Tremellius, Gesenius, Henderson, and others.

2. He sees the Lord not only enthroned but attended by his ministers. *Seraphim*, burning spirits, *standing above it*, the throne, or, *above him* that sat upon it. *Six wings, six wings, to one, i. e.* to each. *With two he covers his face*, as a sign of reverence towards God, *and with two he covers his feet*, for the same purpose, or to conceal himself from mortal view, *and with two he flies*, to execute God's will. The Hebrew word *seraphim* is retained by the Septuagint, Peshito, and Vulgate, but by the Targum paraphrased as *holy ministers*. It is rightly explained by Kimchi and Abulwalid as meaning *angels of fire*, from שָׂרַף to burn, the name being descriptive either of their essence, or, as Clericus supposes, of their ardent love, or according to Grotius, of God's wrath which they execute. Lightfoot supposes a particular allusion to the burning of the temple, which is needless and unnatural. This reference to heat as well as light, to something terrible as well as splendid, does away with Gesenius's objection that the root means to burn, not to shine, and also with his own derivation of the noun from the Arabic شريف *noble*, because angels are the nobility of heaven, and Michael is called one of the chief princes (Dan. x. 13). Still less attention is due to the notion that the word is connected in its origin with *Serapis* (Hitzig) and signifies *serpents* (Umbreit), *sphinxes* (Knobel), mixed forms like the cherubim (Ewald), or the cherubim themselves (Hendewerk). The word occurs elsewhere only as the name of the *fiery serpents* of the wilderness (Num. xxi. 6, 8; Deut. viii. 15), described by Isaiah (xiv. 29; xxx. 6) as *flying serpents*. The transfer of the name to beings so dissimilar rests on their possession of two common attributes. Both are described as *winged*, and both as *burning*. Umbreit considers *standing* as synonymous with *serving*, because servants are often said in the Old Testament to *stand before* their masters.—But it is better to retain the proper meaning, not as implying necessarily that they rested on the earth or any other solid surface, but that they were stationary, even in the air. This will remove all objection

to the version *above him*, which may also be explained as describing the relative position of persons in a standing and sitting posture.   There is no need therefore of the rendering *above it*, which is given in our Bible, nor of taking the compound preposition in the unusual sense of *near* (Grotius, Henderson), or *near above* (Junius), *around* (Sept. Gesen. Ewald), or *around above* (Targ. Cocceius, Arg. Umbr.)   The repetition of the phrase *six wings* supplies the place of a distributive pronoun (Gesen. § 118, 5.)   The version *six pairs of wings* rests on an entire misconception of the Hebrew dual, which is never a periphrasis of the number two, but is simply a peculiar plural form belonging to nouns which denote things that naturally exist in pairs.   Hence the numeral prefixed always denotes the number, not of pairs, but of individual objects.   (See Ewald's Heb. Gr. § 365).   The future form of the verbs denotes continued and habitual action.   According to Origen, there were only two seraphs, and these were the Son and Holy Spirit, who are here described as covering, not their own face and feet, but the face and feet of the Father, to imply that although they are his revealers, they conceal the beginning and the end of his eternity.   Jerome denounces this ingenious whim as impious, but retains the same construction (faciem ejus, pedes ejus).   The Chaldee paraphrase is, "with two he covered his face, *lest he should see;* with two he covered his body, *lest he should be seen;* and with two he *served.*"   The covering of the feet may, however, according to oriental usage, be regarded as a reverential act, equivalent in import to the hiding of the face.

3. He now describes the seraphim as praising God in an alternate or responsive doxology.   *And this cried to this, i. e.* to one another, *and said, Holy, Holy, Holy, (is) Jehovah of hosts, the fulness of the whole earth,* that which fills the whole earth, *is his glory!*   It was commonly agreed among the Fathers, that only two seraphim are mentioned here, and this opinion is maintained by Hendewerk.   It cannot be proved, however, from the words *this to this*, which are elsewhere used in reference to a greater number.   (See Exod. xiv. 20 ; xxxvi. 10 ; Jer. xlvi. 16.)   Clericus explains *this to this* as relating not to the *cry* but the position of those crying, *alter ad alterum conversus.*   Rosenmüller understands the triune repetition as implying that the words were uttered first by one choir, then by another, and lastly by the two together, which is a very artificial hypothesis.   The allusion to the Trinity in this τϱισάγιον is the more probable because different parts of the chapter are referred in the New Testament to the three persons of the Godhead.   Calvin and Cocceius admit that the doctrine of the Trinity cannot be proved from this expression, and that a like repetition is used elsewhere simply for the sake of emphasis.   See for example Jer. vii. 4, xxii. 9 ; Ezek. xxi. 27.   But according to J. H. Michaelis, even there the idea of trinity in unity was meant to be suggested (cum unitate conjuncta triplicitas).   *Holy* is here understood by most interpreters as simply denoting moral purity, which is certainly the prominent idea.   Most probably, however, it denotes the whole divine perfection, that which *separates* or distinguishes between God and his creatures.   " I am God and not man, the Holy One in the midst of thee," Hos. xi. 9.   On the etymology and usage of this word, see Hengstenberg on Ps. xxii. 4, and xxix. 9.   Grotius strangely restricts its import by referring it in this case to God's righteousness in dealing with the king and people.   Umbreit supposes the idea of a separate or personal God, as opposed to the pantheistic notion, to be included in the meaning of the term.   Grotius and Junius understand by כָּל־הָאָרֶץ *all the land;* Luther and Hendewerk, *all lands;* the last of which, although inaccurate in form, is

really synonymous with *all the earth,* and the former is forbidden by the strength of the expressions in the text and context. Clericus makes *glory* not the subject but the predicate : *the fulness of the earth,* all that the earth contains, *is thy glory,* or promotes it. But the common construction is sustained by the analogy of chap. viii. 8, where *fulness of the earth* is the predicate, and that of the prayer and prediction in Ps. lxxii. 19 (let the whole earth be filled with his glory), and Num. xiv. 21 (all the earth shall be filled with the glory of Jehovah). The words may have reference not only to the present but the future, implying that the judgments about to be denounced against the Jews, should be connected with the general diffusion of God's glory. There may also be allusion to the cloud which filled the temple, as if he had said, the presence of God shall no longer be restricted to one place, but the whole earth shall be full of it. By the *glory* of God J. H. Michaelis understands his essence (Wesen) or God himself. But the idea of special manifestation seems to be not only expressed but prominent. The same writer renders יהוה צבאות, here and elsewhere, *God of gods.* Clericus as usual makes it mean *God of armies* or *battles.* The Hebrew word is retained by the Septuagint, Luther, Augusti, and Umbreit. The use of the preterite at the beginning of the verse is probably euphonic. The *Vav* has no conversive influence, because not preceded by a future verb (Nordh. § 219).

4. The effect of this doxology, and of the whole supernatural appearance, is described. *Then stirred,* or shook, *the bases of the thresholds at the voice that cried,* or *at the voice of the one crying, and the house is filled with smoke.* The words אמות הספים are explained to mean the *lintel* or upper part of the door-frame, by the Septuagint, Luther, and J. D. Michaelis. The Vulgate gives the second word the sense of *hinges* (superliminaria cardinum). It is now commonly admitted to mean *thresholds,* and the other word *foundations.* The common version, *posts,* is also given by Clericus and Vitringa. The door may be particularly spoken of, because the prophet was looking through it from the court without into the interior. The participle *crying* may agree with *voice* directly, *voce clamante* (Junius and Tremellius), or with *seraph* understood. Clericus makes it a collective, at the voice of those crying, in which he is followed by Gesenius and others ; but Hendewerk supposes the singular form to intimate that only one cried at a time. Cocceius and J. H. Michaelis understand it to mean *every one* that cried. By *smoke* Knobel and others understand a cloud or vapour shewing the presence of Jehovah. Most interpreters, however, understand it in its proper sense of *smoke,* as the natural attendant of the fire which blazed about the throne of God, or of that which burned upon the altar, as in Lev. xvi. 13, the mercy-seat is said to be covered with a " cloud of incense." In either case it was intended to produce a solemn awe in the beholder. The reflexive sense, *it filled itself,* given to the last verb by Hitzig, Hendewerk, Ewald, and Umbreit, is not so natural as the simple passive, *it was filled* or *it became full.*

5. The Prophet now describes himself as filled with awe, not only by the presence of Jehovah, but also by a deep impression of his own sinfulness, especially considered as unfitting him to praise God, or to be his messenger, and therefore represented as residing in the organs of speech. *And I said,* when I saw and heard these things, then I said, *Woe is me,* woe to me, or alas for me, a phrase expressing lamentation and alarm, *for I am undone,* or destroyed, *for a man of impure lips,* as to the lips, *am I, and in the midst of a people impure of lips,* of impure lips, *I am dwelling,* and am

therefore undone, *for the King, Jehovah of hosts, my eyes have seen.* The allusion is not merely to the ancient and prevalent belief that no one could see God and live (Gen. xxxii. 30 ; Judges vi. 22–24, xiii. 22 ; Exod. iv. 10, 12 ; xxxiii. 20 ; 1 Sam. vi. 19), but to the aggravation of the danger arising from the moral contrast between God and the beholder.—According to an old interpretation, נִדְמֵיתִי is a statement of the reason why he was alarmed, to wit, because he had kept silence, *quia tacui* (Vulgate), either when he heard the praises of the seraphim, or when it was his duty to have spoken in God's name. The last sense is preferred by Grotius, the first by Lowth (I am struck dumb), and with some modification by J. D. Michaelis (that I must be dumb). This sense is also given to the verb by Aquila, Symmachus, Theodotion, the Peshito, and in some copies of the Septuagint, the common text of which has κατανένυγμαι, I am smitten with compunction. Most other writers, ancient and modern, understand the word as meaning *I am 'ruined* or *destroyed.* It is possible, however, as suggested by Vitringa, that an allusion was intended to the meaning of the verb in its ground-form, in order to suggest that his guilty silence or unfitness to speak was the cause of the destruction which he felt to be impending. Above sixty manuscripts and several editions read נדמתי, which, as Henderson observes, is probably a mere orthographical variation, not affecting the sense. The lips are mentioned as the seat of his depravity, because its particular effect, then present to his mind, was in capacity to speak for God or in his praise. That it does not refer to official unfaithfulness in his prophetic office, is apparent from the application of the same words to the people. The preterite form of the verb implies that the deed was already done and the effect already certain. The substitution of the present, by Luther and many of the late writers, weakens the expression.

6. He now proceeds to describe the way in which he was relieved from this distress by a symbolical assurance of forgiveness. *And there flew* (or then flew) *to me one of the seraphim, and in his hand a live coal* (or a hot stone) ; *with tongs he took it from off* (or *from upon*) *the altar ;* of incense, according to Hendewerk and others, but according to Grotius, that of burnt-offering, which stood without the temple in the court where the Prophet is supposed to have been stationed. Both these interpretations take for granted the necessity of adhering to the precise situation and dimensions of the earthly temple, whereas this seems merely to have furnished the scenery of the majestic vision. Knobel understands by the altar the golden altar seen by John in heaven, Rev. viii. 3, ix. 13. All that is necessary to the understanding of the vision is, that the scene presented was a temple, and included an altar. The precise position of the altar or of the Prophet is not only unimportant, but forms no part of the picture as here set before us. As רִצְפָּה elsewhere means a *pavement*, and its verbal root *to pave*, and as the Arabs call by the same name the heated stones which they employ in cooking, most modern writers have adopted Jerome's explanation of the word, as meaning a hot stone taken from the altar, which was only a consecrated hearth or fire-place. The old interpretation *coal* is retained by Hendewerk, who denies that stones were ever used upon the altar. In the last clause either personal or the relative pronoun may be supplied, *he took it*, or *which he took;* but the former (which is given by Hendewerk, De Wette, and Umbreit) seems to agree better with the order of the words in Hebrew. The word translated *tongs* is elsewhere used to signify the *snuffers* of the golden candlestick, and tongs are not named among the furniture of the altars ; but such an implement seems to be indispensable, and the Hebrew

word may be applied to anything in the nature of a forceps.—Hitzig and others, who regard the seraphim as serpents, sphinxes, or mixed forms, are under the necessity of explaining *hand* to mean *forefoot* or the like.   Nothing in the whole passage implies any variation from the human form, except in the addition of wings, which are expressly mentioned.

7. *And he caused it to touch* (*i. e.* laid it on) *my mouth, and said, Lo, this hath touched thy lips, and thy iniqui'y is gone, and thy sin shall be atoned for* (or forgiven).   In the Chaldee Paraphrase the *coal* from off the *altar* is transformed into a *word* from the *shechinah*, which is put into the Prophet's mouth, denoting his prophetic inspiration.   So Jeremiah says : " The Lord put forth his hand, and touched my mouth ; and the Lord said unto me, Behold, I have put my words in thy mouth" (Jer. i. 9).   And Daniel : " One like the similitude of the sons of men touched my lips, then I opened my mouth and spake" (Dan. x.ᵃ16).   Hence the Rabbins and Grotius understand the act of the seraph in the case before us as a symbol of prophetic inspiration.   But this leaves unexplained the additional circumstance, not mentioned in the case of Jeremiah or Daniel, that the Prophet's lips were not only touched, but touched with fire.   This is explained by Jerome as an emblem of the Holy Spirit, and by others as a symbol of purification in general.   But the mention of the altar and the assurance of forgiveness, or rather of atonement, makes it far more natural to take the application of fire as a symbol of expiation by sacrifice, although it is not necessary to suppose, with J. D. Michaelis, that the Prophet actually saw a victim burning on the altar.   The fire is applied to the lips for a twofold reason : first, to shew that the particular impediment of which the Prophet had complained was done away ; and secondly, to shew that the gift of inspiration is included, though it does not constitute the sole or chief meaning of the symbol.   The gift of prophecy could scarcely be described as having taken away sin, although it might naturally accompany the work of expiation.   The preterite and future forms are here combined, perhaps to intimate, first, that the pardon was already granted, and then that it should still continue.   This, at least, seems better than arbitrarily to confound the two as presents.

8. The assurance of forgiveness produces its usual effect of readiness to do God's will. *And I heard the voice of the Lord saying, Whom shall I send, and who will go for us ?   And I said, Here am I* (literally, *behold me,* or *lo I* am), *send me.*   The form of expression in the first clause may imply that the speaker was now invisible, perhaps concealed by the smoke which filled the house.   According to Jerome, the question here recorded was not addressed to Isaiah himself, because it was intended to elicit a spontaneous offer upon his part.   " Non dicit Dominus quem ire præcipiat, sed proponit audientibus optionem, ut voluntas præmium consequatur."   The same idea is suggested by J. H. Michaelis and Umbreit.   *For us* is regarded by Vitringa as emphatic, " Who will go for us, and not for himself, or any other object ?"   But the phrase is probably equivalent to saying, "Who will be our messenger ?"   This is the version actually given by Luther, J. D. Michaelis, and Gesenius.   Most of the other German writers follow the Vulgate version, *quis nobis ibit ?*   The plural form *us,* instead of *me,* is explained by Gesenius, Barnes, and Knobel, as a mere *pluralis majestaticus,* such as kings and princes use at this day.   Hitzig denies the existence of that idiom among the orientals, either ancient or modern, and undertakes to give a metaphysical solution, by saying that the speaker looks upon himself as both the subject and object of address.   Kimchi and

Grotius represent the Lord as speaking, not in his own name merely, but in that of his angelic council (tanquam de sententia concilii angelorum), and the same view is taken by Clericus and Rosenmüller. The Peshito omits *for us* while the Septuagint supplies instead of it the words *to this people,* and the Targum, *to teach*—"Whom shall I send to prophesy, and who will go to teach ?" Jerome's explanation of the plural, as implying a plurality of persons in the speaker, is approved by Calvin, who was doubtful with respect to the τρισάγιον in ver. 3. This explanation is the only one that accounts for the difference of number in the verb and pronoun— "Whom *shall I send,* and who will go *for us* ?" Jerome compares it with the words of Christ, "Ego et Pater unum sumus ; *unum* ad naturam referimus, *sumus* ad personarum diversitatem." The phrase הִנְנִי is the usual idiomatic Hebrew answer to a call by name, and commonly implies a readiness for service. J. D. Michaelis translates it *I am ready.* A beautiful commentary upon this effect of pardoned sin is afforded in David's penitential prayer, Ps. li. 12-15.

9. The Prophet now receives his commission, together with a solemn declaration that his labours will be fruitless. This prediction is clothed in the form of an exhortation or command addressed to the people themselves, for the purpose of bringing it more palpably before them, and of aggravating their insanity and wickedness in ruining themselves after such a warning. *And he said, Go and say to this people, Hear indeed,* or hear on, *but understand not ; and see indeed,* or continue to see, *but know not.* In most predictions some obscurity of language is required to secure their full accomplishment. But here where the blindness and infatuation of the people are foretold, they are allowed an abundant opportunity of hindering its fulfilment if they will. Not only is their insensibility described in the strongest terms, implying extreme folly as well as extreme guilt, but, as if to provoke them to an opposite course, they are exhorted, with a sort of solemn irony, to do the very thing which would inevitably ruin them, but with an explicit intimation of that issue in the verse ensuing. This form of speech is by no means foreign from the dialect of common life. As J. D. Michaelis well observes, it is as if one man should say to another in whose good resolutions and engagements he had no faith, " Go now and do the very opposite of all that you have said. A similar expression is employed by Christ himself when he says to the Jews (Mat. xxiii. 32), *Fill ye up then the measure of your fathers.* The Septuagint version renders the imperatives as futures, and this version is twice quoted in the New Testament (Mat. xiii. 14, Acts xxviii. 26), as giving correctly the essential meaning of the sentence as a prophecy, though stripped of its peculiar form as an ironical command. J. H. Michaelis and Gesenius make even the original expression a strict prophecy, by rendering the future forms as futures proper (nec tamen intelligetis) on the ground that אַל is sometimes simply equivalent to לֹא, or that the second of two imperatives sometimes expresses the result dependent on the act denoted by the first. But even admitting these assertions, both of which may be disputed, the predominant usage is so clear as to forbid any departure from the proper sense of the imperatives without a strong necessity, which, as we have seen, does not exist. Another mode of softening the apparent harshness of the language is adopted by the Targum, which converts the sentence into a description of the people, " who hear indeed, but understand not, and see indeed but know not." Ewald and some older writers understand *this people* as a phrase expressive of displeasure and contempt intentionally substituted for the

phrase *my people*, not only here but in several other places. See for example Exod. xxxii. 9 ; Isa. ix. 16, xxix. 13 ; Jer. vii. 16. The idiomatic repetition of the verbs *hear* and *see* is disregarded in translation by Luther, Clericus, and De Wette, and copied more or less exactly, by the Septuagint (ἀκοῇ ἀκούσετε, βλέποντες βλέψετε), the Vulgate (audite audientes, videte visionem), Calvin, Cocceius, and Vitringa. Neither of these methods conveys the true force of the original expression, which is clearly emphatic, and suggests the idea of distinctness, clearness (J. D. Michaelis), or of mere external sight and hearing (Augusti), or of abundant sight and hearing (J. H. Michaelis, *sufficientissime*), or of continued sight and hearing (Junius, *indesinenter*), probably the last which is adopted by Gesenius, Hitzig, Hendwerk, Henderson, and Ewald. Maurer makes the prominent idea that of repetition (iterum iterumque). The idea of hearing and seeing without perceiving may have been proverbial among the Jews, as it seems to have been among the Greeks, from the examples given by Wetstein in his note on Mat. xiii. 13. Demosthenes expressly cites it as a *proverb* (παροιμία) ὁρῶντας μὴ ὁρᾶν καὶ ἀκούοντας μὴ ἀκούειν, and the Prometheus of Æschylus employs a like expression, in describing the primitive condition of mankind on which one of the Greek scholiasts observes, διότι νοῦν καὶ φρόνησιν οὐκ εἶχον.

10. As the foregoing verse contains a prediction of the people's insensibility, but under the form of a command or exhortation to themselves, so this predicts the same event, as the result of Isaiah's labours, under the form of a command to him. *Make fat*, gross, callous, *the heart of this people*, *i. e.* their affections or their minds in general, *and its ears make heavy*, dull or hard of hearing, *and its eyes smear*, close or blind, *lest it see with its eyes*, *and with its ears hear, and its heart understand*, perceive or feel, *and it turn to me, i. e.* repent and be converted, *and be healed*, or literally *and one heal it*, the indefinite construction being equivalent in meaning to a passive. The thing predicted is judicial blindness, as the natural result and righteous retribution of the national depravity. This end would be promoted by the very preaching of the truth, and therefore a command to preach was in effect a command to blind and harden them. The act required of the Prophet is here joined with its ultimate effect, while the intervening circumstances, namely, the people's sin and the withholding of God's grace, are passed by in silence. But although not expressed, they are implied, in this command to *preach the people callous*, blind, and deaf, as J. D. Michaelis phrases it. The essential idea is their insensibility, considered as the fruit of their own depravity, as the execution of God's righteous judgment, and as the only visible result of Isaiah's labours. " Deus sic præcipit judicialiter, populus agit criminaliter, propheta autem ministerialiter ' (J. H. Michaelis). In giving Isaiah his commission, it was natural to make the last of these ideas prominent, and hence the form of exhortation or command in which the prophecy is here presented. Make them insensible, not by an immediate act of power, nor by any direct influence whatever, but by doing your duty, which their wickedness and God's righteous judgments will allow to have no other effect. In this sense the prophet might be said to *preach them callous*. In other cases, where his personal agency no longer needed to be set forth or alluded to, the verse is quoted, not as a command, but a description of the people, or as a declaration of God's agency in making them insensible. Thus in Mat. xiii. 15, and in Acts xxviii. 26, the Septuagint version is retained, in which the people's own guilt is the prominent idea—" for this people's heart is waxed gross, and their ears are dull of hearing, and their eyes they have closed, lest," &c. In John

xii. 40, on the other hand, the sentence takes a new form, in order to bring
out distinctly the idea of *judicial* blindness—" he hath blinded their eyes
and hardened their heart, lest," &c. Both these ideas are in fact included
in the meaning of the passage, though its forms are different, in order to
suit the occasion upon which it was originally uttered. There is no need,
therefore, of supposing, with Cocceius, that the verbs in the first clause are
infinitives with preterites understood (impinguando impinguavit—aggra-
vando aggravavit—oblinendo oblivit), to which there is besides a philological
objection (*vide supra*, chap. v. 5). The paraphrase in John no more proves
that the verse must be directly descriptive of God's agency, than that in
Acts and Matthew proves that it must be descriptive of the people's own
agency, which sense is actually put upon Cocceius's construction by Abarbenel, who first proposed it, and who thinks that the verbs must either be
reflexive—" the heart of this people has made itself fat, their ears have
made themselves heavy, their eyes have shut themselves,"—or must all
agree with לְבּו—" the heart of this people has made itself fat, it has made
their ears heavy, it has closed their eyes." That a divine agency is really
implied, though not expressed as Cocceius supposes, is clear from the
paraphrase in John xii. 40, and creates no difficulty here that is not common to a multitude of passages, so that nothing would be gained by explaining it away in this one instance. " Absque hoc testimonio," says Jerome,
" manet eadem quæstio in ecclesiis, et aut cum ista solventur et ceteræ,
aut cum ceteris et hæc indissolubilis erit."—The same considerations which
have been presented render it unnecessary to suppose, with Henderson and
others, that the command to blind and harden is merely a command to predict that the people will be blind and hard ; a mode of explanation which
may be justified in certain cases by the context or by exegetical necessity,
but which is here gratuitous and therefere inadmissible.—Gesenius, Augusti,
and De Wette, understand by *heart* the seat of the affections, and accordingly translate יָבִין by *feel ;* but the constant usage of the latter in the sense
of understanding or perceiving seems to require that the former should be
taken to denote the whole mind or rational soul. The ancient versions take
לְבָבוֹ as an ablative of instrument, in which they are followed by Luther,
the English Version (with their heart), Junius, Vitringa, J. D. Michaelis,
Lowth, Augusti, and Henderson. Calvin makes it the subject of the verb
(cor ejus intelligat), in which he is followed by Gesenius, Hitzig, De Wette,
Ewald, Umbreit. The last construction is more simple in itself, but breaks
the uniformity of the sentence, as the other verbs of this clause all agree
with *people* as their subject.—Clericus takes רְפָא as a noun and reads *lest
there be healing*, and the same sense is put upon it as a verb by Junius and
Vitringa. The Septuagint and Vulgate substitute the first for the third
person, *and I heal them.* Cocceius refers the verb to God directly, *lest he
heal them*, in accordance with his explanation of the first clause. Most of
the modern writers assume an impersonal or indefinite construction, which
may either be resolved into a passive (Gesenius. De Wette, Henderson), or
retained in the translation (Hitzig, Maurer, Hendewerk, Ewald). Kimchi
explains the healing mention to be pardon following repentance. The representation of sin as a spiritual malady is frequent in the Scriptures.
Thus David prays (Ps. xli. 4), " Heal my soul, for I have sinned against
thee." Instead of *heal*, in the case before us, the Targum and Peshito
have *forgive*, which is substituted likewise in the quotation or rather the
allusion to this verse in Mark iv. 12.

11. *And I said, How long, Lord ? And he said, Until that cities are*

*desolate for want of an inhabitant, and houses for want of men, and the
land shall be desolated, a waste,* or utterly desolate. The spiritual death of
the people should be followed by external desolation. Hitzig understands
the Prophet to ask how long he must be the bearer of this thankless message; but the common explanation is no doubt the true one, that he asks
how long the blindness of the people shall continue, and is told until it
ruins them and drives them from their country. Grotius supposes a particular allusion to Sennacherib's invasion, Clericus to that of Nebuchadnezzar; but as the foregoing description is repeatedly applied in the New
Testament to the Jews who were contemporary with our Saviour, the
threatening must be equally extensive, and equivalent to saying that
land should be completely wasted, not at one time but repeatedly.
Kimchi, who also understands the verse as referring to the Babylonian conquest, finds a climax in the language, which is much more appropriate
however when applied to successive periods and events.—The acumulation
of particles עַד אֲשֶׁר אִם is supposed by Henderson to indicate a long lapse
of time; but it seems to differ from the simple form only as *until* differs
from *until that* or *until when.* On the meaning of מָאֵין *vide supra,*
chap. v. 9.

12. This verse continues the answer to the Prophet's question in the
verse preceding. *And* (until) *Jehovah shall have put far off* (removed to a
distance) *the men* (or people of the country), *and great* (much or abundant)
shall be that which is left (of unoccupied forsaken ground) *in the midst of
the land.* This is little more than a repetition, in other words, of the declaration in the verse preceding. The Septuagint and Vulgate make the
last clause not a threatening but a promise that those left in the land shall
be multiplied. Clericus and Lowth understand it to mean " there shall be
many a deserted woman in the land." Gesenius, " many ruins." Ewald,
" a great vacancy or void (Leere)." Most other writers take עֲזוּבָה as an
abstract, meaning desolation or desertion. But the simplest construction
seems to be that of Henderson and Knobel, who make it agree with the
land itself, and understand the clause as threatening that there shall be a
great extent of unoccupied forsaken land. The terms of this verse may be
applied to all the successive desolations of the country, not excepting that
most extreme and remarkable of all which exists at the present moment.

13. The chapter closes with a repetition and extension of the threatening,
but in such a form as to involve a promise of the highest import. While it
is threatened that the stroke shall be repeated on the remnant that survives
its first infliction, it is promised that there shall be such a remnant after every
repetition to the last. *And yet*—even after the entire desolation which had
first been mentioned—*in it*—the desolated land—(there shall remain) *a tenth*
or *tithe*—here put indefinitely for a small proportion—*and* (even this tenth)
shall return and be for a consuming—*i. e.* shall again be consumed—but still
not utterly, for—*like the terebinth and like the oak*—the two most common
forest trees of Palestine—*which in falling*—in their fallen state, or when
felled—*have substance* or vitality *in them*—so *a holy seed* shall be, or is *the
substance*—vital principle—*of it*—the tenth or remnant which appeared to be
destroyed. However frequently the people may seem to be destroyed, there
shall still be a surviving remnant, and however frequently that very remnant
may appear to perish, there shall still be a remnant of the remnant left, and
this indestructible residuum shall be the holy seed, the true Church, the
λεῖμμα κατ' ἐκλογὴν χάριτος (Rom. xi. 5). This prediction was fulfilled, not
once for all, but again and again; not only in the vine-dressers and husband-

men left by Nebuchadnezzar and afterwards destroyed in Egypt; not only in the remnant that survived the destruction of the city by the Romans, and increased until again destroyed by Adrian; but in the present existence of the Jews as a peculiar people, notwithstanding the temptations to amalgamate with others, notwithstanding persecutions and apparent extirpations; a fact which can only be explained by the prediction that "all Israel shall be saved" (Rom. xi. 26). As in many former instances, throughout the history of the chosen people, under both dispensations, "even so, at this present time also, there is a remnant according to the election of grace." The reference of *holy seed* to Christ (as in Gal. iii. 16) restricts the verse to the times before the advent, and is here forbidden by the application of the Hebrew phrase to Israel in general (Ezra ix. 2, Comp. Isaiah iv. 3, lxv. 9), a meaning which is here not changed but only limited, upon the principle that "they are not all Israel which are of Israel" (Rom. ix. 6). As thus explained, the threatening of the verse involves a promise. There is no need therefore of attempting to convert it into a mere promise, by giving to בָּעַר the active sense of consuming or destroying enemies (De Dieu), or by making שָׁבָה signify *return* from exile (Calvin), and connecting לְבָעֵר with what follows—"be destroyed like the terebinth and oak," *i.e.* only destroyed like them. The passive sense of הָיְתָה לְבָעֵר is fixed by the analogy of Num. xxiv. 22, and Isaiah xliv. 15. The idiomatic use of the verb *return* to qualify another verb by denoting repetition is of constant occurrence, and is assumed here by almost all interpreters, ancient and modern. Besides, the tenth left *in* the land could hardly be described as returning *to* it. That בָעַר denotes purification is a mere rabbinical conceit. מַצֶּבֶת has been variously explained to mean the sap (Targum), root (De Wette), trunk (Gesenius), germ (Hitzig), &c. But the sense which seems to agree best with the connection and the etymology is that of *substance* or *subsistence*, understanding thereby the vitality, or that which is essential to the life and reproduction of the tree. שַׁלֶּכֶת occurs elsewhere only in 1 Chron. xxvi. 16, where it seems to be the name of one of the temple gates. Hence Aben Ezra supposes the Prophet to allude to two particular and well-known trees at or near this gate, while other Jewish writers understand him as referring to the timber of the gate or of the causeway leading to it (1 Kings x. 5). The same interpretation is adopted by Junius, and Cocceius explains the word in either case as an appellative meaning *causeway*. But with these exceptions, all interpreters appear to be agreed in making the word descriptive of something in the condition of the trees, the spreading of their branches (Vulgate), the casting of their leaves (Targum) or of their fruit (Septuagint), or the casting down or felling of the tree itself, which last is commonly adopted. Instead of בם, referring to the trees, more than a hundred manuscripts read בה, referring to the tenth or to the land. The suffix in the last word of the verse is referred to the land or people by Ewald and Maurer, but with more probability by others to the tenth, which is the nearest antecedent and affords a better sense.

Chapter 7

HERE begins a series of connected prophecies (chaps. vii.–xii.), belonging to the reign of Ahaz, and relating in general to the same great subjects, the deliverance of Judah from Syria and Israel, its subsequent subjection to Assyria and other foreign powers, the final destruction of its enemies, the advent of Messiah, and the nature of his kingdom. The series admits of different divisions, but it is commonly agreed that one distinct portion is contained in the seventh chapter. Hendewerk and Henderson suppose it to include two independent prophecies (vers. 1–9 and 10–25), and Ewald separates the same two parts as distinct portions of the same prophecy. The common division is more natural, however, which supposes vers. 1–16 to contain a promise of deliverance from Syria and Israel, and vers. 17–25 a threatening of worse evils to be brought upon Judah by the Assyrians in whom they trusted.

The chapter begins with a brief historical statement of the invasion of Judah by Rezin and Pekah, and of the fear which it excited, to relieve which Isaiah is commissioned to meet Ahaz in a public place, and to assure him that there is nothing more to fear from the invading powers, that their evil design cannot be accomplished, that one of them is soon to perish, and that in the mean time both are to remain without enlargement, vers. 1–9.

Seeing the king to be incredulous, the prophet invites him to assure himself by chosing any sign or pledge of the event, which he refuses to do, under the pretext of confidence in God, but is charged with unbelief by the Prophet, who nevertheless renews the promise of deliverance in a symbolical form, and in connection with a prophecy of the miraculous conception and nativity of Christ, both as a pledge of the event, and as a measure of the time in which it is to take place, vers. 10–16.

To this assurance of immediate deliverance, he adds a threatening of ulterior evils, to arise from the Assyrian protection which the king preferred to that of God, to wit, the loss of independence, the successive domination of foreign powers, the harassing and predatory occupation of the land by strangers, the removal of its people, the neglect of tillage, and the transformation of its choicest vineyards, fields, and gardens, into wastes or pastures, vers. 17–25.

1. Rezin, the king of Damascene Syria or Aram, from whom Uzziah had taken Elath, a port on the Red Sea, and restored it to Judah (2 Kings xiv. 22), appears to have formed an alliance with Pekah, the murderer and successor of Pekahiah, king of Israel (2 Kings xv. 27), during the reign of Jotham (ib. ver. 37), but to have deferred the actual invasion of Judah until that king's death, and the accession of his feeble son, in the first year of whose reign it probably took place, with most encouraging success, as the army of Ahaz was entirely destroyed, and 200,000 persons taken captive, who were afterwards sent back at the instance of the prophet Oded (2 Chron. xxviii. 5–15). But notwithstanding this success, they were unable to effect their main design, the conquest of Jerusalem, whether repelled by the natural strength and artificial defences of the place itself, or interrupted in the siege by the actual or dreaded invasion of their own dominions by the king of Assyria (2 Kings xvi. 7–9). It seems to be at a point of time between their first successes and their final retreat, that the Prophet's narrative begins. *And it was*—happened, came to pass—*in the days of Ahaz, son of Jotham, son of Uzziah, king of Judah, that Rezin king of Aram*—or Syria—*and Pekah, son of Remaliah, king of Israel, came up to*—or against—*Jerusalem to war against it; and he was not able to war against it.* As *war* is both a verb and a noun in English, it may be used to represent the Hebrew verb and noun in this sentence. Some give a different meaning to the two, making one mean to fight and the other to conquer (Vulgate) or take (Henderson); but this distinction is implied, not expressed, and the simple meaning of the words is that *he* (put by a com-

mon licence for *they*, or meaning *each of them*, or referring to Rezin as the principal (confederate) *could not* do what he attempted.   There is no need of taking יָכֹל in the absolute sense of *prevailing* (Vitringa), which would require a different construction.   It is sufficient to supply the idea of *success* in either case; they wished of course to war successfully against it, which they could not do.   Gesenius sets the first part of this chapter down as the production of another hand, because it speaks of Isaiah in the third person, and because the first verse nearly coincides with 2 Kings xvi. 5. But as that may just as well have been derived from this—a supposition favoured by the change of יָכֹל into יְכֹלוּ—and as the use of the third person is common among ancient writers, sacred and profane, Isaiah himself not excepted (chap. xx. 37, 38), there is no need even of supposing with Vitringa, that the last clause was added at a later period, by the sacred scribes, or with Hengstenberg and Ewald, that the verse contains a general summary, in which the issue of the war is stated by anticipation.   It is not improbable, indeed, that this whole prophecy was written some time after it was first delivered ; but even this supposition is not neecessary for the removal of the alleged difficulty, which arises wholly from assuming that this verse and the next relate to the beginning of the enterprise, when Rezin and Pekah first invaded *Judah*, whereas they relate to the attack upon *Jerusalem*, after the country had been ravaged, and the disappointment with which they are threatened below is the disappointment of their grand design upon the royal city, which was the more alarming in consequence of what they had already effected.   This view of the matter brings the two accounts in Kings and Chronicles into perfect harmony, without supposing what is here described to be either the first (Grotius, Usher), or second (Jerome, Theodoret, Jarchi, Vitringa, Rosenmüller), of two different invasions, or that although they relate to the same event (Lightfoot), the account in Chronicles is chargeable with ignorant exaggeration (Gesenius). Another view of the matter, which also makes the two accounts refer to one event, is that of Hengstenberg, who supposes the victory of Pekah described in Chronicles to have been the consequence of the unbelief of Ahaz, and his refusal to accept the divine promise.   But the promise, instead of being retracted, is renewed, and the other supposition that Pekah's victory preceded what is here recorded, seems to agree better with the terror of Ahaz, and with the comparison in ver. 3.   Either hypothesis, however, may be entertained, without materially affecting the details of the interpretation. The invaders are said to have *come up* to Jerusalem, not merely as a military phrase (Vitringa), nor with exclusive reference to its natural position (Knobel), its political pre-eminence (Henderson), or its moral elevation (C. B. Michaelis), but with allusion, more or less distinct, to all the senses in which the holy city was above all others.   On the construction of *Jerusalem* directly with the verb of motion, see Gesenius, § 116, 1.

2. *And it was told the house of David*—the court, the royal family, of Judah—*saying, Syria resteth*—or is resting—*upon Ephraim : and his heart*—i. e. the king's, as the chief and representative of the house of David—*and the heart of his people shook, like the shaking of the trees of a wood before a wind.*   This is commonly applied to the effect produced by the first news of the coalition between Rezin and Pekah or the junction of their forces.   The oldest writers understand the news to be that *Syria is confederate* or joined *with Ephraim* (Septuagint, Targum, Peshito, Vulgate, Calvin, English Version, &c.).   Some, however, read in violation of the accents נָחָה, and translate thus—*Syria is marching* or *leading his forces to*

wards Ephraim (J. D. Michaelis), or *with Ephraim* (Henderson). Others, *Syria relies upon*—or *is supported by*—*Ephraim* (Lowth, Barnes). Others, *Syria influences* or *controls Ephraim* (Vitringa). But most interpreters, especially the latest, *Syria is encamped upon* (the territory of) *Ephraim*, or, as Steudel understands it, *near* (the city of) *Ephraim*. It is equally natural, and more consistent with the history, to understand the words as having reference to a later date, *i. e.* either the time of the advance upon Jerusalem, or that of the retreat of the invaders, laden with the spoil of Judah, and with two hundred thousand captives. In the one case, *Syria, i. e.* the Syrian army, may be said to *rest upon* (the army of) *Ephraim*, in the modern military sense, with reference to their relative position on the field of battle; in the other, *Syria* may be described as literally *resting* or reposing in the territory of Ephraim, on its homeward march, and as thereby filling Ahaz with the apprehension of a fresh attack. Although neither of these explanations may seem altogether natural, they are really as much so as any of the others which have been proposed, and in a case where we have at best a choice of difficulties, these may claim the preference as tending to harmonize the prophecy with history as given both in Kings and Chronicles. We read in 2 Kings xix. 7–9, that Ahaz applied to Tiglathpileser king of Assyria, to help him against Syria and Israel, which he did. At what precise period of the war this alliance was formed, it is not easy to determine; but there seems to be no doubt that Ahaz, at the time here mentioned, was relying upon some human aid in preference to God.—The construction of the feminine verb נחה with the masculine ארם is to be explained, not by supplying מלכות (Jarchi) or עדת (Rosenmüller) before the latter, but by the idiomatic usage which connects the names of countries, where they stand for the inhabitants, with verbs of this form, as in Job. i. 15, 1 Sam. xvii. 21, and 2 Sam. viii. 6, where this very name is so construed.

3. From this alarm Isaiah is sent to free the king. *And Jehovah said to Isaiah son of Amoz, Go out to meet Ahaz, thou and Shearjashub thy son, to the end of the conduit of the upper pool, to the highway of the fuller's field.* The mention of these now obscure localities, although it detracts nothing from the general clearness of the passage, is an incidental proof of authenticity, which no later writer would or could have forged. The Upper Pool, which has been placed by different writers upon almost every side of Jerusalem, is identified by Robinson and Smith with a large tank at the head of the Valley of Hinnom, about seven hundred yards west north-west from the Jaffa gate. It is full in the rainy season, and its waters are then conducted by a small rude aqueduct to the vicinity of the gate just mentioned, and so to the Pool of Hezekiah within the walls. This aqueduct is probably the *conduit* mentioned in the text, and the *end* of this conduit the point where it enters the city, as appears from the fact, that when Rabshakeh afterwards conferred with the ministers of Hezekiah at this same spot, he was heard by the people on the city wall (chap. xxxvi. 2, 12.) From the same passage it may be inferred that this was a frequented spot, which some suppose to be the reason that Isaiah was directed to it, while others understand the direction as implying that Ahaz was about to fortify the city, or rather to cut off a supply of water from the invaders, as Hezekiah afterwards did when besieged by Sennacherib (2 Chron. xxxii. 4); an example often followed afterwards, particularly in the sieges of Jerusalem by Pompey, Titus, and Godfrey of Bouillon. The Prophet is therefore commanded to *go out*, not merely from his house, but from the city, *to meet*

Ahaz, which does not imply that the king was seeking him, or coming to him, but merely specifies the object which he was to seek himself. For the various opinions with respect to the position of the Upper Pool—so called in relation to the Lower Pool, mentioned in chap. xxii. 9, and situated lower down in the same valley, south of the Jaffa gate—see Rosenmüller, Gesenius, and Hitzig on this passage, Winer's Realwörterbuch s. v. Teiche, and Robinson's Palestine, vol. i. pp. 352, 483. The Fuller's Field was of course without the city, and the highway or causeway mentioned may have led either to it or along it, so as to divide it from the aqueduct. The command to take his son with him might be regarded merely as an incidental circumstance, but for the fact that the name *Shear-jashub* is significant, and as we may suppose it to have been already known, and the people were familiar with the practice of conveying instruction in this form, the very sight of the child would perhaps suggest a prophecy, or recall one previously uttered, or at least prepare the mind for one to come ; and accordingly we find in chap. x. 21 this very phrase employed, not as a name, but in its proper sense, *a remnant shall return*. Cocceius assigns two other reasons for the presence of the child—that he might early learn the duties of a prophet—and that the sight of him might prove to all who heard the ensuing prophecy, that the mother mentioned in ver. 14 could not be the Prophet's wife. But this precaution would have answered little purpose against modern licence of conjecture ; for Gesenius does not scruple to assume a second marriage.

4. The assurance, by which Ahaz is encouraged, is that the danger is over, that the fire is nearly quenched, that the enemies, who lately seemed like flaming firebrands of war, are now mere smoking ends of firebrands ; he is therefore exhorted to be quiet and confide in the divine protection. *And thou shalt say to him, Be cautious and be quiet*—or take care to be quiet— *fear not, nor let thy heart be soft, before*—or on account of—*these two smoking tails of firebrands, in the heat of the anger of Rezin and Syria and the son of Remaliah.* The comparison of Rezin and Pekah to the tails or ends of firebrands, instead of firebrands themselves, is not a mere expression of contempt, as most interpreters suppose, nor a mere intimation of their approaching fate, as Barnes and Henderson explain it, but a distinct allusion to the evil which they had already done, and which should never be repeated. If the emphasis were only in the use of the word *tails*, the tail of anything else would have been equally appropriate. The smoking remnant of a firebrand implies a previous flame, if not a conflagration. This confirms the conclusion before drawn, that Judah had already been ravaged, and that the narrative in Kings and Chronicles are perfectly consistent and relate to the same subject. The older versions construe the demonstrative with *firebrands*—" the tails of these two smoking firebrands ;" the moderns more correctly with *tails*—" these two tails or ends of smoking firebrands."—The last clause of the verse is not to be construed with עָשֵׁנִים— " smoking in the anger of Rezin," &c., but with the verbs preceding—" fear not, nor let thy heart be faint in the anger," &c. The reason implied in the connection is that the hot fire of their anger was now turned to smoke and almost quenched.—The distinct mention of Rezin and Syria, while Pekah is simply termed the son of Remaliah, is supposed by some to be intended to express contempt for the latter, though the difference may after all be accidental, or have only a rhythmical design. The patronymic, like our English surname, can be used contemptuously only when it indicates ignoble origin, in which sense it may be applied to Pekah, who was a

usurper, as the enemies of Napoleon always chose to call him Buonaparte, because the name betrayed an origin both foreign and obscure.

5. *Because Syria has devised,* meditated, purposed, *evil against thee, also Ephraim and Remaliah's son, saying.* Hendewerk, and most of the early writers, connect this with what goes before, as a further explanation of the king's terror—"fear not, nor let thy heart be faint, because Syria," &c. But Gesenius, Hitzig, Henderson, Ewald and Umbreit, make it the beginning of a sentence, the apodosis of which is contained in ver. 7—" because (or although) Syria has devised, &c., therefore (or nevertheless) thus saith the Lord," &c. The constructions may be blended by regarding this verse and the next as a link or connecting clause between the exhortation in ver. 4, and the promise in ver. 7. " Fear not because Syria and Israel thus threaten, for on that very account the Lord declares," &c. Here again Syria appears as the prime agent and controlling power, although Ephraim is added in the second clause. The suppression of Pekah's proper name in this clause, and of Rezin's altogether in the first, has given rise to various far-fetched explanations, though it seems in fact to shew, that the use of names in the whole passage is rather euphonic or rhythmical than significant.

6. The invaders themselves are now introduced as holding counsel or addressing one another, not at the present moment, but at the time when their plan was first concerted. *We will go up,* or let us go up, *into Judah,* or *against it,* although this is rather implied than expressed, *and vex* (*i.e.* harass or distress) *it, and make a breach in it,* (thereby subduing it) *to ourselves, and let us make a king in the midst of it, to wit, the son of Tabeal* or *Tabeel,* as the name is written out of pause, Ezra iv. 7. The feminine suffixes probably refer, not to Judah (Henderson) but to Jerusalem (Gesenius, Rosenmüller), although the same terms are applied to the whole country elsewhere (2 Chron. xxi. 17). The reference to Jerusalem is required by this history, according to which they did succeed in their attack upon the kingdom, but were foiled in their main design of conquering the royal city. The entrance into Judah was proposed only as a means to this end, and it is the failure of this end that is predicted in the next verse. The reference to the city is also recommended by the special reference to the capital cities of Syria and Ephraim in vers. 8, 9. נְקִיצֶנָּה is explained to mean *let us arouse her* by the Vulgate (suscitemus eam), Luther (auf-wecken), Calvin and others, which supposes the verb to be derived from הֵקִיץ (יָקַץ) *to awaken.* Others, deriving it from קָצַץ *to cut off,* explain it to mean *let us dismember* or *divide it* (Vitringa, Augusti), or *subvert, destroy it* (Peshito, J. D. Michaelis, Schroeder, Henderson). The simplest etymology, and that most commonly adopted, derives it from קוּץ to be distressed or *terrified,* and in the Hiphil to *alarm* (Hitzig), or to *distress,* with special reference to the hardships of a siege (Kimchi, Aben Ezra, Cocceius, Rosenmüller, Gesenius, Ewald, &c.). *Oppress* (Barnes) is too indefinite. The other verb has also been variously explained, as meaning let us level it (from בִּקְעָה, a plain), let us tear it away (Vulgate: avellamus ad nos), let us divide or rend it (Luther, Cocceius, Alting, J. W. Michaelis, Vitringa, Barnes). It is now commonly agreed, however, that it means to *make a breach* or *opening* (Calvin: faire bresche ou ouverture, Hendewerk, Henderson), and thereby *take* or *conquer* (Ewald, Knobel). The creation of tributary kings by conquerors is mentioned elsewhere in the sacred history (*e.g.* 2 Kings xxiii. 34, xxiv. 17). *Son of Tabeal* like *Son of Remaliah,* is

commonly explained as a contemptuous expression, implying obscurity or mean extraction. But such an expression would hardly have been put into the mouths of his patrons, unless we suppose that they selected him expressly on account of his ignoble origin or insignificance, which is a very improbable assumption. They would be far more likely to bestow the crown on some prince, either of Ephraim or Syria, which some suppose to be implied in the Syriac form of the name, equivalent to the Hebrew *Tobijah* (Neh. ii. 15), and analogous to *Tabrimmon*, from whom Benhadad king of Syria was descended (1 Kings xv. 18). So in Ezra iv. 7. *Tabeel* is named as one of those who wrote to the king *in the Syrian* (Aramean) *tongue.* This whole speculation, though ingenious, and illustrated by Gesenius with a profusion of etymological learning (Comm. vol. i. p. 281, note), is probably fanciful, and certainly of no exegetical importance, which last is also true of Calvin's suggestion that the *Son of Tabeal* may have been a disaffected Jew. There is something curious in the Jewish explanation of the name by that form of the *cabbala* called *Albam* (because it puts *a* for *l*, *b*, for *m*, and so forth, as identical with רמלא (*i. q.* רמליה). A more important observation is, that this familiar reference *en passant* to the names of persons now forgotten, as if familiar to contemporary readers, is a strong incidental proof of authenticity.

7. *Thus saith the Lord Jehovah, it shall not stand*—or it shall not arise —*and it shall not be*, or come to pass. This, as was said before, is taken by Gesenius and others as the conclusion of a sentence beginning in ver. 5, but may just as naturally be explained as the commencement of a new one. The feminine verbs may be referred to *counsel* (עֵצָה) understood or taken indefinitely, which is a common Hebrew construction. (*Vide supra*, chap. i. 6.) As קוּם means both to *rise* and *stand*, the idea here expressed may be either that the thing proposed shall not even come into existence (Hitzig), or that it shall not continue or be permanent (Gesenius, Hengstenberg, Hendewerk, Ewald, Umbreit). The general sense is clear, viz., that their design should be defeated. The name יהוה, being here preceded by אֲדֹנָי takes the vowels of אֱלֹהִים. The accumulation of divine names is, as usual, emphatic, and seems here intended to afford a pledge of the event, derived from the supremacy and power of the Being who predicts it.

8, 9. The plans of the enemy cannot be accomplished, because God has decreed that while the kingdoms of Syria and Israel continue to exist, they shall remain without enlargement, or at least without the addition of Jerusalem or Judah to their territories. It shall not stand or come to pass, *because the head* (or capital) *of Aram is Damascus* (and shall be so still), *and the head* (chief or sovereign) *of Damascus is Rezin* (and shall be so still—and as for the other power there is as little cause of fear) *for in yet sixty and five years* (in sixty-five years more) *shall Ephraim be broken from a people* (*i. e.* from being a people, so as not to be a people—and even in the mean time, it shall not be enlarged by the addition of Judah) *for the head* (or capital) *of Ephraim is Samaria, and the head* (chief or sovereign) *of Samaria is Remaliah's son. If you will not believe* (it is) *because you are not to be established.* Here again Syria is the prominent object, and Ephraim subjoined, as if by an afterthought. The order of ideas is that Syria shall remain as it is, and as for Ephraim it is soon to be destroyed, but while it does last, it shall remain as it is likewise; Pekah shall never reign in any other capital, nor Samaria be the capital of any other kingdom. To this natural expression of the thought corresponds the rhythmical arrangement of the sentences, the first clause of the eighth verse answering exactly to the first clause of the ninth, while the two last clauses, though dissimilar, complete the measure.

> For the head of Syria is Damascus—
> And the head of Damascus Rezin—
> And in sixty-five years more, &c.
> And the head of Ephraim is Samaria—
> And the head of Samaria Remaliah's son —
> If ye will not believe, &c.

Whether this be poetry or not, its structure is as regular as that of any other period of equal length in the writings of Isaiah. As to the substance of these verses, the similar clauses have already been explained, as a prediction that the two invading powers should remain without enlargement. The first of the uneven clauses, *i.e.* the last of ver. 8, adds to this prediction, that Ephraim, or the kingdom of the ten tribes, shall cease to exist within a prescribed period, which period is so defined as to include the three successive strokes by which that power was annihilated—first, the invasion of Tiglath-pileser, two or three years after the date of this prediction (2 Kings xv. 29 ; xvi. 9)—then, the conquest of Samaria, and the deportation of the ten tribes, by Shalmaneser, about the sixth year of Hezekiah (2 Kings xvii. 6)—and finally, the introduction of another race by Esar-haddon in the reign of Manasseh (2 Kings xvii. 24 ; Ezra iv. 2 ; 2 Chron. xxxiii. 11). Within sixty-five years all these events were to occur, and Ephraim, in all these senses, was to cease to be a people. It seems then that the language of this clause has been carefully selected, so as to include the three events which might be represented us destructive of Ephraim, while in form it balances the last clause of the next verse, and is therefore essential to the rhythmical completeness of the passage. And yet this very clause has been rejected as a gloss, not only by Houbigant, and others of that school, but by Gesenius, Hitzig, Maurer, and Knobel, expressly on the ground that it violates the truth of history and the parallelism of the sentence. In urging the latter reason none of these critics seem to have observed that the omission of the clause would leave the verses unequal ; while the puerile suggestion that the similar clauses ought to come together, would apply to any case in Greek, Latin, or modern poetry, where two balanced verses are divided by a line of different length or termination, as in the *Stabat Mater* or Cowper's Ode to Friendship. Such an objection to the clause is especially surprising on the part of those who insist upon subjecting even Hebrew prose to the principles, if not the rules, of Greek and Latin prosody.—As to the more serious historical objection, it is applicable only to the theory of Usher, Lowth, Hengstenberg, and Henderson, that the conquest of Israel by Tiglath-pileser and Shalmaneser are excluded from the prophecy, and that it has relation solely to what took place under Esar-haddon ; whereas all three are included. If a historian should say that in one and twenty years from the beginning of the nineteenth century, the Emperor Napoleon had ceased to be, he could not be charged with the error of reckoning to the time of his death, instead of his first or second abdication, because all these would be really included, and the larger term chosen only for the purpose of embracing every sense in which the Emperor ceased to be. So in the case before us, the invasion by Tiglath-pileser, and the deportation by Shalmaneser are included, but the term of sixty-five years is assigned, because with it expired every possible pretension of the ten tribes to be reckoned as a state or nation, though the

real downfall of the government had happened many years before. Nor is
it improbable that if the shorter periods of three or twenty years had been
named, the same class of critics would have made the exclusion of the winding up under Esar-haddon a ground of similar objection to the clause.
The propriety of including this event is clear from the repeated mention of
Israel as a people still subsisting until it took place (2 Kings xxiii. 19, 20;
2 Chron. xxxiv. 6, 7; xxxv. 18), and from the fact that Esar-haddon placed his
colonists in the cities of Samaria, *instead of the children of Israel* (2 Kings
xxvii. 24), thereby completing their destruction as a people. The same
considerations furnish an answer to the objection that the time fixed for the
overthrow of Ephraim is too remote to allay the fears of Ahaz; not to mention that this was only one design of the prediction, and that the encouragement was meant to be afforded by what follows, and which seems to have
been added for the very purpose, as if he had said, "Ephraim is to last but
sixty-five years at most, and *even while it does last* the head," &c. That the
order of the numerals, *sixty and five* instead of *five and sixty* is no proof of
later origin (Gesenius), may be inferred from the occurrence of the same
collocation at least three times in Genesis (iv. 24, xviii. 28, xlvi. 15). The
alleged inconsistency between this clause and ver. 16 rests on a gratuitous
assumption that the desolation threatened there and the destruction here
are perfectly identical. To allege that בְּעוֹד is elsewhere used to denote the
precise time of an event (Gen. xl. 13, 19; Josh. i. 11, iii. 2; Jer. xxviii.
3, 11), is only to allege that a general expression admits of a specific application. The Hebrew phrase corresponds exactly to the English phrase *in
sixty-five years more*, and like it may be either applied to something happening at the end of that period, or to something happening at any time within
it, or to both, which is really its application here. To the objection that
the precise date of the immigration under Esar-haddon is a matter of conjecture, the answer is, that since this event and the sixty-fifth year from
the date of the prediction both fall within the reign of Manasseh, the supposition that they coincide is less improbable than the supposition that they
do not. To reject the clause on such a ground is to assume that whatever
is not proved (or rather twice proved) must be false, however probable.
Enough has now been said, not only to vindicate the clause as genuine, but
to preclude the necessity of computing the sixty-five years from any other
period than the date of the prediction, as for instance from the death of
Jeroboam II., with Cocceius, or from the leprosy of Uzziah with the Rabbins,
both which hypotheses, if necessary, might be plausibly defended. It also
supersedes the necessity of emendation in the text. Grotius and Cappellus
drop the plural termination of ששים and thus convert it into *six*. But even
if Isaiah could have written *six and five* instead of *eleven*, the latter number
would be too small, as Capellus in his computation overlooks an interregnum
which the best chronologers assume between Pekah and Hoshea. See
Gesenius *in loc*. Vitringa supposes ששים וחמש to have arisen out of ששי
וחמש (a common abbreviation in Hebrew manuscripts, and this out of ״ שש
וחמש, *six, ten, and five*, the exact number of years between the prophecy and
Shalmaneser's conquest, viz. sixteen of Ahaz and five of Hezekiah, which he
therefore supposes to be separately stated. But even if letters were used
for ciphers in Isaiah's time, which is highly improbable, it is still more improbable that both modes of notation would have been mixed up in a single
number. Gesenius sneers at Vitringa's thanking God for the discovery of
this emendation; but it is more than matched by two of later date and German origin. Steudel proposes to read שָׁנֹה (for שָׁנָה) in the sense of *repeatedly*,

and to supply *days* after *sixty-five!* Hendewerk more boldly reads בְּעוֹד שִׁשִּׁים וְחֹמֵשׁ שֵׁנָה *while the robbers and the murderer are a sleep* (*i. e.* asleep)! This he thinks so *schön und herrlich*, and the light which it sheds so *ganz wunderbar*, that he even prefers it to Hensler's proposition to read *six or five*, (*i. q.* five or six,) *i. e.* a few. Luzzato give this latter sense to the common text, which he explains as a round number, or rather as two round numbers, *sixty* being used in the Talmud indefinitely for a large number, and *five* even in Scripture for a small one. Ewald seems willing to admit that *sixty-five* itself is here put as a period somewhat shorter than the term of human life, but rejects the clause as a quotation from an older prophecy, transferred from the margin to the text of Isaiah. Besides these emendations of the text, the view which has been taken of the prophecy enables us to dispense with various forced constructions of the first clause—such as Aben Ezra's —" it shall not come to pass (with respect to you) but (with respect to) the head of Syria (which is) Damascus, &c." Or this—" Though the head of Syria is Damascus (a great city), and the head of Damascus is Rezin (a great prince), yet in sixty-five years, &c." Hitzig reverses this, and makes it an expression of contempt—" for the head of Syria is (only) Damascus, and the head of Damascus (only) Rezin (a smoking fire-brand)."—The last clause of the verse has also been variously construed. J. D. Michaelis supposes a threatening or indignant pause in the midst of it—" If ye will not believe—for (I see that) ye will not believe." Grotius makes it interrogative—" will ye not believe, unless ye are confirmed " or assured by a sign ? The construction now most commonly adopted makes כִּי a participle of asseveration (Rosenmüller, Henderson) or even of swearing (Maurer), or supposes it to introduce the apodosis and to be equivalent to *then* (Gesenius). Luther's version of the clause, thus understood, has been much admired, as a successful imitation of the paronomasia in Hebrew : *Gläubet ihr nicht, so bleibet ihr nicht.* This explanation of the clause is strongly favoured by the analogy of 2 Chron. xx. 20; but another equally natural is the one already given in translation—" if ye do not believe (it is) because ye are not to be established." For other constructions and conjectural emendations of the several clauses, see Gesenius and Rosenmüller on the passage.

10. *And Jehovah added to speak unto Ahaz, saying,*—which, according to usage, may either mean that *he spoke again*, on a different occasion, or that *he spoke further*, on the same occasion, which last is the meaning here. This verse, it is true, is supposed to commence a new division of the prophecy by Ewald, and an entirely distinct prediction by Hendewerk, who connects it with the close of the fifth chapter, and by Henderson, who regards all that follows as having reference to the invasion of Judah by Assyria. A sufficient refutation of the two last hypothesis is involved in the admission made by both these writers, that the offer of a sign has reference to nothing in the context, but to something not recorded ; whereas it was naturally called forth by the incredulity which some suppose to have been betrayed by the king's silence (Hengstenberg) or his looks (Rosenmüller), and which is certainly referred to in the last clause of ver. 9.

11. *Ask for thee* (*i. e.* for thy own satisfaction) *a sign from Jehovah thy God* (literally *from with him*, *i. e.* from his presence and his power) —*ask deep or high above*—or *make deep thy request or make it high*— *i. e.* ask it either above or below. A *sign* is not necessarily a miracle, nor necessarily a prophecy, but a sensible pledge of the truth of something else,. whether present, past, or future ; sometimes consisting in a miracle (Isa. xxxviii. 8; Judges vi. xxxvii.; Exod. iv. 8), but sometimes

in a mere prediction (Exod. iii. 12 ; 1 Sam. ii. xxxiv. ; 2 Kings xix. 29), and sometimes only in a symbol, especially a symbolical name or action (Isa. xxxviii. 18, xx. 3 ; Ezek. iv. 8). The sign here offered is a proof of Isaiah's divine legation, which Ahaz seemed to doubt. He is allowed to choose, not only the place of its exhibition (Plüschke), but the sign itself. The offer is a general one, including all the kinds of signs which have been mentioned, though the only one which would have answered the purpose of accrediting the Prophet, was a present miracle, as in the case of Moses (Exod. iv. 30). Aquila, Symmachus, and Theodotion, seem to have read שְׁאָלָה *to the grave or lower world* (βάθυνον εἰς ᾅδην), which is adopted by Jerome, Michaelis, Lowth, and also by Ewald but without a change of text, as he supposes שְׁאָלָה to be simply a euphonic variation for שְׁאָלָה intended to assimilate it to לְמָעְלָה. Thus understood, the word may refer to the opening of the earth or the raising of the dead, in opposition to a miracle in heaven. But as heaven is not particularly mentioned, there is no need of departing from the old explanation of שְׁאָלָה as a paragogic imperative (comp. Dan. ix. 19 ; Ps. xli. 4), signifying *ask thou*. The two preceding verbs may then be taken also as imperatives, *go deep, ask, i. e.* in asking, or as infinitives equivalent to adverbs, *ask deep, ask high;* or the construction may be simplified still further by explaining שְׁאָלָה as a noun equivalent to שְׁאָלָה, and governed directly by the two verbs as imperatives—*make deep (thy) request, make (it) high*. There may either be a reference to the distinction between signs in heaven and signs on earth (Mat. xvi. 1), which Jerome illustrates by the case of the Egyptian plagues, or the words may be more indefinitely understood as meaning *any where*, up or down, above or below (Calvin). The phrase *thy God* is emphatic and intended to remind Ahaz of his official relation to Jehovah, and as it were to afford him a last opportunity of profiting by the connection.

12. *And Ahaz said, I will not ask, and I will not tempt Jehovah.* Some regard this as a contemptuous irony, implying a belief that God would not be able to perform his promise (Grotius, Gesenius, &c.), or a disbelief in the existence of a personal God (Umbreit). We have no reason to doubt, however, that Ahaz believed in the existence of Jehovah, at least as one among many gods, as a local and national if not a supreme deity. It is better, therefore, to understand the words as a hypocritical excuse for not obeying the command, with obvious allusion to the prohibition in Deut. vi. 6, which is of course inapplicable to the case of one who is exhorted to choose. His refusal probably arose not from speculative doubts or politic considerations, but from the state of his affections, his aversion to the service of Jehovah, and his predilection for that of other gods, perhaps combined with a belief that in this case human aid would be sufficient and a divine interposition superfluous ; to which may be added a specific expectation of assistance from Assyria, for which he had perhaps already sued (2 Kings xvi. 7–9). To *tempt* God is not to try him in the way of trusting him (Hoheisel), nor simply to call in question his power, knowledge, or veracity (Gesenius, Hitzig), but to put him practically to the test. The character of Ahaz is illustrated by a comparison of this refusal with the thankful acceptance of such signs by others, and especially by his own son Hezekiah, to whom, as Jerome observes, signs both in heaven and on earth were granted.

13. At first Ahaz seemed to doubt only the authority and divine legation of the Prophet ; but his refusal to accept the offered attestation was

an insult to God himself, and is therefore indignantly rebuked by the Prophet. *And he said, hear, I pray you, oh house of David! is it too little for
you* (is it not for you) *to weary men* (*i. e.* to try mens' patience) *that you*
(must) *weary* (or try the patience of) *my God?* The meaning is not merely
that it is worse to weary God than man (Chrysostom), or that it was not
man but God whom they were wearying (Jerome); but that having first
wearied man, *i. e.* the Prophet by disputing his commission, they were now
wearying God, by refusing the offered attestation. הַלְאוֹת is not to
regard as weak or impotent (Kimchi), but to try or exhaust the patience
of another. The plural form of the address does not imply that the Prophet
turned away from Ahaz to others (Jerome), but that members of his family
and court were, in the Prophet's view, already implicated in his unbelief.

14. The king having refused to ask a sign, the Prophet gives him one,
by renewing the promise of deliverance (vers. 8, 9), and connecting it with
the birth of a child, whose significant name is made a symbol of the divine
interposition, and his progress a measure of the subsequent events. Instead of saying that God would be present to deliver them, he says the
child shall be called *Immanuel* (God-with-us); instead of mentioning a
term of years, he says, before the child is able to distinguish good from
evil; instead of saying that until that time the land shall lie waste, he
represents the child as eating *curds and honey*, spontaneous products,
here put in opposition to the fruits of cultivation. At the same time,
the form of expression is descriptive. Instead of saying simply that the
child shall experience all this, he represents its birth and infancy as
actually passing in his sight; he sees the child brought forth and named
Immanuel; he sees the child eating curds and honey till a certain age.
Therefore (because you have refused to choose) *the Lord himself will give
you a sign. Behold! the virgin pregnant and bringing forth a son, and she
calls his name Immanuel* (God-with-us)—*curds and honey shall he eat*
(because the land lies waste) *until he shall know* (how) *to reject the evil and
choose the good* (but no longer); *for before the child shall know* (how) *to
reject the evil and to choose the good, the land, of whose two kings thou art
afraid,* (*i. e.* Syria and Israel), *shalt be forsaken, i. e.* desolate), which of
course implies the previous deliverance of Judah.—All interpreters appear
to be agreed that these three verses contain a threatening of destruction
to the enemies of Judah, if not a direct promise of deliverance, and that
this event is connected, in some way, with the birth of a child, as the
sign or pledge of its certain occurrence. But what child is meant, or who
is the Immanuel here predicted? The various answers to this question
may be all reduced to three fundamental hypotheses, each of which admits of several minor variations.

I. The first hypothesis is that the only birth and infancy referred to in
these verses are the birth and infancy of a child born (or supposed to be
born) in the ordinary course of nature, and in the days of Isaiah himself.
The unessential variations, of which this hypothesis is susceptible, have
reference chiefly to the question what particular child is intended. 1. The
Jews of old supposed it to be Hezekiah; but this was exploded by Jerome's
suggestion, that he was already at least nine years old, since his father
reigned but sixteen years, and he succeeded him at twenty-five (2 Kings
xvi. 2, xviii. 2). 2. Kimchi and Abarbenel suppose Immanuel to be a
younger son of Ahaz, by a second marriage. 3. Isenbiehl, Bauer, Cube,
Steudel, and Hitzig, understand by הָעַלְמָה, a woman who was present, and
at whom the Prophet pointed. 4. J. D. Michaelis, Eichhorn, Paulus,

Hensler, Ammon, understand the Prophet to predict not a real but an ideal birth, as if he had said, should one now a virgin conceive and bear a son, she might call his name Immanuel, &c. 5. Aben Ezra, Jarchi, Faber, Plüschke, Gesenius, Maurer, Hendewerk, Knobel, suppose him to be speaking of his own wife, and the birth of his own son; and as Shear-jashub was already born, Gesenius assumes a second marriage of the Prophet, and supposes two events to be predicted; first, the deliverance of Judah at the birth of the child, and then the desolation of Syria and Israel before he should be able to distinguish good and evil. To this last supposition, it is justly objected by Hengstenberg that it assumes too great an interval between the deliverance of Judah and the desolation of the other countries, as well as between the former and the resumption of agricultural employments. It is besides unnecessary, as the interposition denoted by the name Immanuel need not be restricted to the time of the child's birth, and as the desolation of Syria and Israel is said to take place *before*, but not *immediately* before the child's attaining to a certain age; to which it may be added that the age itself is left somewhat indefinite. But besides these objections to Gesenius's assumption of a twofold prophecy, his whole hypothesis, with all the others which have been enumerated, except perhaps the fourth, may be justly charged with gratuitously assuming facts of which we have no evidence, and which are not necessary to the interpretation of the passage; such as the second marriage of Ahaz, or that of Isaiah, or the presence of a pregnant woman, or the Prophet's pointing at her. A further objection to all the variations of this first hypothesis is, that although they may afford a *sign*, in one of the senses of that term, to wit, that of an emblem or symbol, they do not afford such a sign as the context would lead us to expect. Ahaz had been offered the privilege of choosing any sign whatever, in heaven or on earth. Had he actually chosen one, it would no doubt have been something out of the ordinary course of nature, as in the case of Gideon (Judges vi. 37–40) and Hezekiah (Isa. xxxviii. 7, 8). On his refusal to choose, a sign is given him unasked, and although it does not necessarily follow that it was precisely such as he would have selected—since the object was no longer simply to remove his doubts, but to verify the promise and to mark the event when it occurred as something which had been predicted—yet it seems very improbable that after such an offer, the sign bestowed would be merely a thing of every day occurrence, or at most the application of a symbolical name. This presumption is strengthened by the solemnity with which the Prophet speaks of the predicted birth, not as a usual and natural event, but as something which excites his own astonishment, as he beholds it in prophetic vision. This may prove nothing by itself, but is significant when taken in connection with the other reasons. The same thing may be said of the address to Immanuel, in chap. viii. 8, and the allusion to the name in ver. 11, which, although they may admit of explanation in consistency with this first hypothesis, agree much better with the supposition that the prophecy relates to something more than a natural and ordinary birth. A still stronger reason for the same conclusion is afforded by the parallel passage in chap. ix. 5, 6, occurring in the same connected series of prophecies. There, as here, the birth of a child is given as a pledge of safety and deliverance, but with the important addition of a full description, which, as we shall see below, is wholly inapplicable to any ordinary human child, however high in rank or full of promise. If led by these remarkable coincidences to examine more attentively the terms of the prophecy itself, we find the mother of the promised child described, not as *a woman* or as any particular woman merely, but as הָעַלְמָה a term which has been variously derived from עלם to conceal, and from غَلِم to grow up, but which, in the six places where it occurs elsewhere, is twice applied to young unmarried females certainly (Gen. xxiv. 43; Exod. ii. 8) and twice most probably (Ps. lxviii. 25; Sol. Song i. 3), while in the two remaining cases (Sol. Song i. 8; Prov. xxx. 19) this application is at least as probable as any other. It would therefore naturally suggest the idea of a virgin, or at least of an unmarried woman. It is said, indeed, that if this had been intended, the word בְּתוּלָה would have been employed; but even that word is not invariably used in its strict sense (see Deut. xxii. 19; Joel i. 8), so that there would still have been room for the same cavils, and perhaps for the assertion that the idea of a virgin could not be expressed except by a periphrasis. It is enough for us to know that a virgin or unmarried woman is designated here as distinctly as she could be by a single word. But why should this description be connected with a fact which seems to render it inapplicable, that of parturition? That the word means simply a *young woman*, whether married or unmarried, a virgin or a mother, is a subterfuge invented by the later Greek translators who, as Justin Martyr tells us, read νεᾶνις, instead of the old version πάρθενος, which had its rise before the prophecy became a subject of dispute between the Jews and Christians. That the word denotes one who is a virgin or unmarried *now*, without implying that she is to remain so, is certainly conceivable; but, as we said before, its use in this connection, especially when added to the other reasons previously mentioned, makes it, to say the least, extremely probable that the event foretold is something more than a birth in the ordinary course of nature. So too, the name *Immanuel*, although it might be used to signify God's providential presence merely (Ps. xlvi. 8, 12, lxxxix. 25; Joshua i. 5; Jer. i. 8; Isa. xliii. 2), has a latitude and pregnancy of meaning which can scarcely be fortuitous, and which, combined with all the rest, makes the conclusion almost unavoidable, that it was here intended to express a *personal* as well as a *providential* presence. If to this we add the early promise of salvation through the *seed of the woman* (Gen. iii. 15), rendered more definite by later revelations, and that remarkable expression of Isaiah's contemporary prophet Micah (ver. 2), *until the time that she which travaileth hath brought forth*, immediately following the promise of a *ruler*, to be born in Bethlehem, but *whose goings forth have been of old, from everlasting*—the balance of probabilities, as furnished by the Old Testament exclusively, preponderates decidedly in favour of the supposition, that Isaiah's words had reference to a miraculous conception and nativity. When we read, therefore, in the gospel of Matthew, that Jesus Christ was actually born of a virgin, and that all the circumstances of his birth came to pass that this very prophecy might be fulfilled, it has less the appearance of an unexpected application, than of a conclusion rendered necessary, by a series of antecedent facts and reasons,—the last link in a long chain of intimations more or less explicit. The same considerations seem to shew that the prophecy is not merely transferred or accommodated to another subject by the evangelist, which is, moreover, clear from the emphatic form of the citation (τοῦτο ὅλον γέγονεν ἵνα πληρωθῇ κ. τ. λ.), making it impossible to prove the existence of any quotation, in the proper sense, if this be not one, and from the want of any similarity between the two events, viz., a natural and miraculous conception, upon which a mere illustrative accommodation of the words could have been founded. The idea, insidiously suggested by J. D. Michaelis, that the first two chapters of Matthew may be spurious, is so far from deriving any countenance from this application of the prophecy, that, on the contrary, its wonderful agreement with the scattered but harmonious intimations of the Old Testament, too numerous and too detached to be fortuitous, affords a strong though incidental proof that these very chapters are genuine and authentic. The rejection of Matthew's authority *in toto*, as an interpreter of the prediction, is not only inconsistent with the proofs of his inspiration drawn from other quarters, but leaves unexplained the remarkable coincidence between his interpretation and the original form of expression, the context, and the parallel passages. That these should all conspire to recommend an ignorant or random explanation of the prophecy, is more incredible than that the explanation should be true, and the words of Isaiah a prediction of something more than the birth of a real or ideal child in the ordinary course of nature, and in the days of the Prophet himself. The question, however, still arises, how the birth of Christ, if here predicted, is to be connected with the promise made to Ahaz, as a sign of the event, or as a measure of the time of its fulfilment?

II. The second hypothesis removes this difficulty, by supposing that the prophecy relates to two distinct births and two different children. Of this general theory there are two important modifications. 1. The first supposes one child to be mentioned in ver. 14, and another in ver. 16. As to ver. 15, some connect it with the one before and some with the one after it. Thus Junius understands ver. 14 to refer to Christ, but vers. 15, 16 to Shearjashub; Usher applies vers. 14, 15 to Christ, and ver. 16 to Shearjashub; Calvin, vers. 14, 15 to Christ, but ver. 16 to *a child, i.e.* any child indefinitely. They all agree that the prophecy contains two promises. First, that Christ should be born of a virgin, and then that Judah should be delivered before Shearjashub (or before any child born within a certain time) could distinguish good from evil. To such of these interpretations as refer ver. 15 to the infancy of Christ, it may be objected that they put a sense upon that verse which its expressions will not bear, and which is inconsistent with the use of the same terms in ver. 22. It will be seen below that the eating of curds and honey is predicted as a sign of general desolation, or at least of interrupted tillage. Another objection which applies to all the forms of this interpretation is the sudden change of subject, in the fifteenth or sixteenth verse, from Immanuel to Shearjashub, or to any child indefinitely. Nothing but extreme exegetical necessity could justify the reference of vers. 15, 16 to any person not referred to in ver. 14. 2. This difficulty is avoided in the second modification of the general hypothesis that the passage, as a whole, refers to two distinct births and to different children, by assuming that both are mentioned in the fourteenth verse itself. This is the supposition of a double sense, though some refuse to recognise it by that name. The essence of the theory is this, that while ver. 14, in its obvious and primary sense, relates to the birth of a child in the ordinary course of nature, its terms are so selected as to be descriptive, in a higher sense, of the miraculous nativity of Christ. This theory is mentioned by Jerome as the opinion of a certain Judaizing Christian, whom he does not name (quidam de nostris judaïzans), and by Calvin as a compromise between the orthodox and Jewish expositions, but it has since had many eminent and able advocates. The minor variations of this general hypothesis have reference chiefly to the particular child intended by the prophecy in its lower sense, whether a son of Isaiah himself, as Grotius, Clericus, and Barnes suppose, or any child born within a certain time, as Lowth, with more probability, assumes. The advantage of these interpretations is, that they seem to account for the remarkable expressions which the prophet uses, as if to intimate a deeper meaning than the primary and obvious one, and at the same time answer the conditions both of the context in Isaiah and of the application in Matthew, presenting a sign analogous to others given before and after by this very prophet (chap. vii. 3, viii. 2), and at the same time furnishing believers with a striking prophecy of the Messiah. The objections to it are its complexity, and what seems to be the arbitrary nature of the assumption upon which it rests. It seems to be a feeling common to learned and unlearned readers, that although a double sense is not impossible, and must in certain cases be assumed, it is unreasonable to assume it when any other explanation is admissible. The improbability in this case is increased by the want of similarity between the two events, supposed to be predicted in the very same words, the one miraculous, the other not only natural, but common, and of everyday occurrence. That two such occurrences should be described in the same words, simply because they were both *signs* or pledges of a promise, though not impossible, can only be made probable by strong corroborating proofs, especially if any simpler mode of exposition be at all admissible. Another objection, which lies equally against this hypothesis and the one first mentioned is, that in its primary and lower sense it does not afford such a sign as the context and the parallel passages would lead us to expect, unless we suppose that the higher secondary sense was fully understood at the time of the prediction, and in that case, though the birth of the Messiah from a virgin would be doubtless a sufficient sign, it would, for that very reason, seem to make the lower one superfluous. Dathe's courageous supposition, that the primary reference is to a *miraculous* conception and birth in the days of Isaiah, only aggravates the difficulty which it would diminish, though it certainly escapes the force of some of the objections to the supposition of a double sense, to wit, those founded on the inadequacy of the sign and the dissimilarity of the events. None of these reasons seem, however, to be decisive against the supposition of a double sense, as commonly understood, unless there be some other way in which its complexity and arbitrary character may be avoided, and at the same time the connection between the birth of the Messiah and the deliverance of Judah satisfactorily explained.

III. The third general hypothesis proposes to effect this by applying all three verses directly and exclusively to the Messiah, as the only child whose birth is there predicted, and his growth made the measure of the subsequent events. The minor variations of this general hypothesis relate to the time when these events were to occur, and to the sense in which the growth of the Messiah is adopted as the measure of them. 1. The simplest form in which this theory has been applied, is that exhibited by J. H. Michaelis and others, who suppose the prediction to relate to the real time of Christ's appearance, and the thing foretold to be the desolation which should take place before the Saviour reached a certain age. To this it is an obvious objection that it makes the event predicted too remote to answer the conditions of the context, or the purpose of the prophecy itself. A similar objection has, indeed, been urged by the Rabbins and others, to a prophecy of Christ's birth as a *sign* of the promise made to Ahaz. But the cases are entirely dissimilar. The promise of immediate deliverance might be confirmed by an appeal to an event long posterior, if the one necessarily implied the other, as included in it, or as a necessary previous condition.   Thus the promise that Israel should worship God at Sinai, was a *sign* to Moses, that they should first be delivered from Egypt (Exod. iii. 12), and the promise that the tillage interrupted by Sennacherib's invasion should be resumed, was a sign to Hezekiah, that the invasion was itself to cease (Isa. xxxvii. 30).   In like manner, the assurance that Christ was to be born in Judah, of its royal family, might be a *sign* to Ahaz, that the kingdom should not perish in his day ; and so far was the remoteness of the sign in this case from making it absurd or inappropriate, that the further off it was, the stronger the promise of continuance to Judah, which it guaranteed.   Especially is this the case, if we suppose it to have been a familiar doctrine of the ancient Church, that the Messiah was to come, and that for his sake, Israel existed as a nation.   But, according to the theory now in question, not only is the *sign* remote, but also the thing signified ; not only the pledge of the event, but the event itself.   The Prophet's contemporaries might have been encouraged to expect deliverance from present danger by the promise of Christ's coming ; but a promise of deliverance before the end of seven hundred years could afford no encouragement at all.   That this objection to the theory in question has been felt by some of its most able advocates, may be inferred from several facts.   One is, that J. H. Michaelis is obliged to insert the words *long since* (dudum deserta erit), and yet to leave the promise wholly indefinite.   Another is, that Henderson departs from the ancient and almost universal explanation of the passage as a promise, and converts it into a threatening, not only against Israel, but against Judah ; both of which kingdoms were to lose their kings before the twelfth year of our Saviour, when Archelaus was banished from Judea.   A third is, that Cocceius, though one of the most accurate philologists of his own or any other age, and only too decided in his exegetical judgments, hesitates between the interpretation now in question and the ungrammatical and arbitrary reference of ver. 16 to a different child.   At all events, it may be safely assumed, that the application of these three verses to the time of Christ's actual appearance has no claim to be received, if there is any other form of the same general hypothesis, by which the connection of the promise with the context can be made more natural. 2. This end Vitringa has attempted to secure, by supposing the language to be hypothetical, or that the Prophet, while he views the birth of Christ as a remote event, makes it the measure of the events at hand—*q. d.* before the Messiah, *if he were born now*, could know how to distinguish good from evil, &c.   The only objection to this ingenious explanation is, that the conditional expression on which all depends, *if he were born now*, is precisely that which is omitted, and of which the text contains no intimation.   And that the Prophet, without such intimation, would make this use of an event which he distinctly saw to be remote, though not incredible, ought surely not to be assumed without necessity.   3. Another modification of the hypothesis which refers the three verses all to the Messiah, is that proposed by Rosenmüller, in the second and subsequent editions of his Scholia, and substantially renewed by Ewald, viz., that Isaiah really expected the Messiah to be born at once, and therefore naturally made the progress of his infancy the measure of a proximate futurity.   Neither of these writers supposes any reference to Christ, both regarding the prediction as a visionary anticipation. But Hengstenberg has clearly shewn that such a positive belief and expectation, on Isaiah's part, is not only inconsistent with other prophecies, but with the sequel of this, in which a series of calamitous events is described as intervening between the approaching deliverance and the nativity of the

Messiah. To the merely negative assumption that the time of the advent formed no part of this particular revelation, he thinks there is not the same objection. 4. Accordingly, his own interpretation of the passage is, that the birth of the Messiah being presented to the Prophet in connection with the proximate deliverance of which it was the sign or pledge, without regard to chronological relations, and seen by him in prophetic ecstacy as actually present, he naturally makes the one the measure of the other. As if he had said, I see the virgin bringing forth a son, and calling his name Immanuel; I see him living in the midst of desolation till a certain age; but before that time arrives, I see the land of our invaders lying desolate. The only objection to this ingenious improvement on Vitringa's ingenious exposition, is that it rests upon a certain theory as to the nature of prophetic inspiration, or of the mental state in which the prophets received and uttered their communications, which, however probable, is not at present generally current with believers in the plenary inspiration of the Scriptures, nor perhaps maintained by Hengstenberg himself.

In expounding this difficult and interesting passage, it has been considered more important to present a tolerably full view of the different opinions, arranged according to the principles on which they rest, than to assert the exclusive truth of any one interpretation as to all its parts. In summing up the whole, however, it may be confidently stated, that the first hypothesis is false; that the first modifications of the second and third are untenable; and that the choice lies between the supposition of a double sense and that of a reference to Christ exclusively, but in connection with the promise of immediate deliverance to Ahaz. The two particular interpretations which appear to be most plausible and least beset with difficulties, are those of Lowth and Vitringa, with which last Hengstenberg's is essentially identical. Either the Prophet, while he foretells the birth of Christ, foretells that of another child, during whose infancy the promised deliverance shall be experienced; or else he makes the infancy of Christ himself, whether foreseen as still remote or not, the sign and measure of that same deliverance. While some diversity of judgment ought to be expected and allowed, in relation to this secondary question, there is no ground, grammatical, historical, or logical, for doubt as to the main point, that the Church in all ages has been right in regarding this passage as a signal and explicit prediction of the miraculous conception and nativity of Jesus Christ.

As to the form of the expression, it will only be necessary further to remark that הָרָה is not a verb or participle (Vitringa, Rosenmüller), but a feminine adjective, signifying *pregnant*, and here connected with an active participle, to denote that the object is described as present to the Prophet's view. *Behold, the virgin, pregnant and bringing forth a son, and she calls his name Immanuel.* The future form adopted by the Septuagint (ἕξει, λήψεται, τέξεται) is retained in the New Testament, because the words are there considered simply as a prophecy; but in order to exhibit the full force which they have in their original connection, the present form must be restored. The form of the sentence is evidently copied from the angel's address to Hagar (Gen. xvi. 11), and so closely that the verb קָרָאת remains unchanged; not, however, as the second person feminine (though all the other Greek versions have καλέσεις, and Junius likewise, who supplies *o virgo* to remove the ambiguity), but as the third person feminine, analogous to עָשָׂת (Lev. xxv. 21), נִפְלְאָת (Ps. cxviii. 23), הִבָּאת (Gen. xxxiii. 11). The form קָרָאת itself occurs (Deut. xxxi. 29; Jer. xliv. 23), but in another sense (See Nordheimer, § 422). Calvin, with a strange lapse of memory, alleges

that in Scripture mothers never name their children, and that a departure
from the constant usage here is a prophetic intimation that the child would
have no human father. The error of fact is easily corrected by referring
to the exercise of this prerogative by Eve, Leah, Rachel, Hannah, and
others (Gen. iv. 1–25 ; xix. 37 ; xxix. 32–35 ; xxx. 6–24 ; 1 Sam. i. 20 ;
1 Chron. iv. 9 ; vii. 16). That the same act is frequently ascribed to the
father, needs of course no proof. In the case before us, it is so far from
being an important question, who was to impose the name, that it matters
very little whether it was ever imposed at all ; or rather, it is certain that
the name is merely descriptive or symbolical, and that its actual use in real
life was no more necessary to the fulfilment of the prophecy, than that the
Messiah should be commonly known by the titles of Wonderful, Counsellor,
the Prince of Peace (Isa. ix. 6), or the Lord our Righteousness (Jer. xxiii. 6).
Hence in Mat. i. 23, the singular קָרָאת is changed into the plural καλέσουσι,
they shall call, i. e. they indefinitely, as in our familiar phrase *they say*,
corresponding to the French *on dit* and the German *man sagt*, which last construction is adopted by Augusti in his version of this sentence (man wird
nennen seinen Namen). With equal adherence to the spirit, and equal departure from the letter of the prophecy, the Peshito and Vulgate give the
verb a passive form, *his name shall be called.* As to the meaning of the
name itself, its higher sense is evident from Matthew's application, notwithstanding Hitzig's paradoxical denial, and its lower sense from the usage
of analogous expressions in Ps. xlvi. 8, 12, lxxxix. 25 ; Josh. i. 5, Jer.
i. 8, Isa. xliii. 2.

15. This verse and the next have already been translated in connection
with the fourteenth, upon which connection their interpretation must depend. It will here be necessary only to explain one or two points more
distinctly. *Butter* (or curds) *and honey shall he eat, until he knows (how)
to reject the evil and to choose the good.* The simple sense of the prediction
is that the desolation of Judah, caused by the invasion of Rezin and Pekah,
should be only temporary. This idea is symbolically expressed by making
the new-born child subsist during his infancy on curds and honey, instead
of the ordinary food of an agricultural population. This is clearly the
meaning of the same expression in ver. 22, as we shall see below ; it cannot
therefore here denote the real humanity of the person mentioned (Calvin,
Vitringa, Henderson, &c.), which is besides sufficiently implied in his being
born of a human mother, and could not be asserted here without interrupting the connection between the fourteenth and sixteenth verses. It cannot
denote his poverty or low condition (Calovius), or that of the family of
David (Alting), because no such idea is suggested by the words. It cannot,
on the other hand, denote abundance or prosperity in general (Grotius,
Cocceius, Junius, &c.), because such a diet is no proof of that condition,
and because, according to ver. 22, the words are descriptive only of such
abundance as arises from a sparse population and neglected tillage. That
this desolation should be temporary, is expressed by representing it as co-
extensive with the early childhood of the person mentioned. לְדַעְתּוֹ is explained by Jarchi, Lowth, Hitzig, Henderson, and Ewald, to mean *when he
knows* ; by most other writers, *till* or *before he knows* (LXX. πρὶν ἢ γνῶναι).
The Vulgate, Luther, Junius, and Clericus refer it, not to time at all, but
to the design or effect of his eating curds and honey, *that he may know.* It
is clear, however, from the next verse, that this one must contain a specification of time, however vague. The difference between the versions *when*
and *till*, and also in relation to the age described—which J. D. Michaelis

puts as high as twenty-one, Ewald from ten to twenty, Henderson at twelve, but Kimchi and most others at about three years—is not so important as might at first sight seem, because the description was probably intended to be somewhat indefinite. The essential idea is that the desolation should not last until a child then born could reach maturity, and probably not longer than his first few years. Clericus supposes *good* and *evil* to mean pleasant and unpleasant food, as in 1 Sam. xix. 35 ; but the same words elsewhere constantly relate to moral distinctions and the power to perceive them (Gen. iii. 5 ; Deut. i. 39 ; 1 Kings iii. 9 ; Jonah iv. 2). Nothing short of the strongest exegetical necessity could justify the reference of this verse to Shearjashub (Junius, Usher), or to any other subject than the one referred to in the verse preceding, namely, Immanuel, the child whose birth the Prophet there describes as just at hand, and whose infancy he here describes as passed in the midst of surrounding desolation. To the explanation of this verse as having reference to Isaiah's own son or a son of Ahaz on the one hand, or to the time of our Saviour's actual appearance on the other, sufficient objections have already been adduced in the interpretation of the fourteenth verse.

16. The desolation shall be temporary—*for before the child shall know* (how) *to reject the evil and to choose the good, the land, of whose two kings thou art afraid* (or *by whose two kings thou art distressed*) *shall be forsaken, i. e.* left by its inhabitants and given up to desolation, in which sense the same verb is used elsewhere by Isaiah (chap. xvii. 2, xxvii. 10, lxii. 12. Comp. vi. 12). Instead of taking תֵּעָזֵב thus absolutely, most of the older writers, and a few of later date, connect it with מִפְּנֵי, and קָץ with אֲשֶׁר. *The land which thou abhorrest* (or *for which thou fearest*) *shall be forsaken by both its kings*—*i. e.* Judah shall be forsaken by Rezin and Pekah, whom Steudel supposes to be called its kings *de facto*—or Syria and Israel shall be deprived of Rezin and Pekah—or Canaan (including Israel and Judah) shall lose both its kings. This last is the interpretation given by Henderson, who also reads *the land which thou destroyest.* Clericus takes תֵּעָזֵב absolutely, in the sense of being desolate, but translates the rest, *which thou abhorrest on account of its two kings.* To some of these constructions it may be objected that they make the land and not the kings the object of abhorrence, and to all, that they construe קָץ directly with אֲשֶׁר which is contrary to usage, and disjoin it from מִפְּנֵי, by which it is followed in at least two other places (Ex. iii. 12, Num. xxii. 3) ; to which may be added that according to the Hebrew idiom, this construction is the only one that could be used to signify *before* (or *on account of*) *whose two kings thou art in terror.* This construction, which is given by Castalio and De Dieu, is adopted by Cocceius, Vitringa, J. D. Michaelis, Rosenmüller, Gesenius, Ewald, and most other modern writers, who are also agreed that *the land* here meant is Syria and Israel, spoken of as one because confederate against Judah. The wasting of these kingdoms and the deportation of their people by Tiglath-pileser (2 Kings xv. 29, xvi. 9), is here predicted, which of course implies the previous deliverance of Judah and the brief duration of its own calamity, so that this verse assigns a reason for the representation in the one preceding. There is no need, therefore, of imposing upon כִּי at the beginning of the verse, the sense of *nay* (Piscator), *indeed* (Calvin), *although* (Alting), or *but* (Umbreit), or any other than its usual and proper one of *for, because.* Nor is it necessary to regard the fifteenth verse as a parenthesis, with Cocceius and Rosenmüller ; much less to reject it as a gloss, with Hitzig, and as breaking the connection between the name Immanuel

in ver. 14, and the explanation of it in ver. 16. The true connection of the verses has been well explained by Maurer and Knobel to be this, that Judah shall lie waste for a short time, and *only* for a short time, *for* before that short time is expired, its invaders shall themselves be invaded and destroyed. This view of the connection is sufficient to evince, that the reference of this verse to Shearjashub (Lowth) or to *any child* indefinitely (Calvin), is as unnecessary as it is ungrammatical. *A child* is born—*he* learns to distinguish good and evil—but before *the child* is able to distinguish good and evil, something happens. If these three clauses, thus succeeding one another, do not speak of the same child, it is impossible for language to be so employed as to identify the subject without actually saying that it is the same.

17. Again addressing Ahaz, he assures him that although he shall escape the present danger, God will inflict worse evils on himself and his successors, by means of those very allies whose assistance he is now seeking. *Jehovah will bring upon thee*—not merely as an individual, but as a king——*and on thy people—and on thy father's house*—or family—the royal line of Judah—*days which have not come since the departure of Ephraim from Judah, to wit, the king of Assyria.* It is possible to construe the sentence so as to make it refer to the retreat of the invaders—*Jehovah will bring upon thee days which have not come* (never come before), *from the day that Ephraim departs from Judah, i. e.* as soon as this invasion ceases, worse times shall begin. This construction, which is permitted, if not favoured, by the Masoretic accents, has the advantage of giving to מֵעַל its strict sense, as implying the removal of a burden or infliction (see Exod. x. 28, and Gesenius s. v.) rather than a mere revolt or schism, and also that of making the expression stronger (*days which have not come* at all, or *never come*), and at the same time less indefinite by specifying when the days were to begin. But as the absolute use of the phrase *which have not come* is rather harsh and unusual, and as the compound forms לְמִיּוֹם and לְמִימֵי are elsewhere used only in relation to the past (Judges xix. 30 ; 2 Sam. vii. 6 ; 2 Kings xix. 25 ; Mal. iii. 7), although the simple forms מִיּוֹם and מִימֵי sometimes denote the future (Exod. xii. 15 ; Lev. xxii. 27 ; Ezek. xxxviii. 8), it is safer to adhere to the unanimous decision of all versions and interpreters, so far as I can trace it, and understand the verse as declaring the days threatened to be worse than any which had come upon Judah since the revolt of the ten tribes, here called Ephraim, from the largest and most powerful tribe, that to which Jeroboam belonged, and within which the chief towns of the kingdom were situated. This declaration seems at first sight inconsistent with the fact, demonstrable from sacred history, that the injuries sustained by Judah, during the interval here specified, from other foreign powers, as for example from the Egyptians in the reign of Rehoboam (2 Chron. xii. 2–9), from the Philistines and Arabians in the reign of Jehoram (2 Chron. xxi. 16, 17), from the Syrians in the reign of Joash (2 Chron. xxiv. 23, 24), not to mention the less successful attacks of the Ethiopians in the reign of Asa (2 Chron. xiv. 8–15, and of Moab and Ammon in the reign of Jehoshaphat (2 Chron. xx. 1–30), or the frequent incursions of the ten tribes, must have greatly overbalanced the invasion of Sennacherib, by far the most alarming visitation of Judah by the armies of Assyria. This apparent discrepancy is not to be explained by regarding the prophecy before us, with Gesenius, as a mere threat (blosses Drohwort), nor by alleging that the days here threatened are not described as *worse* than any former days, but only as different

from them. Even granting that the prophecy implies not merely change of condition, but a change for the worse, it may be justified in either of two ways. According to Cocceius, Vitringa, Henderson, and others, the *king of Assyria* may here include the kings of Babylon, to whom the title is applied in 2 Kings xxiii. 29, if not in Neh. ix. 32, as it is to the kings of Persia in Ezra vi. 22, considered as successors to the Assyrian power, in accordance with which usage, Herodotus calls Babylon a city of Assyria. But even this supposition, although highly probable, is not here necessary. Let it be observed that the days here threatened were to be worse, not simply with respect to individual suffering or temporary difficulties of the state itself, but to the loss of its independence, its transition to a servile state, from which it was never permanently freed, the domination of Assyria being soon succeeded by that of Egypt, and this by that of Babylon, Persia, Syria, and Rome, the last ending only in the downfall of the state, and that general dispersion of the people which continues to this day. The revolt of Hezekiah and even longer intervals of liberty in later times, are mere interruptions of the customary and prevailing bondage. Of this critical change it surely might be said, even though it were to cost not a single drop of blood, nor the personal freedom of a single captive, that the Lord was about to bring upon Judah days which had not been witnessed from the time of Ephraim's apostasy, or according to the other construction of the text, at any time whatever; since none of the evils suffered, from Solomon to Ahaz, had destroyed the independence of Judah, not even the Egyptian domination in the reign of Rehoboam, which only lasted long enough to teach the Jews the difference between God's service and *the service of the kingdoms of the countries* (2 Chron. xii. 8). This view of the matter is abundantly sufficient to reconcile the prophecy with history, whether Assyria be understood to mean the kingdom properly so called, or to include the empires which succeeded it; and whether the threatening be referred exclusively to Ahaz and his times, as Gesenius and Rosenmüller say it must be, or to him and his successors jointly, which appears to be the true sense of *thy people and thy father's house* as distinguished from himself and his own house; but even on the other supposition, as the change of times, *i. e.* the transition from an independent to a servile state, took place before the death of Ahaz, the expressions used are perfectly consistent with the facts. It is implied, of course, in this interpretation, that Sennacherib's invasion was not the *beginning* of the days here threatened, which is rather to be sought in the alliance between Ahaz and Tiglath-pileser, *who came unto him and distressed him and strengthened him not* (2 Chron. xxviii. 19, 20), but exacted repeated contribution from him as a vassal; which degrading and oppressive intercourse continued till his death, as appears from the statement (2 Kings xviii. 7), that *Hezekiah rebelled against the king of Assyria, and served him not*, clearly implying that he did at first, as he offered to do afterwards, on Sennacherib's approach, with confession of his fault, renewal of his tribute, and a repetition of his father's sacrilege (2 Kings xviii. 13–16). That during the whole term of this foreign ascendancy, Judah was infested by Assyrian intruders, and by frequent visitations for the purpose of extorting their unwilling tribute, till at last the revolt of Hezekiah, no longer able to endure the burden, led to a formal occupation of the country, is not only probable in itself, but seems to be implied in the subsequent context (verses 18–20). The abrupt commencement of this verse, without a connecting particle, led Alting to regard it as the apodosis of the sentence beginning with ver. 16—" before the child shall know, &c., and *before* the land shall

be forsaken, Jehovah will bring upon thee," &c.   But besides the unusual
length and involution of the sentence, and the arbitrary repetition of *before*
with *and*, it cannot be explained, on this hypothesis, to what desolation
ver. 16 alludes, as the overthrow of Israel *preceded* the invasion of Judah
by Assyria.   The abrupt commencement of the sentence is regarded by
Maurer as a proof that the remainder of the chapter is of later date ; by
Hitzig as marking the commencement of the prophecy itself, what precedes
being introductory to it.   Vitringa supposes that the Prophet paused, as
if unwilling to proceed ; Houbigant, as usual, amends the text by inserting
vav; while Lowth and others follow the Septuagint by supplying *but.*
According to Hendewerk, however, the adversative particle is out of place,
as he denies that what now follows is a threatening appended to a previous
promise, and regards it as an amplification of the threatening in ver. 15 ;
but that relates to the Syrian invasion, this to the Assyrian domination.
Alting's translation of עָלָיִד by *against thee*, though it does not change the
general sense, destroys its figurative dress, in which there is an obvious
allusion to the bringing of water or the like *upon* a person, so as to destroy
him.   Compare Joshua xxiii. 15 and xxiv. 7.—The last words of this verse
(את מלך אשור) have been rejected as a gloss by Houbigant, Secker,. Lowth,
Eichhorn, Gesenius, Hitzig, Maurer, Hendewerk, Umbreit, and Knobel,
on the ground that they contain an inelegant anticipation of what follows,
and an explanation of what goes before, at once superfluous and incorrect,
since Egypt as well as Assyria is mentioned afterwards.   That Assyria
might be naturally named alone, as first in time and in importance, is admitted by Eichhorn, who rejects the clause on other grounds ; and Maurer,
who does the same, speaks with contempt of the objection founded on the
days being explained to mean the *king* (id nihil est).   As for the rhetorical
objection that the words are too prosaic, it is founded on the modern notion
that the prophets were mere poets.   The objections to the explanation
which the clause contains, as superfluous and incorrect, may cancel one
another, as both cannot well be true.   Gesenius thinks the supposition of
a gloss the more probable because he has detected several others in this
prophecy ; while Ewald, on the other hand, retains the words as genuine,
because they recur below in ver. 20 and in chap. viii. 7.   The external
evidence is all in favour of the clause.   There is no need of making אֵת a
preposition meaning *by, though,* or *from*, as Jerome, Luther, Grotius, and
Clericus do ; nor is it necessary to regard the words as in apposition to
יָמִים, since they are rather a second object to the verb יָבִיא, which may be
considered as repeated before אֵת, as Hengstenberg suggests—*he shall bring
upon thee days*, &c. (he shall bring upon thee) *the king of Assyria.*

18. The evil times just threatened are here more explicitly described as
arising from the presence and oppression of foreigners, especially Assyrians
and Egyptians, whose number and vexatious impositions are expressed by
comparing them to swarms of noxious and annoying insects, pouring into
the country by divine command.   *And it shall be* (or come to pass) *in that
day* (in the *days* just threatened) *that Jehovah will hiss* (or *whistle*) *to* (or
for) *the fly which* (is) *in the end* (or *edge*) *of the rivers of Egypt, and to* (or
for) *the bee which is in Assyria.*   The fly is peculiarly appropriate to
Egypt, where the marshy grounds produce it in abundance, and there may
be a reference, as Barnes supposes, to the plague of flies in Exodus.
Knobel and others think there may be also an allusion to the abounding of
bees in Assyria ; but the Prophet probably intended only to combine two

familiar and annoying kinds of insects, and not to describe the distinctive qualities of the two nations, the fierceness and boldness of the Assyrians, the filth (Basil), cowardice (Jerome), or buzzing speech (Cyril), of the Egyptians. The *end of the streams* of Egypt is referred by some to the adjacent countries (Junius, Piscator) ; but it evidently means something belonging to Egypt itself, viz. the arms of the Delta (Vitringa, Clericus, J. D. Michaelis, Rosenmüller, Hendewerk, Henderson), or the remotest streams (Gesenius, Maurer, Ewald), implying that the flies should come from the very extremities, or from the whole land (Barnes). By making קצה denote the lateral extremity or edge, and rendering it *brink* or *border*, as the common version does in Joshua iii. 8, Exod. xvi. 35, an equally good sense is obtained, viz. that the flies shall come from the banks of the streams, where they are most abundant.—The hiss or whistle, denoting God's control over these enemies of Judah, has the same sense as in chap. v. 26. Assyria and Egypt are not here named indefinitely (Hendewerk), but as the two great rival powers who disturbed the peace of Western Asia, and to whom the land of Israel was both a place and subject of contention. The *bee* cannot of itself denote an *army* (Barnes), nor is the reference exclusively to actual invasion, but to the annoying and oppressive occupation of the country by civil and military agents of these foreign powers. It was not merely attacked but infested, by the flies and bees of Egypt and Assyria. *Fly* is understood as a generic term including gnats, mosquitoes, &c., by Henderson, and *bee* as including wasps and hornets by Hitzig and Umbreit.

19. Carrying out the figures of the preceding verse, the Prophet, instead of simply saying that the land shall be infested by foreigners, represents it as completely filled with bees and flies, who are described as settling upon all the places commonly frequented by such insects. *And they come and rest* (or settle) *all of them in the desolate* (or precipitous) *valleys, and in the clefts of rocks, and in all thorn-hedges, and in all pastures.* According to Clericus, the places mentioned are those suited for the encampment of troops; but this supposes a different meaning of the words translated *desolate valleys* and *thorn-hedges.* The exclusive reference to invading armies is assumed by other writers also ; but although this may have been the prominent idea, the words seem naturally to express the general notion of a country overrun, infested, filled with foreigners and enemies, not only by military occupation but in other ways. The opinion of Kimchi and Forerius, that the sites of towns are here described, overlooks the beautiful allusion to the habits of the insects mentioned. The same objection lies in part against the supposition of an antithesis between deserted and frequented places (Cocceius), or between worthless and valuable products, " thorns and shrubbery of pleasure " (Barnes), which rests moreover upon etymologies now commonly abandoned. Grotius suggests that these four terms have reference to the two kinds of insects alternately, the first and third denoting customary haunts of flies, the second and fourth of bees. The version above given is the one adopted by the latest writers (Gesenius, Hitzig, Ewald, Hendewerk, Henderson, Umbreit, Knobel). For a great variety of older explanations see Rosenmüller on the passage and Gesenius's Thesaurus s. v.

20. Had the Prophet, as Hendewerk suggests, represented the invaders as *locusts*, he would probably have gone on to describe them as devouring the land ; but having chosen bees and flies as the emblem, he proceeds to express the idea of their spoliations by a different figure, that of a body

closely shorn or shaven by a razor under the control of God and in his service. *In that day* (the same day mentioned in ver. 19) *will the Lord shave, with a razor hired in the parts beyond the river* (Euphrates), (that is to say) *with the king of Assyria, the head and the hair of the feet* (*i. e.* of both extremities, or of the whole body), *and also the beard will it* (the razor) *take away.* The words במלך אשור are rejected by Gesenius, Maurer, Umbreit, Knobel, for the same reason, or rather with as little reason, as in ver. 17. They are retained by Hendewerk and Ewald. Aben Ezra and Abarbenel follow the Targum and Peshito in making the king of Assyria the subject of the operation here described, and suppose the destroying angel to be called a hired razor, *i. e.* one of the best temper and condition. Theodoret also understands the king of Assyria to be here described as shaved, but by the Medes and Persians as a razor. These constructions wholly disregard the preposition before מֶלֶךְ, or take it in the sense of *in*—"will shave in the king of Assyria, the head," &c. Some understand בְּעֶבְרֵי נָהָר as an additional description of the razor—"with a hired razor, with those beyond the river with the king of Assyria." But as בְּעֶבְרֵ and בְּעֵבֶר are never used in reference to persons, the former no doubt here denotes the place of hiring—"a razor hired in the parts beyond the river." If so, שְׂכִירָה cannot be a noun (novacula conductionis), but must be taken as a verbal adjective, equivalent to a passive participle, of which this is a common form in Chaldee. There is no need of changing the division of the words, so as to read תַּעֲרָה שְׂכִירָה, since the article before the noun may be omitted by poetic licence, and תַּעַר is construed as a feminine with תִּסְפֶּה. Instead of *hired* (μεμισθωμένῳ), the Alexandrian MS. of the Septuagint reads *drunken* (μεμεθυσμένῳ), which is also the version of Aquila, Symmachus, and Theodotion ; and accordingly J. D. Michaelis would read שְׁכִירָה understanding by a *drunken razor* one employed as a drunkard would employ it, *i. e.* recklessly and rashly. The same reading seems to be implied in the common text of the Peshito, though Ephrem Syrus gives the Syriac adjective the sense of *sharp.* According to the common reading, which is no doubt genuine, the king of Assyria is called a hired razor, not because men use what is hired more unsparingly than if it were their own (Calvin)—nor simply because he was allured or hired by the hope of conquest (Jerome, Grotius, J. D. Michaelis, &c.)—nor simply because Ahaz had already hired him (Junius, Piscator, Glassius, &c.)—but for the last two reasons put together, that as Ahaz had profaned and robbed God's house to hire a foreign razor, with which Israel and Syria might be shaven, so God would make use of that self-same razor to shave Judah, *i. e.* to remove its population, or its wealth, or both. The rabbinnical interpretation of שֵׂעַר רַגְלִים is a poor conceit, the adoption of which by Gesenius, if indicative of nothing worse, says but little for the taste and the "æsthetic feeling" which so often sits in judgment on the language of the Prophet. The true sense is no doubt the one expressed by Ewald (von oben bis unten), and before him by Clericus, who justly says of the Rabbinical expounders of the phrase "rem turpiculam de suo Prophetæ admetiri videntur." The separate mention of the *beard* may have reference to the oriental fondness for it and associations of dishonour with the loss of it. The specific explanation of the beard as meaning the ministers of religion (Vitringa), or Sennacherib (Vatablus), &c., and a like explanation of the other terms, are not only arbitrary and capricious, but destructive of a beautiful and simple metaphor, which represents the spoiling of Judah by foreign invaders and intruders as the shaving of the hair from the whole body. The same remark

applies to Hendewerk's suggestion, that the parts of a country are often
represented by those of a human body, and that the hair of the head may
possibly denote the wooded hills of Palestine. Lowth applies *Vav* before
נָהָר ; but the latter may be poetically used for the Euphrates, even without
the article (Jer. ii. 18). Barnes explains תִּסְפֶּה in a passive sense ; but
this requires וְקַן, as well as תַּעַר, to be taken as a feminine noun contrary to
usage, a concurrence of anomalies by no means probable. Henderson
makes תִּסְפֶּה a stronger expression than יְגַלַּח, and translates it *shall scrape
off*, which is given by Gesenius as the primary sense, but that of *causing to
cease* or *removing* is the one best sustained by usage. The Targum paraphrases תַּעַר as denoting various kinds of weapons used in war, and the
Vulgate almost seems to make the razor itself the object to be shaved.

21, 22. In consequence of these spoliations, the condition of the country
will be wholly changed. The population left shall not be agricultural but
pastoral. Instead of living on the fruits of the soil, they shall subsist upon
spontaneous products, such as milk and honey, which shall be abundant
only because the people will be few and the uncultivated grounds extensive.
And it shall be in that day (that) a man shall save (or *keep*) *alive a young
cow and two sheep ; and it shall be (that) from the abundance of the making*
(yielding or production) *of milk, he shall eat butter* (or *curds* or *cheese* or
cream); *for butter and honey shall every one eat that is left in the midst of*
(or *within*) *the land.* There is no need of assuming a conditional construction—" *q. d.* if one should keep "—as J. H. Michaelis, Maurer, and De
Wette do—since this idea is sufficiently implied in an extract translation.
אִישׁ does not necessarily mean *every man*, implying that the poorest of the
people should have so much cattle (Gesenius), or that the richest should
have no more (Calvin), but simply *one* indefinitely (Hitzig, Ewald). The
piel of חָיָה nowhere else signifies to "keep, own, feed" (Barnes), nor to
hold, possess (Gesenius, Ewald, &c.). Its primary meaning is to *give life*
originally (Job xxxiii. 4), or to *restore* it after death (1 Sam. ii. 6) ; whence
by a natural transition it is used to denote the *preservation* of one's life in
danger (Ps. xxx. 4) ; so that unless we depart from its proper meaning
here, it must denote not merely the *keeping* or *raising* of the cow and sheep,
but their being *saved* from a greater number, and preserved with difficulty,
not for want of pasture, which was more than ever plentiful, but from the
presence of invaders and enemies. Thus understood, the word throws light
upon the state of the country, as described in the context. Hendewerk
thinks it not improbable that by *a cow* and *two sheep* we are to understand
a *herd* of cows and two *flocks* of sheep, because so small a number would
not yield *abundance* of milk. But the abundance is of course to be relatively understood, with respect to the small number of persons to be fed,
and is therefore an additional and necessary stroke in the prophetic picture
—few cattle left, and yet those few sufficient to afford milk in abundance
to the few inhabitants. This abundance is expressed still more strongly by
describing them as eating, not the milk itself, but that which is produced
from it, and which of course must bear a small proportion to the whole ;
and as this is the essential idea meant to be conveyed by mentioning the
חֶמְאָה, it matters little whether it be understood to mean butter (Septuagint, &c.), cheese (Hendewerk), cream (Hitzig, De Wette, Ewald, Umbreit,
Knobel), or curds (Gesenius, &c.), though the last seems to agree best
with what we know of oriental usages. It is here mentioned neither as a
delicacy nor as plain and ordinary food, but as a kind of diet independent
of the cultivation of the earth, and therefore implying a neglect of tillage

and a pastoral mode of life, as well as an unusual extent of pasturage, which may have reference, as Barnes suggests, not only to the milk, but to the honey. The rabbinical interpretation of these verses, as a promise of abundance in the reign of Hezekiah after Sennacherib's retreat (2 Chron. xxii. 27–29), and the adaptation of the same exposition to the time of Christ (Grotius, Cocceius, &c.), appear to have arisen from confounding what is here said of *butter and honey* with a frequent description of the promised land as *flowing with milk and honey*. But not to insist upon the circumstance, that this is a literal and that a metaphorical description, and that even in the latter the idea of abundance is conveyed by the *flowing* of the land with milk and honey, which is not here mentioned; let it be observed that even the abundance thus asserted of the promised land is not fertility, but the abundance of spontaneous products, not dependent upon tillage; and that after Israel was possessed of Canaan, and had become an agricultural people, the natural emblem of abundance would no longer be *milk and honey*, but *corn and wine*, or *flesh and fruits*, so that the prospect of subsisting on the first two, if it did not suggest the idea of personal privation, would suggest that of general desolation, or at least that of interrupted or suspended cultivation. Thus Boswell, in the Journal of his tour with Dr Johnson to the Hebrides, observes of the inhabitants of one of the poor islands, that " they lived all the spring *without meal*, upon *milk and curds and whey* alone." This verse, then, is descriptive of abundance only as connected with a paucity of people and a general neglect of tillage. It was designed, indeed, to be directly expressive neither of abundance nor of poverty (Barnes), but of a change in the condition of the country and of the remaining people, which is further described in the ensuing context. The older interpreters were probably misled by the peculiar mode in which a threatening is here uttered in the tone of a promise, or as Knobel expresses it, the words sound promising (klingen verheissend), but contain a threat. The same thing had been observed before by Henderson, and most of the recent writers are agreed in giving to the 22d verse its true sense as a prophecy of desolation. This of course determines that of the fifteenth, to which Hendewerk supposes Isaiah to refer directly, as if he had said, " This is what I meant by saying that the child should eat curds and honey, *for curds and honey shall every one eat that is left in the midst of the land.*"

23. Having described the desolation of the country indirectly, by saying what the food of the inhabitants should be, the Prophet now describes it more directly, by predicting the growth of thorns and briers even in spots which had been sedulously cultivated, for example the most valuable vineyards. *And it shall be* (or come to pass) *in that day* (that) *every place where there shall be a thousand vines at* (or *for*) *a thousand silverlings* (pieces or shekels of silver), *shall be for* (or *become*) *thorns and briers*, or *shall be* (given up) *to the thorn and to the brier*. Kimchi reverses the prediction, so as to make it mean that every place *now* full of thorns and briers shall *hereafter* abound in valuable vines, which is of course an impossible construction. Calvin supposes the *thousand silverlings* or *shekels* to be mentioned as a very low price, and understands the verse to mean that every place planted with a thousand vines should, in these days of desolation, be sold for only so much, *on account of* the thorns and briers which had overrun them. All other writers seem to confine the threatening to the thorns and briers, and to regard בְּאֶלֶף כֶּסֶף as a part of the description of a valuable vineyard, though they differ on the question whether this was the price for which the vineyard might be sold, or its annual rent, as in Sol. Song viii.

11, where, however, it is said to be the price of the *fruit*, and the number of vines is not mentioned. The vines of the Johannisberg are valued at a ducat each, according to J. D. Michaelis, who thinks, however, that, allowance being made for the change in the value of money, the price mentioned in the text was probably a high one even for a valuable vineyard. Henderson computes that it was nearly one-half more than the price at which the vineyards of Mount Lebanon were sold in 1811, according to Burckhardt, namely, a piastre for each vine.—The substantive verb with ל may signify either "to belong to" (Hitzig, Ewald), "to be given up to" (Umbreit), "or to become" (De Wette, Knobel), which last is its most usual meaning. The irregular repetition of the verb is occasioned by the length of the parenthetical clause. The construction of the sentence is entirely changed in Henderson's version—*in every place, &c., there shall be briers and thorns.*

24. So complete shall be the desolation of these once favoured spots, that men shall pass through them armed, as they would through a wilderness. *With arrows and with bow shall one* (or *shall a man*) *go thither, because thorns and briers shall the whole land be.* The essential idea, as the last clause shews, is that of general desolation; there is no need, therefore, of supposing that the bows and arrows have exclusive reference to protection against enemies (Kimchi), or beasts (Jarchi), or robbers (Clericus), or to hunting (Calvin), as neither is particularly mentioned, and as it would be natural to carry weapons into such a region both for protection and the chase (Lowth, Gesenius). It is no objection to the mention of the latter, that the people had just been represented as subsisting upon milk and honey, since these two methods of subsistence often co-exist, as belonging to the same state of society, and both imply a general neglect of tillage. The exact sense of the last clause is not that the land shall *become thorns and briers* (English version), as in ver. 24, but that it shall actually *be* thorns and briers.

25. Not only the fields, not only the vineyards, shall be overrun with thorns and briers, but the very hills, now laboriously cultivated with the hand, shall be given up to like desolation. *And all the hills* (*i.e.* even all the hills) *which are digged with the hoe* (because inaccessible to the plough) *—thou shalt not go* (even) *there, for fear of briers and thorns, and* (being thus uncultivated) *they shall be for a sending-place of cattle and a trampling-place of sheep* (*i.e.* a place where cattle may be sent to pasture, and which may be trodden down by sheep). The reference is probably to the hills of Judea, anciently cultivated to the very top, by means of terraces that still exist, for an account of which by eye-witnesses, see Keith's Land of Israel, chapter xii., and Robinson's Palestine, vol. ii. p. 187. Thus understood, the verse merely strengthens the foregoing description, by declaring that even the most carefully-cultivated portions of the land should not escape the threatened desolation. It is not necessary, therefore, to give הָאָרֶץ in ver. 24 the arbitrary sense of *lowlands*, as distinguished from the mountains mentioned here (Henderson); much less to understand הָרִים itself as meaning mounds or hillocks formed by the hoe (Forerius). It is equally gratuitous, and therefore inadmissible, to take *thorns and briers* in a different sense from that which they have in the preceding verses, *e.g.* in that of a *thorn hedge*, implying that the vineyard should no longer be enclosed (Grotius, Cocceius, Vitringa), an arbitrary change which cannot be justified by Matthew Henry's epigrammatic observation, that the thorns, instead of growing where they would be useful, should spring up in abundance where they were not wanted. With this explanation of *thorns and briers* is con-

nected an erroneous construction of תָּבוֹא as a verb in the third person, agreeing with יְרָאַת as its subject—" the fear of thorns and briers shall not come thither"—*i. e.* there shall be no hindrance to their growth (Ewald), or no regard to them (Junius), or no thorn hedges (Grotius). Kimchi and Abarbenel connect this same construction with the natural and proper sense of *thorns and briers*, and thus convert the verse into a promise that in the mountains there should be no fear of desolation ; while Cyril and Calvin make it a threatening in the form of a promise (like ver. 22), by explaining it to mean that even if the hills where the remaining inhabitants take refuge should be tilled, and thus escape the fear of thorns and briers, it would only be because the rest of the country should be desolate. The simplest and most satisfactory construction is the one now commonly adopted, which takes תָּבוֹא as the second person used indefinitely (*thou* for *any one*), and יְרָאַת as a noun used adverbially to denote *for fear of*, which is more agreeable to Hebrew usage than to suppose an ellipsis of the preposition מִן (Rosenmüller). Thus understood, the verse continues and completes the description of the general desolation, as manifested first by the people's living upon milk and honey, then by the growth of thorns and briers in the choicest vineyards and the terraced hills, and by the conversion of these carefully-tilled spots into dangerous solitudes, hunting-grounds, and pastures.

Chapter 8

THE prediction of the overthrow of Syria and Israel is now renewed in the form of a symbolical name, to be inscribed on a tablet and attested by two witnesses, and afterwards applied to the Prophet's new-born son, whose progress as an infant is made the measure of the event, vers. 1–4. It is then foretold that the judgment denounced upon Syria and Israel should extend to Judah, as a punishment for distrust of God and reliance upon human aid, in consequence of which the kingdom should be imminently threatened with destruction, yet delivered for the sake of Immanuel, by whom the strength and wisdom of all enemies should be alike defeated, vers. 5–10. The Messiah himself is then introduced as speaking, warning the Prophet and the true believers neither to share in the apprehensions nor to fear the reproaches of the people, but to let Jehovah be an object of exclusive fear and reverence to them, as he would be an occasion of destruction to the unbelievers, from whom the true sense of this revelation was to be concealed, and restricted to his followers, who, together with the Prophet and the Son of God himself, should be for signs and wonders to the multitude, while waiting for the manifestation of his presence, and refusing to consult any other oracle except the word of God, an authority despised by none but those doomed to the darkness of despair, which is described as settling down upon them ; with a sudden intimation, at the close, of a change for the better, especially in reference to that part of the country which had been most afflicted and despised, vers. 11–23.

The Hebrew and English text differ here in the division of the chapters. A better arrangement than either would have been to continue the eighth without interruption to the close of what is now the sixth (or seventh) verse of the ninth chapter, where a new division of the prophecy begins.

1. The prediction of the overthrow of Syria and Israel, contained in chap. vii. 8, 9, is here repeated, and as before in a symbolical form. In order to excite immediate attention, and at the same time to verify the pro-

phecy, Isaiah is required to inscribe an enigmatical name on a large tablet in a legible character, with a view to present exhibition and to subsequent preservation. The name itself includes a prophecy of speedy spoliation. *And Jehovah said to me, take thee* (or *for thyself*) *a great tablet, i. c.* great in proportion to the length of the inscription, *and write upon it with a man's pen* (or *stylus, i. e.* in an ordinary and familiar hand), *To Maher-shalal-hash-baz* (*i. e.* Haste-spoil-quick-prey). The name may also be read as a sentence—*Hasten spoil! Prey hastens.* (So Cocceius : propera spolium, festinavit direptio.) Others take מַהֵר, as an infinitive (either used as such or instead of a preterite), on account of the לְ prefixed, which, however, has no more connection with this than with the other words, being joined to it merely as the first word in the sentence, just as the English *to* might be prefixed to an inscription. Here as in ver. 3, *Maher-shalal-hash-baz* is a name, and the exhibition of the tablet, in the temple (Barnes), or the market-place (Ewald), or the Prophet's house (Knobel), was intended to suggest the question, who is meant ? It is therefore less correct to say that the inscription is afterwards transferred to the child, than that the name of the child is anticipated here. These four words are not merely the heading or title of the writing (Barnes), but the writing itself. The modern lexicographers explain גִּלָּיוֹן not as a derivative of גָּלַל, to roll, and a synonyme of מְגִלָּה, a volume, but as a derivative of גָּלָה, to polish, and as meaning a tablet of metal, or as Knobel supposes, of wood covered with wax. חֶרֶט the stylus used in writing on such tablets. *Human* is here explained by Hendewerk as meaning common or ordinary in opposition to *divine*, but by others more probably in opposition to a mode of writing only known to some, and not to men in general ; whether the allusion be to a *sacred* character (Henderson), or simply to the letters used in books as distinguished from those used in common life (Ewald). Both the kind of writing and the size of the tablet (admitting larger characters), have reference to its being legible, *so that he may run that readeth it.* (Hab. ii. 2.)

2. In order to preclude all suspicion of its having been uttered after the event, the prophecy is not only recorded, but attested by two witnesses. *And I* (Jehovah) *will take to witness for me credible witnesses, to wit, Uriah the priest, and Zechariah, son of Jeberechiah.* These were not to be witnesses of the Prophet's marriage (Luther, Grotius), but of his having written and exhibited the prophecy long before the event. Uriah is probably the same who connived at the king's profanation of the temple (2 Kings xvi. 10–16). The word נֶאֱמָנִים does not relate to their true character or standing in the sight of God, but to their credit with the people, especially perhaps with the king, in which view, as well as on account of his official rank, Uriah was a very suitable witness. The same consideration makes it not improbable that the Zechariah mentioned here was the father-in-law of Ahaz (2 Kings xviii. 2 ; 2 Chron. xxix. 1), perhaps the same that is mentioned as a Levite of the family of Asaph (2 Chron. xxix. 13). The Zechariah mentioned in 2 Chron. xxvi. 5, seems to have died before Uzziah. Zechariah the son of Jehoiada was put to death between the porch and the altar (Mat. xxiii. 35) long before this, in the reign of Joash (2 Chron. xxiv. 20, 21). Zechariah the Prophet was the son of Berechiah, but he lived after the Babylonish exile. The Rabbins and Lightfoot give to עֵדִים the emphatic sense of *martyrs* (μάρτυρες), witnesses for the truth, and suppose Uriah to be the person who prophesied against Judah, and was put to death by Jehoiakim, about 130 years after the date

of this prediction. But such an attestation would have been wholly irrelevant and useless. The Vulgate takes the verb as a preterite (et adhibui
mihi testes) and Gesenius, Maurer, Knobel read accordingly וָאָעִידָה with *Vav*
conversive. The Septuagint, Targum, and Peshito make it imperative
(μάρτυράς μοι ποίησον), and Hitzig accordingly reads הָעִידָה. Gesenius formerly preferred an indirect or subjunctive construction, which is still retained by Henderson, *and that I should take as witnesses.* The true construction is no doubt the obvious one, *and I will cite as witnesses* (Hendewerk, Ewald, Umbreit)—God being still the speaker, and the matter being
one in which the Prophet was concerned only as his representative, so that
the ascription of the act to God himself is not only admissible but necessary.
This construction also accounts best for the paragogic form of the verb, as
expressing strong determination or fixed purpose.

3. The significant name, before inscribed upon the tablet, is now applied
to the Prophet's new-born son, that the child, as well as the inscription,
might remind all who saw them of the prophecy. The execution of the
previous command is here, as in many other cases, tacitly included in the
record of the command itself. (*Vide supra*, chap. vii. 4). *And I approached unto the Prophetess, and she conceived and bare a son, and Jehovah
said to me, Call his name Maher-shalal-hash-baz.* Calvin's supposition
that this passed in vision is entirely gratuitous. This name, like *Immanuel*,
may be understood as simply descriptive or symbolical, but its actual imposition is inferred by most interpreters from ver. 18, where the Prophet
speaks of himself and his children as signs and wonders in Israel, with
reference, as they suppose, to the names *Shear-jashub and Maher-shalal-
hash-baz.* The four ancient versions all translate the name, and all, except
the Targum, with some variations from the rendering in ver. 1. Most of
the later German writers adopt Luther's version, *Raubebald Eilebeute*, but
instead of the first word Ewald has *Schnellraub.* The pluperfect construction, *I had approached*, &c., given by Junius, Gesenius, and others, is not
only needless but, according to Ewald, Maurer, and Hitzig, ungrammatical.
The strange opinion of Tertullian, Basil, Cyril, and Jerome, that the Prophetess is the Virgin Mary, and that this verse is the language of the Holy
Spirit, though adopted by Œcolampadius and others, is rejected even by
Thomas Aquinas. The *Prophetess* is probably so called, not because she
was inspired (Grotius), or because she was to give the name *Immanuel*
(Hendewerk), or because she bore a part in this prophetical transaction
(Calvin), but because she was a prophet's wife, as *queen* usually means a
royal consort, not a queen *suo jure.* A remarkable series of prophetic
names, imposed upon three children, is recorded in the first chapter of Hosea.

4. It is not merely by its name that the child is connected with the prophecy. The date of the event is determined by a reference to the infant's
growth, as in the case of Immanuel. *For before the child shall know (how)
to cry my father and my mother, one* (or *they* indefinitely) *shall take away
the wealth of Damascus and the spoil of Samaria before the king of Assyria,*
i. e. into his presence, to deliver it to him (Gesenius), or in triumphal procession (Calvin), or before him, *i. e.* before he marches homeward himself
(Hendewerk), or simply *in his presence*, that is by his command and under
his direction. The construction of יִשָּׂא is indefinite, so that there is no
need of supplying יְהֹוָה as the subject. The time fixed is that of the child's
capacity not to recognise its parents, or to talk, but to utter the simple
labial sounds by which in Hebrew, as in many other languages, *father* and
mother are expressed. The time denoted has been fixed by Vitringa and

Rosenmüller at three years, by Junius and most later writers at one. But this very difference of judgment seems to show that the description was intended to be somewhat indefinite, equivalent perhaps to our familiar phrase *a year or two*, within which time we have reason to believe that the event occurred. Gesenius alleges that the prophecy in reference to Israel was not fulfilled for eighteen years (2 Kings xvii. 6), to which Hengstenberg replies that Samaria is here put for the kingdom and not for the capital city. But even if the name be strictly understood, there is no reason to doubt that Samaria was plundered by Tiglath-pileser (2 Kings xv. 29) although not destroyed, which idea is in fact not conveyed by the terms of the description. חַיִל properly means *strength*, but is specifically applied to *military* strength and to *wealth*, which last is the meaning here. The carrying away of its wealth does not necessarily imply anything more than such a spoiling of the capital as might be expected in the course of a brief but successful invasion. Barnes's construction of the second clause—" Damascus shall be borne away as regards its riches "—is inconsistent with the form of the original.

5. *And Jehovah added to speak to me again* (or *further*) *saying*. Here, as in chap. vii. 10, an interval of time may be assumed. Hendewerk supposes that in the mean time the Assyrians had approached and the invaders been compelled to withdraw from Judah.

6. The Assyrian invasion is now represented as a punishment of Judah for distrusting the divine protection and seeking that of the Assryians themselves. The immediate relief thus secured was to be followed by a worse calamity produced by those in whom they now confided. *Because this people* (Judah, so called in token of divine displeasure) *hath forsaken* (or rejected with contempt) *the waters of Shiloah* (or Siloam, the only perennial fountain of Jerusalem, here used as a symbol of the divine protection) *that go softly* (or flow gently, unaccompanied by noise or danger), *and* (because there is) *joy with respect to Rezin and the son of Ramaliah* (*i. e.* because the Jews are exulting in the retreat of their invaders, caused by the approach of the Assyrians), *therefore*, &c., the apodosis of the sentence being given in the next verse. Steudel supposes the invasion itself to be represented by the waters of Siloam, and contrasted with a worse invasion yet to come. Because they despised the gentle fountain, God would bring upon them a mighty river. But to this there are several objections. 1. The fountain of Siloam would hardly have been used as the emblem of a foreign invasion merely because weak and unsuccessful. 2. The verb מָאַס does not mean simply to despise, but to reject with contempt something once esteemed or entitled to esteem, and is therefore inapplicable to an invasion. 3. God himself had taught them to despise it (chap. vii. 4), and would not therefore have assigned their doing so as a reason for the punishment to be inflicted. Calvin understands by the waters of Siloam the mild and peaceful government of God, compared with the powerful military sway of foreign monarchs. Because the Jews despised their own advantages, and admired the conquests of Pekah and Rezin, therefore God would cause them to experience the hardships of Assyrian domination. But the only feelings which the Jews can be supposed to have experienced with respect to their invaders, are fear at their approach, and joy at their departure. That they rejoiced at their success, is a gratuitous assumption contradicted by the history. The same objection lies, with almost equal force, against the supposition of Gesenius, Maurer, Ewald, and Knobel, that this sympathy with the invaders is not asserted of the whole nation, but of a disaffected party

who rejected the authority of the family of David (the waters of Siloam), and rejoiced in the success of the enemy. However plausible such a supposition may appear, it is not to be assumed without necessity, or in preference to an explanation which involves no such imaginary facts. Henderson and others understand by *this people*, the kingdom of the ten tribes, whose apostasy from the true religion, and their rejection of the theocracy, are here assigned as reasons for the evils threatened. A Jewish prophet, speaking or writing to the Jews, would of course be understood to mean by *this people* those whom he addressed. It may be said indeed that *this* has reference to the mention of Ephraim in the foregoing context (ver. 4). But this would prove too much, by requiring Syria to be included in the charge of rejecting the waters of Siloam (Umbreit), in which case we must either suppose the words to be used in a twofold sense, or take מָאַס in that of simply *despising*, which is inadmissible. The same objection lies, in a less degree, against the opinion of Barnes and others, that by *this people* we are to understand Israel and Judah as a race. This is favoured by the fact that both these kingdoms are included in the threatenings of the subsequent context. But the exclusion of Syria is still more unnatural if Ephraim is included. The true sense seems to be that given by Hitzig, except that he regards מְשׂושׂ as an incorrect orthography for מְסוֹס, the infinitive of מָסַס to melt, to be dissolved with fear. "Because this people has rejected the waters of Siloam, gently flowing, and is afraid of Rezin and the son of Remaliah," &c. This explanation is unnecessary, as the same people who were terrified by the approach of the invaders would of course rejoice in their departure. The particle אֵת simply denotes the direct occasion of the joy. The more definite idea of rejoicing *over* is suggested by the context. For a full description of the fountain of Siloam, and the localities connected with it, see Robinson's Palestine, vol. i. pp. 501–505.

7. *Therefore* (because the people had thus ceased to trust in the divine protection, and rejoiced in the success of their application to Assyria), *behold* (as if the event were actually present), *the Lord* (is) *bringing up upon them the waters of the river* (*i. e.* the Euphrates, as an emblem of the Assyrian power), *its strong and many* waters) here contrasted with the gently flowing waters of Siloam), *to wit*, the *king of Assyria and all his glory* (with particular reference to military strength and display), *and it* (the river) *shall come up over all its channels and go over all its banks*, which may either mean, that it shall transcend its usual limits, or that, after submerging Israel, it shall overflow into Judah also. In favour of this last interpretation is the language of the next verse, and the fact that otherwise the punishment of Ephraim or the ten tribes is not expressly mentioned.—The copulative conjunction is used by a common Hebrew idiom to introduce the apodosis of the sentence. The figure of an overflowing river is peculiarly appropriate, not only as affording a striking antithesis to the fountain mentioned in the sixth verse, but because הַנָּהָר is often used absolutely to denote the Euphrates, the great river of the Assyrian and Babylonian empires. Clericus supposes that it here denotes the Tigris, as a river of Assyria Proper. But, according to the usage of the Greek and Roman writers, Assyria extended to the bank of the Euphrates, which Arrian describes as rising above its banks and overflowing τὴν γῆν ᾽Ασσυρίαν. The beauty of the metaphor is rendered still more striking by the frequent allusions, both in ancient and modern writers, to the actual inundations of this river. Here, as in chap. vii. 17, 18, the figures are explained in literal expressions by the Prophet himself. Here, too, the explanation has been questioned as a gloss

on grounds exclusively rhetorical. But every repetition, as Ewald well observes, makes the hypothesis of an interpolation more and more improbable. Its alleged incongruity, if it did not exclude it in the first place, must have struck the most uncritical reader on its second or third recurrence. Some suppose an allusion in כְּבוֹדוֹ to the pomp of the oriental kings in their marches. But this is not known to have been an Assyrian usage, and the supposition is at least unnecessary.—Some understand by *its channels* and *its banks* the channel and banks of Judah ; but this construction agrees neither with the proper meaning of the words nor with the metaphor of which they form a part. According to Junius, the overflowing of the banks were designed to represent the king of Assyria's violation of his own engagements in oppressing those for whose relief he had come forth.

8. *And it* (the river) *shall pass over* (from Syria and Israel) *into Judah, overflow and pass through* (so as nearly to submerge it), *to the neck shall it reach* (but not above the head), *and the spreadings of its wings shall be the filling of the breadth of thy land, O Immanuel !* The English Version disturbs the metaphor by using the person pronoun *he* so as to refer this verse directly to the king, and not to the river which represented him. It also makes חָלַף mean to *pass through*, which is really expressed by עָבַר, while the former verb denotes a change of direction, and subjoins a threatening against Judah to the threatening against Israel. By the neck, the Targum understands Jerusalem, in which it is followed by Calvin, Junius, Piscator, Vitringa, Henderson and Barnes, the last of whom supposes a distinct allusion to the elevated site of the Holy City. Most probably, however, the expression was intended to denote nothing more than the imminency of the danger by figures borrowed from a case of drowning, the head alone being left above the water. Most writers suppose the figure of a stream to be exchanged in the last clause for that of a bird, or for the description of an army ; but Umbreit and Knobel understand *wings* to be used here, as often elsewhere, in the sense of sides or lateral extremities, and applied to the river itself. Some of the Jewish writers make עִמָּנוּאֵל a proposition, *God (is) with us*, in favour of which is the analogy of ver. 9 below, and the fact that the words are separately written in most manuscripts. In favour of making it a proper name is the analogy of chap. vii. 16, and the pronoun of the second person joined to the preceding word, *thy land, Immanuel !* Some of the Rabbins make the Prophet the object of address, " thy land (O Isaiah)." But this is arbitrary, and renders the connection of the clauses very harsh. If this had been the meaning, the Prophet would probably have said, " *but* God is with us." Those who regard *Immanuel* as the name of a contemporary child, understand by *thy land* thy native land (as in Gen. xii. 1 ; John i. 8), and to the question why this child should be specially addressed, reply because he was a *sign* to the people, and his name prophetic. But as we have seen that *Immanuel* is the Messiah, *thy land* must mean *the land belonging to thee*, thy dominion ; or rather both ideas are included. Thus understood, this brief apostrophe involves a prayer and promise of deliverance, *acsi dixisset, terra nihilominus erit tua o Immanuel !* (Calvin).

9. He now turns to the enemies of Judah, and assures them of the failure of their hostile plans. The prediction, as in chap. vi. 9, is clothed in the form of an ironical command or exhortation. *Be wicked* (*i. e.* indulge your malice, do your worst) *and be broken* (disappointed and confounded), *and* (that not only Syria and Israel, but) *give ear all remote parts of the earth* (whoever may attack the chosen people), *gird yourselves* (*i. e.* arm and

equip yourselves for action), *and be broken, gird yourselves and be broken* (the repetition implying the certainty of the event). The first verb (רֹעוּ) has been variously derived from רָעָה, רוּעַ, and רָעַע, and explained to mean *associate yourselves* (Targum, Vulgate, &c.), *break and be broken* (Aben Ezra, Kimchi, &c.), *make a noise* or *rage* (Henderson). This last is given by Gesenius in the second edition of his German version; in the first, and in his latest Lexicons, he gives the verb its usual sense of being evil or malignant, which is also expressed by Luther (seyd böse ihr Völker!). It is here equivalent to *do your worst*. Secker and Lowth, on the authority of the Septuagint, read דְּעוּ *know ye*, corresponding to תַּאֲזִינוּ, *hear ye*. Hendewerk and Knobel suppose Assyria and Israel to be exclusively addressed; but this is directly contradicted by the second clause. The failure or disappointment threatened is of course that of their ultimate design to overthrow the kingdom of Judah, and does not exclude the possibility of partial and temporary successes.

10. Not only their strength but their sagacity should be confounded. *Devise a plan, and it shall be defeated* (nullified or brought to nought); *speak a word* (whether a proposition or an order), *and it shall not stand* (or be carried into execution): *for (Immanuel) God (is) with us.* Junius and Tremellius make the last word a proper name, as in ver. 8—" Loquimini verbum et non existet, nam Himmanuelis (existet verbum)." This construction is too forced to be even called ingenious. The truth is, that even as a name Immanuel contains a proposition, and that here this proposition is distinctly announced, but with a designed allusion to the person whom the name describes. As if he had said, "The assurance of your safety is the great truth expressed by the name of your deliverer, to wit, that God is with us." The mere retention of the Hebrew word could not convey its sense in this connection to the English reader.

11. The triumphant apostrophe in ver. 10 is now justified by an appeal to the divine authority. I have reason to address our enemies in this tone, *for thus said Jehovah to me in strength of hand* (*i.e.* when his hand was strong upon me, when I was under the influence of inspiration), *and instructed me away from walking in the way of this people* (*i. e.* warned me not to follow the example of the unbelieving Jews). When one is spoken of in Scripture as inspired, it is said not only that the *spirit* was upon him (Ezek. xi. 5), but also that the *hand* of Jehovah was upon him (Ezek. i. 3; iii. 22; xxxiii. 32; xxxvii. 1), and in one case at least that it was *strong* upon him (Ezek. iii. 14). Hence *strength of hand* may have the sense of inspiration, and the whole phrase here employed be equivalent in meaning to the New Testament expressions ἐν πνεύματι (Rev. i. 10), ἐν ἐκστάσει (Acts xi. 5), ἐν δυνάμει καὶ πνεύματι ἁγίῳ (1 Thes. i. 5). Henderson is right in saying that the translation *taking me by the hand* cannot be justified, but wrong in representing it as " the rendering of our common version," the text of which has *with a strong hand*, and the margin *in strength of hand*, the literal translation. יִסְּרֵנִי is explained by Gesenius as a future Kal of unusual form, by Ewald as a preterite Piel with an unusual union-vowel. Gesenius connects it with a phrase before it (" when his hand was strong upon me, and he warned me." &c.). Others more probably with כֹּה אָמַר (" thus spake Jehovah and warned me," &c.). The author of this communication is supposed by some interpreters to be the Son of God, for reasons which will be explained below.

12. The words of God himself are now recorded. *Saying, ye shall not call conspiracy (or treason) every thing which this people calleth conspiracy*

(*or treason*), *and its fear ye shall not fear nor be afraid.* קֶשֶׁר, according to etymology and usage, is a treasonable combination or conspiracy. It is elsewhere constantly applied to such a combination on the part of subjects against their rulers (2 Kings xi. 14, xii. 21, xiv. 19, xv. 30). It is not strictly applicable, therefore, to the confederacy of Syria and Israel against Judah (Gesenius, Rosenmüller, Henderson, &c.), nor to that of Ahaz with the king of Assyria (Barnes, &c.). It would be more appropriate to factious combinations among the Jews themselves (Aben Ezra, Kimchi), if there were any trace of these in history. The correct view of the passage seems to be this. The unbelieving fears of the people led them to seek foreign aid. From this they were dissuaded by the Prophet and his followers, who regarded it as a violation of their duty to Jehovah. This opposition, like the conduct of Jeremiah during the Babylonian siege, was regarded by the king and his adherents as a treasonable combination to betray them to their enemies. But God himself commands the Prophet and the true believers not to be affected by this false reproach, not to regard the cry of treason or conspiracy, nor share in the real or pretended terrors of the unbelievers.

13. *Jehovah of hosts, him shall ye sanctify* (*i. e.* regard and treat as a Holy God, and as the Holy One of Israel); *and he shall be your fear, and he your dread, i. e.* the object of these feelings. If they felt as they ought towards God, as supreme and almighty, and as their own peculiar God, with whom they were united in a national covenant, they could not so distrust him as to be alarmed at the approach of any earthly danger. מַעֲרִיץ may either be an active participle (that which terrifies you) or a verbal noun resembling מוֹרָא in its mode of derivation. The collocation of the words makes the sentence more emphatic. *Him shall ye fear* is substantially equivalent to *Him alone shall ye fear.* Thus explained, the passage is at once a condemnation of the terror inspired by the approach of the two kings, and of the application, which it had occasioned, to Assyria for aid against them.

14. *And he* (Jehovah) *shall be for* (or become) *a holy thing* (an object to be sanctified) *and for a stone of stumbling and for a rock of offence* (*i. e.* a stone to strike against and stumble over) *to the two houses of Israel* (Ephraim and Judah); *for a gin* (or trap) *and for a snare to the inhabitants of Jerusalem.* מִקְדָּשׁ is by many understood to mean a *sanctuary,* in the specific sense, or with the accessory idea, of a *refuge* or *asylum* (Paulus, Gesenius, Rosenmüller, Winer, Maurer, Hendewerk, Barnes, Ewald, Umbreit, Henderson). But although the temples of the gods were so regarded by the Greeks and Romans, no such usage seems to have prevailed among the Christians till the time of Constantine (Bingham's Orig. Eccles. viii. 11, 1). As to the Jews, the only case which has been cited to establish such a practice seems to prove the contrary. So far was the altar from protecting Joab, that he was not even dragged away but killed upon the spot (2 Kings ii. 28). J. D. Michaelis supposes an allusion to the stone which Jacob called *Bethel* or the residence of God (Gen. xxviii. 19), the same object being here described as a *sanctuary* and as a *stone* of stumbling. But although this idea may be included, the word has probably a wider meaning, and was meant to bear the same relation to תקדישו (in ver. 13) that מוֹרָא bears to תיראו and מעריץ to תעריצו. God was the only proper object to be dreaded, feared, and sanctified, *i. e.* regarded as a holy being in the widest and most emphatic sense. Thus explained, the Hebrew מִקְדָּשׁ corresponds almost exactly to the Greek τὸ ἅγιον, the term applied to Christ by

the angel who announced his birth (Luke i. 35). In 1 Peter ii. 7, where this very passage is applied to Christ, ἡ τιμή seems to be employed as an equivalent to מִקְדָּשׁ as here used. To others he is a stone of stumbling, but to you who believe he is ἡ τιμή, something precious, something honoured, something looked upon as holy. The same application of the words is made by Paul in Rom. ix. 33. These quotations seem to shew that the Prophet's words have an extensive import, and are not to be restricted either to his own times or the time of Christ. The doctrine of the text is, that even the most glorious exhibitions of God's holiness, *i. e.* of his infinite perfection, may occasion the destruction of the unbeliever. The most signal illustration of this general truth was that afforded in the advent of the Saviour. It was frequently exemplified, however, in the interval, and one of these exemplifications was afforded by the conduct of the unbelieving Jews in the reign of Ahaz, to whom the only power that could save them was converted by their own unbelief into a stone of stumbling and a rock of offence. The same idea is then expressed by another simple and familiar figure, that of a snare or trap. Both figures naturally suggest the idea of inadvertence and unforeseen ruin. The two houses of Israel are not the two schools of Hillel and Shammai, or the kingdom of Israel and the faction that favoured it in Judah, both which are rabbinical conceits, but the two rival kingdoms of Judah and Ephraim, here put together to describe the whole race or nation of Israel. The sense is not that Jehovah would be sanctified by Judah, and become a stumbling-block to Israel; but that to some in either house or family these opposite events would happen. The inhabitants of Jerusalem are distinctly mentioned as the most conspicuous and influential members of the nation, just as Jerusalem itself is sometimes mentioned in connection with Judah, which really included it (*vide supra*, chap. i. 1).

15. This verse completes the threatening by an explicit declaration that Jehovah would not only be a stumbling-block and snare to the houses of Israel, but that many should actually fall and be ensnared and broken. *And many shall stumble over them* (the stone and snare)—or *among them* (the children of Israel)—*and fall and be broken and be snared, and be taken.* Gesenius and most of the later writers refer בָּם to the stone, rock, &c.; but Ewald and most of the older writers to the people. The first construction points out more distinctly the occasion of the threatened ruin, the last the persons whom it should befall; the general sense remains the same in either case.

16. *Bind up the testimony, seal the law, in my disciples.* These are not the words of the Prophet speaking in his own person, but a command addressed to him by God, or as some suppose by the Messiah, the מִקְדָּשׁ mentioned in the foregoing verse. Vitringa explains צֹר as the imperative of צוּר to form, delineate, inscribe. The command will then be to inscribe the revelation in the hearts of the disciples. It is commonly agreed, however, that the root is צָרַר to bind, and that the Prophet is commanded to tie up a roll or volume, and to seal it, thereby closing it. By law and testimony here we may either understand the prophetic inscription in ver. 1, or the whole preceding context, considered as included in the general sense of *revelation*, as God's *testimony* to the truth and as a *law* or declaration of his will. The *disciples*, or those taught of God, are supposed by some to be Uriah and Zechariah, the two witnesses named in ver. 2; by others, the sons of the prophets or literal disciples of Isaiah; but it probably means the better portion of the people, those truly enlightened because

taught of God (chap. liv. 13), to whom the knowledge of this revelation, or at least of its true meaning, was to be restricted. It is probable, therefore, that the preposition before לְמִדַּי does not mean *to* or *for* or *with* or *through ;* but either *among* or *in, i. e.* in their minds or hearts. The act described is not that of literally binding and sealing up a material record, but that of spiritually closing and depositing the revelation of God's will in the hearts of those who were able and willing to receive it, with allusion at the same time to its concealment from all others. Kimchi regards these as the words of the Prophet—nothing now remains but *to bind and seal the testimony.* This, however, even if we make צֹר an infinitive, is a very harsh construction.

17. *And I* (the Messiah) *will wait for Jehovah, that hideth his face from the house of Jacob, and will expect him.* Most writers make these the words of the Prophet ; but since he is addressed in the verse preceding, without any intimation of a change of speaker here, and since the next verse is quoted in Heb. ii. 13, as the words of the Messiah, it seems better to assume with Cocceius and Henderson, that throughout this passage the Messiah is the speaker. The phrase *to wait upon* has changed its meaning since the date of the English version, the prominent idea being now that of service and attendance, not as of old, that of expectation, which is the meaning of the Hebrew verb. God's hiding his face from the house of Jacob implies not only outward troubles but the withholding of divine illumination, indirectly threatened in the verse preceding. The house of Jacob is the whole race of Israel, perhaps with special reference to Judah. The thing to be expected is the fulness of time when the Messiah, no longer revealed merely to a few, should openly appear. For a time the import of God's promises shall be concealed from the majority, and during that interval Messiah shall wait patiently until the set time has arrived.

18. *Behold, I and the children which Jehovah hath given me* (are) *for signs and for wonders in Israel from Jehovah of hosts, the (One) dwelling in mount Zion.* Luther supplies a verb in the first clause—" Behold, here am I and the children," &c. Augusti repeats a verb from the preceding verse—" I and my children trust in the Lord." Most writers supply *are* after *given me*—" I and my children are for signs," &c. *From Jehovah, i. e.* sent and appointed by him. Of the whole verse there are two distinct interpretations. 1. According to Kimchi, Rosenmüller, Gesenius, Ewald, Barnes, and others, Isaiah is the speaker, and the children meant are his two sons, *Shear-Jashub* and *Maher-shalal-hash-baz* to which some add *Immanuel*. As all these names, and that of the Prophet himself, are significant, it is supposed that for this reason he and his children are said to be *signs and wonders*, personified prophecies to Israel, from Jehovah, who had caused the names to be imposed. 2. According to Henderson and many older writers, these are the words of the Messiah, and the children are his spiritual seed (Isa. liii. 10), whom the Father had given him (John vi. 37, 39, x. 29, xvii. 6, 7, 9, 11, 12.) The great argument in favour of this last interpretation is the application of the verse to Christ by Paul (Heb. ii. 13), not as an illustration but an argument, a proof, that Christ partook of the same nature with the persons called his *children* and his *brethren*. It is true that many who regard Isaiah as the speaker, suppose him to have been a type of Christ in this transaction. But a double sense ought not to be assumed where a single one is perfectly consistent with the context, and sufficient to explain all apparent contradictions, as in this case, where, admitting that the Messiah is the speaker, we have no ellipsis to supply, and no occasion to resort to the hypothesis either of a type or an accommoda-

tion. It is not necessary, however, to restrict the terms, with Henderson, to the period of the advent, and to our Saviour's personal followers. Even before he came in the flesh, he and his disciples, *i. e.* all who looked for his appearing, were signs and wonders, objects of contemptuous astonishment, and at the same time pledges of the promise.

19. *And when they* (indefinitely *any one*, or definitely the unbelievers) *shall say to you* (the disciples and children of Messiah, who is still speaking), *Seek unto* (*i. e.* consult as an oracle) *the spirits* (or the spirit-masters, those who have subject or *familiar* spirits at command) *and to the wizards* (wise or knowing ones), *the chirpers and the mutterers* (alluding to the way in which the heathen necromancers invoked their spirits, or uttered their responses): *should not a people seek to* (or consult) *its God, for the living* (*i. e.* in behalf of the living should it resort) *to the dead?* Grotius explains the last clause as a continuation of the speech of the idolaters —" Consult familiar spirits; ought not a people to consult its gods?" But since Jehovah was the God of Israel, such an argument would defeat itself. It is better to regard this clause as the reply of the believing Jews to those who tempted them. Ewald and others give בְּעַד the meaning of *instead*— " Should a people consult the dead instead of the living God?" It is more consistent with the usage of the language to take the preposition in the sense of *for, i. e. for the benefit* or *in behalf of.* " When you, my disciples, are invited by superstitious sinners to consult pretended wizards, consider (or reply) that as the heathen seek responses from their gods, so you ought to consult Jehovah, and not be guilty of the folly of consulting senseless idols or dead men for the instruction of the living." Henderson supposes the Prophet to be speaking in his own person; but if the Messiah is the speaker in ver. 18, it is gratuitous and therefore arbitrary to suppose another speaker to be introduced without any intimation of the change.

20. Instead of resorting to these unprofitable and forbidden sources, the disciples of Jehovah are instructed to resort *to the law and to the testimony* (*i.e.* to divine revelation, considered as a system of belief and as a rule of duty)—*if they speak* (*i.e.* if any speak) *not according to this word* (another name for the revealed will of God), it is he *to whom there is no dawn* or morning (*i. e.* no relief from the dark night of calamity).—The first clause is elliptical. Cocceius alone connects it immediately with what precedes, and understands ל as meaning *besides*—" in addition to the law and the testimony which we have already." Others supply a new verb *return, adhere, come, go,* &c. It is best, however, to repeat יִדְרְשׁוּ from the preceding verse, especially as this verb is elsewhere followed by ל in the same sense. (See 2 Chron. xvii. 3, 4. Comp. Job x. 6).—Piscator violates the accents by separating אִם לֹא from יֹאמְרוּ. " If not (*i. e.* if they will not come to the law and the testimony), let them say," &c. Junius takes אִם לֹא as equivalent to הֲלֹא, which it never is, unless another interrogation precedes. Knobel refers to the הֲלֹא in ver. 19; but this is too remote, and is moreover separated from אִם לֹא by the first clause of ver. 20. Kimchi, Abarbenel, Cocceius, Hitzig, Maurer, make אִם לֹא the common elliptical formula of swearing—" if they will not say," *i. e.* they surely will say. Ewald adopts the same construction, and explains the verse to mean that when they are reduced to extremity (as those who have no dawn) they will begin too late to *speak according to this word, i.e.* join in the appeal *to the law*

and to the testimony, which they now despise. Umbreit modifies this interpretation by giving אִם its strict conditional meaning, and continuing the sentence through the next verse—" If they do not thus speak, to whom there is no morning, then they must pass through the land," &c.—אֲשֶׁר, which is properly the relative pronoun, is omitted by the Vulgate, and explained in the English Version and by Barnes as a causal particle. De Dieu, Vitringa, and some others make it a particle of asseveration, *certainly; surely ;* Gesenius the sign of the apodosis, *then there is no dawn to them ;* J. H. Michaelis, a substitute for כִּי, but in the sense of *that*, " know ye that." So the Dutch Version, " it shall come to pass that." All these are needless and therefore inadmissible departures from the ordinary usage. Of those who give the word its proper meaning as a relative pronoun, some refer it to the noun immediately preceding—*this word which* (Lowth)—others to the people or to some individual among them—*they who have* or *he who has no morning* (Hitzig, Ewald, Umbreit). But the best construction seems to be that of Hendewerk, who supplies the substantive verb before the relative, " they are as one who has no morning," or better still, " it is he who has (or they who have) no morning." None can speak inconsistently with God's word—or, none can refuse to utter this word, viz. to the law and to the testimony—but one whom God has abandoned—" If our gospel be hid, it is hid to them that are lost " (2 Cor. iv. 3). Quem Deus vult perdere prius dementat. Lowth renders שַׁחַר *obscurity*, from the analogy of שָׁחֹר, *black*, and שְׁחוֹר, *blackness*. J. H. Michaelis, Dathe, and Augusti, make it equivalent to the Arabic ساحِر, meaning *magic*—" His word in which there is no magic," *i. e.* no deception. But the Hebrew word is never used in this sense. Calvin, the English Version, Barnes and others, give it the general sense of *light*—" it is because there is no light (*i. e.* knowledge or sound judgment) in them." But according to usage, the word means specifically morning-light, the dawn of day succeeding night, and is so rendered by the Vulgate (matutina lux), Luther (Morgenröthe), and most modern writers. By this Vitringa understands the morning of the resurrection, and J. H. Michaelis the epiphany of Christ. But as night is a common figure for calamity, the dawn will naturally signify its termination, the return of better times. (See chap. lviii. 8, xlvii. 11 ; Job xi. 17.) They may be said to have no *dawn*, for whom there is nothing better in reserve.

21. *And they* (the people) *shall pass through it* (the land) *hardly bestead* (*i. e.* distressed) *and hungry : and it shall be* (or come to pass) *that when they are hungry they shall fret themselves, and curse their king and their God, and shall look upward*. Those interpreters who make the whole of the preceding verse conditional, explain the וְ at the beginning of this as the sign of the apodosis—" If they speak not, &c., *then* shall they pass," &c. So J. D. Michaelis, Dathe, and Augusti. The latter supplies *people* as the subject of עָבַר; Lowth and the Dutch Version, *every one of them ;* but this is unnecessary. The verbs, though singular in form, like לֹ in the preceding verse, refer to the subject of the plural יֹאמְרוּ. Jerome repeats שַׁחַר as the subject of עָבַר (lux pertransibit), light shall pass through the land, but not continue in it.—*Through it*, not the condition just described (Schroeder), nor the *law* (either in the sense of *searching* or in that of *transgressing* it), nor the *earth* or the gentile part of it (as some of the Jews explain it), nor *Zion* mentioned in ver. 18 (Cocceius), but the *land* of Judah, which, though not expressly mentioned till the next verse, is tacitly referred to by a com-

mon Hebrew idiom. (See Ps. lxviii. 16; lxxxvii. 1). Grotius repeats his favourite suggestion, that the Prophet pointed to the ground when he said בָּהּ, so that the gesture and the word together meant *this land*—נָקְשָׁה is not *hardened* in a moral sense, but *hardly treated* or *distressed*, as appears from the addition of רָעֵב. This last is not expressive of bodily hunger (Gesenius, Hitzig, Maurer), nor of spiritual famine (Cocceius); nor is it a mere figure for the absence of all comfort and tranquillity of mind (Vitringa), but a term implying destitution both of temporal and spiritual good (J. H. Michaelis). Calvin, Lowth, and Barnes, understand הִתְקַצֵּף as expressing self-reproach or anger with themselves; but this is not consistent with the subsequent description of their desperate impenitence. The reflexive form, which occurs nowhere else, more probably denotes to excite one's self to anger. *His king* is not his earthly sovereign, the king of Judah (Grotius), of Judah or Israel as the case might be (Hitzig), or his idol, particularly *Moloch* or *Milcom*, names derived from מֶלֶךְ (Targum, Calvin, Junius), but Jehovah considered as the king of Israel. So too אֱלֹהָיו is not his false god, his idol, but the God whom he was bound to serve, his God, who at the same time was -his king (Henderson), As the verb to *curse* does not elsewhere take the preposition בּ as a connective, Cocceius proposes to translate the phrase *he shall curse by his king and by his God*, by which he seems to understand the conduct of the Jews, who at one time cursed Cæsar in Jehovah's name, and at another time rejected Christ saying, We have no king but Cæsar! Thus they alternately cursed their king in God's name, and cursed God in their king's. The art of *looking up* is by some regarded as a sign of penitence or of conversion from idols to the true God; but this is inconsistent with the terms of the next verse. Junius, Piscator, and the Dutch annotators, connect it with the cursing as an accompanying gesture —"they shall curse their king and their God, looking up." But this clause is really in close connection with the first of the next verse, and both together must be understood as indicating utter perplexity and absolute despair of help from God or man, from heaven or earth, from above or below.

22. *And to the earth he shall look; and behold distress and darkness, dimness of anguish, and* into *darkness (*he shall be*) driven—or, the dimness of anguish and of darkness* is *dispelled.* Heaven and earth are here opposed to one another, as sea and land are in chap. v. 30. *Distress* and *darkness* are here identified, as *distress* and *light* are there contrasted. Junius and Henderson explain מָעוּף as a participle, corresponding to מְנֻדָּח in the last clause (darkened with distress, driven into gloom); but there is no such participal form. Cocceius explains it as a noun denoting the dizziness and dimness of sight produced by great distress (vertigo arctationis), which may also be the meaning of the Septuagint version (σκότος ωστε μὴ βλέπειν). The true sense of the Hebrew word is outward and inward gloom, distress of circumstances and despair of mind. It is separated from what follows by Calvin (caligo, augustia) and Barnes (gloom, oppression), but is really a construct form governing צוּקָה. As the latter originally signifies pressure or compression, Gesenius explains the phrase to mean *darkness of compression, i. e.* dense or compact darkness. But צוּקָה is here (as in Isa. xxx. 6; Prov. i. 27) a synonyme of צָרָה, both denoting straitened circumstances and a corresponding state of mind.—The Peshito translates מְנֻדָּח as an active verb, and the Vulgate as an active participle (caligo persequens). The Targum, Cocceius, and Vitringa, suppose the passive participle to be here used as an abstract noun (caligo, impulsio). Saadias, Munster, Barnes, and others, make מְנֻדָּח an epithet of אֲפֵלָה ("obscuritas

impulsa," "deepened darkness"), but the latter word is feminine. Lowth as usual cuts the knot by proposing to read either אפל or מנדחה, and Kocher by taking the latter as a neuter noun in apposition with the former. Jarchi, Kimchi, Calvin, Junius, Rosenmüller, Gesenius, Ewald, and others refer מֻנְדָּח to the people or the person who is the subject of the verb יָבִּיט, and either supply a preposition before אֲפֵלָה, or explain it as an accusative after a verb of motion. The meaning will then be *thrust* or *driven into darkness.* The objections to this construction are, first, the necessity of supplying both a verb and preposition ; and secondly, the unusual collocation of the words אפלה מנדח for מנדח אל אפלה. On the other hand, it is strongly recommended by the analogy of Jer. xxiii. 12, where the same idea is expressed by the union of the same verb and noun. Another construction is the one proposed by J. D. Michaelis, who connects מנדח with מעוף, and puts the latter in construction not only with צוקה but also with אפלה, " the dimness of anguish and of gloom is dissipated." This construction is recommended by its freedom from grammatical anomalies, and by its rendering the use of כִּי at the beginning of the next verse altogether natural. The objections to it are, that it violates the accents ; that it makes the Prophet speak of the darkness of darkness (but see Exod. x. 22) ; and that the transition from the threatening to the promise is, on this supposition, too abrupt. Either of the two constructions last proposed may be preferred without materially affecting the interpretation of the passage. Hitzig modifies that of Michaelis by taking the last word separately—*it is dispelled !*

23. This darkness is to be dispelled, *for* (there shall) *not* (be) *darkness* (for ever) *to her who is now distressed* (literally, to whom there is distress). The present calamity, or that just predicted, is not to be perpetual. The future state of things shall exhibit a strange contrast with the former. *As the former time degraded the land of Zebulon and the land of Naphtali, so the latter glorifies the way of the sea, the bank of the Jordan, Galilee of the Gentiles.* The same region is described in both clauses, namely, the northern extremity of the land of Israel. This is designated, first, by the tribes which occupied it, then, by its relative position with respect to the Jordan and the sea of Tiberias. This part of the country, from being the most degraded and afflicted, should receive peculiar honour. Its debasement and distress both arose from its remote and frontier situation, proximity to the heathen, intercourse and mixture with them, and constant exposure to the first attacks of enemies, who usually entered Canaan from the north. To the former of these reasons may be traced the expressions of contempt for Galilee recorded in the books of the New Testament (John i. 46, vii. 52 ; Mat. xxvi. 69 ; Acts i. 11, ii. 7). How this disgrace was to be exchanged for honour, is explained in the next verse. Besides this, which seems to be the most satisfactory interpretation, there are several others, more or less at variance with it. The English version supposes a contrast not merely between הֵקַל and הִכְבִּיד, but between these two and the subsequent deliverance. This requires הֵקַל to be taken in the sense of *lightly afflicting,* as distinguished from הִכְבִּיד, to *afflict more grievously.* But this distinction is unauthorised by usage. The Vulgate renders הֵקַל *alleviata est.* Some of the Jewish writers make it mean to *lighten* the country by removing its inhabitants ; but then הִכְבִּיד must mean to bring them back again. Koppe makes Judah the subject of the promise. As Galilee was first afflicted, then delivered, so should Judah be ; but this is wholly

arbitrary. Cocceius converts the promise into a threat by reading *there was not* (or has never been) *such darkness*. Gesenius, Rosenmüller, Ewald, and others, give to כִּי the sense of *but*, because what immediately precedes is understood by them not as a promise but a threatening. Vitringa and Junius retain the proper meaning *for*, but connect it with ver. 16 or ver. 18. The necessity of either supposition is removed by explaining the last clause of ver. 22, with J. D. Michaelis and Hitzig, as the beginning of the promise. The Vulgate connects לֹא מוּעָף with ver. 22 and translates it *non poterit avolare*, as if from עוּף, to fly; but it is obviously a cognate form to מְעוּף in the preceding verse. Hitzig explains לֹא מוּעָף as a compound, meaning the negative or opposite of darkness, *i. e.* light, as לֹא עֵץ (chap. x. 15) means that which is not wood. Some regard כְּ as a temporal particle, *at* or *in the former time*. Junius, Rosenmüller, Gesenius, and others make it a conjunction, *as the former time debased*, &c. The original construction seems to be *like the former time* (which) *debased*, &c. Of those who regard הֵקַל and הִכְבִּיד as descriptive of different degrees of affliction, some suppose the invasion of Tiglath-pileser to be compared with that of Shalmaneser; or the invasion of Israel with that of Judah; or the Assyrian with the Babylonian conquest; or the Babylonian with the Roman. The *sea* mentioned in the last clause is not the Mediterranean but the sea of Galilee, as appears from Mat. iv. 15, 16. עֵבֶר is here used in the sense of *side* or *part adjacent*. The region spoken of was that *along the Jordan* (on one or both sides), near the sea of Galilee. According to Junius, *Galilee of the Gentiles* means *Galilæa populosa*. Gesenius admits that Isaiah has reference to the times of the Messiah in this promise of deliverance and exultation to the Galileans.

Chapter 9

The change for the better, which was promised at the close of the eighth chapter, is described in the ninth as consisting in the rise of the great light upon the darkness, in the increase of the nation and their joy, excited by deliverance from bondage and the universal prevalence of peace, arising from the advent of a divine successor to David, who should restore, establish, and enlarge his kingdom without any limitation, vers. 1-6.

From the times of the Messiah, the Prophet suddenly reverts to his own, and again predicts the punishment of Ephraim by repeated strokes. The people had been warned both by messages from God and by experience, but had continued to indulge their proud self-confidence, in consequence of which God allowed the Assyrians, after overthrowing Rezin, to attack them also, while at the same time they were harassed by perpetual assaults from their hostile neighbours, vers. 7–11.

Still they did not repent and return to God, who therefore cut off suddenly many of all classes, but especially the rulers of the nation and the false prophets, the flattering seducers of the wretched people, from whom he must now withhold even the ordinary proofs of his compassion, vers. 12–16.

All this was the natural effect of sin, like a fire in a thicket, which at last consumes the forest, and involves the land in smoke and flame. Yet amidst these strokes of the divine displeasure, they were still indulging mutual animosities and jealousies, insomuch that Israel was like a famished man devouring his own flesh. Manasseh thus devoured Ephraim and Ephraim Manasseh, while the two together tried to devour Judah, vers. 17–20.

The recurrence of the same clause at the end of vers. 11, 16, 20, and the fourth verse of the next chapter, has led the modern Germans to regard this as a case of regular strophical arrangement; and as the same form occurs above in chap. v. 25, Ewald interpolates that verse between the sixth and seventh of this chapter, as a part of the same context. The objection to these critical hypotheses will be stated in the exposition.

It has been observed already that the division of the chapters is in this part of the book peculiarly unfortunate; the first part of the ninth (vers. 1–6) containing the conclusion of the eighth, and the first part of the tenth (vers. 1–4) the conclusion of the ninth.

The numbers of the verses in this chapter differ in the Hebrew and English Bibles; what is the last verse of the eighth in the former is the first of the ninth in the latter. The references in the commentary are all to the divisions of the Hebrew text.

1. *The people* (just described, *i. e.* the people of Galilee), *those walking in the dark* (expressive both of spiritual blindness and extreme distress), *have seen a great light* (the change being presented to the Prophet's view as already past): *the dwellers in the land of the shadow of death* (*i. e.* of intense darkness), *light has beamed upon them.* These words, in a general sense, may be descriptive of any great and sudden change in the condition of the people, especially of one from ignorance and misery to illumination and enjoyment. They are still more appropriate to Christ as the *light of the world* (John viii. 12), *a light to the nations* (Isa. xlii. 6, xlix. 6), and the *Sun of righteousness* (Mal. iv. 2), which rose upon the world when he *manifested forth his glory* by his teachings and his miracles in Galilee (John ii. 11). It was in this benighted and degraded region that he first appeared as a messenger from God; and in that appearance we are expressly taught that this prediction was fulfilled (Mat. iv. 12–17). Cocceius needlessly supposes these to be the words of a new speaker. There is nothing to intimate a change of subject, and this verse is really a mere specification in positive form of the negative prediction in the first clause of the verse preceding. By *the people* we are not to understand all Israel (Maurer), nor the Jews as distinguished from the ten tribes (Kimchi, Calvin), nor the people of Jerusalem (Jarchi, Aben Ezra, Grotius), nor the people of God, the spiritual Israel (Cocceius), but the Galileans who had just been mentioned (Junius, J. H. Michaelis, Vitringa, Hendewerk). By *darkness* Piscator understands sorrow; Gesenius, calamity in general; the Targum, Israel's sufferings in Egypt; Jarchi, Kimchi, and Grotius, those of Judah during Sennacherib's invasion; Calvin, those of the Jews; and Hendewerk those of the ten tribes, in exile. But it rather expresses the complex idea of a state of sin and misery (Ps. cvii. 10, 11), including outward and inward darkness, the darkness of ignorance and the darkness of distress. De Dieu and Fürst make צלמות a simple derivative of צלם with a feminine termination, like מלכות from מלך. The more common and probable opinion is that it is a compound of צל and מות. It is not the proper name of a particular valley (Hitzig), but a poetical designation of the most profound obscurity—as dark as death—deadly darkness—with a special allusion here to the spiritual death, under whose shade the Galileans sat. Instead of *have seen*, Luther, J. H. Michaelis, Gesenius, and others, have

the present *see*, as if the Prophet while speaking beheld a sudden flash. *Light* is not merely an emblem of joy (Piscator), or deliverance (Gesenius), but of outward and inward illumination. Knobel understands by *the people* the exile of the ten tribes, and by the *land of the shadow of death* Assyria as the place of their captivity.

2. The Prophet now, by a sudden apostrophe, addresses God himself, who, by bestowing on the Galileans this *great light*, would not only honour them, but afford occasion of great joy to all the true Israel, including those who should be gathered from the gentiles. *Thou hast enlarged the nation* (*i. e.* Israel in general), *thou hast increased its joy* (literally, to it thou hast increased the joy) : they *rejoice before thee like the joy in harvest, as men rejoice when they divide the spoil.* Luther and Umbreit explain—ﬡﬡ to mean the Gentiles, and regard this not as a description of deliverance but of oppression. Hitzig supposes ﬡﬡ to mean the returning exiles. All other writers seem to be agreed that it means the Israelites in general. The increase of the nation has been variously explained to mean the gathering of a great army by the king of Assyria, to whom the verse is then addressed (Grotius)—or the crowding of the Jews into Jerusalem during Sennacherib's invasion (Aben Ezra)—or an increase in the number of the Israelites while in captivity (Hitzig)—or the general diffusion of the Jewish race after the exile (Vitringa). It really means the increase of the people in their own land, not a mere growth of population (Gesenius), but an increase of the true Israel by the calling of the Gentiles (Hengstenberg, Christol. vol. i., part 2, p. 110). Symmachus separates הגדלת from what follows (ἐπλήθυνας τὸ ἔθνος ὃ οὐκ ἐμεγάλυνας), in which he is followed by J. D. Michaelis and Maurer. But this requires a change in the punctuation and division of the words to render it grammatical. De Dieu takes לא as equivalent to הלא—"hast thou not increased the joy?"—which is forced and arbitrary. Another construction is, *thou hast increased the nation* of the Jews, but *thou hast not increased the joy* of their enemies (Jarchi), or of the Gentiles (Luther). But this assumes two different subjects in the two successive clauses. Hitzig and Hengstenberg thus construe it—*thou dost increase the nation* whose *joy thou hast not* heretofore *increased.* But this requires a relative to be supplied, and, arbitrarily refers the verbs to different times. If the textual reading (לא) be retained, as it is by Hengstenberg, Maurer, Hitzig, Henderson, Umbreit, and the older writers, the best construction is that given by Calvin and Cocceius—*thou hast increased the nation* but *thou hast not increased the joy* as thou art now about to do. It is best, however, to read לו instead of לא, with the Masora, several ancient versions, Gesenius, De Wette, and Knobel, or to regard the latter as a mere orthographical variation for the former (Ewald *ad loc.* and Heb. Gr. § 555). The same emendation is required by the context in several other places (*e. g.* chap. xlix. 5, lxiii. 9). Junius and Tremellius suppose the former joy or prosperity of Israel, acquired ʰy toil and bloodshed, as in a harvest or a battle, to be here contrasted with the joy which the Messiah would impart. Knobel supplies a relative before שמחו, gives כאשר the sense of *when*, and supposes the joy of actual victory to be compared with that of harvest—*thou hast increased the joy* wherewith *they rejoice before thee, like the joy of harvest, when they rejoice in their dividing the spoil.* But this makes the structure of the sentence artificial and complex. *Rejoicing before God* Calvin explains to mean rejoicing with a real or a reasonable joy ; Piscator with a secret spiritual joy, nut before man

but God; Cocceius, Vitringa, Hitzig, Hengstenberg, and Ewald, more correctly, as an act of religious worship, either simply in allusion to the rejoicing of the people before God at the tabernacle or temple under the law of Moses (Deut. xii. 7, xiv. 26), or in reference to an actual performance of that duty. The Targum explains *harvest* as a metaphor for war or battle, which destroys the Prophet's beautiful comparison of the joy of victory, or joy in general, to that which accompanies the harvest in all countries, and especially in the East (Ps. iv. 8, cxxvi. 6).—Kimchi makes the Assyrians the subject of יגילו, Knobel the Israelites themselves, but it is better to take it indefinitely or to supply *men* as in the English Version. בקציר is not a false reading for קציר or הקציר, which we find in a few manuscripts (Lowth), but another instance of the idiomatic use of the construct form before a preposition, as in the preceding verse (ישבי בארץ). See Gesenius, § 114, 1; Ewald, § 510. To the promise here given there is probably allusion in the language of the angel who announced the birth of Jesus to the shepherds (Luke ii. 10): *Behold, I bring you good tidings of great joy, which shall be to all the people* (παντὶ τῷ λαῷ), *i. e.* to the whole nation, all the Israel of God.

3. This verse assigns the reason or occasion of the promised joy. They shall rejoice before thee, *that* (or because) *the yoke of his burden* (his burdensome yoke), *and the rod of his shoulder* (or back), *and the staff of the one driving him* (his task-master, slave-driver) *thou hast broken like the day* (as in the day) *of Midian*, as Gideon routed Midian, *i. e.* suddenly, totally, and by special aid from heaven. This promise was not fulfilled in the deliverance of the Jews from Babylon (Calvin), which bore no resemblance to the victory of Gideon; nor in the destruction of Sennacherib's army (Grotius), the benefits of which events were only temporary; nor in the destruction of Jerusalem by Titus (J. D. Michaelis), to which there is no allusion in the context; but in the glorious deliverance of the Galileans (the first converts to Christianity), and of all who with them made up the true Israel, from the heavy burden of the covenant of works, the galling yoke of the Mosaic law, the service of the devil, and the bondage of corruption. Outward deliverance is only promised, so far as it accompanied spiritual change or was included in it. Cocceius refines too much when he distinguishes between the rod and staff, as denoting the civil and the ceremonial law. The meaning, on the other hand, is lowered by restricting the prophetic figures to Sennacherib's siege of Jerusalem (Grotius), or the tribute paid to Assyria by Hezekiah (Jarchi) or Ahaz (Gesenius), or to mere dependence on a foreign power (Hitzig). The application of the terms by J. D. Michaelis to the persecution of the Galileans or first Christians by the Jews, seems altogether fanciful. Barnes refers the pronoun in *his burden* to the oppressor (*which he made you bear*), and Forerius in like manner explains *the rod of his shoulder* to mean the rod carried on the tyrant's shoulder. But the suffix in both cases relates not to the oppressor but to the oppressed, and שכם includes not merely the shoulders but the space between them, the upper part of the back. Forerius also refers בו to the oppressor—"thou hast broken the rod of the oppressor with himself." Munster refers it to the rod—"with which he oppressed them." Maurer refers it correctly to the sufferer, but gives the preposition the distinct sense of *against* or *upon*, because the tyrant presses or rushes upon his victim. It is no doubt, as Gesenius and Ewald hold, a mere connective, taken here by נֶשׁ as it is elsewhere by עָבַד (Exod. i. 14, Lev. xxv. 39). The *day* of any one in Hebrew often means the day in which something memor-

able happens to him, or is done by him (*vide supra*, chap. ii. 12), and in Arabic is absolutely used for a day of battle. The rout of the Midianites, recorded in the seventh chapter of Judges, is here referred to, not because it took place in a single night, like the destruction of Sennacherib's army (Jarchi)—nor because the foes of Israel, like those of the Church, destroyed each other (Cocceius)—nor because the truth, which overcomes the world, is in earthen vessels, like the lamps of Gideon (Vitringa)—nor because the preaching of the Gospel may be likened to the blowing of trumpets (Dutch annotations)—but because it was a wonderful display of divine power, without the use of any adequate human means; and also, as suggested by Herder (Heb. Poes. vol. ii. p. 496), because it took place in the same part of the country which this prophecy refers to. Jezreel, where the battle was fought (Judges vi. 33), was in the territory of Manasseh, to which tribe Gideon himself belonged (Judges vi. 15); but he was aided by the neighbouring tribes of Asher, Zebulon, and Naphtali (Judges vi. 35).— Junius, in order to sustain his interpretation of the second verse, continues the construction into this, and gives to כ the sense of *when*—"they rejoiced before thee, &c., when (whenever) thou didst break their yoke," &c. —*i. e.* in every case of former deliverance. (See also the margin of the English Version.) The Septuagint and Targum supply a verb in the first clause (ἀφῄρηται, אעדית), which is unnecessary, as the nouns in that clause are governed by the verb in the last part of the sentence. That verb does not mean to scatter (Septuagint), or to conquer (Vulgate), or to frighten (Cocceius), but to break, to break off, or to break in pieces. Vitringa takes מַטֶּה as a synonyme of מֹטָה a yoke; but it no doubt denotes here, as in every other case, a staff or rod. Gesenius, in his Commentary, supposes an ellipsis of the proposition before יוֹם; but, in the last edition of his grammar, he agrees with Maurer in supposing the noun itself to be used adverbially or absolutely in answer to the question *when?* The absolute form of סְבֳלוֹ is written by Gesenius סַבֶל, by Ewald סְבֹל. The Daghesh is euphonic, and the Sheva anomalous.

4. The destruction of the oppressing power shall be followed by profound and universal peace. To express this idea, the Prophet describes the equipments of the soldier as consumed with fire. *For all the armour of the armed man* (or the man-at-arms, who mingles) *in the tumult* (of battle), *and the garment rolled in blood, shall be for burning* (and for) *food* (or fuel), *of fire.* In other words, the usual accompaniments of battle shall be utterly destroyed, and by implication, war itself shall cease. There is no need of supposing, with Vitringa, Lowth, Hitzig, Hendewerk, and Henderson, an allusion to the ancient custom of burning the armour and equipments of the slain upon the field of battle as an act of triumph. It is not the weapons of the enemy alone, but all weapons of war, that are to be consumed; not merely because they have been used for a bad purpose, but because they are hereafter to be useless. It is not so much a prophecy of conquest as of peace; a peace, however, which is not to be expected till the enemies of God are overcome; and therefore the prediction may be said to include both events, the final overthrow of all opposing powers and the subsequent prevalence of universal peace. This last is uniformly spoken of in Scripture as characteristic of Messiah's reign, both internal and external, in society at large and in the hearts of his people. With respect to the latter, the prediction has been verified with more or less distinctness, in every case of true conversion. With respect to the former, its fulfilment is inchoate, but will one day be complete, when the

lion and the lamb shall lie down together, and He who is the Prince of peace shall have dominion from sea to sea, and from the river to the ends of the earth. An allusion to this promise and its final consummation may be found in the words of the heavenly host who celebrated the Saviour's birth (Luke ii. 14), *Glory to God in the highest, and on earth* PEACE, *good will to men.* According to Jarchi, Kimchi, Calvin, and Grotius, this verse contains two distinct propositions, one relating to the *day of Midian* or to wars in general, and the other to the slaughter of Sennacherib's army or the deliverance of the Jews from exile. The sense would then be that while other battles are accompanied with noise and bloodshed, this shall be with burning and fuel of fire. But this construction, besides assuming a change of subject, of which there is no intimation in the text, departs from the natural and ordinary meaning of the words. The *fire* mentioned in the last clause has been variously explained as a poetical description of the Assyrian slaughter (Jarchi, Kimchi, Aben Ezra, Grotius), or of the angel by whom it was effected (Abarbenel)—of the destruction of Jerusalem (Vatablus, J. D. Michaelis), or of the world (Diodati)—or as an emblem of the Holy Ghost (Forerius)—or of our Saviour's zeal for man's salvation (Gill). It is mentioned simply as a powerful consuming agent, to express the abolition of the implements of war, and, as a necessary consequence, of war itself. The verse, then, is not a mere description of Gideon's victory (Junius)—nor a comparison between that or any other battle and the slaughter of Sennacherib's army (Grotius)—nor a prediction of the fall of Jerusalem in spite of an obstinate and bloody defence (J. D. Michaelis)—but a prophecy of changes to take place when the *great light* and deliverer of *the nation* should appear. The כִּי at the beginning is translated *when* by Junius and Tremellius and in the margin of the English Bible; but it really means *for*, and assigns a second reason for the joy predicted in ver. 2. סְאוֹן, which occurs nowhere else, is taken in the sense of war or battle, by David Kimchi, Luther, Calvin, and Grotius; in that of a military greave or sandal, boot or shoe, by Joseph Kimchi, Rosenmüller, Gesenius, Maurer, Hengstenberg, Hendewerk, Henderson, and Ewald; and in that of armour or equipment in general, by Hitzig, De Wette, Umbreit, and Knobel. סֹאֵן is a participle formed from this noun, and signifies a person thus equipped. The whole phrase therefore means *the armour of the armed man, the equipment of the soldier.* The obscurity of these terms to the old translators is sufficiently apparent from the στολὴν ἐπισυνηγμένην of the Septuagint, the *violenta praedatio* of the Vulgate, and the unintelligible version of the whole sentence given in the Targum. Hoheisel and Rosenmüller understand by רַעַשׁ the *noise* or *clatter* of the military shoe or sandal armed with nails; but it rather means noise in general, or more specifically, the shock and tumult of battle, the *melée*. The phrase בְּרַעַשׁ qualifies סֹאֵן—*the armour of him* who mingles *armed in the tumult* of battle, and whose שִׂמְלָה or upper garment is described as *rolled in blood*, not merely dyed of a red colour (Hitzig), but literally stained with the blood of conflict. J. D. Michaelis makes the first clause, by a harsh and ungrammatical construction, mean that he who arms himself arms himself only to tremble or to make to tremble. There is no need of supplying a verb in the first clause, with Calvin (fit) and Grotius (solet esse), much less two with Barnes. The nouns in this clause are the subjects of the verb at the beginning of the second, which agrees grammatically with the second, but logically with both. The Vav is conversive, and at the same time introduces the apodosis of the sentence (Gesenius, § 152, 1, *a*).

There is no need therefore of adopting J. D. Michaelis's construction of the last clause, that *whatever is destined for the fire* (מאכלת אש) *will certainly be burned* (היתה לשרפה).

5. This verse gives a further reason for the joy of the people, by bringing into view the person who was to effect the great deliverance. *For a child is born to us* (or *for us, i. e.* for our benefit)—*a son is given to us* (*i. e.* by Jehovah, an expression frequently applied in the New Testament to Christ's incarnation), *and the government is upon his shoulder* (as a burden or a robe of office)—*and his name is called Wonderful* (literally *Wonder*)—*Counsellor—Mighty God—Everlasting Father—Prince of Peace.* The figure of a robe or dress is preferred by Grotius and Hengstenberg, that of a burden by Gesenius, Hitzig, and Knobel, who cites analogous expressions from Cicero (rempublicam universam vestris humeris sustinetis), and the younger Pliny (bene humeris tuis sedet imperium). When it is said that his name should be called, it does not mean that he should actually bear these names in real life, but merely that he should deserve them, and that they would be descriptive of his character. The verb יקרא may agree with יהוה, or be construed indefinitely—*he* (*i. e.* any one) *shall call his name*—which is equivalent to saying *they shall call his name*, or in a passive form, *his name shall be called.* The child here predicted or described is explained to be Hezekiah, by Jarchi, Kimchi, Aben Ezra, Grotius, Hensler, Paulus, Gesenius, Hendewerk. This explanation is rejected, not only by the older writers, but among the modern Germans, by Bauer, Eichhorn, Rosenmüller, Maurer, Hitzig, Ewald, Umbreit, Knobel. The Vav conversive renders the futures וַתְּהִי and וַיִּקְרָא perfectly equivalent, in point of time, to the preterites יֻלַּד and נִתַּן; so that if the latter refer to an event already past, the former must refer to past time too, and *vice versa.* The verse then either represents Hezekiah as unborn, or as already invested with the regal office, at the date of the prediction, neither of which can be historically true. The attempt to escape from this dilemma, by referring the two first verbs to something past, and the two next to something future, is a direct violation of the laws of Hebrew syntax. Besides, the terms of the description are extravagant and false, if applied to Hezekiah. In what sense was he *wonderful*, a *mighty God*, an *everlasting Father*, a *Prince of peace?* The modern Jews, in order to sustain their antichristian exegesis, have devised a new construction of the sentence, which applies all these epithets, except the last, to God himself, as the subject of the verb יקרא. *And* (he who is) *Wonderful, the Counsellor, the mighty God, the Everlasting Father, calls his* (*i. e.* Hezekiah) *name the Prince of peace.* This construction, which is given by Jarchi and Kimchi, is supposed by some to have been suggested by the Chaldee Paraphrase, while others cite the latter as a witness in favour of applying all the names to the Messiah. (See the opposite statements in Vitringa and Henderson.) But how could even the last of these distinctive titles be applied to Hezekiah? Neither actively nor passively could he be called, at least with any emphasis, a Prince of peace. He waged war against others, and was himself invaded and subjected to a foreign power, from which he afterwards revolted. To this it is replied by Gesenius and Maurer, that the Prophet may have entertained a groundless expectation. But even this bold conjecture is of no avail against a second objection of a different kind, viz. that a long enumeration of titles belonging to God himself is utterly irrelevant in speaking of a name which should be borne by Hezekiah. And this objection lies, with still more force, against Abarbenel's construction, which

includes even *Prince of peace* among Jehovah's titles, and takes יקרא שמו
absolutely in the sense of giving a name or making famous. The hypothesis first mentioned is exposed moreover to the fatal grammatical objection, urged by Calvin and Cocceius, that, according to invariable usage,
שמו must have stood between the names of God and the name of Hezekiah.
These constructions are accordingly abandoned now, even by some who
still identify the child with Hezekiah. These assume the ground, maintained of old by Aben Ezra, that there is nothing in the epithets which
might not be applied to Hezekiah. In order to maintain this ground,
the meaning of the epithets themselves is changed. פלא is either
made to mean nothing more than *remarkable, distinguished* (Grotius,
Gesenius, Knobel), or is ungrammatically joined with יועץ in the sense of a
wonderful counsellor (Ewald), or *wonderfully wise* (Hendewerk). יועץ itself
is joined with אל נבור, as meaning a *consulter of the mighty God*; a construction which is equally at variance with the Masoretic interpunction
and the usage of the word יועץ, which never means one who *asks*, but
always one who *gives advice*, and more especially a public counsellor or
minister of state. (*Vide supra*, chap. i. 26, iii. 3). But some who admit
this explain the next title, אל נבור, to mean a *mighty hero* or a *godlike
hero* (Gesenius, De Wette, Maurer), although they grant that in another
part of this same prophecy it means the *mighty God*. (*Vide infra*, chap.
x. 21; cf. Deut. x. 17, Jer. xxxii. 18). אבי עד is explained to mean a
father of spoil, a plunderer, a victor (Abarbenel, Hitzig, Knobel)—or a *perpetual father*, i. e. benefactor of the people (Hensler, Doederlein, Gesenius,
Maurer, Hendewerk, Ewald)—or at most, the *founder of* a new or *everlasting age* (Lowth), or the *father of a numerous offspring* (Grotius). All this
to discredit or evade the obvious meaning of the phrase, which either signifies *a father* (or possessor) *of eternity*, i. e. an eternal being—or an author
and bestower of eternal life. Possibly both may be included. The necessity of such explanations is sufficient to condemn the exegetical hypothesis involving it, and shews that this hypothesis has only been adopted
to avoid the natural and striking application of the words to Jesus Christ,
as the promised *child*, emphatically *born for us* and *given to us*, as the *Son*
of God and the *Son* of man, as being *wonderful* in his person, works,
and sufferings—a *counsellor*, prophet, or authoritative teacher of the truth,
a wise administrator of the church, and confidential adviser of the individual believer—a real man, and yet the *mighty God*—*eternal* in his own
existence, and the *giver of eternal life* to others—the great *peace-maker*
between God and man, between Jew and Gentile, the umpire between
nations, the abolisher of war, and the giver of internal peace to all who
being justified by faith have peace with God through our Lord Jesus Christ
(Rom. v. 1). The doctrine that this prophecy relates to the Messiah, was
not disputed even by the Jews, until the virulence of antichristian controversy drove them from the ground which their own progenitors had
stedfastly maintained. In this departure from the truth they have been
followed by some learned writers who are Christians only in the name,
and to whom may be applied, with little alteration, what one of them
(Gesenius) has said with respect to the ancient versions of this very text,
viz. that the general meaning put upon it may be viewed as the criterion
of a Christian and an antichristian writer. It has been already mentioned
that some writers even of this class have been compelled to abandon the
application of this text to Hezekiah, and that one of the latest and most
eminent interpreters by whom it is maintained, admits that there may be

some allusion to the nascent doctrine of a personal Messiah. These concessions, partial and reluctant as they are, serve to strengthen the most ancient and most natural interpretation of this signal prophecy.

6. The reign of this king shall be progressive and perpetual, because founded in justice and secured by the distinguishing favour of Jehovah. *To the increase of the government* (or power) *and to the peace* (or prosperity of this reign) *there shall be no end, upon the throne of David and upon his kingdom, to establish it and to confirm it, in justice and in righteousness from henceforth and for ever. The zeal of Jehovah of hosts shall do this.* According to Luther, Cocceius, Castalio, Gesenius, Maurer, Hitzig, De Wette, Ewald, the proposition at the beginning of the verse connects it with what goes before. He is born, or called by these names, *for the increase of power and for prosperity without end.* To this it may be objected, first, that the means and the end thus stated are incongruous, and then that אין, according to usage, is not a mere particle of negation, but includes the substantive verb. Rosenmüller, Hengstenberg, Umbreit, and Knobel, retain the old and common construction, which supposes a new sentence to begin here and connects the preposition with what follows. The government or power thus to be enlarged is of course that of the *child*, who is described as born and given in the foregoing verse. A striking parallel is furnished by the prophecy in Micah v. 3. There, as here, a king is promised who should be the son of David, and should reign over all the earth in peace and righteousness for ever. It is there expressed, and here implied, that this king should re-unite the divided house of Israel, although this is but a small part of the increase promised, which includes the calling of the gentiles also. *Peace*, though included in שלום, is not a full equivalent. The Hebrew word denotes not only *peace* as opposed to war, intestine strife, or turbulence, but welfare and prosperity in general as opposed to want and sorrow. The reign here predicted was to be not only peaceful but in every respect prosperous. And this prosperity, like the reign of which it is predicted, is to have no limit, either temporal or local. It is to be both universal and eternal. There is nothing to preclude the very widest explanation of the terms employed. Ewald explains על as meaning *for the sake of, on account of;* but there is no need of departing from the sense of *on*, which is its proper one, and that which it always has in other cases when prefixed to the noun כסא. A verb is introduced before על כסא by the Vulgate (sedebit) and Gesenius (komme), but without necessity. The construction is what the grammarians call a pregnant one. The endless increase of power and prosperity *on the throne of David* means of course that the Prince, whose reign was to be thus powerful and prosperous, would be a descendant of David. This is indeed a repetition and explanation of a promise given to David (2 Sam. vii. 11–16; 1 Kings viii. 25), and repeatedly referred to by him (2 Sam. xxiii. 1–5; Ps. ii., xlv., lxxii., lxxxix., cxxxii.). Hence the Messiah is not only called the *Branch* or *Son of David* (2 Sam. vii. 12, 13; Jer. xxiii. 5, xxxiii. 15), but David himself (Jer. xxx. 9; Ezek. xxxiv. 23, 24; xxxvii. 24; Hosea iii. 5). The two reigns are identified, not merely on account of an external resemblance or a typical relation, but because the one was really a restoration or continuation of the other. Both kings were heads of the same body, the one a temporal head, the other spiritual, the one temporary, the other eternal. The Jewish nation, as a spiritual body, is really continued in the Christian Church. The subject of the prophecy is the reign of the Messiah; the effect predicted, its

stability and increase; the means to be employed, judgment and justice; the efficient cause, the zeal of Jehovah. Grotius distinguishes between *judgment* and *justice*, as denoting righteous government on one hand, and righteous subjection to it on the other. The justice spoken of is that of the Messiah and his subjects. All the acts of his administration will be righteous, and the effect of this upon his people will be righteousness on their part and this prevalence of righteousness will naturally generate the increase and stability here promised. The preposition בְּ does not merely mean *with* justice, as an accompanying circumstance, but *by* it, as a necessary means. The phrase מֵעַתָּה cannot mean *from that time*, as explained by Junius and Tremellius (ab isto tempore), but must have its ordinary sense, *from this time*. It is possible, however, that the Prophet, as in many other cases, takes his stand upon a point of future time, and speaks of it as actually present. Having spoken of the promised child in ver. 5 as already *born* and *given*, he may now look forward from its birth into the future, and in this sense use the phrase *from henceforth*. Cocceius understands the words more strictly as meaning " from the date of the prediction," and referring to the whole series of events, from that time onwards, which are mentioned in this prophecy—the deliverance of Judah—the destruction of Ephraim and the overthrow of Syria—the deportation of the ten tribes—Sennacherib's invasion—Nebuchadnezzar's conquest—the Babylonish exile—the return—the subsequent vicissitudes—the rising of the *great light* upon Galilee—the increase of the church by the accession of the Gentiles—the breaking of the yoke and staff of spiritual bondage—the destruction of the implements of war—the establishment and gradual enlargement of the Messiah's kingdom. These form a chain of great events succeeding one another without any interruption from the date of the prediction to the end of time. Whatever be the *terminus a quo* intended by the Prophet, it is clear that he describes the reign of the Messiah as an endless one. The word עוֹלָם, though properly denoting mere indefinite duration, and therefore frequently applied to terms and periods of time, such as the length of human life, is always to be taken in its largest meaning, unless limited by something in the context or the nature of the case; much more in such an instance as the one before us, where the context really precludes all limitation by the strength of its expressions. To explain *for ever* here, with Jarchi and Grotius, as meaning till the end of Hezekiah's life, is simply ludicrous, unless the other phrases, both in this verse and the fifth, are mere extravagant hyperboles. The Masoretic interpunction requires this phrase to be connected with what follows—" from henceforth and for ever the zeal of Jehovah of hosts will do this." It is so read by Junius, Cocceius, and Gill ; but most interpreters suppose it to qualify what goes before, and take the remaining words as a short independent proposition. The difference is little more than one of punctuation. Both constructions make the reign of the Messiah an eternal one. The word קִנְאָה expresses the complex idea of strong affection, comprehending or attended by a jealous preference of one above another. It is used in the Old Testament to signify not only God's intense love for his people but his jealousy in their behalf, that is to say, his disposition to protect and favour them at the expense of others. Sometimes, moreover, it includes the idea of a jealous care of his own honour, or a readiness to take offence at anything opposed to it, and a determination to avenge it when insulted. There is nothing in this idea of the divine jealousy incongruous or unworthy, as Umbreit supposes. The expressions are derived from the dialect of human passion, but describe something absolutely right on God's part for the very reasons which demonstrate its absurdity and wickedness on man's. These two ideas of God's jealous partiality for his own people, and his jealous sensibility respecting his own honour, are promiscuously blended in the usage of the word, and are perhaps both included in the case before us. Both for his own sake and his people's, he would bring these events to pass. Or rather the two motives are identical, that is to say, the one includes the other. The welfare of the church is only to be sought so far as it promotes God's glory, and a zeal which makes the glory of the church an object to be aimed at for its own sake, cannot be a zeal for God, or is at best *a zeal for God, but not according to knowledge.* The mention of God's jealousy or zeal as the procuring cause of this result affords a sure foundation for the hopes of all believers. His zeal is not a passion, but a principle of powerful and certain operation. . The astonishing effects produced by feeble means in the promotion, preservation, and extension of Christ's kingdom, can only be explained upon the principle that the zeal of the Lord of hosts effected it. The reign here described cannot be that of Hezekiah, which was confined to Judah, and was neither peaceful, nor progressive, nor perpetual. It cannot be the joint reign of himself and his successors ; for the line was broken at the Babylonish exile. It cannot be the reign of the Maccabees or Hasmonean princes, for these were not the sons of David but of Levi. The prediction, if fulfilled at all, could only be fulfilled in a reign which, after it began, was never interrupted, and has ever since been growing in extent and power. Is not this the reign of Christ? Does it not answer all the requisite conditions? The evangelists take pains to prove by formal genealogies his lineal descent from David, and his reign, unlike all others, still continues and is constantly enlarging. Hendewerk and other modern German writers have objected that this prophecy is not applied to Christ in the New Testament. But we have seen already, that the first verse of the chapter and the one before it are interpreted by Matthew as a prophecy of Christ's appearing as a public teacher first in Galilee ; and no one has denied that this is part of the same context. Nor is this all. The expressions of the verse before us were applied to Christ, before his birth, by Gabriel, when he said to Mary (Luke i. 32–34), *He shall be great, and shall be called the Son of the Highest ; and the Lord God shall give unto him the throne of his father David, and he shall reign over the house of Jacob for ever ; and of his kingdom there shall be no end.* The historical allusions in these words shew clearly that the person spoken of was one expected, or in other words a subject of prophecy ; and though the terms are not precisely those used by Isaiah, they agree with them more closely than with any other passage. Indeed, the variations may be perfectly accounted for, upon the supposition that the angel's message was intended to describe the birth of Christ as a fulfilment, not of this prediction only, but of several others also which are parallel with this, and that the language was so framed as to suggest them all, but none of them so prominently as the one before us and the earlier promise upon which it was founded. (Compare 2 Sam. vii. 11, 12 ; Dan. vii. 14, ·27; Micah iv. 7, &c.). The objection that Christ's kingdom is not of this world, and that the mention of the throne of David shews that a temporal monarchy was meant, proceeds upon the supposition that there is no such thing as figurative language, or at least that it is never used in prophecy. The objection of the Jews, that wars have not ceased since Christ came, lies with still greater force against their application of the text to Hezekiah. It is founded moreover on a misconception of the promise, which was not made to the world but to the church, and not even to that, as something to be realized at once, but by a gradual process of pacification. The reference to Christ is not a mere typical and secondary one, but primary and positive. Some who refer this whole prediction, in its proper sense, to Hezekiah, at the same time grant that it has a higher reference to Christ. Why then assume a lower sense without necessity or warrant? The violence thus done to the expressions of the text will be sufficiently evinced by stating that according to this view of the matter, as exhibited by Grotius, the *increase* here promised means continuance for nine and twenty years (*multiplicabitur ejus imperium*, id est, durabit per annos XXIX.)—*from henceforth and for ever* is from Hezekiah's birth until his death (*a modo et usque in sempiternum, ab initio ad finem vitæ*)—and when the Prophet says the zeal of God shall do this, what he means is that his zeal will lead him to bestow upon his people such a prince as Hezekiah (*zelus Domini exercituum faciet hoc*, id est, ardens amor Dei erga pios, qui insunt populo, dabit nobis ac servabit tam bonum principem). This forced attenuation of the Prophet's meaning might be natural enough in the rabbinical expositors, whose only aim was to avoid the application of the prophecy to Christ; but it was utterly unworthy of a man like Grotius, who had nothing to gain by it, and who after all admits the very thing which he appears to be denying, but admits it in the questionable shape of a twofold fulfilment and a double sense, by which proceeding he gratuitously multiplies the very difficulties which interpretation is intended to remove. Upon the whole, it may be said with truth that there is no alleged prophecy of Christ, for which it seems so difficult with any plausibility to find another subject; and until that is done which all the Rabbins and a Grotius could not do, we may repose upon the old evangelical interpretation as undoubtedly the true one.—In nearly all editions and manuscripts, the first letter of the word מרבה presents the final form ם, an orthographical anomaly mentioned in the Talmud, and perhaps very ancient, but not to be regarded as a relic of Isaiah's autograph, and therefore involving some mysterious meaning. By different Jewish writers it has been explained as an allusion to the recession of the shadow on the dial—to the enclosing of Jerusalem with walls again after the captivity—to the captivity itself, as an enclosure—to the stability of Messiah's kingdom, as the open ם is said to have the opposite meaning in Neh. ii. 13. Some Christian writers have followed this rabbinical example by suggesting what may possibly have been intended by the unusual orthography, supposing it to be both ancient and intentional—*e. g.* the exclusion of the unbelieving Jews from the kingdom of Christ—the secret inward progress of that kingdom among men—the perpetual virginity of Mary—the concealment of the time when the prediction should be verified—the spread of the gospel to the four corners of the world—the birth of Christ six hundred years (of which ם is the cipher) after the prediction—the opening to the Gentiles of the church which had been previously shut up and restricted to the Jews—the perfection of Christ's kingdom, as denoted by the perfect or square form—and its mystical nature—as denoted by the unusual form of the letter. It is suggested by Cocceius, that the unusual mode of writing may have been intended to attract attention to this signal prophecy. But why should it have been resorted to in this one passage, and in this particular part of it? Hengstenberg, Hitzig, Hendewerk, and Henderson regard it as an accidental anomaly, occasioned by mistake and preserved by superstition; the only objection to which is the extreme care of the Jews as to all points of orthography, and the improbability of such an error, if it could occur, becoming general. Some have accordingly supposed the singularity to be connected, in its origin, with the criticism of the Hebrew text. Hiller (de Arcano Chethib et Keri) conjectures that the final *mem* was meant to shew that the first two letters of למרבה, according to some ancient reading, ought to be omitted, and the word read simply רבה. Gesenius, Maurer, and Knobel adopt the supposition of Elias Levita, that it indicates a different division of the words, which is also noticed in the Masora, viz., לם רבה המשרה—*to them the dominion shall be great or multiplied.* There is, however, no example of the abbreviation לָם for לָהֶם, corresponding to the common one of בָּם for בָּהֶם.

7. Having repeatedly interchanged the three great subjects of this prophecy—the deliverance of Judah from the power of Syria and Israel—its subsequent punishment by means of the Assyrians—and the reign of the Messiah, for whose sake the kingdom was to be preserved—the Prophet passes here abruptly from the last to the first, and again predicts the punishment of Ephraim. He reverts to this event, which had already been repeatedly foretold, for the purpose of declaring that the blows would be repeated as often and as long as might be needed for the absolute fulfiment of God's threatenings. He begins by shewing that Israel had already been sufficiently forewarned. *The Lord sent a word into Jacob, and it came down into Israel.* Calvin supposes an antitheses between the clauses, and explains the verse to mean that what had been *predicted* as to Israel should be *fulfilled* in Israel; but there is no such usage of נָפַל. Grotius adopts the same construction, with the additional error of applying *Jacob* to the whole race, and *Israel* to the ten tribes, which is altogether arbitrary. Equally groundless is the supposition that *Jacob* and *Israel* denote the rival kingdoms. The two names of the patriarch are here used as equivalents, denoting his descendants, and especially the larger part, the kingdom of the ten tribes, to which the national name *Israel* is wont to be distinctively applied. Another false antithesis is that between the verbs, referring one to past time and the other to the future. This is adopted even by Ewald; but according to the usage of the language, *Vav* is conversive of the preterite only when preceded by a future, expressed or implied. (See Nordheimer, § 219, 1.) The LXX. seem to have read דֶּבֶר a pestilence, instead of דָּבָר a word. Castalio gives it here the sense of *thing* (rem mittet), Vitringa that of *threatening*, which is not expressed by this word, but suggested by the context. The true sense is that of a *dictum* or authoritative declaration, not that which follows, nor that which goes before, but the whole series of threatenings and warnings which God has sent *by all the prophets and by all the seers* (2 Kings xvii. 13), perhaps with special reference to that respecting Pekah in the seventh chapter. The sending of the word here mentioned had either actually taken place, or was regarded by the Prophet in his vision as already past. The preposition does not mean *against*, or simply *to*, but *into*, as usual, after verbs of motion. The Septuagint renders נפל *came*, the Targum *was heard.* In Josh. xxi. 45, and 1 Kings viii. 56, this same verb is used with דָּבָר *word* in the sense of *failing*, or not coming to pass. Adopting this sense here, the meaning of the verse would be, that God had sent a word of warning, but that it had not yet been fulfilled. But in both the places cited, the idea expressed is not that of mere delay, but of entire failure, implying the falsity of the prediction. To give it the contrary sense of coming to pass

or taking effect, as Jarchi and Calvin do, is altogether arbitrary. The great majority of writers take it in its usual and proper sense of falling or descending. There is no need, however, of supposing an allusion to the falling of an arrow, or of seed into the earth, or of rain upon it. A more obvious and natural association would be that of a thunderbolt, suggested by Gill and J. D. Michaelis, in reference to the threatening nature of the revelation; especially as ב נפל is elsewhere used in the sense of *falling upon, i. e.* attacking (Joshua xi. 7). The essential import of the phrase is to describe the word as coming down from God in heaven (compare Daniel iv. 28), or, as Hendewerk supposes, from Jerusalem, his earthly residence, motion from which is always spoken of as downward in the Hebrew idiom. The word which God had uttered against Israel had reached them as a message from him, as a revelation, so that there could be no doubt as to its authority and genuineness. Gesenius and Hitzig render the verbs in the present tense, and regard this verse as a title or inscription of the following prophecy, because it makes the strophe and antistrophe unequal. But if this proves any thing, it is that the strophical arrangement is itself a fanciful misapplication of the principles of Greek and Latin prosody to the measured prose of the Hebrew prophets. The solemn repetition of the last clause of ver. 8 would be just as natural in an oration as in an ode or a dramatic chorus. The injurious effects of this exaggerated theory of Hebrew versification on the criticism and interpretation of the sacred text have been already stated in the general introduction, pp. 32, 33.

8. The word which God had sent had reached the people; they had heard and understood it, but continued to indulge their pride and self-security. *And they know* (the divine threatening), *the people, all of them,* (literally *all of it; the* noun being singular but used collectively), *Ephraim and the inhabitant of Samaria* (a limitation of the general terms preceding, so as to prevent their application to Judah), *in pride and in greatness of heart* (an equivalent expression), *saying* (the words recorded in the next verse.) The apparent inversion in the last clause is well explained by Hendewerk, as arising from the fact that לאמר always stands immediately before the words spoken. Most writers understand the verbs as futures; but this is a question of no moment, as the past time which the Prophet has in view upon the other supposition, was actually future at the date of the prediction. Lowth arbitrarily translates the *vav* at the beginning of this verse *because,* and that at the beginning of ver. 10 *therefore,* making one long sentence. Luther, Hendewerk, and Ewald, render it by *that,* and make the construction a subjunctive one—" that they may know or feel it "—which is at least unnecessary. Umbreit not only gives the same construction, but takes ידעו in the absolute sense of having or obtaining knowledge (das zu Erkentniss komme), which is less consistent both with usage and the context than the common opinion that the דבר of ver. 7 is the object of the verb. Vitringa, Gesenius, and many others, understand the clause to mean that they should know the truth of these predictions by experience. It rather means that they had known and understood God's warning message. By *the people* we are not to understand the whole race (Junius), but the ten tribes, or perhaps the whole race and especially the ten tribes (J. H. Michaelis). The suffix in כלו, is referred by Gill to דבר—the people shall know all of it, *i. e.* all the word—" they shall find that the whole of it will be accomplished, every punctilio in it." Gesenius, Hendewerk, and Umbreit render it *his* (sein ganzes Volk), as if referring to the names in ver. 7. Its real antecedent is העם, as the construction is the common Hebrew one

in all such cases—*the people, all of it, i. e. all the people.* The Septuagint makes *people* govern *Ephraim* (πᾶς ὁ λαὸς τοῦ 'Εφραΐμ); but in Hebrew this construction is forbidden by the article. The inhabitant of Samaria is distinctly mentioned, as the inhabitants of Jerusalem are in chap. viii. 14. Schultens (in his Animadv. Philol. ad Jer. l. 11) gives to ‫ב‬ the sense of *for, because of,* and connects it with what goes before. It really means *in* or *with,* and connects the noun with what follows. ‫גֹּדֶל‬ is inaccurately rendered as an adjective, agreeing with ‫לְבָב‬, by the Septuagint (ὑψηλῇ καρδίᾳ) and Hendewerk (stolzem Herzen). Greatness of heart in Hebrew does not mean magnanimity, but pride and arrogance. (*Vide infra,* chap. x. 12). The feeling here described is not "a desire of splendour, power, and magnificence, a purpose to be distinguished" (Barnes), but a misplaced confidence in the stability of their condition. ‫לֵאמֹר‬, although an infinitive in form, is not incorrectly rendered as a gerund (dicendo) by Pagninus, Montanus, and Cocceius. A relative construction is preferred by Luther (die da sagen), Calvin (qui dicunt), J. H. Michaelis (dum dicunt), and many others. The participial form of the English Version is given also by the Septuagint, Vulgate, and Dutch Versions, by Vitringa, and by Lowth. There is no necessity or ground for the interrogative construction given by De Dieu (an in superbia dicendum fuit?). Forerius strangely understands the Prophet as sarcastically saying that the people shall be taught to *say,* in their pride and arrogance, what follows. Hitzig, without the irony—the people shall be made conscious of their own pride and arrogance in saying, &c. But this construction seems to overlook the preposition. ‫אמר‬ is not to be taken in the sense of purposing or thinking, which it sometimes obtains from an ellipsis of ‫אל לבו‬, *in his heart,* or *to himself* (Gen. xxvii. 41), but in its proper sense of speaking, as the usual expression of intention and desire. The conjectural emendation of the text by changing ‫ידעו‬ to ‫ירעו‬ (Houbigant), ‫ידברו‬ (Secker), or ‫יגבהו‬ (Lowth), is perfectly gratuitous.

9. The very words of the self-confident Ephraimites are now recorded. Instead of being warned and instructed by what they had already suffered, they presumptuously look for greater prosperity than ever. *Bricks are fallen, and hewn stone will we build; sycamores are felled, and cedars will we substitute.* The oriental bricks are unburnt, so that most of their brick structures are as little durable as mud walls. The sycamore is durable, but too light and spongy to be used in solid building. The latter is accordingly contrasted with the cedar, and the former with hewn stone, the two most highly valued building materials. By some interpreters these words are literally understood. According to J. H. Michaelis, they refer to the cities of the ten tribes which the Syrians destroyed; according to Gill, to the houses outside of the cities and peculiarly exposed to the invaders. So Knobel understands the sense to be, that instead of the mean houses which the Assyrians had destroyed, the people of the ten tribes were determined to build better. Hitzig and De Wette suppose that sycamores and cedars are here mentioned, not as timber, but as living trees, and give ‫נחליף‬ the specific sense of planting anew. Thus Calvin understands the people to be here represented as regarding the devastations of the enemy only as occasions for increasing the beauty of their houses and plantations. But as this implies a protracted process, we must either suppose it to be put into the mouth of the presumptuous Israelites as a foolish boast, or understand it figuratively. So indeed the whole verse is explained by many, of whom some regard the brick, stone, and trees as figures for great men in general (Targum), or for the kings of Israel in particular (Jarchi), or for the State

considered as a building or a tree (Hendewerk), while others more correctly understand both clauses as a metaphorical description of a change from worse to better, by a substitution of the precious for the vile, without specific reference to the literal rebuilding of towns or houses. Bricks and sycamores are then mere proverbial expressions for that which is inferior, and cedars and hewn stones for that which is superior. An illustrative parallel is found in chap. lx. 17, where the same general idea is expressed by the exchange of stones for iron, iron for silver, wood for brass, brass for gold, of course without allusion to a literal exchange or mutual substitution. Jerome refers this verse to the low condition of Judah under Ahaz, and the boastful determination of the ten tribes to subdue and then restore it to its former splendour ; but it really relates to what the ten tribes had themselves endured, and expresses their belief that these reverses would be followed by a better state of things than they had ever known. Cocceius understands the sense to be that the prosperity enjoyed already would be followed by still greater ; but even an inferior degree of prosperity would hardly have been represented by the metaphor of fallen bricks and prostrate trees.

10. Here begins a second stage in the progress of God's judgments. He had sent a warning prophecy before (ver. 7), and they had been taught its meaning by experience (ver. 8), but without effect upon their proud self-confidence. *And* (now) *Jehovah raises up above him* (*i. e.* Ephraim) *the* (victorious) *enemies of Rezin* (his late ally), *and* (besides these) *he will instigate his own* (accustomed) *enemies* (to wit, those mentioned in the next verse). The suffix in עָלָיו, refers, not to Rezin, but to Jacob, Israel, Ephraim, the inhabitant of Samaria, mentioned in vers. 8, 9. They who were to conquer Israel are called the *enemies of Rezin*, to remind the Israelites of their alliance with him, and to intimate that they who had so lately conquered Syria were soon to conquer Israel. There is no need therefore of the emendation שָׂרֵי, *princes*, which is found in many manuscripts, and approved by Houbigant and Ewald, but which seems to be a mere attempt to escape the supposed difficulties of the common reading צָרֵי, which has here no doubt its usual sense of enemies, with a particular allusion to its etymology as meaning those who press, oppress, and overcome, so that in this connection it would really suggest the idea of Rezin's *conquerors*, which is expressed by Hitzig. Still less is it necessary to exchange רְצִין for צִיוֹן or הַר צִיוֹן, as J. D. Michaelis is disposed to do, on the authority of the Septuagint (ἐπὶ ὄρος Σιών).—עָלָיו may be properly translated, as it usually is, *against him*, which idea is undoubtedly included ; but connected as it is with the verb יִשְׂגַּב, the preposition may be taken in its original and proper sense of *over* or *above*. " Then he exalted Rezzin's enemies above him." By אֹיְבָיו we are to understand *his own foes*, those to whose attacks he was accustomed, in addition to the *enemies of Rezin*, the Assyrians. יְסַכְסֵךְ is rendered by the Septuagint *scatter* (διασκεδάσει), and by the Vulgate *confound* (in tumultum vertet), misprinted in the London Polyglot *in tumulum*. It is taken in the sense of *mixing* or combining by Calvin (conturbabit), Grotius (conglomeravit), Munster, Castalio, and others. J. H. Michaelis, who adopts this version, explains אֵת as a preposition meaning *with* (eosque cum hostibus Israelis commiscebit). Others suppose an allusion to the mixture of nations in the Assyrian army (Calvin), or to the mixture of Assyrians with the Syrian population (Vatabulus). Gesenius, in his Commentary, and in the earlier editions of his Lexicon, follows Schultens and J. D. Michaelis in attaching to this word the sense of *arming*, which is adopted by Rosenmüller in the abridgment of his Scholia, and by Hitzig,

Maurer, Hendewerk and De Wette. But Gesenius himself, in his Thesaurus, now explains the word as meaning to excite, raise up, or instigate, an explanation given in the Targum (עיר) and by Saadias, Abulwalid, and Cocceius (instigat).

11. This verse contains a more particular description of Ephraim's *own enemies* who were to be stirred up against him, with a declaration that this was not to be the end of the infliction. *Aram (or Syria in the widest sense) before, and Philistia (or the Philistines) behind, and they devour Israel with open mouth,* (*i.e.* ravenously). *For all this* (or notwithstanding all this) *his wrath does not turn back* (from the pursuit or the attack), *and still his hand is stretched out.* On the meaning of this clause, *vide supra,* chap. v. 25. The Syrians and Philistines are supposed by some to be referred to, as forming part of the Assyrian army. The reference may, however, be to separate attacks from these two powers. *Before* and *behind* may simply mean on opposite sides, or more specifically to the east and west, which are often thus described in Hebrew. בכל פה does not mean *in every place* (Targum) or *on all sides* (Lowth)—nor does it mean *with all their mouths* (Peshito), *i.e.* the mouths of all their enemies—but *with the whole mouth,* with the mouth wide open, as expressed by Luther (mit vollem Maul), Calvin (a pleine bouche), and most modern writers. J. H. Michaelis makes בכל זאת mean *on account* or *in consequence of all this.* It is clear, however, from the first clause and the whole connection, that the reference is not to the people's sin but to their punishment.

12. These continued and repeated strokes are still without effect in bringing the people to repentance. *And the people has not turned to him that smote them, and Jehovah of hosts they have not sought.* Sin is described in Scripture as departing from God. Repentance, therefore, is returning to him. To *seek* God, in the idiom of Scripture, is to pray to him (Isa. lv. 6), to consult him (Isa. viii. 19), to resort to him for help (Isa. xxxi. 1), to hold communion with him (Amos v. 4, 5). Hence it is sometimes descriptive of a godly life in general (Ps. xiv. 2). So here it includes repentance, conversion, and new obedience. Calvin, followed by the English version, makes the *vav* at the beginning mean *because* or *for.* This verse, however, does not assign the reason of the fact recorded in the one preceding, but continues the description. God went on punishing, *and* the people went on sinning. The strict sense of the particle may therefore be retained. The first verb agrees with עם in form as a singular; the second agrees with it in sense as a collective. The preposition עד, which strictly means *until, as far as,* is regarded by Cocceius as emphatic, and as signifying that the people, if they turned at all, did not turn far enough. But as this preposition often follows שב when used in the sense of returning to God by repentance, it may be regarded merely as an idiomatic substitute for אל. A single manuscript reads על for עד. The unusual combination of the article and suffix in המכהו is regarded by Gesenius (Lehrg. p. 658) as a simple anomaly, and by Nordheimer (vol. ii. p. 13) as an emphatic form; but Ewald (§ 516, 3) explains it by supposing הו to be not a possessive but an objective suffix, governed by the participle. The difference of construction is the same as in the English phrases *his smiter* and *the* (one) *smiting him.* God is thus described, as Aben Ezra has observed, in order to intimate that he was the inflicter of their punishment—the Assyrian being merely *the rod of his anger* (chap. x. 5)—and also that his stroke sought to lead them to repentance.

13. The next stroke mentioned is a sudden destruction among all ranks

of the people, the extremes being designated by two figures drawn from the animal and vegetable world. *And Jehovah has cut off from Israel head and tail, branch and rush, in one day.* כִּפָּה does not mean a root (Aben Ezra), nor a branch in general (Kimchi), but a branch of the palm-tree (Gesenius in Comm.), or the tree itself (Gesenius in Thes.). This tree, though now rare in the Holy Land, abounded there of old, especially in the southern part, where several places were named after it (Deut. xxxiv. 3 ; 2 Chron. xx. 2). Hence it appears on Roman coins as the symbol of Judea. It is highly esteemed in the East, both for beauty and utility. Its branches grow near the top of its lofty trunk and bend towards the ground, as its leaves do also, with a gentle curvature, resembling that of a hand partly closed, from which peculiarity the Hebrew name כפה and the Latin *palma* seem to be derived. It is here contrasted with the אגמון, not a smaller branch or twig (Jarchi), but a rush or reed, so called from אגם, a marsh, because it is in such ground that it chiefly grows. The Targum seems to treat the figure as synonymous, not opposite in meaning, perhaps with some allusion to the Greek word ἡγεμών. *Palm* and *rush* are explained to mean the strong and weak by Kimchi and Cocceius, who refer them specifically to the young men and warriors, as contrasted with the widows and orphans in ver. 16. It is best, however to understand them as denoting more generally that which is superior and inferior, including every class in the community. The figures are correctly resolved by the Septuagint (μέγαν καὶ μικρόν), and strangely rendered by the Vulgate (incurvantem et refrænantem), perhaps with some allusion to the derivation of the Hebrew words. It is a singular conceit of Gill's that the use of the terms *head* and *tail* was intended to imply that the people had become beasts, which no more follows than it does from the use of the terms *branch* and *rush* that they had become plants.

14. To the descriptive figures of the preceding verse, the Prophet now adds a specific application of the first. Jehovah had cut off from Israel, not only in a general sense, the upper and lower classes of society, but in a more restricted sense, the wicked rulers, who were the corrupt *head* of the body politic, and the false prophets who, as their abject adherents, and on account of their hypocrisy and false pretensions to divine authority, might be regarded as its *tail*, because contemptible and odious, even in comparison with other wicked men, who laid no claim to a religious character. *The elder and the favourite* (or honourable person), *he is the head, and the prophet teaching falsehood, he is the tail.* On the meaning of זקן and נשוא פנים, *vide supra*, chap. iii. 2, 3. That the *head* is not explained to mean the *king*, may be, as Hendewerk suggests, because the prophecy relates to the time which immediately succeeded the death of Pekah. Henderson transposes the conjunction in the last clause—*the prophet and the teacher of lies*—but מורה is properly a participle, and is needed to qualify נביא. It is not the *prophet*, as such, but the *prophet teaching falsehood*, who is called the *tail*. The teaching of falsehood does not mean the teaching of traditions (J. H. Michaelis), or of vice (Septuagint), but teaching in the name of God what he has not revealed. The Targum makes נביא denote a *scribe* (ספר) or doctor of the law ; but it must have its sense of *prophet*, as denoting one who claims to be inspired. The false prophets are called the *tail*, not because they were weak (Targum), or of low extraction (Gill), or of a mean spirit, like a dog which wags its tail upon its master (Musculus), nor because their false doctrine was like the poison in the stings of scorpions (Menochius), nor because the civil rulers and religious teachers

were the two extremes between which the mass of the people was included (Vitringa); but because the false prophets were morally the basest of the people, and because they were the servile adherents and supporters of the wicked rulers. With respect both to the head which they followed and the body of which they were the vilest part, they might be justly be called the tail. This verse has been rejected, as a gloss or interpolation, by Houbigant, Koppe, Cube, Eichhorn, Gesenius, Hitzig, Ewald, and Knobel, on the ground that it interrupts the natural consecution of the passage; that it is too prosaic for a poetical context; that it contains a superfluous explanation of a common proverbial expression; that it explains it in a manner inconsistent with the context, as the figures in ver. 13 obviously mean the high and the low generally; that it explains only one of the two figures in that verse; that it has the very form of an explanatory gloss; that it breaks the strophical arrangement by giving to this strophe a supernumerary verse. To this it may be answered, that correctly understood it does not interrupt the train of thought, but sensibly advances it; that it is not too prosaic for the context, and that if it were, Isaiah was a prophet, not a poet by profession, and was always wise enough to sacrifice rhetoric and rhythm to common sense and inspiration; that if the verse contained an explanation not suggested by the context, it could not be superfluous; that it is not an explanation of the figures in ver. 13, but a more specific application of the first of them; that the Prophet did not make a like use of the second, because it was not equally suited to his purpose of expressing his contempt for the false prophets; that the same form is used in cases where no interpolation is suspected; and lastly, that the strophical arrangement is itself a modern figment, founded on a kind of repetition which is not unusual in animated prose. (*Vide supra ad* ver. 7.) Another answer to the last objection is given in Hendewerk's commentary on the passage, which, with this exception, is an admirable refutation of the adverse argument as stated by Gesenius. The interpolation of these words is ascribed by Gesenius to some very ancient Jewish polemic. But if so old, why may it not be a little older, and the work of Isaiah himself, who was certainly no friend of the false prophets? The rhetorical objections to this obvious conclusion are not only insufficient because they are rhetorical, but because the rhetoric itself is bad.

15. This verse gives a reason, not why all classes were to be destroyed, but why the rulers and false prophets had been specially mentioned. It arises, therefore, naturally out of the fourteenth, and thus incidentally proves it to be genuine. The truth expressed and implied is that the leaders of the people had destroyed them, and should perish with them. *The leaders of this people have been seducers, and the led of them* (are) *swallowed up* (or *ruined*). On the double meaning of מאשרי, and the paronomasia erroneously introduced by some translators, *vide supra*, chap. iii. 12, where the verb בלע occurs in the same connection. On Ewald's supposition, that the fourteenth verse was interpolated from that chapter, the verse before us ought to be rejected also. Luther explains מאשריו as meaning those who suffer themselves to be led (die sich leiten lassen); Hendewerk, those who were to be, or ought to have been rendered happy (seine zu beglückenden). But even supposing that the Hebrew word was intended to suggest both ideas, it cannot be correct to express one in the first clause, and the other in the second, as the original expressions correspond exactly, and the primary sense must be the same in both. The suffix in מאשריו, is omitted as superfluous by the Vulgate and Gesenius. Henderson refers it to מאשרי as its antecedent (*led*

by them); but the true antecedent is הָעָם (such of the people as are thus misled), and is correctly pointed out as such by Calvin (in eo), Vatablus (ex hoc populo), and others.   According to J. D. Michaelis, they are said to be *swallowed up* in sloughs and pitfalls; according to Jarchi, in ways from which there is no exit.   It is more probably, however, a strong figure for losing the way (Luther), or for destruction in general (Calvin).

16. *Therefore* (because the people are thus incorrigibly impenitent) *the Lord will not rejoice over their young men* (literally *chosen ones, i. e.* for military service, the word being used in the general sense of *youths*, but seldom without reference to war), *and on their orphans and their widows* (elsewhere represented as peculiarly the objects of God's care) *he will not have mercy* (expressing in the strongest form the extent and severity of the threatened judgments), *for every one of them* (literally *of it*, referring to the singular noun *people*) *is profane* (or impious) *and an evil doer, and every mouth* (is) *speaking folly* (in the strong Hebrew sense of wickedness).   *For all this his wrath is not turned back, and still is his hand outstretched.*   The Vulgate, Aben Ezra, Calvin, Vitringa, Lowth, and Fürst give to חָנֵף the sense of *hypocrite* or *hypocritical.*   Gesenius, Ewald, and the other modern writers give it the general sense of *impious* or *wicked*, as expressed by the Septuagint (ἄνομοι).   This explanation is supported by etymological analogy, the other by rabbinical tradition.   Lee, from the analogy of Syriac, explains it to mean *heathenish, idolatrous* (Hebrew Lexicon, s. v.).   The מ in מֵרַע is taken as a preposition (*of evil*, made up or consisting of evil) by Hitzig (vom Argen), Ewald (vom Bösen), De Wette and Knobel.   Gesenius, Umbreit, and the older writers treat it as a participle from רֵעַ.   Calvin explains דָּבָר נְבָלָה as implying that they uttered their own wickedness, betrayed themselves; but it probably means nothing more than that they were wicked in speech as well as act.   For אֲדֹנָי Lowth reads יִהְיֶה on the authority of eighteen manuscripts.

17. This verse assigns a reason why God's hand is still stretched out for the destruction of his people, by describing that destruction as the natural effect of their own wickedness, here likened to a fire beginning near the ground among the thorns and briers, then extending to the undergrowth or brushwood of the forest, which, as it consumes away, ascends in a volume of smoke.   *For wickedness burneth as the fire, thorns and briers it consumes, then kindles in the thickets of the forest, and they roll themselves upwards, a column* (literally, *an ascent) of smoke.*   Most of the older writers translate all the verbs as futures, thus converting the whole verse into a threatening.   But the interchange of preterite and future forms, as well as the connection, seems to shew that they should be explained as presents, and as expressing the natural effects of wickedness, in the form of a description or a general proposition.   The Vav conversive before תִּצַּת shews it to be dependent on the foregoing verbs and posterior in point of time, a relation which may be expressed in English by exchanging *and* for *then.*   Henderson gives רִשְׁעָה the specific meaning of idolatry (See Zech. v. 8–11), but Luther more correctly that of wickedness in general, of heart and life (das gottlose Wesen).   Thorns and briers are often used as emblems of the wicked (Micah vii. 4, Neh. i. 10, 2 Sam. xxiii. 6), and their burning as a figure for the punishment of sinners (Isa. xxxiii. 12, Ps. cxviii. 12, 2 Sam. xxiii. 7), especially by means of foreign enemies (Isa. x. 17, xxxii. 13).   Most of the recent German versions render the last Vav *so that*, in order to shew that what precedes is related to what follows as the cause to its effect.   The verb יִתְאַבְּכוּ, which occurs nowhere else, has been variously derived and

explained as meaning to be pulverized (Cocceius, Junius), to move proudly (Castellus, J. D. Michaelis), to ascend (Aben Ezra, Kimchi, Calvin). This last sense is combined with that of spreading out by J. Michaelis (ut expandant et elevent se). Gesenius, Ewald, and other modern Germans, adopt the sense of rolling or being rolled together, which is given in the Vulgate and Peshito, and by Saadias, Abulwalid, Jarchi, and Rabbi Parchon. The Vulgate makes the verb agree with גאות (convolvetur superbia fumi), Eichhorn with העם; but it really agrees with the thickets of the forest —*and they* (the burning thickets) *are rolled* (or roll themselves) *together.* The meaning of גאות is not *pride* (Vulgate), but *elevation* or *ascent*, and in this connection an ascending body, column, cloud, or volume. It may either be governed by the preposition *in* understood, or construed as the object of the verb, or put in apposition with its subject. *They roll upwards (in* or *as) a volume of smoke.*

18. The figure of a general conflagration is continued in this verse, and then exchanged for a literal description of the miseries produced by civil war. *In the wrath of Jehovah of hosts, the land is darkened* with the smoke—or *heated* by the flame—*and the people is like food* (or fuel) *of fire—one another* (literally, *man his brother) they do not spare.* Most writers understand the ב at the beginning in the sense of *by* or *through,* as denoting the cause or the means by which the effect is produced. Thus Hendewerk observes that the displeasure of Jehovah is described as the second source of misery; and Henderson says that "instead of being further represented as resulting from wickedness, the conflagration is resolved into the anger of God as the avenger of sin." But this is not necessarily the meaning of the particle, and in chap. xiii. 13, where the same phrase occurs—*in the wrath of Jehovah of hosts, and in the day of his fierce anger* —the ב in one clause seems to mean the same thing as ביום in the other. It is probable, therefore, that in this case also it denotes not the cause but the time of the event, and should not be rendered *by* or *through,* but simply *in, i.e.* in the time or during. There is then no departure from the import of the figure in ver. 17. That the sufferings of Israel were produced by the divine wrath, is abundantly implied, though not expressed.—נעתם, which occurs only here, has been variously derived, and explained as meaning to tremble (Peshito), to be disturbed (Vulgate), to be smitten (Saadias), to be wasted (Gesenius in Lex. Man.), &c. Kimchi, Luther, Calvin, the English version, Vitringa, Lowth, J. D. Michaelis, Barnes, and Umbreit, make it mean to be *darkened,* which agrees well with the figures of the foregoing verse. But Gesenius (in Thes.), Rosenmüller, Maurer, Hitzig, Hendewerk, Ewald, Knobel, follow the Septuagint and Targum and the Arabic analogy in giving the sense of being *burnt* or *burnt up.* The agreement of ארץ with a masculine verb, here and in a few other cases (*e. g.* Gen. xiii. 6; Ps. cv. 30), may be resolved into the rule of Hebrew syntax, that the verb, when it stands before its subject, often takes the simplest form, without regard to the distinction of genders.—מאכלת, a derivative of אכל, to devour, is peculiar not only to this book, but to this chapter. It denotes not the act of burning or consuming (Lee, Heb. Lex.), but the thing consumed. The particle before it is omitted by Gesenius and De Wette, but is really important, as denoting that the language of the verse is metaphorical. The grammatical subject of יחמלו is not איש, but the people understood. The original construction is retained in the versions of Cocceius, Rosenmüller, Hitzig, Barnes, and Ewald. The word *brother* may have merely its idiomatic meaning of *another person,* or be treated as emphatic, and as meaning that

the nearest ties of blood were disregarded (Calvin). Kimchi supposes that although the figure of a conflagration seems to be dropped in the last clause, there is really a tacit allusion to the mutual ignition of one tree or piece of wood by another.

19. The horrors of civil war are now presented under the fearful image of insatiable hunger, leading men to devour their own flesh. *And he tears on the right hand, and is hungry still, and devours on the left, and still they are not satisfied ; each the flesh of his own arm they devour.* Ewald refers the first clause to the past, and the second to the present ; Umbreit the first to the present, and the second to the future. But the very intermingling of the past and future forms shews that the whole was meant to be descriptive. The first verb has been variously rendered to turn aside (Septuagint, Vulgate), to withdraw one's self (Pagninus, Montanus), to distribute (Schmidius), to plunder (Targum, Jarchi, Kimchi, Luther), to snatch (Calvin, Grotius, English version, Lowth) ; but the true sense seems to be to *cut* or *tear* (Junius, Cocceius, Henderson), particularly with the teeth (De Dieu), and thence to *devour* (Gesenius, De Wette, Ewald, Umbreit, Knobel). The English version seems to make this verb agree with איש in ver. 18 (he shall snatch) ; Calvin, Cocceius, and Vitringa, with a distributive pronoun understood (rapiet quisque) ; J. D. Michaelis and the later Germans better still with an indefinite subject (*one devours*, or *they devour*). The Prophet sees one assailing the other on the right, and the other in turn attacking him upon the left, and this double subject, corresponding to *a man* and *his brother* in verse 18, may have given occasion to the plural forms שבעו and יאכלו, corresponding to יחמלו, the plural verbs referring to the people collectively, the singular nouns to the component individuals. The Targum explains *right* and *left* as meaning *south* and *north ;* but they simply denote that the devouring should be mutual, and extend in all directions. The *flesh of his own arm* is explained to mean the wealth of his kindred by the Targum (כנסי קריביה), and Grotius (res cognatorum) ; but the figures evidently have a stronger meaning. Eating and fighting are cognate ideas in the Hebrew etymology (compare לָחַם and נִלְחַם) ; but in this case the additional idea, that the fighting is between near kinsmen, is expressed by the strong figure of devouring one's flesh, while the special mention of the arm may imply (as Hitzig and Hendewerk suggest) that the mutual destroyers ought to have been mutual protectors. Knobel, indeed, objects to this as a far-fetched explanation, and supposes simply an allusion to the fact, that starving men do actually gnaw their arms, as the most convenient and accessible portion of the body. Gesenius, Rosenmüller, and Maurer give to *arm* itself the sense of *neighbour*, which is hardly justified by Jer. xix. 9. Still less ground is there for an emendation of the text by reading רעו for זרעו, as proposed by Secker, and approved by Lowth, on the authority of the Chaldee paraphrase (קריביה) and the Alexandrian text of the Septuagint (τοῦ ἀδελφοῦ αὐτοῦ), which varies from the common reading (τοῦ βραχίονος αὐτοῦ).

20. The application of the figures in ver. 19 is now made plain by the Prophet himself, who has been drawing no imaginary scene. It is Israel, the chosen race, that feeds on its own flesh. *They devour each the flesh of his own arm—Manasseh* (devours) *Ephraim, and Ephraim Manasseh—and together they* (are) *against Judah. For all this his wrath is not turned back, and still his hand* (is) *stretched out.* The tribes here specified are chosen for two reasons : first, because Judah and Joseph were the most important branches of the stock of Israel, as well before as after the disrup-

tion; and secondly, because the tribes of Ephraim and Manasseh were more nearly related to each other than to any of the rest, and therefore their hostility afforded the most striking illustration of the mutual rancour which the Prophet has described as prevalent. The Targum, followed by Jarchi, greatly weakens the effect of the first clause by explaining את to be the preposition *with*, implying merely the conjunction of these two tribes against Judah, without any intimation of their mutual hostility. The repetition of the names in that case would be perfectly unmeaning. Gesenius, Hitzig, and Umbreit also explain את as a preposition, but in the sense of *against*, which it seldom has, and which is in this case very far from being obvious. Ewald, De Wette, and Knobel, correctly adhere to the old construction given in the Septuagint, which takes את as the sign of the objective or accusative, and repeats the verb *devour* between the two proper names. Vitringa goes still further, and makes all the names accusatives (Ephraimum Manassen, Manassen Ephraimum), which leaves the verb without a subject in the sentence, and wholly overlooks the objective particle. In the next clause various verbs have been supplied—they shall besiege (Septuagint), they shall unite (Targum), they make an attack (Augusti)—but the simplest method is to supply the verb of existence *are* or *shall be*. Hitzig denies that any joint action against Judah is ascribed to Manasseh and Ephraim. But יחדו seldom if ever means *alike* or *equally;* the cases cited by Gesenius (Thes., tom. ii. p. 589) may all be resolved into examples of the usual and proper sense *at once, together*, implying unity of time, place, and action. Eichhorn's proposal to reject this clause as a gloss, upon the ground that it interrupts the sense, and is at variance with the context (Hebr. Proph. ii. p. 219), although not more unreasonable than the other propositions of the same kind which have been already stated, is nevertheless sufficiently absurd. Not only is it common for intestine wars to give occasion and give place to foreign ones, as Gesenius most truly says, but this clause really continues the description, and adds greatly to its force, by suggesting the idea that the mutual enmity of these two kindred tribes could only be exceeded by their common hatred to their common relative, the tribe of Judah.— Grotius and Junius would refer this verse to the time of Sennacherib's invasion; but the kingdom of the ten tribes was then no longer in existence, and there seems to be no ground for Junius's assertion or conjecture, that the conquered Israelites were forced to serve in the Assyrian army against Judah. The allusions of the verse are not to one exclusive period, but to a protracted series of events. The intestine strifes of Ephraim and Manasseh, although not recorded in detail, may be inferred from various incidental statements. Of their ancient rivalry we have examples in the history of Gideon (Judges viii. 1-3) and Jephthah (Judges xii. 1-6); and as to later times, it is observed by Vitringa, that of all who succeeded Jeroboam the Second on the throne of Israel, Pekahiah alone appears to have attained it without treachery or bloodshed. That Manasseh and Ephraim were both against Judah, may refer either to their constant enmity or to particular attacks. No sooner did one party gain the upper hand in the kingdom of the ten tribes, than it seems to have addressed itself to the favourite work of harassing or conquering Judah, as in the case of Pekah, who invaded it almost as soon as he had waded to the throne through the blood of Pekahiah.—The repetition in the last clause intimates that even these extreme evils should be followed by still worse; that these were but the beginning of sorrows; that the end was not yet.

Chapter 10

THE Prophet first completes his description of the prevalent iniquity, with special reference to injustice and oppression, as a punishment of which he threatens death and deportation by the hands of the Assyrians, vers. 1–4. He then turns to the Assyrians themselves, God's chosen instruments, whom he had commissioned against Israel to punish and degrade it, but whose own views were directed to universal conquest, to illustrate which, the Assyrian himself is introduced as boasting of his tributary princes and his rapid conquests, which had met with no resistance from the people or their gods, and threatening Judah with a like fate, unaware of the destruction which awaits himself, imputing his success to his own strength and wisdom, and glorying, though a mere created instrument, over his maker and his mover, vers. 5–15. His approaching doom is then described under the figure of a forest suddenly, and almost totally consumed by fire, vers. 16–19. This succession of events is to have the effect of curing the propensity to trust in man rather than God, at least among the elect remnant who survive; for though the ancient promises of great increase shall certainly be verified, only a remnant shall escape God's righteous judgments, vers. 20–23. To these the Prophet now addresses words of strong encouragement, with a renewed prediction of a judgment on Assyria, similar to that on Midian at Oreb, and on Egypt at the Red Sea, which is then described, in the most vivid manner, by an exhibition of the enemy's approach, from post to post, until he stands before Jerusalem, and then, with a resumption of the metaphor before used, his destruction is described as the prostration of a forest —trees and thickets—by a mighty axe, vers. 24–34.

It is commonly agreed that the close of the chapter relates chiefly, if not wholly, to the destruction of Sennacherib's army, recorded in chap. xxxvii. 36. The exceptions to this statement, and the arguments on both sides, will be given in the exposition of ver. 28.

For the best illustration of the geographical details in vers. 28–32, a general reference may here be given to Robinson's Palestine (vol. ii. pp. 104–151).

1. In these four verses, as in the different divisions of the ninth chapter, there is an accusation followed by a threatening of punishment. The sin denounced in the first two verses is that of oppression and injustice. The punishment threatened is desolation by a foreign foe, and its effect, captivity and death. *Woe unto them that decree decrees of injustice, and that write oppression which they have prescribed.* Many interpreters suppose two different kinds of public functionaries to be here described, viz., judges or magistrates, and their clerks or scribes (Aben Ezra, Kimchi, Abarbenel, Grotius, Junius), or evil counsellors and sovereigns, or their secretaries (Clericus), or civil rulers and prophets (Hendewerk). The Piel form כִּתֵּבוּ is explained as a causative by Pagninus, Montanus, Vatablus, and Munster (jubent scribere). Others suppose the distinction to be simply that between enacting and recording. But the more common and probable opinion is, that the parallel verbs are here substantially synonymous, as חקק originally means to engrave, or inscribe by incision, which was probably the oldest mode of writing. Thus the Septuagint renders both γράφουσι. The metaphor of *writing*, is used elsewhere to describe the decrees and providential purposes of God (Isa. lxv. 6, Job xiii. 26). Here the terms may include both legislative and judicial functions, which are not so nicely distinguished

in ancient as in modern theories of government. The divine displeasure is expressed against all abuse of power. The primary sense of אָוֶן seems to be inanity or nonentity; then more specifically, the absence of truth and moral goodness; and still more positively falsehood, injustice, wickedness in general. The primary import of עָמָל is *toil* or painful labour; then (like the Greek and Latin πόνος, *labour*) suffering, vexation. It is related to אָוֶן as the effect to the cause, as the oppression of the subject to the injustice of the ruler. The proper sense of both words is retained by Cocceius in his version *(statuta, vanitatis, laborem scribentibus)*. The Masoretic accents require עָמָל to be governed by מכתבים and separated from כתבו. This makes it necessary to supply a relative before the last verb. Otherwise, it would be more natural to understand מכתבים as a title of office, and to supply the relative before עָמָל. This is pointed out by Aben Ezra as the true construction, and Luther accordingly has *Schriftgelehrte* as the subject of both clauses. Cocceius makes the whole refer to the elders of the people or hereditary magistrates, and the scribes or doctors of the law, by whom all public matters were controlled in our Saviour's time. By the חקקי אָוֶן he understands the traditions of the elders, and by עָמָל the yoke which they imposed upon the conscience. It is evident, however, that the Prophet is still describing the evils which existed in his own day, although not peculiar to it. The Piel form of the last verb, if it has any distinctive meaning, is a frequentative, and indicates repeated and habitual action.

2. As the first verse describes the sinners and their sin, so the second sets forth its effect upon the people. *To turn aside* (or exclude) *from judgment the weak, and to take away* (by violence) *the right of the poor* (or afflicted) *of my people, that widows may be* (or so that widows are) *their spoil, and the fatherless they plunder*. The infinitive indicates the tendency and actual effect of their conduct. The Septuagint omits the preposition and governs judgment by the verb directly (ἐκκλίνοντες κρίσιν πτωχῶν). This form of expression frequently occurs in the sense of perverting justice or doing injustice (Deut. xxvii. 19; Lam. iii. 25; Exod. xxiii. 6; Deut. xxvi. 19, xxiv. 17; 1 Sam. viii. 3). Nearly allied to these, in form and meaning, is the phrase *to turn one aside in judgment* (Prov. xviii. 5) *or in the gate*, as the place where courts were held in eastern towns (Amos v. 12), or with an ellipsis of the second noun to turn the person aside, *i. e.*, to deprive him of his right by false judgment (Mal. iii. 5; Isa. xxix. 21), or with an ellipsis of both nouns (Exod. xxiii. 2). But the phrase here used is to turn one aside *from* the judgment, and seems intended to express not so much the idea or judging wrongfully as that of refusing to judge at all. "Verus sensus est ut arceant pauperes a judicio, vel efficiant ut cadant causâ" (Calvin). The same charge is brought against the rulers of Judah in chap. i. 23. The expression *of my people* intimates, not only that the sufferers were Israelites, but that they sustained a peculiar relation to Jehovah, who is frequently described in Scripture as the protector of the helpless, and especially of widows and orphans (Ps. lxviii. 5). The second verb (גזל) means to take away by violence, and may here be understood either strictly, or figuratively in the sense of *violating* justice, as the Vulgate expresses it (ut vim facerent causæ humilium).

3. The wicked rulers are themselves addressed, and warned of an approaching crisis, when they must be deprived of all that they now glory in. *And* (though you are now powerful and rich) *what will you do in the day of visitation, and in the ruin* (which) *shall come from far* (though all

may appear safe at home) ? *To whom will you flee for help, and where will you leave your glory* (for safe keeping) ? The questions imply negation, as if he had said, You can do nothing to protect yourselves, there is no place of concealment for your glory. Junius and Tremellius make the construction hypothetical—what would you do?—to whom would you fly?—where could you leave ? But as this implies that the contingency alluded to might not occur, it virtually changes a threat into a promise, which would here be out of place, between the woe at the beginning of ver. 1, and the menace at the end of ver. 4. By the *day of visitation* Vitringa understands a day of inspection and examination ; but this is a modern or a technical meaning of the term. Cocceius understands by the phrase, here and elsewhere, even in Ps. viii. 5, the time when God should be incarnate, and literally visit his people as a man. According to the usage of the Old Testament, the *day of visitation* is a time when God manifests his presence specially, whether in mercy or in wrath, but most frequently the latter. שׁוֹאָה originally signifies a noise or tumult, and is therefore peculiarly appropriate to the ruin caused by foreign invasions, such as those of the Assyrians and Babylonians, which appear to be alluded to. ממרחק תבוא is properly an independent clause—*from afar it shall come*—but in order to conform the expression to our idiom, a relative may be supplied as in the English version. The על Kimchi observes, is in this connection simply equivalent to אל. The idea of fleeing for help is expressed by the same verb and noun in chap. xx. 6. By כבוד we are not simply to understand nobility (Musculus, Forerius, Henderson)—or wealth (Clericus, Lowth, Rosenmüller)—much less the gains of oppression and injustice (Jarchi)—least of all their idols (Hendewerk) but whatever they now boasted of and trusted in.

4. *It* (your glory) *does not bow beneath the prisoners, and* (yet) *they shall fall beneath the slain*—i. e. if they do not bow under the captives they shall fall under the slain—or, such of them as do not bow, &c. *Beneath* may either be strictly understood as meaning under their feet, or simply among them. Junius and Piscator understand it to mean *lower than* the captives and the slain. De Dieu and Rosenmüller make it an adverb meaning *down.* Ewald explains it to mean *instead of*, in the place or quality of, equivalent to *as*—as captives and as slain. Cocceius and Umbreit make the first clause interrogative—does he not bow among the captives ? Kimchi, De Dieu, Gesenius, and De Wette, render בלתי *without me, i. e.* having forsaken me, or being forsaken by me (Junius)—without my interposition. Some make it mean *unless*, referring to what goes before—they can do nothing but bow, &c. (Ewald)—or what follows—unless one bow, &c. they shall fall, &c. The Septuagint and Vulgate, Castalio and Clericus, take בלתי in the sense of *lest* or *that not*, and continue the construction from the preceding verse—where will ye leave your glory, that ye bow not, &c. Luther adopts the same construction, but connects כרע with כבוד in ver. 3. Where will you leave your glory, that it bow not ? &c. This agrees well with Henderson's explanation of כבוד as meaning nobility or chief men, which would account also for the change to the plural form in יפלו. De Dieu makes אסיר and הרוגים the subjects of the verbs—taking תחת as an adverb meaning down or beneath—" besides that the captive sinks, they shall fall down slain." Knobel suggests, as a possible construction, that כרע may mean *to bow down* to the slaughter as in chap. lxv. 12, in which case both verbs would express the idea of a violent death.

On the whole, the most natural interpretation of this difficult and much disputed verse is that which explains it as a solemn declaration that their glory and especially their noble chiefs must either go into captivity or fall in battle. The concluding formula—*for all this his wrath is not turned back and still his hand is stretched out*—again suggests the fearful thought that all these accumulated judgments would be insufficient to arrest the progress of the sinner or appease the wrath of God.

5. The Assyrian is now distinctly brought into view, as the instrument which God would use in punishing his people. But instead of simply executing this task, the Assyrians would seek their own ends and exceed their commission, and for this they must themselves be punished. The Prophet begins therefore with a woe against them. *Woe unto Asshur* (the *Assyrian* or *Assyria* itself), *the rod of my anger, and the staff in their* (the Assyrians') *hand is my indignation, i. e.* its instrument. According to Kimchi, הוי is merely a לשון קריאה, or particle of calling, by which God summons the Assyrian to punish Israel. So Munster : O Assur (veni ut sis) virga, &c. It is also rendered *O* by Pagninus, Montanus, Forerius, Vatablus, and Calvin, who suggests, however, that it may be taken as an expression of grief (*alas!*) on God's part, at the necessity of punishing his people. Lowth translates it *Ho!* De Wette *Ha!* But the analogy of ver. 1 and the subsequent threatenings are decisive in favour of the common version. A pronoun of the second person is supplied after הוי by Clericus (vae vobis, Assyrii), and J. D. Michaelis (wehe dir, Assyrien), while De Dieu supplies the substantive verb after אשור (Heus! Assyria est virga, &c.). But it is simpler to connect the particle as usual directly with the noun, as in the Septuagint (οὐαὶ Ἀσσυρίοις) and most other versions. Junius, Piscator, and the margin of the English Bible give to the second *vav* the sense of *for* or *though*, which is needless and unauthorized. The Vulgate, Aben Ezra, Luther, Calvin, De Dieu, Vatablus, and Clericus, take הוא as a demonstrative equivalent to *hic, ille, ipse*, or the like. Pagninus, Cocceius, Schmidius, Vitringa, Rosenmüller, treat it as a relative (*the rod which*), and Gesenius gives the same sense, by supposing an ellipsis of אשר, and making הוא the substitute or index of the verb *to be*. For בידם Secker reads ביום (*in the day of my wrath*), a mere conjecture. The preposition is omitted by Luther and Clericus (est manus eorum). The words הוא בידם are rejected by Hitzig and Ewald as a gloss, on the ground that they render the two clauses inconsistent, one describing Assyria as itself the rod, the other putting a rod into Assyria's own hand, whereas in ver. 14 Assyria is still represented as the rod and not as the rod-bearer. Hendewerk, De Wette, and Knobel, avoid the conclusion by connecting שבט אפי with the verb *to be* supplied in the second clause—" the rod of my anger and the staff of my indignation, it is in their hand." But in ver. 24 (cf. chap. ix. 3) Assyria reappears as a rod-bearer, and the chief point and beauty of the verse before us lie in the alleged inconsistency of representing the Assyrian, by whose rod the Israelites were smitten, as himself a mere rod in the hand of God. Such emendations are as puerile in taste as they are inconsistent with the favourite German canon, that the harder reading is presumptively the true one. Any school-boy can expound the hardest passage in the classics by omitting what he pleases on the score of *inconcinnity*. The disputed words are retained by Gesenius, Maurer, Hendewerk, De Wette, Umbreit, Knobel. According to Junius, Hendewerk, and De Wette, ועמי is governed by מטה (the staff is in their hand of my indignation), and Schmidius, Clericus, Rosenmüller and Gesenius, give the

same sense by repeating מטה before זעמי (*q. d.* the staff in their hand is
the staff of my indignation). The Septuagint connects the last word of
this verse with the next (τὴν ὀργήν μου ἀποστελῶ.

6. *Upon* (or against) *an impious nation* (*i. e.* Israel, including Ephraim
and Judah) *will I send him* (the Assyrians), *and against the people of my
wrath* (*i. e.* the people that provokes it, and deserves it, and is to experience it) *I will commission him* (or give him his orders), *to take spoil and to
seize prey* (literally *to spoil spoil* and *to prey prey*), *and to place* (or render)
it (the people) *a trampling* (a thing to be trodden under foot, a common
figure for extreme degradation), *like the mire of streets.* See the same
comparison in chap. v. 25, and Ps. xviii. 43. According to Cocceius, the
use of the word גוי in application to Israel implies that they had now become
gentiles or heathen. But the word seems to be simply used as a poetical
equivalent to עם. On the meaning of חנף, *vide supra* chap. ix 16. Aben Ezra,
Lowth, Gesenius, and others, explain *people of my wrath* as meaning simply
the people at whom I am angry ; but a stronger meaning seems to be required by the form of the expression and the context. Cocceius, with perverse ingenuity, refers the suffix in עברתי to עם, which could not take it in
construction, and translates the phrase *populum excandescentiæ meum,* implying that they were (or had been) his people, but were now the objects
of his wrath. The Septuagint changes the sense by omitting עברתי (τῷ ἐμῷ
λαῷ). The true sense is not ill expressed in the paraphrase of Forerius,
populum quem duriter tractare decrevi. Piscator understands by גוי הנף the
Jews exclusively, in which he is followed by Henderson, who argues from
vers. 9–11, that the kingdom of the ten tribes is regarded in this passage as
destroyed already. But, as Vitringa had before observed, the Assyrians
did not reduce Judah to an extreme of desolation, and in Sennacherib's invasion, Jerusalem, though pre-eminently guilty, was unharmed. Besides,
the connection between this and the next chapter forbids the exclusive reference to Judah.

7. The Assyrian is now described as an unconscious instrument in
God's hand, and as entertaining in his own mind nothing but ambitious plans
of universal conquest. *And he* (Assyria personified, or the king of Assyria)
not so will think (will not *imagine* for what purpose he was raised up, or
will not *intend* to execute my will), *and his heart not so will think* (or
purpose); *for* (on the contrary) *to destroy* (is) *in his heart, and to cut
off nations not a few, i. e.* by a litotes common in Hebrew, *very many nations.* According to Cocceius, לא כן ידמה (from דמה, to resemble) means *he
will not* (or does not) *think as I do.* But the sense of imagining or purposing appears to be fully justified by usage.

8. This verse introduces the proof and illustration of his selfishness
and pride. *For he will say* (or giving it a descriptive form, *he says*) *are not
my princes altogether kings,* or *at the same time kings,* mere princes with
respect to me, but kings as to all the world besides ? By exalting his tributary princes or the nobles of his court, he magnifies himself the more.
The oriental monarchs, both in ancient and modern times, have affected the
title of *Great King* (Isa. xxxvi. 4 ; Hos. viii. 10), and *King of kings* (Ezek.
xxvi. 7 ; Dan. ii. 37), corresponding to the Greek μέγαλοι βασιλεῖς, βασιλεῖς
βασιλέων, and the Persian شاونشاه This is the more offensive because
such titles properly belong to God alone (Ps. xcv. 3 ; Dan. ii. 47, viii. 25 ;
Mat. v. 35).

9. Having boasted of his princes, he now boasts of his achievements.

Is not Calno like Carchemish? Have they not been equally subdued by
me? *Or* is *not Hammath like Arpad? Or* is *not Samaria like Damascus?*
Similar boastings were uttered by Rabshakeh (chap. xxxvi. 19, 20, xxxvii. 12,
13). These conquests were the more remarkable because so speedily achieved,
and because the Assyrians had before confined themselves within their own
limits. All the towns named were farther north than Jerusalem and probably commanded the navigation of the two great rivers, Tigris and Euphrates. *Carchemish* was a fortified town on an island in the Euphrates.
at the mouth of the Chaboras, called by the Greeks Κιρκήσιον, and in Latin
Cercusium. It had its own king (Isa. xxxvii. 13) and its own gods (Isa.
xxxvi. 19), and was taken by Tiglath-pileser (2 Kings xv. 29). *Calno* was
the *Ctesiphon* of the Greeks, on the east bank of the Tigris opposite Seleucia. It is identified by Kimchi with the *Calneh* of Gen. x. 10, and by
Bochart with the *Canneh* of Ezek. xxvii. 23. *Hamath* was a city of Syria,
on the Orontes, the mouth of which river, according to Keith (Land of Israel, chap. ii. § 3), is the *entering into Hamath,* sometimes mentioned as the
northern boundary of Canaan in its widest extent (Num. xxxiv. 8; Jos. xiii.
5). It was called by the Greeks *Epiphania.* Abulfeda, the Arabian historian, reigned there about the beginning of the fourteenth century. It is
now one of the largest towns in Asiatic Turkey, having about 100,000 inhabitants. *Arpad,* another town of Syria, near Hamath, with which it is
several times named. Junius and Paulus regard it as the name of a region.
Grotius, Döderlein, and others, confound it with *Arvad* in Phenicia (Gen.
x. 8); but none of the ancient versions do so, and ו is not interchangeable
with פ. It is mentioned last in Jer. xlix. 23, and is probably no longer in
existence. According to Jerome, there were two Hamaths, one the same
with Epiphania, the other with Antioch, the Hamath Rabba of Amos vi. 2.
Vitringa supposes the Hamath here mentioned to be, not the Epiphania, but
the Emesa (or Emissa) of the Greek and Roman writers. The latest authorities are all in favour of the other explanation. According to Jarchi,
the Assyrian in this verse is still boasting of his tributaries—"as the sons of
Carchemish are princes and rulers, so are those of Calno"—which is altogether arbitrary. The Targum, followed by Aben Ezra, Calvin, and Gill,
refers the questions of this verse to the future. *Shall not Calno be as
Carchemish?* i. e. as I have subdued Carchemish, shall I not in like manner
subdue Calno? But the great majority of writers understand the passage as
explained above, although they differ in the form of their translations.
Some adhere strictly to the form of the original without supplying anything
(Vulgate, Calvin, Cocceius, Vitringa). Some supply the present of the
verb *to be* (Luther, Piscator, Clericus, Lowth, Barnes, Henderson, Ewald,
Knobel). Some introduce another verb—shall it not perish (Aben Ezra)—
did it not happen (ging's nicht? Gesenius, Hitzig, Hendewerk, Umbreit).
J. D. Michaelis omits the interrogation, and the Peshito substitutes *behold!*
—אם לא, as usual, continues the interrogative introduced by הלא (Nordheimer, § 1090, 4, *a*). It is most exactly rendered *or not* (oder nicht), by
Hendewerk, Ewald, and Umbreit—less exactly, as a simple interrogative
without negation, by Luther, Lowth, Barnes, and Henderson—as a negative
interrogation, but without expressing אם, by Hitzig and Vitringa—as a
mere disjunctive (oder) by Gesenius.

10. *As my hand hath found* (i. e. reached and seized) *the idol-kingdoms*
(worshippers of idols)—*and their images* (Anglice, whose images were more)
than (those of) *Jerusalem and Samaria*—the apodosis of the sentence

follows in the next verse. Barnes explains *found* as meaning *found them helpless;* and J. H. Michaelis, *found strength to subdue them;* both which are forced and arbitrary. Gesenius, Maurer, Umbreit, suppose it to mean *struck,* as an arrow *finds* the mark; but this idea is rather implied than expressed, both here and in Ps. xxi. 9, 1 Sam. xxiii. 17. The ideas naturally suggested are those of detecting and reaching. The original import of אֱלִיל is retained in translation by Coccecius and Vitringa (regna nihili), both of whom however understand it to mean idols. The singular form is retained by Theodotion (τοῦ εἰδώλου), the Vulgate (regna idoli), and Umbreit (des Götzen). Ewald renders the whole phrase *Götzen-Länder.* Coccecius supposes that in using this expression, the king of Assyria is made to speak rather in the person of a Jew than in his own (pro eo quod requirebat τὸ πρέπον personae, substituitur quod requirit veritas rei). Grotius understands him to express contempt of these foreign gods as in their nature inferior to his own; but the reference is rather to their having proved unable to protect their votaries. The heathen nations of antiquity do not seem to have denied the real existence and divinity of one another's gods, but merely to have claimed superior honours for their own.—Instead of the comparative sense *than,* the Vulgate gives to מִן its local sense of *from* (de), which seems to mean that the idols of the kingdoms were derived from Israel, a fact which Jarchi does not scruple to assert, though not only unsupported but directly contradicted by all history. Vatablus gives the same construction but refers the words, with less improbability, to the inferior and dependent towns of Israel, as having learned idolatry from the royal cities. On the whole, however, though the sentence is at best obscure, the most satisfactory construction, both in a grammatical and historical point of view, is that adopted by the great majority of writers, not excepting the most learned of the Rabbins, David Kimchi, and which takes מִן as a particle of comparison. Kimchi and Calvin govern *Samaria* and *Jerusalem* directly by the preposition; most other writers repeat *images* before them. The point of the comparison is not expressed in the original; those versions are too definite which render it more numerous, more precious, or more powerful, as all these particulars may be included. The second clause is parenthetical, and disturbs the structure of the sentence by leaving the comparison, with which it opens, incomplete, although the remainder is sufficiently implied in the parenthesis itself. *As my hand hath found the idol-kingdoms* [*so shall it find Samaria and Jerusalem*]. This, which would seem to be the natural apodosis, is formerly excluded but substantially supplied by the last clause of the sentence as it stands. As if he had said, "Since my hand has found the idol-kingdoms whose images exceeded those of Jerusalem and Samaria, much more shall it find Jerusalem and Samaria themselves." But instead of protasis without an apodosis, Gesenius and Maurer describe the sentence as a double protasis with one apodosis. "As my hand has found the idol-kingdoms (whose images exceeded those of Jerusalem and Samaria), and as I have done to Samaria itself, shall I not, &c." This supposes Samaria to be regarded, even in ver. 10, as already conquered.

11. *Shall I not, as I have done to Samaria and to her idols, so do to Jerusalem and her gods?* The interrogative particle, which properly belongs to the second verb, is placed at the beginning of the sentence, in order to give prominence to its interrogative form, which involves an affirmation of the strongest kind. This effect is wholly neutralized by rendering הֲלֹא *much more* (Piscator), *furthermore* (Hendewerk), *yes* (Ewald), or *behold* (Gesenius, Hitzig). Because an interrogative construction is employed in

Hebrew where in other tongues a simple exclamation would be used, it does not follow that the one can be substituted for the other without doing violence to the usage and genius of the language. The facts alleged by Gesenius (in his Thesaurus, s. v.), that הלא, as used in the Books of Kings, is generally changed in Chronicles to הנה, and that the Septuagint frequently translates the former ἰδού, may prove a change of idiomatic usage, but cannot change the meaning of הלא itself, or make that meaning less acceptable to every unsophisticated taste than the arbitrary substitute proposed. Still more objectionable is the omission of הלא altogether. Luther, Vitringa, and J. D. Michaelis, give the verb in this interrogation, a subjunctive form,—*may, might, could, or should I not do?* It is best, however, to retain the simple future, as most writers do.—The English Version and some others use the same word to translate אלילי and עצביה, which are in fact synonymous, although the latter signifies originally *trouble, sorrow,* with reference perhaps to the ultimate effect of image worship on the worshippers. The two words are differently rendered by the Septuagint (χειροποιήτοις, εἰδώλοις), the Vulgate (idolis, simulacris), the Targum, Junius, Vitringa, Gesenius, Ewald, Lowth (idols, images).

12. To the boastful speech of the Assyrian succeeds a prediction of his fate. Although he had been suffered to proceed so far, and would be suffered to proceed still further, in the work of subjugation, till he reached the very verge of Zion and the portals of Jerusalem; God had determined that the work should go no further, but be there cut short by the infliction of a signal vengeance on the selfishness and pride of the invader. *And it shall be (i. e. the end of all his glorying shall be) that the Lord will cut all his work short at mount Zion and at Jerusalem.* (Yes, even there) *will I visit* (i. e. manifest my presence for the purpose of inflicting punishment) *on the fruit* (or outward exhibition) *of the greatness of heart* (i. e. arrogance and pride) *of the king of Assyria, and on the ostentation* (or display) *of his loftiness of eyes* (or looks, a common Scriptural expression for great haughtiness. *His work* may mean the Assyrian's work of conquest, or the Lord's own work of punishment, in reference either to Assyria or Israel. Either of these senses may be preferred without effect upon the meaning of the sentence. By the destruction of Sennacherib's army, God may be said to have cut short the work of that invader, or to have cut short his own work by accomplishing his purpose of destruction, or to have cut short his own work of punishing his people, by relieving them from danger. The last of these senses may, however, be retained, and yet the general meaning of the first clause wholly altered, as is actually done by nearly all interpreters, who take כי in the sense of *when,* and read the clause as it is rendered in the English Bible. *It shall come to pass, when the Lord hath performed his whole work on mount Zion and in Jerusalem, that I will punish* &c., *i. e.* the instrument of punishment shall be destroyed as soon as it has done its work. According to this view of the passage, the completion of God's work upon mount Zion is a previous condition of his punishing Assyria; according to the other, the completion and the punishment are one and the same thing. The former interpretation is that unanimously given by all writers known to me, excepting Hitzig, who adopts a singular construction of his own, disregarding the accents and connecting *in mount Zion and Jerusalem* with the second clause. He gives to כי, however, like the rest, its more unfrequent sense of *when,* whereas the first interpretation above stated makes it as usual equivalent to ὅτι. The principal

objection to this new construction, next to the great weight of authority against it, is the meaning which it puts upon the preposition before *Zion* and *Jerusalem*. This, it is said, can only mean *within* the walls, and cannot therefore have respect to the destruction of the host *without*. But the preposition sometimes denotes mere proximity, even when prefixed to nouns denoting place, *e.g.* בעין at the fountain, 1 Sam. xxix. 1, בנהר כבר by the river of Chebar, Ezek. x. 15, and בצור ערב at the rock Oreb, in this very chapter, ver. 26. (See Gesenius's Thesaurus, tom. i. p. 172.) To the common explanation it may be objected that יבצע does not mean simply to finish, but to finish abruptly or cut short (Isa. xxxviii. 12; Job. vi. 9), which is certainly not so appropriate to the deliberate execution of a purpose as to its sudden interruption. It is true that according to Cocceius, Vitringa, and Gesenius (in Thesauro), there is an allusion to the weaver's cutting out the web when it is finished; but there seems to be no sufficient ground for this assertion. J. D. Michaelis and Gesenius translate אפקד as a third person, which removes the appearance of grammatical irregularity, but only by the sacrifice of strict adherence to the form of the original, which, when attainable, adds greatly to the value of a version, but in point of utility and taste. In this case the enallage is highly emphatic—"the Lord will cut short"—yes, "I will visit." There is the same objection to the gratuitous omission of והיה by Luther, Clericus, Piscator, J. D. Michaelis, Gesenius, Henderson, and Ewald. That phrase is not an idiomatic pleonasm, or intended to determine the futurity of what directly follows—but an emphatic clause connecting this verse with the one before it—*q. d.* such are the boasts and such the expectations of Assyria, *but it shall be, i. e.* the end shall be, the end of all this glorying and of all these threats shall be, *that the Lord will cut short*, &c. J. D. Michaelis is singular in giving to the verb אפקד the sense of *looking down upon* (wird er herabblicken). Here, as in chap ix. 8, *greatness of heart* is a temper opposite to that of the *lowly in heart* and the *poor in spirit*, who are represented in the New Testament as peculiarly acceptable to God (Mat. v. 3; xi. 29). According to Henderson, there is an implied antithesis between the looks considered as the *leaves* and the actions as the *fruit* of the same tree, all which is more ingenious than natural. Gesenius and Maurer seem to restrict the meaning of תפארת to mere ostentation and parade; but it is best to take it in a wider sense, as including all the outward manifestations of an arrogant spirit.

13. The Assyrian is again introduced as speaking, and as arrogating to himself the two most necessary qualities of a successful ruler, to wit, energy and wisdom, military prowess and political sagacity. The last clause gives the proofs of the assertion in the first, and mentions three things which the boasters had disposed of at his pleasure, political arrangements, money, and men. *For he saith* (in heart and life, if not in words) *by the strength of my* (own) *hand I have done* (all this), *and by my* (own) *wisdom, for I am wise* (as well as strong), *and* (in the exercise of these two attributes) *I remove the bounds of the nations, and rob their hoards, and bring down, like a mighty man* (as I am), *the inhabitants.* J. H. Michaelis takes עשיתי in the sense of *making* gain or profit, as in Ezek. xxviii. 4; but it is better to translate it, *I have done,* and understand it as referring to the series of successes just before enumerated. — Cocceius and Vitringa make the next clause mean, *it is through my wisdom that I have acted prudently,* a construction far inferior, in simplicity and strength, to the obvious and common one proposed above. The removing of the bounds appears to be explained

in the Targum as descriptive of his conquering progress from one province to another (ממדינא למדינא) ; but the true sense is the more specific. one of destroying the distinctions between nations by incorporation in a single empire. עתידותיהם is variously rendered by the Septuagint (τὴν ἰσχὺν αὐτῶν), Junius (instructissima loca eorum), and Cocceius (et fixa eorum), but according to its etymology denotes things *laid up* or kept in store for future use ; hence treasures, with particular reference to their being hoarded. The Keri כביר for כאביר is unnecessary, as the כ in the latter is a *caph veritatis*, denoting comparison, not with something wholly different, but to the class to which the thing itself belongs. Thus *like a mighty man* does not imply that the person spoken of was not of that description, but that he was—" *like a mighty man or hero* as I am." As the primary meaning of ישב is to *sit*, some writers explain ישבים as meaning those who sit on high (Vulgate, J. D. Michaelis), or on thrones (Gesenius, Hendewerk, Ewald, Umbreit, Knobel), and הורדתי in the sense of displacing or dethroning. There is no necessity, however, for departing from the less poetical but more familiar sense, *inhabitants* and *bringing down*, i.e. subduing.

14. The rapidity and ease of the Assyrian conquests is expressed by a natural and beautiful comparison. In seizing on the riches of the nations, the conqueror had encountered no more difficulty than if he had been merely taking eggs from a forsaken nest, without even the impotent resistance which the bird, if present, might have offered, by its cries and by the flapping of its wings. *My hand has found* (i.e. reached and seized) *the strength* (or more specifically, the pecuniary strength, the *wealth*) *of the nations, and like the gathering of* (or as one gathers) *eggs forsaken, so have I gathered all the earth* (i.e. all its inhabitants and their possessions), *and there was none that moved a wing, or opened a mouth, or chirped.*—The present form, which Hendewerk adopts throughout the verse, is equally grammatical, but less in keeping with the context, which seems to represent the speaker as describing not his habits but his past exploits. Clericus renders חיל by *moenia*, as being the strength or defences of a besieged city, and the Vulgate takes it as an abstract meaning *strength* itself, which is its primary import ; but interpreters are generally agreed in giving it the more specific sense of *wealth*, or strength derived from property, an idea which seems to be more fully expressed by our word *substance*. The meaning of עמים is here again obscured in the English Version by the use of the singular form *people*, for which Lowth has substituted *peoples*, thereby conveying the true sense of the original, but at the same time violating the prevalent usage of the English language. Hitzig gives to מצא ל the sense of reaching after ; but according to usage and the common judgment of interpreters, the particle is here a mere connective of the verb and object. The infinitive construction כאסף is expressed in the passive form by the Vulgate (sicut colliguntur), Calvin, Clericus, and Vitringa, and as a verb of the first person by Junius (quasi reciperem), and Cocceius (quasi auferrem), but as an indefinite construction by Luther (wie man aufrafft), and most modern writers. The pronoun before אספתי is omitted in some versions as unnecessary to the sense, but it is for that very reason emphatic, and adds to the boastful tone of the Assyrian's language. Fürst and Ewald follow some of the Rabbins in making נדד, which is elsewhere intransitive, agree with כנף (flatterden Flügels), which is itself construed adverbially by Calvin (qui abigeret alâ) and Cocceius (divagans alâ). The construction of

מצפצף as a gerund by Clericus (ad pipiendum), and Gesenius (zum Gezirp), is a needless departure from the form of the original. The word *peeped* (pipio) used in the English Version is not only obsolete, but liable to be confounded with another of like form from another root. (See Richardson's English Dictionary, vol. i. p. 1433.) The terms of the last clause may be understood as having reference to young birds; but in that case there are two distinct comparisons confusedly mingled in one sentence. In either case the language is designed to be descriptive of entire non-resistance to the progress of the Assyrian conquests, and although designedly exaggerated in expression, agrees well with the historical statements, not only of the Scriptures, but of Ctesias, Berosus, Herodotus, Diodorus, Justin, and Trogus.

15. Yet in all this the Assyrian was but an instrument in God's hand, and his proud self-confidence is therefore as absurd as if an axe, or a saw, or a rod, or a staff, should exalt itself above the person wielding it. *Shall the axe glorify itself above the* (person) *hewing with it? Or shall the saw magnify itself above the* (person) *handling it?* (This is indeed) *like a rod's wielding those who wield it, like a staff's lifting* (that which is) *no wood* (viz. a man). The idea is not merely that of boastful opposition but of preposterous inversion of the true relation between agent and instrument, between mind and matter.—The potential form *may* or *can the axe* (Luther, Clericus, J. D. Michaelis), and the present form *does the axe* (Gesenius, Hitzig, Hendewerk, De Wette, Ewald), although not incorrect, are less emphatic than the future proper, *shall the axe glorify itself? i. e.* shall it be suffered so to do? Would not such assumption, if it were possible, be intolerable? Barnes corrects the common version by omitting the reflexive pronoun after *boast;* but יתפאר does not simply mean to use boastful language, but by boasting to exalt one's self in comparison with others (Judges vii. 2). The preposition על therefore does not mean merely *in the presence of* (Hitzig), nor even *against* (English Bible), but should have its proper sense of *over* or *above.* Lowth, Barnes, and Henderson omit the *or* before the second question, perhaps because the English Bible gives it in italics; but the Hebrew word has often a disjunctive meaning, when preceded in construction by the common interrogative particle. A figurative sense is put upon יתגדל by Luther (trotzen), Gesenius (brüstet), and the later German writers; but the literal version *magnify itself* is perfectly intelligible, and retains the precise form of the original. הניף is variously rendered *draw* (Septuagint, Vulgate), *shake* Calvin), *guide* (Cocceius), *move* (Clericus), &c. The essential idea is that of motion, determined and qualified by the nature of the thing moved. The Hebrew verb is specially appropriated to denote the handling or wielding of a tool or implement (Deut. xxiii. 25, xxviii. 5; Exod. xx. 25). Piscator, Gataker, and others take the כ before the verbs of the last clause as a specification of time—*when one shakes a rod or when a staff is lifted up*—but this construction, although not ungrammatical, introduces several very harsh ellipses. A writer quoted by Vatablus takes the double כ as the sign of a comparison, *as—so,* but this would be comparing a thing merely with itself. Most interpreters follow the Septuagint version in rendering the particle *as if.* This is no doubt the sense, but the precise construction is *like the lifting of a staff,* not in the passive sense of being lifted (ὡς ἄν τις ἄρῃ ἑάβδον), but in the active one of lifting something else, *like a rod's lifting those who lift it.* The construction which makes את a preposition meaning *in the power of, dependent on,* is arbitrary in itself and does not yield so good a sense. The Vulgate, the Peshito, and the English Version, give הרים a reflexive

sense, and either read על for את, or take the latter in the sense of *against*, as Calvin and Piscator do. The margin of the English Bible gives another version, which is that of Junius and Cocceius, and the one now commonly adopted as the simplest and most natural.—Gesenius, Hitzig, De Wette, Ewald, Umbreit, Knobel, make מרימיו a *pluralis majestaticus* designed to enhance the contrast between mind and matter. It is much more natural, however, to explain it as a plural proper, as is done by Maurer, Hendewerk, and Henderson.—As examples of misplaced ingenuity I add, that J. D. Michaelis (in his Notes for the Unlearned) explains שבט as the stock or handle in distinction from the iron of the axe or saw, and that De Dieu proposes to take הרים as the plural of הר, a mountain—" as if the staff were *mountains*, not a piece of wood "—a construction which is not only forced, but inconsistent with the strict correspondence of כהניף and כהרים. The same objection lies against Forerius's construction of the last clause—" as if the lifting of a staff (were) not (the lifting of) *a piece of wood*."—Junius, Cocceius, and most later writers, understand לא־עץ as a peculiar idiomatic compound (like לא־אל and לא־עם, Deut. xxxii. 21, לא־איש and לא־אדם Isa. xxxi. 8, comp. Jer. v. 7), meaning that which is very far from being wood, of an opposite nature to wood, *i. e.* according to Cocceius and Henderson, *God* himself, but more correctly *man*, since the case supposed is that of a man brandishing a rod or staff, the relation between them being merely used to *illustrate* that between Jehovah and Assyria, considered as his instrument. The last clause of this verse has not only been very variously explained by modern writers, but given great difficulty to the old translators, as appears from their inconsistent and unmeaning versions of it.

16. *Therefore* (on account of this impious self-confidence), *the Lord, the Lord of hosts, will send upon his fat ones leanness, and under his glory shall burn a burning like the burning of fire.* The accumulation of divine names calls attention to the source of the threatened evil, and reminds the Assyrian that Jehovah is the only rightful Sovereign and the God of Battles. This combination occurs nowhere else, and even here above fifty manuscripts and twelve printed editions read יהוה for אדני, and thereby assimilate the form of expression to that used in chap. i. 24, iii. 1, x. 33, xix. 5. This emendation is approved by Lowth, Ewald, and Henderson, who says that "in consequence of Jewish superstition, the divine name has been tampered with by some copyist." It is much more probable, however, that an unusual form was exchanged for a common one in a few copies, than that Jewish superstition tampered with the divine name in a single place, and left it untouched in at least four others.—Gesenius and De Wette use the present form *sends;* but in a case of threatening, the future proper is far more appropriate. This particular form of the Hebrew verb is often used with the same preposition to denote the infliction of penal sufferings. The best translation, therefore, is not *send among* but *send upon*, implying the action of a higher power (compare Ezek. vii. 3 and v. 7). Hitzig regards משמניו as an abstract meaning *fatnesses* or *fatness*, and Cocceius, Vitringa, and J. H. Michaelis translates it by a plural neuter (pinguia) meaning fat things or parts ; Ewald more explicitly, *his fat limbs ;* which supposes an allusion to a body. Most interpreters, however, understand it as an epithet of persons (fat ones), as in Ps. lxxviii. 31, viz., the Assyrian warriors or their chiefs, so called as being stout and lusty. The sending of leanness upon them seems to be a figure for the reduction of their strength, with or without allusion to the health of individuals. Some suppose an exclusive

reference to the slaughter of Sennacherib's army, others a more general one to the decline of the Assyrian power. Both are probably included, the first as one of the most striking indications of the last. By *glory* we are not to understand the splendid dress of the Assyrian soldiers (Jarchi), nor the army (Vitringa), nor the great men of the army or the empire (Lowth), nor the glorying or boasting of the king (Kimchi), but magnificence and greatness in the general, civil and military, moral and material. The preposition תחת may either mean *instead of, in exchange for* (Peshito), or *in the place of, i. e.* in the place occupied by Junius), or literally *under*, which is probably the true sense, as it agrees best with the figure of a fire, which is then described as kindled at the bottom of the splendid fabric, with a view to its more complete destruction.—Luther, Calvin, the English Version, and some others, make יקד a transitive verb meaning to kindle and agreeing with Jehovah, or the king of Assyria ; but in all the other places where it occurs it is intransitive, and is so rendered by the Vulgate (ardebit) and the recent writers, agreeing with יקד, which is not here an infinitive, though so explained by Cocceius (ardebit ardendo), but a noun. Cocceius is singular in supposing that this last clause is descriptive of the rage and spite excited in Sennacherib by his first repulse from Judah. Other interpreters regard it as descriptive of the slaughter of Sennacherib's army, as caused by a burning disease or pestilential fever (Junius, J. H. Michaelis, J. D. Michaelis) —others more naturally as a lively figure for the suddenness, completeness, and rapidity of the destruction, without direct allusion to the means or cause (Calvin, Clericus, Vitringa, Rosenmüller, Barnes, Henderson). Gesenius, who excludes any special reference to Sennacherib's army, understands by the fire here described the flames of war in general.

17. *And the light of Israel shall be for a fire* (*i. e.* shall become one, or shall act as one), *and his Holy One for a flame, and it shall burn and devour his* (the Assyrian's) *thorns and briers in one day* (*i. e.* in a very short time). —אור always denotes *light*, literal or figurative. In the places cited by Barnes (chap. xliv. 16, xlvii. 14 ; Ezek. v. 2), the idea of *fire* is denoted by a cognate but distinct form (אוּר). According to Jarchi, the Light of Israel is the Law of God, while another rabbinical tradition applies it to Hezekiah. It is no doubt intended as an epithet of God himself, so called because he enlightened Israel by his Word and Spirit, and cheered them by the light of his countenance. There may be an allusion to the pillar of cloud, and some think to the angel of God's presence who was in it. The Vulgate even renders לאש *in igne*, which is wholly unauthorised. There seems to be no sufficient reason for supposing with Vitringa that the Prophet alludes to the worship of Light or the God of Light among the heathen under the names Ὧρος, *Horus*, probably derived from אוֹר. There seems to be an antithesis between light and fire. He who was a light to Israel was a fire to Assyria. Some of the early Jews read קדושו as a plural, meaning *his saints, i. e.* the pious Jews in the days of Hezekiah. The thorns and the briers are explained by Jarchi as a figure for the chiefs of the Assyrians—by Lowth, Ewald, Umbreit and others, for the common soldiers as distinguished from the officers and princes, the forest-trees of the ensuing context—but by most interpreters, with more probability, as a figure for the whole body, either in allusion to their pointed weapons (Gesenius, Henderson), or to their malice and vexation of the Jews (Kimchi, Grotius, Hitzig), or to their combustible nature and fitness for the fire (Clericus, Barnes). Vitringa supposes a threefold allusion to their number and confusion as a great mixed multitude, their mischievous hostility, and their

impending doom.   Here, as in the foregoing verse, fire is mentioned as a rapid and powerful consuming agent, without express allusion to the manner or the means of the destruction threatened.

18. *And the glory* (i. e. beauty) *of his* (the Assyrian's) *forest and his fruitful field, from soul to body* (i. e. totally), *will he* (the Lord) *consume, and it shall be like the wasting away of a sick man.*—Clericus reads *their forest*, but the reference is not so much to the Assyrians collectively as to the king who was their chief and representative.   By *his forest* some writers understand *his host* collectively, his individual soldiers or their arms being the *trees* which composed it ; others the chief men as distinguished from the multitude, the *thorns and briers* of the verse preceding.—The Vulgate, Clericus, Rosenmüller and Augusti, take כרמלו as a proper name (*his Carmel*), the mountain or mountains of that name being noted for fertility. The name, however, is itself significant, being derived by some of the older writers from כר, *a pasture*, and מלא, *full* (Vitringa), or מול, *to cut* (Bochart) —by others from כרם, *a vineyard*, and אל, the name of God, *a vineyard of God*, i. e. a choice or fruitful vineyard (Lowth, Lee)—but by most of the recent lexicographers from כרם a vineyard, with the addition of ל, making it diminutive (Gesenius, Winer, Fürst).   In its primary import it may be applied to any highly cultivated or productive spot, a garden, vineyard, orchard, or the like, and its appropriation as a proper name is altogether secondary.   Henderson renders it *plantation*.   Here it may either be equivalent and parallel to forest, in which case it would signify a park stocked with choice and noble trees (Gesenius, Hitzig, Hendewerk, De Wette)—or it may be in antithesis to *forest*, and denote a cleared and cultivated field (Ewald, Umbreit, &c.).   Kimchi would understand by *forest* the chief men, and by *fruitful field* their wealth and especially their military stores. Vitringa thinks it possible that the *forest* is Nineveh the royal city, the *fruitful field* the country at large, and the *glory* of both, the wealth and magnificence of the whole empire, as concentrated and displayed in Sennacherib's army.   The obvious and true interpretation is, that the Prophet meant to represent the greatness of Assyria under figures borrowed from the vegetable world, and for that purpose uses terms descriptive of the most impressive aspects under which a fruitful land presents itself, forests and harvest-fields, the two together making a complete picture, without the necessity of giving to each part a distinctive import.   The *forest* and the *fruitful field*, here applied to Assyria, are applied by Sennacherib himself to Israel (chap. xxxvii. 24).   Cocceius and Vitringa construe כבוד as an absolute nominative—*and as to the glory*—but it is rather governed by the verb in the next clause.—As the terms *soul* and *flesh* are strictly inapplicable to the trees and fields, we must either suppose that the Prophet here discards his metaphor, and goes on to speak of the Assyrians as men, or that the phrase is a proverbial one, meaning *body and soul*, i. e. altogether, and is here applied without regard to the primary import of the terms, or their agreement with the foregoing figures.   Either of these explanations is better than to understand the clause with Vatablus, as meaning that the fire would not only take away the lives (נפש) of the Assyrians, but consume their bodies (בשר)—or with the Dutch Annotators, that the destruction would extend both to men (נפש) and to beasts (בשר)—or with Musculus, that the progress of the fatal stroke would be not *ab extra* but *ab intra*, which J. D. Michaelis regards as an exact description of the plague.—In the English Version, the construction is continued from the preceding verse, as if יכלה and the verbs

of that verse had a common subject. But as those verbs were feminine to agree with להבה, so this is masculine to agree with Jehovah, or the Light of Israel, or the Angel of his Presence. Henderson restores the Hebrew collocation, but makes *it* the subject of the verb consume. Lowth and Barnes more correctly supply *he*. This verb is rendered by a passive or a neuter in the Vulgate, Luther, and Augusti, as if it were the Kal and not the Piel. The same construction is ascribed to the Peshito in the Latin version of the London Polyglot; but as the Syriac verb (ﻧﺼﻤﯩ)has both an active and a neuter sense, and as the rest of the clause is in exact accordance with the Hebrew text, this translation does injustice to the faithfulness and skill of that celebrated version.—Some of the recent versions render והיה *so that it is* (Ewald, Umbreit), or *so that he is* (Hende-werk). Cocceius makes נסס the nominative before היה, Junius the nomi-native after it. The most natural construction is to read with Hendewerk, *he shall be* (i. e. the king of Assyria), or with the English Bible, *they shall be, i.e.* the Assyrians collectively, or with Hitzig indefinitely, *it shall be, i.e.* the end, issue, consequence, shall be, or the final state of things shall be.—— The remaining words of the verse have been very variously explained. Junius takes כ as a particle of time, which sense it often has before the infinitive : *as* (i. e. when) *he decays.* All other writers seem to give it its usual com-parative meaning. Aben Ezra makes מְסֹס a noun analogous in form to יְקוֹד, in ver. 16. All other writers seem to make it the infinitive of מָסַס to *melt*, dissolve, or waste away, literally or figuratively, with fear, grief, or disease.—Jarchi explains נֹסֵס as a cognate form to סָס and as being the name of a worm or insect which corrodes wood—*he shall be like the wasting of a wood-worm*—i.e. pulverised. The ancient versions make נֹסֵס the participle of נָסַס (i. q. נוּס) *to flee*, and Junius reads the whole clause thus —*and it shall be* (i. e. this shall come to pass) *when the fugitive shall melt away* (or be destroyed)—i.e. when Sennacherib, fleeing from Judah, shall be murdered at home. Cocceius explains נֹסֵס to mean that which is lofty or eminent, and takes it as the subject of הָיָה—*that which is lofty shall be like corruption or decay.* Kimchi derives the meaning of נֹסֵס from נֵס, an ensign or standard—*like the fainting of an ensign* or *as when a standard-bearer falls* (the soldiers fly). This is followed by Calvin, by the French, Dutch, and English Versions, by Vatablus, Piscator, Gataker, and Clericus (who explains מְסֹס of the standard-bearer's heart failing him). To this it has been objected, that נֵס never means a military standard, but a signal or a signal-pole, and that no such effect as that supposed would necessarily follow from the flight or the fall of an ensign. The first of these objections applies also to the very different interpretation of Tremellius—*and he shall be a standard-bearer* (to the Assyrians) *at the time of* (their) *decline.* The most recent writers are agreed in adopting the derivation of נֹסֵס proposed by Hezel and Schelling, who compare it with the Syriac ﻧﺴﻰ to be sick (whence the adjective ﻧﺴﯩﺴﺎ), and explain the clause to mean *it* (or *he*) *is* (or *shall be*) *like the fainting* (or *wasting away*) *of a sick man.* None of the ancient version give a literal translation of this clause. The Septuagint renders both מְסֹס and נֹסֵס by ὁ φεύγων, and adds ἀπὸ φλογὸς χαιομένης, upon which Lowth does not hesitate to found a change of text. The Chaldee paraphrase is, *and he shall be broken and a fugitive*; the Syriac, *he shall be as if he had not been* ; the Latin, *erit terrore profugus.* To these may be added Luther's—*he shall waste away and disappear;* and Augusti's —*there shall remain a wasted body.* This disposition to paraphrase the clause instead of translating it, together with the various ways in which it is explained, may serve to shew how difficult and doubtful it has seemed to all interpreters, ancient and modern. The paronomasia in the original is not very happily copied by Gesenius—*wie einer hinschmachtet in Ohnmacht.*

19. *And the rest* (or *remnant*) *of the trees of his forest shall be few, and a child shall write them,* i. e. make a list or catalogue, and by implication *number* them.—The singular form of עֵץ is retained in translation by the Vulgate and Calvin (reliquiæ ligni), and the sense of wood, though in the plural, by Junius (reliqua ligna). *His forest* is omitted by Hendewerk, changed to *this forest* by J. D. Michaelis, to *the forest* by Gesenius, and to *their forest* by Clericus. The Septuagint substitutes ἀπ' αὐτῶν, and the Targum an explanatory paraphrase, *the rest of his men of war.*—In the Hebrew idiom, *number*, when absolutely used, has an opposite meaning to its usual sense in English and in Latin. By a *number*, we generally mean a considerable number; Horace says, *nos numerus sumus*, meaning, *we are many* (numerous); but in Hebrew, *men of number* is a few men (Gen. xxxiv. 30; Deut. iv. 27, xxxiii. 6). The idea seems to be that small amounts may easily be reckoned, with some allusion, Rosenmüller thinks, to the ancient usage of weighing large, and counting only small sums. Thus Cicero speaks of treasures so vast *ut jam appendantur non numerentur pecuniæ*, and Ovid says, of another kind of property, *pauperis est numerare pecus.* The same idiom exists in Arabic, the *numbered days* often mentioned in the Koran being explained by the commentators to mean *few*. —The plural יהיו may either agree with שְׁאָר as a collective, or with a plural understood—as for *the rest, they shall be few.* So J. H. Michaelis and Rosenmüller. In order to remove the ambiguity, the words יהיו מספר are paraphrastically rendered by the Vulgate (præ paucitate numerabuntur), Luther, Vitringa, J. D. Michaelis, Ewald, Umbreit. The English version and some others simply substitute for מספר its peculiar idiomatic sense of *few*.—According to Rosenmüller, there is an allusion in the last clause to a child just beginning to count, and as yet only able to reckon on its fingers, which he thinks will account for the rabbinical tradition that a definite number (ten) is here predicted, and that just this number of Sennacherib's army did in fact escape. Gill quotes another Jewish legend which reduces the number to five and specifies the persons. The first of these traditions is explained by Jarchi as involving an allusion to the letter *yodh* (the alphabetic representative of 10), as the smallest and simplest of the Hebrew characters, so that a child who was barely able to form this one would be competent to write down the number of those who should escape the slaughter. According to Gataker and Knobel, the idea is, that there would be no need of an inspector or a muster-master, any child would be able to discharge the office.

20. *And it shall be* (or come to pass) *in that day* (that is, after these events have taken place), *that the remnant of Israel, and the escaped of the house of Jacob, shall no longer add* (i. e. continue) *to lean upon their smiter* (him that smote them), *but shall lean upon Jehovah, the Holy One of Israel, in truth.* There is here an allusion to the circumstances which gave rise to this whole prophecy. Ahaz, renouncing his dependence upon God, had sought the aid of Assyria, which secured his deliverance from present danger, but subjected the kingdom to worse evils from the very power to which they had resorted. But even these oppressions were to have an

end in the destruction of the hostile power; and when this should take place, Judah, now instructed by experience, would no longer trust in tyrants, but sincerely in Jehovah. Cocceius, Brentius, and Schmidius, refer this promise to the times of Christ exclusively, because this is the usual application of the phrase *that day:* because reliance upon God in truth is a peculiar promise of the new dispensation; because Israel did continue to rely on foreign aid, even after the decline of the Assyrian power; and because vers. 22, 23, are referred by Paul (Rom. ix. 27, 28) to the times of the New Testament. But since this prophecy immediately follows and precedes predictions of the downfall of Assyria, and since that power seems distinctly mentioned in the phrase מַכֵּהוּ, it is not unreasonable to conclude, that *in that day* means *after that event,* and that the reference is not to a sudden and immediate effect, but to a gradual result of the divine dispensations, so that what is here predicted, though it began to be fulfilled from the time of that catastrophe, did not receive its final consummation before Christ's appearance. On this supposition, we are better able to explain the *remnant of Israel,* as meaning not merely those left in Judah after the carrying away of the ten tribes—nor the Jews themselves who should outlive the Assyrian oppressions, and to whom the same phrase is applied, 2 Kings xix. 4, 31; xxi. 14—nor merely the Jews who should return from the Babylonish exile, and to whom it is applied, Hag. i. 2, Zech. viii. 6—nor merely the spiritual Israel, the *remnant according to the election of grace,* Rom. xi. 5—but all these at once, or rather in succession, should be taught the lesson of exclusive reliance upon God, by his judgments on his enemies.—The verbal form יוֹסִיף, *shall add* (expressing continued or repeated action), is suppressed not only in the English Version, but in many others, including the most recent. It is retained in the ancient versions and by Calvin and Cocceius, and accommodated to the idiom of other languages by Junius (pergat) Augusti (fortfahren), Hendewerk (aufhören).—The verb *stay,* used in the English Version to translate נִשְׁעַן is equivocal, like *peep* in ver. 14, because now employed chiefly in another sense. The idea expressed by the Hebrew word is simply that of leaning for support.—Calvin renders the ו at the beginning of the last clause *for,* and Hitzig *no!* Its true force may be best conveyed in English by the simple adversative *but.* For the usage of the phrase קְדוֹשׁ יִשְׂרָאֵל, *vide supra,* chap. i. 9. By the phrase *in truth,* Cocceius understands that the elect should trust in the *reality,* as distinguished from the types and shadows of the old economy. The common and obvious interpretation is, that they should trust God in *sincerity,* as opposed to a mere hypocritical profession, and with *constancy,* as opposed to capricious vacillation.

21. *A remnant shall return, a remnant of Jacob, to God Almighty.* There is an obvious allusion in these words to the name of the Prophet's son *Shear-Jashub,* mentioned in chap. vii. 3. As the people were probably familiar with this name, its introduction here would be the more significant. The Targum expounds the *remnant of Jacob* to mean " those who have not sinned, or have turned from sin." It really means those who should survive God's judgments threatened in this prophecy, not merely the Assyrian invasion or the Babylonish exile, but the whole series of remarkable events, by which the history of the chosen people would be marked, including the destruction and dispersion of the nation by the Romans. There is no need, as Henderson supposes, of supplying the words *and only* in the text or in translation. That idea, as Hitzig well observes, is suggested by the repetition. The return here spoken of is one that was to take place at various

times and in various circumstances. Under the old dispensation, the prophecy was verified in the conversion of idolatrous Jews to the worship of Jehovah, or of wicked Jews to a godly life, by means of their afflictions—under the new, in the admission of believing Jews to the Christian Church, and prospectively in the general conversion of Israel to God, which is yet to be expected. Grotius imagines that the return here mentioned is that of the Jews, whom Sennacherib's invasion had assembled in Jerusalem, to their own homes ; but this is directly contradicted by the words that follow, *to the mighty God*, which in that case would mean nothing. These words are understood by Gesenius, Hitzig, and De Wette, here as in chap. ix. 5, to mean *mighty hero*. Hendewerk, Umbreit, and Knobel, with all the early writers, give the words their proper sense. They shall return to Him who has thus shewn himself to be the mighty God. Jarchi supposes a special allusion to the slaughter of Sennacherib's army; Clericus, to the impotence of idols, from whose worship they would turn to that of the true God, the God truly and exclusively omnipotent. The present form given to the verb *turn* by the recent German writers, is less suited to so manifest a promise than the proper future.—The definite article (*the* remnant), which is used in the English Version and by Barnes, is less exact than the indefinite one employed by Lowth and Henderson,

22. The Prophet now explains his use of the word *remnant*, and shews that the threatening which it involves is not inconsistent with the ancient promises. *For though thy people, O Israel* (or Jacob), *shall be like the sand of the sea* (in multitude), *only a remnant of them shall return. A consumption is decreed, overflowing* (with) *righteousness*. The first clause is explained by Augusti, Hitzig, Hendewerk, De Wette, Ewald, Umbreit, as expressive only of a possible contingency (*were thy people*, or *even if thy people were*)—by Luther, Gesenius, and Barnes, as referring to their actual condition (*though thy people be now numerous*)—but more correctly by Calvin, Cocceius, and Lowth, as relating to a certain event, but one still future (*though thy people shall be* or *is to be*). There seems, as Calvin says, to be allusion to the promises given to the Patriarchs (*e. g.* Gen. xiii. 16, xxii. 17), and repeated by the Prophets (*e. g.* Hos. ii. 1), the fulfilment of which might have seemed to be precluded by the threatening in ver. 21—to prevent which false conclusion, Isaiah here repeats the threatening with the promise—"though thy people shall indeed be numerous, *yet*," &c. This particle, supplied in the English Version, though unnecessary, does not " evidently obscure the sense " (Barnes), but makes it clearer by rendering more prominent the apparent opposition between the threatening and the promise.—*Israel* is taken in the Septuagint and English Version, and by Henderson, as a nominative in apposition with *thy people*, God himself being the object of address ; but the better and more usual construction regards *Israel* as a vocative. The name may be understood as that of the nation ; but there is more force in the language of (we suppose, with Calvin), an apostrophe to Israel or Jacob as the common ancestor, thus keeping up a distinct allusion to the ancient promises. *Thy people* will then mean *thy posterity*—not the ten tribes exclusively, nor Judah exclusively, but the whole race without distinction.—*Like the sand of the sea* does not mean scattered and despised, as Augusti strangely imagines, but innumerable as in every other case where the comparison occurs (*e. g.* Gen. xxii. 17 ; Ps. cxxxix. 18 ; Hos. ii. 1 ; cf. Gen. xiii. 16). Henderson explains בּוֹ *to him*, *i. e.* to God, as in Hos. xii. 6 ; but it rather means *in it*, *i. e.* in thy people, as we express proportion by saying " one *in* ten." It is retained

by Cocceius (in eo), Umbreit (darin), and Ewald (darunter) ; but in order to avoid the ambiguity arising from a difference of idiom, the *in* may be exchanged for *of* or *from*, as in the ancient versions and by most modern writers. Gesenius, Hitzig, Hendewerk, and De Wette, use the present form *returns*, which is not so natural in this connection as the future given by Ewald, Umbreit, and all the older writers. The return predicted is not merely that from the Babylonish exile, but a return to God by true repentance and conversion, as the only means of salvation—*reliquiae convertentur* (Vulgate). That a remnant only should escape, implies of course a general destruction, which is positively foretold in the last clause. Grotius and Clericus explain כליון to mean a *reckoning*, or a *sum* as determined by a reckoning, here applied to the remnant of Israel as a small number, easily computed. This, according to Clericus, is also the meaning of the Vulgate version, *consummatio*. Forerius and Sanctius understand by it the remnant itself, as having been almost consumed ; De Dieu, a decree or determination ; J. D. Michaelis, the accomplishment or execution of a purpose ; but the simple and true meaning is consumption or destruction, as in Deut. xxviii. 65. Forerius strangely understands חרוץ to mean a *harrow* or a *threshing-machine*, figuratively applied to the sufferings of the people. Some explain it as an adjective, meaning *severe* (Umbreit) or *certain* (Vatablus)—the Vulgate as a participle, meaning *shortened*. Aben Ezra gives the true explanation of the word, as a participle meaning *decreed*, *determined* (1 Kings xx. 40). Henderson supposes an allusion to the primary meaning of the verb (to cut, carve, or engrave), implying permanence and immutability. Junius and Clericus make this phrase dependent on שׁטֵף as a transitive verbal form ; but it is rather to be construed with the substantive verb understood—*a consumption is decreed*—or as a subject with שׁטֵף as a predicate—*the consumption decreed (is) overflowing, i. e.* overflows—a metaphor frequently applied to invading armies (chap. viii. 8, xxviii. 15, 18; Dan. xi. 20, 22)—so that there is no need of attaching to שׁוטֵף the Chaldee sense of *hastening*, as proposed by Clericus. He also makes it agree with the name of God, as Grotius does with *remnant ;* but it really agrees with *consumption*. Righteousness, according to De Dieu, here means goodness in general and mercy in particular. Calvin and Grotius too explain it to mean piety or virtue ; but Vitringa and others take it more correctly in its strict sense of retributive and punitive justice. A preposition is supplied before it by the Septuagint (ἐν δικαιοσύνῃ) and Umbreit (mit Gerechtigkeit), making it merely an attendant circumstance. Gesenius, Hitzig, Maurer, Hendewerk, De Wette, make it the object of שׁטֵף considered as an active verb—floating righteousness in, *i. e.* bringing it in like a flood. Ewald and others make the noun an adverbial accusative—*flowing or overflowing* (with) *righteousness*. The sense is not that the remnant of Israel should be the means of flooding the world with righteousness (Calvin), nor that they should be full of it themselves (Grotius), but that the destruction of the great mass of the people would be an event involving an abundant exhibition of God's justice. This clause is therefore not, as De Dieu alleges, a direct promise of deliverance to the elect, but a threatening of destruction to the reprobate.

23. This verse contains a further explanation of the כִּלָּיוֹן חָרוּץ. *For a consumption even (the one) determined, (is) the Lord, Jehovah of hosts, making (or about to make) in the midst of all the earth.*—Augusti makes בָלָה a verb (abgemessen ist), Vitringa a participle (consummatum. Clericus takes it as a noun, but in the sense of *sum* or *reckoning*, Lowth in that

of *full decree.* Castellio has *slaughter*, which is too specific; Gesenius *wasting*, which is not strong enough. Most writers follow the ancient version in translating it *consumption* or *destruction.* Castalio and Umbreit make נחרצה an adjective, meaning *cruel* or *severe.* The Targum seems to treat it as an adjective without a substantive, used as a noun, synonymous with כָּלָה . Cocceius, Junius, Gesenius, Ewald, and others, give it the sense of *something decreed*, a decree, a judgment. It may, however, be more strictly understood as a passive participle agreeing with כָּלָה—*a consumption, even a decreed* (consumption).—כֹּל is omitted by the Targum, Lowth and Barnes, and rendered *all this* by Junius and Piscator, so as to give אֶרֶץ the restricted sense of *land*, which is the common explanation, although Ewald has *earth*, like Septuagint (οἰκουμένη). This verse and the one before it are quoted by Paul (Rom. ix. 27, 28), to shew that the Jews, as such, were not the heirs of the promise, which was intended for the remnant, according to the election of grace. The words are quoted from the Septuagint with a slight variation. The sense of the Greek is correctly given in the English Version.

24. The logical connection of this verse is not with that immediately preceding, but with ver. 19. Having there declared the fate impending over the Assyrian, the Prophet, as it were, turned aside to describe the effect of their destruction on the remnant of Israel, and now, having done so, he resumes the thread of his discourse, as if there had been no interruption. *Therefore thus saith the Lord Jehovah of hosts* (since this is soon to be the fate of the Assyrians), *Be not afraid, O my people inhabiting Zion, of Asshur* (or *the Assyrian*). *He shall smite thee* (it is true) *with the rod, and shall lift up his staff upon* (or *over*) *thee in the way of Egypt.* There is consequently no need of departing from the ordinary meaning of לְךָ and rendering it *but*, as Gesenius, Hitzig, Henderson and Umbreit do.—Instead of *saith*, Clericus and J. H. Michaelis read *hath said* in the past tense, which seems to make the verse the record of a former revelation.—According to Aben Ezra and Kimchi, Zion is here put simply for Jerusalem, and the address is to the population of that city, whether permanent or temporary, during Sennacherib's invasion. But as Zion was the seat of the true religion, and the people of God are often said to inhabit Zion, not in a local but a spiritual sense, most interpreters understand the object of address to be Israel in general, while some restrict it to the pious and believing Jews, the remnant of Israel, who were now to be consoled and reassured amidst the judgments which were coming on the nation.—אַשּׁוּר is properly the name of the whole people, and denotes the Assyrians in the strict sense, and not, as Cocceius suggests, the Syro-Grecian kings who succeeded Alexander, or the Babylonians under Nebuchadnezzar, though the terms of the consolation are so chosen as to be appropriate to other emergencies than that by which they were immediately occasioned. Gesenius, Hitzig, De Wette, Hendewerk, and Umbreit make יַכֶּכָּה a description of the past (*he smote thee*), which is wholly arbitrary, if not ungrammatical. Ewald and Knobel translate it as a present, and supply a relative (*who smites thee*). Henderson has *he may smite thee*, which appears to render it too vague and dubious. By far the simplest and most natural construction is that which gives the future form its strict sense (*he shall smite thee*), and explains the clause as a concession of the fact, that Israel was indeed to suffer at the hand of Assyria—*q. d.* true, he shall smite thee with the rod, &c. Aben Ezra supposes this to mean, that Assyria should

smite them only in design, *i. e.* try to smite them—others, that he should do no more than smite them, he should smite, but not kill, as a master treats his slave or a rider his beast. It seems more natural, however, to explain it in a general way, as simply conceding that they should be smitten, the necessary qualification or restriction being afterwards expressed.—Here, as in chap. ix. 3, Vitringa understands by מַטֶּה, a yoke, and by the whole phrase, *he shall lift up* (and impose) *his yoke upon thee*. This does not materially change the sense, but makes a distinction between the parallel expressions, which, to say the least, is needless and gratuitous. The best interpretation is the common one, which takes *rod* and *staff* as equivalent figures for oppression.—The last words, *in the way of Egypt*, are ambiguous, and admit of two distinct interpretations. Some early writers, quoted by Calvin, make the phrase to mean, *on the way to* (or *from*) *Egypt*, in allusion to the fact, that Sennacherib attacked Judea in the course of an expedition against Egypt. This view of the passage is adopted by Jerome, Clericus, J. D. Michaelis, and Augusti, and has much to recommend it, as it seems to adhere to the literal import of the terms, and introduces a striking coincidence of prophecy with history. The principal objection is derived from the analogy of ver. 26. The weight of exegetical authority preponderates in favour of a figurative exposition, making *in the way* synonymous with *in the manner, after the example*, as in Amos iv. 10. The sense will then be this: "Assyria shall oppress thee, as Egypt did before." An entirely different construction of this whole clause is that given by Junius and Tremellius, who make God himself the subject of the verbs יַכֶּה and יִשָּׂא. *He shall smite thee with the rod* (*i.e.* with the Assyrian, so called in ver. 5), *but his staff he will lift up for thee* (*i.e.* for thy deliverance), *as he did in Egypt* (when the Red Sea was divided by the rod of Moses). This construction, though ingenious, is to be rejected, on the ground that it supposes an antithesis, and changes *and* to *but* without necessity, refers the *rod* and *staff* to different subjects, although both are applied to the Assyrian in ver. 5, and gives the preposition עַל the sense of *for* or *in behalf of*, which it cannot naturally have in this connection, especially when following the verb יִשָּׂא.

25. This verse assigns a reason for the exhortation not to fear in ver. 24. *For yet a very little, and wrath is at an end, and my anger* (shall go forth, or tend) *to their destruction, i.e.* the destruction of the enemy. Interpreters are not agreed upon the question whether the first clause has reference to that destruction also, or to the restoration of God's people to his favour. Kimchi, Luther, Calvin, Clericus, J. H. Michaelis, Augusti, Rosenmüller, Hitzig, and Hendewerk, refer both זַעַם and אַפִּי to God's displeasure with Assyria, and this seems to be the sense designed to be conveyed by the English version. כָּלָה will then mean to exhaust or sate itself. But Jarchi Junius, Cocceius, Vitringa, J. D. Michaelis, Gesenius, Maurer, Barnes, De Wette, Ewald, Umbreit, Knobel, refer זַעַם to God's anger against Israel, and אַפִּי to his wrath against Assyria. "For yet a very little, and the indignation, which has caused these sufferings to my people, shall be ended, and my wrath shall turn to the destruction of their enemies." The only objection to this exposition is, that it supposes an ellipsis of some verb in the last clause, and in that respect is not so simple as the other, which construes both the nouns with כָּלָה. In favour of it, may be urged, not only the authorities already cited, but the fact that it makes the connection with the foregoing verse much more natural and easy—that it gives כָּלָה its usual sense of being terminated, coming to an end—and זַעַם its appropriated sense of God's dis-

pleasure with his own people. (*Vide supra*, ver. 5; also chap. xxx. 27, xxviii. 20; Dan. viii. 19.) The preterite form of בָּלָה is beautifully expressive of the change as already past in the view of the Prophet. This effect is greatly weakened by a substitution of the future (*shall cease*) for the past (*has ceased already*). For תבליתם (from בלה) some MSS. read תבליתם from בלה, and Luzzatto תבל יתם (my wrath against the world shall cease).

26. The suddenness and completeness of the ruin threatened are expressed by a comparison with two remarkable events in sacred history, the slaughter of the Midianites by Gideon, and the overthrow of Pharaoh in the Red Sea. *And Jehovah of hosts shall raise up against him* (the Assyrian) *a scourge* (or instrument of vengeance) *like the smiting of Midian at the rock Oreb*, and his *rod* (Jehovah's) shall again be *over the sea, and he shall lift it up* (again) *as he did in Egypt* (literally, *in the way of Egypt*, as in ver. 24). The *rock Oreb* is particularly mentioned, because one of the Midianitish princes, who had escaped from the field of battle, was there slain by Gideon; and so Sennacherib, although he should survive the slaughter of his host, was to be slain at home (chap. xxxvii. 38).—In the last clause there is a beautiful allusion to ver. 24. As the Assyrians lifted up the rod over Israel in the manner of Egypt, so God would lift up the rod over them in the manner of Egypt. As they were like the Egyptians in their sin, so should they now be like them in their punishment.— According to the Rabbins, שׁוֹט is something more than שֵׁבֶט, as *flagellum* is distinguished from *scutica* by Horace. They had lifted a *rod* over Israel, but God would raise up a *scourge* against them.—The construction of the last clause in the English Bible—*and* (as) *his rod was upon the sea*, (so) *shall he lift it up*, &c.—puts an arbitrary meaning on the particles. According to the first construction given, *his rod* (shall be again) *upon the sea* is a poetical expression for " his power shall again be miraculously displayed."—Cocceius refers the suffix in מַטֵּהוּ to אַשּׁוּר, by which he understands the Syro-Grecian kings, and especially Antiochus Epiphanes, who invaded Cyprus, and made an attempt upon Egypt, but was driven back by the Romans. Hence he reads—*and his* (the Assyrian's) *rod shall be over the sea, and he shall lift it up* (or *one shall take it away from him*) *in the way to Egypt*.

27. *And it shall be* (happen, or come to pass) *in that day* (when this prediction is fufilled) *that his burden* (the burden imposed by him, the heavy load of Assyrian oppression, perhaps with special reference to the tribute imposed upon Hezekiah) *shall depart* (be removed) *from thy shoulder, and his yoke* (a poetical equivalent to *burden*) *from thy neck* (O Israel!), *and the yoke* (itself) *shall be destroyed* (or broken off) *because of* (literally, *from the face of*) *oil* (or *fatness* or *anointing*). The only difficulty lies in the concluding words, which have been variously understood. Some have attempted to remove the difficulty by a change of text. Thus Lowth reads שכמכם on the authority of the Septuagint (ἀπὸ τῶν ὤμων); Secker מפני שמי *on account of my name*, or מבני שמן, *by the sons of oil*; J. D. Michaelis (for חֶבֶל) חֵבֶל the *band* of the yoke. Of those who retain the common text, some take שֶׁמֶן in its usual sense of *oil*, and suppose an allusion to the softening of the yoke with oil, or to its preservation by it. " Whereas yokes are commonly preserved by oil, this on the contrary shall be destroyed by it " (Kocher). But in this interpretation, the explanatory fact is arbitrarily assumed. Others take שֶׁמֶן in the sense of

fat or *fatness*, and suppose an allusion to the rejection of the yoke by a fat bullock, Deut. xxxii. 15 ; Hos. iv. 16, x. 11 (Gesenius), or to the bursting of the yoke by the increasing fatness of the bullock's neck (Hitzig, Hende-werk, or to the wearing away of the yoke by the neck, instead of the neck by the yoke (Kimchi). Of those who give this sense to שֶׁמֶן, some give to פָּנָיו its strict sense, *face.* Thus Döderlein—*the yoke shall be destroyed from off the fat faced,* *i. e.* prosperous. Others read *the yoke shall be de-stroyed by the fatness* (*i. e.* the excessive wealth and prosperity of the Assy-rian empire)—or *before the increasing prosperity of Judah.* Knobel sup-poses the face of the bullock to be meant (compare Job xli. 6). and with J. D. Michaelis reading חֵבֶל, understands the verse as meaning that the yoke shall first slip from the *shoulder* of the animal, then from its *neck,* and lastly from its *fat face* or head. Jerome and Vitringa understand by שֶׁמֶן the *unction* of the Holy Ghost, as a spirit of grace and supplications, with allusion to the influence of Hezekiah's prayers. Grotius and Dathe follow Jarchi and Kimchi in explaining שֶׁמֶן as an abstract used for a con-crete, *anointing* for *anointed one,* which they apply to Hezekiah. The Targum gives the same construction, but applies the word to the Messiah, in which it is followed by Calvin and Henderson. The general mean-ing of the verse is plain, as a prediction of deliverance from Assyrian bondage.

28. From the time of the Assyrian's overthrow the Prophet now reverts to that of his invasion, which he describes in the most vivid manner by rapidly enumerating the main points of his march from the frontier of Judah to the gates of Jerusalem. From the geographical minuteness and precision of this passage, Eichhorn and Hitzig have inferred that it was written after the event, because Isaiah could not know what route Sennacherib would take. Ewald supposes the description to be drawn from what had actually taken place in former cases, *i. e.* from the route of the Assyrians on previous occasions, but applied to an event still future. Gesenius and Hende-werk regard the description as ideal and intended to express, in a poetical manner, the quarter from which the invasion was to come and its general direction, by rapidly enumerating certain places as the points through which it was to pass. The same position is maintained in Robinson's Researches (vol. ii. p. 149), on the ground that the road here traced could never have been commonly used, because impracticable from the nature of the ground. If passable at all, however, it may well have been adopted in a case of bold invasion, where surprise was a main object. The difficulties of the route in question must be slight compared with those by which Hannibal and Na-poleon crossed the Alps. It is therefore not impossible nor even improbable, that Isaiah intended to delineate the actual course taken by Sennacherib. At the same time this is not a necessary supposition, since we may conceive the Prophet standing in vision on the walls of Jerusalem, and looking to-wards the quarter from which the invasion was to come, enumerating cer-tain intervening points without intending to predict that he would really pass through them. In this case, the more difficult the route described, the better suited would it be to express the idea that the enemy would come in spite of all opposing obstacles. J. D. Michaelis supposes the invasion here described to be that of Nebuchadnezzar—partly because that supposi-tion, as he thinks, makes the connection between this and the next chapter clearer and more natural—partly because the Babylonian army did pursue this course, whereas Sennacherib came against Jerusalem from the south (Isa. xxxvi. 2). That there is no weight in the former argument, will be

shewn in the proper place. That there is little in the other, will appear from the consideration, that the history contains no account of Sennacherib's own march upon the city, but only of Rabshakeh's embassy from Lachish, and it is expressly said that when that officer rejoined his master, he had already advanced further to the north. It is easy to imagine, therefore, that he may have chosen a circuitous and difficult approach, in order to take the city by surprise. Besides the inconclusiveness of these objections to the old interpretation, that of J. D. Michaelis is exposed to very serious objections, for example, that the foregoing context has relation to Assyria, without any intimation of a change of subject; that there is no hint of the city's being taken, much less destroyed; that the description in the text is not one of a deliberate, protracted occupation, but of a rapid and transient incursion; that the march is immediately followed by a great reverse and sudden overthrow, whereas Nebuchadnezzar was entirely successful. On these and other grounds, the passage is applied by most interpreters to the Assyrians, although some suppose Sennacherib's personal approach to be described, and others that of his representative (Junius, Robinson, &c.)—The places here enumerated seem to have belonged chiefly or wholly to the tribes of Benjamin and Judah. Some of them are still in existence, and the site of several has been recently determined by the personal observations and inquiries of Robinson and Smith. The catalogue begins at the frontier of the kingdom of Judah, and, as J. D. Michaelis suggests, at the first place conquered by the Israelites on taking possession of the land. The language is precisely that of an eye-witness describing at the moment what he actually sees. *He is come to Aiath—he is passed to Migron—to Michmash he entrusts his baggage.* Although the form *Aiath* nowhere else occurs, it is commonly supposed to be the same with *Ai*, the ancient royal city of the Canaanites, destroyed by Joshua (Josh. viii. 1), and afterwards rebuilt (Ezra ii. 28; Neh. viii. 32). It is unnecessary, therefore, to suppose that the name here denotes the spot or the region in which Ai once stood, as explained by Junius (Hajanam regionem versus). The ancient Ai was situated on a height to the north-east of Jerusalem. Eusebius describes it as in ruins when he wrote, and Jerome says its remains were scarcely visible in his day. According to Robinson, its site is probably still marked by certain ruins, south of Deir Diwan, an hour from Bethel.—The present form, *he passes*, represents the thing as actually taking place; the preterite, *he has passed*, implies that he has scarcely reached a place before he leaves it, and is therefore more expressive of his rapid movements. Either is better than the future form adopted by the ancient versions. According to J. D. Michaelis, *he passes by Migron* without entering; according to others, *he passes to Migron* from Ai; according to Gessenius and the other recent versions, *he passes through Migron*, as the second landmark on the route of the invaders. The precise situation of this place is now unknown, as it is mentioned only here and in 1 Sam. xiv. 2, from which text it would seem to have been near to Gibeah.—*Michmash* is still in existence under the almost unchanged name of Mukhmas, to the north-east of Jeba, on the slope of a steep valley. The place is now desolate, but exhibits signs of former strength, foundations of hewn stone and prostrate columns. Some give to יַפְקִיד here its secondary sense of *depositing* his baggage, stores, &c. (called in old English, *carriages*), *i. e.* merely while he halted (Barnes), or leaving them behind to expedite his march (Grotius), or because not needed for the taking of Jerusalem (Jerome), or on account of the difficult passage mentioned in the next verse (Hendewerk).

29. *They have passed the pass*, a narrow passage between Michmash and Geba (1 Sam. xiii. 3, 5, &c.), a spot no doubt easily maintained against an enemy. Their passing it implies that they met with no resistance, or had overcome it, and that there was now little or nothing to impede their march. *In Geba they have taken up their lodging* (literally, lodged a lodging). *Geba* appears, from 1 Kings xv. 22, to have been on or near the line between Benjamin and Judah. There is a small village now called *Jeba*, half in ruins, with large hewn stones and the remains of a square tower, on the opposite side of the valley from the ancient Michmash. This place Robinson and Smith supposed at first to be *Geba*, but afterwards concluded that it must be *Gibeah* of Saul, and that the site of Geba must be farther down, where they heard of ruins, but had not time to explore them (vol. ii. pp. 114, 115). Knobel alleges that Geba and Gilbeah of Saul were one and the same place, and adopts the Vulgate version of the phrase מָלוֹן לָנוּ (Gaba sedes nostra), which is also retained by Barnes (Geba is a lodging-place for us). This supposes the Assyrians to be suddenly introduced as speaking, to avoid which abrupt change of construction Lowth, Doederlein, and Dathe, adopt the reading of the Targum לָמוֹ for לָנוּ. Most interpreters, however, follow Aben Ezra in explaining לָנוּ as a verb from לוּן. The construction of the verb with its derivative noun is analogous to that of *dreaming a dream*, and other like expressions. The form of the original is imitated by Junius and Tremellius (in diversorium diverterunt). This construction of לָנוּ as a verb is favoured by the parallelism, עברו מעברה being a similar combination of a noun with its verbal root. Thus far he has described what the Assyrians themselves do—they cross the line at Ajath—pass through Migron—leave their baggage at Michmash—lodge at Geba. Now he describes what the places themselves do—*Ramah trembles; Gibeah of Saul flees*. Ramah was a city of Benjamin, near Geba, but farther from Jerusalem. It is still in existence as *Er-ram*, which is the masculine form of the one here used, with the Arabic article prefixed. It is about half a mile nearly due west of Jeba, but hidden from it by intervening heights (Robinson, vol. ii. pp. 108–114). It is two hours north of Jerusalem, on the eastern side of the road to Nablus. Eusebius and Jerome describe it as a small village, six Roman miles from Jerusalem. The identity of this place with the ancient Ramah was long lost sight of, but has been clearly ascertained by Smith and Robinson. *Ramah trembles* (or *is afraid*) at the enemy's approach, a strong and beautiful personification, or the place may be simply put for its inhabitants, as in the Targum. The trembling and flight of these towns are naturally represented as occurring while the enemy was resting at Geba. It may imply either that Ramah was not in the direct line of the march, but within sight and hearing of it, or on the contrary, that it was the next place to be reached, and was trembling in apprehension of it. A still stronger metaphor is used as to the next place. *Gibeah of Saul*—so called because it was his birth-place and residence, and to distinguish it from others of the same name—*is fled*. There is here a rapid but marked climax. While Ramah trembles, Gibeah flees.

30. To terror and flight he now adds an audible expression of distress, representing one place as crying, another as listening, and according to some writers, a third responding. At the same time he exchanges the language of description for that of direct personal address. *Cry aloud, daughter Gallim* (or *daughter of Gallim*); *hearken Laishah, ah poor Anathoth!* The site of Gallim is no longer known, but it was no doubt somewhere in the

neighbourhood of Gibeah. The personification is made more distinct by the use of the word *daughter*, whether employed simply for that purpose and applied to the town itself, as explained by J. D. Michaelis (Stadt Gallim) and Rosenmüller (oppidum Gallim), with or without allusion to its beauty (Barnes)—or, as in many other cases, to the population, as an individual. The Targum and Augusti read the name *Bath-gallim*. Grotius and others render הַקְשִׁיבִי לַיְשָׁה *cause it* (thy voice) *to be heard to Laish* (with ה directive), *i. e.* to the northern extremity of the country, where stood the town of Dan, anciently called *Laish*, and often coupled with Beersheba to' express the whole extent of Canaan—or to *Laish*, a town near the others here mentioned, but no longer in existence. Others suppose the name to be *Laishah*, and govern it directly by the verb—*cause Laishah to hear*—but הַקְשִׁיב always means to *listen*. Luther, Lowth, Augusti, Henderson, and Umbreit, suppose an apostrophe to Laishah itself—*hearken, O Laishah!* Cocceius, Vitringa, Maurer, and De Wette, *hearken to* (or towards) *Laish*, which is then supposed to be crying itself, and the call to listen is addressed to Gallim or the next place mentioned, which implies a close proximity. *Anathoth*, now *Anâta*, a sacerdotal city of Benjamin, built upon a broad ridge, an hour and a quarter from Jerusalem. Ecclesiastical tradition has assigned another site to Anathoth, between Jerusalem and Ramleh; but the true site has been clearly ascertained and fixed by Robinson and Smith (vol. ii. p. 109). There are still remains of an ancient wall of hewn stone, old foundations, and fragments of columns. It commands an extensive view, and from it the travellers just mentioned beheld several of the places here enumerated. Lowth and Ewald take עֲנִיָה as a verb with a suffix, Hendewerk as a verb with a paragogic letter, meaning *answer* or *answer her*, O Anathoth! Lowth supposes an allusion to the primary meaning of the name, viz. answers, *i. e.* echoes or reverberations from the hills by which the city was surrounded. Hitzig takes עֲנִיָה as a proper name with בֵּית, left out or understood before it, of which ellipsis there are several examples, and denoting *Bethany*, now called *Elaziriyah* (or the town of Lazarus), and situated on the eastern declivity of the mount of Olives. (See Robinson's Palestine, vol. ii. p. 101). But the majority of writers, old and new, make עֲנִיָה, as in other places where it occurs, the feminine of עָנִי *poor, afflicted, miserable*, and descriptive, not of its ordinary state, as a poor mean village, but of the Prophet's sympathy in view of the danger with which Anathoth was threatened. The introduction of the epithet in this case only may perhaps be ascribed to a designed paronomasia between the cognate forms עֲנִיָה and עֲנָתוֹת. The position of the adjective, though certainly unusual, is not unparalleled, there being instances enough to justify its explanation as a case of emphatic inversion. These two words are construed as an independent clause by Doederlein (misera est Anathoth), which Gesenius thinks admissible, although he prefers the vocative construction of the Vulgate (paupercula Anathoth!).

31. *Madmenah wanders* (or removes from her place); *the inhabitants of Gebim flee* (or *cause to flee, i. e. carry off* their goods). These places are no longer in existence, nor are they mentioned elsewhere. The *Madmen* spoken of by Jeremiah (xlviii. 2), was a town of Moab, and *Madmannah* (Jos. xv. 21) was too far south. In this verse, for the first time, the inhabitants are expressly mentioned and distinguished from the place itself. But Hiller (in his Onomasticon) makes יֹשְׁבֵי a part of the proper name (*Joshebehaggebim*), and Jerome, on the contrary, makes גֵּבִים an appellative (inhabitants of the hills). The Vulgate renders הֵעִיזוּ by *confortamini*,

deriving it apparently from עוּז, and a similar version is given in the Peshito. The English Version *gather themselves to flee*, is substantially the same with that of Calvin and Junius. According to Vitringa, it means to flee with violence and haste. Gesenius, in his Commentary, gives it the simple sense of fleeing ; but in the second edition of his German Version, and in his Thesaurus, he explains it as a causative, in which he is followed by Hitzig, Maurer, and Knobel.

32. This verse conducts him to the last stage of his progress, to a point so near the Holy City that he may defy it thence. *Yet to-day in Nob* (he is) *to stand ;* (and there) *will he shake his hand* (a gesture of menace and defiance) *against the mountain of the house* (or daughter) *of Zion (i. e.* mount Zion itself) *the hill of Jerusalem.* Nob was a sacerdotal city of Benjamin, near Anathoth (Neh. xi. 32), and according to the Talmud and Jerome, within sight of Jerusalem. Robinson and Smith explored the ridge of Olivet for traces of this town, but without success. The Nob here mentioned is no doubt the same that Saul destroyed, although there was another in the plain towards Lydda, which Jerome seems to identify with this.—The first clause has been variously explained, according to the sense put upon עֲמֹד as signifying rest or arrival, and upon הַיּוֹם as an indefinite expression for *a day*, or a specific one for *this day* or *to-day.* Joseph Kimchi, J. D. Michaelis, and Rosenmüller, understand the clause to mean that *yet to-day* (but no longer, it will be safe for the inhabitants) *to stay in Nob.* Maurer and Henderson explain it to mean *yet a day* (or one day longer, he is) *to remain in Nob.* Of these and other constructions which have been proposed, the best is that which makes the clause mean that *to-day* (before to-morrow) *he shall stand (i. e.* arrive) *in Nob*—or that which makes it mean *yet this day* (he is) *to stand (i. e.* rest) *in Nob* (before commencing his attack). This last, which is given by the latest writers, is supposed to be most in accordance with the usage of the Hebrew verb.—According to the common explanation of the phrase בַּת צִיּוֹן as meaning Jerusalem itself (*vide supra* chap. i. 8), the mountain of the daughter of Zion coincides exactly with the parallel phrase, *hill of Jerusalem.* The kethib בית ציון can only mean the temple, taking Zion in the widest sense as meaning the whole eminence on which Jerusalem was built. This reading is sustained by none of the ancient versions but the Targum, and although הר בית יהוה is no unusual combination, the phrase הר בית ציון does not occur elsewhere.—In this verse the Targum introduces a description of Sennacherib's army, and a soliloquy of Sennacherib himself, neither of which has the slightest foundation in the original.

33. To the triumphant march and proud defiance now succeeds abruptly the tremendous downfall of the enemy himself, in describing which, the Prophet resumes the figure dropped at ver. 19, and represents the catastrophe as the sudden and violent prostration of a forest. *Behold, the Lord, Jehovah of hosts,* (is) *lopping* (or about to lop) *the branch* (of this great tree) *with terror* (or tremendous violence), *and the* (trees) *high of stature* (shall be) *felled, and the lofty ones brought low.* According to Knobel, the excision of the ornamental crown or head-dress of the tree is mentioned first, because the destroying power is to be conceived as darting down from heaven like a thunderbolt, not creeping upwards from the earth, like the spreading fire in ver. 17, and in the same verse of the foregoing chapter. Jerome applies these two last verses to the death of Christ, and the consequent downfall of the Jewish State ; Calvin, Cocceius, and J. D. Michaelis, to the destruction of Jerusalem by Nebuchadnezzar. But these interpretations,

although recommended by a seeming coherence with the following chapter,
are at variance with the foregoing context, where Sennacherib's invasion is
described, and with the scope of the whole passage, which is to console the
Jews in view of that event.—הִגֵּה, when followed by an active participle,
commonly indicates a proximate futurity, at least with respect to the perceptions of the writer.—According to Kimchi, the divine names introduced
imply that Sennacherib had hitherto supposed himself to be without a master, but was now to learn his error.—Hendewerk supplies *appears* before
מְסָעֵף; but is simpler and therefore better to supply the present of the verb
to be.—פֻּארָה (from פָּאַר, to adorn) means an ornamental branch, or the
branches considered as the *beauty* of the tree.—מַעֲרָצָה properly means terror,
and in this case sudden and terrific violence. It is more vigorously rendered by Henderson (*a tremendous blow*), and Lowth (*a dreadful crash*).
The ב denotes not so much the manner as the means, not only violently,
but by violence. *Lofty of stature* is not to be applied to men directly, as
descriptive either of their pride or their appearance, but to trees as representing the Assyrians in general, or their chief men in particular. For the
same cause, נבהים should not be rendered *haughty*, an epithet which cannot
be applied to trees, but *high* or *lofty.*

34. *And he* (Jehovah) *shall cut down* (or away) *the thickets of the forest*
(the Assyrian army) *with iron*, (*i. e.* with an instrument of iron, as an axe),
and this Lebanon (this wooded mountain, this enormous forest, still referring to the host of the Assyrians) *with* (or by) *a mighty one shall fall.* It
is clear that the *iron* of this verse, and the *fire* of ver. 17, denote one and
the same thing, both implying that the forest was to perish, not by slow
decay, but by sudden violence, which shews the absurdity of giving a specific sense to all the particulars in such a picture. Thus the *thickets* are
probably mentioned only to complete the picture of a forest totally destroyed,
though Kimchi understands this as an emblem of Sennacherib's counsellors,
by whose devices he had been entangled, while Grotius, Vitringa, and others,
make it signify the common soldiers as distinguished from the chiefs before
described as trees, and Hitzig applies it to the whole mixed multitude of
the Assyrians.. The general figure of a forest is made more specific by referring to Lebanon, a mountain celebrated for its woods. Ezekiel represents
Sennacherib himself as a cedar of Lebanon (Ezek. xxxi. 3). The name is
not here put for the land of Israel, of which mount Lebanon was the northern boundary, nor for Jerusalem or the temple, in allusion to the cedar-
wood employed in their construction.—Calvin and others understand בְּאַדִּיר
as an adverbial phrase, meaning *mightily* or *violently ;* but most interpreters
explain it to mean *by a mighty one.* This is applied by Gesenius and
Maurer to God himself—by Cocceius, Schmidius, Alting, and J. D. Michaelis,
to Nebuchadnezzar—by Grotius, to the son of Sennacherib who slew him
—by several of the Rabbins to the destroying angel—by Rosenmüller and
Hitzig to the Messiah—by Vitringa and J. D. Michaelis to the Messiah and
the angel considered as identical. To these interpretations may be added,
as a mere suggestion, that אַדִּיר is possibly an epithet descriptive of בַּרְזֶל in
the preceding clause—*and he shall cut down the thickets of the forest with
iron* (*i. e.* with the axe), *and this Lebanon shall fall by a mighty one* (*i. e.*
by a mighty axe). This would be perfectly in keeping with the figurative
caste of the whole sentence, while at the same time it would leave the
application of the terms as open as it can be upon any other supposition.
—נִקַּף is taken as a passive form by Luther, J. D. Michaelis, Hitzig, Hendewerk, De Wette, Ewald. Its agreement with the plural סֻבְכֵי may in that

case either be resolved into a common licence of Hebrew syntax, or explained by supposing the agreement to be really with יַעַר. It is best, however, to take נֹקֵף as a Piel of less usual form (Nordheimer, § 238) governing סֻבְכֵי and indefinitely construed (*one shall cut*), or agreeing with *Jehovah* understood.

Chapter 11

THIS chapter is occupied with promises of restoration and deliverance, external safety and internal peace, to God's own people, as contrasted with the ruin previously threatened to their enemies. Borrowing his imagery from the fall of the Assyrian forest, just before predicted, the Prophet represents a shoot as springing from the prostrate trunk of Jesse, or rather from his roots, and invested by the Spirit of Jehovah with all the necessary attributes of a righteous judge and ruler, vers. i. 4. The pacific effect of the Messiah's reign is then described by the beautiful figure of wild and domestic animals dwelling and feeding together, and of children unhurt by the most venomous reptiles; to which is added an express prediction that all mutual injuries shall cease in consequence of the universal prevalence of the knowledge of Jehovah, vers. 5–9. To these figures borrowed from the animal creation, the Prophet now adds others from the history of Israel, but intended to express the same idea. The Messiah is here represented as a signal set up to the nations, gathering the outcasts of his people from all quarters, and uniting them again into one undivided body, free from all sectional and party animosities, vers. 10–13. Under figures of the same kind, the triumph of the church is then represented as a conquest over the old enemies of Israel, especially those nearest to the Holy Land; while the interposition of God's power to effect this and the preceding promises is vividly described as a division of the Red Sea and Euphrates, and a deliverance from Egypt and Assyria, vers. 14–16.

The evidently figurative character of some parts of this chapter seems to furnish a sufficient key to the interpretation of those parts which in themselves would be more doubtful.

1. The figure of the preceding verse is continued but applied to a new subject, the downfall of the house of David and the Jewish State, which is contrasted with the downfall of Assyria. The Assyrian forest was to fall for ever, but that of Judah was to sprout again. *And there shall come forth a twig* (or shoot) *from the stock* (or stump) *of Jesse, and a Branch from his roots shall grow.* According to Aben Ezra, Hendewerk and others, this refers to Hezekiah exclusively, and according to Grotius as a type of Christ. But Hezekiah was already born, and the house from which he sprang was not in the condition here described. Others refer it to Zerubbabel, and others to the Maccabees, who were not even descendants of Jesse. The Targum explicitly applies it to the Messiah (משיחא מלכא). Eichhorn, Bauer, Rosenmüller, Gesenius, De Wette, Hitzig, Ewald, also apply it to an ideal Messiah whom Isaiah looked for. The modern Jews of course suppose it to be yet unfulfilled. The only application of the passage that can be sustained is that to Jesus Christ, who sprang from the family of Jesse when reduced to its lowest estate, and to whom alone the subsequent description is literally applicable. Abarbenel objects that Christ was not a descendant of Jesse unless he was really the son of Joseph. But even if Mary had been of another tribe, her marriage would entitle her

offspring to be reckoned as a Son of David ; much more when she herself was of the same lineage. It is enough to know, however, that the fact of Christ's descent from David is not only repeatedly affirmed, but constantly presupposed in the New Testament, as a fact too notorious to be called in question or to call for proof.—גֶּזַע is not the seed (Aben Ezra), nor the root (Septuagint), nor even the trunk or whole stem of a tree (Gesenius, Hitzig, Hendewerk), but the *stump* or part remaining above ground when the tree is felled, as translated by Aquila, Symmachus and Theodotion (κόρμον). and explained by Kimchi (מַה הכשׁאר מן הֵעֵץ עַל הֵאָרֶץ). Together with the parallel term *roots*, it is an emblem not of mere descent or derivation, as alleged by Hitzig and Hendewerk, but of derivation from a reduced and almost extinct family, as explained by Calvin, Cocceius, Vitringa, Hengstenberg, Ewald and Umbreit. Jesse is supposed by Hitzig and Hendewerk to be named instead of David for the purpose of excluding the latter, or of intimating a correlative descent from the same ancestor. According to Kimchi, he is named as the last progenitor before the family attained to royal rank ; according to Umbreit, simply to indicate the antiquity of the house. Vitringa's explanation is more probable, viz. because Jesse resided at Bethlehem where Christ was to be born, and because the family is here considered as reduced to the same obscure condition in which Jesse lived, as contrasted with that to which David was exalted, and which the mention of the latter would naturally have recalled to mind. This last reason is also given by Calvin and Hengstenberg.

2. The person, whose origin and descent are metaphorically described in the preceding verse, is here described by his personal qualities, as one endowed with the highest intellectual and moral gifts by the direct influences of the Holy Spirit. *And upon him shall rest the Spirit of Jehovah, a Spirit of wisdom and understanding, a Spirit of counsel and strength, a Spirit of knowledge and of the fear of Jehovah.* The Targum seems to explain רוּחַ יְהֹוָה as the first item in the catalogue, meaning the Spirit of prophecy or inspiration. Gataker takes it as the cause of which the others are effects. But Kimchi more correctly understands it as a general designation of the self-same spirit which is afterwards described in detail. So Saadias and Aben Ezra understand it—" the Spirit of Jehovah which is a Spirit of wisdom," &c. Hengstenberg understands the *Spirit of Jehovah*, a stronger expression than the *Spirit of God*, the former having more explicit reference to the government and edification of the church. Gesenius, as usual, explains the *Spirit of Jehovah* as an influence, but it obviously means a person. The following genitives do not denote qualities but effects of the Spirit. The Spirit of Jehovah is not here described as being himself wise, &c., but as the author of wisdom in others. This is evident from the last clause, where the fear of Jehovah cannot be an attribute of his Spirit, but must be a fruit of his influence. The qualities enumerated are not to be confounded as mere synonymes, nor on the other hand distinguished with metaphysical precision. That the latter process must be an arbitrary one may be seen by a comparison of any two or more attempts to define the terms precisely. On the same etymological basis have been founded the most opposite interpretations. Thus the gift of prophetic inspiration is supposed to be intended both by the *Spirit of Jehovah* (Vitringa), and the *Spirit of counsel* (Reinhard), both suppositions being perfectly gratuitous. When Hengstenberg, who takes a just view of the principle on which the passage ought to be interpreted, departs so far from it in practice as to attempt a precise discrimination between חָכְמָה and בִּינָה, he proposes one directly opposite to that

proposed by Hendewerk, though both agree that one relates to theoretical and the other to practical wisdom. The truth is that none of these terms is entirely exclusive of the others. Wisdom, understanding, the knowledge of God, the fear of God, are all familiar Scriptural descriptions of religion or piety in general. Wisdom and understanding are often joined as equivalent expressions. The latter, according to its etymology, strictly denotes the power of discernment or discrimination. Both are applied to theoretical and practical wisdom, and especially to moral and religious subjects. Counsel and strength are the ability to plan and the ability to execute, neither of which can avail without the other. The knowledge of God does not in itself mean the love of him (Vitringa), although it may infer it as a necessary consequence. The correct knowledge of him certainly produces godly fear or holy reverence, and the two are probably put here for religion in the general, and are so explained in the Septuagint (γνώσεως καὶ εὐσεβείας) and Vulgate (scientiæ et pietatis). The six attributes here enumerated are grouped in three distinct pairs ; the first and last of which, as Hengstenberg supposes, have respect to personal qualities, the second to such as are official ; but Ewald distinguishes the first as theoretical, the second as practical, the third as spiritual or religious. Hendewerk ingeniously and earnestly maintains that all these epithets relate to Hezekiah, and are verified in his history—the wisdom in 2 Kings xviii. 7, *he acted wisely* (ישׂכיל) *whithersoever he went*—the spirit of counsel and might in 2 Kings xviii. 20, and in his subduing the Philistines (2 Kings xviii. 8), &c. The simple statement of this exposition is sufficient to refute it. The only person in whom the terms of this prediction have been verified is Jesus Christ, whose wisdom displayed itself in early life, and is expressly ascribed to a special divine influence ; who proved himself a " discerner of the thoughts and intents of the heart ; " whose ministry was not only characterised by fortitude and boldness, but attested by miracles and mighty deeds ; whose knowledge of divine things far surpassed that of all other men ; and who was himself a living model of all piety. This application is maintained, not only by the older Christian writers, and by Hengstenberg and Henderson, but also by Umbreit. It is an old opinion that the *seven spirits* of the Apocalypse have reference to the sevenfold רוּחַ of this passage.

3. The Messiah is now described as taking pleasure in true piety and recognizing its existence by an infallible sagacity or power of discerning good and evil, which would render him superior to the illusions of the senses and to every external influence. This faculty is figuratively described as an exquisite olfactory perception, such as enables its possessor to distinguish between different odours. *And his sense of smelling* (*i. e.* his power of perception, with a seeming reference to the pleasure it affords him) shall be exercised *in* (or upon) *the fear of Jehovah* (as an attribute of others), *and* (being thus infallible) *not by the sight* (or *according to the sight*) *of his eyes shall he judge, and not by the hearing of his ears shall he decide.* The Septuagint (followed by J. D. Michaelis, Doederlein, Hensler, Koppe, Kuinöl, Cube), takes הריחו as a preterite with a suffix, and explains the verb as meaning to fill with the Spirit or inspire. Forerius, Clericus, Herder, Van der Palm, Hendewerk, and Ewald, make it mean to breathe. " His breath is in the fear of Jehovah." *Nihil nisi pietatem spirabit* (Forerius). Reinhard makes it mean to blow, as an expression of anger. But the only sense confirmed by usage is to smell—his smell is in the fear of Jehovah. Schmidius applies this to the sweet smelling savour of our Lord's atoning sacrifice, and J. H. Michaelis to his sacerdotal functions. Sanctius and

Paulus understand it to denote *his odour* as perceived by others. But it rather denotes actively his smelling or olfactory perception. This is understood by Jarchi, Kimchi, Eichhorn, Henderson and Umbreit, as a figure for discernment or discrimination between false and true religion; and by Rosenmüller, Gesenius, Maurer, Hitzig, De Wette, Barnes, and Knobel, for the act of taking pleasure as the sense does in a grateful odour. But these two meanings are perfectly consistent, and the phrase is therefore best explained by Cocceius, Vitringa, Lowth, and Hengstenberg, as comprehending an infallible discernment and a feeling of complacency. He shall take delight in goodness, and be able to distinguish it without fail from its counterfeits. Gataker understands בִּרְאַת יְחוֹה as denoting that this power of discernment should be exercised in sacred, not in secular affairs ; Junius, Piscator, and Vatablus, that it should be joined with, or attended by, the fear of God. But the ב is really a connective, which the verb הֵרִיחַ commonly takes after it, and adds no more to the meaning of the phrase than the English prepositions when we speak of *smelling to* or *of* a thing instead of simply smelling it. The meaning therefore must be that the fear of God or piety in others would itself be the object upon which this faculty was to exert itself. Grotius, Clericus, Gesenius, and Henderson, understand by *the hearing of his ears* reports or rumours, Hitzig and others complaints and arguments before a judge, both which interpretations are too much restricted. The sight of the eyes and the hearing of the ears, are put for the testimony of those senses by which men are chiefly governed in their judgments. The same erroneous view of the passage, which led Hitzig to restrict the hearing of the ear to forensic litigation, has led Barnes and Umbreit to apply the whole of the last clause to judicial partiality or respect of persons. Hendewerk extends this application only to the sight of the eye, and makes the hearing of the ear relate to actual deception of the judge by arguments or testimony. All this is implicitly included in the text, but it includes much more. It is no doubt true, that as a judge the Messiah would be equally exempt from all disposition to favour the rich and the great at the expense of the poor, and from all liability to imposition ; but it is also true, and here declared, that he should not judge of character at all by the senses, but by an infallible sagacity or power of discerning good and evil.—According to Cocceius, the mention of eyes and ears implies the real humanity of the Messiah. Aben Ezra explains the clause to mean that he would rely upon the sense of smelling rather than that of sight or hearing, and Kimchi even says *instead of* sight and hearing. This interpretation is connected with an old Jewish notion, that the Messiah may be known, when he appears, by his power to distinguish moral character through the sense of smell. In this way the famous false Messiah Bar Kokba (son of a star), is said to have been proved an impostor, and his name changed to Bar Kozba (son of a lie). The original authorities are cited by Gill in his Commentary on this place. Traces of this opinion have been found by some in the New Testament (Luke vii. 39, John i. 49), but on very insufficient grounds. Grotius applies the verse to Hezekiah in the following manner. *His consolation* (הֲרִיחוֹ) *shall be in the fear of the Lord* (*i. e.* afforded by religion). *He shall not judge according to the sight of his eyes* (*i. e.* shall not despair even under the most discouraging appearances). *He shall not reason* (יוֹכִיחַ) *according to the hearing of his ears* (*i. e.* he shall draw no conclusions from the rumours that may reach him, but believe the declarations of the Prophets). Thus explained, the passage is certainly an accurate description of that good king's conduct during the time of the Assyrian invasion. In the English Version and by Lowth, יוכִיחַ is explained as meaning to *reprove ;* by Luther, Junius, Clericus and Hengstenberg, to *punish ;* by the Septuagint, Vulgate, Calvin, Cocceius, and Vitringa, to *convince* or *convict ;* but by J. H. Michaelis, Gesenius, Ewald, and others, to *decide ;* and as this includes the others, and makes the parallelism more exact, it is undoubtedly to be preferred.

4. The Messiah, as a righteous judge, is now exhibited in contrast with the unjust magistrates of Judah, as described in chaps. i. 23 ; x. 2 ; v. 23. *And he shall judge in righteousness the weak* (or poor) *and do justice with equity* (or impartiality) *to the meek of the earth ; and shall smite the earth with the rod of his mouth, and with the breath of his lips shall slay the wicked.* By the *earth* to be smitten, Gesenius and others understand the inhabitants of the earth. But the expression seems at least to include the smiting of the earth itself, which is elsewhere represented as the object of God's wrath, and is here described as cursed on man's account. By a *breath of his lips*, some understand a sentence of death, or command to kill (Cocceius, Clericus, Hitzig, Hendewerk)—others a natural expression of anger (Gesenius, De Wette)—others a secret, imperceptible influence, producing conviction (Kimchi, Abarbenel, Vitringa). But the true sense' seems to be the one expressed by Calvin and Ewald—a mere word, or a mere breath, as something even less than a word, and yet sufficient to effect his purpose. The Targum adds to רָשָׁע the word ארמילוס, used by the old Jews to denote the last great enemy of their religion, who is to kill Messiah the son of Joseph, but to be killed by Messiah the son of David. Paul, in 1 Thess. ii. 8, applies these words, with little change, to the destruction of antichrist at the coming of Christ. It does not follow, however, that this is a specific and exclusive prophecy of that event, but only that it comprehends it, as it evidently does. If one of the Messiah's works is to destroy his enemies, it cannot be fulfilled without the destruction of the last and greatest of those enemies to whom the Scriptures make allusion. But as Hengstenberg observes, if the promise in the first clause is of general import, the threatening in the last must be coextensive with it.

5. *And righteousness shall be the girdle of his loins, and faithfulness the girdle of his reins, i. e.* he shall be clothed or invested with these attributes, and they shall adhere closely to him. The metaphor of putting on or clothing one's self with moral attributes is not unfrequent in the Scriptures. The girdle is mentioned as an essential part of oriental dress, and that which keeps the others in their proper place, and qualifies the wearer for exertion. Calvin supposes a particular reference to decoration, and Hendewerk to the military use of the girdle as a sword-belt. Lowth imagines אזור in one of the clauses to be an error for חגור, because all the ancient versions vary the expression except that of Symmachus, and because the common text is an inelegant tautology. But Gesenius gives a number of analogous examples from this very book, and the recurrence of the word has in fact a good effect, and none the less because the other words are varied. According to Hendewerk, the insertion of חגור would do violence to usage, because that is a generic term for all belts or girdles, including the אזור or military sword-belt, the קשר or female sash, and the אבנט or sacerdotal cincture. These distinctions are not noticed in the lexicons. The Septuagint takes אֵזוֹר in both clauses as a passive participle (אָזוּר) agreeing with the subject of the verb (ἐζωσμένος). The Chaldee paraphrase of this verse makes it mean that the Messiah would be constantly surrounded by just and faithful men.

6. Here, as in chap. ii. 4, and ix. 5, 6, universal peace is represented as a consequence of the Messiah's reign, but under a new and striking figure. —*And the wolf shall dwell with the lamb, and the leopard shall lie down with the kid, and the calf and young lion and fatling together, and a little child shall lead them.* The נָמֵר, so called from its spots, includes the leopard and the panther, and perhaps the tiger. The כְּפִיר is a lion old enough to roar and raven. The מְרִיא rendered *ox* by the Septuagint and Peshito, and explained to be a particular kind of wild ox by Aben Ezra and Bochart, denotes more probably any fatted beast, and may here be mentioned because beasts of prey select such as their victims. The wolf is introduced as the natural enemy of the lamb, and the leopard, as Bochart tries to prove from Aelian, sustains the same relation to the kid. גּוּר does not mean to dwell in general, but to sojourn as a stranger or a guest, and implies that the lamb should, as it were, receive the wolf into its home. The verb רָבַץ is specially appropriated to express the lying down of sheep and other animals. Here it may denote that the leopard, accustomed to crouch while waiting for its prey, shall now lie down peaceably beside it; or there may be an allusion to the restlessness and fleetness of the wild beast, now to be succeeded by the quiet habits of the ruminating species. The unusual construction נֹהֵג בָּם has led some to take בְּ in the sense of *among*, and others to regard נֹהֵג as a noun, meaning leader or conductor. But the truth is that the insertion of בְּ between words which seem to cohere most closely, is a common idiom of Hebrew syntax. (*Vide supra*, chap. ix. 1, 2). נָהַג is properly to *lead*, but may include the idea of *driving*, as a shepherd does his flock. Some supply the substantive verb with יַחְדָּו — shall be together—but a similar construction is to connect it with the verb in the preceding clause—the leopard and the kid shall lie down together, the calf, the young lion, and the fatted beast together. Jerome speaks of the Jews and some judaizing Christians as believing that the literal change in the nature of wild beasts is here predicted. Kimchi regards it as a promise of immunity from wild beasts, to be enjoyed by the Jews alone in the days of the Messiah. Most Christian writers, ancient and modern, with Aben Ezra and Maimonides among the Jews, explain the prophecy as wholly metaphorical, and descriptive of the peace to be enjoyed by God's people— according to Grotius, after Sennacherib's retreat—but according to the rest, under the new dispensation. Cocceius and Clericus apply the passage to the external peace between the church and the world, but it is commonly regarded as descriptive of the change wrought by Christianity in wicked men themselves. Vitringa gives a specific meaning to each figure in the landscape, making the lamb, the calf, and the fatted beast, denote successive stages in the Christian's progress, the lion open enemies, the leopard more disguised ones, the wolf treacherous and malignant ones, the little child the ministry. This kind of exposition not only mars the beauty, but obscures the real meaning of the prophecy. Calvin and Hengstenberg suppose the passage to include a promise of a future change in the material creation, restoring it to its original condition (Rom. viii. 19–22), while they agree with other writers in regarding the pacific effects of true religion as the primary subject of the prophecy.

7. *And the cow and the bear shall feed—together shall their young lie down—and the lion like the ox shall eat straw.* According to Vitringa, there is here a climax, not in form but in sense; not only shall the nobler lion be at peace with the domesticated animals, but even the less generous and more ferocious bear. The Septuagint and Peshito repeat יַחְדָּו, in which

they are followed by most interpreters, and Lowth inserts it in the text. But according to Hitzig, the wonder is not that the bear grazes *with the cow*, but that it grazes at all, the cow being mentioned only to shew what kind of pasture is intended.　The sense will then be simply that the bear grazes *like the cow*, the very form of expression used in the last clause with respect to the lion.　He mentions straw as a common kind of fodder— *hordei stipulam bubus gratissimam—palea plures gentium pro fœno utuntur.* (Pliny, Nat. Hist. xviii. 30).　The lion's eating straw implies not only cohabitation with domestic cattle, but a change of his carnivorous habits. Vitringa carries out his allegorical hypothesis by making the cow the representative of Christians who have reached the point of giving as well as receiving instruction, of yielding milk as well as drinking it.　He apologizes for the use of straw as an emblem of divine truth or the gospel, on the ground that its doctrines are so simple and uninviting to fastidious appetites. The arbitrary character of such interpretations is betrayed by Gill's remark that straw here means true doctrine, elsewhere false (1 Cor. iii. 12).　The truth is that neither the straw nor the lion means anything by itself; but the lion's eating straw denotes a total change of habit, and indeed of nature, and is therefore a fit emblem for the revolution which the gospel, in proportion to its influence, effects in the condition of society, with some allusion possibly, as before suggested, to the ultimate deliverance of the κτίσις or irrational creation from that bondage of corruption, to which, for man's sake, it is now subjected.

8. To express the idea still more strongly, venomous serpents are represented as innoxious, not to other beasts, but to the human species, and to the most helpless and unthinking of that species.　*And the sucking child shall play on* (or over) *the hole of the asp, and on the den of the basilisk* (or *cerastes*) *shall the weaned child stretch* (or *place*) *its hand.*—חֻר is omitted by the Septuagint, and explained by Ewald as denoting the *feelers* of a horned snake, and the same sense is ascribed to מְאוּרָה by J. D. Michaelis.　But both words really denote a hole or cavity, מְאוּרָה properly a light-hole or aperture admitting light.　Gesenius in his Commentary follows Bochart in deriving it by permutation from מְעוּרָה; but in his Thesaurus, he admits the derivation from אוֹר.　Aben Ezra and Kimchi make it mean the eye of the serpent itself, and Hitzig the shield between the eyes of the basilisk. The precise discrimination of the species of serpents here referred to, is of no importance to the exegesis.　All that is necessary to a correct understanding of the verse is that both words denote extremely venomous and deadly reptiles.　The weaned child means of course a child just weaned, which idea is expressed in translation by Vitringa (nuper depulsus a lacte), Lowth (the new-weaned child), and Gesenius (der kaum Entwöhnte).　The parallel terms are rendered by Henderson the *suckling* and the *weanling*.　According to Jerome, this verse predicts the casting out of devils by our Lord's disciples; according to Vitringa, the conversion or destruction of heretical teachers; while Cocceius makes it a specific prophecy of Luther, Calvin, and Huss, as the children who were to thrust their hands into the den of the antichristian serpents.　It is really a mere continuation of the metaphor begun in ver. 7, and expresses, by an additional figure, the change to be effected in society by the prevalence of true religion, destroying noxious influences and rendering it possible to live in safety.

9. The strong figures of the foregoing context are now resolved into literal expressions.　*They* (indefinitely, men in general) *shall not hurt nor destroy in all my holy mountain, because the land is full of the knowledge of*

Jehovah (literally, of knowing him) *like the waters covering the sea.*—Aben Ezra seems to think that the verbs in the first clause must agree with the nouns in the preceding verse—*they* (the animals just mentioned) *shall not hurt,* &c. But the absence of the copulative shews that this is not so much a direct continuation of the previous description as a summary explanation of it. The true construction, therefore, is indefinite. Rosenmüller distinguishes the two verbs as meaning to injure others and to injure themselves; but they are evidently used as mere equivalent expressions. *My holy mountain* does not mean the whole land of Israel, so called as being higher than all other countries (Kimchi)— nor the mountainous part of it (Jahn), to which there could be no reason for specially alluding, and of which the singular form הַר is not descriptive—but Zion, or Moriah, or the city built upon them, not considered simply as a capital city, in which a reformation was particularly needed (Hitzig), but as the seat of the true religion, and at that time the local habitation of the church. What was true of the church there, is true of the church everywhere. The first clause clearly shews that the foregoing description is to be figuratively understood. That the wolf and the lamb should lie down together, means in other words, that none should hurt or destroy in the Messiah's kingdom. The reason is given in the last clause. אֶרֶץ may mean the land of Israel as the abode of the true religion, and the whole earth so far as the church was to become coextensive with it. For the syntax of the verbal noun with the accusative, see Gesenius § 130, 1. *The sea,* according to Kimchi and Gesenius, means the bottom or the basin of the sea. The construction of this clause by Luther and Augusti (as if covered with the waters of the sea) is very inexact. The ל is used instead of the more usual עַל. The strict sense of the words is, *covering with respect to the sea.* The point of comparison is not the mere extent of surface (Vatablus), nor the depth (Vitringa), but the fulness of the land to the extent of its capacity. This passage is descriptive of the reign of the Messiah, not at any one period, but as a whole. A historian, as Vitringa well observes, in giving a general description of the reign of David, would not use language applicable only to its beginning. The prophecy is therefore one of gradual fulfilment. So far as the cause operates, the effect follows, and when the cause shall operate without restraint, the effect will be complete and universal. The use of the future in the first clause and the preterite in the second may imply, that the prevalence of the knowledge of Jehovah must precede that of universal peace. It is not till the land *has been filled* with that knowledge, that men *will cease* to injure and destroy.—It will be sufficient to record without comment, that according to Cocceius the holy mountain is the reformed church, as the basilisk's den was the Church of Rome, and that the reconciliation here predicted is a mere external one between the people of God and their oppressors.

10. Having described the Messiah's reign and its effects, he now brings his person into view again. *And in that day shall the root of Jesse which* (is) *standing* (or set up) *be for a signal to the nations—unto him shall the Gentiles seek, and his rest* (or residence) *shall be glorious.*—Almost all interpreters take הָיָה in the indefinite sense, *it shall be* or *come to pass,* as a mere idiomatic introduction to what follows, leaving שֹׁרֶשׁ to be construed as a nominative absolute. But Ewald makes שֹׁרֶשׁ itself the subject of הָיָה, which is a simpler construction.—*The root of Jesse* is explained by Kimchi and most other writers to be put by metonymy for that which grows

out of his roots and therefore equivalent to חֹטֶר and נֵצֶר in ver. 1. So the ῥίζα Δαβίδ of Rev. v. 5 and xxii. 16 is explained by Stuart as meaning "not *root* of David, but a *root-shoot* from the trunk or stem of David." But Vitringa supposes the Messiah to be called the *root of Jesse*, because by him the family of Jesse is sustained and perpetuated; Cocceius, because he was not only his descendant but his Maker and his Saviour. Hitzig understands by the root that in which the root is reproduced and reappears. But Umbreit takes the word in its proper sense, and understands the prophecy to mean that the family of Jesse now under ground should reappear and rise to the height of a נֵס, not a military standard, but a signal, especially one raised to mark a place or rendezvous, for which purpose lofty trees are said to have been sometimes used. A signal of the nations then is one displayed to gather them. עֹמֵד describes it as continuing or permanently fixed. The reference is not to Christ's crucifixion, but to his manifestation to the Gentiles through the preaching of the gospel. עַמִּים is here used as a synonyme of גוים, meaning not the tribes of Israel but other nations. To *seek to* is not merely to inquire about, through curiosity—or to seek one's favour in the general—or to pay religious honours—but more specifically to consult as an oracle or depositary of religious truth. By *his rest* we are not to understand his grave, or his death, or his Sabbath, or the rest he gives his people, but his place of rest, his residence. There is no need of supplying a preposition before *glory*, which is an abstract used for a concrete—glory for glorious. The church, Christ's home, shall be glorious from his presence and the accession of the Gentiles. Forerius and J. D. Michaelis needlessly read מִנְחָתו his offering.

11. *And it shall be* (or come to pass) *in that day*—not the days of Hezekiah (Grotius), not the days of Cyrus and Darius (Sanctius), nor the days of the Maccabees (Jahn), but the days of the Messiah—*the Lord shall add his hand* (or add to apply his hand) *a second time*—not second in reference to the overthrow of Pekah and Rezin (Sanctius), or the return from Babylon (Forerius), or the first preaching of the gospel to the Jews (Cocceius), but to the deliverance from Egypt. שֵׁנִית is not pleonastic (Gesenius), but emphatic. *His hand*—not his arm (Hitzig)—as a symbol of strength (Targum)—not in apposition with *the Lord*, the Lord even his hand (Hitzig, Hendewerk), nor governed by *show* understood (τοῦ δεῖξαι), nor qualifying לקנות (Grotius), but either governed by לִשְׁלֹחַ understood (Luther ausstrecken) or directly by יוֹסִיף (Vul. adjiciet manum). קנית is not the infinitive of קָנָא (LXX. ζηλῶσαι, Clericus), but of קָנָה. It does not mean merely to possess (Vulgate), but to acquire (Luther), especially by purchase, and so *to redeem* from bondage and oppression (Vitringa), as מָכַר is to subject them to it (Gesenius), although the true opposite of the latter verb seems to be פָּדָה (Hendewerk). *The remnant of his people*—not the survivors of the original captives (Aben Ezra, Hendewerk)—but those living at the time of the deliverance, or still more restrictedly, the remnant according to the election of grace (Calvin).—*From Assyria, &c.*, to be construed, not with לקנות (Abarbenel), but with יִשְׁאָר, as appears from ver. 16. The countries mentioned are put for all in which the Jews should be scattered.—There is no importance to be attached to the order in which they are enumerated (Cocceius), nor is the precise extent of each material. Assyria and Egypt are named first and together, as the two great foreign powers, with which the Jews were best acquainted. *Pathros* is not Parthia (Calvin), nor Arabia Petræa (Forerius), nor Pharusis in Ethiopia (Grotius), nor Patures in the Delta of the Nile (Brocard, Adrichomius),

but Thebais or Upper Egypt, as appears not only from a comparison of Scriptures (Bochart), but also from the Egyptian etymology of the name (Jablonsky), as denoting the region of the south (Gesenius). It is distinguished from Egypt by the classical writers also.—מִצְרַיִם is a dual form, properly denoting either upper and lower or middle and lower Egypt.— *Cush* is not merely Ethiopia proper (Gesenius), or the land of Midian (Bochart), or Babylonia (Septuagint), or India (Targum), but Ethiopia, perhaps including part of Arabia, from which it appears to have been settled (Calvin, J. D. Michaelis).—*Shinar* is properly the plain in which Babylon was built, thence put for Babylonia. *Elam* is not the rising of the sun (Septuagint), but Elymais, a province of Persia, contiguous to Media, sometimes put for the whole country. *Hamath* is not Arabia (Septuagint), but a city of Syria on the Orontes (*vide supra*, chap. x. 9). *Islands of the sea*, not regions (Henderson), which is too vague, nor coasts in general (J. D. Michaelis), nor islands in the strict sense (Clericus), but the shores of the Mediterranean, whether insular or continental, and substantially equivalent to Europe (Cocceius), meaning the part of it then known, and here put last, according to Cocceius, as being the most important.—This prophecy does not relate to the Gentiles or the Christian Church (Cocceius), but to the Jews (Jerome). The dispersions spoken of are not merely such as had already taken place at the date of the prediction (Gesenius), but others then still future (Hengstenberg), including not only the Babylonish exile, but the present dispersion. The prophecy was not fulfilled in the return of the refugees after Sennacherib's discomfiture (Grotius), nor in the return from Babylon (Sanctius), and but partially in the preaching of the Gospel to the Jews. The complete fulfilment is to be expected when *all Israel shall be saved*. The prediction must be figuratively understood, because the nations mentioned in this verse have long ceased to exist. The event prefigured is, according to Keith and others, the return of the Jews to Palestine ; but according to Calvin, Vitringa, and Hengstenberg, their admission to Christ's kingdom on repentance and reception of the Christain faith.

12. *And he* (Jehovah) *shall set up a signal to the nations, and shall gather the outcasts of Israel, and the dispersed of Judah shall he bring together from the four wings of the earth.*—נֵס is not necessarily a *banner* (Luther), but a sign or signal (LXX. σημεῖον, Vulg. signum), displayed for the purpose of assembling troops or others at some one point.—*To the nations*, not *among them* (Luther), nor *for them* (English Version), which though essentially correct, is not so simple and exact as *to the nations*, *i. e.* in their sight. The nations thus addressed are not the Jews but the Gentiles, and, as most interpreters suppose, those Gentiles among whom the Jews were scattered, and who are summoned by the signal here displayed to set the captives free, or to assist them in returning, or, according to the rabbins, actually to bring them as an offering to Jehovah, a figure elsewhere used in the same book (chap. lxvi. 19, 20). Hitzig, indeed, with double assurance pronounces that passage to be not only written by another hand, but founded upon a misapprehension of the one before us. But the very same idea is expressed in chap. xiv. 2, xlix. 22. There is, however, another view of the passage, which supposes the *nations* or Gentiles to be here mentioned as distinct from the Jews, and unconnected with them. The verse then contains two successive predictions, first, that the Gentiles shall be called, and then that the Jews shall be restored, which agrees exactly with Paul's account of the

connection between these events. *Blindness in part is happened to Israel until the fulness of the Gentiles be come in* (Rom. xi. 25, 26). On this hypothesis, the signal is displayed to the Gentiles, not that they may send or bring the Jews back, but that they may come themselves, and then the gathering of Israel and Judah is added, as a distinct, if not a subsequent event. This last interpretation is favoured by the analogy of a New Testament prophecy, the first by an analogous prophecy of Isaiah himself.— Israel and Judah are put together to denote the race in general. *Outcasts* and *dispersed* are of different genders. The latter, which is feminine in form, is supposed by the older writers to agree with some word understood —such as souls (Pagninus), members (Junius), sheep (Piscator), families (Clericus), women (Gataker)—implying that no sex or rank would be passed by. According to Gesenius, the construction is an idiomatic one, both predicates belonging to both subjects, the exiled men of Israel, and the scattered women of Judah, meaning the exiled men and scattered women both of Israel and Judah. (For other examples of this merismus or *parallage elliptica*, see chap. xviii. 6 ; Zech. ix. 17 ; Prov. x. 1). At the same time he regards it as an example of another idiom which combines the genders to express totality (*vide supra*, chap. iii. 1). But these two explanations are hardly compatible, and Henderson, with more consistency, alleges that there is no distinct allusion to the sex of the wanderers, and that the feminine form is added simply to express universality. Ewald, on the contrary, makes the distinction of the sexes prominent by adding to the participles *man and wife.* כָּנָף is properly the wing of a bird, then the skirt or edge of a garment, then the extremity of the earth, in which sense it is used both in the singular and plural. The same idea is expressed by the *four winds,* with which, in the New Testament, are mentioned the *four corners,* and this last expression is used even here by Clericus and in the old French Version. The reference of course is to the cardinal points of the compass, as determined by the rising and setting of the sun.—If this verse be understood as predicting the agency of the Gentiles in restoring the Jews, it may be said to have been partially fulfilled in the return from Babylon under the auspices of Cyrus, and again in all efforts made by Gentile Christians to convert the Jews ; but its full accomplishment is still prospective, and God may even now be lifting up a signal to the Gentiles for this very purpose.—Hendewerk's notion that this prophecy was fulfilled when *many brought gifts unto the Lord to Jerusalem, and presents to Hezekiah, king of Judah, so that he was lifted up* (וַיִּנָּשֵׂא) *in the sight of all nations from thenceforth* (2 Chron. xxxii. 23), neither requires nor admits of refutation. The same may perhaps be said of Cocceius's opinion, that this verse relates wholly or chiefly to the healing of divisions in the Christian Church.

13. *And the envy of Ephraim shall depart* (or cease), *and the enemies of Judah shall be cut off. Ephraim shall not envy Judah, and Judah shall not vex* (oppress or harass) *Ephraim.* Jacob, in his prophetic statement of the fortunes of his sons, disregards the rights of primogeniture, and gives the pre-eminence to Judah and Joseph (Gen. xlix. 8–12, 22–26), and in the family of the latter to the younger son Ephraim (Gen. xlviii. 19). Hence from the time of the exodus, these two were regarded as the leading tribes of Israel. Judah was much more numerous than Ephraim (Num. i. 27–33)—took precedence during the journey in the wilderness (Num. ii. 3, x. 14)—and received the largest portion in the promised land. But Joshua was an Ephraimite (Num. xiii. 8), and Shiloh, where the taber-

nacle long stood (Joshua xviii. 1 ; 1 Sam. iv. 3), was probably within the limits of the same tribe. The ambitious jealousy of the Ephraimites towards other tribes appears in their conduct to Gideon and Jephthah (Judges viii. 1, xii. 1). Their special jealousy of Judah showed itself in their temporary refusal to submit to David after the death of Saul—in their adherence to Absalom against his father—and in the readiness with which they joined in the revolt of Jeroboam, who was himself of the tribe of Ephraim (1 Kings xi. 26). This schism was, therefore, not a sudden or fortuitous occurrence, but the natural result of causes which had long been working. The mutual relation of the two kingdoms is expressed in the recorded fact, that *there was war between Rehoboam and Jeroboam, and between Asa and Baasha, all their days* (1 Kings xiv. 30, xv. 16). Exceptions to the general rule, as in the case of Ahab and Jehoshaphat, were rare, and a departure from the principles and ordinary feelings of the parties. The ten tribes, which assumed the name of Israel after the division, and perhaps before it, regarded the smaller and less warlike State with a contempt which is well expressed by Jehoash in his parable of the cedar andⱼ the thistle (2 Kings xiv. 9), unless the feeling there displayed be rather personal than national. On the other hand, Judah justly regarded Israel as guilty, not only of political revolt, but of religious apostasy (Ps. lxxviii. 9–11), and the jealousy of Ephraim towards Judah would of course be increased by the fact that Jehovah had *forsaken the tabernacle of Shiloh* (Ps. lxxviii. 60), that he *refused the tabernacle of Joseph, and chose not the tribe of Ephraim, but chose the tribe of Judah, the mount Zion which he loved* (ib. vers. 67, 68). To these historical facts Gesenius refers, as shewing the incorrectness of De Wette's assertion, that the hatred and jealousy existed only on the part of Judah—a paradox which may indeed be looked upon as neutralized by the counter-paradox of Hitzig that they existed only on the part of Ephraim ! They were no doubt indulged on both sides, but with this difference, that Ephraim or Israel was in the wrong from the beginning, and as might have been expected, more malignant in its enmity. This view of the matter will serve to explain why it is that when the Prophet would foretell a state of harmony and peace, he does so by declaring that the hereditary and proverbial enmity of Judah and Israel should cease. It also explains why he lays so much more stress upon the envy of Ephraim than upon the enmity of Judah, viz. because the latter was only an indulgence of unhallowed feeling, to which, in the other case, were superadded open rebellion and apostasy from God. Hence the first three members of the verse before us speak of Ephraim's enmity to Judah, and only the fourth of Judah's enmity to Ephraim ; as if it had occurred to the Prophet, that although it was Ephraim whose disposition needed chiefly to be changed, yet Judah also had a change to undergo, which is therefore intimated in the last clause, as a kind of after-thought. The envy of Ephraim against Judah shall depart—the enemies of Judah (in the kingdom of the ten tribes) shall be cut off—Ephraim shall no more envy Judah—yes, and Judah in its turn shall cease to vex Ephraim. There is indeed another construction of the verse, ancient and sanctioned by very high authority, which makes the Prophet represent the parties as precisely alike, and predict exactly the same change in both. This construction supposes צֹרְרֵי יְהוּדָה to mean, not the *enemies of Judah* (whether foreign, as Cocceius thinks, or in the sister kingdom), but the *enemies (of Ephraim) in Judah*, or *those of Judah who are enemies* to Ephraim. This construction, which is copied by Rosenmüller and Gesenius from Albert

Schultens, is really as old as Kimchi, who remarks upon the clause, *for of old there were in Judah enemies to Ephraim*. Against it may be urged, not only the general principle of Hebrew syntax, that a noun in regimen with an active participle denotes the object of the action, but the specific usage of this very word. Haman is called צֹרֵר הַיְּהוּדִים, *the enemy* (or oppressor) *of the Jews* (Esther iii. 10), and Amos (v. 12) speaks of those who treat the righteous as an enemy (צֹרְרֵי צַדִּיק). In all the cases where a different construction of the participle with a noun has been alleged, either the usual one is precluded by the connection or the nature of the subject, or the syntax is more doubtful than in the case before us (*e. g.* Exod. v. 14; 1 Sam. xix. 29; 1 Kings ii. 7, v. 32). Knobel's assertion that the participle is used as a noun, and does therefore signify the object of the action, is contradicted by the usage of צֹרֵר, already stated. A still more arbitrary method of attaining the same end is that proposed by Secker and approved by Lowth, who read צֹרְרֵי as an abstract meaning *enmity*, or the modification suggested by Gesenius, of taking the active participle itself as an abstract noun. These constructions are so violent, and the contrary usage so plain, that the question naturally arises, why should the latter be departed from at all ? The answer is, because the favourite notion of exact parallelism requires it. All the writers who maintain this opinion assume that the second clause must express the same idea with the first, and in the same order. Luther indeed was satisfied with an inverted order, and by giving to the first phrase the sense of *envy against Ephraim* (which is not more unauthorized than to make the other mean *enemies in Judah*), has contrived to make the first clause correspond to the fourth, and the second to the third (und der Neid *wider* Ephraim wird aufhören, u. s. w.). But the modern writers must have a parallelism still more exact, and to this rhetorical chimera both the syntax and the true sense of the passage must be sacrificed. In this case we are able to produce an instance from another prophet, an older contemporary of Isaiah, in which the structure of the sentence coincides precisely with the one before us, that is to say, there are several successive clauses relating to one of the parties mentioned, and then a final one relating to the other. This example is found in Hosea iii. 3, *And I said to her, thou shalt abide for me many days—thou shalt not play the harlot—and thou shalt not be another man's—and I will also* (act thus) *to thee*. So here, the jealousy of Ephraim shall cease—the enemies of Judah among them shall be cut off—Ephraim shall then no longer envy Judah—and Judah in return shall no longer be the enemy of Ephraim. The objection that the passage in Hosea is mere prose, is not only gratuitous, but concedes the liberty of assuming the same thing in the case before us. The influence exerted on interpretation by this theory of perfect parallels is clear in this case, from the fact that Hengstenberg follows Gesenius without any hesitation, and that Ewald (though he modifies the meaning of צֹרֵר) adopts the same construction, in direct opposition to his own authority (Heb. Gr. § 208), which Hitzig had cited in defence of the true interpretation. The tendency of this theory is moreover apparent from the conclusion to which Hitzig himself comes, that although צֹרְרֵי יְהוּדָה can only mean the *enemies of Judah*, the second clause evidently puts the other sense upon it, and is therefore an interpolation ! Umbreit alone of the recent German writers has the good sense and taste to reject at once this wanton mutilation of the text and the forced construction of the sentence, and to understand the sentence in the simple and obvious meaning put upon it by the ancient versions and by the older writers who have not been mentioned.—The fulfilment of this prophecy is found by Hendewerk in Hezekiah's efforts to reclaim the Israelites to the worship of Jehovah (2 Chron. xxx.). That it was not fulfilled in the return from exile, is sufficiently notorious. That it had not been fulfilled when Christ came, is plain from the continued enmity between the Jews, Samaritans, and Galileans. The only fulfilment it has ever had is in the abolition of all national and sectional distinctions in the Christian Church (Gal. iii. 27, 29, v. 6), to which converted Jews as well as others must submit. Its full accomplishment is yet to come, in the re-union of the tribes of Israel under Christ their common head (Hosea i. 11).—Jarchi explains the verse to mean that Messiah the son of Joseph, and Messiah the son of Judah shall not envy one another; Aben Ezra, that Ephraim shall not be jealous because the Messiah is to come of Judah. Cocceius applies the prophecy exclusively to future reconciliations in the Christian Church. —צָרַר is not to *envy*, as Schulten argues from the Arabic analogy, nor to be *turbulent*, as Ewald gives it, but to treat in a hostile manner. סָרָה is strictly to *depart, i. e.* cease or be removed, as in chap. x. 27.

14. Instead of assailing or annoying one another, they are represented as making common cause against a common enemy. *And they* (Ephraim and Judah, undivided Israel) *shall fly* (like a bird of prey) *upon the shoulder of the Philistines towards the sea* (or *westwards*)—*together they shall spoil the sons of the east* (the Arabians and perhaps the Assyrians)— *Edom and Moab the stretching out of their hand* (*i. e.* the object of that action) *and the children of Ammon their obedience* (*i. e.* their subjects). All the names are those of neighbouring nations with whom the Hebrews were accustomed to wage war. Edom, Moab, and Ammon, may be specially named for an additional reason, viz., that they were nearly related to Israel, and yet among his most inveterate enemies. The Jews explain this as a literal prediction having respect to the countries formerly possessed by the races here enumerated. Most Christian writers understand it spiritually of the conquests to be achieved by the true religion, and suppose the nations here named to be simply put for enemies in general, or for the heathen world; this method of description being rendered more emphatic by the historical associations which the names awaken.—To *fly upon* means here to *fly at*, or, as Henderson expresses it, to *pounce upon*, the figure being that of an eagle or other bird of prey. The almost innumerable meanings put upon this verse and its peculiar expressions, may be found in Poole, Rosenmüller, and Gesenius.

15. To the destruction of the enemies of Israel is added a prediction that all obstacles, even the most formidable, to the restoration of God's people, shall be overcome or taken away by his almighty power. This idea is naturally expressed by the dividing of the Red Sea and Euphrates, because Egypt and Assyria are the two great powers from which Israel had suffered and was yet to be delivered. *And Jehovah will destroy* (by drying up) *the tongue* (or bay) *of the sea of Egypt* (*i. e.* the Red Sea), *and he will wave his hand* (as a gesture of menace or a symbol of miraculous power) *over the river* (Euphrates), *in the violence of his wind* (or breath), *and smite it* (the Euphrates) *into seven streams, and make* (his people) *tread* (it) *in shoes* (*i. e.* dry-shod). The meaning of הֶחֱרִים is not to split, divide (Knobel), for which there is nothing but an Arabic analogy and a doubtful interpretation of חָרֻם, Lev. xxi. 18,—but properly to consecrate by an irrevocable vow, and then by implication to destroy, which in this case could be done only by *drying up*. This last idea, therefore, is

included, but there is no need of reading החריב, as Houbigant, Lowth, and Rosenmüller do, on the authority of the ancient versions.—*Tongue*, which is applied in other languages to projecting points of land, is here descriptive of a bay or indentation in a shore. The *sea of Egypt* is not the Nile, as some suppose, although the name *sea* has been certainly applied to it from the earliest times—but the Red Sea, called the Sea of Egypt for the same reason that it is called the Arabian Gulf. The *tongue* of this sea is the narrow gulf or bay in which it terminates to the north-west near Suez, called by the old writers the *Sinus Heroopolitanus*, to distinguish it from the *Sinus Elaniticus*, the north-east extremity. Through the former the Israelites passed when they left Egypt, and it is now predicted that it shall be utterly destroyed, *i. e.* dried up. At the same time the Euphrates is to be smitten into seven streams, and so made fordable, as Cyrus is said to have reduced the Gyndes by diverting its waters into 360 artificial channels. Vitringa supposes a specific overthrow of Egypt and Assyria to be here predicted ; Grotius, the division of the latter into several kingdoms. But the terms are probably strong figures drawn from the early history and experience of Israel. Gesenius, in the last edition of his Lexicon, appears to favour the reading of עצם for עים (in the strength of his wind), suggested by Luzzatto, on the ground of the resemblance between ' and צ in the old Hebrew alphabet. The other reading, which occurs only here, is commonly explained to mean *violent heat*, and then secondarily violence in general.

16. *And there shall be a highway for the remnant of his people, which shall be left, from Assyria, as there was for Israel, in the day of his coming up from the land of Egypt.* This verse admits of two interpretations. According to one, it is a comparision of the former deliverance from Egypt with the future one from Assyria and the neighbouring countries, where most Jewish exiles were to be found. According to the other, it is a repetition of the preceding promise, that previous deliverances, particularly those from Egypt and Assyria, should be repeated in the future history of the Church. The fulfilment has been sought by different interpreters, in the return from Babylon, in the general progress of the gospel, and in the future restoration of the Jews. The first of these can at most be regarded only as a partial or inchoate fulfilment, and against the last lies the obvious objection that the context contains promises and threatenings which are obviously figurative, although so expressed as to contain allusions to remarkable events in the experience of Israel. Such is the dividing or drying up of the tongue of the Red Sea, which must either be figuratively understood or supposed to refer to a future miracle, which last hypothesis is certainly not necessary, and therefore can be fully justified by nothing but the actual event.—מְסִלָּה is not simply a *way*, as the ancient versions give it, nor a fortified way as Cocceius explains it (via munita), but a highway as explained by Junius (agger) and Henderson (causey), an artificial road formed by casting up the earth (from סָלַל to raise), and thus distinguished from a path worn by the feet (דֶּרֶךְ or נְתִיבָה). Knobel, and some other of the later writers, suppose an allusion to the desert after the crossing of the water, whereas all the older writers understand a way through the water itself. Grotius and Knobel connect מֵאַשּׁוּר with מְסִלָּה, others with תִּשָּׁאֵר, as in ver. 11. The ambiguity of the Hebrew construction is skilfully retained in the English version.

Chapter 12

TAKING occasion from the reference to Egypt and the exodus in the close of the preceding chapter, the Prophet now puts into the mouth of Israel a song analogous to that of Moses, from which some of the expressions are directly borrowed. The structure of this psalm is very regular, consisting of two parts, in each of which the Prophet first tells the people what they will say, or have a right to say, when the foregoing promises are verified, and then addresses them again in his own person and in the usual language of prediction. In the first stanza, they are made to acknowledge the divine compassion and to express their confidence in God as the source of all their strength, and therefore the rightful object of their praise, vers. 1–3. In the second stanza, they exhort one another to make known what God has done for them, not only at home but among all nations, and are exhorted by the Prophet to rejoice in the manifested presence of Jehovah, vers. 4–6.

Ewald rejects this chapter, as an addition made by some reader or transcriber of Isaiah later than the exile. His reasons are, that the prophecy is wound up and complete at the close of the eleventh chapter, and that the style, phraseology, and tone, are not those of Isaiah. The first of these reasons he refutes himself by saying that the reference to Egypt in chap. xi. 16, probably suggested this addition to the later writer ; a hypothesis which we are equally at liberty to apply to Isaiah himself, unless the passage is manifestly from another hand. This reduces Ewald's arguments to one, and to that one Umbreit gives a sufficient answer when he says that the Prophet, intending to wind up his prophecy with a composition in the nature of a psalm, adopts of course the general style, which from the time of David had been used for that purpose. That he did not rather copy the manner of Moses, may be explained, not only on the ground that the other style had now become familiar to the people, but also on the ground that such an imitation might have made the comparison with Egypt and the exodus too prominent for the Prophet's purpose, which was to express thanksgiving in a manner appropriate to all the deliverances of the Church from evil, whether natural or spiritual. Hence too the indefiniteness of the language, and a seeming want of intimate connection with the foregoing prophecy.

1. *And thou*—Israel, the people of God—*shalt say in that day*—when the foregoing promise is accomplished—*I will praise thee*—strictly *acknowledge thee* as worthy, and as a benefactor—*for thou wast angry with me, but thine anger is turned away, and thou comfortest me.*—The English version renders כִּי *though*, but according to the Masoretic interpunction, it must be read with the preceding words. The apparent incongruity of thanking God because he was angry, is removed by considering that the subject of the thanksgiving is the whole complex idea expressed in the remainder of the verse, of which God's being angry is only one element. It was not simply because God was angry that the people praise him, but because he was angry and his anger had ceased. The same idea is expressed by the English version in another form, by intimating early in the sentence the relation of its parts, whereas it is characteristic of the Hebrew style to state things absolutely first, and qualify them afterwards. The same mode of expression is used by Paul in Greek, when he says (Rom. vi. 17), " God be thanked that ye were the servants of sin, but ye have from the heart obeyed,

&c." This view of the matter precludes the necessity of taking אוֹדְךָ in the sense of *I acknowledge thee* to have been just in being angry at me. The force of the particle at the beginning of the second clause can be fully represented only by the English *but.*—יָשֹׁב is the abbreviated form of the future, commonly used to express a wish or a command, in which sense some explain it here, taking this clause as a prayer for deliverance. But this would confine the expression of thanksgiving to God's being angry, the very incongruity which has just been shown not to exist. It must be taken either as a poetical substitute for יָשׁוּב with a present meaning, or as contracted for וַיָּשָׁב in a past sense, which is given in most versions. The force of the verb in this connection is enhanced by a comparison with chap. x. 4, and the parallel verse of the foregoing context, where it is said repeatedly that God's wrath had not turned back or away (לֹא שָׁב). *Thou comfortest me*, not by words only, but by deeds, which may seem to justify the version *thou hast mercy on me*, given by some writers.

2. *Behold God is my salvation. I will trust, and not be afraid; for my strength and song is Jah Jehovah, and he is become my salvation.* Some exchange the abstract for the concrete, *my Saviour*, but with a great loss of strength in the expression. The first verb may be rendered in the present *(I trust)*, as describing an actual state of mind; but the future form, while it sufficiently implies this, at the same time expresses a fixed determination, I will trust, be confident, secure. The next words contain a negative expression of the same idea. In certain connections, עֹז seems to denote power as an element of glory, an object of admiration, and a subject of praise. Hence Gesenius and others assign *praise* as a secondary meaning of the word itself, which is pushing the deduction and distinction of senses to extremes. Jarchi observes that עָזִּי, with ŏ in the first syllable is never used except in combination with זִמְרָה, the orthography elsewhere being always עֻזִּי. This variation may, however, be euphonic, and have no connection with a difference of meaning. *My praise and my song* gives a good sense, but no better, and assuredly no stronger, than *my strength and my song*, i. e. the source of my protection and the subject of my praise. Kimchi and others regard זִמְרָת, here, and in the parallel passages, as an abbreviation of זִמְרָתִי; but the modern writers make it a collateral or cognate form of זִמְרָה, and supply the suffix from the preceding word.—Cocceius derives יָהּ from יָאָה to be suitable, becoming, and considers it an abstract denoting the divine perfection. It is much more probably an abbreviation of יְהוָה, and as such occurs at the end of many compound proper names. In the song of Moses, from which this expression is borrowed, יְהוָה is omitted (Exod. xv. 2), as also in Ps. cxviii. 14, which is copied from the same. Nor does the combination יָהּ יְהוָה occur elsewhere, except in Isa. xxvi. 4. Some of the modern writers, therefore, have contended that יְהוָה is superfluous. But the fact of its occurrence in another passage of this very book precludes this emendation in the absence of external evidence. There is really nothing more surprising in the combination than in the frequent accumulation of the other divine names.

3. *And ye shall draw water with joy from the springs of salvation.*— This is a natural and common figure for obtaining and enjoying divine favour. There is no need of supposing a particular allusion to the doctrines of religion. By this verse the Talmudists explain and justify the custom of pouring out water from the fountain of Siloam at the feast of tabernacles, a ceremony no doubt long posterior to the time of Isaiah.

4. *And ye shall say* (to one another) *in that day, praise* (or give thanks

to) *Jehovah, call upon his name* (proclaim it), *make known among the nations his exploits* (or achievements), *remind* (them) *that his name is exalted.* Some take הַזְכִּירוּ in the sense of praising, celebrating, and translate כִּי for, because, in which case what follows is not the subject but the reason of the praise. The English Bible has *make mention ;* but the strict sense of the Hiphil as a causative is perfectly appropriate and suits the context. *Name* is here used in the pregnant sense of that whereby God makes himself known, including explicit revelation and the exhibition of his attributes in all. On the usage of this word in the Psalms, see Hengstenberg on Ps. viii. 1.

5. *Praise Jehovah* (by singing, and perhaps with instruments) *because he has done elevation* (or sublimity, *i. e.* a sublime deed). *Known is this* (or *be* this) *in all the earth.*—זמר means properly to play upon stringed instruments, then to sing with an accompaniment, then to sing in general, then to praise by singing or by music generally. In this last sense it may govern the noun directly.—The English Version, *excellent things*, is too indefinite for the singular form גֵּאוּת.—The Kethib מידעת is the Pual, the Keri מוּדַעַת the Hophal participle, of ידע, *to know.* Both forms are causative and passive, *made known*, caused to be known. Knobel conjectures that מֵידַעַת may have been a noun, synonymous with מוֹדַעַת, and analogous in form to מִיפַּעַת from יָפַע.—The English Version supplies *is*, and makes the last clause an appeal to the whole world for the truth of the thing celebrated. Most of the recent versions make it an imperative expression, exhorting to a general diffusion of the truth.

6. *Cry out and shout* (or sing), *oh inhabitant of Zion* (the people or the Church personified as a woman), *for great in the midst of thee* (residing in thee by a special manifestation of his presence) *is the Holy One of Israel* (that Holy Being who has bound himself to Israel, in a peculiar and extraordinary manner, as their covenant God).

Chapters 13 & 14

HERE begins a series of prophecies (chaps. XIII.—XXIII.) against certain foreign powers, from the enmity of which Israel had been more or less a sufferer. The first in the series is a memorable prophecy of the fall of the Babylonian empire and the destruction of Babylon itself (chaps. XIII., XIV.) The Medes are expressly named as the instruments of its subjection, and the prophecy contains several other remarkable coincidences with history, both sacred and profane. Hence it was justly regarded by the older writers, both Jews and Christians, as an extraordinary instance of prophetic foresight. As such, even J. D. Michaelis defends it against the hypothesis (then a novel one) of an *ex post facto* prophecy invented for the purpose of inducing Cyrus to befriend the Jews. He argues conclusively against this supposition, on the ground that the literary merit of the passage is too exquisite for such an origin, and that the writer, in the case supposed, could not have represented the destruction of Babylon as total without defeating his own purpose. The last objection also lies against Eichhorn's supposition of a prophecy written after the event but without any fraudulent design, the form of prediction being merely a poetical costume. Rosenmüller holds that it was written towards the close of the Babylonish exile, while the events which it describes were in progress, or so near at hand as to be readily foreseen. This view of the matter is also taken by Gesenius and the later German writers on Isaiah. The arguments in favour of it, as recently stated by Knobel, may be reduced to three : (1) a spirit unworthy of Isaiah, *i. e.* one of bitter hatred and desire of revenge ; (2) a want of resemblance in the style and diction to the genuine writings of Isaiah, and a strong resemblance to some later compositions ; (3) a constant allusion to historical events and a state of things which did not exist for ages after Isaiah.   The answer to the first reason is that it is false.   Such is not the natural impression which the prophecy would make on an unbiassed reader. This perversion has been unintentionally aided by a rhetorical mistake of Calvin and other Christian interpreters in representing the fourteenth chapter as taunting and sarcastic in its tone, which, on the contrary, is characterized by pathos.   But even on this erroneous supposition, there is nothing to justify the charge of bitter vengefulness, brought for the first time by the latest German writers, with an obvious design to strengthen their weak arguments derived from other sources.   The second argument is unsound in principle and precarious in application.   On the ground that every writer always writes alike, only one composition of any author can be certainly proved genuine.   The Satires of Horace must be spurious because he was a lyric poet—the Georgics of Virgil because he was an epic poet —the Plaideurs of Racine because he was a tragic poet.   One half of Aristophanes and Shakspeare might be thus made to prove the other half a forgery.   This mode of criticism is peculiarly German, and will never commend itself to the general taste and judgment of the learned world. The same thing may be said of the attempt to ascertain the age of ancient writings by a comparison of words and phrases.   One critic singles out whatever, taken by itself, appears to favour his own foregone conclusion, and leaves the rest unnoticed.   Another, with another end in view, might prove the contrary by the self-same process.   This is not only possible but actually done.   Thus Gesenius and Hitzig prove that Isaiah could not have written the fifteenth and sixteenth chapters, by an enumeration of diversities in diction, phraseology, grammatical construction, style, &c. Hendewerk just as clearly proves, by a specification of minute but remarkable coincidences, that Isaiah must have been the author.   Admitting that the second demonstration is worth no more than the first, they may at least serve to cancel one another, and to shew the fallacy of all such reasoning. This argument proves nothing by itself, because it proves, or may be made to prove, too much.   The true strength of the doctrine now in question lies not in the *moral* or *philological* arguments which have been noticed, but in the *historical* one, that these chapters contain statements and allusions which imply a knowledge of what happened long after Isaiah's death. Hitzig says expressly that a prophecy against Babylon before the time of Jeremiah is impossible.   This of course is tantamount to saying that prophetic inspiration is impossible.   And this is, after all, the only question of importance.   If there cannot be prophetic foresight, then of course a reference to subsequent events fixes the date of the writing which contains it.   If, on the other hand, there is such a thing as inspiration and prophetic foresight, there is nothing to weaken the presumption created by a uniform tradition, the immemorial position of this prophecy, and the express terms of a title not less ancient than the text, of which, according to oriental usage, it is really a part.   The point at issue, therefore, between Christian and infidel interpreters has reference not to words and phrases merely, but to the possibility and reality of inspiration.   Assuming this, we can have no hesitation in regarding the prophecy before us as a genuine production of Isaiah.—Of those who take this ground, Cocceius seems to stand alone in questioning the literal application of the prophecy to Babylon in the proper sense. He refers it partly to ancient Israel, partly to Antichrist, a theory which condemns itself, as equally arbitrary and inconsistent. Grotius, as usual, goes to the opposite extreme, of supposing that this is a hyperbolical description of evils which were to be experienced by Babylon before it reached the zenith of its greatness under Nebuchadnezzar,—a hypothesis as arbitrary as the other, and, moreover, chargeable with contradicting history. Some particular absurdities of both these schemes will be brought to view in the exposition. The great majority of Christian writers understand these chapters as a specific prophecy of the downfall of the Babylonian empire occasioned by the conquests of the Medes and Persians. To this event there are repeated unequivocal allusions. There are some points, however, in which the coincidence of prophecy and history on this hypothesis is not so clear. This is especially the case with respect to the total destruction and annihilation of the city itself, which was brought about by a gradual process through a course of ages. The true solution of this difficulty is, that the prediction is generic, not specific ; that it is not a detailed account of one event exclusively, but a prophetic picture of the fall of Babylon considered as a whole, some of the traits being taken from the first, and some from the last stage of the fatal process, while others are indefinite or common to all. The same idea may be otherwise expressed by saying that the king of Babylon, whose fall is here predicted, is neither Nebuchadnezzar nor Belshazzar, but the kings of Babylon collectively, or rather an ideal king of Babylon, in whom the character and fate of the whole empire are concentrated. Some of the terms applied to him may therefore be literally true of one king, some of another, some individually of none, although descriptive of the whole. This hypothesis, while it removes all discrepancies, still retains the wonderful coincidences of the prophecy with history, and makes them more remarkable, by scattering them through so vast a field. Even if the allusions to the conquest of Cyrus could be resolved into conjecture or contemporary knowledge, how shall we account for a description of the fate of the great city, not once for all, but down to the present moment ? Even supposing that the writer of this prophecy lived at the time of Cyrus, how will the infidel interpreter account for his prediction of that total desolation, which was not consummated for ages afterwards, but which now exists to the full extent of the prophetic description in its strongest sense. On the one hand, we have only to believe that Isaiah was inspired of God ; on the other, we must hold that a writer of the very highest genius either personated the Prophet, or was confounded with him by the ancient Jews, and that this anonymous writer, whose very name is lost, without any inspiration, uttered a prediction which then seemed falsified by the event, but which has since been accidentally fulfilled !—It is universally admitted that the thirteenth chapter, and the greater part, if not the whole, of the fourteenth, constitute a single prophecy. The division of the chapters is, however, not a wrong one. Both parts relate to the destruction of Babylon, setting out from God's decree, and winding up with the threatening of total desolation. Chap. xiv. is therefore not a mere continuation of chap. xiii., but a repetition of the same matter in another form. The difference of form is chiefly this, that while chap. xiii. is more historical in its arrangement, chap. xiv. is dramatic, or at least poetical. Another point of difference is, that in chap. xiii. the downfall of Babylon is represented rather as an act of divine vengeance, in chap. xiv. as a means of deliverance to Israel, the denunciations of divine wrath being there clothed in the form of a triumphant song, to be sung by Israel when Babylon is fallen.—Cocceius, as we have already seen, applies this part of the prediction secondarily but strictly to the fall of Antichrist. Many other of the older writers make this the mystical or secondary sense of the whole prophecy, because they understand it to be so explained in the Apocalypse. The truth, however, seems to be, first, that the downfall of Babylon, as a great anti-theocratic power, an opponent and persecutor of the ancient church, affords a type or emblem of the destiny of all opposing powers under the New Testament; and secondly, that in consequence of this analogy, the Apocalyptic prophecies apply the name Babylon to the Antichristian power. But these Apocalyptic prophecies are new ones, not interpretations of the one before us.

Chapter 13

AFTER a title, the prophecy opens with a summons to the chosen instrument of God's righteous judgments upon Babylon, who are described as mustered by the Lord himself, and then appearing, to the terror and amazement of the Babylonians, who are unable to resist their doom, vers. 1–9. The great catastrophe is then described in a series of beautiful figures, as an extinction of the heavenly bodies, and a general commotion in the frame of nature, explained by the Prophet himself to mean a fearful visitation of Jehovah, making men more rare than gold, dispersing the strangers resident at Babylon, and subjecting the inhabitants to the worst inflictions at the hands of the Medes, who are expressly mentioned as the instruments of the divine vengeance, and described as indifferent to gain and relentless in their cruelty, vers. 10–18. From this beginning of the process of destruction, we are then hurried on to its final consummation, the completeness of which is expressed by a comparison with the overthrow of Sodom and Gomorrah, and by a prediction that the site of Babylon shall not be frequented, even by the wandering Arab, or by shepherds and their flocks, but only by solitary animals, whose presence is itself a sign of utter desolation, vers. 19–22.

1. *The burden of Babylon* (or threatening prophecy respecting it), *which Isaiah, the son of Amoz saw* (received by revelation). There are two interpretations of מַשָּׂא, both very ancient. The one makes it simply mean a *declaration* (from נָשָׂא to utter), or more specifically a divine declaration, a prophecy, oracle, or vision. The Septuagint translates it by ὅρασις, ὅραμα and sometimes by λῆμμα (from נָשָׂא to receive). The Vulgate has *visio.* This interpretation is adopted by Cocceius, Vitringa, J. D. Michaelis, Lowth, and all the recent German writers. Henderson has *sentence.* The other explanation gives the word the sense of a minatory prophecy. So Luther, Calvin, and, in our own day, Hengstenberg, who denies that the word is ever applied to any prediction but a minatory one, even Zech. xii. 1 being no exception. (See his exposition of Zech. ix. 1, in his Christologie, vol. ii. p. 102.) He also alleges that the word is never joined like נְאֻם with the name of God or of any other person but the subject of the prophecy. For these reasons, and because מַשָּׂא, in other connections always means a *burden*, it is best to retain the common explanation, which is also given by Barnes. This word occurs in the titles of all the distinct prophecies of this second part. The one before us is rejected by Hitzig and Ewald, as the addition of a copyist or compiler, but without the least external evidence or sufficient reason.

2. The attack of the Medes and Persians upon Babylon is now foretold,

not in the proper form of a prediction, nor even in that of a description, which is often substituted for it, but in that of an order from Jehovah to his ministers to summon the invaders, first, by an elevated signal, and then as they draw nearer, by gestures and the voice. *Upon a bare hill* (*i. e.* one with a clear summit, not concealed by trees) *set up a signal, raise the voice,* (shout or cry aloud) *to them* (the Medes and Persians), *wave the hand, and let them enter the gates of the* (Babylonian) *nobles.*—Forerius takes נשפה as the proper name of a mountain, dividing Chaldea from Persia and Media. The Vulgate renders it *caliginosum,* which Jerome applies to the spiritual darkness of the Babylonians, and Grotius to the fogs and mists arising from the marshy situation of the city. The Targum paraphrases the expression as denoting a city secure and confident of safety. Kimchi, Luther, Calvin, and most of the early Christian writers, with Augusti, Barnes, and Lee, in later times, give it the sense of *lofty.* But the latest lexicographers and commentators seem to be agreed that the true sense is that of *bare* or *bald.* The Septuagint version (ὄρους πεδινοῦ) is explained by Gesenius as descriptive of a mountain with a flat or level top, but the older writers understand it as denoting a mountain surrounded by a plain, a metaphorical description of Babylon. It is not, however, a description of the city, but an allusion to the usual method of erecting signals on a lofty and conspicuous spot. As the expression is indefinite—a mountain—there is no need of supposing with Vitringa a particular allusion to the Zagrian mountains between Media and Babylonia. Jerome and Cocceius suppose the angels to be here addressed ; Knobel and others, the captive Jews ; but it is best to understand the words indefinitely, as addressed to those whose proper work it was to do the thing commanded. Jehovah being here represented as a military leader, the order is of course to be conceived as given to his heralds or other officers. They are not commanded to display a banner as a sign of victory (Cyril), but to erect a signal for the purpose of collecting troops. There is no need of supposing with Vitringa and Henderson that קול means the sound of the trumpet. The subjunctive construction of ויבאו given by most writers *(that they may enter),* is not only unnecessary, but much less expressive than the obvious construction which supposes the command to be continued. The nobles are not those of Media and Persia, to whose doors Clericus supposes the soldiers to be summoned for the purpose of enlisting in this service, but those of Babylon. The specific sense of *tyrants,* which Gesenius and the later Germans put upon this word, is wholly unauthorized by the analogy of Job xxi. 28, unless we assume that parallel terms must always be synonymous. Other constructions of the last clause have been given by the Septuagint (ἀνοίξατε οἱ ἄρχοντες)—the Vulgate (ingrediantur portas duces) —Schmidius (ut veniant portae principum)—Koppe (voluntarii portas aperite)—Döderlein (ut veniant enses evaginati voluntariorum)—J. D. Michaelis (dass meine Freywillige·sich vor meiner Pforte versammeln) &c. All these involve a change of text or a harshness of construction. Lowth omits להם, as of no use, and rather weakening the sentence. On the contrary, it strengthens it by an abrupt reference to the invaders without naming them, as being too well known already.

3. The enemies thus summoned are described as chosen, designated instruments of the divine vengeance, and as already exulting in the certainty of their success. *I* (myself) *have given command* (or a commission) *to my consecrated* (chosen and appointed instruments). *Yes* (literally, *also*), *I have called* (forth) *my mighty ones* (or heroes) *for* (the execution of) *my wrath, my proud exulters.*—The insertion of אני is not an idiom of the later Hebrew,

as explained by Gesenius (Lehrg. p. 801), but as Maurer has correctly stated, an emphatic designation of God as the sole efficient agent, *I myself*, or *I even I.* מקדשי has no reference to the moral character or purpose of the instruments, but simply to God's choice and preparation of them for their work. The Chaldee Paraphrase makes the last of these ideas, that of preparation, too exclusively prominent. Henderson and Knobel suppose a special reference to the religious ceremonies practised before going out to war (1 Sam. vii. 9, xiii. 9 ; 2 Chron. xiii. 12. Comp. Gen. xiv. 14). But as this would not be strictly applicable to the Medes and Persians, it seems more natural to suppose that קדש is here used in its primary and proper sense of separating, setting apart, or consecrating to a special use or service. The גם at the beginning of the second clause is arbitrarily omitted by Gesenius and De Wette, but retained by Ewald and Umbreit. To *call* out is here explained by Rosenmüller as denoting specially a call to military service. It may, however, have the general sense of summoning or calling upon by name. גבורי is commonly regarded as simply equivalent to מקדשי ; but Knobel understands the former as a specific epithet of chiefs or officers. Augusti, Barnes, and most of the older writers, understand the last words of the verse as meaning *those who exult in my greatness*, or *in my great plan* (Barnes) ; Kimchi and Jarchi, those by whom I glorify myself. But the other modern writers have adopted the construction of Cocceius and Vitringa, who refer the suffix to the first word or the whole phrase, a common Hebrew idiom (Gesen. § cxix. 5)—*my exulters of pride*, (*i. e.* my proud exulters). This may be understood as a description of the confidence with which they anticipated victory ; but most interpreters suppose an allusion to the natural character of the Persians as described by Croesus in Herodotus (φύσιν ἐόντες ὑβρισταί)—by Herodotus himself (νομίζοντες ἑαυτοὺς εἶναι ἀνθρώπων μακρῷ τὰ πάντα ἀρίστους)—by Æschylus (ὑπέρκομποι ἄγαν)—and by Ammianus Marcellinus (abundantes inanibus verbis insanumque loquentes et ferum, magnidici et graves ac tetri, minaces juxta in adversis rebus ac prosperis, callidi, superbi). The same idea is expressed by the Septuagint version (χαίροντες ἅμα καὶ ὑβρίζοντες.

4. The Prophet, in his own person, now describes the enemies of Babylon, who had just been summoned, as actually on their way. He hears a confused noise, which he soon finds to be that of confederated nations forming the army of Jehovah against Babylon. *The voice* (or sound) *of a multitude in the mountains ! the likeness of much people ! the sound of a tumult of kingdoms of nations gathered* (or gathering themselves)! *Jehovah of hosts mustering* (*i.e.* inspecting and numbering) *a host of battle* (*i. e.* a military host) ! The absence of verbs adds greatly to the vividness of the description. The sentence really consists of a series of exclamations, describing the impressions made successively upon the senses of an eye and ear witness. The expression is weakened by supplying *is heard* (Junius), or *there is* (Cocceius). Gesenius and Ewald insert *hark !* at the beginning of the sentence, which is better, though unnecessary. By the mountains some suppose Media to be meant, to which Henderson adds Armenia and the other hilly countries from which Cyrus drew his forces. This supposes the movement here described to be that of the levy or conscription. But it seems more natural to understand it, as most writers do, of the actual advance of the invaders. The mountains then will be those dividing Babylonia from Media or Persia.—The symbolical interpretation of mountains as denoting states and kingdoms (Musculus), is entirely out of place here. דמות is commonly explained here as equivalent to *as* or *like;*

but J. D. Michaelis and Rosenmüller seem to take it in its proper sense of *likeness* or similar appearance, and refer to the indistinct view of a great multitude approaching from a distance. The reference to sound before and afterwards, makes the reference of this clause to the sense of sight improbable.—The rendering of קול שאון *tumultuous noise*, is not only a gratuitous departure from the form of the original, but a weakening of the description. The object presented is not a tumultuous noise merely, but the noise of an actual tumult.—Calvin, Gesenius, and others, separate *kingdoms* from *nations*, as distinct particulars. The construction *kingdoms of nations*, which is retained by Ewald, is the one required by the Masoretic accents, and affords a better sense.—The Niphal participle may be taken in a reflexive sense, in which case the description would refer to the original assembling of the troops. There is no necessity however for departing from the ordinary usage, according to which it describes the nations as already assembled.—It is commonly agreed that there is here a direct reference to the mixture of nations in the army of Cyrus. Besides the Persians and the Medes, Xenophon speaks of the Armenians, and Jeremiah adds the names of other nations (Jer. l. 9, li. 27). Most interpreters suppose the event here predicted to be subsequent in date to the overthrow of Croesus, while Knobel refers it to the first attack of Cyrus upon Babylonia, recorded in the third book of the Cyropedia. But these distinctions seem to rest upon a false view of the passage as a description of particular marches, battles, &c., rather than a generic picture of the whole series of events which ended in the downfall of Babylon. For a just view of the principles on which such prophecies should be explained, with particular reference to that before us, see Stuart on the Apocalypse, vol. ii. p. 143. The title *Jehovah of hosts*, may here seem to be used unequivocally in the sense of *God of battles*, on account of the obvious allusion to the word *host* following. But as this explanation of the title is not justified by scriptural usage (*vide supra*, chap. i. 9), it is better to understand the words as meaning that the Lord of the hosts of heaven is now mustering a host on earth. Lowth, on the authority of a single manuscript, reads למלחמה *for the battle* or *for battle*. But the last word appears to be added simply for the purpose of limiting and qualifying that before it. This was the more necessary as the same word had been just used in another sense. He who controls the *hosts of heaven* is now engaged in mustering a *host of war*, *i. e.* an army. The Septuagint and Vulgate construe these last words with the following verse—the Lord of hosts has commanded an armed nation to come, &c.—which is a forced and ungrammatical construction.—The substitution of the present for the participle in the English Version (*mustereth*) and most others, greatly impairs the force and uniformity of the expression by converting a lively exclamation into a dispassionate assertion. Hendewerk carelessly omits the last clause altogether.

5. *Coming from a distant land* (literally, *a land of distance*), *from the* (visible or apparent) *end of the heavens—Jehovah and the instruments* (or weapons) *of his wrath—to lay waste* (or destroy *the whole land* (of Babylonia).—Junius and most of the later writers construe באים as a present (*they come*, &c.). It is better to make it agree with צבא as a collective, and to continue the construction from the foregoing verse, as above.—The *end of heaven* is of course regarded by Gesenius as a proof of ignorance in the writer. Others more reasonably understand it as a strong but natural hyperbole. The best explanation is that given by J. D. Michaelis and Barnes, who suppose the Prophet to refer to the *horizon* or *bounding line*

of vision. He is not deliberately stating from what region they set out, but from what point he sees them actually coming, viz. from the remotest point in sight. This view of the expression, not as a geographical description, but as a vivid representation of appearances, removes the necessity of explaining how Media or Persia could be called a distant land or the extremity of heaven. Schmidius evades this imaginary difficulty by applying the terms to the distant nations from which Cyrus drew his forces; Clericus by referring *distant* not to Babylonia but Judea, and supposing the Prophet to be governed in his use of language by the habitual associations of his Jewish readers. Cocceius, partly for this very reason, understands the whole passage as a threatening against Judah.—*Jehovah and the weapons of his wrath.* According to the Michlol Jophi, *and* is here put for *with*, and some translators actually make the substitution, which is wholly unnecessary. The host which Jehovah was before said to be mustering is now represented as consisting of himself *and* the weapons of his wrath. This intimation of his presence, his co-operation, and even his incorporation, with the invading host, adds greatly to the force of the threatening. The Hebrew word כֵּלִים corresponds to our *implements* in its widest sense, as including *instruments* and *vessels*. It has here the active sense of weapons, while in Rom. ix. 22, Paul employs a corresponding Greek phrase in the passive sense of vessels. *Weapons of wrath* are the weapons which execute it, *vessels of wrath* the vessels which contain it.—The ambiguous phrase כָל הָאָרֶץ is explained by the Septuagint as meaning the whole world (πᾶσαν τὴν οἰκουμένην), and this interpretation is approved by Umbreit, on the ground that Babylon was a type or symbol of human opposition to divine authority. In its primary import it no doubt denotes the land of Babylonia or Chaldea. Cocceius alone understands the land of Israel or Judah to be meant, in accordance with his singular hypothesis already mentioned.

6. *Howl* (ye Babylonians, with distress and fear), *for the day of Jehovah* (his appointed time of judgment) *is near. Like might* (*i. e.* a mighty stroke or desolation) *from the Almighty it shall come.*—Calvin points out a *lusus verborum* in the combination of שַׁדַּי almighty, and שֹׁד desolation or destruction, both derived from שָׁדַד. As if he had said, you shall know with what good reason God is called שַׁדַּי. This is described by Calvin as a *concinna allusio ad etymologiam*, by Barnes as a "paronomasia or pun, a figure of speech quite common in the Scriptures." *Paronomasia* and *pun* are not synonymous, and the application of the latter term in this case, if not irreverent, is inexact. Gesenius denies that it is even a paronomasia in the proper sense. He also takes כ as a *caph veritatis*—"like a destruction from the Almighty (as it is)." But Hendewerk takes it in its proper sense—a destruction as complete and overwhelming *as if* it were an act of reckless violence. Kimchi explains the clause to mean, as a destruction (not from man, but) from a mighty one who cannot be resisted or avoided. Vitringa labours to explain and justify the derivation of a divine name from a root of evil import like שָׁדַד to plunder or destroy. But this etymological difficulty is removed by the latter lexicographers, who give the root the general sense of being strong or mighty, as in Arabic. The specific sense of tempest or destructive storm, which Gesenius puts upon שֹׁד here and in Joel i. 15, is perfectly gratuitous. Jehovah's days are well defined by Cocceius: In genere dies Domini dicuntur *divinitus constitutae opportunitates* quibus judicium suum exercet. (*Vide supra*, chap. ii. 12). This day is said to be *near*, not absolutely with respect to the date of the prediction, but rela-

tively, either with respect to the perceptions of the Prophet, or with respect
to what had gone before. For ages Babylon might be secure ; but after
the premonitory signs just mentioned should be seen, there would be no
delay. The words of the verse are supposed to be uttered in the midst of
the tumult and alarm of the invasion.

7. *Therefore* (because of this sudden and irresistible attack) *all hands
shall sink* (fall down, be slackened or relaxed), *and every heart of man shall
melt.* Clericus supposes an allusion to the etymology of אנוש as denoting
frailty and infirmity (omne ægrorum mortalium cor); but most interpreters
explain the phrase as simply meaning *every mortal heart,* or the heart of
every mortal. Cocceius understands by the sinking of the hands the loss
of active power, and by the melting of the heart, the fear of coming evil.
Junius supposes an antithesis between the *hands* or body, and the *heart* or
mind. But both the clauses, in their strict sense, are descriptive of bodily
effects, and both indicative of mental states. Each of the figures is repeatedly used elsewhere. (See Josh. vii. 5, Ps. xxii. 13, Jer. l. 43, Job. iv. 3.)
Knobel quotes from Ovid the analogous expression, *cecidere illis animique
manusque.*

8. *And they* (the Babylonians) *shall be confounded—pangs and throes
shall seize* (them)—*like the travailing* (woman) *they shall writhe—each at
his neighbour, they shall wonder—faces of flames* (shall be) *their faces.*—
The Vulgate, Peshito, and Lowth, connect the first word with the verse
preceding, which is, to say the least, unnecessary.—The translation *fear* or
tremble, is too weak for נבהלו, which includes the ideas of violent agitation
and extreme perplexity. The Septuagint strangely gives to צירים here the
sense of ambassadors or messengers (*vide infra,* chap. xviii. 2, lvii. 9),
which is precluded by the whole connection, and especially by the combination with חבלים. Solomon ben Melech explains ן in יאחזון as an anomalous
suffix used instead of ם. Lowth as usual corrects the text by reading
יאחזום, on the alleged authority of the Septuagint, Targum, and Peshito,
which supply the suffix. Gesenius, Hitzig, Ewald, and Knobel, adopt a
construction mentioned by Kimchi, which makes *pangs and throes* the object
not the subject of the verb—they shall take pangs and throes—as we speak
of a house *taking fire* or a person *taking a disease,* and as Livy says *capere
metum.* This form of expression occurs, not only in Arabic, but in Job
xviii. 20, xxi. 6. The construction is also recommended by its rendering
the suffix unnecessary, and by its giving to יאחזון the same subject with the
verbs before and after it. The objection to it, strongly urged by Hendewerk,
is that the construction, even in Job, is Arabic, not Hebrew, the idiom of
the latter being clear from other cases where the same verb and nouns are
combined (Isa. xxi. 3, Jer. xiii. 21), or the same nouns with other verbs
(1 Sam. iv. 19, Isa. lxvi. 7, Jer. xxii. 23, Dan. x. 16, Hos. xiii. 13), or
other nouns and verbs of kindred meaning (Exod. xv. 14, Isa. xxxv. 10,
Deut. xxviii. 2), but in all without exception the noun is the subject, not the
object, of the verb. The construction thus proved to be the common one,
may at least be safely retained here, the rather as the collocation of the
words is evidently in its favour. The sense of *trembling* given to יחילון by
several of the recent writers is too weak. The best translation seems to be
that of Henderson—*they shall writhe—i. e.* with pain. The expression
wonder at each other occurs once in historical prose (Gen. xliii. 33). It
seems here to denote not simply consternation and dismay, but stupefaction
at each other's aspect and condition—*q. d. each man at his friend shall*

stand aghast.—The last clause is referred by J. H. Michaelis to the Medes and Persians, and explained as a description of their violence and fierceness, in which sense the same figures are employed in Isaiah lxvi. 15, and Rev. ix. 17. It is commonly and much more naturally understood as a continued description of the terror and distress of the Chaldeans. Aben Ezra mentions an interpretation of להבים as the proper name of an African race descended from Mizraim the son of Ham (Gen. x. 13, 1 Chron. i. 11), and probably the same with the *Lubim* (2 Chron. xvi. 8) or *Libyans.* "Their faces shall be (like) the faces of Africans," *i.e.* black with horror and despair. This explanation is approved by Gataker; but all other writers seem to take להבים as the plural of להב a flame. The point of comparison, according to Kimchi, is *redness,* here referred to as a natural symptom of confusion and shame. But as this seems inappropriate in the case before us, Hitzig and Knobel understand the aspect indicated to be one of *paleness,* as produced by fear. Calvin, Gesenius, and many others, understand the *glow* or *flush* produced by anguish and despair to be intended. For the classical usage of fire and flame as denoting a *red* colour, see Gesenius's Thesaurus, tom. ii. p. 743. In the last edition of his Lexicon by Robinson, the phrase before us is explained to mean "ruddy and burning with *eagerness*," an expression applicable only to the conquerors. Instead of *eagerness*, the Thesaurus has *internum animi œstum.*—Cocceius refers this, as well as the preceding verses, to the Assyrian and Babylonian invasions of the Holy Land. He also makes the verbs descriptive presents, in which he is followed by J. D. Michaelis and the later Germans. There is, however, no need of departing from the strict sense of the future.

9. All this must happen and at a set time—for *behold the day of Jehovah cometh*—*terrible*—*and wrath and heat of anger*—*to place* (or make) *the land a waste*—*and its sinners he* (or *it,* the day) *will destroy from it* (or *out of it*). According to Cocceius, the mention of Jehovah throughout this passage, sometimes in the first person, sometimes in the third, has reference to the plurality of persons in the Godhead.—He also renders אכזרי as an abstract noun (immanitas), in which he is followed by Vitringa, while Ewald gives it an adverbial sense (grausamer Art), but most interpreters regard it as an adjective synonymous with אכזר. The application of this term to God, or to his judgments, seems to have perplexed interpreters. *Crudelem diem vocat* (says Jerome) *non merito sui sed populi. Non est enim crudelis qui crudeles jugulat, sed quod crudelis patientibus esse videatur. Nam et latro suspensus patibulo crudelem judicem putat.* "The word (says Barnes) stands opposed here to *mercy*, and means that God would not spare them." It is dubious, however, whether the word in any case exactly corresponds to the *crudelis* of the Vulgate or the English *cruel.* The essential idea is rather that of vehemence, destructiveness, &c. It is rendered accordingly in various forms, without any implication of a moral kind, by the Septuagint (ἀνίατος), Lowth (inexorable), Gesenius (furchtbar), and others.—The following words, as well as אכזרי, are construed by Cocceius as in apposition with יום יהוה—the day itself being described as cruelty, wrath, &c. Gesenius, in his Commentary, repeats יום *fearful, and* (a day of) *wrath,* &c. In his translation he supplies another word—*full of anger,* &c. Ewald and others supply a preposition—*with wrath,* &c.—Another possible construction would be to suppose a change of subject—"The day of Jehovah is coming and (so is) his wrath," &c. In that case, יהוה is of course the subject of ישמיד. Upon the other supposition it may agree with יום, but without a change of meaning. The most vigorous though not the

most exact translation of these epithets is Luther's (*grausam, grimmig, zornig*). Most interpreters, from Jarchi downwards, understand הארץ to be Babylonia ; but the Septuagint makes it mean the earth or world (οἴκου μέ·ην) as in ver. 5. This explanation is revived by the three latest writers whom I have consulted, Ewald, Umbreit, and Knobel, the last of whom understands the term as an allusion to the universal sway of the Babylonian empire.—The moral causes of the ruin threatened are significantly intimated by the Prophet's calling the people of the earth or land *its sinners*. As the national offences here referred to, Vitringa enumerates pride (v. xi. 14, 11 ; xlvii. 7, 8), idolatry (Jer. l. 38), tyranny in general (xiv. 12, 17), and oppression of God's people in particular (xlvii. 6).—In the laying of the land waste, Junius supposes a particular allusion to the submerging of the Babylonian plains, by the diversion of the waters of Euphrates.

10. The day of Jehovah is now described as one of preternatural and awful darkness, in which the very sources of light shall be obscured. This natural and striking figure for sudden and disastrous change is of frequent occurrence in Scripture (see Isa. xxiv. 23, xxxiv. 4 ; Ezek. xxxii. 7, 8 ; Joel ii. 10, iii. 15 ; Amos viii. 9 ; Mat. xxiv. 29). Well may it be called a day of wrath and terror—*for the stars of the heavens and their signs* (or constellations) *shall not shed their light—the sun is darkened in his going forth—and the moon shall not cause its light to shine.*—It can only be from misapprehension of the connection between this verse and the ninth, that Lowth translates כִּי *yea !*—According to Hitzig and Knobel, the darkening of the stars is mentioned first, because the Hebrews reckoned the day from sunset.—Vitringa and J. D. Michaelis understand the image here presented to be that of a terrific storm, veiling the heavens, and concealing its luminaries. But grand as this conception is, it falls short of the Prophet's vivid description, which is not that of transient obscuration but of sudden and total extinction.—The abrupt change from the future to the preterite and back again, has been retained in the translation, although most modern versions render all the verbs as presents. From simply *foretelling* the extinction of the stars, the Prophet suddenly *describes* that of the sun as if he saw it, and then adds that of the moon as a necessary consequence.—Clericus explains כסילים as a synonyme of כסל in the sense of *hope* or *confidence*, and refers the suffix to the Babylonians, who were notoriously addicted to astrology and even to astrolatry. *The stars of heaven which are* (literally *and* or *even*) *their confidence*, &c. This ingenious exposition seems to have commended itself to no other writer, though Malvenda does likewise suppose a special allusion to the astrological belief and practice of the Babylonians. Theodotion and Aquila retain the Hebrew word (χεσιλεέμ). Jerome gives the vague sense *splendour*, the Peshito that of *strength* or *host*. Calvin and others render it by *sidera*. Vitringa makes it mean the *planets*, Junius the *constellations*, as distinguished from the *stars*. Rabbinical and other writers make כסיל the name of a particular star, but differ as to its identity. The latest writers have gone back to the version of the Septuagint (ὁ Ὠρίων) and Luther (sein Orion), except that they restore the plural form of the original.—The proofs of the identity of Nimrod and Orion, as hunters transferred to the heavens, in the oriental and classical mythology, have been arrayed, with a minuteness of detail and a profusion of learning out of all proportion to the exegetical importance of the subject, by J. D. Michaelis, in his Supplement ad lexx. Hebr. p. 1319 *seq.*—Gesenius on the passage now before us—and Lee on Job. ix. 9. It is commonly agreed that the word which occurs elsewhere only in the singular (Job ix. 9, xxxviii. 31 ;

Amos v. 8), is here used in the plural to give it a generic sense—*Orions, i. e.* Orion and other brilliant constellations. To express this idea most of the recent versions exchange the proper name for an appellative. The word *Bilder*, used by the latest German writers, seems to have reference to the *signs* of the Zodiac. Ewald alone retains the primary meaning (seine Orionen). In this, as in many other cases, the spirit of the passage is nowhere more felicitously given than in Luther's energetic paraphrase. *Die Sterne am Himmel und seine Orion scheinen nicht helle ; die Sonne gehet finster auf, und der Mond scheinet dunkel.*

11. The Prophet, according to his custom (*vide supra*, chap. i. 22, v. 7, xi. 9), now resolves his figures into literal expressions, shewing that the natural convulsions just predicted are to be understood as metaphorical descriptions of the divine judgments. *And I will visit upon the world* (*its*) *wickedness* (*i. e.* manifest my presence for the purpose of punishing it)—*and upon the wicked their iniquity—and I will cause to cease the arrogance of presumptuous sinners—and the pride of tyrants* (or oppressors) *I will humble.* The primary meaning of תֵּבֵל is retained in the versions of Junius (orbis habitabilis) and Cocceius (frugiferam terram), who regards the use of this word as a proof that the prophecy relates to Israel (populus per verbum Dei cultus). It is no doubt a poetical equivalent to אֶרֶץ, and is here applied to the Babylonian empire, as embracing most of the known world. Thus the Roman empire, as Lowth shews, was called *universus orbis Romanus*, and Minos, in Ovid, speaks of Crete as *meus orbis.* Hitzig makes תֵּבֵל רָעָה mean *the evil world*, but the parallel expression which immediately follows, and the analogy of Jer. xxiii. 2, Exod. xx. 5, are decisive in favour of the usual construction.—The Septuagint makes עריצים synonymous with זדים (ὑπερηφάνων), and the Vulgate makes it simply mean the powerful (fortium). But active violence is an essential part of the meaning. The English Version and some others adopt the sense of *terrible* (from עָרַץ to terrify); but the latest interpreters prefer the meaning given by Calvin, Clericus, and others (tyrannorum).

12. To the general description in the foregoing verse he now adds a more specific threatening of extensive slaughter, and a consequent diminution of the population, expressed by a strong comparison. *I will make man more scarce* (or rare) *than pure gold, and a human being than the ore of Ophir.*— אנוש and אדם cannot here denote a difference of rank, as איש and אדם sometimes do, because neither of them is elsewhere used in the distinctive sense of *vir* or ἀνήρ. They are really poetical equivalents, like *man* and *mortal* or *human being*, which last expression is employed by Henderson. פָּז is regarded as a proper name by Bochart, who applies it to the Coromandel coast, and by Huet, who supposes it to be a contraction of אוּפָז, and this a variation of אופיר. Gill speaks of some as identifying פ with Fez, and איפיר with Peru. פז and כתם are either poetical synonymes of זהב, or emphatic expressions for the purest, finest, and most solid gold. The Septuagint version of the last words is ὁ λίθος ὁ ἐν Σουφίρ, instead of which the Arabic translation founded on it has *the stone which* (*comes*) *from India.* The disputed question as to the locality of Ophir, although not without historical and archæological importance, can have no effect upon the meaning of this passage. Whether the place meant be Ceylon, or some part of continental India, or of Arabia, or of Africa, it is here named simply as an *Eldorado*, as a place where gold abounded, either as a native product or an article of commerce, from which it was brought, and with which it was associated in the mind of every Hebrew reader. For the various opinions and the

arguments by which they are supported, see the geographical Works of Bochart and Rosenmüller, Winer's Realwörterbuch, Gesenius's Thesaurus, and Henderson's note upon the verse before us.—Instead of making *rare* or *scarce*, the meaning put upon אוקיר by Jerome and by most modern writers, some retain the original and strict sense of *making dear* or *costly*, with allusion to the impossibility of ransoming the Babylonians from the Medes and Persians. This interpretation, which Henderson ascribes to Grotius, was given long before by Calvin, and is indeed as old as Kimchi. Barnes, and some older writers understand the words as expressive of the difficulty with which defenders could be found for the city. Henderson speaks of some as having applied the verse, in an individual sense, to Cyrus and to the Messiah. The latter application is of Jewish origin, and found in the book Zohar. Jarchi explains the verse as having reference to the honour put upon the prophet Daniel as the decipherer of the writing on the wall. The Targum makes it a promise of protection to the godly and believing Jews in Babylon. Cocceius, while he gives the words the sense now usually put upon them, as denoting paucity of men in consequence of slaughter, still refers them to the small number of Jews who were carried into exile.—From the similar forms אוקיר and אופיר at the beginning and the end of the sentence, Gesenius infers that a paronomasia was intended by the writer, which, as usual, he imitates, with very indifferent success, by beginning his translation with *seltener* and ending it with *seltene Schätze*. Henderson, with great probability, denies that the writer intended any assonance at all. On the modern theory of perfect parallelisms, it would be easy to construct an argument in favour of understanding אופיר as a verb, and thereby rendering the clauses uniform. Such a conclusion, like many drawn from similar premises in other cases, would of course be worthless.

13. The figurative form of speech is here resumed, and what was before expressed by the obscuration of the heavenly bodies is now denoted by a general commotion of the frame of nature. *Therefore I will make the heavens tremble, and the earth shall shake* (or be shaken) *out of its place in the wrath of Jehovah of hosts and in the day of the heat* (or *fierceness*) *of his anger.* Henderson translates עַל־כֵּן *because*, which is not only inconsistent with the usage of the words, but wholly unnecessary. *Therefore* may either mean because of the wickedness mentioned in ver. 11, or for the purpose of producing the effect described in ver. 12. In the last clause some give ב the sense of *by* or *on account of* in both members. Others explain the first ב thus, but take the other in its proper sense of *in*. It is highly improbable, however, that the particle is here used in two different senses, and the best construction, therefore, is the one which lets the second ב determine the meaning of the first—*in the wrath, i. e.* during (or in the time of) the wrath.

14. *And it shall be* (or come to pass, that) *like a roe* (or antelope) *chased* (or driven by the hunters) *and like sheep with none to gather them* (literally, *like sheep, and there is no one gathering*)—*each to his people, they shall turn—and each to his country they shall flee.*—The English Version seems to make the *earth* the subject of הָיָה, with which, however, it does not agree in gender. Gesenius and Hitzig make the verb indefinite, *one shall be.* Aben Ezra and Jarchi supply Babylon or the Babylonians. The best construction is that given by De Wette, Umbreit, and Knobel, who take הָיָה in its common idiomatic sense of coming to pass, happening. Kimchi refers the verse to the foreign residents in Babylon (בבבל העם הנכרי אשר)—what Jeremiah calls the *mingled people* (l. 37), and Æschylus the πάμμικτον

ὄχλον of Babylon. Calvin supposes an allusion, not to foreign residents, but mercenary troops or allies. Clericus applies the last clause to these strangers, and the first to the Babylonians themselves, which is needless and arbitrary. The צְבִי, according to Bochart and Gesenius, is a generic term including all varieties of roes and antelopes. The points of comparison are their timidity and fleetness. The figure of scattered sheep, without a gatherer or shepherd, is a common one in Scripture. Junius connects this verse with the twelfth, and throws the thirteenth into a parenthesis, a construction complex in itself, and so little in accordance with the usage of the language, that nothing short of exegetical necessity can warrant its adoption.

15. The flight of the strangers from Babylon is not without reason, for *every one found* (there) *shall be stabbed* (or thrust through), *and every one joined* (or joining himself to the Babylonians) *shall fall by the sword.* All interpreters agree that a general massacre is here described, although they differ as to the precise sense and connection of the clauses. Some suppose a climax. Thus Junius explains the verse to mean that not only the robust but the decrepit (נִסְפָּה from סָפָה to consume) should be slain, and the same interpretation is mentioned by Kimchi. Hitzig takes the sense to be that every one, even he who joins himself (*i. e.* goes over to the enemy), shall perish ; they will give no quarter. Others suppose an antithesis, though not a climax. Gesenius, in the earlier editions of his Lexicon, explains the verse as meaning that he who is found in the street, and he who withdraws himself into the house, shall perish alike. Lowth makes the antithesis between one *found alone* and one *joined* with others. Umbreit supposes an antithesis not only between נמצא and נספה, but also between ידקר and יפול בחרב—the one clause referring to the first attack with spears, the other to the closer fight with swords hand to hand. J. D. Michaelis changes the points, so as to make the contrast between him who *remains* and him who *flees,* and Henderson extracts the same sense from the common text, avowedly upon the ground that נספה must denote the opposite of נמצא. But even the most strenuous adherent of the theory of perfect parallelisms must admit that they are frequently synonymous, and not invariably antithetical. In this case there is no more need of making the participles opposite in meaning than the nouns and verbs. And as all except Umbreit (and perhaps Knobel) seem agreed that to be thrust through, and to fall by the sword, are one and the same thing, there is every probability that both the clauses have respect to the same class of persons. Upon this most natural and simple supposition, we may either suppose נמצא and נספה to denote the person *found* and the person *caught,* as Ewald and Gesenius do, or retain the old interpretations found in Kimchi, which connects the verse directly with the one before it, and applies both clauses to the foreigners in Babylon, every one of whom still *found* there, and still *joined* with the besieged, should be surely put to death.

16. The horrors of the conquest shall extend not only to the men, but to their wives and children. *And their children shall be dashed to pieces before their eyes, their houses shall be plundered and their wives ravished.* The same thing is threatened against Babylon in Ps. cxxxvii. 9, in retaliation for the barbarities practised in Jerusalem (2 Chron. xxxvi. 17, Lam. v. 11). The horror of the threatening is enhanced by the addition of *before their eyes.* (Compare chap. i. 7, and Deut. xxviii. 31, 32.) Hitzig coolly alleges that the last clause of this verse is copied from Zech. xiv. 2, to which Knobel adds, that the spoiling of the houses is here out of place.—For the

textual reading תשגלנה the Keri, here and elsewhere, substitutes תשכבנה as a euphemistic emendation.

17. The Prophet now, for the first time, names the chosen instruments of Babylon's destruction. *Behold I (am) stirring up against them Madai* (Media or the Medes) *who will not regard silver and (as for) gold, they will not take pleasure in it* (or desire it). Here, as in Jer. li. 11, 28, the Medes alone are mentioned, as the more numerous and hitherto more powerful nation, to which the Persians had long been subject, and were still auxiliary. Or the name may be understood as comprehending both, which Vitringa has clearly shewn to be the usage of the classical historians, by citations from Herodotus, Thucydides, and Plutarch. Indeed, all the names of the great oriental powers are used, with more or less latitude and licence, by the ancient writers, sacred and profane. As the Medes did not become an independent monarchy till after the date of this prediction, it affords a striking instance of prophetic foresight, as J. D. Michaelis, Keith, Barnes, and Henderson, have clearly shewn. It is chiefly to evade such proofs of inspiration that the modern Germans assign these chapters to a later date.—מָדַי is properly the name of the third son of Japhet from whom the nation was descended. At the date of this prediction, they formed a part of the Assyrian empire, but revolted at the time of the Assyrian invasion of Syria and Israel. Their first king Dejoces was elected about 700 years before the birth of Christ. His son Phraortes conquered Persia, and the united Medes and Persians, with the aid of the Babylonians, subdued Assyria under the conduct of Cyaxares I. The conquest of Babylon was effected in the reign of Cyaxares II. by the Median army, with an auxiliary force of thirty thousand Persians, under the command of Cyrus, the king's nephew. In the last clause of the verse, Hitzig and Knobel understand the Medes to be described as so uncivilised as not to know the value of money. Others suppose contempt of money to be mentioned as an honourable trait in the national character, and Vitringa has pointed out a very striking coincidence between this clause and the speech which Xenophon ascribes to Cyrus. Ἄνδρες Μῆδοι, καὶ πάντες οἱ παρόντες, ἐγὼ ὑμᾶς οἶδα σαφῶς, ὅτι οὔτε χρημάτων δεόμενοι σὺν ἐμοὶ ἐξήλθετε κ. τ. λ. The most natural interpretation is, however, that the thirst of blood would supersede the thirst of gold in the conquerors of Babylon, so that no one would be able to secure his life by ransom. Even Cocceius admits that this verse relates to the conquest of Babylon, but only, as he thinks, by a sudden change of subject, or at least a transition from God's dealings with his people to his dealings with their enemies.

18. *And bows shall dash boys in pieces, and the fruit of the womb they shall not pity ; on children their eye shall not have mercy.*—Augusti needlessly continues the construction from the foregoing verse—" they shall not delight in gold, but in bows which," &c. The Septuagint has the *bows of the young men* (τοξεύματα νεανίσκων) which is inconsistent with the form of the original. The Vulgate, Luther, and Calvin, " with their bows they shall dash in pieces." But the feminine form תְּרַטַּשְׁנָה must agree with קְשָׁתוֹת, as Aben Ezra has observed. Clericus and Knobel think that *bows* are here put for *bowmen*, which is a forced construction and unnecessary. Hendewerk supposes the bow to be mentioned, as in many other cases, as one of the most common and important weapons. Other interpreters appear to be agreed that there is special allusion to the large bows and skilful archery of the ancient Persians, as described by Herodotus, Xenophon, and Ammianus Marcellinus. Kimchi's extravagant idea that the Medes are here

described as shooting children from their bows instead of arrows, is strangely copied by some later writers. There is more probability in the opinion, that they are represented as employing their large massive bows instead of clubs. There is no serious objection, however, to the common supposition, that the effect described is that of arrows, or of bows used in the ordinary manner. The strong term *dash in pieces* is employed instead of one more strictly appropriate, with evident allusion to its use in ver. 16. There is no need of giving נערים the sense of *young men*. It rather denotes *children* of both sexes, as בנים does when absolutely used. Hendewerk and some older writers understand by the *fruit of the womb* the unborn child (see Hosea xiv. 1; Amos i. 13; 2 Kings viii. 12, 15, 16). Gesenius and others make it simply equivalent to *children*, as in Gen. xxx. 2; Deut vii. 13; Lam. ii. 20. The cruelty of the Medes seems to have been proverbial, in the ancient world. Diodorus Siculus makes one of his characters ask, " What destroyed the empire of the Medes ? 'Their cruelty to those beneath them.' " Compassion is ascribed to the eye, says Knobel, because it is expressed in the looks. Kimchi observes that this is the only case in which the future of חוס has *u* instead of *o*.

19. From the very height of splendour and renown, Babylon shall be reduced not only to subjection but to annihilation. *And Babylon, the beauty* (or *glory*) *of kingdoms, the ornament, the pride of the Chaldees, shall be like God's overthrowing Sodom and Gomorrah—i. e.* shall be totally destroyed in execution of a special divine judgment. According to Kimchi, צבי means *delight* (חפץ), and צבי ממלכות that in which the nations delighted. It is now agreed, however, that its meaning, as determined both by etymology and usage, is *beauty*. The same Hebrew word is applied as a distinctive name to a class of animals, remarkable for grace of form and motion. (*Vide supra* ver. 14). The *beauty of kingdoms* is by most writers understood comparatively as denoting the most beautiful of kingdoms, either in the proper sense, or in that of royal cities (see 1 Sam. xxvii. 5). But Knobel understands the words more strictly as denoting the ornament of an empire which included various tributary kingdoms. This agrees well with the next clause, which describes the city as the ornament and pride of the Chaldees. The origin of this name, and of the people whom it designates, is doubtful and disputed. But whether the Chaldees were of Semitic origin or not, and whether they were the indigenous inhabitants of Babylonia or a foreign race imported from Armenia and the neighbouring countries, it is plain that the word here denotes the *nation* of which Babylon was the capital. For a statement of the archaeological question, see Gesenius's Thesaurus, tom. ii. p. 719—Winer's Realwörterbuch, vol. i. p. 253—and Henderson's note on Isaiah xxiii. 13. By most interpreters תפארת גאון are construed together as denoting *ornament of pride*, i. e. *proud ornament*. The same sense, with a slight modification, is expressed in the Vulgate (inclyta superbia), and by Luther (herrliche Pracht). Equally simple, and perhaps more consistent with the Masoretic interpunction, is the separate construction of the words by Junius and Tremellius (ornatus excellentiaque), still better expressed, without supplying *and*, by the Dutch Version (de heerlickheyt, de hoovaerdigheyt)—and in English by Barnes (the ornament, the pride).—In the last clause, the verbal noun מהפכת is construed with the subject in the genitive and the object in the accusative (Gesen. Lehrg. p. 688). It has been variously paraphrased—as *when* God overthrew Sodom and Gomorrah—like Sodom and Gomorrah *which* God overthrew— like the overthrow *with which* God *overthrew* Sodom and Gomorrah—like

the overthrow of God *with which he overthrew* Sodom and Gomorrah—but the exact sense of the Hebrew words is that already given—like God's overthrowing Sodom and Gomorrah. This is a common formula in Scripture for complete destruction, viewed as a special punishment of sin. (*Vide supra*, chap. i. 7, 9). The allegation of the Seder Olam, as cited both by Jarchi and Kimchi, that Babylon was suddenly destroyed by fire from heaven in the second year of Darius, is a Jewish figment designed to reconcile the prophecy with history. It is certain, however, that the destruction of the city was by slow degrees, successively promoted by the conquests of Cyrus, Darius Hystaspes, Alexander the Great, Antigonus, Demetrius, the Parthians, and the founding of the cities of Seleucia and Ctesiphon. Strabo calls Babylon μεγάλην ἐρημίαν. Pausanias says that in his day οὐδὲν ἔτι ἦν εἰ μὴ τεῖχος. In Jerome's time this wall only served as the enclosure of a park or hunting ground. From this apparent disagreement of the prophecy with history, Cocceius seems disposed to infer that it relates not to the literal but spiritual Babylon. The true conclusion is that drawn by Calvin, that the prophecy does not relate to any one invasion or attack exclusively, but to the whole process of subjection and decay, so completely carried out through a course of ages, that the very site of ancient Babylon is now disputed. This hypothesis accounts for many traits in the description which appear inconsistent only in consequence of being all applied to one point of time, and one catastrophe exclusively.

20. *It shall not be inhabited for ever* (*i. e.* it shall never again, or no more, be inhabited) *and it shall not be dwelt in from generation to generation* (literally to generation and generation)—*neither shall the Arab pitch tent there—neither shall shepherds cause* (their flocks) *to lie there.* The conversion of a populous and fertile district into a vast pasture-ground, however rich and well frequented, implies extensive ruin, but not such ruin as is here denounced. Babylon was not even to be visited by shepherds, nor to serve as the encamping ground of wandering Arabs. The completeness of the threatened desolation will be seen by comparing these expressions with chap. v. 5, 17, vii. 21, xvii. 2, where it is predicted that the place in question should be *for flocks to lie down, with none to make them afraid.* So fully has this prophecy been verified that the Bedouins, according to the latest travellers, are even superstitiously afraid of passing a single night upon the site of Babylon. The simplest version of the first clause would be, *she shall not dwell for ever, she shall not abide*, &c. And this construction is actually given by Calvin and Ewald. But the great majority of writers follow the Septuagint and Vulgate in ascribing to the active verbs a passive or intransitive sense. Kimchi explains this usage on the ground that the city is made to represent its inhabitants—*she dwells* for *her people dwell*. This intransitive usage of the verbs is utterly denied by Hengstenberg on Zechariah xii. 6 (Christol. ii. 286), but maintained against him by Gesenius in his Thesaurus (ii. 635). The result appears to be, that in a number of cases, the intransitive version is required by the context. The only objection to it in the case before us, is that it does not here seem absolutely necessary. The choice therefore lies between the general usage of ישׁב and שׁכן as active verbs, and their special usage in connection with prophecies of desolation. The sense of *sitting on a throne*, ascribed to ישׁב here by Gataker, and elsewhere by Hengstenberg, does not agree so well with that of the other verb and with the general import of the threatening. On the whole, the passive or neuter construction, though not absolutely necessary, is the most satisfactory and natural.—יָהֵל is explained by the rabbinical interpreters as a

contraction of יֶאֱהַל, the Kal of which is used in the sense of pitching a tent or encamping, Gen. xiii. 12, 18. (See Gesenius § 67, Rem. 2). This explanation is adopted by most modern writers. Rosenmüller and Ewald, however, make the form a Hiphil one for יַאֲהִיל. Hitzig takes it likewise as a Hiphil, but from נָהַל *to lead* (flocks) *to water*, which is also found connected with the Hiphil of רָבַץ in Ps. xxiii. 2. Hendewerk objects that although this verb is repeatedly used by Isaiah, it is always in the Piel form (chap. xl. 11, xlix. 10, li. 18). The Hiphil occurs nowhere else, and the contraction assumed by Hitzig rarely if at all. The derivation from אהל is assumed in the Chaldee Paraphrase and Vulgate Version.—Barnes applies this clause to the encampment of caravans, and supposes it to mean that wayfarers will not lodge there even for a night. But the mention of shepherds immediately afterwards renders it more probable that the allusion is to the nomadic habits of the Bedouins, who are still what Strabo represents them, half shepherds and half robbers (σκηνῖται λῃστρικοί τινες καὶ ποιμενικοί), passing from one place to another when their plunder or their pasture fails. Gesenius suggests that ערבי may here be used generically to denote this class of persons or their mode of life. There can be no doubt, however, that Arabians, properly so called, do actually overrun the region around Babylon with their flocks and herds, although, as we have seen, they refuse to take up their abode upon the doomed site of the vanished city.

21. Having excluded men and the domesticated animals from Babylon, the Prophet now tells how it shall be occupied, viz. by creatures which are only found in deserts, and the presence of which therefore is a sign of desolation. In the first clause these solitary creatures are referred to in the general; the other clause specifies two kinds out of the many which are elsewhere spoken of as dwelling in the wilderness. *But there* (instead of flocks) *shall lie down desert creatures—and their houses* (those of the Babylonians) *shall be filled with howls or yells—and there shall dwell the daughters of the ostrich—and shaggy beasts* (or *wild goats*) *shall gambol there.* The contrast is heightened by the obvious allusion in רבצו and שכנו to the תשכן and ירביצו of ver. 20. As if he had said, flocks shall not lie down there, but wild beasts shall; man shall not dwell there, but the ostrich shall. The meaning evidently is, that the populous and splendid city should become the home of animals found only in the wildest solitudes. To express this idea, other species might have been selected with the same effect. The endless discussions therefore as to the identity of those here named, however laudable as tending to promote exact lexicography and natural history, have little or no bearing on the interpretation of the passage. The fullest statement of the questions in detail may be found in Bochart's Hierozoicon and in Gesenius's Thesaurus, under the several words and phrases. Nothing more will be here attempted than to settle one or two points of comparative importance. Many interpreters regard the whole verse as an enumeration of particular animals. Thus ציים has been rendered *wild-cats, monkeys, vampyres;* אחים *owls, weasels, dragons,* &c., &c. This has arisen from the assumption of a perfect parallelism in the clauses. It is altogether natural, however to suppose that the writer would first make use of general expressions and afterwards descend to particulars. This supposition is confirmed by the etymology and usage of ציים, both which determine it to mean those belonging to or dwelling in the desert. In this sense, it is sometimes applied to men (Ps. lxxii. 9, lxxiv. 14), but as these are here

excluded by the preceding verse, nothing more was needed to restrict it to wild animals, to which it is also applied in chap. xxxiv. 14, and Jer. l. 39. This is now commonly agreed to be the meaning, even by those who give to אֹחִים a specific sense. The same writers admit that אֹחִים properly denotes the howls or cries of certain animals, and only make it mean the animals themselves, because such are mentioned in the other clauses. But if צִיִּים has the generic sense which all now give it, the very parallelism of the clauses favours the explanation of אֹחִים in its original and proper sense of *howls* or *yells*, viz. those uttered by the צִיִּים. The common version (*doleful creatures*) is too indefinite on one of these hypotheses, and too specific on the other. The *daughter of the ostrich* is an oriental idiom for ostriches in general, or for the female ostrich in particular. The old translation *owls* seem to be now universally abandoned. The most interesting point in the interpretation of this verse has reference to the word שְׂעִירִים. The history of its interpretation is so curious as to justify more fulness of detail than usual. It has never been disputed that its original and proper sense is *hairy*, and its usual specific sense *he-goats*. In two places (Lev. xvii. 7 ; 2 Chron. xi. 15), it is used to denote objects of idolatrous worship, probably images of goats, which according to Herodotus were worshipped in Egypt. In Chronicles especially this supposition is the natural one, because the word is joined with עֲגָלִים *calves*. Both there and in Leviticus, the Septuagint renders it ματαίοις, *vain things, i. e.* false gods, idols. But the Targum on Leviticus explains it to mean *demons* (שֵׁדִין), and the same interpretation is given in the case before us by the Septuagint (δαιμόνια), Targum (שֵׁדִין), and Peshito (ܫܐܕ̈ܝܢ). The Vulgate in Leviticus translates the word *daemonibus*, but here *pilosi*. The interpretation given by the other three versions is adopted also by the Rabbins, Aben Ezra, Jarchi, Kimchi, &c. It appears likewise in the Talmud and early Jewish books. From this traditional interpretation of שְׂעִירִים, here and in chap. xxxiv. 14, appears to have arisen, at an early period, a popular belief among the Jews, that *demons* or *evil spirits* were accustomed to haunt desert places in the shape of goats or other animals. And this belief is said to be actually cherished by the natives near the site of Babylon at the present day. Let us now compare this Jewish exposition of the passage with its treatment among Christians. To Jerome, the combination of the two meanings, *goats* and *demons*, seems to have suggested the Pans, Fauns, and Satyrs of the classical mythology, imaginary beings· represented as a mixture of the human form with that of goats, and supposed to frequent forests and other lonely places. This idea is carried out by Calvin, who adopts the word *satyri* in his version, and explains the passage as relating to actual appearances of Satan under such disguises. Luther, in like manner, renders it *Feldgeister*. Vitringa takes another step, and understands the language as a mere concession or allusion to the popular belief, equivalent to saying, the solitude of Babylon shall be as awful *as if* occupied by Fauns and Satyrs—there *if anywhere*, such beings may be looked for. In explaining how שְׂעִירִים came to be thus used, he rejects the supposition of actual apparitions of the evil spirit, and ascribes the usage to the fact of men's mistaking certain shaggy apes (or other animals approaching to the human form), for incarnations of the devil. Forerius and J. D. Michaelis understand the animals themselves to be here meant. The latter uses in his version the word *Waldteufel* (wood-devils, forest-demons), but is careful to apprise the reader in a note that it is the German name for a species of ape or monkey, and that the

Hebrew contains no allusion to the devil. The same word is used by Gesenius and others in its proper sense. Saadias, Cocceius, Clericus, and Henderson, return to the original meaning of the Hebrew word, to wit, *wild goats.* But the great majority of modern writers tenaciously adhere to the old tradition. This is done, not only by the German neologists, who lose no opportunity of finding a mythology in Scripture, but by Lowth, Barnes, and Stuart, in his exposition of Rev. xi. 2, and his Excursus on the Angelology of Scripture (Apocal. ii. 403). The arguments in favour of this exposition are : (1) the exegetical tradition of the Jews ; (2) their popular belief, and that of the modern orientals, in such apparitions ; (3) our Saviour's allusion (Mat. xii. 43) to the unclean spirit, as walking through dry places, seeking rest and finding none ; (4) the description of Babylon in Rev. xviii. 2, as the abode of demons, and the hold (or prison house) of every foul spirit and of every unclean and hateful bird, with evident allusion to the passage now before us. Upon this state of the case it may be remarked : (1) That even on the supposition of a reference to evil spirits, there is no need of assuming any concession or accommodation to the current superstitions. If שעירים denotes demons, this text is a proof, not of a popular belief, but of a fact, of a real apparition of such spirits under certain forms. (2) The Jewish tradition warrants the application of the Hebrew term *to demons,* but not to the *fauns* or *satyrs* of the Greek and Roman fabulists. (3) The fauns and satyrs of the classical mythology were represented as grotesque and frolicsome, spiteful, and mischievous, but not as awful and terrific beings, such as might naturally people horrid solitudes. (4) The popular belief of the Jews and other orientals may be traced to the traditional interpretation of this passage (see Stuart *ubi supra*), and this to the Septuagint Version. But we do not find that any of the modern writers adopt the Septuagint Version of בנות יענה (σειρῆνες) or of אײם in the next verse (ὀνοκενταύροι). If these are mere blunders or conceits, so may the other be, however great its influence on subsequent opinions. (5) There is probably no allusion in Mat. xii. 43 to this passage, and the one in Rev. xviii. 2, is evidently founded on the Septuagint Version, which was abundantly sufficient for the purpose of a symbolical accommodation. What the Greek translators incorrectly gave as the meaning of this passage might be said with truth of the spiritual Babylon. (6) The mention of *demons* in a list of beasts and birds is at variance not only with the favourite canon of parallelism, but with the natural and ordinary usage of language. Such a combination and arrangement as the one supposed—ostriches —demons—wolves—jackals—would of itself be a reason for suspecting that the second term must really denote some kind of animal, even if no such usage existed. (7) The usage of שעירים, as the name of an animal, is perfectly well defined and certain. Even in Lev. xvii. 7, and 2 Chron. xi. 15, this, as we have seen, is the only natural interpretation. The result appears to be that if the question is determined by tradition and authority, שעירים denotes *demons ;* if by the context and the usage of the word, it signifies *wild goats,* or more generically *hairy, shaggy* animals. According to the principles of modern exegesis, the latter is clearly entitled to the preference ; but even if the former be adopted, the language of the text should be regarded, not as " a touch from the popular pneumatology " (as Rev. xviii. 2, is described by Stuart *in loc.*), but as the prediction of a real fact, which, though it should not be assumed without necessity, is altogether possible, and therefore if alleged in Scripture, altogether credible. The argument in favour of the strict interpretation, and against the traditional and current one, is presented briefly, but with great strength and clearness, in Henderson's note upon the passage.

22. *And wolves shall howl in his* (the king of Babylon's) *palaces, and jackals in the temples of pleasure. And near to come is her* (Babylon's) *time, and her days shall not be prolonged.*—The names אִיִּים and תַּנִּים have been as variously explained as those in ver. 21. The latest writers seem to be agreed that they are different appellations of the jackal, but in order to retain the original variety of expression, substitute another animal in one of the clauses, such as *wolves* (Gesenius), *wild-cats* (Ewald), &c. As אִיִּים, according to its etymology, denotes an animal remarkable for its cry, it might be rendered *hyenas*, thereby avoiding the improbable assumption that precisely the same animal is mentioned in both clauses. But whatever be the species here intended, the essential idea is the same as in the foregoing verse, viz. that Babylon should one day be inhabited exclusively by animals peculiar to the wilderness, implying that it should become a wilderness itself. The contrast is heightened here by the particular mention of palaces and abodes of pleasure, as about to be converted into dens and haunts of solitary animals. This fine poetical conception is adopted by Milton in his sublime description of the flood—

> And in their palaces
> Where luxury late reigned, sea-monsters whelped
> And stabled.

The meaning of אַלְמָנוֹת, in every other case where it occurs, is *widows*, in which sense some rabbinical and other writers understand it here. But as it differs only in a single letter from אַרְמְנוֹת *palaces*, and as ל and ר are sometimes interchanged, it is now commonly regarded as a mere orthographical variation, if not an error of transcription. It is possible, however, that the two forms were designedly confounded by the writer, in order to suggest both ideas, that of palaces and that of widowhood or desolation. This explanation is adopted in the English Version, which has *palaces* in the margin, but in the text *desolate houses,* Henderson avoids the repetition of *palaces*, by rendering the second phrase *temples of pleasure*, which affords a good sense, and is justified by usage. The older writers explain עָנָה as denoting a responsive cry; but the latest lexicographers make *answer* a secondary meaning of the verb, which they explain as properly denoting to sing, or to utter any inarticulate sound, according to the nature of the subject. Hence it is translated *howl.*—The last clause of the verse may be strictly understood, but in application to the Jewish captives in the Babylonian exile, for whose consolation the prophecy was partly intended. Or we may understand it as denoting proximity in reference to the events which had been passing in the Prophet's view. He sees the signals erected —he hears a noise in the mountains—and regarding these as actually present, he exclaims, *her time is near to come!* It may, however, mean, as similar expressions do in other cases, that when the appointed time should come, the event would certainly take place, there could be no postponement or delay.

Chapter 14

THE destruction of Babylon is again foretold, and more explicitly connected with the deliverance of Israel from bondage. After a general assur-

ance of God's favour to his people, and of an exchange of conditions between
them and their oppressors, they are represented as joining in a song of
triumph over their fallen enemy.   In this song, which is universally admitted to possess the highest literary merit, they describe the earth as again
reposing from its agitation and affliction, and then breaking forth into a
shout of exultation, in which the very trees of the forest join, vers. 1–8.
By a still bolder figure, the unseen world is represented as perturbed at the
approach of the fallen tyrant, who is met, as he enters, by the kings already
there, amazed to find him sunk as low as themselves, and from a still greater
height of actual elevation and of impious pretensions, which are strongly
contrasted with his present condition, as deprived not only of regal honours
but of decent burial, vers. 9–20.   The threatening is then extended to the
whole race, and the prophecy closes as before with a prediction of the total
desolation of Babylon, vers. 21–23.

Vers. 24–27 are regarded by the latest writers as a distinct prophecy,
unconnected with what goes before, and misplaced in the arrangement of
the book.   The reasons for believing that it is rather an appendix or conclusion, added by the Prophet himself, will be fully stated in the exposition.

Vers. 28–32 are regarded by a still greater number of writers as a distinct prophecy against Philistia.   The traditional arrangement of the text,
however, creates a strong presumption that this passage stands in some close
connection with what goes before.   The true state of the case may be, that
the Prophet, having reverted from the downfall of Babylon to that of Assyria,
now closes with a warning apostrophe to the Philistines who had also suffered from the latter power, and were disposed to exult unduly in its overthrow.   If the latter application of the name Philistia to the whole land of
Canaan could be justified by Scriptural usage, these verses might be understood as a warning to the Jews themselves not to exult too much in their
escape from Assyrian oppression, since they were yet to be subjected to the
heavier yoke of Babylonian bondage.   Either of these suppositions is more
reasonable than that this passage is an independent prophecy subjoined to
the foregoing one by caprice or accident.

1. This verse declares God's purpose in destroying the Babylonian
power.   *For Jehovah will pity* (or *have mercy upon*) *Jacob, and will again*
(or *still*) *choose Israel and cause them to rest on their* (*own*) *land—and the
stranger shall be joined to them—and they* (the strangers) *shall be attached
to the house of Jacob.*   Jacob and Israel are here used for the whole race.
The plural pronoun *them* does not refer to Jacob and Israel as the names of different persons, but to each of them as a collective.   For the same reason נִסְפְּחוּ
is plural, though agreeing with הַגֵּר.   By God's *still choosing* Israel we are to
understand his continuing to treat them as his chosen people.   Or we may
render עוֹד *again,* in which case the idea will be, that having for a time or in
appearance cast them off and given them up to *other lords,* he would now
take them to himself again.   Gesenius gives two specimens in this verse of
his disposition to attenuate the force of the Hebrew words by needlessly departing from their primary import.   Because בָּחַר is occasionally used where
we should simply speak of loving or preferring, and because the Hiphil of
נוּחַ to rest, is sometimes used to signify the act of *laying down* or *placing,*
he adopts these two jejune and secondary senses here.——In this he is closely
followed by De Wette.   Hitzig, Hendewerk, and Umbreit, have the good
taste to give בָּחַר its distinctive sense, but Ewald alone among the later
Germans has done full justice to the meaning of both words, by translating
the first *choose* and the other *give them rest.*   The Vulgate takes the בְּ after

בָּחַר as a partitive (eliget de Israel), whereas it is the usual connective particle between this verb and its object. It is allowable, but not necessary, to give the Niphals in the second clause a reflexive meaning, as some writers do. נִלְוָה is followed by עַל as in Numbers, xviii. 2. Knobel understands by הַגֵּר the surviving Canaanites, some of them who went into captivity with Israel (Ezek. xiv. 7, xlvii. 22), and others remained in possession of the land (Ezra ix. 1, *seq.*). But there seems to be no reason for restricting the meaning of the word, especially as a general accession of the Gentiles is so often promised elsewhere. According to Cocceius and Gill, the maxim of the Talmud, that *proselytes are like a scab*, is founded on the affinity of the verb נספח with the noun ספחת.—Umbreit correctly understands this not as a mere promise of temporal deliverance and increase to Israel as a nation, but as an assurance that the preservation of the chosen people was a necessary means for the fulfilment of God's purposes of mercy to mankind in general.—The literal fulfilment of the last clause, in its primary sense, is clear from such statements as the one in Esther viii. 17.

2. *And nations shall take them and bring them to their place—and the house of Israel shall take possession of them on Jehovah's land for male and female servants—and* (thus) *they* (the Israelites) *shall be the captors of their captors, and rule over their oppressors.* The first clause is rendered somewhat obscure by the reference of the pronoun *them* to different subjects, first the Jews and then the Gentiles. Umbreit renders עַמִּים tribes (Stämme), and seems to refer it to the Jews themselves, and the first suffix to the Gentiles, thereby making the construction uniform. The sense will then be, not that the Gentiles shall bring the Jews home, but that the Jews shall bring the Gentiles with them. Most interpreters, however, are agreed that the first clause relates to the part taken by the Gentiles in the restoration of the Jews.—To a Hebrew reader the word הִתְנַחֲלוּ would convey the idea, not of bare possession merely, but of permanent possession, rendered perpetual by hereditary succession. The word is used in this sense, and with special reference to slaves or servants, in Lev. xxv. 46.—It is curious to observe the meanings put upon this promise by the different schools and classes of interpreters. Thus Grotius understands it of an influx of foreigners after Sennacherib's invasion in the reign of Hezekiah, an interpretation equally at variance with the context and with history. Cocceius, as the other pole or opposite extreme, applies it to the final deliverance of the Christian Church from persecution in the Roman empire, and its protection by Constantius and establishment by Constantine. Clericus and others find the whole fulfilment in the number of foreign servants whom the Jews brought back from exile (Ezra ii. 65). Calvin and others make the change predicted altogether moral, a spiritual conquest of the true religion over those who were once its physical oppressors. It is scarcely possible to compare these last interpretations without feeling the necessity of some exegetical hypothesis by which they may be reconciled. Some of the worst errors of interpretation have arisen from the mutual exclusion of hypotheses as incompatible, which really agree, and indeed are necessary to complete each other. The simple meaning of this promise seems to be that the Church, or chosen people, and the other nations should change places, the oppressed becoming the oppressor, and the slave the master. This of course admits both an external and internal fulfilment. In a lower sense, and on a smaller scale, it was accomplished in the restoration of the Jews from exile; but its full accomplishment is yet to come, not with respect to the Jews as a people, for their pre-eminence has ceased for ever, but with respect to the

Church, including Jews and Gentiles, which has succeeded to the rights and privileges, promises and actual possessions, of God's ancient people. The true principle of exposition is adopted even by the Rabbins. Jarchi refers the promise to the *future* (לעתיד), to the period of *complete redemption*. Kimchi more explicitly declares that its fulfilment is to be sought partly in the restoration from Babylon, and partly in the days of the Messiah.

3. *And it shall be* (or come *to pass*) *in the day of Jehovah's causing thee to rest from thy toil* (or *suffering*), *and from thy commotion* (or *disquietude*), *and from the hard service which was wrought by thee* (or *imposed upon thee*). The precise construction of the last words seem to be, *in which* (or *with respect to which*) *it was wrought with thee*, *i.e.* they (indefinitely) wrought with thee, or thou wast made to work. The nominative of עֻבַּד is not עֲבֹדָה nor the relative referring to it, but an indefinite subject understood. This impersonal construction makes it unnecessary to account for the masculine form of the verb as irregular. Aben Ezra refers עצב and רגז to pain of body and pain of mind, and Cocceius to outward persecutions and internal divisions of the Church. But they are much more probably equivalent expressions for pain and suffering in general. In this verse and the following context, the Prophet, in order to reduce the general promise of the foregoing verse to a more graphic and impressive form, recurs to the downfall of Babylon, as the beginning of the series of deliverances which he had predicted, and describes the effect upon those most concerned, by putting into the mouth of Israel a song of triumph over their oppressor. This is universally admitted to be one of the finest specimens of Hebrew, and indeed of ancient, composition.

4. *That thou shalt raise this song over the king of Babylon and say*, *How hath the oppressor ceased, the golden* (*city*) *ceased!* The *Vav* at the beginning continues the construction from וְהָיָה in ver. 3, and can only be expressed in our idiom by *that* —נָשָׂא is not merely to *begin* or to *utter*, but to *raise*, as this word is employed by us in a musical sense, including the ideas of commencement, utterance, and loudness.—מָשָׁל is not so called from מָשַׁל to rule, but from מָשַׁל to resemble or compare. Its most general sense seems to be that of tropical or figurative language. The more specific senses which have been ascribed to it are for the most part suggested by the context. Here it may have a special reference to the bold poetical fiction following. If so, it may warn us not to draw inferences from the passage with respect to the unseen world or the state of departed spirits. Calvin's description of the opening sentence as sarcastic, has led others to describe the whole passage as a *satire*, which is scarcely consistent with its peculiar merit as a song of triumph.—אֵיךְ is an exclamation of surprise, but at the same time has its proper force as an interrogative adverb, as appears from the answer in the following verse.—נֹגֵשׂ is properly a task-master, slave-driver, or tax-gatherer. מַדְהֵבָה is derived by the Rabbins and many modern writers from דְּהַב, the Chaldee form of זָהָב *gold*, in which Junius sees a sarcasm on the Babylonians, and Gesenius an indication that the writer lived in Babylonia! According to this etymology, the word has been explained by Vitringa as meaning a golden sceptre—by others the golden city—the place or repository of gold—the exactress of gold, taking the word as a participial noun—the exaction of gold, taking it as an abstract —or gold itself, considered as a tribute. From dubious Arabic analogies, Schultens and others have explained it to mean the destroyer or the plunderer. J. D. Michaelis and the later Germans are disposed to read

מרהבה *oppression*, which is found in one edition, appears to be the basis of the ancient versions, and agrees well with the use of נְגַשׂ and יִרְהֲבוּ in chap. iii. 5. Ewald gives it the strong sense of tyrannical rage.— The meaning of the first clause is of course that Israel would have occasion to express such feelings. There is consequently no need of disputing when or where the song was to be sung. Equally useless is the question whether by the king of Babylon we are to understand Nebuchadnezzar, Evilmerodach, or Belshazzar. The king here introduced is an ideal personage, whose downfall represents that of the Babylonian monarchy.

5. This verse contains the answer to the question in the one before it. *Jehovah hath broken the staff of the wicked, the rod of the rulers.* The meaning *tyrants*, given to the last word by Gesenius and the later Germans, is implied, but not expressed. The rod and staff are common figures for dominion, and their being broken for its destruction. There is no need of supposing a specific reference either to the rod of a task-master, with Gesenius, or to the sceptre of a king, with Ewald and the older writers.

6. *Smiting nations in anger by a stroke without cessation—ruling nations in wrath by a rule without restraint*—literally, which *he* (or *one* indefinitely) *did not restrain.*—The participles may agree grammatically either with the *rod* or with the king who wields it. Junius and Tremellius suppose the punishment of the Babylonians to be mentioned in both clauses. "As for him who smote the nations in wrath, his stroke shall not be removed—he that ruled the nations in anger is persecuted, and cannot hinder it." The English Version, Lowth, Barnes, and others, apply the last clause only to the punishment; but the great majority both of the oldest and the latest writers make the whole descriptive of the Babylonian tyranny. Kimchi, Calvin, and Vatablus read the last clause thus—(if any one was) *persecuted, he did not hinder it.* Dathe reads מרדף as an active participle (מְרַדֵּף), and this reading seems to be likewise supposed in the Chaldee, Syriac, and Latin versions. Some make מֻרְדָּף a verbal noun, meaning *persecution*, though the passive form is singular, and scarcely accounted for by Henderson's suggestion, that it means persecution as experienced rather than as practised. All the recent German writers have adopted Doederlein's proposal to amend the text, by changing מרדף into מרדת, a construct form like מכת, and derived, like it, from the immediately preceding verb. Striking a stroke without cessation, swaying a sway without restraint, will then correspond exactly, as also the remaining phrases, *peoples* and *nations*, *wrath* and *anger*. Of all the emendations founded on the principle of parallelism, there is none more natural or plausible than this, the rather as the letters interchanged are much alike, especially in some kinds of Hebrew writing, and as the sense is very little affected by a change of *persecution* into *domination*. Henderson, however, though he admits the plausibility, denies the necessity of this emendation. It may also be observed that a general application of this principle of criticism would make extensive changes in the text. For although there may be no case quite so strong as this, there are doubtless many where a slight change would produce entire uniformity. And yet the point in which the parallelism fails may sometimes be the very one designed to be the salient or emphatic point of the whole sentence. Such emendations should be therefore viewed with caution and suspicion, unless founded on external evidence, or but slightly affecting the meaning of the passage, as in the case before us. Umbreit, who adopts Doederlein's suggestion, gives to רדה and מרדת what is supposed to be

their primary sense, that of *treading* or *trampling* under foot.—Cocceius, who applies this to the tyranny of Antichrist, explains בְּלְתִּי סָרָה as a compound noun (like לֹא־עֵץ, chap. x. 15), meaning *non-apostasy*, and having reference to the persecution of true Christians on the false pretence of heresy, schism, or apostasy. By the side of this may be placed Abarbenel's interpretation of the whole verse as relating to God himself.

7. *At rest, quiet, is the whole earth. They burst forth into singing* (or a shout of joy). Jarchi seems to make the first clause the words of the song or shout mentioned in the second. There is no inconsistency between the clauses, as the first is not descriptive of *silence*, but of tranquillity and rest. *The land had rest* is a phrase employed in the book of Judges (*e. g.* chap. v. 31) to describe the condition of the country after a great national deliverance.—There is no need of supposing an ellipsis of יֹשְׁבֶיהָ to agree with the plural פָּצְחוּ, as Henderson does, since it may just as well be construed with הָאָרֶץ as a collective, or indefinitely, *they* (*i.e.* men in general) *break forth into singing*. Ewald, who gives the whole of this מָשָׁל in a species of blank verse, is particularly happy in his version of this sentence. (*Nun ruht, nun rastet die ganze Erde, man bricht in Jubel aus.*) The verb to *burst* is peculiarly descriptive of an ebullition of joy long suppressed or suddenly succeeding grief. Rosenmüller quotes a fine parallel from Terence. *Jamne erumpere hoc licet mihi gaudium?* The Hebrew phrase is beautifully rendered by the Septuagint, βοᾷ μετ᾽ εὐφροσύνης. It is a curious illustration of the worth of certain arguments, that while Gesenius makes the use of this phrase a proof that this prediction was not written by Isaiah, Henderson with equal right adduces it to prove that he was the author of the later chapters, in which the same expression frequently occurs.

8. Not only the earth and its inhabitants take part in this triumphant song or shout, but the trees of the forest. *Also* (or *even*) *the cypresses rejoice with respect to thee—the cedars of Lebanon* (saying) *now that thou art fallen* (literally *lain down*), *the feller* (or woodman, literally *the cutter*) *shall not come up against us.* Now that we are safe from thee, we fear no other enemy. The ברוש has been variously explained to be the fir, the ash, and the pine; but the latest authorities decide that it denotes a species of cypress. According to J. D. Michaelis, Antilibanus is clothed with firs, as Libanus or Lebanon proper is with cedars, and both are here introduced as joining in the general triumph. Vitringa makes עָלֵינוּ a noun with a suffix, meaning *our leaves* or *our tops* (cacumina nostra). Among other reasons, he alleges that כָּרַת is not construed with עַל elsewhere. But the accents might have taught him that עָלֵינוּ is dependent on יַעֲלֶה, and that הַכֹּרֵת is to be construed as a noun. Forerius reads *on us*, and supposes an allusion to the climbing of the tree by the woodman, in order to cut off the upper branches. Knobel refers the words in the same sense to the falling of the stroke upon the trees. It is much more natural, however, to regard the words as meaning simply *to us*, or more emphatically *against us*. The preposition in לְךָ, here as elsewhere, strictly denotes general relation, *as to*, *with respect to*. The specific sense of *over* or *against*, in all the cases which Gesenius cites, is gathered from the context. Instead of *liest*, Pagninus has *sleepest*, which might be metaphorically applied to death, but is not really the meaning of the word, which denotes a sleeping posture, but not sleep itself. As to the meaning of the figures in this verse, there are three distinct opinions. The first is, that the trees are emblems of kings and other great men. This is the explanation given in the Targum, and by Cocceius,

Vitringa, and other interpreters of that school. The second opinion is, that
the trees, as such, are introduced rejoicing that they shall no more be cut
down to open roads, or to supply materials for barricades or forts, or for
luxurious buildings. This prosaic exposition, proposed by Aben Ezra, and
approved by Grotius, is a favourite with some of the writers at the present
day who clamour loudest about Hebrew poetry, and insist most rigorously
on the application of the so-called laws of versification. The third opinion,
and the only one that seems consistent with a pure taste, is the one proposed by Calvin, who supposes this to be merely a part of one great picture,
representing universal nature as rejoicing. The *symbolical* and *mechanical*
interpretations are as much out of place here as they would be in a thousand
splendid passages of classical and modern poetry, where no one yet has ever
dreamed of applying them. Both here and elsewhere in the sacred books
inanimate nature is personified, and speaks herself, instead of being merely
spoken of.

> Ipsi lætitia voces ad sidera jactant
> Intonsi montes ; ipsæ jam carmina rupes,
> Ipsa sonant arbusta.

The Septuagint version of עָלָה as a preterite (ἀνέβη), which is followed by
all the early writers, is not only arbitrary and in violation of the *usus
loquendi*, but also objectionable on the ground that it implies too long an
interval between the utterance of the words and the catastrophe which called
them forth. The trees are not to be considered as historically stating what
has happened or not happened since a certain time, but as expressing, at
the very moment of the tyrant's downfall, or at least soon after it, a confident assurance of their future safety. In such a connection מֵאָז corresponds
exactly to the English *now that*. The present form given to both verbs
(now that thou liest, no one comes, &c.) by Luther and most of the later
Germans, approaches nearer to the true construction, but is neither so
exact nor so poetical as the literal translation of the future given by Rosenmüller and Ewald, and before them by the Vulgate (non ascendet qui
succidat nos). It is characteristic of Cocceius and his whole scheme, that
he makes the firs and cedars mean not only great men in general, but
ecclesiastical rulers in particular, and, in his exposition of the verse, refers
expressly to the English bishops who became reformers, and to the case
of the Venetians when subjected to a papal interdict in 1606. Such expositions have been well described by Stuart (Apocal. ii. p. 147) as
attempts to convert prophecy into a syllabus of civil and church history.

9. The bold personification is now extended from the earth and its forests
to the invisible or lower world, the inhabitants of which are represented as
aroused at the approach of the new victim and as coming forth to meet
him. *Hell from beneath is moved* (or *in commotion*) *for thee* (*i. e.* on
account of thee) *to meet thee* (*at*) *thy coming ; it rouses for thee the giants*
(the gigantic shades or spectres), *all the chief ones* (literally, *he-goats*) *of
the earth ; it raises from their thrones all the kings of the nations.*—שְׁאֹל
has already been explained (*vide supra*, chap. v. 14) as meaning first *a
grave* or individual sepulchre, and then *the grave* as a general receptacle, indiscriminately occupied by all the dead without respect to character, as
when we say, the rich and the poor, the evil and the good, lie together in
the grave, not in a single tomb, which would be false, but *under ground* and
in a common state of death and burial. The English word *hell*, though
now appropriated to the condition or the place of future torments, corresponds, in etymology and early usage, to the Hebrew word in question.

Gesenius derives it, with the German *Hölle*, from *Höhle* hollow, but the English etymologists from the Anglo-Saxon *helan*, to cover, which amounts to the same thing, the ideas of a *hollow* and a *covered* place being equally appropriate. The modern English versions have discarded the word *hell* as an equivocal expression, requiring explanation in order to be rightly understood. But as the Hebrew word *Sheol*, retained by Henderson, and the Greek word *Hades*, introduced by Lowth and Barnes, require explanation also, the strong and homely Saxon form will be preferred by every unsophisticated taste, not only to these Greek and Hebrew names, but also to the periphrases of Gesenius (Schattenreich), and Hendewerk (Todtenreich), and even to the simpler and more poetical expression (Unterwelt), employed by Hitzig and De Wette. Ewald and Umbreit have the good taste to restore the old word *Hölle* in their versions.—Two expressions have been faithfully transcribed by interpreters from one another, in relation to this passage, with a very equivocal effect upon its exposition. The one is that it is full of biting sarcasm, an unfortunate suggestion of Calvin's, which puts the reader on the scent for irony and even wit, instead of opening his mind to impressions of sublimity and tragic grandeur. The other, for which Calvin is in no degree responsible, is that we have before us not a mere prosopopœia or poetical creation of the highest order, but a chapter from the popular belief of the Jews, as to the locality, contents, and transactions of the unseen world. Thus Gesenius, in his lexicon and commentary, gives a minute topographical description of *Sheol*, as the Hebrews believed it to exist. With equal truth a diligent compiler might construct a map of hell, as conceived of by the English Puritans, from the descriptive portions of the Paradise Lost. The infidel interpreters of Germany regard the Scriptural and classical mythology precisely in the same light. But when Christian writers copy their expressions or ideas, they should take pains to explain whether the popular belief, of which they speak, was true or false, and if false, how it could be countenanced and sanctioned by inspired writers. This kind of exposition is moreover chargeable with a rhetorical incongruity in lauding the creative genius of the poet, and yet making all his grand creations commonplace articles of popular belief. The true view of the matter, as determined both by piety and taste, appears to be, that the passage now before us comprehends two elements, and only two, religious verities or certain facts, and poetical embellishments. It may not be easy to distinguish clearly between these ; but it is only between these that we are able or have any occasion to distinguish. The admission of a *tertium quid*, in the shape of superstitious fables, is as false in rhetoric as in theology. —Gesenius, in the earlier editions of his lexicon, and in his commentary on Isaiah, derives רפאים from רָפָה to be weak, and makes it a poetical description of the manes, shades, or phantoms of the unseen world. In the last edition of his lexicon, he derives it from רפא, to be still or quiet, a suppositious meaning founded on an Arabic analogy. By this new derivation he destroys the force of the argument derived from the expression in the next verse, " Thou art become *weak* (חלית) as we," to which it may also be objected that if the author designed any such allusion he would probably have used the word רפית from רפה. The ancient versions and all the early writers understand it to mean *giants*, to avoid which Gesenius makes רפאים in the prose books a mere proper name derived from רפא or רפה, their ancestor. But this last always has the article, and no exegetical tradition is more uniform than that which gives to *Rephaim* the sense of *giants*. Its application to the dead admits of several explanations, equally plausible with that of Gesenius, and entitled to the preference according to the modern laws of lexicography, because instead of multiplying they reduce the number of distinct significations. Thus the shades or spectres of the dead might naturally be conceived as actually larger than the living man, since that which is shadowy and indistinct is commonly exaggerated by the fancy. Or there may be an allusion to the Canaanitish giants who were exterminated by divine command and might well be chosen to represent the whole class of departed sinners. Or in this particular case, we may suppose the kings and great ones of the earth to be distinguished from the vulgar dead, as giants or gigantic forms. Either of these hypotheses precludes the necessity of finding a new root for a common word, or of denying its plain usage elsewhere. As to mere poetical effect, so often made a test of truth, there can be no comparison between the description of the dead as *weak* or *quiet ones*, and the sublime conception of gigantic shades or phantoms.—Aben E'zra and Kimchi call attention to the fact that שְׁאוֹל, in this one verse, is construed both with a masculine and feminine verb. Hitzig explains this on the ground that in the first clause Sheol is passive, in the second active ; Maurer, with more success, upon the ground that the nearest verb takes the feminine or proper gender of the noun, while the more remote one, by a common licence, retains the masculine or radical form, as in chap. xxxiii. 9. (See Gesenius, § 141, Rem. 1). Another method of removing the anomaly is afforded by an ingenious conjecture of J. D. Michaelis, who detaches בּוֹאֲךָ from what precedes, and makes it the subject of the verb עוֹרֵר. *Thy coming rouses the gigantic shades.* This is also recommended by its doing away with the somewhat harsh construction of בּוֹאֲךָ adverbially after לִקְרָאתְךָ. There is nothing indeed to hinder the adoption of this simple change, but the general expediency of adhering to the Masoretic interpunction wherever it is possible. Some of the older writers refer עוֹרֵר to the King of Hell, the objection to which is not its inconsistency with *Hebrew mythology*, but its being wholly arbitrary.—Because מִתַּחַת is sometimes simply equivalent to תַּחַת, Gesenius here prefers this secondary and diluted meaning to the one which he himself gives as the primary and proper one, and which is really demanded by the figure of hell's being roused and coming forth (or as it were, coming up) to meet him. The appropriateness of the strict sense here is recognized by Knobel, who renders it " *von unten her*, nämlich entgegen dem von oben kommmenden Chaldäer-könige."—Kings are poetically called עַתּוּדִים as the leaders of the flocks. J. D. Michaelis adopts another reading, on the ground that his readers might have laughed at the idea of he-goats rising from their thrones. But as this combination is at variance with the accents, the laugh might have been at the translator's own expense. Hitzig indeed proposes to change the interpunction, but he translates עַתּוּדִים the mighty ones (Mächtigen).—According to Clericus, the dead kings are here represented as arising from their ordinary state of profound repose upon their subterranean thrones, a supposition not required by the terms of the description, though it adds to its poetical effect. The same may be said of the opinion, that the kings here meant are specifically those whom the king of Babylon had conquered or oppressed. Kimchi seems to think that they are first represented as alarmed at the approach of their old enemy, but afterwards surprised to find him like themselves. רָגְזָה, however, does not necessarily imply fear, but denotes agitation or excitement from whatever cause. Cocceius of course finds a reference in this clause to the history of the Reformation.

10. *All of them shall answer and say to thee—thou also art made weak*

as we—to us art likened! Calvin persists in saying *haec sunt ludibria*, and his successors go beyond him in discovering severe taunts, bitter irony, and biting sarcasm, in this natural expression of surprise that one so far superior to themselves should now be a partaker of their weakness and disgrace. The idiomatic use of *answer*, both in Hebrew and in Greek, in reference even to the person speaking first, is so familiar that there can be no need of diluting it to *say* with Calvin (loquentur), or transforming it into *accost* with Lowth and Barnes, or *commence* with Henderson and the modern Germans. Nor is it necessary to suppose, with Œcolampadius, that they *answer* his thoughts and expectations of welcome with a taunting speech. Luther seems to adopt the old interpretations of responsive or alternate speech (um einander reden). Gesenius makes *answer* a secondary sense, but a different deduction is proposed by Winer, who makes reference to another person an essential part of the meaning. Pagninus translates it here *vociferabuntur*.—The interrogative form given to the last clause by Calvin and all the English versions is entirely arbitrary, and much less expressive than the simple assertion or exclamation preferred by the oldest and latest writers. Augusti supposes the words of the רפאים to extend through ver. 11, Rosenmüller through ver. 13, and some have even carried it through ver. 20 ; but Vitringa, Lowth, Gesenius, and the later writers, more correctly restrict it to the verse before us, partly because such brevity is natural and appropriate to the case supposed, partly because the termination is otherwise not easily defined. It is perfectly conceivable, however, that in such a piece of composition, the words of the chief speaker and of others whom he introduces, might insensibly run into one another without altering the sense.—As נמשל does not elsewhere take אל after it, Knobel supposes a *constructio praegnans* (Gesen. § 138), " thou art made like and actually brought to us," but this supposition is entirely gratuitous.

11. *Down to the grave is brought thy pride* (or *pomp*)—*the music of thy harps—under thee is spread the worm—thy covering is vermin.* That שאול is here used in its primary sense of *grave*, is clear from the second clause. גאון, like the English *pride*, may either signify an affection of the mind or its external object. The size and shape of the נבלים are of no exegetical importance here, as the word is evidently put for musical instruments or music in general, and this for mirth and revelry. (*Vide supra*, chap. v. 12). Both the nouns in the last clause are feminine, while the verb and participle are both masculine. This has led the latest writers to explain מכסיך as a noun. Lowth reads מכסך in the singular, on the authority of several manuscripts, versions, and editions. According to Gesenius and the later Germans, מכסיך is itself a singular form peculiar to the derivatives of לה roots. (See his Heb. Gr. § 90). But even if it be a plural, *coverings* may as well be said as *clothes*. Luther יצע also a noun meaning *bed*. De Wette makes it an impersonal verb ; a bed is made under thee with vermin (gebettet ist unter dir mit Gewürm). Gesenius treats it as a mere anomaly or idiomatic licence of construction. (See his Heb. Gr. § 144, *a*). Kimchi's explanation is that collective nouns admit both of a masculine and feminine construction. Junius and others suppose an allusion to the practice of embalming ; but the words seem naturally only to suggest the common end of all mankind, even the greatest not excepted. The imagery of the clause is vividly exhibited in Gill' homely paraphrase—" nothing but worms over him and worms under him, worms his bed and worms his bedclothes "—or as Ewald expresses it, with a curious allusion to the domestic usages of Germany, " worms, instead of silk, becoming his *under* and his

upper bed."—The expression is not strengthened but weakened by Lowth's interrogations, which are besides entirely arbitrary. As the Hebrew language has a form to express interrogation, it is not to be assumed in the absence of this form without necessity.

12. *How art thou fallen from heaven, Lucifer, son of the morning— felled to the ground, thou that didst lord it over the nations.* In the two other places where הֵילֵל occurs (Ezek. xxi. 17, xi. 2), it is an imperative signifying *howl.* This sense is also put upon it here by the Peshito, Aquila, Jerome in his commentary, and J. D. Michaelis. "Howl, son of the morning, for thy fall." Von Cölln makes the clause a parenthetical apostrophe—"How art thou fallen from heaven, O king—howl, son of the morning, for his fall!" The first construction mentioned was originally given by Rosenmüller and Gesenius, both of whom afterwards adopted another, found in all the ancient versions but the Syriac, in all the leading Rabbins, and in most of the early Christian writers. This interpretation makes the word a derivative of הָלַל to shine, denoting *bright one,* or more specifically *bright star,* or according to the ancients more specifically still the *morning star* or harbinger of daylight, called in Greek ἑωσφόρος and in Latin *lucifer.* The same derivation and interpretation is adopted by the latest German writers, except that they read הֵילָל to avoid the objection, that there is no such form of Hebrew nouns as הֵילֵל, and that where this form does occur, as we have seen, it is confessedly a verb. Tertullian and other fathers, Gregory the Great, and the scholastic commentators, regarding Luke x. 18 as an explanation of this verse, apply it to the fall of Satan, from which has arisen the popular perversion of the beautiful name *Lucifer* to signify the Devil. Erroneous as this exposition is, it scarcely deserves the severe reprehension which some later commentators give it who receive with great indulgence exegetical hypotheses much more absurd. In the last clause Knobel makes the Prophet represent the morning star as cut out from the solid vault of heaven, a convincing proof, of course, that the sacred writers entertained absurd ideas of the heavenly bodies. All other writers seem agreed that in the last clause the figure of a prostrate tree succeeds that of a fallen star. Clericus, Vitringa, and several other Latin writers, introduce another verb between נגדעת and לארץ (*excisus dejectus in terram*), on the ground that these do not cohere. In our idiom, however, there is no need of supplying any thing, to *fell* or *cut down to the ground* being equally good Hebrew and English. Junius and Tremellius give to חוֹלֵשׁ a passive or neuter sense, as in Job xiv. 10, and make the clause comparative—weakened above (*i. e.* more than) the nations. It is commonly explained, however, as a description of the Babylonian tyranny. Hitzig and Hendewerk understand the image to be that of a tree overspreading other nations, as in Ezek. xxxi. 6, 17. Gesenius and Umbreit, with the older writers, give חלש the sense of weakening, subduing, or discomfiting, as in Exod. xvii. 13. The עַל is then a mere connective like the English preposition in the phrase to *triumph over* or to *lord it over.* Cocceius regards it as an elliptical expression for אשר על— oppressing those who were over the nations—and applies it to the tyranny of the papal see over the monarchies of Europe, after specifying some of which he adds with great naïveté, *longum esset in omnia ire.* Vitringa adopts the same construction of חלש על, but applies the verse to the literal king of Babylon. J. H. Michaelis takes חוֹלֵשׁ as a noun (debilitator), which removes the difficulty as to the construction. The Peshito and J. D. Michaelis gives

to חלש the unauthorised sense of despising, looking down upon.   Calvin adopts an ancient Jewish opinion that it means *casting lots* upon the nations, as to the time or order of attack, or as to the treatment of the conquered.

13. His fall is aggravated by the impious extravagance of his pretensions.   *And* (yet) *thou hadst said in thy heart* (or to thyself)—*the heavens will I mount* (or *scale*)—*above the stars of God will I raise my throne—and I will sit in the mount of meeting* (or *assembly*)—*in the sides of the north.* It is universally agreed that he is here described as aiming at equality with God himself.   Grotius understands by *heaven* the land of Judah, and by *stars* the doctors of the law.   Vitringa explains *heaven* to be the sanctuary, and *stars* the priests.   Cocceius applies the whole verse to the usurpations of the Roman See.   But most interpreters receive the first clause in its natural meaning.   As to the other, there are two distinct interpretations, one held by the early writers, the other by the modern since John David Michaelis.   According to the first, הַר־מוֹעֵד is analogous to אֹהֶל־מוֹעֵד, and denotes the mountain where God agreed to meet the people, to commune with them, and to make himself known to them (Exod. xxv. 22, xxix. 42, 43). Calvin indeed gives to מוֹעֵד the sense of *testimony* or *covenant*, but does not differ from the rest as to the application of the phrase.   All the interpreters, who are now referred to, understand by הַר־מוֹעֵד mount Zion or mount Moriah.   Those who adopt the former explanation are under the necessity of explaining *sides of the north* by the assumption that Zion lay upon the north side of Jerusalem, which is expressly taught by Kimchi (כי ציון לצפון ירושלם).   Grotius, Junius, Clericus, and Lightfoot.   Others, admitting the notorious fact that Zion was on the south side of the city, suppose the mountain meant to be Moriah, lying on the north side of Zion.   So Cocceius, Vitringa, Gataker, and others.   On the same hypothesis, both Zion and Moriah might have been included, one as the mount of congregation and the other as the sides of the north, in reference to the tabernacle and temple, as the places where God's presence was successively revealed.   According to this view of the passage, it describes the king of Babylon as insulting God by threatening to erect his throne upon those consecrated hills, or even affecting to be God, like antichrist, of whom Paul says, with obvious allusion to this passage, that he " opposeth and exalteth himself above all that is called God, or that is worshipped, so that he, as God, sitteth in the temple of God, shewing himself that he is God" (2 Thess. ii. 4).   To this interpretation three objections have been urged.   1. The first is that it involves an anticlimax unworthy of Isaiah. After threatening to ascend the heavens and surmount the stars, something equally or still more aspiring might have been expected; but instead of this, he simply adds, I will sit upon mount Zion and mount Moriah north of it.   This by itself can have little weight, partly because it is a mere rhetorical objection, partly because it supposes Zion and Moriah to be mentioned as mere hills, whereas they are referred to as the residence of God, and by his presence invested with a dignity equal at least to that of clouds and stars.   2. But in the next place it is urged that although this allusion to the sacred mountains of Jerusalem would be perfectly appropriate if uttered by a Jew, it is wholly misplaced in the mouth of a heathen, the rather as Isaiah makes the heathen speak elsewhere in accordance with their own superstitions, and not in the language of the true religion.   (See chap. x. 10 ; xxxvi. 18, 19 ; xxxvii. 12). In weighing this objection, due allowance should be made for the facts, that the writer is himself a Hebrew, writing for the use of Hebrew readers, and

that the conqueror, in uttering such a threat, would of course have reference to the belief of the conquered, and might therefore naturally threaten to rival or excel their God upon his chosen ground. 3. The third objection is that the failure of these impious hopes is obviously implied, whereas the threatening to take possession of mount Zion and Moriah was abundantly fulfilled before the time at which we must suppose this song of triumph to be uttered. This is true, so far as the mere possession of the ground is concerned, but not true as to the equality with God which the conqueror expected to derive from it, as the first clause clearly shews. He had said, I will sit upon the sacred hills, and thereby be the equal of Jehovah; but instead of this he is brought down to the grave. Whether the weight of argument preponderates in favour of the old interpretation or against it, that of authority is now altogether on the side of the new one. This, as originally stated by J. D. Michaelis, makes the Babylonian speak the language of a heathen, and with reference to the old and wide-spread oriental notion of a very high mountain in the extreme north, where the gods were believed to reside, as in the Greek Olympus. This is the Meru of the Hindoo mythology, and the Elborz or Elborj of the old Zend books. The details of this belief are given by Gesenius in the first appendix to his Commentary. According to J. D. Michaelis, there is also an allusion to this figment in the mention of the stars, which were supposed to rest upon the summit of the mountain. The meaning of the clause, as thus explained, is, " I will take my seat among or above the gods upon their holy mountain." This interpretation is supposed to be obscurely hinted in the Septuagint Version (ἐν ὄρει ὑψηλῷ, ἐπὶ τὰ ὄρη τὰ ὑψηλὰ τὰ πρὸς βοῤῥᾶν) and in the similar terms of the Peshito. Theodoret remarks upon the verse, that the highest mountains upon earth are said to be those separating Media and Assyria, meaning the highest summits of the Caucasus. The Targum also, though it renders הַר־מוֹעֵד *mountain of the covenant*, translates the last words סִיפֵי צְפוֹנָא *extremities of the north*. As the mythological allusion is in this case put into the mouth of a heathen, there is not the same objection to it as in other cases where it seems to be recognised and sanctioned by the writer. It may be made a question, however, whether the difficulty of an anticlimax is not as real here as in the other case. How is the oriental Olympus any more in keeping with the skies and stars, than Zion and Moriah, considered as the dwelling of Jehovah? It may also be objected that the usual meaning of מוֹעֵד is here departed from, and that, according to Gesenius's own shewing the sacred mountain of the Zend and Hindoo books is not in the extreme north, but in the very centre of the earth. It might even be doubted whether צפון ירכתי means the extreme north at all, were it not for the analogous expression in ver. 15, which will be explained below. Notwithstanding these objections, all the recent writers have adopted this hypothesis, including Hengstenberg, who gives the same sense to ירכתי צפון in his commentary on Ps. xlviii. 3. Ewald translates הַר־מוֹעֵד the mountain of all the gods (im Berge aller Götter). The general meaning of the verse is of course the same on either hypothesis. It is characteristic of Knobel's eagerness to convict the sacred writers of astronomical blunders, that he makes the simple phrase *above the stars* mean on the upper side of the vault as the stars are on the under side. The expression *stars of God* does not merely describe them as his creatures, but as being near him, in the upper world or heaven.

14. *I will mount above the cloud-heights; I will make myself like the Most High.* This is commonly regarded as a simple expression of unbounded arrogance; but Knobel thinks there may be an allusion to the oriental cus-

tom of calling their kings gods, or to the fact that Syrian and Phenician kings did actually so describe themselves (Ezek. xxviii. 2, 6, 9 ; 2 Macc. ix. 12). According to Grotius and Vitringa, the singular noun עָב is here used to designate the cloud of the divine presence in the tabernacle and temple. This would agree well with the old interpretation of ver. 13 ; but, according to the other hypothesis, עָב is a collective, meaning clouds in general. Hendewerk describes this as a literal explanation of the foregoing figures. It is commonly regarded as a continuation of them. Some understand him to mean that he will ride upon the clouds as his chariot ; but Gesenius, that he will control the clouds, as conquerors are elsewhere said to ride on the heights of the earth (chap. lviii. 14; Deut. xxxii. 13, xxxiii. 29; Micah. i. 3). Some suppose *cloud* to denote a multitude, as in the phrase a *cloud of witnesses* (Heb. xii. 1), and so understand the Chaldee Paraphrase (כל עמא), which appears, however, to be only another method of expressing the idea of superiority. Gill thinks that the *clouds* may be the ministers of the word. Cocceius makes it mean the word itself, and the ascent above them the suppression of the Scriptures and their subordination to tradition by the Church of Rome, from which he draws the inference that the Pope is not the vicar of Christ, but the king of Babylon, and adds with great simplicity, " non morabimur in his, *quæ sunt evidentia*, diutius." As אֲדַמֶּה is a reflexive form (Gesen. § 53, 2), it means not merely *I will be like*, but *I will make myself like*, or as Michaelis supposes, *I will act like*. Sanctius understands him as declaring that he will work miracles as God had done so often from the clouds. As עֶלְיוֹן was a term also used by the Phenicians to denote the supreme God, Henderson regards it here as specially emphatic. " Not satisfied with making himself equal to any of the inferior deities, his ambition led him to aspire after an equality with the supreme." He also observes that the use of this term does not imply that the king of Babylon was a monotheist, since in all the modifications of polytheism, one god has been regarded as superior to the rest.

15. But instead of being exalted to heaven, *thou shalt only be brought down to hell*—(not to the sides of the north, but) *to the depths of the pit*. אַךְ has its proper sense of *only* (Winer s. v.) but in order to accommodate the idiom of other tongues variously rendered *but* (Lowth), *yes* (J. D. Michaelis), *no* (Ewald) &c. Some interpreters observe that שְׁאוֹל is here confounded with the grave—others that בּוֹר must have the sense of שְׁאוֹל, opposite deductions from the same parallelism. The correct view of the matter is taken by Knobel, who observes that the idea of שְׁאוֹל itself is originally nothing more than that of the grave, so that the two run into one another, without any attempt to discriminate precisely what belongs exclusively to either. (*Vide supra*, ad v. 9.) Against the strict application of the last clause to the grave is the subsequent description of the royal body as unburied. But the imagery is unquestionably borrowed from the grave.—Clericus and Barnes understand by *sides* the horizontal excavations in the oriental sepulchres or catacombs. But according to its probable etymology the Hebrew word does not mean *sides* in the ordinary sense, but rather *hinder parts* and then *remote parts* or *extremities*, as it is explained by the Targum here and in ver. 13. The specific reference may be either to extreme height, extreme distance, or extreme depth, according to the context. Here the last sense is required by the mention of the *pit*, and the word is accordingly translated in the Vulgate *profundum*, and in the Septuagint more freely τὰ θεμέλια.

16. *Those seeing thee shall gaze* (or stare) *at thee, they shall look at thee*

attentively, (and say) *Is this the man that made the earth shake, that made kingdoms tremble?* Umbreit, Knobel, and others suppose the Prophet to be still describing the reception of the king in the world below. Gill, on the contrary, says "these are the words of the dead, speaking of the living, when they should see the carcase of the king of Babylon lying on the ground." This agrees much better with the subsequent context; but the simplest and most natural supposition is that the scene in the other world is closed, and that the Prophet, or triumphant Israel, is now describing what shall take place above ground. The gazing mentioned in the first clause is not merely the effect of curiosity, but of incredulous surprise. The Vulgate gives יַשְׁגִּיחוּ the specific sense of *stooping down* (inclinabuntur) in order to examine more attentively. J. D. Michaelis strangely ascribes to it the sense of regarding with tender sympathy, which is as arbitrary as Calvin's favourite notion of derision, here repeated (iterum propheta regem deridet), and faithfully copied by the later writers. The prominent if not the only feeling here expressed is neither scorn nor pity, but astonishment. יִתְבּוֹנָנוּ is supposed to be descriptive of the salutary influence on the spectators, by Clericus (prudente se gerent) and Augusti (an deinem Beyspiele klug werden), and the same idea seems to be expressed by Aben Ezra (סילמדו ביכס בעַנְוְרֶן). But the usual sense of paying strict attention is much more appropriate. Henderson's idea that the Hithpael of בִּין means to *consider and reconsider*, as if unable to believe one's senses, is not justified by usage, and appears to be founded on a misapprehension of a remark by Hitzig, who attaches the same meaning not to the peculiar form of one verb but to the junction of the two. Gesenius and De Wette weaken the second clause by changing its idiomatic form for a more modern one, *before whom the earth shook, kingdoms trembled.* Ewald, Umbreit, and Hendewerk, restore the original construction.

17. *Made a* (fruitful or habitable) *world like the desert, destroyed its cities, and its captives did not set free homewards.* These are still the words of the astonished spectators as they behold the body of the slain king. The contrast in the first clause is heightened by supposing an intentional allusion to the primary meaning of תֵּבֵל, as expressed by Cocceius (frugiferam) and Junius (orbem habitalem). The version *inhabited land,* given by J. D. Michaelis and Augusti, would be still better but for the constant usage of תֵּבֵל as an equivalent to אֶרֶץ in its widest sense. Hitzig observes that תֵּבֵל must be taken as a masculine noun, in order to account for the suffix in עָרָיו, which cannot be referred to the king like that in אֲסִירָיו. If so, it is better to refer the latter also to the same antecedent for the sake of uniformity, as Knobel does, since they may just as well be said to belong to the world as the cities. But the same end may be gained, and the anomaly of gender done away, by referring both the pronouns to the king himself, who might just as well be said to have destroyed *his own cities* as his own *land* and his own *people* (ver. 20), the rather as his sway is supposed to have been universal. The construction of the last clause is somewhat difficult. The general meaning evidently is that he did not release his prisoners, and this is expressed in a general way by the Septuagint and Peshito. The Targum reads, *who did not open the door to his captives;* the Vulgate more exactly, *the prison* (carcerem). This construction supplies a preposition before *captives,* and regards the termination of ביתה as merely paragogic. Junius and Tremellius understand it as the *local* or *directive* ה, and make the word mean *home* or *homewards* (non solvebat reversuros domum). This construction is adopted by Henderson and others, who suppose the

same ellipsis of the verb *return* or *send* before the last word. But the other recent versions follow De Dieu in connecting פתח directly with ביתה, without supplying anything, and giving to the verb itself the sense of releasing or dismissing. This construction is also given in the margin of the English Bible (*did not let his prisoners loose homewards*), while the text coincides with the Vulgate (*opened not the house of his prisoners*).

18. *All kings of nations, all of them, lie in state* (or *glory*), *each in his house.* There is here a special reference to the peculiar oriental feeling with respect to burial. Diodorus says that the Egyptians paid far more attention to the dwellings of the dead than of the living. Some of the greatest national works have been intended for this purpose, such as the pyramids, the temple of Belus, and the cemetery at Persepolis. The environs of Jerusalem are full of ancient sepulchres. The want of burial is spoken of in Scripture as disgraceful even to a private person (1 Kings xiii. 22), much more to a sovereign (2 Chron. xxi. 20, xxxiv. 24). The ancient oriental practice of burying above ground and in solid structures, often reared by those who were to occupy them (*vide infra*, chap. xxii. 16) will account for the use of *house* here in the sense of *sepulchre*, without supposing any reference to the burial of kings within their palaces. בַּיִת is not used elsewhere absolutely in the same sense, but the grave is called בית עולם (Eccles. xii. 5) and בית מועד לכלחי (Job xxx. 23), the first of which phrases is copied in the Chaldee Paraphrase of that before us (בבית עלמיה). Henderson's version, *lie in state*, may seem appropriate to burial, but is in fact happily descriptive of the oriental method of sepulture. Lowth's version, *lie down*, gives too active a meaning to the verb, which is intended to describe the actual condition of the dead. The words of this verse might possibly be understood to describe the generality of kings as dying in their beds and at home—*they have lain down*, (*i. e.*) died *each in his own house.* But there is no need of dissenting from the unanimous judgment of interpreters, that the verse relates to burial. Knobel supposes a specific allusion to the kings whom the deceased had conquered or oppressed; but nothing more is necessarily expressed by the words than the general practice with respect to royal bodies.

19. With the customary burial of kings he now contrasts the treatment of the Babylonian's body. *And thou art cast out from thy grave—like a despised branch, the raiment of the slain, pierced with the sword, going down to the stones of the pit,* (even) *like a trampled carcass* (as thou art). Gesenius and the other modern writers understand the Prophet as contrasting the neglect or exposure of the royal body with the honourable burial of the other slain, those who are (soon) to go down to the stones of the grave, *i. e.* to be buried in hewn sepulchres. Hitzig understands by the stones of the pit, the stones which closed the mouths of the sepulchres, —Henderson, stone coffins or sarcophagi—Knobel, the ordinary stone tombs of the east resembling altars. All these interpreters follow Cocceius in explaining לְבֻשׁ as a passive participle, *clothed* (*i. e.* covered) *with the slain*, which may also be the meaning of the Vulgate version, *obvolutus cum his qui interfecti sunt gladio*. But this form of expression, *covered with the slain who are buried in stone sepulchres*, is rather descriptive of a common burial than of any invidious distinction. It is much more natural to understand יוֹרְדֵי אֶל אַבְנֵי בור as a description of the indiscriminate interment of a multitude of slain in a common grave, such as a pit containing stones or filled with stones to cover the bodies. The reference assumed by the Dutch

Annotators and Doederlein, to the covering of the slain with stones upon the surface of the earth, is forbidden by the terms *going down* and *pit*. The explanation just proposed would be consistent either with Cocceius's interpretation of לְבֻשׁ or with the older one which makes it as usual a noun meaning raiment, and supplies the particle of comparison before it. In the latter case, the direct comparison is not with the bodies of the common dead, but with their blood-stained garments, as disgusting and abhorrent objects. As מָעַן occurs elsewhere only in Gen. xlv. 17, where it means to *load*, Cocceius here translates it *onustis gladio,* and Junius *onustorum (crebris ictibus) gladii.* The latter writer adopts the Rabbinical derivation of the word from a cognate root in Arabic, which means to *pierce* or *perforate*. The kind of death is supposed by some to be particularly mentioned, in order to account for the staining of the garments. By גֵּזֶר נִתְעָב Lowth understands a tree on which a malefactor had been hung, and which was therefore looked upon as cursed (Deut. xxi. 23 ; Gal. iii. 13), and according to Maimonides was buried with him. This ingenious combination accounts for the use of the strong word נִתְעָב, which is scarcely applicable to the useless or even troublesome and noxious branches that are thrown aside and left to rot. To remove the same difficulty, J. D. Michaelis gives גֵּזֶר the supposititious sense of *ulcer,* here put for a leprous body. Some suppose גֵּזֶר to be here used, as in chap. xi. 1, with a genealogical allusion, the despised branch or scion of a royal stock. מִקִּבְרֶךָ is explained by Gesenius and Maurer to mean simply *without a grave,* by Hitzig and Knobel *away from thy grave,* on the ground that he had not been in it. This prosaic objection has not hindered Ewald from using the expressive phrase *out of thy grave,* which is no more incorrect or unintelligible than it is to speak of an heir as being deprived of his estate, or a king's son of his crown, before they are in actual possession. Henderson even goes so far as to deny that מִן depends upon the verb at all, a statement equally at variance with usage and the Masoretic accents. In order to reconcile this verse with the history of Nebuchadnezzar, to whom they exclusively apply it, the Jews have an old tradition, given not only in the Seder Olam but by Jerome in almost the same words, that when Nebuchadnezzar recovered his reason, he found Evilmerodach his son upon the throne, and threw him into prison. When the father died, the son refused to become king again, lest his predecessor should again return ; and in order to convince him of the old man's death, the body was disinterred and exposed to public view. That the terms of the prediction were literally fulfilled in the last king of Babylon, Nabonned or Belshazzar, is admitted by Gesenius to be highly probable, from the hatred with which this ἀνόσιος βασιλεύς (as Xenophon calls him) was regarded by the people. Such a supposition is not precluded by the same historian's statement that Cyrus gave a general permission to bury the dead ; for, as Henderson observes, his silence in relation to the king rather favours the conclusion that he was made an exception, either by the people or the conqueror. There is no need, however, as we have already seen, of seeking historical details in this passage, which is rather a prediction of the downfall of the empire than of the fate of any individual monarch.

20. *Thou shalt not be joined with them* (the other kings of the nations) *in burial, because thy land thou hast destroyed, thy people thou hast slain. Let the seed of evil-doers be named no more for ever.* Gesenius and other recent writers think the reference to the kings in ver. 18 too remote, and this is one principal reason for interpreting ver. 19 in the way already

mentioned, as exhibiting a contrast between those who receive burial and those who do not. The sense of this verse then will be, *thou shalt not be joined with them, i. e.* with those who go down to the stones of the grave. But the remoteness of the antecedent in ver. 18, ceases to occasion any difficulty when the whole of the nineteenth verse is a description of the king's unburied and exposed condition. On this hypothesis, ver. 18 describes the state of other deceased kings; ver. 19, the very different state of this one, and ver. 20 draws the natural inference, that the latter cannot be joined in burial with the former. Instead of *thy land* and *thy people*, the Septuagint has *my land* and *my people*, making the clause refer directly to the Babylonian conquest and oppression of Judea. Jerome suggests, that the same sense may be put upon the common text by making *thy land* and *thy people* mean the land and people subjected to thy power in execution of God's righteous judgments. But the only natural interpretation of the words is that which applies them to the Babylonian tyranny as generally exercised. The charge here brought against the king implies that his power was given him for a very different purpose. The older writers read the last clause as a simple prediction. Thus the English Version is, the seed of evil-doers shall never be renowned. But the later writers seem to make it more emphatic by giving the future the force of an imperative or optative. For the sense of זֶרַע מְרֵעִים *vide supra*, chap. i. 4. Hitzig and Henderson take זֶרַע even here in the sense of a race or generation, and suppose יִקָּרֵא to refer to monumental inscriptions. Some of the older writers understand the clause to mean that the names of the wicked shall not be perpetuated by transmission in the line of their descendants. Others explain the verb as meaning to be called, *i. e.* proclaimed or celebrated. It is now pretty generally understood to mean, or to express a wish, that the posterity of such should not be spoken of at all, implying both extinction and oblivion.

21. That the downfall of the Babylonian power shall be perpetual, is now expressed by a command to slaughter the children of the king. *Prepare for his sons a slaughter, for the iniquity of their fathers. Let them not arise and possess the earth, and fill the face of the world with cities.* This verse is regarded by Gesenius, Rosenmüller, Maurer, and Umbreit, as the close of the triumphal song beginning in ver. 4. Hitzig and Hendewerk suppose it to have closed in the preceding verse, as the address is no longer to the king of Babylon. Ewald extends it through ver. 23. But these distinctions rest upon a false assumption of exact and artificial structure. The dramatic form of the prediction is repeatedly shifted, so that the words of the triumphant Jews, of the dead, of the Prophet, and of God himself, succeed each other, as it were, insensibly, and without any attempt to make the points of the transition prominent. The command in the first clause is not addressed specifically to the Medes and Persians, but more indefinitely to the executioners of God's decree against Babylon, or, as Calvin calls them, his *lictores aut carnifices*. The reference is not to the children of Nebuchadnezzar or Belshazzar, as the Rabbins and others have assumed, but to the progeny of the ideal being who here represents the Babylonian monarch. Hitzig, Umbreit, and Hendewerk, make מַטְבֵּחַ mean a place of slaughter (Schlachtbank), after the analogy of the cognate form מִזְבֵּחַ. Gesenius and Ewald give it the general sense of massacre (Blutbad). There are three constructions of the last clause authorised by usage. מָלְאוּ may agree either with עָרִים, or with פְּנֵי, or with בָּנָיו. The last is entitled to the preference, because it is the subject of the two preceding verbs. Cocceius,

Hendewerk, Umbreit, and others make this last clause the expression of a hope or a promise—and (then) the world will (again) be full of cities—or, that the world may (again) be full of cities. Gesenius, who ascribes this construction to Von Cölln, objects that it gives to בַּל one half of its meaning (*that*), and rejects the other half (*not*). But the subjunctive construction of the clause is a mere assimilation to the forms of occidental syntax. The Hebrew construction is, they shall not arise (or let them not arise), and the negative may either be confined to the first two verbs or extended to the third. The last, however, is more natural on account of the exact resemblance in the form of the two members, מָלְאוּ פְנֵי־תֵבֵל and יָקֻשׁוּ אָרֶץ.— The Targum, followed by the Rabbins, gives to עָרִים the sense of *enemies*, as in 1 Sam. xxviii. 16, Ps. cxxxix. 20, and fill the face of the world with enemies—or enemies fill the face of the world. This meaning of the word is adopted by Vitringa, Gesenius, Rosenmüller, and others. Hitzig reads עִיִּים, ruins ; Ewald, עָרִיצִים, tyrants ; Knobel, רָעִים, wicked ones. The best sense, on the whole, is afforded by the old interpretation given by the Vulgate and Saadias, and retained by Umbreit and Hendewerk, which takes עָרִים in its usual sense as the plural of עִיר, and understands the clause to mean, lest they overspread and colonise the earth. The objection that the Babylonians had been just before described as wasters and destroyers, cannot weigh against the constant usage of the word.

22. This verse contains an intimation that the destruction just predicted is to be the work not of man merely but of God, and is to comprehend not only the royal family but the whole population. *And I (myself) will rise up against them* (or *upon them*), *saith Jehovah of hosts, and will cut off from Babylon* (literally, *with respect to Babylon*) *name, and remnant, and progeny, and offspring, saith Jehovah*. The last four nouns are put together to express posterity in the most general and universal manner. נִין and נֶכֶד occur together in Gen. xxi. 31, Job xviii. 19. The specific meaning *son* and *nephew* (*i. e.* nepos, grandson), given in the English version and most of the early writers, and retained by Umbreit, is derived from the Chaldee paraphrase (בַּר וּבַד בַּר). Aben Ezra makes the language still more definite by explaining שֵׁם to be a man himself, שְׁאָר a father, נִין a son, and נֶכֶד a grandson. This supposes שְׁאָר to be equivalent in meaning to שְׁאֵר בָּשָׂר, used in Lev. xviii. 6, xxv. 49, for a blood relation. So Montanus renders it here, *consanguineum*. But the word which has that sense is of a different form, and according to Gesenius, of a different origin. The more general meaning of the terms, now held to be correct, is given in the Septuagint (ὄνομα καὶ κατάλειμμα καὶ σπέρμα) and the Vulgate (nomen et reliquias et germen et progeniem). Doederlein's version, *the fruitful and the barren*, is entirely unauthorised. Grotius remarks upon the threatening of this verse, *nempe ad tempus !* Cocceius applies this verse and the one preceding to the civil and ecclesiastical dignitaries subject to the Roman see, and thinks it probable that נִין and נֶכֶד may be distinctive terms for bishops and kings. The threatening is applied by other classes of interpreters to Nebuchadnezzar and Belshazzar, but most correctly to the king of Babylon, not as a collective appellation merely, but as an ideal person representing the whole line of kings. The agreement of the prophecy with history is shewn by J. D. Michaelis from the facts, that none of the ancient royal family of Babylon ever regained a throne, and that no Babylonian empire ever rose after the destruction of the first, Alexander the Great's project of restoring it having been defeated by his death.

23. *And I will render it* (literally, *place it for*) *a possession* (or *inheri-*

tance) of the porcupine, and pools of water, and will sweep it with the broom (or besom) of destruction. קִפֹּד has been variously explained to be the tortoise, beaver, bittern, &c., but since Bochart it is commonly agreed to mean the porcupine or hedgehog. It is here mentioned only as a solitary animal frequenting marshy grounds. The construction is not, I will make the pools of water a possession, &c., by drying them up—nor, I will make it a possession for pools of water—but I will make it a possession for the porcupine and (will convert it into) pools of water. The exposure of the level plains of Babylonia to continual inundation without great preventive care, and the actual promotion of its desolation by this very cause, are facts distinctly stated by the ancient writers. Some suppose this evil to have had its origin in the diversion of the waters of the Euphrates by Cyrus. The Septuagint version of the last clause (καὶ θήσω αὐτὴν πηλοῦ βάραθρον εἰς ἀπώλειαν), adopted with little variation by Clericus (demergam eam in profundum lutum ut eam perdam), and by Lowth (I will plunge it in the miry gulf of destruction), supposes וְטֵאטֵאתִיהָ to be derived from טִיט, clay or mire. J. D. Michaelis refers it to an Arabic root meaning to sink or plunge, and thus excludes the allusion to mire (in den Abgrund des Nichts versenken). Three of the ancient versions, followed by the Talmud and rabbinical interpreters, make it mean to *sweep*, which is adopted by the latest writers. Gesenius formerly derived it from an obsolete root טוא, but in his Thesaurus from טִיט, supposing the verb properly to mean the removal of dirt. Thus Aben Ezra explains מטאטא to be an instrument with which dirt is removed (זֶּטֶן שֶׁמְסִירוּ בוֹ הַזֻּחַן). Lee, from an Arabic root, explains the clause to mean, I will humble it with the humiliation of destruction (Heb. Lex. s. v). The Vulgate renders הִשְׁמֵד as a participle (*terens*), in which it is followed by Calvin (*evacuans*), while others more correctly make it an infinitive or verbal noun.

24. From the distant view of the destruction of Babylon, the Prophet suddenly reverts to that of the Assyrian host, either for the purpose of making one of these events accredit the prediction of the other, or for the purpose of assuring true believers, that while God had decreed the deliverance of his people from remoter dangers, he would also protect them from those near at hand. *Jehovah of hosts hath sworn, saying, Surely* (literally, *if not*) *as I have planned* (or imagined) *it has come to pass, and as I have devised, it shall stand* (or be established). On the elliptical formula of swearing, *vide supra*, chap. v. 9. We may either supply before אִם לֹא, with Calvin and Vitringa, let me not be recognised as God—or as Junius briefly and boldly expresses it, *mentiar*—or else we may suppose the elliptical expression to have been transferred from man to God, without regard to its original and proper import. Kimchi explains הָיְתָה to be a preterite used for a future (עָבַר בִּמְקוֹם עָתִיד), and this construction is adopted in most versions, ancient and modern. It is, however, altogether arbitrary and in violation of the only safe rule as to the use of the tenses, viz. that they should have their proper and distinctive force unless forbidden by the context or the nature of the subject, which is very far from being the case here, as we shall see below. Gesenius and De Wette evade the difficulty by rendering both the verbs as presents, a construction which is often admissible and even necessary in a descriptive context, but when used indiscriminately or inappropriately, tends both to weaken and obscure the sense. Ewald and Umbreit make the first verb present and the second future, which is scarcely if at all less objectionable. The true force of the preterite and future forms, as here employed, is recognised by Aben Ezra, who explains the clause to mean that according

to God's purpose, it has come to pass and will come to pass hereafter (בֶן הִיה וּבֵן יִהְיֶה לְעַתִּיד). The antithesis is rendered still more prominent by Jarchi, by whom the verse is paraphrased as follows—" Thou hast seen, O Nebuchadnezzar how the words of the prophets of Israel have been fulfilled in Sennacherib, to break Assyria in my land, and by this thou mayest know that what I have purposed against thee shall also come to pass." (Compare Ezek. xxxi. 3–18). This view of the matter makes the mention of Assyria in this connection altogether natural, as if he had said, of the truth of these predictions against Babylon a proof has been afforded in the execution of the threatenings against Assyria. The only objection to it is, that the next verse goes on to speak of the Assyrian overthrow, which would seem to imply that the last clause of this verse, as well as the first, relates to that event. Another method of expounding the verse, therefore, is to apply הִיתה and תקום to the same events, but in a somewhat different sense—" As I intended, it has come to pass, and as I purposed, it shall continue." The Assyrian power is already broken, and shall never be restored. This strict interpretation of the preterite does not necessarily imply that the prophecy was actually uttered after the destruction of Sennacherib's army. Such would indeed be the natural inference from this verse alone, but for reasons which will be explained below, it is more probable that the Prophet merely takes his stand in vision at a point of time between the two events of which he speaks, so that both verbs are really prophetic, the one of a remote, the other of a proximate futurity, but for that very reason their distinctive forms should be retained and recognised. Yet the only modern writers who appear to do so in translation, are Calvin and Cocceius, who have *factum est*, and J. D. Michaelis, who has *ist geschehen*. The acute and learned, but superficial Clericus jumps to the conclusion that this verse begins an entirely new prophecy, a dictum eagerly adopted by the modern German critics. who are always predisposed to favour new views of the connection and arrangement of the text. Rosenmüller represents these verses as a fragment of a larger " poem " on the Assyrian overthrow. Gesenius confidently sets it down as the conclusion or continuation of the tenth chapter, with which it exhibits several verbal coincidences. Hendewerk, with still more precision, gives it place between vers. 27 and 28 of that chapter. Hitzig and Knobel put it after the twelfth chapter, and regard it as a prophecy of later date, but having direct reference to that in chaps. x.–xii. Ewald assigns it the same relative position, but interpolates the last three verses of the seventeenth chapter and the whole of the eighteenth between the twelfth or rather the eleventh (for he looks upon the twelfth as spurious) and the paragraph before us, which he takes to be the winding up of the whole prophecy. The first thing that will strike the reader in this statement is the principle assumed by all the hypotheses, viz., that similar passages must belong together, which is tantamount to saying that whatever a writer had to say upon a certain point, or in a certain manner, he must have said once for all in a single and continuous composition. On the same ground all those passages in the odes of Horace, which contain the praises of Augustus or Mæcenas, might be brought together into a cento of endless repetitions. To an ordinary reader it is scarcely more surprising that an author should use the same expressions in two different productions, than that he should repeat them in the same. But even if the principle assumed were less unreasonable than it is, the different and inconsistent ways in which it is applied, and the assurance with which each new-comer puts his predecessors in the wrong, will satisfy most readers that conjectures which admit of being varied and multiplied *ad libitum* must needs be worthless. This conclusion is confirmed by the existence of a strong and very obvious motive, on the part of neological interpreters, for severing this paragraph, if possible, from what precedes. The resemblance of these verses to the undisputed writings of Isaiah is too strong to leave a doubt as to their origin. If left then in connection with the previous context, they establish the antiquity and authenticity of this astonishing prediction against Babylon, beyond the reach of cavil. And if this be admitted, we have here a signal instance of prophetic foresight exercised at least two centuries before the event. This conclusion must be avoided at all cost and hazards, and the sacrifice of taste and even common sense is nothing in comparison with such an object. A remote design of this kind may frequently be traced in critical decisions, which, to superficial observation or to blinded admiration, seem to be determined solely by the unbiassed application of universal laws. In the case before us, the unsoundness of the principle, its arbitrary application, and the evident appearances of sinister design, all conspire to recommend the old view of the passage, as immediately connected with the previous context, which is further recommended by the uniform authority of Hebrew manuscripts, a constant tradition, the grammatical construction, and the perfectly coherent and appropriate sense which it puts upon the passage. It need scarcely be added that the explanation of the name Assyria, by Lowth and others, as denoting or at least including the Babylonian dynasty, is here entirely untenable, because it is unnecessary. Where the proper meaning of the term is so appropriate, it is worse than useless to assume one which at least is rare and dubious.

25. He now declares what the purpose is, which is so certainly to be accomplished, namely God's determination *to break Assyria* (or the Assyrian) *in my land, and on my mountains I will trample him; and his yoke shall depart from off them, and his burden from off his back* (or *shoulder*) *shall depart.* The infinitive depends upon יָעַצְתִּי in the verse preceding, and is followed by a finite verb, as in many other verses. (See for example chap. v. 24). Barnes continues the infinitive construction in the next clause (*to remove*, &c.), while Gesenius, on the other hand, assimilates the first clause to the second (*Assyria is broken*, &c.), both which are gratuitous departures from the form of the original. Forced constructions of the clause are given by Junius (when by breaking Assyria, &c. I shall have trampled on him, then shall his yoke, &c.) and by Gataker (as by breaking Assyria, &c. I trampled on him, so that his yoke and burden were removed, in like manner Babylon shall be destroyed). Hendewerk makes a frivolous objection to the translation of אשור by *Assyria*, viz., that Assyria never was in Palestine. The use of the names of countries to denote their governments and even their armies is sufficiently familiar, even without supposing עשׁור to be really the name of the progenitor, like *Israel* and *Canaan*. *My mountains* some have understood to be Mount Zion, others more generally the mountains of Jerusalem; but it seems to be rather a description of the whole land of Israel, or at least of Judah, as a mountainous region. (See Ezek. xxxviii. 21, xxxix. 2, 4; Zech. xii. 15; 1 Kings x. 23). Calvin's idea that this term is used because the country was despised as a mere range of mountains, seems extremely forced. Umbreit, however, also understands the words *in my land* as an allusion to the contempt of foreigners for Palestine. The expressions of this verse bear a strong resemblance to those of chaps. ix. 3, x. 27, xxx. 30, 31, xxxi. 8. Aben Ezra refers the plural suffix in עליהם to *land* and *mountains*, Grotius

to the latter only ; but the true construction is no doubt the common one, which refers it to the people of Israel collectively, and the suffix in שכמו to the same people as an individual. The place here assigned to the destruction of Assyria sufficiently refutes the application of the name for Babylonia by Calvin, Lowth, and others. Gill thinks that " the Assyrian here may represent the Turks, who now possess the land of Israel, and shall be destroyed." Cocceius understands by Assyria the Turks and Saracens, and by the mountains the once Christian regions which they have usurped, in Armenia, Mesopotamia, Asia, Syria, Palestine, Egypt, Africa, Greece, Thrace, Illyria, Hungary. (Hi sane sunt montes Dei et terra ipsius atque ecclesiæ . . . . . . suspicio igitur est prophetiam hanc loqui de hisce, qui nunc Assyria nominari possunt.

26. The Prophet now explains his previous conjunction of events so remote as the Assyrian overthrow and the fall of Babylon, by declaring both to be partial executions of one general decree against all hostile and opposing powers. *This is the purpose that is purposed upon all the earth, and this the hand that is stretched out over all the nations.* On the supposition that this relates to Babylon alone, or to Assyria alone, we are obliged to understand *the whole earth* and *all nations* as describing the universal sway of these great powers respectively. Henderson applies the terms to Assyria, with an indefinite reference to any other powers that might set themselves in opposition. The true interpretation of the words as comprehending Assyria and Babylon, with reference to what goes before, is given by Aben Ezra, Jarchi, and J. D. Michaelis. Aben Ezra seems indeed to make this the apodosis of the sentence, which is wholly unnecessary. Clericus regards the combination of the cognate noun and participle (*purpose, purposed*) as emphatic, and implying settled immutable determination. Vitringa explains *purpose* and *hand* as meaning wisdom and strength ; Gill, more correctly, plan and execution. The outstretched hand, as Knobel observes, is a gesture of threatening. Hitzig gratuitously changes *hand* to *arm*, as in chap. v. 25. *All the earth* is, with as little reason, changed to *all lands* by Gesenius and the later Germans except Ewald.

27. As the preceding verse declares the extent of God's avenging purpose, so this affirms the certainty of its execution, as a necessary consequence of his almighty power. *For Jehovah of Hosts hath purposed* (this), *and who shall annul* (his purpose) ? *And his hand* (*is*) *the one stretched out, and who shall turn it back ?*—Instead of *Jehovah of Hosts*, the Septuagint has here *the Holy God*, or *God the Holy One*. יָפֵר has been variously translated, scatter (LXX.), weaken (Vulgate), avert (Luther), dissolve (Calvin), change (J. D. Michaelis), hinder (Gesenius), break (Ewald); but its sense is that given in the English Version (disannul), and by De Wette (vereiteln). The meaning of the last clause is not simply that *his hand is stretched out*, as most writers give it, but that *the hand stretched out is his*, as appears from the article prefixed to the participle נטויה. (See Gesenius § 108, 3. Ewald § 560). The construction is given by Cocceius, Lowth, Maurer, Henderson, Knobel, and Ewald (seine Hand ist die ausgereckte). Hitzig's attempt to strengthen the last verb by rendering it *frightened back* (zurückschrecken) has the opposite effect. Ewald's translation (hemmen) also fails to convey the exact sense of the Hebrew verb, which is correctly given in the Vulgate (avertet), and still more precisely by Cocceius (retroaget). Clericus modernizes the construction of the whole verse (cum consilium ceperit, &c.), and Gesenius that of the second clause (ist seine Hand gestreckt u. s. w.). Here again Gill is felicitous in paraphrase. " There's

nothing comes to pass but he has purposed, and everything he has purposed does come to pass."

28. *In the year of the death of King Ahaz, was this burden*, or threatening prophecy, against Philistia. Junius begins the fifteenth chapter here, and Calvin says it would have begun here, but for the preposterous division or rather laceration of the chapters. Jerome notes this as the first prophecy belonging to the reign of Hezekiah, and J. H. Michaelis accordingly makes this the beginning of the fourth division of the book. According to Cocceius's arrangement, it is the beginning of the seventh part, extending to the twentieth chapter, and distinguished by the fourfold recurrence of the title מַשָּׂא, as to the sense of which *vide supra*, chap. xiii. 1. Gesenius, Hendewerk, and Henderson, suppose the words of this verse to refer to a period anterior to the death of Ahaz, Maurer to a period after it. J. D. Michaelis thinks that the title at least was written afterwards. Hitzig and Knobel regard the title as the work of a compiler, and the former supposes the entire passage to have been reduced to writing long after the alleged date of the prophecy, while Knobel throws the whole back to the year 739, near the beginning of the reign of Ahaz. These are mere conjectures, which can have no weight against a title forming part of the text as far as we can trace it back. One manuscript instead of *Ahaz* has *Uzziah*, a mere emendation intended to remove a supposed chronological difficulty. Henderson points out an erroneous division of the text in some editions of the English Bible, by prefixing the paragraph mark to ver. 29, so as to apply the date here given to what goes before, whereas the dates are always placed at the beginning. Augusti's translation of the second clause (*the threatening prophecy was this*) mistakes the form of the original, which can only mean *this threatening prophecy*.

29. *Rejoice not, O Philistia, all of thee* (or all Philistia), *because the rod that smote thee is broken, for out of the root of the serpent shall come forth a basilisk, and its fruit a flying fiery serpent.* The name פלשת is applied in Hebrew to the south-western part of Canaan on the Mediterranean coast, nominally belonging to the tribe of Judah, but for ages occupied by the פלשתים or Philistines, a race of Egyptian origin who came to Canaan from Caphtor, *i. e.* according to the ancients Cappadocia, but according to the moderns either Cyprus or Crete, most probably the latter. The name is now traced to an Ethiopic root meaning to wander, and probably denotes wanderers or emigrants. Hence it is commonly rendered in the Septuagint ἀλλόφυλοι. The Philistines are spoken of above in chaps. ix. 11, xi. 14, and throughout the historical books of the Old Testament as the hereditary enemies of Israel. They were subdued by David (2 Sam. v. 17–25, xxi. 15), and still paid tribute in the reign of Jehoshaphat (2 Chron. xvii. 11), but rebelled against Jehoram (2 Chron. xxi. 16, 17), were again subdued by Uzziah (2 Chron. xxvi. 6), and again shook off the yoke in the reign of Ahaz (2 Chron. xxviii. 48). The Greek name Παλαιστίνη, a corruption of פלשת, is applied by Josephus and other ancient writers to the whole land of Israel, from which comes our *Palestine*, employed in the same manner.

The expression כֻּלֵּךְ is explained by Lowth to mean *with one consent*, while Henderson connects it with the negative in this sense, *let not any part of thee*. Most writers make it simply mean *the whole of thee*, perhaps with reference to Philistia as a union of several principalities. All interpreters agree that the Philistines are here spoken of as having recently escaped from the ascendancy of some superior power, but at the same

time threatened with a more complete subjection. The first of these
ideas is expressed by the figure of a broken rod or staff, for the meaning of which *vide supra* ad. v. 5. The other is expressed by the very
different figure of an ordinary serpent producing or succeeded by other
varieties more venomous and deadly. On the natural history of the passage, see the Hebrew Lexicons, Bochart's Hierozoicon, and Rosenmüller's
Alterthumskunde. Whatever be the particular species intended, the essential idea is the same, and has never been disputed. Some, indeed, suppose
a graduation or climax in the third term also, the fiery flying serpent
being supposed to be more deadly than the basilisk, as this is more so
than the ordinary serpent. But most writers refer the suffix in פריו to
נחש, and regard the other two names as correlative or parallel. The transition in the last clause from the figure of an animal to that of a plant may serve
the double purpose of reminding us that what we read is figurative, and of
shewing how unsafe it is to tamper with the text on the ground of mere
rhetorical punctilios. As to the application of the figures, there are several
different opinions. Jerome, and a long line of interpreters, including
Hendewerk, suppose the broken staff to be the death of Ahaz. But he, so
far from having smitten the Philistines, had been smitten by them. Kimchi,
Abarbenel, Vitringa, and others, understand the first clause as referring to
the death of Uzziah. But this had taken place more than thirty years
before. Vitringa endeavours to remove this difficulty by supposing an
ellipsis ; rejoice not in the death of him who smote you, and in the prosperity which you have since enjoyed for many years. But this is wholly
arbitrary. Others suppose Tiglath-pileser to be meant by the rod which
smote them ; but for this there is no sufficient ground in history. Gesenius
applies the figures not to an individual, but to the Jewish power, which
had been broken and reduced during the reign of Ahaz. The still more
formidable domination threatened in the last clause he explains, not with
the older writers to be that of Hezekiah (2 Kings xviii. 18), but the recovered strength of Judah. Hitzig and Ewald make the last clause a prediction of Assyrian invasion. Knobel adopts the same interpretation, but
with this addition, that he understands the figure of the basilisk coming
forth from the serpent as referring to the agency of Judah in procuring the
Assyrian invasion of Philistia. Rosenmüller refers this clause to the
Messiah, in which he follows the Chaldee Paraphrase. " From among the
sons of the sons of Jesse, the Messiah shall come forth, and his works shall
be among you as fiery serpents." Some of the old writers suppose נחש to
contain an allusion to one of the names of Jesse (2 Sam. xvii. 25).

30. *And the first-born of the poor shall feed, and the needy in security lie
down, and I will kill thy root with famine, and thy remnant it shall slay.* The
future condition of the Jews is here contrasted with that of the Philistines.
The figures in the first clause are borrowed from a flock, in the second from
a tree, but with obvious allusion to a human subject. The first-born of the
poor is explained by the Targum and the Rabbins to mean the nobles of
Judah, now despised by the Philistines. Calvin makes it a superlative expression for the poorest and most wretched (quasi suis miseriis insignes),
and this sense is approved by most of the later writers, some of whom refer
to Job xviii. 13, for an analogous expression. Gesenius, however, is disposed to admit an allusion to the next generation, which would make the
promise too remote, and leaves the expression of *first-born* unexplained.
Some writers needlessly amend the text. Thus J. D. Michaelis makes the ב
in בכרי a preposition, and reads *in my pastures*, a conjecture recently re-

newed by Ewald, who would point the word בְּכֹרֵי and make כֹּר a synonyme of כַּר. But an exposition which involves a change of text and the invention of a word to suit the place, and both without necessity, seems to have a twofold claim to be rejected. Equally gratuitous is Lowth's reading בִּכֻּרֵי, *my choice first-fruits.* Gesenius and De Wette supply לבטח in the first clause from the second, *shall feed quietly.* But the threat of famine in the other clause seems to shew that the prominent idea is *abundance*, as expressed by the older writers. There is no need of taking *root* in the sense of *stock* or *race.* The figurative part of the last clause is borrowed from a tree, here divided into two parts, the *root* and the *rest* or remainder. Gesenius distinguishes between המית and הרג as terms which usage has appropriated to the act of God and man respectively. Hitzig makes the one mean *kill* in general, and the other more specifically kill with the sword (Jer. xv. 3). The third person יהרג is by some regarded as a mere enallage personæ, and referred like המתי to God himself. Others refer it to the enemy mentioned in ver. 31, or the fiery serpent in ver. 30. Others prefer an indefinite construction, which is very common, and would here be entitled to the preference, were there not another still more simple. This makes רעב the subject of the last verb, so that what is first mentioned as an instrument in God's hand, reappears in the last member of the sentence as an agent.

31. *Howl, O gate! cry, O city! dissolved, O Philistia, is the whole of thee; for out of the north a smoke comes, and there is no straggler in his forces.* The Philistines are not only forbidden to rejoice, but exhorted to lament. The object of address is a single city representing all the rest. There is no ground for the opinion that Ashdod is particularly meant. It is rather a case of poetical individualisation. *Gate* is not here put for the judges or nobles who were wont to sit there—nor is it even mentioned as the chief place of concourse—but rather with allusion to the defences of the city, as a parallel expression to *city* itself. The insertion of a preposition by the Targum and Kimchi—*howl for the gate, cry for the city*—is entirely unauthorised, and changes the whole meaning. The masculine form נָמוֹג seems to have greatly perplexed interpreters. Some of the older writers supply איש, others עם, and even Ewald says that we must be content to make it an infinitive. Knobel regards it as a mere anomaly or idiomatic licence of construction. Hitzig supposes a sudden transition from the third to the second person—it is dissolved, O whole Philistia. The true solution is that נָמוֹג agrees regularly with כֹל in כֻּלֵּךְ. This explanation, which Hendewerk admits to be as old as Maurer, is distinctly given by Cocceius (liquefactum est, Palæstina, universum tui), and copied by Vitringa and J. H. Michaelis. Another idea ascribed to Maurer by Knobel—viz. that the *smoke* here meant is that of conflagrations kindled by the enemy—is at least as old as Clericus. Some of the older writers understood it simply as an emblem for wrath or trouble. Lowth cites Virgil's *fumantes pulvere campos*, and supposes an allusion to the clouds of dust raised by an army on the march. This is adopted by Gesenius, Rosenmüller, Hendewerk, and others; but Hitzig and Knobel object to this interpretation of עָשָׁן as unauthorised by Hebrew usage. Hitzig refers it to the practice of literally carrying fire in front of caravans to mark the course; but this is objected to by others as peculiar to the desert and to straggling or divided bodies. It may be doubted, notwithstanding the allusion in the last clause, whether עָשָׁן was intended to refer to an army at all. If not, we may suppose with Calvin that smoke is mentioned merely as a sign of distant and approaching

fire, a natural and common metaphor for any powerful destroying agent.—
בּוֹדֵד has been conjecturally explained in various ways, but is agreed by all
the modern writers to mean properly *alone* or *separated*, and to be descriptive of the enemy with which Philistia is here threatened. Some give to
מוֹעָדָיו the sense of the cognate מוֹעָדִים, viz. appointed times, and understand
it as referring to the orders under which the invading army acts. Most
writers now, however, give it another sense of מוֹעָדִים, viz. assemblies, here
applied specifically to an army. Thus understood the clause is descriptive
of a compact, disciplined, and energetic host A similar description we
have had already in chap. v. 26–29, from which resemblance some infer
that this passage *must* relate to the Assyrians. Aben Ezra refers it to the
Babylonians under Nebuchadnezzar, Kimchi to the Jews under Hezekiah,
and Cocceius to the Romans as the final conquerors of *whole Palestina*, by
which he understands the whole of what we now call Palestine, or at least
Judea. Vitringa, who usually quotes the strangest notions of Cocceius with
indulgent deference, appears to lose his patience at this point, and exclaims,
" Hanc ego interpretationem totam suo relinquam loco, nec ejus amplius
meminero ; est enim plane paradoxa et a communi sensu aliena." The
diversity of judgments as to the particular enemy here meant, and the
slightness of the grounds on which they severally rest, may suffice to shew
that the prophecy is really generic, not specific, and includes all the agencies
and means by which the Philistines were punished for their constant and
inveterate enmity to the chosen people, as well as for idolatry and other
crimes.

32. *And what shall one answer* (what answer shall be given to) *the
ambassadors of a nation? That Jehovah has founded Zion, and in it the
afflicted of his people shall seek refuge.* The meaning of the last clause is
too clear to be disputed, viz., that God is the protector of his people. This
is evidently stated as the result and sum of the whole prophecy, and as such
is sufficiently intelligible. It is also given, however, as an answer to ambassadors or messengers, and this has given rise to a great diversity of explanations. Instead of ambassadors (מַלְאֲכֵי) kings (מַלְכֵי) is given by all the old
Greek Versions except Symmachus, who has ἀγγέλοις. The older writers
for the most part make ambassadors the subject of the verb—*what will the
ambassadors answer?* Thus understood, the words have been applied to the
report carried back by the ambassadors of friendly powers, or by those sent
out by the Jews themselves, on the occasion of Hezekiah's victory over the
Philistines, or of his delivery from the Assyrian invasion. In order to avoid
the irregularity of giving גּוֹי a plural meaning, some have supposed the sentence to relate to the report carried back by a Philistine embassy, sent to
ascertain the condition of Jerusalem after the Assyrian attack. The
irregular concord of the plural noun with מַלְאֲכֵי was explained by supplying
a distributive pronoun, *every one* of the ambassadors, a form of speech quite
foreign to the Hebrew language. Hendewerk, who retains this old construction, understands this as the answer of the Assyrian ambassadors, when
asked by the Philistines to attack Jerusalem. It is now commonly agreed,
however, that מַלְאֲכֵי גּוֹי is the object of the verb, which is repeatedly construed with a noun directly, and that its subject is either Hezekiah or more
probably indefinite. As to גּוֹי, some still give it a collective meaning: others
refer it to the Philistines, suing for peace, or proposing a joint resistance to
Assyria; others to Judah itself, an application contrary to usage. All this
seems to shew that the expression is indefinite, as the very absence of the

article implies, and that the whole sense meant to be conveyed is this, that such may be the answer given to the inquiries made from any quarter.   Of all the specific applications, the most probable is that which supposes an allusion to Rabshakeh's argument with Hezekiah against trusting in Jehovah. But this seems precluded by the want of any natural connection with Philistia, which is the subject of the previous context.   I shall only add, that Cocceius is not only true to his original hypothesis, but so far carried away by it as to lay aside his usual grammatical precision (which often contrasts strangely with his exegesis) and translate יענה as a preterite.   He understands the verse as accounting for the ruin of the Jews by the reception which they give to the apostles of Christ.   *What answer was given to the messengers of the nation* (*i. e.* the messengers sent to them) *when Jehovah founded Zion,* (or the Christian Church) *and the afflicted of his people sought refuge in it?*   The same sense might have been as well attained without departing from the strict sense of the future.   As to the sense itself, it needs no comment to evince that it is purely arbitrary, and that a hundred other meanings might be just as well imposed upon the words.

Chapters 15 & 16

THESE chapters contain a prediction of the downfall of Moab.   Most of the recent German writers deny that any part of it was written by Isaiah, except the last two verses of chap. xvi., which they suppose him to have added as a postscript to an older prophecy.   The reasons for ascribing the remainder of the passage to another writer are derived from minute peculiarities of phraseology, and from the general character and tone of the whole composition.   Hitzig regards this as the prophecy of Jonah mentioned in 2 Kings xiv. 25.   In this conclusion Maurer acquiesces, and Knobel thinks it not improbable.   The grounds on which such hypotheses must be rejected, when not only destitute of external evidence but contradicted by it, have been already stated in the general introduction.   Hendewerk combats Hitzig's doctrine on his own ground and with his own weapons, deducing from the verbal minutiæ of the passage proofs of its poetical excellence and of its genuineness.   Some of the older writers regard the last two verses of chap. xvi. as an addition made by Isaiah to an earlier prediction of his own.   Henderson thinks them an addition made to a prophecy of Isaiah by a later prophecy,   If we set aside the alleged internal evidence of a different origin, the simplest view of the passage is that which regards the whole as a continuous composition, and supposes the Prophet at the close to fix the date of the prediction which he had just uttered.   The particular event referred to in these chapters has been variously explained to be the invasion of Moab by Jeroboam II., king of Israel; by Tirhakah, king of Ethiopia; by Tiglath-Pileser, king of Assyria; by his successors Shalmaneser, Sennacherib, and Esarhaddon; by Nebuchadnezzar, king of Babylon, &c. The safest conclusion seems to be, that the prediction is generic, and intended to describe the destruction of Moab, without exclusive reference to any one of the events by which it was occasioned or promoted, but with special allusions possibly to all of them.   Compare the introduction to chap. xiii., xiv.   According to Cocceius, the Moab of this prophecy is Israel, the hostile power Rome, and the time that of the downfall of Jerusalem. To such hypotheses the answer still is, that they might be indefinitely multiplied and varied, with as much or rather with as little reason.

Chapter 15

This chapter is occupied with a description of the general grief, occasioned by the conquest of the chief towns and the desolation of the country at large. Its chief peculiarities of form are the numerous names of places introduced, and the strong personification by which they are represented as grieving for the public calamity. The chapter closes with an intimation of still greater evils.

1. (This is) *the burden of Moab, that in a night Ar-Moab is laid waste, is destroyed; that in a night Kir-Moab is laid waste, is destroyed.* The English Version, Rosenmüller, and Hitzig, understand the first verse as assigning a reason for the second. *Because in a night*, &c., *he ascends*, &c. But so long a sentence is at variance not only with the general usage of the language, but with the style of this particular prophecy. Gesenius supposes an ellipsis at the beginning, and takes כִּי in its usual sense of *that.* "(I affirm) that," &c. The same construction occurs where a verb of swearing is understood (vii. 9, xlix. 18). In the absence of the governing verb, the particle may be translated *surely.* Most of the recent German versions render it by *yea* (ja!). *In a night* may be literally understood, as assaults are often made by night (chap. xxi. 4), or figuratively, as the phrase is sometimes used to denote sudden destruction. *Ar* originally meant a *city,* and *Ar-Moab* the city of Moab, *i. e.* the capital city, or, as Gesenius says, the only real city of the Moabites. It was on the south side of the Arnon (Num. xxii. 36). The Greeks called it *Areopolis,* or city of Mars, according to their favourite practice of corrupting foreign names, so as to give them the appearance of significant Greek words. Ptolemy calls it *Rhabmath-mom,* a corruption of the Hebrew *Rabbath-Moab, i. e.* chief city of Moab. Jerome says that the place was destroyed in one night by an earthquake when he was a boy. The Arabs call it *Mab* and *Errabba.* It is now in ruins. In connection with the capital city, the Prophet names the principal or only fortress in the land of Moab. *Kir* originally means a *wall,* then a walled town or fortress. The place here meant is a few miles southeast of Ar, on a rocky hill, strongly fortified by nature, and provided with a castle. The Chaldee paraphrase of this verse calls it *Kerakka de Moab,* the fortress of Moab, which name it has retained among the orientals, who extend it to the whole of ancient Moab.

2. The destruction of the chief cities causes general grief. *They* (indefinitely) *go up to the house* (*i. e.* the temple), *and Dibon* (*to*) *the high places for* (the purpose of) *weeping. On Nebo and on Medeba, Moab howls—on all his heads baldness—every beard cut off.* Luther, Gesenius, and others, make the verb indefinite. Lowth, Rosenmüller, Hitzig, and Maurer, regard *Moab* as the subject. Vitringa makes בַּיִת a contracted proper name for *Bethmeon* (Jer. xlviii. 23) or *Beth-baal-meon* (Josh. xiii. 19), on the south side of the Arnon, now called *Maein.* Ewald makes it a contraction of בֵית דבלתים (Jer. xlviii. 22), which was not far from Dibon (Num. xxxiii. 46). The same explanation was once approved by Rosenmüller, but in the Compendium of his Scholia, he adopts the opinion of Kimchi, that בֵית is here used in the sense of *temple,* and is equivalent to מקדש, which occurs below (xvi. 12) as a parallel to בָמוֹת. The ancient heathen built their temples upon heights (chap. lxv. 7). Solomon built one to the Moabitish god Chemosh on the mountain before Jerusalem (1 Kings xi. 1). This explanation is approved by Gesenius and all the later Germans except

Ewald. Some who take בית as a proper name, make במות one also, regarding it as a contracted form of *Bamoth-Baal* (Josh. xiii. 17). *Dibon*, a town north of the Arnon, rebuilt by the tribe of Gad, and thence called *Dibod-gad* (Num. xxxiii. 45), although it had formerly belonged to Moab, and would seem from this passage to have been recovered by them. The same place is called *Dimon* in ver. 9, in order to assimilate it to דם, blood. The modern name is Diban. There is no preposition before בית and דיבון in the Hebrew. Hence the latter may be taken either as the object or the subject of the verb. The first construction is preferred by the older writers ; those of modern date are almost unanimous in favour of the other, which makes Dibon itself go up to the high places. The only objection is, that the writer would hardly have coupled this one place with the country at large, and this is not sufficient to exclude it. The objection to the other is, that Dibon was situated in a plain, to which it may be answered that the phrase *go up* has reference in many cases not to geographical position, but to sacredness and dignity.

3. *In its streets, they are girded with sackcloth ; on its roofs and in its squares* (or broad places) *all* (literally, *all of it*) *howls, coming down with weeping* (from the house-tops or the temples). In this verse there is a singular alternation of masculine and feminine suffixes, all relating to Moab, sometimes considered as a country, and sometimes as a nation. The last clause is explained by most modern writers to mean melting into tears, as the eye is elsewhere said to run down tears or water (Jer. ix. 17; Lam. iii. 48). But as the eye is not here mentioned, and the preposition is inserted, making a marked difference between this and the alleged expressions, it is better to adhere to the old construction, which supposes an antithesis between this clause and the ascent to the temples or the house-tops. Sackcloth is mentioned as the usual mourning dress and badge of deep humiliation.

4. *And Heshbon cries and Elealeh—even to Jahaz is their voice heard—therefore the warriors of Moab cry—his soul is distressed to him* (or *in him*). Heshbon, a royal city of the Amorites, assigned to Reuben and to Gad at different times, or to both jointly, famous for its fish-pools, was a celebrated town in the days of Eusebius, the ruins of which are still in existence, under the slightly altered name of *Hesbân*. Elealeh, often mentioned with it, was also assigned to the tribe of Reuben. Eusebius describes these towns as near together in the highlands in Gilead, opposite to Jericho. Robinson and Smith, while at the latter place, conversed with an Arab chief, who pointed out to them the Wady Hesbân, near which, far up in the mountain, is the ruined place of the same name, the ancient Heshbon. Half an hour north-east of this lies another ruin called El Al, the ancient Elealeh (Palestine, ii. 278). The names יחץ and יָחְצָה are treated by Gesenius as identical, but Hitzig understands them to denote two different places, one described by Jerome as overhanging the Dead Sea, the other further to the south-east, on the edge of the desert, the scene of the battle between Sihon and Israel. In either case, the preposition seems to imply that the place meant was a frontier town. The same form of expression that is here used occurs also chap. x. 30.—Vitringa and Gesenius give עַל־כֵּן the rare and doubtful sense *because*, and understand the Prophet to describe the cities or people in general as lamenting because even the warriors were dismayed. Most writers give the words their usual méaning, and suppose the terror of the warriors to be here described as the effect, not the cause of the general lamentation. According to Knobel, *therefore* has reference to

the cry of Heshbon and Elealeh which had just been mentioned; according to Hitzig and others, to the downfall of the capital (ver. 1). For חֲלֻצֵי the Septuagint seems to have read חֲלָצָי, which it renders ἡ ὀσφύς. This reading and translation, which is also favoured by the Peshito, is adopted by Lowth: *the very loins of Moab cry out.* Other interpreters agree that it is the passive participle of חָלַץ, used as a noun in the sense of warriors or heroes, whether so called because drawn out for military service, or as being strong, or girded and equipped, or disencumbered of unnecessary clothing. Aquila has ἔξωμοι, with the arms or shoulders bare. There is peculiar significance in thus ascribing an unmanly terror to the very defenders of the country. Vitringa supposes an additional emphasis in the use of the verb יָרִיעוּ, which may either mean a joyful or a mournful cry, and by itself might here denote a battle-cry or war-shout. As if he had said, the warriors of Moab raise a cry, not of battle or defiance, but of grief and terror. The same natural expression of distress is ascribed by Homer to his heroes. (*Vide infra*, chap. xxxiii. 7). Cocceius is singular in making this an exhortation : let them raise the war-cry (vociferentur, classicum canant, barritum faciant, clamorem tollant, ut in praelio). For ירעה the Septuagint reads ידעה (γνώσεται), probably a mere inadvertence. The English Version and Lowth take נפש in the sense of *life*, other interpreters in that of *soul*. Rosenmüller, Gesenius, and Ewald, give to ירעה the sense of *trembling*, from a kindred root in Arabic ; others with more probability that of *being evil, i. e.* ill at ease or suffering, in which the future corresponding to this preterite is frequently used elsewhere. Gesenius indeed refers that future to another root, but one of kindred origin, in which the essential idea is probably the same. The paronomasia in יריעו and ירעה is copied in Gesenius's translation by combining the words *klagen* and *verzaget*. The similar terms are confounded by the Vulgate (ululabit sibi), and by Calvin, who understands the sense to be, that every one will be so occupied with his own grief as to disregard that of his neighbours.

5. *My heart for Moab cries out—her fugitives* (are fled) *as far as Zoar— an heifer of three years old—for he that goes up Luhith with weeping goes up by it—for in the way of Horonaim a cry of destruction they lift up.* Every part of this obscure verse has given rise to some diversity of exposition. It has been made a question whose words it contains. Junius connects it with the close of the preceding verse and understands it to contain the words of the warriors there mentioned, endeavouring to rally and recall the fugitives. Others suppose the Moabites in general, or some individual among them, to be here the speaker. Cocceius doubts whether these are not the words of God himself. Calvin supposes the Prophet to be speaking in the person and expressing the feelings of a Moabite. All these hypotheses appear to have arisen from an idea that the Prophet cannot be supposed to express sympathy with these sinners of the Gentiles. But such expressions are not only common elsewhere, but particularly frequent in this part of Isaiah. (*Vide infra* chaps. xvi. 11, xxi. 3, 4, xxii. 5). Hitzig suggests, as a possible but not as a probable construction of the first words, *My heart* (is) *towards Moab* (who) *is crying*, &c., as in Judges ver. 9. Some older writers understand the words to mean *my heart cries to Moab*, as in 1 Chron. ver. 20. Gesenius gratuitously cites other cases in which ל has the sense of *for*, on account of, given to it here by Aben Ezra (בעבור מואב). The particle is here used in its proper sense as indicating general relation, *as to*, with respect to, and simply points out Moab as the subject or occa-

sion of the cry.   Ewald and others make יזעק mean—to complain or lament,
which is neither so exact nor so expressive as the literal translation.   Instead
of *my heart* some read *his heart*, others simply *heart*.   Thus Lowth ; *the
heart of Moab crieth in her*, after the Septuagint (ἐν αὐτῇ).   The Peshito
seems to have read ברוחו *in his spirit*.   The common text itself is variously
explained.   According to the usual analogy, it means *her bars*, and the
Vulgate accordingly has *vectes ejus*.   By this some understand the cities of
Moab, others its barriers or frontier posts, others its guardians or protectors.
Most of the modern writers follow Saadias and Kimchi, who explain the
word to mean *her fugitives*.   The only objection to this explanation is
the absence of the long vowel under the first letter.   Zoar, one of the
cities of the plain, preserved by Lot's intercession, is now ascertained
to have been situated on the eastern shore of the Dead Sea, near its southern extremity, and at the foot of the mountains. (Robinson's Palestine, ii. 480,
648).   It is here mentioned as an extreme southern point, but not without
allusion, as Vitringa with great probability suggests, to Lot's escape from
the destruction of Sodom.   The next phrase (עגלה שלשיה) is famous as the
subject of discordant explanations.   These may however be reduced to two
classes, those which regard the words as proper names, and those which
regard them as appellatives.   J. D. Michaelis supposes two places to be
mentioned, *Eglath* and *Shelishiyyah;* but of the latter there is no trace in
geography or history.   Doederlein conjectures that the city *Eglath* consisted of three towns, and that the Hebrew שְׁלִשִׁיָּה is the same as the Greek
τρίπολις or *triple city*.   But the former no where else means *threefold*, but
always *third*.   According to Lightfoot, the phrase means *Eglah*, or *Eglath
the Third*, so called to distinguish it from *Eglaim* or *En-eglaim*, a place in
the same region, mentioned in Ezek. xlvii. 10, " where Eglaim is plainly of
the dual number and seems to intimate that there were two Egels, with relation to which our Eglah may be called Eglah the Third." (Lightfoot's Cho-
rographical Inquiry, chap. iii. § 8).   With this may be compared *Ramathaim*
which is also dual (1 Sam. i. 2), and *Upper* and *Nether Beth-horon* (Josh.
xvi. 3, 5).   Lightfoot compares this Eglath the Third with the Νέκλα
of Ptolemy, and the Ἄγαλλα of Josephus, both mentioned in connection
with Zoar, (Ζώαρα) and the latter with Horonaim (Ὡρώναι).   The *Ejlun*
(عجلون) of Abulfeda, meaning *calves* or *heifers*, may be another name for
the same place, which must then have been situated beyond the northern
boundary of Moab, and be mentioned here in order to convey the idea that
the fugitives had fled in opposite directions.   Of the late translators, De Wette,
Henderson, and Ewald retain the Hebrew words as a proper name, *Eglath-
Shelishiyah*.   On the other hand, all the ancient versions, and the great
majority of modern writers, regard the words in question as appellatives, and
all agree in rendering the first of the two *heifer*.   The other is explained
by Jarchi to mean the third in the order of birth, with reference to some
supposed superiority in that class.   Hitzig, Hendewerk, and Umbreit, understand it to mean *third-rate*, of the third order, *i. e.* inferior (compare Dan.
v. 29 ; 1 Sam. xv. 9), and as here applied to a heifer, *lean, ill-favoured*,
a figure borrowed from the pastoral habits of the people in that region to
express the smallness of the city Zoar, which was so called because it was
a little one (Gen. xix. 20, 22).   It is plain however that *third* can have
this meaning only in case of a direct comparison with something of the first
and second rank.   Besides, what has the size of Zoar to do with this
pathetic description of the flight of Moab ?   The great majority of voices

is in favour of the meaning *three years old*, or retaining the form of the original more closely, *a heifer of the third* (year). A cognate participle (משלשת) is used in this sense and in connection with this very noun (Gen. xv. 9). By *a heifer three years old*, Gesenius understands one that has never yet been tamed or broken, according to Pliny's maximum, *domitura boum in trimatu, postea sera, antea præmatura*. Now as personal afflictions are sometimes likened to the taming of animals (Jer. xxxi. 18; Hosea x. 11), and as communities and governments are often represented by the figure of a heifer (Jer. xlvi. 20, l. 11; Hosea iv. 16), the expressions thus interpreted would not be inappropriate to the state of Moab, hitherto flourishing and uncontrolled, but now *three years old* and subjected to the yoke. Some of the older interpreters suppose this statement of the age to have reference to the voice of the animal, which is said by Bochart to be deepest at that age, and according to Aristotle, stronger in the female than the male. There is still a doubt, however, with respect to the application of the simile, as last explained. Bochart refers it to the Prophet himself. " My heart cries for Moab (for her fugitives to Zoar), as a heifer three years old." Vitringa refers it to the fugitives of Moab, who escape to Zoar, crying like a heifer three years old.—מעלה is commonly a noun denoting an ascent or rising ground. It is translated *hill* in the English version of 1 Sam. ix. 11, and *ascent* in that of Num. xxxiv. 4, and 2 Sam. xv. 30, which last place is strikingly analogous to this. The construction commonly adopted makes מעלה an absolute nominative : " The ascent of Luhith (or as to the ascent of Luhith) with weeping one ascends it." It is possible, however, to make מעלה a participle or a participial noun—"the ascender of Luhith (*i. e.* he who ascends it) with weeping ascends by it." The parallel passage (Jer. xlviii. 5) instead of בּוֹ repeats בְּכִי. This is regarded by the latest writers as an error in transcription of בכי for בו כי. The Septuagint has πρὸς σὲ ἀναβήσονται, which implies still another reading (בך). It is a curious and instructive fact that J. D. Michaelis corrects the text of Isaiah by comparison with Jeremiah, while Lowth, with equal confidence, inverts the process and declares the text in Jeremiah to be unmeaning. Luhith is mentioned only here and in Jer. xlviii. 5. Eusebius describes it as a village still called Λουειθ, between Areopolis and Zoar, which Jerome repeats but calls it *Luitha*. The article before לוחית is explained by Gesenius as having reference to the meaning of the name as an appellative, *the boarded* (town), but by Henderson with more probability as properly belonging to מעלה. (See Gesenius, § 109, 1). Horonaim is mentioned only here and in Jer. xlviii. 3, 5, 34. The name originally means *two caverns*, and is near akin to Beth-horon, *locus civitatis* (Gesenius, Thes. I. 195, 459). As Jeremiah instead of דֶּרֶךְ *way*, has מוֹרַד *descent*, it is not improbable that Luhith and Horonaim were on opposite faces of the same hill, so that the fugitives on their way to Zoar, after going up the ascent of Luhith, are seen going down the descent of Horonaim. A *cry of breaking* is explained by some of the rabbinical interpreters as meaning the explosive sound produced by clapping the hands or smiting the thigh. Others understand it to mean *a cry of contrition*, *i. e.* a penitent and humble cry. Gill suggests that it may mean a *broken cry*, *i. e.* one interrupted by sighs and sobs. Gesenius makes it mean a cry as of destruction, *i. e.* a loud and bitter cry ; Knobel, a cry (on account) of destruction. It is possible, however, that שֶׁבֶר may be mentioned as the very word uttered, like תָּמָם in other cases. The very unusual form יעערו is by some regarded as a transposition for ירעעו from רעע. But

the rabbins and the latest writers are agreed that it is a derivative of עור.
The former suppose an anomalous reduplication of the first radical. The
latter regard it as a Pilpel for יערעו, either by error of transcription or
euphonic change. (See Ewald, § 237, 1.) There is no absurdity in the
conjecture of Cocceius that this strange form was employed here in allusion
to the names עָר and עֲרֹעֵר, Moabitish cities. Junius supposes, still more
boldly, that the Prophet wishing to say *cry*, instead of using any ordinary
word, invented the cacophonous one now in question, as in keeping with
the context and the feelings it expresses.

6. *For the waters of Nimrim* (are and) *shall be desolations ; for withered
is the grass, gone is the herbage, verdure there is none.* According to Vitringa, this verse gives a reason for the grief described in ver. 5 as prevailing in the south of Moab. Maurer makes it an explanation of the flight in
that direction. Hendewerk supposes the description to be here at an end,
and a statement of the causes to begin. It seems more natural, however,
to suppose, with Ewald and some older writers, that the description is
itself continued, the desolation of the country being added to the cap-
ture of the cities and the flight of the inhabitants. Aurivillius, in his dissertation on this passage, explains נמרים as an appellative, meaning as in
Arabic clear, limpid waters. But all other writers understand it as a proper
name. Grotius takes מי in the sense of *pastures*, which it never has.
Lightfoot suggests that the *waters* meant may be the hot springs of this
region, mentioned by Josephus, and perhaps the same with those of which
Moses speaks in Gen. xxxvi. 24, according to the best interpretation of
that passage. It is more probably explained by Junius as the name of
streams which met there (rivorum confluentium), and by others still more
generally as denoting both the springs and running streams of that locality.
Junius supplies a preposition before *waters* (ad aquas Nimrimorum desola-
tiones erunt), but the true construction makes it the subject of the verb.
The same writer understands the plural form as here used to denote the
waters meeting at Nimrah or Beth-nimrah. But it is now agreed that
Nimrim is another name for the town itself, which is mentioned in Num.
xxxii. 3, 36, and Josh. xiii. 27 as a town of Gad. Vitringa's assumption
of another town in the south of Moab rests on his misconception of the
nexus between this verse and the fifth. Bochart derives the name from
נָמֵר a panther, but the true etymology is no doubt that already mentioned.
Forerius explains משמות as denoting an object of astonishment and horror,
but the common sense of desolations is no doubt the true one. Most
writers since Vitringa understand the Prophet as alluding to the practice of
stopping fountains and wasting fields in war. (Compare 2 Kings iii. 19, 25.)
But Ewald and others suppose an allusion to the effects of drought. This
is a question which the Prophet's own words leave undecided. The second
כִּי is translated *so that* by Luther, *and* by the Septuagint, *because* by the
Vulgate, *yea* by Augusti, while Calvin omits both. The translation of the
first verb as a future and the others as preterites seems to make the desolation of the waters not the cause but the effect of the decay of vegetation.
It is better, therefore, to adopt the present or descriptive form throughout
the verse, as all the latest writers do. חציר is not *hay*, as Luther and the
English version give it, but mature *grass*, דשא the springing herbage, ירק
greenness or verdure in general. Ewald and Henderson neglect the distinction between the last two words. The whole is given with great precision
in the Vulgate : *herba, germen, viror.* The Septuagint also has χόρτος
χλωρός.

7. *Therefore* (because the country can no longer be inhabited) *the remainder of what (each) one has made (i. e.* acquired), *and their hoard* (or store), *over the brook of the willows they carry them away.* Not one of the ancient versions has given a coherent or intelligent rendering of this obscure sentence. Jerome suggests three different interpretations of נחל ערבים ; first, the brook of the Arabians or of the Ravens (עֹרְבִים) who fed Elijah ; then, the brook of the willows in the proper sense ; and lastly, Babylon, the plains of which were full of willows (Ps. cxxxvii. 2). The first of these is adopted by J. D. Michaelis, who translates it *Rabenbach* (Ravenbrook) ; the last by Bochart, Vitringa, and others ; the second by most interpreters. A new interpretation is proposed by Hitzig, viz. brook or valley of the deserts, supposed to be the same with the brook or valley of the plain mentioned, Amos vi. 14. It is now commonly agreed that whatever be the meaning of the name, it denotes the Wady el Ahsa of Burckhardt (the Wady el Ahsy of Robinson and Smith), running into the Dead Sea near its southern extremity, and forming the boundary between Kerek and Gebal, corresponding to the ancient Moab and Edom.—יתרה may either mean what is left by the enemy, or the surplus of their ordinary gains. The ם in ישאום is regarded by Henderson as the old termination of the verb. All other writers seem to look upon it as the suffix referring to יתרה and פקדה, which are then to be construed as nominatives absolute. The older writers make the enemy the subject of the verb ; the moderns the Moabites themselves. On the whole, the most probable meaning of the verse is that the Moabites shall carry what they can save of their possessions into the adjacent land of Edom.—Kimchi points out an ellipsis of the relative before עשה, precisely similar to that in our colloquial English. Clericus coolly inserts *not* and *enemies* in the first clause, both which he says are necessary to the sense.

8. The lamentation is not confined to any one part of the country. *For the cry goes round the border of Moab (i. e.* entirely surrounds it) ; *even to Eglaim* (is) *its howling* (heard), *and to Beer Elim its howling.* The meaning, as Hendewerk observes, is not that the land is externally surrounded by lamentation, but that lamentation fills it. Vatablus understands the cry here spoken of to be the shout of battle, contrary to usage and the context. Piscator makes אֶגְלַיִם mean the confluence of the Arnon or the streams that form it, called הנחלים ארנון in Num. xxi. 14, and connected there with Beer. All others understand it as the name of a town. Rosenmüller and Gesenius identify it with the Ἀγαλλείμ of Eusebius, eight miles south of Areopolis, and not far from the southern boundary of Moab. Josephus also mentions Ἄγαλλα in connection with Zoar. As these, however, must have been within the Moabitish territory, Hitzig and the later German writers make *Eglaim* the same with *En-eglaim* (Ezek. xlvii. 10). The different orthography of the two names is noticed by none of these interpreters ; and Henderson, who adopts the same opinion, merely says that " the change of א and ע is too frequent to occasion any difficulty."—*Beer Elim*, the well of the mighty ones or heroes, the same that " the princes and nobles of the people digged with their staves " (Numb. xxi. 18). This explanation, suggested by Junius, is adopted by Vitringa and the later writers, as the situation in Numbers agrees well with the context here. The word באלי (substantially equivalent to שרים and נדיבים, the words used in Numbers) may have been specially applied to the chiefs of Moab, as the phrase אֵלֵי מוֹאָב occurs in the song of Miriam, Exod. xv. 15. The map-

pik in the final letter of יללתה is wanting in some manuscripts and editions.
Aurivillius regards it as a paragogic termination (compare Ps. iii. 3, cxxv.
3), but other interpreters follow the ancient versions in making it a suffix referring to Moab. Henderson needlessly departs in two points from the form
of the original, by introducing a masculine pronoun (his wailing), and by
varying the last noun (wailing, lamentation) on the ground that the repetition would have a bad effect in English. The suffix in יללתה may possibly
refer to זעקה and mean the howling sound of it (*i. e.* the cry).

9. The expressions grow still stronger. Not only is the land full of
tumult and disorder, fear and flight; it is also stained with carnage and
threatened with new evils. *For the waters of Dimon are full of blood ; for
I will bring upon Dimon additions (i. e.* additional evils), *on the escaped*
(literally, *the escape) of Moab a lion ; and on the remnant of the land*
(those left in it, or remaining of its population). It is an ingenious conjecture of Junius that the *Dimon* is the stream mentioned 2 Kings iii.
20, 22, in which case the meaning of the clause would be, this stream
shall not be merely red as it then was, but really full of blood. Jerome says,
however, that the town *Dibon*, mentioned in ver. 2, was also called *Dimon*
in his day, by a common permutation of the labials. The latter form may
have been preferred, in allusion to the word דם following. According to
this view, the Prophet here returns to the place first named, and ends
where he began. By the waters of Dimon or Dibon, most writers understand the Arnon, near the north bank of which the town was built, as the
river Kishon is called *the waters of Megiddo* (Judges v. 19). Hitzig thinks
it more probable that there was a pool or reservoir at Dibon, as there was
at Heshbon according to Cant. vii. 5, and according to modern travellers at
Mâb and Medeba likewise. Those who take Dimon as the name of a river
give to נוספות the specific meaning of *more blood*. Grotius explains it, I
will give a new reason for its being called Dimon *(i. e.* bloody). Gesenius
also admits the probability of such an allusion, on the ground that the verb
יָסַף, from which נוֹסָפוֹת is derived, often includes the meaning of some preceding word (Job xx. 9, xxxiv. 32). Grotius and Bochart understand the
last clause literally as a threat that God would send lions (or according to
Piscator, wild beasts in general) to destroy the people, a judgment elsewhere threatened (Lev. xxvi. 22 ; Jer. xv. 3) and inflicted (2 Kings xvii.
25, 26). But the later writers seem agreed that this is a strong figurative
expression for the further evils to be suffered at the hand of human enemies.
Hitzig supposes Judah to be called a lion in allusion to the prophecy in
Gen. xlix. 9. Cocceius and Vitringa understand it to mean Nebuchadnezzar, whose conquest of the Moabites, though not historically recorded,
may be gathered from such passages as Jer. iv. 7, xlix. 28, xxv. 11-21,
xxvii. 3, 6. In itself the figure is applicable to any conqueror, and may
be indefinitely understood, not in reference however to the same inflictions
just described, as Rosenmüller and Gesenius think, but with respect to
new inflictions not specifically mentioned though distinctly intimated in the
word נוֹסָפוֹת. The Septuagint makes אריה and אדמה both proper names,
Ariel and *Admah*. According to Jerome and Theodoret, Ar or Areopolis
was sometimes called Ariel, while Moab as descended from Lot might be
described as the remnant or survivor of Admah, one of the cities of the
plain. Both these interpretations are adopted by Lowth, and the last by
Cocceius and J. D. Michaelis.

Chapter 16

THIS chapter opens with an exhortation to the Moabites to seek protection from their enemies by renewing their allegiance to the house of David, accompanied by an intimation that this prospect of deliverance would not in fact be realised, vers. 1–6. From this transient gleam of hope, the prophecy reverts to a description of the general desolation and distress, in form almost identical with that in the foregoing chapter, vers. 7–12. The prophecy then closes with a specification of the time at which it was to be fulfilled, vers. 13, 14.

The needless division of the prophecy at this point seems to have some connection with an old opinion that the lamb mentioned in ver. 1 is Christ. A similar cause appears to have affected the division of the second, third, and fourth chapters.

1. In their extremity, the Moabites exhort one another to return to their allegiance to the family of David, by whom they were subdued and rendered tributary (2 Sam. viii. 2). When the kingdom was divided, they continued in subjection to the ten tribes till the death of Ahab, paying yearly, or perhaps at the accession of every new king, a tribute of a hundred thousand lambs and as many rams with the wool (2 Kings iii. 4, 5). After the kingdom of the ten tribes was destroyed, their allegiance could be paid only to Judah, who had indeed been all along entitled to it. *Send ye the lamb* (*i. e.* the customary tribute) *to the ruler of the land* (your rightful sovereign) *from Sela* (or *Petra*) *to the wilderness, to the mountain of the daughter of Zion.* Hitzig and Maurer regard these as the words of the Edomites, with whom they suppose the Moabites to have taken refuge. Petra, it is true, was an Idumean city (2 Kings xiv. 7); but it may at this time have been subject to the Moabites, by one of the fluctuations constantly taking place among these minor powers, or it may be mentioned as a frontier town, for the sake of geographical specification. The older writers understand these as the words of the Prophet himself; but Knobel objects that both the Prophet and the Edomites must have known that the course here recommended would be fruitless. It is best to understand them, therefore, as the mutual exhortations of the Moabites themselves in their confusion and alarm. This is also recommended by its agreement with what goes before and after. The verse then really continues the description of the foregoing chapter. The Septuagint and Peshito render the verb in the first person singular, *I will send.* The latter also instead of כר reads בר. This reading is approved by Lowth and J. D. Michaelis, who understand the verse as meaning that even if the son of the ruler of the land (*i. e.* of the king of Moab) should go upon an embassy of peace to Jerusalem, he would not obtain it. Others suppose the flight of the king's son to be mentioned as an additional trait in the prophetic picture. But this departure from the common text is wholly unnecessary. Forerius and Malvenda suppose כר to mean a battering-ram, or take it as a figurative term for soldiery or military force. Calvin understands by it a sacrificial lamb to be offered to Jehovah as the *ruler of the earth*, in token of repentance and submission. Most other writers understand the tribute of lambs paid by Moab to the kings of Israel, and Barnes combines this sense with that before it, by supposing that the Jews exacted lambs from tributary powers, in order to supply the altar with victims. Jerome puts משל

in apposition with כר, and understands the verse as a prayer or a prediction, that God would send forth Christ, *the lamb, the ruler of the land* (or earth). Others take משל as a vocative, used collectively for משלים ; *send, O ye rulers of the land.* Most modern writers make it either a genitive (the *lamb of the ruler*), *i. e.* due, belonging to him, or a dative (*to* or *for* the *ruler of the land*), a common construction after verbs expressing or implying motion. Clericus supposes the ruler of the land to be Nebuchadnezzar as the conqueror of Judah. *Sela,* which properly denotes a *rock,* is now commonly agreed to be here used as the name of the city *Petra,* the ancient capital of Idumea, so called because surrounded by impassable rocks, and to a great extent hewn in the rock itself. It is described by Strabo, Diodorus, and Josephus as a place of extensive trade. The Greek form Πέτρα is supposed to have given name to *Arabia Petræa* in the old geography. If so, the explanation of that name as meaning *stony,* and as descriptive of the soil of the whole country, must be incorrect. Petra was conquered by Trajan, and rebuilt by Hadrian, on whose coins its name is still extant. It was afterwards a bishop's see, but had ceased to be inhabited before the time of the crusades. It was then entirely lost sight of, until Burckhardt, in 1812, verified a conjecture of Seetzen's, that the site of Petra was to be sought in the valley called the *Wady Musa,* one or two days' journey south-east of the Dead Sea. It was afterwards explored by Irby and Mangles, and has since been often visited and described. See in particular Robinson's Palestine, ii. 573–580. Grotius supposes Petra to be mentioned as an extreme point, *from Petra to the wilderness, i. e.* throughout the whole extent of Moab. Ewald understands it to be named as the most convenient place for the purchase of the lambs required. Vitringa supposes that the Moabites fed their flocks in the wilderness by which Petra was surrounded. Luther's translation, *from the wilderness,* is wholly inconsistent with the form of the original. The construction given by some of the old writers, *Sela of the wilderness,* disregards the local or directive ה. That of Gesenius and other recent writers, *through* or *along the wilderness,* is also a departure from the form of the original, which can only mean *from Petra to the wilderness* (and thence) *to mount Zion* (or Jerusalem.) Jerome explains the whole verse as a prediction of Christ's descent from Ruth the Moabitess, the *lamb, the ruler of the land, sent forth from the rock of the wilderness!* The Targum paraphrases *ruler of the land* by the *Messiah* (or *anointed*) *of Israel,* which may possibly mean nothing more than king.

2. This verse assigns the ground or reason of the exhortation in the one before it. *And it shall be* (or come to pass) *like a bird wandering,* (like) *a nest cast out, shall be the daughters of Moab, the fords of Arnon.* The construction *cast out from the nest* is inconsistent with the form of the original. *Nest* may be understood as a poetical term for its contents. The *nidi edaces* of Virgil are analogous. There are three interpretations of בנות מואב. 1. The first gives the words the geographical sense of villages or dependent towns. (*Vide supra,* chap. iii. 16, iv. 4.) To this it has been objected that בת has this sense only when it stands in connection with the metropolis or mother city. Ewald and Hitzig modify this interpretation by making *daughters* mean the several communities or neighbourhoods of which the nation was composed. 2. The second explanation makes it mean the people generally, here called *daughters,* as the whole population is elsewhere called *daughter.* 3. The third gives the words their strict sense as denoting the female inhabitants of Moab, whose flight

and sufferings are a sufficient index to the state of things. In the absence of any conclusive reason for dissenting from this strict and proper sense of the expressions, it is entitled to the preference. מעברות is not a participle agreeing with בנות, passing (or when they pass) the Arnon; nor does it mean the two sides of the river, but its fords or passes. Ewald supposes it to be put for the dwellers near the river, which is arbitrary. Some suppose it to be governed by a preposition understood, or to be used absolutely as a noun of place, while others put it in apposition with בנות, " the daughters of Moab, the fords of Arnon." The ל in the last word denotes possession—the fords which belong to Arnon. This is mentioned as the principal stream of Moab. Whether at this time it ran through the country, or was its northern boundary, is doubtful.

3. Most of the older writers, from Jerome downwards, understand this verse as a continuation of the advice to the Moabites, in which they are urged to act with *prudence* as well as *justice*, to take counsel (*i. e.* provide for their own safety) as well as execute judgment (*i. e.* act right towards others). In other words, they are exhorted to prepare for the day of their own calamity, by exercising mercy towards the Jews in theirs. Calvin adopts this general view of the meaning of the verse, but interprets it ironically as he does the first, and understands the Prophet as intending to reproach the Moabites sarcastically for their cruel treatment of the Jewish fugitives in former times. This forced interpretation, which is certainly unworthy of its author, seems to have found favour with no other. It is not the first case in which Calvin has allowed his exposition to be marred by the gratuitous assumption of a sarcastic and ironical design. Gesenius and most of the later writers follow Saadias in regarding this verse as the language of the Moabitish suppliants or messengers, addressed to Judah. הביאו עצה they explain to mean *bring counsel, i. e.* counsel us, and *execute justice, i. e.* treat us justly. Hitzig takes פלילה in the sense of intervention (interpose between the parties), Maurer in that of intercession, Hendewerk in that of decision. According to Aben Ezra, הביאו עצה means apply or exercise your understanding (Ps. xc. 12); according to Vitringa, apply prudence to your conduct, *i. e.* regulate it prudently. The explanation of the verse as the words of the Moabites addressed to the Jews, is favoured by the foregoing context, which relates throughout to the sufferings of Moab, whereas on the other supposition, the Prophet suddenly exhorts the sufferers to harbour the fugitives of that very nation, with whom they had themselves been exhorted to seek refuge. This interpretation also relieves us from the necessity of determining historically what particular affliction of the Israelites or Jews is here referred to, a question which has occasioned much perplexity, and which can be solved only by conjecture. According to Vitringa, the passage refers to the invasion of Reuben, Gad, and Manasseh, by Tiglath-Pileser in the fourth year of Ahaz (2 Kings xv. 29), and also to the invasion of Judah by the Edomites about the same time (2 Chron. xxviii. 17). Others refers the passage to Sennacherib's invasion of Judah, and others to that of Nebuchadnezzar. Knobel supposes the object of address to be the Edomites. As noonday heat is a common oriental figure to denote distress (Isa. iv. 6, xxv. 4, xxxii. 2), so a shadow is relief from it. Possibly, however, the allusion here is to the *light* of noonday, and the shadow dark as night denotes concealment. If so, the clause is equivalent in meaning to the one which follows. Some of those who adopt the other sense suppose a climax in the sentence. Relieve, refresh the sufferers—or at least conceal them—or if that is too much to ask, at least do not betray them.

4. *Let my outcasts, Moab, sojourn with thee ; be thou a covert* (refuge or hiding-place) *to them from the face* (or presence) *of the spoiler* (or oppressor) : *for the extortioner is at an end, oppression has ceased, consumed are the tramplers out of the land.* Here, as in the preceding verse, the sense depends upon the object of address. If it be Moab, as the older writers held, the outcasts referred to are the outcasts of Israel. If the address be to Israel, the outcasts are those of Moab. The latter interpretation seems to be irreconcileable with the phrase נִדְחֵי מוֹאָב. Gesenius disregards the accent and supposes an ellipsis before Moab : my outcasts, even those of Moab. So also Rosenmüller and Hendewerk. The other recent German writers follow Lowth in reading נִדְחֵי מוֹאָב *outcasts of Moab*, a construction found in all the ancient versions. Maurer, without a change of vowels, explains נִדְחַי as an old form of the plural construct. Calvin gives the verbs in the last clause a past or present sense, and supposes the first clause to be ironical. As if he had said, " Yes, give them shelter and protection now, now when their oppressor is destroyed, and they have no need of assistance. Ewald also takes the preterite strictly, but understands the second clause to mean that the Moabites were encouraged thus to ask aid of Judah, because the former oppressive government had ceased there, and a better reign begun, more fully described in the next verse. But most interpreters, ancient and modern, give the verbs in this last clause a future sense. As if he had said, " Give the fugitives a shelter ; they will not need it long, for the extortioner will soon cease," &c. This gives an appropriate sense, whether the words be addressed to Israel or Moab. Some who adopt the same construction supply the ellipsis in another way. " Fear not to shelter them, for the oppressor will soon cease," &c. Knobel explains the clause as an assurance, on the part of the Moabites, that they would no longer vex or oppress Edom, to whom he imagines that the words are addressed. The collective construction of רֹמֵס with תַּמּוּ is not uncommon in the case of participles. (Ewald, § 599.)

5. This verse contains a promise, that if the Jews afforded shelter to the fugitives of Moab, their own government should be strengthened by this exercise of mercy, and their national prosperity promoted by the appearance of a king in the family of David, who should possess the highest qualifications of a moral kind for the regal office. *And a throne shall be established in mercy ; and one shall sit upon it in truth in the tent of David, judging and seeking justice, and prompt in equity.* Knobel supposes the throne here meant to be that of the Jewish viceroy in Edom, called a שֹׁפֵט, to distinguish him from the מֹשֵׁל or lord paramount. Clericus fancies an allusion to Gedaliah, who was appointed viceroy of Judah by Nebuchadnezzar. Barnes, who follows the old writers in making Moab the object of address, understands this as a promise that the Jewish government would hereafter exercise kindness towards the Moabites. Grotius understands this verse as a promise to the Moabites that their throne should be established (if they harboured the Jewish refugees) *in the tabernacle of David, i. e.* under the shadow or protection of his family. But the tabernacle of David has no doubt the same meaning here as the analogous expression in Amos ix. 11. Barnes's translation, *citadel of David*, is entirely gratuitous. Most writers understand it as a promise of stability to Judah itself. Some suppose a reference to Hezekiah ; but the analogy of other cases makes it probable that the words were intended to include a reference to all the good kings of the house of David, not excepting the last king of that race, to whom God was to give the throne of his father David, who was to reign over the house

of Jacob for ever, and of whose kingdom there should be no end" (Luke i. 32, 33). Hence the indefinite expression *one shall sit, i. e.* there shall always be one to sit on David's throne. It is true that J. D. Michaelis and the later Germans make יָשַׁב agree with שֹׁפֵט as a noun—there shall sit thereon a judge, &c. But this construction is forbidden by the position of the latter word, and by its close connection with דֹּרֵשׁ, which can only be construed as a participle.

6. *We have heard the pride of Moab, the very proud, his haughtiness, and his pride, and his wrath, the falsehood of his pretensions.* Those writers who suppose Moab to be addressed in the preceding verses, understand this as a reason for believing that he will not follow the advice just given. As if he had said, "It is vain to recommend this merciful and just course, for we have heard," &c. But the modern writers who regard what immediately precedes as the language addressed by the Moabitish fugitives to Judah, explain this as a reason for rejecting their petition. In the second clause the English Version supplies the substantive verb, *he is very proud.* A simpler construction is adopted by most writers, which connects it immediately with what precedes. Knobel makes it agree with גָאוֹן, but Ewald more naturally with מוֹאָב. The four derivatives of one root in this sentence are imitated in Henderson's paraphrase : *haughtiness, haughty, high-mindedness, hauteur.* Most modern writers are agreed that כֵּן is here an adjective meaning *right* or *true*, and that in combination with the negative it forms a compound noun meaning *vanity* or *falsehood.* בדִּים is variously explained as denoting lies, vain pretensions, plausible speeches, idle talk, all which ideas are perhaps included. Barnes introduces an interjection in the second clause (*ah ! his haughtiness !* &c.), but the true construction is no doubt the common one, which governs these nouns by שׁמענו. This is also the simplest construction of the last clause : "we have heard the falsehood of his vain pretensions." It is unnecessary, therefore, to supply either *are* or *shall be.*

7. *Therefore* (because thus rejected) *Moab shall howl for Moab ; all of it shall howl ; for the grapes* (or raisin-cakes) *of Kir-hareseth shall ye sigh* (or moan), *only* (i. e. altogether) *smitten.* Umbreit and others make יֶלִיל a descriptive present (Moab howls). Others, as De Wette, read *must howl ;* Henderson, *may howl ;* Ewald, *let Moab howl.* There is, however, no sufficient reason for departing from the strict sense of the future.—Jerome and Clericus take ל in the sense of *to*, Knobel in that of *as to* or *as for,* making מוֹאָב an absolute nominative—*as for Moab, it shall howl*—equivalent in emphasis to *Moab, yes, Moab shall howl.* For an example of the same construction, he refers to chap. xxxii. 1 ; but as it is confessedly a rare one, and as there is no necessity for assuming it in this case, it is better to adhere to the common interpretation of לְמוֹאָב, as denoting the subject or occasion of the lamentation. By *Moab howling for Moab,* Jerome understands the mutual lamentations of the city and the provinces, or town and country ; Barnes, the alternate responses of one part to another in their lamentation ; others simply the mourning of one Moabite for another. The idea may be that the nation of Moab mourns for the land of Moab, but the simplest supposition is that *Moab for Moab* means *Moab for itself.* The English version of כֻּלֹּה (*every one*), overlooks the suffix, which is also the case with the simple version *all*, and the distributive paraphrase of Clericus (*quotquot sunt*). The form of the original is retained by Ewald (ganz es jammre), *let it all lament.* The next clause Clericus translates, *to* (or *at*) *the walls of Kir-hareseth ye shall talk* (ad muros colloquemini). But all

the later writers give the particle the sense of *for*, as in the first clause, and the verb that of *sigh* or *moan*. The word אֲשִׁישֵׁי seems to have perplexed the old translators, some of whom confound it with the verb יָשִׁישׁוּ, or one of its derivatives. Thus the Vulgate has *his qui laetantur super muros cocti lateris*. Lowth and Dathe read אַנְשֵׁי on the authority of Jer. xlvii. 31. But in all such cases of imitation or reconstruction which occur in Scripture, there are many intentional and significant changes of one word for another similar in form but different in sense. For a clear and ample illustration of this practice, see Hengstenberg's comparison of Psalm xviii. with 2 Sam. xxii. in his Commentary on the former. Vitringa takes אֲשִׁישֵׁי in the sense of wine-flagons, and this interpretation is approved by most of the early writers, who suppose אֲשִׁישֵׁי to have here the same sense as אֲשִׁישִׁים and אֲשִׁישׁוֹת elsewhere (Hosea iii. 1; Cant. ii. 5; Comp. 2 Sam. vi. 19; 1 Chron. xvi. 3). J. D. Michaelis and the later Germans give the word in this one case the sense of *foundations* (equivalent in this connection to *ruins*) derived from an Arabic analogy. Cocceius curiously combines the two ideas by explaining the word to mean the props or supports of the vines (*sustentacula uvarum*). Ewald and Knobel have returned to the old interpretation, except that they explain the word wherever it occurs to mean, not flasks or flagons, but cakes of grapes or raisins pressed together. This allusion to grapes agrees well with the subsequent mention of the vines of Moab. The other interpretation is favoured by the meaning of the name *Kir-hareseth* (a wall of earth or brick). The same place is mentioned in 2 Kings iii. 25, and is no doubt identical with *Kir-Moab* (chap. xv. 1), which latter form may have been used to correspond with the parallel name *Ar-Moab*. The particle אַךְ, which is variously rendered *but* (Clericus), *for* (Barnes), *surely* (English Version), *wholly* (Henderson), strictly means, *only, nothing but*, and is so translated by Knobel (nur zerschlagen), and Ewald (nichts als betrübt). Knobel applies the last word in the sentence to the grapes or raisin-cakes, as being all consumed or gone, implying the desolation of the vineyards. It is more natural, however, to refer it to the people, as being smitten, downcast, and distressed.

8. *For the fields of Heshbon are withered—the vine of Sibmah—the lords of the nations broke down its choice plants—unto Jazer they reached—they strayed into* (or *through*) *the desert—its branches—they were stretched out— they reached to* (or *over*) *the sea*. Clericus renders אָמְלָל as a future, which destroys the force of the description. On the construction of אָמְלָל with שְׁדֵמוֹת, *vide supra*, chap. iii. 12. *Sibmah* is mentioned, Num. xxxii. 38, Joshua xiii. 19, and in the former place joined with Nebo, which occurs above, chap. xv. 2. It had been taken by the Amorites, but was probably again recovered. Eusebius speaks of it as a town of Gilead, and Jerome describes it as not more than half a mile from Heshbon. For בַּעֲלֵי the LXX. have καταπίνοντες, confounding it, as Clericus observes, with בָּלַע. *Heathen*, in the modern sense, is not a correct version of גוֹיִם, as the Moabites themselves were heathen. According to the English Version, it would seem to be the lords of the nations who came to Jazer, wandered through the wilderness, &c. All this, however, is really predicted of the vines, the luxuriant growth of which is the subject of the following clauses. As the verb הָלַם is used, chap. xxviii. 1, to express the intoxicating power of wine, Cocceius gives it that sense here, and makes it agree with שְׁרוּקָה as its subject: the choice vines of Sibmah overcame the rulers of the nations, *i. e.* the wine was drunk at royal tables. This ingenious exposition is adopted

by Vitringa, Lowth, Hitzig, Maurer, Hendewerk, De Wette, Knobel, on the ground of its agreement with the subsequent praises of the vine of Sibmah. Gesenius objects that there is then no mention of the wasting of the vineyards by the enemy, unless this can be supposed to be included in אמלל. Besides Gesenius, Rosenmüller, Ewald, Umbreit, and most of the older writers, make שרוקיה the object of the verb. On the meaning of the noun itself compare what is said of the cognate from שורק, *supra*, chap. v. 2. Jazer is mentioned Num. xxi. 32, and described by Eusebius as fifteen miles from Heshbon, and ten west of Philadelphia, on a stream running into the Jordan. It is here mentioned as a northern point, the desert and the sea representing the east and the west or south. Knobel infers from this that Sibmah was a well-known centre of wine-culture. In the absence of a preposition before מדבר, it may be rendered either *through the wilderness*, or simply *into it*. Knobel supposes the word *stray* or *wander* to be used because the wilderness is pathless. The exact sense of שְׁלֻחֹת is *things sent forth*, or as Clericus expresses it, *missiones*. עבר without a preposition sometimes denotes the act of passing simply *to* a place, and this sense is adopted here by the Septuagint and Henderson. But most writers adhere to the more usual sense of *passing over*, which may either mean that the vines covered the shore and overhung the water, or that the luxuriant vineyards of Moab really extended beyond the northern point of the Dead Sea. In the parallel passage, Jer. xlviii. 32, we read of the *sea of Jazer*. Henderson regards the ים in that phrase as an interpolation, a conclusion not sufficiently supported by the authority of two Hebrew manuscripts and one ancient version. The *sea of Jazer* may have been a lake in its vicinity, or even a reservoir, such as Seetzen found there. The same traveller found an abundant growth of vines in the region here described, while at Szalt (the ancient Ramoth) Burckhardt and Buckingham both speak, not only of the multitude of grapes, but of an active trade in raisins.

9. *Therefore I will weep with the weeping of Jazer (for) the vine of Sibmah. I will wet thee (with) my tears, Heshbon and (thee) Elealeh! For upon thy fruit and upon thy harvest a cry has fallen.* Some suppose these to be the words of a Moabite bewailing the general calamity. There is no objection, however, to the supposition that the Prophet here expresses his own sympathy with the distress of Moab, as an indirect method of describing its intensity. The emphasis does not lie merely in the Prophet's feeling for a foreign nation, but in his feeling for a guilty race, on whom he was inspired to denounce the wrath of God. Most of the modern writers give the verbs a present form; but Ewald makes them expressive of entreaty, *let me weep*, &c. There is no sufficient cause, however, for departing from the strict sense of the future, which is still retained by Barnes and Henderson. Clericus takes אבכה בבכי together, and translates it *flebo in fletu*; but the accents join the second word, no doubt, correctly, with what follows. The sense is not that he will weep for the vine of Sibmah as he does for Jazer, the construction given by Clericus and Barnes, but that he will weep for the vines of Sibmah as Jazer (*i. e.* the inhabitants of Jazar) did, who were particularly interested in them. There is no need of supposing, with Hendewerk, a reference to the destruction of Jazer by the Israelites in the times of Moses (Num. xxi. 32, xxxii. 35). אריוך is strongly rendered by Jerome (inebriabo), Clericus (irrigabo), Hendewerk (überströme), but strictly means to saturate with moisture. On the anomalous form, see Gesenius, § 74, 17, § 71, 7. קיץ, which elsewhere means the fruit of summer (Jer. xl. 12, Amos viii. 1), is used here and in chap. xxviii. 4, to denote the ingathering

of the fruit. This peculiar usage of the term is urged by Hendewerk as a proof that the passage was written by Isaiah. In like manner, he maintains that if הלם in ver. 8 has the same sense as in chap. xxviii. 1, as Hitzig alleges, it is an incidental proof that Hitzig is mistaken in denying the genuineness of this prophecy. These arguments are mentioned, not on account of their intrinsic weight, but as effective arguments *ad hominem*, and as illustrations of the ease with which the weapons of a fanciful criticism may be turned upon itself. הידד, according to its etymology and usage, may be applied to any shout or cry whatever, and is actually used to denote both a war-cry or alarm (Jer. li. 14), and a joyful shout, such as that which accompanies the vintage (Jer. xxv. 30). In the next verse, it has clearly the latter sense, which some retain here also, giving to נפל the sense of *ceasing*, as in the text of the English Version. Others prefer the former sense, as given in the margin of the English Bible, and take נפל על in that of *falling upon* suddenly, attacking by surprise, which is sometimes expressed elsewhere by נפל ב (*e. g.* Josh. xi. 7). The latest writers are agreed, however, that there is here an allusion to both senses or applications of the term, and that the thing predicted is, that instead of the joyful shout of vintage or of harvest, they should be surprised by the cry of battle. This idea is beautifully clothed in another form by Jeremiah (xlviii. 33), *their shouting shall be no shouting*, *i. e.* not such as they expected and designed, or, as De Wette vigorously renders it, *war-cry, not harvest-cry* (Schlachtruf, nicht Herbstruf). On the strength of the parallelism, Knobel gives to קציר the sense of *vintage* or *fruit-harvest*, as in chap. xviii. 5. Ewald retains the strict sense, and supposes the two kinds of ingathering to be distinctly specified. For קציר and הידד, Lowth reads בציר and שדד, in imitation of Jer. xlviii. 32. But the insecurity of such assimilations has been shewn already in the exposition of ver. 7. The ancient versions, and especially the Septuagint, are so confused and unintelligible here, that Clericus, not without reason, represents them as translating *audacter æque ac absurde*.

10. *And taken away is joy and gladness from the fruitful field : and in the vineyards shall no (more) be sung, no (more) be shouted ; wine in the presses shall the treader not tread ; the cry have I stilled* (or *caused to cease*). Hendewerk translates the *vav* at the beginning *so that*, in order to shew that this verse describes the effect of what is threatened in ver. 9. Henderson omits the particle entirely. It is best, however, to give it its proper sense of *and*. There is no need of departing from the future meaning of the verbs ; but most of the later writers prefer the descriptive present. The strict sense of נאסף is *gathered*, and by implication *taken away* from its former place. On the masculine form of the verb, see Gesenius, § 144, *a*. Jerome and Clericus take כרמל as a proper name, denoting a cultivated hill like Carmel ; but it is no doubt an appellative, as in chap. x. 18. De Wette and Knobel give it here the specific sense of *orchard*, others that of *fruitful field*, or cultivated ground in general. According to Clericus, the verbs in the next clause are active, and לא equivalent to לא איש (nemo vociferabitur). They are really passive, both in form and meaning, and indefinitely construed. Barnes and Henderson resolve it into our idiom by employing a noun and the substantive verb ; *there shall be no cry or shouting*. The later Germans retain the original construction. Hendewerk explains ירעע as the Pual of רעע, Gesenius as the Palul of רוע. In the next clause, Barnes, De Wette, and Ewald, read *no treader*, Henderson and Umbreit more exactly *the treader*, leaving the לא to qualify the verb. The English Version, on

the other hand, by using the expression *no wine*, seems to imply that the treading of the grapes would not be followed by its usual result, whereas the meaning is that the grapes would not be trodden at all. The same Version needlessly puts *treaders* in the plural. The idiomatic combination of the verb and its participle or derivative noun (יִדְרֹךְ הַדֹּרֵךְ) is not uncommon in Hebrew. (See for example, Ezek. xxxiii. 4, 2 Sam. xvii. 9, Deut. xxii. 8.) The word *vats*, used by Barnes and Henderson in rendering this clause, is less appropriate than the common version *presses*. (*Vide supra*, chap. v. 2.) The ancient mode of treading grapes is still preserved in some of the monuments of Egypt. Umbreit gives הֵידָד the general sense of tumult (Getümmell), Ewald that of wild noise (den Wilden Lärm) ; but most writers understand it here as specifically meaning the vintage or harvest-shout. הִשְׁבַּתִּי may be rendered either as a preterite or present. It signifies not merely to bring to an end, but to still or silence. This prediction of course implies the failure of the vintage, if not the destruction of the vineyards.

11. *Therefore my bowels for Moab like the harp shall sound, and my inwards for Kirhares.* The viscera are evidently mentioned as the seat of the affections. Modern usage would require *heart* and *bosom*. Barnes correctly applies to this verse the distinction which philologists have made between the ancient usage of *bowels* to denote the upper viscera and its modern restriction to the lower viscera, a change which sufficiently accounts for the different associations excited by the same or equivalent expressions, then and now. Ewald goes too far in softening the expression when he translates מֵעִים *feelings*. The comparison is either with the sad notes of a harp, or with the striking of its strings, which may be used to represent the beating of the heart or the commotion of the nerves. *Sound* is not an adequate translation of יֶהֱמוּ, which conveys the idea of tumultuous agitation. Clericus understands the mention of the bowels as intended to suggest the idea of a general commotion (totus commovebor). He also gives to לְ as in ver. 7, the sense of *ad*. *Kir-hares* is another variation of the name written *Kir-hareseth* in ver. 7, and *Kir-Moab* in chap. xv. 1.

12. From the impending ruin Moab attempts in vain to save himself by supplication to his gods. They are powerless and he is desperate. *And it shall be* (or come to pass), *when Moab has appeared* (before his gods), *when he has wearied himself* (with vain oblations) *on the high place*, *then* (literally *and*) *he shall enter into his sanctuary to pray, and shall not be able* (to obtain an answer). Another construction, equally grammatical, though not so natural, confines the apodosis to וְלֹא יוּכָל : "when he has appeared, &c., and enters into his sanctuary to pray, he shall not be able." A third gives to its more usual sense of *that;* but this requires נִרְאָה and נִלְאָה to be taken as futures, which is inadmissible. Luther and Castalio, on the other hand, refer even יוּכַל to the past: "and has accomplished nothing." Some regard נִרְאָה as impersonal, *it shall be seen*, or *when it is seen*. But the phrase would then add nothing to the sense, and נִרְאָה is the technical term for the appearance of the worshipper before his god. (*Vide supra*, chap. i. 12.) Lowth reads רָאָה (*when Moab shall see*) on the authority of the Targum and Peshito. At the same time he pronounces it "a very probable conjecture" of Secker, that נִרְאָה is a various reading for נִלְאָה, inadvertently inserted in the text. To this opinion Gesenius also is inclined, though he retains both words, and copies the paronomasia by rendering them *man sieht* and *sich mühet*. For the first, Knobel substitutes *zieht*. Ewald has *erscheint* and

umsonst weint. Henderson translates כִּי *though*, which is unnecessary, but does not affect the sense. Vitringa regards בָּמָה as identical with βωμός, and quotes Diodorus's description of the vast altars sometimes erected by the ancients, the ascent to which must of course have been laborious. That the Hebrew word does not mean a hill, he argues from the fact that בָּמוֹת were sometimes erected in cities (2 Chron. xxviii. 25, Jer. xxxii. 35). But the word means a *height* or *high place*, whether natural or artificial. The singular form may be regarded as collective, but need not be translated in the plural. The *weariness* here spoken of is understood by some as referring to the complicated and laborious ritual of the heathen worship; by others, simply to the multitude of offerings; by others, still more simply, to the multitude of prayers put up in vain. J. D. Michaelis reads *my sanctuary*, changes לֹא to לוֹ, and takes יוּכַל in the sense of the corresponding root in Arabic: "then shall he come to my sanctuary, and in it shall trust." מִקְדָשׁ is also explained to mean the temple at Jerusalem, by Ephraem Syrus, Clericus, Schmidius and Gill, the last of whom asserts, that "the house or temple of an idol is never called a sanctuary." But see Ezek. xxviii. 18, Amos vii. 9, 13. The same explanation of מקדש is erroneously ascribed by Barnes to Kimchi. Solomon Ben Melech makes it mean the palace of the king, and Jarchi applies נלאה על הבמה to the weariness of the defenders with fighting from the towers. According to the true interpretation of the verse, the last clause may either represent the worshipper as passing from the open high place to the shrine or temple where his god resided, in continuation of the same religious service, or it may represent him as abandoning the ordinary altars, and resorting to some noted temple, or to the shrine of some chief idol, such as Chemosh (1 Kings xi. 17). The Septuagint refers יוכל to the idol (he shall not be able to deliver him), but as this had not been previously mentioned, the construction is a harsh one. As applied to Moab, it does not mean that he should not be able to reach or to enter the sanctuary on account of his exhaustion, but that he should not be able to obtain what he desired, or indeed to effect anything whatever by his prayers. Ewald imagines the apodosis of the sentence to have been lost out of the text, but thinks it may have been preserved by Jeremiah in the words, *Moab shall be ashamed of Chemosh* (Jer. xlviii. 13).

13. *This is the word which Jehovah spake concerning Moab of old.* The reference is not to what follows but to what precedes. מֵאָז does not mean since the date of the foregoing prophecy, or since another point of time not specified—such as the time of Balak, or of Moab's subjection to Israel, or of its revolt—but more indefinitely, heretofore of old. It may be applied either to a remote or a recent period, and is frequently used by Isaiah elsewhere, in reference to earlier predictions. The same contrast between מֵאָז and עַתָּה occurs in 2 Sam. xv. 34. דבר does not mean a *sentence* but a prophecy. Some give to אל its usual sense *to*, and suppose it to point out Moab as the object of address. Others give it the strong sense of *against*. But it is best to understand it as indicating merely the theme or subject of the declaration.

14. *And now Jehovah speaks* (or *has spoken*), *saying, In three years, like the years of an hireling, the glory of Moab shall be disgraced, with all the great throng, and the remnant shall be small and few not much.* By the years of an hireling most writers understand years computed strictly and exactly, with or without allusion to the eager expectation with which hirelings await

their time, and their joy at its arrival, or to the hardships of the time of servitude. J. D. Michaelis supposes a specific reference to the lunar years of the ancient calendar, as being shorter than the solar years. Knobel supposes three years to be put for a small number, but this indefinite interpretation seems to be precluded by the reference to the years of a hireling. The glory of Moab is neither its wealth, its army, its people, nor its nobility exclusively, but all in which the nation gloried. The ב before כל does not mean *consisting in*, or *notwithstanding*, but *with, including*. המון denotes not merely a great number, but the tumult and confusion of a crowd. לוא כביר is by some understood to mean *not strong*. It was possibly intended to include the ideas of diminished numbers and diminished strength.—As the date of this prediction is not given, the time of its fulfilment is of course uncertain. Some suppose it to have been executed by Tirhakah, king of Ethiopia (2 Kings xix. 9); others by Shalmaneser; others by Sennacherib; others by Esarhaddon; others by Nebuchadnezzar. These last of course suppose that the verses are of later date than the time of Isaiah. Henderson regards them as the work of an inspired writer in the following century. That the final downfall of Moab was to be effected by the Babylonians, seems clear from the repetition of Isaiah's threatenings by Jeremiah (chap. xlviii.). Some indeed suppose that an earlier invasion by Assyria is here foretold, as a pledge of the Babylonian conquest which had been predicted in the foregoing chapter. But this supposition of a twofold catastrophe appears to be too artificial and complex. Barnes understands the thirteenth verse to mean that such had been the tenor of the prophecies against Moab from the earliest times, which were now to receive their final accomplishment. A majority of writers look upon vers. 13, 14, as a postscript or appendix by Isaiah to an earlier prediction of his own or of some older prophet, whom Hitzig imagines to be Jonah, on the strength of 2 Kings xiv. 25. The only safe conclusion is that these two verses were added by divine command in the days of Nebuchadnezzar, or that if written by Isaiah they were verified in some of the Assyrian expeditions which were frequent at that period, although the conquest of Moab is not explicitly recorded in the history.

Chapter 17

This chapter is chiefly occupied with a prophecy of desolation to the kingdoms of Syria and Ephraim, vers. 1–11. It closes with a more general threatening against the enemies of Judah, vers. 12–14. Most of the modern writers regard ver. 12 as the beginning of a new and distinct prophecy, extending through the eighteenth chapter, and relating to the destruction of Sennacherib's host. Some of the older writers explain vers. 12–14 as a direct continuation of the prophecy concerning Syria and Israel. Others treat it as a fragment, or an independent prophecy, connected neither with the seventeenth nor eighteenth chapter. In favour of connecting it with chap. xvii. is the absence of any distinctive title or intimation of a change of subject. In favour of connecting it with chap. xviii., is the similarity of form in the beginning of xvii. 12 and xviii. 1. The still stronger resemblance between xvii. 11 and xviii. 15, seems to shew that the whole is a continuous composition. This is, at least, a safer conclusion, and one more favourable to correct interpretation, than the extreme of mutilation and division, to which the modern criticism uniformly tends. Less exegetical error is likely to arise from combining prophecies really distinct than from separating the parts of one and the same prophecy. The most satisfactory view of the whole passage is, that it was meant to be a prophetic picture of the doom which awaited the enemies of Judah, and that while many of its expressions admit of a general application, some traits in the description are derived from particular invasions and attacks. Thus Syria and Ephraim are expressly mentioned in the first part, while the terms of the last three verses are more appropriate to the slaughter of the Assyrian host; but as this is not explicitly referred to, there is no need of regarding it as the exclusive subject even of that passage. The eighteenth chapter may then be treated as a part of the same context. In the first part of chap. xvii. the Prophet represents the kingdoms of Syria and Ephraim as sharing the same fate, both being brought to desolation, vers. 1–3. He then describes the desolation of Ephraim especially, by the figures of a harvest and a gathering of olives, in which little is left to be afterwards gleaned, vers. 4–6. As the effect of these judgments, he describes the people as renouncing their idols and returning to Jehovah, vers. 7, 8. He then resumes his description of the threatened desolation, and ascribes it to the general oblivion of God, and cultivation of strange doctrines and practices, vers. 9–11. This last might be regarded as a simple repetition of the threatenings in vers. 4–6, interrupted by the promise in vers. 7, 8. But as the desolation of Syria and Israel was actually effected by successive strokes or stages, as Shalmaneser accomplished what Tiglath-pileser had begun, and as history records a partial conversion of the Israelites from their apostasy between these two attacks, it is altogether natural to understand the prophecy as exhibiting this sequence of events. In the close of the chapter, the Prophet first describes a gathering of nations, and then their dispersion by divine rebuke, which he declares to be the doom of all who attack or oppress God's people, vers. 12–14.

1. *The burden of Damascus. Behold, Damascus is removed from (being) a city, and is a heap, a ruin.* On the meaning of *burden, vide supra*, chap. xiii. 1. The modern Germans suppose the first words to have been added by a copyist or compiler, on the ground that they are appropriate, as a title, only to the first few verses. Some have defended the correctness of the title, on the ground that Ephraim is only mentioned as an ally of Syria, or that Damascus is again included in the threatenings of vers. 9–11. The true answer seems to be, that the objection confounds these prophetic inscriptions with the titles or headings of modern composition. The latter are comprehensive summaries, entirely distinct from the text; the former are an original part of it. The one before us is equivalent to saying, " I have a threatening to announce against Damascus." Such an expression would not imply that no other subject was to be introduced, nor would the introduction of another subject justify the rejection of the prefatory formula as incorrect and therefore spurious. Not a little of the slashing criticism now in vogue rests upon a forced application of modern or occidental usages to ancient and oriental writings. The idiomatic phrase *removed from a city* is not to be explained as an ellipsis for *removed from* (the number of) *cities*, in which case the plural form would be essential. It rather means *removed from* (the state or condition of) *a city*, or, as Jarchi completes the construction, *from* (being) *a city*. Compare chap. vii. 8, and 1 Sam. xv. 26. Knobel needlessly and harshly explains *Damascus* as the name of the people, who are then described as being literally *removed from the city*. J. D. Michaelis, still more extravagantly, makes מוסר a noun and מעיר a particle. *Behold,*

Damascus ! punishment awakes ! מֵעִי occurs only here, and seems to have been used instead of the cognate עִי on account of its resemblance to מְעִיר. The last two words are propably in apposition rather than in regimen (acervus ruinæ) or in concord as an adjective and substantive (a ruinous heap). The radical idea in the first is that of *overturning*, in the other that of *falling*. Some regard this and the next two verses as a description of the past, and infer that the prophecy is subsequent in date to the conquest of Damascus and Syria. But as the form of expression leaves this undetermined, it is better to regard the whole as a prediction. Damascus is still the most flourishing city in Western Asia. It is also one of the most ancient. It is here mentioned as the capital of a kingdom, called *Syria of Damascus* to distinguish it from other Syrian principalities, and founded in the reign of David by Rezon (1 Kings xi. 23, 24). It was commonly at war with Israel, particularly during the reign of Benhadad and Hazael, so that a three years' peace is recorded as a long one (1 Kings xxii. 1). Under Rezin, its last king, Syria joined with Ephraim against Judah, during which confederacy, *i. e.* in the first years of the reign of Ahaz, this prophecy was probably uttered. From the resemblance of the names *Rezon* and *Rezin*, Vitringa takes occasion to make the following extraordinary statement. " Omnis docet historia mundi passim accidere, lusu quodam singulari Providentiæ Divinæ, ut regna et imperia iisdem vel similibus nominibus oriantur et occidant." Damascus appears to have experienced more vicissitudes than any other ancient city except Jerusalem. After the desolation here predicted it was again rebuilt, and again destroyed by Nebuchadnezzar, notwithstanding which it reappears in the Old Testament as a flourishing city and a seat of government. In the verse before us, the reference may be chiefly to its downfall as a royal residence.

2. *Forsaken (are) the cities of Aroer ; for flocks shall they be, and they shall lie down, and there shall be no one making (them) afraid.* There are three Aroers distinctly mentioned in the Bible : one in the territory of Judah (1 Sam. xxx. 28), one at the southern extremity of the land of Israel east of Jordan (Jos. xii. 2, xiii. 6), a third farther north and near to Rabbah (Jos. xiii. 25, Num. xxxii. 24). Some suppose a fourth in Syria, in order to explain the text before us, while others understand it as the name of a province in that kingdom. Vitringa thinks it either means the plain or valley of Damascus or Damascus itself, so called because divided and surrounded by the Chrysorroas, as one of the Aroers was by the Arnon (Josh. xii. 2). It is now commonly agreed that the place meant the northern Aroer east of Jordan, and that *its cities* are the towns around it and perhaps dependent on it. An analogous expression is the *cities of Heshbon* (Josh. xiii. 17). Knobel, however, understands the phrase to mean *the cities Aroer, i. e.* both the towns of that name, put for all the towns east of Jordan, on account of the resemblance of the name to עִיר, and perhaps with allusion to the sense of *nakedness*, belonging to the root. Thus understood, this verse predicts the desolation of Ephraim and not of Syria. It is possible, however, as well on account of their contiguity, as of the league between them, that they are here, as in chap. vii. 16, confounded or intentionally merged in one. At all times, it is probable, the boundaries between these adjacent states were fluctuating and uncertain. This accounts for the fact that the same place is spoken of at different times as belonging to Israel, to Moab, to Ammon, or to Syria. *Forsaken* probably means emptied of their people and left desolate. There is then a specific reference to deportation and exile.

3. *Then shall cease defence from Ephraim and royalty from Damascus and the rest of Syria. Like the glory of the children of Israel shall they be, saith Jehovah of hosts.* מבצר may be taken in its usual specific sense of a fortified place, meaning either Damascus (as a protection of the ten tribes) or Samaria (Micah i. 5). Some disregard the Masoretic interpunction, and connect *the rest of Syria* with the verb in the last clause : *the rest of Syria shall be*, &c. שאר may either mean the whole of Syria besides Damascus, or the *remnant* left by the Assyrian invaders. The latter agrees best with the terms of the comparison. What was left of Syria should resemble what was left of the glory of Israel. Houbigant and Lowth gratuitously read שאת *pride*, in order to obtain a parallel expression to כבוד. The *glory of Israel* is not Samaria, nor does it denote wealth or population exclusively, but all that constitutes the greatness of a people. (*Vide supra*, chap. v. 14). Jerome and others regard *glory* as an ironical and sarcastic expression ; but it seems to mean simply what is left of their former glory.

4. *And it shall be* (or *come to pass*) *in that day, the glory of Jacob shall be brought low* (or *made weak*), *and the fatness of his flesh shall be made lean.* This is not a mere transition from Syria to Ephraim, nor a mere extension of the previous threatenings to the latter, but an explanation of the comparison in the verse preceding. The remnant of Ephraim was to be like the glory of Israel; but how was that ? This verse contains the answer. *Glory*, as before, includes all that constitutes the strength of a people, and is here contrasted with a state of weakness. The same idea is expressed in the last clause by the figure of emaciation. The image, as Gill says, is that of " a man in a consumption, that is become a mere skeleton, and reduced to skin and bones." *Jacob* does not mean Judah (Eichhorn) but the ten tribes. Hendewerk refers the suffix in the last clause to כבוד, and infers that the latter must denote a human subject. Junius regards the sentence as unfinished : " in the day when the glory, &c., then shall it be (ver. 5), &c." Cocceius makes this the beginning of a promise of deliverance to Judah : "in that day, it is true (quidem), the glory of Jacob shall be reduced," &c., but (ver. 5) &c. Both these constructions supply something not expressed, and gratuitously suppose a sentence of unusual length.

5. *And it shall be like the gathering* (or *as one gathers*) *the harvest, the standing corn, and his arm reaps the ears. And it shall be like one collecting ears in the valley of Rephaim.* The first verb is not to be rendered *he shall be* (*i. e.* Israel, or the king of Assyria), but to be construed impersonally, *it shall be* or *come to pass.* Some suppose the first clause to describe the act of reaping, and the second that of gleaning. Others regard both as descriptive of the same act, a particular place being mentioned in the last clause to give life to the description. The valley of Rephaim or the Giants extends from Jerusalem to the south-west in the direction of Bethlehem. There is a difference of opinion as to the purpose for which it is here mentioned. Aben Ezra and Ewald suppose it to be named as a barren spot, producing scanty harvests, and gleanings in proportion. Most writers, on the contrary, assume it to have been remarkably fertile. Vitringa imagines at the same time an allusion to the level surface, as admitting of a more complete and thorough clearing by the reaper than uneven grounds. If we consider the passage without reference to imaginary facts, the most natural conclusion is that the valley of Rephaim was mentioned as a spot near to Jerusalem, and well known to the people, for the purpose of giving a specific character to the general description or allusion of the first clause. There

is no proof that it was remarkable either for fertility or barrenness. Some of the commentators represent it as now waste ; but Robinson speaks of it *en passant*, as " the cultivated valley or plain of Rephaim." (Palestine, i. 323). Some refer אסף to the act of gathering the stalks in one hand, in order to cut them with the other ; but this is a needless refinement. The Hebrew verb probably denotes the whole act of reaping. There are several different ways of construing קציר. Some make קמה agree with it as a feminine noun (*the standing harvest*), which is contrary to usage. Umbreit explains it as an adverb of time (*in harvest*), which is very forced. Gesenius adopts Aben Ezra's explanation of the word as equivalent in meaning to קצר or איש קציר. Some make קציר itself a verbal noun analogous in form and sense to שריד פליט, &c. Ewald makes the season of harvest (Erntezeit) the subject of the verb ; *as when the harvest-season gathers*, &c. Perhaps the simplest supposition is that קמה is in apposition with קציר, not as a mere synonyme, but as a more specific term, *the crop, the standing corn*. The suffix in זרעו then refers to the indefinite subject of the first clause. According to Cocceius, the point of the comparison is the care and skill with which the grain is gathered to be stored away ; in like manner God would cause his people to be gathered for their preservation. All other writers understand the figures as denoting the completeness of the judgment threatened against Israel.

6. *And gleanings shall be left therein like the beating* (or *shaking*) *of an olive tree, two* (or) *three berries in the top of a high bough, four* (or) *five in the branches of the fruit-tree, saith Jehovah, God of Israel.* There is here an allusion to the custom of beating the unripe olives from the tree for the purpose of making oil. Those described as left may either be the few left to ripen for eating, or the few overlooked by the gatherer or beyond his reach. The common version of עללות (*gleaning grapes*) is too restricted, and presents the incongruity of grapes upon an olive-tree. The transition from the figure of a harvest to that of an olive-gathering may be intended simply to vary and multiply the images, or, as Hitzig supposes, to complete the illustration which would otherwise have been defective, because the reaper is followed by the gleaner who completes the ingathering at once, whereas the olive-gatherer leaves some of course. The verb נשאר is masculine and singular, as in many other cases where the subject follows. The suffix in בו refers of course to Jacob or Israel, *i. e.* the ten tribes. Two, three, four, and five, are used, as in other languages, for an indefinite small number or *a few*. All interpreters agree that the idea of height is essentially included in אמיר. Aben Ezra connects it with the Arabic أَمِير (Emir) from which, says Gill, " the word amiral or admiral comes." Most writers give the Hebrew the specific sense of high or highest branch ; Henderson that of lofty tree ; Gesenius the more general sense of top or summit, in order to accommodate his explanation of the same word in ver. 9. The combination *head of the top* would then be emphatic, though unusual and scarcely natural. The suffix in סעפיה is treated by Gesenius as superfluous, and by others as belonging proleptically to the next word. Some of the older writers make פריה agree with it (*in its fruitful branches*), but the words differ both in gender and number. The latest writers seem to be agreed that the expression literally means *in the branches of it, the fruit-tree*, the *it* being unnecessary in any other idiom. The irregularity is wholly but arbitrarily removed by Hitzig's division of the words סעפי הפריה. This verse is regarded by Cocceius as a promise to the people, by others

as a promise to the pious Jews and especially to Hezekiah, but by most interpreters as describing the extent to which the threatened judgment would be carried. The gleanings, then, are not the pious remnant, but the ignoble refuse who survived the deportation of the ten tribes by the Assyrians.

7. *In that day man shall turn to his Maker, and his eyes to the Holy One of Israel shall look.* Grotius and Junius make this an advice or exhortation—*let him look*—but there is no ground for departing from the strict sense of the words as a prediction. שעה על occurs again below (chap. xxxi. 1) in the sense of looking to any one for help, which implies trust or confidence. The Septuagint accordingly has here πεποιθώς. Jarchi explains the phrase as equivalent to יפנה אל. The article before אדם gives it a generic, not a specific, sense. It does not therefore mean *every man* or the people in general (Barnes), but *man* indefinitely. It is commonly agreed that *Maker* is here used in a pregnant sense to describe God, not merely as the natural creator of mankind, but as the maker of Israel, the author of their privileges, and their covenant God. (Compare Deut. xxxii. 6.) The same idea is expressed by the parallel phrase, *Holy One of Israel*, for the import of which *vide supra*, chap. i. 4. Some refer this verse partially or wholly to the times of the New Testament, others more correctly to the effect of the preceding judgments on the ten tribes of Israel. It is matter of history, that after the Assyrian conquest and the general deportation of the people, many accepted Hezekiah's invitation and returned to the worship of Jehovah at Jerusalem (2 Chron. xxx. 11); and this reformation is alluded to as still continued in the times of Josiah (2 Chron. xxxiv. 9). At the same time the words may be intended to suggest, that a similar effect might be expected to result from similar causes in later times.

8. *And he shall not turn* (or *look*) *to the altars, the work of his own hands, and that which his own fingers have made shall he not regard, and the groves* (or *images of Ashtoreth*) *and the pillars* (or *images*) *of the sun.* The positive declaration of the preceding verse is negatively expressed in this, with a particular mention of the objects which had usurped the place of God. Kimchi's superficial observation, that even God's altar was the work of men's hands, and that this phrase must therefore denote idols, is adopted by Clericus (aras erectas operi manuum) and by Lowth, who observes that "all the ancient versions and most of the modern have mistaken it," and then goes on to say that מעשה is not in apposition with המזבחות, but governed by it; a construction precluded by the definite article before the latter word. The true explanation is that given by Calvin, and adopted by most later writers, viz. that idol-altars are described as the work of men's hands, because erected by their sole authority, whereas the altar at Jerusalem was, in the highest sense, the work of God himself. Vitringa arbitrarily explains the next clause (*what their fingers have made*) as synonymous neither with what goes before nor with what follows, but as denoting the household *gods* of the idolaters. The old writers take אשרים always in the sense of *groves*, *i. e.* such as were used for idol-worship. It has been shewn, however, by Selden, Spencer, Gesenius, and others, that in some places this sense is inadmissible, as when the אשרה is said to have stood upon an altar, or under a tree, or to have been brought out of a temple (1 Kings xiv. 23, 2 Chron. xxxiv. 4). The modern writers, therefore, understand it as denoting the goddess of fortune or happiness (from אשר, to be prosperous), otherwise called *Ashtaroth*, the Phenician Venus, extensively worshipped in

conjunction with Baal. But according to Movers, the Hebrew word denotes a straight or upright pillar. Ewald adheres to the old interpretation (Götzenhainer). חמנים is a derivative of חַמָּה, which properly means solar heat, but is poetically used to denote the sun itself. This obvious etymology, and the modern discovery of Punic cippi inscribed to בעל חמן, *Baal the Sun* (or *Solar*), lead to the conclusion that the word before us signifies images of Baal, worshipped as the representative of the sun. From the same etymology, Montanus derives the meaning, *loca aprica*, and Junius that of *statuas subdiales*. The explanation of the word, as meaning suns or solar images, is as old as Kimchi.

9. *In that day shall his fortified cities be like what is left in the thicket and the lofty branch*, (namely the cities) *which they leave* (as they retire) *from before the children of Israel, and* (the land) *shall be a waste.* It is universally agreed that the desolation of the ten tribes is here described by a comparison, but as to the precise form and meaning of the sentence there is great diversity of judgment. Some suppose the strongest towns to be here represented as no better defended than an open forest. Others on the contrary understand the strong towns alone to be left, the others being utterly destroyed. עזובת is variously understood to mean *what is left of* and *what is left in.* Hitzig and Hendewerk make *Horesh* and *Amir* proper names, the former identical with *Harosheth-goim* (Judges iv. 2, 13, 16), the latter with the 'Aμήϱυθα of Josephus or the 'Aνέϱθ of Eusebius. Symmachus, Aquila, and Theodotion all retained the word אמיר, and Theodotion חרש also. The Septuagint renders the words οἱ 'Aμοϱϱαῖοι ϰαὶ οἱ Εὐαῖοι. For the first the Peshito has *Heres.* The last two versions Vitringa connects by a reference to the statement (Judges i. 35) that the *Amorites would dwell in Mount Heres.* Ewald explains the Septuagint version on the ground that the old Canaanites divided themselves into the two great classes of Amorites (mountaineers), and Hittites (lowlanders) or Hivites (villagers). Jerome translates the words *aratra et segetes.* Capellus also has *arationis.* Most writers give אמיר the sense it has in ver. 6, and חרש that of a thick forest, or more specifically its underwood or thickets. Here as before, Henderson understands by אמיר a high tree, and Gesenius the summit of a hill. From the combination of these various verbal explanations have arisen two principal interpretations of the whole verse, or at least of the comparison which it contains. The first supposes the forsaken cities of Ephraim to be here compared with those which the Canaanites forsook when they fled before the Israelites under Joshua, or with the forests which the Israelites left unoccupied after the conquest of the country. The same essential meaning is retained by others who suppose the Prophet to allude to the overthrow of Sisera by Deborah and Barak. The other interpretation supposes no historical allusion, but a comparison of the approaching desolation with the neglected branches of a tree or forest that is felled, or a resumption of the figure of the olive tree in ver. 6. This last is strongly recommended by its great simplicity, by its superseding all gratuitous assumptions beyond what is expressed, and by its taking אמיר in the same sense which it has above. Another disputed point is the construction of אשר which some refer to the immediate antecedent, others less simply but more correctly to ערי מעוזו.

10. *Because thou hast forgotten the God of thy salvation, and the rock of thy strength hast not remembered, therefore thou wilt plant plants of pleasantness* (or pleasant plantations), *and with a strange slip set it.* Some render כי at the beginning *for*, and understand the first clause as giving a reason for

what goes before; but the emphatic על כן in the second clause seems to require that כי should have the meaning of *because*, and introduce the reason for what follows. The sense, then, is not merely that because they forgot God they were desolate, but that because they forgot God they fell into idolatry, and on that account were given up to desolation. Some regard the second clause of this verse and the whole of the next as a description of their punishment. Because they forgot God, they should sow and plant, but only for others; the fruit should be gathered not by themselves, but by their enemies (*Barbarus has segetes et culta novalia habebit*). Others suppose the description of the sin to be continued through this verse and the first clause of the next. Because they forgot God, they planted to please themselves, and introduced strange plants into their vineyard. On the latter hypothesis, the planting is a metaphor for the culture and propagation of corrupt opinions and practices, especially idolatry and illicit intercourse with heathen nations. According to the other view, the planting is to be literally understood, and the evil described is the literal fulfilment of the threatening in Deut. xxviii. 39. The latter sense is given by most of the early writers. Cocceius, who seems first to have proposed the other, thought it necessary to translate תטעי as a preterite (*plantabas*), which is ungrammatical and arbitrary. The same general sense may be attained without departing from the future form, by making the last clause of ver. 10 a prediction of what they would hereafter do, without excluding the idea that they had done so already, and were actually doing it. It is not even necessary to read with Grotius *quamvis plantaveris*, or with Henderson *thou mayest plant*, or with Umbreit *lass nur wachsen*, although these translations really convey the true sense of the clause. It is urged as an objection to the older and more literal interpretation, that the evil threatened is too insignificant for such a context. This objection might be abated by supposing the fruitless cultivation to be not strictly literal, but a figure for disappointment, or labour in vain generally. On the whole, however, it seems best to acquiesce in the opinion now very commonly adopted, that the planting here described is the sin of the people, not their punishment. Jerome confounds נעמנים with נאמנים, *fideles*, *i. e.* not disappointing expectation. The Septuagint strangely gives an opposite meaning (φύτευμα ἄπιστον), which is regarded by some as a mere blunder, by others as an arbitrary change, and by others as an error in the text. The older writers make the Hebrew word an adjective agreeing with *vines, fruits*, or some other noun understood. It is now commonly explained as an abstract, meaning pleasantness, and the whole phrase as equivalent to pleasant or favourite plants. A similar construction occurs in the last clause, where *slip* or *shoot of a stranger* is equivalent to a *strange slip* or *shoot*. Those who think a literal planting to be meant, understand *strange* to signify exotic, foreign, and by implication valuable, costly; but upon the supposition that a moral or spiritual planting is intended, זר has its frequent emphatic sense of *alien from God*, *i. e. wicked*, or more specifically *idolatrous*. Cocceius takes תזרע as the third person, which is forbidden by the preceding second person תטעי. The suffix in the last word may be most naturally referred to *vineyard, garden*, or a like word understood. J. D. Michaelis and others suppose an allusion in this last clause to the process of grafting, with a view to the improvement of the stock. The foreign growth introduced is understood by some to be idolatry, by others foreign alliance; but these two things, as we have seen before, were inseparably blended in the history and policy of Israel (*vide supra*, chap. ii. 6–8).

11. *In the day of thy planting thou wilt hedge it in, and in the morning thou wilt make thy seed to blossom,* (but) *away flies the crop in a day of grief and desperate sorrow.* The older writers derive תשגשגי from שגג, and explain it to mean *cause to grow.* The modern lexicographers assume a root שוג equivalent to שׂוּךְ, to enclose with a hedge. Either sense is appropriate as describing a part of the process of culture. *In the morning* is commonly explained as an idiomatic phrase for *early,* which some refer to the rapidity of growth, and others to the assiduity of the cultivator, neither of which senses is exclusive of the other. גֵד is elsewhere a noun meaning a *heap,* and is so explained here by the older writers : *the harvest* (shall be) *a heap,* *i.e.* a small or insufficient one. Vitringa derives גֵד from נוד, to lament, and translates it *comploratio.* Others give it the sense of *shaking, agitation.* Gesenius and the later writers make it the preterite of נוד, to flee (in form like מֵת). נַחֲלָה as pointed in the common text, is a noun meaning inheritance, possession, and most of the older writers understand ביום נהלה to mean *in the day of expected possession.* The latest writers, for the most part, read נַחְלָה which is properly the passive participle of חָלָה, but is used as a noun in the sense of *deadly wound* or *disease,* here employed as a figure for extreme distress. Even Jarchi explains it by the phrase יום צרה. The same idea is expressed by כְּאֵב אָנוּשׁ, which the Seventy seem to have read כְּאָב אֱנוֹשׁ, *like the father of a man.* Kimchi appears to assume an antithesis in each of these verses between the original and degenerate state of Israel : at first thou didst plant pleasant plants, but now thou hast set strange slips; at first thou didst make it to flourish, but now the harvest, &c. This, though ingenious, is entirely arbitrary and gratuitous. The usual and simple construction of the sentence gives a perfectly good sense.

12. *Hark! the noise of many nations! Like the noise of the sea they make a noise. And the rush of peoples! Like the rush of many waters they are rushing.* The diversity of judgments, as to the connection of the verses (12–14) with the context, has been already stated in the introduction. By different interpreters they are explained, as a direct continuation of the foregoing prophecy (J. D. Michaelis)—as a later addition or appendix to it (Hitzig)—as a fragment of a larger poem (Rosenmüller)— as an independent prophecy (Lowth)—as the beginning of that contained in the next chapter (Gesenius)—and as equally connected with what goes before and follows (Vitringa). That the passage is altogether broken and detached, and unconnected with what goes before (Barnes), it is as easy to deny as to affirm. On the whole, the safest ground to assume is that already stated in the introduction, viz., that the two chapters form a single prophecy or prophetic picture of the doom awaiting all the enemies of Judah, with particular allusion to particular enemies in certain parts. הוי is variously explained as a particle of cursing (Luther), of pity for the sufferings of God's people (Calvin), of wonder (Hitzig), or of simple invocation (Vitringa). Henderson understands it as directing attention to the sound described, which the Prophet is supposed to be actually hearing, an idea which Augusti happily expresses by translating the word *hark!* This descriptive character of the passage allows, and indeed requires, the verbs to be translated in the present tense. המון most frequently denotes a *multitude;* but here, being connected with the future and infinitive of its root (המה), it seems to have its primary sense of *noise* or *tumult.* רבים may either denote *great* (Luther) or *many* (Calvin); but the latter is preferred by most interpreters, and is most in accordance with the usage of the word. שאון is not simply noise or sound (Montanus), but more specifically a *roaring* (Lowth) or a *rushing*

(Augusti). The sense of *storm* (Cocceius) is not sufficiently sustained by usage. The nations meant are not Gog and Magog (Castalio), nor Syria and Israel (Clericus), nor their allies and abettors (Grotius), but all the hostile nations by whom Israel was scourged (Jarchi), with particular reference to Assyria, and especially to the army of Sennacherib. The application of the verse by most interpreters to these last alone is too exclusive; much more that of Gill to the " hectoring, blustering, and blaspheming speeches of Sennacherib and Rabshakeh." To the poetical images of this verse a beautiful parallel is adduced by Clericus from Ovid's Metamorphoses (xv. 604):

> Qualia fluctus
> Aequorei faciunt, si quis procul audiat ipsos,
> Tale sonat populus.

13. *Nations, like the rush of many waters, rush; and he rebukes it, and it flees from afar, and is chased like the chaff of hills before a wind, and like a rolling thing before a whirlwind.* The genuineness of the first clause is questioned by Lowth and Gesenius, because it is a repetition of what goes before, and is omitted in the Peshito and several manuscripts. Hendewerk and Knobel, on the contrary, pronounce it not only genuine, but full of emphasis, and Henderson describes it as a pathetic repetition. Thus the same expressions, which one critic thinks unworthy of a place in the text, are regarded by another as rhetorical beauties, an instructive illustration of the fluctuating and uncertain nature of conjectural criticism founded on the taste of individual interpreters. Luther and Augusti insert *yes* (ja) at the beginning of the verse, which, though unnecessary, indicates the true connection. The verb גָּעַר is often used in reference to God's control of the elements, denoting, as Gataker observes, a real rather than a verbal rebuke. Ewald, on the contrary, supposes the emphasis to lie in God's subduing the elemental strife by a bare word. The suffix in בּוֹ, and the verbs נָס and רָדַף, being all in the singular number, are referred by Hitzig to שָׁאוֹן, but more naturally by most other writers to Sennacherib, or his host considered as an individual. Knobel makes the suffix collective, as in chap. v. 26, and regards the singular verbs as equivalent to plurals. By using the neuter pronoun *it* in English, and making the verbs agree with it in number, the peculiar form of the original may be retained without additional obscurity. The subjunctive construction given by Junius (ut fugiat) and some others, is a needless departure from the idiomatic form of the original. The expression *from afar* is explained by Kimchi as meaning that the fugitive, having reached a distant point, would flee *from it* still farther. Vitringa understands it to mean that he would flee while human enemies were still at a distance. Most of the modern writers suppose *from* to be used, by a peculiar Hebrew idiom, as *to* would be employed in other languages. (See Nordheimer, § 1046, iv. 1.) Kimchi sees in רָדַף an allusion to the destroying angel. (Comp. Ps. xxxv. 5, 6.) מֹץ is not dust or straw, but chaff or stubble. Mountains, according to Gataker, are here contrasted with threshing-floors; but these were commonly on hills or knolls, where the wind blows freely. According to Jarchi, גַּלְגַּל is a ball of thistle-down; according to Gill, "a round wisp of straw or stubble." Junius translates it *rota*, Cocceius *vortex*, Lowth *gossamer*. All these interpretations are too definite. Calvin explains it, in accordance with its etymology, as meaning *rem volubilem*, anything blown round by the wind. This is also not improbably the meaning of the Vulgate version, *sicut turbo coram tempestate*. The common version, *rolling thing*, may therefore be retained. While there

seems to be an obvious allusion to the flight of Sennacherib and the remnant of his host (chap. xxxvii. 36, 37), the terms are so selected as to admit of a wider application to all Jehovah's enemies, and thus prepare the way for the general declaration in the following verse.

14. *At evening-tide, and behold terror; before morning he is not. This is* (or *be*) *the portion of our plunderers, and the lot of our spoilers.* According to Piscator, these are the words of the people; according to Henderson, their shout of exultation in the morning of their deliverance. Gill says the Prophet and the people speak together. There is no need, however, of departing from the simple supposition that the Prophet is the speaker, and that he uses the plural pronouns only to identify himself with the people. On account of the ו before הנה, some think it necessary to supply a verb before לעת, (they shall come) in the evening. The English Version, on the same ground, transfers *and behold* to the beginning of the sentence. But nothing is more common in the Hebrew idiom than the use of *and* after specifications of time. (See Gesenius, § 152, *a.*) In many cases it must be omitted in English, or exchanged for *then;* but in the present instance it may be retained. Luther renders ל *about* (um), Ewald *towards* (gegen), but Gesenius and most other writers *at* (zu), which is the simpler version, and the one most agreeable to usage. *Tide* is an old English word for *time*, identical in origin with the German *Zeit*. Lowth awkwardly substitutes *at the season of evening.* בַּלָּהָה is not merely *trouble*, but *terror, consternation.* Vitringa renders it still more strongly *horror*, and Ewald *Todesschrecken.* Cocceius has *nebula*, founded on an erroneous etymology. The reference of אֵינֶנּוּ to בַּלָּהָה, it (the terror) is no more, is ungrammatical, the latter being feminine. Gesenius, Hitzig, and Henderson have *they are no more.* Most writers suppose a specific allusion to Sennacherib or his host. It is best, at all events, to retain the singular form of the original, as being more expressive and poetical. The paraphrastic versions, *he shall no more be present* (J. H. Michaelis), *he is vanished* (Ewald), *there is no more any trace of him* (Augusti), and the like, are all not only less exact, but weaker than the literal translation, *he is not.* Lowth inserts ו before אֵינֶנּוּ, on the authority of several manuscripts and three ancient versions, thereby restoring, as he says, "the true poetical form," by obtaining a more exact parallel to והנה. Umbreit and others suppose night and morning to be here combined in the sense of a very short time, as in Ps. xxx. 5, *Weeping may endure for a night, but joy cometh in the morning.* (Compare Ps. xc. 6.) Most interpreters, however, suppose an allusion to the destruction of Sennacherib's army in a single night. Of these some, with Aben Ezra, understand by בַּלָּהָה the terror of the Jews on the eve of that event, relieved in the morning by the sight of the dead bodies. Others, with Jarchi, understand by it the sudden consternation of the Assyrians themselves when attacked by the destroying angel. Jarchi seems, moreover, to refer this panic to the agency of demons (שרים). The allusion to Sennacherib is denied by Grotius, Clericus, and Rosenmüller, the first two supposing Syria, or Syria and Israel, to be the only subject of the prophecy. Gesenius and Knobel arbitrarily assert that the history of the slaughter of Sennacherib's army is a *mythus* founded on this prophecy. The only reason why this assertion cannot be refuted is because it is a mere assertion. Before such licence of conjecture and invention, neither history nor prophecy can stand a moment. The correct view of the verse before us seems to be, that while the imagery is purposely suited to the slaughter of Sennacherib's army, the

description is intended to include other cases of deliverance granted to God's people by the sudden and complete destruction of their enemies. Calvin supposes this more general sense to be expressed by the figure of a storm at night which ceases before morning. " Quemadmodum tempestas, vesperi excitata et paulo post sedata, mane nulla est amplius, ideo futurum ut hostibus dispulsis redeat subito praeter spem laeta serenitas.'' Not content with this comprehensive exposition, Cocceius, true to his peculiar principles of exegesis, specifies as subjects of the prophecy the whole series of Assyrian and Babylonian kings, Antiochus Epiphanes, the persecuting Jews, Nero, Domitian, Chosroes king of Persia, and the persecuting kings of France and England, adding, not without reason after such a catalogue, "utile est, cumprimis studiosis theologiae, historiam ecclesiæ et hostium ejus non ignorare.'' The substantive verb being suppressed, as usual, in the last clause of the verse, it may be either an affirmation of a general fact, or an expression of desire, as in the close of Deborah and Barak's song, *so let all thine enemies perish, O Jehovah* (Judges v. 31). The first explanation is in this case more obvious and natural, and is accordingly preferred by most interpreters.

Chapter 18

THE two great powers of western Asia, in the days of Isaiah, were Assyria, and Egypt or Ethiopia, the last two being wholly or partially united under Tirhakah, whose name and exploits are recorded in Egyptian monuments still extant, and who is expressly said in Scripture (2 Kings xix. 9) to have come out against Sennacherib. With one or the other of these great contending powers, Judah was commonly confederate, and of course at war with the other. Hezekiah is explicitly reproached by Rabshakeh (Isa. xxxvi. 9) with relying upon Egypt, *i. e.* the Ethiopico-Egyptian empire. These historical facts, together with the mention of Cush in ver. 1, and the appropriateness of the figures in vers. 4, 5, to the destruction of Sennacherib's army, give great probability to the hypothesis now commonly adopted, that the Prophet here announces that event to Ethiopia, as about to be effected by a direct interposition of Jehovah, and without human aid. On this supposition, although not without its difficulties, the chapter before us is much clearer in itself and in its connection with the one before it, than if we assume with some interpreters, both Jews and Christians, that it relates to the restoration of the Jews, or to the overthrow of the Egyptians or Ethiopians themselves, as the enemies of Israel. At the same time, some of the expressions here employed admit of so many interpretations, that it is best to give the whole as wide an application as the language will admit, on the ground before suggested, that it constitutes a part of a generic prophecy or picture of God's dealings with the foes of his people, including illustrations drawn from particular events, such as the downfall of Syria and Israel, and the slaughter of Sennacherib's army.

The Prophet first invites the attention of the Ethiopians and of the whole world to a great catastrophe as near at hand, vers. 1–3. He then describes the catastrophe itself, by the beautiful figure of a vine or vineyard suffered to blossom and bear fruit, and then, when almost ready to be gathered, suddenly destroyed, vers. 4–6. In consequence of this event, the same people, who had been invoked in the beginning of the chapter, are described as bringing presents to Jehovah at Jerusalem, ver. 7.

1. *Ho! land of rustling wings, which art beyond the rivers of Cush* (or Ethiopia)! הוֹי is rendered *woe!* by the Septuagint, Cocceius, and Paulus, *hark!* by Augusti, but by most other writers, as a particle of calling, *ho!* or *ha!* צִלְצַל is explained by some as an intensive or frequentative form of צֵל, a *shadow*, in which sense it is rendered by the Peshito and Aquila (σκιὰ πτερύγων)—here used as a figure for protection (Calvin)—or in allusion to the shadow cast by a double chain of mountains (Saadias, Abulwalid, Grotius, Junius, Vitringa, Dathe)—or to the opposite direction of the shadows in winter and summer under the tropics (Vogt, Aurivillius, Eichhorn, Knobel)—a circumstance particularly mentioned in connection with Meroe by Pliny (in Meroe his anno absumi umbras), Lucan (donec umbras extendat Meroe), and other ancient writers. Knobel takes כְּנָפִים in the sense of *sides* (chap. xxx. 20, xi. 12; Ezek. vii. 2), and supposes the expression to have been suggested by the common phrase *shadow of wings* (Ps. xvii. 8, xxxvi. 8, lvii. 2, lxiii. 8). But as the double form צִלְצַל in every other case has reference to sound, some suppose an allusion to the noise made by the locusts, one of the names of which in Hebrew is צְלָצַל (Paulus, J. D. Michaelis)—some to the rushing sound of rivers (Umbreit)—others to the clash of arms or other noises made by armies on the march, here called *wings* by a common figure (Gesenius, Rosenmüller, Hitzig, Maurer, Hendewerk). But Knobel denies that כָּנָף, absolutely used, can signify an army. The plural צְלָצְלִים is elsewhere used in the sense of *cymbals*, and the Vulgate here has *terrae cymbalo alarum.* Bohart, Huet, Clericus, and Lowth, suppose the word to be here applied to the Egyptian *sistrum*, a species of cymbal, consisting of a rim or frame of metal, with metallic rods or plates passing through and across it, the extremities of which might be poetically called wings. From the resemblance of the ancient ships to cymbals, or of their sails to wings, or from both together, the phrase before us is applied to ships by the Septuagint (πλοίων πτέρυγες), Targum, Kimchi, and Ewald (O Land geflügelter Kähne!) The relative אֲשֶׁר is construed with the nearest antecedent כְּנָפִים by Cocceius and J. H. Michaelis, but by most other writers with the remoter antecedent אֶרֶץ. מֵעֵבֶר לְ is understood to mean *on this side* by Vitringa, Hitzig, and Hendewerk—*on that side* or *beyond* by Gesenius, Rosenmüller, Maurer, Umbreit, and most of the older writers— *at the side* or *along* by Saadias, Grotius, Junius, Lowth, Barnes, Ewald, Knobel, and others. *Cush* is supposed by Wahl to mean *Chusistan* or *Turan*, both here and in Gen. ii. 13—by Bochart, Ethiopia and the opposite part of Arabia, but by Gesenius and the later writers, Ethiopia alone. The *rivers of Cush* are supposed by some to be the Nile and its branches— by others, the Astaboras, Astapus, and Astasobas, mentioned by Strabo as the rivers of Meroe, which last name Knobel traces to the Ethiopic root רוּי as he does the Hebrew *Saba* to the synonymous סְבָא, both implying an abundant irrigation. The country thus described is understood by Cyril, Jerome, Bochart, Vitringa, and Lowth, to be Egypt; by most other writers Ethiopia; but by Knobel, Saba or Meroe, a region contiguous to Ethiopia, and watered by its rivers, often mentioned with it, but distinguished from it (Gen. x. 7; Isa. xliii. 3; xlv. 14). Besides the usual construction of the first clause, may be mentioned that of Döderlein, Hensler, and Dereser, who make צִלְצַל a verb (er schwirrt), and that of Augusti; "hearken, oh land, to the rushing of his wings who is beyond the rivers of Ethiopia."

2. *Sending by sea ambassadors, and in vessels of papyrus on the face of the waters. Go ye light* (or *swift*) *messengers, to a nation drawn and shorn,*

*to a people terrible since it existed and onwards, a nation of double strength,
and trampling, whose land the streams divide.* Nearly every word and
phrase of this difficult verse has been the subject of discordant explanations.
הַשֹּׁלֵחַ is translated in the second person (thou that sendest) by Cocceius,
Clericus, Vitringa, and Henderson ; by most other writers in the third.
It refers not to God, but to the people mentioned in ver. 1. Vitringa
construes it with עַם understood, Gesenius with אֶרֶץ in the sense of עַם, and
therefore masculine. יָם is variously explained to mean the Red Sea, the
Mediterranean, and the Nile (Isa. xix. 5 ; Nahum iii. 8). Bochart takes
צִירִים in the sense of *images,* supposing an allusion to the Egyptian prac-
tice, mentioned by Cyril, Procopius, and Lucian, of sending an image of
Osiris annually on the surface of the sea to Byblus in Phenicia. The
Septuagint renders the word hostages (ὅμηρα) ; but all the latest writers
are agreed in giving it the sense of ambassadors, to wit, those sent to
Ethiopia, or from Ethiopia to Judah. The next phrase is rendered in the
Septuagint, ἐπιστολὰς βιβλίνας, but is now universally explained to mean
vessels made of the papyrus plant, the use of which upon the Nile is expressly mentioned by Theophrastus, Pliny, Lucan, and Plutarch. The
second clause of the verse (לְכוּ &c.) is regarded by some writers as the
language of the people who had just been addressed, as if he had said,
" sending ambassadors (and saying to them) go," &c. More probably,
however, the Prophet is still speaking in the name of God. The following
epithets are applied by some to the Jews, and supposed to be descriptive
of their degraded and oppressed condition. Gesenius and the later writers
apply them to the Ethiopians, and make them descriptive of their warlike
qualities. מְמֻשָּׁךְ, according to usage, means drawn or drawn out, which
is applied by some to the shape of the country, by others to the numbers
engaged in foreign war, by the Septuagint and Hitzig to the stature of the
people. This meaning is rejected by Gesenius in his Commentary, but
approved in his Thesaurus. The meanings convulsed (Vulgate), and torn
(Luther), are not justified by usage. Those of ancient, inaccessible, and
scattered, are entirely conjectural. מוֹרָט for מְמוֹרָט properly denotes shorn
or shaven, and is applied by some to the Ethiopian and Egyptian practice
of shaving the head and beard, while others understand it as a figure for robbery and spoliation. Some understand it to mean smoothed or smooth, and
by implication beautiful. Others apply it to the character, and take it in the
sense of brave or fierce. מִן הוּא is by some applied to time, from the first and
hitherto, from the earliest time, from this time ; by others to place, from this
place and onward. Many interpreters make it comparative, more terrible than
this, or any other, more terrible than this and farther off. In favour of applying it to time, are the analogous expressions in 1 Sam. xviii. 9, while 1 Sam.
xx. 22 justifies the local sense. קַו־קָו is explained by Clericus to be the
proper name of the Egyptian plant called *kiki.* Most writers take it in its
usual sense of line, *i. e.* as some suppose, a rule or precept, the people
being described as burdened with superstitious rites ; according to others,
a measuring line, meted or meting out others to destruction ; according to
a third class, a boundary line, enlarging its boundaries. Some make it
mean *on every side,* and others *by degrees,* in both cases qualifying that
which follows. But the latest German writers make the word identical
with the Arabic قُوَّة, meaning power, the reduplication signifying double
strength. מְבוּסָה must then have an active sense, a people of trampling,
i. e. trampling on their enemies. Those who apply the description to the

Jews give the word of course a passive sense, a people trampled on by their oppressors. By rivers, in the last clause, some suppose nations to be meant, or the Assyrians in particular; but most writers understand it literally as a description of the country. בזא is explained by the Rabbins as a synonyme of בזז, to spoil or plunder, and a few manuscripts read בזזו. Others give the verb the sense of nourishing, watering, overflowing, washing away, promising; but the best sense is that of cutting up, cutting through, or simply dividing, in allusion to the abundant irrigation of Ethiopia. Vitringa supposes this clause to refer to the annual overflowing of the Nile, and the one before it to the Egyptian practice of treading the grain into the soil when softened by the inundation.

3. *All ye inhabitants of the world, and dwellers on the earth, shall see as it were the raising of a standard on the mountains, and shall hear as it were the blowing of a trumpet.* Another construction, more generally adopted, makes the verbs imperative, and the כ a particle of time, as it usually is before the infinitive. So the English Version: *see ye when he lifteth up an ensign on the mountains, and when he bloweth a trumpet hear ye.* There seems, however, to be no sufficient reason for departing from the strict translation of the verbs as future; and if this be retained, it is better to make כ a particle of comparison. In either case, the verse invites the attention of the world to some great event. The restricted explanation of תבל and ארץ, as meaning *land* or *country*, is entirely arbitrary. According to Vitringa, Gesenius, Rosenmüller, and Maurer, the signals meant are those of the Assyrian invader, or those announcing his destruction; but according to Döderlein, Hitzig, Hendewerk, and Knobel, the signals by means of which the Ethiopians would collect their forces.

4. *For thus said* (or *saith*) *Jehovah to me, I will rest* (remain quiet) *and will look on* (as a mere spectator) *in my dwelling-place, like a serene heat upon herbs, like a cloud of dew* (or dewy cloud), *in the heat of harvest* (*i. e.* the heat preceding harvest, or the heat by which the crop is ripened). This verse assigns a reason for the preceding invitation to attend. The obvious meaning of the figure is, that God would let the enemy proceed in the execution of his purposes until they were nearly accomplished. Gesenius and the later writers explain כ before חם and עב as a particle of time, "during the heat and dewy cloud," *i. e.* the summer season. This use of the particle, which is very common before the infinitive, is rare and doubtful before nouns, and ought not to be assumed without necessity. According to this construction, the words merely indicate the time of God's apparent inaction. If we give the כ its proper sense as a comparative particle, the meaning seems to be, that he would not only abstain from interfering with the enemy, but would even favour his success to a certain point, as dew and sunshine would promote the growth of plants. The latest writers give to אור the sense of sunshine, and explain the whole phrase to mean the clear or genial heat which accompanies the sunshine, and is produced by it. But as this requires the preposition (עֲלֵי) to be taken in an unusual sense, it is better perhaps to regard אור as synonymous with אוֹרָה, herb or herbage. Some of the Rabbins explain אור, here and in Job xxxvi. 22, xxxvii. 11, as meaning *rain* (*like clear heat after rain*); but of this sense there are no decisive examples. Junius and Lowth make מְכוֹנִי the object of the contemplation, whereas it is merely added to express the idea of *rest at home*, as opposed to activity abroad. It is not necessary, therefore, to explain the noun as meaning *heaven*, although this is better than its application to the earthly sanctuary.

5. *For before the harvest, as the bloom is finished, and the flower becomes a ripening grape, he cuts down the branches with the pruning knives, and the tendrils he removes, he cuts away.*   The obvious meaning of the figure is, that although God would suffer the designs of the enemy to approach completion, he would nevertheless interfere at the last moment, and destroy both him and them.   Some writers give to כִּי the sense of *but*, in order to make the antithesis clearer ; but in this, as in many other cases, the particle refers to something more remote than the immediately preceding words, and is correctly explained by Knobel as correlative and parallel with the כִּי at the beginning of ver. 4.   As if he had said, let all the world await the great catastrophe—*for* I will let the enemy almost attain his end—but let them still attend—*for* before it is attained, I will destroy him.   The verbs in the last clause may either be referred directly to *Jehovah* as their subject, or construed indefinitely, one shall cut them down.   Jarchi supplies the participle or cognate noun (כרת הכורת) as in chap. xvi. 10.   The form הֵתַז is derived by Gesenius from תִּיז, by Hitzig from תָּזַז, and by Knobel from נָתַז, but all agree as to the meaning.   The verb יִהְיֶה receives its form from the predicate, and not from the subject, which is feminine.   (See Gesenius, § 134.)

6. *They shall be left together to the wild birds of the mountains, and to the wild beasts of the earth* (or *land*), *and the wild bird shall summer thereon, and every wild beast of the earth* (or *land*) *thereon shall winter.*   It is commonly supposed that there is here a transition from the figure of a vineyard to that of a dead body, the branches cut off and thrown away being suddenly transformed into carcasses devoured by beasts and birds.   For a like combination, *vide supra*, chap. xiv. 19.   But this interpretation, though perhaps the most natural, is not absolutely necessary.   As the act of devouring is not expressly mentioned, the reference may be, not to the carnivorous habits of the animals, but to their wild and solitary life.   In that case, the sense would be, that the amputated branches, and the desolated vineyard itself, shall furnish lairs and nests for beasts and birds which commonly frequent the wildest solitudes, implying abandonment and utter desolation.   This seems to be the meaning put upon the words by Luther, who translates the verbs *shall make their nests* and *lie therein* (darinnen nisten, darinnen liegen).   The only reason for preferring this interpretation is that it precludes the necessity of assuming a mixed metaphor, or an abrupt exchange of one for another, both which, however, are too common in Isaiah to excite surprise.   On either supposition, the general meaning of the verse is obvious.   The form of the last clause is idiomatic, the birds being said to spend the summer and the beasts the winter, not with reference to any real difference in their habits, but for the purpose of expressing the idea, that beasts and birds shall occupy the spot throughout the year.   According to the common explanation of the verse as referring to dead bodies, it is a hyperbolical description of their multitude, as furnishing repast for a whole year to the beasts and birds of prey.

7. *At that time shall be brought a gift to Jehovah of hosts, a people drawn out and shorn, and from a people terrible since it has been and onward* (or still more terrible and still farther off), *a nation of double power and trampling, whose land streams divide, to the place of the name of Jehovah of hosts, mount Zion.*   Here, as in ver. 2, the sense of some particular expressions is so doubtful, that it seems better to retain, as far as possible, the form of the original, with all its ambiguity, than to attempt an explanatory paraphrase.   All are agreed that we have here the prediction of an act

of homage to Jehovah, occasioned by the great event described in the preceding verses. The Jews, who understand the second verse as a description of the sufferings endured by Israel, explain this as a prophecy of their return from exile and dispersion, aided, and as it were presented as an offering to Jehovah, by the heathen. (*Vide infra*, chap. lxvi. 20.) The older Christian writers understand it as predicting the conversion of the Egyptians or Ethiopians to the true religion. Whoever, says Gesenius, is fond of tracing the fulfilment of such prophecies in later history, may find this one verified in Rev. viii. 26, *seq.*, and still more in the fact that Abyssinia is at this day the only great Christian power of the East. Gesenius himself, with the other recent Germans, understands the verse as describing a solemn contemporary recognition of Jehovah's power and divinity, as displayed in the slaughter of Sennacherib's army. According to Gesenius, two different nations are described both here and in ver. 2, an opinion which he thinks is here confirmed by the insertion of the copulative ו before the second עם. But Knobel refers to chap. xxvii. 1, and Zech. ix. 9, as proving that this form of expression does not necessarily imply a plurality of subjects. A stronger argument in favour of Gesenius's hypothesis is furnished by the insertion of the preposition before the second עם. The most natural construction of the words would seem to be that the gift to Jehovah should consist of one people offered by another. Most interpreters, however, including Gesenius himself, infer that מן must be supplied before the first עם also—a gift shall be brought (*from*) *a people*, &c., *and from a people*, &c.—whether the latter be another or the same. If another, it may be Ethiopia as distinguished from Egypt, or Meroe as distinguished from Ethiopia. If the same, it may either be Egypt, or more probably the kingdom of Tirhakah, including Ethiopia and Upper Egypt. The substitution of עם here for גוי in ver. 2, and the antithesis between them there, are regarded by Cocceius as significant, and founded on the constant usage of גוי to denote a heathen and עם a believing people. Most other writers seem to regard them as poetical equivalents. The place of God's name is not merely the place called by his name, as explained by Clericus and J. D. Michaelis, but the place where his name, *i. e.* the manifestation of his attributes, resides.

Chapter 19

THIS chapter admits of a well-defined division into two parts, one of which contains threatenings (vers. 1–17), and the other promises (vers. 18–25). The first part may again be subdivided. In vers. 1–4, the Egyptians are threatened with a penal visitation from Jehovah, with the downfall of their idols, with intestine commotions, with the disappointment of their superstitious hopes, and with subjection to hard masters. In vers. 5–10 they are threatened with physical calamities, the drying up of their streams, the decay of vegetation, the loss of their fisheries, and the destruction of their manufactures. In vers. 11–17, the wisdom of their wise men is converted into folly, the courage of their brave men into cowardice, industry is universally suspended, and the people filled with dread of the anger of Jehovah. The second part may be also subdivided. In vers. 18–21, the Egyptians are described as acknowledging the true God, in consequence of what they had suffered at his hand, and the deliverance which he had granted them. In vers. 22–25, the same cause is described as leading to an intimate union between Egypt, Assyria, and Israel, in the service of Jehovah, and the enjoyment of his favour.

Cocceius takes *Egypt* in what he calls its mystical sense, as meaning Rome, or the Roman empire, and explains the chapter as a synopsis of Church history from the conversion of Constantine to the latest time. Both the fundamental hypothesis and the details of his exposition are entirely arbitrary. He also violates the obvious relation of the parts by making the whole chapter minatory in its import. A similar objection lies against the theory of Cyril, Eusebius, Jerome, and others, who understand the whole as a prediction of the conversion of the Egyptians to Christianity. But the first part (vers. 1–17) cannot be explained, except by violence, either as a promise or a figurative description of conversion. Junius errs in the opposite extreme, by applying the first part in a literal sense to events in the early history of Egypt, and the last in a figurative sense to the calling of the gentiles, without sufficiently explaining the transition or connection of the parts. Grotius applies the whole to events which occurred before the advent. He regards the first part as a description of the troubles in Egypt during the dodecarchy which preceded the reign of Psammetichus, the last part as a prophecy of the diffusion of the true religion by the influx of Jews into Egypt. Clericus agrees with him in principle, but differs in detail by referring the first part of the chapter to the conquest of Egypt by Nebuchadnezzar. J. D. Michaelis takes the same general view, but applies the first part to the troubles in Egypt under Sethos, and the last part to the recognition of Jehovah as a true God by the Egyptians themselves, but without abjuring heathenism. Vitringa more ingeniously explains the first part as a prediction of the conquest of Egypt by the Persians, and the second as a promise of deliverance by Alexander the Great, and of general peace and friendly intercourse, as well as religious advancement under his successors, the Syrian and Egyptian kings, by which the way would be prepared for the introduction of the Gospel. This view of the passage is substantially adopted by Lowth, Barnes, and Henderson. Of the modern German writers, some explain the difference between the two parts of the chapter by supposing an interpolation. Thus Koppe and Eichhorn regard vers. 18–25 as a distinct prophecy, and even Gesenius doubts the genuineness of vers. 18–20. Hitzig supposes vers. 16–25 to have been forged by Onias, when he induced Ptolemy to build a temple for the Jews at Leontopolis. These absurd suppositions have been fully and triumphantly refuted by later writers of the same school, and especially by Hendewerk and Knobel. The notion of Koppe and Eichhorn, that even the first part is later than the times of Isaiah, has also been exploded. Ewald admits a peculiarity of manner, but ascribes it to the old age of Isaiah, when this prophecy was written. Gesenius, Rosenmüller, Hendewerk, and Knobel, proceeding on the twofold supposition, that the first part must describe the events of a particular period, and that prophetic foresight is impossible, are under the necessity of finding something in the contemporary history of Egypt, corresponding to the terms of the description. Gesenius and Knobel, in particular, have taken vast pains to combine and reconcile the contradictory accounts of Herodotus, Diodorus, and Manetho, as to the dynasties of Egypt, the succession of the several monarchs, and especially the date of the accession of Psammetichus. Ewald and Umbreit, much more rationally, reject the hypothesis of specific historical allusions, and regard the whole as an indefinite anticipation. On the same general principle, but with a far closer approximation to the truth, Calvin and J. D. Michaelis understand the chapter as a prophetic picture of the downfall of the old Egyptian empire, and of the subsequent conversion of its people.   The most correct view of the matter seems to be as follows :   The Prophet, wishing to announce to the Jews the decline and fall of that great heathen power, in which they were so constantly disposed to trust (xxx. 1, xxxi. 1), describes the event under figures borrowed from the actual condition of Egypt.   As a writer, who should now predict the downfall of the British empire, in a poetical and figurative style, would naturally speak of its fleets as sunk or scattered, its colonies dismembered, its factories destroyed, its railways abandoned, its universities abolished, so the Prophet vividly portrays the fall of Egypt, by describing the waters of the Nile as failing, its meadows withering, its fisheries ceasing, and the peculiar manufactures of the country expiring, the proverbial wisdom of the nation changed to folly, its courage to cowardice, its strength to weakness.   Whether particular parts of the description were intended to have a more specific application, is a question not affecting the truth of the hypothesis, that the first part is a metaphorical description of the downfall of the great Egyptian monarchy.   So too in the second part, the introduction of the true religion, and its effect as well on the internal state as on the international relations of the different countries, is expressed by figures drawn from the civil and religious institutions of the old economy. The comparative merits of this exegetical hypothesis and those which have been previously stated, will be best exhibited in the detailed interpretation of the chapter.   It will only be necessary here to add that there is no abrupt transition, but a natural and intimate connection between the downfall of a heathen power and the growth of the true religion, and also that nothing can be more arbitrary than the exposition of the first part as a literal, and of the other as a metaphorical prediction.

1. *The Burden of Egypt.   Behold ! Jehovah riding on a light cloud, and he comes to* (or *into*) *Egypt, and the idols of Egypt move at his presence, and the heart of Egypt melts within him.*   This verse describes God as the author of the judgments afterwards detailed.   His visible appearance on a cloud, and the personification of the idols, prepare the mind for a poetical description.   Lowth, Barnes, and Henderson, translate the suffix in the last word *her*.   But מִצְרַיִם is here the name of the ancestor (Gen. x. 6) put for his descendants.   The English Version has the neuter *it*.   The act of riding on a light cloud implies that he comes from heaven, and that he comes swiftly.   On the contemptuous import of the word translated *idols, vide supra,* chap. ii. 8 ; on the meaning of מַשָּׂא, chap. xiii. 1.

2. *And I will excite Egypt against Egypt, and they shall fight, a man with his brother, and a man with his fellow, city with city, kingdom with kingdom.* The first verb is by some rendered *arm*, by others *join* or engage in conflict ; but the sense of *stirring up* or *rousing* is preferred both by the oldest and the latest writers.   The version usually given, *Egyptians against Egyptians*, though substantially correct, is neither so expressive nor so true to the original as that of J. D. Michaelis and Augusti, *Egypt against Egypt*, which involves an allusion to the internal divisions of the kingdom, or rather the existence of contemporary kingdoms, more explicitly referred to in the other clause.   The last words are rendered in the Septuagint, νόμος ἐπὶ νόμον, meaning no doubt the thirty-six *nomes* or provinces of ancient Egypt. Grotius, J. D. Michaelis, Gesenius, and others, understand this verse as referring specifically to the civil wars of Egypt in the days of Sethos or Psammetichus.   But while the coincidence with history adds greatly to the propriety and force of the description, there is no sufficient reason for

departing from its obvious import, as a description of internal strife and anarchy in general. The expressions bear a strong resemblance to those used in the description of the state of Judah, chap. iii. 5. Junius regards these as the words to be uttered by Jehovah when he enters Egypt. It may, however, be a simple continuation of the prophecy, with a sudden change from the third to the first person, of which there are many other examples.

3. *And the spirit of Egypt shall be emptied out* (or *exhausted) in the midst thereof, and the counsel* (or *sagacity) thereof I will swallow up* (annihilate or render useless), *and they will seek to the idols, and to the mutterers, and to the familiar spirits, and to the wizards.* By *spirit* we are not to understand courage but intellect. Gesenius, in his Lexicon, reads מְקִרְבּוֹ and renders it *out of* or *from the midst of it.* The original and proper sense of אָטִים seems to be *murmurs* or *mutterings,* here applied to the mutterers themselves, in allusion to the ancient mode of incantation, as to which, and the meaning of אוֹבוֹת and יִדְּעֹנִים, *vide supra,* chap. viii. 19. נִבְקָה is variously rendered by the early writers, *troubled, decayed, destroyed,* &c., but the etymology is decisive in favour of the sense now commonly adapted. Augusti expresses the contemptuous import of אֱלִילִים by translating it *their wretched gods.*

4. *And I will shut up Egypt in the hands of a hard master, and a strong king shall rule over them, saith the Lord Jehovah of hosts.* As סָכַר means to shut up wherever it occurs, the intensive form here used cannot have the weaker sense of *giving up, delivering,* in which some take it. קָשֶׁה and עַז do not mean *cruel* or *fierce,* but *stern* or *rigorous.* The first of these Hebrew words is singular in form but construed with a plural noun. The Septuagint renders both phrases in the plural. Junius makes the first plural and refers it to the dodecarchy which intervened between the reigns of Sethos and Psammetichus. Cocceius makes קָשֶׁה agree with something understood (*dominorum gravis dominationis*), and refers to examples of a similar construction in Exod. xxviii. 17, Judg. v. 13, 1 Kings vii. 42, 2 Kings iii. 4. Most of the later writers are agreed in explaining אֲדֹנִים as a *pluralis majestaticus,* elsewhere applied to individual men (2 Kings xlii. 30, 33, 2 Kings ii. 3, 5, 16). The king here mentioned is identified, according to their various hypotheses, by J. D. Michaelis with Sethos, by Grotius, Gesenius, and others with Psammetichus, by the Rabbins with Sennacherib, by Hitzig and Hendewerk with Sargon, by Clericus with Nebuchadnezzar, by Vitringa with Cambyses or Ochus, by Cocceius with Charlemagne. The very multiplicity of these explanations shews how fanciful they are, and naturally leads us to conclude, not with Ewald that the Prophet is expressing mere conjectures or indefinite anticipations (reine Ahnung), but with Calvin that he is describing in a general way the political vicissitudes of Egypt, one of which would be subjection to an arbitrary power, whether foreign or domestic, or to both at different periods of its history.

5. *And the waters shall be dried up from the sea, and the river shall fail and be dried up.* Three distinct verbs are here used in the sense of drying up, for which our language does not furnish equivalents. As the Nile has in all ages been called a sea by the Egyptians (Robinson's Palestine, i. 542), most interpreters suppose it be here referred to, in both clauses. Gesenius and others understand the passage as foretelling a literal failure of the irrigation upon which the fertility of Egypt depends. Vitringa, Knobel, and others, explain it as a figurative threatening of disorder and calamity. Grotius supposes an allusion to the decay of the Egyptian commerce as conducted on the Nile and the adjacent seas; Calvin to the loss of the

defence and military strength afforded by these waters. According to the exegetical hypothesis laid down in the introduction to the chapter, this is a prediction of Egypt's national decline and fall, clothed in figures drawn from the characteristic features of its actual condition. As the desolation of our own western territory might be poetically represented as the drying up of the Mississippi and its branches, so a like event in the history of Egypt would be still more naturally described as a desiccation of the Nile, because that river is still more essential to the prosperity of the country which it waters. In favour of this figurative exposition is the difficulty of applying the description to particular historical events, and also the whole tenor of the context, as will be more clearly seen hereafter. The Septuagint treats נִשְׁתּוּ as an active form of שָׁתָה, to drink, the Egyptians shall drink water from the sea. Aquila makes it a passive from the same root, shall be drunk up or absorbed. Hitzig derives it from שָׁתַת, in the sense of settling, subsiding, and so failing. Gesenius and most other writers make it a derivative of נָשַׁת. Junius understands this verse as relating to the diversion of the waters of the Nile to form the lake Moeris, and Luzzatto proposes to take יָם as the name of the lake itself. By the drying up of the seas and rivers, Cocceius understands the irruption of the Saracens and Turks into Europe.

6. *And the rivers shall stink*, (or become putrid), *the streams of Egypt are emptied and dried up, reed and rush sicken* (pine or wither). The streams meant are the natural and artifical branches of the Nile. יְאֹר is an Egyptian word meaning *river*, and is specially appropriated to the Nile itself. The older writers take מָצוֹר in its usual meaning of defence or fortification, and understand the whole phrase as denoting either the moats and ditches of fortified places, or walled reservoirs. The modern writers regard מָצוֹר as the singular of מִצְרַיִם, denoting either Lower Egypt or the whole country indiscriminately. Ewald translates it *Angstland*, in allusion to the supposed root צוּר or צָרַר, to press. הֶאֶזְנִיחוּ is explained by the older writers as meaning to depart or to be turned away, but is now commonly understood to denote the stench or putrescence produced by the failure of the Nile to fill its branches or canals. Gesenius explains it as a mixed form compounded of the Chaldee and Hebrew Hiphil; Ewald, Maurer, Hitzig, and Knobel, as a verb, derived from an adjective אָזְנֵח, and meaning fetid or putrescent. The reed and rush are mentioned as a common growth in marshy situations. The Septuagint makes סוּף mean the papyrus, Vitringa and Lowth the lotus.

7. *The meadows by the river, by the mouth of the river, and all the sown ground of the river, shall wither, being driven away, and it is not* (or shall be no more). The Septuagint for עָרוֹת has ἄχι, which it elsewhere gives as the equivalent of אָחוּ, an Egyptian word meaning, according to Jerome, everything green that grows in the marshes of the Nile. Luther, Calvin, and others, explain it to mean *grass*. Gesenius derives it from עָרָה to be naked, and explains it to mean bare or open places, *i. e.* meadows, as distinguished from woodland. The English and some other Versions treat it as the name of the papyrus, but without authority. The English version also takes יְאֹר as a collective (*brooks*), and Barnes errroneously observes that the Hebrew word is here in the plural number. It is the word already mentioned as the common name in Scripture for the Nile, nor is there any need of departing from this sense in the case before us by translating it *canals*, as Lowth does. Calvin explains *mouth* to mean source or fountain, which is wholly arbitrary. J. H. Michaelis, Gesenius, and others regard it as synonymous with *lip*, used elsewhere (Gen. xli. 3, Exod. ii. 3) to denote

the brink or margin of the Nile. Knobel gives the same sense to the Hebrew word in Prov. viii. 29. Hendewerk and some of the older writers give the word its geographical sense, as denoting the place where the waters of a stream are discharged into another, or the sea. מִזְרָע is not *produce* (Henderson), but a local noun meaning the *place of seed* or *sowing, i. e.* cultivated grounds here distinguished from the meadows or uncultivated pastures. נִדַּף is commonly supposed to refer to the driving away of the withered and pulverized herbage by the wind. The Vulgate seems to take עָרוּת as a verb, and the first clause as describing the disclosure of the bed of the river by the sinking of the water (nudabitur alveus rivi a fonte suo). The decay of vegetation here predicted, Cocceius explains to be the dying out of Christianity in those parts of Europe conquered by the Saracens and Turks.

8. *And the fishermen shall mourn, and they shall lament, all the throwers of a hook into the river* (Nile), *and the spreaders of a net upon the surface of the water, languish.* Having described the effect of the drought on vegetation, he now describes its effect upon those classes of the people who were otherwise dependent on the river for subsistence. The multitude of fishes in the Nile, and of people engaged in catching them, is attested both by ancient and modern writers. The use of fish in ancient Egypt was promoted by the popular superstitions with respect to other animals. The net is said to be not now used in the fisheries of Egypt. It is remarkable, however, that the implement itself appears on some of the old monuments. This verse is not to be applied to an actual distress among the fishermen at any one time, but to be viewed as a characteristic trait in the prophetic picture. When he speaks of a wine-growing country, as Calvin well observes, the Prophet renders vineyards and vine-dressers prominent objects. So here, when he speaks of a country abounding in fisheries and fishermen, he describes their condition as an index or symbol of the state of the country. In like manner, a general distress in our southern States might be described as a distress among the sugar, cotton, or tobacco planters. By the fishermen of this verse, Cocceius understands the bishops, archbishops, and patriarchs, whose sees became subjected to the Moslem domination, with sarcastic allusion to the seal of the Fishermen by which the Pope authenticates his briefs.

9. *And ashamed* (disappointed or confounded) *are the workers of combed* (or hatchelled) *flax, and the weavers of white* (stuffs). The older writers suppose the class of persons here described to be the manufacturers of nets for fishing, and took חוֹרִי in the sense of perforated open-work, or net-work. The moderns understand the verse as having reference to the working of flax and manufacture of linen. Knobel supposes חוֹרִי to mean *cotton*, as being white by nature and before it is wrought. Some of the older writers identified שְׂרִיקוֹת with *sericum*, the Latin word for silk. Calvin supposes an allusion in the last clause to the diaphanous garments of luxurious women. Cocceius applies the verse to those who would force all men into one church or commonwealth, like fish collected in a net.

10. *And her pillars* (or *foundations*) *are broken down, all labourers for hire are grieved at heart.* Many of the older writers suppose the allusion to the fisheries to be still continued, and arbitrarily make שָׁתוֹת mean *nets*, and נֶפֶשׁ *fish*. Others take שָׁתוֹת in the sense of *looms* or *weavers*, and עֹשֵׂי שֶׂכֶר in that of *brewers* or makers of strong drink, which last interpretation is as old as the Septuagint version (οἱ ποιοῦντες τὸν ζῦθον). The simplest exposition of the verse is that proposed by Gesenius and adopted

by most succeeding writers, which regards this as a general description of distress extending to the two great classes of society, the pillars or chief men, and the labourers or commonality. Hendewerk less naturally understands by the שָׁתוֹת or foundations, the agricultural class as distinguished from manufacturers and traders. All the late writers explain אַגְמֵי, not as the plural of אַגם, a pool, but of an adjective signifying *sorrowful*, from one of the senses of the same root in Chaldee. This explanation of אַגְמֵי removes all necessity and ground for taking נֶפֶשׁ, in any other than its usual sense.

11. *Only foolish* (*i. e.* entirely foolish) *are the princes of Zoan, the sages of the counsellors of Pharaoh,* (their) *counsel is become brutish* (or irrational). *How can ye say to Pharaoh, I am the son of wise* (fathers), *I am the son of kings of old?* The reference is not merely to perplexity in actual distress, but also to an unwise policy as one of the causes of the distress itself. The meaning of אַךְ is not *for* or *surely*, but *only*, nothing else, exclusively. Zoan, the Tanis of the Greeks, was one of the most ancient cities of Lower Egypt (Num. xiii. 22), and a royal residence. The name is of Egyptian origin, and signifies a low situation. *Pharaoh* was a common title of the Egyptian kings. It is originally an Egyptian noun with the article prefixed. חַכְמֵי cannot agree directly as an adjective with עַצְי (*wise counsellors*)—but must either be in apposition with it (*the wise men, counsellors of Pharaoh,* 2 Kings x. 6)—or be understood as a superlative (*the wisest of the counsellors of Pharaoh*). The statesmen and courtiers of ancient Egypt belonged to the sacerdotal caste, from which many of the kings were also taken. The *wisdom of Egypt* seems to have been proverbial in the ancient world (1 Kings iv. 30 ; Acts vii. 22). The last clause is addressed to the counsellors themselves. The interrogation implies the absurdity of their pretensions. The question is not, how can you say this *of* Pharaoh (Luther), or how can you *dictate* this *to* Pharaoh, *i. e.* put these words into his mouth (Junius), but how can *you* say it, each one for himself? Hence the use of the singular number. מַלְכֵי does not mean *sages* or *counsellors* (Vitringa), but *kings* as elsewhere. Cocceius applies the last clause to the popish claim of apostolical succession. His comment on the first clause may be quoted as a characteristic specimen of his exegesis. " Concilium certe stultum fuit in Belgio novos episcopatus instituere, quod factum A. 1562. Eodem anno primum bellum civile religionis causa motum est in Gallia, duce inde Francisco Guisio, hinc Ludovico Condaeo. Exitus fuit ut regina religionis reformatae exercitium permitteret sequenti anno 19 Martii. An principes Galliae per principes Tsoan intelligi possint, fortasse magis patebit ex ver. 13."

12. *Where* (are) *they? Where* (are) *thy wise men? Pray let them tell thee, and* (if that is too much) *let them* (at least) *know, what Jehovah of Hosts hath purposed against* (or *concerning*) *Egypt.* It was a proof of their false pretensions that so far from being able to avert the evil, they could not even foresee it. Knobel thinks there may be an allusion to the belief of the Egyptians, as recorded by Herodotus, that supernatural foresight of the future is impossible, an article of faith which they could not more devoutly hold than Knobel himself appears to do. נָא is not an adverb of time equivalent to *nunc* (Vulgate), or *jam* (Junius), but a particle of exhortation or entreaty not unlike the Latin *age* (Cocceius). יֵדְעוּ is not synonymous with יַגִּידוּ (Sept. Vulg. Luther, Clericus, Augusti, Barnes) ; nor does it mean *inquire* or *investigate* (Hitzig) ; nor is the true text יוֹדִיעוּ (Secker) ;

but the word is to be taken in its usual sense with emphasis, *or let them even know*, as well expressed by Calvin (aut etiam sciant), and by Maurer (quin sciant). The repetition of the interrogative *where* is highly emphatic, through neglect of which the expression is materially weakened in the ancient versions, and by Luther, Hitzig, Hendewerk, Henderson, De Wette, Ewald, Umbreit. The construction is assumed to be subjunctive by Calvin (ut annuncient), relative by Junius (qui indicent), conditional by J. H. Michaelis (wenn sie wissen), and indefinite by Gesenius (dass man's erfahre) ; but the simple imperative, retained by Ewald, is at once more exact and more expressive. The sense of עַל is not *upon* but either *concerning* or *against*.

13. *Infatuated are the chiefs of Zion, deceived are the chiefs of Noph, and they have misled Egypt, the corner* (or *corner-stone*) *of her tribes.* There is no need of supplying *but* at the beginning of the sentence (Luther). The first verb does not mean to *fail* (Septuagint), or to *act lightly* (Cocceius), or to act foolishly (Junius, Vitringa, Rosenmüller), but to be rendered or become foolish (Vulgate), to be infatuated (Calvin). The translation *they are fools* (De Wette) is correct, but inadequate. *Noph* is the *Memphis* of the Greek geographers, called *Moph*, Hosea ix. 6. It was one of the chief cities of ancient Egypt, the royal seat of Psammetichus. After Alexandria was built it declined. Arabian writers in the twelfth and thirteenth centuries speak of its extensive and magnificent ruins, which have now almost wholly disappeared. נִשְׁאוּ is explained as if from נָשָׂא to lift up, by the Septuagint (ὑψώθησαν), the Peshito and Cocceius (elati sunt). The Vulgate renders it *emarcuerunt*. All others make it the passive of נָשָׁא, to *deceive*. פִּנַּת is not to be read פִּנֵּת (Grotius), nor is it the object of the preceding verb (Vulgate, J. H. Michaelis, Luther), nor governed by a preposition understood (Cocceius *quoad angulum*, Clericus *in angulo*), but construed collectively with הִתְעוּ (Calvin, Vitringa, Gesenius, &c.). It is a figure not for the nomes (Clericus, Vitringa, Rosenmüller), nor for the noble families (Luther), nor for the wise men (Calvin), or the king (J. H. Michaelis), but for the chief men of the different castes (Hitzig, Ewald). Knobel conjectures that the military caste may have been predominant at Memphis, as the sacerdotal was at Tanis. The view which Cocceius takes may be gathered from a single observation. "Gallia et Belgium extremae orae spiritualis Aegypti sunt."

14. *Jehovah hath mingled in the midst of her a spirit of confusion, and they have misled Egypt in all its work, like the misleading of a drunkard in his vomit.* This verse describes the folly before mentioned as the effect not of natural causes or of accident, but of a judicial infliction. מָסַךְ may be either a preterite or a present, but not a future. It does not strictly mean to *pour out*, but in usage is nearly equivalent, from its frequent application to the mixing or preparation of strong drinks. (*Vide supra*, chap. v. 22.) There is no need of reading קִרְבָּם with Secker, on the authority of the ancient versions, which evidently treat the singular suffix as a collective. The antecedent of the suffix is not פִּנָּה (Hitzig), but אֶרֶץ (Knobel). The translation *breast* or *bosom* is too specific. *Spirit* here means a supernatural influence. עִוְעִים is not *error* or *perverseness*, but *subversion*, turning upside down, and thence perplexity, confusion. It is strongly expressed by the Vulgate (spiritum vertiginis), and by Luther (Schwindelgeist). The plural הִתְעוּ may possibly agree with עִוְעִים, but it may be more naturally construed with the Egyptians understood, or taken indefinitely, as equivalent to a passive form, *they have misled them, i. e. they have been misled.* By *work*

we are here to understand affairs and interests. The masculine form of the suffix here returns, with the usual reference to the national ancestor. הַתְעוֹת does not directly denote staggering, much less rolling or wallowing, but the act of wandering from the straight course ; or retaining the passive form, that of being made to wander from it; or, assuming the reflexive sense of Niphal, that of making one's self to wander, leading one's self astray. The same verb is elsewhere used in reference to the unsteady motions of a drunken man (Job xii. 25 ; Isa. xxviii. 7).

15. *And there shall not be to Egypt a work which head and tail, branch and rush, may do.* לְ is neither *for* nor *in*, but *to*, as usual denoting possession, *Egypt shall not have.* The translation *shall not succeed* or *be completed* is not a version, but a paraphrase of the original. מַעֲשֶׂה is not merely a deed (Gesenius), much less a great deed (Hendewerk), nor does it refer exclusively to the acts or occupations before mentioned ; but it means anything done or to be done, including private business and public affairs. The figures of head and tail, branch and rush, are used, as in chap. ix. 13, to denote all classes of society, or rather the extremes between which the others are included. The Septuagint translates the last two *beginning and end.* The Targum makes them all mean chiefs and rulers. The Peshito, by a strange repetition and inversion, has *head and tail, tail and head.* Cocceius thinks it easy to trace the fulfilment of this prophecy in the history of Europe from 1590 to 1608.

16. *In that day shall Egypt be like women, and shall fear and tremble from before the shaking of the hand of Jehovah of hosts, which he (is) shaking over it.* The comparison in the first clause is a common one for terror and the loss of courage. מִפְּנֵי may be rendered *on account of,* which idea is certainly included, but the true force of the original expression is best retained by a literal translation. תנופת יד is not the act of beckoning for the enemy, but that of threatening or preparing to strike. The reference is not to the slaughter of Sennacherib's army, but more generally to the indications of divine displeasure. At this verse Hitzig supposes the forgery of Onias to begin, but admits that it cannot be proved from the use of the masculine suffix in reference to Egypt, which occurs several times in what he assumes to be the genuine part of this very chapter, nor does it follow from the repetition of the phrase *in that day* at the beginning of vers. 15, 18, 23, 24, as this formula occurs with equal frequency in the seventh chapter. Knobel observes, moreover, that this verse and the next bear the same relation to ver. 4 that vers. 11–15 do to 1–3, and are therefore necessary to complete the context.

17. *And the land of Judah shall be for a terror* (or *become a terror*) *unto Egypt, every person to whom one mentions it* (or *every one who recalls it to his own mind*) *shall fear before the purpose of Jehovah of Hosts, which he is purposing against it.* This verse relates, not to the destruction of Sennacherib's army in Judah, nor to the approach of the Assyrians from that quarter, nor to an attack upon Egypt by Judah itself, but to the new feelings which would be entertained by the Egyptians towards the God of the Jews and the true religion. Judah, in a political and military sense, might still appear contemptible ; but in another aspect, and for other reasons, it would be an object of respect and even fear to the Egyptians. A different sense is put upon the verse by Schultens, J. D. Michaelis, and Dathe, who take חָגָּא in the sense of *refuge,* deduced from an Arabic analogy. עָלָיו is referred by some interpreters to Judah, but the change of gender renders it more probable that it relates to Egypt. The sense will then be that the

knowledge of God's purpose against Egypt will dispose its inhabitants to look with awe upon the chosen people. There is no need of taking אֲדָמָה with Hendewerk in the strict sense of soil or ground, as distinguished from the people. אֵלָיו is not to be construed with יִפְחָד but with יַזְכִּיר. This last verb Ewald takes in the strict sense of causing to remember, or recalling to mind; most other writers in the secondary but more usual sense of mentioning. According to Cocceius, the Judah of this verse is the northern part of Europe, in which the Reformation was successfully established, and which holds the same relative position with respect to the unreformed regions, that Judea occupied in reference to Egypt.

18. *In that day there shall be five cities in the land of Egypt speaking the lip (i. e.* language) *of Canaan, and swearing to Jehovah of hosts. The city of destruction shall be said to one (i. e.* shall one be called). *In that day,* according to prophetic usage, is a somewhat indefinite expression, and may either mean *during* or *after* the distresses just described. *Canaan* is here put for the land of Canaan (as in Exod. xv. 15), and the *language of Canaan* for the Hebrew language, not because it was the language of the old Canaanites, but because it was spoken in the land which they once occupied. Some of the later writers understand what is here said, strictly as denoting an actual prevalence of the Hebrew language, while others take it as a strong expression for such intimate union, social, commercial, and political, as would seem to imply a community of language. The older writers very generally apply the terms to religious union and communion. Calvin explains *lip* or *language* as a figure for confession or profession, and the speaking of the language of Canaan for a public profession of the true religion. Vitringa gains the same end by a reference to the phrase *speaking the same things*, used in the New Testament to signify conformity of feeling and opinion. (See 1 Cor. i. 10.) He also admits the possibility of allusion to the dialect of saints or believers, as distinguished from that of the world, and to the study of the literal Hebrew as promoted by the spread of the true religion. Cocceius and some others understand directly by the use of the language of Canaan, the study of the Bible, or rather the reception and promulgation of its doctrines. The simplest interpretation of the phrase is, that in itself it denotes intimate intercourse and union generally, but that the idea of religious unity is here suggested by the context, and especially by the following clause. Many interpreters appear to regard the phrases *swearing by* and *swearing to* as perfectly synonymous. The former act does certainly imply the recognition of the deity by whom one swears, especially if *oaths* be regarded as they are in Scripture as solemn acts of religious worship. But the phrase *swearing to* conveys the additional idea of doing homage, and acknowledging a sovereign by swearing fealty or allegiance to him. This is the only meaning that the words can bear in 2 Chron. xv. 14, and in Isa. xlv. 23 the two phrases seem to be very clearly distinguished. The distinction intended in Zeph, i. 5, is not so clear. The act of thus professing the true faith and submitting to the true God is ascribed in the verse before us to *five towns* or *cities*. Of this phrase there are three distinct interpretations. Gesenius, Ewald, Knobel, and others, understand five as a round or indefinite number, meaning few or many, and derived either from Egyptian usage (Gen. xliii. 34; xlv. 22; xlvii. 2), or from the practice of counting on the fingers. Thus understood, the sense is simply that *a number of cities* shall do so and so. Another class of writers understand the words strictly as denoting five, and neither more nor less. The five cities meant are supposed by Vitringa to be Heliopolis,

Memphis, Sais, Bubastis, Alexandria; by Clericus, Migdol, Tahpanhes, Memphis, Heliopolis, and one in Pathros, probably No-ammon or Diospolis; by Hitzig the same, except the last, for which he substitutes Leontopolis; by Hendewerk, the five cities of the Philistines, which he supposes to be here considered as belonging to Egypt. Among the five cities perhaps referred to, Barnes includes *Pathros* or *Thebais*, which was not a city at all. A third interpretation understands the words as expressive not of absolute number but proportion; five out of the twenty thousand cities which Herodotus says Egypt contained; or out of the one thousand which Calvin thinks a more reasonable estimate; or five out of ten, *i. e.* one half; or five out of six, which is Calvin's own interpretation. The objection to the first or indefinite construction is the want of any clear example of this number being used in that way without something in the context to afford a standard of comparison. (See Lev. xxvi. 8, 1 Cor. xiv. 19.) The objection to the second or absolute construction is the impossibility of fixing certainly what five are meant, or of tracing the fulfilment of so definite a prophecy, or even of ascertaining from the context any reason why just five should be distinguished in this manner. Of the third class or relative constructions, that of Calvin is to be preferred, because the others arbitrarily assume a standard of comparison (twenty thousand, ten thousand, ten, &c.), whereas this hypothesis finds it in the verse itself, *five* professing the true religion to *one* rejecting it. Most of the other interpretations understand the one to be included in the five, as if he had said *one of them.* As אֶחָת admits either of these senses, or rather applications, the question must depend upon the meaning given to the rest of the clause. Even on Calvin's hypothesis, however, the proportion indicated need not be taken with mathematical precision. What appears to be meant is that five-sixths, *i. e.* a very large proportion, shall profess the true religion, while the remaining sixth persists in unbelief. *It shall be said to one, i. e.* one shall be addressed as follows, or called by the following name. This periphrasis is common in Isaiah, but is never applied, as Gesenius observes, to the actual appellation, but always to a description or symbolical title (See Isa. iv. 3, lxi. 6, lxii. 4.) This may be urged as an argument against the explanation of הַהֶרֶס as a proper name. The Hebrew form is retained in the Complutensian text of the Septuagint ('Αχερές) by Theodotion and Aquila ('Αρές), by the Peshito (ܐܚܪܣ), and by Luther (Irheres). Sixteeen manuscripts and several editions read הַחֶרֶס, and this is adopted as the true text by most of the modern writers. It is also supposed to be confirmed by the Greek form 'Αχερές above quoted. Jerome compares it with חֶרֶשׂ, a potsherd, and refers to the town which the Greeks called 'Οστραχίνη (*i. e.* earthen). Others suppose an allusion to Tahpanhes, the brick-kilns of which are mentioned, Jer. xliii. 9. Gesenius, in his Commentary, derives the meaning of the name from the Arabic حرس and renders it *deliverance* (Errettung). Ewald, with reference to the same root, renders it *fortune* or *happiness* (Glückstadt). But most of those who adopt this reading give to חֶרֶם the sense of *sun*, which it has in several places (Judges viii. 13, xiv. 18; Job ix. 7), and regard the whole phrase as equivalent to the Hebrew *Bethshemesh* (dwelling of the sun), and the Greek *Heliopolis* (city of the sun), the name of a famous town of Lower Egypt, in the Heliopolitan Nome, so called from it. In this nome, Onias, a fugitive priest from Palestine, about 150 years before Christ, prevailed upon Ptolemy Philometor to erect a temple for the Jews of Egypt, an event which some suppose to be predicted here. The exact site of this temple, although in the nome just mentioned, was at *Leontopolis* (or city of the lion), and this name also has been found by some interpreters in the prediction. J. D. Michaelis and Dathe, following a suggestion made by Iken, identify the common reading הרם with the Arabic هرس. But this has been shewn by later writers to be merely a poetical epithet of the lion, denoting its voracity. Rosenmuller, in his larger Scholia, agrees with Hezel in explaining הרם from the Syriac analogy as signifying safety or salvation. But Gesenius has shewn that there is no such Syriac word, and that the Syriac writers quoted merely give conjectural explanations of the Hebrew word before us. Rosenmüller, therefore, in the Compendium of his Scholia, adopts Gesenius's interpretation given above, while Gesenius himself, in his Thesaurus, adopts that of Vitringa and the Vulgate (civitas solis). This is also given by Hitzig, who identifies חֶרֶם the sun with חֶרֶם, a scab (Deut. xxviii. 27), the disk of the former being so called on account of its scratched, scraped, or smooth appearance, an etymological deduction of which Umbreit gravely signifies his approbation. All the interpretations which have now been mentioned either depart from the common text, or explain it by some forced or foreign analogy. If, however, we proceed upon the only safe principle of adhering to the common text and to Hebrew usage, without the strongest reasons for abandoning either or both, no explanation of the name can be so satisfactory as that given by Calvin (civitas desolationis) and the English Version (city of destruction). It is very remarkable that both the readings (הרם and חרם) appear to be combined in the Chaldee Paraphrase: "the city of Bethshemesh (*i. e.* Heliopolis), which is to be destroyed." This would seem to imply that the text or the meaning of the word was already doubtful and disputed at the date of that old Version. It has been objected to the common reading and the sense just put upon it, that a threatening of destruction would here be out of place. But on Calvin's hypothesis, there is a promise of salvation to five-sixths. It is also a favourite idea with some writers, that the text was corrupted by the Jews of Palestine, in order to convert what seemed at least to be an explicit prediction of the temple of Onias into a threatening of its destruction. To the same source some ascribe the reading החרם which is found in a few manuscripts. On the other hand, the common text of the Septuagint Version has ἀσεδέκ (הצדק), which is supposed to have been introduced (from chap. i. 26) by the Egyptian Jews in order to put honour on their temple. Even this, however, is pressed into the service of other hypotheses by Iken, who identifies ἀσεδέκ with an Arabic word used by the poets in describing the appearance of a lion, and by Le Moyne, who argues from Mal. iii. 20, that צדק and צדקה were applied to the sun. Thus the same blunder of the Seventy is made to prove that the Hebrew word means Heliopolis and Leontopolis. Hitzig, as we have seen already, looks upon this whole passage from the sixteenth verse as a fabrication of Onias, intended to facilitate the rearing of his temple. But in that case he would surely have made it more explicit, or at least have prevented its conversion into an anathema against himself. It is not even true that he interpreted this clause as pointing out the place for the erection, as alleged by Lowth and others after him. Josephus merely says that he appealed to the prediction of an altar to Jehovah in the land of Egypt, which would hardly have contented him if he had understood the verse before us as expressly naming either Heliopolis or Leontopolis. These facts, when taken in connection with the usage of יֵאָמֵר לְ already stated, make it altogether probable that עִיר הַהֶרֶם is not a proper name, but a descriptive and prophetic title, meaning (in accordance with the constant usage of the verb הָרַם) *the city of destruction*. Kimchi, who puts this sense upon the words, but is puzzled by the threatening against one of the five towns, as he supposes it to be, absurdly makes the words to mean that the five cities would be so devoted to the true religion that if either of them should apostatise the others would destroy it. Scarcely more natural is the explanation of the words by Junius and Tremellius, as meaning a city almost destroyed, or saved from destruction. Schmidius more ingeniously evades the difficulty by taking הָרֶם in an active sense, *a city of destruction, i.e.* to its enemies or those of the true religion. Both the hypotheses last mentioned give to אַחַת the distributive sense of *each* or *every one*, which it sometimes derives from repetition or context. (See Ezek. i. 6). Hendewerk, who supposes the five towns of the Philistines to be meant, understands this as a prophecy that one of them (Ashdod) should be destroyed, but afterwards rebuilt, with an allusion to the derivation of the name from שָׁדַד, to destroy. But of all the explanations of the common text, the simplest is the one proposed by Calvin, which supposes the whole verse to mean that for one town which shall perish in its unbelief, five shall profess the true faith and swear fealty to Jehovah. The simplicity of this interpretation, and its strict agreement with a general tenor of the passage as a prophetic picture of great changes in the State of Egypt, serve at the same time to commend the common reading as the true one. By the five cities Cocceius understands the five States in which the Reformation was permanently established (Great Britain, Denmark, Sweden, Holland, and northern Germany), and by *desolation* or *destruction* what they subsequently suffered by war and otherwise from the popish powers.

19. *In that day there shall be an altar to Jehovah in the midst of the land of Egypt, and a pillar at* (or *near*) *its border to Jehovah*. It has been disputed whether we are here to understand an altar for sacrifice, or an altar to serve as a memorial (Josh. xxii. 26, 27). It has also been disputed whether the prohibition of altars and consecrated pillars (Lev. xxvi. 1 ; Deut. xii. 5, xvi. 22) was applicable only to the Jews or to Palestine, leaving foreign Jews or proselytes at liberty to rear these sacred structures as the Patriarchs did of old (Gen. xxviii. 18, xxxv. 14). The necessity of answering these questions is removed by a just view of the passage, as predicting the prevalence of the true religion and the practice of its rites, in language borrowed from the Mosaic or rather from the patriarchal institutions. As we might now speak of a missionary *pitching his tent* at Hebron or at Shechem, without intending to describe the precise form of his habitation, so the Prophet represents the converts to be the true faith as erecting an altar and a pillar to the Lord in Egypt, as Abraham and Jacob did of old in Canaan. A still more exact illustration is afforded by the frequent use among ourselves of the word *altar* to denote the practice of devotion, especially in families. There is a double propriety and beauty in the use of the word מַצֵּבָה, because while it instantly recalls to mind the patriarchal practice, it is at the same time finely descriptive of the obelisk, an object so characteristic of Egypt that it may be regarded as its emblem. Both the obelisk and the patriarchal pillar, being never in the human form, are to be carefully distinguished from statues or images, although the latter word is sometimes used to represent the Hebrew one in the English Version (see 2 Kings iii. 2, x. 26 ; Micah v. 13). Those explanations of the verse which suppose the altar and the pillar, or the centre and the border of the land, to be contrasted, are equally at variance with good taste and the usage

of the language, which continually separates in parallel clauses, words and things which the reader is expected to combine. See an example of this usage in the sixth verse of the preceding chapter. As the wintering of the beasts and the summering of the birds are there intended to denote the presence of both beasts and birds throughout the year, so here the altar in the midst of the land, and the pillar at its border, denote altars and pillars through its whole extent. This is much more natural than Ewald's supposition that the words are expressive of a gradual progress or extension of the truth.

20. *And it shall be for a sign and for a testimony to Jehovah of hosts in the land of Egypt, that they shall cry to Jehovah from the presence of oppressors, and he will send them a deliverer and a mighty one, and save them.* The older writers for the most part construe וְהָיָה with what goes before: " and it (or they) shall be," &c. In that case we must either suppose an enallage of gender (so as to make מַצֵּבָה the subject of the verb), or an enallage of number (so as to construe it with both the nouns), or else refer it to the remoter antecedent מִזְבֵּחַ. Any of these constructions would be admissible if absolutely necessary; but in the case before us they are all superseded by a simpler one now commonly adopted. This refers וְהָיָה not at all to what precedes but to what follows, taking כִּי in its proper sense of ὅτι, *that.* " This shall be a sign and a witness to (*i. e.* with respect to, in behalf of) Jehovah in the land of Egypt, viz. that when they cry," &c. He will afford a providential testimony in behalf of his own being, presence, and supremacy, by saving those who cry to him. Those who refer וְהָיָה to what goes before, either take the other verbs in the past tense (a sign and a testimony that they cried), which is entirely arbitrary, or give to כִּי its usual sense of *for, because* (for they shall cry), in which case the connection is not obvious between their crying and the altar's being a sign and witness for Jehovah. Even then, however, we may understand the Prophet to mean that when they cry *at the altar* of Jehovah, he will answer and deliver them, and thus the altar will bear witness to him. But as nothing is said of crying at the altar, the other construction is to be preferred, which makes the hearing of their prayers, and their deliverance from suffering, the sign and witness in behalf of Jehovah. רָב may be either an adjective meaning *great*, or the participle of רִיב, to strive, especially at law, and then to plead the cause or take the part of any one, the participle of which might well be used to signify an advocate, patron, or defender. Calvin and others, adopting the former explanation of the word (salvatorem et principem), apply it to Christ. Vitringa, laying stress upon the word as meaning *great*, regards it as a proof that the deliverer here mentioned was Alexander the Great, or his Egyptian successor Ptolemy, also called the Great, and, by a singular coincidence, *Soter* or the Saviour. The whole force of this ingenious combination lies in the explanation of רָב as an adjective. It cannot, therefore, be consistently maintained by those who adopt the other supposition, as Henderson does. Barnes also weakens the argument in favour of Vitringa's exposition by exchanging *great* for *powerful.* The other explanation of רָב as a participle is found in all the ancient versions, and is adopted by most modern writers. It is also favoured by the fact that the adjective is usually written רַב when not in pause, although some cases of the other pointing do occur (*e. g.* Gen. xxxvi. 7; Joshua xi. 4), and Hitzig thinks the form here sufficiently accounted for by the accompanying accent. As to the application of the term in either case, besides that adopted by Vitringa and others, may be mentioned the

rabbinical opinion that it means the angel who destroyed Sennacherib's army, and the opinion of some modern writers that it denotes Psammetichus. A name, which admits of being plausibly applied to things so far apart and unlike, may safely be regarded as generic in its import. Even if the language of this verse by itself might seem to point to a particular deliverer, the comprehensive language of the context would forbid its reference to any such exclusively. If, as we have seen reason to believe, the chapter is a prophecy, not of a single event, but of a great ·progressive change to be wrought in the condition of Egypt by the introduction of the true religion, the promise of the verse before us must be, that when they cried God would send them a deliverer, a promise verified not once but often, not by Ptolemy or Alexander only, but by others, and in the highest sense by Christ himself. The assertion, that the meaning of the prophecy was exhausted by events before the advent, is as easily contradicted as advanced. It is admitted that the rise of Alexander's power was contemporaneous with a great increase of Jewish population and Jewish influence in Egypt, and also with a great improvement in the social and political condition of the people. This was still more remarkably the case when Christianity was introduced, and who shall say what is yet to be witnessed and experienced in Egypt under the influence of the same Gospel? In the language of this verse there is an obvious allusion to the frequent statement in the book of Judges, that the people cried to God, and he raised them up deliverers who saved them from their oppressors (Judges ii. 16, iii. 9, &c.). Cocceius applies these terms to the various deliverers who were raised up to free the Reformed Church from its enemies.

21. *And Jehovah shall be known to Egypt, and Egypt* (or the Egyptians) *shall know Jehovah in that day, and shall serve (with) sacrifice and offering, and shall vow a vow to Jehovah, and perform it.* This is not the prediction of a new event, but a repetition in another form of the preceding promise. The first clause may be understood as containing an emphatic repetition, or נוֹדַע may be taken in a reflexive sense as meaning *he shall make himself known*, in which case each of the parties is the subject of an active verb. The second clause is still but another variation of the same idea. What is first described as the knowledge of the true God, is afterwards represented as his service, the expressions being borrowed from the ancient ritual. If the last clause be literally understood, we must either regard it as an unfounded expectation of the Prophet which was never fulfilled, or suppose that it relates to an express violation of the law of Moses, or assume that the ancient rites and forms are hereafter to be re-established. On the other hand, the figurative explanation is in perfect agreement with the usage of both testaments, and with the tenor of the prophecy itself. Bloody and unbloody sacrifice is here combined with vows, in order to express the totality of ritual services as a figure for those of a more spiritual nature. The express mention of the Egyptians themselves as worshipping Jehovah, shews that they are also meant in the preceding verse, and not, as Hitzig imagines, the Jews resident in Egypt, whose example and experience of God's favour were to be the means of bringing those around them to the knowledge and reception of the truth. Gesenius explains עֲבָדוּ to be a synonyme of עָשׂוּ, and makes it govern the noun directly in the sense of *performing* or *offering* sacrifice, &c. Hitzig adopts the same construction, and moreover makes this use of עָבַד symptomatic of a later writer. Hendewerk justly condemns this reasoning as exceedingly unfair, when the common acceptation of the term gives a perfectly good sense, and

the absolute use of עֲבַד in the sense of serving God occurs elsewhere (Job xxxvi. 11), and the same ellipsis in this very chapter (ver. 23).

22. *And Jehovah shall smite Egypt (or the Egyptians), smiting and healing, and they shall return unto Jehovah, and he shall be entreated of them, and shall heal them.* Here again the second clause contains no advance upon the first, and the whole verse no advance upon the foregoing context, but an iteration of the same idea in another form. This verse may indeed be regarded as a recapitulation of the whole preceding prophecy, consisting as it does of an extended threatening (vers. 1–17), followed by an ample promise (vers. 18–21). As if he had said, Thus will God smite Egypt and then heal it. That great heathen power, with respect to which the Jews so often sinned both by undue confidence and undue dread, was to be broken and reduced : but in exchange for this political decline, and partly as a consequence of it, the Egyptians should experience benefits far greater than they ever before knew. Thus would Jehovah *smite and heal*, or smite but so as afterwards to heal, which seems to be the force of the reduplicated verb. (See Ewald, § 540.) The meaning is not simply that the stroke should be followed by healing, nor is it simply that the stroke should itself possess a healing virtue ; but both ideas seem to be included. Returning to Jehovah is a common figure for repentance and conversion, even in reference to the heathen. (See Psalm xxii. 28.)

23. *In that day there shall be a highway from Egypt to Assyria, and Assyria shall come into Egypt and Egypt into Assyria, and Egypt (or the Egyptians) shall serve with Assyria.* No translation will convey the precise form of the original, in which the ancestral names מִצְרַיִם and אַשּׁוּר are put not only for their descendants, but for the countries which they occupied. Thus in one clause we read of coming into מִצְרַיִם, while in the next the same name is construed with a plural verb. No one, it is probable, has ever yet maintained that a road was literally opened between Egypt and Assyria, or that Isaiah expected it. All classes of interpreters agree that the opening of the highway is a figure for easy, free, and intimate communication. This unanimous admission of a metaphor in this place not only shews that the same mode of interpretation is admissible in the other parts of the same prophecy, but makes it highly probable that what is said of altars and sacrifices is to be likewise so understood. The Chaldee Paraphrast alone seems to have understood the second clause as having reference to hostile communication. Some understand it as relating only to commercial intercourse ; others confine it to religious union. But the same thing is true here and in ver. 18, that while the language itself denotes intimate connection and free intercourse in general, the context renders the idea of spiritual union prominent. The last clause admits of two constructions, one of which regards את as the objective particle, and understands the clause to mean that *the Egyptians shall serve the Assyrians:* the other makes את a preposition, and explains the clause to mean that *the Egyptians shall serve* (God) *with the Assyrians.* In favour of the first is the constant usage of עבד with את (Gen. xiv. 4, xxvii. 40, xxxi. 6; Exod. xiv. 12, &c.), and the unanimous agreement of the ancient versions. But the sense thus yielded is at variance with the context, what precedes and follows being clearly expressive of a union so complete and equal as to exclude the idea of subjection or superiority. Some have attempted to evade this difficulty by attaching to עבד the sense of serving by benevolence (Gal. v. 13), or of simply treating with respect or reverence. But even if this explanation of the word were justified by usage, why should this difference be confined to one party

instead of being mutual, especially when what precedes and follows so emphatically expresses the idea of reciprocity? In favour of the other construction is the constant use of עבד to denote the service of Jehovah, and the omission of the divine name after it, not only in Job xxxvi. 11, but in ver. 21 of this very chapter. For although the latter place admits, as we have seen, of two interpretations, the very fact that the elliptical construction is appropriate in both, and that no other sense but that of *serving God* is equally appropriate to both, would seem to be decisive in favour of this sense and this construction as the true one. Some understand the clause to mean that the Egyptians should *serve* with the Assyrians in the same army, under the same leader, viz., Alexander the great or his successors. But עבד is nowhere absolutely used, if at all, in this modern military sense, which is moreover wholly inadmissible in ver. 21. The sense of *serving God together* is adopted by Luther and all the later German writers except Hitzig who agrees with Cocceius and the ancient versions. Some remove the ambiguity by supplying the ellipsis, others by giving a specific meaning to the verb, as Lowth (worship), and Ewald (huldigen).

24. *In that day shall Israel be a third with respect to Egypt and Assyria, a blessing in the midst of the earth.* The meaning obviously is that Israel should be *one of three*, or a party to a triple union. שְׁלִישִׁיָּה therefore does not agree with יִשְׂרָאֵל, considered as a feminine noun, because intended to denote not the country but the nation. This explanation, the one suggested by Gesenius, is directly contrary to usage, which makes countries feminine, and nations masculine, as stated by Gesenius himself in his comment on the next verse. Nor is it necessary to suppose a reference to עֶרֶץ or any other noun understood. "As the fractional numerals are all abstract nouns, the feminine form of the ordinals is employed exclusively for their representation." (Nordheimer, § 627. Compare Gesenius, § 96.) The word therefore means a third part, or one equal part out of three. The idea meant to be conveyed, however, is not, as Cocceius supposes, merely that of equality in magnitude or power, but also that of intimate conjunction, as in the preceding verse. *Blessing* is here used in a comprehensive sense, as denoting at the same time a source of blessing, a means of blessing, and an object to be blessed. Luther supplies a preposition before it and a relative after it (though the blessing which is in the midst of the earth). Knobel simply supplies the verb of existence (blessing shall be in the midst, &c.). The simplest construction is to put it in apposition with ישראל or שלישיה, a blessing in the midst of the earth, which is equivalent to saying, *as a blessing,* or (as Ewald has it) *for a blessing* in the midst of the earth. The restricted sense of *land*, whether understood to mean the land of Israel or the land of the three united powers, now reckoned as one, is not only arbitrary, *i. e.* assumed without necessity, but greatly impairs the strength of the expressions.

25. *Which Jehovah of hosts has blessed* (or *with which Jehovah of hosts has blessed it*) *saying, Blessed be my people Egypt, and the work of my hands Assyria, and my heritage* (or peculiar people) *Israel.* The perfect union of the three great powers in the service of God and the enjoyment of his favour is now expressed by a solemn benediction on the three, in which language commonly applied to Israel exclusively is extended to Egypt and Assyria. The force of the expressions would be much enhanced by the habitual associations of a Jewish reader. It arises very much from the surprise excited by the unexpected termination of the clauses. Instead of

Blessed be my people Israel, the formula is *blessed be my people Egypt*. That *the work of my hands* does not merely mean *my creature*, or a creature perfectly at my disposal, but my creature in a special and a spiritual sense, the same in which God is said to be the maker or founder of Israel (Deut. xxxii. 6; Isa xliii. 6, 7), is evident from this consideration, that the clause would otherwise say nothing peculiar or distinctive of Assyria, as those before and after it do of Egypt and Israel. Some writers understand the last clause as still making a distinction in favour of Israel, as if he had said, Egypt is indeed my people and Assyria my handiwork, but Israel after all and alone is my inheritance. The objections to this interpretation are, first, that it is wholly arbitrary; that is, it assumes a peculiar emphasis in the word *inheritance* which neither usage nor the context warrants; and secondly, that it contradicts or makes unmeaning the varied and reiterated forms of speech by which the Prophet had before expressed the ideas of equality and union. Where his very object seems to be to represent the three united powers as absolutely one in privilege, it cannot be supposed that he would wind up by saying that they are not absolutely equal after all. Much less is such a meaning to be put upon his words when there is nothing in the words themselves to require or even authorize it. The correct view of the verse seems to be this: In order to express once more and in the most emphatic manner the admission of Egypt and Assyria to the privileges of the chosen people, he selects three titles commonly bestowed upon the latter exclusively, to wit, *God's people*, the *work of his hands*, and his *inheritance*, and these three he distributes to the three united powers without discrimination or invidious distinction. If this view of the matter be correct, the meaning of the whole will be distorted by attaching any undue emphasis to the concluding words. As to the application of the prophecy, there are three distinct opinions. One is that the Prophet here anticipates a state of peace and international communion between Egypt, Israel, and Assyria in his own times, which may or may not have been actually realized. Another is that he predicts what actually did take place under the reign of Alexander and the two great powers that succeeded him, viz. the Graeco-Syrian and Egyptian monarchies, by which the true religion was protected and diffused, and the way prepared for the preaching of the gospel. A third is that Egypt and Assyria are here named as the two great heathen powers known to the Jews, whose country lay between them, and was often the scene, if not the subject, of their contests, so that for ages they were commonly in league with the one against the other. To describe these two great belligerent powers as at peace with Israel and one another, was not only to foretell a most surprising revolution in the state of the world, but to intimate at least a future change in the relation of the Jews and Gentiles. When he goes still further and describes these representatives of heathenism as received into the covenant, and sharing with the church of God its most distinctive titles, we have one of the clearest and most striking predictions of the calling of the Gentiles that the word of God contains. One advantage of this exposition is, that while it thus extends and elevates the scope of the prediction, it retains unaltered whatever there may be of more specific prophecy or of coincidence with history. If Alexander is referred to, and the spread of Judaism under him and his successors, with the general pacification of the world and progress of refinement, these are so many masterly strokes added to the great prophetic picture; but they cannot be extracted from it and made to constitute a picture by themselves. As to the construction of the first clause, it may be observed that most writers refer the relative pronoun to הָאָרֶץ, or give אֲשֶׁר the sense of *for, because,* but Ewald and Knobel make בְּרָכָה the antecedent, the blessing wherewith God has blessed it, as in Deut. xii. 7, xv. 14. In either case, the suffix בְּרֵכוֹ refers not to הָאָרֶץ as a masculine, because denoting people, but to Egypt, Assyria, and Israel, considered as a single nation. The preterite form of the verb has reference to the benediction as preceding and occasioning the union just before described. When Egypt, Assyria, and Israel are thus united, it will be because God *has already blessed them, saying,* &c. There is therefore no necessity or ground for an arbitrary change of the preterite into a future, nor even for evading an exact translation by the substitution of the present form. How far the early Jews were below the genuine spirit of the Prophecies, may be gathered from the fact that both the Septuagint and Targum make this a promise to Israel exclusively, Assyria and Egypt being mentioned merely as the places where they had experienced affliction.

Chapter 20

About the time of the Assyrian attack on Ashdod, the Prophet is directed to walk naked and barefoot, as a sign of the defeat and captivity of the Egyptians and Ethiopians who were at war with Assyria. The first verse fixes the date of this symbolical transaction; the second contains the divine command and the record of its execution; the third and fourth explain the meaning of the symbol; the fifth and sixth predict its effect, or rather that of the event which it prefigured. The questions which have been raised, as to the date of the composition and the fulfilment of the prophecy, will be most conveniently considered in the course of the detailed interpretation. It may be added here, however, that Cocceius, with all other interpreters, applies this chapter to the literal Egypt, but instead of admitting any inconsistency between this hypothesis and that which supposes chap. xix. to relate to the mystical Egypt, he ingeniously converts the juxtaposition into an argument for his own opinion, by alleging that the chapter now before us was added for the very purpose of shewing that the foregoing promises and threatenings did not belong to the literal Egypt.

1. *In the year of Tartan's coming to Ashdod, in Sargon king of Assyria's sending him* (*i. e.* when Sargon, king of Assyria, sent him), *and he fought with Ashdod* (*i. e.* besieged it) *and took it.* Ashdod was one of the five cities of the Philistines (Josh. xi. 22, xv. 46; 1 Sam. v. 1), considered on account of its strong fortifications (from which its name is supposed to be derived) the key of Egypt, and therefore frequently attacked in the wars between Egypt and Assyria. According to Herodotus, Psammetichus besieged it twenty-nine years. This, if not an exaggeration, is the longest siege in history, and probably took place after what is here recorded, in order to recover Ashdod from Assyria. Its site is marked by a village still called *Esdúd* (Robinson's Palestine, ii. 368.) The name of Sargon nowhere else occurs. Tartan appears again as a general under Sennacherib (2 Kings xviii. 17). From this Usher, Grotius, Lowth, and Doederlein infer that Sargon and Sennacherib are one and the same person. According to Jerome, this king had seven names; according to Kimchi and the Talmud, eight. This looks very much like a Jewish figment designed to render the alleged identity more probable. Marsham and J. D. Michaelis identify Sargon with Esarhaddon; Sanctius, Vitringa, and Eichhorn, with Shalmaneser. All these

suppositions are less probable than the obvious one, that Sargon was a king of Assyria mentioned only here, because his reign was very short, and this was the only occurrence that brought him into contact with the Jews. That he was not the immediate successor of Sennacherib, is clear from chap. xxxvii. 38, and from the fact which seems to be implied in 2 Chron. xxxii. 21, that Tartan perished in the great catastrophe. The most plausible hypothesis, and that now commonly adopted, is, that he reigned three or four years between Shalmaneser and Sennacherib (according to Knobel's computation, from 718 to 715 B.C.). It is said indeed in one of the Apocryphal books (Tob. i. 15) that Sennacherib was the son of Enemessar (*i. e.* Shalmaneser) ; but even allowing more weight to this authority than it deserves, Sargon may have been an elder brother. In the Vatican text of the Septuagint this name is written 'Αρνᾶ, in the Complutensian Ναρνᾶ, by Aquila and Theodotion Σαραγών, The immediate succession of these two kings readily accounts for Tartan's being named as an officer of both, as Vitringa observes that Abner served under Saul and Ishbosheth, and Benaiah under David and Solomon. So the Duke of Wellington, in our day, has served under four successive sovereigns. Nothing, therefore, can be proved in this way as to the identity of Sargon and Sennacherib. Hendewerk even questions the propriety of inferring that they reigned in immediate succession, on the ground that *Tartan*, like *Rabshakeh* and *Rabsaris* (2 Kings xviii. 17), was not a proper name but an official title. Hendewerk himself, however, acquiesces in the common chronological hypothesis, although he questions this mode of proving it. The name Tartan is written in the Alexandrian text of the Septuagint Νάθαν, in the Vatican Τανάθαν. Here, as in chap. vi. 1, it is disputed whether *in the year of Tartan's coming* means before or after that occurrence. The truth is, it means neither, but leaves that question undetermined, or at most to be determined by the context. Those who refer the last two verses of the chapter to the Philistines, and suppose the prophecy to have been intended to forewarn them of the issue of the siege of Ashdod, and of the folly of relying on Egyptian or Ethiopian aid against Assyria, must of course assume that this symbolical transaction took place before the arrival of Tartan, or at least before the end of the siege. Those, on the other hand, who suppose it to refer to the Jews themselves, find it more natural to assume that the prophecy was uttered after the fall of Ashdod. In this case, the recording of the prophecy may have been contemporaneous with its publication. In the other case, we must suppose it to have been reduced to writing after the event. Here, as in chap. vii. 1–16, Gesenius infers from the use of the third person, that the chapter was not written by Isaiah himself, but by a scribe or amanuensis. Here too, as in chap. vii. 1, Ewald regards the last clause as a parenthetical anticipation, and the next verse as continuing the narrative directly. As if he had said, " In the year that Tartan came to Ashdod (which he besieged and finally took), at that time," &c. But this supposition is at least unnecessary. On the change of construction from the infinitive to the future, and the collocation of the subject and the object in the first clause, *vide supra*, chap. v. 24.

2. *At that time spake Jehovah by the hand of Isaiah the son of Amoz, saying, Go, and thou shalt open* (*i. e.* loose) *the sackcloth from upon thy loins, and thy shoe thou shalt pull off from upon thy foot. And he did so, going naked and barefoot.* Maimonides, Kimchi, Stäudlin, and Hendewerk, suppose this to have been done merely in vision. This supposition

is not altogether arbitrary, *i.e.* without any intimation in the text, but is rendered more improbable by the expression *that he did so*, as well as by the statement in the next verse, that the act required was to be a sign or symbol to the spectators, which certainly implies that it was really exhibited. This supposition of an ideal exposure seems to have been resorted to, in order to avoid the conclusion that the Prophet really appeared before the people in a state of nudity. It is commonly agreed, however, that this was not the case. The word *naked* is used to express partial denudation in all languages. The examples quoted by Vitringa from Seneca, Suetonius, and Aurelius Victor, have been copied or referred to by most later writers. As biblical examples, may be cited 1 Sam. xix. 24, 2 Sam. vi. 20, Amos ii. 16, John xxi. 7. In the case before us we may either suppose that the שַׂק was an upper garment which he threw entirely off, or an inner garment which opened by ungirding it, or a girdle itself which he loosened and perhaps removed. Sackcloth was a common mourning dress, and some suppose that Isaiah was now wearing it in token of his grief for the exile of the ten tribes (Kimchi, Lightfoot). Others understand it as an official or ascetic dress worn by the prophets (Zech. xiii. 4), as for instance by Elijah (2 Kings i. 8), and by John the Baptist (Matt. iii. 4). Others again suppose that it is mentioned as a cheap coarse dress worn by the Prophet in common with the humbler class of the people. The name שַׂק appears to have reference merely to the coarseness of the texture; but the cloth would seem to have been usually made of hair, and, in later times at least, of a black colour (Rev. vi. 12). The expression *by the hand* denotes ministerial agency or intervention, and is often used in reference to communications made to the people *through* the prophets. (Exod. iv. 13; 1 Sam. xvi. 20; Jer. xxxvii. 2.) So in this case the divine communication was really addressed to the people, though the words immediately ensuing are addressed to the Prophet himself. There is no ground, therefore, for suspecting, with Hendewerk, that the words בְּיַד, &c., were interpolated afterwards as an explanatory gloss, or for assuming, with Gesenius, that בְּיַד is here used like a corresponding phrase in Arabic to mean *before* or *in the presence of*, as some suppose it does in 1 Sam. xxi. 14, and Job xv. 27. It is not even necessary to suppose that the phrase has exclusive reference to the symbolical action. Gill: "He spoke *by* him by the sign he used according to his order, and he spoke *to* him to use the sign." The simplest and most natural solution is, that what was said *to* the Prophet was obviously said *through* him to the people. Above thirty manuscripts and several editions read רַגְלָיו in the plural, but of course without a change of meaning.

3. *And Jehovah said, As my servant Isaiah has gone naked and barefoot three years a sign and symbol concerning Egypt and concerning Ethiopia.* Here begins the divine explanation of the symbolical act before commanded. Although the design of this transaction was to draw attention by exciting surprise, מוֹפֵת does not merely mean a *wonder*, but a *portent* or extraordinary premonition. עַל might here be taken in the more specific sense of *against*, but the more general meaning is sufficient, and agrees well with the context. *Cush* has been variously explained to mean a part of Arabia on the coast of the Red Sea (Bochart), or this part of Arabia with the opposite part of Africa (Vitringa); but the latest authorities confirm the ancient explanation of the word as meaning *Ethiopia*. In the prophecies belonging to the reign of Hezekiah, Egypt and Ethiopia are frequently combined, either because they were in close alliance, or because an Ethiopian dynasty

then reigned in Upper Egypt.   It has been a question with interpreters whether the words *three years* are to be connected with what follows or what goes before.   The Septuagint gives both solutions by repeating τρία ἔτη.   The Masoretic interpunction throws the words into the second clause, *three years a sign*, &c.   This construction is adopted by some modern writers for the purpose of avoiding the conclusion that Isaiah walked naked and bare-foot for the space of three years, which is certainly the obvious and *prima facie* meaning of the words.   Those who adhere to the Masoretic accents, understand the second clause to mean *a three years' sign and wonder, i. e.* either a sign of something to occur in three years, or to continue three years, or a sign for three years of a subsequent event.   Those who connect *three years* with what precedes, either understand the language strictly as denoting that the Prophet continued to go naked and barefoot for that space of time, or palliate the harshness of this supposition by assuming that he only appeared thus when he went abroad, or at certain set times, or occasionally. The most improbable hypothesis of all is that of a transposition in the text, שלש שנים אות for אות שלש שנים (Gesenius), unless the preference be due to that of Lowth, that the original reading was *three days*, or to that of Vitringa, that *three days* was meant to be supplied by the reader.   On the whole, the simplest and most satisfactory solution is that proposed by Hitzig, who sup-poses the Prophet to have exposed himself but once in the way described, after which he continued to be a sign and wonder for three years, *i. e.* till the fulfilment of the prophecy.   This explanation avoids the difficulty as to the three years' exposure, and at the same time adheres to the Masoretic interpunction.   The three years have been variously understood,—as the duration of the siege of Ashdod, as the duration of the exile threatened in the next verse, and as the interval which should elapse between the pro-phecy and its fulfilment.   Of these three hypotheses the second is the least probable, while the first and third may be combined.

4. *So shall the king of Assyria lead the captivity* (i. e. *the captives*) *of Egypt and the exiles of Ethiopia, young and old, naked and barefoot, with their buttocks uncovered, the nakedness* (or *disgrace*) *of Egypt.*   This verse completes the comparison begun in that before it.   נָהַג is commonly applied to flocks and herds, and, like the Latin *ago*, corresponds both to *lead* and *drive* in English.   Our language does not furnish two equivalents to שְׁבִי and גָּלוּת as abstract nouns, *exile* being never used as a collective for *exiles*.   The sense of the original is expressed, with a change of form, in the English Version (*the Egyptians prisoners, and the Ethiopians captives*), and by Luther (*das gefangene Egypten und vertriebene Mohrenland*).   The phrase נְעָרִים וּזְקֵנִים is not meant to exclude men in the prime of life because already slain in battle (Musculus), but comprehends all ages.   It is clear from this verse that Isaiah's exposure did not prefigure the spoliation of the Egyptians (Barnes), but their personal captivity.   It is also clear, from a comparison of the type and antitype, that the nakedness of ver. 2 was a par-tial one, since captives were not commonly reduced to a state of absolute nudity.   This is confirmed by the addition of the word *barefoot* in both cases, which would be superfluous if *naked* had its strictest sense.   The last clause is separately construed by Ewald: they who are thus uncovered are the shame of Egypt.   Other interpreters continue the construction from the previous clause.   עֶרְוַת is not to be taken in its strict sense, as in appo-sition with the phrase before it, but in its secondary sense of *shame* or *igno-miny*, with or without a preposition understood.   The omission of Ethiopia in this last clause is no ground for supposing it to be interpolated in the other

(Hitzig), nor is there an allusion to the greater sensitiveness of the Egyptians (Vitringa). The omission is, so to speak, an accidental one, *i. e.* without design or meaning. Even Hendewerk exclaims against the tasteless and unmeaning maxim, that a writer who repeats his own expressions must do it with servile exactness, or be suspected of some deep design in the omission. Connected as Egypt and Ethiopia were in fact and in the foregoing context, either name includes the other. The *king of Assyria* here meant is neither Nebuchadnezzar (Cocceius), nor Esarhaddon, nor Shalmaneser, but either Sennacherib or Sargon himself. The modern German writers suppose this prediction to have been fulfilled in the conquest of No-Ammon (*i. e.* Diospolis or Thebes), mentioned in Nahum iii. 8 as a recent event. How long beforehand the prediction was uttered is a question of small moment, and one which cannot be decided. There is no ground, however, for the supposition that the interval was so short as to convert the prophecy into a mere conjecture or an act of sagacious forecast. Equally vain are the attempts to determine whether the king of Assyria remained at home during the siege of Ashdod, or was then engaged in his attack upon Egypt. The chronological hypotheses of Usher, Marsham, and Vitringa, all assume that Sargon was identical either with Shalmaneser, Esarhaddon, or Sennacherib. חֲשׂוּפַי is explained by Jarchi as a singular with a supernumerary syllable, by Kimchi and Gesenius as an old form of the plural absolute, by Ewald as an old form of the plural construct. On the construction with the following noun, *vide supra*, chap. i. 4, iii. 16.

5. *And they shall be afraid and ashamed of Ethiopia their expectation, and of Egypt their boast.* This is the effect to be produced by the catastrophe just threatened. Both the Hebrew verbs take מִן after them, as *afraid* and *ashamed* take *of* in English; but the full sense of חַתּוּ is, that they shall be confounded, filled with consternation, at the fate of those in whom they trusted for deliverance. מַבָּט is that to which they *look* for help. It is used in the same sense Zech. ix. 5. According to Hitzig, מַבָּט properly belongs to מִצְרַיִם, but was taken from it to be joined with the interpolated כּוּשׁ, its place being supplied by the inappropriate word תִּפְאֶרֶת. Knobel, on the contrary, sees a peculiar beauty in the distinction between Ethiopia, to which they merely looked for help, and Egypt, from which they had formerly received it, and in which they therefore gloried. The verbs in this verse are indefinite. Some refer them to the Philistines, others to the Jews, and a third class to an Egyptian faction in Jerusalem. These are mere conjectures, nor can anything more be ascertained from the intentionally vague terms of the text. That the words refer to the Philistines, is inferred from the mention of the siege of Ashdod in the first verse. But this is by no means a necessary inference, since Ashdod was attacked and taken, not as a town of the Philistines, but as a frontier post of great importance to both parties in the war. So far, then, as the Jews were interested in the war at all, they were interested in the fate of Ashdod, and the mention of this siege as one of the principal events of the campaign is altogether natural. In favour of the reference to Judah may be also urged the want of any clear example in Isaiah of a prophecy exclusively intended for the warning or instruction of a foreign power. In either case, the meaning of the verse is, that they who had relied on Egypt and its ally Ethiopia for aid against Assyria, whether Jews or Philistines, or both, should be confounded at beholding Egypt and Ethiopia themselves subdued.

6. *And the inhabitant of this isle* (or *coast*) *shall say in that day, Be-*

hold, thus (or *such*) *is our expectation, whither we fled for help, to be delivered from the presence of the king of Assyria. And how shall we* (*ourselves*) *escape?* The disappointment described in the foregoing verse is now expressed by those who felt it. The argument is one *a fortiori*. If the protectors were subdued, what must become of the protected? The pronoun in the last clause is emphatic, as it usually is when not essential to the sense. The Hebrew אִי has no exact equivalent in English. Three distinct shades or gradations of meaning seem to be clearly marked in usage. The first is that of *land*, as opposed to water; the second that of *coast*, as opposed to inland; the third that of *island*, as opposed to mainland. The last, although commonly expressed in most translations, is perhaps the least frequent of the three. The word here denotes, not Lower Egypt, or the Delta of the Nile (Clericus), but the south-eastern shore of the Mediterranean, here called *this coast*, as Hendewerk observes, in order to distinguish it from *that coast*, viz. Ethiopia and Egypt, which had just before been mentioned. As to the extent of country meant to be included, nothing of course can be determined from the word itself, which is designedly indefinite. Hitzig, in accordance with his view of the whole prophecy, restricts the application to the land of the Philistines, as the maritime tract in the south-west of Palestine, adjacent to Egypt. Others with more probability regard it as denoting Palestine itself, in the large modern sense, but with particular reference to Judah.—*Thus* or *such is our expectation, i.e.* this is the end of it, you see what has become of it, you see the fate of that to which we looked for help (מִבְּטֵנִי); how then can we ourselves (אֲנַחְנוּ) be delivered or escape? See a similar expression, 2 Kings x. 4.

Chapter 21

As three of the verses of this chapter begin with the word מַשָּׂא (vers. 1, 11, 13), it is now commonly supposed to consist of three distinct prophecies. It is also agreed that the first of these (vers. 1–10) relates to the conquest of Babylon by the Medes and Persians; the second (vers. 11, 12) either to Edom, or the Arabian tribe Dumah; and the third (vers. 13–17) to another Arabian tribe, or to Arabia in general. The second and third of these divisions are admitted by the recent German writers to be genuine, that is to say, composed by Isaiah himself, while the first is with almost equal unanimity declared to the product of a later age. This critical judgment as in other cases, is founded partly on alleged diversities of phraseology, but chiefly on the wonderful coincidences with history, both sacred and profane, which could not be ascribed to Isaiah or to any contemporary writer, without conceding the reality of prophetic inspiration. The principle involved in this decision is consistently carried out by Paulus, Eichhorn, and Rosenmüller, who regard the passage as an *ex post facto* prophecy, while Gesenius, Maurer, Hitzig, Ewald, Umbreit, and Knobel, arbitrarily reject this supposition, and maintain that it was written just before the event, when Isaiah, as a politician or a poet, could foresee what was to happen. Upon this we may observe, first, that all such reasoning proceeds, not upon the want of satisfactory evidence, but upon the impossibility of inspiration or prophetic foresight, so that even supposing it to have existed, no proof could establish it. There is nothing, therefore, in the reasoning of such writers to shake the faith of any who do not hold their fundamental principle of unbelief. In the next place, this hypothesis entirely fails to account for the minute agreement of the prophecy with history in circumstantials, which must therefore be explained away by forced constructions and interpretations. Taking the language in its obvious meaning, and excluding all gratuitous assumptions, we shall be constrained to look upon this passage as one of the most striking instances of strict agreement between prophecy and history. As to the remainder of the chapter, while it cannot be denied that the connection of the parts, and the meaning of each in itself, are exceedingly obscure, it may be doubted whether there is sufficient ground for their entire separation as distinct and independent prophecies. The extreme brevity, especially of the second part (vers. 11, 12), makes this very dubious, and the doubt is strengthened by the recurrence of the figure of a watchman in ver. 11. The conclusion drawn from the use of the word מַשָּׂא rests upon the dubious assumption that it is to be regarded as a formal title or inscription. It is worthy of remark, that some of the same writers who reject these *titles* as no part of the text, appeal to their authority in settling the division and arrangement of the chapter. The truth is, that this formula, in many cases, seems to indicate at most the subdivisions of an unbroken context. In the case before us, as in chap. xiv. 20, it is safer to assume the unity of the composition than rashly to dismember it. However difficult it may be, therefore, to determine the connection of these parts, they may safely be regarded as composing one obscure but continuous prediction. This is the less improbable, because they can all be brought into connection, if not unity, by simply supposing that the tribes or races, to which vers. 11–17 relate, were sharers with the Jews in the Babylonian tyranny, and therefore interested in its downfall. This hypothesis, it is true, is not susceptible of demonstration; but it is strongly recommended by the very fact that it explains the juxtaposition of these prophecies, or rather entitles them to be considered one.

The first part of the prophecy opens with an emphatic intimation of its alarming character, vers. 1–4. We have then a graphic representation of the march of the Medes and Persians upon Babylon, vers. 5–9. This is followed by a hint of the effect which this event would have upon the people of Jehovah, ver. 10.

The remainder of the chapter represents the neighbouring nations as involved in the same sufferings with the Jews, but without any consolatory promise of deliverance, vers. 11–17.

1. *The burden of the desert of the sea. Like whirlwinds in the south, as to rushing* (or *driving*) *from the wilderness it comes, from a terrible land.* By the desert of the sea, Grotius understands the country of the Edomites, extending to the Red Sea, as it did in the days of Solomon (1 Kings ix. 26). Other interpreters are agreed that the phrase is an enigmatical description of Babylonia as a great plain (Gen. xi. 1; Isa. xxiii. 13), watered by a great river, which, like the Nile (chap. xix. 5), is sometimes called a sea (chap. xxvii. 1). This designation was the more appropriate because the plain of Babylon, according to Herodotus, was often overflowed before Semiramis took measures to prevent it, and Abydenus says expressly that it then had the appearance of a sea. The threatened danger is compared to the approach of a tempest from the south, *i. e.* from the great Arabian desert, in which quarter the most violent winds are elsewhere represented as prevailing. ל before חלוף denotes relation in general, and indicates the

point of the comparison. בָּא is indefinite, and may either be referred to the enemy or made to agree with *something*, or the like understood. As מִמִּדְבָּר cannot be referred to the countries through which Cyrus passed, Knobel disregards the accents and connects it with what goes before. " Like south-winds sweeping from the wilderness, one comes (or they come) from a terrible land." This, however, is unnecessary, as the phrase מִמִּדְבָּר may be figurative, and refer to the foregoing comparison, as if he had said, they come as storms come from the desert.

2. *A hard vision, it is revealed to me ; the deceiver deceiving and the spoiler spoiling. Go up, O Elam ; besiege, O Media : all sighing* (or *all its sighing) have I made to cease.* The first phrase of course means a vision of severe and awful judgments. The feminine form of the noun is connected with a masculine verb, as Henderson imagines, to intimate the dreadful nature of the judgment threatened. It is hard to see how this end is attained by an irregularity of syntax. Others regard it as a mere enallage, which is the less probable, however, as the noun precedes the verb. Perhaps the simplest explanation is that הֻגַּד is indefinite, and governs the preceding words; as if he had said, A revelation has been made to me (consisting of) a grievous vision. The older writers understand the next clause as a description of the Babylonian tyranny, and give בּוֹגֵד its usual meaning of a *treacherous dealer.* The late writers apply the clause to the conquerors of Babylon, and make בּוֹגֵד nearly synonymous with שׁוֹדֵד. But this sense of the word cannot be justified by usage. Nor is it necessary, even if the clause be applied to Cyrus, since one of the terms may describe the stratagems of war, as the other does its violence. This is the more natural, as Babylon was actually taken by stratagem. *Go up, i. e.* against Babylon, either in reference to its lofty defences (chap. xxvi. 5), or according to a more general military usage of the phrase. (*Vide supra*, chap. vii. 1.) The Medes and Persian were united under Cyrus, but the latter are here named first, as Knobel thinks, because they were now in the ascendant. The final letter of אַנְחָתָה is commonly regarded as a suffix, though without mappik, *all its sighing,* sc. Babylon's, *i. e.* all the sighing it has caused by its oppression, or all the sighing of it, sc. the גָּלוּת, or captivity. Some, however, make the letter paragogic, and read *all sighing,* which amounts to the same thing, the limitation which is expressed in one case being understood in the other. Elam, a province of the Persian empire, is here put for the whole. Knobel sees a designed paronomasia in the similar forms עֲלִי עֵילָם.

3. *Therefore my loins are filled with pain ; pangs have seized me like the pangs of a travailing (woman) ; I writhe* (or *am convulsed) from hearing ; I am shocked* (or *agitated) from seeing.* Some regard these as the words of a captive Jew, or of a Babylonian ; but there is no objection to explaining them as expressive of the Prophet's own emotions, a very common method of enhancing the description even of described and righteous judgments. The reduplicated form חַלְחָלָה is intensive. Lowth's translation, *convulsed,* is perhaps too strong, as the common version, *bowed down,* is too weak. The older writers give the מִן a causal meaning, *from, i. e.* by, or on account of. The later writers make it privative, *away from hearing, i. e.* so as not to hear. Ewald obtains the same sense by making it comparative, *too much confounded to hear, too much frightened to see.*

4. *My heart wanders* (reels, or is bewildered) ; *horror appals me ; the twilight* (night or evening) *of my pleasure* (or *desire) he has put for* (or converted into) *fear* (or *trembling) for me.* Compare the combination תְּעֵי לֵבָב Ps. xcv 10. There are two interpretations of the last clause. One sup-

poses it to mean that the night desired as a time of rest is changed into a time of terror; the other, that a night of festivity is changed into a night of terror. As this last brings the prophecy into remarkable coincidence with history, the modern Germans commonly prefer the former. That the court was revelling when Cyrus took the city, is stated in general by Herodotus and Zenophon, and in full detail by Daniel. That the two first, however, did not derive their information from the prophet, may be inferred from their not mentioning the writing on the wall,—a prodigy which would have seemed incredible to neither of them.

5. *Set the table, spread the cloth, eat, drink : arise, ye chiefs, anoint the shield!* The Hebrew verbs are not imperatives but infinitives, here used in the first clause for the historical tense in order to give brevity, rapidity, and life to the description. For the same purpose the English imperative may be employed, as the simplest form of the verb, and unencumbered with the personal pronouns. The sense, however, is, that while the table is set, &c., the alarm is given. Luzzatto makes the whole verse antithetical : they 'set the table, they had better set a watch ; they eat and drink, they had better arise and anoint the shield. צָפֹה הַצָּפִית is commonly explained to mean *watching the watch, i.e.* setting a guard to prevent surprise. But the context implies that they were surprised. Ewald refers it to the watching of the stars, which agrees well with the Babylonian usages, but, like the first explanation, seems misplaced between the setting of the table and the sitting at it. Hitzig and Knobel give צָפָה the usual sense of צָפָה, to overspread or cover, and צָפִית (which occurs only here) that of the thing spread, whether it be the cloth or skin which serves the orientals for a table, or the carpet upon which they sit at meals. The anointing of the shield is supposed by some to be a means of preserving it or of repelling missiles from its surface, by others simply a means of cleansing and perhaps adorning it. Both agree that it is here poetically used to express the idea of arming or preparing for battle. There are two interpretations of the last clause. One makes it an address by Jehovah or the Prophet to the Medes and Persians, as in the last clause of ver. 2 ; the other a sudden alarm to the Babylonians at their feast. Both explanations, but especially the last, seem to present a further allusion to the surprise of the king and court by Cyrus. This coincidence with history can be explained away only by giving to the verse a vague and general meaning, which is wholly at variance with the graphic vividness of its expressions.

6. *For thus saith the Lord to me : Go set* (or *cause to stand*) *the watchman* (or *sentinel*) *; that which he sees let him tell.* Instead of simply predicting or describing the approach of the enemy, the Prophet introduces an ideal watchman, as announcing what he actually sees. According to Knobel, he is himself the watchman (Hab. i. 8), which is hardly consistent with the language of this verse. The last clause may be also construed thus—*who may see* (and) *tell ;* but the first construction seems more natural.

7. *And should he see cavalry—a pair* (or *pairs of horsemen*)—*ass-riders—camel-riders—then shall he hearken with hearkening a great hearkening (i. e.* listen attentively). This is Ewald's construction of the sentence, which supposes the divine instructions to be still continued. All other writers understand the Prophet as resuming his own narrative ; and he saw (or he sees), &c. Against this construction, and in favour of the first, is the form of the verbs, which are all in the preterite with *vav conversive,* because following the futures of the foregoing verse (Nordheimer, § 219). Besides, if the usual construction be adopted, ver. 9 is a mere repetition of ver. 7, and

ver. 8 is obviously misplaced between them.   But on the other supposition, this verse contains the order, and the ninth its execution, while the eighth, as a preface to the latter, is exactly in its proper place.   צֶמֶד is properly a *yoke* of oxen, then a *pair* in general.   It is here collective, and means *pairs* of horsemen, *i. e.* horsemen in pairs, or marching two and two.   The sense of steeds or riding-horses (as opposed to סוּסִים, chariot-horses), given to פָּרָשִׁים by Gesenius, is extremely rare and doubtful, and ought not to be assumed without necessity.   רֶכֶב in a very great majority of cases means a chariot.   But as this would seem to make the Prophet speak of chariots drawn by asses and camels, most of the late writers either take the word in the sense of rows or troops, which seems entirely arbitrary, or in that of mounted troops or cavalry, which seems to be easily deducible from רָכַב, to ride, and may be justified by the analogy of 1 Sam. viii. 4, x. 18, where the word must mean either riders, or the beasts on which they rode, although the English translators, in order to retain the usual sense of *chariot*, supply *horses* in one place and *men* in the other.   On the first of these hypotheses, the camels and asses would be mentioned only as beasts of burden ; but we know from Herodotus and Xenophon that the Persians also used them in their armies for riding, partly or wholly for the purpose of frightening the horses of the enemy.   It is a slight but obvious coincidence of prophecy and history, that Xenophon represents the Persians advancing two by two (εἰς δύο).

8. *And he cries—a lion—on the watch-tower, Lord, I am standing always by day, and on my ward* (or *place of observation*) *I am stationed all the night* (*i. e. all night*, or *every night*, or *both*).   That the setting of this watch is an ideal process, seems to be intimated by the word אֲדֹנָי one of the divine names (not אֲדֹנִי, *my lord* or *sir*), and also by the unremitted vigilance to which he here lays claim.   From the first of these particulars, Knobel infers that the Prophet is himself the watchman stationed by Jehovah.   But see ver. 7, and the comment on it.   Another view of the passage may be suggested as possibly the true one, viz., that the Prophet, on receiving the order to set a watch, replies that he is himself engaged in the performance of that duty.   According to the usual interpretation, these are the words of the delegated watchman, announcing that he is at his post, and will remain there, and announce whatever he may see.   There are two explanations of וַיִּקְרָא אַרְיֵה.   The first makes אַרְיֵה the beginning of the watchman's speech—*he cries, a lion!* *i. e.* I see a lion coming, meaning the invader.   The objection to this is not, as Henderson alleges, that the usage of the language does not authorize such an application of the figure of a lion ; but rather that this abrupt and general announcement of the enemy would hardly have been followed by a prefatory declaration of the watchman's diligence.   This, it is clear, must come before, not after, the announcement of the enemy, and accordingly we find that announcement in the next verse, corresponding exactly to the terms of the instructions in the seventh.   These considerations seem decisive in favour of the other hypothesis, now commonly adopted, viz. that אַרְיֵה forms no part of the sentinel's report, but is rather a description of the way in which he makes it.   The true sense of the words is given in a paraphrase in Rev. x. 3, *he cried with a loud voice as when a lion roareth.* As to the syntax, we may either supply כְּ before אַרְיֵה, of which ellipsis there are some examples, or still more simply read *the lion cries*, thus converting the simile into a metaphor.   The first construction agrees best, however, with the Masoretic accents.   Luzzatto explains אַרְיֵה as the usual cry of shepherds when they saw wild beasts approaching.

9. *And behold, this comes* (or this is what is coming), *mounted men, pairs of horsemen.   And he answers* (*i. e.* speaks again) *and says, Fallen, fallen is Babylon, and all the images of her gods he has broken* (or *crushed*) *to the earth.*   The last verb is indefinitely construed, but obviously refers to the enemy as the instrument of Babylon's destruction rather than to God, as the efficient cause.   The omission of the asses and camels in this verse is explained by Knobel on the ground that the enemy is now to be conceived as having reached the city, his beasts of burden being left behind him. But the true explanation seems to be that the description given in ver. 7 is abbreviated here, because so much was to be added.   Still the correspondence is sufficiently exact.   רֶכֶב אִישׁ is supposed by some to mean chariots containing men ; but according to the analogy of ver. 7, it rather means *mounted men.*   As the phrases *camel-riders, ass-riders,* there used, from the nature of the case can only mean riders upon camels and asses, so here *man-riders,* from the nature of the case, can only mean men who are riders themselves.   The structure of the passage is highly dramatic.   In the sixth verse, the Prophet is commanded to set a watch.   In the seventh, the sentinel is ordered to look out for an army of men, mounted on horses, camels, and asses.   In the eighth, he reports himself as being at his post.   In the ninth, he sees the very army which had been described approaching.   *Answer* is used, both in Greek and Hebrew, for the resumption of discourse by the same speaker, especially after an interval.   It is here equivalent to *spoke again.*   During the interval implied, the city is supposed to have been taken, so that when the watchman speaks again, it is to say that Babylon is fallen.   The omission of all the intermediate details, for the purpose of bringing the extremes together, is a masterly stroke of poetical description, which would never have occurred to an inferior writer.   The allusion to idols in the last clause is not intended merely to remind us that the conquest was a triumph of the true God over false ones, but to bring into view the well known aversion of the Persians to all images.   Herodotus says they not only thought it unlawful to use images, but imputed folly to those who did it.   Here is another incidental but remarkable coincidence of prophecy even with profane history.

10. *O my threshing, and the son of my threshing-floor !   What I have heard from Jehovah of hosts, the God of Israel, I have told you.*   This part of the prophecy closes with an apostrophe, showing at once by whose power and for whose sake the downfall of Babylon was to be brought about. *Threshing* here means that which is threshed, and is synonymous with the following phrase, *son of the threshing-floor, i. e.* (according to the oriental idiom which uses *son* to signify almost any relation) *threshed grain.*   The comparison of severe oppression or affliction to threshing is a common one, and though the terms here used are scarcely intelligible when literally rendered into English, it is clear that they mean, *oh my oppressed and afflicted people,* and must therefore be addressed not to the Babylonians but the Jews, to whom the fall of Babylon would bring deliverance, and for whose consolation this prediction was originally uttered.   The last clause assures them that their own God had sent this message to them.

11. *The burden of Dumah.   To me* (one is) *calling from Seir.   Watchman, what of the night ?   Watchman, what of the night ?*   It has been already stated that most interpreters regard this and the next verse as an independent prophecy ; but that the use of the word מַשָּׂא is an insufficient reason, while the extreme brevity of the passage, and the recurrence of the figure of a sentinel or watchman, seem to indicate that it is a continuation of

what goes before, although a new subject is here introduced. Of *Dumah* there are two interpretations. J. D. Michaelis, Gesenius, Maurer, Hitzig, Ewald, Umbreit, understand it as the name of an Arabian tribe descended from Ishmael (Gen. xxv. 14 ; 1 Chron. i. 30), or of a place belonging to that tribe, perhaps the same now called *Dumah Eljandil* on the confines of Arabia and Syria. In that case, Seir, which lay between Judah and the desert of Arabia, is mentioned merely to denote the quarter whence the sound proceeded. But as Seir was itself the residence of the Edomites or children of Esau, Vitringa, Rosenmüller, and Knobel, follow the Septuagint and Jarchi, in explaining דוּמָה as a variation of the name אֱדוֹם, intended at the same time to suggest the idea of *silence*, solitude, and desolation. This enigmatical name, as well as that in ver. 1, is ascribed by Knobel to the copyist or compiler who added the inscriptions. In favour of the first interpretation is the mention of Arabia and of certain Arabian tribes in the following verses. But even Edom might be said to form a part of Arabia. Jerome also mentions Dumah as a district in the south of Edom. The greater importance of Edom, and the frequency with which it is mentioned in the prophets, especially as an object of divine displeasure, also recommend this exegetical hypothesis. Knobel adds that the Edomites were subject to Judah till the year B.C. 743, and would therefore naturally take part in its sufferings from Babylonian tyranny. Clericus understands the question to be, what has happened since last night ? The English Version seems to mean, what have you to say of the night ? Interpreters are commonly agreed, however, that the מִן is partitive, and that the question is, what part of the night is it, equivalent to our question, what o'clock ? This may have been a customary method of interrogating watchmen. קֹרֵא is indefinite, or may agree with קוֹל understood. (*Vide infra*, chap. xl. 3). Night is a common metaphor to represent calamity, as daybreak does relief from it. Some regard this as a taunting inquiry addressed to Judah by his heathen neighbours. It is much more natural, however, to explain it as an expression of anxiety arising from a personal concern in the result.

12. *The watchman says, Morning comes and also night ; if ye will inquire, inquire ; return, come.* Grotius understands this to mean that though the natural morning might return, the moral or spiritual night would still continue. Gesenius explains it as descriptive of vicissitude : morning comes, but night comes after it. Most writers understand it as relating to different subjects : morning comes (to one) and night (to another) ; which would seem to mean that while the Jewish night was about to be dispelled, that of Edom or Arabia should still continue. Those who regard these verses as genuine, but deny the inspiration of the writer, are under the necessity of referring them to something which took place in the days of Isaiah. Knobel, for example, understands him here as threatening Edom with a visit from the Assyrians on their return from Egypt. But connected as the words are with the foregoing prophecy, it is far more natural to understand them as referring to the Babylonian conquest of Judea and the neighbouring countries. The last clause intimates that the event was still uncertain. Henderson and others give to שֻׁבוּ the spiritual sense of repentance and conversion ; but there seems to be no need of departing from the literal import of the word. The true sense of the clause is that given by Luther. If you wish to know you must inquire again ; you are come too soon ; the time of your deliverance is not at hand ; return or come again. On any hypothesis, however, these two verses still continue enigmatical and doubtful in their meaning.

13. *The burden of Arabia. In the forest in Arabia shall ye lodge, oh ye caravans of Dedanim.* The genuineness of this verse and of those which follow is questioned by Eichhorn, Paulus, Baur, and Rosenmüller, but defended by Knobel on the ground that שְׂאָר כָּבוּד, and שְׁנֵי שָׂכִיר are expressions belonging to Isaiah's dialect. Hitzig and Hendewerk, with the older writers, regard these verses, and vers. 11, 12, as forming one prophecy. But Knobel maintains that vers. 11, 12 are of a later date, for the singular reason that they speak with uncertainty of that which is confidently foretold in the others. He also alleges that the title or inscription was taken from the word בַּעְרַב in the next clause, even the preposition being retained. But בְּ is often interposed between words most closely connected, and this very combination occurs in Zech. ix. 1, where no such explanation can be given. The Prophet here passes from Edom to Arabia, or from one Arabian tribe or district to another. The answer in ver. 12, that the dawn was approaching for the Jews but not for them, is here explained. The country was to be in such a state that the caravans which usually travelled undisturbed would be obliged to leave the public road, and pass the night among the bushes or thickets, which seems to be here (and perhaps originally) the meaning of יַעַר. Forests properly so called do not exist in the Arabian desert. Gesenius explains אֹרְחוֹת as the participle of אֹרַח, used as a noun in the sense of travelling companies or caravans. The Dedanim are mentioned elsewhere in connection with Edom and Teman (Jer. xlix. 8 ; Ezek. xxv. 13), to whom they were probably contiguous. Their precise situation is the less important as they are not the subjects of the prophecy, but spoken of as strangers passing through, the interruption of whose journey is mentioned as a proof of the condition of the country. For בַּעְרַב the ancient versions seems to read בָּעֶרֶב, in which they are followed by Lowth, Hitzig, Hendewerk, and Knobel, the last of whom defends the emendation on the twofold ground, that עֲרָב is a name found only in the later Hebrew writers, and that the addition of this name would be superfluous, as the caravans of Dedanim must pass of course through the desert of Arabia. The first of these arguments admits the easy answer that this place is itself a proof of earlier usage. To the second it may be replied, that *Arabia* is not half so superfluous as *evening* in connexion with תָּלִינוּ which strictly means to spend the night. How easy it would be to retort upon such criticism by demanding whether they could pass the night in the day-time.

14. *To meet the thirsty they bring water, the inhabitants of the land of Tema ; with his bread they prevent (i. e.* meet or anticipate) *the fugitive.* The men of Tema, another Arabian tribe, also engaged in trade (Jer. xxv. 23 ; Job vi. 19), are described as bringing food and drink, not to the Dedanim mentioned in ver. 13, but to the people of the wasted country. *His bread* is rendered in the English Version as a collective (*their bread*) referring to the men of Tema ; but the suffix relates rather to the fugitive himself, and the whole phrase means his portion of food, the food necessary for him, his *daily bread*. The ancient versions make the verbs imperative and understand the sentence as an exhortation to the people of Tema. This construction, which is adopted by Henderson, requires a change in the pointing of the text, for which there is no sufficient authority, much less a necessity. On the contrary, the context makes it far more natural to understand the Prophet as describing an act than as exhorting to it.

15. *Because* (or *when*) *from the presence of swords they fled, from the presence of a drawn sword and from the presence of a bended bow, and from the presence of a weight of war.* This verse describes them as not only plun-

dered but pursued by a blood-thirsty enemy. נְטוּשָׁה, according to usage, seems to mean not only *drawn* or *thrust forth*, but *given up*, abandoned to itself, and as it were allowed to do its worst. כֹּבֶד is properly weight, pressure, burden, or oppression. The corresponding verb is connected with the same noun in 1 Sam. xxxi. 3.

16. *For thus saith the Lord to me, In yet a year* (or *in a year longer*) *like the years of a hireling* (*i. e.* strictly computed) *shall fail* (or *cease*) *all the glory of Kedar.* This verse seems to fix a time for the fulfilment of the foregoing prophecy. Here, as in chap. xvii. 3, glory comprehends all that constitutes the dignity or strength of a people. On the meaning of the phrase כִּשְׁנֵי שָׂכִיר, *vide supra*, chap. xvi. 14. Kedar was the second son of Ishmael (Gen. xxv. 13). The name is here put either for an Arab tribe or for Arabia in general (Isa. xlii. 11, lx. 7; Ezek. xxvii. 21). The Rabbins call the Arabic the *language of Kedar*. The chronological specification in this verse makes it necessary, either to assume a later writer than Isaiah, as some do in chap. xvi. 14, or a *terminus a quo* posterior to his time, as if he had said, within a year after something else before predicted; or an abrupt recurrence from the days of Nebuchadnezzar or Cyrus to those of Hezekiah. The last would be wholly in accordance with the usage of the prophets; but the best solution seems to be afforded by the second hypothesis. The sense will then be that the Arabians who suffered with the Jews, so far from sharing their deliverance, should, within a year after the event, be entirely destroyed. At the same time, due allowance should be made for diversity of judgment in a case so doubtful.

17. *And the remnant of the number of bows* (or *archers*), *the mighty men* (or *heroes*), *of the children of Kedar, shall be few* (or *become few*), *for Jehovah God of Israel hath spoken it.* קשת is here collective and may either be in regimen or apposition with the words which follow. The latter construction is favoured by the accents. We read elsewhere of the archery of Ishmael (Gen xxi. 20) and Kedar (Ps. cxx. 4). Another construction, which refers the first clause to the remnant left by the bows of the enemy, is possible, but should not be assumed without necessity. The last clause intimates that God, as the God of Israel, has a quarrel with Kedar, and at the same time that his power and omniscience will secure the fulfilment of the threatening. It is not impossible that future discoveries may yet throw light upon these brief and obscure prophecies.

Chapter 22

THIS chapter naturally falls into two parts. The first describes the conduct of the people of Jerusalem during a siege, vers. 1–14. The second predicts the removal of Shebna from his post as treasurer or steward of the royal household, vers. 15–25. The modern critics are of course inclined to treat these parts as independent prophecies, although they admit that both are by Isaiah, and that both were written probably about the same time. Against this supposition, and in favour of regarding them as one connected composition, we may argue, first, from the want of any title to the second part. This, it is true, is not conclusive, but creates a presumption which can only be rebutted by strong direct evidence. Another reason is that the second part of this chapter is the only example in Isaiah of a prophecy against an individual. This again is not conclusive, since there might be one such prophecy, if no more. But the presumption is against it, as analogy and usage give the preference to any exegetical hypothesis which would connect this personal prediction with one of a more general nature. A third reason is that in the second part the ground or occasion of the threatening is not expressed, and it is certainly less probable that the design was meant to be conjectured or inferred from the prophecy itself, than that it is explained in the passage which immediately precedes it. The result appears to be, that by considering the parts as independent prophecies we leave the second incomplete and *sui generis*, whereas by combining them, we make the one explain the other; and as no philological or critical objection has been urged against this supposition, it is probably the true one. The whole may then be described as a prophecy against the people of Jerusalem in general, and against Shebna in particular, considered as their leader and example.

It has been disputed whether the description in the first part of this chapter was intended to apply to the siege of Jerusalem by Sennacherib, or by Esarhaddon in the reign of Manasseh, or by Nebuchadnezzar, or by Titus. An obvious objection to the last two is that they leave the prediction against Shebna unconnected with the one before it. Cocceius ingeniously suggests that Eliakim and his family were to retain their official rank and influence until the city was destroyed, and the kingdom of Judah at an end; but this, though possible, will scarcely be preferred to any more natural and simple supposition. The objection to Sennacherib's invasion is that no such extremities were then experienced as the Prophet here describes. The objection to Nebuchadnezzar's is, that vers. 9–11 contain an exact description of the measures taken by Hezekiah, as recorded in 2 Chron. xxxii. 3–5. Moved by this consideration, some have assumed a reference to both events, the siege by Sennacherib, and that by Nebuchadnezzar. According to Vitringa, the Prophet first describes the later event (vers. 1–5), and then recurs to one nearer at hand (vers. 6–14), this being placed last partly for the purpose of bringing it into juxtaposition with the threatening against Shebna. According to Calvin, vers. 1–5 predict the siege by Nebuchadnezzar, while vers. 6–11 describe that by Sennacherib as already past. These suppositions, though admissible in case of necessity, can be justified by nothing short of it. As the measures described in vers. 9–11 were temporary ones which may have been frequently repeated, it is not absolutely necessary to apply that passage to the times of Hezekiah. If the whole must be applied to one specific point of time, it is probably the taking of Jerusalem by the king of Assyria in the days of Manasseh, when the latter was himself carried captive with his chief men, and Shebna possibly among the rest. The choice seems to lie between this hypothesis and that of a generic prediction, a prophetic picture of the conduct of the Jews in a certain conjuncture of affairs which happened more than once, particular strokes of the description being drawn from different memorable sieges, and especially from those of Sennacherib and Nebuchadnezzar.

1. *The burden of the Valley of Vision. What (is) to thee* (what hast thou? or what aileth thee?) *that thou art wholly* (literally, *the whole of thee*) *gone up on the house tops?* The first clause is not an inscription of later date, erroneously copied from ver. 5 (Hitzig, &c.), but the original commencement of the prophecy, or of this part of it. The modern Germans pronounce all the titles in this form spurious, and then make the use of the word מַשָּׂא in each particular case a proof of later date. It is just as easy and far more reasonable to assert that the use of this word in such connections is a characteristic of Isaiah's manner. The enigmatical form is inten-

tional.   By the valley of vision we are not to understand Babylon, nor
Judea (Calvin, Lightfoot), but Jerusalem, as being surrounded by hills with
valleys between them.   There is no allusion to the degradation which
awaited Jerusalem (Kimchi), nor to the name Moriah (J. D. Michaelis),
nor to the school of the prophets in the valley at its foot (Vitringa), nor to
the spectacle which was soon to be there exhibited (J. H. Michaelis), but
to Jerusalem as the seat of revelation, the abode of the prophets, and the
place where God's presence was manifested.   מַה־לָּךְ as usual expresses both
surprise and disapprobation.   (*Vide supra*, chap. iii. 15).   The oriental
roofs are flat and used for various purposes.   The ascent here mentioned
has been variously explained, as being designed to gratify curiosity by gazing at the approaching enemy or the crowds of people seeking refuge in Jerusalem, or to assail the invaders, or take measures for resisting them, or to
indulge in grief, or to engage in idolatrous worship, or to celebrate a feast.
The truth probably is, that the expression is here used as a lively description of an oriental city in commotion, without any intention to intimate as
yet the cause or the occasion, just as we might say that the streets of our
own cities were full of people, whether the concourse was occasioned by
grief, joy, fear, or any other cause.   Some suppose the Prophet to inquire
as a stranger what is the matter; but he seems rather to express disapprobation of the stir which he describes.

2.   *Full of stirs, a noisy town, a joyous city, thy slain are not slain with
the sword nor dead in battle.*   The first clause is commonly explained by the
older writers as a descriptive of the commotion and alarm occasioned by
the enemy's approach.   But this makes it necessary either to give עֲלִיָּה
a sense not justified by usage, or to refer to a past time, while the other
epithets are applied to the present.   Thus Junius makes the Prophet ask,
how is it that the city is *now* full of confusion and alarm which was *once* so
joyous?   But this distinction of times is altogether arbitrary.   The same
remark applies, but in a less degree, to another construction which refers
the whole clause to past time.   The latest writers are agreed in making it
descriptive of the present, not in reference however to alarm and agitation,
but to the opposite condition of joyous excitement, frivolous gaiety, and
reckless indifference, described in ver. 13.   Kennicott and Tingstad make
חֲלָלַיִךְ mean *thy warriors*, but it is now universally taken in its usual sense.
The expression *thy slain are not slain with the sword* cannot mean that
none were slain, but necessarily implies mortality of another kind.   The
allusion is supposed by some to be to pestilence, by others to famine, such
as prevailed in the siege of Jerusalem by Nebuchadnezzar, and also that by
the Romans.   As neither is specified, the words may be more generally
understood as describing all kinds of mortality incident to sieges, excepting
that of actual warfare.

3.   *All thy chiefs fled together—from the bow—they were bound—all that
were found of thee were bound together—from afar they fled.*   This verse
describes the people, not as crowding from the country into Jerusalem,
nor as fleeing from the public places in Jerusalem to hide themselves, but
as flying from the enemy, and being nevertheless taken.   קָצִין is neither a
civil nor a military chief exclusively, but may be applied to either.   נָדַד is
not to *wander*, but to *flee*.   The Masoretic accents connect מִקֶּשֶׁת with
אֻסָּרוּ, according to which construction we may either read *they are bound*
(*i. e.* made prisoners) *by the bow* (*i. e.* the archers, as light-armed troops),
or *without the bow* (*i. e.* not in battle, as the slain were not slain with the

sword) ; or it may mean *without resistance*, without drawing a bow. Some understand it to mean, *they are restrained* (by fear) *from* (using) *the bow*. Ewald and some older writers disregard the accent, and connect מקשת with נדדו, they fled from the bow, but are nevertheless taken prisoners together. *All that were found of thee* may be in antithesis to *thy chiefs ;* as if he had said, not only thy chiefs, but all the rest. Some understand this as describing the voluntary confinement of the people in Jerusalem during a siege ; others apply it to their vain endeavours to escape from its privations and dangers. It is best to give the verse its largest meaning as descriptive of the hardships and concomitant evils, not of one siege merely, but of sieges in general.

4. *Therefore I said* (or say), *Look away from me ; let me be bitter in weeping* (or *weep bitterly*) *; try not to comfort me for the desolation of the daughter of my people.* These are not the words of Jerusalem in answer to the question in ver. 1 (Junius), but those of the Prophet expressing his sympathy with sufferings which he foresees and foretells, as in chaps. xvi. 11, xxi. 3. תָּאִיצוּ seems to include the idea of obtruding consolation upon one who is unwilling to receive it. *The daughter of my people* does not mean the towns dependent on Jerusalem (Junius), nor Jerusalem itself as built by the people (Clericus), nor the sons of the people expressed by a feminine collective (Gesenius), but the people itself, poetically represented as a woman, and affectionately spoken of as a daughter.

5. *For there is a day of confusion and trampling and perplexity to the Lord Jehovah of hosts, in the valley of vision—breaking the wall and crying to the mountain.* לאדני does not mean *from* or *by the Lord*, as the efficient cause, but *to the Lord* as the possessor. It is equivalent to our phrase *the Lord has*, which cannot be otherwise expressed in Hebrew. *He has a day*, *i. e.* he has it appointed, or has it in reserve. (*Vide supra*, chap. ii. 12.) *Trampling* does not refer to the treading down of the fields and gardens, but of men in battle, or at least in a general commotion and confusion. מקרקר has been variously explained as a participle and a noun, and as expressing the ideas of breaking down, shouting, and placing chariots or waggons in array. שוע is not simply a cry but a cry for help. *To the mountain* are not the words of the cry but its direction. The mountain is not Jerusalem or Zion as the residence of God, but the mountains round about Jerusalem (Ps. cxxv. 1). The meaning is not that the people are heard crying on their way to the mountain, but rather that their cries are reverberated from it. The whole verse is a vivid poetical description of the confusion of a siege.

6. *And Elam bare a quiver, with chariots, men (i.e. infantry), horsemen, and Kir uncovered the shield.* Elam was a province of Persia, often put for the whole country. Its people were celebrated archers. Some read *chariots of men*, *i.e.* occupied by men, which would seem to be a superfluous description. Others read *cavalry* or *riding of men*, *i. e.* mounted men as in chap. xxi. 5, but in that case פרשים would be superfluous. Others give רכב, here and in chap. xxi. the sense of row, line, troop, or column, which is not sufficiently sustained by usage. Others give ב its usual sense of *in*, which cannot however be applied to *horsemen*. The sense of *horses*, doubtful at best, is entirely unnecessary here. On the whole, the simplest and most natural construction seems to be that which supposes three kinds of troops to be here enumerated : cavalry, infantry, and men in chariots. Kir is now agreed to be identical with Κῦρος, the name of a river rising in the Caucasus, and emptying into the Caspian sea, from which Georgia

(Girgistan) is supposed to derive its name. Kir was subject to Assyria in the time of Isaiah, as appears from the fact that it was one of the regions to which the exiles of the ten tribes were transported. It may here be put for Media, as Elam is for Persia. The uncovering of the shield has reference to the *involucra clypeorum* and the *tegimenta scutis detrahenda*, of which Cicero and Cæsar speak, leathern cases used to protect the shield or keep it bright. The removal of these denotes preparation for battle. The ancient versions and some modern writers make קיר an appellative and translate the clause, *the shield leaves the wall bare* by being taken down from the place where it hung, or the enemy *deprives the wall of its shield, i. e.* its defenders. Some even suppose an allusion to the *testudo* or covered way of shields, under which the Roman soldiers used to advance to the walls of a besieged town. All the latest writers are agreed in making קיר a proper name. The verbs are in the past tense, which proves nothing however as to the date of the events described.

7. *And it came to pass* (that) *the choice of thy valleys* (thy choicest valleys) *were full of chariots, and the horsemen drew up* (or took up a position) *towards the gate.* The most obvious construction of the first clause, and the one indicated by the accents, is, *the choice of thy valleys was,* or *it was the choice of thy valleys;* but as this seems forbidden by the following words, most writers either omit וַיְהִי as a pleonasm, or give it the usual idiomatic meaning when it introduces or continues a narrative. It seems here to mark the progress of events. The Prophet sees something which he did not see before. He had seen the chariots and horsemen coming; but now he sees the valleys around full of them. The future form adopted by some versions is entirely unauthorised. Whatever be the real date of the events described, the Prophet evidently meant to speak of them as past or present, and we have neither right nor reason to depart from his chosen form of expression. The address is to Jerusalem. The valleys are mentioned as the only places where the cavalry or chariots could be useful, or could act at all. As the only level approach to Jerusalem is on the north, that quarter may be specially intended, and the *gate* may be a gate on that side of the city. Otherwise it would be better to take שערה indefinitely as denoting the direction of the movement. שת may either be explained as an emphatic infinitive, in which case the verb will be reflexive or govern something understood, or as a verbal noun equivalent in this connection to our *post* or *station.* Another admissible construction is to make הפרשים the object of the verb, and the verb itself indefinite, " They station the horsemen opposite the gate."

8. *And he removed the covering of Judah, and thou didst look in that day to the armour of the house of the forest.* The first verb, which some connect with *the enemy* and others with *Jehovah* understood, is really indefinite and may be resolved into an English passive, *the covering was removed.* This expression has been variously explained to mean the disclosure of long hidden treasures—the taking of the fortified towns of Judah by Sennacherib —the disclosure of the weak points of the country to the enemy—the opening of the eyes of the Jews themselves to their own condition—the ignominious treatment of the people, represented by the oriental figure of an unveiled virgin. The analogous expression of taking away the veil from the heart (2 Cor. iii. 15, 16), and the immediate mention of the measures used for the defence of the city, are perhaps decisive in favour of explaining the words to mean that the Jews' own eyes were opened. As תְּפַּט cannot well agree יְהוּדָה, which as the name of the people must be masculine, it is best

to understand it as the second person, and to suppose an abrupt apostrophe to Judah, a figure of perpetual occurrence in Isaiah. בית היער is not a proper name, but the designation of a house built by Solomon, and elsewhere called the house of the forest of Lebanon, because erected on that mountain, as some writers think, but according to the common opinion, because built of cedar-wood from Lebanon. This house is commonly supposed to have been either intended for an arsenal by Solomon himself, or converted into one by some of his successors, and to be spoken of in Neh. iii. 19 under the name of נשק. There is no need of supposing that the house contained only the golden shields of Solomon and Rehoboam. The fact that these were there deposited might naturally lead to a more extensive use of the building for the purpose mentioned. *Looking to* this arsenal implies dependence on its stores as the best means of defence against the enemy, unless we understand the words to signify *inspection*, which agrees well with what follows, but is not sufficiently sustained by the usage of the verb and preposition. *In that day* seems to mean *at length, i. e.* when made aware of their danger.

9. *And the breaches of the city of David ye saw, that they were many, and ye gathered the waters of the lower pool.* The breaches meant are not those made by the enemy in the siege here described, but those caused by previous neglect and decay. The city of David may be either taken as a poetical name for Jerusalem at large, or in its strict sense as denoting the upper town upon mount Zion, which was surrounded by a wall of its own, and called the city of David because he took it from the Jebusites and afterwards resided there. *Ye saw* may either mean, ye saw them for the first time, at length became aware of them, or, ye looked at them, examined them, with a view to their repair. The last is more probably implied than expressed. כי may with equal propriety be rendered *for,* implying that they could no longer overlook or fail to see them, because they were so many. The last clause describes a measure of defence peculiarly important at Jerusalem where there are very few perennial springs. This precaution (as well as the one previously hinted at) was actually taken by Hezekiah in the prospect of Sennacherib's approach (2 Chron. xxxii. 4), and has perhaps been repeated in every siege of any length which Jerusalem has since experienced. The *lower pool* is probably the tank or reservoir still in existence in the valley of Hinnom opposite the western side of mount Zion. This name, which occurs only here, has reference to the *upper pool* higher up in the same valley near the Jaffa gate (*vide supra*, chap. vii. 3. Compare Robinson's Palestine, I. 483–487).

10. *And the houses of Jerusalem ye numbered, and ye pulled down the houses to repair* (rebuild or fortify) *the wall.* The numbering of the houses probably has reference, not to the levying of men or of a tax, but to the measure mentioned in the last clause, for the purpose of determining what houses could be spared, and perhaps of estimating the expense. The houses are destroyed, not merely to make room for new erections, but to furnish materials. Ancient Jerusalem, like that of our day, was built of stone.

11. *And a reservoir ye made between the two walls* (or *the double wall*) *for the waters of the old pool, and ye did not look to the maker of it, and the former of it ye did not see.* מִקְוָה according to its etymology is a place of gathering, and according to usage a place where waters are collected. As the Hebrew dual is not a mere periphrasis for *two* (*vide supra*, chap. vi. 2), חֹמֹתַיִם cannot simply mean *two walls*, but must denote a *double wall* in

some situation where but one had been before, or might have been expected. The reference is probably to a wall built out from that of the city and returning to it, so as to enclose the tank or reservoir here mentioned. As this was a temporary measure, perhaps often repeated, there is no need of tracing it in other parts of history or in the present condition of Jerusalem. It is altogether probable, however, that the *old pool* here mentioned is the same with the *upper pool* of chap. vii. 3. Some have identified it with the *lower pool* of the ninth verse, but this would hardly have been introduced so soon by another name. The last clause shews that the fault, with which the people of Jerusalem were chargeable, was not that of guarding themselves against attack, but that of relying upon human defences, without regard to God. The verbs *look* and *see* are evidently used in allusion to the last clause of ver. 8 and the first of ver. 9. They looked to the arsenal but not to God. This seems to put the clause before us in antithesis to the whole foregoing context from ver. 8. If so, the suffixes in עשיה and יצרה cannot refer merely to the pool or reservoir, but must have respect either to the city or to the calamity now coming on it. In the latter case, the feminine pronoun may be indefinitely understood as a neuter in Greek or Latin, *it*, *i. e.* this crisis or catastrophe, or the whole series of events which led to it. *Maker* and *former* are not distinctive terms referring to God s purpose or decree on one hand, and the execution of it on the other, but are poetical equivalents both denoting the efficient cause.

12. *And the Lord Jehovah of hosts called in that day to weeping, and to mourning, and to baldness, and to girding sackcloth.* The meaning is not that he called or summoned grief to come, but that he called on men to mourn, not only by his providence, but by his word through the prophets. By *baldness* we may either understand the tearing of the hair, or the shaving of the head, or both, as customary signs of grief. The last phrase, rendered in the English Bible *girding with sackcloth*, does not mean girding up the other garments with a sackcloth girdle, but girding the body with a sackcloth dress, or girding on, *i.e.* wearing sackcloth. The providential call to mourning here referred to must be the siege before described.

13. *And behold mirth and jollity, slaying of oxen and killing of sheep, eating of flesh and drinking of wine; eat and drink, for to-morrow we die.* This verse presents the contrast of their actual behaviour, with that to which God called them by his providence. The construction in the common version is ambiguous, as *slaying*, &c., seem to be participles agreeing with joy and gladness, whereas the Hebrew verbs are all infinitives. Some suppose the words of the revellers to begin with הָרֹג (let us kill, &c.), others with אָכֹל (let us eat flesh, &c.) ; but the common division of the sentence is most natural, because there is then no repetition or tautology. In the one case, the people themselves, say, *let us eat flesh and drink wine, let us eat and drink.* In the other it is said that they do eat flesh and drink wine, and they are then introduced as saying, *let us eat and drink.* On the same ground, the common interpretation is to be preferred to Hendewerk's idea, that the whole verse contains the words of the Prophet, and that those of the people are not introduced at all. " Slaying of oxen, killing of sheep, eating of flesh, drinking of wine, eating, drinking, though to-morrow we die ! " Another objection to this construction is, that it supposes the event to be still future, even to the Prophet's view ; whereas the whole foregoing context represents it as already past, if not in fact, at least in his perceptions. The common version, *let us eat and drink*, is perfectly correct as to sense, but needlessly departs from the peculiar and

expressive form of the original. I have substituted *eat and drink,* not as imperatives, but as the simplest forms of the English verbs. (*Vide supra,* chap. xxi. 5.) *To eat and to drink* might be considered more exact, but would not exhibit the compression and breviloquence of the original. It has been disputed whether these last words are expressive of contemptuous incredulity or of a desperate determination to spend the residue of life in pleasure. It is by no means clear that these two last feelings are exclusive of each other, since the same man might express his disbelief of the threatening, and his resolution, if it should prove true, to die in the enjoyment of his favourite indulgences. At all events, there can be no need of restricting the full import of the language, as adapted to express both states of mind, in different persons, if not in the same.

14. *And Jehovah of hosts revealed himself to my ears* (*i. e.* made a revelation to me, saying) *If this iniquity shall be forgiven you* (*i. e.* it certainly shall not be forgiven you) *until you die.* Some take נִגְלָה as a simple passive, and supply a preposition before יְהֹוָה, it was revealed in my ears by Jehovah of hosts. This is no doubt the true sense ; but the construction of the verb as a reflexive with יְהֹוָה for its subject, is fully justified by the analogy of 1 Sam. ii. 27, iii. 21. It is wholly unnecessary, therefore, to read אָזְנָי, " in the ears of Jehovah of hosts," or to supply אָמַר, " in my ears, saith Jehovah of hosts." (*Vide supra,* chap. v. 9.) The וֹ before נִגְלָה is not conversive, as it does not connect it with the future נְמוּת, which is merely a quotation, but with the infinitives in the first clause of ver. 13, which represent historical or descriptive tenses. (Nordheimer, § 219.) The conditional form of expression, so far from expressing doubt or contingency, adds to the following declaration the solemnity of an oath. What is said is also sworn, so that " by two immutable things in which it is impossible for God to lie," the truth of the threatening may be confirmed. On the elliptical formula of swearing, *vide supra,* chap. v. 9. *This iniquity* of course means the presumptuous contempt of God's messages and providential warnings, with which the people had been charged in the preceding verse. This offence is here treated as the sin against the Holy Ghost is in the New Testament, and is indeed very much of the same nature. יְכֻפַּר strictly means *shall be atoned for* or expiated. *Until you die* is equivalent to *ever,* the impossibility of expiation afterwards being assumed. This use of *until* is common in all languages. Some of the Jewish writers understand the words to mean *at death but not before,* and draw the inference that death does or may atone for sin. But the Targum has *the second death* (מוֹתָא תִנְיָנָא), a phrase found also in the Greek of the New Testament (ὁ δεύτερος θάνατος), and constantly employed in modern religious phraseology to signify eternal perdition. In this case, however, there is no ground for departing from the simple and ordinary meaning of the words. " As long as you live you shall not be forgiven," is equivalent to saying, " you shall never be forgiven."

15. *Thus said the Lord Jehovah of hosts, Go, go into this treasurer* (or steward, or chamberlain), *to Shebna who* (*is*) *over the house.* From the people in general the threatening now passes to an individual, no doubt because he was particularly guilty of the crime alleged, and by his influence the means of leading others astray likewise. The word סֹכֵן has been variously derived and explained to mean a *Sochenite* (from *Sochen* in Egypt), a sojourner or dweller (*i. q.* שֹׁכֵן) in the sanctuary, a steward or provider, a treasurer, and an *amicus regis* or king's friend, *i. e.* his confidant and

counsellor. Some understand the last words of the verse as simply explanatory of this title; while others argue that the Prophet would hardly have described the man by two titles meaning the same thing. A third class deny that סֹכֵן is here applied to Shebna at all, and understand the words to mean *this steward of Shebna's*, or *this (person) labouring for Shebna*, *i. e.* making his monument. But Shebna himself is undoubtedly the object of address in the remainder of the chapter. Whatever סֹכֵן may denote, it must be something compatible with the description in the last clause of the verse. Whatever Shebna may have been as סֹכֵן, he was certainly *over the house*. Some of the ancient versions give to *house* here the sense of *temple* or the house of God, and infer that Shebna, if not High Priest or a Priest at all, was at least the treasurer of the temple. But the phrase here used is nowhere else employed in reference to the temple, whereas it repeatedly occurs as the description of an officer of state or of the royal household, a major-domo, chamberlain, or steward. As the modern distinction between State and household officers is not an ancient or an oriental one, it is not unlikely that the functionary thus described, like the mediæval *maires du palais*, was in fact prime minister. This would account for the influence tacitly ascribed to Shebna in this chapter, as well as for his being made the subject of a prophecy. The phrase *this treasurer* may either be expressive of disapprobation or contempt, or simply designate the man as well known to the Prophet and his readers. These familiar allusions to things and persons now forgotten, while they add to the obscurity of the passage, furnish an incidental proof of its antiquity and genuineness. The double imperative לֶךְ־בֹּא admits of different explanations. The second may perhaps mean *go*, and the first be a particle of exhortation like the Latin *age*. It might then be rendered *come go*, although this would be really an inversion of the Hebrew phrase, which strictly means *go come*. On the whole, however, it is better to give לֶךְ the sense of *go*, and בֹּא that of *enter* or *go in*, meaning into Shebna's house, or into the sepulchre which he was preparing, and in which some suppose him to have been accosted by the Prophet. The use of עַל for אֶל before שֶׁבְנָא is supposed by some to imply the unfavourable nature of the message; but the interchange of the particles is not so unusual as to make this explanation necessary. Some manuscripts and versions add *and say to him*, which any reader can supply for himself without an emendation of the text.

16. *What hast thou here, and whom hast thou here, that thou hast hewn thee here a sepulchre? Hewing on high his sepulchre, graving in the rock a habitation for himself!* The negation implied in the interrogation is not that he had none to protect and aid him, or that none of his kindred should be buried there because they should be banished with him, but rather that he had none buried there before him; it was not his birth-place, or the home of his fathers. What interest, what part or lot, what personal or hereditary claim hast thou in Judah? *Here* then refers not to the sepulchre, but to Jerusalem. The foreign form of the name *Shebna*, which occurs only in the history of Hezekiah, and for which no satisfactory Hebrew etymology has been proposed, seems to confirm this explanation of the first clause as representing him to be a foreigner, perhaps a heathen. Another confirmation is afforded by the otherwise unimportant circumstance, that the name of Shebna's father is nowhere added to his own, as in the case of Eliakim and Joah (ver. 20, chap. xxxvi. 3). These seem to be sufficient reasons for concluding that the Prophet is directed to upbraid him, not

with seeking to be buried in the royal sepulchres although of mean extraction, but with making provision for himself and his posterity in a land to which he was an alien, and from which he was so soon to be expelled. The third person in the last clause is not to be gratuitously changed into the second (*thy* sepulchre, a habitation for *thyself*), nor is the syntax to be solved by introducing a comparison (*as* he that heweth), but rather by supposing that the Prophet, after putting to him the prescribed question, was to express his own contemptuous surprise at what he saw, or as Maurer says, to let his eyes pass from the man to the sepulchre which he was hewing. It is not necessarily implied, however, in this explanation, that the conversation was to take place at the sepulchre. מָרוֹם is properly a noun, and means *a high place*, but is here and elsewhere used adverbially. The labour and expense bestowed on ancient sepulchres (of far later date however than Isaiah's time) is still attested by the tombs remaining at Jerusalem, Petra, and Persepolis, where some are excavated near the tops of lofty rocks in order to be less accessible, to which practice there may be allusion in the מָרוֹם of the verse before us, as well as in the words of 2 Chron. xxxii. 33, as explained by most interpreters, viz. that Hezekiah was buried in the *highest* of the tombs of the sons of David. (See Robinson's Palestine, I. 516–539, II. 525.) The מִשְׁכָּן is supposed by some to have allusion to the oriental practice of making tombs in shape (and frequently in size) like houses, by others more poetically to the idea of the grave, as a *long home*, (בֵּית עוֹלָם), the very name applied to it by Solomon (Eccles. xii. 5). In this case, as in many others, the ideal and material allusion may have both been present to the writer's mind. *What* (*is*) *to thee* and *who is to thee* are the usual unavoidable periphrases for *what and whom hast thou*, the verb to *have* being wholly wanting in this family of languages.

17. *Behold, Jehovah is casting thee a cast, O man! and covering thee a covering.* The addition of the infinitive or verbal noun as usual adds emphasis to the expression, while the participle denotes a present act or a proximate futurity. The idea that he is *certainly* about to cast and cover thee, or to do it *completely* and with violence. מְטַלְטֶל is by some rendered *casting out*, by others *casting down*. The latter agrees best with the etymology and with the rest of the description. Those who give the other sense are under the necessity of assuming, that the Prophet, after saying that the Lord would cast him off, goes back to the preliminary acts of seizing him and rolling him. The other explanation gives the natural order. First he is thrown upon the ground, then rolled into a ball, and then violently thrown away. Some of the latest writers give עטה the sense of seizing, grasping, founded on an Arabic analogy, and justified, as they suppose, by the usage of the Hebrew word in 1 Sam. xiv. 32, xv. 19, xxv. 14. But except in these few doubtful cases the word uniformly signifies to veil or cover. As this is the term used in the law which requires the leper to cover his upper lip (Lev. xiii. 45), Grotius, with perverse ingenuity, infers that Shebna was to be smitten with leprosy, excluded from the city on that account, and afterwards restored, but not reinstated in his former office. Gesenius gives עטה the sense of wrapping up, and makes it thus synonymous with צָנַף. As both the terms have reference to the figure of a ball, the distinction seems to be that the first denotes the imposition of a covering or wrapper, and the second the formation of the whole into a regular and compact shape. There are several different ways of construing גבר with the words before it. Some suppose it to be governed by טַלְטֵלָה—*with the*

cast of a man, i. e. a manly, vigorous, or powerful cast. In this case we must either suppose טלטלה to be an absolute form put for the construct—or טלטלת to be understood after it—or גבר to be in apposition with it, or in agreement with it as an adjective—all which are gratuitous and forced assumptions. A better method of obtaining the same sense is by translating גֶּבֶר—*like a man, i. e.* a mighty man. (Compare Job xxxviii. 3.) According to Hendewerk, טלטלה is a verbal noun construed as an infinitive, and governing גבר as דעה does יהוה in chap. xi. 9. The sense is then *with the casting of a man, i. e.* as a man is cast or thrown. But the throwing of a man is the very thing here likened to the throwing of a ball. The simplest construction is the one given by Ewald and by many older writers, which takes גבר as a vocative. J. D. Michaelis reads גֹּבֵר, and translates it *oh robber!* But this is not the meaning even of that word. Others take גֶּבֶר in its proper sense of mighty man, others in the simple sense of man as distinguished from God, of which use there are several unequivocal examples. (Job xxii. 2, x. 5 ; Prov. xx. 4.)

18. *Rolling he will roll thee in a roll, like a ball* (*thrown*) *into a spacious ground—there shalt thou die—and there the chariots of thy glory—shame of thy master's house.* The ejection of Shebna from the country is compared to the rolling of a ball into an open space where there is nothing to obstruct its progress. The ideas suggested are those of violence, rapidity, and distance. Maurer supposes צנף to denote a rolling motion ; but most interpreters apply it to the act of *rolling up* into a ball, which agrees better both with usage and the context. The ellipsis of *thrown* or *cast* before אל is altogether natural and easily supplied. Instead of *spacious* the original has רחבת ידים, *wide on both hands* or *sides, i. e.* extended and open in every direction. All the interpreters appear to apply this directly to Shebna, and are thence led to raise the question, what land is meant ? Some say Assyria, some Mesopotamia, Ewald the wilderness, Grotius the open fields out of Jerusalem where lepers were obliged to dwell. It seems to me, however, that the phrase in question, has relation, not to Shebna as a man, but to the ball with which he is compared, and that ארץ should be taken in the sense of *ground.* To the three derivatives of צנף in the first clause Henderson cites as illustrative parallels chaps. xxvii. 7, x. 16, xxix. 14 ; Micah ii. 4 ; and from the classics, the πόνος πόνῳ πόνον φέρει of Sophocles and the δόσιν κακὰν κακῶν κακοῖς of Æschylus. There are several different constructions of the last clause. The oldest versions make מרכבות the subject, and קלון the predicate of the same proposition : " the chariots of thy glory (shall be) the shame of thy lord's house." This can only mean that the king would be disgraced by having honoured such a man, chariots being then put as an outward sign of dignity and wealth. Most writers make קלון, and what follows, a description of Shebna addressed to himself (" thou shame of thy master's house"), and construe מרכבות either with תמות (" and there shall thy splendid chariots perish"), or with the verb of existence understood (" there shall thy splendid chariots be"). As שמה properly means *thither*, it may be so taken here, the construction with תמות being then a pregnant one : *thither shalt thou die* (i. e. thither shalt thou go to die), *and thither shall thy splendid chariots* (*convey thee*). The allusion will then be simply to Shebna's return to his own country (whether Syria, Phœnicia, Mesopotamia, or Assyria), and not to captivity in war or to suffering in exile, of which there is no intimation in the text. All that the Prophet clearly threatens Shebna with, is the loss of rank and influence

in Judah, and a return to his own country. An analogous incident in modern history (so far as these circumstances are concerned) is Necker's retreat from France to Switzerland at the beginning of the French Revolution.

19. *And it shall come to pass in that day that I will call for my servant, for Eliakim, the son of Hilkiah, i. e.* will personally designate him. Eliakim appears again in chap. xxxvi. 3, and there, as here, in connection with Shebna. There is probably no ground for the rabbinical tradition that Eliakim is identical with Azeriah, mentioned, 2 Chron. xxxi. 13, as the ruler of the house of God. The epithet *my servant* seems to be intended to describe him as a faithful follower of Jehovah, and, as such, to contrast him with Shebna, who may have been a heathen. The employment of such a man by such a king as Hezekiah is explained by some upon the supposition that he had been promoted by Ahaz, and then suffered to remain by his successor. It is just as easy to suppose, however, that he had raised himself by his abilities for public business.

20. *And I will thrust thee from thy post, and from thy station shall he pull thee down.* The verb in the last clause is indefinite, and really equivalent to a passive (thou shalt be pulled down). It should not therefore be translated in the first person as a mere enallage, nor made to agree with *Jehovah* understood, which would be a very harsh construction, and though not without example, should be assumed only in case of necessity.

21. *And I will clothe him with thy dress, and with thy girdle will I strengthen him, and thy power will I give into his hand, and he shall be for a father* (or *become a father*) *to the dweller in Jerusalem, aud to the house of Judah.* We may either suppose a reference to an official dress, or a metaphor analogous to that of filling another's shoes in colloquial English. The Piel of חזק may simply mean to bind fast, but the strict sense of strengthening agrees well with the oriental use of the girdle to confine the flowing garments, and to fit the wearer for active exertion. *Father* is not a mere oriental synonyme of *ruler*, but an emphatic designation of a wise and benevolent ruler. It seems, therefore, to imply that Shebna's administration was of an opposite character. The inhabitants of Jerusalem and the family of Judah comprehend the whole nation.

22. *And I will put the key of the house of David on his shoulder; he shall open, and there shall be no one shutting, he shall shut, and there shall be no one opening.* In other words, he shall have unlimited control over the royal house and household, which, according to oriental usages, implies a high political authority. Some suppose a reference to the actual bearing of the key by the royal steward or chamberlain, and explains its being carried on the shoulder by the fact, that large wooden locks and keys of corresponding size are still used in some countries, the latter being sometimes curved like a sickle, so as to be hung around the neck. Against this explanation it may be objected, that the phrase *house of David* seems to imply a metaphorical, rather than a literal palace, and that שכם does not mean the shoulder merely, but includes the upper part of the back, as the place for bearing burdens. (*Vide supra*, chaps. ix. 3, x. 27.) There is still less to be said in favour of supposing an allusion to the figure of a key embroidered on the dress. The best interpreters appear to be agreed that the government of administration is here represented by the figure of a burden, not merely in the general, as in chap. ix. 5, but the specific burden of a key, chosen in order to express the idea of control *over the royal house*, which was the title of the office in question. The application of the same terms

to Peter (Mat. xvi. 19), and to Christ himself (Rev. iii. 7), does not prove that they here refer to either, or that Eliakim was a type of Christ, but merely that the same words admit of different applications.

23. *And I will fasten him a nail in a sure place, and he shall be for a throne of glory to his father's house.* The figure in the first clause naturally conveys the idea of security and permanence. The reference is not to the stakes or centre-post of a tent, but to the large pegs, pins, or nails often built into the walls of oriental houses for the purpose of suspending clothes or vessels. The last clause is obscure. Some suppose the figure of a pin or peg to be still continued, and that it is here represented as so large that men may sit upon it. Others suppose the nail to be here described as fastened in a throne; it shall be (attached) to the glorious throne of his father's house. This would seem to warrant Calvin's supposition that Eliakim was of the blood royal. But such a construction, if not wholly ungrammatical, is very forced, and כסא is the Hebrew name for any seat (answering to stool or chair), and denotes a throne or chair of state only as being a seat *par eminence.* The most natural interpretation of the words, and that most commonly adopted, is, that the figure of a nail is here exchanged for that of a seat, this being common to the two, that they alike suggest the idea of support, though in different ways. Those whom Eliakim was the means of promoting might be said, with a change of figure, but without a change of meaning, both to sit and hang upon him. He was to be not only a seat, but a *seat of honour,* which is nearer to the meaning of the Hebrew phrase than *throne of glory.*

24. *And they shall hang upon him all the honour of his father's house— the offspring and the issue—all vessels of small quantity—from vessels of cups even to all vessels of flagons.* Here the figure of a nail is resumed. The dependents of Eliakim are represented as suspended on him as their sole support. צאצאים and צפעות are expressions borrowed from the vegetable world. Henderson imitates the form of the original by rendering them *offspring and offset.* It is commonly assumed by interpreters that the two words are in antithesis, denoting either different sexes (sons and daughters), or different generations (sons and grandsons), or different ranks, which last is the usual explanation, and derives some countenance from the etymology of צפעה and the analogy of Ezek. iv. 15. The next phrase is designed to shew that even the least are not to be excepted. In the last clause אגנות and נבלים may either be taken as equivalent expressions, or as contrasting the gold and silver vessels of the altar (Exod. xxiv. 6) with common earthen utensils (Jer. xlviii. 12; Lam. iv. 2). The old interpretation of נבלים, as denoting musical instruments, though justified by usage, is forbidden by the context. The Targum explicitly applies the clause to the priests who served the altar, and the Levites who conducted the music of the temple. This explanation is connected with that of בית in ver. 1, as denoting the temple or the house of God.

25. *In that day, saith Jehovah of hosts, shall the nail fastened in a sure place be removed, and be cut down, and fall, and the burden which was on it shall be cut off, for Jehovah speaks.* The most natural and obvious application of these words is to Eliakim, who had just been represented as a nail in a sure place. But as this would predict his fall, without the slightest intimation of the reason, and in seeming contradiction to the previous context, most interpreters reject this exposition as untenable. Hitzig indeed maintains that this is the only meaning which the words will bear, but assumes that these two verses were added at a later date, shortly before or

after Eliakim's own disgrace. Hendewerk adopts the same hypothesis, but applies it to the last verse only. J. H. Michaelis alone gives a favourable meaning to the figures of ver. 25, as signifying that Eliakim should die in peace, to the irreparable loss of Judah, and of his own dependents in particular. Another exegetical expedient is to apply even ver. 23 to Shebna, not as a promise of what God would do, but as a narrative of what he had done. The obvious objections are, that the verbs in that verse are as certainly future as those in the one before it; and that both verses must be referred to the same subject, unless the supposition of a change be absolutely necessary. Such a necessity does seem to exist in ver. 25, and is the more easily assumed because the grammatical objection is not applicable there. Most writers, therefore, seem to be agreed, that the twenty-fifth verse relates to Shebna, and that the Prophet, after likening Eliakim to a nail fastened in a sure place, tacitly applies the same comparison to Shebna, and declares that the nail which now seems to be securely fastened shall soon yield to make way for the other. Those who refer the verse to Eliakim suppose his fall to have been occasioned by his nepotism or excessive patronage of his relations, a conjectural inference from ver. 24. The partial fulfilment of this prophecy is commonly supposed to be recorded in chap. xxxvi. 3, where Eliakim actually fills the place here promised to him, and Shebna appears in the inferior character of a scribe or secretary. Some indeed suppose two persons of the name of Shebna, which is not only arbitrary in itself, but rendered more improbable by this consideration, that Shebna is probably a foreign name, and certainly occurs only in these and the parallel places, whereas Hilkiah is of frequent occurrence, and yet is admitted upon all hands to denote the same person. It seems improbable no doubt that Shebna, after such a threatening, should be transferred to another office. But the threatening may not have been public, and the transfer may have been merely the beginning of his degradation. But even supposing that the Shebna of chap. xxxvi. 2 is a different person, and that the execution of this judgment is nowhere explicitly recorded, there is no need of concluding that it was revoked, or that it was meant to be conditional, much less that it was falsified by the event. It is a common usage of the Scriptures, and of this book in particular, to record a divine command and not its execution, leaving the latter to be inferred from the former as a matter of course. Of this we have had repeated examples, such as chap. vii. 4, and viii. 1. Nay, in this very case, we are merely told what Isaiah was commanded to say to Shebna, without being told that he obeyed the order. If the execution of this order may be taken for granted, so may the fulfilment of the prophecy. If it had failed, it would not have been recorded or preserved among the prophecies.

Chapter 23

THIS prophecy consists of two parts. The first predicts the fall of Tyre, vers. 1–14. The second promises its restoration and conversion, vers. 15–18. The fall of Tyre is predicted, not directly, but in the form of apostrophes, addressed to her own people or her colonies, vers. 1–7. The destruction is referred to God as its author, and to the Chaldees as his instruments, vers. 8–14. The prediction in the latter part includes three events. Tyre shall be forsaken and forgotten for seventy years, ver. 15. She shall then be restored to her former activity and wealth, vers. 16, 17. Thenceforth her gains shall be devoted to the Lord, ver. 18.

Tyre, one of the chief cities of Phenicia, was situated partly on a rocky island near the coast, and partly in a wide and fertile plain upon the coast itself. It was long a current opinion that the insular Tyre had no existence before the time of Nebuchadnezzar; but Hengstenberg has made it probable that from the beginning the chief part of the city was situated on the island, or rather a peninsula connected with the mainland by a narrow isthmus. (See his elaborate and masterly tract, *De Rebus Tyriorum*, Berlin, 1832). The name *Palætyrus* (Old Tyre), given by the ancient writers to the continental city, he supposes to have come into use after that part of Tyre was destroyed, and while the other was still standing. Tyre is remarkable in history for two things : its maritime trade, and the many sieges it has undergone. The first of these on record was by Shalmaneser king of Assyria, who, according to Menander, a historian now lost, but quoted by Josephus, blockaded Tyre for five years, so as to cut off the supply of water from the mainland, but without being able to reduce the city. The next was by Nebuchadnezzar king of Babylon, who besieged it thirteen years ; with what result is not expressly mentioned either in profane or sacred history. A third siege was by Alexander the Great, who, after seven months and with the utmost difficulty, finally reduced it. It was afterwards besieged by the Syrian king Antigonus, and more than once during the Crusades, both by Franks and Saracens. After this period it entirely decayed, and has now disappeared, its site being marked by the insulated rock, by the causeway between it and the mainland still existing as a bar of sand, and by columns and other architectural remains mostly lying under water.

It has been much disputed which of these events is the subject of the prophecy before us. Grotius, as usual, sees the fulfilment, in the days of Isaiah himself, and refers the prediction to the siege by Shalmaneser. Clericus gives it a wider scope, and seems to make the siege by Alexander its main subject. But the great body of the older writers refer it to an intermediate event, the siege by Nebuchadnezzar. The arguments in favour of this application are stated with great learning, force, and clearness, by Vitringa on the passage.

The German writers of the new school are divided on this question. Eichhorn, Rosenmüller, Hitzig, and others, admit the reference to Nebuchadnezzar, but ascribe the prophecy of course to a contemporary writer. Gesenius, Maurer, Umbreit, and Knobel, admit its genuineness, but refer it to the siege by Shalmaneser. Hendewerk also admits the genuineness of the passage, but denies its having reference to any particular historical event. Ewald refers it to the siege of Shalmaneser, but infers from the inferiority of the style that it may be the production of a younger contemporary and disciple of Isaiah. The discussion of the subject by these writers is in one respect interesting and instructive. In most other cases they occupy common ground against the truth. But here they are reduced to a dilemma, and by choosing different horns of it, are placed in opposition to each other, clearly betraying, in the conflict that ensues, the real value of their favourite style of criticism. Thus while Ewald thinks the style unlike that of Isaiah, and Eichhorn, and Hitzig see the clearest indications of a later age, Gesenius and Hendewerk are struck with the tokens of antiquity and with the characteristics of Isaiah. So, too, with respect to the literary merit of the passage : Hitzig treats it almost with contempt, while Hendewerk extols it as a masterpiece of eloquence. There could not be a stronger illustration of the fact, already evident, that the boasted diagnosis of this school of critics is always dependent on a foregone conclusion. Had there been no siege of Tyre in the days of Isaiah, Gesenius would easily have found abundant proofs that the chapter was of later date. But this not being necessary for his purpose here, he treats as inconclusive even stronger proofs than those which he himself employs in other cases.

To the reference of this prophecy to Shalmaneser there are two main objections. The first is the express mention of the Chaldees in ver. 13. Ewald easily disposes of this difficulty by reading כנענים instead of כשדים. Gesenius and the rest maintain that the Chaldees are mentioned only as tributaries or auxiliaries of Assyria. As this, though arbitrarily assumed, is not impossible, the first objection cannot be regarded as decisive. The second is that Shalmaneser's attempt upon Tyre was perfectly abortive. This argument of course has no effect upon Gesenius and others who deny the inspiration of the Prophet. Even such, however, must admit that if the descriptions of the prophecy were actually realised in another case, it is more likely to have been the one intended. They allege, however, that the very same objection lies against the supposition of a reference to Nebuchadnezzar, on the ground that no historian, sacred or profane, records the fact of his having taken Tyre. To account for this omission, and to shew by various incidental proofs that the event did nevertheless happen, is the main design of Hengstenberg's tract already mentioned, in which he has performed his task with a rare combination of minute learning, ingenuity, and good sense, although not to the satisfaction of contemporary German writers. His argument from the nature of the case turns in a great measure on minute details, and sometimes on intricate calculations in chronology. It will be sufficient therefore to record the result, which is that the actual conquest of Tyre by Nebuchadnezzar, even leaving out of view the prophecy before us, and the more explicit one in Ezekiel, chap. xxvi., is much more probable than the contrary hypothesis. But there is still another difficulty in the way of applying the prophecy to Nebuchadnezzar's siege and conquest. Isaiah intimates and Ezekiel explicitly foretells an entire desolation of Tyre, which did not take place till the Middle Ages. Hengstenberg's solution of this difficulty is, that the prophets constantly connect the immediate consequences of the events which they predict with their remoter and more gradual results. On the same general principal of interpretation, but with a difference of form, it may be said that the prophecy before us is generic, not specific, a panoramic picture of the downfall of Tyre, from the beginning to the end of the destroying process, with particular allusion to particular sieges, as for instance to that of the Chaldees in ver. 13, and perhaps to that of Alexander in ver. 6. Antiquarian research and discovery may yet bring to light coincidences still more striking.

While the great majority of writers understand the passage as referring to the literal Tyre, a few prefer to take it in a mystical sense. Some of the older Jewish writers say that whenever the literal Tyre is meant, the name is fully written (צור), but that when it is defectively written, as it is here, (צר) it signifies *Rome*. Abarbenel refutes this dictum by shewing that both forms occur in the same context, but himself makes Tyre here mean *Venice*. But these hypotheses are modest in comparison with that of Cocceius, who understands by Tyre the Church of Rome, by Egypt Germany, by Chittim Spain, by Tarshish France, by Assyria Turkey, by the land of the Chaldees Hungary, and by the whole passage a chapter from the history of the Reformation. Of such interpretations it may surely be said without undue severity : "Hariolationes hæ sunt ; sequamur certa ; incerta æquo animo ignoremus ; neque etiam hanc prophetiam cum quibusdam veterum allegorice interpretabimur, nam si Scriptura non indicet debere nos in re una cernere imaginem alterius, etiamsi res diversæ a Scriptura explicatæ similitudinem et conformitatem aliquam habeant, non possumus tamen asserere hoc illius typum et figuram esse, nisi quatenus illa conformitas ex Scripturarum comparatione demonstratur.' These are the words of Cocceius himself, reproving Grotius for his groundless hypothesis of Shebna's leprosy in chap. xxii., and declaring his own dissent from the old interpretations of that chapter.

1. *The burden of Tyre. Howl, ships of Tarshish ; for it is laid waste, no house, no entrance ; from the land of Chittim it is revealed to them.* Here, as in chap. xiii. 1, xv. 1, xvii. 1, xix. 1, xxi. 1, xi. 13, xxii. 1, there is not the slightest reason for rejecting the first words as the addition of a copyist or compiler. The command or exhortation to howl implies that those to whom it is addressed have peculiar cause for grief. By ships of Tarshish we are not to understand merchant ships in general, but strictly those which carried on the trade between Phenicia, and its Spanish colony Tartessus. For the other meanings which have been attached to תַּרְשִׁישׁ, *vide supra*, chap. ii. 15. Rosenmüller condemns the generic explanation of the phrase as unpoetical, but does not scruple to make ships mean sailors, which is wholly unnecessary. The masculine form שֻׁדַּד may either be referred to צֹר by a common licence, or indefinitely taken to mean *desolation has been wrought*, or *something has been desolated*, without saying what. Ewald resolves it into an indefinite active verb (zerstört hat man) without a change of meaning. The preposition in מִבַּיִת and מִבּוֹא has a privative effect. The meaning strictly is, *away from house, away from entrance.* It may be less concisively rendered, *so that there is no house*, &c. Some make the two expressions strictly parallel and correlative, *so that there is neither house nor entrance,* in which case the latter may have reference to the entering of ships into the harbour. Others make the second dependent on the first, *so that there is no house left to enter.* This may refer particularly to the mariners returning from their long voyage and finding their homes destroyed. *Chittim* is neither Macedonia (Clericus), Italy (Vitringa), Susiana (Bochart), Cilicia (Junius), nor a region in Arabia (Hensler), but the island of Cyprus (Josephus), in which there was a city *Citium*, which Cicero explicitly refers to as a Phenician settlement. The wider explanation of the name, as denoting other islands or the Mediterranean coasts in general, though not without authority from usage, is uncertain and in this case needless. These words are connected with what goes before by Calvin (ut non sit commeatus e terra Cittim) and others ; but most interpreters adhere to the Masoretic interpunction. *It is revealed* (*i. e.* the event announced in the preceding clause) *to them* (the Tyrian mariners on their way home from Tarshish). The meaning seems to be, that the news of the fall of Tyre has reached the Phenician settlements in Cyprus, and through them the Tyrian mariners that touch there.

2. *Be silent, O inhabitants of the isle* (or *coast*), *the merchants of Sidon crossing the sea filled thee.* This may either be addressed to the coast and islands of the Mediterranean which had long been frequented by the Phenician traders, or to Phenicia itself, which foreign commerce had enriched. The last explanation is commonly preferred ; but the first is recommended

by the fact that it assigns a reason for the mention of the foreign trade of Sidon, as accounting for the interest which other nations are supposed to feel in the fall of Tyre. On either supposition, Sidon, the other great city of Phenicia, is put for the whole country. The plural verb in the last clause agrees with סֹחֵר as a collective.

3. *And in great waters (was) the seed of the Nile; the harvest of the river (was) her revenue; and she was a mart of nations.* שָׁחֹר and יְאוֹר are the Hebrew and Egyptian names of the Nile. The first, according to its etymology, means *black*, and corresponds to Μέλας and *Melo*, Greek and Latin names of the same river, all derived from the colour of the water or the mud which it deposits. The use of the word שָׁחֹר is one of the proofs, adduced by Eichhorn and Rosenmüller, that the chapter is of later date. It is true the name occurs in Joshua xiii. 13; but that is also classed among the later books. Gesenius observes, however, that an inference can hardly be drawn from one or two examples. Of the whole verse there are three interpretations. The first supposes an allusion to the fact that the grain of Egypt was exported in Phenician vessels *on the great waters*, *i.e.* over the sea. The objection that Phenicia is described by Ezekiel as trading not with Egypt but with Palestine in grain, though entitled to some weight, is not conclusive. A stronger objection may be drawn from the apparent incongruity of naming this one branch of commerce as a proof that Tyre was *a mart of nations*. A second interpretation understands what is said of Egypt figuratively, or as a comparison; as if he had said that the wealth which Egypt derived from the Nile, Phenicia derived from the great waters, *i.e.* by her maritime trade. The third differs from this only by supposing a distinct allusion to the insular situation of Tyre, which, though planted on a rock and girt by many waters, reaped as rich a harvest as the fertile land of Egypt. This last interpretation, which is that of J. D. Michaelis and Hengstenberg, is much more poetical than either of the others, and at least in that respect entitled to the preference.

4. *Be ashamed* (or *confounded*), *Zidon; for the sea saith, the strength of the sea, saying, I have not travailed, and I have not borne, and I have not reared young men* (or) *brought up virgins.* One of the great cities of Phenicia is here called upon to be confounded at the desolation of the other; or Zidon may be put for the whole country, as in the preceding verse. The Targum gives to יָם its geographical sense of *west* (מערבא). Some writers understand the sea itself as the ideal speaker, and explain מָעוֹז as an allusion to the turret-like appearance of the waves when in commotion. The correct view of the case seems to be this: the Prophet hears a voice from the sea, which he then describes more exactly as coming from the stronghold or fortress of the sea, *i.e.* insular Tyre as viewed from the mainland. The rest of the verse is intended to express the idea that the city thus personified was childless, was as if she had never borne children. Here, as in chap. i. 2, Hendewerk takes רוֹמַמְתִּי in the sense of *exalting*, making great, which is at once a violation of usage and of the Prophet's metaphor. Interpreters are commonly agreed that the negative force of the last לֹא extends to both of the following verbs. Cocceius alone seems to to make the last clause affirmative (*non educavi juvenes; extuli virgines*) as if she were complaining that she had not borne sons, but daughters. But the whole metaphor is clearly intended to express the idea of depopulation.

5. *When the report (comes) to Egypt, they are pained at the report of Tyre.* There are three distinct interpretations of this verse. The first

refers יְחִילוּ to the Sidonians or Phenicians generally, and understands the verse to mean that they would be as much grieved to hear of the fall of Tyre as if they should hear of that of Egypt. The second makes the verb indefinite, or understands it of the nations generally, who are then said to be as much astounded at the fall of Tyre, as they once were at the judgments of Jehovah upon Egypt. The third, which is the one now commonly adopted, makes Egypt itself or the Egyptians the subject of the verb, and explains כ and כַּאֲשֶׁר as particles of time, not of comparison. The first of these senses is expressed by Vitringa (*ut fama de Egypto commoveret animos, sic dolebunt ad famam Tyri*), the second by Luther (*gleichwie man erschrak da man von Egypten hörete, also wird man erschrecken wenn man von Tyrus hören wird*), the third by the Vulgate (*cum auditum fuerit in Egypto, dolebunt cum audient de Tyro*). This last supposes the Egyptians to lament for the loss of their great mart and commercial ally. The idea expressed by the second construction is a much more elevated one, and it seems more agreeable to usage to take כ before a noun as a particle of comparison. (*Vide supra*, chap. xviii. 4.) כַּאֲשֶׁר equally admits of either explanation. Either of these interpretations appears preferable to the first, which yields an unnatural and inappropriate sense.

6. *Pass over to Tarshish; howl, ye inhabitants of the isle* (*or coast*). The mother country is exhorted to take refuge in her distant colonies. J. D. Michaelis compares the resolution of the Dutch merchants in 1672 to remove to Batavia if the mother country could not be delivered. According to Diodorus, Curtius, and Justin, the Tyrians when besieged by Alexander, sent their old men, women, and children, to Carthage. Aben Ezra gratuitously makes אִי a collective, and supposes the address to be to all the islands where the Tyrians traded.

7. *Is this your joyous city* (literally, *is this to you a joyous one*)? *from the days of old is her antiquity; her feet shall carry her afar off to sojourn.* Some adopt a relative construction, and continue the interrogation through the verse; *whose feet*, &c. Of those who read the sentence thus, some understand the last clause as descriptive of the colonial and commercial activity of Tyre. But this requires יוֹבִילוּ to be arbitrarily explained as a preterite. Most writers understand the clause as applying, either to the flight of the Tyrians to their colonies, or to their being carried into exile. To the first, Gesenius objects that they could not cross the sea on foot. Umbreit replies that they must have feet to go on board the ships. Knobel rejoins that in that case it would not be their feet that carried them far off. It does not seem to have occurred to either, that a city can no more cross the sea in ships than dry-shod; that the verse contains a bold personification; and that having once converted Tyre into a woman, the writer may naturally represent her as going anywhere on foot, without respect to the actual method of conveyance used by individual emigrants. Grotius avoids the difficulty mentioned by Gesenius, by making *feet* mean sails and oars. The epithet עַלִּיזָה has reference to the bustle of commercial enterprise, and also to the luxury and pride of Tyre. Hendewerk refers to the use of this word in chap. xxii. 2, as an incidental proof that Isaiah wrote both chapters. The resemblance between קַדְמָה and קֶדֶם is imitated by Gesenius in his version (*Ursprung* and *Urzeit*). These expressions may be referred either to the real antiquity of Tyre, or to the exaggerated boastings of the Tyrians, of which we have examples in Herodotus and other profane writers.

8. *Who hath purposed this against Tyre the crowning (city), whose merchants (are) princes, her traffickers the honoured of the earth?* The Vulgate gives מעטירה a passive sense (*quondam coronatam*), which Sanctius applies to the pinnacles and turrets of the city. Hitzig makes it mean the *crown-wearer*. Most writers seem to be agreed that it denotes the *crowner* or *crown-giver*, in allusion to the fact that crowned heads were among the tributaries of Phenicia, according to the testimony of the Greek historians. Gesenius refers to the oriental crowns dispensed by the East India Company, and to the crown of Corsica once subject to the Genoese Republic. He also illustrates the use of the name *Canaan* to denote a trader, by the analogous usage of *Chaldean* for astrologer, and that of *Swiss, Savoyard, Jew*, in modern parlance, to denote certain callings or professions. The question in this verse implies that no ordinary power could have done it. The sense of *rich* which Gesenius gives to נכבדי in this place is entirely arbitrary. That of *land*, which some writers put instead of *earth*, though it does not change the sense of the expression, weakens it.

9. *Jehovah of hosts hath purposed it, to profane the elevation of all beauty, to degrade all the honoured of the earth.* This is the answer to the question in ver. 8. The suffix in יעצה refers to זאת. The supposition of a chorus, or of choruses responding to each other, is gratuitous and artificial, and better suited to a Greek play than a Hebrew prophecy. Not only in poetry, but in animated prose, the writers of all languages ask questions to be answered by themselves. צבי includes all that was splendid and beautiful in Tyre. The exclusive reference of the word to the people can be justified by nothing but the parallelism, and even that will admit of an antithesis between an abstract and a concrete term. חלל means strictly to profane or desecrate that which is reckoned holy, but is here used to express the making common of that which was distinguished by magnificence or beauty. The force of the antithesis between הקל and נכבדים cannot be fully expressed in a translation, as the roots respectively mean *light* and *heavy*. They are also contrasted, but in a different application and connection, in chap. viii. 23.

10. *Pass through thy land like the river (Nile); Daughter of Tarshish, there is no girdle (any) longer.* Some read, pass over to thy land, and make the verse an exhortation to the strangers from Tartessus to go home. Others understand כיאר to mean as (*one would cross*) the Nile or any other stream, *i. e.* naked or without a girdle, as in the other clause. It is commonly agreed, however, that the phrase means, *as the Nile passes, i. e.* quickly or without restraint. Some suppose the figure to be still continued in the last clause, and take מזח in the sense of a dam, mound, or embankment. Others, giving it its proper sense of *girdle*, apply it to the fortifications of Tyre which were now dismantled. *The daughter of Tarshish* is not Tyre, nor Phenicia now considered as dependent on her colonies; nor the population of Tarshish; but Tarshish itself. *There is no more girdle* may be taken in opposite senses, as denoting the failure of strength and general dissolution, or the absence of restraint and freedom from oppression. The former is preferred by Hengstenberg; but it does not seem appropriate to Tarshish, though it might be so if addressed to the mother country.

11. *His hand he stretched out over the sea; he made kingdoms tremble; Jehovah commanded respecting Canaan to destroy her strongholds.* The subject of the verbs in the first clause is the same as in the last. The stretching out of God's hand, followed by the trembling of the earth or its inhabitants, is urged by Hendewerk as a favourite expression of Isaiah (see particularly

chap. v. 25). Eichhorn and Rosenmüller, on the other hand, make מְעֹנִיָה
a Chaldaism and a proof of later origin. Gesenius denies that there is anything analogous in Chaldee or Syriac usage, and regards it as either an
anomalous case of epenthesis or an orthographical error. The feminine
suffix at the end refers to Canaan as the name of a country.

12. *And he said, Thou shalt not add longer (or continue) to triumph, oppressed (or violated) virgin daughter of Zidon ; to Chittim arise, pass over ;
there also there shall be no rest to thee.* The address is not to Chittim (or the
Macedonians); nor to Tyre as a daughter of the older city ; but to Zidon
itself. The fact that בְּתוּלַת is in apposition with בַּת (as to sense), makes
it altogether probable that בַּת sustains the same relation to צִידֹון. The
reading בַת צִיוֹן, though found in sixteen manuscripts and several ancient
versions, is probably a mere mistake, arising from the frequent occurrence
of the combination elsewhere. Zidon is here put for Phenicia in general.
יָנוּחַ is impersonal. This exhortation corresponds exactly to the one in ver. 6,
Tarshish and Chittim being both Phenician colonies. The last clause implies, either that the colonists would not receive them, or that the enemy
would still pursue them, probably the latter. The figure of a violated virgin,
for a conquered city or country, is alleged by Eichhorn as a proof of later
origin ; but it is used by the contemporary prophet Nahum (iii. 5), and as
Knobel observes, occurs nowhere else in Isaiah because he nowhere has
occasion to employ it.

13. *Behold the land of the Chaldees ; this people was not ; Assyria
founded it for dwellers in the wilderness ; they have set up his towers ; they
have roused up her palaces ; he has put it for (or rendered it) a ruin.* This
difficult verse has been variously understood. Some apply it exclusively to
the destruction of Tyre by the Assyrians ; but this can only be effected by
an arbitrary change of text. Thus J. Olshausen (in his emendations of
the text of the Old Testament) omits the words from ארץ to אשור as a gloss,
changes ציים into עיים, and explains the rest to mean that Assyria converted Tyre into a heap of ruins. The origin of the gloss he supposes to
be this, that some one wrote upon the margin by way of correction, ארץ
כשדים, meaning that it was not Assyria but Babylonia that destroyed Tyre,
and then added more explicitly, זה העם לא היה, all which afterwards found
its way into the text. This piece of criticism is too extravagant even for
the Germans, who accordingly reject it with contempt. Ewald, however,
also tampers with the text by reading כנענים for כשדים. His version of the
whole is : "behold the land of the Canaanites (*i. e.* Phenicia) ; this nation
is no more ; Assyria has converted it into a wilderness ; they (the Phenicians) set up their towers (and) build their palaces ; he (the Assyrian) has
turned it to ruin." Besides the arbitrary change of text, this explanation
gives to ציים and עוררו senses which cannot be sustained by usage. The
great majority, both of the older and the later writers, leave the text unaltered, and suppose that the Prophet here brings the Chaldees into view
as the instruments of Tyre's destruction. The words from זה to לציים will
then be a parenthesis, containing an allusion to a historical fact not expressly mentioned elsewhere, but agreeing well with other facts of history,
viz. that the Chaldees were not the aboriginal inhabitants of Babylonia,
but were brought thither from the mountains of Armenia or Kurdistan by
the Assyrians in the days of their supremacy. This accounts for the fact,
that Xenophon speaks of the Chaldees as northern mountaineers, while in
the sacred history we find them in possession of the great plain of Shinar.
The former statement has respect, no doubt, to that portion of the people

who were left behind in their original territory. This incidental statement, it may also be observed, is in strict accordance with the Assyrian policy of peopling their own provinces with conquered nations. The construction commonly adopted, by interpreters who thus explain the sentence, is as follows : "Behold the land of the Chaldees; this people (the people now inhabiting it) was not (*i. e.* had no existence until lately) ; Assyria founded (or established) it (the country) for dwellers in the wilderness (*i. e.* for the Chaldees who before had led a wild nomadic life)." To this construction Knobel, though he acquiesces in the exposition as a whole, makes two objections : first, that while it explains ארץ as denoting the *people*, it refers the suffix in יסדה to the *country;* secondly, that ציים is really descriptive of the Chaldees, not before but after their transportation to the plains of Babylonia. Knobel himself refers both ארץ and the suffix to the people considered as possessors of the land, and takes יסד ל in the sense of appointing, constituting, as in Hab. i. 12. " Behold the nation of the Chaldees ; this people was not (*i. e.* was unknown) till Assyria changed them into inhabitants of the wilderness (or plain)."—But why should this history of the Chaldees be referred to here ? The answer usually given to this question is, because the recent origin and present insignificance of the chosen instruments made the conquest more humiliating to the Tyrians. A kindred feeling would have been excited in the ancient Romans by a prediction of their subjugation and destruction by the Goths. If the reason assigned for the incidental mention of the Chaldee migration be the true one, it has evidently far more force upon the supposition that the prophecy relates to the Babylonian conquest under Nebuchadnezzar, than upon the supposition that it relates to the attack of Shalmaneser. Indeed, the whole assumption, that the Chaldees are here mentioned as auxiliaries only, is so perfectly arbitrary, that it would never have occurred to any writer, who had not determined upon other grounds, that the event predicted took place under the Assyrian domination. Even Umbreit, who assents to this hypothesis, admits that it is only probable, not certain ; and that this verse taken by itself would rather prove the contrary, by mentioning the Chaldees as the principal assailants, and Assyria only in a parenthesis containing a historical allusion. According to the usual interpretation which has now been given, the *towers* mentioned are those used in ancient sieges ; the masculine suffix refers to עם; the feminine suffix to Tyre ; and עורר may be taken either in the sense of *raising* (from ערר), or in that of *rousing* (from עור), that is, filling with confusion and alarm. Besides the interpretations which have now been given, there is another that deserves at least to be recorded. Schleyer, a recent German writer on this prophecy and that against Babylon in chaps. xiii. xiv., gives the same sense to the words from זה to אשור that is put upon them by Olshausen, but instead of rejecting them as a marginal correction, retains them as a necessary part of the text. " Behold, the nation of the Chaldees; this people (it was not Assyria) has assigned it (*i. e.* Tyre) to the dwellers in the wilderness (*i. e.* made it desolate). Umbreit, without dwelling on the violation of the Masoretic accents, objects to this interpretation, that it fails to account for the use of the word ארץ before כשדים, but especially that no reason can be given for the negative assertion that it was not Assyria that desolated Tyre. If the interpretation, however, were otherwise tenable, this, so far from being an objection, would in fact recommend it. When Isaiah wrote, Assyria was the ruling power of the world ; whatever changes were expected, were expected from that quarter.

But here the conquest of Phenicia is ascribed to a people then but little known, if known at all. It was perfectly natural therefore to say negatively, that it was not to be effected by Assyria, as well as positively, that it was to be effected by Chaldea. In like manner if the fall of the Roman State had been foretold during the period of the Punic wars, how naturally would the prophet have said that it should fall, *not before the Carthaginians*, but before the Goths. The sense therefore yielded by Schleyer's construction is a good sense in itself, and appropriate to the context. It cannot, however, be affirmed that there is any sufficient reason for departing from the Masoretic tradition as to the interpunction of the sentence. But let it be observed, that on either of these suppositions, the reference of the verse to the siege of Tyre by Nebuchadnezzar is far more natural than any other.

14. *Howl, ships of Tarshish, for destroyed is your stronghold.* The first part of the prophecy here closes very much as it began. The description of Tyre is the same as in ver. 4, except that it was there called the fortress of the sea, and here the fortress of the Tyrian ships.

15. *And it shall come to pass in that day that Tyre shall be forgotten seventy years, as the days of one king; from the end of seventy years shall be* (or *happen*) *to Tyre like the harlot's song.* The remainder of the chapter predicts the restoration of Tyre, not to its former dignity, but to its wealth and commercial activity, the fruits of which should thenceforth be consecrated to Jehovah. There is no difference of opinion with respect to the meaning of the words or the grammatical construction of the sentence ; but the utmost diversity of judgment in relation to the general sense and application of the whole, and especially of the words, *seventy years as the days of one king.* Vitringa and others take the seventy years strictly. Gesenius and the later German writers make it a round number, as in Gen. l. 3, Exod. xv. 27, xxiv. 1. The following words are rejected by Umbreit as a gloss. J. D. Michaelis and Paulus read אַחֵר (another) for אֶחָד (one). Grotius reads *seven* for *seventy*, forgetting that the following noun must then be in the plural, and assuming that Shalmaneser reigned seven years, or was seven years at Tyre. Jarchi understands by the *one king*, David, who died at the age of threescore and ten, though he cannot explain why it should be here referred to. Kimchi suggests that it may be in allusion to the treaty between David and Hiram, the breach of which was the occasion of this judgment. Kimchi prefers, however, to explain the words as a description of the ordinary length of human life, in which he is followed by Gesenius and Maurer, who account for the mention of *one king* rather than *one man*, upon the ground that kings and kingdoms are the subject of the prophecy. The same interpretation is suggested by the double version of the Septuagint (ὡς χρόνος βασιλέως, ὡς χρόνος ἀνθρώπου), which is found in all the manuscripts, though some modern critics reckon only part of it as genuine, Gesenius considering the first phrase as an emendation of the second, Rosenmüller the second as a later explanation of the first. Hitzig pretends that this form of expression was borrowed from Jeremiah's expectation that Zedekiah was to be restored at the end of seventy years. Movers supposes that the things compared are not two periods of time, but two cases of oblivion, and understands the clause as meaning that Tyre should be forgotten as completely as Jehoahaz and his three months' reign. Henderson, more generally, makes the sense to be that Tyre should be forgotten as completely as a king when he is dead, in illustration of which general fact he strangely cites the case of Napoleon. Knobel understands the verse to mean that the oblivion of Tyre

for a time should be as fixed and unalterable as the decrees of an oriental
monarch during his own reign. Eichhorn and Ewald understand the phrase
as opposite in meaning to the one employed in chap. xvi. 14, xxi. 16.   As
the years of a hireling mean years computed strictly, so the days of a king
may mean days computed freely.   Hengstenberg, without attempting to
explain the phrase (quomodcunque illa explicentur), understands it to
imply that *seventy years* is here to be indefinitely understood, and carefully
distinguished from the seventy years of Jeremiah and from the other specifications of time contained in the writings of Isaiah himself.   Those, on the
other hand, who give the words their strict sense, for the most part follow
Aben Ezra and Vitringa in supposing that the reigns of Nebuchadnezzar
and his successors are here computed *as one*.   It is no sufficient answer to
say that מֶלֶךְ never means a *dynasty*.   That idea may of course be implied
even if it is not expressed.   The chronological hypothesis of this interpretation has, however, been denied by J. D. Michaelis, who puts the end of the
prescribed term thirty-three or four years later than the fall of Babylon.
That Tyre was a flourishing city in the time of Alexander the Great, is matter of history.   When it again became so, is not.   But since the fact is
certain and the prophecy explicit, the most rational conclusion is that they
chronologically coincide, or in other words, that Tyre did begin to recover
from the effects of the Babylonian conquest about seventy years after the
catastrophe itself.   This of course supposes that the words are to be definitely understood.   If, on the other hand, they are indefinite, there can be
still less difficulty in supposing their fulfilment.   In either case, the words
כִּימֵי מֶלֶךְ אֶחָד remain so enigmatical, and all the explanations of them so
unsatisfactory, that some may be tempted to refer them to the future, and to
look for their development hereafter.   Hengstenberg's view of the connection
between this prediction of Isaiah and the parallel prophecies of Ezekiel
(chaps. xxvi. and xxvii.) and Zechariah (chap ix.) is this, that the last should
be regarded as a supplement or sequel to the other two.   When Zechariah
wrote, the Babylonian conquest predicted by Isaiah and Ezekiel had already
taken place.   The change for the better, predicted by Isaiah alone, was then
already visible.   The prophecies of both respecting the total destruction of
the city are renewed by Zechariah, and referred to a period still future, with
particular reference, as Hengstenberg supposes, to the time of Alexander,
but it may be with a scope still more extensive.—The last clause foretells
the restoration of Tyre in a very peculiar and significant form.   Instead of
a queen reinstated on the throne, she now appears as a forgotten harlot,
suing once more for admiration and reward.   Although this metaphor, as we
shall see below, does not necessarily imply moral turpitude, it does necessarily impart a contemptuous tone to the prediction.   The best explanation
of this change of tone is not, as Eichhorn imagined, that these verses are a
later addition, but that the restoration here predicted was to be a restoration to commercial prosperity and wealth, but not to regal dignity or national
importance.   The *song of a harlot* (or *the harlot*) is now commonly agreed
to mean a particular song well known to the contemporaries of the Prophet.
It shall be to her like this song can only mean that what the song presents
as an ideal situation should be realised in the experience of Tyre.   The
Hebrew words will scarcely bear the meaning put upon them in the text of
the English Version.

16. *Take a harp, go about the city, O forgotten harlot; play well, sing
much, that thou mayest be remembered.*   These are now commonly explained
as the words of the song itself, describing the only way in which the harlot

could recover her lost place in the memory of men, viz., by soliciting their notice and their favour. The application of the song to Tyre implies not only that she had lost her former position in the sight of the nations, but that exertion would be needed to recover it. The literal meaning of the words translated *play well, sing much*, is *make good playing, multiply song*. See Gesenius, § 139, 1.

17. *And it shall be* (or *come to pass*), *from* (or *at*) *the end of seventy years, Jehovah will visit Tyre, and she shall return to her hire* (or *gain*), *and shall play the harlot with all the kingdoms of the earth upon the face of the ground.* As God is said to *visit* men both in wrath and mercy, and as the figure here employed is at first sight a revolting one, some of the older writers understand this verse as describing the continued wickedness of Tyre requiring further judgments. But this makes it necessary to explain the next verse as referring to a still remoter future, which is done by inserting *tandem* or the like at the beginning. It is evident, however, from the repetition of the word אתנגה in the next verse, that the prediction there has reference to the very course of conduct here described. From this again the inference is plain, that notwithstanding the apparent import of the figure, the conduct is not in itself unlawful. The figure indeed is now commonly agreed to denote nothing more than commercial intercourse without necessarily implying guilt. In ancient times, when international commerce was a strange thing and nearly monopolized by a single nation, and especially among the Jews, whose law discouraged it for wise but temporary purposes, there were probably ideas attached to such promiscuous intercourse entirely different from our own. Certain it is that the Scriptures more than once compare the mutual solicitations of commercial enterprise to illicit love. That the comparison does not necessarily involve the idea of unlawful or dishonest trade, is sufficiently apparent from the following verse.

18. *And her gain and her hire shall be holiness* (or *holy, i. e.* consecrated) *to Jehovah; it shall not be stored and it shall not be hoarded; for her gain shall be for those who sit* (or *dwell*) *before Jehovah, to eat to satiety, and for substantial clothing.* By those who dwell before Jehovah we are probably to understand his worshippers in general and his official servants in particular. Henderson's objection, that the priests were not allowed to sit in the temple, is applicable only to the primary meaning of the verb. There may be an allusion to the chambers around the temple which were occupied by priests and Levites when in actual service. עתיק, according to the Arabic analogy, means *ancient* as an epithet of praise, and is accordingly resolved by the modern writers into *fine* or *splendid*. The older interpreters deduced perhaps from the same original idea that of durable, substantial, wearing long and well. The latter agrees better with the application of the words to private dress, the former to official robes, in which magnificence was more important than solidity, and which might be transferred from one incumbent to the next, and so be represented even in the stricter sense as old or ancient. The general sense of the prediction evidently is, that the commercial gains of Tyre should redound to the advantage of the servants of Jehovah.

Chapter 24

HERE begins a series of prophecies (chaps. xxiv.–xxxv.), having reference chiefly to Judah. It is not divided into parts by any titles or express intimations of a change of subject. The style is also homogeneous and uniform. The attempts which have been made to subdivide this portion of the book, are for the most part arbitrary. The conventional division into chapters may be retained as a matter of convenience. The first four chapters (xxiv.–xxvii.) are now universally regarded as forming one continuous composition. What is said of chap. xxiv. is therefore in some degree applicable to the whole. This chapter contains a description of a country filled with confusion and distress, by a visitation from Jehovah in consequence of its iniquities, vers. 1–12. It then speaks of a remnant scattered among the nations and glorifying God in distant lands, vers. 13–16. The Prophet then resumes his description of the judgments coming on the same land or another, winding up with a prophecy of Jehovah's exaltation in Jerusalem, vers. 16–23. Eusebius and Jerome explained this chapter as a prediction of the end of the world, in which they have been followed by Œcolampadius and some later writers. Cyril referred it to the same event, but understood it in its primary meaning, as a summary of the foregoing prophecies against foreign nations. The older Jews (as we learn from Jarchi and Aben Ezra) applied the first part of the chapter to the Assyrian invasions of the Holy Land, and the last to the wars of Gog and Magog in the days of the Messiah. But Moses Haccohen referred the whole to the former period, Kimchi and Abarbenel the whole to the latter. Luther applied it to the desolation of Judea by the Romans. Calvin agreed with Cyril in regarding it as a summary of the preceding prophecies both against Israel and foreign nations, but denied any reference to the day of judgment. Grotius adhered to Moses Haccohen, in applying the whole to the Assyrian invasions. He referred the first part to the wasting of the ten tribes by Shalmaneser, and the second to Sennacherib's invasion of Judah. Cocceius is as usual in the opposite extreme, applying the chapter to the German and Bohemian war, Gustavus Adophus, Wallenstein, the taking of Ratisbon, the battle of Norlingen, and the conflicts between Charles I. of England and the Parliament. Clericus understood the chapter as a prophecy of the Babylonian conquest of Judea, the captivity, and the restoration of the Jewish commonwealth. Vitringa explained it as relating, in its primary sense, to the persecution of the Jews by Antiochus Epiphanes and his successors, and their deliverance by the Maccabees, but in its mystical or secondary sense to certain changes which await the Christian Church in future times. Lowth differed little in reality from Calvin, except that he confined the prediction more exclusively to Judah and its sufferings at the hands of the Assyrians, Babylonians, and Romans. None of the writers who have now been mentioned entertained the least doubt as to the genuineness of the prophecy. The turning-point between the old and new school of criticism is occupied by J. D. Michaelis, who, without suggesting any doubt as to the age or author, pronounces the passage the most difficult in the book, and is altogether doubtful whether it has ever been fulfilled. Koppe divides the chapter into two independent prophecies. Eichhorn approves of this division, and infers from the style and phraseology, that the chapter was written after the destruction of Babylon. Bertholdt determines in the same way, that it was composed immediately after the destruction of Jerusalem by Nebuchadnezzar. Rosenmüller, in the first edition of his Scholia, agrees with Eichhorn, but in the second, he maintains that Isaiah was the author, and that he here expresses a general anticipation of approaching changes. Gesenius pronounces the style far inferior to that of Isaiah, and ascribes the passage to a writer in the Babylonian exile just before the fall of Babylon. Hitzig on the other hand ascribes it to an Ephraimite captive in Assyria, and supposes the destruction of Nineveh to be foretold. Ewald thinks the prophecy was written in Palestine after the restoration of the Jews, and in anticipation of Cambyses' attack on Egypt. Umbreit agrees substantially with Gesenius, and Knobel with Bertholdt. We have here another illustration of the value of the boasted modern criticism. Gesenius is confident that the prophecy was written in Babylon; Ewald and Knobel are equally confident that it was written in the Holy Land. Gesenius disparages the style as cold and artificial; Hitzig speaks of it with contempt as awkward, feeble, and inelegant; Ewald treats it with respect as poetical and skilful, although not original; while Umbreit lauds it as a noble specimen of Hebrew poetry. In this case, as in others, each writer first determines upon general grounds the age of the production, and then confirms it by internal proofs. The points of resemblance to the undisputed writings of Isaiah are set down as plagiarisms or imitations. Ewald even goes so far as to mark certain passages as borrowed from older writers no longer extant. The paronomasias and other verbal peculiarities of the passage, instead of proving it the work of Isaiah, in whose acknowledged writings they are also found, prove the contrary because they are so numerous. In this way all proof of the genuineness of a disputed passage is rendered impossible. If it has not the usual characteristics of the author, it is therefore spurious; if it has, it is evidently an imitation. It is true, distinctions are made as to the number, good taste, and connection; but they are always made at will, and so as to confirm the previous conclusion. Setting aside this empirical criticism as unworthy of attention, we may observe that the endless diversity of judgment, both among the older and later writers, shews that the prediction is generic. Henderson observes indeed on Lowth's suggestion that the prophecy refers to more than one invasion of the Holy Land, that "this hypothesis, though supplying an easy mode of interpreting all its parts, is to be rejected, having been obviously framed for the purpose of getting rid of the difficulties;" as if hypotheses were ever framed for any other purpose, and as if there could be a stronger proof that a hypothesis is true, than the fact of its getting rid of the difficulties and supplying an easy mode of interpreting all the parts. In this case, as in many others, the exclusive restriction of the prophecy to one event is wholly arbitrary. What the Prophet has left indefinite we have no right to make specific. Particular allusions there may be; but this, as we have seen in other cases, does not limit the application of the whole.

1. *Behold Jehovah (is) pouring out the land and emptying it, and he will turn down its face, and he will scatter its inhabitants.* The figure is that of a bottle or other vessel drained of its contents by being turned upside down. The face is not the soil or ground (Hendewerk), but the upper part or mouth of the vessel. The last clause resolves the figure into literal expressions. הֵפִיץ is not to cause to flow, as in Arabic, but to scatter, according to the uniform Hebrew usage. The allusion may be both to flight and deportation. Gesenius admits that הִנֵּה with the participle commonly indicates present or future time; but nevertheless applies this verse to the Babylonian conquest of Judea, which was long past at the time when he supposes the chapter to have been written. Ewald and Hitzig, who refer it to events still future at the date of the prediction, insist upon the future form. The simple truth is, that Isaiah here speaks of the Babylonian conquest as still distant, but at the same time as infallibly certain. To avoid this conclusion, Gesenius denies that Isaiah was the author, and violates the usage of the language by translating this whole passage in the past tense.

2. *And it shall be, as the people so the priest, as the servant so his master, as the maid so her mistress, as the buyer so the seller, as the lender so the borrower, as the creditor so the debtor.* That is, all ranks and classes shall fare alike. The double כ to express the idea *as-so* is like the use of *et-et* in Latin, where we say *both-and*, or *aut-aut* where we say *either-or*. Kimchi says that each term includes a double comparison, (the people) *like the priest* (and the priest) *like the people*, (the servant) *like the master* (and the master) *like the servant*. On the form נשּׁא see Gesenius, § 74, 20. The mention of the priest is no more a proof of later date in this case than in Hosea iv. 9. Saadias makes כהן mean a prince or ruler, which is also given in the margin of the English Bible.

3. *The land shall be utterly emptied and utterly spoiled, for Jehovah speaks (or hath spoken) this word.* Gesenius arbitrarily translates the verbs as preterites, in which he is followed by Hendewerk. Ewald explains them as descriptive presents. De Wette as usual disregards the reduplication of the Hebrew verbs. It is no doubt emphatic, however, and may be expressed by a simple repetition, *emptied emptied* (Ewald), or by combining a verb and adjective, *empty and emptied* (Hitzig), or by introducing an intensive adverb, *utterly, wholly*, as in the English Version and most others. According to Knobel, תּבּוֹק is put for the more usual form תּבּק in order to assimilate it to the infinitive. The full orthography with ו is mentioned by Gesenius as a sign of later date, although he does not deny that it also occurs in the older books. The *land* here mentioned is supposed by Hitzig to be Assyria; by all other interpreters Palestine. In order to justify his reference of this part of the chapter to past time, Gesenius explains the last clause as relating to the divine purpose or decree (for so Jehovah had commanded), whereas it elsewhere denotes the certainty of the event because predicted by Jehovah. The necessity of this departure from the usage of the phrase is a strong objection to his interpretation of the chapter, as written during the Babylonian exile by a captive Jew.

4. *The earth mourneth, fadeth; the world languisheth, fadeth; the highest of the people of the earth languish.* הארץ is not *the land* (Gesenius), as appears from the parallel expression תבל. *Earth* and *world*, however, are not to be taken in their widest sense (Rosenmüller), but as poetical descriptions of a country (Ewald); not Assyria (Hitzig), but Palestine. Jerome refers the whole description to the end of the world. For מרום Koppe reads מֵרוֹם *from the height* (*i. e.* cast down from it), for which there is neither authority nor necessity. J. D. Michaelis inserts *and* after מרום (the high ones *and* the people of the land), which is also unnecessary. The Septuagint and Peshito omit עם, but it is found in all manscripts. מרום is an abstract used for a concrete, *height* for *highest part* or *high ones*. Henderson supposes an allusion to the two thousand nobles carried away by Nebuchadnezzar. The figures are borrowed from the vegetable world. Several of the German writers amuse themselves with trying to copy the paronomasia in the first clause. Gesenius has *ächzet und lechzet*, Ewald *es welkt es verwelkt*, Knobel *welkt und fällt die Welt*. It is curious to observe the pains laid out upon these useless and unsuccessful imitations by writers who often disregard the idiomatic form of the construction.

5. *And the land has been profaned under its inhabitants, because they have transgressed the laws, violated the statute, broken the everlasting covenant.* Knobel reads, *and so the land*, as if the verse contained the punishment and not the sin of the chosen people. In accordance with this hypothesis, he explains the profaning of the land to be its invasion and subjection by

the Babylonians. *Under its inhabitants* will then mean nothing more than the land with those upon it. All other writers seem to apply the passage to the Jews, and to understand it as referring their calamities to their transgressions. The land is said to be profaned as being a holy land or consecrated to Jehovah. Most interpreters suppose a special reference to pollution by blood, or the guilt of murder, in accordance with Symmachus's version ἐφονοκτονήθη. The ancient versions give תַּחַת the sense of *for*, on *account of;* but the proper meaning *under* is far more appropriate and expressive. The ancient versions also make חק a plural, and this reading is found in one manuscript and one edition. Aben Ezra explains the unusual plural תורת as denoting not the law of Moses, but the laws common to all nations. Vitringa in like manner makes it synonymous with the *jus gentium* of the Roman writers. Hitzig understands by it the Noachic precepts, on account of the allusion to the flood in ver. 8. There seems to be no sufficient reason for departing from the ordinary meaning of the Hebrew words as denoting the divine law generally. The three terms used are substantially synonymous, *law, statute, covenant*, being continually interchanged. Henderson needlessly refers the last to the covenant of Sinai, and Hendewerk distinguishes between the moral and ceremonial parts of the Mosaic law. The simple meaning of the verse is that they disobeyed the will of God. In the phrase, *they changed the ordinance*, Gill finds a reference not only to the popish corruptions of the eucharist, but to the substitution of infant sprinkling for adult immersion.

6. *Therefore a curse devoured the earth, and those dwelling in it were reckoned guilty* (and so treated). *Therefore the inhabitants of the earth burned, and there are few men left.* אָלָה does not here mean false swearing, as explained in the Targum and by Jarchi and Kimchi, but the curse of God, attending the violation of his law. The mention of this penalty is absurdly represented by Gesenius and Knobel as a proof of the late date of the prophecy. אשם is taken by some of the early writers in the sense of being *desolate*. Its true sense is that of being recognised as guilty, and treated accordingly. It therefore suggests the ideas both of guilt and punishment. Twenty-eight manuscripts and three editions with the Peshito read אבלה instead of אכלה, a variation probably derived from ver. 4, or from Jer. xliii. 10. The Septuagint makes חרו mean *they shall be poor;* Symmachus, *they shall be exhausted;* J. D. Michaelis, *they shall be diminished.* The Targum gives the word the general sense of being consumed or destroyed; but the latest writers all prefer the more specific sense of burning or being burnt, either by internal heat like that of fever, or by the fire of outward persecutions. Houbigant and Lowth, without the least authority, read חרבו for חרו. Gesenius supposes the imagery to be copied from Joel i. 8–20.

7. *The new wine mourneth; the vine languisheth; all the merry-hearted do sigh.* Gesenius, Hitzig, and Henderson understand תירוש as denoting the juice of the grape while on the vine; Knobel by synecdoche the grape itself. But as the whole description is figurative, there is no need of departing from the usual sense of *sweet* or new wine. Rosenmüller and Barnes think the wine is here described as mourning because none drink it; Hendewerk, because it is drunk by foreigners and not by natives. This is changing a natural and beautiful figure into a frigid conceit. Gesenius informs us that this verse was also copied from Joel (chap. i. 10–12), where he says it stands in a much more natural connection.

8. *Still is the mirth of drums; ceased is the noise of revellers; still is*

the mirth of the harp. Music is here mentioned as a common token and accompaniment of mirth. Three manuscripts, instead of שָׁאוֹן, read גָּאוֹן.

9. *With the song they shall not drink wine; bitter shall strong drink be to them that drink it.* Hitzig understands this to mean that they shall not drink wine at all; Knobel, that it shall not be accompanied with music. שכר is neither beer (J. D. Michaelis) nor palm-wine (Lowth) specifically, but intoxicating drinks in general. The last clause means of course that they should lose the appetite for such enjoyments.

10. *Broken down is the city of confusion* (emptiness or desolation), *shut up is every house from entering,* (*i. e.* so that it is not or cannot be entered). The city meant is neither Nineveh (Hitzig), nor cities in general (Rosenmüller), but Jerusalem. Hitzig and Knobel prefer the construction, *it is broken down into* (*i. e.* so as to be) *a city of desolation*, but the common construction is more natural which makes קרית תהו the subject of the verb. The last clause might be understood to refer to the closing of the houses by the inhabitants against the enemy, or to their being left unoccupied; but the first clause seems to shew that it rather relates to the obstruction of the entrance by the ruins. Rosenmüller's explanation of קרית תהו, as denoting *city of idols*, or idolatrous city, is very unnatural. Hitzig and others make the מן before בית simply equivalent to *without*. Compare the similar expression in chap. xxiii. 1.

11. *A cry for wine in the streets—darkened is all joy—departed is the gladness of the earth.* To the critical acumen of Gesenius this verse stands confessed as a plagiarism from Joel i. 15. To the exquisite taste of Hitzig it is not only an *unda redundans*, but completely lame and flat (*vollends lahm und matt*). One ground of objection to it is that a calling for wine, though perfectly appropriate in Joel, is entirely out of place in this description of a conquered and dismantled town. The later writers have had taste enough to see that the cry meant is not that of drunkards for more liquor, but of the perishing inhabitants for necessary refreshment (Hendewerk), perhaps with special reference to the sick and wounded (Henderson) or to children (Hitzig). Knobel gives the words the still more general sense of lamentation for the blasted vintage. Hendewerk points out that wine alone is mentioned here, as bread is in Lam. iv. 4, while in Lam. ii. 12 both are combined. There is no need of taking צוחה in the sense of a call to the wine-sellers from their customers (Kimchi), much less of supplying a negative, so as to make it mean that there is *no call* for wine in the streets (Clericus). Houbigant and Lowth for ערבה read עברה (has passed away). Rosenmüller gives the same or nearly the same sense to the common text. But all the latest writers acquiesce in Buxtorf's definition of the word as meaning to grow dark, with special reference to the setting of the sun or the coming on of twilight. This beautiful figure is itself an answer to the æsthetical sneers of certain critics. נגלה may either have the general sense of *gone, departed* (Henderson), or the more specific one of banished (Gesenius), expatriated (J. D. Michaelis), carried captive (Umbreit). The first clause is rendered more expressive in the versions of De Wette, Umbreit, and Hendewerk, by the omission of the verb. The last-mentioned writer understands by the joy of the land, the population of Jerusalem. Nine manuscripts have כל before הארץ, and the Septuagint supplies it before משוש.

12. What is *left in the city is desolation, and into ruins is the gate beaten down.* The first clause is in apposition to the last of ver. 11. Joy is gone and desolation is left behind. All the modern writers take שאיה as an ad-

verbial accusative qualifying יכת by describing the effect or result of the action. The gate is here named as the most important part of the city ; but it does not directly mean the city itself. On the form יִפַּת see Gesenius, § 66. Rem. 8.

13. *For so shall it be in the midst of the earth among the nations, like the beating of an olive-tree, like gleanings when the gathering is done.* There is no need of rendering כִּי *but* (Rosenmüller) or *yet* (Henderson), as the Prophet is stating more distinctly the extent of the desolation which he had before described. The fact that some survive is indeed referred to, but only indirectly and by implication, so that the verse is not properly an antithesis to that before it. Instead of saying that Isaiah here repeats his beautiful comparison in chap. xvii. 5, 6, Gesenius and his followers set this down as the plagiarism of a later writer. The Prophet is thus reduced to a dilemma ; if he does not repeat his own expressions, he is a stranger to himself and his own writings ; if he does, he is an imitator of a later age. Rosenmüller supposes an allusion not only to paucity but to inferiority of quality. *In the midst of the nations* is explained by Hitzig as contrasting the condition of the country with that of its neighbours. Others understand it of actual dispersion among foreign nations.

14. *They shall raise their voice, they shall sing* (or *shout*), *for the majesty of Jehovah they cry aloud from the sea.* The pronoun at the beginning is emphatic. *They*, not the nations (Schelling) or the Jews left in the land (Barnes), but the few dispersed survivors of these judgments. The ב before גָּאוֹן is not a particle of time (Rosenmüller), but points out the subject (Maurer) or the occasion of the praise (Gesenius). Ewald supposes the words of the song itself to be begun in the last clause of this verse and continued through the next. But this compels him to change the pointing of צָהֲלוּ, and make it an imperative. The Septuagint and Theodotion have the *waters of the sea*, as if instead of מִיָּם they read מַיִם or מֵי יָם. Dathe gives the מִן its comparative sense : more (*i. e.* louder) than the sea. Jarchi had before given the same construction but a different sense : *more than* (*at*) *the sea, i. e.* more than they rejoiced at the deliverance from Egypt. Many render the phrase *from the west*, which is rather implied than expressed. Hitzig denies that there is here a transition to another subject, as admitted by almost all interpreters.

15. *Therefore in the fires glorify Jehovah, in the islands of the sea the name of Jehovah God of Israel.* Ewald supposes the words of the song or shout to be continued. Hendewerk and Barnes understand the Prophet as here turning from the remnant of Israel in Palestine to the scattered exiles. But it seems to be really an address to the persons who had already been described as praising God, exhorting them to do so still. אֻרִים has been variously explained as meaning valleys, caverns, doctrines, fires of affliction, exile, Urim (and Thummim), Ur (of the Chaldees), &c. Clericus makes בָּאֻרִים the passive participle of בָּאר. It is now commonly agreed to be a local designation. Doederlein deduces from an Arabic analogy the meaning *in the north*. Barnes suggests that ארים may denote the northern lights or aurora borealis. Henderson thinks the Prophet means the region of volcanic fires, viz. the Mediterranean coasts and islands. But the weight of exegetical authority preponderates in favour of the meaning *in the east* (as the region of sunrise, or of dawning light) in opposition to the sea or west. Various attempts have been made to mend the text by reading בָּאִיִּם (Lowth), בְּאֻמִּים or בְּיָמִּיב (Houbigant), בְּהָרִים or בִּיאֻרִים (Calmet). Hensler reads בְּאֻרִים as a contraction for בִּיאֹרִים, like כָּאֹרִים, Amos. viii. 8.

16. *From the wing (skirt or edge) of the earth we have heard songs, praise to the righteous ; and I said, Woe to me, woe to me, alas for me ! The deceivers deceive, with deceit the deceivers deceive.* We hear promises and praise to the righteous, but our actual experience is that of misery. צדיק is not an epithet of God (Henderson) or Cyrus (Hendewerk), but of righteous men in general. Gesenius infers from the second clause that the writer was involved in the miseries of Babylon ; but the same use might be made of every ideal situation which the book presents. Several of the ancient versions and of the rabbinical interpreters take רזי in the sense of *secret :* my secret is to me, and I must keep it, *i. e.* I cannot utter what I know. Aben Ezra and Kimchi, followed by Vitringa, gave it the specific sense of *leanness.* But the latest writers understand it as denoting ruin, misery, or woe, and the whole exclamation as substantially equivalent to that which follows. Here, as in chap. xxi. 2, the latest writers make בגד express, not fraud, but violence, which is contrary to usage and entirely unnecessary. Ewald takes בֶּגֶד in its usual sense of garment, and explains the clause to mean, that robbers strip off the very clothes. צבי לצדיק is commonly regarded as the very language of the song referred to ; but it may as well be a description of it, (a song of) *praise* or *honour to the righteous.*

17. *Fear and pit and snare upon thee, O inhabitant of the land !* This may be either a warning (*are upon thee*) or the expression of a wish (*be upon thee*). It is a probable though not a necessary supposition, that the terms here used are borrowed from the ancient art of hunting. פחד would then denote some device by which wild beasts were frightened into snares and pitfalls. It is at least a remarkable coincidence that the Romans gave the name *formido* to an apparatus used for this purpose. Henderson explains the Hebrew word to mean a *scarecrow.* The paronomasia is copied by Gesenius, Ewald, Umbreit, and Hitzig, in as many different forms. It is of course regarded as a proof of recent origin, though no one undertakes to say at what precise period the paronomasia became a favourite with the Hebrew writers.

18. *And it shall be (that) the (one) flying from the voice of the fear shall fall into the pit, and the (one) coming up from the midst of the pit shall be taken in the snare ; for windows from on high are opened, and the foundations of the earth are shaken.* The first clause carries out the figures of the foregoing verse ; and the second introduces those of a deluge and an earthquake. One manuscript instead of מקול reads מפני, and some interpreters regard קול as a mere idiomatic pleonasm. But it much more probably denotes the voice of the hunter or the noise made by the instrument called פחד. The allusion to the flood is acknowledged by all writers except Knobel, who objects that the Hebrews did not believe that there could be a second deluge ; as if this belief could prevent their understanding or employing such a figure of speech. There are thousands now who have the same belief, but who do not for that reason feel debarred from representing overwhelming evils as a deluge of misfortune or of wrath. Akin to this is the assertion of the same writer, and of Gesenius before him, that the early Hebrews actually thought that there were windows in the solid vault of heaven. In the same way it might be proved that Milton held the stars and planets to be burning lamps, and that Gesenius himself, when he speaks of a *column* of smoke, means a solid piece of masonry. It seems to be a canon with some critics, that all the prosaic language of the Bible is to be interpreted as poetry, and all its poetry as prose, especially when any colour is afforded for the charge of ignorant credulity. Kimchi imagines that windows are here mentioned as the apertures through which God looks upon the earth ; Knobel, as those through which he sends down thunder-bolts and lightning. But the allusion to the flood is rendered certain by the resemblance of the language to that used in Gen. vii. 11.

19. *Broken, broken is the earth ; shattered, shattered is the earth ; shaken, shaken is the earth.* This striking verse is pronounced by Gesenius and Hitzig, in accordance with some mystical canon of criticism, very inelegant and in bad taste. They both assign the reason that the word *earth* is repeated. Hitzig adds that the verse contains an anticlimax, which is not the case, as no natural phenomenon can be more impressive than an earthquake. The reduplication of the Hebrew verbs is as variously expressed by the different translators as in ver. 3.

20. *The earth reels, reels like a drunken man, and is shaken like a hammock. And heavy upon her is her guilt, and she shall fall and rise no more.* The ideas *earth* and *land*, both which are expressed by the Hebrew ארץ, run into one another and are interchanged in a manner not to be expressed in a translation. The old translation of the second clause (*removed like a cottage*) is now commonly abandoned. מלונה is properly a temporary lodging-place. In chap. i. 8, it was applied to a watch-shed in a melon-field. Here it seems to signify something more moveable and something suspended in the air. The latest writers are accordingly agreed in retaining the interpretation put upon the word by the Targum, the Peshito, and Saadias, which makes it mean a cloth or mat suspended between trees or boughs of trees for the use of nocturnal watchers. Such are described by Niebuhr as common in Arabia, and are known throughout the East by a name essentially identical with those used in the versions above cited. The readers of this verse would never have discovered, without Hitzig's aid, that its figures are extravagant and overstrained.

21. *And it shall be in that day that Jehovah shall visit* (for the purpose of inflicting punishment) *upon the host of the high place in the high place, and upon the kings of the earth upon the earth.* Interpreters have commonly assumed that the *host of the high place* is the same with the *host of heaven*, and must therefore mean either stars (Jerome), or angels (Aben Ezra), or both (Gesenius). Grotius understands by it the images of the heavenly bodies worshipped in Assyria. Gesenius finds here an allusion to the punishment of fallen angels, and then makes this a proof of recent origin, because the Jewish demonology was later than the time of Isaiah. It may be doubted whether there is any reference to the host of heaven at all. מרום is a relative expression, and although applied to heaven in ver. 18, is applied to earth, or to human society in ver. 4. The former sense may seem to be here required by the antithesis of אדמה ; but it is not clear that any antithesis was intended, which is the less probable because אדמה is not the customary opposite of heaven. The sense may simply be that God will judge the high or lofty host, viz. the kings of the land upon the land. But even if there be an antithesis, and even if the host of heaven in the usual sense of the expression be alluded to, the analogy of this whole context would seem to indicate that this is merely a strong figure for different ranks or degrees of dignity on earth. It is not indeed probable that the Jewish hierarchy is specifically meant, as Barnes supposes ; but it is altogether natural to understand the words more generally as denoting kings and potentates. And even on the supposition that the contrast here intended is between the hosts of heaven and earth, the obvious meaning is

that God will judge the principalities and powers of both worlds, in order to accomplish his declared designs. To pronounce the passage spurious because it seems to speak of evil spirits and their doom, is to assume that nothing is ever mentioned for the first time, but that all allusion to a doctrine must be simultaneous. Even in the later books of Scripture, how few and incidental and obscure are the allusions to this subject! In the same taste and spirit, and of equal value, are Gesenius's attempts to connect this verse with the doctrines of Zoroaster. It is not unworthy of remark that Hitzig, who delights in all such demonstrations of a later date and lower standard of opinion in the sacred books, foregoes that pleasure here, and flatly denies that there is any reference to demons in the text, because he had assumed the ground that it was written in Assyria before the fall of Nineveh.

22. *And they shall be gathered with a gathering as prisoners in a pit, and shall be shut up in a dungeon, and after many days they shall be visited.* Whether אֲסֵפָה be construed with אַסִּיר (*the gathering of a prisoner*), or explained as an emphatic reduplication, the sense of the first clause evidently is that they shall be imprisoned. The persons meant are of course the principalities and powers of the verse preceding. The affinity between סגרו and מסגר cannot well be expressed in English, as it is in the German version of Gesenius (verschlossen ins Verschloss). There are two interpretations of the verb יפקדו. According to one, it means *they shall be punished*, or at least brought forth to judgment. This is the sense put upon it by Eichhorn, Rosenmüller, Gesenius, Maurer, Umbreit, and Hendewerk. The other is, *they shall be visited in mercy.* This explanation is as old as Rabbi Joseph Kimchi, if not as the Peshito. Calvin seems to favour it, and it is adopted by Hitzig, Henderson, and Ewald. Barnes, who refers these verses to the Jewish priests, gives the verb the specific meaning, *shall be mustered*, with a view to their return from exile.

23. *And the moon shall be confounded, and the sun ashamed, for Jehovah of hosts is king in mount Zion, and in Jerusalem, and before his elders there is glory.* Before the splendour of Jehovah's reign all lesser principalities and powers shall fade away. There is no need of supposing an allusion to the worship of the sun and moon. Some give to כִּי the sense of *when*, which is admissible, but needless and indeed inadequate It was not merely *when* Jehovah reigned, but *because* he reigned, that all inferior luminaries were to be eclipsed. The *elders* are the rulers of Israel as the church. Henderson sees a distinct allusion to the form of government by elders, as that which shall prevail in the last and best days of the church. The simple meaning of the verse appears to be that Jehovah's reign over his people shall be more august than that of any created sovereign. This is true of the church in various periods of history, but more especially in those when the presence and power of God are peculiarly manifested. The affinity between this verse and the last of the preceding chapter seems to shew that their juxtaposition is by no means fortuitous. The Septuagint renders the first clause thus, *the brick shall moulder and the wall shall fall.* They evidently read לְבֵנָה and חֹמָה, although Grotius imagines that the deviation from the true sense was intentional, in order to avoid offending the Platonists of Egypt by disparaging the sun and moon. If such a motive could have influenced the authors of the version, its effects would not have been confined to one or a few comparatively unimportant passages.

Chapter 25

THIS chapter consists of three distinguishable parts. The first is a thanksgiving to God for the destruction of Babylon and the deliverance of the Jews, vers. 1–5. The second is a promise of favour to the Gentiles and the people of God, when united on mount Zion, vers. 6–9. The third is a threatening of disgraceful ruin to Moab, vers. 10–12.

It may be mentioned as a specimen of Ewald's bold and arbitrary criticism, that he connects vers. 6–11 directly with chap. xxiv., puts the first four verses together as a *strophe*, and the fifth, twelfth, and first four verses of the next chapter, as another strophe.

It is worthy of remark that, though the modern German writers all regard this chapter as the work of the same period, and indeed of the same author as the one before it, they find here none of those strong proofs of deteriorated taste and diction which are so abundant in the other case. To be consistent, they should either ascribe the passages to different authors, or admit that the twenty-fifth was written at a time and by a man not incapable of pure and lofty composition. It ought to be observed, however. that the admirable figure in ver. 10 strikes the delicate taste of Gesenius as low (*unedel*), and of Ewald as dirty (*schmutzig*).

Cocceius, in his exposition of this chapter, still enjoys his old hallucination that it is a chapter of church history, referring the first part to the great rebellion in England, and the last to the destruction of the Turks, &c.

1. *Jehovah my God (art) thou; I will exalt thee; I will praise thy name; for thou hast done a wonder, counsels from afar off, truth, certainty.* The song of praise opens in the usual lyric style. (See Exodus xv. 2, 11; Ps. cxviii. 28, cxlv. 1.) Cocceius, Vitringa, and some others, read *O thou my God*, without supplying the substantive verb; but the latter construction is more agreeable to usage. אוֹדְךָ strictly means *I will acknowledge* or confess. The whole phrase may either mean, I will acknowledge thy goodness towards me, or I will confess thee to be what thy name imports, I will acknowledge thy acts to be consistent with the previous revelations of thine attributes. Some render פֶּלֶא simply as a plural. Rosenmüller explains it as a collective implying that many particular wonders were included. Vitringa more naturally makes it an indefinite expression, *something wonderful* (mirabile quid). What wonder is especially referred to, the next verse explains. The last clause admits of several different constructions. Ewald, with many of the older writers, makes it an independent proposition, of which עֵצוֹת is the subject and אֱמוּנָה the predicate. Thus the English Version: *thy counsels of old are faithfulness and truth.* · Barnes supplies another verb: *thou hast shown to be faithful and true.* Gesenius makes עֵצוֹת as well as פלא the object of the verb עָשִׂיתָ, and supplies a preposition before אמונה, or regards it as an adverbial accusative: *thou hast executed ancient plans (with) faithfulness and truth.* Hitzig simplifies the same construction still more by making all the nouns in the last clause objects of the verb in the first: thou hast brought to pass a wonder, ancient counsels, faithfulness, and truth. *From afar off* seems to imply, not only that the plans were formed of old, but that they were long ago revealed. Even long before the event they are certain. Hitzig, who applies the whole prophecy to Nineveh, is disposed to understand this clause as referring to the earlier prophecies of its destruction by Nahum and Zephaniah. The Septuagint, followed by J. D. Michaelis, reads אָמֵן *Amen* (γένοιτο), which

would here be out of place. אמן and אמונה are cognate forms, both denoting truth or certainty, and here combined, according to a very common Hebrew idiom, for emphasis.

2. *For thou hast turned (it) from a city to a heap, a fortified town to a ruin, a palace of strangers from (being) a city; for ever it shall not be built.* According to Rosenmüller, *city* is here put for cities in general, and the verse contains a promise or prophetic description of the golden age when fortifications should no longer be needed, as Virgil says of the same ideal period, that there shall then no more be *oppida muris cincta*. Most interpreters, however, are agreed that it refers to a particular city; Grotius says Samaria; Cappellus, Jerusalem; Hitzig, Nineveh; the others, Babylon. Cocceius applies the first clause to the overthrow of episcopacy in England, and especially to the exclusion of the bishops from the House of Lords. (*Sensus hic est: ex ecclesia episcopali fecisti acervum, hoc est eam totam diruisti.*) The other clause he applies to the subsequent change of the republic into a tyranny (from a city to a palace of strangers). שַׂמְתָּ means strictly *thou hast placed*, but is often used with ל to denote the conversion of a thing into something else. Here it is separated from לַגָּל by מֵעִיר, an unusual collocation, which led Houbigant to read עִיר or הָעִיר, in which he is followed by Lowth, Döderlein, Dathe, Gesenius, and Knobel. J. D. Michaelis reads עִיר שַׂמְתָּם, which, instead of easing the construction, makes it still more harsh. The difficulty is entirely removed, without a change of text, by supposing the object of the verb to be עִיר or קִרְיָה understood. *Thou hast changed (a city) from a city to a heap.* So Vitringa, Rosenmüller, and others. Gesenius doubts whether such an ellipsis is admissible; but it is surely more so than an arbitrary change of text. Another solution of the syntax is proposed by Hitzig, "thou hast turned from a city to a heap, a fortified town to a ruin," in which case לְמַפֵּלָה is an unmeaning repetition of לַגָּל, without even parallelism or rhythm to sanction it. The same construction had substantially been given long before by De Dieu. Hendewerk goes still further and connects למפלה with ארמון זרים: "thou changest the fortified town from a city to a heap, the palaces of strangers from a city to ruins." Gesenius gives בְּצוּרָה here its primary and proper sense of *inaccessible*. Most of the modern writers understand by *a palace of strangers* the royal city mentioned in the first clause, called a *palace* on account of its splendour, or as being a collection of *palaces*, or because the palace was the most important part of it. מֵעִיר must then be taken in a privative sense (*so as not to be a city*). But as the same phrase in the first clause means *from being a city*, some give it that sense here, and understand the clause to mean that God had changed it from a city to a palace (or royal residence) of strangers. But if it ceased to be a city, how could it become a palace? There is in fact no inconsistency between the senses put upon מֵעִיר by the usual interpretation. Even in the first clause it means strictly *from* or *away from a city*, which can be clearly expressed in our idiom only by using a negative expression. For זרים, Houbigant proposes to read זדום, wholly without reason or authority. זרים has the same sense as in chap. i. 7. For the use of *stranger* in the sense of *enemy*, Gesenius cites the authority of Ossian. Grotius explains it to mean *strange gods*, or their worshippers, and applies the whole phrase to the idolatrous temple of Samaria. The Targum in like manner makes it mean an idol-temple in Jerusalem itself.

3. *Therefore a powerful people shall honour thee, a city of terrible nations*

shall fear thee. The destruction of Babylon, and the fulfilment of prophecy thereby, shall lead even the boldest and wildest of the heathen to acknowledge Jehovah as the true God. It is usual to apply the terms of this verse specifically to the Medes and Persians as the conquerors of Babylon. Hitzig refers them to the Medes and Babylonians as the conquerors of Nineveh. To this it may be objected, that the epithets, according to usage, imply censure, rather than praise, and that עֲרִיצִים is applied in the next verse to the conquered Babylonians themselves as having once been tyrants or oppressors. There seems to be no need of applying the verse to a cordial voluntary recognition of Jehovah. It may just as well denote a compulsory extorted homage, *fear* being taken in its proper sense. The verse will then be an apt description of the effect produced by Jehovah's overthrow of Babylon on the Babylonians themselves. There is still another explanation, namely that which understands the verse more indefinitely as descriptive of an effect produced upon the nations generally. This, however, does not agree so well with the use of the terms *people* and *city* in the singular number, for although they may be taken as collectives, such a construction should not be assumed without necessity. But even on the other supposition, there is something unusual in the expression *city of nations.* It must either be explained as implying a plurality of subject nations, or גּוֹיִם must be taken in its secondary sense of *gentiles, heathen,* as applied to individuals or to one community.

4. *For thou hast been a strength* (or *stronghold*) *to the weak, a strength* (or *stronghold*) *to the poor, in his distress, a refuge from the storm, a shadow from the heat, when the blast of the terrible* (or *of the tyrants*) *was* like *a storm against a wall.* The nations shall reverence Jehovah, not merely as the destroyer of Babylon, but as the deliverer of his people, for whose sake that catastrophe was brought about. מָעוֹז is not merely *strength* in the abstract, but a *strong place* or fortress. דַּל and אֶבְיוֹן are epithets often applied to Israel considered as a sufferer. The two figures of extreme heat and a storm of rain are combined to express the idea of persecution or affliction. כִּי may also be taken in its usual sense of *for,* as pointing out the reason why protection was required. רוּחַ does not directly denote *wrath,* but *breath,* and here a violent breathing, as indicative of anger. It is thus explained by Gesenius (Zornhauch), while Ewald gratuitously lowers the tone of the descriptions by translating the word snorting (Schnauben). Jarchi explains זרם קיר (wall-storm), as denoting a storm which overthrows or destroys a wall. The same idea is expressed in the Targum, Peshito, and Vulgate, and approved by most of the recent writers. Knobel objects that the phrase does not naturally suggest the idea of subversion or destruction, and on that account adopts the reading וְקֹר proposed by Cappellus, and approved by Vitringa, Lowth, and Dathe. The phrase would then mean a *cold* or *winter storm.* There is no need, however, of a change in the text, although Knobel's objection to the common explanation is well founded. The Hebrew phrase naturally signifies precisely what the English Version has expressed, to wit, *a storm against a wall,* denoting the direction and the object of the violence, but not its issue. As a storm of rain beats upon a wall, so the Babylonian persecution beat upon the captive Jews. The simple but striking and impressive imagery of this verse is very far from indicating an inferior writer or a recent date of composition. It is not strange, however, that this fine passage should be deemed unworthy of Isaiah or his times by those who look upon Macpherson's Ossian as a relic of antiquity.

5. *As heat in a drought* (or *in a dry place*), *the noise of strangers wilt thou bring down;* (as) *heat by the shadow of a cloud,* (so) *shall the song of the tyrants be brought low.* The sufferings of Israel under oppression shall be mitigated and relieved as easily and quietly as the intense heat of the sun by an intervening cloud. The *noise* mentioned in the first clause is probably the tumult of battle and conquest, and the *song* in the last clause the triumphal song of the victorious enemy. The meaning *branch* is more agreeable to usage, but not so appropriate in this connection. De Dieu's translation of the last words, *the pruning* (or *excision*) *of the tyrants shall bear witness*, is extremely forced. Still worse is that of Junius and Tremellius : *it* (the heat) *answered* (or *favoured*) *the branch of the oppressors*. The same idea is expressed in both the clauses, though the first is elliptical, and the idea of a shadowy cloud must be supplied from the second. Gesenius makes יענה intransitive ; the later Germans take it as a Hiphil form (*he shall bring low*), corresponding to תכניע in the other clause. Barnes removes the enallage by rendering יענה in the second person. Koppe and Bauer most gratuitously read it as a passive, וְעֻנָּה. As צִיּוֹן is properly an abstract, it may be applied either to time or place, a dry season or a desert, without affecting the sense. The Seventy appear to have read צִיּוֹן *Zion*, which would change the sense entirely.

6. *And Jehovah of hosts will make, for all nations, in this mountain, a feast of fat things, a feast of wines on the lees, of fat things, full of marrow, of wines on the lees well refined.* Jerusalem, hitherto despised and oppressed, shall yet be a source of attraction, nourishment and exhilaration to mankind. This verse resumes the thread of the discourse, which was interrupted at the end of the last chapter, for the purpose of inserting the triumphal song (vers. 1–5). Having there said that Jehovah and his elders should appear in glory on mount Zion, he now shews what is there to be bestowed upon the nations. שמנים properly means *fatnesses*, here put for rich and dainty food. Clericus strangely supplies *sheep*, as if שמנים were an adjective. שמרים means the lees of wine, as being the *keepers* (from שמר, to keep), or preservers of the colour and flavour. It is here put for wine kept long upon the lees, and therefore old and of superior quality. מזקקים probably means strained or filtered. מְמֻחִים from מָחָה is put for the more usual form מְמֻחִים, in order to assimilate it to the other word. This verse contains a general statement of the relation which Jerusalem or Zion should sustain to the whole world, as a source of moral influence. There is nothing to indicate the time when the promise should be fulfilled, nor indeed to restrict it to one time exclusively. As the ancient seat of the true religion, and as the cradle of the church which has since overspread the nations, it has always more or less fulfilled the office here ascribed to it.

7. *And he will swallow up* (i. e. destroy) *in this mountain the face of the veil, the veil upon all peoples, and the web, the* (one) *woven over all the nations*. The influence to go forth from this centre shall dispel the darkness both of ignorance and sorrow which now broods over the world. The subject of the verb is of course Jehovah. By the *face of the veil*, some understand the veil itself. Others suppose a metathesis for the *veil of the face*. Lowth adopts the reading in one manuscript, which sets פְּנֵי before כָּל־הָעַמִּים. Gesenius, with more probability, infers from the analogous expression in Job xli. 5, that the veil or covering is here described as being the *surface*, or upper side of the object covered. Most interpreters suppose an allusion to the practice of veiling the face as a sign of mourning, which agrees well with the next verse, and is no doubt included, but the words

seem also to express the idea of a veil upon the understanding. (*Vide supra*, chap. xxii. 8.) Some have explained the words as relating to the covering of the faces of condemned criminals; but this is neither justified by usage nor appropriate in this connection. Gesenius makes the second לוט an active participle of unusual form, chosen in order to assimilate it to the foregoing noun (*the cover covering*). But as the language contains traces of the usual form לָט, and as the forms here used are not only similar, but identical, it seems more natural to suppose an emphatic repetition of the noun itself, especially as such repetitions are so frequent in the foregoing chapter. Some of the ancient versions, deriving מַסֵּכָה from a verbal root meaning to *anoint*, explain the cause as threatening the fall of a tyrannical power. Thus the Targum has "the face of the chief who rules over all peoples, and the face of the king who rules over all kingdoms." Henderson deduces from the Arabic analogy the specific and appropriate sense of *web* or *weaving*.

8. *He has swallowed up death for ever, and the Lord Jehovah wipes away tears from off all faces, and the reproach of his people he will take away from off all the earth, for Jehovah hath spoken (it).* The people of God, who seemed to be extinct, shall be restored to life, their grief exchanged for joy, and their disgrace for honour in the presence of the world, a result for which he pledges both his power and foreknowledge. The preterite form בִּלַּע may either be explained as a descriptive present, or as indicating something previous in point of time to what is mentioned afterwards. Henderson objects to the rendering of the Piel by the English *swallow up;* but the sense of *destroying*, which he prefers, is evidently secondary and derivative. Barnes, on the other hand, supposes a specific allusion to a *maelstrom*, which is erring in the opposite extreme. Rosenmüller understands the first clause as a promise, that in the golden age which Isaiah anticipated wars and mutual violence should cease; Gesenius as a promise of immortality, like that which man enjoyed before the fall. Hendewerk applies it to the death and immortality of Israel as a nation. The true sense seems to be, that all misery and suffering, comprehended under the generic name of *death*, should be completely done away. It is, then, a description of the ultimate effects of the influence before described as flowing from mount Zion, or the church of God. In its higher sense this may never be realised by any individual till after death. Paul says accordingly (1 Cor. xv. 54), that when this corruptible shall have put on incorruption, and this mortal shall have put on immortality, then shall be brought to pass the saying that is written, κατεπόθη ὁ θάνατος εἰς νῖκος. As this is not an explanation of the text before us, nor even a citation of it in the way of argument, but merely a sublime description, all that it was necessary to express was the final, perpetual, triumphant abolition of death. The phrase εἰς νῖκος, therefore (which is also found in Theodotion's Version), although not a strict translation of לָנֶצַח, is no departure from its essential meaning. In its primary import, the clause is a promise to God's people, corresponding to the foregoing promise to the nations. While, on the one hand, he would lift the veil from the latter, and admit them to a feast upon Zion, on the other, he would abolish death, and wipe tears from the faces of his people. The restriction of these last expressions to the pains of death, or to the sorrow of bereavement, detracts from the exquisite beauty of the passage, which the poet Burns (as Barnes informs us) could not read without weeping, a sufficient proof that he was not aware of the German discovery, that

this prediction is an exceedingly lame and flat composition, quite unworthy of the Prophet to whom it has from time immemorial been erroneously ascribed.

9. *And one shall say* (or *they shall say*) *in that day, Lo, this is our God; we have waited for him, and he will save us; this is Jehovah; we have waited for him; let us rejoice and be glad in his salvation.* When these gracious promises shall be fulfilled, those who have trusted in them shall no longer be ashamed of their strong confidence, because it will be justified by the event, and they will have nothing left but to rejoice in the fulfilment of their hopes. *This is our God, this is Jehovah;* as if they had said, This is the God of whom we have spoken, and for trusting in whom we have so often been derided. We have waited long, but he has come at last, to vindicate his truth and our reliance on him. The augmented futures at the close may either denote fixed determination (*we will rejoice, we will be glad*), or a proposition (*let us then rejoice*), for which the language has no other distinct form.

10. *For the hand of Jehovah shall rest upon this mountain, and Moab shall be trodden down under him* (or *in his place*) *as straw is trodden in the water of the dunghill.* While Israel shall thus enjoy the permanent protection of Jehovah, his inveterate enemies shall experience ignominious destruction. God's hand is the symbol of his power. Its resting on an object is the continued exercise of that power, whether for good or evil. This is determined by the nature of the object, as *this mountain* cannot well mean anything but what is meant in vers. 6, 7, to wit, mount Zion, or the Church of God, and the promise of the foregoing context must of course be continued here. Moab and Edom were the two hereditary and inveterate enemies of Israel, their hatred being rendered more annoying and conspicuous by their affinity and neighbouring situation. Hence they are repeatedly mentioned, separately or together, as the representatives of obstinate and maligant enemies in general. Henderson insists upon the word's being taken in its literal import; but this is not excluded in the usual interpretation. As the name *British*, in our own revolutionary war, became equivalent to *hostile*, without losing its specific sense, so might the Prophets threaten Moab with God's vengeance, without meaning to exclude from the denunciation other like-minded enemies. This wide interpretation, both of Moab and Edom, is confirmed by the fact that one of them is often mentioned where both would seem to be equally included. The figure in the last clause is strongly expressive, both of degradation and destruction. Moab is likened not only to straw, but to straw left to rot for the dunghill. The idea of subjection and ruin is expressed by the figure of treading down or trampling under foot. דוּשׁ is commonly translated *thresh*; but as the oriental threshing was performed for the most part by the feet of cattle, this sense and that of *treading down* are really coincident. In reference to the same usage, the Septuagint, Peshito, and Vulgate, introduce the word *waggons*, meaning the heavy carts or threshing machines of the East. Lowth conjectures that they read מרכבה for מדמנה; but the former word denotes a chariot, especially a chariot of war, and the versions in question do not necessarily imply a difference of text. According to some writers, מדמנה is the name of a city, *Madmenah*, which may at one time have belonged to Moab, and be mentioned here on account of some local peculiarity. Henderson thinks there can be no allusion to this place; but it is perfectly accordant with the usage of the sacred writers to suppose that the word was

here intended to convey a contemptuous allusion to the primary meaning of the name in question. As an appellative, it is a noun of place derived from רמן, and denoting either a manured field or a dunghill. The *keri*, or Masoretic reading in the margin, has במו, a poetical equivalent of ב, the preposition *in*. The *kethib*, or textual reading, which is probably more ancient, is במי, *in the water*. This, with the next word, may denote a pool in which the straw was left to putrefy. In Job ix. 30 we have an opposite correction, במו in the text, and במי in the margin. *Under him* may either mean *under Jehovah* or *under himself*, that is, in his own place, in the country of Moab, or wherever he is found.

11. *And he shall spread forth his hands in the midst of it, as the swimmer spreadeth forth his hands to swim; and he shall humble his pride, together with the spoils* (or *devices*) *of his hands.* From this ignominious doom Moab shall in vain try to save himself; his pride shall be humbled, and his struggles only serve to precipitate his ruin. Having compared the fall of Moab to the treading down of straw in a filthy pool, the Prophet carries out his figure here, but with a change so slight and at the same time so natural, as almost to escape observation, while it greatly adds to the life of the description. The down-trodden straw now becomes a living person, who struggles in the filthy pool to save himself from drowning, but in vain. The older writers for the most part make *Jehovah* the subject of the verb at the beginning of the sentence. But the image then becomes incongruous, not only as applied to God, but as failing to express any appropriate action upon his part. It is, indeed, explained to mean that God will strike him here and there, or in every part, as a swimmer strikes the waves in all directions; but this idea might have been expressed more clearly by a hundred other images. So too בקרבו is explained to mean that God would strike, not merely on the surface or extremities of Moab, but in the very midst of him, or to his very centre, which is still more forced and arbitrary. The only idea naturally suggested by the images employed, is that of a drowning man struggling in the water. The latest writers therefore follow Grotius in referring פרש to מואב, and the suffix in בקרבו to the pool or dunghill. ארבות has been variously explained as meaning *strength, spoils, arms, armpits, joints,* &c. The sense *by the strength of his hands* (*i.e.* God's) is precluded by the preposition עם, which does not indicate the instrument or means, but signifies *together with*. Rosenmüller and Ewald prefer the meaning *joints,* founded on an Arabic analogy. Gesenius adheres to Hebrew usage and explains the word to mean *devices, plots* (*insidiis* which Robinson translates *ambuscades,* a word of less extensive import than the Latin one). The mention of the hands is explained by Gesenius from the fact that ארב primarily means to knit, spin, or weave. It is hard, however, to resist the impression, that these last words have respect to the image in the first clause, and describe the movements of the swimmer's hands in endeavouring to save himself. Eichhorn, Umbreit, and Knobel carry the figure through the verse, explaining גאותו to mean *his back* or *his rising,* and the last words either *his arms* or the motions of his hands. But most interpreters suppose the figure to be dropped in this clause, and the humbling of Moab to be here foretold in literal terms. Lowth's proposition to read שׁחֶה for שׂחֶה (*he that sinks* for *he that swims*) is not only needless, but injurious to the force of the expression, puts an unusual sense upon the word supposed, and does away with an example of a very common Hebrew idiom, that of combining verbs with their particles and derivative nouns.

12. *And the fortress of the high fort of thy walls he hath cast down,*

humbled, brought to the ground, to the very dust (or *even to the dust*). Many interpreters suppose that the Prophet here reverts from Moab to the city mentioned in the second verse. Others more naturally understand this as the close of the prediction against Moab ; first, because abrupt transitions should not be assumed without necessity ; and secondly, because the verse appears to be an amplification of the phrase השפיל גאותו in that before it. מבצר and משגב are equivalent in usage, though distinct in etymology. Both are local nouns, and mean a place of safety ; but the prominent idea in the first is that of fortification, in the second that of loftiness. Some manuscripts read הֹמֹתַיִךְ in the feminine, in which case the city or country is the object of address, in the other the nation, or Moab represented as a man. The specific fulfilment of this prophecy cannot be distinctly traced in history. It was certainly verified, however, in the downfall of the Moabitish nation, whenever it took place.

Chapter 26

THIS chapter contains a song of praise and thanksgiving, to be sung by Israel after his deliverance, vers. 1–19. To this is added a postscript, intimating that the time for such rejoicing was not yet at hand, vers. 20, 21.

The song opens with an acknowledgment of God's protection and an exhortation to confide therein, vers. 1–4. This is founded on the exhibition of his righteousness and power in the destruction of his foes and the oppressors of his people, vers. 5–11. The Church abjures the service of all other sovereigns, and vows perpetual devotion to him by whom it has been delivered and restored, vers. 12–15. Her utter incapacity to save herself is then contrasted with God's power to restore his people to new life, with a joyful anticipation of which the song concludes, vers. 17–19. The additional sentences contain a beautiful and tender intimation of the trials, which must be endured before these glorious events take place, with a solemn assurance that Jehovah is about to visit both his people and their enemies with chastisement, vers. 20, 21.

1. *In that day shall this song be sung in the land of Judah* : *We have a strong city ; salvation will he place* (*as*) *walls and breastwork.* The condition and feelings of the people after their return from exile are expressed by putting an ideal song into their mouths. Though the first clause does not necessarily mean that this should actually be sung, but merely that it might be sung, or that it would be appropriate to the times and to the feelings of the people, it is not at all improbable that it was actually used for this purpose, which could more readily be done as it is written in the form and manner of the Psalms, with which it exhibits many points of resemblance. The day meant is the day of deliverance which had just been promised. Lowth connects *in the land of Judah* with what follows, in violation of the accents and without the least necessity. Nor can it be supposed that the song itself would have begun with such a formula, unless the singers are assumed to be the Jews still in exile, which is hardly consistent with the following verse. Knobel, on the other hand, asserts that the singers are *no doubt* the Jews left by the Babylonians in the land of Judah. This is necessarily involved in his hypothesis, that chaps. xxiv.–xxvii. were written immediately after Nebuchadnezzar's conquest. (See the introduction to chap. xxiv.) Another inference from this supposition is, that the verse before us describes Jerusalem in its dismantled state, as still protected by the divine

favour, whereas it is rather a description of the divine help and favour, as the city's best defence, or as that without which all others would be useless. Ewald, however, makes it mean that walls and bulwarks give salvation (*Heil geben Mauern und Graben*), which, besides the harsh construction, yields a sense directly opposite to that intended. The obvious and natural construction of ישׁית is with יהוה understood. The future form implies that the description is prospective. חֵל is the outer and lower wall protecting the trench or moat of a fortification. The whole phrase is rendered by the Septuagint τεῖχος καὶ περίτειχος. Junius adds to his translation of this verse the word *dicendo* so as to make the next words those of God himself.

2. *Open ye the gates, and let the righteous nation enter, keeping truth* (or *faith*). The supposition of responsive choruses gives a needless complexity to the structure of the passage. The speakers are the same as in the first verse, and the words are addressed to those who kept the doors. Knobel understands this as the language of the remaining Jews, exhorting themselves or one another to receive the returning exiles. These are described as *righteous* and as *keeping faith*, probably in reference to the cessation of idolatry among the Jews during the exile. Lowth connects אֱמֻנִים שֹׁמֵר with the first clause of the next verse. J. D. Michaelis makes it an independent proposition (*he preserves the faithful*). Knobel says that the use of גּוֹי in application to the Jews is a later usage, which assertion is undoubtedly true if every place where it occurs is assumed to be of recent date.

3. *The mind stayed (on thee) thou wilt preserve in peace (in), peace (i. e. in perfect peace), because in thee (it is) confident (literally confided).* This is a general truth deduced from the experience of those who are supposed to be the speakers. Lowth adds the last words of the foregoing verse *constant in the truth, stayed in mind*, by which nothing is gained, and the Masoretic interpunction needlessly violated. Calvin makes the first two words an independent clause (*cogitatio fixa*), and Ewald seems to adopt the same construction (*die Einbildung steht fest*), probably meaning that what follows is a just thought or a certain truth. Luther seems to refer it to God's promise (nach gewisser Zusage). But the best construction is the common one, which connects יֵצֶר סָמוּךְ with the following words. יֵצֶר is the *invention* (or perhaps the *constitution*) of the mind, put for the mind itself. The elliptical construction in the English Bible (*him whose mind is stayed on thee*) is not very natural; still less so that of Knobel, who refers סָמוּךְ to the person understood, and makes יֵצֶר a qualifying noun (*stayed as to mind*), citing as examples of a similar inversion chap. xxii. 2; Nahum iii. 1. Barnes omits יֵצֶר altogether in his version (*him that is stayed on thee*). Henderson gives the true construction, making תִּצֹּר govern יֵצֶר directly, though he renders סָמוּךְ *firm*, which is hardly an adequate translation, as the word necessarily includes the idea of *reliance, i. e.* upon God. Ewald derives תִּצֹּר from יָצַר instead of נָצַר, translates it *thou wilt form* (or *create*) *peace*. For this no reason can be given, except that it evolves a new paronomasia, both in sense and sound, between the noun and verb. The mere assonance exists of course, however the words may be explained; and though Gesenius was so unhappy as to overlook it, Knobel has copied it by the combination *Festen festigest*. The idiomatic iteration, *peace, peace*, to express a superlative, is perfectly in keeping with the frequent reduplications of the twenty-fourth chapter, and may serve to shew, that the accumulation of such idioms there arises from difference of subject or of sentiments to be expressed, and not from want of genius or corruption of

taste. There is no need of explaining בָּטוּחַ as a passive substituted for an active participle. The word corresponds both in form and meaning to *assured* in English.

4. *Trust ye in Jehovah for ever* (literally, *even to eternity*), *for in Jah Jehovah is a rock of ages* (or *an everlasting rock*). To the general truth stated in ver. 3, a general exhortation is now added, not addressed by one chorus to another, but by the same ideal speakers to all who hear them or are willing to receive the admonition. This is one of the few places in which the name *Jehovah* is retained by the common English version. On the origin and usage of the name יָהּ *vide supra*, chap. xii. 2. The occurrence of the combination here confirms its genuineness there. In this place it is at least as old as Aquila, who has ἐν τῷ κυρίῳ κύριος. Knobel, however, chooses to reject יְהֹוָה as a mere explanation or correction of יָהּ, added by a later hand. Cocceius, in accordance with his own etymology of יָהּ, translates it *in decentia Jehovæ*, which is very much like nonsense. Vitringa makes these names the subject of the proposition (*Jah Jehovah est rupes sæculorum*), according to De Dieu's observation, that the preposition בְּ is often pleonastic. The same construction is adopted by Gesenius, on the ground that בְּ is frequently a *beth essentiæ*, corresponding to the French *en* in the phrase *en roi*, *i.e.* in (the character or person of) a king. The existence of this idiom in Hebrew is denied, both by Winer in his Lexicon, and Ewald in his grammar, but maintained against them by Gesenius in his Thesaurus. It is evident, however, that in all cases where it is assumed, this conclusion can only be defended on the ground of exegetical necessity, and that such analogies cannot require, or even authorize, the preference of this obscure and harsh construction where the obvious and simple one is perfectly admissible. In the case before us, Gesenius is obliged to create a necessity for his construction, by gratuitously making יָהּ the subject, and יְהֹוָה the predicate, of the proposition. This he chooses to translate *Jehovah is God*, but it ought to have been *Jah is Jehovah*, and as one of these names is explained by himself to be a mere abbreviation of the other, the clause becomes an identical proposition, meaning nothing more than that *Jehovah is himself*. All that is gained by the supposition of a *beth essentiæ* may be secured, without departing from the ordinary meaning of the preposition, by supplying an active verb, as in Augusti's Version, *in him (ye have) an everlasting rock*. But the simplest and most accurate of all constructions is the common one, retained by Ewald, who omits neither *Jah* nor the particle before it, but translates the clause, *for in Jah Jahve, is an everlasting rock*. This figurative name, as applied to God, includes the two ideas of a *hiding-place* and a *foundation*, or the one complex idea of a *permanent asylum*. Barnes translates the whole phrase, *everlasting refuge*. Lowth's *never-failing protection* is correct in sense, but in form a diluted paraphrase.

5. *For he hath brought down the inhabitants of the high place, the exalted city; he will lay it low, he will lay it low, to the very ground; he will bring it to the very dust.* He has proved himself able to protect his people, and consequently worthy to be trusted by them, in his signal overthrow of that great power by which they were oppressed. נִשְׂגָּבָה means *lofty* in the sense of being inaccessible, and is especially applied to fortresses, as we have seen with respect to the derivative noun מִשְׂגָּב, chap. xxv. 12. Hitzig explains יֹשְׁבֵי to mean *those enthroned;* but its connection with מָרוֹם requires it to be taken in the sense of inhabitants. The alternation of the tenses here is somewhat remarkable. Henderson translates them all as

preterites ; Barnes uses first the present, then the preterite ; both which constructions are entirely arbitrary. The English Version more correctly treats them all as presents, which is often allowable where the forms are intermingled, and is also adopted by the latest German writers. But in this case, a reason can be given for the use of the two tenses, even if strictly understood. The Prophet looks at the events from two distinct points of observation, his own and that of the ideal speakers. With respect to the latter, the fall of Babylon was past ; with respect to the former it was still future. He might therefore naturally say, even in the same sentence, *he has brought it low* and *he shall bring it to the dust.* Cocceius, as usual, reproduces the precise form of the Hebrew sentence. No two things can well be more unlike than the looseness of this writer's exegesis and the critical precision of his mere translation. Henderson thinks the Masoretic inter-punction wrong, and throws ישפילנה into the first clause, to which arrange-ment there are three objections : first, that it is arbitrary and against the textual tradition ; second, that it makes the suffix in the verb superfluous, the object having been expressed before ; and third, that it renders less effective, if it does not quite destroy, the idiomatic iteration of the verb, which is characteristic of this whole prediction. עד strictly means *as far as,* and may be expressed in English, either by the phrase *even to,* or by the use of the intensive *very,* as above in the translation.

6. *The foot shall trample on it, the feet of the afflicted, the steps of the weak.* The ruins of the fallen city shall be trodden under foot, not only by its conquerors, but by those whom it oppressed. Neither עני nor דל strictly signifies *poor.* The prominent idea in the first is that of *suffering,* in the second that of *weakness.* They are here used, like דל and אביון in chap. xxv. 4, as epithets of Israel while subjected to the Babylonian tyranny. פעמי, which Luther translates *heels* (Ferse), and Junius *footsteps* (vestigia), is here a poetical equivalent to *feet.* Henderson here translates the verbs in the present, Barnes more exactly in the future.

7. *The way for the righteous is straight* (or *level*)*; thou most upright wilt level* (or *rectify*) *the path of the righteous.* A man's way is a common Scriptural figure for his course of life. A straight or level way is a pros-perous life. It is here declared that the course of the righteous is a prosperous one, because God makes it so. מישרים strictly denotes *straight-ness,* the plural being used as an abstract. The moral sense of *uprightness* does not suit the connection. ישר may either be construed as a vocative, or with the name of God understood (*as a righteous God*). Knobel makes it an adverbial accusative, thou dost rectify the path of the righteous straight, *i. e.* so as to make it straight. The primary idea of פלס is to render even ; it is therefore applied both to balances and paths ; but the two applications are not to be confounded ; paths may be made even, but they cannot be weighed.

8. *Also in the way of thy judgments, O Jehovah, we have waited for thee ; to thy name and thy remembrance (was our) soul's desire.* For this manifestation of thy righteousness and goodness we have long been waiting *in the way of thy judgments, i. e.* to see thee come forth as a judge, for the vindication of thy people and the destruction of their enemies. *Name* and *remembrance* or *memorial* denote the manifestation of God's attributes in his works. Ewald translates the second fame or glory (Ruhm). J. D. Michaelis connects the first words with the seventh verse, " thou dost regulate the path of the righteous, but also the way of thy judgments."

Lowth takes מִשְׁפָּטֶיךָ in the sense of *laws* and קִוִּינוּ in that of *trusting*. It is more probable, however, that the same idea is expressed here as in chap. xxv. 9.

9. (*With*) *my soul have I desired thee in the night; yea* (*with*) *my spirit, within me will I seek thee early: for when thy judgments* (*come*) *to the earth, the inhabitants of the world learn righteousness.* The desire here expressed is not a general desire for the knowledge and favour of God, but a special desire that he would manifest his righteousness by appearing as a judge. This explanation is required by the connection with what goes before and with what follows in this very verse. Gesenius takes *my soul* as a periphrasis for *I.* Maurer supposes this to be in apposition with the pronoun. Ewald and Knobel retain the old construction, which supplies a preposition before נֶפֶשׁ, or regards it as an adverbial accusative or qualifying noun, corresponding to the ablative or instrument of cause in Latin. The night is mentioned, not as a figure for calamity or ignorance, nor as a time peculiarly appropriate to meditation, but for the purpose of expressing the idea, that he feels this wish at all times, by night and by day. This shews that the recent lexicographers are wrong in excluding from the Piel of שׁחר the sense of seeking *in the morning*, seeking *early*, to which exclusion it may also be objected, that the soundest principles of lexicography tend to the union and not to the multiplication of roots. The question whether these are the words of the Prophet, or of each of the people, or of a choir or chorus representing them, proceeds upon the supposition of an artificial structure and a strict adherence to rhetorical propriety, which have no real existence in the writings of the Prophet. The sentiments, which it was his purpose and his duty to express, are sometimes uttered in his own person, sometimes in that of another, and these different forms of speech are interchanged, without regard to the figments of an artificial rhetoric. Some give to כַּאֲשֶׁר its strict sense as a particle of comparison, and understand the clause to mean that men learn how to practise righteousness by imitating God's example. By *judgments*, here as in the foregoing context, we can only understand judicial providences. The doctrine of the verse is, that a view of God's severity is necessary to convince men of his justice. The Septuagint has μάθετε in the imperative, which gives a good sense, but is forbidden by the obvious address to God himself throughout the verse.

10. *Let the wicked be favoured, he does not learn righteousness ; in the land of right he will do wrong, and will not see the exaltation of Jehovah.* The reasoning of the preceding verse is here continued. As it was there said that God's judgments were necessary to teach men righteousness, so it is here said that continued prosperity is insufficient for that purpose. The wicked man will go on to do wickedly, even in the very place where right conduct is peculiarly incumbent. Though the verse is in the form of a general proposition, and as such admits of various applications, there is obvious reference to the Babylonians, who were not only emboldened by impunity to do wrong in the general, but to do it even in the *land of right* or rectitude, the holy land, Jehovah's land, where such transgressions were peculiarly offensive. There are other two explanations of אֶרֶץ נְכֹחוֹת which deserve attention. The first understands the phrase to mean, in the midst of a righteous population, surrounded by examples of good conduct. The other supposes an allusion, not to moral but to physical rectitude or straightness, as a figure for prosperity. This last would make the clause a repetition of the sentiment expressed before it, viz., that favour and in-

dulgence do not teach men righteousness. But neither of these latter explanations agrees so well with the last words of the verse as the one first given, according to which they represent the wrong-doer as not knowing or believing or considering that the land in which he practises his wickedness, belongs to the most High God. J. D. Michaelis explains the closing words to mean that God is too exalted to be seen by them (*den zu erhabenen Gott*).

11. *Jehovah, thy hand is high, they will not see ; (yes) they will see (and be ashamed) thy zeal for thy people ; yea, the fire of thine enemies shall devour them.* The tenses in this verse have been very variously and arbitrarily explained. Some make them all past, others all future, and a few all present. Even the double future (יחזיון and יחזו) is referred to different tenses, past and future, past and present, present and future. They have not seen, but they shall see ; they do not see, but they shall see; they did not see, but they do see. Some make יחזו an optative ; *but may they see !* All these constructions are grammatical, but the very fact that so many are possible, makes it advisable to adhere somewhat rigorously to the proper meaning of the forms. As to רמה, it matters little whether it be rendered as a preterite or present, as the one implies the other ; but as to יחזיון and יהזו, the safest course is to translate them both alike as simple features. The seeming contradiction instantly explains itself, as being a kind of after-thought. *They will not see,* (but yes) *they will see.* There are two ways of connecting קנאת עם with what precedes. The obvious construction found in most of the old versions, makes it the object of the verb immediately before it : " they shall be ashamed of their zeal against (or envy of) the people." This of course supposes קנאת עם to denote the envy of the heathen against Israel, or which is much less probable, the jealousy of Israel with respect to the accession of the Gentiles. But as usage is decidedly in favour of interpreting the phrase to mean the jealousy or zeal of God himself in behalf of his own people, Gesenius and several later writers construe it with יחזו and throw ויבשו into a parenthesis, " they shall see (and be ashamed) the zeal &c.," which is equivalent to saying, " they shall see with shame, &c." Another construction, given independently by Henderson and Knobel, construes the phrase in question, not as the object of a verb preceding, but as the subject of the verb that follows, " zeal for thy people, yea, fire against thine enemies, shall devour them (or may it devour them)." In favour of this construction is the strict agreement of the sense which it affords with many other passages, in which the same divine acts are described as acts of mercy to the righteous, and of wrath to the wicked. (See for example chap. i. 27, and the commentary on it.) It is also recommended by the strong emphatic meaning which it gives to אף. Knobel, moreover, makes צריך the object of the verb תאכל, and regards the suffix to the latter as an idiomatic pleonasm, which is not only arbitrary and extremely harsh (and therefore not required by a few examples where no other solution of the syntax is admissible), but destructive of a beautiful antithesis between God's *zeal for his people* and *fire for his enemies*. Of the two constructions, therefore, Henderson's is much to be preferred. *Fire* does not simply denote war (Gesenius) or sudden death (J. D. Michaelis), but the wrath of God, as a sudden, rapid, irresistible, and utterly destroying agent.

12. *Jehovah, thou wilt give us peace, for even all our works thou hast wrought for us.* This is an expression of strong confidence and hope, founded on what has already been experienced. God certainly would favour them in future, for he had done so already. The translation of the first

verb as a preterite or present, though admissible if necessary, cannot be justified in such a case as this, where the strict translation gives a perfectly good sense. תשפת לנו literally means *thou wilt place to us*, which some understand to mean *appoint* or *ordain for us;* but Gesenius more correctly explains it as the converse of the idiomatic usage of נתן to *give* in the sense of *placing.* Peace is, as often elsewhere, to be taken in the wide sense of prosperity or welfare. גם, though omitted in translation by Gesenius and others, is emphatic, and should be connected, not with the pronoun or the verb, as in the English Version, but as in Hebrew with the phrase *all our works*, as if he had said, *even all our works, i. e.*, all without exception. It is commonly agreed among interpreters, that *our works* here means not *the works done by us* but *the works done for us, i. e.* what we have experienced, or as Calvin expresses it in French, *nos affaires.* The version of the last clause in the text of the English Bible (thou hast wrought all our works *in us*) is connected with an old interpretation of the verse, as directly teaching the doctrine of human dependence and efficacious grace. This translation, however, is equally at variance with the usage of the Hebrew preposition (לנו) and with the connection here. The context, both before and after, has respect, not to spiritual exercises, but to providential dispensations. It is not a little curious that while Cocceius, in his Calvinistic zeal, uses this verse as an argument against the Arminian doctrine of free-will, Calvin himself had long before declared that the words cannot be so applied. " Qui hoc testimonio usi sunt ad evertendum liberum arbitrium, Prophetæ mentem assecuti non sunt. Verum quidem est Deum solum bene agere in nobis, et quicquid recte instituunt homines esse ex illius Spiritu ; sed hic simpliciter docet Propheta omnia bona quibus fruimur ex Dei manu adeptos esse : unde colligit nullum fore beneficentiæ finem donec plena felicitas accedat." This brief extract is at once an illustration of the great Reformer's sound and independent judgment, and of the skill with which he can present the exact and full sense of a passage in a few words.

13. *Jehovah, our God, (other) lords beside thee have ruled us; (but hence-forth) thee, thy name, only will we celebrate.* In this verse again there is great diversity as to the explanation of the tenses. Clericus renders both the verbs as preterites, and understands the verse as saying, that even when the Jews were under foreign oppression, they maintained their allegiance to Jehovah. Ewald gives the same sense, but in reference to the present fidelity of Israel under present oppression. Gesenius, more correctly, distinguishes between the verbs as preterite and present. There is no good ground, however, for departing from the strict sense of the forms as preterite and future, which are faithfully expressed in all the English versions. The usual construction of the last clause understands בך as meaning *through thee, i. e.* through thy favour, by thy help, we are enabled now to praise thy name. But Ewald, Barnes, and Henderson regard the pronoun as in apposition with *thy name*, and the whole clause as describing only the object of their worship, not the means by which they were enabled to render it. The construction of בך is in that case somewhat singular, but may have been the only one by which the double object of the verb could be distinctly expressed without the repetition of the verb itself. As to the *lords* who are mentioned in the first clause, there are two opinions. One is, that they are the Chaldees or Babylonians, under whom the Jews had been in bondage. This is now the current explanation. The other is, that they are the false gods or idols, whom the Jews had served before the exile. Against the former, and in favour of the latter supposition it may be suggested, first, that

the Babylonian bondage did not hinder the Jews from mentioning Jehovah's name or praising him; secondly, that the whole verse looks like a confession of their own fault and a promise of amendment, rather than a reminiscence of their sufferings; and, thirdly, that there seems to be an obvious comparison between the worship of Jehovah as *our God*, with some other worship and some other deity. At the same time let it be observed, that the ideas of religious and political allegiance and apostasy, or of heathen rulers, and of idol gods, were not so carefully distinguished by the ancient Jews as by ourselves, and it is therefore not impossible that both the kinds of servitude referred to may be here included, yet in such a manner that the spiritual one must be considered as the prominent idea, and the only one, if either must be fixed upon to the conclusion of the other. An additional argument, in favour of the reference of this verse to spiritual rulers, is its exact correspondence with the singular fact in Jewish history, that since the Babylonish exile they have never even been suspected of idolatry. That such a circumstance should be adverted to in this commemorative poem, is so natural that its omission would be almost unaccountable.

14. *Dead, they shall not live: ghosts, they shall not rise: therefore thou hast visited and destroyed them, and made all memory to perish with respect to them.* Those whom we lately served are now no more; thou hast destroyed them and consigned them to oblivion, for the very purpose of securing our freedom and devotion to thy service. Most of the recent writers follow Clericus in referring this verse to the Babylonians exclusively. Hitzig, Ewald, and Umbreit apply it to the forefathers of the supposed speakers, who had perished on account of their idolatry. It seems best, however, to refer it to the strange lords of the foregoing verse, *i. e.* the idols themselves, but with some allusion, as in that case, to the idolatrous oppressors of the Jews. The reason for preferring this interpretation to that of Hitzig is, that the latter introduces a new subject which had not been previously mentioned. The first clause may indeed be rendered as a general proposition, *the dead live not,* &c.; but this still leaves the transition an abrupt one, and the allusion to the departed Israelites obscure. The disjunctive accents which accompany מתים and רפאים also show that, according to the Masoretic tradition, these words are not the direct subject of the verb, but in apposition with it. The sense is correctly given in the English Version, *they are dead, they shall not live; they are deceased, they shall not rise.* An attempt, however, has been made above to imitate more closely the concise and compact form of the original. For the meaning of רפאים, *vide supra,* chap. xiv. 9. It is here a poetical equivalent to מתים, and may be variously rendered, shades, shadows, spirits, or the like. The common version (*deceased*) leaves too entirely out of view the figurative character of the expression. *Giants,* on the contrary, is too strong, and could only be employed in this connection in the sense of gigantic shades or shadows. The Targum strangely makes these terms denote the *worshippers* of dead men and giants, *i. e.* probably of heroes. The Septuagint gives a curious turn to the sentence by reading רפאים *physicians* (ἰατροὶ οὐ μὴ ἀναστήσουσι). Gesenius needlessly attaches to לכן the rare and dubious sense *because,* which Ewald regards as a fictitious one, deduced from a superficial view of certain passages, in which the meaning *therefore* seems at first sight inappropriate. The other sense is certainly not to be assumed without necessity. In this case the apparent necessity is done away by simply observing, that *therefore* may be used to introduce, not only the cause, but the design of an action. Though the words cannot mean, thou hast destroyed them *be-*

cause they are dead and powerless, they may naturally mean, thou hast destroyed them *that they might be* dead and powerless. The same two meaning are attached to the English phrase *for this reason*, which may either denote cause or purpose. The meaning of the verse, as connected with the one before it is, that the strange lords who had ruled them should not only cease to do so, but, so far as they were concerned, should cease to exist or be remembered.

15. *Thou hast added to the nation, O Jehovah, thou hast added to the nation; thou hast glorified thyself; thou hast put far off all the ends of the land.* By this deliverance of thy people from the service both of idols and idolaters, thou hast added a great number to the remnant who were left in the Holy Land, so that larger territories will be needed for their occupation; and in doing all this, thou hast made an exhibition of thy power, justice, truth, and goodness. Thus understood, the whole verse is a grateful acknowledgement of what God had done for his suffering people. Some, on the contrary, have understood it as relating wholly to his previous judgments. Thus De Dieu, with his usual ingenuity and love of paradox, confounds the idea of *adding to the nation* with that of *gathering* a person *to his people* or his fathers, a common idiomatic periphrasis for death. This is founded on the etymological affinity of יסף and אסף. To match this in the other clause, he makes קצוי ארץ mean the *extremities* of the land, *i. e.* its *highest extremities* or chief men, whom Nebuchadnezzar carried into exile. A more common explanation of the verse is that which supposes the last clause to describe the exile, and the first the restoration. To remove the ὕστερον πρότερον which thus arises, it becomes necessary to make רחקת a pluperfect, as in the English Version, which moreover supplies a pronoun as the object of the verb, and a preposition before *ends*. A much simpler construction of the last clause is the one now commonly adopted, which supposes no ellipsis, makes קצוי ארץ itself the object of the verb, and identical in meaning with the Latin *fines terræ* in the sense of boundaries, the removing of which farther off denotes of course territorial enlargement. Junius supplies *life* after *added* in the first clause; J. D. Michaelis and others supply *gifts* or *favours*; but the obvious meaning seems to be that God had added to the number of the people, not by an aggregate increase of the whole nation, but by the reunion of its separated parts, in the restoration of the exiles from Babylon. The word גוי, as Knobel well observes, may here denote the remnant left in Judah, to which the analogous term עם is repeatedly applied by Jeremiah. The enlargement of the boundaries may either be explained as a poetical description of the actual increase and expected growth of the nation (chap. xlix. 19), or literally understood as referring to the fact, that after the return from exile the Jews were no longer restricted to their own proper territory, but extended themselves more or less over the whole country. Knobel gives נכבדת the specific meaning, thou hast made thyself great, *i. e.* the king of a great nation; but the wider and more usual sense is much to be preferred. The translation of the verb as a reflexive, rather than a simple passive, greatly adds to the strength of the expression.

16. *Jehovah, in distress they visited thee; they uttered a whisper; thy chastisement was on them.* It was not merely after their deliverance that they turned from idols unto God. Their deliverance itself was owing to their humble prayers. *Visit* here used in the unusual but natural sense of seeking God in supplication. Hitzig and Hendewerk prefer the secondary sense of לחש, *incantation* (Beschwörung); but the primary meaning is not only admissible, but beautifully expressive of submissive humble prayer,

like that of Hannah when *she spake in her heart and only her lips moved, but her voice was not heard*, although, as she said herself, *she poured out her soul before God*, which is the exact sense of צָקוּן in this place. A like expression is applied to prayer in the title of Psalm cii. Barnes explains לַחַשׁ here to mean *a sighing, a calling for help*, as if the two things were identical, whereas the idea of a call or cry is at variance with the figurative import of the language. This is one of the few cases in which the plural of the preterite takes a paragogic nun. Whether it was meant to be intensive, as Henderson supposes, or to affect the sense in any way, may be doubted. Knobel supplies a preposition before מוּסָרְךָ, and says that the Prophet would have written מוּסָרָם, but for the necessity of adding the suffix of the second person, which required that of the third to be separately written with a preposition. It is simpler, however, to supply the substantive verb and take the words as a short independent clause. It is implied, though not expressed, that their prayer was humble and submissive *because* they felt that what they suffered was a chastisement from God. Ewald, who usually makes an advance upon his predecessors, in the way of simple and exact translation, is here misled by his fondness for critical emendation, and proposes to read לָחַשׁ as a verb, and צָקוּן as a noun derived from צוּק to press. (*In*) *distress it was lisped* (or *whispered*) *by them* (לָמוֹ) *Thy chastisement!* The construction thus obtained is as harsh and infelicitous as the correction of the text is arbitrary.

17. *As when a pregnant* (*woman*) *draws near to the birth, she writhes, she cries out in her pangs, so have we been, from thy presence, O Jehovah!* Before we thus cast ourselves upon thy mercy in submissive prayer, we tried to deliver ourselves, but only to the aggravation of our sufferings. The comparison here used is not intended simply to denote extreme pain, as in many other cases, but as the next verse clearly shews, the pain arising from ineffectual efforts to relieve themselves. כְּמוֹ, like the corresponding English *as*, is properly a particle of comparison, but constantly applied to time, as a synonyme of *when*. The full force of the term may be best expressed in this case by combining the two English words. The future is here used to denote a general fact which not only does, but will occur. Hendewerk translates the last verb as a present; but it seems clear that the Prophet is reverting to the state of things before the deliverance which had just been acknowledged. Knobel, in accordance with his general hypothesis as to the date and subject of the prophecy, applies this verse to the condition of the Jews who were left behind in Palestine, but the great majority of writers, much more probably, to that of the exiles. There are three explanations of the phrase מִפָּנֶיךָ. Clericus and Hitzig take it in its strictest sense as meaning *from thy presence*, *i. e.* cast out or removed far from it. Knobel, on the contrary, excludes the proper local sense of the expression and translates it *on account of thee*, *i. e.* because of thine anger. Gesenius and Ewald give the intermediate sense *before thee, in thy presence*. Even in the cases cited by Knobel, the evils experienced are described as coming from the presence of Jehovah. Some of the older writers even give פָּנִים itself the sense of *anger*, which is wholly unnecessary and unauthorised. The only way in which the question can be settled is by the application of the general principle, that where a choice of meaning is presented, that is entitled to the preference which adheres most closely to the strict sense of the terms. On this ground the translation *from thy presence* is to be preferred; but whether with the accessory idea of

removal, alienation, or with that of infliction, is a question not determined
by the phrase itself, but either left uncertain or to be decided by the context.

18. *We were in travail, we were in pain, as it were we brought forth
wind. Deliverances we could not make the land, nor would the inhabitants
of the world fall.* The figure introduced in the preceding verse is here
carried out and applied. Ewald makes כְּמוֹ mean *as if*, but neither this
nor *as it were* is fully justified by usage. Gesenius renders it *when* as in
ver. 17, but this requires a verb to be supplied, *when we brought forth* (it
was) *wind.* The general sense is evident. The next clause admits of
several different constructions. The simplest supplies a preposition before
אָרֶץ, *in* or *for the land.* The one now commonly adopted is, *we could not
make the land safety, i. e.* could not make it safe or save it. The same
writers generally make נעשה the passive participle, in which case it must
agree, either with אָרֶץ which is usually feminine, or with ישועות which is
both feminine and plural. The possibility of such constructions does not
warrant them, much less require them, when as here the obvious one is
perfectly appropriate and in strict agreement with the parallel יפלו. The
objection urged to making נעשה a future is that the people could not save
the country, which is the very thing the future was intended to assert. The
future form of the verb has respect to the period described. As the people
then might have said, *we shall not save the land,* so the same expression is
here put into their mouths retrospectively. The best equivalent in English
is the potential or subjunctive form, *we could not.* Gesenius and the other
recent German writers understand this as a description of the Holy Land
after the return from exile. We cannot save the country, and the inhabitants of the land will not be born, (יפלו) *i. e.* it is still very thinly peopled.
This is far from being an obvious or natural interpretation. The foregoing
context, as we have seen, relates to the period of captivity itself. The
meaning given to נפל, though sustained by analogies in other languages,
derives no countenance from Hebrew usage. Nor is it probable that the
figure of parturition would be here resumed, after it had been dropped in
the preceding member of the sentence. The way in which the metaphors
of this verse have been treated by some commentators furnishes an instance
of the perversion and abuse of archæological illustration. J. D. Michaelis
imagined that he had discovered an allusion to a certain medical phenomenon of very rare occurrence. This suggestion is eagerly adopted by
Gesenius, who, not content with naming it in his text, pursues the subject
with great zest in a note, and appears to have called in the assistance of
his colleague, the celebrated medical professor Sprengel. From one or
the other of these sources the details are copied by several later writers,
one of whom, lest the reader's curiosity should not be sated, says that the
whole may be seen fully described in the books on obstetrics. It is a
curious fact that some, who are often reluctant to recognise New Testament
doctrines in the prophecies, can find there allusions to the most extraordinary medical phenomena. The best comment upon this obstetrical elucidation is contained in Hitzig's caustic observation, that by parity of
reasoning the allusion in chap. xxxiii. 11 is to an actual bringing forth
of straw (eine wirkliche Strohgeburt). Knobel has also pointed out, what
any reader might discover for himself, that *wind* is here used, as in chap.
xli. 29 ; Hosea xii. 2, as a common metaphor for failure, disappointment.
תֵּבֵל is variously explained according to the sense put upon the whole
verse. Those who refer it to the period after the return from exile

regard תבל as equivalent to ארץ. Those who suppose the exile itself to be the time in question, understand by תבל the Babylonian empire as in chap. xiii. 11.

19. *Thy dead shall live, my corpses shall arise; (awake and sing ye that dwell in the dust!) for the dew of herbs is thy dew, and (on) the earth (on) the dead, thou wilt cause it to fall.* This verse is in the strongest contrast with the one before it. To the ineffectual efforts of the people to save themselves, he now opposes their actual deliverance by God. They shall rise because they are *thy dead, i. e.* thy dead people. The construction of נבלתי with יקומון is not a mere grammatical anomaly. The noun and suffix are singular, because the words are those of Israel as a body. The verb is plural, because the corpse of Israel included in reality a multitude of corpses. The explanation of the suffix as a parogogic syllable is contrary to usage, which restricts paragoge to the construct form. Kimchi supplies a preposition (*with my dead body*) which construction is adopted in the English version and in several others, but is now commonly abandoned as incongruous and wholly arbitrary. Neither the Prophet, nor the house of Israel, in whose name he is speaking, could refer to their own body as distinct from the bodies of Jehovah's dead ones. *Awake,* &c. is a joyful apostrophe to the dead, after which the address to Jehovah is resumed. There are two interpretations of אורת, both ancient, and supported by high modern authorities. The first gives the word the usual sense of אור *light;* the other that of *plants,* which it has in 2 Kings. iv. 39. The first is found in the Targum, Vulgate, and Peshito, and is approved by Grotius, Ewald, Umbreit, and Gesenius in his Commentary. The other is given by Kimchi, Clericus, Vitringa, Rosenmüller, Maurer, Hitzig, and Gesenius in his Lexicon. To the former it may be objected, that it leaves the plural form unexplained, that it arbitrarily makes *light* mean *life,* and that it departs from the acknowledged meaning of אורת in the only other place where it occurs. The second interpretation, on the other hand, assumes but one sense of the word, allows the plural form its proper force, and supposes an obvious and natural allusion to the influence of dew upon the growth of plants. In either case the reference to the dew is intended to illustrate the vivifying power of God. Gesenius and Ewald both explain the verbs as optatives and the verse as expressive of a wish that God would raise the dead and thus repeople the now empty country. This construction, though admissible in case of necessity, has nothing to entitle it to preference, when the strict interpretation yields a perfectly good sense. The obvious meaning of the words is an expression of strong confidence and hope, or rather of prophetic foresight, that God *will* raise the dead, that his life-giving influence will be exerted. The use of תַּפִּיל here is certainly obscure. Gesenius, Ewald, and the other late interpreters, suppose it to denote the act of *bearing, bringing forth,* as the Kal in ver. 18 means, according to the same writers, *to be born.* But if it there seems unnatural to suppose a resumption of that figure, it is much more so here, where another figure, that of vegetation, goes before. The mere rhetorical objection to mixed metaphors, as we have seen in other cases, ought to weigh but little where the sense is clear; but in determining a doubtful sense, we are rather to presume that a figure once begun is continued, than that it is suddenly changed for another. An additional objection to this exposition is the incongruity of making the earth *bring forth the dead,* and thus putting the two extremes of life into juxta-

position. To avoid this incongruity, Gesenius and Ewald are obliged to give נפל, both here and in ver. v. 18, not only the precarious sense of *bearing* and of *being born*, but the arbitrary and specific one of *bearing again* and being *born again*. Some of the older writers make תַּפִּיל the second person (which agrees well with the previous address to God) and understand the words to mean *thou wilt cause the giants to fall to the earth*. But the combination of רפאים with מתים in ver. 14, and the repetition of the latter here, decides the meaning of the former, as denoting the deceased, the dead. Retaining the construction of תפיל as a second person, and supposing the allusion to the influence of dew upon the growth of plants to be continued, we may render the words thus : (*upon*) *the earth*, (*upon*) *the dead thou wilt cause it to fall*. As if he had said, thou hast a life-giving influence and thou wilt exert it ; as thy dew makes plants to grow, so shall it make these dead to live. That the ellipsis of the preposition before ארץ and רפאים, although not without analogy, is somewhat harsh, must be admitted, and the only view with which this construction is proposed is, that its difficulties and advantages may be compared with those of the translation given by Gesenius and Ewald, *the earth brings forth the dead*. All these interpretations coincide in applying the verse to a resurrection of the dead, and the question now arises, what resurrection is referred to ? All the answers to this question may be readily reduced to three. The first is, that the Prophet means the general resurrection of the dead, or according to an old rabbinical tradition, the exclusive resurrection of the righteous at the last day. The second is, that he refers to a resurrection of the Jews already dead, not as an actual or possible event, but as a passionate expression of desire that the depopulated land might be replenished with inhabitants. The third is, that he represents the restoration of the exiles and of the theocracy under the figure of a resurrection, as Paul says the restoration of Israel to God's favour will be *life from the dead*. The obvious objection to the first of these opinions is, that a prediction of the final resurrection is as much out of place in this connection as the same expectation seemed to Martha as a source of comfort for the loss of Lazarus. But as our Saviour, when he said to her, *thy brother shall rise again*, designed to console her by the promise of an earlier and special resurrection, so in this case what was needed for the comfort of God's people was something more than the prospect of rising at the day of judgment. The choice therefore lies between the other two hypotheses, that of a mere wish that the dead might literally rise at once, and that of a prediction that they should rise soon but *in a figure* (ἐν παραβολῇ) as Paul says of Isaac's resurrection from the dead (Heb. xi. 19). The objection to the first of these interpretations is, that the optative construction of the verbs, as we have seen already, is not the obvious and natural construction, and ought not to be assumed unless it yields a better sense and one more appropriate in this connection. But so far is this from being the case, that the mere expression of a wish which could not be fulfilled would be a most unnatural conclusion of this national address to God, whereas it could not be more suitably wound up, or in a manner more in keeping with the usage of the prophecies, than by a strong expression of belief, that God would raise his people from the dust of degradation and oppression, where they had long seemed dead though only sleeping. On these grounds the figurative exposition seems decidedly entitled to the preference. Upon this allusion to a resurrection Gesenius fastens as a proof that the prophecy could not have been written until after the doctrine of the resurrection had been borrowed by the Jews from Zoroaster. To this it may be answered, first, that the alleged derivation of the doctrine is a figment, which no authoritative writer on the history of opinion would now venture to maintain ; secondly, that the mention of a figurative resurrection, or the expression of a wish that a literal one would take place, has no more to do with the doctrinal belief of the writer, than any other lively figure or expression of strong feeling ; thirdly, that if a knowledge and belief of the doctrine of a general resurrection is implied in these expressions, the text, instead of being *klassisch* as a proof of later Jewish opinions, is *klassisch* as a proof that the doctrine was known to Isaiah, if not to his contemporaries. If Gesenius, believing this prediction to belong to the period of the exile, is entitled to adduce it as a proof of what opinions were then current, those who believe it to be genuine are equally entitled to adduce it as a proof of what was current in the days of Isaiah. It is easy to affirm that the prophecy is known on other grounds to be of later date ; but it is just as easy to affirm that the alleged grounds are sophistical and inconclusive. Holding this to be the truth, we may safely conclude that the text either proves nothing as to a general resurrection of the dead, or that it proves the belief of such a resurrection to be at least as old as the prophet Isaiah.

20. *Go, my people, enter into thy chambers, and shut thy doors after thee, hide thyself for a little moment, till the wrath be past.* Having wound up the expectations of the people to a full belief of future restoration from their state of civil and religious death, the Prophet by an exquisite transition intimates, that this event is not yet immediately at hand, that this relief from the effects of God's displeasure with his people must be preceded by the experience of the displeasure itself, that it is still a time of indignation, and that till this is elapsed the promise cannot be fulfilled. This painful postponement of the promised resurrection could not be more tenderly or beautifully intimated than in this fine apostrophe. The inferences drawn by certain German writers, as to the date of the composition, can have no effect on those who believe that Isaiah was a *prophet*, not in the sense of a quidnunc or a ballad-singer, but in that of an inspired revealer of futurity. The similar conclusion drawn by Knobel from the form חבי is equally frivolous, it being commonly agreed at present that what are called Aramaean forms may just as well be archaisms as neologisms, since they may have arisen, not from later intercourse with neighbouring nations, but from an original identity of language. Gesenius and others understand this verse as an exhortation to the Jews in Babylon to keep out of harm's way during the storming of the city. A more prosaic close of a poetical context could not be imagined. Those who refer ver. 19 to the general resurrection understand the verse before us as an intimation that they must rest in the grave until the time is come. Such an allusion is of course admissible on the supposition of a figurative resurrection. It is more natural, however, to suppose that the people of God are here addressed as such, and warned to hide themselves until God's indignation *against them* is past. On this specific usage of the word זעם, *vide supra*, chap. x. 5. On the idiomatic usage of the verbs קך and בא, *vide supra*, chap. xxii. 15. The textual variation דלתיך and דלתך is of no exegetical importance. בעדך strictly means *without thee* or *outside of thee*, implying that the person is *shut in.* It first occurs in Gen. vii. 16, where it is said that God shut Noah in the ark. Knobel explains כמעט רגע as meaning *like the smallness of a moment.* The כ is a particle of time, equivalent, or nearly so, to our *about.* The

English Version (*as it were*) is therefore incorrect. The period of suffering is described as very small in comparison with what had gone before and what should follow it, as Paul says (Rom. viii. 18), that *the sufferings of this present time are not worthy to be compared with the glory which shall be revealed in us.*

21. *For behold, Jehovah (is) coming out of his place, to visit the iniquity of the inhabitant of the earth upon him, and the earth shall disclose her blood, and shall no more cover her slain.* This is a reason both for expecting ultimate deliverance and for patiently awaiting it. The reason is that God has a work of chastisement to finish, first upon his own people, and then upon their enemies. During the former process, let the faithful hide themselves until the wrath be past. When the other begins, let them lift up their heads, for their redemption draweth nigh. This large interpretation of the verse is altogether natural and more satisfactory than those which restrict it either to the judgments upon Israel or to those upon Babylon. On the latter, the eye of the Prophet of course chiefly rests, especially at last, so that the closing words may be applied almost exclusively to the retribution which awaited the Chaldean for the slaughter of God's people. On the idiomatic usage of the plural דמים where the reference is to murder, *vide supra*, chap. i. 15. Rosenmüller and Hitzig understand the last clause as a prediction that the dead should actually come out of the graves, Knobel as a poetical anticipation of the same event. But it seems far more natural to understand the clause, with Gesenius and Umbreit, as a simple variation of the one before it. The blood, which the earth had long since drunk in, should as it were be vomited up, and the bodies of the murdered, which had long been buried should be now disclosed to view. It agrees best with the wider meaning put upon this verse, and is at the same time more poetical to give ארץ in both clauses its generic sense of *earth*, rather than the specific one of *land*. Instead of the simple version *slain*, Gesenius employs with good effect the strong expression *murdered* (die Gemordeten), as one of the French versions had done long before (ses massacrés). Without laying undue stress on the mere rhetorical aspect of the sacred writings, it may safely be affirmed that at the bar of the most elevated criticism, the concluding verses of the chapter now before us would at once be adjudged to possess intrinsic qualities of beauty and sublimity (apart from the accident of rhythm and parallelism, in which some writers find the essence of all poetry) sufficient to brand with the stigma of absurdity the judgment that can set the passage down as the work of a deteriorated age or an inferior writer.

Chapter 27

THIS chapter is an amplification of the last verse of the one preceding, and contains a fuller statement both of Israel's chastisements and of Jehovah's judgments on his enemies. The destruction of the latter is foretold as the slaughter of a huge sea-monster, and contrasted with God's care of his own people even when afflicting them, vers. 1–5. Hereafter Israel shall flourish, and even in the meantime his sufferings are far less than those of his oppressors, vers. 6, 7. The former is visited in moderation, for a time, and with the happiest effect, vers. 8, 9. The latter is finally and totally destroyed, vers. 10, 11. This shall be followed by the restoration of the scattered Jews, vers. 12, 13.

1. *In that day shall Jehovah visit, with his sword, the hard, the great, the strong (sword), upon Leviathan the swift (or flying) serpent, and upon Leviathan the coiled (or crooked) serpent, and shall slay the dragon which (is) in the sea.* It is universally agreed that this is a prediction of the downfall of some great oppressive power, but whether that of a single nation or of several, has been much disputed. Clericus supposes two, Vitringa and many others three, to be distinctly mentioned. In favour of supposing a plurality of subjects may be urged the distinct enumeration and description of the monsters to be slain. But the same form of expression occurs in many other places where there can be no doubt that a single subject is intended. To the hypothesis of three distinct powers it may be objected, that two of them would scarcely have been called leviathan. To the general hypothesis of more than one, it may be objected that by parity of reasoning three swords are meant, viz., a hard one, a great one, and a strong one. But even if three powers be intended, it is wholly impossible to identify them, as may be inferred from the endless variety of combinations, which have been suggested : Egypt, Assyria, and Babylonia ; Egypt, Babylonia, and Tyre ; Assyria, Babylonia, and Rome ; Babylonia, Media, Persia, &c., &c. Gill thinks the three meant are the devil, the beast, and the false prophet ; Cocceius, the emperor, the pope, and the devil. What is common to all the hypotheses is, that the verse describes a power or powers hostile and oppressive to the people of God. The most probable opinion, therefore, is, that this was what the words were intended to convey. Or if a more specific reference must be assumed, it is worthy of remark that nearly all the hypotheses, which apply the words to two or more of the great powers of the ancient world, make Babylonia one of them. From this induction we may safely conclude, that the leviathan and dragon of this verse are descriptive of a great oppressive power, with particular allusion to the Babylonian empire, a conclusion perfectly consistent with the previous allusions to the fall of Babylon and the restoration of the Jews from exile. Assuming this to be the general meaning of the verse, that of its mere details becomes either easy or comparatively unimportant. The word *leviathan*, which, from its etymology, appears to mean *contorted*, *coiled*, is sometimes used to denote particular species (*e.g.* the crocodile), and sometimes as a generic term for huge aquatic animals, or the larger kinds of serpents, in which sense the corresponding term תַּנִּין is also used. They both appear to be employed in this case to express the indefinite idea of a formidable monster, which is in fact the sense now commonly attached to the word *dragon*. The second epithet עֲקַלָּתוֹן means *tortuous*, either with respect to the motion of the serpent, or to its appearance when at rest. Bochart regarded the 'Εγκέλαδος of the Greek mythology as a corruption of this Hebrew word. The other epithet בָּרִחַ has been variously explained. Some of the ancients confound it with בְּרִיחַ, *a bar*, and supposes the serpent to be so described either in reference to its length, or stiffness, or straightness, or strength, or its penetrating power, or the configuration of its head. J. D. Michaelis gives it the sense of *northern*, and supposes the three objects here described to be the three constellations which exhibit the appearance and bear the name of *serpents* or *dragons*. This explanation, founded on Job xxiii. 16, does not materially change the meaning of the verse, since the constellations are supposed to be referred to, as connected in some way with the fortunes of great states and empires. The allusion, however, is so far-fetched and pedantic, that, although it suits the taste of Michaelis and Hitzig, who delight in recondite interpretations, it will scarcely satisfy the

mind of any ordinary reader. The only explanation of בְּרִחַ which is fully
justified by Hebrew usage is that of *fugitive* or *fleeing*, which may either be
a poetical equivalent to *fleet*, or descriptive of the monster as a *flying* serpent.
Hitzig objects to the supposition of a single monster, on the ground that
these two epithets, *flying* and *coiled*, are incompatible, as if the same serpent
could not be described both in motion and at rest, not to mention that the
second term, as Umbreit suggests, may itself be descriptive of motion. The
omission of any descriptive epithet with תַּנִּין makes it probable at least that
it is not a new item in the catalogue. There is no need of explaining יָם to
mean Babylonia, as in chap. xxi. 1 since the expression relates to the type,
not to the antitype, and must be joined with תַּנִּין to express the complex
idea of a *sea-serpent*. For the meaning of the phrase to *visit upon*, vide
supra, chap. xiii. 11. The sword is a common emblem for the instruments
of the divine vengeance. The explanation of קָשָׁה as meaning *heavy* is not
justified by usage : *severe* or *dreadful* does not suit the context, as the other
two epithets denote physical qualities of a literal sword. The word no
doubt means *hard-edged*, or, as Lowth expresses it, *well-tempered*.

2. On the explanation of this verse depends that of a large part of the
chapter. The two points upon which all turns, are the meaning of עֲנוּ and the
reference of the suffix in לָהּ. The modern writers solve the latter by supposing כֶּרֶם to be feminine in this one place, and when expressions afterwards
occur which are inapplicable to a vineyard, regard them as inaccuracies
or perhaps as proofs of an uncultivated taste, whereas they only prove
that the assumed construction is a false one. The only supposition which
will meet the difficulties, both of the syntax and the exegesis, is the one
adopted by most of the older writers, to wit, that לָהּ refers, not directly to
כֶּרֶם, but to Jerusalem or the daughter of Zion, *i. e.* to the Church or people
of God considered as his spouse (chap. i. 21). This reference to a subject
not expressly mentioned might be looked upon as arbitrary, but for the fact
that the assumption of it is attended with fewer difficulties than the construction which it supersedes, as will be seen below. As to the other word,
tradition and authority are almost unanimous in giving it the sense of *sing*.
Assuming that the primary meaning of the verb is to *answer*, and that the
derivative strictly denotes responsive singing, Lowth, Dathe, Schnurrer, and
others, have converted the whole context to the end of ver. 5, into a dialogue
between Jehovah and his vineyard. This fantastic arrangement of the text
has been rejected by most later writers as artificial, complex, and at variance
with the genius and usage of Hebrew composition, Lowth's eloquent
plea to the contrary notwithstanding. But the same interpreters, who have
relieved the passage from this factitious burden and embarrassment, continue
for the most part to regard what follows as a *song* though not a dramatic
dialogue, because the people are commanded in ver. 2 to sing, and the song of
course must follow. To this exposition, which is really a relic of the old
dramatic one, there are several objections. In the first place, no one has
been able to determine with precision where the *song* concludes, some
choosing one place for its termination, some another. This would of course
prove nothing in a clear case, but in a case like this it raises a presumption
at least that a song, of which the end cannot be found, has no beginning.
But in the next place, it is easy to see why the end cannot be easily defined,
to wit, because there is nothing in the next three, four, or five verses to distinguish them as being any more a *song* than what precedes and follows,
whether with respect to imagery, rhythm, or diction. In the third place,
the presumption thus created and confirmed is corroborated further by the

obvious incongruity of making the song, which the people are supposed to sing, begin with *I Jehovah keep it*, &c. It is in vain that Grotius, with his usual ingenuity, explains עַנּוּ as meaning " sing in the name or person of Jehovah," and that other writers actually introduce *thus saith the Lord* at the beginning of the song. This is only admitting indirectly that the supposition of a song is wholly arbitrary in a case so doubtful, whatever it might be if the mention of the song were more explicit. For in the fourth place, there is this striking difference between the case before us and those which are supposed to be analogous (*e. g.* chaps. v. 1, xxvi. 1), that in these the verb שִׁיר and its derivative noun of the same form are employed, whereas here the verb is different, and the noun *song* does not appear at all. Under these circumstances it would seem to be sufficient to take עַנּוּ as a general exhortation to sing, without supposing that the words of the song actually follow, which is surely not a necessary supposition. But in the fifth place, out of fifty-six cases in which the *piel* of עָנָה occurs, there are only three in which the sense of *singing* is conceivable, and of these three, one (Ps. lxxxviii. 1) is the enigmatical title of a Psalm, another (Exod. xxxii. 18) is so dubious that the one sense is almost as appropriate as the other, and the third is that before us. It is true the concordances and lexicons assume two different roots, but this is merely to accommodate the difficulties of these three texts, and the multiplication of roots is now universally regarded as at best a necessary evil. On such grounds the assumption of the meaning *sing* could hardly be justified, even if it were far more appropriate to the context than the common one. But in the last place, while the supposition of a song, as we have seen, embarrasses the exposition, the usual meaning of the verb עָנָּה is perfectly appropriate. This meaning is to *afflict*, and especially to afflict in an humbling and degrading manner. This may seem to be utterly at variance with the context as it is commonly explained ; but the common explanation rests on the supposititious meaning of the verb, and cannot therefore be alleged in favour of that meaning. On the usual hypothesis, the verse exhorts the people to sing to the vineyard or the Church ; on the one now proposed it challenges her enemies to do their worst, declaring that God still protects her. This explanation of the verse agrees well with the distinct allusions to the punishment of Israel in vers. 4, 7, 8, 9, which would be comparatively out of place in a song of triumph or gratulation. Against this explanation of עַנּוּ, and of the whole verse, lies the undivided weight of tradition and authority ; so far as I can trace the exposition of the passage, the only writer who adopts the sense *afflict* being Gousset (or Gussetius) in his Comment. Ebr., as cited by Gill. So unanimous a judgment might be looked upon as perfectly decisive of the question but for two considerations ; first, that the proposed interpretation removes a variety of difficulties, not by forsaking usage but by returning to it ; and secondly, that none of the interpreters consulted seem to have adverted to the facts already stated, with respect to the usage of עָנָּה. But besides the objection from tradition and authority, another may be urged of a grammatical nature, viz. the unusual connection of the verb with its object, not directly, but by means of the pre-position לְ. To this it can only be replied, in the first place, that the choice presented is a choice of difficulties, and that those attending the construction now in question seem to be less than those attending any other ; in the next place, that although this verb does not elsewhere take the preposition לְ after it, there are many cases in which other active verbs are separated from their objects by it, the verb then denoting the mere action, and the לְ pointing out the object *as to* which, or *with respect to* which, it is performed ; and in the last place, that the ל may have been rendered necessary here because the nouns before the verb are also in some sense its objects. The latest German writers, it is true, construe כֶּרֶם חֶמֶר as an absolute nominative (*as to the vineyard of wine*), or as the subject of a verb understood (*there shall be a vineyard of wine*), but these are mere expedients to explain the לָהּ, and must of course give way to any simpler method of accomplishing that purpose. As the result of this investigation, we may now translate the verse as follows : *In that day, as a vineyard of wine, afflict her*, or *in that day afflict for her the vineyard of wine*. It is then a defiance or permission of the enemies of the Church to afflict her, with an intimation that in carrying out this idea, the expressions will be borrowed from the figure of a vineyard, as in chap. v. 1–6. חֶמֶר strictly denotes *fermentation*, then fermented liquor, and is used as a poetical equivalent to יַיִן. It has been objected that this idea is involved in that of a vineyard, but such apparent pleonasms are common in all languages, as when we speak of a *well of water* or a *coal of fire*. Besides, כרם seems to have originally had a latitude of meaning not unlike that of *orchard* in English, and we actually read of a כֶּרֶם זַיִת (not a vineyard but an olive-yard), Josh. xv. 5. חֶמֶר may therefore have been added to complete the phrase, or to preclude all doubt as to the meaning, either of which suppositions renders it superfluous to borrow the sense *red wine* from the Arabic, as Kimchi does, and to assume that the Hebrews set a special value upon this sort. Much less is it necessary to amend the text by reading כרם חמד, *pleasant* or *beloved vineyard*. The analogous expression כרמי חמד, Amos v. 11, only makes a change in this place more improbable, not to mention the endless licence of conjecture, which would be introduced into the criticism of the text, by adopting the principle that phrases, which partially resemble one another, must be made to do so altogether. As a closing suggestion, not at all necessary to the exposition, but tending to explain in some degree the form of the original, it may here be added, that the Masoretic interpunction may have been intended to suggest an interval of time between the clauses, as if he had said, *in that day* (shall this come to pass, but in the meantime) *afflict her*, &c.

3. *I Jehovah* (am) *keeping her ; every moment I will water her ; lest any hurt her, night and day will I keep her.* That is, in spite of the afflictions which befall her I will still preserve her from destruction. The antecedent of the pronouns is the same as in ver. 2, viz. the Church or nation considered as a vineyard. לִרְגָעִים literally means *at moments* or *as to moments*, but its sense is determined by the analogous לִבְּקָרִים, *every morning*. Kimchi takes עָלֶיהָ as a noun, in which he is followed by some later writers, who explain the clause to mean, *lest one hurt a leaf of her*, or *lest a leaf of her be wanting*. But the want of any usage to justify such an explanation of יִפְקֹד, and the construction of the same verb in ver. 1 with the preposition עַל, leave no doubt that the usual explanation is the true one. To *visit upon* has here its common meaning of *inflicting evil upon*, but without any special reference to crime or punishment. As the expression is a relative one, it must here be understood, according to the context, as denoting at least excessive injury.

4. Of all the senses put upon this difficult verse, there are only two which can be looked upon as natural or probable. The first may be paraphrased as follows : It is not because I am cruel or revengeful that I thus afflict my people, but because she is a vineyard overrun with thorns or

briers, on account of which I must pass through her and consume her
(*i. e.* burn them out of her). The other is this : I am no longer angry with my
people ; O that their enemies (as thorns and briers) would array themselves against me, that I might rush upon them and consume them. This
last is preferred by most of the later writers. The objection that *no longer*
has to be supplied is of little weight. A more important one is that the
feminine suffix is referred to the masculine nouns שָׁמִיר and שָׁיִת. To this
it may be answered, first, that the feminine in Hebrew often corresponds
to the Greek and Latin neuter ; and secondly, that a free use of the feminine, where the masculine might have been expected, is characteristic of
this passage. See particularly ver. 11 below, to which some would add the
application of the feminine pronoun throughout the passage to the masculine noun כֶּרֶם. This grammatical peculiarity, under other circumstances,
would no doubt have been alleged as the mark of a different writer. But
if the author of chaps. xxiv.–xxvii. can use expressions in chap. xxvii.
which he does not use in the others, why may not Isaiah, as the author of
the whole book, exhibit similar peculiarities in different parts of a collection so extended ? It is important that the reader should take every
opportunity to mark the arbitrary nature of the proofs, by which the genuineness of the prophecies has been assailed, and the strange conclusions to
which they would lead, if applied with even-handed justice. The objection
to the first interpretation of the verse is, that it puts a forced construction on
the words חמה אין לי, and explains מי יתנני in a manner not consistent with
the usage of the phrase. Lowth, and the others who suppose a dramatic
structure, are obliged to read חֵמָה with the Seventy, and to make this verse
a complaint of the vineyard that it has no wall, and an expression of its
wish that it had a thorn-hedge, to which God replies that he would still
pass through it. Schnurrer, however, makes even the last clause the
words of the vineyard, by arbitrarily supplying *when they say, i. e.* when my
enemy says, I will march against it, &c.

5. *Or let him lay hold of my strength and make peace with me ; peace let
him make with me.* The verbs are properly indefinite (let one take hold,
&c.), but referring to the enemy described in the preceding verse as thorns
and briers. מָעוֹז commonly denotes a strong place or fortress, and is here
understood by most interpreters to signify a refuge or asylum, with allusion
to the practice of laying hold upon the altar. Vitringa even goes so far as
to suppose that the horns of the altar are themselves so called because the
strength of certain animals is in their horns. Lowth gives the word the
sense of strength afforded or *protection.* The general meaning is the same
in either case, viz. that the alternative presented to the enemy is that of
destruction or submission. The abbreviated future is employed as usual
to express a proposition. By varying the translation of the futures, the
sentence may be made more pointed ; let him make peace (or if he will
make peace), he shall make peace. But there is no sufficient reason for the
variation, and the imperative meaning of יעשה seems to be determined by
that of יחזק. Of the various senses ascribed to אֹ (such as *unless, oh that
if*, &c.), the only one justified by usage is the disjunctive sense of *or.*
Lowth's dramatic arrangement of the text assigns the first clause to
Jehovah and the second to the vineyard. *J. Ah ! let her rather take hold
of my protection. V. Let him make peace with me ! Peace let him make
with me.* If the thorns and briers of ver. 4 be referred to the internal condition of the Church, this may be understood as having reference to the
Church itself, which is then called upon to make its peace with God as the

only means of escaping further punishment. Gesenius speaks of the repetition and inversion in the last clause as a very imperfect kind of parallelism extremely common in the Zabian books!

6. (*In*) *coming* (*days*) *shall Jacob take root, Israel shall bud and blossom, and they shall fill the face of the earth with fruit.* The construction of the first clause in the English Bible (*them that come of Jacob shall he cause to take root*) is forbidden by the collocation of the words, and by the usage of the verb, which always means to *take root.* The same remark applies to another construction (*them that come to Jacob*), which applies the words to the conversion of the Gentiles. If there were any sufficient reason for departing from the Masoretic interpunction, the sentence might be thus arranged with good effect: *they that come* (*i. e.* the next generation) *shall take root; Jacob shall bud; Israel shall blossom,* &c. It is best, however, to retain the usual construction indicated by the accents. מְלְאוּ may possibly agree with יִשְׂרָאֵל as a collective; but as the other verbs are singular, the plural form of this appears to imply a reference to both names, though belonging to one person. Or as מָלֵא is both an active and a neuter verb, it may be construed with the plural noun פְּנֵי, *the face of the world shall be filled with fruit.* תֵּבֵל does not mean the land of Israel, but the world, the whole expression being strongly metaphorical.

7. *Like the smiting of his smiter did he smite him, or like the slaying of his slain was he slain?* Having declared in the preceding verse that Israel should hereafter flourish, he now adds that even in the meantime he should suffer vastly less than his oppressors. Negation, as in many other cases, is expressed by interrogation. Did the Lord smite Israel as he smote his smiters or slay him as his murderers were slain? This is now commonly agreed to be the meaning, although some of the older writers understand the verse as asking, whether God smote Israel as his oppressors smote him, which would yield a good sense, but one less suited to the context. To make the parallelism perfect, הֲרֻגָיו (his slain) should be הֹרְגָיו (his slayers); but this, so far from being a defect, is a beauty, since Israel could not have been said to be slain without destroying the force of the comparison. The suffix in הֲרֻגָיו is to be referred to the oppressors, or the enemy.

8. *In measure, by sending her away, thou dost contend with her. He removes* (her) *by his hard wind in the day of the east wind.* The negation implied in the preceding verse is here expressed more distinctly. The Prophet now proceeds to shew that Israel was not dealt with like his enemies, by first describing what the former suffered, then what the latter. Israel was punished moderately, and for a time, by being removed out of his place, as if by a transient storm or blast of wind. Of the numberless senses put upon סַאסְּאָה, none is so good in itself, or so well suited to the context as the one handed down by tradition, which explains it as a reduplicated form of סְאָה, strictly denoting a particular dry measure, but here used to express the general idea of measure, *i. e.* moderation. The meaning *measure for measure, i. e.* in strict justice, is preferred by some, but this would either do away with the comparison of Israel and his enemies, or imply that the latter suffered more than they deserved. The feminine suffixes must be referred to the Church or nation as a wife, which agrees well with the verb שלח, used in the law to denote repudiation or divorce. The same verb is also used to signify the sending down of judgments upon men, which sense some prefer in this case, and refer the suffix both in this word and the next to the stroke or punishment. *In sending*

it upon them thou dost strive with it, or try to mitigate it. But the other explanation is more natural, and has the advantage of explicitly intimating the precise form of the punishment endured. The change of person in the last clause is abrupt, but of too frequent occurrence to excite surprise. הָגָה is interpreted by Kimchi as synonymous with הֵסִיר, to remove or take away. Its object is to be supplied from the first clause ; its subject is *Jehovah*. The east wind is mentioned as the most tempestuous in Palestine. The *day* of the east wind is supposed by some to denote the season of the year when it prevails ; but it is rather used to intimate the temporary nature of the chastisement, as if he had said, one day when the east wind chanced to blow. The first רוּחַ is by some translated *spirit*, and supposed to be expressive of the divine displeasure ; but it is not probable that the word would be so soon used in a different sense, and the very repetition adds to the force and beauty of the sentence, *a strong wind in the day of the east wind.* תריב might be taken as a future proper ; but the use of the preterite in the next clause seems to shew that both were meant to be descriptive presents.

9. *Therefore* (because his chastisement was temporary and remedial in design) *by this* (affliction) *shall Jacob's iniquity be expiated (i. e.* purged away), *and this is all* (its) *fruit* (or intended effect) *to take away his sin,* (as will appear) *in his placing all the stones of the* (idolatrous) *altar like limestones dashed in pieces* (so that) *groves and solar images* (or images of Ashtoreth and Baal) *shall arise no more.* The contrast between Israel and Babylon is still continued. Having said that the affliction of the former was but moderate and temporary, he now adds that it was meant to produce a most beneficent effect, to wit, the purgation of the people from the foul stain of idolatry. יְכֻפַּר, though it strictly means *shall be atoned for*, is here metonymically used to denote the effect and not the cause, purification and not expiation. In the very same way it is applied to the cleansing of inanimate objects. There is no need of rendering לָכֵן either *but* or *because*, as the strict and usual meaning, though less obvious, is perfectly appropriate. As the punishment was moderate and temporary, it was *therefore* not destructive but remedial. Some understand by *this*, the act described in the last clause, viz., that of destroying the idolatrous altar. But the preference is always due in such constructions to an antecedent literally going before, *i. e.* already mentioned. Besides, the destruction of the idols could not be the cause of the purification which produced it, unless we take יכפר in the strict sense of *atonement*, which would be incongruous, and inconsistent with the teachings of Scripture elsewhere, not to mention that in that case the moral effect of the captivity is not described at all. The sense required by the connection is, not that the breaking of the altars, as a spontaneous act, atoned for Israel's previous idolatry, but that the exile cured them of that vice, and thereby led to the breaking of the altars. The construction, *this is all the fruit of the removal of his sin,* affords an incongruous and inappropriate sense, viz., that the only effect of this great revolution was the breaking of the idol altars. The true construction is the one pointed out by the disjunctive accent under פְּרִי, which marks it as the subject of the proposition of which הָסִר is the predicate. Some refer the suffix in בְּשׂוּמוֹ to Jehovah, or the enemy, and the whole clause to his demolition of the altar at the conquest of Jerusalem. But besides the arbitrary change of subject, this would seem to refer the moral improvement of the exiles, not to their affliction but to the destruction of their idols at Jerusalem, which, even if consistent with the fact, would be irrele-

vant in this connection, where the Prophet is shewing the beneficent effects of the removal of the people. That the altar is not the altar of Jehovah, is apparent from the mention of the idol in the last clause. (For the meaning of חַמָּנִים and אֲשֵׁרִים, *vide supra*, chap. xvii. 8.) Cocceius seems to understand the verse as a prediction that the Jews should no longer pay a superstitious regard to the temple at Jerusalem. By אַבְנֵי־גִר we may either understand some kind of stone commonly used in building, or the fragments of stone and mortar scattered by the demolition of an altar. לֹא יָקֻמוּ may either mean *shall not rise again*, or *shall stand no more*, both implying their complete destruction. The prophetic description which this verse involves was fully and gloriously verified in history.

10. *For a fenced* (or *fortified*) *city shall be desolate, a dwelling broken up and forsaken like the wilderness. There shall the calf feed, and there shall it lie and consume her branches.* Here begins the other part of the comparison. While Israel is chastised in measure and with the happiest effect, his oppressors are given up to final desolation. This explanation of the verse, as referring to Babylon, is strongly recommended by the fact, that the comparison otherwise remains unfinished, only one side of it having been presented. Apart from this consideration, there are certainly strong reasons for supposing the city meant to be Jerusalem itself. One of these reasons is, that the figure of a vineyard seems to be still present to the writer's mind, at the close of this verse and throughout the next, although the terms used admit of a natural application to the figure of a tree. Another reason is, that the desolation here described is not so total as that threatened against Babylon in chap. xiii. 19–22, where, instead of saying it shall be a pasture, it is said expressly that it shall not even be frequented by flocks or herds. But these two places may have reference to different degrees of desolation. In favour of the reference to Babylon may be alleged the natural consecution of the twelfth verse upon that hypothesis. On the whole, the question may be looked upon as doubtful, but as not materially affecting the interpretation of the chapter, since either of the two events supposed to be foretold would be appropriate in this connection. מְשֻׁלָּח properly means *sent away*, but seems to be applied in chap. xvi. 1 to a bird's nest, the occupants of which are scattered. The whole phrase here may suggest the idea of a family or household which is broken up and its residence forsaken. סְעִפֶיהָ is by some understood to mean *its heights* or *hills;* but the more usual sense of *branches* is entirely appropriate. This may be understood of the vegetation springing up among ruins; but it seems best to refer it to the image of a tree, which is distinctly presented in the following verse. According to Vitringa, *the calf* means pious men who grow in spiritual strength, to which interpretation we may apply the words of the same excellent writer, in commenting upon Jerome's notion, that the devil in ver. 1 is called a *bar* because he *imprisons* many souls. Saepe mihi mirari contingit, homines ejusmodi cogitationes aut loquendi formas imputare Spiritui Sancto, quas sibi vir sapiens imputare nollet.

11. *In the withering of its boughs* (or *when its boughs are withered*) *they shall be broken off, women coming and burning them; because it is not a people of understanding, therefore its Creator shall not pity it, and its Maker shall not have mercy on it.* The destruction of Babylon is still described, but under the figure of a tree, whose branches are withered and cast into the fire. Women are mentioned, not in allusion to the weakness of the instruments by which Babylon was to be destroyed, but because the gathering of firewood in the East is the work of women and children. מְאִירוֹת is not

simply *setting on fire*, but *making a fire of*, or *burning up*. The construction of this last clause bears a strong resemblance to the absolute genitive in Greek, and ablative in Latin. The last clause contains a double instance of litotes or meiosis. According to the usage of the Scriptures, *not wise* here means foolish in the strongest sense, and God's *not pitying* and not having mercy is equivalent to his being very wroth and taking vengeance. קְצִיר, which usually means a harvest, in a few places seems to have the sense of a bough, or of boughs collectively. The feminine pronouns in the first clause must refer to עִיר or בָּבֶל understood; the masculine pronouns of the last clause refer of course to עָם.

12. *And it shall be in that day, that Jehovah shall beat off* (or gather in his fruit) *from the channel of the river to the stream of Egypt, and ye shall be gathered one by one* (or *one to another*) *O ye children of Israel.* To the downfall of Babylon he now adds, as in chap. xi. 1, its most important consequence, viz., the restoration of the Jews. חָבַט is to beat fruit (and particularly olives) from the tree. (*Vide supra*, chap. xvii. 6.) Henderson here translates יַבְחֹט, *shall have an olive harvest.* The idea meant to be conveyed is that of a careful and complete ingathering. נַחַל מִצְרַיִם is explained by some of the older writers as denoting the great valley of the Nile; by others, the Nile itself; but is now commonly agreed to signify the Wady el-Arish, anciently called *Rhinocorura*, which name is given to it here by the Septuagint. *The river* is as usual the Euphrates. The simple meaning of the whole expression is, *from Assyria to Egypt*, both which are expressly mentioned in the next verse. אַחַד is properly the construct form, but occurs in several places as the absolute. One of these places is Zech. xi. 7, from which it cannot be inferred, however, that this use of the form betrays a later age, for it occurs not only in 2 Sam. xvii. 22, but in Gen. xlviii. 22. Gesenius puts upon this verse the forced construction, that the whole land, as possessed of old by David and Solomon, should be repeopled as abundantly and suddenly as if men fell from the trees like olives. Having given this gratuitous perversion of a natural and simple metaphor, he then apologises for it as *offensive to our taste* (für unseren Geshmack anstössig), no unfair sample of the way in which the sacred writers are sometimes made to suffer for the erroneous judgment and bad taste of their interpreters. The later writers are almost unanimous in setting this construction of the words aside and giving them their true sense, which is not only the obvious one, but absolutely required by the phrase לְאַחַד אֶחָד, which cannot mean the sudden streaming in of a great multitude, but must denote the thorough and complete ingathering of what might otherwise be lost or left behind. The precise sense of this Hebrew phrase is not well expressed by the English *one by one*, which seems to represent the process as a gradual one. It rather denotes *one to one, i. e.* in our idiom, *one to another*, all together, or without exception. From what has been already said it will be seen, that the boundaries named are not intended to define the territory which should be occupied by those returning, but the regions whence they should return, which explanation is confirmed, moreover, by the explicit terms of the next verse.

13. *And it shall be* (or *come to pass*) *in that day*, (*that*) *a great trumpet shall be blown, and they shall come that were lost* (or *wandering*) *in the land of Assyria, and those cast out* (or *exiled*) *in the land of Egypt, and shall bow down to Jehovah, in the holy mountain, in Jerusalem.* The same event is here described as in the verse preceding, but with a change of figure. What is there represented as a gathering of olives by beating the tree, is

now represented as a gathering of men by the blast of a trumpet, which here takes the place of a signal-pole or flag in chap. xi. 12. This variety of forms, in which the same idea is expressed, clearly shows the whole description to be figurative. Assyria and Egypt may be either put for foreign countries generally, or with particular allusion to the actual emigration and dispersion of the Jews in these two regions. Assyria may here be used as a comprehensive term, in order to include both the Assyrian and Babylonian deportations. For although the ten tribes never were restored, individual members of them found their way back with the Jews from Babylon. On the whole, however, it is probable that Egypt and Assyria are here named, just as Babylonia and the islands of the sea might have been named instead of them, and just as all these names and others are connected elsewhere, to denote the various lands where Jews were scattered. The emigration of the people, especially after Nebuchadnezzar's conquests, was of course not confined to their actual deportation by the enemy, nor was the restoration merely that of such as had been thus carried captive, but of all who, in consequence of that catastrophe or any other, had been transferred to foreign parts by exile, flight, or voluntary expatriation. The application of this verse to a future restoration of the Jews can neither be established nor disproved. If such a restoration can be otherwise shewn to be a subject of prophecy, this passage may be naturally understood at least as comprehending it. But in itself considered, it appears to contain nothing which may not be naturally applied to events long past, or which has not found in those events an adequate fulfilment. יִתָּקַע is an impersonal verb, *it shall be blown on the trumpet.* According to Gesenius this verb denotes a single blast, as opposed to a continuous winding of the trumpet. He finds no difficulty in reconciling his hypothesis, as to the date of the prediction, with the mention of Assyria, on the ground that Assyria still formed a part of the Babylonian empire, that the name was used with latitude not only by the classical but the sacred writers, that the Prophet perhaps designedly avoided to name Babylon expressly, and that this verse *perhaps* was partly taken from an older composition belonging to the times of the Assyrian ascendancy. How much hypotheses, as plausible as these, are allowed by Gesenius himself to weigh, in behalf of the genuineness of the prophecies, we have already had occasion to observe, and shall yet have occasion to observe hereafter.

Chapter 28

SAMARIA, the crown of Ephraim, shall be cast down by a sudden and impetuous invasion, as a just judgment upon sensual and impious Israel, vers. 1–4. To the remnant of Israel, Jehovah will himself be a crown and a protection, a source of wisdom and of strength, vers. 5, 6. Yet even these imitate the example of apostate Israel, and in their self-indulgence cast off the authority of God and refuse the instructions of his prophet, to their own undoing, vers. 7–13. But their impious contempt of God and self-reliance shall but hasten their destruction. All who do but build upon the sure foundation laid in Zion, must inevitably perish, as the enemies of Israel were destroyed of old, vers. 14–22. The delay of judgment no more proves that it will never come, than the patience of the husbandman, and his preparatory labours, prove that he expects no harvest; and the difference of God's dealings with different men is no more inconsistent with his general purposes of wrath or mercy, than the husbandman's treatment of the different grains is inconsistent with his general purpose of securing and enjoying them, vers. 23–29.

This chapter is by most of the late writers joined with chaps. xxix.–xxxiii., as belonging to the same date and subject.   Ewald without sufficient ground regards it as a later composition.   The elaborate attempts, made by Hitzig and others, to determine the precise date of the composition, as they rest on no sufficient data, are of course unsatisfactory and inconclusive.   It was obviously written before the downfall of Samaria, but how long before is neither ascertainable nor of importance to the exposition of the prophecy.

1. *Woe to the high crown of the drunkards of Ephraim, and the fading flower, his ornament of beauty, which (is) on the head of the fat valley of the wine-smitten.*   Here, as in chap. ix. 9, 21, xi. 13, we are to understand by *Ephraim* the kingdom of the ten tribes, by the *drunkards of Ephraim* its vicious population, and by the *lofty crown* the city of Samaria, so called as the chief town and the royal residence, but also with allusion to its local situation on an insulated hill overlooking a rich plain or valley.   "It would be difficult to find, in all Palestine, a situation of equal strength, fertility, and beauty combined" (Robinson's Palestine, iii. 146).   Most interpreters assume a further allusion to the practice of wearing wreaths or garlands at feasts.   Lowth and Gesenius suppose this to be the only reason why the men of Ephraim are here called *drunkards*, q. d. like the crown which drunkards wear at feasts, so is Samaria a crown to Ephraim.   Others, with more probability, invert the process, and suppose the figure of a garland to have been suggested by the description of the people as drunkards.   Ewald combines the two hypotheses by saying that as Samaria was in its situation like a crown, and as the people were habitually drunk, the city is poetically represented as a reveller's crown.   The reference to literal intoxication appears plain from a comparison of Amos iv. 1, 6, i. 6.   Drunkenness is mentioned, not as the only prevalent iniquity, but as a crying one, and one contributing to many others.   The moral and spiritual consequences of this vice must be taken into view ; but the exclusive reference of the words to spiritual drunkenness, whether delusion, or stupidity, or both, seems entirely untenable.   No such conclusion can be drawn, as we shall see below, from chap. xxix. 9, on the authority of which the Septuagint seems to have translated חַלְמֵי יַיִן, in the verse before us, μεθύοντες ἄνευ οἴνου.   The same Version has confounded שָׂבְרֵי with שְׂכִירֵי and rendered it μισθωτοί.   This verse contains three examples of the Hebrew idiom, which, instead of an adjective, uses one substantive to qualify another ; *crown of elevation* for lofty crown, *beauty of glory* for glorious beauty, and *valley of fatnesses* for fat valley. Yet no one has alleged this accumulation of peculiar idioms as a proof of bad taste or a later age.   Cocceius greatly adds to the beauty of the first clause, by explaining גֵּאוּת of physical elevation rather than of pride.   Hitzig supposes two distinct comparisons, that of the city to a crown, and that of the population to a flower.   It is far more natural, however, to apply both clauses to Samaria, and to suppose that the figure of a crown is exchanged for that of a flower, or that the idea throughout the verse is that of a wreath or garland, which is really included under the name crown. The latter member of the first clause is by some construed thus, *and the flower whose glorious beauty fades ;* by others, for example the English Version (*Ephraim*) *whose glorious beauty is a fading flower.*   The analogy of ver. 4 seems to shew, however, that this member of the sentence is in apposition with עֲטֶרֶת גֵּאוּת in the one before it, which construction is, more-

over, the most obvious and simple. The English Version also mars the beauty of the first clause, by making שִׁכֹּרֵי אֶפְרַיִם not a genitive but a dative. The *fading flower* implies that the glory of Samaria was transient, with particular allusion to its approaching overthrow by Shalmaneser. Hitzig and Ewald render הוי as a mere exclamation (O!), and suppose the verse to speak of Samaria as already fallen. Vatablus strangely understands by גֵּיא־שְׁמָנִים the head of the reveller, drenched with unguents and perfumes. Augusti likewise renders it, *dem Sammelplatze der Salben.* שְׁמָנִים, as being a mere qualifying term, retains the absolute form, although the phrase, considered as a whole, is in regimen with the one that follows. Examples of a similar construction may be found in chap. x. 12, and 1 Chron. ix. 13. *Wine-smitten* or *wine-stricken* is a strong description of the intellectual and moral effects of drunkenness. Gill's lively paraphrase is : smitten, beaten, knocked down with it as with a hammer, and laid prostrate on the ground, where they lie fixed to it, not able to get up. Analogous expressions are the Greek οἰνοπλήξ, and the Latin *saucius mero* and *percussus vino.* Barnes sets this verse down as a proof, that the inhabitants of wine countries are *as certainly* intemperate as those which make use of ardent spirits.

2. *Behold, there is to the Lord (i. e. the Lord has) a strong and mighty one, like a storm of hail, a destroying tempest, like a storm of mighty rushing waters, he has brought (it) to the ground with the hand.* As הִנֵּה very commonly denotes a proximate futurity, Clericus explains it as equivalent to *mox ;* but in this case it appears to be intended merely to invite attention to the following description, as of a scene or action present to the senses. The oldest editions of the Hebrew text, and a large number of manuscripts, read יהוה instead of אדני. Lowth understands *to the Lord* as expressing a superlative, like the analogous expression *before the Lord* in Gen. x. 9, and translates accordingly, *the mighty one, the exceedingly strong one.* Henderson supposes לְ to denote possession, and translates *of Jehovah.* Luther has *from,* which is retained by Gesenius, who, moreover, introduces the verb *comes.* Hitzig explains the לְ as denoting efficient agent, as it is said to do after passive verbs, corresponding to the English *by.* But this use of the particle is very doubtful, and at least unnecessary in the case before us. The simplest construction, and the one most agreeable to usage, is that given by Hendewerk, Ewald, and Knobel, *there is to Jehovah, i. e.* Jehovah has, has ready, has in reserve. (*Vide supra,* chaps. ii. 12, xxii. 5). The English Version therefore (*the Lord hath*) is in sense entirely correct. J. D. Michaelis follows the Peshito in taking חָזָק and אַמִּץ as abstracts meaning *power* and *strength.* Of those versions which translate them strictly as adjectives, the Vulgate makes them epithets of God himself, (*validus et fortis Dominus*) and so overlooks the לְ altogether ; Jarchi construes them with *wind,* Kimchi with *day,* and others with *army* understood ; Cocceius and Vitringa make them neuter or indefinite, meaning *something strong and mighty ;* the Targum and Rosenmüller construe them with strokes or visitations understood ; but most interpreters, including the most recent, understand them as descriptive of a person, and apply them directly to Shalmaneser or to the kings of Assyria indefinitely. For *tempest of destruction* Cocceius has *horror excidii,* in reference to the meaning of the root שָׁעַר and some of its derivatives. De Dieu reads שַׁעַר and translates it, *in the gate there is destruction ;* others, *through the gate* it enters. But the common version (*a destroying storm*) may now be looked upon as settled. The last clause is strangely paraphrased by Jonathan so as to mean, that the enemy shall take the people from their own land to another, on account of

the iniquity found in their hand. The meaning *to the earth* or *to the ground* is clear from chap. lxiii. 6, and other cases. The Vulgate confounds the phrase with יָדַיִם אֶרֶץ (chap. xxii. 18), and translates it *super terram spatiosam.* בְּיָד is commonly explained to mean *with power*, as in the Septuagint (βίᾳ). Gesenius gives this sense to יָד itself; Rosenmüller supposes an ellipsis of *strong*, Hitzig, of *outstretched*, Hendewerk, an allusion to a rod held in the hand. Junius explains the phrase to mean *with one hand, i. e.* easily. There seems, however, to be no need of departing from the strict sense of the words as given in the English Version (*with the hand*), and by Ewald with a needless change of *hand* to *fist*. It then completes the picture by describing the crown of Ephraim as torn from his head and thrown upon the ground by the hand of a victorious enemy. To this explanation no objection can be drawn from the previous mention of the hail and rain ; for these are mere comparisons, descriptive of the violence with which the enemy should make his attack. It is as if he had said, a strong and mighty enemy, rushing upon you like a hail-storm or a driving rain, shall cast your crown upon the earth with his hand. That the crown is the object of the verb הִנִּיחַ, may be safely inferred from the foregoing and the following verses, though some interpreters have made it govern the strong and mighty one himself, or the rain and storm with which he is compared, as being sent upon the earth by Jehovah. Though הִנִּיחַ should be rendered as a preterite, it does not follow of necessity that the event described had already taken place, but merely that in this case it is so presented to the Prophet's view.

3. *With the feet shall be trodden the lofty crown of the drunkards of Ephraim.* It is cast down by the hand and trampled under foot. This antithesis makes it almost certain that יָד in the preceding verse is to be taken in its proper sense. The plural form of the verb has been variously explained. The ancient versions all translate it as a singular. The Rabbins make עֲטֶרֶת a collective. Lowth reads עֲטָרוֹת in the plural. Cocceius refers the verb to the crown and flower separately. Junius puts *drunkards*, not in construction but in apposition with *crown*, which is also the case of the English Version (*the crown of pride, the drunkards of Ephraim*). Vitringa explains the plural form upon the ground, that while the verse literally relates to the downfall of Samaria, it mystically relates to the downfall of Jerusalem. Clericus simply says that the *crown* meant was that of many persons ; Rosenmüller that the feminine verb is used as neuter ; Hendewerk that it is a pluralis majestaticus, or refers to Samaria as the representative of the other towns of Israel. Gesenius, Hitzig, and Knobel, seem to be agreed that it is an anomalous or rather idiomatic use of the plural for the singular, as in Exod. i. 10; Judges v. 26; Job xvii. 16. There is great probability in Henderson's suggestion that the נָה in all such cases is not a feminine but a paragogic or intensive termination, analogous to that of the antithetic future in Arabic.

4. *And the fading flower of his glorious beauty, which is on the head of the fat valley, shall be like a first-ripe fig before summer, which he that sees it sees, and while it is yet in his hand swallows it.* This comparison expresses the avidity with which the enemy would seize upon Samaria, and perhaps the completeness of its desolation. The fruit referred to is the early fig of Palestine which ripens in June, while the regular season of ingathering is from August to November, so that the former is regarded as a rarity and eaten with the greater relish. The figure is not here intended to express either ease or rapidity of conquest, for the seige of Samaria lasted three years (2 Kings xvii. 5). To suppose, with J. D. Michaelis and Henderson,

that a siege of this length was considered short compared with those of Tyre and Askelon, seems very forced. The immediate eating of the fruit is only mentioned as a sign of eagerness or greediness. Vitringa understands the simile as meaning that Samaria when taken would be instantly destroyed, as the first ripe fruit is eaten and not stored away. This would also remove the apparent discrepancy, and is in itself not improbable, although less obvious and natural than the explanation first proposed. The last clause, though singularly worded, evidently means that as soon as one sees it and lays hold of it he swallows it without delay, or as Gill expresses it in homespun English, " as soon as he has got it into his hand, he can't keep it there to look at, or forbear eating it, but greedily devours it and swallows it down at once." בְּעוֹד, however, does not literally mean *as soon as*, but *while yet*, which renders the expression stronger still, as strictly denoting that he eats it while it is yet in his hand. The Septuagint expresses the same meaning with a change of form, by saying that before one has it in his hand he *wishes* to devour it. The same Version renders בְּכּוּרָה πρόδρομος σύκου, and Pliny says, *ficus et praecoces habet quas Athenis prodromos vocant.* Joseph Kimchi explained כַּף to mean a *branch*, and this sense is expressed by Luther, who understands the clause to mean, that the fig spoils or perishes (verdirbt) while one still sees it hanging on the branch. As בְּעוֹד means literally *in yet*, so בְּטֶרֶם, strictly means *in not yet*, two examples of a peculiar Hebrew idiom in a single-sentence. Hitzig, in order to refer this verse to the conquest of Samaria as already past, denies that the ו at the beginning is conversive, and refers to other cases where it is simply conjunctive, but in this case its conversive power is determined by the foregoing future תְּרָמַסְנָה, whereas in the others there is either no preceding future, or it is contained in a quotation and not in the regular order of discourse. It may also be objected to Hitzig's hypothesis, that the הוֹי in ver. 1 and the בַּיּוֹם הַהוּא in ver. 5, both imply that the event described is future. צִיצַת seems to be a more euphonic variation of צִיץ in ver. 4. In solving its construction with what follows, Gesenius and most of the late writers take נֹבֵל to be an adjective used as a substantive and governed regularly by צִיצַת *flower of fading* for *fading flower*, of which construction there are some examples elsewhere. (See chap. xxii. 24; Prov. vi. 24, xxiv. 25). The next clause may then be relatively understood (*which was his glorious beauty*), or in apposition (*the fading flower, his glorious beauty*); but Ewald and many of the older writers regard this phrase as in regimen with what follows (*the fading flower of*, &c.) The English Version, as in ver. 1, makes צִיצַת נֹבֵל the predicate (*shall be a fading flower, and as*, &c.) Hendewerk supposes נֹבֵל, *the fading one*, to be an epithet of Ephraim himself. קַיִץ is the fruit-harvest, and especially the ingathering of figs. The modern critics are agreed that the final syllable of בכורה, although written in most manuscripts with *mappik*, is not a suffix, but a feminine termination. This name of the early fig is still retained, not only in Arabic, but in Spanish, into which it was transplanted by the Moors. Lowth's decision, that יראה הראה is a *miserable tautology*, is worth about as much as his decision, that Houbigant's emendation (יארה for יראה) is a *happy conjecture*. The tautology, at all events, is no more miserable here than in chaps. xvi. 10, or xxviii. 24, not to mention 2 Sam. xvii. 9, or Ezek. xxxiii. 4. The liberties which critics of this school took with the text, and the language which they used in self-justification, must be considered as having contributed in some degree to the subsequent revolution of opinion with respect to points of more intrinsic moment.

5. *In that day shall Jehovah of Hosts be for* (or *become*) *a crown of beauty and a diadem of glory to the remnant of his people.* By the remnant of the people Jarchi understands those of the ten tribes who should survive the destruction of Samaria ; Knobel the remnant of Judah itself, which should escape Shalmaneser's invasion expected by the Prophet ; Hendewerk the remnant of Israel, again considered as one body after the fall of the apostate kingdom ; Kimchi the kingdom of the two tribes, as the remnant of the whole race. This last approaches nearest to the true sense, which appears to be, that after Samaria, the pride of the apostate tribes, had fallen, they who still remained as members of the church, or chosen people, should glory and delight in the presence of Jehovah as their choicest privilege and highest honour. The expressions are borrowed from the first verse, but presented in a new combination. As our idiom admits in this case of a close imitation of the Hebrew, the common version, which is strictly literal, is much to be preferred to Lowth's (*a beauteous crown and a glorious diadem*). Of the versions which exchange the nouns for adjectives, the most felicitous is Luther's (*eine liebliche Krone und herrlicher Kranz*). Instead of *Jehovah of Hosts*, the Targum has *the Messiah of Jehovah.*

6. *And for a spirit of judgment to him that sitteth in judgment, and for strength to them that turn the battle to the gate.* This, which is the common English Version, coincides with that of the latest and best writers. עַל הַמִּשְׁפָּט may either be explained as meaning *on the judgment-seat*, with Calvin (super tribunal), or *in judgment, i. e.* for the purpose of judging, with Clericus (juris dicundi causa) and most other writers. In illustration of the first sense may be cited Ps. ix. 5, *thou sittest on the throne judging right;* in illustration of the other, 1 Sam. xx. 24, xxx. 24, where יָשַׁב עַל indicates the purpose for which, or the object with respect to which, one sits. The last words of the verse are applied to those who return home safe from war by Symmachus, the Targum, and the Vulgate (revertentibus de bello ad portam) ; to those who repel the battle *from* the gate by the Peshito, Clericus, and Augusti ; but by all the later writers to those who drive the war back to the enemy's own gates, or, as it were, carry it into his own country. J. D. Michaelis gives to *gate* the specific sense of boundary, or frontier, which is wholly unnecessary, as it is usual to mention towns, if not their gates, in such connections. (See, for example, 2 Sam. xi. 23 ; 2 Kings xviii. 8.) The war meant is therefore wholly defensive. The two great requisites of civil government are here described as coming from Jehovah. Even Gesenius adverts to the fact, that the *Spirit* of this verse is not a mere influence, but God himself.

7. *And (yet) these also* (or *even these*) *through wine have erred, and through strong drink have gone astray. Priest and prophet have erred through strong drink, have been swallowed up of wine, have been led astray by strong drink, have erred in vision, have wavered in judgment.* Having predicted in the foregoing verse that when Ephraim fell Judah should continue to enjoy the protection of Jehovah, the Prophet now describes even this favoured remnant as addicted to the same sins which had hastened the destruction of the ten tribes, viz., sensual indulgence, and the spiritual evils which it generates. The drunkenness here mentioned is taken in a moral and spiritual sense even by Calvin and others, who understand ver. 1 as relating to literal intoxication ; but this mode of exposition seems entirely arbitrary. All that is necessary is to suppose the moral or spiritual effects of drunkenness to be included. Many interpreters suppose the Prophet to

revert at this point to the state of Judah in his own day. Of such transitions there are numerous examples; but the supposition is unnecessary here, where the obvious construction of the passage, as continuous in point of time, yields a good and appropriate sense. The meaning then is, that the Jews, although distinguished from the ten tribes by God's sparing mercy, should nevertheless imitate them in their sins. There is great probability in Henderson's suggestion, that the prophecy refers to the national deterioration in the reign of Manasseh. The גַּם at the beginning is emphatic, not only Ephraim, but *also these*, or *even these*. Ewald arbitrarily translates אֵלֶּה *here*, and makes the verbs indefinite (*taumelt man*). The priest and prophet are named as the leaders of the people, and as those who were peculiarly bound to set a better example. The reference to *judgment* in the last clause may be explained either on the ground that the priest and prophet represent the rulers of the people in general, or because the priests themselves exercised judicial functions in certain prescribed cases (Deut. xvii. 9, xix. 17). Junius and others needlessly take כֹּהֵן in the general sense of *ruler*. Another not improbable solution is, that פְּלִילִיָּה does not mean judgment in the technical sense, but more generally. the declaration of the will of God. There seems to be no sufficient ground for Gesenius's explanation of the word as meaning *judgment-seat*. Maurer gives the same sense, and explains the whole phrase, *they stagger* (or *reel*) *into the judgment-seat*. Most of the late interpreters, instead of the more general sense of *erring, wandering*, explain שָׁגָה and תָּעָה as specifically meaning to reel or stagger, which adds to the vividness of the description, but does not seem to be entirely justified by usage. Hendewerk takes שֵׁכָר as an abstract, meaning *intoxication*. J. D. Michaelis translates it *beer*. Hitzig explains בַּיִּין as meaning *in the act of drinking wine;* but most other writers, with more probability, regard both מִן and בְּ as here denoting the means or cause of the intoxication. Henderson's version of נִבְלְעוּ (*overpowered*), leaves out of view the obvious allusion to literal deglutition; for, as Gill suggests, they swallowed the wine down, and it swallowed them up. Here again Barnes sees his favourite image of a *maelstrom*. Maurer suggests, as a possible construction, that the last words may cohere with the first of the next verse, and פָּקוּ have the meaning of the Chaldee and Syriac נפק: they go out of the judgment-seat because all the tables, &c. But שֻׁלְחָן is a dining-table, not a writing-desk. Nor is there any such improvement in the sense as would seem to justify such a departure from the traditional arrangement of the text. The use of strong drinks was expressly forbidden to the priests in the discharge of their official functions (Lev. x. 9; Ezek. xliv. 21). רֹאֶה is commonly explained as a participle used for an abstract noun, *seeing* or *seer* for *sight*, an explanation which is certainly favoured by the analogous use of חֹזֶה in ver. 18. It is possible, however, that בָּרֹאֶה may mean in the office, character, or functions of a seer, as Junius explains it (in functione videntis).

8. *For all tables are full of vomit, of filth, without a place* (*i. e.* a clean place). Grotius understands by *tables* the tribunals, and by filth and vomit the injustice practised there, which he says was likewise called *sordes* by the Latins. How arbitrary such expositions must be, will appear from the fact, that Vitringa makes the *tables* mean the schools or places of public instruction, and the *vomit* the false doctrine there taught and again reproduced to the injury of others. The only natural interpretation is that

which supposes *tables* to denote the places where men eat and drink, and the other terms the natural though revolting consequences of excess. Cocceius, who takes *tables* in its proper sense, explains the filth to mean corrupt or unprofitable conversation; but this is a most unreasonable mixture of literal and figurative exposition. Whether the intoxication thus described is wholly spiritual, depends of course upon the meaning given to the preceding verse. Most writers suppose צֹאָה to be governed by קִיא, and resolve the phrase into an adjective construction by translating it *filthy vomit*. Augusti makes the first word the qualifying term, and renders it *vomited filth*. As the words, however, are distinct in origin, the best construction is that which makes them both dependent on the verb : full of vomit, full of filth. There is no more need of supplying a preposition before צֹאָה than before קִיא. The introduction of the copulative *and* is needless, and impairs the force of the expression. בְּלִי is properly a noun meaning *failure* or *defect*, but is constantly used as a negative adverb or preposition. The sense of this clause is correctly though diffusely given in the English Version (*so that there is no place clean*). Luther gives the sense, but with a change of form, by rendering it *in all places*. So too one of the French Versions (tellement que tout en est plein). It is somewhat remarkable that the Septuagint translation of this verse does not exhibit any trace of the original.

9. *Whom will he teach knowledge? And whom will he make to understand doctrine? Those weaned from the milk and removed from the breasts.* The Targum makes this a description of Israel as the favoured people to whom the law was exclusively given. In like manner some of the older Christian writers understand it as descriptive of the persons whom Jehovah, or the Prophet acting in his name, would choose as proper subjects of instruction, viz., simple and child-like disciples, who *as new-born babes desire the sincere milk of the word* (1 Pet. ii. 2). But the children here described are weanlings, not sucklings, and on this hypothesis the weaning, which is so particularly mentioned, would have no significancy. Besides, this explanation of the words would not suit the context, either before or after. It is therefore commonly agreed, that the last clause must be taken in a contemptuous or unfavourable sense, as denoting children not in malice merely but in understanding (1 Cor. xiv. 20). On this assumption some have explained the verse as meaning, that the priest and the prophet, mentioned in ver. 7, were utterly unfit to teach the people, being themselves mere children in knowledge and in understanding. This explanation supposes the singular verbs of the first clause, and the plural adjectives of the second, to refer to the same persons. Another interpretation makes the words descriptive not of the teachers but the taught, as being no more fit to receive instruction than a child just weaned. J. D. Michaelis applies the last clause not to their incapacity but to their unwillingness to be instructed, as being *long since weaned* and now too old to return to the breast. This ingenious explanation has the advantage of taking עָתִיק in its usual sense of *old*, whereas all others give it one derived from עָתַק to remove. But the comparative meaning, which it puts upon the preposition following, is excluded by its obvious use in the foregoing phrase in its proper local sense of *from*. A new turn was given to the exposition of the verse by Lowth, who, adopting an obscure suggestion of Jerome, explains it as the language not of the Prophet but of the wicked men before described, expressing their indignation and contempt at the Prophet's undertaking to instruct them as if they were mere children. Whom does he

undertake to teach ? and whom would he make to understand his doctrine? Children weaned from the milk and removed from the breast ?   This interpretation has in substance been adopted by all later writers, as affording a good sense and one admirably suited both to the foregoing and the following context.   It seems to be liable to only two objections : first, that it gratuitously gives the passage a dramatic form by supposing a new speaker to be introduced without any intimation in the text; and then, that it arbitrarily continues the interrogation through the sentence.   The last objection may be obviated by adopting Henderson's modified construction, which supposes them to ask not whom he *would* but whom he *ought* to teach, and then to answer, little children just weaned from the breast, not men of mature age and equal to himself.   The other objection, being wholly negative, must yield of course to the positive arguments in favour of an exposition which is otherwise coherent, satisfactory, and suited to the context.   Rosenmüller seems indeed to think that the space between this verse and that before it in the Hebrew manuscripts denotes a change of subject; but these mechanical arrangements of the text can have no authoritative influence upon its exposition.   The verbs in the first clause may either be indefinitely construed or referred to the Prophet, without a material change of meaning.   שְׁמוּעָה properly denotes something heard, and here means that which the Prophet heard from God and the people from the Prophet; in other words, divine revelation, whether general or special.   There are few examples of a more exact translation than the Vulgate version of this verse, in which the very form of the original is happily retained, not excepting the etymological import of the word שְׁמוּעָה. So rigid is the version, that Montanus has retained it in his own unchanged. *Quem docebit scientiam ? et quem intelligere faciet auditum? ablactatos a lacte, avulsos ab uberibus.*

10. *For (it is) rule upon rule, rule upon rule, line upon line, line upon line, a little here, a little there.*   The interpretation of this verse varies of course with that of the one before it.   Those who understand ver. 9 as descriptive of God's favour to the Jews, explain this in like manner as relating to the abundance of the revelations made to them, including rules and counsels suited to every emergency of life.   Henderson's remark, that the words are often preposterously quoted in application to the abundant possession of religious privileges, rests of course on the assumption that his own interpretation of ver. 9 is certainly the true one.   But this is far from being so clear as to justify the branding of an opposite opinion with absurdity.   Those who apply ver. 9 to the incapacity of the *people* for high attainments in spiritual knowledge, regard ver. 10 as a description of the elementary methods which were necessary for them.   Those who apply ver. 9 to the incapacity of the religious *teachers* of the Jews, explain ver. 10 as a description of their puerile method of instruction.   The words are thus understood by Vitringa and applied to the Scribes and Pharisees in the time of Christ.   But as all the latest writers make ver. 9 the language of the Jews themselves, complaining of the Prophet's perpetual reproofs and teachings, they are equally agreed in making ver. 10 a direct continuation of the same complaint.   Aben Ezra explains צַו לָצַו as meaning *rule after rule* or *rule (joined) to rule.*   Equally good is the construction in the English Version (*precept upon precept*) except that the word *precept* is too long to represent the chosen monosyllables of the original.   The same objection may be made to Gesenius's imitation of the paronomasia (Gebot auf Gebot, Verbot auf Verbot), which is much

inferior to that of Ewald (Satz zu Satz, Schnur zu Schnur). Paulus, Gesenius, Maurer, Hitzig, and Ewald, understand this peculiar clause as the people's scoffing imitation of the Prophet's manner; Koppe, Eichhorn, Umbreit, and Knobel, as the Prophet's own derisive imitation of their drunken talk. Koppe even goes so far as to imagine that צו and קו are here intentionally given as half-formed words, if not as inarticulate unmeaning sounds. But קו is in common use, and צו occurs in the sense of *rule* or *precept* in Hos. v. 11. The Peshito and J. D. Michaelis treat these words as cognate forms and synonymes of צוֹאָה and קיא in ver. 8, and translate accordingly, *vomit upon vomit, filth upon filth.* Michaelis, moreover, gives זְעֵיר the sense of spot or stain. Both שָׁם and זְעֵיר are referred by some to time, and by others to quantity or space; but the simplest and best explanation seems to be the one given in the English Version (*here a little, there a little*), as expressive of minuteness and perpetual repetition. Gesenius understands this verse as having reference to the constant additions to the law of Moses in Isaiah's time, the design of which interpretation is to fortify the doctrine that the Pentateuch, as we now have it, is long posterior to the days of Moses. Rosenmüller, Hitzig, and Knobel, all admit that the allusion is not to the written law, but to the oral admonitions of the Prophets. The Targum contains a diffuse paraphrase of this verse, in which the principal words are retained, but so combined with others as to make the whole relate to the captivity of Israel, as the consequence of his despising the appointed place of worship and practising idolatry.

11. *For with stammering lips and with another tongue will he speak unto this people.* As לעגי שפה may denote either *foreign* or *scoffing* speech (the former being usually described in the Old Testament as *stammering*), some suppose a double allusion here, to wit, that as they had mocked at the divine instructions by their stammering speech, so he would speak to them in turn by the stammering lips of foreigners in another language than their own. This, though by no means an obvious construction in itself, is preferred by the latest writers and countenanced by several analogous expressions in the subsequent context. Ewald understands by the stammering speech of this verse the inarticulate language of the thunder, which is very unnatural. Of the older writers some explain this verse as descriptive of God's tenderness and condescension in accommodating his instructions to the people's capacity as nurses deal with children. Others understand it to mean that through their own perverseness those instructions had been rendered unintelligible and of course unprofitable, so that their divine teacher had become as it were a barbarian to them.

12. *Who said to them, This is rest, give rest to the weary, and this is quiet, but they would not hear.* The judgments threatened in the foregoing verse were the more evident, just because he who threatened them had warned the people, and pointed out to them the only way to happiness. אֲשֶׁר should not be taken in the rare and doubtful sense *because*, but in its proper sense as a relative pronoun. This construction, far from being *intolerably harsh* (Henderson), is the only natural and simple one, as well as the only one entirely justified by usage. The pronoun may either be connected with אֲלֵיהֶם in the sense of *to whom* (for which there is no other Hebrew expression), or referred to *Jehovah* as the subject of the following verb. Who was it that should speak to them with another tongue? He who had so often said to them, &c. Although admissible, it is not necessary to take מְנוּחָה in the local sense of *resting-place* (Ewald). The sense is not, that the true way to rest is to give rest to the weary; the latter ex-

pression is a kind of parenthesis, as if he had said, This is the true rest, let the weary enjoy it. By *this* we are therefore to understand, not compassion and kindness to the suffering, but obedience to the will of God in general. This is the true rest which I alone can give, and the way to which I have clearly marked out. *Rest* is not quiet submission to the yoke of the Assyrians (Hitzig), but peace, tranquillity. To *give rest to the weary* does not mean to cease from warlike preparations, or to relieve the people from excessive burdens, whether of a civil or religious kind, but simply to reduce to practice the lesson which God had taught them. This is the way to peace, let those who wish it walk therein. In the last clause, *would* is not a mere auxiliary, but an independent and emphatic verb, *they were not willing*. The form אָבוּא (from the root אָבָה), though resembling the Arabic analogy, is not a proof of recent date, but rather of the fact, that some forms, which are prevalent in the cognate dialects, were known, if not common, in the early periods of Hebrew composition.

13. *And the word of Jehovah was to them rule upon rule, rule upon rule ; line upon line, line upon line ; a little here, a little there ; that they might go, and fall backwards, and be broken, and be snared, and be taken.* The law was given that sin might abound. The only effect of the minute instructions, which they found so irksome, was to aggravate their guilt and condemnation. The terms of the first clause are repeated from ver. 10, and have of course the same meaning in both places. The *Vav* at the beginning of the verse is not conversive, as the verbs of the preceding verse relate to past time. There is neither necessity nor reason for translating the particle *but, so that*, or anything but *and*, as it introduces a direct continuation of the foregoing description. יֵלְכוּ does not simply qualify the following verbs (go on, or continue to fall backwards), but expresses a distinct act. כָּשְׁלוּ includes the two ideas of stumbling and falling. Some give to וְנִשְׁבָּרוּ the more specific sense, *and break their limbs*. לְמַעַן according to its etymology denotes design (*in order that*), but may here be used simply to express an actual result (*so that*), unless we refer it, in its strict sense, to the righteous purpose or design of God's judicial providence.

14. *Therefore* (because your advantages have only made you more rebellious) *hear the word of Jehovah, ye scornful men* (literally *men of scorn*, i. e. despisers of the truth), *the rulers of this people which is in Jerusalem* (or ye rulers of this people who are in Jerusalem). The אֲשֶׁר may refer grammatically either to הָעָם or to מֹשְׁלֵי. *This people*, here as elsewhere, may be an expression of displeasure and contempt. Jerusalem is mentioned as the seat of government and source of influence. The whole verse invites attention to the solemn warning which follows.

15. *Because ye have said* (in thought or deed, if not in word) *we have made a covenant with death, and with hell* (the grave, or the unseen world) *have formed a league ; the overflowing scourge, when it passes through, shall not come upon us, for we have made falsehood our refuge, and in fraud we have hid ourselves.* The meaning evidently is, that if their actions were translated into words, this would be their import. There is no need, therefore, of throwing the words כזב and שקר into a parenthesis (J. D. Michaelis) as the Prophet's comment on the scoffer's boast. שאול is here nothing more than a poetical equivalent to מות. The textual reading שיט is probably an old cognate form and synonyme of שוט, which is given in the margin. The mixed metaphor of an *overflowing scourge* combines two natural and common figures for severe calamity. Some interpreters

apologise for the rhetorical defect of the expression on the ground that Hebrew ears were not as delicate as ours. Barnes throws the blame upon the English version, and explains the Hebrew word to mean *calamity*, but in ver. 18 gives the meaning *scourge*, and says that three metaphors are there combined, which makes it less incredible that two are blended here. חֹזֶה is properly a participle (*seeing*) often used as a noun to denote a *seer* or prophet. Here the connection seems distinctly to require the sense of *league* or covenant. That there is no error in the text, may be inferred from the substitution of the cognate form חזות in ver. 18. Hitzig accounts for the transfer of meanings by the supposition that in making treaties it was usual to consult the seer or prophet. Ewald supposes an allusion to the practice of necromantic art or divination as a safeguard against death, and translates the word *orakel*. The more common explanation of the usage traces it to the idea of an *interview* or *meeting* and the act of looking one another in the face, from which the transition is by no means difficult to that of mutual understanding or agreement. (Calvin: visionis nomine significat id quod vulgo dicimus *avoir intelligence*.) The marginal reading יעבר was probably intended to assimilate the phrase to that employed in ver. 18, but without necessity, since either tense might be used in this connection to express contingency. As the other variations (שׁיט and שׁוט, חֹזֶה and חוזת) shew that the two verses were not meant to be identical in form, the reading in the text (עבר) is probably the true one. בוא, when construed directly with the noun, means to *come upon*, in the sense of attacking or invading. The *falsehood* mentioned in the last clause is not a false profession of idolatry in order to conciliate the enemy (Grotius), nor idols, nor false prophets, but falsehood or unfaithfulness to God, *i. e.* wickedness in general, perhaps with an allusion to the falsity or treacherous nature of the hopes built upon it. The translation *under falsehood*, which is given in the English Bible and in some other versions, is neither justified by usage nor required by the connection. On the other hand, the reflexive version, *we have hid ourselves*, is much more expressive than the simple passive.

16. *Therefore thus saith the Lord Jehovah, Behold I lay in Zion a stone, a stone of proof, a corner stone of value, of a firm foundation; the believer will not be in haste.* To the words of the scoffers are now opposed the words of God himself. Because you say thus and thus, therefore the Lord says in reply what follows. You trust for safety in your own delusions; on the contrary, I lay a sure foundation, and no other can be laid. This foundation is neither the temple (Ewald), nor the law (Umbreit), nor Zion itself (Hitzig), nor Hezekiah (Gesenius), but the Messiah, to whom it is repeatedly and explicitly applied in the New Testament (Rom. ix. 33, x. 11; 1 Peter ii. 6). The same application of the text is made by Jarchi, and according to Raymund Martini (in his Pugio Fidei) by the Targum of Jonathan, although the word *Messiah* is now wanting in the Chaldee text. The objection, that the stone here mentioned was already laid, has no weight, as the whole theocracy existed with a view to the coming of Messiah. The reference of the words to Hezekiah is an old one, as Theodoret pronounces it an instance of extreme folly (ἀνοίας ἐσχάτης). Hitzig and Knobel, in order to make Zion itself the sure foundation, make the particle a *beth essentiæ*, as if he had said, You have *in Zion* (*i. e.* Zion is to you) a sure foundation. All other writers seem to give the ב its proper local sense. The phrase literally rendered *stone of proof* admits of two interpretations. Calvin understands by it a stone which was to be the test or standard of comparison for others;

but the common explanation is more natural, which makes it mean a stone
that has itself been proved or tried and found sufficient. A kindred idea is
expressed by the phrase מוּסָד מוּסָד, a cognate noun and participle, literally
meaning a *founded foundation, i. e.* one entirely firm and safe. The peculiar form of the original, arising from the repetition of the construct state,
has been retained in the translation above given. There is no need of supposing, with Kimchi and others, that יקרת is an absolute form in apposition
with what follows. The writer's purpose seems to have been to unite the
members of the sentence in construction by a very intimate and close articulation. מאמין may either be referred specifically to the corner-stone or
taken in the general sense of trusting or believing, sc., God. The objection to the former that the prophets never exhort men to trust in men or
mere localities, is valid as an argument against the reference to Hezekiah,
or the temple, or mount Zion, but not against the reference to the Messiah,
who is constantly presented as an object of faith, and a ground of trust.
Will not be in haste, i. e. will not be impatient, but will trust the promise,
even though its execution be delayed. This suits the connection better
than the sense preferred by the modern German writers, *will not flee,* or
have occasion to flee, in alarm or despair. The Septuagint version adopted
in the New Testament (*shall not be ashamed*), agrees essentially with that
first given, though it makes more prominent the fact that the believer's
hopes shall not be disappointed. If it be true, as Gesenius thinks probable,
that the Hebrew verb, like a kindred one in Arabic, not only meant to
hasten but to be ashamed, the Septuagint version is fully justified, and the
authority of the New Testament should be regarded as decisive in favour
of that meaning here. But as it cannot be traced in Hebrew usage, it is
better to regard the Greek as paraphrasing rather than translating the
original expression. At all events, there is no need of reading יביש with
Grotius, Houbigant, and Lowth. The force of the figures in this verse is
much enhanced by the statements of modern travellers in relation to the
immense stones still remaining at the foundation of ancient walls. (See
particularly Robinson's Palestine, i. 343, 351, 422.

17. *And I will place judgment for a line and justice for a plummet, and
hail shall sweep away the refuge of falsehood, and the hiding-place waters
shall overflow.* The meaning of the first clause is, that God would deal with
them in strict justice; he would make justice the rule of his proceedings,
as the builder regulates his work by the line and plummet. The English
Version seems to make judgment or justice not the measure but the
thing to be measured. The verb שֹוּם with the preposition לְ means to
place a thing in a certain situation, or to apply it to a certain use. (See
chap. xiv. 23.) Hail and rain are here used, as in ver. 2 above, to denote
the divine visitations. The refuge and the hiding-place are those of which
the scornful men had boasted in ver. 15. To their confident assurance
of safety God opposes, first, the only sure foundation which himself had
laid, and then the utter destruction which was coming on their own chosen
objects of reliance. Hitzig thinks that שקר must have dropped out after
סתר, as if there were no examples of even greater variation in the repetitions
of the prophets. The truth is, that slavish iteration of precisely the same
words is rather the exception than the rule.

18. *And your covenant with death shall be annulled, and your league with
hell shall not stand, and the overflowing scourge—for it shall pass through,
and ye shall be for it to trample on.* כפר seems to be here used in its
primary sense of *covering,* or perhaps more specifically *smearing over,*

so as to conceal if not to obliterate, applied in this case to a writing, the image in the mind of the Prophet being probably that of a waxen tablet, in which the writing is erased by spreading out and smoothing the wax with the stylus. In the last clause, the construction seems to be interrupted. This supposition at least enables us to take both the כ and the ו in their natural and proper sense. Supposing the construction of the clause to be complete, it may be explained as in the English Version, which makes both the words in question particles of time meaning *when* and *then*. מרמס is properly a place or object to be trodden down or trampled on. (See chap. v. 5.) The construction above given is the one proposed by Henderson, except that he has *him* instead of *it*, in order to avoid the application of the words to the *scourge*. There can be no doubt that the idea of a human invader was before the Prophet's mind ; but the mere rhetorical incongruity is not at all at variance with the Prophet's manner, and is the less to be dissembled or denied, because the scourge will still be described as *overflow-ing*. The attempt to reconcile the language with the artificial rules of composition is in this case rendered hopeless by the combination of expressions which cannot be strictly applied to the same subject. An army might trample, but it could not literally overflow ; a stream might overflow, but it could not literally trample down. The time perhaps is coming when, even as a matter of taste, the strength and vividness of such mixed metaphors will be considered as outweighing their inaccuracy in relation to an arbitrary standard of correctness or propriety.

19. *As soon (or as often) as it passes through, it shall take you (or carry you away) ; for in the morning, in the morning, (i. e.* every morning*), it shall pass through, in the day and in the night, and only vexation (or dis-tress) shall be the understanding of the thing heard.* The primary meaning of the noun די is sufficiency ; but the phrase מדי is used in reference to time, both in the sense of *as soon* and *as often as.* The meaning may be that the threatened visitation shall come soon and be frequently repeated. There are three interpretations of the last clause, one of which supposes it to mean, that the mere report of the approaching scourge should fill them with distress ; another, that the effect of the report should be unmixed distress ; a third, that nothing but a painful experience would enable them to understand the lesson which the Prophet was commissioned to teach them. שמועה meaning simply what is heard, may of course denote either rumour or revelation.. The latter seems to be the meaning in ver. 9, where the noun stands connected with the same verb as here. Whether this verb means simply to perceive or hear, may be considered doubtful ; if not, the preference is due to the third interpretation above given, viz., that nothing but distress or suffering could make them understand or even attend to the message from Jehovah.

20. *For the bed is too short to stretch one's self, and the covering too narrow to wrap one's self.* This is probably a proverbial description of a perplexed and comfortless condition. Jerome absurdly makes the verse a description of idolatry considered as a spiritual adultery. The כ before the last infinitive may be a particle of time, meaning *when one would wrap himself in it,* which is the explanation given by Cocceius. The connection with the foregoing verse is this : you cannot fully understand the lessons which I teach you now until your bed becomes too short, &c.

21. *For like mount Perazim shall Jehovah rise up, like the valley in Gibeon shall he rage, to do his work, his strange work, and to perform his task, his strange task.* Into such a condition as that just described they

shall be brought, for some of the most fearful scenes of ancient history are yet to be repeated. Interpreters are not agreed as to the precise events referred to in the first clause. The common opinion is, that it alludes to the slaughter of the Philistines, described in 2 Sam. v. 18–25, and 1 Chron. xiv. 9–16, in the latter of which places *Gibeon* is substituted for *Geba*. The valley meant will then be the valley of Rephaim. Ewald, on the contrary, applies the clause to the slaughter of the Canaanites by Joshua, when the sun stood still on Gibeon, and the moon in the valley of Ajalon (Joshua x. 7–15). Still another hypothesis is that of Hendewerk, who applies the first part of the clause to the *breach of Uzzah* (פֶּרֶץ עֻזָּה) described in 2 Sam. vi. 6–8, and the last to the slaughter of Israel in the valley of Achor (Joshua vii. 1–26). The only argument in favour of this forced interpretation is, that these were cases in which God took vengeance, not of strangers merely, but of his own people. But as there is no mention of a mountain in the case of Uzzah, nor of Gibeon in that of Achan, nor of Perez or Perazim in that of Joshua, neither Hendewerk's hypothesis nor Ewald's is so probable as that of Gesenius and most other writers, which refers the whole clause to the double slaughter of the Philistines by David. That these were foreigners and heathen, only adds to the force of the threatening, by making it to mean that as God had dwelt with these in former times, he was now about to deal with the unbelieving and unfaithful sons of Israel. It is indeed not only implied but expressed, that he intended to depart from his usual mode of treating them, in which sense the judgments here denounced are called *strange works*, *i. e.* foreign from the ordinary course of divine providence. The English word *strange* is here the only satisfactory equivalent to the two Hebrew adjectives זָר and נָכְרִיָּה. The idea that punishment is God's strange work because at variance with his goodness, is not only less appropriate in this connection, but inconsistent with the tenor of Scripture, which describes his vindicatory justice as an essential attribute of his nature. The unusual collocation of the words זָר and נָכְרִיָּה has led some to explain them as the predicates of short parenthetical propositions (*strange will be his work*, &c.). But most interpreters, with greater probability, suppose the adjectives to be prefixed for the sake of emphasis. *Like mount Perazim* is a common idiomatic abbreviation of the phrase *as in* (or *at*) *mount Perazim.*

22. *And now scoff not, lest your hands be strong; for a consumption and decree* (or *even a decreed consumption*) *I have heard from the Lord Jehovah of hosts, against* (or *upon*) *the whole earth.* Some versions retain the reflexive form of the first verb ; others make it a frequentative ; but it seems to be simply intensive or emphatic. *Bands*, *i. e.* bonds or chains, is a common figure for afflictions and especially for penal sufferings. To strengthen these bands is to aggravate the suffering. The last clause represents the threatened judgments as inevitable, because determined and revealed by God himself. The form of expression is partly borrowed from chap. x. 23.

23. *Give ear and hear my voice ; hearken and hear my speech.* This formula invites attention to what follows as a new view of the subject. The remainder of the chapter contains an extended illustration drawn from the processes of agriculture. Interpreters, although agreed as to the import of the figures, are divided with respect to their design and application. Some regard the passage as intended to illustrate, in a general way, the wisdom of the divine dispensations. Others refer it most specifically to the delay of judgment on the sinner, and conceive the doctrine of the passage to

be this, that although God is not always punishing, any more than the husbandman is always ploughing or always threshing, he will punish at last. A third interpretation makes the prominent idea to be this, that although God chastises his own people, his ultimate design is not to destroy but to purify and save them. To these must be added, as a new hypothesis, the one maintained by Hitzig and Ewald, who reject entirely the application of the passage to God's providential dealings, and apply it to the conduct of men, assuming that the Prophet's purpose was to hold up the proceedings of the husbandman as an example to the scoffers whom he is addressing. As the farmer does not always plough or always thresh, nor thresh all grains alike, but has a time for either process and a method for each case, so should you cease now from scoffing and receive instruction. To this explanation it may be objected, first, that the comparison contained in the passage does not really illustrate the expediency of the course proposed; and secondly, that even if it did, the illustration would be too extended and minute for a doctrine so familiar and intelligible. The objection to the third interpretation is, that the obvious design for which the comparison is introduced is not to comfort but alarm and warn. The first interpretation is too vague and unconnected with the context. The preference is therefore, on the whole, due to the second, which supposes the Prophet to explain by this comparison the long forbearance of Jehovah, and to shew that this forbearance was no reason for believing that his threatenings would never be fulfilled. As the husbandman ploughs and harrows, sows and plants, before he reaps and threshes, and in threshing employs different modes and different implements, according to the nature of the grain, so God allows the actual infliction of his wrath to be preceded by what seems to be a period of inaction but is really one of preparation, and conforms the strokes themselves to the capacity and guilt of the transgressor.

24. *Does the ploughman plough every day to sow? Does he open and level his ground?* The common version *all day*, though it seems to be a literal translation, does not convey the sense of the original expression, which is used both here and elsewhere to mean *all the time* or *always*. (Gill : he may plough a whole day together when he is at it, but he does not plough every day in the year ; he has other work to do besides ploughing.) The interrogation may be confined to the first clause, and the second construed as an exhortation : (*no*) *let him open and level his grounds.* But as there is a difficulty then in explaining what is meant by *opening* the ground, as distinct from opening the furrows with the plough, most interpreters suppose the interrogation to extend through the verse, and make the second clause a repetition of the first, with an additional reference to harrowing. As if he had said, Is the ploughman always ploughing? is he always ploughing and harrowing? Kimchi explains the last clause thus, as an answer to the question in the first : (*no*) *he will loose* (*his oxen*) *and harrow his ground.*

25. *Does he not, when he has levelled the surface of it, cast abroad dill, and scatter cummin, and set wheat in rows, and barley* (*in the place*) *marked out, and spelt in his border?* That is to say, he attends to all these processes of husbandry successively, with due regard to time and place, and to the various crops to be produced. The words שׂורה and נסמן are by some explained as epithets of the grain ; *principal wheat, appointed or sealed barley.* Ewald makes them descriptive of the soil ; wheat in the best ground, barley in the rough ground. But the explanation best sustained

by usage and analogy is that of Gesenius, who takes נסמן in the sense of appointed, designated, and שורה in that of a row or series. This agrees well with the verb שם as denoting, not an indiscriminate sowing, but a careful planting, which is said to be still practised in the oriental culture of wheat, and is thought by Gesenius and others to have been one of the causes of the wonderful fertility of Palestine in ancient times. The suffix in גבלתו probably relates to the farmer, and the noun to the edge of the field in which the other grains are sown or planted. The reference of the suffix to נסמן, or to the several preceding nouns, is very forced. Gesenius, in order to retain the supposed paronomasia of שורה ושערה, gives his version of this clause the form of doggerel—(Waizen in Reihen und Gerste hinein.)

26. *So teaches him aright his God instructs him.* This is the form of the Hebrew sentence, in which *his God* is the grammatical subject of both the verbs between which it stands. The English idiom requires the noun to be prefixed, as in the common version, and by Lowth, Barnes, and Henderson. למשפט means *according to what is right, i.e.* correctly. The verse refers even agricultural skill to divine instruction. As parallels the commentators quote, from the Wisdom of Solomon, (vii. 16) γεωργίαν ὑπὸ ὑψίστου ἐκτισμένην, and from the Georgics, (i. 157), Prima Ceres ferro mortales vertere terram instituit. Joseph Kimchi thus explains the verse: so he (the husbandman) chastises it (the ground, as) his God teaches him.

27. *For not with the sledge must dill be threshed, or the cart-wheel turned upon cummin; for with the stick must dill be beaten, and cummin with the rod.* Having drawn an illustration from the husbandman's regard to times and seasons, he now derives another from his different modes of threshing out the different kinds of grain. The *semina infirmiora*, as Jerome calls them, are not to be separated by the use of the ponderous sledge or waggon, both of which are common in the East, but by that of the flail or switch, as better suited to their nature. The minute description of the oriental threshing-machines belongs more properly to books of archaeology, especially as nothing more is necessary here to the correct understanding of the verse than a just view of the contrast intended between heavy and light threshing. The כי at the beginning of the verse might be translated *that*, and understood as introducing an explicit statement as to what it is that God thus teaches him. *His God instructs him that,* &c. This arrangement of the sentences, though certainly not necessary, makes them clearer, and is favoured by the otherwise extraordinary brevity of ver. 26, as well as by its seeming interruption of the intimate connection between vers. 25 and 27. An objection to it, drawn from the analogy of ver. 29, will be stated in the exposition of that verse.

28. *Bread-corn must be crushed, for he will not be always threshing it; so he drives the wheel of his cart (upon it), but with his horsemen (or horses) he does not crush it.* The sense of this verse is obscured by an apparent inconsistency between the opening and the closing words. Ewald cuts the knot by reading יודש in the former place. Umbreit takes לֶחֶם in its proper sense of *bread,* and understands the clause to mean that bread is broken by the teeth! Others make the first clause interrogative, and thus conform it to the express negation in the last clause. The translation above given supposes a climax beginning in ver. 27 and completed here. Dill and cummin must be threshed out with the flail; wheat and barley may be more severely dealt with; they will bear the wheel, but not the hoofs of horses. The first words and the last are then in strict agreement; bread-

corn must be bruised, but not with horses' hoofs. This is merely suggested as an additional attempt to elucidate a passage in detail, the general sense of which is clear enough. The reading פרסיו *his hoofs* (*i. e.* the hoofs of his cattle) is unnecessary, as the use of פרש in the sense of *horse* appears to be admitted by the best philological authorities. The historical objection, that the horse was not in common use for agricultural purposes, seems to be likewise regarded by interpreters as inconclusive.

29. *Even this* (or *this also*) *from Jehovah of hosts comes forth; he is wonderful in counsel, great in wisdom.* The literal translation of the last clause is, *he makes counsel wonderful, he makes wisdom great.* The Hiphils may, however, be supposed to signify the *exhibition* of the qualities denoted by the nouns, or taken as intransitives. The antithesis which some suppose the last clause to contain between plan and execution (*wonderful in counsel and excellent in working*) is justified neither by the derivation nor the usage of תּוּשִׁיָה. As to the meaning of the whole verse, some suppose that the preceding illustration is here applied to the divine dispensations; others, that this is the conclusion of the illustration itself. On the latter hypothesis, the meaning of the verse is, that the husbandman's treatment of the crop, no less than his preparation of the soil, is a dictate of experience under divine teaching. In the other case, the sense is, that the same mode of proceeding, which had just been described as that of a wise husbandman, is also practised by the Most High in the execution of his purposes. Against this, and in favour of the other explanation, it may be suggested, first, that *coming forth* from God is a phrase not so naturally suited to express his own way of acting as the influence which he exerts on others; secondly, that this verse seems to correspond, in form and sense, to ver. 27, and to bear the same relation to the different modes of threshing that ver. 27 does to the preparation of the ground and the sowing of the seed. Having there said of the latter, that the husbandman is taught of God, he now says of the former, that it also comes forth from the same celestial source. This analogy may also serve to shew that ver. 27 is not a part of ver 28, and thereby to make it probable that כִּי at the beginning of the latter is to be translated *for, because.* According to the view which has now been taken of ver. 29, the general application of the parable to God's dispensations is not formally expressed, but left to the reflection of the reader.

Chapter 29

THIS chapter consists of two parts, parallel to one another, *i. e.* each containing the same series of promises and threatenings, but in different forms. The prophetic substance or material of both is that Zion should be threatened and assailed, yet not destroyed, but on the contrary strengthened and enlarged. These ideas are expressed in the second part much more fully and explicitly than in the first, which must therefore be interpreted according to what follows. In the first part, the threatening is that Zion shall be assailed by enemies and brought very low, vers. 1–4. The promise is that the assailants shall be scattered like dust and chaff, vanish like a dream, and be wholly disappointed in their hostile purpose, vers. 5–8. In the second part, the Prophet brings distinctly into view, as causes of the threatened judgments, the spiritual intoxication and stupor of the people, their blindness to revealed truth, their hypocritical formality, and their presumptuous contempt of God, vers. 9–16. The judgment itself is described as a confounding of their fancied wisdom, ver. 14. The added promise is that of an entire revolution, including the destruction of the wicked, and especially of wicked rulers, the restoration of spiritual sight, joy to the meek and poor in spirit, and the final recovery of Israel from a state of alienation and disgrace, to the service of Jehovah and to the saving knowledge of the truth, vers. 17–24. The attempts to explain the first part of the chapter as relating to the siege of Jerusalem by Sennacherib, Nebuchadnezzar, or Titus, have been unsuccessful, partly because the description is not strictly appropriate to either of these events, and partly because the connection with what follows is, on either of these suppositions, wholly obscure. Those who deny the inspiration of the writer regard the last part as a visionary anticipation which was never fully verified. Those who admit it are obliged to assume an abrupt transition from the siege of Jerusalem to the calling of the Gentiles. The only key to the consistent exposition of the chapter as a whole is furnished by the hypothesis already stated, and that the two parts are parallel, not merely successive, and that the second must explain the first. That the second part describes not physical but spiritual evils, is admitted on all hands, and indeed asserted by the Prophet himself. This description is directly and repeatedly applied in the New Testament to the Jews contemporary with our Saviour. It does not follow from this, that it is a specific and exclusive prophecy respecting them ; but it does follow that it must be so interpreted as to include them, which can only be effected by regarding this last part of the chapter as descriptive of the Jews, not at one time merely, but throughout the period of the old dispensation,—an assumption fully confirmed by history. The judgment threatened will then be the loss of their peculiar privileges, and an exchange of state with others who had been less favoured, involving an extension of the church beyond its ancient bounds, the destruction of the old abuses, and the final restoration of the Jews themselves. If this be the meaning of the second part, it seems to determine that of the first as a figurative expression of the truth, that the church should suffer but not perish, the imagery used for this purpose being borrowed from the actual sieges of Jerusalem. Thus understood, the chapter is prophetic of two great events, the seeming destruction of the ancient church, and its reproduction in a new and far more glorious form, so as not only to include the Gentiles in its bounds, but also the converted remnant of God's ancient people.

1. *Woe to Ariel* (or *alas for Ariel*), *Ariel, the city David encamped ! Add year to year ; let the feasts revolve.* All interpreters agree that *Ariel* is here a name for Zion or Jerusalem, although they greatly differ in the explanation of the name itself. Besides the explanation which resolves the form into הַרְאֵל (mountain of God), there are two between which interpreters are chiefly divided. One of these makes it mean *lion of God, i. e.* a lion-like champion or hero (2 Sam. xxiii. 20, Isa. xxxiii. 7), here applied to Jerusalem as a city of heroes which should never be subdued. This explanation is retained not only by Gesenius, but by Ewald, who, to make the application more appropriate, translates it *lioness of God.* The other hypothesis explains it, from an Arabic analogy, to mean the *hearth* or *fire-place of God,* in which sense it seems to be applied to the altar by Ezekiel, (xliii. 15, 16), and the extension of the name to the whole city is the more natural because Isaiah himself says of Jehovah that *his fire is in Zion and his furnace in Jerusalem* (chap. xxxi. 9). Hitzig supposes the name to be

here used in the first sense, but with an allusion to the other in the following verse.   This double usage is the less improbable, because the name is evidently meant to be enigmatical.   The Rabbins combine the two explanations of the Hebrew word by supposing that the altar was itself called the lion of God, because it devoured the victims like a lion, or because the fire on it had the appearance of a lion, or because the altar (or the temple) was in shape like a lion, that is, narrow behind and broad in front!   *The city David encamped* is an elliptical expression, not unlike the Hebrew one, in which the relative must be supplied, or קִרְיַת supposed to govern the whole phrase חָנָה דָוִד as a noun.   Here again there seems to be a twofold allusion to David's siege and conquest of Zion (2 Sam. v. 7), and to his afterwards encamping, *i. e.* dwelling there (2 Sam. v. 9).   *Add year to year* is understood by Grotius to mean that the prophecy should be fulfilled in two years, or in other words, that it was uttered just two years before Sennacherib's invasion.   Upon this clause Hitzig founds an ingenious but complex and artificial theory as to the chronology of this whole passage (chaps. xxviii.–xxxi.).   Most interpreters explain the words as simply meaning, let the years roll on with the accustomed routine of ceremonial services.   Many of the older writers take the last words of the verse in this sense, *let them kill* (or more specifically, *cut off the heads of*) *the sacrificial victims;* but it is more in accordance both with the usage of the words and with the context, to give חַגִּים its usual sense of *feasts* or *festivals*, and נָקַף that of moving in a circle or revolving, which it has in Hiphil.   The phrase then corresponds exactly to the one preceding, *add year to year.*

2. *And I will distress Ariel, and there shall be sadness and sorrow, and it shall be to me as Ariel.*   Let the years revolve and the usual routine continue, but the time is coming when it shall be interrupted.   The words translated *sadness and sorrow* are collateral derivatives from one root.   The best imitation of the form of the original is that given by Vitringa (*moeror ac moestitia*).   The last clause may be either a continuation of the threatening or an added promise.   If the former, the meaning probably is, *it shall be indeed a furnace* or *an altar, i. e.* when the fire of affliction or divine wrath shall be kindled on it.   If the latter, *it shall still be a city of heroes,* and as such withstand its enemies.   Or, combining both the senses of the enigmatical name, it shall burn like a furnace, but resist like a lion.

3. *And I will camp against thee round about* (literally, *as a ring* or *circle*), *and push against thee* (or *press upon thee with*) *a post* (or *body of troops*), *and raise against thee ramparts* (or *entrenchments*).   The siege of Ariel is now represented as the work of God himself, which although it admits of explanation as referring merely to his providential oversight and control, seems here to be significant, as intimating that the siege described is not a literal one.   The dubious phrase וצרתי עליך מצב is understood by Ewald as meaning, *I enclose thee with a wall,* or literally, *close a wall around thee.*   To the supposition that these words relate to Sennacherib's attack upon Jerusalem, it has been objected that the history contains no record of an actual siege.   Henderson, indeed, says that *there cannot be a doubt* that they occupied themselves with hostile demonstrations while the negotiations were going forward; but, in spite of this assurance, there is still room for suspicion that this verse does not, after all, relate to the Assyrian incursion.

4. *And thou shalt be brought down, out of the ground shalt thou speak, and thy speech shall be low out of the dust, and thy voice shall be like* (*the voice of*) *a spirit, out of the ground, and out of the dust shall thy speech mutter.*   Grotius understands this of the people's hiding themselves in subterranean

retreats during Sennacherib's invasion, while Vitringa shews from Josephus that such measures were actually adopted during the Roman siege of Jerusalem. But the simple meaning naturally suggested by the words is, that the person here addressed, to wit, the city or its population, should be weakened and humbled. Some suppose the voice to be compared with that of a dying man or a departing spirit; others, with that of a necromancer who pretended to evoke the dead. To this last the terms of the comparison would be the more appropriate if, as the modern writers commonly suppose, the ancient necromancers used ventriloquism as a means of practising upon the credulous. The last verb properly denotes any feeble inarticulate sound, and is applied in chap. x. 14, and xxxviii. 14, to the chirping or twittering of birds.

5. *Then shall be like fine dust the multitude of thy strangers, and like passing chaff the multitude of the terrible ones, and it shall be in a moment suddenly.* Calvin understands by *strangers* foreign allies or mercenary troops, which he supposes to be here described as powerless and as enduring but a moment. Others among the older writers take *strangers* more correctly in the sense of enemies, but understand the simile as merely descriptive of their numbers and velocity. It is now very commonly agreed, however, that the verse describes their sudden and complete dispersion. The absence of *but* at the beginning, or some other indication that the writer is about to pass from threats to promises, although it renders the connection more obscure, increases the effect of the description. Ewald, instead of *multitude* has *tumult*, which is the primary meaning of the word; but the former is clearly established by usage, and is here much more appropriate, since it is not the noise of a great crowd, but the crowd itself, that can be likened to fine dust or *flitting chaff*, as Lowth poetically renders it. The terms of this verse readily suggest the sudden fall of the Assyrian host, nor is there any reason for denying that the Prophet had a view to it in choosing his expressions. But that this is an explicit and specific prophecy of that event is much less probable, as well because the terms are in themselves appropriate to any case of sudden and complete dispersion, as because the context contains language wholly inappropriate to the slaughter of Sennacherib's army. To the Babylonian and Roman sieges, which were both successful, the verse before us is entirely inapplicable. These considerations, although negative and inconclusive in themselves, tend strongly to confirm the supposition founded on the last part of the chapter, that the first contains a strong metaphorical description of the evils which Jerusalem should suffer at the hands of enemies, but without exclusive reference to any one siege, or to sieges in the literal sense at all. That the evils which the last part of the chapter brings to light are of a spiritual nature, and not confined to any single period, is a fact which seems to warrant the conclusion, or at least to raise a strong presumption, that the Ariel of this passage is Zion or Jerusalem considered only as the local habitation of the church.

6. *From with (i. e.* from the presence of*) Jehovah of hosts shall it be visited with thunder, and earthquake, and great noise, tempest and storm, and flame of devouring fire.* Vitringa refers this to the singular phenomena which are said to have preceded and accompanied the taking of Jerusalem by Titus. This application may be admitted, in the same sense and on the same ground with the allusion to Sennacherib's host in the foregoing verse. But that the prophecy is not a prophecy of either catastrophe, may be inferred from the fact that neither is described in the context. Indeed, the direct application of this verse to the fall of Jerusalem is wholly inadmis-

sible, since the preceding verse describes the assailants as dispersed, and this appears to continue the description.   As תִּפְקֹד can be either the third person feminine or the second masculine, the verse may be considered as addressed directly to the enemy ; or the verb may agree with המון as a feminine noun, in which way it is construed elsewhere (Job xxxi. 34), although evidently masculine in ver. 8 below.   The city cannot be addressed, because the verb must then be feminine, and the preceding verse forbids the one before us to be taken as a threatening against Ariel.

7. *Then shall be as a dream, a vision of the night, the multitude of all the nations fighting against Ariel, even all that fight against her and her munition, and distress her.* Calvin understands this to mean that the enemy shall take her unawares, as one awakes from a dream.   The modern writers generally understand both this verse and the next as meaning that the enemy himself should be wholly disappointed, and his vain hopes vanish as a dream. But the true sense appears to be the one proposed by Grotius and others, who regard the comparisons in these two verses as distinct though similar, the enemy being first compared to a dream and then to a dreamer.   He who threatens your destruction shall vanish like a dream, *par levibus ventis volucrique simillima somno.* He who threatens your destruction shall awake as from a dream, and find himself cheated of his expectations, for, as Grotius beautifully says, *spes sunt vigilantium somnia.*   These seem to be the two comparisons intended, both of which are perfectly appropriate, and one of which might readily suggest the other.   The feminine pronouns may refer to *Ariel* as itself a feminine, or to the city which it represents.

8. *And it shall be as when the hungry dreams, and lo he eats, and he awakes, and his soul is empty ; and as when the thirsty dreams, and lo he drinks, and he awakes, and lo he is faint and his soul craving : so shall be the multitude of all the nations that fight against mount Zion.* The meaning of this beautiful comparison seems so clear, and its application to the disappointment of the enemies of Ariel so palpable, that it is hard to understand how such an interpreter as Calvin could say, *Nihil hic video quod ad consolationem pertineat.*   His explanation of the verse as meaning that the Jews should be awakened by the enemy from their dream of security and find themselves wholly unprovided with the necessary means of defence, is forced and arbitrary in a high degree, and seems the more so when propounded by a writer who is characteristically free from all propensity to strained and far-fetched expositions.   In this verse *soul* is twice used in the not uncommon sense of *appetite*, first described as *empty* (*i.e.* unsatisfied), and then as *craving*.   This is much better than to take the word, with Grotius, as a mere periphrasis for the man himself.   To this verse Lowth quotes a beautiful but certainly inferior parallel from Lucretius :

> Ac velut in somnis sitiens quum quærit, et humor
> Non datur, ardorem in membris qui stinguere possit,
> Sed laticum simulacra petit, frustraque laborat,
> In medioque sitit torrenti flumine potans.

The passage quoted from Virgil by the same accomplished critic is not so opposite because more general.   A less poetical but not less striking and affecting parallel from real life is found in one of Mungo Park's journals, and pertinently quoted here by Barnes.   " No sooner had I shut my eyes than fancy would convey me to the streams and rivers of my native land. There, as I wandered along the verdant bank, I surveyed the clear stream with transport, and hastened to swallow the delightful draught; but alas !

disappointment awakened me, and I found myself a lonely captive, perishing of thirst amid the wilds of Africa."

9. *Waver and wonder! be merry and blind! They are drunk, but not
with wine; they reel, but not with strong drink.* Here begins the description
of the moral and spiritual evils which were the occasion of the judgments
previously threatened. In the first clause, the Prophet describes the condition of the people by exhorting them ironically to continue in it; in the
second, he seems to turn away from them and address the spectators. The
terms of the first clause are very obscure. In each of its members two
cognate verbs are used, but whether as synonymous, or as expressing
different ideas, appears doubtful. Ewald adopts the former supposition,
and regards the first two as denoting wonder (*erstaunt und staunt*), the last
two blindness (*erblindet und blindet*). Gesenius, on the contrary, supposes
verbs alike in form but different in sense to be designedly combined. To
the first he gives the sense of lingering, hesitating, doubting; to the second,
that of wondering; to the third, that of taking pleasure or indulging the
desires; to the fourth, that of being blind. The second imperative in either
case he understands as indicating the effect or consequence of that before
it: refuse to believe, but you will only be the more astonished; continue
to enjoy yourselves, but it will only be the means of blinding you. The
express description of the drunkenness as spiritual, shews that where no
such explanation is added (as in chap. xxviii. 1, 7), the terms are to be
literally understood. By spiritual drunkenness we are probably to understand unsteadiness of conduct and a want of spiritual discernment.

10. *For Jehovah hath poured out upon you a spirit of deep sleep, and hath
shut your eyes; the prophets and your heads (or even your heads) the seers
hath he covered.* On the agency here ascribed to God, see the exposition
of chap. vi. 9, 10. The two ideas expressed in the parallel clauses are
those of bandaging the eyes and covering the head so as to obstruct the
sight. In the latter case, the Prophet makes a special application of the
figure to the chiefs or religious leaders of the people, as if he had said, he
hath shut your eyes, and covered your heads, viz. the prophets'. Some
have proposed to make the clauses more symmetrical by changing the
division of the sentence, so as to read thus, *he hath shut your eyes, the
prophets, and your heads, the seers, hath he covered.* Others, because the
Prophet did not use a commonplace expression or conform to the petty
rules of rhetoric, reject *prophets* and *seers* as a gloss accidentally transferred
from the margin. One of the reasons given for this bold mutilation of the
text is, that the subject of the previous description is not the prophets but
the people; as if the former were not evidently mentioned as the leaders of
the latter. The people were blinded by rendering the revelations of the
prophets useless. To produce the usual confusion, Ewald, though he strikes
out נביאים, insists upon retaining חזים as an adjective agreeing with ראשיכם
(*your seeing heads*). This amendment of Gesenius's amendment has the
good effect of making both ridiculous, and shewing that the common text,
with all its difficulties, is best entitled to respect and confidence.

11. *And the vision of all (or of the whole) is (or has become) to you like
the words of the sealed writing, which they give to one knowing writing, saying,
Pray read this, and he says, I cannot, for it is sealed.* The *vision of all* may
either mean *of all the prophets,* or collectively *all vision,* or the *vision of all
things, i. e.* prophecy on all subjects (Ewald: Weissagung über alles).
Gesenius arbitrarily takes *vision* in the sense of *law.* If we depart from

that of *prophecy*, the most appropriate sense would be the primary one of *sight*. The English word *book* does not exactly represent the Hebrew סֵפֶר, which originally signifies writing in general, or anything written (Hende-werk : Schrift), and is here used as we might use *document*, or the still more general term *paper*. J. D. Michaelis employs the specific term *letter*, which the Hebrew word is some cases denotes. In the phrase ידע ספר, the last word seems to mean writing in general, and the whole phrase one who understands it, or knows how to read it. The application of the simile becomes clear in the next verse.

12. *And the writing is given to one who knows not writing, saying, Pray read this, and he says, I know not writing.* The common version, *I am not learned*, is too comprehensive and indefinite. A man might read a letter without being learned, at least in the modern sense, although the word was once the opposite of illiterate or wholly ignorant. In this case it is necessary to the full effect of the comparison, that the phrase should be distinctly understood to mean, *I cannot read.* The comparison itself re-presents the people as alike incapable of understanding the divine communi-cations, or rather as professing incapacity to understand them, some upon the general ground of ignorance, and others on the ground of their obscurity.

13. *And the Lord said, Because this people draws near with its mouth, and with its lips they honour me, and its heart it puts* (or *keeps*) *far from me, and their fearing me is* (or *has become*) *a precept of men, (a thing) taught.* The apodosis follows in the next verse. Some read נֻשָּׁא for נִגַּשׁ, and understand the clause to mean, they are *compelled* to honour me, they serve me by compulsion ; or, when they are *oppressed* and afflicted, then they honour me. The common reading is no doubt the true one. Ewald makes רָחַק an intransitive verb (*wanders far from me*), which is contrary to usage. The singular and plural pronouns are promiscuously used in this verse with respect to Israel considered as a nation and an individual. At the end of the verse the English Version has, *taught by the precepts of men :* but a simpler construction, and one favoured by the accents, is to take מלמדה as a neuter adjective without a substantive in apposition with מצוה. This clause might be simply understood to mean, that they served God merely in obedience to human authority. It would then of course imply no censure on the persons thus commanding, but only on the motives of those by whom they were obeyed. In our Saviour's application of the passage to the hyprocrites of his day (Mat. xv. 7- 9), he explains their teachings as human corruptions of the truth, by which the commandment of God was made of none effect. The expressions of the Prophet may have been so chosen as to be applicable either to the reign of Hezekiah, when the worship of Jehovah was enforced by human authority, or to the time of Christ, when the rulers of the people had corrupted and made void the law by their additions. It is unnecessary to suppose, with Henderson, that this corruption had already reached a great height when Isaiah wrote. The apparent reference, in this description, to the Jews, not at one time only but throughout their history, tends to confirm the supposition, that the sub-ject of the prophecy is not any one specific juncture, and that the first part of the chapter is not a prediction of any one siege of Jerusalem exclusively.

14. *Therefore, behold, I will add* (or *continue*) *to treat this people strangely, very strangely, and with strangeness, and the wisdom of its wise ones shall be lost* (or *perish*), *and the prudence of its prudent ones shall hide itself, i. e.* for shame, or simply *disappear*. This is the conclusion of the sentence which begins with the preceding verse. *Because they draw near, &c.,*

therefore I will add, &c. יוֹסִיף is explained by some as an unusual form of the participle for יוֹסֵף; but the latest interpreters make it as usual the third person of the future, and regard the construction as elliptical. *Behold, I (am he who) will add,* &c. See a similar construction of the preterite in chap. xxviii. 16. הַפְלִיא is strictly to *make wonderful,* but when applied to persons, to *treat wonderful, i. e.* in a strange or extraordinary manner. The idiomatic repetition of the verb with its cognate noun (הַפְלֵא וָפֶלֶא) cannot be fully reproduced in English. The literal translation (*to make wonderful and wonder*) would be quite unmeaning to an English reader. The nature of the judgment here denounced seems to shew that the corruption of the people was closely connected with undue reliance upon human wisdom. (Compare chap. v. 21.)

15. *Woe unto those* (or *alas for those*) *going deep from Jehovah to hide counsel* (*i. e.* laying their plans deep in the hope of hiding them from God), *and their works (are) in the dark, and they say, Who sees us, and who knows us?* This is a further description of the people or their leaders, as not only wise in their own conceit, but as impiously hoping to deceive God, or elude his notice. The absurdity of such an expectation is exposed in the following verse. In the last clause of this, the interrogative form implies negation.

16. *Your perversion! Is the potter to be reckoned as the clay* (and nothing more), *that the thing made should say of its maker, He made me not, and the thing formed say of its former, He does not understand?* The attempt to hide anything from God implies that he has not a perfect knowledge of his creatures, which is practically to reduce the maker and the thing made to a level. With this inversion or perversion of the natural relation between God and man, the Prophet charges them in one word (הׇפְכְּכֶם). The old construction of this word as nominative to the verb (*your turning of things upside down shall be esteemed,* &c.) appears to be forbidden by the accents and by the position of the אִם. That of Barnes (*your perverseness is as if the potter,* &c.) arbitrarily supplies not only an additional verb but a particle of comparison. Most of the recent writers are agreed in construing the first word as an exclamation, *oh your perverseness! i. e.* how perverse you are! in which sense it had long before been paraphrased by Luther (*wie seyd ihr so verkehrt?*). Both the derivation of the word, however, and the context here seem to demand the sense *perversion* rather than *perverseness.* The verse seems intended not so much to rebuke their perverse disposition, as to shew that by their conduct they subverted the distinction between creature and Creator, or placed them in a preposterous relation to each other. Thus understood, the word may be thus paraphrased: (*this is*) *your (own) perversion (of the truth,* or of the true relation between God and man). The English Version puts the following nouns in regimen (*like the potter's clay*), but the other construction (*the potter like the clay*) is so plainly required by the context, that Gesenius and others disregard the accents by which it seems to be forbidden. Hitzig, however, denies that the actual accentuation is at all at variance with the new construction. The preposition לְ is here used in its proper sense as signifying general relation, *with respect to, as to.* By translating כִּי *for,* the connection of the clauses becomes more obscure.

17. *Is it not yet a very little while, and Lebanon shall turn* (or *be turned*) *to the fruitful field, and the fruitful field be reckoned to the forest* (*i. e.* reckoned as belonging it, or as being itself a forest)? The negative interrogation is one of the strongest forms of affirmation. That הַכַּרְמֶל is not

the proper name of the mountain, may be inferred from the article, which is not prefixed to *Lebanon*. The mention of the latter no doubt suggested that of the ambiguous term *Carmel*, which is both a proper name and an appellative. For its sense and derivation see the commentary on chap. x. 18. The metaphors of this verse evidently signify a great revolution. Some suppose it to be meant that the lofty (Lebanon) shall be humbled, and the lowly (Carmel) exalted. But the comparison is evidently not between the high and the low, but between the cultivated and the wild, the field and the forest. Some make both clauses of the verse a promise, by explaining the last to mean that what is now esteemed a fruitful field shall then appear to be a forest in comparison. But the only natural interpretation of the verse is that which regards it as prophetic of a mutual change of condition, the first becoming last and the last first. If, as we have seen sufficient reason to believe, the previous context has respect to the Jews under the old dispensation, nothing can be more appropriate or natural than to understand the verse before, as foretelling the excision of the unbelieving Jews, and the admission of the Gentiles to the church.

18. *And in that day shall the deaf ear hear the words of the book* (or *writing*)*, and out of obscurity and darkness shall the eyes of the blind see.* This is a further description of the change just predicted under other figures. As the forest was to be transformed into a fruitful field, so the blind should be made to see, and the deaf to hear. There is an obvious allusion to the figure of the sealed book or writing in vers. 13, 14. The Jews could only plead obscurity or ignorance as an excuse for not understanding the revealed will of God. The Gentiles, in their utter destitution, might be rather likened to the blind who cannot read, however clear the light or plain the writing, and the deaf who cannot even hear what is read by others. But the time was coming when they, who would not break the seal or learn the letters of the written word, should be abandoned to their chosen state of ignorance, while on the other hand, the blind and deaf, whose case before seemed hopeless, should begin to see and hear the revelation once entirely inaccessible. The perfect adaptation of this figurative language to express the new relation of the Jews and Gentiles after the end of the old economy, affords a new proof that the prophecy relates to that event.

19. *And the humble shall add joy* (*i. e.* shall rejoice more and more) *in Jehovah, and the poor among men in the Holy One of Israel shall rejoice.* As the preceding verse describes the happy effect of the promised change upon the intellectual views of those who should experience it, so this describes its influence in the promotion of their happiness. Not only should the ignorant be taught of God, but the wretched should be rendered happy in the enjoyment of his favour. The *poor of men, i. e.* the poor among them.

20. *For the violent is at an end, and the scoffer ceaseth, and all the watchers for injustice are cut off.* A main cause of the happiness foretold will be the weakening or destruction of all evil influences, here reduced to the three great classes of violent wrong-doing, impious contempt of truth and goodness, and malignant treachery or fraud, which watches for the opportunity of doing evil, with as constant vigilance as ought to be employed in watching for occasions of redressing wrong and doing justice. This is a change which, to some extent, has always attended the diffusion of the true religion. Gesenius connects this verse with the foregoing as a statement of the cause for which the humble would rejoice, viz. *that the oppressor is no more*, &c. But this construction is precluded by the fact, that wherever men are said to rejoice *in God*, he is himself the subject of their joy. It is,

however, a mere question of grammatical arrangement, not affecting the general import of the passage.

21. *Making a man a sinner for a word, and for him disputing in the gate they laid a snare, and turned aside the righteous through deceit.* An amplification of the last phrase in the foregoing verse. Some understand the first clause to mean, *seducing people into sin by their words.* It is much more common to explain דָּבָר as meaning a judicial cause or matter, which use of the word occurs in Exodus xviii. 16. The whole phrase may then mean unjustly condemning a man in his cause, which agrees well with the obvious allusion to forensic process in the remainder of the verse. Ewald, however, takes בְּדָבָר in the same sense with the English and many other early versions, which explain the clause to mean accusing or condemning men for a mere error of the tongue or lips. The general sense is plain, viz. that they embrace all opportunities and use all arts to wrong the guiltless. Another old interpretation, now revived by Ewald, is that of מוֹכִיחַ as meaning one that reproves others. Most of the modern writers take it in the sense of arguing, disputing, pleading, *in the gate, i.e.* the court, often held in the gates of oriental cities. The other explanation supposes the gate to be mentioned only as a place of public concourse. Ewald translates it *in the market-place.* By the *turning aside* of the righteous (*i.e.* of the party who is in the right), we are here to understand the depriving him of that which is his due. For the meaning and usage of the figure, see the commentary on chap. x. 2. בַּתֹּהוּ has been variously understood to mean *through falsehood* (with particular reference to false testimony), or by means of a judgment which is null and void, or for nothing, *i.e.* without just cause. In either case the phrase describes the perversion or abuse of justice by dishonest means, and thus agrees with the expressions used in the foregoing clauses.

22. *Therefore thus saith Jehovah to the house of Jacob, he who redeemed Abraham, Not now shall Jacob be ashamed, and not now shall his face turn pale.* The Hebrew phrase *not now* does not imply that it shall be so hereafter, but on the contrary, that it shall be so no more. Gesenius and others render אֶל *of* or *concerning*, because Jacob is immediately afterwards mentioned in the third person; but this might be the case consistently with usage, even in a promise made directly to himself. That אֲשֶׁר refers to the remoter antecedent, must be obvious to every reader; if it did not, Jacob would be described as the redeemer of Abraham. There is consequently not the slightest ground for Lowth's correction of the text by reading אֵל instead of אֶל (*the God of the house of Jacob*). There is no need of referring the redemption of Abraham to his removal from a land of idolatry. The phrase may be naturally understood, either as signifying deliverance from danger and the divine protection generally, or in a higher sense as signifying Abraham's conversion and salvation. Secker and Lowth read יֶחְפְּרוּ for יֶחֱוָרוּ, because paleness is not a natural indication of confusion. Other interpreters affirm that it is; but the true explanation seems to be that shame and fear are here combined as strong and painful emotions from which Jacob should be henceforth free. Calvin and others understand by Jacob here the patriarch himself, poetically represented as beholding and sympathizing with the fortunes of his own descendants. Most interpreters suppose the name to be employed like *Israel* in direct application to the race itself. The reasons for these contrary opinions will be more clear from the following verse.

23. *For in his seeing (i.e.* when he sees) *his children, the work of my hands, in the midst of him, they shall sanctify my name, and sanctify (or yes, they shall sanctify) the Holy One of Jacob, and the God of Israel they shall*

fear. The verse thus translated, according to its simplest and most obvious sense, has much perplexed interpreters. The difficulties chiefly urged are, first, that Jacob should be said to see his children *in the midst of himself* (בְּקִרְבּוֹ); secondly, that *his* thus seeing them should be the occasion of *their* glorifying God. The last incongruity is only partially removed by making the verb indefinite, as Ewald does (wird man heiligen); for it may still be asked why Jacob is not himself represented as the agent. To remove both difficulties, some explain the verse to mean, when *he* (that is) *his children see the work of my hands* (viz., my providential judgments), *they shall sanctify*, &c. It is evident, however, that in this construction the mention of the children is entirely superfluous, and throws the figures of the text into confusion. Ewald accordingly omits ילדיו as a gloss, which is merely giving up the attempt at explanation in despair. Gesenius, on the other hand, in his translation, cuts the knot by omitting the singular pronoun, and making *his children* the sole subject of the verb. What follows is suggested as a possible solution of this exegetical enigma. We have seen reason, wholly independent of this verse, to believe that the immediately preceding context has respect to the excision of the Jews and the vocation of the Gentiles. Now the latter are described in the New Testament as Abraham's (and consequently Jacob's) spiritual progeny, as such, distinguished from his natural descendants. May not these adventitious or adopted children of the patriarch, constituted such by the electing grace of God, be here intended by the phrase, *the work of my hands?* If so, the whole may thus be paraphrased: when he (the patriarch, supposed to be again alive, and gazing at his offspring) shall behold his children (not by nature, but), created such by me, in the midst of him (*i.e.* in the midst, or in the place, of his natural descendants), they (*i.e.* he and his descendants jointly) shall unite in glorifying God as the author of this great revolution. This explanation of the verse is the more natural, because such would no doubt be the actual feelings of the patriarch and his descendants, if he should really be raised from the dead, and permitted to behold what God has wrought, with respect both to his natural and spiritual offspring. To the passage thus explained a striking parallel is found in chap. xlix. 18–21, where the same situation and emotions here ascribed to the patriarch are predicated of the church personified, to whom the Prophet says, "Lift up thine eyes round about and behold, all these gather themselves together, they come to thee. The children which thou shalt have after thou hast lost the others shall say, &c. Then shalt thou say in thine heart, Who hath begotten me these, seeing I have lost my children, and am desolate, a captive, and removing to and fro? And who hath brought up these? Behold, I alone was left; these, where were they?" For the use of the word *sanctify*, in reference to God as its object, see the note on chap. viii. 13. The *Holy One of Jacob* is of course identical in meaning with the *Holy One of Israel*, which last phrase is explained in the note on chap. i. 4. The emphatic mention of the Holy One of Jacob and the God of Israel as the object to be sanctified, implies a relation still existing between all believers and their spiritual ancestry, as well as a relation of identity between the Jewish and the Christian church.

24. *Then shall the erring in spirit know wisdom, and the murmurers* (or *rebels*) *shall receive instruction*. These words would be perfectly appropriate as a general description of the reclaiming and converting influence to be exerted upon men in general. But under this more vague and comprehensive sense, the context, and especially the verse immediately preceding,

seems to shew that there is one more specific and significant included. **If** the foregoing verse predicts the reception of the Gentiles into the family of Israel, and if this reception, as we learn from the New Testament, was connected with the disinheriting of most of the natural descendants, who are, nevertheless, to be restored hereafter, then the promise of this final restoration is a stroke still wanting to complete the fine prophetic picture now before us. That finishing stroke is given in this closing verse, which adds to the promise that the Gentiles shall become the heirs of Israel, another that the heirs of Israel according to the flesh shall themselves be restored to their long-lost heritage, not by excluding their successors in their turn, but by peaceful and brotherly participation with them. This application of the last part of the chapter to the calling of the Gentiles and the restoration of the Jews has been founded, as the reader will observe, not on any forced accommodation of particular expressions, but on various detached points, all combining to confirm this exegetical hypothesis as the only one which furnishes a key to the consistent exposition of the chapter as a concatenated prophecy, without abrupt transitions or a mixture of incongruous materials.

Chapter 30

THIS chapter contains an exposure of the sin and folly of ancient Israel in seeking foreign aid against their enemies, to the neglect of God, their rightful sovereign and their only strong protector. The costume of the prophecy is borrowed from the circumstances and events of Isaiah's own times. Thus Egypt is mentioned in the first part of the chapter as the chosen ally of the people, and Assyria in the last part as the dreaded enemy. There is no need, however, of restricting what is said to that period exclusively. The presumption, as in all such cases, is, that the description was designed to be more general, although it may contain allusions to particular emergencies. Reliance upon human aid, involving a distrust of the divine promises, was a crying sin of the ancient church, not at one time only, but throughout her history. To denounce such sins, and threaten them with condign punishment, was no small part of the prophetic office. The chronological hypotheses assumed by different writers with respect to this chapter are erroneous, only because too specific and exclusive. Thus Jerome refers it to the conduct of the Jews in the days of Jeremiah, Kimchi to their conduct in the reign of Ahaz, Jarchi to the conduct of the ten tribes in the reign of Hoshea. Vitringa takes a step in the right direction, by combining Israel and Judah as included in the censure. Some of the later writers assume the existence of an Egyptian party in the reign of Hezekiah, who negotiated with that power against the will or without the knowledge of the king. But even if this fact can be inferred from Rabshakeh's hypothetical reproach in chap. xxxvi. 6, it does not follow that this was the sole subject or occasion of the prophecy. It was clearly intended to reprove the sin of seeking foreign aid without divine permission; but there is nothing in the terms of the reproof confining it to any single case of the offence. This chapter may be divided into three parts. In the first, the Prophet shews the sin and folly of relying upon Egypt, no doubt for protection against Assyria, as these were the two great powers between which Israel was continually oscillating, almost constantly at war with one and in alliance with the other, vers. 1–7. In the last part, he describes the Assyrian power as broken by an immediate divine inter-

position, precluding the necessity of any human aid, vers. 27–33. In the
larger intervening part, he shews the connection of this distrust of God and
reliance on the creature with the general character and spiritual state of the
people, as unwilling to receive instruction, as dishonest and oppressive,
making severe judgments necessary, as a prelude to the glorious change
which God would eventually bring to pass, vers. 8–26.

1. *Woe to the disobedient children, saith Jehovah,* (so disobedient as)
to form (or execute) *a plan and not from me, and to weave a web, but not* (of)
my Spirit, for the sake of adding sin to sin. Here, as in chap. i. 2, Israel's
filial relation to Jehovah is particularly mentioned as an aggravation of his
ingratitude and disobedience. The infinitives express *the respect in which,*
or the *result with which,* they had rebelled against Jehovah. The relative
construction of the English Version does not materially change the sense.

The phrase לִנְסֹךְ מַסֵּכָה has been variously explained. The Peshito makes
it mean *to pour out libations,* probably with reference to some ancient mode
of ratifying covenants, and the Septuagint accordingly translates it ἐποιήσατε
συνθήκας. Cocceius applies it to the casting of molten images (*ad fundendum fusile*), De Dieu to the moulding of designs or plots. Kimchi and
Calvin derive the words from the root to *cover,* and suppose the idea here
expressed to be that of concealment. Ewald follows J. D. Michaelis in
making the phrase mean to *weave a web,* which agrees well with the context,
and is favoured by the similar use of the same verb and noun in chap. xxv.
7. Knobel's objection, that this figure is suited only to a case of treachery,
has no force, as the act of seeking foreign aid was treasonable under the
theocracy, and the design appears to have been formed and executed
secretly. (Compare chap. xxix. 15, where the reference may be to the
same transaction.) Vitringa, who refers the first part of the chapter to the
kingdom of the ten tribes, supposes the sin of seeking foreign aid to be
here described as added to the previous sin of worshipping the golden calf.
Hitzig supposes the first sin to be that of forsaking Jehovah, the second that
of seeking human aid. The simple meaning seems, however, to be that of
multiplying or accumulating guilt. סוֹרְרִים is strongly rendered by the Septuagint *apostates,* and by the Vulgate *deserters,* both which ideas may be
considered as involved in the translation *rebels* or *rebellious,* disobedient or
refractory.

2. *Those walking to go down to Egypt, and my mouth they have not consulted* (literally *asked*), *to take refuge in the strength of Pharaoh, and to trust
in the shadow of Egypt.* Motion towards Egypt is commonly spoken of in
Scripture as downward. הֹלְכִים is commonly explained to mean *setting out*
or *setting forward ;* but De Wette and Ewald omit it altogether, or consider it as joined with the other verb to express the simple idea of descent.
Hendewerk takes *mouth* as a specific designation of the Prophet, which is
wholly unnecessary. To *ask the mouth,* or *at the mouth,* of the Lord, is a
phrase used elsewhere in the sense of seeking a divine decision or response.

3. *And the strength of Egypt shall be to you for shame, and the trust in the
shadow of Egypt for confusion.* הָיָה לְ may here be taken in its frequent
sense of *becoming* or being *converted into.* The common version of the first
ו by *therefore* changes the idiomatic form of the original without necessity.

4. *For his chiefs are in Zoan, and his ambassadors arrive at Hanes.*
For the site and political importance of *Zoan* or *Tanis,* see the commentary
on chap. xix. 11. For חָנֵס יַגִּיעוּ, the Seventy seem to have read חִנָּם יִגְעוּ,
they shall labour in vain. This reading is also found in a few manuscripts

and approved by Lowth and J. D. Michaelis. The latter thinks it possible, however, that חנם may denote the Pyramids. The Targum changes *Hanes* into *Tahpanhes*, and Grotius regards the former as a mere contraction of the latter, which is also the conjecture of Champollion. Vitringa identifies the חָנֵם of Isaiah with the Ἄνυσις of Herodotus. This combination is approved by Gesenius and the later writers, who, moreover, identify the Greek and Hebrew forms with the Egyptian *Hnés* and the Arabic *Ehnés*. The city so called was in Middle Egypt, south of Memphis. The older writers almost unanimously understand this verse as relating to the envoys of Israel and Judah. Clericus indeed refers the suffixes to Egypt or to Pharaoh, but without a change of meaning, as he supposes the Egyptian envoys to be such as were sent to meet the others, or to convey the answer to their applications. But some of the late interpreters adopt the same construction with a total change of meaning. Hitzig regards the verse as a contemptuous description of the narrow boundaries and insignificance of Egypt. *His* (Pharaoh's) *princes are in Zoan* (the capital), *and his heralds* (the bearers of his royal mandates) *only reach to Hanes* (a town of Middle Egypt.) The unnatural and arbitrary character of this interpretation will appear from the curious fact that Ewald, who adopts the same construction of the pronouns, makes the whole verse a concession of the magnitude and strength of the Egyptian monarchy. *Although his princes are at Zoan* (in Lower Egypt) *and his heralds reach to Hanes* (much further south). Knobel objects to these constructions, that the phrase, *his princes are at Zoan*, is unmeaning and superfluous. He therefore resuscitates the Septuagint reading חנם יגעו, and makes the whole mean, that the chiefs of Pharaoh are still at Zoan (*i. e.* remain inactive there), and that his messengers or commissaries labour in vain to raise the necessary forces. From these ingenious extravagances it is satisfactory to fall back on the old interpretation, which is also that of Gesenius, Umbreit, and Hendewerk, with this modification in the case of the latter, that he supposes Zoan and Hanes to be mentioned as the royal seats of Sevechus and Tirhakah, to both of whom the application may have been addressed.

5. *All are ashamed of a people who cannot profit them (a people) not for help and not for profit, but for shame, and also for disgrace.* Lowth inserts אם after כי, on the authority of four manuscripts. But the כ is itself here equivalent to an adversative particle in English, although it really retains its usual meaning, *for, because*. The Hebrew construction is, they are not a profit or a help, *for* (on the contrary) they are a disgrace and a reproach. Gesenius regards הִבְאִישׁ as an incorrect orthography for הוֹבִישׁ ; but Maurer and Knobel read it הִבְאִישׁ, and assume a root בָּאַשׁ synonymous with בּוֹשׁ. The עַל in the first clause has its very frequent meaning of *concerning, on account of*.

6. *The burden of the beasts of the south, in a land of suffering and distress, whence (are) the adder and the fiery flying serpent ; they are carrying* (or *about to carry*) *on the shoulder of young asses their wealth, and on the hump of camels their treasures, to a people* (or *for the sake of a people*) *who cannot profit.* The Prophet sees the ambassadors of Israel carrying costly presents through the waste howling wilderness, for the purpose of securing the Egyptian alliance. Gill applies the description to the emigration of the Jews into Egypt in the days of Jeremiah. This may be alluded to, but cannot be the exclusive subject of the passage. The Septuagint translates מַשָּׂא by ὅρασις, and converts the first clause into a title or inscrip-

tion. Schmidius and J. H. Michaelis regard this as the beginning of a special prophecy, or subdivision of the greater prophecy, against the southern Jews who were nearest to Egypt. Henderson also thinks it *incontrovertible*, that this is the title or inscription of the record which the Prophet is afterwards commanded to made. The latest German writers, as might have been expected, reject the clause as spurious, Hendewerk and Ewald expunging it wholly from the text, while the others include it in brackets as of doubtful authenticity. These critical conclusions all involve the supposition, that some ancient copyist or reader of the Prophet, imagining a new subdivision to begin here, introduced this title, as the same or another hand had done in chaps. xiii. 1, xv. 1, xvii. 1, xix. 1, xxi. 1, 11, 13, xxii. 1, xxiii. 1. The number of these alleged interpolations, far from adding to the probability of the assumption, makes it more improbable in every instance where it is resorted to. In this case there is nothing to suggest the idea of a change of subject or a new division, if the title be omitted. How then can the interpolation be accounted for? If it be said that we are not bound to account for the absurdity of ancient interpolators, the answer is that we are just as little bound to believe in their existence. The truth appears to be that the interpretation of this clause as an inscription is entirely imaginary. Even in the other cases cited we have seen that the assumption of a formal title may be pushed too far. But here it is wholly out of place. It is surely an unreasonable supposition, that the Prophet could not put the word משָׂא at the beginning of a sentence without converting it into a title. The most natural construction of the first clause is to take it as an exclamation (*O the burden of the beasts! what a burden to the beasts!*), or as an absolute nominative (*as to the burden of the beasts*). The beasts meant are not the lions and the vipers of the next clause (Hitzig), but the asses and the camels of the one following, called *beasts of the south* because travelling in that direction. The *land* meant is not Egypt (Vitringa), though described by Ammianus Marcellinus as peculiarly abounding in venomous reptiles (serpentes alit innumeras, ultra omnem perniciem sævientes, basiliscos et amphisbænas et scytalas et acontias et dipsadas et viperas aliasque complures), nor the land of Israel as the nurse of lion-like men or heroes (J. D. Michaelis), but the interjacent desert described by Moses in similiar terms (Deut. i. 19, viii. 15). The preposition בְּ, meaning strictly *in*, might in this connection denote either *through* or *into*, but the former seems to be required by the context. It follows of course that ארץ צרה וצוקה cannot mean a *land of oppression*, in allusion either to the bondage of the Hebrews or to that of the natives (Vitringa), nor a land compressed and narrow in shape (Clericus), but must denote a land of suffering, danger, and privation, such as the great Arabian desert is to travellers. Those who make ארץ to mean Egypt explain מהם as referring rather to the people than the country; but if the land referred to is the desert, it must be explained, with the latest German writers, as either a poetical licence or a grammatical anomaly. The general meaning of the phrase, as all agree, is *whence*. It is also agreed that two designations of the lion are here used; but how they mutually differ is disputed. Calvin has *leo et leo major;* Cocceius, *leo animosus et annosus.* Luther makes the distinction one of sex (*lions and lionesses*), which is now regarded as the true distinction, though the first of the two Hebrew words, since Bochart, has been commonly explained to mean the *lioness.* So Clericus, *leœna et leo violentus,* and all the recent writers except Hitzig, who makes both the words generic (*Leu und Löwe*). אפעה may be translated *adder, viper, asp,* or by any other term denoting a venomous and deadly serpent. For the meaning of שׂרף מעופף, see the note on chap. xiv. 29. The lions and vipers of this verse are not symbolical descriptions of the Egyptians (Junius), but a poetical description of the desert. Clericus makes even בהמות (Behemoth), an emblem of Egypt, and translates the clause (as an inscription), *oratio pronunciata de meridiano hippopotamo!* עורים or עירים, which Lowth translates too vaguely *young cattle*, denotes more specifically *young asses*, or it may be used as a poetical designation of asses in general. That דבשת signifies the hump or bunch of the camel, as explained in the Vulgate (super gibbum cameli), the Peshito, and the Targum, is clear from the context, but not from etymology, as to which interpreters are much divided. The old Jews traced the word to דבשׂ, *honey* (because sometimes applied for medicinal purposes), while Henderson explains it by an Arabic analogy as meaning the natural *furniture* of the animal. The על before עם does not seem to be a mere equivalent to אֶל, but rather, as in ver. 5, to mean *on account of, for the sake of.*

7. *And Egypt* (or *the Egyptians*) *in vain and to no purpose shall they help. Therefore I cry concerning this, their strength is to sit still.* This, which is the common English Version of the last clause, is substantially the same with Calvin's. Later writers have rejected it, however, on the ground, that רהב, according to etymology and usage, does not mean *strength* but *indolence*. On this supposition, the Vulgate version would be more correct (superbia tantum est, quiesce), שבת being then explained as the imperative of שָׁבַת to cease, to rest. This construction is exactly in accordance with the Masoretic accents, which connect הם with רהב and disjoin it from שבת. But the last word, as now pointed, must be either a noun or an infinitive. Since רהב occurs elsewhere as a name of Egypt, most of the modern writers take קראתי in the sense of naming, which is fully justified by usage, and understand the clause as contrasting the pretensions of Egypt with its actual performances; the two antagonist ideas being those of arrogance, or insolence and quiescence, or inaction. Thus Gesenius translates it *Grossmaul das still sitzt*, and Barnes, *the blusterer that sitteth still*. Besides the obscurity of the descriptive epithets, the construction is perplexed by the use, first of the feminine singular (זאת), and then of the masculine plural (הם), both in reference to one subject. The common solution is that the former has respect to the country, and the latter to the people. The general meaning of the clause may be considered as determined by the one before it. הבל and ריק are nouns used adverbially. Ewald introduces in the last clause a paronomasia which is not in the original (*Trotzige das ist Frostige*).

8. *And now go, write it with them on a tablet and inscribe it in a book, and let it be for a future day, for ever, to eternity.* This, like the similar precaution in chap. viii. 1, was intended to verify the fact of the prediction after the event. אִתָּם seems to include the ideas of *before them* and *among them*. Knobel infers from this command, that the Prophet's house must have been upon the street or square, in which the prediction was orally delivered. Most interpreters suppose two distinct inscriptions to be here required, one on a solid tablet for public exhibition, and the other on parchment or the like for preservation. But Gesenius more naturally understands the words לוח and ספר as equivalents, which is the less improbable, because if a distinction were intended, חקק would no doubt have been connected, not with ספר but with לוח. Some of the ancient versions exchange עד for עֵד (a testimony for ever), which is adopted by several interpreters on the authority of Deut. xxxi. 19, 21, 26, where the same combination occurs.

Ewald adds that the idea of testimony is essential, and Knobel that the concurrence of עֵד עַד would be cacophonus.

9. *For a people of rebellion* (a rebellious people) *is it, lying* (or *denying*) *children, children* (*who*) *are not willing to learn the law of Jehovah.* By denying children Kimchi understands such as deny their father, Gill, such as falsely pretend to be his children. Hitzig gives the phrase a more specific meaning, as denoting that they would deny the fact of the prediction without some such attestation as the one required in the preceding verse. The English Version makes this verse state the substance of the inscription, *that this is a rebellious people*, &c.

10. *Who say to the seers, Ye shall not see, and to the viewers, ye shall not view for us right things; speak unto us smooth things, view deceits.* There is great difficulty in translating this verse literally, as the two Hebrew verbs, meaning *to see*, have no equivalents in English, which of themselves suggest the idea of prophetic revelation. The common version (*see not, prophesy not*), although it conveys the true sense substantially, leaves out of view the near relation of the two verbs to each other in the original. In the translation above given, *view* is introduced merely as a synonyme of *see*, both being here used to express supernatural or prophetic vision. With this use of the verbal noun (*seer*) we are all familiar through the English Bible. Clericus translates both verbs in the present (*non videtis*), which would make the verse a simple denial of the inspiration of the prophets, or of the truth of their communications. Most interpreters prefer the imperative form, which is certainly implied ; but the safest because the most exact construction is Luther's, which adheres to the strict sense of the future (*ye shall not see*). This is of course not given as the actual language of the people, but as the tendency and spirit of their acts. It is an ingenious but extravagant idea of Cocceius, that the first clause of this verse condemns the prohibition of the Scriptures by antichristian teachers, *who say to those seeing ye shall not see*, &c. Even if the first clause could be naturally thus explained, the same sense could not possibly be put upon the others. *Smooth things* or *words* is a common figurative term for flatteries. Luther's expressive version is *preach soft to us*.

11. *Depart from the way, swerve from the path, cause to cease from before us the Holy One of Israel.* The request is not (as Gill suggests) that they would get out of the people's way, so as no longer to prevent their going on in sin, but that they would get out of their own way, *i. e.* wander from it or forsake it. This way is explained by Gesenius to be the way of piety and virtue, but by Hitzig more correctly as the way which they had hitherto pursued in the discharge of their prophetic functions. *Cause to cease from before us, i. e.* remove from our sight. It was a common opinion with the older writers, that this clause alludes to Isaiah's frequent repetition of the name *Holy One of Israel*, and contains a request that they might hear it no more. But the modern interpreters appear to be agreed that the allusion is not to the name but the person. Cocceius understands the clause as relating to the antichristian exclusion of Christ from the church as its sanctifier. The form of the preposition (מִפְּנֵי) is peculiar to this place.

12. *Therefore thus saith the Holy One of Israel, Because of your rejecting* (or *despising*) *this word, and* (*because*) *ye have trusted in oppression and perverseness, and have relied thereon.* On the hypothesis already stated, that the people had expressed a particular dislike to the title *Holy One of Israel*, Piscator supposes that the Prophet here intentionally uses it, as if in defiance of their impious belief. Gill even thinks that *this word* may

mean *this name.* But all this seems to limit the meaning of the terms too much. The *word* here mentioned is no doubt the *law* of ver. 9, both being common epithets of revelation generally, and of particular divine communications. (See the note on chap. ii. 3). J. D. Michaelis ingeniously converts the last clause into a description of Egypt, as itself oppressed and therefore unfit to be the protector of Israel. But in order to extract this meaning from the words, he is forced into an arbitrary change of the pointing. Houbigant and Lowth, instead of עשק read עקש, thus making it synonymous with נלוז. The latter word seems to denote perverseness or moral obliquity in general. It is rendered in a strong idiomatic form by Hitzig (*Verschmitztheit*) and Ewald (*Querwege*).

13) *Therefore shall this iniquity be to you like a breach falling* (or *ready to fall*) *swelling out in a high wall, whose breaking may come suddenly, at* (*any*) *instant.* J. D. Michaelis, by another arbitrary change of text, reads *this help* instead of *this iniquity.* The image is that of a wall which is rent or cracked, and, as Gill says, *bellies out and bulges.* The verse is explained with great unanimity by the interpreters until we come to Hitzig, who puts an entirely new face upon the simile. He objects with some truth to the old interpretation that it assumes without authority a future meaning of the participle נפל, and that it makes the breach or chasm swell and fall, instead of the wall itself. He then infers, from the use of פרץ in 2 Sam. v. 20, and of תבעה in Isaiah lxiv. 1, that the former here denotes a *torrent* (Waldstrom), *falling upon* (*i. e.* attacking, as in Josh. xi. 7), *and swelling against a high wall.* The weakest point in this ingenious combination is the necessity of construing נפל with בְּ, from which it is separated by נבעה. To remove this difficulty, Hendewerk, adopting the same general construction, takes the whole phrase פרץ נפל in the sense of *waterfall.* The later German writers, Ewald, Umbreit, and Knobel, have returned to the old interpretation. Ewald, however, to remove the first of Hitzig's objections, applies נפל not to the falling of the wall, but to the sinking or extension downwards of the breach itself (*ein sinkender Riss*); while Knobel gains the same end by explaining פרץ to be not the aperture or chasm, but the portion of the wall affected by it. This last explanation had been previously and independently proposed by Henderson, who says that the word here means properly *the piece forming one side of the breach or rent.* But this is really a mere concession that the strict and usual sense is inappropriate. With respect to the main point, that the figures were intended to express the idea of sudden destruction, there is and can be no diversity of judgment. In favour of the old interpretation, as compared with Hitzig's, it may be suggested, that the former conveys the idea of a gradual yet sudden catastrophe, which is admirably suited to the context. It is also true, as Umbreit well observes, that the idea of a downfall springing from internal causes is more appropriate in this connection, than that of mere external violence, however overwhelming.

14. *And it* (the wall) *is broken like the breaking of a potter's vessel* (any utensil of earthenwhere), *broken unsparingly* (or *without mercy*), *so that there is not found in its fracture* (or *among its fragments*) *a sherd to take up fire from a hearth, and to skim* (or *dip up*) *water from a pool.* The first words strictly mean, *he breaks it,* not the enemy, as Knobel supposes, which would imply an allusion to the breach made in a siege, but *he* indefinitely, *i. e.* some one (Cocceius : *aliquis franget*), which may be resolved into a passive form as in the Vulgate (*comminuetur*). It is wholly gratuitous to read

וְשִׁבְרָהּ. The phrase כָּתוֹת לֹא יַחְמֹל exhibits a construction wholly foreign from our idiom, and therefore not susceptible of literal translation. The nearest approach to it is, *breaking he spareth not* (or will not spare). *Sherd* is an old English word, now seldom used, meaning a broken piece of pottery or earthenware, and found more frequently in the compound form of *potsherd*. A potter's vessel, literally, *vessel of the potters*. חָתָה, except in a single instance, is always applied to the taking up of fire. חָשֹׂף is strictly to remove the surface of a liquid, but may here have greater latitude of meaning. For גֶּבֶא the English version has *pit*, Lowth *cistern*, and most other writers *well;* but in Ezek. xlvii. 11 it denotes a *marsh* or *pool*. Ewald supposes a particular allusion to the breaking of a poor man's earthen pitcher, an idea which had been suggested long before by Gill ; *as poor people are wont to do, to take fire from the hearth, and water out of a well in a piece of broken pitcher.*

15. *For thus saith the Lord Jehovah, the Holy One of Israel, in returning* (or *conversion*) *and rest shall ye be saved, in remaining quiet and in confidence shall be your strength ; and ye would not* (or *were not willing*). This overwhelming judgment would be strictly just because they had been fully admonished of the way of safety. Here again Gill supposes a peculiar significance in the repetition of the *Holy One of Israel*. The rabbinical explanation of שׁוּבָה as a derivative from יָשַׁב is gratuitous and certainly not justified by Num. x. 36. Grotius understands by *returning* retrocession from the unlawful measures and negotiations. The Targum gives it the more general sense of returning to the law, which agrees in substance with the common explanation of the term as meaning a return to God by repentance and conversion. (For the spiritual usage of the verb, see the note on chap. i. 27.) This sense Gesenius mentions as admissible although he prefers to assume a hendiadys, *by returning to repose*, which is needless and unnatural. Hitzig's idea that the word denotes returning to one's self may be considered as included in the other.

16. *And ye said, No, for we will flee upon horses ; therefore shall ye flee ; and upon the swift will we ride ; therefore shall your pursuers be swift.* Calvin points out a double sense of נוּס in this verse, and the modern interpreters express it in their versions, the most successful being that of Ewald, who employs the kindred forms *fliegen* and *fliehen*. This can be perfectly copied in English by the use of *fly* and *flee;* but it may be doubted whether this is not a mere refinement, as the Hebrew verb in every other case means to *flee*, and the hope here ascribed to the people is not simply that of going swiftly, but of *escaping* from the dangers threatened. In קַל and קָלַל, the primary sense of lightness is very often merged into that of rapid motion. Knobel discovers an additional paronomasia in סוּסִים, which he makes perceptible in German by employing the three words, *fliegen*, *fliehen, flüchtigen*. Many of the older writers use a comparative expression in the last clause after the example of the Vulgate (*velociores*). Grotius תְּנוּסוּן the specific sense of *exsulabitis*.

17. *One thousand from before the rebuke* (or *menace*) *of one, from before the rebuke of five shall ye flee, until ye are left like a mast* (or *pole*) *on the top of the mountain, and like the signal on the hill.* From the use of the definite article in the last clause, Junius and Tremellius needlessly infer that the meaning is *this mountain, this hill*, meaning Zion. The pleonastic form *one thousand* is not urged by any of the German writers as a proof of later date. To supply a particle of comparison (*as one*) is of

course entirely unnecessary.   To complete the parallelism, and to conform
the expression to Lev. xxvi. 8, Deut. xxxii. 31, Lowth supposes רְבָבָה (a
myriad) to have dropped out of the text, and finds a trace of this original
reading in the Septuagint version πολλοί.   Instead of a definite expression, Clericus and others supply *omnes*.   The former emendation, although
not adopted, is favoured by Gesenius ; but the later writers reject both,
not only as unnecessary, but because, as Hitzig well observes, such a
change would disturb the connection with what follows, the sense being
plainly this, that they should flee *until* they were left, &c.   תֹרֶן is taken as
the name of a tree by Augusti (Tannenbaum) and Rosenmüller (pinus), by
Gesenius and Ewald as a signal or a signal-pole.   In the only two cases
where it occurs elsewhere, it has the specific meaning of a *mast*.   The
allusion may be simply to the similar appearance of a lofty and solitary tree,
or the common idea may be that of a *flag-staff*, which might be found in
either situation.   The word *beacon*, here employed by Gataker and Barnes,
is consistent neither with the Hebrew nor the English usage.   The idea of
the last clause, as expressed by Hitzig, is that no two of them should
remain together.   (Compare 1 Sam. xi. 11.)

18.   *And therefore will Jehovah wait to have mercy upon you, and
therefore will he rise up* (or *be exalted*) *to pity you, for a God of judgment
is Jehovah ; blessed are all that wait for him*.   The apparent incongruity
of this promise with the threatening which immediately precedes, has led to
various constructions of the first clause.   The most violent and least satisfactory is that which takes לָכֵן in the rare and doubtful sense of *but* or
nevertheless.   This is adopted among recent writers by Gesenius, Barnes,
Henderson.   Another solution, given by Vitringa, leaves לָכֵן to be understood as usual, but converts the seeming promise into a threatening, by
explaining יְחַכֶּה *will delay* (to be gracious), and יָרוּם *will remain afar off*
(Jarchi : יִקְרַק). But this is certainly not the obvious and natural meaning
of the Prophet's words.   חִכָּה elsewhere means to wait with earnest expectation and desire, and the Kal is so used in the last clause of this very verse.
This objection also lies against Maurer's explanation of the clause as
referring to delay of punishment.   Hitzig supposes the connection to be this :
therefore (because the issue of your present course must be so fatal) he will
wait or allow you time for repentance.   Knobel applies the whole to God's
intended dealings with them after the threatened judgments should have
been endured.   On the whole, the simplest and most probable conclusion
seems to be that לָכֵן has its usual meaning, but refers, as in many other
cases, to a remoter antecedent than the words immediately before it.   As if
the Prophet paused at this point and reviewing his denunciations said,
Since this is so, since you must perish if now dealt with strictly, God will
allow you space for repentance, he will wait to be gracious, he will exalt
himself by shewing mercy.   J. H. Michaelis, with much the same effect,
refers לָכֵן to the condition mentioned in ver. 15.   *Therefore* (if you will be
quiet and believe) *Jehovah will wait*, &c.   Another difficulty of the same
kind has arisen from the next clause, where the justice of God seems to be
given as a reason for shewing mercy.   Gill removes the difficulty by translating כִּי *although ;* Henderson by taking משפט in the sense of rectitude,
including as a prominent idea faithfulness or truth in the fulfilment of his
promises.   Another expedient suggested by Gill is to give משפט the sense
of *discretion*.   That the clause does not relate to righteousness or justice in
the strict sense, appears plain from the added benediction upon those who

trust Jehovah.   One point is universally admitted, namely, that somewhere in this verse is the transition from the tone of threatening to that of promise. The question where it shall be fixed, though interesting, does not affect the general connection or the import of the passage as a whole.   Ewald strangely adopts, as absolutely necessary, Houbigant's emendation of the text, by reading ידום for ירום, and explains the former to mean, does not suffer himself to be moved (rührt sich nicht), an explanation scarcely less arbitrary than the criticism on which it is founded.

19. *For the people in Zion shall dwell in Jerusalem ; thou shalt weep no more ; he will be very gracious unto thee at the voice of thy cry ; as he hears it he will answer thee.*   The position of the first verb in this English sentence leaves it doubtful whether it is to be construed with what follows or what goes before.   Precisely the same ambiguity exists in the original, which may either mean that the people who are now in Zion shall dwell in Jerusalem, or that the people shall dwell in Zion, in Jerusalem. This last is the most natural construction, and the one indicated by the accents.   It is adopted in the English Version, but with a needless variation of the particle, *in Zion at Jerusalem.*   According to Henderson, the ב expresses more strongly the relation of the Jews to Zion as their native home. But this assertion is hardly borne out by the places which he cites (chap. xxi. 13, 1 Kings xvi. 24, 2 Kings v. 23).   In the translation above given the Hebrew order is restored.   According to these constructions, *dwell* must be taken in the strong sense of remaining or continuing to dwell (Hendewerk), in allusion to the deportation of the rest of Judah (Grotius), or of the ten tribes (Clericus).   But a very different construction of the first clause is proposed by Döderlein, and approved by Gesenius and Ewald.   These interpreters regard the whole clause as a vocative, or in other words as a description of the object of address.   *For O people in Zion, dwelling in Jerusalem, thou shalt weep no more.*   To obtain this sense, we must either read ישׁב as a participle, or supply the relative before it, and suppose a sudden change of person, as in chap. xxviii. 16, and xxix. 14.   This necessity, together with the collocation of the כי renders the vocative construction less natural and probable than that which makes the first clause a distinct proposition or promise.   Besides, it is not easy to account for so extended a description of the people, as a mere introduction to the words that follow. These words are made emphatic by the combination of the infinitive and finite verb.   De Wette, according to his wont, regards it as an idiomatic pleonasm.   Grotius translates the first phrase, *non diu flebis ;* the English Version, *thou shalt weep no more.*   (For the usage of this combination to express continued action, see the note on chap. vi. 9.)   Ewald adheres more closely to the form of the original by simple repetition of the verb (weinen weinen sollst du nicht, begnadigen begnadigen wird er dich).   Cocceius retains the strict sense of the preterite ענך as an appeal to their experience (cum audivit respondit tibi).   This yields a good sense, but the other agrees better with the context.   The particle of comparison has its usual sense before the infinitive, and is best represented by the English *as.* Lowth, on the authority of the Septuagint, inserts קדוש and changes לא to לו, reading the whole clause thus : *when a holy people shall dwell in Zion, when in Jerusalem thou shalt implore him with weeping.*   For the form יחנך see Gen. xliii. 29.

20. *And the Lord will give you bread of affliction and water of oppression, and no more shall thy teachers hide themselves, and thine eyes shall see thy teachers.*   The first clause is conditionally construed by Calvin (ubi dederit),

Vitringa (siquidem), and Ewald (gibt euch).   Clericus refers it to the past (dedit).   But both usage and the context require that ו should be regarded as conversive, and the condition, though implied, is not expressed.   The Vulgate renders צר and לחץ as adjectives (panem arctum, aquam brevem).   De Dieu supposes them to be in apposition with the noun preceding, affliction (as) bread, and oppression (as) water.   This is favoured by the absolute form of מַיִם ; but the same words are construed in the same way, 1 Kings xxii. 27, where the reference can only be to literal meat and drink.   For other examples of the absolute instead of the construct, see the Hebrew grammars.   Gesenius supplies *in* before affliction and oppression, implying that even in the midst of their distress God would feed them.   Jarchi regards this as a description of the temperate diet of the righteous, and Junius likewise renders it *modice cibaberis*.   The true connection seems to be, that God would afflict them outwardly, but would not deprive them of their spiritual privileges ; or, as Cocceius says, there should be a famine of bread, but not of the word of the Lord (Amos viii. 11).   From the use of כָּנָף in the sense of *wing* and *corner*, the reflexive verb has been variously explained as meaning to fly away (Montanus), and to be removed into a corner (English Version), or shut up in one (Junius).   It is now commonly agreed, however, that the primary sense is that of covering, and that the Niphal means to hide one's self.   The Vulgate renders מוֹרֶיךָ as a singular (doctorem tuum), in which it is followed by Ewald, who explains the Hebrew word as a singular form peculiar to the roots with final ה.   (See the note on chap. v. 12.)   Thus understood, the word must of course be applied to God himself, as the great teacher of his people.   Kimchi's explanation of the word as meaning the early rain (which sense it has in Joel ii. 23, and perhaps in Ps. lxxxiv. 7) has been retained only by Calvin and Lowth.   The great majority of writers adhere, not only to the sense of *teacher*, but to the plural import of the form, and understand the word as a designation or description of the prophets, with particular reference, as some suppose, to their reappearance after a period of severe persecution or oppression.   (See Ezek. xxxiii. 22.)

21. *And thine ears shall hear a word from behind thee, saying, This is the way, walk ye in it, when ye turn to the right and when ye turn to the left.*   The Septuagint makes this the voice of seducers (τῶν πλανησάντων) ; but it is evidently that of a faithful guide and monitor ; according to the Rabbins, the *Bath Kol* or mysterious echo which conducts and warns the righteous.   *Word* is an idiomatic expression used where we should say *one speaking*.   The direction of the voice *from behind* is commonly explained by saying, that the image is borrowed from the practice of shepherds going behind their flocks, or nurses behind children, to observe their motions.   A much more natural solution is the one proposed by Henderson, to wit, that their guides were to be before them, but that when they declined from the right way their backs would be turned to them, consequently the warning voice would be heard behind them.   The meaning of the call is, this is the way which you have left, come back to it.   Lowth follows the Septuagint, Targum, and Peshito, in making כִּי a negative (*turn not aside*), wholly without necessity or warrant.   Interpreters are commonly agreed that the particle is either conditional (*if ye turn*) or temporal (*when ye turn*) ; but the simplest construction seems to be that proposed by Hendewerk (*for ye turn* or *will turn* to the right and to the left).   As if he had said, this warning will be necessary, for you will certainly depart at times from the

path of safety. This idea may, however, be considered as included or implied in the usual translation *when*. Calvin is singular in applying this clause, not to deviations from the right path, but to the emergencies of life in general : wherever you go, whichever way you turn, you shall hear this warning and directing voice. The verbs in the last clause are derived from nouns meaning the right and left hand. The peculiar form of the original is closely and even barbarously copied by Montanus (cum dextraveritis et cum sinistraveritis). תאמינו may be either an inaccurate orthography for תימינו, or derived from a synonymous root אמן.

22. *And he shall defile* (*i. e.* treat as unclean) *the covering of thy idols of silver and the case of thy image of gold, thou shalt scatter them* (or *abhor them*) *as an abominable thing. Away! shalt thou say to it.* The remarkable alteration of the singular and plural, both in the nouns and verbs of this sentence, is retained in the translation. The sense of טִמֵּאתֶם is determined by the analogy of 2 Kings xxiii. 8, 10, 13. The gold and silver, both in Hebrew and English, may qualify either the image or the covering. The latter is more probable, because the covering would scarcely have been mentioned, if it had not been commonly of greater value than the body of the idol. פֶּסֶל and מַסֵּכָה strictly denote *graven* and *molten* images respectively, but are constantly employed as poetical equivalents. The specific meaning given to דָּוָה by the older writers, and by some of them dwelt upon with needless and disgusting particularity, is rejected by Ewald, who makes it synonymous with דְּוַי in Job vi. 7, meaning *loathsomeness* or anything loathsome. He also connects תְּזָרֵם with the noun זָרָא in Num. xi. 20, and renders it *abhor*. The common meaning *scatter* is appropriate, however, and is here recommended by its application to the dust or fragments of the golden calf in Exod. xxxii. 20.

23. *And he shall give the rain of thy seed* (*i. e.* the rain necessary to its growth), *with which thou shalt sow the ground, and bread, the produce of the ground, and it shall be fat and rich ; thy cattle shall feed that day in an enlarged pasture.* Rosenmüller calls this a description of the golden age, and cites a parallel from Virgil. He even mentions, as a trait in the description, *fruges nullo cultu enatœ*, whereas the very next words imply laborious cultivation. · J. D. Michaelis supposes the resumption of tillage in the last years of Hezekiah to be here predicted. Henderson explains it as a promise of increased fertility after the return from exile. All these applications appear too exclusive. The text contains a promise of increased prosperity after a season of privation, and was often verified. That כַּר, which usually has the sense of *lamb*, is ever used in that of *pasture*, is denied by Hengstenberg (on Ps. xxxvii. 20, and lxv. 14). But the latter meaning seems to be absolutely necessary here, and is accordingly assumed by all interpreters. The passive participle נרחב seems to imply, not only that the pastures should be wide, but they had once been narrow.

24. *And the oxen and the asses working the ground shall eat salted provender which has been winnowed* (literally, *which one winnows*) *with the sieve and fan.* The meaning evidently is that the domesticated animals shall fare as well as men in other times. The word *ear*, used in the English Version, is an obsolete derivative of the Latin *aro* to plough. בְּלִיל חָמִיץ properly means *fermented mixture*. The first word is commonly supposed to denote here a mixture of different kinds of grain, and the other a seasoning of salt or acid herbs, peculiarly grateful to the stomachs of cattle. Lowth translates the whole phrase *well-fermented maslin*, which is retained by Barnes, while Henderson has *salted provender*. J. D. Michaelis sup-

poses the grain to be here described as twice winnowed; but the implements mentioned were probably employed in one and the same process. Augusti : *thrown to them* (vorgeworfen) *with the shovel and the fan.*

25. *And there shall be, on every high mountain, and on every elevated hill, channels, streams of waters, in the day of great slaughter, in the falling of towers* (or *when towers fall*). J. D. Michaelis connects this with what goes before, and understands it as a description of the height to which agriculture would be carried, by means of artificial irrigation, after the overthrow of the Assyrians. Grotius regards it as a promise of abundant rains. Clericus calls this a gratuitous conjecture, but immediately proceeds to connect the verse with the figures of ver. 33, and to explain it as referring to the water-courses which it would be necessary to open, in order to purify the ground from the effects of such a slaughter. To this, much more justly than to Grotius's interpretation, we may apply the words of Clericus himself in another place, *præstat tacere quam hariolari.* He also arbitrarily gives עַל the sense of *from.* The simple meaning seems to be that water shall flow where it never flowed before, a common figure in the Prophets for a great change, and especially a change for the better. The same sense is no doubt to be attached to the previous descriptions of abundance and fertility. In allusion to the etymology of פְּלָגִים, Lowth poetically renders it *disparting rills.* For מִגְדָּלִים Clericus reads מַגְדִּלִים, and understands it as descriptive of the Assyrians, *qui magnifice se efferebant.* J. D. Michaelis makes the same application, and translates the word *Grossprecher.* A similar reading is implied in the versions of Aquila and Symmachus (μεγαλυνομένους). Lowth has *the mighty* in imitation of the Targum (רברבין). Calvin applies מִגְדָּלִים, in its usual sense, to Babylon. Hitzig infers from the use of the word הֶרֶג, that the towers meant are living towers, *i. e.* the Assyrian chiefs. Knobel applies הֶרֶג to the slaughter of the Jews themselves, and understands by *towers* their fortifications, of which there would be no further need in the happy period here foretold. The words are referred by some of the Jewish writers to the days of the Messiah; by Vitringa, with a threefold application, to the times of the Maccabees, of Constantine, and of the seventh Apocalyptic period; by Gill, to the slaughter of the antichristian kings described in Rev. xix. 17–21. The diversity and arbitrary nature of these explanations shew that there are no sufficient data in the text itself for any such specific and exclusive application. All that can certainly be gathered from the words is, that a period of war and carnage should be followed by one of abundance and prosperity.

26. *And the light of the moon shall be as the light of the sun, and the light of the sun shall be sevenfold, as the light of seven days, in the day of Jehovah's binding up the breach of his people, and the stroke of his wound he will heal.* Instead of the usual words for sun and moon, we have here two poetical expressions, one denoting *heat* and the other *white.* Lowth renders one simply *moon,* but the other *meridian sun.* Augusti has *pale moon* and *burning sun.* (Ewald, *das bleiche Mondlicht* und *das Gutlicht.*) Lowth pronounces the words *as the light of seven days* to be " a manifest gloss, taken in from the margin; it is not in most of the copies of the LXX.; it interrupts the rhythmical construction, and obscures the sense by a false or at least an unnecessary interpretation." This sentence is remarkable as furnishing the model, upon which the textual criticism of the modern Germans, with respect to glosses, seems to have been moulded. We have here the usual supposition of a transfer from the margin, the usual appeal

to some defective ancient version, the usual complaint of interrupted rhythm, and the usual alternative of needless or erroneous explanation. The liberties which Lowth took with the text, in pursuance of a false but favourite hypothesis, have led, by a legitimate but unforeseen application of his principles, to results from which he would himself have undoubtedly recoiled. As to the history of this particular criticism, it is approved by Gesenius and Hitzig, but rejected by Ewald, and Umbreit, who observes that the addition of these words was necessary to explain the previous words as not describing seven suns, but the light of one sun upon seven days. Maimonides supposes an allusion to the seven days of the dedication of Solomon's temple. The Targum, still more strangely, multiplies the seven twice into itself and reads, *three hundred and forty-three days*, a conceit no doubt founded upon some cabalistic superstition. Grotius explains the figures of this verse as denoting joy, and quotes as a classical parallel, *ipse mihi visus pulchrior ire dies*, to which Vitringa adds, *gratior it dies et soles melius nitent*. It is plain, however, that the Prophet's language is designed, not merely to express great joy, but to describe a change in the face of nature, as an emblem of some great revolution in the state of society (Compare chap. xiii. 10, 13). It is therefore another item added to the catalogue of previous similes or comparisons, all denoting the same thing, yet shewing by their very diversity that they denote it only in a tropical or figurative manner. Hendewerk ironically censures Hengstenberg for not including the improved feed of oxen and asses among the attributes of the Messiah's reign. But the real inconsistency is on the part of those who understand ver. 24 in its strictest sense, and yet explain the verse before us as a mere poetical description or imaginative anticipation. The remark of J. D. Michaelis upon this point may be quoted as characteristic of his mind and manner. "This is not to be literally taken, for it would be very inconvenient to us, if it were as bright by night as it is now by day when the sun shines; and if the sun should shine seven times brighter than now, we must be blinded." According to Gesenius, the wounds referred to in the last clause are the wounds inflicted by false teachers; but there seems to be no reason for restricting the import of the terms as descriptive of suffering in general.

27. *Behold, the name of Jehovah cometh from afar, burning his anger, and heavy the ascent* (of smoke): *his lips are full of wrath, and his tongue as a devouring fire.* Koppe begins a new division here without necessity. By the *name of Jehovah* we are not simply to understand Jehovah himself, but Jehovah as revealed in word or act, and therefore glorious. (Grotius: Deus omni laude dignissimus.) According to Raymund Martini, the expression was applied by the old Jews to the Messiah. Gill thinks it may denote the angel who destroyed Sennacherib's army. J. D. Michaelis takes the name in its strict sense, and translates the verb *erschallet* (the name of Jehovah sounds or echoes from afar). מֵרָחוֹק is by some referred to time, but the proper local sense is more appropriate. Clericus alone translates אַפּוֹ *his face* (ardens facies ejus). The English Version makes בֹּעֵר agree with שֵׁם, and supplies a preposition before אַפּוֹ (*burning with his anger.*) Others supply the preposition before בֹּעֵר (*with his burning anger*). Others make the clause an independent proposition (*burning is his anger*). Ewald adopts a construction similar to that of the ablative absolute in Latin (*his anger burning*). Augusti supposes the next words to mean, *he makes the burden heavy*, which implies a change of text, at least as to the pointing. Most of the late interpreters explain מַשָּׂאָה as synonymous with מַשְׂאֵת, meaning strictly the *ascent* of smoke or flame, and by metonymy the smoke

or flame itself. (Compare the notes on chap. ix. 18, 19.) Barnes : *the flame is heavy.* Henderson : *dense is the smoke.* Hendewerk has *Rauch-säule* (column of smoke), Umbreit *aufstiegender Brand* (ascending fire or conflagration). Ewald and Knobel have reverted to the primary meaning, ascent or elevation. The former has *gewaltiger Erhebung ;* the latter, *heavy* (*i. e.* slow) *is the rising of Jehovah* in the distance. Œcolampadius understands by *lips* and *tongue* the sentence pronounced by the Messiah on his enemies : but the words are to be strictly understood as traits in the prophetic picture of this terrible epiphany.

28. *And his breath* (or *spirit*), *like an overflowing stream, shall divide as far as the neck, to sift the nations in the sieve of falsehood, and a misleading bridle on the jaws of the people.* There are here three metaphors employed to express the same general idea, those of a flood, a sieve, and a bridle. Umbreit is singular in putting a favourable meaning on the last two, as implying that the nations should be purged, not destroyed, by sifting ; and that when they thought themselves misled, they should be brought into the right path by a way they knew not. This is far less natural than the common explanation of the whole verse as a threatening against Jehovah's enemies. Grotius renders רוּחַ *anger,* Luther and the English Version *breath ;* but there is no sufficient reason for excluding an allusion to the Holy Spirit as a personal agent. Junius makes יֶחֱצֶה a preterite, in accordance with his notion that the whole verse has respect to the Assyrian oppression of the tributary nations. The verb means strictly to divide into halves, and is here explained by the English Version in the sense of *reaching to the midst ;* but most interpreters adopt the explanation of Vatablus, that the water, rising to the neck, divides the body into two unequal parts. The metaphor itself, as in chap. viii. 8, denotes extreme danger. The phrase נָפַת שָׁוְא is ambiguous. It may either mean the *sieve of falsehood* (Clericus, cribro mendacii) or of wickedness in general, *i. e.* the instrument by which the wicked, and especially the false, are to be punished ; or the *sieve of ruin,* pointing out the issue of the process, as the other version does the object upon which it acts. This last sense is attained, in a different way, by Calvin, who explains the words to mean in *a useless* (or *worthless*) *sieve,* *i. e.* according to Gill's paraphrase, " they were to be sifted, not with a good and profitable sieve, which retains the corn and shakes out the chaff, or so as to have some taken out and spared, but with a sieve that lets all through, and so be brought to nothing, as the Vulgate Latin Version (*in nihilum*)." Barnes's translation of this clause is, *to toss the nations with the winnowing shovel of perdition.* הֲנָפָה is noted by Gesenius and Knobel as a Chaldee form, but neither of them seems to regard it as a proof that the passage is later than the time of Isaiah. The construction of this verb with רֶסֶן is regarded by some writers as an instance of *zeugma.* Others supply the verb *to put,* others the substantive verb *to be,* or *there shall be,* as in the English Version. The connection is in any case too plain to be mistaken. The last clause is paraphrased by Luther as denoting that Jehovah would drive the nations hither and thither (hin und her treibe). Most interpreters prefer the more specific sense of *leading astray,* or in the wrong direction, with particular allusion, as J. D. Michaelis supposes, to the fact that Sennacherib was misled by a false report respecting Tirhakah, the king of Ethiopia. The equestrian allusion in the text has nowhere, perhaps, been so fully carried out as in the old French Version, *qui les fera trotter à travers champs.*

29. *The song* (or *singing*) *shall be to you* (*i. e.* your song shall be) *like the night of the consecration of a feast, and joy of heart* (*i. e.* your joy shall

be) *like* (that of) *one marching with the pipe* (or *flute*) *to go into the mountain of Jehovah, to the Rock of Israel.* The night may be particularly mentioned in the first clause, either because all the Mosaic festivals began in the evening, or with special allusion to the Passover, which is described in the law (Exod. xii. 42) as *a night to be much observed unto the Lord,* as *that night of the Lord to be observed of all the children of Israel in their generations.* By התקדש we are probably to understand the whole celebration of the feast, and not the mere *proclaiming* of it, as expressed by Lowth and Barnes. This verse gives an interesting glimpse of ancient usage as to the visitation of the temple at the greater yearly festivals. The *Rock of Israel* is not mount Zion or Moriah, but Jehovah himself, to whose presence they resorted, as appears from 2 Samuel xxiii. 3.

30. *And Jehovah shall cause to be heard the majesty of his voice, and the descent of his arm shall he cause to be seen, with indignation of anger and a flame of devouring fire, scattering, and rain, and hailstones* (literally *stone of hail*). There is no more need of explaining Jehovah's voice to be thunder than there is of explaining the stroke of his arm to be lightning, both which explanations are in fact given by Knobel. The image presented is that of a theophany, in which storm and tempest are only accompanying circumstances. נַחַת may be either a derivative of נוּחַ, to *rest,* or of נָחַת, to *descend,* although the latter is more probably itself derived from the noun. Lowth's translation of בְּזַעַף אַף (*with wrath indignant*) is neither so exact nor so impressive as the literal version. נְפֵץ is rendered by the older writers as an abstract noun from נָפַץ, to *scatter;* by Rosenmüller and Knobel as a poetical description of the winds as *scatterers;* but by Gesenius from the Chaldee and Arabic analogy, as meaning a violent or driving rain.

31. *For at the voice of Jehovah shall Assyria* (or *the Assyrian*) *be broken, with the rod shall he smite.* The מִן before קוֹל may denote either the time or the cause of the effect described, and may accordingly be rendered either *at* or *by.* The first may be preferred as more comprehensive, and as really including the other. חָתַת originally means *to be broken,* and is so used in chap. vii. 8 above; but it is commonly applied, in a figurative sense, to the breaking of the spirit or courage by the alarm. Here some translate it, *beaten down,* as in the English version, others *frightened* or *confounded,* as in Luther's (erschrecken). There are two constructions of the last clause, one continuing Assyria as the subject of the verb, the other referring it to *Jehovah.* Forerius amends the text by reading יֻכֶּה in the passive (*he shall be smitten*), which gratuitous suggestion is adopted by Dathe and Koppe. Lowth, not content with supplying the relative before יַכֶּה, inserts it in the text, on the authority of Secker's conjecture that it may have dropped out (*forte excidit*). The past form given to the verb, not only in the English version (*smote*), but by Hitzig (*schlug*), seems entirely unauthorized by usage or the context. Ewald, less violently, reads it as a present (*schlägt*); but even if Assyria be the subject of the clause, it is clear that the Prophet speaks of her oppressions as being, in whole or in part, still future to his own perceptions. A much less simple and successful method of accounting for the future is by making the verb mean that Assyria was *ready* or *about to smite,* with Lowth and Vitringa (*virga percussurus*). But by far the most natural construction of the clause is that which supplies nothing and adheres to the strict sense of the future, by connecting יַכֶּה, not with אַשּׁוּר, but יְהֹוָה, both which are mentioned in the other clause. Gesenius, although right in this respect, mars the beautiful simplicity of the construction, by gratuitously introducing *when* at the be-

ginning of the first clause, and *then* at the beginning of the second. No less objectionable, on the score of taste, is the use of *yea* or *yes*, as an equivalent to כִּי, by De Wette and Ewald. Knobel's translation of the same word by *then* is as arbitrary here as in chap. vii. 9, the only authority to which he appeals. The express mention of Assyria in this verse, though it does not prove it to have been from the beginning the specific subject of the prophecy, does shew that it was a conspicuous object in Isaiah's view, as an example both of danger and deliverance, and that at this point he concentrates his prophetic vision on this object as a signal illustration of the general truths which he has been announcing.

32. *And every passage of the rod of doom, which Jehovah will lay* (or *cause to rest*) *upon him, shall be with tabrets and harps, and with fights of shaking it is fought therein.* There is the same diversity of judgment here as in the foregoing verse, with respect to the question whether the rod mentioned in the first clause is the rod which the Assyrian wielded, or the rod which smote himself. On the former supposition, the sense would seem to be, that in every place through which the rod of the oppressor had before passed, there should now be heard the sound of joyful music. This construction not only involves the necessity of supplying *in* before the first noun, but leaves the words, *which Jehovah will lay upon him*, either unmeaning or irrelevant, or at least far less appropriate than if the reference be to Jehovah's judgments on Assyria, which is further recommended by the reasons above given for applying the last words of ver. 31 to the same catastrophe. Assuming, therefore, that the clause before us was likewise intended to be so applied, the sense would seem to be that every passage of Jehovah's rod (*i. e.* every stroke which passes from it to the object) will be hailed by those whom the Assyrian had oppressed, with joy and exultation. It is an ingenious suggestion of Henderson, though scarcely justified by Hebrew usage, that מעבר is here employed in the peculiar acceptation of the English *pass*, as used to denote a push or thrust in fencing. This combination, however, is not needed to justify his version (*stroke*). For מוּסָדָה, Clericus reads מוּסָרָה or מוּסָר (*supplicii*), on the ground of which conjecture, and the authority of one or two manuscripts, Lowth amends the text, and translates accordingly (*the rod of correction*). In like manner, J. D. Michaelis, in his German Version (*strafenden Stab*). None of the later writers seem to have retained this needless emendation. The common version, *grounded staff*, is almost unintelligible. It may have some connection with Calvin's explanation of the Hebrew phrase as meaning, a staff grounded, that is, firmly planted, in the object smitten, or as J. D. Michaelis (in his Notes) has it, *well laid on* (recht vest und stark auf den Rücken geleget). This, to use a favourite expression of the great Reformer, seems both forced and frigid. It is now very generally agreed that מוּסָדָה denotes the divine determination or decree, and that the whole phrase means the rod appointed by him, or to put it in a form at once exact and poetical, the *rod of destiny* or *doom*. Umbreit attaches to the words the specific sense of *long since determined* (lang verhängte), which is not in the original. The tabrets and harps are not here named as the ordinary military music (Gill), nor as the sacred music which on particular occasions was connected with the march of armies (2 Chron. xx. 21, 22). Nor is the meaning that Jehovah would overcome the enemy as if in sport or like a merry-making (Grotius), which is inconsistent with the words that follow, *battles of shaking, i. e.* agitating or tumultuous battles, or as some explain the words, convulsive, struggling conflicts. The true sense seems to be, that every stroke would

be attended with rejoicing on the part of the spectators, and especially of those who had been subject to oppression. נִלְחָם may agree with יְהוָֹה as an active or deponent verb, or be construed impersonally as by Ewald (wird gekämpft). The keri (בָּם) must of course mean *with them, i.e.* the Assyrians. The kethib (בָּהּ) is commonly explained to mean *with her, i. e.* Assyria, considered as a country. But Ewald takes it to mean *there,* or literally *in it, i.e.* in the Holy Land. This, if we make the verb impersonal, is natural enough, except that it assumes an antecedent not expressly mentioned in the context. Be this as it may, the general sense is plain, to wit, that God would violently overthrow Assyria.

33. *For arranged since yesterday is Tophet; even it for the king is prepared; he has deepened, he has widened (it); its pile fire and wood in plenty; the breath of Jehovah, like a stream of brimstone, kindles it.* It is universally agreed that the destruction of the Assyrian king is here described as a burning of his body at a stake, or on a funeral-pile. But whether the king mentioned be an individual king or an ideal representative of all, and whether this is a mere figurative representation of his temporal destruction or a premonition of his doom hereafter, are disputed questions. Tophet is well known to have been the name of a place in the valley of Hinnom where children were sacrificed to Moloch, and on that account afterwards defiled by the deposit of the filth of the city, to consume which, constant fires were maintained. Hence, by a natural association, Tophet, as well as the more general name, Valley of Hinnom, was applied by the later Jews to the place of future torment. The Chaldee paraphrase of this verse renders תָּפְתֶּה by נהנם. The name *Tophet* has been commonly derived from תּוּף, to *spit upon,* as an expression of abhorrence; but Gesenius derives it from the Persian تافتن to burn, with which he also connects ϑάπτειν, as originally meaning *to burn* and secondarily *to bury.* If this be the correct etymology of תֹּפֶת, it denotes a place of burning in the general, and was only applied to the spot before mentioned by way of eminence, in allusion either to the sacrificial or the purgatorial fires there maintained, or both. On this hypothesis, it would be altogether natural to understand the word here in an indefinite or generic sense, as meaning a place of burning, such as a stake or a funeral pile, and it is so explained accordingly by Gesenius (Brandstätte), Ewald (Scheiterhaufen), and other late interpreters. The question whether it is here used to describe the place of future torments, or as a mere poetical description of the temporal destruction of the king of Assyria, is the less important, as the language must in either case be figurative, and can teach us nothing therefore as to the real circumstances either of the first or second death. Considering, however, the appalling grandeur of the images presented, and our Saviour's use of similar expressions to describe the place of everlasting punishment, and also the certainty deducible from other scriptures, that a wicked king destroyed in the act of fighting against God must be punished in the other world as well as this, we need not hesitate to understand the passage as at least including a denunciation of eternal misery, although the general idea which the figures were intended to express is that of sudden, terrible destruction. As the phrase מֵאֶתְמוּל has been variously explained to mean *long ago,* and *just now* or *a little while ago,* it is best to retain the original expression with Calvin (ab hesterno) and Umbreit (von gestern her). The old Jews have a curious tradition that hell was made on the second day of the creation, or the first that had a yesterday, for which reason God pronounced no blessing on it. The verbs הֶעֱמִיק and הִרְחִב must

be either construed with *Jehovah* or indefinitely. מְדֻרָה means the whole
circumference and area of the place of burning. Gesenius connects it with
the foregoing verbs to make the structure of the sentence more symmetrical
(deep and wide is its pile—fire and wood in plenty) ; but Hitzig vindicates
the Masoretic interpunction on the ground that the foregoing verbs cannot
be applied to the pile, and that the following proposition would in that
case have no predicate. For a similar expression he refers to Jer. xxiv. 2.
Lowth connects מְדֻרָתָהּ with אֵשׁ and renders it *a fiery pyre*, which Barnes
has altered to *a pyre for the flame*, both overlooking the pronominal suffix.
Augusti takes the final ה as a suffix (*his Tophet*) ; but it is commonly regarded as a paragogic letter or a mere euphonic variation of the usual form
תֹּפֶת. J. D. Michaelis, however, thinks that if the present reading is the
true one, it must be a verb meaning *thou shalt be deceived*, another allusion
to the false report about the Ethiopians. De Wette renders כִּי at the beginning *yea ;* but it has really its proper sense of *for, because*, connecting this
verse, either with the one immediately before it, or with the remoter context.
Knobel supposes that the images of this verse were selected because the
burning of the dead was foreign from the Jewish customs and abhorrent to
their feelings. According to Clericus, the *Tophet* of this verse was a place
of burning really prepared by Hezekiah for the bodies of the slain Assyrians,
but entirely distinct from the Tophet near Jerusalem. Luther by rendering
it *pit* (die Grube), and J. D. Michaelis *churchyard* (Kirchhof), destroy its
connection with the real Tophet, and with the ideas of fire and burning.

Chapter 31

RELIANCE upon Egypt is distrust of God, who will avenge himself by
destroying both the helper and the helped, vers. 1–3. His determination and
ability to save those who confide in his protection are expressed by two
comparisons, vers. 4, 5. The people are therefore invited to return to him,
from every false dependence, human or idolatrous, as they will be constrained
to do with shame, when they shall witness the destruction of their enemies
by the resistless fire of his wrath, vers. 6–9.

Hitzig assumes an interval, though not a very long one, between this
and the preceding chapter. To most interpreters and readers, it seems to
be a direct continuation, or at most a repetition, of the threatenings and
reproofs which had just been uttered.

1. *Woe to those going down to Egypt for help, and on horses they lean
(or rely) and trust in cavalry, because it is numerous, and in horsemen, because they are very strong, and they look not to the Holy One of
Israel, and Jehovah they seek not.* The abundance of horses in Egypt is
attested, not only in other parts of Scripture, but by profane writers.
Homer describes Thebes as having a hundred gates, out of each of which
two hundred warriors went forth with chariots and horses. Diodorus speaks
of the whole country between Thebes and Memphis as filled with royal
stables. The horses of Solomon are expressly said to have been brought
out of Egypt. This kind of military force was more highly valued, in comparison with infantry, by the ancients than the moderns, and especially by
those who, like the Hebrews, were almost entirely deprived of it themselves.
Hence their reliance upon foreign aid is frequently identified with confidence
in horses, and contrasted with simple trust in God (Ps. xx. 8). Most
interpreters give רֶכֶב here its usual sense of *chariot*, put collectively for
chariots ; but as such a use of the singular between two plurals would be

somewhat unnatural, it may be taken in the sense which we have seen it to
have in chap. xxi. 7.   To *seek Jehovah* is not merely to consult him, but to
seek his aid, resort to him, implying the strongest confidence.   For the
meaning of the phrase *look to,* see the note on chap. xvii. 8.

2. *And* (yet) *he too is wise, and brings evil, and his words he removes not,
and he rises up against the house of evil-doers, and against the help of the
workers of iniquity.*   The adversative *yet* is required by our idiom in this
connection, but is not expressed by גַּם, which has its usual sense of *too* or
also, implying a comparison with the Egyptians, upon whose wisdom, as
well as strength, the Jews may have relied, or with the Jews themselves,
who no doubt reckoned it a masterpiece of wisdom to secure such powerful assistance.   The comparison may be explained as comprehending both.
God was as wise as the Egyptians, and ought therefore to have been consulted : he was as wise as the Jews, and could therefore thwart their boasted
policy.   There is not only a *meiosis* in this sentence, but an obvious irony.
There is no need of supposing, with Vitringa, that the wisdom, either of
Egypt or of Israel, is here denied, excepting in comparison with that of
God.   The translation of the verbs as futures is arbitrary.   Ewald refers
יָבֵא to previous threatenings, which is hardly justified by usage.   הֵסִיר, in
this connection, seems to have the sense of withdrawing or revoking; as in
Josh. xi. 15, it denotes a practical revocation by neglecting to fulfil.   The
house of evil-doers is their family or race (chap. i. 4), here applied to the
unbelieving Jews.   The Egyptians are called their *help,* and both are
threatened with destruction.   To *rise up* is to shew one's self, address one's
self to action, and implies a state of previous forbearance or neglect.

3. *And Egypt* (is) *man and not God, and their horses flesh and not spirit;
and Jehovah shall stretch out his hand, and the helper shall stumble, and the
helped fall, and together all of them shall cease* (or be destroyed).   This
verse repeats the contrast between human and divine aid, and the threatening that the unbelievers and their foreign helpers should be involved in
the same destruction.   The antithesis of *flesh* and *spirit,* like that of *God*
and *man,* is not metaphysical but rhetorical, and is intended simply to
express extreme dissimilitude or inequality.   Reliance upon Egypt is
again sarcastically represented as reliance upon horses, and as such opposed
to confidence in God.   As Egypt here means the Egyptians, it is afterwards referred to as a plural.   *Stumble* and *fall* are here poetical equivalents.

4. *For thus said Jehovah unto me, As a lion growls, and a young lion,
over his prey, against whom a multitude of shepherds is called forth, at
their voice he is not frightened, and at their noise he is not humbled, so will
Jehovah of hosts come down, to fight upon mount Zion and upon her hill.*
This is still another form of the same contrast.   The comparison is a
favourite one with Homer, and occurs in the eighteenth book of the Iliad, in
terms almost identical.   *Growl* is to be preferred to *roar,* not only for the
reason given by Bochart, that the lion roars before, not after it has seized
its prey, but because הָגָה more properly denotes a suppressed or feeble
sound.   מְלֹא is literally *fulness,* and is rendered by Montanus *plenitudine.*
Other less natural constructions of the second clause are : *when a multitude
is called; who* (*when*) *a multitude is called,* &c.   Some read יִקְרָא, and
translate it either *cries* or *meets.*   Most interpreters have, *for mount Zion,*
in which sense עַל is used with נִלְחַם elsewhere.   But as צָבָא itself, with
this same preposition, means to *fight against* in chap. xxix. 7, Hitzig and
Hendewerk regard this as a threatening that God will take part with the
Assyrians against Jerusalem, the promise of deliverance beginning with the

next verse. Ewald supposes צָבָא to be used in allusion to the name
צְבָאוֹת (the Lord of *hosts* will be present in the *host*) and gives עַל the sense
of *over* or *upon* (über), which may either indicate the place or the subject
of the contest. By supposing the particle to mean *concerning*, we can
explain its use both in a hostile and a favourable sense. The כִּי at the
beginning of this verse introduces the ground or reason of the declaration
that the seeking of foreign aid was both unlawful and unnecessary. The
hill is by some supposed to be Moriah, as an appendage of mount Zion;
but it may just as well be simply parallel to *mountain*, the mountain of
Zion and the hill thereof. The feminine suffix refers not to הַר but to צִיּוֹן.

5. *As birds flying* (over or around their nests), *so will Jehovah cover
over* (or protect) *Jerusalem, cover and rescue, pass over and save*. According to Hitzig, it is not Jehovah but Jerusalem that is here compared to
fluttering birds. But, as Hendewerk properly objects, עָפוֹת means *flying*,
and is inapplicable to young birds in the nest. The feminine עָפוֹת also
indicates a reference to the care of mothers for their young. Gesenius
follows Kimchi in explaining הַצִּיל and הַמְלִיט as unusual forms of the infinitive; but Ewald and Hitzig regard this as an instance of the idiomatic
combination of infinitive and finite forms. פָּסַח is the verb used to denote
the passing over of the houses in Egypt by the destroying angel (hence
פֶּסַח, *passover*), to which there may be an allusion here. There is at least
no ground for making the verb, in either case, mean to *cover* (Vitringa) or
to *leap forward* (Lowth). To *pass over*, in the sense of sparing, is appropriate in both.

6. Since you need no protection but Jehovah's, therefore, *return unto
him from whom* (or *with respect to whom*) *the children of Israe have deeply
revolted* (literally, *have deepened revolt*). The last words may also be read,
from whom they (i. e. men indefinitely) *have deeply revolted, O ye children
of Israel*. The substitution of the second person for the third, in the
ancient versions, and by Barnes (*ye have revolted*), is wholly arbitrary.
Some explain לַאֲשֶׁר to mean *according as* or *in proportion as*, which seems
to be a forced construction. The syntax may be solved, either by supposing *to him* to be understood and giving לַאֲשֶׁר the sense of *with respect to
whom*, or by assuming that, as both these ideas could be expressed by this
one phrase, it was put but once in order to avoid the tautology. *Deep*
may be here used to convey the specific idea of debasement, or the more
general one of distance, or still more generally, as a mere intensive, like
our common phrases *deeply grieved* or *deeply injured*. The analogy of
chap. xxix. 15, however, would suggest the idea of deep contrivance or
design, which is equally appropriate.

7. This acknowledgment you will be constrained to make sooner or
later. *For in that day* (of miraculous deliverance) *they shall reject* (cast
away with contempt), *a man* (i. e. each) *his idols of silver and his idols of
gold, which your sinful hands have made for you*, or, *which your own hands
have made for you as sin*, i. e. as an occasion and a means of sin. In like
manner the golden calves are called the sin of Israel (Deut. ix. 21; Amos
viii. 14). The construction which makes *sin* a qualifying epithet of *hands*,
is preferred by Hendewerk and some older writers, but is not so natural
as that which makes the former denote the object or effect of the action.
For the true construction of *his silver* and *his gold*, see the note on chap.
ii. 20. For the same enallage of person, in a similar connection, see chap.
i. 29. Trust in idols and reliance upon human helpers are here, and often

elsewhere, put together, as identical in principle, and closely connected in the experience of ancient Israel. (See the notes on chap. ii. 8, 22.)

8. This future abandonment of all false confidences is described as springing from the demonstration of Jehovah's willingness and power to save. *And Assyria shall fall by no man's sword, and no mortal's sword shall devour him, and he shall flee from before the sword, and his young men* (or *chosen warriors*) *shall become tributary* (literally, *tribute*). לֹא־אִישׁ and לֹא־אָדָם are commonly explained as emphatic compounds, like לֹא־עֵץ in chap. x. 15, implying not mere negation but contrariety, something infinitely more than man. In such a comparison, the antithesis of *mighty man* and *mean man* seems so entirely out of place, that it is best to explain אִישׁ and אָדָם, according to the ordinary principle of parallelism, as equivalents. In either case, the terms are universal and exclusive. For לוֹ, a few manuscripts and one of the earliest editions read לֹא, *not from the sword*, *i. e.* he shall flee when no man pursueth (Prov. xxviii. 1). But the pleonastic dative after verbs of motion is a common Hebrew idiom. Vitringa and others derive מַס from מָסַס to melt, and explain the whole phrase to mean, *shall be melted, i. e.* either dispersed or overcome with fear. But in every other case the expression means to become tributary, with a special reference to the rendering of service to a superior. The objection that the prophecy, as thus explained, was not fulfilled, proceeds upon the false assumption that it refers exclusively to the overthrow of Sennacherib's host, whereas it describes the decline and fall of the Assyrian power after that catastrophe.

9. *And his rock (i. e.* his strength) *from fear shall pass away, and his chiefs shall be afraid of a standard* (or *signal*, as denoting the presence of the enemy), *saith Jehovah, to whom there is a fire in Zion and a furnace in Jerusalem.* Besides the version above given of the first clause, which is that of Jerome (*fortitudo transibit*), there are two constructions, also ancient, between which modern writers are divided. Kimchi explains the words to mean, that in his flight he should pass by the strongholds on his own frontier, where he might have taken refuge. Grotius quotes in illustration the Latin proverb, *fugit ultra casam.* Hendewerk modifies this explanation by supposing caverns in the hills to be referred to, as customary places of concealment. The other construction is proposed by Aben Ezra: he shall pass (not *by* but) *to* his stronghold, *i. e.* as Calvin understands it, Nineveh. Neither of these explanations seems so obvious and simple as the one just given. Lowth arbitrarily translates מִמָּסוֹ *at his flight.* Zwingle applied this clause to the cowardly desertion of the standards. The last clause, according to Piscator, means, *whose hearth is in Jerusalem*, or as Gill expresses it, *who keeps house there, and therefore will defend it.* But this use of *fire* and *furnace* is not only foreign from the usage of the Scriptures, but from the habits of the orientals, who have no such association of ideas between *hearth* and *home.* The true explanation of the clause seems to be that which supposes an allusion both to the sacred fire on the altar, and to the consuming fire of God's presence, whose altar flames in Zion and whose wrath shall thence flame to destroy his enemies. Compare the explanation of the mystical name *Ariel* in the note on chap. xxix. 1.

COMMENTARY
ON ISAIAH

Volume Two

Chapter 32

THIS chapter consists of two distinguishable parts. The first continues the promises of the foregoing context, vers. 1–8. The second predicts intervening judgments both to Israel and his enemies, vers. 9–20.

The first blessing promised in the former part is that of merciful and righteous government, vers. 1, 2. The next is that of spiritual illumination, vers. 3, 4. As the consequence of this, moral distinctions shall no longer be confounded, men shall be estimated at their real value; a general prediction, which is here applied to two specific cases, vers. 5–8.

The threatenings of the second part are specially addressed to the women of Judah, ver. 9. They include the desolation of the country and the downfall of Jerusalem, vers. 10–14. The evils are to last until a total change is wrought by an effusion of the Holy Spirit, vers. 15–18. But fearful changes are to intervene, for which believers must prepare themselves by diligence in present duty, vers. 19, 20.

1. *Behold, for righteousness shall reign a king, and rulers for justice shall rule.* The usual translation is *in justice* and *in righteousness*, as descriptive epithets of the reign foretold. But as this idea is commonly expressed by the preposition בְּ, the use of לְ here may have been intended to suggest, that he would reign not only justly, but for the very purpose of doing justice. The Hebrew particle denotes relation in its widest sense, but is most frequently equivalent to our *to* and *for*. The cognate noun and verb (rule and rulers) are combined as in the original. The לְ before שָׂרִים is commonly agreed to mean *as to, as for*. It is a question among interpreters whether the king here predicted is Hezekiah or the Messiah. The truth appears to be that the promise is a general one, as if he had said, The day is coming when power shall be exercised and government administered, not as at present (in the reign of Ahaz), but with a view to the faithful execution of the laws. Of such an improvement Hezekiah's reign was at least a beginning and a foretaste. The reference of שָׂרִים to the apostles appears very forced, and is certainly not justified, much less required, by the promise in Mat. xix. 28.

2. *And a man shall be as a hiding-place from the wind, and a covert from the rain* (or *storm*), *as channels of water in a dry place* (or *in drought*), *as the shadow of a heavy rock in a weary land.* Most of the late interpreters give אִישׁ the sense of a distributive pronoun, *each* (*i. e.* each of the chiefs

or princes mentioned in ver. 1) *shall be*, &c.   But the word is seldom if
ever so used except when connected with a plural verb, as in chaps. ix. 19,
20; xiii. 8, 14; xiv. 18; xix. 2; xxxi. 7.   The meaning rather is, that there
shall be a man upon the throne, or at the head of the government, who,
instead of oppressing, will protect the helpless.   This may either be indefinitely understood, or applied, in an individual and emphatic sense, to
the Messiah.   The figures for protection and relief are the same used above
in chap. iv. 6, and xxv. 4.   The phrases *heavy rock*, and *weary land*, are
idiomatic, but require no explanation.

3. *And the eyes of them that see shall not be dim, and the ears of them that
hear shall hearken.*   According to analogy, תִּשְׁעֶינָה is the future of שָׁעָה, a
verb used repeatedly by Isaiah in the sense of *looking* either at or away
from any object.   (See, for example, chap. xvii. 7, 8 ; xxii. 4, xxxi. 1.)
In this case, however, a contrary meaning seems to be so clearly required,
both by the context and the parallelism, that most interpreters, ancient and
modern, concur in deriving it from שָׁעַע, or in supposing שָׁעָה to have been
sometimes used in the sense of blinding, which the former verb has in chap.
vi. 10, and xxix. 9.   Some understand רֹאִים as meaning *seers* or prophets,
and שֹׁמְעִים their *hearers;* but most interpreters apply both words to the
people generally, as those who had eyes but saw not, and had ears but
heard not.   Compare the threatening in chap. vi. 9, and the promise in
chap. xxix. 18.

And the heart (or *mind*) *of the rash* (heedless or reckless) *shall understand
to know* (or *understand knowledge*), *and the tongue of stammerers shall hasten
to speak clear things* (*i. e.* shall speak readily and plainly).   Some interpreters suppose that this last metaphor relates to scoffers at religion, who
are elsewhere represented as stammering in derision of the Prophet's admonitions (chap. xxviii. 11).   But it seems more natural to understand the
bodily defects here mentioned as denoting others of an intellectual and
spiritual nature, neglect and ignorance of spiritual matters.   The minds of
men shall begin to be directed to religious truth, and delivered from ignorance and error in relation to it.

5. When men's eyes are thus opened, they will no longer confound the
essential distinctions of moral character, because they will no longer be
deceived by mere appearances.   Things will then be called by their right
names.   *The fool* (in the emphatic Scriptural sense, the wicked man) *will
no longer be called noble* (men will no longer attach ideas of dignity and
greatness to the name or person of presumptuous sinners), *and the churl* (or
niggard) *will no more be spoken of* (or *to*) *as liberal*.   The sense here given
to כִּילַי rests wholly on the Jewish tradition, as the word occurs nowhere
else in Scripture.   Gesenius derives it by *aphæresis* from נָכַל, and explains
it to mean *cunning*.   The sense will then be, that a crafty policy shall no
longer gain for him who practises it the reputation of magnanimous liberality.
Hitzig derives the word from כָּלָה, to consume, and explains the clause as
meaning that the waster (prodigal or spendthrift) shall no longer be called
generous.   This last agrees best with the parallel clause, in which the outward show of a good quality is distinguished from its actual possession.
But both these versions rest upon dubious etymologies.   On either supposition, it is clear that this clause, like the other, contains a specific illustration of the general truth that men shall be estimated at their real value.
Ewald translates נָבָל and כִּילַי *Taugenichts* (good-for-nothing) and *Windbeutel*
(bag-of-wind).

6. The Prophet now defines his own expressions, or describes the characters which they denote. *The fool (is one who) will speak folly* (in the strongest and worse sense), *and his heart will do iniquity, to do wickedness and to speak error unto* (or *against*) *Jehovah* (while at the same time he is merciless and cruel towards his fellow-men), *to starve* (or *leave empty*) *the soul of the hungry, and the drink of the thirsty he will suffer to fail.* The futures in this verse express the idea of habitual action, he does, and will do so. The infinitives convey the same idea in a different form, by making prominent the design and effect of their unlawful course. The common version, *work* and *practise*, needlessly departs from the form of the original, in which the same verb is repeated. To give it first the sense of *devising*, and then that of *executing*, is still more arbitrary. חֹנֶף, according to the older writers, means *hypocrisy ;* according to the moderns, *wickedness* in general, but in a high degree.

7. Such is the fool : *and as for the churl*, although his making money be not sinful in itself, *his arms* or *instruments*, the means which he employs, *are evil.* He that hastens to be rich can scarcely avoid the practice of dishonest arts and of unkindness to the poor. *He deviseth plots to destroy the oppressed* (or *afflicted*) *with words of falsehood, and (i. e. even) in the poor (man's) speaking right* (i. e. even when the poor man's claim is just, or in a more general sense, *when the poor man pleads his cause*). The variation in the form of the word כִּילַי (כְּלַי) is, with great probability, supposed by Gesenius to have been intended to assimilate the form to כֵּלַיו.

8. As the wicked man's true character is betrayed by his habitual acts, so *the noble* or *generous* man (and according to the Scriptures none is such but the truly good man) reveals his dispositions by his conduct—*devises noble* (or *generous*) *things, and in noble* (or *generous*) *things he perseveres* (literally, on them he stands).

9. Here, as in many other cases, the Prophet reverts to the prospect of approaching danger, which was to arouse the careless Jews from their security. As in chap. iii. 16, he addresses himself to the women of Jerusalem, because to them an invasion would be peculiarly disastrous, and also perhaps because their luxurious habits contributed, more or less directly, to existing evils. *Careless women, arise, hear my voice ; confiding daughters, give ear unto my speech.* Women and daughters are equivalent expressions. Careless and confiding (or secure), *i. e.* indifferent, because not apprehensive of the coming danger.

10. Having called their attention in ver. 9, he now proceeds with the prediction which concerned them. *In a year and more* (literally, *days above a year*), *ye shall tremble, ye confiding ones, for the vintage fails, the gathering shall not come.* The English Version makes the time denoted to be that of the duration of the threatened evil. יָמִים עַל שָׁנָה is by some explained to mean, *during the remainder of the year ;* but the version above given agrees best with the form of the original.

11. He now speaks as if the event had already taken place, and calls upon them to express their sorrow and alarm by the usual signs of mourning. *Tremble, ye careless* (*women*); *quake, ye confiding* (*ones*); *strip you and make you bare, and gird* (sackcloth) *on your loins.* A remarkable anomaly in this verse is the masculine form of the first imperative and the singular form of the others. Ewald explains the latter as contractions for חֲגֹרְנָה, רְגַזְנָה, but admits that there are no analogous forms elsewhere. Knobel thinks it possible that the forms are infinitives with local or directive ה (*to*

trembling, stripping, girding!) but this is equally without example. Gesenius, Hitzig, and others, make them paragogic forms, in which case both the gender and number are anomalous.

12. *Mourning for the breasts* (or *beating on the breasts* as a sign of mourning), *for the pleasant fields, for the fruitful vine.* The older writers explained *breasts* as a figure for productive grounds, or sources of supply. Lowth connects it with ver. 11 (*on your loins, on your breasts*). Gesenius in his Commentary reads שָׂדַים *fields ;* but in his Lexicon, he follows Paulus and the ancient versions in giving סֹפְדִים its primary sense of striking, especially upon the breast in sign of mourning. The same act is described in Nahum ii. 8, but by a different verb. This explanation is also given by Maurer, Henderson, Ewald, Umbreit, and Knobel. It is favoured by the striking analogy of κόπτω and *plango* (the words used by the Septuagint and Vulgate here), both which have precisely the same primary and secondary meaning. The other explanation, which is still retained by Hitzig, Hendewerk, and Barnes, is recommended by the usage of סָפַד, and by the fact that עַל is twice used afterwards in this same sentence, to denote the subject or occasion of the sorrow. The argument founded on the masculine form סֹפְדִים has less weight on account of the anomalies in ver. 11, and the remoteness of the feminine antecedent.

13. *Upon the land of my people thorn* (and) *thistle shall come up, for* (they shall even come up) *upon all* (thy) *houses of pleasure, O joyous city !* or, *upon all houses of pleasure* (in) *the joyous city.* The true sense of the כִּי seems to be that expressed above in the translation. Most interpreters, however, employ *yea* as an equivalent. According to Hendewerk, this predicts only a partial and temporary desolation, and Knobel applies it to the pleasure-grounds and houses without the walls, which is a mere gratuitous assumption.

14. *For the palace is forsaken, the crowd of the city* (or *the crowded city*) *left, hill and watch-tower* (are) *for caves* (or *dens*) *for ever, a joy* (or favourite resort) *of wild asses, a pasture of flocks.* The use of the word *palace*, and that in the singular number, clearly shews that the destruction of Jerusalem itself is here predicted, although Knobel still maintains that *palace* means country-houses. The next clause likewise contains a refutation of his hypothesis. עֹפֶל originally means a hill, but is applied as a proper name (Ophel) to the southern extremity of mount Moriah, overhanging the spot where the valleys of Jehoshaphat and Hinnom meet. " The top of the ridge is flat, descending rapidly towards the south, sometimes by offsets of rock ; the ground is tilled and planted with olive and other fruit-trees " (Robinson's Palestine, i. p. 394). Most writers seem to make בְּעַד here mean *instead of*, which is at best a rare and doubtful sense. In the last edition of Robinson's Gesenius, this explanation is relinquished and a local meaning given to the word, *amid caverns*, i. e. *surrounded by them.* But this reverses the true meaning of the preposition, *about, round about.* If strictly understood, it would rather seem to mean that the hill and tower should *enclose* caves or dens within their limits. Hendewerk, in order to avoid the conclusion that an actual destruction of the city is foretold, explains the verse as meaning that the people should shut themselves and their cattle up within the walls, so that the interior of the city, for a time, would be changed into a pasture-ground.

15. The desolation having been described in ver. 14 as of indefinite duration, this verse states more explicitly how long it is to last. *Until the Spirit is poured out upon us from on high, and the wilderness becomes a*

fruitful field, and the fruitful field is reckoned to the forest. The general meaning evidently is, until by a special divine influence a total revolution shall take place in the character, and as a necessary consequence in the condition, of the people. The attempt to restrict it to the return from exile, or the day of Pentecost, or some great effusion of the Spirit on the Jews still future, perverts the passage by making that its whole meaning which at most is but a part. For the meaning of the figures, see the exposition of chap. xxix. 17. In this connection they would seem to denote nothing more than total change, whereas in the other case the idea of an interchange appears to be made prominent.

16. *And justice shall abide in the wilderness, and righteousness in the fruitful field shall dwell.* This may either mean, that what is now a wilderness and what is now a fruitful field, shall alike be the abode of righteousness, *i. e.* of righteous men; or that both in the cultivation of the desert and in the desolation of the field, the righteousness of God shall be displayed. In favour of the former is the use of the word *dwell*, which implies a permanent condition, rather than a transient or occasional manifestation. It also agrees better with the relation of this verse to that before it, as a part of the same sentence. If this be the meaning of the sixteenth verse, it seems to follow clearly, that the whole of the last clause of the fifteenth is a promise, since the same inhabitation of righteousness is here foretold in reference to the forest and the fruitful field. It is possible indeed that these may be put for the whole land, as being the two parts into which he had just before divided it.

17. As the foregoing verse describes the effect of the effusion of the Spirit to be universal righteousness, so this describes the natural and necessary consequence of righteousness itself. *And the work of righteousness shall be peace, and the effect of righteousness rest and assurance* (or *security*) *for ever.* Both מעשה and עבדה strictly denote *work*, or rather that which is wrought, the product of labour. The translation of the former by *fruit* introduces a figure not in the original, as מעשה is never so employed, although the verbal root is used to denote the generation of plants. The phrase עד־עולם, not being limited in this case as it is in vers. 14, 15, must be taken in its widest sense.

18. *And my people shall abide in a home of peace, in sure dwellings, and in quiet resting-places.* There is something tranquillizing in the very sound of this delightful promise, which, as usual, is limited to God's own people, implying either that all should have become such, or that those who had not should be still perturbed and restless.

19. *And it shall hail in the downfall of the forest* (*i. e.* so as to overthrow it), *and the city shall be low in a low place* (or *humbled with humiliation*), *i. e.* utterly brought down. If this be read as a direct continuation of the promise in verse 18, it must be explained as a description of the downfall of some hostile power, and accordingly it has been referred by most interpreters to Nineveh, by Knobel to the slaughter of Sennacherib's army, and by Henderson to the destruction of the Jewish polity at the beginning of the Christian dispensation. Others, thinking it more natural to assume one subject here and in ver. 13, regard this as another instance of prophetic recurrence from remoter promises to nearer threats; as if he had said, Before these things can come to pass, the city must be brought low. This construction is entirely in keeping with the Prophet's manner, as exemplified already in this very chapter. (See note on ver. 9 above). Most interpreters, however, seem to fall into the usual error of regarding as

specific and exclusive what the Prophet himself has left unlimited and
undefined.   However natural and probable certain applications of the passage may appear, the only sense which can with certainty be put upon it,
is that some existing power must be humbled, either as a means or as a
consequence of the moral revolution which had been predicted.   Knobel
applies the first clause to the slaughter of Sennacherib's army, and the
second to the spiritual humiliation of the Jews, which is very unnatural.
The recent writers find a paronomasia in the phrase ברד ברדת, which
Ewald imitates by combining the words *hageln* and *verhagelt*.

20. *Blessed are ye that sow beside all waters, that send forth the foot of
the ox and the ass.*   The allusion in this verse is supposed by some to be to
pasturage, by others to tillage.   Lowth follows Chardin in applying the
words to the practice of treading the ground by the feet of cattle before
planting rice ; Henderson to the act of setting them at liberty from the
rope with which they were tied by the foot.   There is still more diversity
of judgment with respect to the application of the metaphor.   Of the latest
writers who have been consulted, Knobel understands the verse as contrasting the condition of those who lived at liberty on the sea-side or by
rivers, with theirs who were pent up and besieged in cities.   Hitzig supposes a particular allusion to the case of those who had escaped with their
possessions from Jerusalem.   Hendewerk applies the verse to the happy
external condition of the people in the days of the Messiah.   Henderson
says it beautifully exhibits the free and unrestrained exertions of the
apostles and other missionaries in sowing the seed of the kingdom in every
part of the world.   Ewald explains it exclusively of moral cultivation, as
implying that none can expect to reap good without diligently sowing it.
Of all these explanations the last may be considered as approaching nearest
to the truth, because it requires least to be supplied by the imagination.
Taking the whole connection into view, the meaning of this last verse
seems to be, that as great revolutions are to be expected, arising wholly or
in part from moral causes, they alone are safe, for the present and the
future, who with patient assiduity perform what is required ; and provide;
by the discharge of actual duty for contingencies which can neither be
escaped, nor provided for in any other manner.

Chapter 33

THIS chapter contains a general threatening of retribution to the enemies
of God's people, with particular reference to Sennacherib or the Assyrian
power.   The spoiler shall himself be spoiled in due time, through the
divine interposition, and for the exaltation of Jehovah, vers. 1–6.   The
state of desolation and alarm is followed by sudden deliverance, vers. 7–13.
The same vicissitudes are again described, but in another form, vers.
14–19.   The peace and security of Zion are set forth under the figures of
a stationary tent, and of a spot surrounded by broad rivers, yet impassable
to hostile vessels, vers. 20–22.   By a beautiful transition, the enemy is
described as such a vessel, but dismantled and abandoned to its enemies,
ver. 23.   The chapter closes with a general promise of deliverance from
suffering, as a consequence of pardoned sin, ver. 24.

1. *Woe to thee spoiling and thou wast not spoiled, deceiving and they did
not deceive thee !   When thou shalt cease to spoil thou shalt be spoiled, and
when thou art done deceiving they shall deceive thee.*   The plural verbs in

both clauses are indefinitely construed as equivalents to the passive participles. The two ideas meant to be expressed are those of violence and
treachery, as the crying sins of arbitrary powers. The latest German
writers suppose both the verbs to be expressive of robbery or spoliation,
but without authority from usage. (See the note on chap. xxi. 2.) The
person addressed has been supposed by different writers to be Nebuchadnezzar, Antiochus Epiphanes (Vitringa), Ferdinand II. (Cocceius), Antichrist (Gill), and Satan (Jerome). Most interpreters suppose it to be Sennacherib, either as an individual or as a representative of the Assyrian
power. In themselves, the words are applicable to any oppressive and
deceitful enemy, and may be naturally so explained at the beginning of the
prophecy. This verse describes the enemy as acting without provocation,
and also as having never yet experienced reverses.

2. *Jehovah, favour us; for thee we wait; be their arm in the mornings,
also our salvation in time of trouble.* Instead of *their arm*, Lowth follows
several of the ancient versions in reading *our arm*. The common text has
been variously explained as a prayer of the present for the absent (Vitringa),
of the Jewish for the Christian church (De Dieu), of the Reformed Church
for its defenders (Cocceius), &c., &c. The truth seems to be, as Barnes
well says, that Isaiah here interposes his own feelings, and offers his own
prayer that God would be the strength of the nation, and then, with an
immediate change of form, presents the prayer of the people. *Arm* is a
common Hebrew metaphor for strength or support. (See chap. ix. 19.) *As
to the mornings* is an indefinite expression, understood by some to mean
early or *quickly*, by others *every morning* (Kimchi: בכל בקר ובקר), with
allusion to the daily attacks of the enemy (Henderson), or to the daily morning sacrifice (Piscator). Calvin explains the whole clause thus, Be thou,
who wast their arm (*i.e.* that of our fathers) in the morning (*i.e.* of old),
also our salvation in time of trouble. But this is rather a Latin than a
Hebrew construction.

3. *At a noise of tumult* (or *tumultuous noise*) *the peoples flee; at thy
rising the nations are scattered.* The modern notion, that the voice of
Jehovah always means thunder, seems entirely arbitrary. The voice and
the rising up are parts of the same figure, and the one has no more reference to actual phenomena in nature than the other. Aben Ezra and Lowth
suppose these words to be addressed to Sennacherib, all other writers to
Jehovah himself. Jerome refers the first clause to the voice of the destroying angel, Piscator to the tumult in the camp of the Assyrians. Lowth
reads *thy terrible voice*, in which, as he says, he follows the Septuagint and
Peshito. The same combination occurs in Dan. x. 6. (Compare Rev. i.
10, 15.) The *rising* meant is not the ascent of the judge to the judgment-
seat (Piscator), nor the exaltation of the Assyrian power (Aben Ezra), but
the act of rising from a state of seeming inaction, or as when one rouses
himself to strike (Barnes). These words are commonly applied to the
divine interposition in the case of Sennacherib's attack upon Jerusalem.;
but Ewald understands them more generally as denoting that such had
ever been the effect of Jehovah's presence, and must be so still. Some
arbitrarily translate the verse as a direct prediction (*fugient*), or a prayer
(*fugiant*).

4. *And your spoil shall be gathered* (*like*) *the gathering of the devourer;
like the running of locusts running on it.* By another apostrophe, the
Prophet here addresses the enemy collectively. חסיל is a name of the
locust, so called from its devouring. (See the verb in Deut. xxviii. 38.)

Henderson translates the parallel terms, *devouring locust* and *caterpillar-locusts.* The older writers understand this clause to mean *as locusts are gathered,* for the purpose of destroying them, even by children (Calvin), or by labourers in pits (Jerome), a custom still existing in Africa and Spain (Forerius). Junius explains it to mean *that which locusts have gathered.* But all the modern writers understand the words to mean *as locusts gather,* *i. e.* greedily and thoroughly, not leaving a tree or a field till they have stripped it (Bochart). As אסף is the verb used to denote the gathering of fruits in harvest (chap. xvii. 5), Gesenius supposes a specific allusion to that usage here, *like the harvesting of locusts,* &c. The construction of the last clause is: like the running of locusts (shall one be) running on it (*i. e.* on the spoil). The verb שקק denotes specifically the act of *running eagerly,* or with a view to satisfy the appetite. It is sometimes used to denote desire itself, which Umbreit assumes to be the meaning here (*nach Heus-chrecken-Gier giert man darnach*). Vitringa finds the fulfilment of this threatening in 1 Maccab. iv. 23, vi. 6. There is an old rabbinical tradition, which so explains this verse as to justify the seizure of the spoils of the ten tribes by the Jews, when found in the possession of the Assyrians.

5. *Exalted is Jehovah because dwelling on high* (or *inhabiting a high place); he fills* (or *has filled*) *Zion with judgment and righteousness.* The first word being a passive participle, seems to denote not merely a condition, but a change. *He has been exalted* by the subjection of his enemies (Knobel), or by his mighty deeds in general. The future form adopted in the French Version (*va être magnifié*) is needless and arbitrary. There is no need of making כי a relative (Vitringa), or rendering it *yea* (Barnes), as it introduces an explanation of the statement in the first clause. *High place* is not put specifically for heaven (Gesenius), but for a lofty and commanding position. The last clause probably denotes not the moral effects produced upon the people (Ewald), but the manifestation of Jehovah's attributes. According to Hendewerk, this second clause is the beginning of the Messianic part of the first of the three prophecies contained in the chapter. Lowth introduces here his favourite idea of a chorus or choir of Jews representing the whole people.

6. *And he shall be the security of thy times, strength of salvations, wisdom and knowledge, the fear of Jehovah, that is his treasure.* Most interpreters connect היה either with אמונת or חסן as its subject: there shall be security in thy times; or the security of thy times shall be; or strength of salvations, &c., shall be the security of thy times. But the simplest construction is the one proposed by Henderson, which supplies the subject from the foregoing verse, *he (i. e.* Jehovah, or *it, i. e.* his righteousness) *shall be,* &c. The object of address is supposed by some to be Hezekiah, by others the Messiah, but is most probably the people or the believer as an individual. *His treasure* may refer by an enallage personae to the same, or mean the treasure of Jehovah, that which he bestows. Hitzig supposes an allusion in the last clause to Hezekiah's treasury, emptied by the tribute to Sennacherib, as if he had said, Henceforth the fear of the Lord shall be his treasure. Umbreit makes the first clause, by a forced construction, mean that the evil times should produce or foster *faith,* and that this should be a treasure to the people. חסן, according to its etymology, means strength, but in usage is applied exclusively to that arising from wealth. The original construction is perfectly intelligible, and much more expressive than such paraphrastic versions as *possessio salutaris* (Clericus). According to Hendewerk, this verse proves that the only Messiah of whom Isaiah ever pro-

phesies is Hezekiah! Knobel thinks that it must be addressed to the
people, because Hezekiah was a pious man before.

7. *Behold, their valiant ones cry without ; the ambassadors of peace weep
bitterly.* The Targum and some other ancient version seem to treat אֶרְאֶלָּם
as a contraction of אֶרְאֶה לָם or אֶרְאֶה לֹם. Thus Aquila has ὀραθήσομαι
αὐτοῖς, Symmachus ὀφθήσομαι, the Vulgate *videntes.* But there is no
example of the form לָם for לָהֶם. (See the note on chap. ix. 6.) Ewald reads
אַרְאֵלִים, and explains it as an adjective derived from רָאַל,‎synonymous with
the Arabic عل to fear. *They fearful cry aloud.* This coincides in meaning with the Septuagint Version (ἐν τῷ φόβῳ αὐτῶν). Most of the other
modern writers identify the word substantially with *Ariel* in chap. xxix. 1,
by reading אַרְאֶלָם in the plural, or אַרְאֶלָם with a suffix. The latest investigations, although still unsatisfactory, tend strongly to confirm the version
given in the English Bible. (See Gesenius's Thesaurus s. v.) Some,
however, here as in chap. xxix. 1, give *Ariel* the sense of *altar.* Thus
Grotius translates the words, *behold their altar,* and regards it as a derisive
exclamation of the enemy, while Jarchi makes it a sorrowful ejaculation of
the Jews themselves. Aben Ezra and Kimchi give it the sense of *messengers,* which is plainly a conjectural inference from the parallel expression.
J. D. Michaelis characteristically makes it the name of a species of bird,
and renders it *Rohrdommel.* The messengers mentioned in the other
clause are not those sent by Hezekiah to Isaiah (2 Kings xix. 2), nor the
Maccabees, as being both priests and heroes (Vitringa), nor the ministers
of the gospel, nor the two apocalyptic witnesses (Gill), but probably the
three men sent by Hezekiah to Rabshakeh (2 Kings xviii. 18), or perhaps
the bearers of the tribute, weeping on account of Sennacherib's refusal to
fulfil his promise. Hendewerk supposes them to be called valiant, because
they ventured into the enemy's camp ; others because they were probably
military chiefs. Their weeping is agreed by all interpreters to be in strict
accordance with the ancient usage, as described, for example by Homer.
According to Cocceius, the first clause is an exclamation at the death of
Gustavus Adolphus.

8. *The highways are wasted, the wayfarer ceaseth; he breaks the covenant,
despises cities, values no man.* Those are not the words of the ambassadors
reporting the condition of the country (Grotius), but of the Prophet himself describing it. The scene presented is not that of Protestant cities
seized by Antichrist, and a stop put to a religious course and conversation
(Gill), but the actual condition of Judea during the Assyrian invasion.
(Compare Judges v. 6.) The verbs of the last clause are not to be indefinitely construed (Cocceius), nor do they agree with *wayfarer,* but with
Sennacherib or the Assyrian. They are not to be rendered as pluperfects
(Junius), but as preterites or descriptive presents. The meaning is not that
he rejected the cities offered him by Hezekiah (Lowth), nor that he barbarously disregarded the condition of the conquered country (J. D. Michaelis),
but that he despised its defences as unable to resist him. The last words
may either mean that he has no regard to any man's interest or wishes, or
that he does not value human life. Some have strangely understood this
as an impious reproach on God himself as having broken his engagements.

9. *The land mourneth, languisheth ; Lebanon is ashamed, it pines away ;
Sharon is like a wilderness, and Bashan and Carmel cast* (their leaves).
The most fertile and flourishing parts of the country are described as deso-

late. That the language is figurative, may be inferred from the fact that none of the places mentioned were in Judah. Hitzig and Hendewerk suppose the date of the prediction to be fixed by the allusion to the falling of the leaf. But would this periodical change be represented as a sign of desolation? According to Umbreit, Lebanon (the white mountain) is here described as blushing, but according to Ewald as turning pale. Barnes thinks the reference is to the places through which the Assyrians had passed. J. D. Michaelis follows up his favourite mode of exposition by asserting that נער denotes the buzzing of the gadfly, but is here used in the sense of *swarming*, and applied to the hostile armies. Cocceius takes the same word in the sense of *roaring*. According to Grotius, the Sharon here meant is the one in Bashan (1 Chron. v. 16). According to Clericus, Lebanon is put for mount Niphates, and the other places for places in Assyria.

10. *Now will I arise, saith Jehovah, now will I be lifted up, now will I exalt myself.* The emphasis is not upon the pronoun (Barnes), which in that case would have been expressed in Hebrew, but upon the adverb *now*, which is twice repeated to imply that the time for the divine interposition is arrived, and that there shall be no more delay. According to Gesenius, אֲרוֹמָם is for אֶתְרוֹמָם, but others read אֲרוֹמֵם.

11. *Ye shall conceive chaff, ye shall bring forth stubble; your breath (as) fire shall devour you.* The first clause contains a common Scriptural figure for failure and frustration. (See chap. xxvi. 18.) Chaff and stubble are not named as being dry and innutritious food (Vitringa), which would be wholly out of place in this connection, but as worthless and perishable substances. Lowth follows Secker and the Targum in reading כמו רוחי for רוחכם (*my spirit like fire shall consume you.*) Grotius takes רוח in the sense of *anger*, Clericus in that of *pride*. Calvin understands the clause to mean that their own breath should kindle the fire that destroyed them. As specimens of opposite extremes in exposition, it may be mentioned, that J. D. Michaelis applies this last clause to the infection of the plague as communicated by the breath, Cocceius to the evils arising from the abuse of religious liberty in Germany and Holland, and especially from efforts to reunite the Protestant and Romish Churches.

12. *And nations shall be lime-kilns* (or *burnings of lime*); *thorns cut up, in the fire they shall burn.* By *nations* we are not to understand the different races mingled in Sennacherib's army, but all nations that incur the wrath of God. The same word *burnings* is applied to the aromatic fumigations used at ancient burials (Jer. xxxiv. 5), to which there may be some allusion here. The Hebrew word according to analogy may be a noun of place (Hendewerk), but is commonly supposed to denote burnings. Clericus connects the clauses by supposing that the thorns are described as being burnt in lime-kilns. The ideas expressed are those of quickness and intensity. The thorns are perhaps described as *cut up*, to suggest that they are dry, and therefore more combustible. On this same verse J. D. Michaelis observes, that the Jews at that time burnt the bodies of the dead; Knobel, that they regarded the custom with abhorrence. The former adds that when they burnt the Assyrians they might be said to burn a nation. Gill of course refers the verse to the future destruction of antichristian Rome. (Rev. xvii. 16, xviii. 8.)

13. *Hear, ye far, what I have done, and know, ye near, my might.* By *far* and *near* the Targum understands confirmed saints and repentant sinners; Junius, the Jews and Gentiles; Hendewerk, the ten tribes and the

Jews; but Barnes, more naturally, all without exception. According to Hitzig, the near are commanded to *know*, because they can see for themselves. Henderson retains the common version, *acknowledge*. According to Hendewerk, this is the beginning of a third distinct prediction. It is really an apostrophe, expressing the magnitude of the event predicted in the foregoing context.

14. *Afraid in Zion are the sinners;* not *at* or *near Zion*, meaning the Assyrians (Sanctius), but *in Zion*, i. e. in Jerusalem, referring to the impious Jews themselves; *trembling has seized the impious*, a parallel expression to *sinners*. The meaning *hypocrites* is rejected by the modern lexicographers for that of *impure* or gross sinners. So Calvin, in the margin of his version, has *sceleratos*. The persons so described are the wicked and unbelieving portion of the Jews. Gill applies the terms directly to formal professors in the reformed churches; Grotius, to such of the Jews as had apostatized to heathenism in order to conciliate Sennacherib. On this farfetched hypothesis Vitringa well remarks, that such expedients were unknown in ancient warfare, and that Sennacherib probably cared nothing as to the religion of those whom he attacked. What follows might be understood as the language of the Prophet himself, giving a reason for the terror of the wicked. Interpreters appear to be unanimous, however, in making it the language of the wicked Jews themselves. At the same time, they differ greatly as to the time at which these words must be supposed to have been spoken. Some refer them to the past, and understand the verse to mean that they are now in terror who once said thus and thus. On this hypothesis, the words themselves might be explained as the language of *Who of us is afraid* (יגור) *of the devouring fire? Who of us is afraid of everlasting burnings?* Or with Vitringa, as the language of complaint, *Who of us can dwell with* (this) *devouring fire? Who of us can dwell with* (these) *perpetual burnings? i. e.* with a God of such severity? But the great mass of interpreters, both old and new, suppose this to be given not as the former but the present language of the wicked Jews, when actually seized with terror. Not those *who once said*, but *who now say*, &c. On this supposition, it can be expressive neither of defiance nor complaint, but only of alarm and desperation. Ewald, adopting this interpretation in the general, gives יגור the sense of *protecting*, derived from its primary import of *sojourning* as a guest and a friend; but this is a gratuitous departure from the usage of the language. Those who adhere to it are still divided as to the application of the figures. Grotius understands by the fire the Assyrian host that menaced them. *Who can abide this devouring fire?* Piscator, the fire of God's wrath, as executed by the Assyrians. Aben Ezra, the wrath of God as exercised against the Assyrians themselves. This is the interpretation commonly adopted. It supposes the words to be expressive of the feelings excited by the slaughter of Sennacherib's host. If this be a specimen of God's vindicatory justice, what may we expect? *Who of us can dwell with* (this) *devouring fire? Who of us can dwell with these perpetual burnings?* Many make the language still more emphatic, by supposing that the Prophet argues from the less to the greater. If these are God's temporal judgments, what must his eternal wrath be? If the momentary strokes of his hand are thus resistless, *who of us can dwell with the devouring fire, who of us can dwell with everlasting burnings?* The last words may then be taken in their strongest and most unrestricted sense. Henderson thinks they have no meaning if they do not refer to eternal punishment. לנו does not here mean *for us* or *with us*, but is used in its widest

sense, as expressive of relation in general, to qualify the pronoun—*Who with respect to us*, i. e. *who of us*, as opposed to *men in general.* Gesenius describes it as an emphatic formula, and yet omits it in the translation. Hitzig and Hendewerk take fire and burning as a poetical description of the plague, by which they suppose the Assyrians to have perished. Clericus, *more suo*, understands it of the burning of the villages of Judah by the invaders. Knobel says the burning was called everlasting, because it was everlasting in its consequences, *i. e.* it destroyed what it consumed for ever. But who could or would speak, in any language, of a man's being hung with an everlasting rope, or killed by an everlasting stroke of lightning? De Dieu's construction of the last clause, as containing several distinct propositions (*quis commorabitur nostrum? ignis devorat*, &c.), is ingenious, but unnatural and wholly unnecessary.

15. This verse contains a description of the righteous man, not unlike that in the fifteenth and twenty-fourth Psalms. *Walking righteousnesses i. e.* leading a righteous life. *Walk* is a common Scriptural expression for the course of conduct. The plural form of the other word may either be used to mark it as an abstract term, or as an emphatic expression for fulness or completeness of rectitude. In order to retain the figure of walking, the preposition *in* may be supplied before the noun ; but in Hebrew it seems to be governed directly by the verb, or to qualify it as an adverb. *And speaking right things*, or (taking the plural merely as an abstract) *rectitude* or *righteousness.* The idea is not merely that of speaking truth as opposed to falsehood, but that of rectitude in speech as distinguished from rectitude of action. *Rejecting* or *despising* (or, combining both ideas, *rejecting with contempt*) *the gain of oppressions* or *extortions. Shaking his hands from taking hold of the bribe*, an expressive gesture of indignant refusal, which Forerius compares to Pilate's washing his hands, and Gataker to Paul's shaking off the viper. Malvenda imagines that the terms are so selected as to suggest the idea of a weighty gift. Gesenius and others greatly weaken the expression, and indeed destroy its graphic form, by rendering the phrase, *whose hand refuses to receive a bribe.* The true sense is forcibly conveyed in J. D. Michaelis's version, *shakes his hands that no bribe may stick to them*, and in Gill's homely paraphrase, *that won't receive any, but when they are put into his hands shakes them out.* The Chaldee Paraphrase of this first clause contains the expression *mammon of falsehood*, which may be compared with the *mammon of unrighteousness* in Luke xvi. 9. *Stopping his ears from hearing bloods, i. e.* plans of murder, or as Lowth expresses it, *the proposal of bloodshed.* For the usage of the plural form דמים, see the note on chap. i. 15. *Shutting his eyes from looking at evil, i. e.* from conniving at it, or even beholding it as an indifferent spectator. The ב is then a mere connective, like the English *at* or *on ;* but the combination of this verb and particle appears in many cases to denote the act of gazing at a thing with pleasure, which idea would be perfectly appropriate here. Lowth has *against the appearance of evil*, which does not convey the exact sense of the original. According to the natural connection of the passage, this verse would seem to contain the answer to the question in ver. 14, and is so understood by those who make the question mean, Who can stand before this terrible Jehovah? But on the supposition of an allusion to eternal punishment, the answer is absurd, for it implies that the righteous man can or will endure it. This may either be regarded as a proof that there is no such allusion to eternal punishment in ver. 14, or as a proof that this is not an answer to the ques-

tion there recorded.   The former conclusion is adopted by the latest
German writers, who understand this verse as meaning that God is a consuming fire only to the wicked, and that the righteous man, as here
described, is perfectly secure.   On the other hand, Henderson separates
this verse from the preceding context by a larger space than usual, making
this the beginning, as it were, of a new paragraph.   To this construction
there is the less objection, as the sentence is evidently incomplete in this
verse, the apodosis being added in the next.

16. *He* (the character described in ver. 15) *high places shall inhabit.*
This does not denote exalted station in society, but safety from enemies, in
being above their reach, as appears from the other clause.   *Fastnesses* (or
strongholds) *of rocks* (*shall be*) *his lofty place, i.e.* his refuge or his place
of safety, as in chap. xxv. 12.   To the idea of security is added that of sustenance, without which the first would be of no avail.   *His bread is given,*
including the ideas of allotment or appointment and of actual supply.
His water sure, or, retaining the strict sense of the participle, *secured.*   At
the same time there is evident allusion to the moral usage of the word as
signifying faithful, true, the opposite of that which fails, deceives, or dis-
appoints the expectation, in which sense the same word, with a negative, is
applied by Jeremiah (xv. 18) to *waters that fail.*   Clericus explains the
first clause of this verse as a promise that those living in the plain should
be as safe as if they lived in the mountains.   Grotius explains the second
as a promise of literal deliverance from famine.   Knobel arbitrarily applies
the whole to protection and supply in a time of siege, and then infers that
the passage must have been composed before Sennacherib approached Jerusalem, because the Prophet afterwards was well aware that no siege had
taken place at all.   This charge of false prediction is exploded by the
simple observation, that the verse is an assurance, clothed in figurative
language, of general protection and support to the righteous.   Vitringa's
reference of the words in their lower sense to the support of the Levitical
priesthood, and in their higher sense to the happiness of heaven, goes as
much to an extreme, though in an opposite direction.

17. *A king in his beauty shall thine eyes behold.*   Kimchi, by an
arbitrary syntax, takes the future as a past tense, and refers it to the king
of Assyria, whom their eyes had seen but should see no more.   Besides
the grammatical objection to this version, it is inconsistent with the other
clause, and unless that also be referred to the same subject by supplying
king before *a distant land.*   Of those who take the futures in their proper
meaning, some suppose Jehovah to be meant (Vitringa, J. D. Michaelis),
others the Messiah (Abarbenel), but most writers Hezekiah, either exclusively (Gesenius), or as a type of Christ (Calvin).   For this departure from
his customary mode of exposition, Calvin thinks it necessary to apologise
by saying, *ne quis me hic allegorias sequi putet a quibus sum alienus.*   To
see the king *in his beauty* does not mean in his moral excellence (Hendewerk), but in his royal state, with tacit reference to his previous state of
mourning and dejection (chap. xxxvii. 1).   *They* (*i.e.* thine eyes) *shall
behold a land of distances* or *distant places.*   The most natural explanation
of this phrase would be a *distant land,* in which sense it is used by Jeremiah (viii. 19), and a part of it by Zechariah (x. 9), and by both in reference to exile or captivity.   The verse before us, taken by itself, might be
understood as a threatening that the Jews should see the king of Babylon
in his royal state, and in a distant land.   Interpreters seem to be agreed,
however, that in this connection it can be taken only as a promise.   Grotius

accordingly explains it to mean that after the fall of the Assyrian host, the Jews should be free to go abroad without restraint, and especially to visit the scene of the catastrophe. This explanation he illustrates by a parallel from Virgil. *Panduntur portæ, juvat ire et Dorica castra desertosque videre locos litusque relictum.* Hitzig confines it to their literally *seeing* far and wide from the walls of Jerusalem, their view being no longer obstructed by entrenchments or the presence of the enemy. Luther and others, on the contrary, suppose the land itself to be here described as actually widened by an accession of conquered territory. To all these explanations it may be objected that the Prophet does not speak of *distant boundaries* or frontiers, as in chap. xxvi. 15, but of a *distant land*. The only explanation of the verse as a promise, against which this objection does not lie, is that of Henderson, who translates the clause, *they shall see distant lands*, and explains it to mean that instead of being cooped up within the walls of Jerusalem by the Assyrians, the inhabitants should not only freely traverse their own land, but visit distant nations. Whether the liberty of foreign travel is in this connection an appropriate promise, may be made a question. Piscator understands the clause to mean that their eyes should see ambassadors from a far country, viz. those of Berodach-baladan (2 Kings xx. 12). But in this case the most important word of the sentence is supplied by mere conjecture. Vitringa applies the whole verse, in its lower sense, to the conquest of the Maccabees and their enlargement of the Jewish territory, but in a higher sense to the glorious reign of the Messiah.

18. *Thy heart shall meditate terror.* This does not mean, it shall conceive or experience present terror, but reflect on that which is already past. What follows is explained by some as the language of the Jews in their terror calling for the officers on whom they depended for protection. But the officers here named are not those to whom they would probably have looked in this emergency. Others more naturally understand it therefore as the triumphant exclamation of the people when they found themselves so suddenly delivered from their enemies. *Where is he that counted? where is he that weighed? where is he that counted the towers?* As a noun, ספר means a *scribe*, and is commonly so rendered here. Some even give it the New Testament sense of γραμματεύς, a learned man or doctor of the law. So the Septuagint (γραμματικοί), the Vulgate (*literatus*), Luther (*Schriftgelehrten*), Vitringa (*doctus*). This leads of course to an analogous interpretation of the other terms, as meaning *legis verba ponderans, doctor parvulorum, dialecticus subtilis*, &c., &c. Others, adhering to the Hebrew usage of the noun ספר, understand by it a *secretary*, financial or military, *perhaps a secretary of state, or of war, or an inspector-general* (Barnes). The clause is still more modernized by J. D. Michaelis : *where is the general? where is the engineer?* But as the second ספר is evidently construed as a participle, and in the primary sense of *counting* it is much more natural to understand the first ספר and שקל in like manner, as denoting him who counted, him who weighed. This is Ewald's construction (*wer zählte, wer wog*), and Lowth gives the same sense to the words as nouns (*the accomptant, the weigher of tribute*). Thus explained, they may be applied either to the instruments of the Assyrian domination in Judea, or to certain necessary officers attached to the besieging army. The counting and weighing may be either that of tribute, or of military wages The second ספר denotes the same act as the first, but is applied expressly to another object. The *towers* are of course the fortifications of Jerusalem.

By *counting* them, some understand surveying them, either with a view to garrisoning or dismantling ; others, the act of reconnoitring them from without, which some ascribe particularly to Rabshakeh or Sennacherib himself. The general meaning of the verse is plain, as an expression of surprise and joy, that the oppressor or besieger had now vanished. The Apostle Paul, in 1 Cor. i. 20, has a sentence so much like this, in the threefold repetition of the question *where*, and in the use of the word *scribe*, that it cannot be regarded as a mere fortuitous coincidence. Of the mutual relation of the passages, two views have been taken by interpreters. Junius and Cocceius regard that in Corinthians as a quotation of the one before us, and Vitringa makes the former determine the whole meaning of the latter. He accordingly explains the Hebrew words as all denoting some form of worldly wisdom and sagacity, or its possessors, and the whole verse as implying that the great deliverance had not been wrought by any such means but by God alone. The violence done by this interpretation to the language of the Prophet is enough of itself to make the hypothesis on which it rests a doubtful one. Calvin, on the other hand, denies that Paul has any reference to this place, which is going too far, since it is probable, as Henderson observes, that the structure of the one passage may have suggested the other. The expression *it is written*, in the preceding verse of the epistle, introduces a quotation from chap. xxix. 14, but does not necessarily extend to the next verse, which may therefore be regarded as a mere imitation, as to form and diction, of the one before us.

19. *The fierce* (or *determined*) *people thou shalt not see.* Thou shalt see no more the Assyrians, whose disappearance was implied in the questions of the foregoing verse. The essential idea of נועז seems to be that of firmness and decision, perhaps with the accessory idea of agressive boldness. It is taken in the stronger sense of *impudent* by several of the ancient versions. De Dieu and Capellus (the two Ludovici, as Vitringa calls them) would read לועז so as to secure a parallel to נלעג in the other clause. (Compare Ps. cxiv. 1.) *A people deep of lip from hearing, i. e.* too obscure for thee to understand. Deep is referred to the sound of the voice, the mode of utterance, by the Septuagint (βαθύφωνον) Clericus (*e profundo gutture loquentem*), and Vitringa, who illustrates the expression by the difference between the utterance of the Swiss and the Saxons on the one hand, and the French and English on the other. But the later writers more correctly understand *deep* as denoting obscure or unintelligible. The preposition before *hearing*, though not directly negative, is virtually so, as it denotes *away from*, which is really equivalent to *so as not to hear*, or *be heard*. (See the note on chap. v. 6.) *Barbarous tongue* (or of a barbarous tongue), *without meaning* (literally, *there is no meaning*). The verb לעג, in its other forms, means to mock or scoff, an idea closely connected, in the Hebrew usage, with that of foreign language, either because the latter seems ridiculous to those who do not understand it, or because unmeaning jargon is often used in mockery. Jerome's translation of the last phrase, *in quo nulla est sapientia*, changes the meaning of the clause entirely. Some of the latest German writers understand it to signify not only *unintelligible* but *unmeaning*, and regard the description as an illustration of Jewish narrowness and prejudice. The parallelism might have taught them that no more was meant to be conveyed than the actual want of meaning to the hearers. The whole is a mere paraphrastic description of a people altogether strange and foreign. Henderson supposes the expressions to refer to the Medo-Persian mercenaries in the Assyrian army, but most interpreters apply them directly to the

Assyrians themselves. According to Gill, the language here meant is the Latin; but the people he explains to be both Turks and Papists.

20. *Behold Zion, the city of our festivals.* Instead of the presence of foreign enemies, see Jerusalem once more the scene of stated solemnities. Houbigant and Lowth, on the alleged authority of the Targum, read *thou shalt see,* which is not only unnecessary, but less expressive than the direot command to see the object as already present. The address is to the people as an individual, and not to Zion itself, as Luther and the Targum have it. *Thine eyes shall see Jerusalem a quiet home, a tent (that) shall not be removed* (or *taken down*). The whole of this description is drawn from the usages of the nomadic life. *Its stakes shall not be pulled up for ever, and all its cords shall not be broken,* or in our idiom, *none of its cords shall be broken.* According to Kimchi, לנצח means for a long time (זמן רב); according to Henderson, until the end of the old dispensation. The peculiar beauty of the imagery lies in ascribing permanence to a tent, which, from its very nature, must be moveable. This may either imply a previous state of agitation and instability, or that the church, though weak in herself, should be strengthened and established by the power of God. Gill understands the verse as describing what he calls the *Philadelphian church state.* Conrad Pellican applies it to the rest and peace of heaven; Vitringa, to the state of the Jews under the Maccabees, considered as a type of the Christian Church. He also robs the passage of its beautiful simplicity, by making it the language of a choir of teachers, or of the Prophet speaking in their name, and by giving to each part of the tent a specific spiritual sense, the stakes being the promises, and the ropes the hope and faith of true believers. On this mode of expounding the prophetic figures, see the exposition of chap. v. 3.

21. *But there shall Jehovah be mighty for us* (or *in our behalf*). Some take the particles כי אם separately, as meaning *because certainly.* There is no need, however, of departing from the ordinary sense of *but,* which the phrase has elsewhere after a negation. The connection of the verses is, that Zion shall never be weakened or removed, *but on the contrary* Jehovah, &c. The construction of אדיר as a mere epithet of יהוה is forbidden by the collocation of the words. The sense seems to be that he will there display his power for our protection and advantage. *A place of rivers, streams, broad (on) both hands (or sides),* i. e. completely surrounding her. Cocceius connects this clause with the verb of the preceding verse, (*thine eyes shall see a place,* &c.), and throws the immediately foregoing words into a parenthesis. J. D. Michaelis supplies *we have.* But most interpreters connect these words directly with *Jehovah.* Of these some suppose מקום to be used like the Latin *loco* meaning *in the place, instead.* The promise then is, that Jehovah will supply the place of streams and rivers. Others more boldly put מקום in apposition with יהוה, and explain the clause to mean that Jehovah will himself be a place of streams and rivers to the people. Clericus supposes the allusion to nomadic life to be still continued, and the people to be described as encamping on the banks of noble streams, but without incurring the dangers usually incident to such a situation. According to Gill, the ideas meant to be conveyed are those of abundance, freedom, pleasant situation and security. Many interpreters suppose the situation of Jerusalem to be here compared with that of Nineveh, Memphis, and other cities situated on great rivers, the want of which advantage was abundantly compensated by the divine protection. But the latest German writers understand the clause as meaning that God himself would be to Zion what moats and trenches are to fortified cities. This idea is neither natural in

itself nor naturally suggested by the words *streams* and *rivers*, the plurals of the terms which are commonly applied to the Nile and the Euphrates. The most obvious explanation seems to be that this clause is an amplification of the adverb שָׁם. *Jehovah will be mighty for us there.* What place is meant? A place of rivers and streams broad on both sides, *i. e.* spreading in every direction. There is the less occasion, therefore, to read שָׁם with Lowth or שָׁם with Koppe. The situation described is one which has all the advantages of mighty streams without their dangers. *There shall not go in it an oared vessel* (literally, *a ship of oar*), *and a gallant ship shall not pass through it.* The parallel expressions both refer, no doubt, to ships of war, which, in ancient times, were propelled by oars. The antithesis which some assume between trading ships and vessels of war would here be out of place. The fine old English phrase *gallant ship* is ill exchanged by some translators for *mighty* or *magnificent vessel.*

22. *For Jehovah our Judge, Jehovah our Lawgiver, Jehovah our King, he will save us.* This is a repetition of the same idea, but without the figures of the preceding verse. Ewald agrees with the older writers in making *Jehovah* the subject and the other nouns the predicates of a series of short sentences (*Jehovah is our Judge*, &c.). Gesenius makes them all the complex subject of the verb at the end. The general meaning is the same in either case.

23. *Thy ropes are cast loose; they do not hold upright their mast; they do not spread the sail; then is shared plunder of booty in plenty; the lame spoil the spoil.* Cocceius refers the first clause to the tent (thy cords are lengthened) and the rest to a ship. Clericus makes the whole relate to a tent, and supposes תֹּרֶן to denote the central pole or post. Interpreters are agreed, however, that there is, at the beginning of this verse, a sudden apostrophe to the enemy considered as a ship. This figure would be naturally suggested by those of ver. 21. It was there said that no vessel should approach the holy city. But now the Prophet seems to remember that one had done so, the proud ship of Assyria. But what was its fate? He sees it dismantled and abandoned to its enemies. The first phrase is rendered in Robinson's Gesenius, *thy tacklings are broken in pieces*, an expression which could hardly be applied to ropes. The Rabbins understand it to mean, thy ropes are abandoned by the sailors. The Vulgate version is *laxati sunt.* The last two explanations may be combined by supposing the words to mean that they cast the ropes loose and abandon them. Kimchi explains כֵּן as an adverb meaning *well* or *rightly;* Cocceius as a noun, meaning the base or socket of the mast. This last is adopted by most of the late writers; but an equally natural construction is to make כֵּן an adjective meaning *upright*, which is justified by usage and peculiarly appropriate in this connection. Some take נֵס in its more usual sense of flag or banner, without materially changing that of the whole sentence. אָז marks the transition from abandonment to plunder, whether past or future. עַד שָׁלָל appears to be an emphatic pleonasm or reduplication. The eagerness of the pillage is expressed by making the lame join in it.

24. *And the inhabitant shall not say, I am sick* (or *have been sick*). This may either mean that none shall be sick, or that those who have been so shall be recovered. Some interpreters suppose an allusion to the plague. *The people dwelling in it (is) forgiven (its) iniquity.* Some suppose this to be an explanation of the sickness mentioned in the first clause, as a spiritual malady. Others understand it as explaining bodily disease to be the conse-

quence and punishment of sin. The words may be taken in a wider sense than either of these, namely, that suffering shall cease with sin which is its cause. Thus understood, the words are strictly applicable only to a state of things still future, either upon earth or in heaven. The last clause shews the absurdity of making the first mean merely that no one shall excuse himself from joining in the pillage on the plea of sickness.

Chapter 34

THIS chapter and the next appear to constitute one prophecy, the first part of which (chap. xxxiv.) is filled with threatenings against the enemies of the church, the latter part (chap. xxxv.) with promises to the church itself. The threatenings of chap. xxxiv. are directed, first against the nations in general, vers. 1–4, and then against Edom in particular, vers. 5–15, with a closing affirmation of the truth and certainty of the prediction, vers. 16, 17. The destruction of the enemies of Zion and the desolation of their lands are represented by the figures of a great sacrifice or slaughter, the falling of the heavenly bodies, the conversion of the soil into brimstone and the waters into pitch, and the inhabitation of animals peculiar to the desert.

Rabbi Moses Haccohen applies all this to the desolation of Edom in the days of Isaiah. Grotius, who adopts the same hypothesis, supposes these judgments to have been provoked by the aid which the Edomites afforded to the Assyrians in their invasion of Judea, and to have been executed by the Ethiopians. Schmidius also applies the chapter to the literal desolation of Edom in the days of Isaiah. Eusebius applies it to the day of judgment and the end of the world. Cyril makes the same application of vers. 1–4, but applies the rest to the destruction of Jerusalem and the Jewish commonwealth mystically represented here by Edom. Theodoret extends this explanation to the whole, in which he is followed by Cocceius. The rabbinical interpreters, with one exception which has been already mentioned, explain Edom as a mystical or figurative name for Rome, or rather Christendom, of which Rome was once the representative, and understand the chapter as predicting the future downfall of the Christian powers in the days of the Messiah. On this same rabbinical hypothesis Vitringa rears a Christian exposition, by making Edom the emblem not of Christian but of antichristian (*i. e.* papal) Rome. So J. H. Michaelis, Gill, and others, most of whom, however, give the prophecy a greater latitude of meaning, as a general threatening of destruction to the enemies of Zion, but especially to antichrist here typified as Edom. J. D. Michaelis regards the prophecy as yet to be fulfilled, and thinks it possible that the ancient Idumea may hereafter be possessed by an antichristian power whose destruction is here foretold. Rosenmüller and the other recent German writers regard the whole as an extravagant expression of revengeful malice by a writer long posterior to Isaiah. This gratuitous assumption is sustained by the usual empirical criticism, which, as we have seen before, may be employed on either side of any question. Hitzig, while complaining of the writer's diffuseness and verbosity, heaps up tautological expressions of contempt in his own peculiar style. It is worthy of remark, too, that the spirit of this chapter is extremely shocking to these pious unbelievers. Leaving these prejudiced interpretations out of view, the reference of the prophecy to antichrist may be objected to, upon the ground that the sense which it gives to Edom is a forced one, not sustained by any usage or authority, except certain parts of the book of Revelation, which the older writers used as a key to the ancient prophecies, whereas these alone afford the key to it. The simplest and most satisfactory view of the whole passage is the one proposed by Calvin, who regards it as a general threatening of destruction to the enemies of Zion, Edom being particularly mentioned, as an enemy of ancient Israel, peculiarly inveterate and malignant, and thence used to represent the whole class of such enemies. Thus understood, the prophecy extends both to the past and future, and includes many particular events to which interpreters have erroneously endeavoured to restrict it, not excepting the destruction of antichrist, as the greatest event of this kind which is foretold in prophecy. Compare the note on chap. xi. 4.

1. *Come near, ye nations, to hear; and ye peoples, hearken.* Lowth adds *to me,* on the authority of a single manuscript. *Let the earth hear and its fulness* (that which fills it, all that it contains), *the world and all its issues* (or productions, all that comes forth from it). This may either be explained with Calvin as an appeal to inanimate nature, like the one at the beginning of the book (chap. i. 2), or as an appeal to men, poetically represented as the fruit of the earth, which is the sense given in the ancient versions and adopted by Vitringa. Knobel supposes a climax or anticlimax, the Prophet first invoking men (*nations* and *peoples*), then brutes (the *fulness of the earth*), and then plants (*its productions*). But the sense thus put upon the fulness of the earth is altogether arbitrary. This verse announces, as about to be delivered, a prediction of great moment and deserving the attention of the whole world. Cocceius understands by *nations* the heathen, and by *peoples* the tribes of Israel, a distinction which he makes even in the first verse of the second Psalm. All other writers take the words as poetical equivalents.

2. This verse assigns the reason for the invocation in the one before it. *For (there is) anger to Jehovah.* The English Version has, *the indignation of the Lord is,* an idea which would be otherwise expressed in Hebrew. The construction is the same as in chap. ii. 12. *Jehovah has anger* (or *is angry*) *against all the nations.* The common version is *upon,* which is the primary meaning of the particle, and is appropriate in this case as suggesting the idea of infliction. That of hostility is of course implied, even if not expressed. Vitringa needlessly and arbitrarily distinguishes between the nations mentioned in the first verse and in this, upon the ground that those who were to be destroyed would not be summoned to hear of their destruction. But why not? It is exactly like the case of an individual convict hearing his sentence before its execution. Vitringa also makes גוים mean nations in general, and הגוים these nations, *i. e.* the ones to be destroyed. But כל הגוים is the strongest expression possible in Hebrew for *all nations*. *And wrath* (is to Jehovah) *against all their host.* Not *their armies* in particular, as Clericus suggests, but their whole multitude, all that belong to them. (Compare the same expression in Gen. ii. 1.) *He has doomed them,* or devoted them irrevocably to destruction. For the peculiar usage of the Hebrew verb, see the note on chap. xi. 15. *He has given,* (*i. e.* appointed and abandoned) *them to the slaughter.* The past tense is not a mere *præteritum propheticum,* implying the certainty of the event although still future, but describes the divine determination or decree as really and literally past.

3. *And their slain shall be cast out.* The Hebrew word strictly means *their wounded,* and is so translated in the Septuagint and some other versions. But usage gives it the specific sense of *wounded mortally,* and for

the most part in battle. *Cast out, i. e.* unburied. This suggests the several
ideas of contemptuous neglect, of a multitude too vast to be interred, and
perhaps of survivors too few to perform the duty, (Compare chap. xiv.
18–20.) They shall not lie unburied merely for a time, but until they rot
upon the ground. *And their corpses* (or *carcases*), *their stench shall go up.*
The first noun is construed as an absolute nominative, *as to their carcases,
their stench,* &c., which is equivalent in our idiom to *the stench of their carcases shall go up.* With reference to the same revolting' circumstance,
Lucan calls a battle-field *olentes agros.* (Compare Amos iv. 10, Joel ii.
20.) *And mountains shall be melted with* (or *by*) *their blood,* as they are
sometimes. washed away by rains or torrents. This cannot mean merely
that blood shall run down from the hills (Clericus), but must be taken as a
strong poetical hyperbole descriptive of excessive carnage.

4. *And all the host of heaven* (or *heavenly bodies*) *shall consume away.*
This verb is commonly applied to the pining or consumption occasioned by
disease. In Ps. xxxviii. 6 it means to *run* as a sore, from which analogy
Gesenius deduces here the sense of *melting,* and adopts Vitringa's notion
that the stars are poetically likened to wax candles. Maurer, with a better
taste, supposes the obscuration of the heavenly bodies to be represented as
a pining away. The ideas of *sickly lights* and *dying lights* are not unknown
to modern poetry. *And the heavens shall be rolled up* (or *together*) *like a
scroll, i. e.* like an ancient *volume* (*volumen* from *volvo*), or a modern map.
Grotius explains this as meaning that nothing should be seen in the heavens
any more than a book rolled up or closed. This idea Umbreit carries out
by talking of the sky as God's great book, in which he has written his
eternal name with countless stars. J. D. Michaelis more naturally understands the Prophet as alluding to the phenomena of storms, in which the
sky is first overcast and then covered with clouds, the motion of which gives it
the appearance of being rolled together. The best explanation seems, however, to be that proposed by Pfeiffer in his Dubia Vexata, to wit, that as
God is elsewhere described as having stretched out the heavens like a curtain, their destruction or any total change in their appearance would be
naturally represented as a rolling up of the expanse. In like manner
Horace says, *horrida tempestas contraxit cœlum.* The Targum strangely
makes כספר mean according to the book, *i. e.* the Scriptures. Montanus
no less strangely makes it govern השמים (*sicut liber cœlorum*), a construction utterly precluded by the article. (See a similar mistake of Lowth in
chap. xvii. 8.) *And all their host* (referring to *the heavens*) *shall fade* (or
fall away) *like the fading of a leaf from a vine.* This beautiful comparison
with the decay of plants makes it the more probable that the preceding
clause alludes to that of animal life and not to the melting of wax or tallow.
And like a fading (*leaf*) or *a withered* (*fig*) *from a fig-tree.* Knobel explains נבלת as a feminine collective put for the plural masculine, an idiom
of which there are few if any unambiguous examples. As עלה is masculine,
the feminine adjective may be referred to a noun understood. J. D.
Michaelis imagines that this clause describes the seeming motion of the
stars occasioned by a nocturnal earthquake. Grotius supposes the description of the carnage to be still continued, and the exhalations of the putrid
corpses to be here described as veiling the heavens and producing those
meteoric appearances called shooting stars. This extravagant conceit is justly
condemned by Gesenius as a most infelicitous conception of a poetic image,
and it is certainly worse than his own prosaic supposition of wax candles.
Such exhibitions may enable us to estimate correctly the aesthetic contempt

with which some writers speak of this magnificent passage as plainly belonging to a later age. A similar remark may be applied to Knobel's repetition of Vitringa's indiscreet suggestion as to the popular belief of the
Hebrews respecting the heavens and the heavenly bodies. It would be no
less rational to argue from the foregoing verse, that they believed in streams
of blood so vast as to dissolve whole mountains. If the terms of that verse
are poetical hyperboles, on what ground is this to be explained as a lesson
in natural philosophy? Another notion of Vitringa's, equally unfounded,
although not adopted by the modern Germans, is that the terms of this
verse plainly shew that the prediction has respect to some great body politic
or organised society, the sun being the emblem of the civil power, the moon
of the ecclesiastical, and the stars of distinguished men in Church and State.
The context clearly shews that the terms used are not symbolical but poetical, and that here, as in chap. xiii. 10, the idea which they are all intended
to convey is that of revolution, of sudden, total, and appalling change. The
imagery of the passage has been partially adopted in Matt. xxiv. 29, and
Rev. vi. 13, neither of which, however, is to be regarded either as a repetition or an explanation of the one before us.

5. There is no need of giving כ' the sense of *yea* (Augusti), or of explaining it as a mere connective particle (Knobel), since it may be construed, in
its proper sense, either with ver. 3 (Hitzig), or with the whole of the preceding description. All this shall certainly take place, *for my sword* (the
speaker being God himself) *is steeped* (saturated, soaked) *in heaven*. Most
versions, ancient and modern, take the verb here in the same sense of being
drunk or intoxicated, either with wrath or with the blood of enemies. It is
very improbable, however, that two different figures were intended here and
in ver. 7, where all agree that the earth is described as being soaked or
saturated with blood. Koppe proposes to read מרוטה *sharpened*, after the
analogy of Ezek. xxi. 33. The same sense had long before been put upon
the common text by Clericus, who supposes an allusion to the wetting of
the grindstone or the blade in grinding. The Targum has *revealed*, on the
authority of which loose paraphrase Lowth reads *made bare*, adding with
great *naiveté* in his note, *whatever reading, different I presume from the
present, he might find in his copy, I follow the sense which he has given of it.*
This implies that it is not even necessary to know what a reading is before
it is allowed to supersede the common text. The phrase *in heaven* has been
variously explained. Some of the older writers understand it as expressing the certainty of the event (as firm or sure as the heavens); others as descriptive of the great men who were to be destroyed. Gill says *it may denote
the whole Roman papal jurisdiction*, and Henderson, who rejects all allusion
to Rome, explains it to mean *the Idumean heaven or the ruling power in
Edom*. Gesenius supposes the sword to be here described as drunk with
wrath in heaven before it is drunk with blood on earth; Ewald, as dropping
blood in heaven as if by anticipation (*wie zum voraus*). The best explanation is that of Calvin, who refers the expression to the divine determination
and foreknowledge. In the sight of God the sword, although not yet actually
used, was already dripping blood. The sword is mentioned, neither because
commonly employed in executions (Barnes), nor in the sense of a butcher's
knife (Vitringa), but as a natural and common though poetical expression
for any instrument of vengeance. Knobel is singular in understanding this
clause as referring to the slaughter of the Babylonians, already past, and
now to be succeeded by that of the Edomites. *Behold, upon Edom it shall
come down*. Some translate the future as a present, but there is no sufficient

reason for departing from the proper sense. The Jewish tradition is that Edom in the prophecies means Rome. For this opinion Abarbenel endeavours to secure a historical foundation, by making the Romans actual descendants of Esau. Vitringa justly denounces this as egregious trifling, but adopts the same hypothesis, only applying the name to Pagan and Papal Rome. At the same time, he appears unwilling to abandon altogether its application to the Jews themselves. Now the only thing common to these three distinct subjects is their malignant hatred of God's people. This may serve, therefore, to confirm Calvin's doctrine, that the name is here applied to the inveterate enemies of the church at large, and not to any one of them exclusively. Henderson, in avoiding Vitringa's error, goes to the opposite extreme of confining the prediction to the literal and ancient Edom. Even the German critics grant that Edom is here mentioned as a representative. The same thing is clear from the whole complexion of this prophecy and from the analogy of others like it. The strength of the expressions cannot be explained by the gratuitous assertion that *it was merely adequate to meet the expectations of a patriotic Jew in reference to the infliction of divine judgment on those who had been the ancient and most inveterate enemies of his country.* On the other hand, they are sufficiently accounted for, by the supposition that the passage is a prediction of the downfall not of Edom only, but of others like him. The fulfilment of these threatenings cannot be traced in the history of ancient Edom. They ceased to be a people, not by extirpation, but by incorporation with the Jews. The name *Idumea,* as employed by Josephus, includes a large part of Judea. The Herods, the last royal family of Judah, were of Idumean origin. *And upon the people of my curse* or doom, *i. e.* the people whom I have doomed to destruction (see ver. 2). This is not an extension of the threatening against Edom to other nations (Junius), but a repetition of it in a different form. למשפט is not an adverbial phrase meaning *justly,* but a declaration of the end for which the sword was to come down, viz. *for judgment, i. e.* to execute justice upon Edom.

6. *A sword (is) to Jehovah* (or *Jehovah has a sword); it is full of blood.* The genitive construction (*the sword of Jehovah*), although not ungrammatical, is not to be assumed without necessity. *It is smeared with fat.* The allusion is not to the fatty part of the blood or to the fat combined with it (Gesenius), but to fat and blood as the animal substances offered in sacrifice. *With the blood of lambs and goats,* mentioned as well-known sacrificial animals, *with the fat of the kidneys* (or the kidney fat) *of rams,* mentioned either as remarkable for fatness or as a parallel expression to the foregoing clause. *For there is to Jehovah* (or *Jehovah has) a sacrifice in Bozrah, and a great slaughter in the land of Edom.* זבח is otherwise explained to mean a *victim* (Vulgate), or the preparation for a feast (Cocceius). Bozrah was an ancient city of Edom. Gesenius in his Commentary identifies it with Bostra in Auranitis; but in his Thesaurus he agrees with Raumer and Hitzig in making it the same with the modern *Busaireh,* a village and castle in Arabia Petræa, south-east of the Dead Sea (see Robinson's Palestine, ii. p. 570). Cocceius thinks Jerusalem is here called *Bozrah* as being a *stronghold* of thieves and robbers. Vitringa applies it to Rome, which he derives from רמה, *high.* Hitzig applies this verse to the literal slaughter of the Edomitish flocks and herds, which seems inconsistent with the next verse.

7. *And unicorns shall come down with them, and bullocks with bulls. And their land shall be soaked* (or *drenched*) *with blood, and their dust with*

fat shall be fattened. The ancient versions, with great unanimity and uniformity, explain ראם as meaning the unicorn. This animal has been
commonly regarded as fabulous in modern times ; but of late some traces of
it have been found in Thibet and other parts of Asia. But even supposing
it to be a real animal, we have no reason to believe that it was ever common
in the Holy Land, as the ראם would seem to have been from the frequency
with which it is mentioned. The explanation of the Hebrew word by
Aquila and Saadias, as meaning the rhinoceros, may be considered as exploded by Bochart. The modern writers are divided between a certain
species of gazelle or antelope, and the wild buffalo of Palestine and Egypt.
The name may here be used either as a poetical description of the ox, or
to suggest that wild as well as tame beasts should be included in the
threatened slaughter. Some understand the term as denoting potent and
malignant enemies. Grotius gives a distinctive meaning also to the species
mentioned in the foregoing verse, the lambs being the common people, the
goats the priests, and the fat rams the men of wealth. This mode of exposition is at variance with the very nature of figurative language. For
ראמים in this verse some of the old Jews read רומים, Romans. *Dust* here
denotes *dry soil*, which is said to be enriched by the bodies of the slain.
So Virgil says that Roman blood had twice enriched the soil of Macedonia.
The field of Waterloo (says Barnes) *has thus been celebrated, since the great
battle there, for producing rank and luxuriant harvests.* To *come down* in
the first clause is by some explained as meaning to come down to the
slaughter (Jer. l. 27, li. 40) ; by others to fall or sink under the fatal
stroke (Zech. xi. 2).

8. *For* (there is) *a day of vengeance to Jehovah, a year of recompences for
the cause of Zion, i. e.* to maintain her cause. Some have taken this in an
unfavourable sense as meaning *to contend with Zion.* Cocceius and Umbreit
regard day and year as a climax, but most writers as equivalent indefinite
expressions. This verse connects the judgments threatened against Edom
with the cause of Zion or the church of God, On the construction and
the meaning of the first words of the sentence, compare chap. ii. 12.

9. *And her streams* (those of Idumea or the land of Edom) *shall be
turned to pitch, and her dust to brimstone, and her land shall become burning
pitch.* This verse, as Calvin well observes, announces nothing new, but
repeats the same prediction under other figures, borrowed from the overthrow of Sodom and Gomorrah, which throughout the Bible *are set forth
for an example, suffering the vengeance of eternal fire* (Jude 7). To the
fire and brimstone there mentioned, pitch or bitumen is added, as Hendewerk and Knobel suppose, because the soil of Idumea, lying adjacent to
the Dead Sea, is bituminous, and abounds in veins or springs of naphtha.
According to Sanctius, pitch is mentioned as a substance easily kindled
and burning long. נחליה neither means *her valleys* (Septuagint) nor *her
torrents* (Lowth), but *her streams* in general, as distinguished from *her
dust* or dry ground, both being included in the general term *land* which
occurs in the last clause (Hitzig). According to Knobel, the suffix in ארצה
still refers to Idumea, and the noun means *surface.* Grotius applies this
description to the burning of the Idumean cities. Clericus explains the
first clause as meaning that their streams should be as *turbid* as if turned
to pitch. Barnes correctly understands it as expressing in the strongest
terms the idea of *utter and permanent destruction*, as complete and terrible
as if the streams were turned to pitch. The old editions of the Chaldee
Paraphrase read here *the streams of Rome*, &c. According to the Talmud,

Rome was founded on the day that Jeroboam set up the golden calf, and is to be destroyed like Sodom and Gomorrah. Upon this tradition (which is given at length in Buxtorf's Talmudical Lexicon under the word רומא) Gill seizes with avidity, so far as it is suited to his purpose, and applies it to the future destruction of Rome by fire, as predicted in Rev. xvii. 16, xviii. 8. Vitringa also thinks it not impossible that even this verse may be literally verified in the sulphureous soil of Latium and Campania. He seems indeed to have regarded it as an event likely to happen in his own day, and cites with great solemnity the similar anticipations of Jerome Savonarola, as recorded by Philip de Comines, and the prophecy found, according to Matthew of Paris, in the bed-room of Gregory IX. So little does the failure of these earlier forebodings appear to have taught him their groundless and unprofitable nature ! At the same time he appears to allow ample space for the fulfilment by referring to the great fire under Nero as a prelude to the final conflagration.

10. *Day and night it shall not be quenched ; for ever shall its smoke go up ; from generation to generation shall it lie waste ; for ever and ever there shall be no one passing through it.* The remarkable gradation and accumulation of terms denoting perpetuity can scarcely be expressed in a translation. This is especially the case with the last and highest of the series, which Lowth renders *to everlasting ages,* and Henderson *to all perpetuity,* neither of which is stronger than the common version *for ever and ever,* or approaches much nearer to the strict sense of the Hebrew phrase, *to perpetuity of perpetuities.* The original form of expression, though not the exact sense of the words, is retained by Theodotion, εἰς ἔσχατα ἐσχάτων. Grotius's characteristic explanation is in these words : *id est, diu.* Lowth's disposition to improve the common version by substituting Latin for Saxon words is exemplified in this verse, where he changes *waste* and *quenched* into *desert* and *extinguished.* Grotius supposes an allusion to the long-continued smoking of burnt cities, and quotes parallels from Virgil and Seneca. A much more striking parallel is found in the statement (Gen. xix. 28), that when Abraham looked toward Sodom and Gomorrah, *the smoke of the country went up as the smoke of a furnace.* These sublime and fearful images are copied in the book of Revelation (xiv. 10, 11), but it does not follow that the copy, though inspired and prophetic, was intended to determine the sense of the original. Rosenmüller and Knobel understand the last words as meaning that no one shall *go to it* or *pass into it,* but Gesenius and Ewald with the older writers, that no one shall pass *through* or *over it,* implying that it shall not be a thoroughfare for caravans or single travellers. Keith, in his Evidence of Prophecy, has collected some remarkable illustrations of this passage from the incidental statements of modern travellers, with respect to what was once the land of Edom. Thus Volney speaks of thirty deserted towns within three days' journey ; Seetzen, of a wide tract utterly without a place of habitation, and of his own route through it as one never before attempted ; Burckhardt, of the passage as declared by the people of the nearest inhabited districts to be impossible, in accordance with which notion he was unable to procure guides at any price. These are striking coincidences, and as illustrations of the prophecy important, but are not to be insisted on as constituting its direct fulfilment, for in that case the passage of these very travellers through the country would falsify the prediction which they are cited to confirm. The truth of the prophecy in this clause is really no more suspended on such facts, than that of the first clause and

of the preceding verse upon the actual existence of bituminous streams and a sulphureous soil throughout the ancient Idumea. The whole is a magnificent prophetic picture, the fidelity of which, so far as it relates to ancient Edom, is notoriously attested by its desolation for a course of ages. In this verse Hitzig represents the writer as attaining his highest point of bitterness against the Edomites ; and Knobel, in a kindred spirit, says that the repeated threatening of perpetual desolation, while it makes the prediction more impressive, shews great spite (*verräth grossen Hass*), an expression far more applicable to the comment than the text, which is as little open to the charge of malice as the sentence which a judge pronounces on a convict.

11. *Then shall possess it* (as a heritage) *the pelican and porcupine, the crane and crow shall dwell in it. And he* (or one) *shall stretch upon it the line of confusion and the stones of emptiness.* Having declared that man should no longer pass through it, he now explains who shall be its inhabitants. The first verb is rendered by Cocceius *shall inherit ;* by Junius still more fully, *shall possess by hereditary right ;* but by Gesenius and most later writers, *shall possess,* which, though correct, is scarcely adequate, as the original word could not fail to suggest to a Hebrew reader the idea of *succession.* These animals should not only occupy the land, but occupy it as the successors and to the exclusion of mankind. The קָאַת is no doubt the pelican, as the etymology of the name (from קוֹא, to vomit) agrees with the habits of that bird, and the ancient versions to explain it. In this place, it is true, the Septuagint has not πελεκᾶν, as Henderson quotes it, but the general term ὄρνεα, and the Vulgate not *pellicanus* but *onocrotalus.* The next word has been translated *owl* (Calvin), and *bittern* (English Version), but is now agreed to mean the porcupine or hedgehog, as explained in the Septuagint (ἐχῖνοι). The next word is now understood to denote, not an owl (Bochart), but a heron or crane ; according to the Septuagint, the *ibis* or Egyptian heron. The essential idea, as Calvin observes, is that of wild and solitary animals. (Compare chap. xiii. 21, 22 ; xiv. 23, Rev. xviii. 2.) Here again a remarkable coincidence is furnished by the statements of travellers with respect to the number of wild birds in Edom. Mangles, while at Petra, describes the screaming of the eagles, hawks, and owls, seemingly annoyed at any one approaching their lonely habitation. Burckhardt speaks of Tafyle as frequented by an immense number of crows, and of the birds called *katta,* which fly in such large flocks that the boys often kill two or three at a time merely by throwing a stick among them. In this last case the coincidence is verbal also, as the *katta* bears a strong resemblance to the קָאַת. The apparent inconsistency between this clause and the description of the country in the verse before it only shews that neither can be strictly taken, but that both are metaphorical predictions of entire desolation. In the next clause the same idea is expressed by an entire change of figure. The verb may be construed either with *Jehovah* understood (Kimchi), or indefinitely, as by Junius (*quisquis conabitur*), and Augusti (*manzieht*), which is really equivalent to the passive form adopted in the Vulgate (*extendetur*). In the use of the words תֹהוּ and בֹהוּ, there may be a distinct allusion to Gen. i. 2, as there is in Jer. iv. 23. The *line* meant is a measuring line, mentioned elsewhere not only in connection with building (Zech. i. 16), but also with destroying (2 Kings xxi. 13). The *stones* meant are not the black flints with which the soil of ancient Edom is profusely covered (Burckhardt), but stones used for *weights* (Deut. xxv. 13, Prov. xvi. 11), and here for *plumb-line* or *plum-*

met. This sense, which is given in the Vulgate (*perpendiculum*), is required by the parallelism, and assumed by all interpreters. The same figure is employed by (Amos vii. 7–9) to denote a *moral* test or standard, but in this case as a symbol of destruction. The plummet is here mentioned, not because actually used in the taking down of buildings (Henderson), but as a parallel to *line* (Hitzig), both together expressing the idea of exact and careful measurement. The sense of the whole metaphor may then be either that God has laid this work out for himself and will perform it (Barnes), or that in destroying Edom he will act with equity and justice (Gill), or that even in destroying he will proceed deliberately and by rule (Knobel), which last sense is well expressed in Rosenmüller's paraphrase (*ad mensuram vastabitur, ad regulam depopulabitur*). Ewald seems to understand the clause as meaning that the land should be meted out to new inhabitants, but that these should be only Waste and Chaos. Calvin and others make it mean that all attempts at restoration should be vain; the line and plummet of the builder should only serve as measures of desolation. According to Clericus, the sense is that there should be nothing to prevent one from measuring the ruins. The Septuagint curiously assimilates the clauses by translating this: *Ass-centaurs shall inhabit it.*

12. *Her caves and there is no one there* (*i. e.* her uninhabited or empty caves) *they will* (*still*) *call a kingdom, and all her chiefs will be cessation* (*i. e.* cease to be). Lowth reads בחרריה or על חרריה, connects it with the preceding verse (for which division of the text he cites the authority of the Peshito), and translates the last words of that verse as follows:— *And the plummet of emptiness over her scorched plains.* Such a sense is dearly purchased by an arbitrary change of text, and the introduction of a word of rare occurrence, not to say of doubtful meaning. Not content with this, however, he reads שֵׁם for שָׁם, gives קְרָא the sense which he says it has in Prov. xx. 6, and translates the first clause, *No more shall they boast the renown of the kingdom!* Most other writers take חֹרֶיהָ in the sense given to it by the Septuagint (ἄρχοντες), and Vulgate (*nobiles*). Montanus renders it *heroes*. Gesenius retains the common meaning, but derives it (on the strength of an Arabic analogy) from the primary idea of *free-born*. It is also commonly agreed since Vitringa, that this first word should be construed as a nominative absolute (*as to her nobles*), and the first verb as indefinite. That verb has been variously explained here as meaning to *say* (Augusti), to *cry* (French Version), to *lament* (Castalio), to *propose* (De Dieu), to *name* (Forerius), to *recall* (Grotius), to *proclaim* (Cocceius), and to *call* in the sense of nominating or appointing (Vatablus). No less various are the senses put upon the whole clause, among which, however, three may be particularly mentioned. According to the first, it means that there shall be none to proclaim the kingdom (Ewald), or to call a king (Munster). According to the second, it means that there shall be no kingdom. This idea is variously expressed and combined, so as to mean that their princes will be princes without land (Luther), or that they will lament for the destruction of the kingdom (Castalio), or will cry that it is at an end (French Version), or will call for its restoration (De Dieu); to which may be added Augusti's explanation, that men will say of her princes, They have no kingdom! and Grotius's, that they will call to mind (*memoria recolent*) their ancient royal race now extinct, in favour of which he appeals to the Targum, which is here of very doubtful meaning. A third sense, preferred by most of the late writers, is that there shall be no one

whom they can call *to the kingdom*. The same elliptical construction is supposed to occur in Deut. xxxiii. 19. This great variety of explanations, and the harshness of construction with which most of them are chargeable, may serve as an excuse for the suggestion of a new one, not as certainly correct, but as possibly entitled to consideration. All the interpretations which have been cited coincide in giving to חֹרִים the sense of *nobles*, which it certainly has in several places. (See 1 Kings xxi. 8, 11 ; Neh. ii. 16, iv. 13.) But in several others, it no less certainly means *holes* or *caves*. (See 1 Sam. xiv. 11, Job xxx. 6, Nahum ii. 13.) Now it is matter of history not only that Edom was full of caverns, but that these were inhabited, and that the aboriginal inhabitants, expelled by Esau, were expressly called *Horites* (חֹרִים), as being troglodytes or inhabitants of caverns (Gen. xiv. 6, xxxvi. 20, Deut. ii. 12, 22). This being the case, the entire depopulation of the country, and especially the destruction of its princes, might be naturally and poetically expressed by saying that the kingdom of Edom should be thenceforth a kingdom of deserted caverns. How appropriate such a description would be to the actual condition of the country, and particularly to its ancient capital, may be seen from Robinson's account of Petra (Palestine, ii. pp. 514–537). The supposed parallelism between חריה and שריה, which Henderson urges against Lowth's absurd emendation of the text, can have little weight in a case where the construction is at best so difficult. It is proper to add that this interpretation was suggested by the allusion to the Horites which Hendewerk assumes, although he gives חרים the sense of *nobles* with the great mass of interpreters. Gesenius infers from his own interpretation of this clause, that the kingdom of Edom was elective, and Hitzig adds that they sometimes called a king from foreign parts, of which he finds an instance in Gen. xxxv. 37; but Hendewerk objects that, on the same grounds, Isaiah iii. 6, 7, would prove Judah to have been an elective monarchy. Gill of course applies this verse to the *kingdom of the beast* (Rev. xvi. 10), and שריה to the cardinals.

13. *And her palaces* (or *in her palaces*) *shall come up thorns, nettles, and brambles in her fortresses.* The natural consequence of her depopulation. Here, as in chap. v. 6, Cocceius and Ewald construe the verb with the noun of place (*increscent spinis*); but Gesenius, who adopts the same construction in the other case, rejects it here, where it is much more natural, as it precludes the necessity of supplying a preposition. In the next clause, Ewald supplies *are ;* but the preposition before *fortresses* makes the other construction the more probable. Grotius quotes a beautiful parallel from Virgil. *Carduus et spinis surgit paliurus acutis.* The word *paliurus* is itself used in the Vulgate version of this sentence. In במבצריה Gill supposes an allusion to the name *Bozrah*. Grotius explains the phrase to mean within the limits of her ancient walls. The situation here described would of course be the resort of wild and solitary animals. *And she shall be a home of wolves.* The Septuagint has *sirens* and the Vulgate *dragons*, which is retained in most of the old versions. Gill, who refers it all to Rome directly, understands this to mean that as she had been the abode of figurative dragons, *i. e.* of the old dragon, the devil and the beast, with their creatures, popes and cardinals, so now she shall be occupied by literal dragons, *i. e.* monsters of the wilderness. Gesenius and Ewald render תנים *jackals*, but Henderson's version, *wolves*, is more expressive, and the exact species meant is both dubious and unimportant. *A court* (or *grass-plot*) *for ostriches.* Gesenius explains חָצִיר as an orthographical variation for חָצֵר, a court or enclosure. Hitzig takes it in its usual sense of grass. In

like manner it had been explained as meaning grass or pasture long before by Luther (*Weide*) and Cocceius (*gramen*). The general sense, in either case, is that of an enclosed and appropriated spot, a play-ground or a dwelling-place. The last place is rendered by Augusti, *daughters of howling.* It is now understood to mean, not owls, but female ostriches. (See the note on chap. xiii. 21.)

14. *And wild* (or *desert*) *creatures shall* (there) *meet with howling creatures.* The verb sometimes means to meet or encounter in the sense of attacking (Exodus iv. 24; Hosea xiii. 8); but here it seems to have the general sense of falling in with. These lonely creatures, as they traverse Idumea, shall encounter none but creatures like themselves. Gesenius and Ewald follow Bochart in explaining צִיִּים to mean *wild cats.* Lowth has *jackals.* Most other writers, with greater probability, take it in the general sense of those inhabiting the wilderness. (Compare the note on chap. xiii. 21.) In like manner, אִיִּים may be understood, according to its etymology, as signifying howlers, *i. e.* howling animals. This is less arbitrary, and at the same time better suited to the context, than the explanation of the words as names of particular species. The principal specific meanings put upon אִיִּים are those of vultures (Luther), thoes * (Bochart), mountain cats (Lowth), wild cats (Grotius), wild dogs (Gesenius), and wolves (Ewald). Hendewerk prefers the more general meaning, *beasts of prey* (Raubthiere); for which there seems to be no sufficient ground in etymology. Augusti retains both Hebrew words (*Zihim* and *Ijim.*) Castalio has *Sylvani* and *Faunis.* Next to the explanation first proposed, the most probable is that given by Cocceius and the English Version, *wild beasts of the desert* and *wild beasts of the island.* The antithesis might then be, that between the animals inhabiting dry places and those frequenting marshes or the banks of streams (according to the wide sense of the Hebrew אִי, explained in the note on chap. xx. 6), implying either the existence of such spots in Idumea, or that the whole description is to be tropically understood. By the wild beasts of the desert, Cocceius understands the Saracens and Turks, and by the wild beasts of the island the Crusaders. In the words צִיִּים and אִיִּים there is a *paronomasia* but not a *pun* (Barnes). A pun is the use of one word in two senses. A paronomasia is the likeness of two different words in form or sound. *And the shaggy monster shall call to his fellow.* Hitzig and Ewald give יִקְרָא the sense of *meeting*, as a parallel to פָּגַשׁ, and suppose the Kal to be here construed as the Niphal is in Exodus iii. 18. But as the Kal itself never means to meet, excepting in a figurative application, and as the other explanation gives a perfectly good sense, and adds variety to the description, it is better to explain it as most writers have done since the Septuagint Version (βοήσονται). For the true sense of שָׂעִיר, see the extended comment on the plural form as it occurs in chap. xiii. 21. Ewald, who has *satyrs*, there, has *he-goat* in the case before us; and Henderson, who has *wild goats* there, has here *the shaggy he-goat.* Other writers still give the word, as in the former case, the sense of a hirciform spectre (Bochart), field-spirit (Augusti), field-devil (Luther), wood-devil (J. D. Michaelis and Gesenius), and the Dutch Version makes it flatly mean *de duyvel.* Amidst these various and fanciful interpretations, the most consistent with itself and with the etymology is still that of the Vulgate (*pilosus*). This is preferable even to that given by Henderson and Ewald, on the ground that it corresponds better with the general descriptive meaning, which, as we have seen above, most probably belongs to the words צִיִּים and

* Or Jackals.

אִיִּים in the preceding clause. If that clause speaks of wild and howling beasts, and not of any one class exclusively, it is more natural that this should speak of shaggy monsters generally than of goats. Hendewerk's conjecture that the Prophet here alludes to mount Seir (שֵׂעִיר) is not so felicitous as that respecting the allusion to the Horites in ver. 12. *Only there reposes the night-monster, and finds for herself a resting-place.* אַךְ, which the older writers render *quinimo* (Vitringa), *certe* (Cocceius), &c., properly a particle of limitation meaning *only*. The latest writers connect it with שָׁם as meaning *only there* (Gesenius), or with the verb as meaning *only rest* (De Wette), or with לִילִית as meaning *non nisi spectra nocturna* (Maurer). The word לִילִית, which occurs only here, has experienced very much the same fate with שֵׂעִיר. In itself it means nothing more nor less than *nocturnal*, and would seem to be applicable either to an animal or to any other object peculiarly belonging to the night. The Vulgate renders it by *lamia*, a word used very much like the English *witch*, but derived from the name of a Libyan queen, who, having lost her child, was said to prey upon the children of others. With this may be connected another Roman superstition, that of the *strix* or vampyre, which sucked the blood of children in the cradle. These superstitions were adopted by the later Jews, and connected with the world before us, as denoting a *nocturnal spectre* (or *she-demon* as Gill calls it), preying upon new-born children, against which the German Jews are said to use traditional precautions. This gratuitous interpretation of the Hebrew word was unfortunately sanctioned by Bochart and Vitringa, and adopted with eagerness by the modern Germans, who rejoice in every opportunity of charging a mistake in physics or a vulgar superstition on the Scriptures. This disposition is the more apparent here, because the writers of this school usually pique themselves upon the critical discernment with which they separate the exegetical inventions of the Rabbins from the genuine meaning of the Hebrew text. Gesenius, for example, will not even grant that the doctrine of a personal Messiah is so much as mentioned in the writings of Isaiah, although no opinion has been more universally maintained by the Jews, from the date of their oldest uncanonical books extant. In this case, their unanimous and uninterrupted testimony goes for nothing, because it would establish an unwelcome identity between the Messiah of the Old and New Testament. But when the object is to fasten on the Scriptures a contemptible and odious superstition, the utmost deference is paid, not only to the silly legends of the Jews, but to those of the Greeks, Romans, Zabians, and Russians, which are collated and paraded with a prodigal expenditure of trifling erudition, to prove what never was disputed, that these superstitions have existed and do still exist; as if it followed of course that they were current in the days of Isaiah, and if not believed, are distinctly mentioned by him. But this conclusion would be wholly unauthorized, even if the words of the Prophet at first-sight seemed to bear that meaning; how much more when it can only be attached to them by violence? J. D. Michaelis, who stands among the writers on Isaiah at the turning-point between belief and unbelief, acquits the Prophet of believing in such spectres, but regards it as a case of accommodation to popular errors or illusions, the same principle on which the demoniacal possessions of the gospel are explained away, and as the ultimate result of the same process, the historical existence of Christ himself resolved into a mythus. That a similar mode of exposition was adopted by such men as Bochart and Vitringa, only proves that they lived before its dangerous tendency had been developed. It should also be considered that nocturnal spectres had not then been so decisively referred to the category of ideal beings as they are at present. These remarks are intended merely to prevent an inconsiderate adoption of the views in question, on the authority either of the older writers or the modern Germans. Against the views themselves there are substantive objections of the most conclusive kind. Besides the fact already mentioned, that ליליה strictly means *nocturnal* and that its application to a spectre is entirely gratuitous, we may argue here, as in chap. xiii. 25, that ghosts as well as demons would be wholly out of place in a list of wild and solitary *animals*. That such animals are mentioned in the first clause of this verse and of the next, is allowed by all interpreters, however widely they may differ as to the specific meaning of the terms employed. Taking Gesenius's interpretation, the first item in the catalogue is *wild cats*, the second *wild dogs*, the third *demons*, the fourth *hobgoblins*, and the fifth *arrow-snakes*. Is this a natural succession of ideas ? Is it one that ought to be assumed without necessity ? The only necessity that can exist in such a case is that of meeting the conditions of the context. The third and fourth particulars in this list must of course be something doleful or terrific; but they need not be more so than the other objects in the same connection. It is enough if they belong to the same class, in this respect, with wild cats, jackals, wolves, and arrow-snakes. This is sufficiently secured by making ליליה mean a nocturnal bird (Aben Ezra), or more specifically, an owl (Cocceius), or screech-owl (Lowth). But the word admits of a still more satisfactory interpretation, in exact agreement with the exposition which has been already given of the preceding terms as general descriptions rather than specific names. If these terms represent the animals occupying Idumea, first as belonging to the wilderness (ציים), then as distinguished by their fierce or melancholy cries (איים), and then as shaggy in appearance (שעיר), nothing can be more natural than that the fourth epithet should also be expressive of their habits as a class, and no such epithet could well be more appropriate than that of *nocturnal* or belonging to the night. Another objection to the meaning *spectre* is, that the poetry and legends of all nations have associated with such beings the idea of inquietude. When Hamlet says, *Rest, rest, perturbed spirit!* he virtually tells the ghost to cease to be one. But here, according to the fashionable exegesis, the spectre is described, not as flitting or gliding through the land or among its ruins, but as taking up its lodgings and reposing. Of all the figures that could be employed, that of resting seems to be the least appropriate in the description of a spectre, and especially of such as Gesenius describes to us from Eastern story books and rabbinical traditions. Of this incongruity he seems to have had at least a vague apprehension, as he strangely says that the terms here used imply a restless wandering state, whereas they seem to imply the very contrary, and no less strangely cites Mat. xii. 43, where the evil spirit is expressly said to pass through dry places *seeking rest and finding none*. On these grounds, therefore, that the Hebrew word, according to its derivation, simply means *nocturnal;* that in this sense it suits perfectly the parallelism and the context, as containing names of animals or rather descriptions of their habits ; that the action described is peculiarly unsuited to a ghost or a spectre; that the Scriptures contain no intimations of the real existence of such beings ; that the supposition of a mere accommodation to the popular belief is dangerous, unworthy, and gratuitous ; and that the existence of the popular belief itself so early is exceedingly improbable ; we may safely set aside the spectral interpretation as untenable on philological and historical grounds, and as certainly not worth being taken for granted. The same considerations make it unneccessary to retain the Hebrew word (*lilith*), as Augusti and Henderson have done, as if in obedience to the flippant direction of John David Michaelis, that whoever will not tolerate a ghost here must retain the Hebrew word and imagine it to mean what he pleases (*was ihm beliebt*). The alternatives in such a case are seldom so few as they are sometimes represented by this learned and ingenious, but conceited and dogmatical interpreter. It only remains to observe that the Septuagint Version, the authority of which has done so much to introduce *demons* into chap. xiii. 23, makes use of the word δαιμόνια in this verse too, but as the translation of צִיִּים, while its favourite term ὀνοκένταυροι is employed to represent both אִיִּים and לִילִית. This absurd interpretation is so far consistent with itself, that it makes the whole verse a catalogue of nondescript hobgoblins, demons, and ass-centaurs, and if not a refutation of the current exposition of לִילִית, is at least a severe satire on it.

15. Several manuscripts and one of the oldest editions read קִפּוֹד as in ver. 11 above, and the Septuagint has ἐχῖνος in both places. Jarchi and Kimchi explain the common reading (קִפּוֹז) as a synonyme. It is supposed to denote different kinds of birds by Calvin (*ulula*), Junius (*merula*), Cocceius (*anataria*), &c. Bochart objects that if a bird were meant, its *wings* would have been mentioned in the other clause, and not merely its *shadow*. Most of the modern writers follow Bochart in explaining it to mean the *serpens jaculus* or arrow-snake, so called from its darting or springing motion. The same learned writer shews that the use of the word *nest* in reference to serpents is common in Arabic as well as Greek and Latin. There is no need, therefore, of giving קִנְנָה a wider meaning as Jerome does (*habuit foveam*). The next verb is rendered by the Vulgate, *enutrivit catulos ;* by Castalio, as an adverbial expression meaning *safely, with impunity;* but by the great mass of interpreters, as meaning to *lay eggs*, a sense analogous to that of the cognate form applied in chap. lxvi. 7 to human parturition. Jerome translates the next verb *circumfodit*, but most other writers *hatch*, the primary sense being that of cleaving. (Compare chap. lix. 5.) This meaning Luther seems to give to דָּגְרָה, perhaps by an inadvertent transposition. Others explain it to mean *gather* (Junius), *hide* (Augusti), *take refuge* (Rosenmüller), but the latest writers *brood* or *cherish*, after the Vulgate (*fovet*). It is here applied to the young when hatched, as it is in Jer. xvii. 11 to the eggs of the partridge. Calvin seems to refer the suffix in בְּצִלָּהּ not to the animal but to some other object. Grotius's paraphrase is *sub ruinis*. All the modern writers understand it to mean, *under her own shadow*. דַּיָּה is either the black vulture (Bochart), or the kite (Gesenius). Lowth's translation, *every one her mate*, may convey an incorrect idea, as both the Hebrew words are feminine. Cocceius disregards the gender and translates the phrase, *unus cum altero*. As to the particular species of animals referred to in this whole passage, there is no need, as Calvin well observes, of troubling ourselves much about them. (*Non est cur in iis magnopere torqueamur.*) The general sense evidently is, that a human population should be succeeded by wild and lonely animals, who should not only live but breed there, implying total and continued desolation. So Horace says of Troy : *Priami Paridisque busto insultat armentum, et catulos ferae celant inultæ.*

16. *Seek ye out of the book of Jehovah and read.* Knobel connects דִּרְשׁוּ with the preceding verse (*each one her mate they seek*), and then changes

the remainder of this clause so as to read thus : על מספר יהוה יקרא, *by num-*
ber will Jehovah call (*them*). This bears a strong resemblance to Lowth's
treatment of the first clause of ver. 12, but is still more extravagant. The
book of Jehovah has been variously explained to mean the book of his
decrees (Aben Ezra), his annals or record of events (Forerius), the Scriptures generally, or more particularly the book of Genesis, or that part
which relates to clean and unclean animals (Jarchi), the Mosaic law
relating to that subject (Joseph Kimchi), the law in general (Calvin), the
book of Revelation (Gill), the book of Prophecy in general (Junius), the
Prophecies against Edom in particular (Alting), and finally this very prophecy (David Kimchi). The most natural interpretation seems to be that
which makes this an exhortation to compare the prophecy with the event,
and which is strongly recommended by the fact that all the verbs are in
the past tense, implying that the Prophet here takes his stand at a point
of time posterior to the event. *The book* may then be this particular prophecy, or the whole prophetic volume, or the entire Scripture, without
material change of sense. The persons addressed are the future witnesses
of the event. מעל does not mean *from top* to bottom, as Vitringa imagines,
but simply *from upon*, as we speak of reading a sentence *off* a book or paper.
This expression seems to have been used in anticipation of the verb קראו,
which has here the sense of publishing by reading aloud. *One of them has*
not failed. A very few writers understand this as relating to the evils
threatened ; but the great majority more naturally apply it to the animals
mentioned in the preceding verses, as signs of desolation. As if he had
said, I predicted that Edom should be occupied by such and such creatures,
and behold they are all here, not one of them is wanting. This is a
lively and impressive mode of saying, the prediction is fulfilled. *One*
another they miss not. The verb has here the sense of mustering or reviewing to discover who is absent, as in 1 Sam xx. 6, xxv. 15. The reference
is not to the pairing of animals (Barnes), because both אשה and רעותה are
feminine, and because the context requires an allusion to the meeting of
different species, not of the individuals of one kind. *For my mouth, it has*
commanded ; and his spirit it has gathered them, i. e. the animals aforesaid.
The last phrase is a more specific explanation of the general expression
has commanded. To add a suffix to the latter, therefore, would complete
the parallelism but disturb the sense. The sudden change of person from
my mouth to *his spirit* has led to various explanations. Houbigant reads
פיו and Knobel פיהו, *his mouth*, which is actually found in a few manuscripts. Lowth reads יהוה for הוא, *the mouth of Jehovah*, which is not
only arbitrary but in violation of his favourite principle of parallelism.
The same objection lies against the explanation of הוא, by Glassius and
Simonis, as a divine name, and by Rosenmüller and Dathe, as a substitute
for it. Such an explanation of the second הוא is precluded by the foregoing suffix. A much more plausible solution is the one proposed by Aben
Ezra and Kimchi, who refer the suffix in רוחו to פי (*my mouth* and *its*
breath), and thus makes God the speaker in both clauses. But on the
whole, the simplest course is either to suppose with Vitringa that Jehovah
speaks in one clause and the Prophet in the next, an enallage too frequent
to be inadmissible, or that the Prophet really refers the command to his
own mouth instrumentally, but then immediately names the Divine Spirit
as the efficient agent. This is the less improbable because the first clause
of the verse, as we have seen, contains an appeal to his own written prediction. The Spirit of God is not merely his power but himself, with

special reference to the Holy Ghost, as being both the author and fulfiller of the prophecies.

17. *He too has cast the lot for them, and his hand has divided it to them by line.* An evident allusion to the division of the land of Canaan, both by lot and measuring-line. (See Num. xxvi. 55, 56 ; Josh. xviii. 4–6.) As Canaan was allotted to Israel, so Edom is allotted to these doleful creatures. Having referred to the allotment as already past, he now describes the occupation as future and perpetual. *For ever shall they hold it as a heritage, to all generations shall they dwell therein.* Cocceius, who applies the whole prediction to the unbelieving Jews, thus explains this last clause : *nunquam restituetur respublica Judæorum in illa terra.*

Chapter 35

A GREAT and glorious change is here described under the figure of a desert clothed with luxuriant vegetation, vers. 1, 2. The people are encouraged with the prospect of this change, and with the promise of avenging judgments on their enemies, vers. 3, 4. The same change is then expressed, by a change of figure, as a healing of corporeal infirmities, vers. 5, 6. The former figure is again resumed, and the wilderness described as free from all its wonted inconveniences, particularly those of barrenness and thirst, disappointment and illusion, pathlessness and beasts of prey, vers. 7–9. The whole prediction winds up with a promise of redemption, restoration, and endless blessedness, ver. 10.

This chapter is regarded by Eichhorn, Bertholdt, and Rosenmüller, as entirely distinct from that before it ; by Hitzig as a separate composition of the same writer ; but by most interpreters as a direct continuation of it. According to Rosenmüller, it was written by the author of chaps. xi., xii. ; according to Umbreit, by the author of chaps. xl.–lxvi., according to Ewald, by another in imitation of that writer ; according to Gesenius, by the author of chaps. xiii., xiv., which the passage before us resembles, he says, in its literary merit and its moral defects, especially its spirit of revenge and blood-thirsty hatred. All these writers agree that it cannot be the work of Isaiah. As a sample of the proofs on which their judgment rests, it may be stated that Hitzig makes the use of the form חציר, and of the phrase נמהרי לב, a proof of later date. He authoritatively sets it down as belonging to the period immediately before the termination of the exile. By such assertions and pretended proofs, its genuineness is of course unshaken.

With respect to the subject of the chapter there is no less diversity of judgment. It has been explained with equal confidence as a description of the state of Judah under Hezekiah (Grotius), of the return from exile (Clericus), of the state of Judah after that event (Rosenmüller), of that state and the times of the New Testament together (J. H. Michaelis), of the calling of the Gentiles (Cocceius), of the Christian dispensation (Luther, Calvin), of the state of the church after the fall of antichrist (Vitringa), of the state of Palestine at some future period (J. D. Michaelis), and of a future state of blessedness (Gill). These arbitrary hypotheses refute each other. The best description of the chapter is that given by Augusti in the title to his version of it, where he represents it as the description of a happy condition of the church after a period of suffering. This is no doubt its true import, and when thus explained it may be considered as including various particulars, none of which can be regarded as its specific or exclusive subject. Gesenius says this prophecy was of course never fulfilled; but so far is this from being true, that it has rather been fulfilled again and again. Without any change of its essential meaning, it may be applied to the restoration of the Jews from Babylon, to the vocation of the Gentiles, to the whole Christian dispensation, to the course of every individual believer, and to the blessedness of heaven. The ground of this manifold application is not that the language of the passage is unmeaning or indefinite, but that there is a real and designed analogy between the various changes mentioned which brings them all within the natural scope of the same inspired description.

1. *Desert and waste shall rejoice (for) them.* The verb is translated as an imperative of the second or third person by the Septuagint, Cocceius, and others; and as a descriptive present by Gesenius and some later writers; but there is no sufficient reason for departing from the strict sense of the future. The desert has been variously explained to mean Idumea, Judea, the Jewish Church, the Christian Church, the Gentile world, and the wilderness separating Palestine from Babylonia. The true sense seems to be that given by Gesenius, who supposes the blooming of the desert to be used here, as in many other cases, to express an entire revolution, the subject of the change being not determined by the figure itself but by the whole connection. The final מ has been variously explained, as a suffix, eqivalent to בהם, להם, or עמם ; as a paragogic letter, used instead of ן, on account of the מ following ; and as a mere orthographical mistake, arising from the same cause. Those who make it a suffix, refer it either to the animals described in the close of the preceding chapter, or to the judgments there threatened against Edom, or to the Jewish exiles returning from captivity. The suffix is not expressed in any of the ancient versions. Kennicott supposes the מ to have been added merely to complete the line; but why should such a form have been perpetuated? The idea of the first clause is repeated in the second. *And the wilderness shall rejoice and blossom as the rose.* This explanation of the last word is given by several of the Rabbins, and retained by Junius, Cocceius, Lowth, and Augusti. The later writers object that the word, according to its etymology, must denote a bulbous plant. The ancient versions, with Luther and Calvin, make it mean the *lily*, which is retained by Ewald; but for this flower the language has a different name. Saadias and Abulwalid explain it as the *narcissus*, which is approved by Gesenius in his Commentary, and after him by most of the later German writers. But in his Thesaurus he makes it mean the *colchicum autumnale* or meadow-saffron. Amidst this diversity and doubt, it is best with Barnes to retain the English word *rose*, as more familiar and as conveying a more striking image of beauty. The poetry, if not the botany, of this translation is superior to Henderson's (*and blossom as the crocus*).

2. The same idea of complete and joyful change is again expressed by the same figure, but with greater fulness, the desert being here described as putting on and wearing the appearance of the spots most noted for luxuriant vegetation. (*It shall*) *blossom, it shall blossom and rejoice ; yea, (with) joy and shouting ; or, yea, joy and shouting (there shall be). The glory of Lebanon is given unto it* (the desert), *the beauty of Carmel and of Sharon. They* (who witness this great change) *shall see the glory of Jehovah, the beauty of our God.* The figures here employed are so familiar, and in their obvious meaning so expressive, that we only weaken their effect by treating them as symbols or an allegory. Thus Jarchi understands by the

glory of Lebanon the temple; Gill, *choice and excellent Christians*, &c.
As a change in the relative condition of the Jews and Gentiles is no doubt
included in the prophecy, there is not the same objection to the opinion of
Forerius, that the second clause of the verse denotes the transfer of God's
spiritual presence, and the glory connected with it, from the Jewish to the
Christian Church. According to Œcolampadius, Lebanon, Carmel, and Sharon are here mentioned, as natural boundaries or landmarks of the country.
Schmidius supposes that a mountain, a cultivated field, and an extensive
plain, are given as samples of the whole, to intimate that nothing should be
wanting to the perfection of the state here promised and described. But
Lebanon and Carmel are both mountains, unless we give the latter its generic
sense of *fruitful field*, as Junius and Tremellius do, in obvious violation
of the context, since the preceding and the following word are evidently
proper names. The *glory* or *beauty* of the places named, is not fertility,
as Grotius thinks, but rather its effect as seen in their luxuriant vegetation.
The reduplication of the first verb in the sentence is regarded by almost all
interpreters as emphatic, though they differ greatly as to its precise force.
Calvin and Junius make it expressive of abundant and progressive growth,
as if he had said, *it shall blossom more and more.* Hitzig applies it to the
rankness of the growth (*hoch sprosst sie auf*), Knobel to its universality
(*ganz sprosset sie*). Augusti repeats the verb as in Hebrew (*blühen ja blühen*)
and the Vulgate copies the precise form still more closely (*germinans germinabit*) The future translation of נָתֵּן by Calvin and the English Version
is gratuitous and arbitrary. The preterite form points out the true relation of the cause to its effect. It *shall* rejoice because the glory of
Lebanon *has been* given to it. The pronoun *they* is referred by Vitringa to
the desert, Lebanon, &c. But as these are the immediate antecedents, the
pronoun would hardly have been introduced, except for the purpose of
directing attention to some other nominative than the nearest, as in Ps.
xxii. 18. The true sense is probably that given in the Septuagint (*my
people*) and the Targum (*the house of Israel*), and in a more general form
by Clericus (*qui aderunt*). Instead of וְרֻן, the Seventy seem to have read
יַרְדֵּן (τὰ ἔρημα τοῦ Ἰορδάνου), and this reading with a corresponding change
of the preceding word, is adopted by Houbigant (גְלוֹת הירדן), Kennicott
(גְדוֹת הירדן), and Lowth (*the well watered plain of Jordan*). The words,
as they stand in the common text, may be construed either with a preposition or the substantive verb understood. Eleven manuscripts read לְךָ
(*to thee*) for לה (*to it*), which merely converts the description into an
apostrophe.

3. With the prospect of this glorious change the people are commanded
to encourage themselves and one another. *Strengthen hands* (now) *sinking, and knees* (now) *tottering make firm.* The hands and knees are here
combined, as Vitringa observes, to express the powers of action and endurance. The participial forms represent the hands as actually hanging
down, relaxed, or weakened, and the knees as actually giving way. The
passage explained is far more expressive than if we make the participles
adjectives, denoting a permanent quality or habitual condition. In itself
the language of this verse is applicable either to self-encouragement or to
the consolation of others. It is understood to mean *renew your own
strength*, by Cocceius and Clericus (*reparate vires vestras*). Most of the
older writers, and some moderns, make the other the prominent idea, and
suppose the command to be addressed to those in office (Barnes), or to

ministers (Calvin), or to the prophets (Knobel), or to these and other good men (Grotius), or to the people generally (Junius). Neither of these interpretations is erroneous except in being too exclusive. There is no reason why the words should not be taken in their widest sense, as meaning, let despondency be exchanged for hope. That self-encouragement is not excluded, may be learned from Paul's use of the words in that sense (Heb. xii. 12). That mutual encouragement is not excluded, is sufficiently apparent from the following verse. Thus understood the words may be considered as including, but not as specifically signifying spiritual weakness or inability to do God's will (Targum), and the duty of encouraging the Gentiles with the prospect of admission to his favour (Menochius). The specific application of the passage to the Roman persecutions (Gurtlerus) is gratuitous. Equally so is the idea that the Jews are here encouraged under the depressing recollection of sufferings already past (Grotius), or under the alarm excited by the foregoing threats (Calvin). The same objection lies against the exclusive reference of the words to the exiles in Babylon who distrusted the promises (Hendewerk), or believed themselves to be forsaken by Jehovah (Knobel). As a general exhortation, they are applicable to these and to many other situations, none of which can be regarded as the exclusive subject of the promise. The figures here used are the same with those employed in chap. xiii. 7, and in Job iv. 3, 4. The image presented is that of *persons who can scarcely lift up their hands or stand upon their legs* (Gill). The Septuagint supposes the command to be addressed to the hands themselves (*ἰσχύσατε χεῖρες*). Hitzig gratuitously changes *hands* to *arms*, as in chaps. x. 10, 13, xiv. 27, xix. 16, xxv. 10, xxvi. 11, &c.

4. This verse shews how the command in the one before it is to be obeyed, by suggesting, as topics of mutual encouragement, the vindicatory justice of God, and his certain interposition in behalf of his people. *Say ye to the hasty of heart* (*i. e.* the impatient, those who cannot wait for the fulfilment of God's promise), *Be firm, fear not; behold your God* (as if already present or in sight) ; *vengeance is coming, the retribution of God ; he* (*himself*) *is coming, and will save you.* The connecting link between his vengeance and their safety is the destruction of their enemies. (*Seeing it is a righteous thing with God to recompense tribulation to them that trouble you,* 2 Thes. i. 6.) נמהר, as a passive participle, corresponds, in form and sense, to the English *hurried.* It has been variously explained as meaning inconsiderate (Junius), precipitate (Cocceius), inconstant (Vatablus), faint-hearted (Lowth), palpitating (Rosenmüller), ready to flee (Gesenius), *hasty in drawing black conclusions upon themselves and their state* (Gill). But the true sense seems to be the one expressed by Clericus, to wit, impatient of delay in the execution of God's promises (*qui nullas moras æquo animo ferre possunt.*) This includes the ideas of despondency and unbelieving fear, while at the same time it adheres to the strict sense of the Hebrew word. Compare the analogous expression in chap. xxviii. 16, *he that believeth will not make haste* or be impatient. The construction of the second clause is greatly perplexed by making אלהיכם the subject of יבוא. Thus the English version, which is founded upon Calvin's, supplies two prepositions and assumes an unusual inversion of the terms. *Your God will come (with) vengeance, even God (with) a recompence.* This construction also involves an anticlimax, as the simple name of *God* is of course less emphatic than the full phrase *your God.* Luther has *to vengeance* and *God who recompenses.* Jerome makes the construction still more complex by

translating יבא as a causative (*ultionem adducet retributionis*). The true construction, as given by Junius, Cocceius, Vitringa, and most later writers, makes *behold your God* an exclamation, and *vengeance* the subject of the verb. Vitringa observes that יבא is here used to express both the present and the future, an idea which may be conveyed in English by the idiomatic phrase, *is coming* or *about to come.* The הוא might be grammatically construed with נמול (*it will come*), but as the act of saving is immediately afterwards ascribed to the same subject, it is better to explain the pronoun as an emphatic designation of Jehovah. Not only his vengeance but himself is coming. Grotius, true to his principle of seeking the fulfilment of all prophecies in the days of the Prophet himself, explains *he will save you* as meaning *he will not let the Ethiopians reach you.* The exclusive application of the threatening here implied to the Babylonians, the Jews, Antichrist, or the Devil, is untenable for reasons which have been already given in the exposition of the foregoing verse. While Barnes denies that the phrase *your God* refers to the Messiah, Calovius alleges that the name of *Jesus* is expressly mentioned, being included in the verb ישע. The words are really a promise of deliverance to God's people, and include, as the most important part of their contents, the *unspeakable gift* of Christ and his salvation.

5, 6. The change in the condition of the people is now represented by another figure, the removal of corporeal infirmities. *Then* (when God has thus come) *shall the eyes of the blind be opened, and the ears of the deaf shall be unstopped. Then shall the lame leap* (or *bound*) *as an hart, and the tongue of the dumb shall shout* (*for joy*), *because waters have burst forth in the wilderness and streams in the desert.* The reason assigned in this last clause for the joy to be expressed, shews clearly that the miraculous removal of disease and the miraculous irrigation of the desert are intended to express one and the same thing. The essential idea in both cases is that of sudden and extraordinary change. This precludes Grotius's interpretation of the fifth verse, as meaning that the most obtuse and prejudiced shall see and acknowledge what God has wrought. It also precludes Jonathan's symbolical exposition of the words as predicting the removal of spiritual disabilities, and the opposite hypothesis, maintained by many of the older writers, that Isaiah here explicitly foretells the miracles of Christ. Calovius asserts that Christ himself has so interpreted the passage in Matt. xi. 5; Luke vii. 22. But, as Henderson justly says, there is no proof whatever that Christ refers John the Baptist to this prophecy; he employs none of the formulas which he uniformly uses when directing attention to the Old Testament (*e. g.* in Matt. ix. 16, xi. 10, xii. 17, xiii. 14), but simply appeals to his miracles in proof of his Messiahship: the language is similar, but the subjects different. Another argument is urged by J. D. Michaelis, namely, that the last clause of the sixth verse cannot be applied to the miracles of Christ, and yet it obviously forms a part of the same prophetic picture. The evasion of this difficulty, by assuming, as Vitringa seems inclined to do, a mixture of literal and figurative language in the parallel clauses of the very same description, is one of those arbitrary exegetical expedients, which can only be affirmed on one side and rejected on the other. To the question, whether this prediction is in no sense applicable to our Saviour's miracles, we may reply with Calvin, that although they are not directly mentioned, they were really an emblem and example of the great change which is here described. So, too, the spiritual cures effected by the gospel, although not specifically signified by these words, are included in the glorious revolution which they do denote. The simple meaning of the passage is, that the divine interposition which had just been promised should produce as wonderful a change on the condition of mankind, as if the blind were to receive their sight, the dumb to speak, the deaf to hear, the lame to walk, and deserts to be fertilised and blossom as the rose. In the process of this mighty transmutation miracles were really performed both of a bodily and spiritual nature, but the great change which includes these includes vastly more. Gesenius and others understand the sixth verse as describing the joy of the returning exiles, which might be compared to that of men miraculously healed; but it is far more natural to understand the healing as descriptive of the change itself, which must therefore be much more extensive than the restoration of the Jews from Babylon, although this may be one of the particulars included. To the explanation of נבקעו as a future, there is the same objection as to that of נתן in ver. 2. The original form of expression is not that they *shall* rejoice for waters *shall* burst forth, but that they *shall* rejoice because waters *have* burst forth already; the last event being spoken of as relatively past, *i. e.* as previous to the act of rejoicing which the future verb expresses. The version *when they shall have burst forth* (Cocceius) yields an equally good sense, and indeed the same in substance, but departs, without necessity, from the usual and strict sense of the particle. The suggestion, which Barnes quotes from Campbell's travels in South Africa, that lameness and dumbness (*i. e.* indisposition or inability to speak) are here alluded to as painful incidents to travel in the desert, is striking and ingenious, but a little far-fetched and at variance with the context, which requires changes more extraordinary than the mere relief of taciturnity and footsore weariness. Here, as in chap. xxxiv. 14, J. D. Michaelis first suggests a fanciful interpretation (making lameness denote ill success in war), and then prescribes, as the only alternative, a reference to the paths of virtue and religion, in which those who are deficient may be said to halt or limp. Clericus, who usually follows Grotius in preferring the lowest and the most material sense of which the language is susceptible, applies these words to spiritual changes, but thinks it necessary to apologise for this departure from his usual mode of exegesis, which he does by adding to his note upon the sixth verse, *ex quibus intelligere licebit, quamquam propriam verborum potestatem sectemur quotiescumque licet, nos ubi necesse est ad tralatitium adeoque allegoricum (ut vocatur) sensum devenire.* The only wonder is, that he was able to overcome his scruples in a case where there is no necessity whatever for the so-called allegorical interpretation, but a simple instance of poetical metaphor. The verb רנן, to which the older writers gave the sense of *singing*, is explained by the modern lexicographers as properly denoting the expression of joyous feelings by inarticulate cries or shouts.

7. The idea of complete and joyful change is still expressed by the transformation of a desert, and the consequent removal of its inconveniences, among which the Prophet here particularly mentions the tantalising illusions to which travellers in the wilderness are subject. *And the mirage shall become a pool* (or the sand like a water lake, the seeming lake a real one), *and the thirsty land springs of water,* (even) *in the haunt of wolves, their lair, a court* (or *field*) *for reed and rush.* Instead of the general meaning put upon שרב by the older writers following the Septuagint (ἄνυδρος) and the Vulgate (*quæ erat arida*), it is now agreed that the word denotes the illusive appearance caused by unequal refraction in the lower strata of the atmosphere, and often witnessed both at sea and land, called in English

looming, in Italian *fata morgana*, and in French *mirage*. J. D. Michaelis
thanks God that the German language has no need of such a term; but
Ewald and Umbreit use *Kimmung* as an equivalent. Other equivalents are
employed by Hitzig (*Wasserschein*), De Wette (*Sandmeer*), Hendewerk
(*Sandschimmer*), and Henderson (*vapoury illusion*). In the deserts of
Arabia and Africa, the appearance presented is precisely that of an extensive sheet of water, tending not only to mislead the traveller, but to aggravate his thirst by disappointment. The phenomenon is well described by
Quintius Curtius in his Life of Alexander the Great. (*Arenas vapor æstivi
solis accendit. . . . . . . Camporum non alia quam vasti et profundi æquoris
species est.*) It is thus referred to in the Koran (xxiv. 39): *And as for
those who disbelieve, their deeds are like the mirage* (سراب) *in the desert;
the thirsty reckons it for water, till when he comes he finds it nothing.*
More deceitful than the mirage (or *serab*) is an Arabian proverb. Gesenius
follows Hyde in deriving the Hebrew word from a Persian phrase meaning
a surface of water. Hitzig explains it as an Arabic derivative denoting an
abundant flow or stream. Its introduction here adds a beautiful stroke to
the description, not only by its local propriety, but by its strict agreement
with the context. The etymology of מבוע suggests the idea of a gushing
fountain, which is expressed in some translations, particularly those of Lowth
(*bubbling springs*) and Augusti (*Sprudelquellen*). Gesenius and the other
recent German writers render תנים *jackals*, as in chap. xiii. 21, and xxxiv. 13;
but Henderson's translation (*wolves*) has a better effect in English. The
essential idea is that of wild and solitary animals. נוה and חציר are combined as in chap. xxxiv. 13. The latter word is explained by some as
meaning *grass*, and the whole clause as predicting, that hay *and* reeds *and*
rushes (Luther), or grass *with* reeds and rushes (Junius), shall grow in
what was once the haunt of wild beasts; or that grass shall grow *instead of*
reeds and rushes (Augusti); or that grass shall be converted *into* reeds and
rushes (Cocceius). Most writers now, however, give חציר the sense of
court, enclosure, or the more general one of *place*, and understand the clause
to mean, that what was once the haunt of wild beasts should become a place
for the growth of reeds and rushes, which require a great degree of moisture,
and therefore imply an entire change in the condition of the desert. The
same sense is given by Calvin (*locus erit arundini et junco*) and Vitringa
(*late excrescet calamus et juncus*). Knobel, instead of רבצה, reads יצמח on
the alleged authority of the Peshito and the Vulgate (*orietur*). *In the
haunt of jackals springs up grass to* (the height of) *reeds and rushes*, a
luxuriance of vegetation which of course implies excessive moisture. Even
if this construction of the particle were natural and justified by usage, the
change in the text would still be inadmissible because unnecessary. All
these interpretations understand the last clause as a distinct proposition or
description of a change to be wrought in the haunts and lairs of desert
animals. But Ewald regards the whole as a mere description of the desert
and continues the construction into the next verse. *In the haunt of jackals,
(in) their lair, (in) the place for reeds and rushes, even there shall be a way,*
&c. As this removes the difficulty of explaining the growth of reeds and
rushes as a promise, it would seem to be entitled to the preference, but for
the length of the sentence which it assumes and the conjunction of the
beginning of ver. 8. These objections may be obviated, and the advantages
of the construction still secured, by connecting this, as a descriptive clause,
not with what follows but with what precedes: *fountains shall burst forth in*

the haunt of wolves, (*in*) *their lair* (or *resting place*), (*in*) *the court* (or *grow-ing-place*) *of reeds and rushes.* We may then suppose either that these marshy spots are represented as the favourite resort of certain animals, or that two distinct descriptions of the wilderness are given, first by describ-ing it as the resort of solitary animals and then as susceptible alike of culture and inhabitation. The description, even if inapplicable strictly to the same spot, might correctly be applied to different parts of the same wilder-ness. The suffix in רבצה refers not to ארץ understood (De Dieu), but to תנים as a *pluralis inhumanus* (Gesenius), or to each of the תנים distribu-tively (Junius : *cubili cujusque*) as an individual of the feminine gender (Lam. iv. 31). There is consequently no need of reading רבצים (Kennicott), פרץ (Houbigant), פרצה or פרצי (Lowth). Gesenius supplies a relative be-fore רבצה (*which was its lair* or *where its lair was*) ; but a much more natural construction is proposed by Maurer and Hitzig, who explain it as in simple apposition with נוה תנים. The explanation which has now been given of the verse, as a poetical description of complete and joyful change, excludes of course the allegorical interpretation of the pools as meaning schools, and the fountains teachers (Vitringa), the dragon's den the heathen world (Schmidius), the dragons themselves persecutors, *pagan emperors and papal powers* (Gill), the reeds and rushes persons eminent in spiritual knowledge, authority, and influence (Cocceius). All these particulars may be included in the change described, but none of them can be regarded as specifically much less as exclusively intended.

8. The desert shall cease not only to be barren but also to be pathless or impassable by reason of sand. *And there shall be there a highway and a way ; and there shall not pass through* (or *over*) *it an unclean* (*thing or person*) *; and it shall be for them* (*alone*). Job (xii. 24) speaks of a תהו לא דרך (*a wilderness in which there is no way*), and Jeremiah (xviii. 15), of a דרך לא סלולה (*a way not cast up*), to both which descriptions we have here a contrast. The comparison suggested is between a faint track in the sand and a solid artificial causeway. (Rosenmüller : *via aggerata.* Hen-derson : *a raised road.* Vatablus : *exaltata lapidibus.* Clericus : *munita semita.*) Eighteen manuscripts and several ancient versions omit ודרך, which may be explained, however (with Junius and Tremellius), as a hen-diadys, *highway and way* for *high way.* The way meant is explained by Forerius to be Christ, faith, and the sacraments ; by Gill, *a way cast up by sovereign grace, which is raised above the mire and dirt of sin, and carries over it and from it.* Grotius, as usual, goes to the opposite extreme of making it denote the way to the temple. Gataker seems to apply it to the improve-ment of the roads in Judea. Musculus understands it as ensuring to the exiled Jews a free return to their own country. But even this return seems to be only one of many particulars included in the promise of a general change and restoration, which is really the thing denoted by this whole series of prophetic figures. On the form and import of the phrase *it shall be called*, see chap. i. 26. (J. H. Michaelis : *vocabitur quia erit.*) For the *way of holiness*, Clericus substitutes the classical expression, *via sacra.* The next clause is paraphrased by Grotius as meaning that no Syrian, Assyrian, Ethiopian, or Egyptian, shall be seen there. Hitzig explains it as an exclusion of the heathen generally, and pronounces it a *trace of later judaism.* Knobel goes further, and describes it as an effusion of *national hatred.* The obvious meaning of the words is that the people of Jehovah shall themselves be holy. (Compare chap. i. 25, iv. 3.) This is in fact

the meaning even of those Scriptures which exclude from Zion (or the sanctuary) the Canaanite (Zech. xiv. 21), the uncircumcised (Ezek. xliv. 9), and the stranger (Joel iv. 17). The הוא may be grammatically construed either with מסלול or with דרך, which is sometimes masculine. *It shall be for* is rendered by Hitzig *it belongs to*, without a material change of meaning. The pronoun *them*, which has no expressed antecedent in the sentence, has been variously applied to the blind whose eyes were opened (Junius), to the saints (Gataker), to Israel (Kimchi), to the exiles (Hitzig), to those recovered from idolatry (Henderson), and to those truly reformed by suffering (Knobel). Barnes and Henderson refer it, by prolepsis, to גאולים in the next verse. This is no doubt substantially correct; but the precise import of the original expression seems to be, that the highway shall belong exclusively to them for whose sake it was made, for whose use it was intended. A very different sense is put upon this phrase by Calvin, who connects it with what follows, and translates, *et erit illis ambulans in via*, referring הוא to God himself, and explaining the whole as a promise that he would go before them in the way thus prepared, as he went before Israel of old in the pillar of cloud and of fire. The same construction is adopted by De Dieu (*et erit ipse illis ambulator viæ*), and Clericus (*erit qui prior illis viam ingredietur*), who applies it expressly to Christ as the *dux salutis nostræ*. Lowth says that the old English versions gave the same sense, but that our last translators were misled by the absurd division of the verse in the Masoretic text, destroying the construction and the sense. His own version is, *but He himself shall be with them, walking in the way*, which he explains to mean, that God should dwell among them, and set them an example that they should follow his steps. Among the later writers this construction is approved by Dathe and Ewald (*und da er den Weg ihnen geht*). The objections to it, stated by Gesenius, are, the sense which it puts upon the particle in למו, and the needless violation of the Masoretic accents. He, and most of the other modern writers, give precisely the construction found in Junius and Tremellius (*viator ne stulti quidem poterunt deerrare*), taking הלך דרך as equivalent to עבר ארח (chap. xxxiii. 8), and though singular in form, collective in meaning and construction. The ו before אוילים is not expletive (Henderson), but exegetical and emphatic. The meaning strictly is, *the travellers and the fools*, i. e. the travellers, not excepting such as are ignorant or foolish. אוילים is translated by the Septuagint διεσπαρμένοι, and by Cocceius *leves*. Gataker explains it as denoting simple-minded Christians, while Henderson understands the whole clause as a promise, that the Jewish exiles, *however defective some of them might be in intellectual energy*, should not fail of reaching Zion. Hendewerk comes nearer to the full sense of the words, which he explains to mean that only moral impurity, not ignorance or weakness, should exclude men from this highway. But the words, in their primary and strict sense, are descriptive, not of the travellers, but of the way itself, which should not be a faint or dubious tack through shifting sands, but a highway so distinctly marked that even the most ignorant and inexperienced could not miss it. The straightness or directness of the path, which Grotius and Rosenmüller make a prominent idea, may be implied, but is not expressed.

9. The wilderness, though no longer barren or pathless, might still be the resort of beasts of prey. The promised highway might itself be exposed to their incursions. But immunity from this inconvenience is here promised. *There shall not be there a lion, and a ravenous beast shall not ascend it, nor*

be found there ; and (there) shall walk redeemed (ones). For a similar promise, in a still more figurative dress, see Hosea ii. 18, and for a description of the desert as the home of deadly animals, Isaiah xxx. 6. Hendewerk refers *there* and *it* to the desert, Hitzig and others to the way. Both are consistent with the context, which describes all the inconveniences and dangers of the desert as removed ; but in this place the primary allusion is no doubt to the highway described in the foregoing verse. Hence the phrase *ascend it, i. e.* from the level of the sands, through which the road is supposed to be cast up. This precludes the necessity of referring, with Gesenius, to the use of this verb by Ezra and Nehemiah in reference to the journey from Babylon, or by Job in reference to the wilderness itself as higher than the cultivated country (Job vi. 18). Lowth seems to take פריץ חיות as a poetical description of the lion (*the tyrant of the beasts*). But the first word is an adjective denoting violent, rapacious, ravenous, destructive, deadly. It is translated as a simple case of concord by the Vulgate (*mala bestia*), Luther (*reissendes Thier*), Tremellius (*violenta fera*), the English Bible (*ravenous beast*), and Henderson (*destructive beast*). The original construction is retained by Cocceius (*violenta ferarum*), while Knobel supplies a preposition (*ein zerreissendes unter ihnen*), and Ewald makes it a direct superlative (*das gewaltsamste der Thiere*). These terms are applied by the Targum to persecuting kings and rulers, by Jarchi to Nebuchadnezzar in particular, by Junius to the enemies of the church, and by Augusti to the avenger of blood. But they are rather intended to complete the great prophetic picture of a total change in the condition of the desert, under which general idea we may then include a great variety of suitable particulars, without, however, making any one of them the exclusive subject of the prophecy. The feminine verb תמצא is well explained by Knobel, as agreeing in form with חיות, and in sense with פריץ. There is no need, therefore, of reading ימצא with Lowth on the authority of four Hebrew manuscripts. Knobel gives גאולים its original and proper sense of *bought back, i. e.* out of the bondage into which they had been *sold*. Most other writers give it the more general meaning *freed* or *delivered*. Junius: *vindicati.* Cocceius: *asserti.* Barnes understands it in a double sense, as expressive both of temporal and spiritual redemption. Augusti refers it to the avenger of blood, whom he supposes to be mentioned in the other clause (*von ihm gesichert wandelt man hin*). Calvin construes והלכו as a subjunctive (*ut redempti ambulent.*) Vitringa makes the last clause a distinct proposition, or rather the beginning of the next verse (*et ibunt asserti, et redempti,* &c.). Ewald adopts a construction somewhat similar (*so gehen sie erlöst, und Jahvés losgekaufte u. s. w.*). There is no need, however, of departing from the simpler and more usual construction, which connects it closely with what goes before, supplying *there* as in the English Bible (*the redeemed shall walk there*), and *only* as in the version of Gesenius (*nur Erlöste gehen dort*).

10. The whole series of promises is here summed up in that of restoration and complete redemption. *And the ransomed of Jehovah shall return and come to Zion with shouting, and everlasting joy upon their head ; gladness and joy shall overtake (them), and sorrow and sighing shall flee away.* The first phrase, which is no doubt equivalent in meaning to גאולים in ver. 9, is paraphrased as follows in one of the French versions : *ceux-la desquels l'Eternel aura payé la rançon.* The connection with the preceding context is needlessly though not erroneously expressed in some versions by translating the initial particle *yea* (Lowth), *so* (J. H. Michaelis), or *therefore*

(Calvin). Zion is mentioned as the journey's end; they shall not only move towards it but attain it. The words *everlasting joy* may either be governed by the preposition (*with shouting and everlasting joy upon their head*), or construed with the substantive verb understood (*everlasting joy shall be upon their head*). The latter construction seems to agree best with the Masoretic accents. Jarchi understands by שמחת עולם *ancient joy*, or the *joy of old;* but more seems to be promised. The Chaldee Paraphrase supposes the image here presented to be that of a cloud of glory encompassing the head, or floating over it. Gataker and Lowth suppose an allusion to a crown or wreath, and Umbreit to a sacerdotal crown particularly. Vitringa, Gill, and Rosenmüller understand the Prophet as alluding to the festal use of unguents (see Ps. xlv. 8; Eccles. ix. 8; Luke vii. 46). Paulus combines the figure of a crown with that of unction. Gesenius, Maurer, and Knobel explain *joy upon the head* as meaning its expression in the countenance. According to Sanctius, *head* is put for *person*, or the whole body, which seems altogether arbitrary. Clericus explains the clause to mean that joy shall be *at the head, i. e.* march before them. It deserves to be recorded, as a *monstrum interpretationis*, that Forerius supposes an allusion to the washerwomen's practice of carrying clothes upon their heads. In the last clause, *joy and gladness* may be either the subject or the object of the verb. The later construction is given in the English Bible (*they shall obtain joy and gladness*) after the example of the Targum, Peshito, and Vulgate. In favour of the other, which is given in the Septuagint (καταλήψεται αὐτούς), may be urged the analogy of Deut. xxviii. 2 (*all these blessings shall come on thee and overtake thee*), and of the last clause of the verse, where *sorrow and sighing* are allowed to be the subjects of the verb by all except Cocceius, who consistently translates it, *shall escape sorrow and sighing.* The figures of this verse are applied to the return from exile by the Targum (*from the midst of their captivity*), Henderson thinks that deliverance not too trivial to be thus described, and Junius applies it in a wider sense to the reception of converts into the church. Calvin extends it to the whole course of life and to its close. The Talmud applies it to the world to come, and Gill says that " the highway before described not only leads to Zion, the church below, but to the Zion above, to the heavenly glory; and all the redeemed, all that walk in this way, shall come thither; at death their souls return to God that gave them, and in the resurrection their bodies shall return from their dusty beds and appear before God in Zion." The allusions to the Babylonian exile are correctly explained by Barnes upon the principle that minor and temporal deliverances were not only emblems of the great salvation, but preparatory to it. The devout Vitringa closes his exposition of the cheering promise, with which Isaiah winds up the first great division of his prophecies, by exclaiming to his reader, *Ora mecum Dominum supplex, ut eam suo tempore propitius impleat; interim credens non festinabit.*

Chapter 36

The next four chapters contain a historical appendix to the first part of Isaiah's prophecies, relating chiefly to Sennacherib's invasion and the slaughter of his host, to Hezekiah's sickness and miraculous recovery, and to the friendly intercourse between him and the king of Babylon. The same narrative is found substantially in the second book of Kings (chaps.

xviii.–xx.), and a different account of the same matter in the second book of Chronicles (chap. xxxii.). The close resemblance of the former passage to the one before us has afforded full scope to the German appetite for critical conjecture and ingenious combination. Paulus and Hendewerk adhere to the old opinion of Grotius and Vitringa, that the narrative in Kings is a varied transcript of the one in Isaiah ; but Eichhorn, Gesenius, Maurer, and De Wette regard the latter as an addition, by the hand of a compiler, to the collection of Isaiah's prophecies, abridged and otherwise altered from the book of Kings; while Koppe, Rosenmüller, Hitzig, Umbreit and Knobel consider the two narratives as parallel or collateral abridgments, made by different writers, from the same original, viz., a more extended history, no longer in existence. This last hypothesis is founded on the difficulty of maintaining either of the others, a difficulty springing from the fact that neither of the passages sustains, in all respects, the character of an original or an abridgment. Each contains matter which is not found in the other, and although Gesenius and Knobel have endeavoured to demonstrate that the diction, phraseology, grammatical structure, and even the orthography of the passage before us, are symptomatic of a later origin, neither the principle which they assume, nor its specific application here, is so unquestionable as to satisfy the mind of any ordinary reader, in default of more conclusive evidence. The particular points included in this general statement will be noticed in the exposition. From the strong resemblance of the passages, and the impossibility of fixing upon either as the more ancient and authentic of the two, the natural inference would seem to be, that they are different draughts or copies of the same composition, or at least that they are both the work of the same writer, and that this writer is Isaiah. That the prophets often acted as historiographers, and that Isaiah in particular discharged this office, are recorded facts. Nothing can be more natural, therefore, than the supposition that he inserted the same narrative in one book as a part of the chronicle of Judah, and in the other as an illustrative appendix to his earlier prophecies. To what extent this would make him the author of the books of Kings is here a question of but little moment. Whether these are to be regarded as complete compositions of particular authors, or as continuous official records, formed by successive entries, or as abstracts of such records made for permanent preservation, the supposition that he wrote both passages is equally admissible. As to the variations of the two from one another, they are precisely such as might have been expected in the case supposed, that is to say, in the case of the same writer twice recording the same facts, especially if we assume an interval between the acts, and a more specific purpose in the one case than the other. It must also be considered that on this hypothesis, the writer expected both accounts to be within the reach of the same readers, and might therefore leave them to illustrate and complete each other. That there is nothing in these variations to forbid the supposition of their being from the same pen, is evinced by the circumstance that each of the parallels has been declared, for similar reasons, and with equal confidence, to be a transcript of the other. Against the supposition that Isaiah is the author of both or either, even German ingenuity and learning have been able to adduce no better arguments than one or two flimsy philological cavils, such as the use of *Jewish* in chap. xxxvi. 11, and some others which will be particularly mentioned in the exposition, together with the usual objections founded on the assumed impossibility of miracles and inspiration. Thus the recession of the shadow, the destruction of Sennacherib's army, the prediction of his own death, and of the length of Hezekiah's life, are all alleged with great *naïveté* by the infidel interpreters as proofs that these chapters are of later date, whereas they only prove that their writer was a prophet sent from God. The simple common-sense view of the matter is, that since the traditional position of these chapters among the writings of Isaiah corresponds exactly to the known fact of his having written a part of the history of Judah, the presumption in favour of his having written both the passages in question cannot be shaken by the mere possibility, or even the intrinsic probability of other hypotheses, for which there is not the least external evidence. The specific end, for which the narrative is here appended to the foregoing prophecies, appears to be that of shewing the fulfilment of certain prophecies which had relation to a proximate futurity, and thereby gaining credence and authority for those which had a wider scope and a remoter combination.

1. *And it was* (or *came to pass*) *in the fourteenth year of the king Hezekiah, Sennacherib king of Assyria came up against all the fenced* (or *fortified*) *cities of Judah, and took them.* The parallel passage in Kings is immediately preceded by a summary account of the earlier events of Hezekiah's reign, with particular mention of his religious reformations and his extirpation of idolatry, to which is added an account of the deportation of the ten tribes by Shalmaneser (2 Kings xviii. 1–12). This visitation is referred to the apostasy of Israel as its meritorious cause, and contrasted with the favour of the Lord to Hezekiah as a faithful servant. While Ephraim was carried away never to return, Judah was only subjected to a temporary chastisement, the record of which follows. The verse which directly corresponds to that before us (2 Kings xviii. 13) differs from it only in the omission of the idiomatic formula יהי. The statement in Chronicles (xxxii. 1) is, that he entered into Judah and encamped against the fortified cities and proposed (ויאמר) to subdue them to himself. The same restricted sense is put by some interpreters upon the stronger phrase (*and took them*) which Isaiah uses. Others, with the same view, limit the meaning of the word *all* before *cities*. Gesenius understands the cities here meant to be those which Rehoboam fortified (2 Chron. xi. 5–12). Sennacherib is mentioned, under nearly the same name, by Herodotus, who calls him the king of Assyria and Arabia. This may either be accounted for, as an example of the loose geographical distinctions of the ancient writers, or as implying that the Assyrian conquests really included certain portions of Arabia. Between this verse and the next, as they stand in Isaiah, the narrative in Kings inserts three others, which relate what immediately followed the invasion of the country, and preceded the attack upon Jerusalem. The substance of this statement is that Hezekiah sent to Sennacherib at Lachish, saying, I have offended (*i. e.* in renouncing his allegiance to Assyria), return from me, that which thou puttest on me I will bear ; that Sennacherib accordingly imposed a tribute of three hundred talents of silver and thirty of gold, to pay which Hezekiah gave him all the treasures of the palace and the temple, not excepting the metallic decorations of the doors and pillars (2 Kings xviii. 14–16). This last act seems to be entirely inconsistent with the view which Calvin takes of Hezekiah's conduct in this whole transaction as entirely innocent and laudable, evincing a pacific disposition and a willingness to purchase peace at any price. He seems indeed to have been disposed to buy it far too dearly when he stripped the house of God to pay for it, an act which certainly implies distrust of the divine protection. There is nothing, either in the case before us, or in the general

analogy of Scripture, to forbid the supposition, that the narrative was intended to exhibit the weakness no less than the strength of Hezekiah's faith, in which case there is no need of laboriously vindicating all his acts as perfectly consistent with a strong and lively faith, although his general sincerity and godliness cannot be questioned. Another addition to the narrative is found in the second book of Chronicles (xxxii. 1–8), where we read that Hezekiah, when he saw that Sennacherib was come, and that his face was towards Jerusalem for war, took measures to strengthen the defences of the city, and to cut off the supply of water from the enemy, while at the same time he encouraged the people to rely upon Jehovah, and not to be afraid of the Assyrian host. All this is spoken of as having taken place before what is recorded in the next verse of the chapter now before us. If we suppose it to have followed Hezekiah's message to Sennacherib and payment of the tribute, the inference would seem to be that the invader, having received the money, still appeared disposed to march upon the Holy City, whereupon the king abandoned all hope of conciliation, and threw himself without reserve on the divine protection.

2. *And the king of Assyria sent Rabshakeh from Lachish to Jerusalem, to king Hezekiah, with a strong force, and he stood by the conduit* (or *aqueduct*) *of the upper pool, in the highway of the fuller's field.* Besides Rabshakeh, the narrative in Kings mentions Tartan and Rabsaris; that in Chronicles uses the general expression *his servants.* Rabshakeh may be named alone here as the chief speaker, or as the commander of the expedition. The Jews have a tradition that he was a renegado or apostate Jew, and one absurd story makes him out to have been a son of Isaiah. Others account for his knowledge of Hebrew by supposing him to have acquired it by intercourse with captives of the ten tribes. Lachish was a town of Judah, south-west of Jerusalem on the way to Egypt. This place Sennacherib was now besieging (2 Chron. xxxii. 9), and being probably detained longer than he had expected, he detached a part of his forces to attack Jerusalem, or rather to summon Hezekiah to surrender. That the main body of the army afterwards advanced against Jerusalem is nowhere explicitly recorded, although some infer from chap. x. 28–32 that they did so, making a circuit to the north for the purpose of surprising the city. It is said in Chronicles that Sennacherib was now before Lachish, in the military sense, *i. e.* besieging it, *with all his force*, which some explain to mean *with a large part of it*, others *with his court*, and the usual accompaniments of an Eastern camp, in order to remove a supposed inconsistency with what is here said. But the phrase in Chronicles relates to the Assyrian force at Lachish before Rabshakeh was detached, and is inserted merely to explain the statement that he came *from Lachish*, because Sennacherib had halted there with all his army. The verb יעמד may also be referred to the halt of Rabshakeh's detachment, or to the position which they took up on arriving; but it is simpler to refer it to the spot on which Rabshakeh himself stood during the interview about to be described. The spot was doubtless one of great resort. For the localities here mentioned, see the notes on chap. vii. 3, and xxii. 9–11. The verse in Kings, which corresponds to this, is more redundant in expression, from which Gesenius infers as a matter of course, that it is the original and this the copy, as if amplification were not as easy as abridgment.

3. *Then came forth unto him Eliakim, Hilkiah's son, who was over the house, and Shebna the scribe, and Joah, Asaph's son, the recorder.* The parallel narrative (2 Kings xviii. 18) prefixes to this verse a statement that

he called to (or *for*) *the king*, in answer to which summons these three ministers came out. Eliakim here appears as Shebna's successor, according to the prophecy in chap. xxii. 20, and Shebna himself as an inferior office-bearer. Interpreters have amused themselves with trying to discover equivalents in modern parlance for these three official titles, such as chamberlain, steward, major-domo, secretary, master of requests, master of the rolls, historiographer, &c. It is enough to know that they probably denote three principal officers of state, or of the royal household, which in oriental governments is very much the same thing. Clericus, in his version of this sentence, omits the name of *Joah*, and then notes it as an error of the Hebrew text, to be corrected by a comparison with 2 Kings xviii. 18.

4. *And Rabshakeh said to them: Say now* (or *if you please*) *to Hezekiah, Thus saith the great king, the king of Assyria, What is this confidence which thou confidest in?* He expresses his contempt by withholding the name of king from Hezekiah and calling his own master *the great king*, a common title of the Persian and other oriental monarchs, corresponding to *Grand Seignior*, *Grand Monarque*, and *Emperor* as a distinctive royal title. The interrogation in the last clause implies surprise and scorn at a reliance so unfounded. *Confide* and *confidence* sustain the same etymological relation to each other as the Hebrew noun and verb.

5. *I say* (or *have said*), *only word of lips, counsel and strength for the war; now on whom hast thou confided, that thou hast rebelled against me?* The parallel passage in Kings has *thou hast said*, which Lowth assumes to be the true text here, while others treat the common reading as an error of the writer or abridger. It is much easier, however, to account for אָמַרְתְּ as having arisen from אָמַרְתְּ a defective orthography for אָמַרְתִּי, than to deduce the latter from the former. The truth no doubt is that both the readings are original, since both may be so explained as to express the same idea. Many interpreters regard what follows as a parenthesis (*it is only word of lips, i. e.* mere talk). Others make it interrogative (*is mere talk counsel and strength for the war?*). Others suppose an ellipisis in each member (*I say you have only word of lips*, but there is need of *counsel and strength for the war*). The simplest construction is : *I say, mere word of lips is* (*your*) *counsel and strength for the war, i. e.* your pretended strength and wisdom are mere talk, false pretension. The allusion is not so much to Hezekiah's prayers (Kimchi) as to his addresses to the people, recorded in 2 Chron. xxxii. 6–8. The sense of the other passage (2 Kings xviii. 20) seems to be, *thou hast said* (to thyself, or thought, that) *mere talk is counsel and strength for the war*. The contemptuous import of דבר שפתים is apparent from Prov. xiv. 23. The rebellion mentioned in the last clause is Hezekiah's casting off the Assyrian yoke (2 Kings xviii. 7).

6. *Behold, thou hast trusted in the staff* (or *support*) *of this broken reed, in Egypt, which, (if) a man lean upon it, will go into his hand and pierce it; so is Pharaoh king of Egypt to all those trusting in him.* He answers his own question. The charge of relying upon Egypt may be either regarded as a true one, or as a malicious fabrication, or as a mere inference from the analogy of other cases and the habitual relation of the parties. Egypt may be called a broken reed, either as being always weak, or in allusion to what it had already suffered from Assyria. *Broken* of course does not mean entirely divided, but so bruised or shattered as to yield no firm support but rather to do injury. (See chap. xlii. 3, below.) Neither Gesenius nor any other critic seems to consider על מצרים as a gloss, a strong proof that such explanatory clauses are not quite so un-

natural as they are elsewhere represented.   (See the notes on chaps. vii. 17, viii. 7.)

7. *And if thou say to me, We trust in Jehovah our God, is it not he whose high places and whose altars Hezekiah hath taken away, and said to Judah and to Jerusalem, Before this altar shall ye worship.* The parallel passage (2 Kings xviii. 22) has *ye say* in the plural, which Gesenius regards as the original and proper form, because Hezekiah is afterwards mentioned in the third person.   But what then becomes of the favourite critical canon, that the more difficult reading is commonly the true one, or of the allegation that the author of the text before us is proved to be a copyist by his disposition to remove irregularities and make the form of expression uniform?   Rabshakeh's question evidently refers to Hezekiah's reformation of religious worship (2 Kings xviii. 4), which he erroneously regarded as a change of the national religion.   The parallel passage adds, at the end of the sentence, *in Jerusalem*, which is just as likely to have been added in the one copy, as to have been omitted in the other.

8. *And now, engage, I pray thee, with my lord the king of Assyria, and I will give thee two thousand horses, if thou be able on thy part to set riders upon them.* A contemptuous comparison between the Jews, who were almost destitute of cavalry, and the Assyrians, who were strong in that species of force (chap. v. 28).   התערב is not to *wager*, or to *give pledges*, but simply to *engage with;* whether in fight or in negotiation, must be determined by the context.

9. *And how wilt thou turn away the face of one governor* (or *satrap*) *of the least of my master's servants?   So thou hast reposed thyself on Egypt, with respect to chariots and horses.* As a man is said to turn his face towards an object of attack, so the latter may be said to turn back (or away) the face of his assailant when he repels him.   The last clause is an inference from the first, as the first is from the foregoing verse.   If Hezekiah could not command two thousand horsemen, he·was unprepared to resist even a detachment of the Assyrian force, and if thus helpless, he must be trusting, not in his own resources, but in foreign aid.

10. *And now* (*is it*) *without Jehovah I have come up against this land to destroy it?   Jehovah said to me, Go up to* (or *against*) *this land and destroy it.*   Some interpreters suppose that the Assyrians had heard of prophecies, in which they were described as instruments by which Jehovah meant to punish his own people.   It is much more natural, however, to regard this as a bold attempt to terrify the Jews by pleading the authority of their own tutelary deity for this invasion.   The parallel passage (2 Kings xviii. 25) has *place* instead of the first *land*, a clear case, as Knobel imagines, of assimilation on the part of the transcriber.   But no such inference was drawn from the opposite appearance in ver. 7, nor is any attempt made to explain why the על and   were not assimilated also.

11. *Then said Eliakim, and Shebna, and Joah, unto Rabshakeh, Pray speak unto thy servants in Aramean, for we understand* (*it*), *and speak not to us in Jewish, in the ears of the people who* (*are*) *on the wall.*   This request implies an apprehension of the bad effect of his address upon the multitude.   *Aramean* corresponds very nearly to *Syrian* in latitude of meaning ; but the language meant is not what we call *Syriac*, but an older form, which was probably current, as the French is now, at the courts and among the educated classes of an extensive region.   *Jewish* is *Hebrew*, so called by the Jews, as the language of the whole British empire is called *English*, or as German is sometimes called *Saxon*.   The use of this term

here is urged by some as a proof of later date than the time of Isaiah, on the ground that the distinctive name *Jewish* could not have been common till long after the destruction of the kingdom of the ten tribes, which left Judah the only representative of Israel. But how long after this event may we assume that such a usage became common? The ten tribes were carried into exile by Sennacherib's father, if not by his grandfather. It is altogether probable that from the time of the great schism between Ephraim and Judah, the latter began to call the national language by its own distinctive name. At the period in question, such a designation was certainly more natural in the mouths of Jews, than *Israelitish* or even *Hebrew*. *We understand*, literally, *we (are) hearing*, *i. e.* hearing distinctly and intelligently.

12. *And Rabshakeh said: Is it to thy master and to thee, that my master hath sent me to speak these words? Is it not to the men sitting on the wall to eat their own dung and to drink their own water with you?* The last clause might seem to mean, *is it not appointed to them, necessary for them*, or *are they not doomed?* &c. But since עַל is used in the parallel passage (2 Kings xviii. 27) after שָׁלַח as a simple equivalent to אֶל, it is better to repeat the verb of the first clause at the beginning of the second: *has he not sent me?* The last clause is obviously descriptive of the horrors of famine in their most revolting form. The same idea is conveyed still more distinctly in Chronicles: "Whereon do ye trust that ye abide in the fortress of Jerusalem? doth not Hezekiah persuade you to give over yourselves to die by famine and by thirst, saying, the Lord our God shall deliver us out of the hand of the king of Assyria?" (2 Chron. xxxii. 10, 11). So here the people are described as sitting on the wall, *i. e.* holding out against Sennacherib, only that they may experience these horrors. The Masoretic readings in the margin of the Hebrew Bible are mere euphemistic variations. אֲדֹנֶיךָ might seem to mean *thy masters*, as the singular *my master* is expressed in the same sentence by its proper form. But the fact is that the singular אָדוֹן is never joined with any suffixes but those of the first person. The only form, therefore, in which *thy master* could have been expressed, is that here used. The ambiguity is removed by the connection, which requires the phrase to be applied to Hezekiah.

13. *And Rabshakeh stood and called with a loud voice in Jewish (i. e. Hebrew), and said, Hear the words of the great king, the king of Assyria.* In so doing he not only testified his contempt for the king's messengers by insolently disregarding their request, but made a political appeal to the hopes and fears of the multitude. That *he stood and called*, is explained by some to mean that he assumed a higher position, or came nearer to the wall; but the simplest and most natural explanation is, that he remained where he was before and merely raised his voice.

14. *Thus saith the king: let not Hezekiah deceive you, for he will not be able to deliver you.* The repeated mention of the king reminds them, that he is not speaking in his own name, but in that of a great monarch. The parallel passage (2 Kings xviii. 29) adds, *out of his hand.*

15. *And let not Hezekiah make you trust in Jehovah, saying, Jehovah will certainly save us, this city shall not be given up into the hand of the king of Assyria.* The only difference between this and the parallel passage (2 Kings xviii. 30) is that the latter inserts אֵת before *this city*, a construction of the passive verb which, according to Knobel, was considered incorrect by the transcriber. The idea of *certain* deliverance is expressed by the idiomatic combination of the future and infinitive.

16. *Hearken not to Hezekiah, for thus saith the king of Assyria, make with me a blessing, and come out unto me, and eat ye (every) man his own vine and (every) man his own fig-tree, and drink ye (every) man the waters of his own cistern.* ברכה usually means a *blessing*, but in a few instances a *gift* or *present*, as a token of good will. Hence some explain the phrase here used, *make me a present*, or *make an agreement with me by a present*. Others give the Hebrew word, in this one case, the sense of *peace*, which of course suits the connection, because it is in fact a mere conjecture from the context. If an unusual meaning of the word must be assumed, it might have that of *kneeling*, as a gesture of submission or an act of homage, from בָּרַךְ to *kneel*. It is possible, however, to adhere more closely to the usage of the term, by taking *blessing* in the sense of friendly salutation, which in the East is commonly an invocation of the divine blessing. Thus the verb *to bless* is often used to express the act of greeting or of taking leave. To make a blessing with one then might mean to enter into amicable intercourse. To *come out* is in Hebrew the common military phrase for the surrender of a besieged town. The inducements offered in the last clause are in obvious antithesis to the revolting threat or warning in the last clause of ver. 12. To eat the vine and fig-tree (meaning to eat their fruit) is an elliptical form of speech, which has its analogies in every language.

17. *Until I come and take you away to a land like your own land, a land of corn and wine, a land of bread and vineyards.* The parallel passage (2 Kings xviii. 32), adds, *a land of oil-olive and honey, that ye may live and not die*, which has quite as much the aspect of an amplified copy as of a redundant original. This reference to the deportation of the people as a future event has led some interpreters to the conclusion, that Sennacherib was now on his way to Egypt, and deferred the measure until his return. It has been disputed what particular land is here meant, some saying Mesopotamia, to which others object that it was not a wine-growing country. But, as Knobel observes, there is no need of supposing that the Assyrian's description was exactly true. He may indeed have intended merely to promise them in general a country as abundant as their own.

18. *Let not (or beware lest) Hezekiah seduce you, saying, Jehovah will deliver us. Have the gods of the nations delivered every one his land out of the hand of the king of Assyria?* פֶּ is commonly equivalent to *lest*, and dependent on a foregoing verb, but sometimes (like the Latin *ne*) stands at the beginning of a sentence. Here we may either supply *take heed*, or regard פֶּן as equivalent to אַל, which is actually used in the parallel passage (2 Kings xviii. 32) with a repetition of the verb תשמעו (*hearken not to Hezekiah when he incites*, or, *for he shall incite you, saying*). Had this been the form of expression in Isaiah, we should have seen it noted as an instance of assimilation characteristic of a later writer; but as it unluckily occurs in the other place, it is discreetly overlooked by the interpreters. The Assyrian here, with characteristic recklessness, forsakes his previous position, that he was but acting as Jehovah's instrument, and sets himself in disdainful opposition to Jehovah himself.

19. *Where (are) the gods of Hamath and Arpad? where the gods of Sepharvaim? and* (when or where was it) *that they delivered Samaria out of my hand?* In the rapidity of his triumphant interrogation, he expresses himself darkly and imperfectly. The last clause must of course refer to the gods of Samaria, though not expressly mentioned. כִּי is not an interrogative pronoun (*who have delivered?*) nor an interrogative particle (*have they delivered?*), but a connective particle, dependent upon something not

expressed. For the situation of Hamath and Arpad, see the note on chap. x. 9. Sepharvaim is probably the *Sipphara* of Ptolemy, a town and province in the south of Mesopotamia, already subject to Assyria in the days of Shalmaneser. The parallel passage (2 Kings xviii. 34) adds *Hena* and *Ivvah*, which are also named with Sepharvaim in 2 Kings xix. 13, and Isa. xxxvii. 13. The question (*where are they ?*) seems to imply not only that they had not saved their worshippers, but that they had ceased to be.

20. *Who (are they) among all the gods of these lands, that have delivered their land out of my hand, that Jehovah should deliver Jerusalem out of my hand?* The parallel passage (2 Kings xviii. 35) omits *these* before *lands ;* another exception to the general statement, that the narrative before us is an abridgment of the other. In this argumentative interrogation, he puts Jehovah on a level with the gods of the surrounding nations. This is still more frequently and pointedly expressed in the parallel passage in Chronicles : " Know ye not what I and my fathers have done unto all the nations of the countries ? Were the gods of the nations of the countries able to deliver their country out of my hand ? Who was there among all the gods of these nations, which my fathers utterly destroyed, that was able to deliver his people out of my hand, that your God should be able to deliver you out of my hand ? And now, let not Hezekiah deceive you, and let him not seduce you, neither believe him ; for no god of any nation or kingdom has been able to deliver his people out of my hand, and out of the hand of my fathers ; how much less shall your God deliver you out of my hand ?" (2 Chron. xxxii. 13–15). From the same authority we learn that over and above what is recorded, Sennacherib's servants " spake still more against the God Jehovah and against Hezekiah his servant" (ver. 16), and that " they cried with a loud voice in the Jewish language, to the people of Jerusalem who were on the wall, to affright them, and to trouble them, that they might take the city ; and they spake against the God of Jerusalem as against the gods of the nations of the earth, the work of men's hands " (vers. 18, 19).

21. *And they held their peace, and did not answer him a word, for such was the commandment of the king, saying, Ye shall not answer him.* Some interpreters refer the first clause to Eliakim, Shebna, and Joah ; but the parallel passage (2 Kings xviii. 36) says expressly that *the people held their peace,* which Knobel says is more correct, as if the two were inconsistent, and gravely adds, that *our narrator* was thinking of the messengers. The notion of some of the old writers, that they did confer with him, notwithstanding what is here said, is gratuitous and arbitrary in a high degree.

22. *Then came Eliakim, Hilkiah's son, who (was) over the house, and Shebna the scribe, and Joah Asaph's son, the recorder, unto Hezekiah, with their clothes rent* (literally, *rent of clothes*), *and told him the words of Rabshakeh.* Some of the older writers understand the rending of their garments as a mere sign of their horror at Rabshakeh's blasphemies ; some of the moderns as a mere sign of despondency and alarm at the impending dangers ; whereas both may naturally be included.

Chapter 37

THIS chapter is a direct continuation of the one before it. It describes the effect of Rabshakeh's blasphemies and threats on Hezekiah, his humiliation ; his message to Isaiah, and the answer ; the retreat of Rab-

shakeh, Sennacherib's letter, Hezekiah's prayer, Isaiah's prophecy, and
its fulfilment in the slaughter of Sennacherib's army and his own flight
and murder.

1. *And it was* (or *came to pass*) *when king Hezekiah heard* (the report of
his messengers), *that he rent his clothes, and covered himself with sackcloth, and went into the house of Jehovah.*   Gill's suggestion, that he
rent his clothes because of the Assyrian's blasphemy and put on sackcloth
because of his threats, appears to be a fanciful distinction.   Both acts
were customary signs of mourning, and appropriate to any case of deep distress.   He resorted to the temple, not only as a public place, but with
reference to the promise made to Solomon (1 Kings viii. 29), that God
would hear the prayers of his people from that place when they were in
distress.   Under the old dispensation there were reasons for resorting to
the temple, even to offer private supplications, which cannot possibly apply
to any church or other place at present.   This arose partly from the fact
that prayer was connected with sacrifice, and this was rigidly confined to
one spot.

2. *And he sent Eliakim who was over the household, and Shebna the scribe,
and the elders of the priests, covered with sackcloth, unto Isaiah the son
of Amoz, the prophet.*   While he himself resorted to the temple, he sent to
ask the counsel and the intercessions of the Prophet.   Calvin's supposition,
that Isaiah was directed to remain at home, amidst the general alarm and
lamentation, as a test of Hezekiah's faith, seems at least unnecessary.
Eliakim and Shebna are again employed in this case, as being qualified to
make an exact report of what had happened, and in order to put honour
on the Prophet by an embassy of distinguished men.   In the place of Joah,
he sends the *elders of the priests*, *i. e.* the heads of the sacerdotal families.
The reference of *elders* to personal age by Luther (*den ältesten Priestern*)
and Barnes (*the old men of the priests*), is less consistent with the context,
which describes the other messengers by their official titles only, and with
the usage of זקנים, as denoting the hereditary chiefs of Levi no less than
the other tribes.   The king applies to the Prophet as the authorized expounder of the will of God.   Similar applications are recorded elsewhere
with sufficient frequency to shew that they were customary, and that the
prophets were regarded in this light.   Thus Josiah sent to Huldah (2 Kings
xxii. 14), Zedekiah to Jeremiah (Jer. xxxvii. 3), &c.   The impious Ahab
required Micaiah to come to him, and that only at the earnest request of
king Jehoshaphat (1 Kings xxii. 9).   From the mention of the Prophet's
father two very different but equally gratuitous conclusions are drawn ;
one by Vitringa, who infers that Isaiah was of noble rank ; the other by
Hendewerk, who infers that he cannot be the author of this narrative, as
he never would have called himself *the son of Amoz*.   In the parallel
passage (2 Kings xix. 2) the patronymic follows the official title, whereas
here it precedes it.   As this last is the usual collocation, Gesenius appears
to think that it was substituted for the other by the later writer, while Hitzig, for the very same reason, declares this to be the original reading.   The
plural שׂקים seems to shew that שׂק is not here the name of the material
but of the garment (*covered with sacks, or sackcloth dresses*).   Of the king's
prompt appeal to God in his extremity, Gill quaintly says : *Hezekiah does
not sit down to consider Rabshakeh's speech, to take it in pieces and give an
answer to it, but he applies unto God.*

3. *And they said unto him, Thus saith Hezekiah, a day of anguish and
rebuke and contempt* (*is*) *this day, for the children are come to the birth* (or

to the places of birth), *and there is not strength to bring forth.* The indirect construction of the first words (*that they may say to him*), adopted by some writers, is not only unnecessary but foreign from the Hebrew idiom which, especially in narrative, prefers the most simple and direct forms of expression. That Hezekiah told them thus to speak, is not only implied in their doing so, but expressly asserted by themselves, and need not therefore be recorded. As the execution of a command is often left to be inferred from the command itself (chaps. vii. 3, viii. 1, &c.), so here the details of the command are to be gathered from the record of its execution. The common version of צרה (*trouble*) seems too weak for the occasion and for the figure in the other clause. It is well explained by Vitringa, as denoting, not external danger merely, but the complicated distress, both of a temporal and spiritual nature, in which Hezekiah was involved by the threats and blasphemies of the Assyrian. *Rebuke* is applied by the Septuagint (ὀνειδισμοῦ) and some interpreters to the *reproaches* of Rabshakeh; but it is more agreeable to usage to explain it as signifying the divine rebuke or chastisement, as in Ps. lxxiii. 4, cxlix. 7. It is characteristic of the Scriptures and the ancient saints to represent even the malignity of human enemies as a rebuke from God. The very same phrase (*day of rebuke*) is used in the same sense by Hosea (v. 9). The verb from which נאצה is derived means to treat with contempt, or more specifically, to reject with scorn. It is sometimes used to denote God's rejection of his people (Deut. xxxii. 19 ; Jer. xiv. 21 ; Lam. ii. 6), and Hitzig accordingly translates the noun rejection or reprobation (*Verwerfung*). But as the verb more frequently expresses man's contempt of God (*e. g.* chap. i. 4), interpreters are commonly agreed in making the noun here mean *blasphemy.* The terms employed by Lowth (*contumely*) and Henderson (*calumny*) are too weak, if the reference be to God, as the usage of the verb seems to require. The oral expression of contempt for God is blasphemy. The metaphor in the last clause expresses, in the most affecting manner, the ideas of extreme pain, imminent danger, critical emergency, utter weakness, and entire dependence on the aid of others. (Compare the similar expressions of chap. xxvi. 18.) The reference of the passage to the interrupted reformation of religion, or to the abortive effort to shake off the Assyrian yoke, is equally illogical and tasteless, while the question, whether Judah is here represented as the mother or the child, betrays a total incapacity to appreciate the strength and beauty of the Prophet's metaphor. There is no more need of mooting such points than if he had simply said, the present distress is like the pains of childbirth.

4. *If peradventure Jehovah thy God will hear the words of Rabshakeh, whom the king of Assyria his master hath sent to reproach the living God, and will rebuke the words which Jehovah thy God hath heard, then shalt thou lift up a prayer for the remnant* (that is still) *found* (here). אולי may generally be expressed by our *perhaps*, and this translation is adopted here by most interpreters, who then take ו at the beginning of the last clause in the sense of *therefore.* But by retaining what appears to be the primary and proper force of אולי, as a contingent and conditional expression, and making ו the usual sign of the apodosis, we may throw the whole into one sentence, and make more obvious the connection of the clauses. It was because Hezekiah thought Jehovah might hear, that he asked Isaiah's prayers in his behalf. The meaning given to אולי in this construction is expressed in the English version of Isa. xlvii. 12, and Jer. xxi. 2, and might

be substituted for *perhaps* in all the cases where the latter is employed to represent this particle, in some with great advantage to the clearness or the force of the expression. Lowth's explanation of אולי as an optative particle (*O that Jehovah thy God would hear*) is not justified by usage. The doubt expressed in the first clause, whether God *will hear*, is viewed by some interpreters as inconsistent with the statement in the last clause, that he *has heard*. To remove this imaginary discrepancy, some deny that the first clause really expresses doubt or implies contingency; others allege that *hear* is used in two distinct senses, that of simply hearing, and that of regarding or attending to, and acting accordingly. The true solution seems to be, that the preterite שמע denotes a past time only in relation to the contingency expressed by ישמע. Perhaps he *will hear*, and then punish what he *has heard*. Both verbs may then be understood in one and the same sense, either that of simply hearing, or in that of acting as if one heard. The reproach and blasphemy of the Assyrian consisted mainly in his confounding Jehovah with the gods of the surrounding nations (2 Chron. xxxii. 19), in antithesis to whom, as being impotent and lifeless, he is here and elsewhere called the *living God*. The Septuagint, Vulgate, and most interpreters, ancient and modern, make הוכיח an infinitive, connected by the ו with חרף, and descriptive of Rabshakeh's blasphemies (*and to rebuke me in the words*, &c.). But *reprove* or *rebuke* is a description wholly inappropriate to such a speech, and the Hebrew word nowhere means to *rail at* or *revile*. Usage, moreover, would require the particle to be repeated before this infinitive, and Gesenius (in his Commentary) accordingly assumes that והוכיח is put for ולהוכיח. The grammatical and lexicographical objections may be both avoided by taking הוכיח as a preterite with the ו conversive, as in the English Version (*and will reprove*). The ב may then be either a mere connective of the verb with its object (*rebuke the words*), or denote the occasion and the ground (*rebuke him for the words*, &c.). Maurer, who successfully defends this construction (in his note on 2 Kings xix. 4), in order to shew that he is not alone in his opinion, says, *consentientem habeo Fäsium.* He might have gone a little further back, not only to Junius and Tremellius, but to Jonathan, who paraphrases the expression thus, *and will take vengeance for the words*, &c. The same construction is adopted by Gesenius in his Thesaurus. It is also retained in the modern English versions, among which that of Lowth puts a peculiar sense upon the clause, by making it express a wish that God would *refute* Rabshakeh's words, meaning no doubt by the actual exertion of the power which he called in question. But this specific meaning of הוכיח cannot be sustained by usage. *To lift up a prayer* is not simply to utter one, but has allusion to two common idiomatic phrases, that of lifting up the voice in the sense of speaking loud or beginning to speak, and that of lifting up the heart or soul in the sense of earnestly desiring. The passive participle *found* is often used in Hebrew to denote what is *present* in a certain place, or more generally what is *extant* in existence, or forthcoming. The meaning *left*, which is expressed in the English and some other versions, is suggested wholly by the noun with which the participle here agrees. As to the application of the whole phrase, it may either be a general description of the straits or low condition to which the chosen people were reduced (as the church at Sardis is exhorted to *strengthen the things which remain*, Rev. iii. 2), or be more specifically understood in reference to Judah as surviving the destruction of the ten tribes (compare chap. xxviii. 5), or to Jerusalem as spared amidst the general desolation of Judah (compare chap. i. 8). In either case, the king requests the Prophet to pray for their deliverance from entire destruction. This application was made to Isaiah, not as a private person, however eminent in piety, but as one who was recognized as standing in an intimate relation to Jehovah, and as a constituted medium of communication with him. In like manner God himself said to Abimelech of Abraham, *he is a prophet, and shall pray for thee, and thou shalt live* (Gen. xx. 7). In recognition of the same relation, Hezekiah twice says *thy God, i.e.* thine in a peculiar and distinctive sense. This phrase is therefore not to be regarded as an expression of despondency, or even of humility, on Hezekiah's part, but as a kind of indirect explanation of his reason for resorting to the Prophet at this juncture.

5. *And the servants of king Hezekiah came to Isaiah.* This is a natural and simple resumption of the narrative, common in all inartificial history. It affords no ground for assuming a transposition in the text, nor for explaining ויאמרו in ver. 3 as a subjunctive.

6. *And Isaiah said to them, Thus shall ye say to your master, Thus saith Jehovah, Be not afraid of* (literally *from before* or *from the face of*) *the words which thou hast heard,* (*with*) *which the servants of the king of Assyria have blasphemed me.* The last verb means to *rail at* or *revile,* and when applied to God, must be translated by a still stronger term. The word translated *servants* is not the same with that in the preceding verse, but strictly means *young men* or *boys,* and is so translated in the Targum and Vulgate. Many interpreters regard it as a contemptuous description, and it is so translated by Hitzig (*Knappen*), Umbreit (*Buben*), Henderson (*striplings*), and in other modern versions.

7. *Behold I am putting* (or *about to put*) *a spirit in him, and he shall hear a noise, and shall return to his own land, and I will cause him to fall by the sword in his own land.* Calvin translates the first clause *ecce opponam illi ventum,* and explains it to mean that God would carry him away as with a wind (compare chap. xvii. 13). The English Version renders it, *behold I will send a blast upon him,* meaning either a pestilential blast or a destructive tempest. Others understand by רוח the destroying angel, or an evil spirit by whom he should be haunted and possessed. But most interpreters refer the phrase to an effect to be produced upon the mind of the Assyrian. Thus some explain רוח to mean terror, others courage, others a desire to return home, others simply a change of mind. The most probable conclusion is, that it does not denote a specific change, but divine influence as governing his movements. שמועה strictly means anything *heard,* and Luther accordingly translates the phrase, *he shall hear something.* Most writers understand this as referring to the news mentioned in ver. 9 below. But Henderson observes that this news, far from driving Sennacherib home, led to a fresh defiance of Jerusalem. He therefore ingeniously suggests, that this expression has reference to the news of the destruction of his host before Jerusalem while he himself was absent. But in the next verse Rabshakeh is said to have rejoined his master, nor is there any further mention of an army at Jerusalem. It is possible, indeed, though not recorded, that Rabshakeh left the troops behind him when he went to Libnah. under the command of Tartan or Rabsaris (2 Kings xviii. 17), and this is still more probable if, as some suppose, Rabshakeh was a mere ambassador or herald, and Tartan the real military chief. If it can be assumed, on any ground, that the great catastrophe took place in the absence of Sennacherib, which would account for his personal escape, then Henderson's explanation of שמועה is more satisfactory than any other. The modern Germans are

perplexed by this verse. They would gladly explain the prediction in the last clause as a prophecy *ex eventu ;* but in that case, how could the slaughter of the host have been omitted ? The only escape from this dilemma is by the arbitrary allegation that the prophecy was falsely ascribed to Isaiah by a later writer. If this be so, we may as well reject the whole ; for what assurance have we that a writer, who fabricates miracles and prophecies, is faithful in his history of other matters ? The inconveniences of this attempt to save a part while really discrediting the whole, are curiously apparent from Gesenius's endeavour to explain the first clause of this verse as a sagacious political conjecture, and the other as a subsequent interpolation.

8. *And Rabshakeh returned, and found the king of Assyria fighting against* (i. e. *besieging*) *Libnah, for he heard that he had decamped from Lachish.* Both these towns were in the plain or lowlands of Judea, south-west of Jerusalem (Josh. xv. 39, 42), originally seats of Canaanitish kings or chiefs, conquered by Joshua (Josh. xii. 11, 15). Lachish was one of the fifteen places fortified by Rehoboam (2 Chron. xi. 9), and one of the last towns taken by Nebuchadnezzar (Jer. xxxiv. 7). It was still in existence after the exile (Neh. xi. 30). Libnah was a city of the Levites and of refuge (Josh. xxi. 13), and appears to have been nearer to Jerusalem. Henderson infers that Sennacherib had conquered Lachish, most other writers that he failed in the attempt. Some of the older writers make Libnah an Egyptian city, either because one of the stations of the Israelites in the wilderness bore this name (Num. xxxiii. 20), or because Josephus, in order to reconcile Isaiah's narrative with that of Herodotus, represent's Sennacherib as leaving Lachish to besiege Pelusium. The last verb in this verse properly denotes the removal of a tent or an encampment, an idea happily expressed in Lowth's translation by the military term *decamped.* The sense of this verb can be here expressed in our idiom only by the use of the pluperfect, which form is given by most versions to the verb before it likewise, and Hendewerk extends it even to the verbs of the first clause, which is wholly gratuitous.

9. *And he* (Sennacherib) *heard say concerning Tirhakah king of Ethiopia, He is come forth to make war with thee ; and he heard* (*it*), *and sent* (or *when he heard* it *he sent*) *messengers to Hezekiah, saying* (what follows in the next verse). On the meaning of the Hebrew name כוש, see the notes on chap. xviii. 1, and xx. 3. Tirhakah was one of the most famous conquerors of ancient times. Megasthenes, as quoted by Strabo, puts him between Sesostris and Nebuchadnezzar. He is also named by Manetho as one of the Ethiopian dynasty in Egypt. He was at this time either in close aliance with that country, or more probably in actual possession of Thebais or Upper Egypt. The fact that an Ethiopian dynasty did reign there is attested by the ancient writers, and confirmed by still existing monuments. The Greek forms of the name (Ταραχός, Τάρχος, Τέρχων) vary but little from the Hebrew. Barnes and some of the older writers suppose that Sennacherib had already been driven out of Egypt by this king, and was now afraid of being followed into Palestine; but this conclusion is hardly warranted by the facts of the history, sacred or profane. It is unnecessary to suppose, with J. D. Michaelis, that Tirhakah had crossed the desert to invade Assyria, or even with Rosenmüller, that he was already on the frontier of Judah. The bare fact of his having left his own dominions, with the purpose of attacking Sennacherib, would be sufficient to alarm the latter, especially as his operations in the Holy Land had been so unsuccessful. He was naturally anxious, therefore, to induce Hezekiah to capitulate before the

Ethiopians should arrive, perhaps before the Jews should hear of their approach. That he did not march upon Jerusalem himself is very probably accounted for by Vitringa, on the ground that his strength lay chiefly in cavalry, which could not be employed in the highlands, and that the poliorcetic part of warfare, or the conduct of sieges, was little known to any ancient nation but the Romans, as Tacitus asserts. A peculiar difficulty arose also from the scarcity of water in the environs of Jerusalem,. which has been an obstacle to all the armies that have ever besieged it (see the notes on chap. xxii. 9–11). Gesenius supposes that symptoms of the plague had begun to shew themselves in Palestine. Instead of עַל before *Tirhakah*, the parallel passage (2 Kings xix. 9) has אֶל, which is the more remarkable because the latter particle is represented by some critics as a favourite of the copyist or later writer, to whom they ascribe this portion of Isaiah. Instead of the second *heard*, the parallel passage has *he returned*, which, according to a common Hebrew idiom, may qualify the next verb (*sent*), by giving it the sense of *sent again*. This, which certainly yields an appropriate meaning, is restored by Lowth in this place as the true text, while Gesenius and the later German writers, who are usually bold enough in critical conjecture, choose in this case to regard the reading in Isaiah as a tautology of the later writer. Yet the variation is precisely such as one writer would be apt to make in recording the same matter twice.

10. *Thus shall ye say to Hezekiah, king of Judah, Let not thy God deceive thee, in whom thou trustest, saying, Jerusalem shall not be given into the hand of the king of Assyria.* This recognition of Hezekiah's royal dignity, of which Rabshakeh seemed to take no notice, if significant at all, as some interpreters imagine, may be accounted for upon the ground that in this message the design of the Assyrians was not to destroy the people's confidence in Hezekiah, but the king's own confidence in God. For the same reason, Sennacherib's blasphemy is much more open and direct than that of Rabshakeh. The word *saying* may be referred either to Hezekiah or to God. This English Version makes the last construction necessary, by changing the collocation of the words ; but Luther, Gesenius, and many others understand the sense to be, *in whom thou trustest, saying.* This is in fact entitled to the preference, on the ground that בוטח is the nearest antecedent. On the whole, it is best, in a case so doubtful, to retain the Hebrew collocation with all its ambiguity. The word *surrendered*, used by Henderson in this verse, is not only less simple than the common version *given*, but confines the clause too strictly to the act of the besieged, instead of making it at least include the act of God himself, as the protector of Jerusalem.

11. *Behold, thou hast heard what the kings of Assyria have done to all the lands, by utterly destroying them, and thou shalt be delivered !* The interjection *behold* appeals to these events as something perfectly notorious ; as if he had said, See what has happened to others, and then judge whether thou art likely to escape. The pronoun *thou*, in the first clause, not being necessary to the sense, is, according to analogy, distinctive and emphatic, and may be explained to mean, *thou at least* hast heard, if not the common people. In the last clause, the same pronoun stands in opposition to the other kings or kingdoms who had been destroyed. This clause is, in most versions, rendered as an interrogation, but is properly an exclamation of contemptuous incredulity. *All the lands* may either be an elliptical expression for *all the lands subdued by them*, or, which is more in keeping with the character of the discourse, a hyperbolical expression of

the speaker's arrogance. להחרימם strictly means *to doom them*, or devote them irrevocably to destruction, but in usage commonly includes the idea of execution as well as of design. (Compare the note on chap. xi. 15). From the mention of the *kings* of Assyria in the plural, some writers take occasion to accuse Rabshakeh of intending to arrogate the glory of these conquests to Sennacherib exclusively, whereas the latter did not dare to do so in addressing Hezekiah. But others, with more probability, infer that the singular form, employed by Rabshakeh, is itself to be understood collectively, like *king of Babylon* in the fourteenth chapter.

12. *Did the gods of the nations deliver them, which my fathers destroyed, (to wit,) Gozan, and Haran, and Rezeph, and the children of Eden which is (or who were) in Telassar?* Here again the collocation of the words makes the construction doubtful, though the general sense is clear. אותם may either be referred to *lands* in the preceding verse (the masculine form being then a licence, or perhaps a sign that by the lands we are to understand the people who inhabited them), or to אלהי, or to גוים, or it may be connected with אשר in the sense of *those whom*, which appears to be preferred by Hitzig. The construction then is, *Did the gods of the nations deliver those whom my fathers destroyed?* With respect to the places mentioned in the second clause, all that is absolutely necessary to the just understanding of the sentence is, that they were well known, both to speaker and hearer, as Assyrian conquests. The difficulty of identifying some of them affords an incidental argument in favour of the antiquity and genuineness of the passage. *Gozan* is probably the modern *Kaushan*, the *Gauzanitis* of Ptolemy, a region of Mesopotamia, situated on the Chaboras, to which a portion of the ten tribes were transferred by Shalmaneser. *Haran* was a city of Mesopotamia, where Abraham's father died, the *Carrae* of the Romans, and famous for the great defeat of Crassus. *Rezeph*, a common name in oriental geography, here denotes probably the *Ressapha* of Ptolemy, a town and province in Palmyrene Syria. *Eden* means pleasure or delight, and seems to have been given as a name to various places. Having been thus applied to a district in the region of mount Lebanon, the native Christians have been led to regard that as the site of the terrestial paradise. Equally groundless are the conclusions of some learned critics as to the identity of the place here mentioned with the garden of Eden. In Isa. li. 3, the reference is not *to a country well known and distinguished for its fertility* (Barnes), but to the garden of Eden as a matter of history. Such allusions prove no more, as to the site of the garden, than the similar allusions of modern orators and poets to any delightful region as *an Eden* or *a Paradise*. Even the continued application of the name in prose, as a geographical term, proves no more than the use of such a name as *Mount Pleasant* in American geography. The inference, in this place, is especially untenable, because the word *sons* or *children*, prefixed to Eden, leaves it doubtful whether the latter is the name of a place at all, and not rather that of a person, whose descendants were among the races conquered by Assyria. The relative pronoun may agree grammatically either with *sons* or *Eden*, and the form of the verb to be supplied must be varied accordingly. *Tel-assar*, which Gesenius thinks may be identical with the *Ellasar* of Gen. xiv. 1, where it is substituted for the latter by the Targum of Jerusalem, appears to be analogous in form to the Babylonian names, *Tel-abib*, *Tel-melah*, *Tel-hasha*, in all of which *tel* means *hill*, and corresponds to the English *mount* in names of places.

13. *Where is the king of Hamath, and the king of Arpad, and the king of*

the city Sepharvaim, Henah and Ivvah? The question implies that they were nowhere, or had ceased to be. The first three names occur in the same order in Rabshakeh's speech (chap. xxxvi. 19), and the remaining two also in the parallel passage (2 Kings xviii. 34). As the love of uniformity and assimilation here betrayed is on the part of the pretended older writer, the German critics have discreetly overlooked it. Of Hena, nothing whatever is known, and of Ivvah only that it may be identical with the *Avva* of 2 Kings xvii. 24, from which Assyrian colonists were transferred to Sammaria. The absence of all further trace of these two places, and the peculiar form of the names, led J. D. Michaelis to follow Symmachus and Jonathan in making both words verbs or verbal nouns, implying that the kings just mentioned had been utterly subverted and destroyed. But this interpretation, although highly plausible in this one case, is much less natural, if not wholly inadmissible, in 2 Kings xviii. 34. It would be easy to affirm, no doubt, that the writer of the latter passage misunderstood the one before us ; but from this suggestion even Gesenius and his followers are precluded by their foregone conclusion that the text in Kings is the more ancient of the two. Another explanation of these words is that suggested by Luzzatto, who regards them as the names of the deities worshipped at Hamath, Arpad, and Sepharvaim, and takes מלך in the sense of idol or tutelary god, which last idea is as old as Clericus. This ingenious hypothesis Luzzatto endeavours to sustain by the analogy of *Adrammelech and Anammelech, the gods of Sepharvaim* (2 Kings xvii. 31), the second of which names he regards as essentially identical with *Hena.* In favour of this exposition, besides the fact already mentioned that the names, as names of places, occur nowhere else, it may be urged that it agrees not only with the context in this place, but also with 2 Kings xviii. 34, in which the explanations of the words as verbs or nouns is inadmissible. This explanation, and the grounds on which it rests, are at least entitled to a fair comparison with that first given, as the one approved by most interpreters. Musculus understands the dual form of *Sepharvaim* as denoting that it consisted of two towns, perhaps on different sides of the Euphrates, and that *Hena* and *Ivvah* were the distinctive names of these. The particular mention of the *city* Sepharvaim, and the construction of that word with ל, are peculiarities not easily accounted for. The substitution of איה for אי (2 Kings. xix. 13) is of course ascribed by Gesenius and Knobel to the later writer's fondness for exact uniformity, his own violations of it to the contrary notwithstanding.

14. *And Hezekiah took the letters from the hand of the messengers, and read it, and went up (to) the house of Jehovah, and Hezekiah spread it before Jehovah.* As nothing had been previously said respecting letters, we must either suppose that the preceding address was made not orally but in writing, or that both modes of communication were adopted. The latter is most probable in itself, and agrees best with the statement in 2 Chron. xxxii. 17, that besides the speeches which his servants spake against the Lord God, and against his servant Hezekiah, Sennacherib *wrote letters to rail on the Lord God of Israel and to speak against him.* The singular pronoun (*it*) referring to the plural antecedent (*letters*), is explained by David Kimchi distributively, as meaning *every one of them;* by the Targum, as meaning simply *one of them, i. e.* according to Joseph Kimchi, the one that contained the blasphemy. Luzzatto supposes that it was customary to send duplicate of the same letter, as the modern Samaritans did in their correspondences

with Job Ludolf, and that Hezekiah, though he took both or all, had no occasion to read more than one of them. This is certainly ingenious and plausible; but perhaps the most satisfactory explanation is, that ספרים, like the Latin *literæ*, had come to signify a single letter, and might be therefore treated indiscriminately either as a singular or a plural form. This is the more probable, because it can hardly be supposed that Sennacherib would write more than one letter to Hezekiah on this one occasion, unless in the way suggested by Luzzato, which is not to be assumed without necessity or evidence. That he wrote at the same time to the chief men or the people, is an arbitrary and improbable assumption, and even supposing that he did, why should Hezekiah be described as receiving all the letters? Some versions wholly disregard the difference of number. Thus the Septuagint and Luther make both noun and pronoun singular, while Calvin and the Vulgate make both plural. The parallel passage (2 Kings xix. 14) removes all appearance of irregularity by reading *them* instead of *it*. This is so glaring an exception to the sweeping allegation of a constant disposition, in the text before us, to remove anomalies and seeming incongruities, that Gesenius is under the necessity of finding some expedient for the vindication of his darling theory. This he plausibly accomplishes by saying, that as both texts have the singular form *spread it* in the other clause, the later writer chose to assimilate the phrase in question to this, and not to the preceding plural noun. It does not seem to have occurred to the ingenious special pleader, that the last *it* needs as much to be explained as the first, and that such a copyist as he supposes, instead of saying *read it*, because he was going to say *spread it* afterwards, would naturally first say *read them*, and then say *spread them* for the sake of uniformity. Such explanations appear almost puerile compared with the obvious and simple supposition of two draughts or copies by the selfsame writer. Another characteristic observation of Gesenius on this verse is, that Hezekiah must have spread the letter in the temple in order to let Jehovah read it from the Holy of Holies, and that accordingly in ver. 10, he is called upon to open his eyes, which he says reminds him of the praying machines of Thibet. This specimen of exegetical wit is eagerly caught up and repeated by later and inferior writers. The spreading of the letter before God is supposed by Clericus to have been designed to excite the feelings and the prayers of the people, by Calvin to affect the feelings of the king himself. It seems, however, to have been no studied, calculated movement, but a natural expression of anxiety and trust in God, as a protector and a confidential friend; a state of mind which to an infidel must needs appear ridiculous. As any man would carry an open letter, which troubled or perplexed him, to a friend for sympathy and counsel, so the pious king spreads this blasphemous epistle before God, as the occasion and subject of his prayers. Josephus says he left it afterwards rolled up in the temple, of which there is no record in the narrative before us. He also says that Hezekiah lay prostrate, in the Jewish manner, in the presence of Jehovah, from which it might seem that he took יפרשהו in the sense of *stretched himself*, which would be ungrammatical and contrary to usage. But Vitringa is no doubt correct in his opinion, that Josephus had no reference to this word, but to the signs of mourning mentioned in the first and second verses, with which he would naturally associate prostration as their usual accompaniment. (See for example 1 Chron. xxi. 16.)

15. *And Hezekiah prayed to Jehovah, saying* (what follows in the next verse). Hendewerk observes that this mode of proceeding was charac-

teristic of a person more like David in devotion than in energy and enterprise. With a far superior appreciation of the good king's character, Gill
quaintly says that, instead of answering the letter himself, he prays the
Lord to answer it. Instead of *to*, the parallel passage (2 Kings xix 15) has
before Jehovah.

16. *Jehovah of hosts, God of Israel, dwelling between* (or *sitting upon*) *the
cherubim, thou art he, the God* (*i. e.* the only true God), *thou alone, to all
the kingdoms of the earth ; thou hast made the heavens and the earth.* The
parallel passage (2 Kings xix. 15) omits צבאות, upon which Gesenius
remarks that the combination here used is very common in the prophecies,
while it scarcely occurs at all in the historical books. What can be more
natural, therefore, than that Isaiah should employ it in the case before us,
and the simple prose form in the book of Kings ? This is surely a more
obvious conclusion than the one which Gesenius draws, viz., that the later
copyists and compilers of the books of the Old Testament altered the text
at will, to make it suit the customary form of expression in their own day.
The *cherubim* were visible representations of spiritual beings, or, as Bähr
and Hengstenberg suppose, of the perfection of the creature in its highest
form. The name is most probably derived from כרב, as a synonym of קרב,
to *approach*, or as a transposition of רכב, to *ride*, in allusion to the angels
as the bearers of God's chariots. This last verb is connected with the noun
in Ps. xviii. 11. Eichhorn's attempt to identify the word with the γρύπες or
griffins of Eastern mythology has been repeated by some later writers, but
with small success. Some suppose an allusion, in the case before us, to
Jehovah's riding on the cherubim (Ps. xviii. 11), or angels through the air ;
others to his being enthroned above the material cherubs in the temple.
This sense is given by Luther and the ancient versions, but Calvin and
many later writers understand him to be here described as *dwelling between*
the cherubim. (Compare Exod. xxv. 22.) In either case there is allusion to
his manifested presence over the mercy-seat, called by the later Jews
shechinah, which word is itself used in the Chaldee Paraphrase of the verse
before us. Forerius translates the Hebrew phrase without a preposition,
inhabitant of the cherubim, which would seem, however, to describe God as
dwelling in the images, not over them or under the shadow of their wings.
The pronoun הוא is understood by some as an emphatic or intensive addition, like the Latin *ipse :* thou thyself (art) the God, &c. Others regard it
as an idiomatic substitute for the copula or verb of existence, used with all
the persons, *thou art the God*, &c. But on the general principle of adhering to the strict sense of words where it is possible, it is best to translate it *thou* (*art*) *he*, and to regard what follows as explanatory of this
pregnant and concise expression. *The God of all the kingdoms of the earth*
is not an exact translation of the Hebrew words, in which *the God* stands
by itself as an emphatic phrase, meaning *the only God, the true God*, and
what follows is intended to suggest a contrast with the false gods of the
nations. לכל is not simply *of all, in all, for all*, or *over all*, but *with
respect to all*. Thou art the one true God, not only with respect to us,
but with respect to all the nations of the earth. The reason follows : because thou hast made them all, and not the earth only, but the heavens
also. All this is indirectly a reply to the Assyrian blasphemies, which
questioned the almighty power of Jehovah, and put him on a level with the
idols of the heathen. The same antithesis betwen the impotence of idols
and the power of God as shewn in the creation of the world, occurs in Ps.
xcvi. 5, and Jer. x. 11.

17. *Bow thine ear, O Jehovah, and hear ; open thine eyes, O Jehovah, and see ; and hear all the words of Sennacherib, which he hath sent* (or *who hath sent*) *to reproach the living God.* These expressions are entirely analogous to those in many other places, where God is entreated to see and hear, *i. e.* to act as if he saw and heard. The attempt of Gesenius and his followers to restrict them to the reading of the letter or the hearing it read, neither requires nor deserves refutation. Gesenius also takes עֵינֶךָ as a singular, substituted for the plural עֵינֶיךָ of the parallel passage (2 Kings xix. 16), through the *transcriber's* ignorance of the Hebrew idiom, which always speaks of turning *one* ear, but of opening *both* eyes. If this distinction is as natural and obvious as he represents, it is strange that even a transcriber, to whom the Hebrew was vernacular, should not have been aware of it. Supposing, however, that Isaiah wrote both narratives, there would be nothing more surprising in his saying *eyes* in one and *eye* in the other, than there is in the coexistence of such forms as *word of God* and *words of God*, *his mercy* and *his mercies*, where the predominance of one form does not preclude the occasional occurrence of the other. Gesenius, moreover, did not think it necessary to inform his readers of the fact, which Henderson has brought to light, that more than fifty manuscripts, and nearly twenty editions, have the usual plural form עיניך, an amount of evidence ten times as great as that which Gesenius, in other cases, thinks enough to justify the boldest changes in the text. Still less did he consider himself called upon to mention, that the common reading עֵינֶךָ itself may be a plural form, according to analogy, as stated expressly by himself in his *Lehrgebäude* (p. 215) and his smaller Grammar (§ 35, Remark 3). Least of all did he see cause to state, that this explanation of the form is rendered almost necessary here by the parallelism, because if עֵינֶךָ were written instead of עֵינֶיךָ merely because of a pause in the sentence, then אָזְנֶךָ, which occupies the very same position in the other member, would be written אָזְנֶךָ, and as this is not the case, the obvious conclusion is, that the *seghol* in עֵינֶךָ is the union-vowel of a plural noun before the suffix, with the י omitted as in Exod. xxxiii. 13, and other cases cited by Gesenius in his grammars. The fact that עינך has a stronger disjunctive accent than אזנך, instead of weakening confirms the argument, because if the former were in pause, the structure of the sentence would require the latter to be so too. What Gesenius says in reference to the use of the word *Hosts* in the preceding verse, viz., that it throws light upon other critical phenomena, may be applied with justice to his own style of criticism in the case before us. Instead of assuming, as he often does without a tithe of the same evidence, that עיניך is the true text, or reflecting that עינך itself may be a plural according to his own shewing elsewhere, and must be a plural according to the favourite rule of parallelism, he first takes for granted that it is a singular, and then makes use of it not only as a deviation from the older copy, but as characteristic of an ignorant and therefore a later writer. For by some strange process it has been discovered, that the later Hebrew writers were not only inferior in composition, but in knowledge of the idioms of the language, whereas in Greece and Rome the decline of original composition coincided with the rise and progress of grammatical science. The only end for which these inconsistencies are pointed out, is that the reader may correctly estimate authoritative *dicta* of the same kind elsewhere. The simplest version of אשר שלח is, *who has sent.* To express the idea, *which he has sent*, usage would seem to require a suffix with the verb, and accordingly we read in 2 Kings xix. 16, אשר שלחו, *i. e. which he has sent*, referring irregularly to

the plural *words*, or *who has sent him*, meaning Rabshakeh, which is the construction given in the English version of that passage.

18. *It is true, O Jehovah, the kings of Assyria have wasted all the lands and their land.* The first word in the original is a particle of concession, admitting the truth of what Sennacherib had said, so far as it related merely to his conquest of the nations and destruction of their idols. The repetition, *lands* and *land*, has much perplexed interpreters. Vitringa supplies *nations* or *peoples* before *lands*, as in 2 Chron. xxxii. 13. Others suppose ארצות itself to be here used in the sense of *nations*, as the singular seems sometimes to denote the inhabitants of the earth or land. This supposition would account at the same time for the masculine suffix in ארצם. Gesenius follows J. D. Michaelis and Augusti in giving this suffix a reflexive sense, or referring to the Assyrians themselves (*their own land*). The meaning then is that they had destroyed not only other countries but their own, which agrees exactly with the charge against the king of Babylon in chap. xiv. 20, *thou shalt not be joined with them in burial, because thou hast destroyed thy land and slain thy people.* As this sense, however, is not so appropriate here, where Hezekiah is confirming what Sennacherib himself had said, it is better to adopt one of the other constructions, which brings the sentence into strict agreement, not as to form but as to sense, with the parallel passage (2 Kings xix. 17), where we have the unambiguous term *nations.* This is justly described by Rosenmüller as the easier construction of the two, which would militate against the foregone conclusion of the later Germans, as to the relative antiquity and characteristic features of the two texts. Gesenius, therefore, while he grants that the form of expression in the case before us is harsher and more difficult, alleges, with perverse ingenuity, that this arose from the attempt to remove another incongruity, to wit, the application of the verb חרב to persons, in avoiding which the copyist committed the solecism, *lands and their land.* But this hypothesis, besides its fanciful and arbitrary character as a mere makeshift, and its gratuitous assumption of the grossest stupidity and ignorance as well as inattention in the writer, is sufficiently refuted by the emphatic combination of the same verb and noun in chap. lx. 12. Even if that were a composition of a later writer than Isaiah, it would prove that such a writer could not have been so shocked at the expression as to make nonsense of a sentence merely for the purpose of avoiding it. The reader will do well to observe, moreover, that the same imaginary copyist is supposed, in different emergencies, to have been wholly unacquainted with the idioms of his mother tongue, and yet extremely sensitive to any supposed violation of usage. Such scruples and such ignorance are not often found in combination. A transcriber unable to distinguish sense from nonsense would not be apt to take offence at mere irregularities or eccentricities in the phraseology or diction of his author.

19. *And given* (or *put*) *their gods into the fire—for they* (*were*) *no gods, but wood and stone, the work of men's hands—and destroyed them.* Most interpreters separate the clauses and translate ויאבדום *therefore* (or *so*) *they have destroyed them.* But the true construction seems to be the one proposed by Henderson, who connects this verb directly with the first clause, and throws the intervening member into a parenthesis. Instead of the peculiar idiomatic use of the infinite (נתֹן), the parallel passage (2 Kings xvii. 18) has the preterite (נָתְנוּ) a substitution of an easy for a difficult construction so undeniable that Gesenius can escape from it only by asserting that the form here used belongs to the later Hebrew, an assertion which

not one of his followers has ventured to repeat, while Hendewerk flatly
contradicts it. Knobel strangely imagines that Hezekiah here accuses the
Assyrian of impiety towards those whom he acknowledged to be gods,
whereas throughout this verse, and that before it, he is simply acknowledging that Sennacherib had destroyed the idols of the nations, and assigning
a reason for it, viz. that they were no gods, but material idols. The application of the word *gods* to the mere external image is common in profane
as well as sacred writings, and arises from the fact that all idolaters,
whatever they may theoretically hold as to the nature of their deities,
identify them practically with the stocks and stones to which they pay their
adorations.

20. *And now, O Jehovah our God, save us from his hand, and all the kingdoms of the earth shall know, that thou Jehovah art alone* (or *that thou alone
art Jehovah*) The adverb *now* is here used both in a temporal and logical
sense, as equivalent, not only to *at length*, or *before it is too late*, but also
to *therefore*, or *since these things are so*. The fact that Sennacherib had
destroyed other nations, is urged as a reason why the Lord should interpose to rescue his own people from a like destruction ; and the fact that
he had really triumphed over other gods, as a reason why he should be
taught to know the difference between them and Jehovah. The argument
or motive here presented, although sneered at by the infidel interpreters, is
not only common in the Scriptures, but involved in the very idea of a God.
The considerations which make such a motive unbecoming in the case of
creatures are entirely inapplicable to the Supreme Being. The requisition
of a sentimental modesty on his part only shows that he who makes it has
no higher conception of a God than as a vague sublimation of humanity.
The construction of ידע as an optative (*let all the kingdoms of the earth
know*), or a subjunctive (*that all the kingdoms of the earth may know*),
although admissible, ought not to be preferred to the future proper, where
the latter yields a sense so good in itself and so well suited to the context.
The last words of the verse may either mean, *that thou Jehovah art the only
one* (*i.e.* as appears from the connection, the only true God), or, *that thou
alone art Jehovah*, with particular allusion to the proper import of that name
as signifying absolute, eternal, independent existence. The last construction is preferred by Hitzig ; but the first, which is adopted by Gesenius, is
also recommended by its more exact agreement with the Masoretic accents.
It need scarcely be added that these questions of construction do not affect
the general sense, which is, that the deliverance of his people from Sennacherib would prove Jehovah to be infinitely more than the gods of the nations
whom he gloried in destroying.

21. *And Isaiah, the son of Amoz, sent to Hezekiah, saying, Thus saith Jehovah, the God of Israel,* (*as to*) *what thou hast prayed to me* (*with respect*) *to
Sennacherib king of Assyria,* (the apodosis follows in the next verse). Vitringa's supposition that the communication was in writing, is favoured by the
analogy of ver. 14, and by the length and metrical form of the message itself.
Knobel suggests that the messenger was probably a younger prophet.
Why Isaiah corresponded thus with Hezekiah, instead of speaking with him
face to face, as he did in other cases, both before and after this, none of
the interpreters have been able to explain, except by resolving it into a
positive command of God. J. D. Michaelis connects אשר with אלי in the
sense of *I to whom ;* but this use of the first person in immediate combination with the third, although not unexampled, is too rare to be assumed
without necessity. The same objection lies against the explanation of אשר

as a conjunction meaning *as, whereas, forasmuch,* or the like. The same essential meaning is obtained by making it as usual a relative pronoun, construed adverbially, a form of speech which cannot be transferred to our idiom without the introduction of a proposition. Gesenius regards it as an idiomatic pleonasm, and accordingly omits it in his version, which is simply, *thou hast prayed,* &c. Lowth follows several of the ancient versions in making it the object of the verb שמעתי (*I have heard*), which he inserts in the text on the authority of the parallel passage (2 Kings xix. 20). This emendation would be highly probable but for the fact that the sacred writers often intentionally varied their expressions in repeating the same matter, for the proof and illustration of which usage see Hengstenberg's exposition of the fourteenth and eighteenth Psalms (Commentary, vol. i. pp. 269, 372). Be this as it may, no stretch of ingenuity can make the construction in Isaiah easier or more obvious than the one in Kings. Gesenius therefore contents himself with saying that the later writer omitted שמעתי for the sake of brevity, and yet he makes him use אשר in a sense wholly different from that in which he must have used it if שמעתי were inserted. Another difference between the two texts is the use of אל here in the place of על. This agrees well enough with the hypothesis that אל is a favourite of the later writer, but not at all with the assumption that his changes were intended to remove irregularities and make the construction easy. אל may either be regarded as equivalent to על (*against*) in this connection, or be taken in the wider sense of *as to* or *concerning*.

22. *This is the word which Jehovah hath spoken concerning* (or *against*) *him. The virgin daughter of Zion hath despised thee, she hath laughed thee to scorn, the daughter of Jerusalem hath shaken her head after thee.* There is no need of giving *word* the sense of *decree*, or even *prophecy*. The simple meaning is that what follows is a revelation from God in answer to the vaunting of Sennacherib, and the prayers of Hezekiah. The two explanations of the preposition על, between which interpreters appear to be divided, differ only in extent and definiteness. For the meaning of the phrase בת ציון, see the note on chap. i. 8 ; for the construction of בתולת, that on chap. xxiii. 12. As all interpreters agree that this last word is in apposition (as to sense) with בת, so Hengstenberg supposes the latter to sustain the same relation to ציון, on which supposition the meaning of the whole phrase is, *the virgin daughter of Zion, i. e.* Zion considered as a daughter and a virgin. It may be a personification either of the whole church and nation, or of the city of Jerusalem, which last seems more appropriate in this connection. J. D. Michaelis and Hitzig understand the figure of virginity as meaning that the city was still unconquered. Calvin and Clericus, with strange inattention to the form of the original, take *virgin daughter of Zion* as a vocative, and refer the verb to the Assyrian (*he hath despised thee, O virgin,* &c.), a construction utterly prohibited, not only by the masculine form of the pronoun *thee*, which might be differently pointed, but by the feminine termination of the verbs, which is a necessary part of the text. The sense of אחריך is not merely *at thee*, but *after thee* as thou fleest. Henderson has *behind thee*, which is only defective in not suggesting the idea of his flight. Luzzatto endeavours, but without success, to explain the shaking of the head as a gesture of compassion or condolence, even where it is combined with other tokens of contempt. His argument rests wholly on a supposititious meaning of the cognate נוד. Maurer and Knobel under-

stand by *shaking* a derisive nodding or vertical motion of the head accompanied by laughter. Gesenius supposes that a wagging or lateral motion of the head, although not used by us for such a purpose, may have been common as a gesture of derision in the East, the rather as such signs are to a great extent conventional, and as other derisive gestures mentioned in the Scriptures, such as clapping the hands, are equally foreign from our habits and associations. Hitzig supposes that the shaking of the head, with the Hebrews as with us, was a gesture of negation, and that the expression of scorn consisted in a tacit denial that Sennacherib had been able to effect his purpose. Thus understood, the action is equivalent to saying in words, *no, no! i.e.* he could not do it! A similar explanation of this gesture is given by Hengstenberg in his Commentary on Psalm xxii. 8. The meaning of the whole verse, divested of its figurative dress, is that the people of God might regard the threats of the Assyrian with contempt.

23. *Whom hast thou reproached and reviled, and against whom hast thou raised (thy) voice, and lifted thine eyes (on) high towards (or against) the Holy One of Israel?* This is equivalent to saying, Dost thou know who it is that thou revilest? To raise the voice may simply mean to speak, or more emphatically to speak boldly, perhaps with an allusion to the literal loudness of Rabshakeh's address to the people on the wall (chap. xxxvi. 13). The construction *loftiness of eyes* (meaning *pride*) is inconsistent both with the pointing and accentuation. מרום is a noun of place, here construed as an adverb, and in sense equivalent to *heavenwards* or *towards heaven*. The act described is that of looking up to heaven as he uttered his blasphemies. The English and many other versions make the last words of the second clause an answer to the foregoing question. (*Against whom? &c. Against the Holy One of Israel*). This construction is retained by Gesenius, but Ewald carries the interrogation through the verse, and renders ו, at the beginning of the last clause, *that* or *so that,* while Hitzig makes the whole of that clause an exclamation. This construction is more natural than that which makes the answer begin in the middle of the last clause, instead of the beginning of the next verse, where he is expressly charged with blasphemy against Jehovah.

24. *By the hand of thy servants hast thou reproached the Lord and said, With the multitude of my chariots (or cavalry) I have ascended the height of mountains, the sides of Lebanon, and I will cut down the loftiness of its cedars and the choice of its firs (or cypresses), and I will reach its extreme height (literally, the height of its extremity), its garden-forest (literally, the garden of its forest).* This may be regarded either as the substance of another message actually sent by Sennacherib, or as a translation of his feelings and his conduct into words. *By the hand* may then mean simply *through* (as in chap. xx. 1), or refer particularly to the letters mentioned in ver. 14. The parallel passage has מלאכיך, *thy messengers,* a variation just as likely to be made by the original writer as by a later copyist. The textual reading in that passage has ברכב instead of ברב, which is given in the margin. Gesenius points the former בְּרֶכֶב, and translates the whole phrase *with my chariot of chariots* (רֶכֶב being often used collectively) *i. e.* my innumerable chariots (compare Nahum iii. 17). Ewald points it בְּרֹכֶב, *by the driving of my chariots.* The reading in the text before us, and in the margin of the other, is of course regarded as an attempt to simplify and clear up an obscure expression, a tendency diligently noted when it shews itself on the right or rather the convenient side. Vitringa gives to רֶכֶב, here as in chap. xxi. 7, the sense of *cavalry;* but other interpreters

appear to be agreed, that there is no sufficient reason, in this case, for departing from the usual and proper sense, especially as little would be gained by it, lofty and rugged mountains being scarcely more accessible to horses than to chariots. Some understand the *sides of Lebanon* strictly as denoting its acclivities; others with more probability give it the peculiar idiomatic sense of extremities, whether of length, depth, or height, the latter being here required by the connection. (See the note on chap. xiv. 13.) קומת ארזיו is explained by Clericus to mean *its standing cedars*, but by other interpreters *its lofty cedars*, as the parallel expressions mean its *choice firs* or *cypresses*. (Compare the note on chap. xiv. 8.) The explanation of *Carmel* as a proper name can only be admitted on the supposition that the pronouns in this clause refer to Hezekiah or to Judah. If on the contrary they refer to Lebanon, which seems the only natural construction, כרמל must be taken in its primary and proper sense of *fruitful field, vineyard, garden, orchard,* or the like. It is here combined with *forest,* either for the purpose of describing the cedar groves of Lebanon as similar to parks and orchards, or of designating the spot where the cultivated slope of the mountain is gradually changed into a forest. It was long supposed that the only cedar grove of Lebanon was the one usually visited near the highest summit of the range; but, in 1805, Seetzen discovered two others of greater extent, and the American missionaries have since found many trees in different parts of the mountain. (Robinson's Palestine, iii. 440.) Instead of מְרוֹם קִצוֹ the parallel passage has מְלוֹן קצֹה (*his extreme abode*), a variation both in sense and form, which Gesenius and his followers think decidedly more poetical and difficult than that before us, and of course more ancient, as the inference happens in this case to favour the foregone conclusion. Such assertions are best answered by a counter assertion, in itself at least as plausible, that the diversity is just such as might have been expected in the case of one and the same writer. The reference to Lebanon in this verse is by many interpreters literally understood; but why should the Assyrian attempt or even threaten so absurd a passage with his mounted troops, when a shorter and easier one lay open to him? Others regard Lebanon as a poetical description of the kingdom of the ten tribes, or of Judah, or of Israel in general, with special mention of Jerusalem, of the temple, or the tower of Lebanon, as its extreme height or abode. But if we take into consideration the whole context, and the strongly hyperbolical expressions of the other messages and speeches of Sennacherib, it will be found most natural to understand this verse as a poetical assertion of the speaker's power to overcome all obstacles.

25. *I have digged and drunk water, and I will dry up with the sole of my feet* (literally, *steps*) *all the streams of Egypt*. As in the preceding verse, he begins with the past tense and then changes to the future, to denote that he had begun his enterprise successfully and expected to conclude it triumphantly. The confusion of the tenses, as all futures or all preterites, is entirely arbitrary, and the translation of them all as presents is at least unnecessary, when a stricter version not only yields a good sense, but adds to the significance and force of the expressions. According to Luzzato, קוּר means to spring up or gush forth as a fountain, and the verse is a poetical description of the conqueror under the figure of a stream which drinks in its tributary waters and exhausts all other rivers in its course. This last expression the ingenious rabbin wisely disguises in a paraphrase, as he could scarcely have found any reader, Jew or Gentile, who would

tolerate the figure of one stream drying up others with the *soles of its feet.*
Another original interpretation of the verse is that proposed by Barnes, who
gives the usual explanation of the first word, but applies that clause to the
supply of the Assyrian cities with water.   The obvious objections to this
exposition are, that it does not follow, because digging of wells is a public
benefit in desert countries and among nomadic tribes, that the supply of a
great kingdom like Assyria would be so described ; but secondly and chiefly,
that the parallelism and indeed the whole connection of the clauses is destroyed by this interpretation of the first.   What coherence is there between
the assertions that he had supplied his own kingdom with water, and that his
army was numerous enough to exhaust the streams of Egypt ?   Vitringa
understands the first clause as meaning that he had sated his desire of conquest, he had sought and found, he had dug for water and slaked his thirst.
The objection to this interpretation is, not that it makes the first clause
figurative, which agrees exactly with the style of the whole passage, but
that it makes it too indefinite to match the other clause precisely.   If the
latter, as all except Luzzatto seem to grant, describes the march of a great
army, there is a natural presumption that the other has respect to the same
subject.   The best interpretation, therefore, on the whole, is that which
understands the verse to mean that no difficulties or privations could retard
his march, that where there was no water he had dug for it and found it,
and that where there was he would exhaust it, both assertions implying a vast
multitude of soldiers.   The drying up of the rivers with the soles of the feet
is understood by Vitringa as an allusion to the Egyptian mode of drawing
water with a tread-wheel (Deut. xi. 10).   Others suppose it to mean that
they would cross the streams dry-shod, which does not seem to be a natural
explanation of the words.   Bochart understands the sense to be that the
dust raised by their march would choke and dry up rivers.   In favour of
supposing an allusion to the drawing out of water, is the obvious reference
to digging and drinking in the other clause.   This appears to preclude the
explanation of the language as a boast that the elements themselves were
subject to him, not unlike that which Claudian puts into the mouth of
Alaric.   *Subsidere nostris sub pedibus montes, arescere vidimus amnes.*   Even
there, however, the literal and figurative meanings seem to run into each
other, as the poet adds a few lines lower, *fregi Alpes, galeis Padum victri-
cibus hausi.*   That such hyperboles were wont to be applied to the oriental
armies, we may learn from Juvenal.   *Credimus altos defecisse amnes,
epotaque flumina Medo.*   The old interpretation of יְאֹרֵי מָצוֹר, as meaning
the waters of Jerusalem while in a state of siege, or the moats of fortified
places in general, is now universally abandoned for the meaning which the
same words have in chap. xvi. 6.   (See above, p. 326.)

26. *Hast thou not heard?   From afar I have done it, from the days of
old, and formed it.   Now I have caused it to come, and it shall come* (or *come
to pass*), *to lay waste,* (*as* or *into*) *desolate heaps, fortified cities.*   Clericus
makes this a continuation of the speech ascribed to Sennacherib, who is
here boasting that he (*i. e.* Assyria) had created Egypt, meaning that Egypt
was peopled from Assyria, which was now about to lay it waste.   This
interpretation is refuted at great length by Vitringa, whose main objection
to it is, that Assyria was no more the founder of Egypt than of any other
ancient State.   Vitringa supposes this interpretation to have sprung from
an unwillingness to recognise the doctrine of divine decrees.   But such a
motive cannot be imputed to Calvin, who, although he agrees with most
interpreters in making these the words of God himself, refers them not to

his eternal purpose, but to his having made Jerusalem or Zion what she was, and to his fixed determination to preserve her. In order to sustain this explanation of the first clause, he is obliged to read the second interrogatively, which is altogether arbitrary. Most writers, ancient and modern, are agreed in applying the first clause, either to express predictions, or to the purpose and decree of God. The sense is then substantially the same with that of chap. x. 5, 15, to wit, that the Assyrian had wrought these conquests only as an instrument in the hand of God, who had formed and declared his purpose long before, and was now bringing it to pass. *Hast thou not heard ?* may either be a reference to history and prophecy, or a more general expression of surprise that he could be ignorant of what was so notorious.

Gesenius directs attention to the form למימי in the parallel passage (2 Kings xix. 25) as less usual; but the inference, which he evidently wishes to be drawn from this variation, is precluded by the use of the same combination here in the phrase למרחוק. A writer who, through ignorance or want of taste, took offence at the double preposition in the one word, could not have retained it in the other. Instead of ותהי, Luzzato reads ותהי, which is unnecessary, as the future is entirely appropriate. Most writers take this as the second person of the verb, *and thou shalt be*, or *that thou shouldest be*. Ewald more simply makes it the third person, agreeing with the noun to which the pronoun *it* must be referred, namely, the series of events in which Sennacherib had gloried. The parallel passage has the contracted form להשות, which, as being unusual and irregular, is supposed by Gesenius to have been amended in the later copy. For נלים Lowth reads גוים, and translates the whole phrase, *warlike nations*. Most other writers are agreed in making it mean *ruined* or *desolated heaps*. The construction is that of a double accusative, without an ellipsis of the particle, which may, however, be supplied in English.

27. *And their inhabitants are short of hand; they are broken and confounded; they are grass of the field and green herbage, grass of the house-tops and a field before the stalk* (or *standing corn*), *i. e.* before the grain has grown up. This may be regarded either as a description of the weakness of those whom the Assyrian had subdued, or as a description of the terror with which they were inspired at his approach. In the former case this verse extenuates the glory of his conquest, in the latter it enhances it. A short hand or arm implies inability to reach the object, but does not necessarily suggest the idea of mutilation. In a negative sense, it is applied to God, Num. xi. 23 ; Isa. l. 2, lix. 1. Here, as in many other cases, the particle of comparison is not expressed. *Green herbage*, literally, *the green of herbage*. Barnes supposes an allusion to the ease with which grass is trodden down by an army; but how does this cohere with the mention of grass upon the house-tops? In this last expression there is reference at once to the flat surface, the earthy material, and the various uses of the oriental house-top, in consequence of which seeds would frequently spring up there, but without depth of root, and therefore short-lived. The comparison of human frailty and infirmity to grass is very common in the Scriptures. Instead of שדמה, the parallel passage (2 Kings xix. 26) has שדפה, *blasting* or *blasted corn*, which has led some to regard שדמה either as an error of transcription or as an orthographical variation of the other word. If this be so, the text before us cannot be charged with always giving the preference to regular and familiar forms. But as the plural שדמות is elsewhere used in the sense of *fields*, this may be here retained, the idea of blast-

ing being either supplied by the connection, or omitted altogether. In the latter case, the comparison is simply with the weakness and fragility of immature grain, *field* being put by a common figure for its contents or products. The general meaning of the whole verse evidently is that they were unable to resist him.

28. *And thy sitting down, and thy going out, and thy coming in, I have known, and thy raging* (or *provoking of thyself*) *against me.* The Targum explains *sitting* to mean sitting in council, *going out*—going to war, and *coming in*—the invasion of Judah. It is commonly agreed, however, that these phrases are combined to signify all the actions of his life, like *sitting down* and *rising up* in Ps. cxxxix. 2, *going out* and *coming in*, Deut. xxviii. 6, 1 Kings iii. 7, and elsewhere, the latter especially in reference to military movements (1 Sam. xviii. 16, 2 Sam. v. 2).

29. *Because of thy raging against me, and (because) thy arrogance has come up into my ears, I will put my hook in thy nose, and my bridle in thy lips, and I will cause thee to return by the way by which thou camest.* The sense of *tumult*, given by the English and other versions to שאנן, is founded on the etymology proposed by Rabbi Jonah, who derives it, through שאון, from שאה. The more obvious derivation is from the verb שאן and its root שאן, meaning to *rest* or *be quiet*, from which we may readily deduce the ideas of security, indifference, nonchalance, superciliousness, and arrogance. However dubious the etymology may be, the whole connection makes it certain that the word is expressive of something in the conduct of Sennacherib offensive to Jehovah. In the first clause there is an abrupt change of construction from the infinitive to the finite verb, which is not uncommon in Hebrew, and which in this case does not at all obscure the sense. Another solution of the syntax is to take יע as an elliptical expression for יען אשר or יען כי, as in Num. xx. 12, and 1 Kings xx. 42, and make עלה agree with both the verbal nouns preceding. This is the construction given in the English Version. The figures in the last clause are drawn from the customary method of controlling horses, and from a less familiar mode of treating buffaloes and other wild animals, still practised in the East, and in menageries. (Compare Ezek. xix. 4, xxix. 4, xxxviii. 4, Job xli. 1.) The figure may be taken in a general sense as signifying failure and defeat, or more specifically as referring to Sennacherib's hasty flight.

30. *And this to thee* (O Hezekiah, shall be) *the sign* (of the fulfilment of the promise): *eat, the (present) year, that which groweth of itself, and the second year that which springeth of the same, and in the third year sow ye, and reap, and plant vineyards, and eat the fruit thereof.* The preceding verse closes the address to the Assyrians, begun in ver. 22, and the Prophet now continues his message to Hezekiah. It is commonly agreed that ספיח denotes voluntary growth or products, such as spring from the seed dropped before or during harvest. Most writers give a similar meaning to שחים (2 Kings xix. 29, סחיש), the etymology of which is very doubtful. Hitzig applies it, in a wider sense, to spontaneous products generally, such as milk, honey, &c. Aquila and Theodotion render the two words αὐτόματα and αὐτοφυῆ. Symmachus and Jerome make the second mean *apples.* As to the general meaning of the verse, there are two opinions. Rosenmüller, Augusti, and Gesenius understand the infinitive אכול as referring to the past. The sense will then be that although the cultivation of the land had been interrupted for the last two years, yet now in this third year they might safely resume it. To this interpretation it may be objected, that it

arbitrarily makes *the year* mean the year before the last, and no less arbitrarily assumes that the infinitive is here used for preterite. The later German writers seem to have gone back to the old and obvious interpretation, which refers the whole verse to the future. This is grammatically more exact, because it takes *the year* in a sense analogous to that of *the day*, the common Hebrew phrase for *this day*, and assimilates the infinitives to the imperatives which follow. Thus understood, the verse is a prediction that for two years the people should subsist upon the secondary fruits of what was sown two years before, but that in the third year they should till the ground, as usual, implying that Sennacherib's invasion should before that time be at an end. But why should this event be represented as so distant, when the context seems to speak of Sennacherib's discomfiture and flight as something which immediately ensued? Of this two explanations have been given. The one is, that the year in which these words were utttered was a sabbatical year, and the next the year of Jubilee, during neither of which the Jews were allowed to cultivate the ground, so that the resumption of the tillage was of course postponed to the third. It is no conclusive objection to this theory, that the chronological hypothesis which it involves cannot be possibly proved. The difficulty in all such cases arises from the very absence of positive proof, and the necessity of choosing between different possibilities. A more serious objection is, that the mode of subsistence for the two first years seems to be mentioned, not as a mere preparation for what follows, but as a substantive prediction. Even this, however, would be of no weight in opposition to an hypothesis which accounts for the known facts and explains the language of the passage. The other solution of the difficulty is, that Sennacherib was now on his way to Egypt, and that the Prophet expected his return within a year, by which the Jews would be again deterred from making the usual provision for their own subsistence, and thus the crops of two years would be lost. But such an expectation of the Prophet would have been falsified by the Assyrian's immediate retreat to his own country, and however this may recommend the supposition to those who refuse to admit his inspiration, it can have no weight with those who regard him as a Prophet. The proofs of his divine legation and foreknowledge are so many and various, that when two hypotheses present themselves, the one which clashes with his inspiration is of course to be rejected. The only remaining question is, wherein the sign consisted, or in what sense the word *sign* is to be understood. Some take it in its strongest sense of *miracle*, and refer it, either to the usual divine interposition for the subsistence of the people during the sabbatical years, or to the miraculous provision promised in this particular case. Others understand it here as simply meaning an event inseparable from another, either as an antecedent or a consequent, so that the promise of the one is really a pledge of the other. Thus the promise that the children of Israel would worship at mount Sinai was a *sign* to Moses that they should first leave Egypt, and the promised birth of the Messiah was a *sign* that the Jewish nation should continue till he came. (See above, vol. i. p. 170.)

31. *And the escaped* (literally *the escape*) *of the house of Judah, that is left, shall again take root downward and bear fruit upward.* This verse foretells by a familiar figure, the returning prosperity of Judah. יָסַף usually means to *add*, and is taken here by Hendewerk in the sense of enlarging or increasing. Gesenius seems to make it simply equivalent to the English *take* or *strike* in a similar connection. Ewald and the older writers understand it as implying repetition, an idea which may be expressed in trans-

lation by *again, anew,* or *afresh.* For the peculiar use of the abstract noun
פליטה, see above, chap. iv. 2, x. 20, xv. 9.

32. *For out of Jerusalem shall go forth a remnant, and an escape from mount
Zion; the zeal of Jehovah of hosts shall do this.* For the meaning of the
last clause, see the commentary on chap. ix. 8. The first clause is an explanation of the use of the words פליטה and נשארה in the foregoing verse.
Grotius (on 2 Kings. xix. 31) understands the *going forth* literally of the
people being pent up in Jerusalem, but now set at large by the retreat of
the invaders, and again quotes from Virgil, *Panduntur portæ; juvat ire et
Dorica castra desertosque videre locos.* (See above, on chap. xxxiii. 17).
But it is much more natural to understand it figuratively like the preceding verse, and as denoting simply that some in Jerusalem or Zion shall be
saved.

33. *Therefore* (because Jehovah has determined to fulfil these promises),
*thus saith Jehovah (with respect) to the king of Assyria, He shall not come to
this city, and shall not shoot an arrow there, and shall not come before it with
a shield* (or *a shield shall not come before it*), *and shall not cast up a mound
against it.* Some understand this as meaning simply that he should not
take the city, others that he should not even attack it. מגן has its ordinary sense of *shield,* and not that of συνασπισμός or *testudo.* In favour of
the usual construction of יקדמנה is the fact that all the other verbs have
Jehovah for their subject. Some translate אל *into,* which is favoured
neither by the usage of the particle nor by the context, which relates to
movements of the enemy without the walls. Calvin understands by סללה
the *balista,* or ancient engine for projecting stones and other missiles, a
gratuitous expedient to evade an imaginary difficulty, as to the use of the
verb שפך, which usually means to *pour,* but may also be applied to excavation and the heaping up of earth. This verse seems to shew that Jerusalem was not actually besieged by the Assyrians, or at least not by the
main body of the army under Sennacherib himself, unless we assume that
he had already done so and retreated, and regard this as a promise that
the attempt should not be repeated.

34. *By the way that he came shall he return, and to this city shall he
not come, saith Jehovah.* The first clause may simply mean that he shall
go back whence he came, or more specifically, that he shall retreat without
turning aside to attack Jerusalem, either for the first or second time. The
construction given in the English Bible (*by the same shall he return*) makes
בה emphatic and connects it with the following verb. This is also the
Masoretic interpunction; but according to analogy and usage, it belongs to
what precedes and must be joined with אשר, as the usual Hebrew expression for *in which.*

35. *And I will cover over* (or *protect*) *this city,* (*so as*) *to save it, for
my own sake, and for the sake of David my servant.* This does not mean
that the faith or piety of David, as an individual, should be rewarded in
his descendants, but that the promise made to him respecting his successors, and especially the last and greatest of them, should be faithfully performed. (See 2 Sam. vii. 12, 13). It is equally arbitrary, therefore, to
make *David* here the name of the Messiah, and to infer, as Hitzig does,
from this mention of David, that vers. 32–35 are by a later writer.
Knobel, on the contrary, notes it as characteristic of Isaiah, and refers to
chap. ix. 6, xi. 1, 10; xxix. 1, as parallel examples. Umbreit says the
genuineness of these verses can be called in question only by a perfectly

uncritical scepticism (*Zweifelsucht*).   The terms of the promise in the first clause may be compared with those of chap. xxxiii. 5.

36. *And the angel of Jehovah went forth, and smote in the camp of Assyria an hundred and eighty and five thousand, and they* (the survivors or the Jews) *rose early in the morning, and behold all of them* (that were smitten) *were dead corpses.*   Various attempts have been made to extenuate this miracle, by reading אֵלֶף for אֶלֶף, (*chiefs* instead of *thousands*), or by supposing that the vast number mentioned were in danger of death from the plague or otherwise.   Others, unable to explain it away, and yet unwilling to admit the fact recorded, resort to the cheap and trite expedient of calling it a *myth* or a traditional exaggeration.   Such assertions admit of no refutation, because there is nothing to refute.   Receiving, as these very authors do, the other statements of the context as historical, they have no right to single this out as a fabrication.   If it is one, then the rest may be so too, for we know that fictitious writers do not confine themselves to prodigies and wonders, but often imitate the actual occurrences of real life.   In the fact itself, there is nothing incredible.   Those who reject it themselves refer to the enormous ravages of the plague.   If the population of whole cities may be buried in a night by a flow of lava, or in an instant by an earthquake, what is there to shock the understanding in the statement of the text, especially on the supposition, favoured by these same interpreters, that the *angel of Jehovah* is a Hebraism for the plague, or some other physical cause or means of destruction.   But even if we give the phrase its usual sense, " there is," to use the words of Barnes, " no more improbability in the existence of a good angel than there is in the existence of a good man, or in the existence of an evil spirit than there is in the existence of a bad man ; there is no more improbability in the supposition that God employs invisible and heavenly messengers to accomplish his purposes than there is that he employs men."   There is consequently no need of departing from the strict sense of the words, or of disputing whether by the angel of the Lord we are to understand a storm, a hot wind, or a pestilential fever.   As little necessity or reason is there for attempting to make the verse descriptive of a gradual or protracted mortality, so that every morning when they rose there was nothing to be seen but corpses.   The terms used can naturally signify nothing but a single instantaneous stroke of divine vengeance, and the parallel passage (2 Kings xix. 35) says expressly that the angel smote this number *in that night.*   Sceptical critics would be glad to have it in their power to plead the silence of profane tradition as an objection to the narrative before us.   But although such an inference would be wholly inconclusive, even if the fact were so, it happens in this case that the fact is not so.   The account which Herodotus received from the Egyptian priests, as to Sennacherib's retreat from Pelusium, occasioned by an irruption of field-mice, which Vulcan sent to rescue Sethos, who was priest to that divinity as well as king of Egypt, is admitted by the latest German writers, notwithstanding the denial of Gesenius, to be an evident variation of this history, not more corrupt than in many other cases where the identity of origin has never been disputed.   The transfer of the scene of the event to Egypt, and the substitution of Sethos and Vulcan for Hezekiah and Jehovah, are in strict accordance with the common practice of the ancient nations, to connect the most remarkable events, by their traditions, with their own early history.   Even the figment of the mice may be regarded as a change of no unusual character or magnitude, unless we choose to assume, with J. D. Michaelis, that it was founded on a

misconception of the mouse as the hieroglyphical emblem of destruction. The ancient date of the tradition was attested, in the days of Herodotus himself, by a statue of Sethos in the temple of Vulcan, holding a mouse in his hand, with the inscription ἐς ἐμέ τις ὀρέων εὐσεβὴς ἔστω. The parallel narrative in 2 Chron. xxxii. 21, instead of numbering the slain, says that all the mighty men of valour, and the leaders, and the captains in the camp of the Assyrian were cut off. Where this terrific overthrow took place, whether before Jerusalem, or at Libnah, or at some intervening point, has been disputed, and can never be determined, in the absence of all data, monumental or historical. Throughout the sacred narrative, it seems to be intentionally left uncertain whether Jerusalem was besieged at all, whether Sennacherib in person ever came before it, whether his army was divided or united when the stroke befell them, and also what proportion of the host escaped. It is enough to know that one hundred and eighty-five thousand men perished in a single night.

37. *Then decamped, and departed, and returned, Sennacherib king of Assyria, and dwelt* (or *remained*) *in Nineveh.* The form of expression in the first clause is thought by some writers to resemble Cicero's famous description of Catiline's escape (*abiit, excessit, evasit, erupit*), the rapid succession of the verbs suggesting the idea of confused and sudden flight. His dwelling in Nineveh is supposed by some interpreters to be mentioned as implying that he went forth no more to war, at least not against the Jews. An old tradition says that he lived only fifty days after his return ; but according to other chronological hypothesis, he reigned eighteen years longer, and during that interval waged war successfully against the Greeks, and founded Tarsus in Cilicia.

38. *And he was worshipping* (*in*) *the house of Nisroch his god, and Adrammelech and Sharezer his sons smote him with the sword, and they escaped* (literally, *saved themselves*) *into the land of Ararat, and Esarhaddon his son reigned in his stead.* The Jews have a tradition that Sennacherib intended to sacrifice his sons, and that they slew him in self defence. Another tradition is, that he had fled into the temple of his god as an asylum. A simpler supposition is, that the time of his devotions was chosen by his murderers, as one when he would be least guarded or suspicious. Hendewerk cites, as parallel instances of monarchs murdered while at prayer, the cases of the Caliph Omar, and the emperor Leo V. For the various derivations of the name *Nisroch* which have been proposed, see Gesenius's Thesaurus, tom. ii. p. 892. The name *Adrammelech* occurs in 2 Kings xvii. 31, as that of a Mesopotamian or Assyrian idol. Berosus has *Ardumusanus*, and Abydenus *Adramelus*, which are obvious corruptions of the Hebrew or Aramean name. In like manner *Esarhaddon* is called *Asordanius* by Berosus, and *Axerdis* by Abydenus, who moreover has *Nergilus* instead of *Sharezer*, a discrepancy which seems to be explained by the combination *Nergal-sharezer* (Jer. xxxix. 3, 13). Supposing this to have been the full name of Sennacherib's son, one half would seem to have been preserved by Abydenus, and the other by Isaiah. *Ararat*, both here and in Gen. viii. 4, is the name of a region, corresponding more or less exactly to *Armenia*, or to that part of it in which the ark rested. The Armenians still call their country by this name. From the expression *mountains of Ararat* (Gen. viii. 4), has sprung the modern practice of applying this name to the particular eminence where Noah landed. The country of Ararat is described by Smith and Dwight, in their Researches in

Armenia, vol. ii. p. 73, &c. The original name is retained in the Vulgate, while the Septuagint renders it 'Αρμενία.

Chapter 38

THIS chapter contains an account of Hezekiah's illness and miraculous recovery, together with a Psalm which he composed in commemoration of his sufferings and deliverance. The parallel passage (2 Kings xx. 1–11) varies more from that before us than in the preceding chapter. So far as they are parallel, the narrative in Kings is more minute and circumstantial, and at the same time more exactly chronological in its arrangement. On the other hand, the Psalm is wholly wanting in that passage. All these circumstances favour the conclusion that the text before us is the first draught, and the other a repetition by the hand of the same writer.

1. *In those days Hezekiah was sick unto death, and Isaiah the son of Amoz, the Prophet, came to him, and said to him, Thus saith Jehovah, Order thy house, for thou (art) dying, and art not to live.* As Hezekiah survived this sickness fifteen years (ver. 5), and reigned in all twenty-nine (2 Kings xviii. 2), *those days* must be restricted to the fourteenth year, which was that of the Assyrian invasion. Whether this sickness was before the great catastrophe, as Usher, Lightfoot, and Prideaux suppose, or after it, as Calvin, Vitringa, and Gesenius think, is not a question of much exegetical importance. The first opinion is sustained by the authority of the Seder Olam, the last by that of Josephus. In favour of the first is the promise in ver. 6, according to its simplest and most obvious meaning, though it certainly admits of a wider application. It is also favoured by the absence of allusions to the slaughter of Sennacherib's host in the song of Hezekiah. But on the other hand, his prayer is only for recovery from sickness, without any reference to siege or invasion. Vitringa objects to this hypothesis, that the king of Babylon, who was tributary to Assyria, would not have dared to send a message of congratulation to Hezekiah before the destruction of the host. But even granting this, which might be questioned, and admitting the assumed fact as to the dependence of the king of Babylon, why may we not suppose that the catastrophe occurred in the interval between Hezekiah's sickness and the embassy from Merodach-baladan ? Calvin objects to the hypothesis which makes the sickness previous in date to the destruction of the host, that it would not have been omitted in its proper place. It is altogether natural, however, that the Prophet, after carrying the history of Sennacherib to its conclusion, should go back to complete that of Hezekiah also. לָמוּת strictly means *to die, i. e.* so as to be ready to die, or at the point of death. An analogous Greek phrase (ἀσθένεια πρὸς θάνατον) is used in John xi. 4, to denote a sickness actually fatal. Here it expresses merely tendency or danger, the natural and necessary course of things without a special intervention. *Order thy house* is ambiguous, both in Hebrew and in English. The לְ may express relation in general, or indicate the object of address. In the former case the sense will be, give orders with respect to thy house. (LXX. τάξαι περὶ τοῦ οἴκου σου). In the latter, order or command thy household, *i. e.* make known to them thy last will. Grotius quotes from Plutarch the analogous expression, ἐντέλλεσθαι τοῖς οἰκείοις. In either case, the general idea is that of a final settling of his affairs, in the prospect of death. (Compare 2 Sam. xvii. 23). There is no need of departing from the strict sense of מֵת as an active par-

ticiple. The modern writers infer from the treatment described in ver. 21, and said to be still practised in the East, that Hezekiah had the plague, which would make it less improbable that this was the instrument employed in the destruction of Sennacherib's army. Of those who make the sickness subsequent to this great deliverance, some suppose the former to have been intended, like the thorn in Paul's flesh, to preserve Hezekiah from being *exalted above measure.* That he was not wholly free from the necessity of such a check, may be inferred from his subsequent conduct to the Babylonian envoys.

2. *And Hezekiah turned his face to the wall, and prayed to Jehovah.* Jerome understands by *the wall* that of his heart, Vatablus the side of his bed, Jonathan the wall of the temple, towards which Daniel prayed (Dan. vi. 11). But this last was a practice which arose during the exile, and even the promise in 1 Kings viii. 25 has reference to that condition. The obvious meaning is the wall of the room, towards which he turned, not merely to collect his thoughts, or to conceal his tears, but as a natural expression of strong feeling. As Ahab turned his face toward the wall in anger (1 Kings xx. 2), so Hezekiah does the same in grief. There is no need of supposing with Lowth, that the bed was in the corner of the room, so that he could not turn either way without looking towards the wall. Calvin regards the conduct of Hezekiah in this, and all other parts of the narrative, as an eminent example of pious resignation. Vitringa seems to admit that the effect here described was connected in some degree with Hezekiah's undue attachment to the things of this life. Grotius ascribes it to the indistinct views then enjoyed of a future state. Josephus thinks he was the more distressed because he had as yet no heir, since Manasseh was not born till three years afterwards (2 Kings xxi. 1).

3. *And he said, Ah Jehovah, remember, I beseech thee, how I have walked before thee in truth and with a whole heart, and that which is good in thine eyes I have done; and Hezekiah wept a great weeping.* The figure of *walking before God* includes the ideas of communion with him and subjection to him, and is therefore more comprehensive than the kindred phrase of *walking with* him. By *truth* we are here to understand sincerity and constancy. The explanation of שלם by Gesenius as meaning *devoted* (like the Arabic مسلم *Moslim*) is justified neither by Hebrew etymology nor usage, which require it to be taken in the sense of *whole* or *perfect*, as opposed to any essential defect. The reference of this and the following phrase to freedom from idolatry and zeal for the worship of Jehovah, is too limited. This verse is not an angry expostulation, nor an ostentatious self-praise, but an appeal to the only satisfactory evidence of his sincerity. Calvin supposes Hezekiah to be here resisting a temptation to despondency arising from the sudden intimation of approaching death. אָנָּה is a strong expression of entreaty. It is more regularly written elsewhere אָנָּא. Hitzig supposes it to be a contraction of אַל-נָא (Gen. xix. 7); but as it is also used where there is no negation, it is better to derive it with Gesenius from אָן and נָא.

4. *And the word of Jehovah was* (or *came*) *to Isaiah, saying* (what follows in the next verse). Calvin supposes a considerable time to have elapsed before this second message was sent ; but he seems to have overlooked the more particular statement in the parallel passage (2 Kings xx. 4), that the word of the Lord came to him *before he had gone out of the middle court* (according to the keri), or the *middle city* (according to the kethib). The former reading is found in the ancient versions, but the latter as usual is

supposed to be more ancient by the latest critics. The *middle city* may either mean the middle of the city (*media urbs*), or a particular part of Jerusalem so called, perhaps that in which the temple stood, or more generally that which lay between the *upper city* on mount Zion and the *lower city* on mount Akra. The communication may have been through the *middle gate* mentioned by Jeremiah (xxxix. 3). In either case, the interval could not have been a long one, though sufficient to try the faith of Hezekiah. The omission of these words in the text before us is ascribed by Knobel to ignorance of the localities on the part of a writer, living after the exile. It might have been supposed that even such a writer, living on the spot and with the older Scriptures in his hands, would have enjoyed as good opportunities of understanding such a point as Knobel himself.

5. *Go and say to Hezekiah, Thus saith Jehovah, the God of David thy father, I have heard thy prayer, I have seen thy tears* (or *weeping*); *behold, I am adding* (or *about to add*) *unto thy days fifteen years.* The parallel passage (2 Kings xx. 5) has: *return and say to Hezekiah, the chief* (or *leader*) *of my people, Thus saith Jehovah,* &c. After *tears* it adds: *behold,* (*I am*) *healing* (or *about to heal*) *thee; on the third day thou shalt go up to the house of Jehovah.* David is particularly mentioned as the person to whom the promise of perpetual succession had been given (2 Sam. vii. 12). The construction of הִנְנִי יוֹסֵף is the same as in chap. xxix. 14. Gesenius and the rest of that school set this down of course as undoubtedly a prophecy *ex eventu*, because (says Knobel with great *naïveté*) Isaiah could not know how long Hezekiah was to live. Hendewerk adds that Jehovah is here represented as changing his mind, and directly contradicting himself. To this no further answer is necessary than what Calvin had said long before, to wit, that the threatening in ver. 1 was conditional, and that the second message was designed from the beginning no less than the first. The design of the whole proceeding is well explained by Vitringa to have been to let Hezekiah feel his obligation to a special divine interposition for a recovery which might otherwise have seemed the unavoidable effect of ordinary causes.

6. *And out of the hand of the king of Assyria I will save thee and this city, and I will cover over* (or *protect*) *this city.* Hitzig, Hendewerk, and Knobel, with some of the older writers, infer from this verse that the army of Sennacherib was still in Judah. Gesenius and Rosenmüller follow Calvin and Vitringa in referring it to subsequent attacks or apprehensions. This is really more natural, because it accounts for the addition of this promise to that of a prolonged life. The connection, as explained by Calvin, is, that he should not only live fifteen years longer, but should be free from the Assyrians during that time. The parallel passage (2 Kings xx. 6) adds, *for my own sake and for the sake of David my servant,* as in chap. xxxvii. 35. Had this addition been made in the text before us, it would of course have been an instance of repetition and assimilation symptomatic of a later writer.

7. *And this* (*shall be*) *to thee the sign from Jehovah, that Jehovah will perform this word which he hath spoken.* The English Version has *a sign;* but the article is emphatic, *the* (*appointed*) *sign* (*proceeding*) *from Jehovah* (not merely from the Prophet). The translation *this thing*, although justified by usage, is here inadmissible because unnecessary. The parallel narrative in Kings is much more circumstantial. What occurs below, as the last two verses of this chapter, there stands in its regular chronological order, between the promise of recovery and the announcement of the sign,

so that the latter appears to have been given in compliance with Hezekiah's own request and choice. " And Isaiah said, This (shall be) to thee the sign from Jehovah, that Jehovah will perform the thing which he hath spoken ; shall the shadow advance ten degrees, or shall it recede ten degrees ? And Hezekiah said, It is a light thing for the shadow to decline ten degrees: nay, but let the shadow return backward ten degrees " (2 Kings xx. 9, 10). As to the transposition of vers. 21, 22, see below.

8. *Behold, I* (am) *causing the shadow to go back, the degrees which it has gone down* (or *which have gone down*) *on the degrees of Ahaz with the sun, ten degrees backward; and the sun returned ten degrees on the degrees which it had gone down.* As to the nature of the phenomenon here described, there are three opinions. The first is, that the Prophet took advantage of a transient obscuration, or of some unusual refraction, to confirm the king's belief of what he promised. The second is, that the whole is a myth or legend of a later date. The third is, that Isaiah did actually exhibit a supernatural attestation of the truth of his prediction. This is supposed by some to have consisted merely in the foresight of a natural phenomenon, while others regard the phenomenon itself as miraculous. Of these last, some again suppose a mere miraculous appearance, others an actual disturbance of the ordinary course of nature. This last is not a question of much exegetical or practical importance, since it neither can nor need be ascertained whether the course of the sun (or of the earth around it) was miraculously changed, or the shadow miraculously rendered independent of the sun which caused it. The former hypothesis is favoured by the statement that *the sun went back*, if taken in its strictest and most obvious sense, although it may be understood as a metonymy of the cause for the effect. At any rate, little would appear to be gained by paring down a miracle to certain dimensions, when, even on the lowest supposition, it can only be ascribed to the almighty power of God, with whom all things are not only possible, but equally easy. The choice is not between a greater and lesser miracle, but between a miracle, a myth, and a trick. The last two suppositions are so perfectly gratuitous, as well as impious, that no believer in the possibility of either miracle or inspiration can entertain them for a moment. And if thus shut up to the assumption of a miracle, it matters little whether it be great or small. It is enough that God alone could do it or infallibly predict it. As to the disproportion of the miracle to the occasion, it remains substantially the same on any supposition which involves a real miracle at all. If this be admitted, and the historical truth of the narrative assumed, the safest course is to expound it in its simplest and most obvious sense. Another question in relation to this verse, of far less moment in itself, has given rise to. a vast amount of learned and ingenious controversy. This is the question, whether the *degrees* here mentioned were the graduated scale of a dial or the steps of a staircase. In this dispute, besides the exegetical writers on Isaiah and the second book of Kings, we meet with the great names of Usher, Petavius, Salmasius, Scaliger, and others of eminent repute but later date. It is important to observe that there is no word in the text necessarily denoting such an instrument. By comparing the text and margin of the common English Version, it would seem that the translators were disposed to put this sense upon the words מעלות אחז בשמש, which they render, *the sun-dial of Ahaz*, but which literally mean, *the degrees of Ahaz in* (or *by*) *the sun*. So, too, the Targum has *hour-stone* (אבן שעיא), and the Vulgate *horologium*. The only word corresponding to all this in the original is מעלות, which, like

the Latin *gradus*, first means *steps*, and then *degrees*. The nearest approach to the description of a dial is in the words *degrees of Ahaz*. This circumstance may shew that the reference to a dial, properly so called, is not so obvious or necessary in the Hebrew text as in the English Version. It was further alleged by Scaliger, and other early writers on the subject, that the use of dials was unknown in the days of Hezekiah. Later investigations have destroyed the force of this objection, and made it probable that solar chronometers of some sort were in use among the Babylonians at a very early period, and that Ahaz may have borrowed the invention from them, as he borrowed other things from the Assyrians (2 Kings xvi. 10). There is therefore no historical necessity for assuming, with Scaliger, that the shadow here meant was the shadow cast upon the steps of the palace, called the *stairs of Ahaz*, because he had built them or the house itself. The only question is, whether this is not the simplest and most obvious explanation of the words, and one which entirely exhausts their meaning. If so, we may easily suppose the shadow to have been visible from Hezekiah's chamber, and the offered sign to have been suggested to the Prophet by the sight of it. This hypothesis relieves us from the necessity of accounting for the division into ten or rather twenty degrees, as Hezekiah was allowed to choose between a precession and a retrocession of the same extent (2 Kings xx. 9). These two opinions are by no means so irreconcilable as they may at first sight seem. Even supposing *the degrees of Ahaz* to have been an instrument constructed for the purpose of measuring time, it does not follow that it must have been a dial of modern or of any very artificial structure. A Jewish writer, quoted by Grotius, describes it as a globe within a concave hemisphere, casting its shadow on the concave surface. But besides the arbitrary character of this supposition, it does not account for the description of the shadow as descending with the sun, since the shadow on such an instrument would ascend as the sun descended. Knobel imagines that there may have been an artificial eminence or mound, with steps or terraces surrounding it, on which the shadow cast by an obelisk or gnomon at the summit would grow longer as the day declined, or, in other words, descend with the descending sun. But a still more simple supposition is, that the gnomon was erected on a staircase of suitable exposure, or that a column at the top cast a shadow which was found available for a rude measurement of time. The minor questions, whether the gnomon was designed to be such, or was erected for some other purpose, and whether מַעֲלוֹת means ordinary steps or astronomical degrees, do not affect the essential fact, that the recession of the shadow was perceptible in such a situation and on such a scale as to be altogether incontestable. הַמַּעֲלוֹת may either be connected with what goes before (*the shadow of the degrees*), or construed as an accusative of measure (*the degrees which it has gone down*).

9. *A writing of Hezekiah, king of Judah, when he was sick, and lived* (*i.e.* recovered) *from his sickness*. This is the title or inscription of the following Psalm (vers. 10–20), not inserted by a copyist or compiler, but prefixed, according to the ancient oriental usage, by the author himself, and therefore forming an integral part of the text. The title מִכְתָּם, prefixed to several of the Psalms, is regarded by Gesenius as an orthographical variation of the word (מִכְתָּב) here used. Others derive the former from a different root, but suppose its form to be copied from the one before us. (See Hengstenberg on Psalm xvi. 1.) The specific senses put upon this word by the Septuagint (*prayer*), the Targum (*confession*), and Gesenius (*song*), are inferred from the contents of the passage itself, and do not belong to the

Hebrew word, which simply means a *writing*. The particle prefixed is strictly equivalent neither to *by* nor *of*, but means *belonging to*, as in the frequent formulas לדוד and למנצח in the titles of the Psalms, *belonging to David* (as the author), *belonging to the chief musician* (as the performer). The conjecture of Grotius, that Isaiah dictated the psalm, or put it into Hezekiah's mouth, is perfectly gratuitous. That Hezekiah should compose a psalm, is not more strange than that he should make a collection of Proverbs (Prov. xxv. 1). It would have been far more strange if one so much like David in character and spirit had not followed his example in the practice of devotional composition. The inspiration and canonical authority of this production are clear from its having been incorporated by Isaiah in his prophecies, although omitted in the second book of Kings. The questions raised by some interpreters, as to its antiquity and genuineness, are founded on the mere possibility, that the passage may be of later date and by another writer. So far as we have evidence, either external or internal, there is not the slightest ground for critical misgiving. The ב at the beginning of the last clause does not mean *concerning his sickness*, indicating the subject of the composition, but, as usual before an infinitive, denotes the time of the action. This is by most writers understood to be, *after he had been sick* and *had recovered*, as explained in the Vulgate (cum ægrotasset et convaluisset). The words, in themselves considered, would more naturally seem to mean, *during his sickness and recovery*, and are accordingly explained by Hitzig. There is nothing in the Psalm itself at all inconsistent with the supposition, that it was conceived and perhaps composed, if not reduced to writing, before the complete fulfilment of the promise in the king's recovery. The contrary hypothesis has tended to embarrass and perplex the interpretation, as will be more distinctly seen below. The idiomatic phrase to *live from sickness*, in the sense of convalescence or recovery, occurs repeatedly elsewhere, either fully or in an abbreviated form. (See for example 1 Kings i. 2 ; Gen. xx. 7.)

10. *I said in the pause of my days I shall go into the gates of the grave, I am deprived of the rest of my years.* The pronoun of the first person does not seem to be emphatic or distinctive, as it usually is when separately written, but appears to be expressed for the sake of a euphonic or rhythmical effect. The words בדמי ימי may naturally qualify either the foregoing or the following verb, *I said in the pause of my days*, or, *in the pause of my days I shall go ;* but the latter construction is favoured by the accents, and by the analogy of the following verse, where אמרתי is immediately succeeded by the words which he uttered. The explanation of דמי ימי, as meaning *the blood of my days*, is unnatural in itself, and requires an arbitrary change of pointing. Kimchi gives דמי the sense of *cutting off* (כריתה), derived from נדמה. (See above, the note on chap. vi. 5.) Most interpreters regard it as synonymous with דָמִי silence, stillness, though they differ as to the application of the figures. Schmidius supposes it to mean the standing still of the sun, or its apparent pause at noonday, and then noon itself, or what the Greeks call ἡ μεσημβρία τοῦ βίου, and ourselves, the meridian of life. This may also be the meaning of the Septuagint version (ἐν τῷ ὕψει τῶν ἡμερῶν μου), in the height (or zenith) of my days, although Clericus and others confidentially allege that the Seventy for דמי read רמי, of which there is no example elsewhere. Umbreit understands by the stillness of his days the period of life when the passions cease to govern and the character becomes more calm. Gesenius applies it to the reign of Hezekiah, and supposes him to mean that he was about to be cut off when he had every

prospect of a peaceful reign. Even Kimchi's sense of *cutting off* is reconcilable with this explanation of דמי as meaning silence, then cessation. The general idea is correctly given in the Vulgate (*dimidio*), which Gesenius gratuitously thinks may be a mere conjecture from the Latin *demi*, but which is much more likely to have been suggested by the analogous expression in Ps. cii. 25, *I said, O my God, take me not away in the midst of my days* (בחצי ימי). There is not the slightest ground, however, for supposing this last to be the true text here. The preposition before *gates* may mean either *to, through,* or *into ;* 'but the last is its usual sense after verbs of motion. As parallel expressions, may be mentioned *the gates of death* (Ps. ix. 14), and *the gates of hell* (Mat. xvi. 18). The verb פָּקַד means *to visit,* and especially to visit for the purpose either of *inspection* or *punishment.* From the former of these applications springs the secondary sense of *missing* or finding wanting. This is adopted here by Gesenius, so as to make the last clause mean, *I shall be missed* (by my acquaintances and friends) *during the rest of my years.* But nature and the context shew that Hezekiah's thoughts were running upon what he was to miss himself. Besides, the future meaning given to the preterite is, in this case, gratuitous, and therefore ungrammatical. A much better use of the same general sense is made by those who take the Pual as a causative passive, *I am made to miss* or *lose the rest of my years,* or, as the English Version has it, *I am deprived* of them. It is better still, however, because more in accordance with the tone and spirit of the whole composition, to understand the verb as expressing not mere loss or privation, but penal infliction. It was because Hezekiah regarded the threatened abbreviation of his life as a token of God's wrath, that he so importunately deprecated it. Instead of the *remainder,* Cube and Dathe read *the best part* of my days, but without an adequate authority from usage.

11. *I said, I shall not see Jah, Jah in the land of the living ; I shall not behold man again* (or *longer*) *with the inhabitants of the world.* יה יה is not an error of the text for יהוה (Houbigant), but an intensive repetition similar to those in vers. 17–19. Or the second may be added to explain and qualify the first. He did expect to see God, but not in the land of the living. This is better than to make the second יה the subject of a distinct proposition, as Luzzatto does, *I shall not see Jah,* (*for*) *Jah* (*is only to be seen*) *in the land of the living.* The same writer regards this as the appropriate name of God considered as a gracious being. He supposes it to have been originally an exclamation of delight or joy, corresponding to וָי (*oὐaί, vae*), as an exclamation of distress or fear, from the combination of which arose the name יהוה, denoting an object both of love and fear. For other explanations of the name יָה, see above, on chap. xii. 1, and xxvi. 4. The *land of the living* is not the Holy Land (Hendewerk), but the present life. The preposition עִם may connect what follows either with the subject or the object of the verb ; *I with the inhabitants,* or, *man with the inhabitants.* חדל, which strictly means *cessation,* is regarded by the older writers as a description of this transitory life or fleeting world. Vitringa objects, that he would not have regretted leaving such a world, and therefore applies חדל to the state of death. *I, with* (or *among*) *the inhabitants of* (*the land of*) *stillness, shall no more see man.* This is adopted by Gesenius and the other modern writers. It may be objected, however, that it needlessly violates the parallelism, on which so much stress is elsewhere laid, and which plainly indicates in this case, that the last words of the verse bear the same rela-

tion to *I shall not see man*, that the words *in the land of the living* bear to
I shall not see Jah. If the latter designate the place in which he was no
more to see God, then the former would naturally seem to designate the
place in which he was no more to see man. Another reason for preferring
the old interpretation is afforded by the obvious affinity between the expression here and that in Ps. xlix. 2. *Hear this, all the nations; give ear, all the
inhabitants of the world* (ישבי חלד). That the text in one of these cases is
to be corrected by the other, or that one of them arose from misapprehension of the other, are superficial and uncritical assumptions. That the one
was suggested by the other, but with an intentional change of form, so as to
furnish two descriptions of the present life, alike in sound but not identical
is sense, is not only probable in itself, but perfectly in keeping with the
genius of the language and the usage of the sacred writers. (See above,
chap. xxxvii. 24.) As to the objection, that Hezekiah would not have been
loath to leave a world so transient and unsatisfying, it is not only contradicted by experience, but admits of this solution, that its transitory nature
was the very thing for which he grieved.

12. *My dwelling is plucked up and uncovered by me* (or *away from me*)
*like a shepherd's tent. I have rolled up, like the weaver, my life; from the
thrum he will cut me off; from day to night thou wilt finish me.* The same
thing is here represented by two figures. The first is that of a tent, the
stakes of which are pulled up, and the covering removed, with a view to
departure. The usual sense of דור (*generation*) seems inappropriate here.
For that of *age* or *life* there is no authority in usage. That of *dwelling* is
founded on the Arabic analogy, and yields a good sense, not only here but
in Ps. xlix. 20. Most interpreters explain נגלה as meaning *removed* or *departed*, a sense which it has not elsewhere. Its usual sense, *uncovered*, is
entirely appropriate, and exactly descriptive of a part of the process of striking a tent. The מני may then be understood, either as referring the act
described to the speaker, or as making him the object from which the removal was to take place. On the latter hypothesis, some of the German
writers enter into profound discussions whether Hezekiah meant to identify
the *Ich* or personal principle with his body or his soul, or with both,
or with neither. The second figure is that of a web completed and removed
by the weaver from the loom. The old interpretation of קפדתי makes it
mean *cut off*; the modern one *rolled up*; the allusion in either case being
to a weaver's mode of finishing his work. To make this verb passive or
reflexive, is entirely arbitrary. Still more so is a change of person from
the first to the second, since the same succession of the first, second, and
third persons reappears in the next verse. It is not even necessary to make
the verb causative (*I have caused him to cut out* or *roll up my life*). The
true solution is proposed by Calvin, viz. that he first thinks of himself as
the guilty cause of his own death, and then of God as the efficient agent.
Umbreit imagines that he here describes himself as dying by a voluntary
act, as Schleiermacher is said by one of his biographers to have done, instead of dying like other men, because he could not help it. This is not
only unnatural and irrational in itself, but inconsistent with the context,
where the king is represented as anything rather than a voluntary sufferer.
According to the latest writers, מדלה does not mean *with pining sickness*,
nor *from a state of exaltation*, but *from the thrum* (as in the margin of the
English Bible), *i. e.* the ends of the threads by which the web is fastened
to the beam. Lowth gives the same sense by employing the more general

term *loom*. *From day to night* is commonly explained to mean *before to-morrow*, within the space of one day. The verb in the last clause might, without violence to etymology or usage, be explained to mean *thou wilt* (or *do thou*) *make me whole*. But interpreters appear to be agreed in giving it the opposite sense of *thou wilt make an end of me*. Some suppose, more-over, that the figure of a weaver and his web is still continued, and that the idea expressed in the last clause is that of *finishing* a piece of work.

13. *I set* (*him before me*) *till the morning* (*i. e.* all night) *as a lion* (say-ing), *so will he break all my bones; from day to night thou wilt make an end of me*. Either these last words are repeated in a different sense, or else the repetition shews that they have no special reference, in the foregoing verse, to the process of weaving. Gesenius seems to treat with contempt the suggestion of an inadvertent repetition on the part of some transcriber, though he has no difficulty in adopting it when it can serve a useful purpose. Most writers disregard the Masoretic interpunction, and connect *like a lion* with the second clause. They are then obliged to take שִׁוִּיתִי in the sense of *I reckoned* (*i. e.* counted the hours, or reckoned that as a lion, &c.), or as meaning *I endured*, or *I composed myself*, neither of which has any suffi-cient ground in the usage of the language, and the last of which requires *but* to be arbitrarily applied. Jarchi adheres to the Masoretic accents, and explains the first clause, *I likened myself to* (or *made myself like*) *a lion* (*i. e.* roared) *until the morning*. To this it has been objected, not without reason, that as the crushing of the bones involves an obvious allusion to the lion (compare Ps. vii. 3), we then have the same figure used to represent both the sufferer and the author of his sufferings, which is forced and unnatural. The Masoretic interpunction may, however, be retained without this incon-venience, by explaining שִׁוִּיתִי in accordance with its usage in Ps. xvi. 8, and cxix. 30. In the former case, the Psalmist says, *I have set Jehovah before me always*, *i. e.* I continually recognise his presence, or regard him as present. In the other case, the same idea seems to be expressed by the verb alone, with an ellipsis of the qualifying phrase. *Thy judgments have I placed* (*i. e.* before me). Supposing a similar ellipsis here, the sense will be, *I set him before me*, *i. e.* viewed him as present, imagined or conceived of him *as a lion*, and expected him to act as such, saying, *so* (*i. e.* as a lion) *he will crush all my bones*. If this be the true construction, it removes all ground for making *fear*, or *pain*, or *the disease*, the nominative of the verb *will break*, and leaves it to agree with *Jehovah*, as the natural subject of the sentence. This construction is further recommended by its giving uniformity of meaning to the clauses, as descriptive of the sufferer's apprehensions.

14. *Like a swallow* (or) *a crane* (or *like a twittering swallow*), *so I chirp; I moan like the dove; my eyes are weak* (with looking) *upward* (or *on high*); *O Jehovah, I am oppressed, undertake for me* (or *be my surety*). In the first clause the moanings of the sufferer are compared, as in many other cases, to the voice of certain animals. The dove is often spoken of in such connections, and the mention of it here makes it probable that the parallel expressions are also descriptive of a bird or birds. סוּס is the common Hebrew word for *horse*, and is so explained even here by Aquila, who retains עָגוּר without translation. Theodotion retains both, but writes the first σίς (סִיס), which Jerome thinks is probably the true text. This same reading appears as a Keri in the Masoretic text of Jer. viii. 7, the only other place where the word seems to signify a bird. The old rabbinical interpretation gives to סוּס the sense of *crane*, and to עָגוּר that of *swallow*. Bochart re-

verses them, and undertakes to shew that עָגוּר is the Hebrew word for *crane*.
This word affords a curious instance of the way in which Gesenius sometimes leaves his followers and transcribers in the lurch.   In his Commentary, while he speaks of עָגוּר as a word of doubtful import, he gives
Bochart's explanation as upon the whole the most probable.   Some of his
copyists go further, and allege that it certainly means *crane*.   In the mean
time, Gesenius, in his Manual Lexicon, rejects Bochart's proofs as *invalid*,
and explains עגור as a description of the gyratory motion of the swallow.   In
the Thesaurus, this is abandoned in its turn, and the word explained to mean
chirping or twittering.   Maurer objects to the explanation of עגור as a mere
descriptive epithet, that in Jer. viii. 7 we have סוס ועגור as two independent
substantives.   To this Gesenius replies, that the epithet is there used as a
poetical substitute for the noun, or perhaps the name of a particular species.
On any supposition, the comparison before us is evidently meant to be descriptive of inarticulate moans or murmurs.   The reference of the verbs in
the first clause to past time (*I chirped, I moaned*), though assumed by most
interpreters, is perfectly gratuitous, when the future proper yields so good
a sense.   This violation of the syntax has arisen from assuming that the
clause must be a retrospective description of something already past, and
not an expression of present feeling such as he might have uttered at the
moment.   That this last is no unnatural hypothesis, is certain from the
fact that all interpreters adopt it in the other clause.   But if that may be
the language of the sufferer at the time of his distress, it is equally natural,
or rather more so, to explain the first clause in the same way.   Clericus
understands דַּלּוּ as meaning *lifted up*, which he admits to be a mere conjecture having no foundation in usage, but rendered necessary by the addition of למרום.   Most interpreters regard it as an instance of *constructio
prægnans*, and retain the proper meaning of the verb.   Hitzig makes עשקה
an imperative, and identifies it with the Arabic عشق to love tenderly or
ardently.   *Incline thy heart to me.*   There is, however, no necessity or
warrant for departing from the Hebrew usage of עשק to do violence or oppress.   The older writers supply a definite subject, such as *death, my
disease,* or the like.   Ewald makes it impersonal, *it is oppressed to me, i. e.*
I am oppressed.   Gesenius treats it as a noun (*there is*) *oppression to me,*
and explains the Metheg as a mere sign of the secondary accent.   Junius
and Tremellius render עָרְבֵנִי *weave me through* (pertexe me), *i. e.* do not cut
out the unfinished web.   But this return to the metaphor of ver. 12, after
alluding in the mean time to a lion, to a swallow, to a crane, and to a dove,
would be exceedingly unnatural, and although not impossible can only be
assumed in case of extreme exegetical necessity, which certainly has no
existence here.   The same word is used in Ps. cxix. 122, in the sense of
undertake for me or *be my surety, i. e.* interpose between me and my enemies.
The reference is rather to protection than to justification.   Gill carries out
the metaphor to an extreme by saying that Hezekiah here *represents his
disease as a bailiff that had arrested him, and was carrying him to the prison
of the grave, and therefore prays that the Lord would bail him or rescue him
out of his hands.*

15. *What shall I say !   He hath both spoken to me, and himself hath done
(it) ; I shall go softly all my years for the bitterness of my soul.*   This, which
is substantially the common version, is the one adopted by most modern
writers, who regard the verse as an expression of surprise and joy at the
deliverance experienced.   *What shall I say ! i. e.* how shall I express my

gratitude and wonder ! *He hath said and done it*, he has promised and performed, perhaps with an implication that the promise was no sooner given than fulfilled. The recollection of this signal mercy he is resolved to cherish *all his years*, *i. e.* throughout his life, by *going softly*, solemnly, or slowly, *on account of the bitterness of his soul, i. e.* in recollection of his sufferings. Some, however, understand these last words to mean *in the bitterness of my soul, i. e.* in perpetual contrition and humility. But the preposition עַל is properly expressive, not of the manner of his going, but of its occasion. The verb אֶדַּדֶּה occurs only here and in Ps. xliii. 5, where it is commonly agreed to signify the solemn march of the people in procession to mount Zion. It would here seem to be equivalent to the phrase הלך אט applied to Ahab in 1 Kings xxi. 27. Another interpretation of the verse, which might, at first sight, seem more natural, regards it as the language of Hezekiah during his sickness, and as expressive, not of joy and wonder, but of submission. *What shall I say*, in the way of complaint ? *He hath both said and done it, i. e.* threatened and performed it. But this view of the first clause cannot be reconciled with any natural interpretation of the second, where the phrase *all my years* is consistent with the supposition that he expected to die forthwith.

16. *Lord, upon them they live, and as to everything in them is the life of my spirit, and thou wilt recover me and make me live.* This exceedingly obscure verse is now most generally understood to mean, that life in general, and the life of Hezekiah in particular, was dependent on the power and promise of God. *Upon them*, the promise and performance implied in the verbs *said* and *did* of the preceding verse, *they live, i. e.* men indefinitely live. The sense of עַל, when construed thus with חיה, is clear from such examples as Gen. xx. 27, Deut. viii. 6. Some suppose כל to govern חיי, notwithstanding the intervening word בהן, and the prefix ל, which must then be pleonastic. *All the life of my spirit (is) in them.* A similar construction is to make לכל an adverbial phrase meaning *as to* (or *with respect to*) *every thing.* The other attempts which have been made to explain עליהם as referring to the *bones* of Hezekiah, or his *years*, or his *subjects*, or those *over whom* (God is) *Lord*, are so forced, that the one first given, notwithstanding its obscurity and harshness, seems entitled to the preference. The explanation of the future and imperative in the last clause as referring to past time (*thou hast recovered me and made me live*) is not only arbitrary but gratuitous, as it assumes without necessity that such a prayer or expectation could not have been uttered after Hezekiah's recovery, whereas it is a natural expression of desire that what had been begun might be continued and completed. החייני is not an infinitive, which would here take the construct form, but an imperative. In either case, its meaning is determined by the foregoing future, so that both verbs may take the future form in translation. The original form of expression may, however, be retained in English, by omitting the auxiliary in the second future.

17. *Behold to peace (is turned) my bitter bitterness, and thou hast loved my soul from the pit of destruction, because thou hast cast behind thy back all my sins.* The idea of change or conversion must either be supplied, or supposed to be expressed by מָר, which is then the preterite of מוּר, not elsewhere used in Kal, although the Hiphil is of frequent occurrence. Most of the late writers understand מר לי מר as an emphatic or intensive repetition, of which there are several examples in this passage (vers. 11, 19),

and suppose the verb to be suppressed, or suggested by the preposition לְ.
The English Bible, and some other versions, put an opposite meaning on
the clause, as a description, not of his restoration but of his affliction. *For
peace I had great bitterness,* or, *on my peace (came) great bitterness.* The
other interpretation agrees better with the usage of the preposition, and
makes the parallelism more exact. We have here another instance of pregnant construction, *to love from, i. e. so to love as to deliver from.* This
sense is expressed in the English Bible by a circumlocution. בְּלִי means
properly nonentity, annihilation, here put for perdition or "destruction from
the presence of the Lord and from the glory of his power" (2 Thess. i. 9).
The last clause shews that Hezekiah regarded the threatened destruction as
a punishment of sin. To cast behind one, or behind one's back, in Hebrew
and Arabic, is to forget, lose sight of or exclude from view. The opposite
idea is expressed by the figure of setting or keeping before one's eyes. (See
Ps. xc. 8, cix. 14, 15, Jer. xvi. 17, Hosea vii. 2.)

18. *For the grave shall not confess thee (nor) death praise thee; they that
go down to the pit shall not hope for thy truth.* Here, as often in the
Psalms, the loss of the opportunity of praising God is urged as a reason,
not only why he should be loath to die, but why God should preserve him.
(See Ps. vi. 6, lxxxviii. 11, 12.) It does not follow from these words either
that Hezekiah had no expectation of a future state, or that the soul remains
unconscious till the resurrection. The true explanation of the word is given
by Calvin, viz. that the language is that of extreme agitation and distress,
in which the prospect of the future is absorbed in contemplation of the
present, and also that so far as he does think of futurity, it is upon the
supposition of God's wrath. Regarding death, in this case, as a proof of
the divine displeasure, he cannot but look upon it as the termination of
his solemn praises. The *truth* mentioned in the last clause is the truth of
God's promises, to hope for which is to expect the promised blessing.
לֹא יוֹדֶךָ strictly means, *shall not acknowledge thee,* with special reference to
the acknowledgment of favours, or thanksgiving. The influence of the
negative extends to the second clause, as in chap. xxiii. 4. (See above
p. 870.)

19. *The living, the living, he shall thank thee, like me* (or *as I do*) *to-day;
father to sons shall make known with respect to thy truth, i. e.* the truth of
thy promises, as in the verse preceding. Only the living could praise God
in that way to which the writer was accustomed, and on which his eye is
here fixed, with special reference, no doubt, to the external service of the
temple. The last clause must be taken in a general sense, as Hezekiah
was himself still childless.

20. *Jehovah to save me ! And my songs we will play, all the days of our
life, at the house of Jehovah.* The obvious ellipsis in the first clause may
be variously filled with *came, hastened, commanded, was ready, be pleased,*
or with the verb *is,* as an idiomatic periphrasis of the future, *is to save* for
will save. The reference to the future and the past is equally admissible,
since God, in one sense, had already saved him, and in another was to save
him still. נְגִינָה is properly the music of stringed instruments, or a song
intended to be so accompanied. The word may here be used in the more
general sense of song or music; but there seems to be no need of excluding the original and proper meaning. The singular form, *my song,* refers
to Hezekiah as the author of this composition; the plurals, *we will sing*
and *our lives,* to the multitude who might be expected to join in his public
thanksgiving, not only at first, but in after ages. The use of עַל is explained

by some as an allusion to the elevated site of the temple; but it seems to be rather a licence of construction, similar to our promiscuous use of *at* and *in*, with names of towns. It is a possible but not a necessary supposition, that this particle may here denote upward motion, as in a procession from the lower city to the temple. *We will sing* or *play my songs, all the days of our lives, up to the house of the Lord.* The general sense in either case is that of public and perpetual praise, the promise of which closes this remarkable production.

21. *And Isaiah said, Let him take a lump* (or *cake*) *of figs, and rub them* (or *lay them softened*) *on the boil* (or *inflammation*), *and he shall live* (or *let him live*) i. e. *recover.* The indirect construction, preferred by most of the modern writers, *that they should take*, and *that he might recover*, is entirely unnecessary, since the words may naturally be regarded as the very words spoken by the Prophet himself. מרח seems properly to have the sense of rubbing, either in reference to the application, or to the preparing of the figs by trituration. The latter explanation is now commonly preferred. Grotius follows some of the rabbinical interpreters in the assumption that the natural effect of such an application would have been injurious. But although this may seem to magnify the miracle, it is a gratuitous assumption, and directly contradicted by the modern oriental practice of applying figs to pestilential pustules, for the purpose of maturing their discharge. Such a pustule is commonly supposed to be denoted by שחין, both here and elsewhere, although some choose to adhere to what they think the primary sense of *inflammation*. Hitzig makes this noun the subject of the very יחי (*that it might be healed*) on the authority of Lev. xiii. 10, 14, 15; but the analogy of the first verse of the chapter now before us seems to be decisive in favour of the usual construction, which makes the verb refer to Hezekiah.

22. *And Hezekiah said, What sign that I shall go up* (*to*) *the house of Jehovah?* The ellipsis is easily supplied by reading, *what sign dost thou give*, or *what sign is there*, or more simply still, *what is the sign?* The construction of מה as an exclamation of surprise (*what a miracle!*) is neither natural in itself, nor justified by usage, in a case where the usual interrogative sense is perfectly appropriate. The question is more fully given in 2 Kings xx. 8 as follows. *And Hezekiah said to Isaiah, What sign that Jehovah is about to heal me, and that I shall go up, on the third day, to the house of Jehovah?* The reference is to the promise as recorded in ver. 5 of the same chapter. *Return and say to Hezekiah, the chief of my people, Thus said Jehovah, the God of David thy father, I have heard thy prayer, I have seen thy tears; behold, I am about to heal thee; on the third day thou shalt go up to the house of Jehovah.* The last two verses of this chapter in Isaiah are evidently out of their chronological order, and the question has been raised, whether this transposition is to be ascribed to the original writer, and if so, how it is to be accounted for. The hypothesis which have been proposed may be reduced to three. The first is, that the transposition is an error of transcription, arising from the mere inadvertence of some ancient copyist. Besides the difficulty common to all such suppositions, that errors of the kind supposed, although they might take place, could scarcely become universal, it is here precluded by the fact, that these two verses cannot be inserted in the text above without breaking its continuity, and cannot therefore have dropped out of it, unless we take for granted also, that the text was altered after the omission, which is only adding arbitrarily another to the gratuitous assumptions made before. Some avoid this difficulty by supposing that the verses do not properly belong to this text,

but were added by a later hand, in order to complete the narrative as given in the second book of Kings. Apart from the natural presumption against all such imaginary facts, except where the assuming of them cannot be avoided, it can scarcely be doubted that a copyist or critic, who would use such freedom with the text, would have used more, and inserted this statement in its proper place. It is only necessary to compare these fanciful hypotheses with the obvious and simple supposition that the passage before us is the first draught or original form of Isaiah's narrative, in which the facts recorded in these two last verses were added by a kind of after-thought, and that in re-writing the account, as a part of the national history, he naturally placed them in their chronological order. It would probably be easy to produce many parallel cases from the correspondence of voluminous letter-writers, or from other cases of repeated composition on the same subject by the same writer. However this may be, it seems clear that the explanation now proposed is simpler in itself, and requires less to be imagined or supposed, than any other, and'is therefore, even on the strictest principles of criticism, entitled to the preference.

Chapter 39

THIS chapter contains an account of the Babylonian embassy to Hezekiah, and of his indiscreet and ostentatious conduct, which became the occasion of a threatening message by the hands of Isaiah, predicting the Babylonian conquest and captivity, but with a tacit promise of exemption to the king himself, and to the country, while he lived, which he received with humble acquiescence and thankful acknowledgment.

The chapter is evidently a direct continuation of the narrative before it, nor is there any real ground, internal or external, for suspecting its authenticity, antiquity, or genuineness.

1. *In that time, Merodach Baladan, son of Baladan, king of Babylon, sent letters and a gift to Hezekiah, and he heard that he was sick and was recovered.* The first phrase is used with great latitude of meaning, and may either describe one event as contemporaneous with another, or as following it, at once or more remotely. Knobel supposes it to mean here simply *in the days of Hezekiah.* Most other writers take it for granted that this message of congratulation must have been sent soon after the recovery of Hezekiah. These understand וַיִּשְׁמַע as equivalent in meaning to כִּי שָׁמַע 2 Kings, xx. 12, and explain all the verbs of the last clause as pluperfects (*for he had heard*, &c.). Knobel, on the contrary, gives ו its usual sense, and understands the clause to mean, that the king of Babylon heard of Hezekiah's sickness from his ambassadors on their return. But this is inconsistent with the parallel statement, assumes a needless prolepsis or anticipation, and encumbers the narrative with a fact entirely superfluous. What the ambassadors reported to the king on their return, is of no importance to the history. *Merodach* occurs in Jer. l. 2, as the name of a Babylonian idol. Grotius supposes that a man of that name had been defiled; others, that it was common to name men after gods. Hitzig identifies the name with the Persian diminutive مردك *little man* (as a term of endearment), Gesenius with the *Mars* of classical mythology. In 2 Kings xx. 11, it is written *Berodach*, which Hiller explains as a contraction of *Bar Merodach*, the son of Merodach, while Knobel regards it as a mere mistake, and Gesenius as a customary variation, *b* and *m* being often interchanged. Two manuscripts read

Berodach in the case before us, and a few have the transposed form *Medorach.*
Baladan, according to Von Bohlen, is a Persian word meaning *praised ;*
according to Gesenius, an Aramean compound meaning *Bel (is his) lord.*
Hitzig explains *bal* as a connective syllable, like *pol* in Nabopolassar, *pal*
in Sardanapalus, &c. Most of the modern writers agree with Vitringa in
identifying this king with the *Mardokempad* of Berosus, as preserved in the
Armenian version of Eusebius ; but Knobel understands him as naming
Merodach Baladan distinctly. The same authority describes these Babylonian princes, not as sovereigns, but as viceroys or tributaries subject to
Assyria. In that case, it is not improbable that Merodach Baladan was
meditating a revolt, and sent this embassy to gain Hezekiah's co-operation.
The congratulation on his recovery may have been a secondary object, or
perhaps a mere pretext. In 2 Chron. xxxii. 31, a further design is mentioned, namely, *to inquire of the wonder that was done in the land,* whether
this be understood to mean the destruction of Sennacherib's army, or the
miraculous recession of the shadow. There is no incompatibility between
these different designs. Perhaps an embassy is seldom sent to such a distance with a single undivided errand.

2. *And Hezekiah was glad of them, and shewed them his house of rarities,*
the silver, and the gold, and the spices, and the good oil (or *ointment*), *and*
all his house of arms, and all that was found in his treasures ; there was
not a thing which Hezekiah did not shew them, in his house and in all his
dominion. The parallel passage (2 Kings xx. 13) has וישמע עליהם, which
Knobel understands to mean that he *heard of them,* but which seems to be
more correctly rendered in the English Bible, *and he hearkened unto them.*
There is no need of regarding either as an error of transcription, or as the
correction of a later writer. Nothing could be more natural than such a
variation on the part of the original writer, describing Hezekiah's feelings
in the one case and his conduct in the other. He hearkened to them cour-
teously *because* he was glad of their arrival. Henderson says, *he was de-*
lighted with them ; but the context seems to shew that it was not so much
the company or manners of the men that he was pleased with, as the honour done him by the king of Babylon in sending them. The practice of exhibiting the curiosities and riches of a palace to distinguished visitors,
Vitringa illustrates by the parallel case of Crœsus and Solon, as recorded
by Herodotus. נכת has been commonly regarded as identical with the
נכאות of Gen. xxxvii. 43, and the whole phrase interpreted accordingly, as
meaning properly *a house of spices,* and then by a natural extension of its
import, a depository of rare and precious things in general. The former
meaning is retained by Aquila (τὸν οἶκον τῶν ἀρωμάτων) and the Vulgate
(*cellam aromatum*). The other is given in the Targum and Peshito, and
by most modern writers. The Septuagint retains the Hebrew word (νεχωθᾶ).
Abulwalid derives it from נְכַת, to bite, and applies it to provisions; Lorsbach,
from a Persian verb meaning to deposit ; Hitzig, from a Hebrew root of similar import. בית כלים is not a house of *jewels* or *vessels,* but of *arms, i. e.*
an arsenal, most probably the same that is mentioned in chap. xxii. 8. Luther
has *all his arsenals,* but this would be expressed in Hebrew by the plural.
Lowth more correctly has *whole arsenal,* which is also the meaning of the
common version, *all the house of his armour.* The goodly or precious oil
is supposed by Barnes to have been that used in the unction of kings and
priests, or perhaps applied to more ordinary purposes in the royal household. Knobel explains ממשלתו as meaning *in his power* or *possession.* So

the LXX. (ἐξουσία). It is more commonly explained, however, as a local noun denoting realm or dominions. Hitzig gives איצרית the specific sense of store-rooms or treasure-chambers, which is unnecessary. Even on the usual hypothesis, the ב need not be translated *among*; but may have its usual and proper sense of *in*.

3. *Then came Isaiah the prophet to the king Hezekiah, and said to him, What said these men, and whence came they unto thee? And Hezekiah said, From a far country came they unto me, from Babylon.* The Prophet was not sent for by the king, as in chap. xxxvii. 2; but he was no doubt sent by God, and came in his official character. The older writers seem to regard as the occasion of his visit the vainglory which the king had displayed in his entertainment of the strangers. The moderns lay the chief stress on the political negotiations which had passed between them, and which could not be regarded by the Prophet, but with strong disapprobation. The statement in Chronicles is that *God left him to try him, to know all in his heart* (2 Chron. xxxii. 31). This may include the sins of vain ostentation and of distrust in God, shewing itself in a longing after foreign alliances. There is no sufficient ground for Hendewerk's assumption, that a treaty had actually been concluded. Gesenius observes that Hezekiah answers only the second of the Prophet's questions, as if he shrunk from answering the first. But this mode of replying to the last interrogation, when there is more than one, is natural and common in cases where there can be no motive for concealment. It is unnecessary, therefore, to suppose with Clericus, that a part of Hezekiah's answer is omitted in the narrative. In the last clause, Calvin understands the king as boasting of the distance from which the embassy had come, as implying the extent of his own fame and political importance. Vitringa supposes the distance to be mentioned as an excuse for his hospitable attentions. Knobel thinks it was intended to disarm Isaiah's suspicion of a league, as if he had said, too distant to admit of any intimate communion or alliance. All these interpretations seem to strain the words beyond their natural obvious import, according to which *a far country* is nothing more than a familiar designation of Babylon or Babylonia.

4. *And he said, What have they seen in thy house? And Hezekiah said, All that is in my house have they seen; there is not a thing that I have not shewed them in my treasures.* Some of the later Germans say that Hezekiah, finding evasion and concealment impossible, now frankly tells the truth. But the frankness of the answer here recorded rather shews that there was no attempt at concealment from the first. It was not as Calvin well observes, until the Prophet questioned him, that Hezekiah became aware of the error which he had committed. Knobel gratuitously asserts that the Prophet here shifts his ground from finding fault with what had passed in words to blaming what had passed in act, between the king and the ambassadors.

5. *And Isaiah said to Hezekiah, Hear the word of Jehovah of hosts.* This form of expression gives to what follows the solemnity and authority of a divine decree. The parallel passage (2 Kings xx. 16) omits צבאות, which Vitringa regards as emphatic here, implying a signal exercise of divine providence and power.

6. *Behold days (are) coming, when all that (is) in thy house, and that which thy fathers have hoarded until this day, shall be carried to Babylon; there shall not be left a thing* (literally *a word*), *saith Jehovah.* Jarchi directs attention to the exact correspondence of the punishment with the

offence. As the Babylonians had seen all, they should one day take all; as nothing had been withheld from them now, so nothing should be withheld from them hereafter. The German interpreters are at a loss, whether to make this explicit prophecy a proof of later date, or to explain it as a sagacious conjecture, founded on the previous fate of the ten tribes, and on the actual relations of the Babylonian monarchy to Judah and Assyria. The scale preponderates in favour of the latter supposition, notwithstanding its absurd assumption of a mere political conjecture as to events which did not happen for a hundred years. To those who are under no unhappy necessity of explaining away the clearest proofs of inspiration and prophetic foresight, this passage affords a striking instance of the gradual development of prophecy. The general threatening of expatriation had been uttered seven hundred years before by Moses (Lev. xxvi. 33; Deut. xxviii. 64–67, xxx. 3). Five hundred years later, Ahijah had declared that Israel should be rooted up and scattered *beyond the river* (1 Kings xiv. 15). Within a hundred years, they had been threatened by Amos with *captivity beyond Damascus* (Amos v. 27). Isaiah himself had obscurely intimated a future connection between the fortunes of Israel and Babylon (chap. xiv. 1, xxi. 10). But here, for the first time, the Babylonish exile is explicitly foretold, unless the similar prediction of the contemporary prophet Micah (iv. 10) be considered earlier. The fulfilment of the prophecy began in the deportation of Manasseh (2 Chron. xxxiii. 11), but was described as something still prospective by Jeremiah (xx. 5), in whose days, and in the reign of Zedekiah, it was at length fully accomplished (2 Chron. xxxvi. 18). To the objection, that a national calamity of this description bears no proportion to the fault of Hezekiah, there is no need of any other answer than the one already given by Vitringa, to wit, that Hezekiah's fault was not the cause but the occasion of the punishment which fell upon the people, or rather of its being so explicitly predicted in the case before us. For, as Calvin says, the punishment of Hezekiah's individual fault was included in the punishment of Israel for national offences.

7. *And of thy sons that shall issue from thee, which thou shalt beget, shall they take away, and they shall be eunuchs in the palace of the king of Babylon.* The future form of the expression in the first clause has respect to the fact that Hezekiah had as yet no children. (See above on chap. xxxviii. 2). Hendewerk regards the terms used as inapplicable to any but immediate descendants, in which case the prophecy must be restricted to Manasseh (2 Chron. xxxiii. 11). But Hitzig and Knobel justify the wider application of the terms by the analogy of chap. li. 2, and by the constant use of *father* and *son* in reference to remote descendants or progenitors. The מִן at the beginning of the verse is universally admitted to be partitive. *They shall take* may either be an indefinite construction, or agree with *the Babylonians* understood. סָרִיסִים is strictly understood by the Septuagint (σπά-δοντας), and the Vulgate (*eunuchi*), but explained by the Targum to mean nobles (רברבין absurdly rendered in the London Polyglot, *nutriti*), i. e. courtiers or household-officers, an extension of the meaning which agrees well with the usages of oriental courts. The latter explanation is approved by Gesenius in his Commentary for a specified reason. In his earlier Lexicons he leaves it doubtful; but in the Thesaurus he contends for the strict sense, even in Gen. xxxvii. 36, as well as in the case before us, with respect to which he answers his own argument upon the other side, by a counter-argument of equal strength. Instead of יקחו, the parallel passage (2 Kings

xx. 17) has the singular יִקַּח, which is equally correct and regular, in a case
of indefinite construction. The fulfilment of this prophecy is recorded in
2 Kings xxiv. 12–16 and Dan. i. 1–7, and that so clearly, that the neologists are driven to their usual supposition of an interpolation, or of such
an alteration as to make the terms of the prediction more determinate.

8. *And Hezekiah said to Isaiah, Good is the word of Jehovah which thou
hast spoken. And he said, For there shall be peace and truth in my days.*
The word *good* is here used, neither in the sense of *gracious* nor in that of
just exclusively, but in that of *right*, as comprehending both. While the
king acquiesces in the threatening prophecy as righteous and deserved, he
gratefully acknowledges the mercy with which it is tempered. That he
looked upon the woes denounced against his children as a personal misfortune of his own, is clear from his regarding the postponement of the
execution as a mitigation of the sentence on himself. The expression of
thankfulness at this exemption shews how true the narrative is to nature
and experience. Umbreit has the good sense and feeling to describe it as
a natural and child-like acknowledgment. The purer taste and loftier
morality of other German writers can regard it only as *naiv-egoistisch*
(Gesenius), or as an expression of true oriental *egoismus* (Hitzig). According to these philosophical interpreters, Hezekiah, instead of being thankful
for the mercy which was mingled with God's judgments, ought to have
rejected the promise of peace and truth in his own days, unless extended
to his children also. This sentimental magnanimity may answer well
enough in plays and novels, but is equally at variance with human nature
and the word of God. It was not more clearly Hezekiah's duty to submit
without a murmur to God's threatening, than it was to accept with gratitude the exemption promised to himself. " Quamvis enim hæc pœna aliud
seculum maneret, tamen præsentem gratiam amplecti debuit ; et certe
nostro potissimum seculo servire debemus, ejusque præcipue ratio habenda
est ; futurum non est negligendum, sed quod præsens est atque instat
magis officium nostrum requirit." (Calvin.) Nothing, therefore, as the
same great writer well says, can be further from the spirit of this answer,
than that of the Greek sentence, ἐμοῦ θανόντος γαῖα μιχθήτω πυρί, or the
Latin, *mihi mortuo omnes mortui sunt*. Calvin is also of opinion that the
phrase, *which thou hast spoken*, is emphatic, and intended to recognise
Isaiah as an authoritative messenger from God. There is no need of supposing that the second וַיֹּאמֶר means, he said in his heart (Hitzig), or after
Isaiah was gone (Knobel), much less that it simply means *he thought*
(Hendewerk). The obvious sense of the expression is, that these words
were added to explain his previous acquiescence in the divine determination. The repetition of the verb *he said*, implies a pause or interval,
however short. The various explanations of the particle כִּי, as meaning
well, yes, provided, only, yet, O that, &c., are mere substitutions of what
the interpreters think Hezekiah ought to have said for what he did say,
which is simply this, (*I call it good*) *because there is to be*, &c. This exact
sense of the words is retained in the Targum and the English Version.
The optative meaning is expressed in the Septuagint (γενέσθω δὴ), and the
Vulgate (*fiat tantum*). The Peshito simplifies the syntax by omitting *and
he said*, and connecting the two clauses directly : *good is the word of the
Lord which thou hast spoken, that there shall be peace and truth in my days.*
But this, besides its arbitrary mutilation of the text, impairs the force of
Hezekiah's language, by restricting it wholly to the promise. *Peace* may
be here taken in the wide sense of prosperity, but with special reference to

its proper import, as denoting exemption from war. *Truth* is understood by Henderson and Barnes in its modern religious sense of true religion. Cocceius even restricts it to the preaching of the truth. Hendewerk gives it the sense of *goodness*, as the Septuagint does that of *righteousness*. Hitzig supposes it to mean the mutual fidelity of men in their relations to each other. But the best interpretation seems to be the one approved by Calvin, Vitringa, and Gesenius, who take the word in its primary etymological sense of *permanence, stability*, in which the ideas of fidelity and truth may be included, as effects necessarily imply their cause.

From the foregoing exposition of chapters xxxvi.–xxxix. it may safely be inferred, as a legitimate, if not an unavoidable deduction, that they form a continuous unbroken narrative by one and the same writer; that this writer may as well have been Isaiah as any other person, (if we regard internal evidence,) and can have been no other, if we regard the immemorial tradition of the Hebrew Canon; and that these four chapters, far from having been inserted here at random or through ignorance, are in their proper place, as a connecting link between the Earlier and Later Prophecies, the threatening in chap. xxxix. 6 being really the theme or text of the long prophetic discourse, with which the remainder of the book is occupied.

Chapter 40

A GLORIOUS change awaits the Church, consisting in a new and gracious manifestation of Jehovah's presence, for which his people are exhorted to prepare, vers. 1–5. Though one generation perish after another, this promise shall eventually be fulfilled, because it rests not upon human but divine authority, vers. 6–8. Zion may even now see him approaching as the conqueror of his enemies, and at the same time as the shepherd of his people, vers. 9–11. The fulfilment of these pledges is insured by his infinite wisdom, his almighty power, and his independence both of individuals and nations, vers. 12–17. How much more is he superior to material images, by which men represent him or supply his place, vers. 18–25. The same power which supports the heavens is pledged for the support of Israel, vers. 26–31.

The specific application of this chapter to the return from Babylon has no foundation in the text itself, but is supposed by some to be implied in the relation of this chapter to the one before it which contains a prediction of the exile; and this prediction is regarded by Hengstenberg and others as the text or theme of the prophecies that follow. But the promise in itself considered is a general one of consolation, protection, and change for the better, to be wrought by the power and wisdom of Jehovah, which are contrasted, first, with those of men, of nations, and of rulers, then with the utter impotence of idols. That the ultimate fulfilment of the promise was still distant is implied in the exhortation to faith and patience. The reference to idolatry proves nothing with respect to the date of the prediction, although more appropriate in the writings of Isaiah than of a prophet in the Babylonish exile. It is evidently meant, however, to condemn idolatry in general, and more particularly all the idolatrous defections of the Israelites under the old economy.

1. *Comfort ye, comfort ye my people, saith your God.* This command is not addressed specifically to the priests or prophets, much less to the

messengers from Babylon announcing the restoration of the Jews, but to any who might be supposed to hear the order, as in chap. xiii. 2, or to the people themselves, who are then required to encourage one another, as in chap. xxxv. 3, 4.   The Vulgate even goes so far as to put *my people* in the vocative (*popule meus*).   The imperative form of the expression is poetical. Instead of declaring his own purpose, God summons men to execute it. Instead of saying, *I will comfort*, he says, *comfort ye*.   The same idea might have been conveyed by saying, in the third person, *let them comfort her*, or in the passive voice, *let her be comforted*.   The possessive pronouns are emphatic, and suggest that, notwithstanding what they suffered, they were still Jehovah's people, he was still their God.   There is also meaning in the repetition of the verb at the beginning.   Such repetitions are not unfrequent in the earlier prophecies. (See chaps. xxiv. 16, xxvi. 3, xxix. 1, xxxviii. 11, 17, 19.)   The use of the future יֹאמַר for the preterite אָמַר (*saith*) is peculiar to Isaiah.   Gesenius cites as instances in the other books, Jer. xlii. 20, Zech. xiii. 9, and Hosea ii. 28.   But in the first and second cases, the future has its proper sense, and not that of the present; while in the third, the Hebrew word is not יֹאמַר but נְאֻם.   At the same time, he omits the only real instance not in Isaiah, viz. Ps. xii. 6.   Calvin insists upon the strict translation of the future (*dicet*), as implying that the order to console the people was not to be actually given till a later period, and is only mentioned here by anticipation.   But even if it be explained as at present, it is worthy of remark that this form of expression is not only peculiar to Isaiah, but common to both parts of the book. (See chap. i. 11, 18, xxxiii. 10.)   The prefatory exhortation in this verse affords a key to the whole prophecy, as being consolatory in its tone and purpose.   There is evident allusion to the threatening in chap. xxxix. 7. (See previous page.)   Having there predicted the captivity in Babylon, as one of the successive strokes, by which the fall of Israel as a nation, and the total loss of its peculiar privileges, should be brought about, the Prophet is now sent to assure the spiritual Israel, the true people of Jehovah, that although the Jewish nation should soon cease to be externally identified with the Church, the Church itself should not only continue to exist, but in a far more glorious state than ever.   This is the " people " here meant, and this the " comfort " wherewith they were to be comforted.

2. *Speak to* (or *according to*) *the heart of Jerusalem, and cry to her that her warfare is accomplished, that her iniquity is pardoned, that she hath received from the hand of Jehovah double for all her sins.*   By speaking to the heart, we are to understand speaking so as to affect the heart or feelings, and also in accordance with the heart or wishes, *i. e.* what the person addressed desires or needs to hear.   Jerusalem is here put for the Church or chosen people, whose metropolis it was, and for whose sake the place itself was precious in the sight of God.   Those who refer the passage to the Babylonish exile are under the necessity of assuming (with Rosenmüller) that the consolation was addressed to those left behind in Judah, or (with Gesenius) that Jerusalem means its inhabitants in exile.   *Warfare* includes the two ideas of appointed time and hard service, in which sense the verb and noun are both applied to the routine of sacerdotal functions (Num. iv. 23, viii. 24, 25), but here still more expressly to the old dispensation, as a period of restriction and constraint.   The next phrase strictly means, *her iniquity is accepted*, *i.e.* an atonement for it, or the punishment already suffered is accepted as sufficient, not in strict justice,

but in reference to God's gracious purpose. The same idea is supposed by some to be expressed in the last clause, where כִּפְלַיִם (*double*) is not used mathematically to denote proportion, but poetically to denote abundance, like the equivalent expresssion מִשְׁנֶה in chap. lxi. 7, Job xlii. 10, Zech. ix. 12. The sense will then be that she has been punished abundantly, not more than she deserved, yet enough to answer the design of punishment. But as giving or receiving double, in all the other cases cited, has respect, not to punishment, but to favour after suffering, so this clause may be understood to mean, that she has now received (or is receiving) double favours, notwithstanding all her sins. The ב has then the same sense as in chaps. v. 25, ix. 11, 16, 20, x. 4. Either of these explanations makes it unnecessary to give *sin* the rare and doubtful sense of *punishment*. The verbs are *præterita prophetica*, but for that very reason should not be exchanged for futures, as we have no right to depart without necessity from the descriptive form in which it pleased the Holy Ghost to clothe this prophecy. The continuance of the ceremonial system, and the hardships of the old dispensation, are here and elsewhere represented as chastisements due to the defections of the chosen people, notwithstanding which they should continue to exist, and in a far more glorious character, not as a national Church, but as a spiritual Church, set free from ritual and local fetters.

3. *A voice crying—in the wilderness—clear the way of Jehovah—make straight* (or *level*) *in the desert a highway for our God.* The Septuagint version, retained in the New Testament, is φωνὴ βοῶντος, which amounts to the same thing. Both in the Hebrew and the Greek, the words *in the wilderness* may be connected either with what follows or with what precedes ; but the usual division is more natural, and the other has been insisted upon chiefly for the purpose of rendering the verse inapplicable to John the Baptist, who came preaching in a wilderness, and to whom the words are applied expressly in Mat. iii. 3 ; Mark i. 3 ; Luke iii. 4, as the herald of the new dispensation. Those who deny the inspiration of the Prophet are compelled to reject this as a mere accommodation, and apply the verse exclusively to the return from Babylon, of which there is no mention in the text or context. It is said indeed that God is here represented as marching at the head of his returning people. But in all the cases which Lowth cites as parallel, there is express allusion to the exodus from Egypt. Here, on the contrary, the only image presented is that of God returning to Jerusalem, revisiting his people, as he did in every signal manifestation of his presence, but above all at the advent of Messiah, and the opening of the new dispensation. The verb rendered *prepare* denotes a particular kind of preparation, viz. the removal of obstructions, as appears from Gen. xxiv. 31 ; Lev. xiv. 36, and may therefore be expressed by *clear* in English. The parallel verb means *rectify* or make straight, either in reference to obliquity of course or to unevenness of surface, most probably the latter, in which case it may be expressed by *level*. To a general term meaning *way* or *path* is added a specific one, denoting an artificial causeway, raised above the surface of the earth. There is no need of supposing (with Lowth) that the Prophet here alludes to any particular usage of the oriental sovereigns, or (with Grotius) that the order of the first and second verses is continued (*let there be a voice crying*). The Prophet is describing what he actually hears—*a voice crying !*—or as Ewald boldly paraphrases the expression—*Hark ! one cries.*

4. *Every valley shall be raised, and every mountain and hill brought low, and the uneven shall become level, and the ridges a plain.* This may be con-

sidered an an explanation of the manner in which the way of the Lord was
to be prepared. Grotius supposes the command at the beginning of the
chapter to be still continued (*let every valley*, &c.), and the latest German
writers give the same construction of this verse, although they make a new
command begin in the one preceding. The form of the following verb
(וְהָיָה), though not incompatible with this explanation, rather favours the
strict interpretation of the future, which is of course, on general principles,
to be preferred. The common version (*exalted*) seems to imply that the
valleys and mountains were to exchange places; but this would not facilitate the passing, which requires that both should be reduced to a common
level.—The translation *crooked* is retained and defended by some modern
writers, on the ground that the parallel expression requires it; but as מִישׁוֹר
may denote not only lineal but superficial rectitude, so עָקֹב, as its opposite,
may naturally signify unevenness of surface, which is more appropriate in
this connection than obliquity or irregularity of course.   רְכָסִים, according
to its etymology, denotes gorges or ravines, or rather difficult passes; but
in this case it seems to be the opposite of flat or level ground, and may
therefore be expressed by *ridges*. The application of these several terms
to different moral or spiritual objects, such as various classes in society or
nations of the earth, rests upon the false assumption that the features of a
portrait or the figures in a landscape are to be considered one by one, and
not in their mutual relations, as composing a whole picture. (Compare the
comment on chap. v. 3, vol. i. p. 129). The whole impression here intended
to be made is that of a way opened through a wilderness by levelling the
ground and the removal of obstructions, as a natural image for the removal
of the hindrances to God's revisiting his people.

5. *And the glory of Jehovah shall be revealed, and all flesh shall see* (*it*)
together, for the mouth of Jehovah speaks (or *hath spoken*). The subjunctive construction of the first clause by Junius and Tremellius (*ut reveletur*)
is adopted by Hitzig and Ewald, but without necessity. The idea seems
to be that as soon as the way is opened, the Lord will shew himself.
יַחְדָּו may express either coincidence of time (*at once*), or totality *altogether*),
more probably the latter. Ewald needlessly reads יֵשַׁע, which he supposes
to be implied in the Septuagint version (τὸ σωτήριον τοῦ Θεοῦ), retained by
Luke (iii. 6). But this only shews that *salvation* was included in the *glory*
which should be revealed. Gesenius follows Luther in making the last
clause express the thing to be seen (*shall see that the mouth of Jehovah hath
spoken*); but this construction is precluded by the fact that this is the only
case in which the sense thus put upon the formula is even possible; in all
others the meaning of the clause not only may but must be, *for* (*because*)
the mouth of the Lord hath spoken, as a reason why the declaration should
be credited. (See chap. i. 2, 20, xxii. 25, lviii. 14; Jer. xiii. 15; Joel
iv. 8; Obad. i. 18.) To this, the only tenable construction, all the later
German writers have returned. To see God's glory, is a common expression for recognising his presence and agency in any event. (See Exod.
xvi. 7; Isa. xxxv. 2, lxvi. 18). The specific reference of this verse to the
restoration of the Jews from exile is not only gratuitous but inconsistent
with the strength and comprehensiveness of its expressions. The simple
meaning is, that when the way should be prepared, the glory of God would
be universally displayed; a promise too extensive to be fully verified in that
event or period of history.

6. *A voice saying, Cry! And he said* (or *says*), *What shall I cry? All
flesh is grass, and all its favour like a flower of the field!* Here, as in

ver. 3, the participle is construed in the genitive by the Septuagint (φωνὴ
λέγοντος), and the Vulgate (*vox dicentis*) ; but the simplest construction
makes it agree with *voice* as an adjective.   That two distinct speakers are
here introduced, seems to be granted by all interpreters, excepting Junius
and Tremellius, who refer אֹמֵר and אָמַר to the same subject, and exclude
the interrogation altogether.   *A voice says, Cry, and it also says* (or *tells me*)
what I shall cry.   Cocceius supplies *is heard* at the beginning.   Ewald
adopts the same form of expression in ver. 3.   *Hark! one says, Cry.*   The
force and beauty of the verse are much impaired by any version which does
not represent the writer as actually hearing what he thus describes.   The
Septuagint and Vulgate have *and I said*, either because they read וָאֹמַר,
which is found in one or two manuscripts, or because they understood the
form used in the common text as certainly referring to the Prophet himself.
Augusti supplies *the herald says*, which is unnecessary.   There is a pleasing
mystery, as Hitzig well observes, in the dialogue of these anonymous voices,
which is dispelled by undertaking to determine too precisely who the speakers
are.   All that the words necessarily convey is, that one voice speaks and
another voice answers.   Interpreters are universally agreed that the last
clause contains the words which the second speaker is required to utter.   It
is possible, however, to connect these words immediately with what
precedes, and understand them as presenting an objection to the required
proclamation.   *What shall* (or *can*) *I cry,* (*since*) *all flesh is grass,* &c.   The
advantages of this construction are, that it assumes no change of speaker
where none is intimated in the text, and that it does away with an alleged
tautology, as will be seen below.   According to the usual construction, we
are to supply before the last clause, *and the first voice said again* (or
answered), *Cry as follows: All flesh,* &c.   The last phrase is here used, not
in its widest sense, as comprehending the whole animal world (Gen. vi. 7,
13, 17), but in its more restricted application to mankind, of which some
examples may be found in the New Testament (John xvii. 2 ; Rom. iii. 20).
The comparison of human frailty to grass is common in the Scriptures.
(See chaps. xxxvii. 27, li. 12 ; Ps. ciii. 15, 16 ; James i. 10, 11.)   J. D.
Michaelis supposes an allusion, in the last clause, to the sudden blasting of
oriental flowers by the burning east wind.   The Septuagint and Vulgate
give חַסְדּוֹ the sense of *glory*, which is retained by Peter (1 Pet. i. 24,
25).   From this Grotius, Houbigant, and others infer that the original
reading was הוֹדוֹ.   Gesenius rejects this as altogether arbitrary, but with
as little ground assumes that חֶסֶד, in this one place, is synonymous with
חֵן, when used (like the English *grace* and *favour*) in the sense of beauty.
Hendewerk even goes so far as to say that χάρις, in Luke ii. 40, has an
æsthetic sense.   To assume a new sense of חֶסֶד in this one case is a violation of the soundest principles of lexicography, and instead of letting the
writer express his own ideas, forces upon him what the commentator
thinks he might have said or should have said.   There may be cases where
a word must be supposed to have a peculiar sense in some one place ; but
such assumptions can be justified by nothing but extreme necessity, and
that no such necessity exists in this case is apparent from the fact that the
usual explanation gives a perfectly good sense.   The contrast is then
between the short-lived and precarious favour of man, and the infallible
promise of God.   The quotation in Peter confirms the supposition, here
suggested by the context, that the words have reference to the preaching
of the gospel, or the introduction of the new dispensation.

7. *Dried is the grass, faded the flower; for the breath of Jehovah has blown upon it. Surely the people is grass.* The present form usually given to the verbs conveys the sense correctly as a general proposition, but not in its original shape as a description of what has actually happened, and may be expected to occur again.—The translation *when* (instead of *for*), preferred by Gesenius and some older writers, is only admissible because it is a needless deviation from the usual meaning of the particle, which yields a perfectly good sense in this connection.—If רוּחַ does not here denote a divine agent, which is hardly consistent with the figurative form of the whole sentence, it should b taken in its primary sense of *breath*, not in the intermediate one of u nd; although this, as Gesenius suggests, may be what the figure was inte ded to express, the figure itself is that of a person *breathing* on the grass an flower, and causing them to wither. It is strange that Lowth should have overlooked this natural and striking image, to adopt the unpoetical and frigid notion, that " a wind of Jehovah is a Hebraism, meaning no more than a strong wind."—אָכֵן, which properly means *surely, verily*, is here equivalent to an affirmative particle, *yea* or *yes*, and is so explained by Luther.—The treatment which this last clause has experienced affords an instructive illustration of the real value of the " higher criticism." Koppe, the father of this modern art or science, rejects the clause as spurious, because it violates the parallelism. He is followed, with some hesitation, by Gesenius, who assigns, as additional reasons, that the sense is *watery* and incoherent, and that the clause is wanting in the Septuagint, although he does not hesitate to retain the first clause, which is also omitted in that ancient Version. Hitzig grants that this omission may have been a mere mistake or inadvertence, but still rejects the clause, upon the ground, that it contains a false explanation of what goes before, because הָעָם, when absolutely used, *must* mean the Jews, whereas the reference in this whole context is to the Gentiles; as if the latter allegation did not utterly subvert the other, by determining in what sense הָעָם must here be taken. Instead of arguing that, because the Gentiles are referred to in the context, therefore they must be meant here likewise, he assumes that they are not meant here, and then pronounces the clause inconsistent with the context. The clause is retained as genuine by all the German writers since Hitzig. Another curious instance of the confidence with which the *higher critics* can affirm contradictory propositions, is the fact that while Hitzig says that הָעָם *must* mean Israel, Gesenius quietly assumes that it *must* mean the Babylonians.

8. *Dried is the grass, faded the flower, and the word of our God shall stand for ever.* The comparatively rare use of adversative particles in Hebrew is apparent from this verse, in which the relation of the clauses can be fully expressed in English only by means of the word *but.*—Kimchi explains *word* to mean the word of prophecy, while others give it the specific sense of promise, and others understand it as denoting the gospel, on the authority of 1 Peter i. 25. All these explanations can be reconciled by suffering the Prophet to express his own ideas, without any adventitious limitation, and admitting, as the only sure conclusion, that by *word* he means neither promise, nor prophecy, nor gospel merely, but *every word that proceedeth out of the mouth of God* (Deut. viii. 3; Mat. iv. 4). There is a tacit antithesis between the word of God and man ; what man says is uncertain and precarious, what God says cannot fail. Thus understood, it includes prediction, precept, promise, and the offer of salvation ; and although the latter is not meant exclusively, the apostle makes a perfectly

correct and most important application of the verse when, after quoting it,
he adds, *and this is the word which is preached* (εὐαγγελισθέν) *unto you*, that
is to say, this prophetic declaration is emphatically true of the gospel of
Christ. To *stand for ever* is a common Hebrew phrase for perpetuity,
security, and sure fulfilment. The expression *our God* contains, as usual,
a reference to the covenant relation between God and his people. Even
according to the usual arrangement and construction of these verses, the
emphatic repetition in vers. 7 and 8 can only be thought *watery* by critics
of extreme refinement. It is possible, however, to avoid the appearance of
tautology by means of an arrangement which has been already hinted at as
possible, although it does not seem to have occurred to any of the interpreters. The proposition is to give the passage a dramatic form, by making the last clause of ver. 6 and the whole of ver. 7 a continuation of the
words of the second voice, and then regarding ver. 8 as a rejoinder by the
first voice. The whole may then be paraphrased as follows. A voice
says, " Cry ! " And (another voice) says, " What shall I cry ? " (*i. e.*
to what purpose can I cry, or utter promises like those recorded in vers.
1–5), since all flesh is grass, &c.; the grass withereth, &c.; surely the
people is grass (and cannot be expected to witness the fulfilment of these
promises). But the first voice says again : " The grass does wither, and
the flower does fade ; but these events depend not on the life of man, but
on the word of God, and the word of God shall stand for ever." There
are no doubt some objections to this exegetical hypothesis, especially its
somewhat artificial character; and therefore it has not been introduced into
the text, but is simply thrown out here, as a possible alternative, to those
who are not satisfied with the more obvious and usual construction of the
passage.

9. *Upon a high mountain get thee up, bringer of good news, Zion ! Raise
with strength thy voice, bringer of good news, Jerusalem ! Raise* (it), *fear
not, say to the towns of Judah, Lo, your God!* The reflexive form *get thee
up*, though not a literal translation, is an idiomatic equivalent to the
Hebrew phrase (*ascend for thee* or *for thyself*). Some suppose an allusion
to the practice of addressing large assemblies from the summit or acclivity
of hills. (See Judges ix. 7 ; Deut. xxvii. 12 ; Mat. v. 1.) J. D. Michaelis
compares the ancient practice of transmitting news by shouting from one
hill-top to another, as described by Cæsar (Bell. Gall. vii. 3). *Celeriter
ad omnes Galliæ civitates fama perfertur ; nam ubi major atque illustrior
incidit res, clamore per agros regionesque significant ; hunc alii deinceps excipiunt
et proximis tradunt.* The essential idea is that of local elevation as extending
the diffusion of the sound.—There are two constructions of מְבַשֶּׂרֶת צִיּוֹן and
the parallel expression. The first supposes the words to be in regimen, the
other in apposition. According to the former, which is given in the
Septuagint, Targum, and Vulgate, and retained by Grotius, Lowth, Gesenius, and others, the person addressed is the bearer of good tidings *to*
Zion and Jerusalem (compare chap. lii. 7 ; Nah. ii. 1). The feminine form
is explained by Grotius as an enallage for the masculine, like קֹהֶלֶת, *Preacher*,
an idiom, as Dathe thinks, peculiar to official titles. Gesenius regards it
as an instance of the idiomatic use of the feminine singular as a collective,
like יֹשֶׁבֶת for יֹשְׁבִים (Micah i. 11, 12), and agrees with the Targum in making the prophets the object of address. But this whole theory of collective
feminines is so unnatural, and so imperfectly sustained by the cases which
Gesenius cites (Lehrg. p. 477 ; Heb. Gr. § 105, 2 c.), that if the construction now in question be adopted, it is better to revert to the hypothesis of

Lowth and J. D. Michaelis, that the Prophet alludes to the practice of celebrating victories by the songs of women. (See Exod. xv. 20, 21 ; Judges xi. 34 : 1 Sam. xviii. 6, 7.) But although this explanation is decidedly more natural than that of Grotius and Gesenius, it is perhaps less so than the ancient one contained in the Peshito and the three Greek versions of Aquila, Symmachus, and Theodotion, according to which Zion or Jerusalem herself is represented as the bearer of good tidings to the towns of Judah. This construction is further recommended by the beautiful personification which it introduces of the Holy City as the seat of the true religion and the centre of the church. The office here ascribed to it is the same that is recognised in chap. ii. 3 : *the law shall go forth from Zion, and the word of the Lord from Jerusalem.* Not only in the restoration from captivity, or in the personal advent of the Saviour, but in every instance of the Lord's return to his forsaken people, it is the duty of the church to communicate as well as to receive the joyful tidings. The explanation of Jerusalem and Zion as meaning their inhabitants among the captivity is still more arbitrary here than in ver. 2, because no reason can be given why the exiles from the Holy City should be called upon to act as heralds to the others, whereas there is a beautiful poetical propriety in giving that office to the Holy City itself. Let the reader carefully observe how many exegetical embarrassments arise from the attempt to confine the application of the passage to the period of the exile, or to any other not particularly indicated. The exhortation, *fear not,* does not imply that there was danger in making the announcement, but that there might be doubt and hesitation as to its fulfilment. Barnes thinks it necessary to prevent abuse of this text by affirming that it " will not justify boisterous preaching, or a loud and unnatural tone of voice, alike offensive to good taste, injurious to health, and destructive of the life of the preacher." He also infers from it that " the glad tidings of salvation should be delivered in an animated and ardent manner ; the future punishment of the wicked in a tone serious, solemn, subdued, awful."

10. *Lo, the Lord Jehovah will come* (or *is coming*) *in* (*the person of*) *a strong one, and his arm* (*is*) *ruling for him. Lo, his hire is with him and his wages before him.* The double הִנֵּה represents the object as already appearing or in sight. Of the phrase בְּחָזָק there are several interpretations. All the ancient versions make it mean *with strength ;* but this abstract sense of the adjective is not sustained by usage, and the same objection lies, with still greater force, against Ewald's version, *in victory.* Aben Ezra and Kimchi supply יָד (*with a strong hand*); but wherever the entire phrase occurs, the noun is construed as a feminine. Jarchi makes it mean *against the strong one,* which Vitringa adopts and applies the phrase to Satan. But usage requires that בוא, when it has this sense, should be construed with its object, either directly, or by means of the prepositions עַל, אֶל, or לְ. De Dieu regards the בְּ as pleonastic or a *beth essentiæ,* corresponding to the French construction *en roi,* in (the character or person of) a king. The existence of this idiom in Hebrew is questioned by some eminent grammarians, and is at best so unusual that it should not be assumed without necessity. (See the comment on chap. xxvi. 4, vol. i. p. 421.) The choice, however, seems to lie between this and the construction which explains the words to mean that he will *come with a strong one ;* as in chap. xxviii. 2, the Lord is said to *have a strong and mighty one,* who should cast the crown of Ephraim to the ground with his hand. What God is said to do himself in one case, he is represented in the other as accomplishing by means of a

powerful instrument or agent, which, however, is defined no further. The essential meaning, common to the two constructions, is, that Jehovah was about to make a special exhibition of his power.—The participle *ruling*, in the next clause, is expressive of continuous action. The לֹ cannot refer to *arm*, which Gesenius suggests as a possible construction, because זְרוֹעַ, although sometimes masculine, is here expressly construed as a feminine. The antecedent of the pronoun must be either Jehovah, or the Strong One, according to the sense in which בְּחָזָק is taken, as descriptive of God himself, or of his instrument. Those who understand that phrase to mean *against the strong one*, give the next the sense of *ruling over him*. But although לְ strictly denotes relation in general (*as to, with respect to*), and admits of various equivalents in English, it is never elsewhere used in this sense after מָשַׁל, *to rule*, which, with scarcely an exception, is followed by the preposition בְּ. The true sense of לֹ is probably the obvious one *for him*, and the clause is a poetical description of the arm as acting independently of its possessor, and as it were in his behalf.—Here, as in Lev. xix. 13, Ps. cix. 20, Isa. xlix. 4, פְּעֻלָּה, *work*, is put for its effect, reward, or product. There is no need of assuming with Kimchi, an ellipsis of שָׂכָר before it. The word itself, as Aben Ezra well explains it, is equivalent in meaning to שְׂכַר הַפּוֹעֵל.—J. D. Michaelis considers it as doubtful whether the person here referred to is described as dispensing or receiving a reward, since in either case it would be *his*. The former explanation is preferred by most interpreters, some of whom supposes a specific allusion to the customary distribution of prizes by commanders after victory. Upon this general supposition, Lowth explains the phrase *before him*, as referring to the act of stretching forth the hand, or holding out the thing to be bestowed. Those who restrict the passage to the Babylonish exiles, for the most part understand this clause as promising a recompence to such of the captives as had patiently endured God's will and believed his promises. Knobel, however, understands it as referring to the redeemed people as being themselves the recompence of their deliverer; and Henderson adopts the same construction, but applies it to the recompence earned by the Messiah. This explanation is favoured by what follows in the next verse, where Jehovah or his Strong One is described as a shepherd. The two verses may be readily connected, without any change of figure, by supposing that the lost sheep which he has recovered are the recompence referred to in the verse before us. Thus understood, the passage may have furnished the occasion and the basis of our Saviour's beautiful description of himself as the true shepherd, who lays down his life for the sheep, as well as of the figure drawn from the recovery of a lost sheep to illustrate the rejoicing in heaven over one repentant sinner. But a still more decisive argument in favour of this interpretation is the fact, that in every case without exception where שָׂכָר and פְּעֻלָּה have the same sense as here, the *hire* or *wages of* a person is the hire or wages paid to him, and not that paid by him. To give it the latter meaning in this one case, therefore, would be to violate a usage, not merely general, but uniform ; and such a violation could be justified only by a kind and degree of exegetical necessity which no one can imagine to exist in this case. Upon these grounds it is probable, not only that Jehovah is here represented as receiving a reward, but that there is special reference to the recompence of the Messiah's sufferings and obedience by the redemption of his people. According to the view which has been taken of the nexus between these two verses, *be-*

fore him may possibly contain an allusion to the shepherd's following his flock; but it admits of a more obvious and simple explanation, as denoting that his recompence is not only sure, but actually realised, being already in his sight or presence, and *with him, i. e.* in immediate possession.

11. *Like a shepherd his flock will he feed, with his arm will he gather the lambs, and in his bosom carry (them): the nursing (ewes) he will (gently) lead.* Although the meaning of this verse is plain, it is not easily translated, on account of the peculiar fitness and significancy of the terms employed. The word correctly rendered *feed* denotes the whole care of a shepherd for his flock, and has therefore no exact equivalent in English. To *gather with the arm* coincides very nearly, although not precisely, with our phrase to take up in the arms. A very similar idea is expressed by *bearing in the bosom.* The last clause has been more misunderstood than any other. Most interpreters appear to have regarded עָלוֹת as denoting *pregnant*, whereas it is the active participle of the verb עוּל, to suckle or give suck, and is evidently used in that sense in 1 Samuel vi. 7, 10. The former explanation might appear to have arisen from a misapprehension of the Vulgate version, *fœtas*, which, as Bochart has shewn by quotations from the classics, is sometime applied to animals after delivery, but while still giving suck. But the erroneous explanation is much older, being unambiguously given in the Septuagint (ἐν γαστρὶ ἐχούσας). Aben Ezra also explains עָלוֹת as synonymous with הָרוֹת, whereas Solomon ben Melek gives the correct interpretation (הַבְּהֵמוֹת הַמֵּינִיקוֹת). The essential meaning of יְנַהֵל is admitted to be that of *leading* by all interpreters excepting Hengstenberg, who undertakes to show that it always has reference to sustenance. (Commentary on the Psalms, under Ps. xxiii. 2.) His strongest argument is that derived from Gen. xlvii. 17; but he seems to have overlooked 2 Chron. xxviii. 15; and even Exod. xv. 13, which he owns to be against him, cannot be satisfactorily explained on his hypothesis. In that case, both the parallelism and the construction in the second clause are decidedly in favour of the old opinion, from which there seems, upon the whole, to be no sufficient reason for departing. From the primary and simple sense of leading may be readily deduced that of carefully leading or conducting, which as readily suggests the accessory idea of benignant and affectionate protection. Henderson's statement, that this verse and the one before it exhibit certain attributes of the character and work of Christ, is correct, but too restricted, since the passage is descriptive of the whole relation which Jehovah sustains to his people, as their shepherd, and of which inferior but real exhibitions were afforded long before the advent of the Saviour; for example, in the restoration of the Jews from exile, which is no more to be excluded from the scope of this prophetic picture than to be regarded as its only subject.

12. *Who hath measured the waters in the hollow of his hand, and meted out heaven with the span, and comprehended in a measure the dust of the earth, and weighed in a balance the mountains, and the hills in scales?* There are two directly opposite opinions as to the general idea here expressed. Gesenius and others understand the question as an indirect negation of the possibility of doing what is here described. The implied answer upon this hypothesis, is, No one, and the verse is equivalent to the exclamation, How immense are the works of God! The other and more usual interpretation understands the question thus: Who (but God) has measured or can measure, &c.? Thus understood, the verse, so far from affirming

the immensity of God's works, represents them as little in comparison with him, who measures and distributes them with perfect ease. The first explanation derives some countenance from the analogy of the next verse, where the question certainly involves an absolute negation, and is tantamount to saying, that no one does, or can do, what is there described. But this consideration is not sufficient to outweigh the argument in favour of the other explanation, arising from its greater simplicity and obviousness in this connection. It is also well observed by Hitzig, that in order to convey the idea of immensity, the largest measures, not the smallest, would have been employed. An object might be too large to be weighed in scales, or held in the hollow of a man's hand, and yet very far from being immense or even vast in its dimensions. On the other hand, the smallness of the measure is entirely appropriate, as shewing the immensity of God himself, who can deal with the whole universe as man deals with the most minute and trivial objects.—שֹׁעַל is properly a *handful* (1 Kings xx. 10, Ezek. xiii. 19), but is here put for the receptacle or measure of that quantity.— By *waters* we are not to understand specifically either the ocean (Grotius) or the waters above the firmament (Rosenmüller), but water as a constituent element or portion of the globe.—The primary meaning of תִּכֵּן is supposed by Gesenius to be that of weighing, here transferred to the measure of extension. Maurer, with more probability, regards it as a generic term for measurement, including that of weight, capacity, and extension.—The span is mentioned as a natural and universal measure of length, to which we must likewise apply Jerome's translation (*tribus digitis*), and not, as Gill imagines, to the quantity of dust which " a man can hold between his thumb and two fingers."—In every other place where כָּל occurs, it is the construct or abbreviated form of כֹּל, the nearest equivalent to our *all*, but uniformly construed as a noun, meaning properly the *whole* of anything. The Septuagint translates it so in this case likewise (πᾶσαν τὴν γῆν), and Gesenius, in his Lehrgebäude (p. 675), gives it as one of the cases in which the governing and governed noun are separated by an intervening word. In quoting the Hebrew, he inadvertently inserts a *makkeph* (וְכָל־בַּשָּׁלִישׁ), thus conforming the orthography to the usual analogy. But having afterwards observed that the Hebrew text has כָּל with a conjunctive accent, he corrected the error in his Lexicon and Commentary, and referred the word to the root כּוּל, which does not occur elsewhere in Kal, but the essential idea of which, as appears from the Chaldee and Arabic analogy, as well as from its own derivatives in Hebrew, is that of measuring, or rather that of holding and containing, which agrees exactly with the common English Version (*comprehended*). It is a curious and characteristic circumstance that Hitzig, in his note upon this passage, revives the explanation which Gesenius had given by mistake, and afterwards abandoned, appealing to Ps. xxxv. 10 as an example of the use of כָּל (*all*) with a conjunctive accent, and to Isaiah xxxviii. 16 as an instance of its separation from the dependent noun. To this unexpected defence of his own inadvertent error Gesenius replies, in his Thesaurus (ii. 665), that clear expressions are not to be elucidated by the analogy of dark ones, and that a verb is needed here to balance the verbs *measure, mete,* and *weigh* in the other clauses.—The terms used in the English Bible, *scales* and *balance,* are retained above, but transposed, in order to adhere more closely to the form of the original, in which the first word is a singular (denoting properly an apparatus like the steelyard), while the other is a dual, strictly denoting a *pair* of scales. This is in fact the etymological import of *balance*, according to the usual explanation of the Latin *bilanx*, as denoting a double dish or plate; but be this as it may, the English *balance* does not, like the plural *scales*, at once suggest the form of the instrument intended.—The *dust of the earth* seems to be here put for the earth itself, and is therefore not erroneously, though freely, rendered in the Vulgate *molem terræ.* שָׁלִישׁ is properly a *third, i. e.* the third of another measure, probably the ephah, which is often rendered in the Septuagint τρία μέτρα, while the *seah* is translated μέτρον. The name is analogous to *quart* (meaning *fourth*), and exactly coincident with *tierce*, which Skinner defines to be " a measure so called because the third part (*triens*) of another measure called a pipe," but which is also used in old English writers for the third part of other measures. (See Richardson's Dictionary, p. 1910.) The ephah, according to the best computation, was equivalent to one Italian modius and a half. J. D. Michaelis is probably singular in thinking it necessary to express the value of the measure in translation, by making the Prophet ask, who measures the dust of the earth with the third part of a bushel. This is not only in bad taste, but hurtful to the sense; because the literal comprehension of the earth in this specific measure is impossible, and all that the words were intended to suggest is a comparison between the customary measurement of common things by man, and the analogous control which is exercised by God over all his works. For this end, the general sense of *measure*, which the word has in Ps. lxxx. 6, and which is given to it here by the Targum (מכילא), is entirely sufficient. The exact size of the שָׁלִישׁ is of no more importance to the exposition than that of the balance or the scales.—The idea of accurate exact adjustment, which by some interpreters is thought to be included in the meaning of this verse, if expressed at all, is certainly not prominent, the main design of the description being simply to exhibit, not the power or the wisdom of God as distinguishable attributes, but rather the supreme control in which they are both exercised.—Ewald connects this verse with the argument that follows, by suggesting, as the answer to the question, that certainly no man, and much less the image of a man, could do what is here described.—Umbreit connects it with what goes before, by supposing the Prophet to affirm that the gracious Shepherd, just before described, is at the same time all-wise and omnipotent, and therefore able to make good the promise of protection to his people.

13. *Who hath measured the spirit of Jehovah, and (who, as) the man of his counsel, will teach him* (or *cause him to know*)? According to J. D. Michaelis, the connection between this verse and the one before it is, that he who can do the one can do the other; if any one can weigh the hills, &c., he can also measure the divine intelligence. But the natural connection seems to be, that he who weighs the hills, &c., must himself be independent, boundless, and unsearchable.—The various explanations of תִּכֵּן, as meaning known, instructed, prepared, directed, searched, &c., are mere substitutions of what ought to have been said (in the interpreter's opinion) for what is said. Although not impossible, it is highly improbable that the word should have a different meaning here from that which it evidently has in the foregoing verse, where the sense is determined by the mention of the span. What seems to be denied, is the possibility of either limiting or estimating the divine intelligence.—According to Calvin, we are not to understand by רוּחַ here the Holy Spirit as a person of the Godhead,

but the mind or intellect of God. The Targum arbitrarily explains it as denoting *the Holy Spirit* (*i. e.* inspiration) *in the mouth of all the prophets.*— The last clause is not an answer to the first, but a continuation of the question. Most interpreters suppose the *who* to be repeated. Luther and Rosenmüller make it agree directly with the following phrase. (*What counsellor*, &c.) The latest writers make the construction relative as well as interrogative. *Who was* (or *is*) *the counsellor that taught him?* A simpler construction is that given in our Bible, which supplies neither interrogative nor relative: *and* (*being*) *his counsellor*, or (*as*) *his counsellor, hath taught him.* The translation of the last verb as a preterite is entirely arbitrary. Both tenses seem to have been used, as in many other cases, for the purpose of making the implied negation more exclusive. *Who has, and who will* or *can?*—Ewald, rejecting the usual combination of *man* with *counsel* in the sense of *counsellor*, makes one the subject, and the other the object of the verb, "and reveals—though a man—his counsel to him." The same construction seems to be at least as old as Arias Montanus, who translates the clause *vir consilium ejus scire faciet eum.* In favour of the usual interpretation is its greater simplicity, and the occurrence of the plural form, *the men of my counsel*, in the obvious sense of counsellors, in Ps. cxix. 24.—Lowth's translation (*one of his council*) gives a sense to עֵצָה not sustained by usage, and Barnes's modification of it (*one of his counsel*) introduces an idea wholly modern and irrelevant.—Calvin supposes that the Prophet, having spoken of the goodness of God in ver. 11, and of his power in ver. 12, here proceeds to magnify his wisdom. But both these verses are designed alike to set forth his supremacy and independence, by describing him as measuring and regulating all things, while himself incapable either of measurement or regulation.

14. *Whom did he consult* (or *with whom took he counsel*) *and he made him understand, and taught him in the path of judgment, and taught him knowledge, and the way of understanding* (*who*) *will make him know?* The consecution of the tenses is the same as in the foregoing verse. The indirect construction of the second and following verbs, by Lowth and the later German writers (*that he should instruct him*, &c.), is not only forced, but inconsistent with the use of the conversive future, and a gratuitous substitution of an occidental idiom for the somewhat harsh but simple Hebrew syntax, in which the object of the first verb is the subject of the second. *What man did he* (the Lord) *consult, and he* (the man) *made him* (the Lord) *to understand*, &c. The sense is given, but with little change of form, in the English Version, by repeating the interrogative pronoun. *With whom took he counsel, and* (*who*) *instructed him or made him understand?*— The preposition before *path* is understood by Hitzig, Ewald, and Umbreit, as denoting the subject of instruction: taught him respecting or concerning (*über*) the path of judgment. Gesenius and Hendewerk regard it as a mere connective of the verb with its object: taught him the path, &c. But the most satisfactory explanation is the one proposed by Knobel, who attaches to the verb the sense of guiding, and retains the proper meaning of the particle. This is confirmed by the analogy of the synonymous verb הוֹרָה, which originally means to guide, and is also construed with the same preposition (Ps. xxxii. 8, Prov. iv. 11).—By *judgment* we must either understand *discretion*, in which case the whole phrase will be synonymous with *way of understanding* in the parallel clause; or *rectitude*, in which case the whole phrase will mean the *right way*, not in a moral sense, but in that of a way conducting to the end desired, the right way to attain that end. As these

are only different expressions of the same essential idea, the question is of little exegetical importance.—The plural תְּבוּנוֹת, literally *understandings*, is not an Arabism, as Knobel elsewhere affirms of this whole class of words, but a genuine Hebrew idiom, denoting fulness or an eminent degree of the quality in question, just as חָכְמוֹת is used in the book of Proverbs to denote the highest wisdom, the *sapientia hypostatica*. [See Hengstenberg on the Pentateuch, vol. i. p. 258, and on Psalm xlix. 3 (4).]—Jarchi, with characteristic nationality, regards this as a contrast, not between God and man, but between Israel and other nations : " With which of the Gentiles did he take counsel as he did with the prophets, as it is said of Abraham, The Lord said, Shall I hide from Abraham what I am about to do ?"— Junius and Tremellius make the first verb reciprocal, and all the rest re- flexive (*Cum quo communicavit consilium, ut instruerit se*, &c. ?), which is wholly gratuitous and forced.—The first clause of this verse is quoted in Rom. xi. 34, with the following words added, *or who hath first given to him, and it shall be recompensed unto him again ?* As this addition is also found in the Alexandrian text of the Septuagint, J. D. Michaelis infers that it has dropped out of the Hebrew. It is more probable, however, that the words were introduced into the Septuagint from the text in Romans, where they are really no part of the quotation from Isaiah, but the apostle's own paraphrase of it, or addition to it, the form of which may have been sug- gested by the first clause of Job xli. 3 (in the English Bible, xli. 11). Such allusive imitations occur elsewhere in Paul's writings. (See the remarks on 1 Cor. i. 20, and its connection with Isaiah xxxiii. 18, p. 14). In the present case, the addition agrees fully with the spirit of the passage quoted; since the aid in question, if it had been afforded, would be fairly entitled to a recompence.

15. *Lo, nations as a drop from a bucket, and as dust on scales are reckoned; lo, islands as an atom he will take up.* He is independent, not only of nature and of individual men, but of nations. The Septuagint gives הֵן the Chaldee sense of *if*, leaving the sentence incomplete notwithstanding the attempts of the modern editors to carry the construction through several verses. By supplying *are* in the first clause, the English Version impairs the compact strength of the expression. Both members of the clause are to be con- strued with the verb at the end. This verb De Wette and Hendewerk explain as meaning *are to be reckoned* (*sind zu achten*); but although this future sense is common in the Niphal participle, it is not to be assumed in the preterite without necessity. The sense is rather that they are already so considered. Luther gives מַר מִדְּלִי the sense of a drop remaining in a bucket when the water is poured out, corresponding to the parallel expres- sion of an atom which remains in the balance after anything is weighed. Hitzig also translates the last word *in the bucket* (*im Eimer*). Maurer gives the strict translation *from a bucket*, and supposes *hanging* to be understood (*de situla pendens*). But as this is not an obvious ellipsis, it is better to explain the מִן as simply expressing the proportion of the drop to the con- tents of the bucket, a drop out of a whole bucket. Next to this, the simplest explanation is the one suggested in the English Version, which seems to take the phrase as an indirect expression for a *drop of water*. But as the mention of the bucket would in that case be superfluous, the other explana- tion is entitled to the preference. *Dust of the scales* or *balance, i. e.* dust resting on it, but without sensibly affecting its equilibrium. The Vulgate version (*momentum staterae*) seems directly to reverse the meaning of the phrase, in which the dust is obviously spoken of as having no appreciable

weight. The exegetical tradition is decisive in favour of explaining שַׁחַק to mean fine dust, while the uniform usage of the word in other cases would require the sense of *cloud*. It is possible indeed that the image which the Prophet intended to suggest was that of *a cloud in the balance*, the idea of extreme levity being then conveyed by comparison with the weight of what is commonly regarded as imponderable. The weight of authority is all in favour of the other sense, which may be readily connected with the common one, by supposing שַׁחַק to mean first a cloud in general, then a cloud of dust in particular, and then dust in general, or more specifically fine minute dust. דַּק, from דָּקַק, to crush or pulverize, denotes any minute portion of a solid substance, and in this connection may be well expressed by *atom*. The Seventy seem to have mistaken it for רֹק, *saliva*, spittle, and translates it σίελος. Gesenius gives אִיִּם the general sense of *lands*, and then notes this usage of the word as a sign of later date. But why may not *islands*, in the strict sense, be intended here as much as hills and mountains in ver. 12? The only objection is founded on the parallelism; but this is imperfect, even if we give אִיִּם its widest sense. J. D. Michaelis goes to the opposite extreme, by making it mean Europe and Asia Minor. Rabbi Jonah explains יִטּוֹל as the Niphal of טוּל to throw or cast, and this explanation is retained by Knobel. In like manner, Aquila has λεπτὸν βαλλόμενον. But most interpreters agree in making it the future Kal of נְטַל, which in Syriac and Chaldee means to raise or lift up. On the former supposition, it must either agree irregularly with the plural *islands*, or with a relative to be supplied (like an atom which is cast away). This last construction is consistent also with the other derivation of the verb. Thus Rosenmüller has, *quem tollit tollens*; and Maurer, *which it* (the wind) *carries off*. But the simplest construction is the one which makes אִיִּם the direct object of the verb, as in the English Version. Ewald gives the verb itself the sense of *poising*, weighing, which is too specific.

16. *And Lebanon is not enough for burning, and its beasts are not enough for a sacrifice.* The supremacy and majesty of God are now presented in a more religious aspect, by expressions borrowed from the Mosaic ritual. He is not only independent of the power, but also of the good will of his creatures. This general allusion to oblation, as an act of homage or of friendship, suits the connection better than a specific reference to expiation. The insufficiency of these offerings is set forth, not in a formal proposition, but by means of a striking individualisation. For general terms he substitutes one striking instance, and asserts of that what might be asserted of the rest. If Lebanon could not suffice, what could? The imagery here used is justly described by Umbreit as magnificent: Nature the temple; Lebanon the altar; its lordly woods the pile; its countless beasts the sacrifice. There is a strong idiomatic peculiarity of form in this verse. אֵין and דֵי are properly both nouns in the construct state, the first meaning non-existence and the other sufficiency. The nearest approach in English to the form of the original is *nothing of sufficiency of burning*; but אֵין, as usual, includes or indicates the verb of existence, and דֵי is followed by a noun expressive of the end for which a thing is said to be or not to be sufficient. Clericus and Rosenmüller give בָּעֵר the sense of *kindling*, which it sometimes has (*e. g.* Exod. xxxv. 3, Lev. vi. 5); but as this differs from *burning* only in being limited to the inception of the process, and as it seems more natural to speak of wood enough to burn than of wood enough to kindle, there is no cause of departing from the usual interpretation. The collective חַיָּה (*animal for*

animals), having no equivalent in English, although common in Hebrew, can be represented only by a plural.—עֹלָה is the technical name appropriated in the law of Moses to the ordinary sacrifice for general expiation. It seems to denote strictly an ascension or ascent, being so called, either from the mounting of the vapour, or from the ascent of the whole victim on the altar. As the phrase by which it is commonly translated in the English Bible (*burnt-offering*) is not an exact etymological equivalent, and as no stress seems to be laid here upon the species of oblation, the general term *offering* or *sacrifice* would seem to be sufficiently specific. (Compare with this verse chap. lxvi. 1, 1 Kings viii. 27, 2 Chron. vi. 18, Ps. l. 8–13.)

17. *All the nations as nothing before him, less than nothing and vanity are counted to him.* The proposition of ver. 15 is repeated, but in still more absolute and universal terms. Instead of *nations*, he says *all the nations ;* instead of likening them to grains of sand or drops of water, he denies their very being. *Before him* does not simply mean in his view or estimation, but in comparison with him, the primary import of נֶגֶד being such as to suggest the idea of two objects brought together or confronted for the purpose of comparison. So, too, the parallel expression לֹו does not mean *by him* (which is seldom, if ever, so expressed in Hebrew), but *with respect to him*, or simply *to him* in the same sense as when we say that one thing or person is *nothing to* another, *i. e.* not to be compared with it. The same use of *to*, even without a negative, is clear from such expressions as " Hyperion to a Satyr." That God is the arbiter who thus decides between himself and his creatures, is still implied in both the phrases, although not the sole or even prominent idea meant to be expressed by either.—The structure of the sentence is exactly like that of the first clause of ver. 15, and the same remark is applicable, as to the insertion of the substantive verb in the English Version.—The particle *as* may either be a mere connective, *reckoned as nothing, i. e.* reckoned *for* or reckoned *to be* nothing, which is rather an English than a Hebrew idiom, or it may serve to soften the expression by suggesting that it is not to be literally understood, in which case it is nearly equivalent to *as it were.* So the Vulgate: *Quasi non sint, sic sunt coram eo.*—The etymological distinction between אַיִן and אֶפֶס is that the latter means annihilation or the end of being, the former absolute nonentity. In this case, the weaker term is assimilated to the stronger by the addition of another word, denoting desolation or emptiness, and here used as a formula of intense negation. The preposition before אֶפֶס is explained by some as connective of the verb with its object, *reckoned for nothing ;* which construction seems to be as old as the Septuagint (εἰς οὐδὲν ἐλογίσθησαν), but is not sufficiently sustained by the usage of the Hebrew particle. Others make it an expression of resemblance, like the Vulgate (*quasi nihilum*); which seems to be a mere conjecture from the parallelism, and is equally at variance with usage. Calvin (followed by the English Version, Clericus, Vitringa, Umbreit, and Ewald in the first edition of his Grammar) makes the מִן comparative, and understands the phrase as meaning *less than nothing*. To this it is objected by Gesenius, that it does not suit the parallelism (a virtual assertion that a climax is impossible in Hebrew composition), and that the idea is too far-fetched (*zu gesucht*) ; to which Hitzig adds that there is no word to mean *less*, and that if the מִן were really comparative, the phrase would necessarily mean *more than nothing.* These objections are renewed by Knobel, without any notice of

Umbreit's answer to the last, viz. that the idea of minority is suggested by the context ; that *less than nothing* could not well be otherwise expressed ; and that even if it meant *more than nothing*, it would still be an equivalent expression, meaning more of nothing than nothing itself. Gesenius, in his Commentary, makes the מ an expletive or pleonastic particle, of common use in Arabic, so that the phrase means simply *nothing.* But in his Lexicons he agrees with Hitzig and Maurer in giving it a partitive sense, *of nothing, i. e.* a part of nothing, which, as Hitzig says, is here conceived of as a great concrete or aggregate, of which the thing in question is a portion. But as the whole must be greater than the part, this explanation is essentially identical with Calvin's (*less than nothing*), which Gesenius admits, but still objects to the latter as being less poetical than mathematical. The reader may determine for himself whether it is any more *gesucht* than that preferred to it, or than that proposed by Hendewerk, who seems to understand the מ as indicating the material or source, as if he had said, (*made or produced*) *out of nothing and vanity.* The common ground assumed by all these explanations is, that the verse contains the strongest possible expression of insignificance and even non-existence, as predicable even of whole nations, in comparison with God, and in his presence.

18. *And* (*now*) *to whom will ye liken God, and what likeness will ye compare to him?* The inevitable logical conclusion from the previous considerations is that God is One and that there is no other. From this, the Prophet now proceeds to argue, that it is folly to compare God even with the most exalted creature, how much more with lifeless matter. The logical relation of this verse to what precedes, although not indicated in the text, may be rendered clearer by the introduction of an illative particle (*then, therefore,* &c.), or more simply by inserting *now*, which is often used in such connections. (See for example Ps. ii. 10, and Hengstenberg's Commentary, vol. i. p. 44.) The last clause admits of two constructions, both amounting to the same thing in the end. What *likeness* or resemblance (*i. e.* what similar object) will ye *compare* to him ? Or, what *comparison* will ye *institute* respecting him ? The last agrees best with the usage of the verb, as meaning to arrange, prepare, or set in order (*to compare,* only indirectly and by implication) ; while at the same time it avoids the unusual combination of *comparing a likeness* to a thing or person, instead of comparing the two objects for the purpose of discovering their likeness.—The use of the divine name אל (expressive of omnipotence) is here emphatic and significant, as a preparation for the subsequent exposure of the impotence of idols. The force of the original expression is retained in Vitringa's version (*Deum fortem*).

19. *The image a carver has wrought, and a gilder with gold shall overlay it, and chains of silver* (*he is*) *casting.* The ambiguous construction of the first clause is the same in the original, where we may either supply a relative, or make it a distinct proposition. In favour of the first, which is a frequent ellipsis both in Hebrew and English, is the fact, that the verse then contains a direct answer to the question in the one before it. What have you to set over against such a God ? The image which an ordinary workman manufactures. It enables us also to account for the position of *the image* at the beginning of the sentence, and for its having the definite article, while the following nouns have none, both which forms of expression seem to be significant, *the image* which *a workman* (*i. e.* any workman) can produce.— The consecution of the tenses seems to shew, that the writer takes his stand between the commencement and the end of the process, and

describes it as actually going on. The carver has already wrought the image, and the gilder is about to overlay it.—There is a seeming incongruity between the strict etymological senses of the nouns and verb in this clause : חָרָשׁ is properly a carver, and פֶּסֶל a carved or graven image ; whereas נָסַךְ, as descriptive of a process of art, can only mean to melt, cast, or found. This can only be accounted for upon the supposition, that the verb, or the nouns, or both, have acquired in usage a more extensive or indefinite meaning. In the translation above given, the discrepancy has been removed by giving to the verb the general sense of *wrought*, and to the first noun that of *image*, which it evidently has in other places, where a contrast is exhibited between God and idols, of course without regard to the mode of their formation. (See for example chap. xlii. 8, and the note on chap. xxx. 22, vol. i. p. 482.)—צֹרֵף is properly a *melter*, and is elsewhere applied both to the smelter or finer of metals (Prov. xxv. 4), and to the founder or caster of images (Judges xvii. 4). The word *gilder*, although not an exact translation, has been used above, as more appropriate in this connection than the common version *goldsmith*.—רָקַע, which elsewhere means to beat out metal into thin plates, here denotes the application of such plates as an ornamental covering. Henderson repeats this verb, in its original sense of beating out, before *chains of silver*. Hitzig and Ewald continue the construction of the first clause through the second, and take .. as a noun, repeated for the sake of a sarcastic effect. (*And with silver chains the goldsmith*.) A similar construction had before been given by Cocceius, who supplies the substantive verb (*et sunt catenæ argenteæ aurifabri*). But the different mode of writing the word in the two clauses (צֹרֵף and צוֹרֵף seems to favour the opinion of Gesenius and most other writers, that the latter is a verbal form. Lowth reads צָרַף in the preterite, on the authority of twenty-seven manuscripts and three editions. Maurer explains it as the Præter Poel, of which, however, there is no example elsewhere. Gesenius regards it as a participle used for the present tense. It is really equivalent to our continuous or compound present, denoting what is actually now in progress.—The silver chains may be considered either simply ornamental, or as intended to suspend the image and prevent its falling.

20. (*As for*) *the* (*man*) *impoverished* (*by*) *offering, a tree* (*that*) *will not rot he chooses, a wise carver he seeks for it, to set up an image* (*that*) *shall not be moved.* While the rich waste their gold and silver upon idols, the poor are equally extravagant in wood. None of the usual meanings of סָכַן is here appropriate. From the noun מִסְכְּנוֹת (*treasures, stores*), Rabbi Jonah derives the sense of *rich*, while all the modern writers are agreed in giving it the opposite meaning, although doubtful and divided as to the etymology. As the form is evidently that of a participle passive, the best translation seems to be *impoverished*, and the best construction that proposed by Gesenius in his Lehrgebäude (p. 821), *impoverished by oblation or religious gifts*. It is true, that in his Commentary and Lexicons he abandons this construction, on the ground of an objection made by one of his reviewers, that it does not suit the context, and adopts the one which most succeeding writers have repeated, viz., *poor as to offering*, that is, too poor to make a costly one, or, as Cocceius slightly modifies the sense, *frugalior oblationis*. To this there is a strong philological objection, that תְּרוּמָה, though a very common word, is nowhere else applied to an image, and that an image could not be naturally called an offering. On the other hand, the objection from the context, so submissively allowed by

Gesenius, is not only vague but founded on a superficial view of the connection. To say that the poor man uses wood instead of gold and silver, is coherent and appropriate, but far less significant and striking than to say, that the man who has already reduced himself to want by lavish gifts to his idol, still continues his devotions, and as he no longer can afford an image of the precious metals is resolved at least to have a durable wooden one. Thus understood, the verse adds to the general description a particular trait highly expressive of the folly of idolaters. The desertion by Gesenius of his first opinion differs from that mentioned in the exposi· tion of ver. 12 in this respect, that while he there relinquishes his former ground as having been assumed through inadvertence and mistake, he here continues to assert that what he first proposed is still the most grammatical construction (as evinced by the analogy of chap. i. 20, 1 Kings xxii. 10, Ex. xxviii. 11, &c.), but abandons it in deference to an unmeaning and gratuitous objection. The obscurity of this phrase, even to the ancient writers, is apparent from its omission in the Septuagint and Vulgate, and from Jerome's explanation of *amsuchan* as a kind of wood.—In the next clause, the Vulgate makes חָרָשׁ חָכָם the subject of the verb (*artifex sapiens querit quomodo*, &c.; but the common construction is more natural, because it makes the conduct of the devotee still the subject of description. *Wise* is here used in what appears to be its primary meaning of artistically skilful. (See the note on chap. iii. 3, p. 110.) לוֹ may either be reflexive (*for himself*), as some consider it in ver. 11, and as all admit לָךְ to be in ver. 9, or it may be refered to עֵץ. Having secured the stuff, he seeks *for it* a skilful workman. As עֵץ is an obvious antecedent, and as the reflexive use of the pronouns is comparatively rare, this last construction seems entitled to the preference.—Although *to prepare* is a very common meaning of הָכִין, its primary sense of setting upright or erecting is entitled to the preference, not only upon etymological grounds, but because it agrees better with the following expression, לֹא יִמּוֹט, which stands in antithesis, not to the preparation of the image, but to its erection or establishment, in which the previous preparation is of course implied.—As kinds of wood regarded by the ancients as perfectly durable, Grotius enumerates the cypress, grape-vine, juniper, and mulberry; Rosenmüller the olive, cedar, fir, and oak; to which Gesenius adds the lotus and the fig-tree. There is no need, however, of supposing a specific reference to any one or more of these varieties.

21. *Will you not know? will you not hear? has it not been told you from the first? have you not understood the foundations* (or *from the foundations*) *of the earth?* The tenses of the verbs in the first clause have been variously and arbitrarily explained by different interpreters. The English Version and some others exchange both the futures for praeters (*have ye not known? have ye not heard?*) without any satisfactory reason or authority. So far is such a reason from being afforded by the addition of the preterite הֻגַּד in this place, or the use of the praeters יָדַעְתָּ and שְׁמַעְתָּ in ver. 28, that it rather proves the contrary, and makes it necessary to retain the strict sense of the futures. Still more capricious is the explanation of the first verb as a present, and the second as a praeter, by the Vulgate and some modern writers (*do you not know? have you not heard?*). With as much or as little reason Cocceius combines the present and the future (*do you not know? will you not hear?*). There is less objection to the rendering of both verbs in the present tense by Luther (*know you not? hear you not?*). But the most satisfactory, because the safest and most regular construction, is the

strict one given in the Septuagint (οὐ γνώσεσθε; οὐκ ἀκούσεσθε;), revived by Lowth (*will you not know? will you not hear?*), and approved by Ewald (*o wollt ihr nicht erkennen? o wollt ihr nicht hören?*). The clause is then not a mere expression of surprise at their not knowing, but of concern or indignation at their being unwilling to know. There is no inconsistency between this explanation of the first two questions and the obvious meaning of the third, because the proof of their unwillingness to hear and know was the fact of their having been informed from the beginning.—מֵרֹאשׁ is not a mere indefinite expression meaning *long ago, of old,* or the like, but must refer to some specific *terminus a quo,* which Aben Ezra takes to be the beginning of life. This would be more appropriate if an individual were the object of address. Others understand it to mean, from the beginning of your national existence, which supposes too exclusive a reference to the Jews in exile. Neither of these objections lies against the reference of the words to the beginning of the human race, or of the world itself, which is, moreover, favoured by the subsequent appeal to the creation. Kimchi explains מֵרֹאשׁ as an allusion to the *cabbalah* or Jewish tradition, and Hitzig likewise thinks there is a twofold appeal to nature and tradition, or, as Calvin more scripturally states it, to the word and works of God. But although this affords a good sense, it may perhaps be too great a refinement on the plain import of the words, which would seem to refer simply to the testimony of external nature, and to mean that they who question the existence or supremacy of one God are *without excuse,* as Paul says, *because the invisible things of him from the creation of the world are clearly seen, being understood by the things that are made, to wit, his eternal power and Godhead.* (Rom. i. 20. Compare Acts xiv. 17, xvii. 24.)—In the last clause Gesenius and most of the later writers connect the verb directly with the noun, as meaning, *have you not considered* (or *have you not understood*) *the foundations of the earth?* Others, adhering to the Masoretic accents, which forbid the immediate grammatical conjunction of the verb and noun, prefix a preposition to the latter. *Have you not understood (from) the foundations of the earth?* The particle thus supplied may either be a particle of time, as explained by Junius and Ewald (*since the creation*), or indicate the source of knowledge (*from the creation*), as explained by Calvin. The latter is more obvious and simple in itself; but the other is favoured by the parallelism, as מֵרֹאשׁ is universally allowed to have a temporal meaning. Lowth's emendation of the text, by the actual insertion of the preposition, is superfluous, and therefore inadmissible.—By the *foundations* of the earth we are not to understand a literal description of its structure, nor an allusion to the four elements of earth, air, fire, and water, upon which Kimchi here inserts a dissertation, but as a substitution of the concrete for the abstract, the foundations of the earth being put, by a natural and common figure, for its being founded, *i.e.* its creation.

22. *The (one) sitting on* (or *over*) *the circle of the earth, and its inhabitants (are) as grasshoppers* (or *locusts*); *the one spreading like a veil* (or *awning*) *the heavens, and he stretches them out like the tent to dwell in.* The relative construction, *he that sitteth,* is substantially correct, but it is better to retain, as far as possible, the form of the original, as given above. The words may then be construed with the verb of existence understood, as in the English Version (*it is he that sitteth*), or with the last verb in the preceding verse (*have ye not considered the one sitting?* &c.).—The circle of the earth may either mean the earth itself, or the heavens by which it is surmounted and encompassed. (Solomon Ben Melek, גלגל הסובב הכל.) This

expression has been urged with equal propriety by Gill as a proof that the
Prophet was acquainted with the true shape of the earth, and by Knobel as
a proof that he had a false idea of the heavens. On the absurdity of such
conclusions, see p. 20. As a parallel to this may be mentioned the
remark of Hendewerk, that God is here described as bearing just the same
proportion to mankind that the latter bear to insects! The same comparison
occurs in Num. xiii. 33. חָגָב is now commonly explained to mean a species
of *locust*, which of course has no effect upon the point of the comparison,
the essential idea being that of *bestiolæ* (Calvin) or *minuta animantia*
(Grotius).—דֹּק is properly a fine cloth, here applied, as Lowth supposes, to
the awning spread over the open courts of oriental houses. It has been
disputed whether the last words of the verse mean for himself to dwell in,
or for man to dwell in. But they really form part, not of the direct
description, but of the comparison, like a tent pitched for dwelling in, an
idea distinctly expressed in the translation both by Henderson (*a dwelling-
tent*) and Ewald (*das Wohnzelt*).—With this verse compare chaps. xlii. 5,
xliv. 24; Job ix. 8; Ps. civ. 2.

23. *The* (*one*) *bringing* (literally *giving* or *putting*) *princes to nothing,
the judges* (or *rulers*) *of the earth like emptiness* (or *desolation*) *he has made.*
Not only nature but man, not only individuals but nations, not only nations but their rulers, are completely subject to the power of God. The
Septuagint understands לְאָיִן as meaning so as to rule over nothing (ὡς
οὐδὲν ἄρχειν), implying the loss of their authority. The Vulgate strangely
renders רוֹזְנִים *secretorum scrutatores*, a version probably suggested by the
Chaldee רָז, a secret.

24. *Not even planted were they, not even sown, not even rooted in the
ground their stock, and he just breathed* (or *blew*) *upon them, and they
withered, and a whirlwind like the chaff shall take them up* (or *away*).
The Targum gives אַף בַּל the sense of *though* (אפילו), Aben Ezra and
Kimchi that of *as if* (כאלו), which last is adopted by Luther and Calvin.
Gesenius and the later German writers all agree that the compound phrase
has here the sense of *scarcely*. אַ by itself denotes accession, and may
sometimes be expressed by *yea* or *yes*, sometimes by *also* or *even*. It is not
impossible that in the present case the אַף in one clause, and the corresponding גַּם in the other, were intended to connect the statements of this verse
with the one before it. As if he had said, not only can God ultimately
bring them to destruction, but *also* when they are not yet planted, &c.; not
only by slower and more potent means, but *also* by breathing on them.
Another possible solution is that *yes* and *no* are here combined to express
the idea of uncertainty, as if he had said, they are and are not sown,
planted, &c., *i. e.* when they are scarcely sown, or when it is still doubtful
whether they are sown. But perhaps the simplest and most natural construction is the one assumed above in the translation, where the phrase is
taken as substantially equivalent to our *not even*, yielding the same sense
in the end with the usual modern version *scarcely*. The future form which
some give to the verbs is wholly arbitrary. He is describing the destruction of the great ones of the earth as already effected; and even if the
præters be *præterita prophetica*, there is no more need of giving them the
future form in English than in Hebrew. The transition to the future in
the last clause is analogous to that in ver 19, and has the same effect of
shewing that the point of observation is an intermediate one between the
beginning and the end of the destroying process. The essential meaning

of the whole verse is, that God can extirpate them, not only in the end, but in a moment ; not only in the height of their prosperity, but long before they have attained it. J. D. Michaelis supposes a particular allusion to the frequency with which the highest families became extinct, so that there is not now on earth a royal house which is the lineal representative of any race that reigned in ancient times. It is possible, however, that the words may have reference to the national existence of Israel as a nation, the end of which, with the continued and more glorious existence of the church, independent of all national restrictions, may be said to constitute the great theme of these prophecies.

25. *And now to (whom) will ye liken me, and (to whom) shall I be equal ? saith the Holy One.* He winds up his argument by coming back to the triumphant challenge of ver. 18. This repetition does not seem to have struck any one as indicating a strophical arrangement, although such a conclusion would be quite as valid as in many other cases. The indirect construction of the second verb as a subjunctive (*that I may* or *should be equal*), although preferred by Luther, Calvin, and most modern writers, is much less simple in itself, and less consistent with the genius and usage of the language, than its strict translation as a future, continuing directly the interrogation of the other clause.—The epithet *Holy* is in this connection well explained by J. D. Michaelis as including all that distinguishes between God and his creatures, so that the antithesis is perfect. (Compare chap. vi. 3, vol. i. page 147.)

26. *Lift up on high your eyes and see—who hath created these ?—(and who is) the (one) bringing out by number their host ?—to all of them by name will he call—from abundance of might and (because) strong in power —not one faileth* (literally *a man is not missed* or *found wanting*). The same exhortation to lift up the eyes occurs elsewhere in Isaiah (chap. xxxvii. 23, xlix. 18, lx. 4.—The construction is not, *see (him) who created these*, or, *see who created these*, but, as the accents indicate, *see, behold*, the heavens and the heavenly bodies, and then as a distinct interrogation, *who created these ?* There is more doubt as to the question whether the following words continue the interrogation or contain the answer to it. In the former case, the sense is, *Who created these ? (who is) the (one) bringing out*, &c. ? In the latter case, *Who created these ? The (one) bringing out*, &c. This last is favoured by the analogy of chap. xli. 4, 26, xlii. 24, and other places, where a similar question is immediately succeeded by the answer. But in this case such an answer would be almost unmeaning, since it would merely say that he who rules the heavenly bodies made them. It is much more natural to understand the last clause as completing the description.—To *bring out* is a military term, as appears from chap. xliii. 17, and 2 Sam. v. 2. It is applied as here to the host of heaven in Job. xxxviii. 32.—Instead of *by number*, Zwingle and Henderson understand the phrase to mean *in number, i. e.* in great numbers, just as בְּכֹחַ means *with might* or *mightily*. But the common explanation of the phrase as denoting order and arrangement is favoured not only by the military form of the whole description, but by the parallel expression *by name*, which is not used to qualify the noun but the verb, and to shew in what way the commander of this mighty host exerts his power, in what way he brings out and calls his soldiers, viz., by number and by name. The reference of these clauses to the rising of the heavenly bodies makes them too specific, and confounds direct description with comparison. The sense is that the stars are like an army which its leader brings out and enumerates, the

particular points of the resemblance being left to the imagination. The explanation of אַמִּיץ by Gesenius and others as an abstract meaning *strength* is neither justified by usage nor required by the context, since the word may be applied as a descriptive epithet to God, who is the subject of the sentence. It is an old and singular opinion that the strength here spoken of is that residing in the stars themselves. לֹא נֶעְדָּר may also be regarded as a military phrase. The feminine form of the same expression occurs in a different application, chap. xxxiv. 16. (See p. 31.)

27. *Why wilt thou say, O Jacob, and why (thus) speak, O Israel? Hidden is my way from Jehovah, and from my God my cause will pass (or is about to pass) away.* The future verbs in this verse have been rendered as variously as those in ver. 21. The precise question asked by the Prophet is not *why hast thou said, why dost thou say, or why shouldest thou say*, but why wilt thou still go on to say, implying that it has been said, was still said, and would be said again.—The two names of the patriarch are here combined, as in many other cases, to describe his offspring.—*Hidden* may either mean *unknown*, or *neglected*, or *forgotten*, in which last sense it is used below in chap. lxv. 16. The same verb is applied in Gen. xxxi. 49, to persons who are absent from each other, and of course out of sight. —*Way* is a common figure for the course of life, experience, or what the world calls fortune, destiny or fate.—The figure in the last clause is forensic, the idea being that of a cause or suit dismissed, lost sight of, or neglected by the judge. The expression is analogous to that in chap. i. 23, where it is said of the unjust judges, that the cause of the widow does not come unto them or before them. (See p. 91.) The state of mind described is a sceptical despondency as to the fulfilment of God's promises. Since this form of unbelief is more or less familiar to the personal experience of believers in all ages, and the terms of the expostulation here are not restricted to any single period in the history of Israel, the grave conclusions drawn by Gesenius and Knobel with respect to the prevalence of an epicurean scepticism at the period of the Babylonish exile, have an air of solemn trifling, and the proofs of later date which they afford are "like unto them."

28. *Hast thou not known? hast thou not heard? The God of eternity (or everlasting God), Jehovah, the Creator of the ends of the earth, will not faint, and will not tire; there is no search (with respect) to his understanding.* Most of the modern writers prefer Lowth's construction, *that Jehovah (is) the everlasting God;* but this, by making several distinct propositions, impairs the simplicity of the construction. The translation of the futures in the present or potential form (*does not* or *cannot faint*), though not erroneous, is inadequate, since both these senses are included in the promiscuous form or future proper. That he *will* not faint or tire, implies sufficiently in this case that he neither does nor can, while it expresses his unwillingness to do so. The *ends of the earth* is a common Hebrew phrase for its limits and all that they include. The Septuagint makes the Prophet say that Jehovah will not *hunger* (οὐ πεινάσει).—This verse contains an answer to the unbelieving fears expressed in that before it, which ascribed to God an imperfection or infirmity with which he is not chargeable. The last clause may either be a general assertion that he cannot leave his people unprotected through a want of understanding and of knowledge, or, as Hitzig supposes, a suggestion that his methods of proceeding, though inscrutable, are infinitely wise, and that the seeming inconsistency between his words and deeds, far from arguing unfaithfulness or weakness upon his part, does but prove our incapacity to understand or fathom his pro-

found designs. Even supposing that the former is the strict sense of the
words, the latter is implicitly contained in them.

29. *Giving to the faint* (or *weary*) *strength, and to the powerless might will
he increase.* He is not only strong in himself, but the giver of strength to
others, or, to state it as an argument *a fortiori,* he who is the only source
of strength to others must be strong himself, and able to fulfil his promises.
—The construction is similar to that in vers. 22, 23, not excepting the
transition from the participle to the finite verb. נֹתֵן is not strictly a periphrasis for the present tense, as rendered in the English Version, but
agrees with Jehovah as the subject of the preceding verse. The position
of this word at the beginning and of the corresponding verb at the end of
the verse is emphatic and climactic, the first meaning simply *to give*, the
other *to give more,* or abundantly.—The Septuagint has, *giving to the
hungry strength, and to those that grieve not sorrow.*

30. *And* (*yet*) *weary shall youths be and faint, and chosen* (*youths*) *shall
be weakened, be weakened.* There is here an obvious allusion to the terms
of ver. 28. What is there denied of God is here affirmed, not only of men
in general, but of the stoutest and most vigorous, aptly represented by the
young men chosen for military service, which appears to be a better explanation of בַּחוּרִים than the one given by Gesenius, viz. choice, or chosen,
in reference to personal beauty. (Compare chap. ix. 16, vol. i. p. 216.) Fürst,
with still less probability, supposes the essential meaning to be that of
growth or adolescence. That the prominent idea here conveyed is that of
manly strength and vigour, is not questioned.—For the evidence that נִכְשָׁל
strictly means to grow weak or be weakened, see 1 Sam. ii. 4, Zech.
xii. 8, and Gesenius's Thesaurus, tom. ii. p. 720.—The intensive repetition of the verb may either be expressed by the addition of an adverb, as
in the English Version (*utterly fall*), or retained in the translation as above.

31. *And* (on the other hand) *those waiting for Jehovah shall gain new
strength; they shall raise the pinion like the eagles, they shall run and not
be weary, they shall walk and not faint.* The marked antithesis between
this verse and that before it, justifies the use of *but* in English, although
not in the original. קָוָה is to *wait for* or *expect*, implying faith and patience.
This is also the old English meaning of the phrase *to wait upon*, as applied
to servants who await their master's orders ; but in modern usage the idea
of personal service or attendance has become predominant, so that the
English phrase no longer represents the Hebrew one. *Jehovah's waiters,*
which is Ewald's bold and faithful version (*Jahve's Harrer*), would convey,
if not a false, an inadequate idea to the English reader. The class of
persons meant to be described are those who shew their confidence in God's
ability and willingness to execute his promises, by patiently awaiting their
fulfilment. The restriction of these words to the exiles in Babylon is
entirely gratuitous. Although applicable, as a general proposition, to that
case among others, they admit of a more direct and striking application to
the case of those who under the old dispensation kept its end in view, and
still " waited for the consolation of Israel," and " looked for redemption in
Jerusalem " (Luke i. 25, 38).—The phrase translated *they shall gain new
strength* properly means *they shall exchange strength;* but the usage of the
verb determines its specific meaning to be that of changing for the better
or improving. The sense is therefore correctly given in the English Version (*they shall renew their strength*).—Of the next phrase there are three
distinct interpretations. 1. The English Bible follows Luther in explaining יַעֲלוּ as the future Kal, and אֵבֶר as a qualifying noun, equivalent to the

ablative of instrument in Latin (*they shall mount up with wings*). This construction is also adopted by Junius, Cocceius, Vitringa, Augusti, Henderson, and Barnes. 2. The second opinion is expressed in Lowth's translation: *they shall put forth fresh feathers like the moulting eagle.* The reference is then to the ancient belief of the eagle's great longevity, and of its frequently renewing its youth (Ps. ciii. 5). The rabbinical tradition, as recorded by Saadias, is, that the eagle, at the end of every tenth year, soars so near the sun as to be scorched and cast into the sea, from which it then emerges with fresh plumage, till at the end of the tenth decade, or a century complete, it sinks to rise no more. This explanation of the phrase before us is given not only by the Septuagint (πτεροφυήσουσιν), and the Vulgate (*assument pennas*), but by the Targum and Peshito, although more obscurely. In later times it is approved by Grotius, Clericus, J. D. Michaelis, Rosenmüller, Ewald, and De Wette. The principal objections to it are, that יַעֲלוּ has nowhere else the sense of putting forth (although the root does sometimes mean to sprout or grow), and that אֵבֶר does not denote *feathers* in general, but a *wing-feather* or a *pinion* in particular. 3. A third construction, simpler than the first, and more agreeable to usage than the second, gives the verb its ordinary sense of causing to ascend or raising, and the noun its proper sense of pinion, and connects the two directly as a transitive verb and its object, *they shall raise the pinion* (or *the wing*) *like the eagles.* This construction is adopted by Calvin, Hensler, Gesenius, Maurer, Hitzig, Umbreit, Hendewerk, and Knobel ; and, though charged by Beck with enormous flatness, is even more poetical than that which supposes an allusion, not to the soaring, but the moulting of the eagle. In the last clause the verbs יָגַע and יָעַף are introduced together for the third time in a beautiful antithesis. In ver. 28 they are applied to Jehovah, in ver. 30 to the strongest and most vigorous of men, as they are in themselves, and here to the waiters for Jehovah, the believers in his promises, who glory in infirmity that his strength may be made perfect in their weakness (2 Cor. xii. 9).—Knobel's comment on this promise is characteristic of his age and school. After condescendingly shewing that the thought is a correct one (*der Gedanke ist richtig*), he explains himself by saying, that trust in divine help does increase the natural powers, and that this effect is viewed by the pious writer (*i. e.* Isaiah) as a direct gift of God in requital of the confidence reposed in him. All this, though absolutely true, is relatively false, so far as it implies superiority in point of elevation and enlargement, on the part of the expounder as imagining himself to be *more than a prophet* (Luke xi. 9).

Chapter 41

UNTIL the ends of Israel's national existence are accomplished, that existence must continue in spite of hostile nations and their gods, who shall all perish sooner than the chosen people, vers. 1–16. However feeble Israel may be in himself, Jehovah will protect him, and raise up the necessary instruments for his deliverance and triumph, vers. 17–29.

1. *Be silent to me, O islands, and the nations shall gain new strength ; they shall approach, then shall they speak, together to the jadgment-seat will we draw near.* Having proved the impotence of idols in a direct address to Israel, Jehovah now summons the idolaters themselves to enter into controversy with him. The restriction of *islands* here to certain parts of Europe and Asia seems preposterous. The challenge is a general one

directed to the whole heathen world, and *islands* is a poetical variation for
lands or at the most for maritime lands or sea-coasts. *Silence* in this connection implies attention or the fact of listening, which is expressed in Job
xxxiii. 31. The imperative form at the beginning gives an imperative sense
likewise to the future, which might therefore be translated *let them approach*,
&c. There is an obvious allusion in the first clause to the promise in chap.
xl. 31. As if he had said : they that hope in Jehovah shall renew their
strength ; let those who refuse, renew theirs as they can.—The particle
then makes the passage more graphic by bringing distinctly into view the
successive steps of the process. This seems to recommend the explanation
of מִשְׁפָּט as a local rather than an abstract noun. The same judicial or
forensic figure is applied to contention between God and man by Job (ix.
19, xx. 82). Lowth's paraphrase of this verse is more than usually languid
and diluted : *e. g. let the distant nations repair to me with new force of
mind . . . . . . let us enter into solemn debate.* The same writer reads
החרישו on the authority of the Septuagint (ἐγκαινίζεσθε), and says that the
same mistake occurs in Zeph. iii. 17. But the Hiphil of חָרַשׁ does not occur
elsewhere, and the common text is confirmed by Aquila (κωφεύσατε) and
Symmachus (σιλήσατε), as well as by the other ancient versions.

2. *Who hath raised up* (or *awakened*) *from the east ? Righteousness
shall call him to its foot ; it shall give nations before him, and cause him to
tread upon kings ; it shall give* (*them*) *as dust to his sword, and as driven
stubble to his bow.* The simplest construction of the first clause is that
which assumes an abrupt transition from the form of interrogation to that
of prediction. The speaker, as it were, interrupts his own question before
it is complete in order to supply what must otherwise be presupposed.
Instead of going on to ask who brought the event to pass, he pauses to
describe the event itself. The same sense is obtained, but with a change
of form, by supplying a relative and continuing the interrogation. *Who
raised up from the east* (*him whom*) *righteousness*, &c. The old construction,
which makes *righteousness* the object of the verb, and regards it as an abstract used for a concrete (*righteousness* for *righteous one*), is wholly arbitrary
and at variance with the Masoretic accents. Gesenius and the later German writers understand the clause to mean *whom victory meets at every step.*
This new sense of צֶדֶק is entirely gratuitous, and violates the fundamental
laws of lexicography, by multiplying senses without any necessity and confounding the definition of a term with its application. Here and elsewhere
צֶדֶק means the righteousness of God as manifested in his providence, his
dealings with his people and their enemies. (See chap. i. 27, vol. i. p. 93.)
Because it suggests, in such connections, the idea of its consequences
or effects, it no more follows that this is the proper meaning of the word,
than that *wrath* means *suffering*, because the wrath of God causes the sufferings of the guilty. Another objection to this version of the clause is its
giving קָרָא the less usual sense of *meet*, and לְרַגְלוֹ that of *at every step*,
which is certainly not justified by the obscure and dubious analogy of Gen.
xxx. 30, especially when taken in connection with the usage of the same
phrase elsewhere to mean in the footsteps, train, suite, or retinue of any
one. (See 1 Sam. xxv. 42 ; Job xviii. 11 ; Hab. iii. 5.) In his lexicons,
Gesenius admits the idea to be that of *following*, and actually introduces
that verb into the clause, a virtual concession that his own translation of
יִקְרָא is at variance not only with usage but the context. To *call to one's
foot* is a Hebrew idiom for calling to one's service, or summoning to take a
place among one's followers. This act is here ascribed to the divine right-

eousness as a personified attribute. The other verbs may agree with the same subject or directly with Jehovah.—In the last clause Gesenius and the later Germans make the suffixes collective, and by *his sword, his bow,* understand the sword and bow of the nations or their kings. As the modern writers are so much accustomed to reject the old interpretations with contempt, it may not be amiss to mention here, that this construction is as old as Kimchi, and that it is set aside by Vitringa as an *expositio violenta quæ nihil sani præfert.* The enallage of number is in fact too violent to be assumed without necessity. Vitringa himself supposes the sword and bow to be those of the conqueror, and to be described as like dust or chaff in rapidity of motion. But the image, which is that of dust or chaff driven by the wind, is always used elsewhere in a passive and unfavourable sense, never as expressive of activity or energy. On the whole, there seems to be no construction more free from objection than the old one of the English Version, the Targum and the Vulgate, which gives יִתֵּן the same sense, the same subject, and the same object as in the preceding clause. The difficulty which arises from supposing an ellipsis of the preposition before *sword* and *bow,* may be removed by taking these words as adverbial or qualifying nouns, a Hebrew idiom of constant occurrence. This construction becomes still more natural if we understand the clause to mean that he makes the enemy like dust or chaff *with* or *by means* of his sword and bow. In that case, the verb may be construed either with צֶדֶק יְהוָה or the conqueror himself. The construction may be rendered clearer by restoring the Hebrew collocation. *Kings he shall subdue (and) shall make like dust (with) his sword and like driven chaff (with) his bow.*—The explanation of the futures as preterites is wholly arbitrary, and even the descriptive present appears inadmissible when the strict sense is so perfectly appropriate.—The question, whose appearance is predicted in this verse, has been always a subject of dispute. Eusebius, Theodoret, and Procopius understand it as describing the triumphs of the true religion, or the gospel, here called *righteousness.* Cyril and Jerome apply it to the Lord Jesus Christ himself, as the Righteous One, or the Lord our Righteousness. Cocceius stands alone in his application of the verse to the apostle Paul. The Jews make Abraham the subject of the passage, excepting Aben Ezra, who, with Vitringa and all the latest writers, understands it as a prophecy of Cyrus. The inappropriateness of the terms employed to our Saviour or the gospel, to Abraham or Paul, is almost self-evident, and equally clear is its appropriateness to the case of Cyrus. The argument in favour of the latter application, drawn from the analogy of chaps. xlv. 1, xlvi. 11, is less conclusive, because he is there expressly named. The truth appears to be that this is a more general intimation of a great eventful movement from the East, which is afterwards repeated with specific reference to Cyrus and his conquests. It might even be suppposed without absurdity that there is here an allusion to the general progress of the human race, of conquest, civilization, and religion, from the East to the West. Umbreit supposes a specific reference to the course of the sun, from which the name of Cyrus was derived, as we shall see.

3. *He shall pursue them; he shall pass (in) peace (or safety); a path with his feet he shall not go.* There is the same objection here as in the preceding verse to the explanation of the verbs as preterites; but most interpreters, not content with this, make the future in the last clause a pluperfect (*the way that he had not gone with his feet*). This method of translation involves the whole subject in uncertainty. If the past and the future

senses may be interchanged at pleasure and without necessity, the interpreter may make the author say what he pleases. In the case before us, J. D. Michaelis adheres to the proper future sense, and explains the clause to mean that he shall not have occasion to retrace his steps. But as this, like the common explanation before mentioned, leaves the phrase *with his feet* pleonastic and unmeaning, the preference is due to Ewald's supposition that the clause describes the swiftness of his motions, as flying rather than walking on foot. This, which would be natural and striking, even in itself considered, is confirmed by the analogy of Daniel viii. 5, where we read that *an he-goat came from the west on the face of the whole earth, and touched not the ground.*

4. *Who hath wrought and done it, calling the generations from the beginning? I Jehovah, the first and with the last, I (am) he.* Another construction of the verse, preferred by the latest writers, includes the last part of the first clause in answer to the question. *Who hath wrought and done it? He that calleth the generations,* &c. But besides the unequal distribution of the verse which thus arises, this construction makes the answer speak of God both in the first and second person, and gives to the indefinite קֹרֵא the sense of the emphatic הַקֹּרֵא, neither of which departures from the *usus loquendi*, though admissible in case of necessity, ought to be assumed without it.—*Calling the generations* may either mean calling them into existence or proclaiming them, *i.e.* predicting them; probably the latter, since the event itself, although it proved a superhuman agency, did not prove it to be that of Jehovah, which could only be established by the fulfilment of predictions uttered in his name. *With the last,* does not simply mean *the last,* which is the form employed in chap. xli. 21–25, xlvi. 8–10, but coexistent with the last, a mode of expression which would seem to imply that although Jehovah existed before all other beings, he will not outlast them all. אֲנִי הוּא is explained by some of the older writers as meaning *I am God;* by the latest, *I am the same* (*i.e.* unchangeable); but the simplest construction is the common one, *I am he, i.e.* the being to whom the interrogation has respect, *I am he who he has wrought and done it.*

5. *The isles have seen it and are afraid, the ends of the earth tremble; they have approached and come.* Some regard this as a description of the effect produced by the foregoing argument, but others as a part of the argument itself, drawn from the effect of the appearance of the person mentioned in ver. 2. As an instance of the length to which specific historical interpretation can be carried by the new as well as by the old school of interpreters, it may be mentioned that Hendewerk, with the first book of Herodotus before him, explains *islands* here to mean the Greek states in the west of Asia Minor,—their approach,—the message which they sent to Cyrus after the defeat of Crœsus,—the mutual encouragement described in the next verse,—the deliberations of the *Panionion!* All this, however, he supposes to be here described, not by a prophet in the proper sense, but by a contemporary writer.

6. *A man his neighbour* (*i.e.* one another) *they will help, and to his brother* (*one*) *will say, Be strong!* This general description is then filled up, or carried out into detail in the next verse, both containing a sarcastic description of the vain appeal of the idolaters to the protection of their tutelary deities.

7. *And the carver has strengthened the gilder, the smoother with the hammer, the smiter on the anvil; he says* (or *is saying*) *of the solder, It is good; and he has strengthened it with nails; it shall not be moved.* The

sarcasm consists in making the idolaters dependent upon idols, which are themselves dependent upon common workmen and the most trivial mechanical operations for their form and their stability. Hence the particular enumeration of the different artificers employed in the manufacture of these deities. J. D. Michaelis explains חֲלֶק פַּעַם to mean the treader on the bellows, *i. e.* the bellows-blower.—The text of the English Version has, *it is ready for the soldering;* but the other construction is now universally adopted. The last clause implies that the strength of the idol is not in itself, but in the nails that keep it in its place, or hold its parts together.

8. *And thou Israel my servant, Jacob whom I have chosen, the seed of Abraham my friend.* The prominent idea is still that of the contrast between Israel as the people of God, and the heathen as his enemies. The insertion of the substantive verb in the first clause, *thou art Israel my servant* (Vitringa), or *thou Israel art my servant* (English Version), is unnecessary. This whole verse with the next may be understood as a description of the object of address, or of the person to whom the exhortation in ver. 10 is directed. The two names of Jacob are again combined in application to his progeny. The race is described as God's *servant* and his *elect*, or, combining the two characters, his chosen servant, chosen to be his servant. Vitringa understands this last term as including the idea of a worshipper or votary; and Hitzig compares it with *Abdastartus*, a servant of Astarte, and the favourite Arabic name *Abdallah* or a worshipper of Allah.—The people are here described not only as the sons of Jacob, but of Abraham. אֹהֲבִי cannot of itself denote an object of divine love, as it is explained in the Septuagint (ὅν ἠγάπησα), nor can it be both active and passive, *amans* and *amatus*, as Vitringa supposes. The latter idea is implied but not expressed. The same honourable title is bestowed on Abraham in 2 Chron. xx. 7: James ii. 23, and in the common parlance of the Arabs, by whom he is usually styled خليل الله the friend of God, or absolutely, الخليل the Friend.

9. *Thou whom I have grasped from the ends of the earth, and from its joints* (or *sides*) *have called thee, and said to thee, My servant* (*art*) *thou I have chosen thee and not rejected thee.* The description of the object of address is still continued. The essential idea here expressed is that of election and separation from the rest of men, a bringing near of those who were afar off. Interpreters have needlessly disputed whether the vocation of Israel in Abraham, or at the exodus, is here particularly meant; since both are really included in a general description of the calling and election of the people. The objection that Israel distinguished from Abraham in ver. 8, is of no weight except against the supposition (if maintained by any) that Abraham himself is here the object of address. The application of analogous expressions to the exodus from Egypt, in Deut. xxxix. 10; Ezek. xx. 5, only proves that this was one of the great crises or junctures in the progress of the people, at which their election or vocation was declared, and as it were renewed. The question in what sense Egypt could be called the ends of the earth, is as trifling as the answer which some give it, that it was remote from Babylon. The phrase in question is a common idiomatic expression for remoteness, often used without reference to particular localities (see chap. v. 26, xiii. 2). The idea meant to be conveyed is identical with that expressed by Paul when he says (Eph. ii. 13), ὑμεῖς οἱ ποτὲ ὄντες μακρὰν ἐγγὺς ἐγενήθητε. The translation *I have taken* is inadequate, the Hebrew verb meaning *to hold fast*, and the idea of removal being

rather implied than expressed. The parallel expression (אֲצִילֶיהָ) is explained by Gesenius from the analogy of אֵצֶל, *side*, by Maurer from that of
אַצִּיל, *a joint*, which seems to be also presupposed in the version of Symmachus (ἀγκώνων). The rabbinical interpretation, *chief men*, is founded on
the analogy of Exod. xxiv. 11. Some of the Jewish writers understand מִן
as meaning *in spite of*, others *in preference to*, but both without authority.—
Lowth's translation of מְאָסְתִּיךָ as a future is entirely arbitrary, and overlooks the peculiar Hebrew idiom of saying the same thing positively and
negatively. (See chap. iii. 9, vol. i. p. 114.)

10. *Fear thou not, for I* (am) *with thee; look not around, for I* (am) *thy
God; I have strengthened thee, yea I have helped thee, yea I have upheld
thee with my right hand of righteousness.* This may be regarded as the
conclusion of the sentence beginning in ver. 8, as the address to which the
two preceding verses are an introduction.—Vitringa derives תִּשְׁתָּע from שׁוּע.
Ewald makes it an orthographical variation of תִּשְׁתָּאֶה (Gen. xxiv. 21).
Gesenius and most other modern writers make it the Hithpael of שָׁעָה, and
explain it to mean, do not look around fearfully as if for help. Hitzig
compares it with the Homeric verb παπταίνω.—The אַף, which might be
rendered *nay more*, seems to give the last clause the form of a climax,
although such a progression cannot easily be traced in the thoughts. The
English Version, which adheres to the strict translation of the preterites in
ver. 9, here gratuitously employs the future form, which wholly changes the
complexion of the sentence. It is not a simple promise, but a reference to
what God had already done and might therefore be expected to do again.
The present form employed by Rosenmüller (*corroboro te*) is less objectionable than the future, but in no respect preferable to the strict translation.—
Equally arbitrary is the introduction by the later Germans of their favourite
idea that צֶדֶק in these prophecies means prosperity or success, whereas it
does not even suggest that notion, except so far as it flows from the righteousness of God as an effect from its cause. Hitzig's translation *gracious
arm* is at once a departure from the old and the new interpretation. It is
not even necessary to assume with Lowth that צֶדֶק here denotes the faithfulness of God, and to translate accordingly *my faithful right hand*. The
true sense is the strict one of *righteousness* or *justice*, the appeal to which
in such connections has already been explained. (See above, on ver. 2.)
The right hand of my righteousness supposes the attribute to be personified;
a supposition which may be avoided by referring the suffix to the whole
complex phrase, *my right hand of righteousness* or *just right hand*.—As
specimens of ultra-specific exposition, without any foundation in the text,
it may be mentioned that Knobel understands this as an exhortation to the
Jewish exiles not to be afraid of Cyrus.

11. *Lo, ashamed and confounded shall be all those incensed* (or *inflamed*)
against thee; they shall be as nothing (or *as though they were not*), *and
destroyed shall be thy men of strife* (or *they that strive with thee*). Not only
shall Israel himself escape, but his enemies shall perish. To be ashamed
and confounded, here as usual, includes the frustration of their plans and
disappointment of their hopes. On the meaning of *as nothing*, see above,
p. 108. The construction of the phrase *thy men of strife*, is the same as
that of *my right hand of righteousness* in ver. 10.

12. *Thou shalt seek them and not find them, thy men of quarrel; they
shall be as nothing and as nought, thy men of war*, (*i. e.* they who quarrelled
and made war with thee). The first clause contains a common Hebrew

figure for complete disappearance and destruction. (See Ps. xxxvii. 36; Jer. l. 20; Amos viii. 12; Hos. v. 6). אַיִן and אֶפֶס strictly denote non-existence and annihilation. (See above, on chap. xl. 17).

13. *For I, Jehovah thy God, (am) holding fast thy right hand; the (one) saying to thee, Fear not, I have helped thee, i. e.* I, who command thee not to fear, have already helped thee, or secured thy safety. J. D. Michaelis gives מַחֲזִיק the causative sense of strengthening; but this sense is rare, except in a few of the later books, and the other is recommended here, not only by the general agreement of interpreters, but by the analogy of ver. 9.

14. *Fear not, thou worm Jacob and ye men of Israel; I have helped thee, saith Jehovah, and thy Redeemer, the Holy One of Israel.* The same encouragement is here repeated, but with a direct contrast between Israel's weakness and the strength of God.—The feminine form of the verb has reference to that of the noun תּוֹלַעַת. This epithet expresses not merely the contempt of others, as in Ps. xxii. 7, much less the Babylonian oppression of the Jews, as J. H. Michaelis and others think, but the real meanness and unworthiness of man, as in Job xxv. 6. As the parallelism seems to require an analogous expression of contempt in the next clause, some either read מְתֵי (*dead men*) with Aquila (τεθνεῶτες), Theodotion (νεκροί), and Jerome (*qui mortui estis ex Israel*), or regard מְתֵי as a modification of that word denoting *mortals.* Vitringa and Hitzig gain the same end by explaining it as an ellipsis for מְתֵי מִסְפָּר, *men of number,* i. e. few men, Ps. cv. 12. So the Septuagint has ὀλιγοστός, but omits *worm* altogether. Ewald completes the parallelism in a very summary manner, by reading רִמַּת יִשְׂרָאֵל, and translating it *gekrummtes Israel.* Maurer, on the other hand, discovers that the parallelism is not always perfect, and advises the reader to translate it boldly (*redde intrepide*) men of Israel, which seems to be the simplest and most obvious course, leaving the accessory idea of fewness or weakness to suggest itself.—The word גּאָל, *redeemer,* would suggest to a Hebrew reader the ideas of a near kinsman (Lev. xxv. 24, 25) and of deliverance from bondage by the payment of a ransom. Its highest application occurs here and in Job xix. 25. The reference to the Son of God, although it might not be perceptible of old, is now rendered necessary by the knowledge that this act, even under the old dispensation, is always referred to the same person of the Trinity. The substitution of the future for the preterite by the English and some other Versions has already been seen to be gratuitous and arbitrary.

15. *Behold I have placed thee for* (i. e. appointed thee to be, or changed thee into) *a threshing-sledge, sharp, new, possessed of teeth* (or *edges*); *thou shalt thresh mountains and beat* (*them*) *small, and hills like the chaff shalt thou place* (or *make*). The erroneous idea that he simply promises to furnish Israel with the means of threshing mountains, has arisen from the equivocal language of the English Version, *I will make thee,* which may either mean, *I will make for thee,* or *will make thee to become,* whereas the last sense only can by any possibility be put upon the Hebrew, as literally translated above. The oriental threshing machine is sometimes a sledge of thick planks armed with iron or sharp stones, sometimes a system of rough rollers joined together like a sledge or dray. Both kinds are dragged over the grain by oxen. (See Robinson's Palestine, iii. p. 143.)—דָּקַק is properly to crush, pound fine, or pulverize; פִּיפִיּוֹת strictly denotes *mouths;* but like the primitive noun from which it is derived, it is sometimes applied to the *edge* of a sharp instrument, perhaps in allusion to the figure of

devouring. Here it signifies the edges, blades, or teeth, with which the threshing-wain is armed. The reduplicated form is supposed to denote the number of such parts by Ewald (*vielspitzig*) and Knobel (*vielschneidig*). The literal sense of בַּעַל is possessor, owner. There seems to be no ground for the common assumption that *hills* and *mountains* are specific emblems here for States or governments. The image presented is the strange but strong one of a down-trodden worm reducing hills to powder, the essential idea being that of a weak and helpless object overcoming the most disproportionate obstacles, by strength derived from another.

16. *Thou shalt fan* (or *winnow*) *them, and a wind shall take them up, and a whirlwind shall scatter them, and thou shalt joy in Jehovah, in the Holy One of Israel shalt thou boast* (or *glory*). The figure of the preceding verse is here carried out and completed. The mountains, having been completely threshed, are winnowed, in the usual oriental mode, by being thrown to the wind. Israel, on the other hand, is safe, not through his own strength but in that of his protector, *in whom, i. e.* in his relation to whom, he finds his highest happiness and honour. The writer's main design is evidently still to exhibit the contrast between God and his people on the one hand, and the idols and their people on the other.

17. *The suffering and the poor* (are) *seeking water, and it is not* (*there is none*); *their tongue with thirst is parched. I Jehovah will hear* (or *answer*) *them*, (*I*) *the God of Israel will not forsake them.* The first clause describes the need of a divine interposition, the last the interposition itself. The images are so unlike those of the foregoing verse that they might seem to be unconnected, but for the fact that the whole passage is entirely metaphorical. Thirst is a natural and common metaphor for suffering. Those who restrict the verse to the Babylonish exile are divided on the question whether it literally describes the hardships of the journey through the wilderness, or metaphorically those of the captivity itself. Both suppositions are entirely arbitrary, since there is nothing in the text or context to deprive the passage of its genuine and full sense as a general promise, tantamount to saying, When my people feel their need, I will be present to supply it. Such a promise those in exile could not fail to find appropriate in their case; but it is equally appropriate in others, and especially to the glorious deliverance of the church from the fetters of the old economy. עָנָה is not to hear in general, but to hear prayer in a favourable sense, to answer it. The conditional turn given to the sentence in our version (*when the poor and needy seek*, &c.) is substantially correct, but a needless departure from the form of the original.

18. *I will open upon bare hills streams, and in the midst of valleys fountains; I will place the desert for* (*i. e.* convert it into) *a pool of water, and a dry land for* (or *into*) *springs of water.* The same figure for entire and joyful change occurs in chap. xxx. 25, and chap. xxxv. 7, and with its opposite or converse in Ps. cvii. 33, 35. It is now commonly admitted that שְׁפָיִים includes the idea of barrenness or nakedness. Compare נִשְׁפָּה from the same root (chap. xiii. 2).

19. *I will give in the wilderness cedar, acacia, and myrtle, and oil-tree; I will place in the desert fir, pine, and box together.* The main idea, common to all explanation of this verse, is that of trees growing where they never grew before. It is comparatively unimportant therefore to identify the species, although J. D. Michaelis supposes them to have been selected because such as do not naturally grow together. With respect to the cedar and the myrtle there is no doubt. Vitringa regards שִׁטָּה (which has

no *and* before it) as an epithet of אֶרֶז, and translates it *cedrus præstantissima.* Since Lowth, however, it has been commonly regarded as the Hebrew name of the *acacia*, a thorny tree growing in Arabia and Egypt. (See Robinson's Palestine, vol. ii. p. 349).—By the *oil-tree* is meant the *oleaster* or wild olive, as distinguished from the זַיִת or cultivated tree of the same species. For the different explanations of בְּרוֹשׁ, see vol. i. p. 290. According to the latest authorities, תִּדְהָר is neither the pine, the elm, nor the plane-tree, but the ilex, holm, or hard oak, so called from דָּהַר to endure or last. By the same writers תְּאַשּׁוּר is understood to be a species of the cedar of Lebanon, so called from its erectness and loftiness.

20. *That they may see, and know, and consider, and understand together, that the hand of Jehovah hath done this, and the Holy One of Israel hath created it.* The verbs in the first clause may refer to men in general, or to those immediately concerned as subjects or spectators of the change described. יָשִׂימוּ, *they may place*, seems to be an elliptical expression for יָשִׂימוּ לֵב *may place their heart, i. e.* apply their mind, or give attention. There is no need of introducing לֵב into the text, as Lowth does, since the very same ellipsis has been pointed out by Kocher in Judges xix. 20. Still less ground is there to amend the text with Houbigant by reading יָשֹׁמּוּ (*may be astonished*).—There is a climax in the last clause : he has not only *done* it but *created* it, *i. e.* produced a new effect by the exertion of almighty power.

21. *Present your cause* (literally *bring it near* or *cause it to approach, i. e.* into the presence of the judge), *saith Jehovah ; bring forward your defences* (or *strong reasons), saith the king of Jacob.* The Septuagint changes the whole meaning of the sentence, by making it a simple affirmation (*your judgment draweth near).*—Jerome applies the last clause to their idols : *accedant idola vestra quæ putatis esse fortissima.* But most interpreters refer it to the arguments by which they were to maintain their cause. The metaphor is commonly supposed to be that of bulwarks or entrenchments ; but this, as Knobel has observed, is hardly consistent with the call to bring them forward. It is better therefore to give the word its wider sense of strength or strong thing.

22. *They shall bring forward* (or *let them bring forward*) *and shew forth to us the* (things) *which are to happen ; the former things, what they were, shew forth, and we will set our heart* (apply our mind, or pay attention to them), *and know their issue ; or* (else) *the coming* (events) *make us to hear.* The prescience of future events is here appealed to as a test of divinity. (Compare Deut. xviii. 22, Jer. xxviii. 9, and chap. xliii. 12, below). Vitringa, Lowth, and others, understand by *former things* a proximate futurity ; but the antithesis between this and *coming things* shews that the former must mean prophecies already fulfilled, or at least already published. They are required to demonstrate their foreknowledge, either by shewing that they had predicted something, or by doing it now. Knobel's question whether *we* and *us* mean God alone or God and the Prophet together, is not in the best taste or particularly reasonable, since the whole idea which the text conveys is that of two contending parties at a judgment-seat. *They* means the party of the false gods and their worshippers, *we* that of Jehovah and his people.

23. *Shew forth the* (things) *to come hereafter, and we will know that ye are gods ; yes, ye shall do good or evil, and we will look about and see together.* The subjunctive construction, *that we may know*, gives the sense of

the original, but with a needless change of form. The same remark applies to the imperative translation of the futures in the next clause (*do good, do evil*). The use of the disjunctive, on the other hand, is rendered almost unavoidable by an entire difference of idiom, the Hebrews constantly employing *and* where *or* in English seems essential to the sense. The verbs in this clause are strictly and distinctly understood by Vitringa, as relating to the reward of worshippers and the punishment of enemies. Henderson explains the clause as challenging the false gods to perform a miracle. But most interpreters retain the idiomatic meaning of the same expressions elsewhere, namely, that of doing anything whatever, good or bad. (See Jer. x. 5, Zeph. i. 12.) Lowth and Henderson understand נִשְׁתָּעֶה as denoting terror, and change the pointing so as to derive the following verb from יָרֵא to fear. Gesenius makes the former verb synonymous with נִתְרָאֶה (2 Kings. xiv. 8), let us look one another in the face, *i. e.* confront one another in dispute or battle. It is much more probable, however, that the word has the same sense as in ver. 10 above, where it seems to express the act of looking round or about upon those present, in that case with the secondary notion of alarm (as looking round for help), but in this case with that of inspection or consideration (we will look about us). Hitzig refers the word *together* to the two acts which the verbs express; but it is much more natural to understand it as denoting that the two contending parties unite in the same act.

24. *Lo, ye are of nothing* (or *less than nothing*) *and your work of nought* (or *less than nought*) ; *an abomination* (*is he that*) *chooseth* (or *will choose*) *you*. This is the conclusion drawn from their failure or refusal to accept the challenge, and to furnish the required proof of their deity. For the meaning of מֵאַיִן, see above, on chap. xl. 17. The parallel term אֶפַע is regarded by some of the Rabbins as synonymous with אֶפְעֶה (*worse than a viper*) ; but the context requires an expression not of quality but of non-entity. Solomon Ben Melek makes it a synonyme of אֶפֶס, Vitringa an orthographical variation of the same; either of which is better than the supposition now most commonly adopted of an error in the text, the retention of which, even supposing its occurrence, it would not be very easy to account for. Augusti and Hitzig understand the phrase to mean *of nothing* or *belonging to nothing*, which Knobel explains as tantamount to saying that they had no work, or in other words, that they could do nothing.—תּוֹעֵבָה is a strong expression often used to describe an object of religious abhorrence. On the choosing of gods, compare Judges v. 8.

25. *I have raised up* (*one*) *from the north, and he has come ; from the rising of the sun shall he call upon my name ; and he shall come upon princes as upon mortar, and as a potter treadeth clay.* This is correctly understood by Knobel as a specific application of the general conclusion in ver. 24. If the gods of the heathen could do absolutely nothing, it was impossible that they should be the authors of any one remarkable event, and especially of that on which the Prophet has his eye. The expressions are remarkably similar to those in ver. 2, so that the Prophet may be here said to resume the train of thought which had been interrupted at the end of ver. 4. Having taken occasion to describe the effect of the event foretold upon the worshippers of idols, and from that to shew the impotence of the gods themselves, he returns to the event which he had been describing, and continues his description. As before, he takes his stand at an intermediate point between the beginning and the end of the whole process, as appears from the successive introduction of the preterite and future. This peculiar

feature of the passage is obscured if not effaced by rendering them all alike, or by arbitrarily distinguishing between the tense of הֵעִירוֹתִי and וַיֵּאת. With the single substitution of *he has come* for *he shall come*, the common version is entirely correct. The mention of the north and east together has been variously explained. Jerome and Luther understand the clause to mean, that he was called from the north, but came from the east. Eusebius, Cyril, and Jerome refer the first clause to the nations, and the last to Christ, which is entirely gratuitous. Calvin refers the first to the Chaldees and the last to Cyrus, which is better, but still arbitrary. J. D. Michaelis supposes the two subjects of the clause to be Darius or Cyaxares the Mede and Cyrus the Persian, whose respective countries lay to the north and east of Babylonia. The later writers modify this explanation by referring all to Cyrus, here considered at the same time as a Persian and a Mede. A still more satisfactory hypothesis, perhaps, is that the subject of this passage is not a determinate individual, but *the conqueror* indefinitely, who is not identified till afterwards. The use of the word סְגָנִים, which is the appropriate description of the Babylonian nobles, contains a covert intimation of the particular events in view. Instead of shewing that the passage is of later date, as some imagine, it affords a remarkable example of prophetic foresight. The act of calling on the name of Jehovah is commonly regarded as an allusion to the profession of the true religion, or at least the recognition of Jehovah as the true God, on the part of Cyrus (Ezra i. 2).—Compare the figures of the last clause with chaps. x. 6, xxv. 10.

26. *Who declared from the beginning? (Say) and we will know ; and beforehand, and we will say, Right* (or *True*). *Nay, there was none that told; nay, there was none that uttered ; nay, there was none that heard your words.* Because the adverbs of time do not necessarily express remote antiquity, Knobel infers that they here mean *since the first appearance of Cyrus*. But such an appeal to the prediction of what one man could foresee as well as another would be simply ridiculous. The sense of צַדִּיק is determined by that of אֱמֶת in chap. xliii. 9. The meaning of the whole verse is that the events in question had been foretold by Jehovah and no other.

27. *First to Zion, Behold, behold them ! and to Jerusalem a bringer of good news will I give.* This very peculiar idiomatic sentence may be paraphrased as follows : *I am the first to say to Zion, Behold, behold them ! and to give Jerusalem a bringer of good news.* The simplest construction is to make the verb at the end govern both clauses ; but in English the sense may be expressed more clearly by supplying the verb *say*. The common version of the last clause is correct, but that of the first appears to have no meaning. The sense is not *the first* shall say, but *I first, i. e.* before any other god or prophet.

28. *And I will look, but there is no man ; and of these, but there is no one advising* (or *informing*) ; *and I will ask them, and they will return a word* (or *answer*). He allows them as it were another opportunity of proving their divinity. In the first two clauses, the expectation and the disappointment are described together; in the third, the expectation only is expressed, the result being given in the following verse. First he looks, but finds not what he seeks. Then again, but with the same result. Once more he interrogates them and awaits an answer, but (as the next verse adds) discovers them to be impostors. There is something singularly beautiful in this peculiar structure of the sentence, which is wholly marred by the indirect constructions that are commonly adopted, *that when I asked them*

they could answer a word, or, *that I should question them and they return an answer.* The verse is full of laconic and elliptical expressions, which, however, may be easily completed, as will appear from the following brief paraphrase. *I will look* (once more to see whether any of these idols or their prophet can predict the future), *but there is no one* (who attempts it). *From among* (all) *these* (I seek for a response, but there is none). Yet once more *I will ask them, and* (perhaps) *they will return an answer.* The same application of the verb יִשְׁ to the prediction of the future occurs below in chap. xliv. 26. The form here used is to be strictly construed as a participle.

29. *Lo, they (are) all nought, nothing their works, wind and emptiness their molten images.* This is, at once, the termination of the sentence begun in the last clause of the verse preceding, and the summary conclusion of the whole preceding controversy as to the divinity of any gods except Jehovah. To the usual expressions of nonentity the Prophet adds two other strong descriptive terms, viz. wind and emptiness.

Chapter 42

THIS chapter exhibits to our view the Servant of Jehovah, *i. e.* the Messiah and his people, as a complex person, and as the messenger or representative of God among the nations. His mode of operation is described as being not violent but peaceful, vers. 1–5. The effects of his influence are represented as not natural but spiritual, vers. 6–9. The power of God is pledged for his success, notwithstanding all appearances of inaction or indifference on his part, vers. 10–17. In the latter portion of the chapter, the Church or Body of Christ, as distinguished from its Head, and representing him until he came, is charged with unfaithfulness to its great trust, and this unfaithfulness declared to be the cause of what it suffered, vers. 18–25. Several important exegetical questions with respect to the Servant of Jehovah will be fully canvassed in the exposition of the chapter.

1. *Behold my servant! I will hold him fast; my chosen One (in whom) my soul delights; I have given* (or *put*) *my Spirit upon him; judgment to the nations shall he cause to go forth.* There is no need of assuming (with the English Version) an ellipsis of the relative twice in the same clause. The separate construction of the first two words, as an introduction to the following description, makes them far more impressive, like the *ecce homo* (ἴδε ὁ ἄνθρωπος) of John xix. 5.—The first verb, construed as it is here, signifies to hold fast, for the most part with the accessory idea of holding up, sustaining, or supporting. *Elect* or *chosen* does not mean choice or excellent, except by implication; directly and strictly it denotes one actually chosen, set apart, for a definite purpose.—רָצָה is the verb applied in the Law of Moses to the acceptance of a sacrifice, from which some have inferred that there is here an allusion to expiatory merit; but this, although admissible, is not an obvious or necessary supposition.—By *Spirit*, as in all such cases, we are to understand, not only divine influence, but the divine person who exerts it. (See vol. i. pp. 123, 249.)—The use of the phrase *on him*, where *in him* might have seemed more natural, is probably intended to suggest the idea of descent, or of an influence from heaven.— The last clause is understood by Grotius as denoting that the person here described should denounce the penal judgments of Jehovah on the Medes

and Babylonians. But besides the unreasonable limitation of the words to these two nations, this explanation is at variance with the usage of the singular מִשְׁפָּט and with the context, which describes the servant of Jehovah as a source of blessing to the Gentiles. The same objection does not lie against an explanation of מִשְׁפָּט by Clericus as meaning justice or just government; but this is too restricted, as appears from the subsequent context. The most satisfactory interpretation is the common one, which understands this word as a description of the true religion, and the whole clause as predicting its diffusion. The office thus ascribed to the servant of Jehovah, both here and in the following context, as a teacher of the truth, makes the description wholly inappropriate to Cyrus, who is nevertheless regarded as the subject of the prophecy, not only by Saadias among the Jews, but by Hensler, Koppe, and even Ewald, though the last- combines this application with another which will be explained below. Aben Ezra, Grotius, and some later writers, understand the passage as descriptive of Isaiah himself; and this hypothesis is modified by De Wette, and Gesenius in his Commentary, so as to embrace all the prophets as a class. Besides the objection to the first of these opinions, somewhat flippantly alleged by J. D. Michaelis, that if Isaiah had thus spoken of himself, he would have proved himself a madman rather than a prophet, it may be objected to the whole hypothesis, that the prophets of the old dispensation are invariably represented as the messengers of God to the Jews and not the Gentiles. And the same thing is still more emphatically true of the Levitical priesthood. Of some, but much less weight is the objection to the later form of the same theory, that the collective sense which it puts upon the phrase is neither natural nor countenanced by any satisfactory analogy. There is, indeed, as all admit, such a collective use of the phrase, *servant of Jehovah*, in application not to any rank or office or profession, but to Israel, the chosen people, as such considered. Of this usage we have already had an example in chap. xli. 8, and shall meet with many more hereafter. The distinction between this application of the title and the one which De Wette proposes, is, that in the former case the national progenitor is put by a natural metonymy for his descendants, whereas there is no such individual prophet (not even Moses) in whom the whole succession is concentrated, either by natural association or by established usage. A third objection to this theory may be drawn from the analogy of other places, where the same great servant of Jehovah is described, not only as a sufferer, but as an atoning sacrifice. Even admitting the gratuitous assumption, that the prophets, as a class, were habitually subject to malignant persecution, the representation of these sufferings as vicarious and expiatory would be forced and arbitrary in itself, as well as contradicted by the tenor of Scripture. This last objection also lies against the exclusive application of the title to Israel as a people, or to the pious and believing portion of them, which has been maintained by various writers from Solomon Jarchi down to Knobel, who supposes that the servant of Jehovah sometimes means the whole body of the Jews in exile who externally adhered to the worship of Jehovah, sometimes the real spiritual Israel included in this number. But the representation of the Jewish nation as atoning for the sins of the Gentiles, or of the pious Jews as atoning for the sins of the whole nation, is without analogy in any other part of the Old Testament. The objections which have now been stated to these various hypotheses may negatively serve to recommend the one adopted in the Targum and by Kimchi and Abarbenel, who represents the champions of the others as struck with judicial blindness. This ancient doctrine of the Jewish Church, and of the great majority of Christian writers, is that the servant of the Lord is the Messiah. The lengths of paradoxical extravagance to which the unbelieving critics are prepared to go rather than admit this supposition, may be learned from Knobel's positive assertion, that the Old Testament Messiah is nowhere represented either as a teacher or a sufferer, and that the later chapters of Isaiah contain no allusion to a Messiah at all. In favour of the Messianic exposition may be urged not only the tradition of the Jewish Church already cited, and the perfect facility with which this hypothesis at once accommodates itself to all the requisitions of the passages to which it is applied, but also the explicit and repeated application of these passages to Jesus Christ in the New Testament. These applications will be noticed *seriatim* as the texts successively present themselves. To this first verse there are several allusions more or less distinct and unequivocal. Besides the express citation of it, with the next three verses in Mat. xii. 19–21, there is an obvious allusion to its terms, or rather a direct application of them made by God himself, in the descent of the Holy Spirit on our Saviour at his baptism, and in the words pronounced from heaven then and at the time of his transfiguration : *This is my beloved Son in whom I am well pleased* (Mat. ii. 17, xvii. 5). The connecting link between the *Servant* of Isaiah and the *Son* of Matthew, is afforded by the παῖς of the Septuagint, which includes both ideas. According to the explanation which has just been given, υἱὸς is neither a translation of עֶבֶד, nor a perversion of its meaning, but a clearer designation of the subject of the prophecy. That Christ was sent to the Jews and not the Gentiles, is only true of his personal ministry and not of his whole work as continued by his followers, who were expressly commissioned to go into all the world, to make disciples of all nations, the only restriction imposed being that of *beginning at Jerusalem*. It only remains to be considered, whether this application of the title and the description to our Saviour is exclusive of all others, as its advocates commonly maintain. This inquiry is suggested by the fact, which all interpreters admit, that Israel, the chosen people, is not only called by this same name, but described as having some of the same attributes, not only elsewhere, but in this very context, and especially in vers. 19, 20, of this chapter, where any other explanation of the terms, as we shall see, is altogether inadmissable. Assuming, then, that the Messiah is the servant of Jehovah introduced at the beginning of the chapter, there are only two ways of accounting for the subsequent use of the same language with respect to Israel. The first way is by alleging a total difference of subject in the different places ; which in fact though not in form is to decline all explanation of the fact in question, as being either needless or impossible. That such a twofold application of equivalent expressions to entirely different subjects is conceivable, and must in certain cases be assumed, there is no need of denying. But unless we abandon all attempt to interpret language upon any settled principle, we cannot but admit that nothing short of exegetical necessity can justify the reference of the same descriptive terms to different subjects in one and the same context. If then there is an exegetical hypothesis by which these applications can be reconciled, without doing violence to usage or analogy, it seems to be clearly entitled to the preference. Such a hypothesis, it seems to me, is one obscurely stated by some older writers, but which may be more satisfactorily propounded thus, that by the *servant of Jehovah* in these Later Prophecies of Isaiah, we are to understand the church with its Head, or rather the Messiah with the church which is his body, sent by Jehovah to reclaim the world from its apostacy and ruin. This agrees exactly with the mission both of the Redeemer and his people as described in Scripture, and accounts for all the variations which embarrass the interpretation of the passages in question upon any more exclusive exegetical hypothesis. It is also favoured by the analogy of Deut. xviii. where the promised Prophet, according to the best interpretation, is not Christ exclusively, but Christ as the Head of the prophetic body who possessed his spirit. Another analogy is furnished by the use of the phrase *Abraham's seed*, both individually and collectively. He whom Paul describes as the seed of Abraham, and Moses as a prophet like unto himself, in a personal but not an exclusive sense, is described by Isaiah as the servant of Jehovah, in his own person, but not to the exclusion of his people, so far as they can be considered his co-workers or his representatives. Objections founded on the want of agreement between some of these descriptions and the recorded character of Israel, are connected with a superficial view of Israel, considered simply as a nation and like other nations, except so far as it was brought into external and fortuitous connection with the true religion. An essential feature in the theory proposed is that this race was set apart and organised for a specific purpose, and that its national character is constantly subordinate to its ecclesiastical relation. There is precisely the same variation in the language used respecting it as in the use and application of the term ἐκκλησία in the New Testament. Israel is sometimes described as he was meant to be, and as he should have been; sometimes as he actually was. The name is sometimes given to the whole race and sometimes to the faithful portion of it; or, which amounts to the same thing, it is sometimes used to denote the real, sometimes the nominal Israel. The apparent violence of applying the same description to an individual person and a body, will be lessened by considering, that the former, *i. e.* Christ was in the highest and truest sense the servant of Jehovah and his messenger to man, but that his body, church, or people, was, and is, a sharer in the same vocation, under the gospel as an instrument or fellow-worker, under the law as a type or representative of the one who had not yet become visible. Hence the same things might be predicated to a great extent of both. As the Messiah was the servant and messenger of God to the nations, so was Israel. It was his mission also to diffuse the true religion and reclaim the nations. From the very first it was intended that the law should go forth from Zion and the word of the Lord from Jerusalem. (Chap. ii. 3.) The national restrictions of the old economy were not intended to exclude the Gentiles from the church, but to preserve the church from assimilation to the Gentiles. All the world might have come in if they would, by complying with the terms prescribed; and nothing is more clear from the Old Testament than the fact that the privileges of the chosen people were not meant to be restricted even then to the natural descendants of Israel, for this would have excluded proselytes entirely. Multitudes did embrace the true religion before Christ came; and that more did not, was partly their own fault, partly the fault of the chosen people, who neglected or mistook their high vocation as the Messiah's representative and as Jehovah's messenger. If it be asked, how the different applications of this honourable title are to be distinguished so as to avoid confusion or capricious inconsistency, the answer is as follows:

Where the terms are in their nature applicable both to Christ as the Head and to his church as the Body, there is no need of distinguishing at all between them. Where sinful imperfection is implied in what is said, it must of course be applied to the body only. Where a freedom from such imperfection is implied, the language can have a direct and literal reference only to the Head, but may be considered as descriptive of the body, in so far as its idea or design is concerned, though not in reference to its actual condition. Lastly, when anything is said implying deity or infinite merit, the application to the Head becomes not only predominant but exclusive. It may further be observed that as the church, according to this view of the matter, represents its Head, so it is represented by its leaders, whether prophets, priests, or kings; and as all these functions were to meet in Christ, so all of them may sometimes be particularly prominent in prophecy. With this explanation, the hypothesis proposed may be considered as approaching very nearly to the one maintained by Umbreit in his work upon the *Servant of God* (*Knecht Gottes*, Hamburg, 1840), as well as in his Commentary on Isaiah. A similar theory is broached by Ewald, but with this essential difference, that he excludes all reference to Christ, and identifies the Messiah of these prophecies with Cyrus. A correct view of the manifold and variable usage of the title עֶבֶד יְהוָה is given by Gesenius in his Thesaurus and the later editions of his Lexicon. How far the theory here stated with respect to the עֶבֶד יְהוָה is either necessary to explain the prophecies or really consistent with their terms can only be determined by a specific application of the principle to the successive parts of the description. If applied to this first verse, it would determine its interpretation, as describing Israel, the ancient church, to be in a peculiar sense the servant of Jehovah, protected and sustained by Him, enlightened by a special revelation, not for his own exclusive use, but as a source of saving light to the surrounding nations. At the same time it would shew him to possess this character, not in his right, but in that of another, as the representative and instrument of one who, though he was with God and was God, took upon him the form of a servant, and received the Spirit without measure, that he might be *a light to lighten the Gentiles as well as the glory of his people Israel.* (Luke ii. 32.) The reference to Christ is here so evident, however, that there is no need of supposing any distinct reference to his people at all, nor any advantage in so doing, except that of rendering the subsequent verses still more significant, as descriptive, not only of his personal ministry, but of the spirit and conduct of his people, both before and after his appearance.

2. *He shall not cry* (or *call aloud*), *and he shall not raise* (his voice), *and he shall not let his voice be heard in the street* (or abroad, without). The Vulgate strangely supplies פָּנִים after יִשָּׂא (*non accipiet personam*), and so obtains the customary technical expression for respect of persons or judicial partiality. This construction, which was probably suggested by the supposed analogy of chap. xi. 3, 4, is precluded by its want of agreement with what goes before and follows. The same objection lies, though in a less degree, against Cocceius's construction of the verb as a reflexive (*se efferet*), which is, moreover, not grammatically tenable. It is not even necessary to assume an ellipsis of the noun *voice* in the first clause, although this may be required to make the sense clear in a version. The Hebrew construction is continued through both clauses, *i. e.* both verbs govern the same noun. *He shall not raise nor suffer to be heard in the street his voice.* The simple meaning of the verse is, he shall not be noisy, but quiet. Grotius supposes an allusion to the fact, that angry persons often speak so loud

at home as to be heard in the street. Clericus justly denies any special reference to anger, but perhaps goes too far when he translates יַשְׂמִיעַ, *dabit operam ut audiatur*. The idea seems rather to be that of suffering the voice to be heard in public places. As applied both to Christ and to the church, this verse describes a silent, unostentatious method of proceeding. The quotation in Mat. xii. 18 is commonly explained as referring to our Saviour's mild and modest demeanour ; but it rather has respect to the nature of his kingdom, and to the means by which it was to be established. His forbidding the announcement of the miracle is not recorded simply as a trait of personal character, but rather as implying that a public recognition of his claims was not included in his present purpose.

3. *A bruised* (or *crushed*) *reed he will not break, and a dim wick he will not quench ; by the truth will he bring forth judgment.* The verbs of the first clause have no exact equivalents in English. The first appears to mean broken but not broken off, which last is denoted by the other. Clericus supposes an allusion to the growing plant, which may be broken and yet live, but if entirely broken off must die.—The common version, *smoking flax*, is that of the Septuagint and Vulgate. The Hebrew noun really denotes flax (Exod. ix. 31), but the adjective means faint or dim ; so that in order to convey the meaning in translation, the former must be taken in the specific sense of *wick*, which it also has in chap. xliii. 17. The application of these figures to the sparing of enemies, or the indulgence of weak friends, or the sustentation of sincere but feeble faith, is too specific and exclusive. The verse continues the description of the mode in which the Messiah and his people were to *bring forth judgment to the nations*, or in other words, to spread the true religion. It was not to be by clamour or by violence. The first of these ideas is expressed in the preceding verse, the last in this. That such is the true import of the words is clear from the addition of the last clause, which would be unmeaning if the verse re· lated merely to a compassionate and sympathetic temper. That this verse is included in Matthew's quotation (chap. xii. 19), shews that he did not quote the one before it as descriptive of a modest and retiring disposition. For although such a temper might be proved by Christ's prohibiting the publication of his miracles, this prohibition could not have been cited as an evidence of tenderness and mildness. The only way in which the whole quotation can be made appropriate to the case in hand, is by supposing that it was meant to be descriptive, not of our Saviour's human virtues, but of the nature of his kingdom and of the means by which it was to be established. That he was both lowly and compassionate is true, but it is not the truth which he established by his conduct upon this occasion, nor the truth which the evangelist intended to illustrate by the citation of these words. As well in their original connection as in Matthew's application of them, they describe that kingdom which was not of this world ; which came "not with observation" (Luke xvii. 20); which was "neither meat nor drink, but righteousness and peace, and joy in the Holy Ghost" (Rom. xiv. 17); which was founded and promoted, not by might nor by power, but by the Spirit of the Lord ; and of which its Founder said (John xviii. 36), *If my kingdom were of this world, then would my servants fight, that I should not be delivered to the Jews, but now is my kingdom not from hence.* And again (John xviii. 27), when Pilate said unto him, Art thou a king then? Jesus answered, *Thou sayest* (rightly) *that I am a king ; to this end was I born, and for this cause came I into the world, that I should bear witness to the truth ; every one that is of the truth heareth my voice.* How perfectly does this august descrip-

tion tally with the great prophetic picture of the Servant of Jehovah who was to bring forth judgment to the nations, and in doing so was not to cry, or raise his voice, or let men hear it in the streets, not by brutal force to break the crushed reed or quench the dim wick, but to conquer by healing and imparting strength.   This passage also throws light on the true sense of the somewhat obscure phrase לֶאֱמֶת, by showing that it means *with re-spect to the truth,* which is here equivalent to saying *by the truth.*   This con-struction, by presenting an antithesis between the true and false way of bringing forth judgment to the Gentiles, is much to be preferred to those constructions which explain the phrase as simply meaning *in truth,* (*i. e.* truly), or *in permanence,* (*i. e.* surely), or *unto truth,* (*i. e.* so as to establish and secure it).   All these may be suggested as accessory ideas; but the main idea seems to be the one first stated, namely, that the end in question is to be accomplished not by clamour, not by violence, but by the truth.

4. *He shall not be dim, and he shall not be crushed, until he shall set judgment in the earth, and for his law the isles shall wait.*   He shall neither conquer nor be conquered by violence.   This verse is a new proof that the one before it does not describe mere tenderness and pity for the weak.   The antithesis would then be, he shall neither be unkind to the infirm nor infirm himself.   On the other hand, the sense is clear and per-tinent, if ver. 3 means that he shall not use violence towards those who are weaker than himself, and ver. 4 that he shall not suffer it from those who are more powerful; or rather that he shall not subdue others, nor himself be subdued by force.   Some interpreters have been misled, by not observing the exact correspondence of the verbs יִכְהֶה and יָרוּץ with the adjectives כֵּהָה and רָצוּץ.   The same oversight has led Cocceius and Vitringa to derive יָרוּץ from רוּץ, *to run,* and to understand the clause as meaning that he shall neither be remiss nor precipitate.   This construction, it is true, makes the clause itself more antithetical and pointed, but only by the sacrifice of an obvious and beautiful antithesis between it and the first clause of ver. 3.— To *set* or *place judgment in the earth* is to establish and confirm the true religion.—By *his law* we are to understand his word or revelation, con-sidered as a rule of duty.—Here again *the islands* is a poetical expression for the nations, or more specifically for the transmarine and distant nations. The restriction of the term to Europe and Asia Minor (J. D. Michaelis) is as false in geography as it is in taste.—On the ground that the heathen could not wait or hope for that of which they were entirely ignorant, some understand the last verb as meaning *they shall trust* (*i.e.* after they have heard, they shall believe it).   Besides the preference thus given to a second-ary over a primary and proper sense, the general meaning of the clause, and its connection with what goes before, appear to be misapprehended. The hope meant is not so much subjective as objective.   The thing de-scribed is not the feeling of the Gentiles towards the truth, but their de-pendence on it for salvation, and on Christ for the knowledge of the truth itself.   *For his law the isles are waiting* (or *must wait*), and till it comes, they must remain in darkness.

5. *Thus saith the mighty (God), Jehovah, creating the heavens and stretching them out, spreading the earth and its issues, giving breath to the people on it, and spirit to those walking in it.*   Ewald refers *thus saith* to the preceding verses, which he supposes to be here described as the words of God himself.   But as the following verses also contain the words of God, there is no need of departing from the ordinary usage of the Scriptures, according to which the name of the speaker is prefixed to the report of what

he says. We may indeed assume an equal connection with what goes before and follows, as if he had said, *Thus hath Jehovah spoken, and he speaks still further.*—The appeal is so directly to the power of Jehovah, that the name הָאֵל, which is expressive of that attribute, ought not to be resolved into the general term *God.* (See chap. v. 16, vol. i. p. 136.)—The substitution of the preterite for the participle in the English Version (*he that created the heavens, and stretched them out*) is not only a gratuitous departure from the form of the original, but hides from the English reader the allusion to the creative power of God, as constantly exercised in the continued existence of his works. The same figure is exhibited more fully in chap. xl. 22, and the places there referred to. (See above, p. 112, 113.)—This clause is not a scientific, but a poetical description. To the eye, the heavens have the appearance of a canopy or curtain, and the verdant surface of the earth that of a carpet. There is no need, therefore, of supplying a distinct verb to govern *its issues.* רָקַע, though originally used to signify the beating out of metal into thin plates, has acquired in usage the more general sense of spreading or expanding, and is equally applicable to the earth as an apparently flat surface, and to its vegetation as the tapestry which covers it. The Prophet's picture is completely marred by making רָקַע mean *consolidating,* which is wholly inappropriate to צֶאֱצָאֶיהָ, and has no etymological foundation. Even רָקִיעַ in the first chapter of Genesis means an *expanse;* the idea of a *firmament* comes not from the Hebrew, but the ancient versions. No single English word is so appropriate as *issues* to express both the meaning and the derivation of the corresponding one in Hebrew, which denotes the things that come out of the earth, its produce, growth, or vegetation, with particular allusion here to grass.—Here, as in chap. xl. 7, the word *people* is evidently used in application to the whole human race, a fact of some importance in the exposition of what follows. Cocceius alone supposes an antithesis between *the people* (*i. e.* Israel) and the rest of men. If this had been intended, the word *spirit* would no doubt have been connected with the former. By the side of this may be placed Kimchi's notion, that a contrast was intended between men and brutes, on the ground that נְשָׁמָה is limited in usage to the former. נוֹטֵיהֶם in the first clause of this verse is explained by some as a *pluralis majesticus,* by others as a singular form peculiar to the לה verbs and their derivatives. (See vol. i. p. 134.) —The enumeration of Jehovah's attributes in this verse is intended to accredit the assurances contained in the context.

6. *I Jehovah have called thee in righteousness, and will lay hold of thy hand* (or *hold it fast*), *and will keep thee, and will give thee for a covenant of the people, for a light of the Gentiles.*—The act of calling here implies selection, designation, and providential introduction to God's service.—*In righteousness, i. e.* in the exercise of righteousness on God's part, including the fulfilment of his promises as well as of his threatenings. — *Unto righteousness, i. e.* to be righteous, is an idea foreign from the context, and one which would not have been thus expressed in Hebrew. Lowth's translation (*for a righteous purpose*), although too paraphrastical, may be considered as substantially identical with that first stated. Those of Gesenius (*to salvation*) and Hitzig (*in grace*) are equally gratuitous, and contrary to usage.— *I will hold thee fast,* and thereby hold thee up, sustain thee. (See above, ver. 1.)—Lowth and Barnes esteem it an improvement of the common English Version, to change *keep* into *preserve.*—*I will give thee for, i. e.* create, appoint, or constitute thee.—Hitzig understands by בְּרִית עָם a *covenant-people* (Bundesvolk), Ewald a mediatorial people (Mittelsvolk), both

denoting a people called or sent to act as a mediator or a bond of union between God and the nations. But this, although it yields a good sense, is a German and English rather than a Hebrew construction, the instances in which a prefixed noun qualifies the other being very rare and dubious. This objection is sufficient, without adding that the phrase as thus explained would be inapplicable to an individual, whereas the other epithets employed are equally appropriate to persons and communities. Most other writers are agreed in adhering to the obvious construction and in understanding by *a covenant of the people* a negotiator between God and the people. This use of *covenant*, although unusual, is in itself not more unnatural or forced than that of *light* in the next phrase. As *light of the nations* must mean a source or dispenser of light to them, so *covenant of people*, in the very same sentence, may naturally mean the dispenser or mediator of a covenant with them. The only reason why the one appears less natural and simple than the other, is that *light* is habitually used in various languages both for the element of light and for its source or a luminous body, whereas no such twofold usage of the other word exists, although analogies might easily be traced in the usage of such words as *justice* for judge, *counsel* for counsellor, in both which cases the functionary takes the name of that which he dispenses or administers.—But supposing this to be the true construction of the phrase, the question still arises, who are the contracting parties, or in other words, what are we to understand by *people?* The great majority of writers make it mean the *Jews*, the chosen people of Jehovah, and the *covenant* the mediator or negotiator of a new covenant between them and Jehovah, according to the representation in Jer. xxxi. 31–33. To this it may be objected that עַם has not the article as usual when employed in that sense, and that even with the article it is applied in the preceding verse to mankind in general. To this it may be added that the word *nations* in the next clause may as well be exegetical of *people* as in contrast with it. The first supposition is indeed much more natural, because the words are in such close connection, and because there is no antithesis between the correlative expressions, *light* and *covenant*. To this it is replied, that the reference to Israel in this case is determined by the clear unambiguous analogy of chap. xlix. 8, where the phrase recurs and in a similar connection. This conclusion not only rests upon a false assumption as to the meaning of the context there, but is directly contradicted by the language of ver. 6, where it is expressly said that it was not enough for Christ to be the restorer of Israel, he must also be a *light to the Gentiles;* and in direct continuation of this promise it is added in ver. 8, without the show of a distinction or antithesis, that he should be *a covenant of the people*, (*i. e.* of the nations), *to restore or re-establish the earth* (not the land, which is a perfectly gratuitous restriction), *to cause to be inherited the desolate heritages*, (*i. e.* the ruins of an apostate world), *and to say to the prisoners, Go forth*, the arbitrary reference of which words to the Babylonish exile is in fact the only ground for the opinion now disputed. So far is this passage, then, from disproving the wide explanation of the word עַם in the place before us, that it really affords a very strong analogical reason in its favour, and we need no longer hesitate to understand the clause as a description of the *servant of Jehovah* in the character, not only of a light (or an enlightener) to the nations, but of a mediator or negotiator between God and the people, *i. e.* men in general. These are epithets applying in their highest sense to Christ alone, to whom they are in fact applied by Simeon (Luke ii. 32), and Paul (Acts xiii. 47). That neither of these quotes the phrase *a covenant of the people*, does not prove that it has no relation to the Gentiles, but only that it does not relate to them exclusively, but to the whole human race; whereas the other phrase, as applying specifically to the Gentiles, and as being less ambiguous, was exactly suited to Paul's purpose.—At the same time let it be observed that this description is entirely appropriate, not only to the Head but to the Body also in subordination to him. Not only the Messiah but the Israel of God was sent to be a mediator or connecting link between Jehovah and the nations. The meaning put upon בְּרִית עָם by Hitzig and Ewald, although not philologically accurate, is perfectly consistent with the teachings of the Old Testament respecting the mission and vocation of Israel, the ancient Church, as a covenant-race or middle-people between God and the apostate nations.

7. *To open blind eyes, to bring out from prison the bondman, from the house of confinement the dwellers in darkness.* This was the end to be accomplished by the Servant of Jehovah in the character or office just ascribed to him. The spiritual evils to be remedied are represented under the figures of imprisonment and darkness, the removal of the latter having obvious allusion to the *light of the nations* in ver. 6. The fashionable explanation of these words, which refers them to the restoration of the Jews from exile, is encumbered with various and complex difficulties. What is said of bondage must be either strictly understood or metaphorically. If the former be preferred, how is it that the Prophet did not use expressions more exactly descriptive of the state of Israel in Babylon? A whole nation carried captive by its enemies could hardly be described as prisoners in dark dungeons. Knobel, with readiness almost rabbinical, supplies the necessary fact by saying that a part of the Jews were imprisoned. But even granting that they were in prison, were they also blind? If it be said that this is a figurative representation of confinement in the dark, the principle of strict interpretation is abandoned, and the imprisonment itself may be a metaphor for other evils. There is then left no specific reason for applying this description to the exile any more than to a hundred other seasons of calamity. Another and more positive objection to this limitation is that it connects this verse with only part of the previous description, and that the part to which it bears the least resemblance. Even supposing what has been disproved, that *covenant of the people* has respect to Israel alone, how is it that the other attribute, *a light to the Gentiles*, must be excluded in interpreting what follows? It was surely not in this capacity that the Servant of Jehovah was to set the Jewish exiles free. If it be said that this verse has respect to only one of these two characters, this supposition is not only arbitrary, but doubly objectionable; first, because it passes over the nearest antecedent (אוֹר גּוֹיִם) to connect the verse exclusively with one more distant (בְּרִית עָם), and then, because it passes by the very one to which the figures of this verse have most analogy. The opening of the eyes and the deliverance of those that sit in darkness are correlative expressions to the *light of the Gentiles*, which on this account, and as the nearest antecedent, must decide the sense of this verse, if that sense depend on either of these attributes exclusively. *I will make thee a light to the Gentiles, to open the blind eyes*, &c., cannot mean, I will make thee an instructor of the heathen to restore the Jews from captivity in Babylon. Whether the verse before us therefore be strictly or figuratively understood, it cannot be applied to the captivity without doing violence at once to the text and context. The very same reasoning applies to the analogous expressions used in chap. xlix. 9, and thus corroborates our previous conclusion, that

the context in neither of these places favours, much less requires, the restriction of בְּרִית עָם to the Jews. The only natural interpretation of the verse before us is that which makes it figurative like the one preceding it, and the only natural interpretation of its figures is the one which understands them as descriptive of spiritual blindness and spiritual bondage, both which are metaphors of constant application to the natural condition of mankind in the Old as well as the New Testament. The removal of these evils is the work of Christ, as the revealer of the Father who "has brought life and immortality to light;" but in subordination to him, and as his representative, his church may also be correctly represented as a covenant of the people and a light of the nations; since the law, though a divine revelation, was to go forth from Zion, and the word of the Lord from Jerusalem.

8. *I am Jehovah, that is my name, and my glory to another will I not give, and my praise to graven images.* The name Jehovah is here used with emphasis in reference to its etymological import as descriptive of a self-existent, independent, and eternal being. There is no sufficient ground for the opinion that the pronoun הוּא is ever used as a divine name, cognate and equivalent to *Jehovah.* In this case, the obvious and usual construction is entirely satisfactory. *Graven images* are here put, as in many other cases, for idols in general, without regard to the mode of their formation. The connection of this verse with what precedes may seem obscure, but admits of an easy explanation. From the assertion of Jehovah's power and perfection as a ground for his people's confidence, the Prophet now proceeds, by a natural transition, to exhibit it in contrast with the impotence of those gods in whom the Gentiles trusted. These are represented not only as inferior to God, but as his enemies and rivals, any act of worship paid to whom was so much taken from what he claimed as his own, and as his own exclusively. The general doctrine of the verse is that true and false religion cannot co-exist; because, however tolerant idolatry may be, it is essential to the worship of Jehovah to be perfectly exclusive of all other gods. This is included in the very name *Jehovah*, and accounts for its solemn proclamation here.

9. *The first (or former) things—lo, they have come, and new things I (am) telling; before they spring forth (sprout or germinate) I will make (or let) you hear (them).* This is an appeal to former prophecies already verified, as grounds of confidence in those yet unfulfilled. The attempts which have been made to give specific meanings to *former things* and *new things*, as denoting certain classes of prophecies, are unsuccessful, because perfectly gratuitous. The most plausible hypothesis of this kind is Vitringa's, which applies the one term to the prophecies respecting Cyrus and the Babylonish exile, the other to the prophecies respecting the Messiah and the new dispensation. But the simple meaning of the words appears to be, that as former prophecies (not of Isaiah but of older prophets) had come to pass, so those now uttered should be likewise verified. The strong and beautiful expression in the last clause can only mean that the events about to be predicted were beyond the reach of human foresight, and is therefore destructive of the modern notion, that these prophecies were written after Cyrus had appeared, and at a time when the further events of his history could be foreseen by an observer of unusual sagacity. Such a prognosticator, unless he was also a deliberate deceiver, a charge which no one brings against this writer, could not have said of what he thus foresaw, that he announced it before it had begun to germinate, *i. e.* while the seed

was in the earth, and before any outward indications of the plant could be perceived. As this embraces all the writer's prophecies, it throws the date of composition back to a period before the rise of Cyrus, and thereby helps to invalidate the arguments in favour of regarding it as contemporaneous with the Babylonish exile.

10. *Sing to Jehovah a new song, his praise from the end of the earth, (ye) going down to the sea and its fulness, isles and their inhabitants !* To sing a new song, according to Old Testament usage, is to praise God for some new manifestation of his power and goodness. It implies, therefore, not only fresh praise, but a fresh occasion for it. Reduced to ordinary prose style, it is a prediction that changes are to take place joyfully affecting the condition of the whole world. That this is a hyperbole, relating to the restoration of the Jews from Babylon is too gratuitous and forced a supposition to be imposed upon any reader of the prophecy against his will. Let those who can, receive and make the most of it. The great majority of readers will be apt to reject an assumption which has no foundation in the text, and which reduces a sublime prediction to an extravaganza.—Gesenius, for some reason not explained, chooses to read *at* instead of *from* the end. The obvious meaning of the phrase is, that the sound of praise should be heard coming *from* the remotest quarters. *Its fulness* may either be connected with *the sea*, and both dependent on *go down* (to the sea and its fulness), or regarded as a distinct object of address. In the latter case, the marine animals would seem to be intended ; in the former, the whole mass of water with its contents ; the last is more poetical and natural. The antithesis is then between the sea with its frequenters on the one hand, and the isles with their inhabitants on the other.

11. *The desert and its towns shall raise (the voice), the enclosures* (or *en-campments*, in which) *Kedar dwells ; the dwellers in the Rock shall shout, from the top of mountains shall they cry aloud.* This is a direct continuation of the previous description, in which the whole world is represented as exulting in the promised change. The reference of this verse to the course of the returning exiles through the intervening desert is forbidden by the mention of the sea and its fulness, the isles, and the ends of the earth, in the preceding and following verses. If these are not all parts of the same great picture, it is impossible to frame one. If they are, it is absurd to take the first and last parts in their widest sense as an extravagant hyperbole, and that which is between them in its strictest sense as a literal description. The only consistent supposition is, that sea, islands, deserts, mountains, towns, and camps, are put together as poetical ingredients of the general conception, that the earth in all its parts shall have occasion to rejoice.—The mention of cities as existing in the wilderness appears less strange in the original than in a modern version, because both the leading words (מִדְבָּר and עִיר) have a greater latitude of meaning than their usual equivalents ; the first denoting properly a pasture-ground, and being applicable, therefore, to any uncultivated region, whether uninhabited or not, the other answering to *town* in its widest English sense, inclusive of both villages and cities. There is no need, therefore, of supposing a particular allusion to *oases* in the arid desert, or of assuming, as Gesenius does in his Thesaurus, that עִיר sometimes means nothing more than a military station, post, or watch-tower (See chap. i. 8.)—The translation of חֲצֵרִים by *villages* is too restricted, since the Hebrew word is applicable also to collections of tents or nomadic encampments, which appears to be the prominent idea here. Kedar

was the second son of Ishmael (Gen. xxv. 13). Here, as in chap. xxi. 16, the name is put for his descendants, or by a natural metonymy for the Arabians in general. The rabbinical name for the Arabic language is *the tongue of Kedar*. The Septuagint takes it as the name of the country (*and those inhabiting Kedar*). The Vulgate makes this clause a promise (*Kedar shall dwell in houses*), and the preceding verb a passive (*let the desert and its towns be exalted*). Cocceius has the same construction, but gives both the verbs an imperative meaning, and follows the Septuagint in explaining Kedar (*efferat se desertum et oppida ejus ; per pagos habitetur Kedarena*). Most writers, ancient and modern, have regarded a relative construction as more natural (*which Kedar doth inhabit.*) The use of Kedar as a feminine is contrary to general usage, which distinguishes between the name of the country as feminine and that of the nation possessing it as masculine. The rabbins explain it by supposing an ellipsis of עֲרַת before it. More probably, however, it is an irregularity or licence of construction, such as we have seen already in chap. xxi. 2, and elsewhere.—Vitringa, J. D. Michaelis, and some later writers, explain סֶלַע as the proper name of Petra ; but the whole connection renders it more natural to take it in its general sense of *rock*, and as corresponding, not so much to Kedar as to the appellatives, desert, towns, encampments, mountains.

12. *They shall place* (or *give*) *to Jehovah honour, and his praise in the islands they shall shew forth* (or *declare*). Still another mode of saying, the whole world shall praise him. The islands are again mentioned, either as one out of several particulars before referred to, or with emphasis, as if he had said, *even in the islands*, beyond sea, and by implication in the furthest regions.—As the verb to *give*, in Hebrew usage, has the secondary sense of *placing*, so the verb to place is occasionally used as an equivalent to that of giving. (See vol. i. p. 425.) The translation of the verbs in this verse as imperatives (*let them give glory and declare*), although substantially correct, is a needless departure from the form of the original, in which the idea of command or exhortation in sufficiently implied, though not expressed. The verbs do not agree with the series of nouns in the foregoing verse (desert, towns, &c.), for these could not celebrate Jehovah *in the islands*. The construction is indefinite, *they, i. e.* men in general, a form of speech of far more frequent occurrence in Hebrew than would be suspected by a reader of the English Bible.

13. *Jehovah, like a strong one, will go forth ; like a warrior* (literally *a man of battle*) *he will rouse* (*his*) *zeal ; he will shout, yea, he will cry ; against his foes will make* (or *shew*) *himself strong.* From the effect he now reverts to the efficient cause. The universal joy before described is to arise from Jehovah's triumph over his enemies. The martial figures of the verse are intelligible in themselves, and all familiar to the usage of the Scriptures. Lowth and Barnes amend the common version of the first clause by reading, he *shall march forth like a hero.* The modern Germans also use the word *Held* (hero). Luther and Calvin prefer *giant*. It may be doubted whether any English word is more appropriate or striking than the strict translation *strong* or *mighty*. To *go forth* is the common Hebrew phrase for going out to war or battle. (See above, on chap. xl. 26.) Junius and Tremellius understand the plural *battles* as a superlative expression, and translate the phrase *vir bellicosissimus evigilans zelo.* The versions of Clericus (*vir militaris*), and Vitringa (*peritus bellator*) greatly weaken the expression. קִנְאָה may either have its general sense of ardour, strong and violent affection of whatever kind, or its more specific sense of jealousy, or

sensitive regard for his own honour and for the welfare of his people.
(See vol. i. p. 206.) The idea is that of an ancient warrior exciting
his own courage by a shout or war-cry. The last clause may be understood to mean, *he shall prevail over his enemies;* but although this idea
is undoubtedly included, it is best to retain the reflexive form and import
of the verb, as far as may be, in translation.

14. *I have long been still,* (saying) *I will hold my peace, I will restrain
myself.* (But now), *like the travailing (woman) I will shriek, I will pant
and gasp at once.* The consecution of the tenses in the first clause has
occasioned the most opposite constructions. Of these the most violent and
ungrammatical is that of Augusti, who translates all the verbs of the verse
as preterites. With this exception, it appears to be agreed on all hands
that the verbs of the last clause are either futures proper, or descriptive
presents, and the only question is in reference to those of the first. According to Luther, these are all presents; while the Vulgate, followed by
most modern writers, makes them all refer to past time. That such assimilations do occur, is certain; but a general maxim of interpretation makes
it highly desirable to regard the distinction of the tenses, where we can, as
intentional and significant. Lowth and Ewald accordingly follow the Septuagint in retaining the future form of the second and third verbs, but read
them interrogatively (I have long been silent; shall I hold my peace and
restrain myself for ever?) This involves the necessity of reading הַלְעוֹלָם
(*for ever?*) and connecting it against the accents with what follows. It is
true that interrogative sentences, without the interrogative particle expressed, are not unknown to Hebrew usage; but their occurrence is comparatively rare, and ought not to be assumed without necessity, which of
course has no existence if the clause can be affirmatively read without
abandoning the strict sense of the future. This can be done, as may be
seen in the translation above given, by regarding the second and third verbs
as the expression of his own determination or intention while the silence
lasted. The omission of the verb *to say* before such repetitions or citations
is not only frequent in general usage, but the more natural in this case from
the fact that this whole verse is universally regarded as the words of God
himself, although he is not expressly introduced as the speaker. The
necessity of supplying (at least in thought) the words *but now* before the
last clause, is not peculiar to this view of the passage, but common to it
with all others, except Augusti's paradoxical construction. The word אֶפְעֶה
is twice used elsewhere by Isaiah (xxx. 6, lix. 5) as a noun meaning a viper
or some other venomous serpent, in which sense it is also used by Job (xx.
16). The general principles of analogical interpretation would require this
sense to be retained here; but the only writers who have ventured so to do
are Junius and Tremellius, who translate the clause, *ut parturientem viperam
desolabo.* Even the Rabbins give the word the sense of *crying,* which is
plainly a conjecture from the context. Bochart attempts a compromise
between the two opinions, by supposing that the word originally means *to
hiss* like a serpent; and Gesenius connects it with נָפַח *to blow.* The only
objection to the common version, *shriek* or *scream,* is that it seems too strong
both for the etymology and the analogy of the verbs which follow, and which
seem to denote a suppressed sound rather than a loud one, *I will pant and
gasp at once.* There is indeed another very ancient explanation of these
two verbs, given in the Vulgate and by Calvin, Grotius, Hitzig, and Hendewerk, as well as in the English Version, *I will destroy and devour at once.*
This refers אֶשֹּׁם to the root שָׁמֵם *to lay waste* (and more generally *to destroy*),

and gives שָׁאַף the sense of swallowing, and then (like בְּלַע) that of destroying.   But שָׁאַף means elsewhere *to pant* or *gasp;* and אֶשֹּׁם may be readily
regarded as a synonyme, if derived from נָשַׁם *to breathe,* of which it would be
the natural future.   It is true that this verb does not occur elsewhere, but
its derivative נְשָׁמָה *breath* is of perpetual occurrence ; and the very same
writers who reject the derivation from נָשַׁם on this ground, assume that of
אֶפְעֶה from פָּעָה, not only in the absence of any other instance, but in opposition to the usage which determines it to be a noun.   The authority of
Gesenius may be cited upon both sides of this question, not only from his
earlier and later works, but from the last edition of his Lexicon, in which
the two explanations of this clause are separately given as correct, the one
under שָׁאַף, which is explained as meaning to breathe hard, to pant, to blow,
" *e. g.* of an angry person, Isa. xlii. 14," the other under שָׁמֵם, where the two
verbs are translated, "I will destroy and gulp down together."   The paraphrase added in the latter case, "my wrath, long restrained, I will now
let break forth," is no doubt the true sense of the verse on either supposition.

15. *I will lay waste mountains and hills, and all their herbage will I dry
up; and I will turn* (literally *place*) *streams to islands, and pools* (or *lakes*)
will I dry up.   Having described the effect and the cause of the great
future change, he now describes the change itself, under the common form
of a complete revolution in the face of nature, sometimes with special reference to the heavens (chap. xiii. 10), sometimes (as here and in chap.
xxxv. 6, 7) to the earth.   It is strange that, with these analogies in view,
and after such descriptions as those previously given, any should still suppose that by mountains and hills we are here to understand States and
governments, and by their *herbs* the citizens or subjects.   There is more
probability in the opinion that the verse contains an allusion to the
ancient cultivation of the hills of Palestine, by means of terraces, many
of which are still in existence.   (See vol. i. p. 182.)   Houbigant
and Lowth read צִיִּים (*dry deserts*), which is not only needless but contrary
to usage, as צִיִּים nowhere signifies deserts themselves, but always their inhabitants.   Gesenius and the other modern writers suppose אִיִּים to be here
used in the sense of dry land as opposed to water.   The necessity of this
explanation may, however, be avoided by adopting the ingenious suggestion of
Clericus, that what is here described is the actual appearance of islands in
the channels of the streams on the subsiding of the water.—The drying of
the bed of the Euphrates by Cyrus can at the utmost only be the subject
of an indirect allusion.   A literal prophecy of that event would be entirely
misplaced in a series of bold metaphorical descriptions.   Rosenmüller goes
to an extravagant length in attempting to connect this verse with the preceding context by explaining it to mean that the excited warrior will dry up
vegetation with his burning breath.

16. *And I will make the blind walk in a way they knew not, in paths
they knew not I will make them tread ; I will set* (or *turn*) *darkness before
them to light, and obliquities to straightness.   These are the words ; I have
made them* (or *done them*) *and have not left them.*   The particle before the
first verb is conversive, *i. e.* gives a future meaning to the preterite, because
preceded by the future proper.   (See Nordheimer, § 219.)   The ellipsis of
the relative, which twice occurs in this clause, is precisely the same both in
Hebrew and in English.—מַעֲקַשִּׁים may be translated crooked or uneven
places, as opposed to what is level, or to superficial rectitude.   (See above,
on chap. xl. 4, p. 95.)   The combination of these two antitheses (light and
dark, crooked and straight) shews clearly that they are both metaphorical

expressions for the same thing that is represented under other figures in the verse preceding, viz., total change; in what respect and by what means, the metaphors themselves do not determine. And yet some writers understand the first clause as specifically meaning that the exiles in Babylon should be delivered at a time and in a manner which they had not expected; while another class apply the words exclusively to spiritual exercise or religious experience. To both these objects the description admits of an easy application; but neither of them is to be considered its specific subject. It is impossible, without the utmost violence, to separate this one link from the chain of which it forms a part, that is to say, from the series of strong and varied metaphors, by which the Prophet is expressing the idea of abrupt and total change. The same thing that is meant by the wasting of cultivated hills, the withering of herbage, and the drying up of streams and lakes, is also meant by the leading of blind men in a new path, *i. e.* causing them to witness things of which they had had no previous experience.—The usual construction of the last clause supplies a relative before the leading verb and takes it suffix as a dative—" these are the words or things which I have done for them and have not left them." Another construction separates the members as distinct propositions—" these are the words (or the things which I have promised to the people); I have made them and have not forsaken them." The simplest and most regular construction is that given by Jerome and Cocceius, which refers the pronouns not to a noun understood, but to the expressed antecedent: *These are the words* (*i. e.* my promises), *I have performed them and have not abandoned them,* that is to say, I have not relinquished my design until it was accomplished. (Compare the last clause of Ezekiel, xvii. 24.) The translation of these verbs as futures has arisen merely from a feeling on the part of the interpreter that the words *ought* to contain a promise; whereas the promise is implied, or rather superseded by the declaration that the work is done already, or at least that the effect is already secured. The usual construction, which makes one a preterite and one a future, is doubly arbitrary and capricious.

17. *They are turned back, they shall be ashamed with shame* (*i. e.* utterly ashamed), *those trusting in the graven image, those saying to the molten image, Ye are our gods.* This verse describes the effect to be produced by the expected changes on the enemies of God and the worshippers of idols. *They are turned back,* utterly defeated, foiled in their malignant opposition. Nor is this all; for they are yet to be utterly ashamed, confounded, disappointed, and disgraced. In the last clause it is plain that the graven and molten image are separated only by the parallelism, because the address at the end is in the plural form, not *thou art,* but *ye are our gods.* On the usage of these two nouns, see vol. i. p. 482.

18. *Ye deaf, hear! and, ye blind, look to see!* From the connection, this would seem to be a call upon the worshippers of idols, to open their eyes and ears, and become conscious of their own delusions.—The infinitive at the end of the sentence does not express the manner but the purpose of the act required. Vitringa's version therefore (*videndo intuemini*) is less correct than that of Jerome (*intuemini ad videndum*).

19. *Who (is) blind but my servant, and deaf like my messenger (whom) I will send? Who (is) blind like the devoted one and blind like the servant of Jehovah?* Why should he call the heathen blind and deaf, when Israel himself, with all his honours and advantages, refused to see or hear? The very people whose mission and vocation it was to make the Gentiles see

and hear, seemed to emulate their insensibility.   The most difficult expression in this verse is מְשֻׁלָּם, which the Seventy seem to have read מֹשְׁלִים
and understood as meaning those that have dominion over them.   The
various explanations of the common text may all be reduced to two distinct senses of the verbal root, viz., that of being at peace and that of being
perfect or complete.   The latter meaning is assumed by Luther, Calvin,
Cocceius, and Vitringa ; while Clericus modifies it so as to mean *a man of
consummate wisdom*, and Lowth one *perfectly instructed*.   On the other
hypothesis, Junius renders it *donatus pace;* Gesenius, *the friend of God;*
Hitzig, Ewald, and Umbreit, the *devoted* or the *God-devoted*.   This last is
favoured by the analogy of مسلم in Arabic, the name by which the
Mohammedans describe themselves, and which denotes one who gives himself to God.   From the use of the Piel in the sense of completing, making
good, repaying, are derived the Vulgate version (*venundatus*) and that of
Rosenmüller (*redemptus*).   As to the application of the term here, Clericus
supposes that it means the High Priest or some eminent person of the
sacerdotal order.   But the great majority of writers understand it as descriptive of Israel, the chosen people.   The objections arising from the use
of similar expressions at the beginning of the chapter with respect to the
Messiah is usually set aside by arbitrarily assuming entire diversity of subject.   Henderson alone has the intrepidity to understand this verse of the
Messiah likewise, accounting for the application of such epithets to such a
subject by assuming that it expresses the opinion of the unbelieving Jews
respecting Christ.   The obvious objection to this mode of exposition is,
that it opens the door to endless licence of interpretation, by admitting
that a passage may be referred at will to the subject which it is least
adapted to describe, by simply making it express the mind not of the
writer, as it seems to do, but of another party not expressly mentioned.   A
purely arbitrary supposition cannot be justified by the assumption of another
like it.   The true solution of the difficulty seems to be the one already
given in explaining the first verse, viz., that the Servant of Jehovah is a
title applying not only to the Head but to the Body also.   Here, where
the language implies censure and reproach, the terms must be referred exclusively to Israel, the messenger whom God had sent to open the eyes of
the other nations, but who had himself become wilfully blind.   The future
אֶשְׁלַח implies that the mission was not yet fulfilled.   Jerome's construction,
unto whom I sent my messengers, is wholly ungrammatical, and a mere
expedient to avoid a seeming difficulty.   It is scarcely credible that Clericus
seems half inclined to take מַלְאָכִי as the proper name of *Malachi*.

20. *Thou hast seen many things and wilt not observe.* (Sent) *to open
ears! and he will not hear.*   In the first clause he turns to Israel and
addresses him directly; in the last he turns away from him again, and, as
it were, expresses his surprise and indignation to the by-standers.   The
sense of the whole, leaving out of view this difference of form, is the same
as in the foregoing verse, namely, that Israel had eyes but saw not, and
instead of opening the ears of others was himself incapable of hearing.   The
sentence may be said to exhibit a climax.   In the first clause the contrast
is between the blindness of the people and the light which they enjoyed; in
the last it is between their deafness and their high vocation to open the ears
of others.   Hence the abrupt and impassioned form of expression in the
latter case.   The marginal reading רָאוֹת, though susceptible of explanation

as an infinitive, is an unnecessary emendation of the textual רָאִיתָ. The infinitive פֹּקֵחַ might be considered as deriving a preterite sense from the preceding verb; but a better explanation is afforded by the analogy of ver. 7, where the same infinitive describes the end for which the Servant of Jehovah was sent.

21. *Jehovah (is) willing for his righteousness' sake; he will magnify the law and make it honourable.* The people, being thus unfaithful to their trust, had no claim to be treated any longer as an object of Jehovah's favour; and yet he continues propitious, not on their account, but out of regard to his own engagements, and for the execution of his righteous purposes. For these reasons he will still put honour on the chosen people and the system under which they lived. Gesenius and Hitzig arbitrarily construe חָפֵץ with יַגְדִיל, *is pleased to magnify*, of which construction there is no example elsewhere, and then make this an idiom of the later Hebrew. Still less grammatical is the construction of the ancient versions, " it pleased God to justify or sanctify him," whether this be understood to imply the reading צַדְּקוֹ, or taken as a paraphrase of the common text. The application of the words to the righteousness of Christ is inconsistent with the terms of censure and disapprobation which precede and follow.

22. *And (yet) it (is) a people spoiled and robbed, ensnared in holes all of them, and in houses of confinement they are hidden. They have become a spoil; and there is none delivering; a prey, and there is none saying, Restore.* Here another contrast is brought into view. As the conduct of the people did not answer to their high vocation, so their treatment does not answer to the preceding declaration of God's purpose. If he still designed to honour them, though not for their own sake, how was this to be reconciled with what they suffered at the hands of their enemies? The terms are no doubt metaphorical, and therefore not exclusively descriptive of literal captivity. At the same time it may be admitted that the sufferings of Israel in exile furnished one of the most memorable instances of what is here described in general.—בַּחוּרִים is explained in the ancient versions, and by many modern writers, to mean *youths* or *chosen men*, as it does above in chap. xl. 30. But why should this class be described as in captivity? Cocceius and Vitringa change the meaning of the clause by making הָפֵחַ the infinitive of פּוּחַ, to *blow* or *puff*, and explaining the whole phrase, "they are all the puffing of the young men," *i. e.* objects of derision and contempt. But this construction violates the parallelism for the sake of an extremely forced and far-fetched meaning. Most of the modern writers follow Luther in explaining בַּחוּרִים to mean *in holes* or *pitfalls*, corresponding to בָּתֵּי כְּלָאִים in the other member.

23. *Who among you will give ear to this, will hearken and hear for the time to come?* By *this* we are not to understand merely the fact recorded in the foregoing verse, but the doctrine of the whole preceding context as to the vocation and mission of Israel, and as to his actual condition. God had appointed him to be a source, or at least a medium, of light and blessing to the nations; but instead of acting up to this high character, he not only left the nations without light, but was wilfully blinded and insensible himself. Yet God would still be true to his engagements, and put honour on the special revelation which he had already given. Why, then, it might be asked, was Israel suffered to fall before his enemies? The answer to this question is introduced by an indirect caution to consider it and bear it in mind. The interrogative form implies the possibility of their neglecting

or refusing to obey it.—The last phrase is explained to mean *behind* or *backwards* by Vitringa (*a tergo*) and Ewald (*zurückwärts*), who seem to understand it as denoting reflection on the past, or the act of meditating upon what they heard.—Most other writers understand it as relating either to the time of hearing (*henceforth* or *hereafter*) on the subject of the declarations to be heard (*concerning the future*).

24. *Who has given Jacob for a prey, and Israel to spoilers? Has not Jehovah, against whom we have sinned, and they were not willing in his ways to walk, and did not hearken to his law?* This was what they were to bear in mind, viz., that what they suffered was ordained of God and on account of their iniquities. The errors of which this verse is the negation are those of supposing that they suffered without fault, and that they suffered, as it were, in spite of God's protection, or because he was unable to prevent it. The interrogation makes the statement more emphatic : Who else can be imagined to have done it, or for what other cause except our sins ? The change of person in the last clause is a common Hebrew idiom, and does not seem to be significant. (See vol. i. p. 94.) If the Prophet identifies himself with the people in the first phrase, he cannot be supposed to exclude himself in that which follows.—Hitzig's translation of the last word (*his instruction*) is too weak, as it fails to suggest the idea of obligation. It is also at variance with usage, which requires תּוֹרָה to be taken not in its etymological sense merely, but in that of *law*.— This verse is strictly applicable to the sufferings of the Jews in Babylon, and it was no doubt so applied by them ; but in itself it is a general declaration of a fact which has been often verified and was especially exemplified in ancient Israel, viz., that the sufferings even of God's people are the consequence of sin.

25. *And he (Jehovah) poured upon him (Israel) fury (even) his wrath and the strength* (or *violence*) *of war : and it set him on fire round about, and he knew (it) not ; and it burned him, and he will not lay it to heart.* This continues and concludes the description of God's judgments and of Israel's insensibility. Most writers explain חֵמָה as an absolute form used for the construct (*fury of his anger*). Junius and Vitringa make it an adverbial expression qualifying אַפּוֹ (*excandescentiá* or *cum excandescentiá iram*). The simplest construction is to put the nouns in apposition, either as mere equivalents (*my anger as fury*), or as exegetical the one of the other (*fury, to wit, my anger*).—*He knew not* does not here mean *unawares*, without his knowledge, but, as the parallel clause shews, implies extreme insensibility. The translation of the last verb as a preterite is ungrammatical, and the assimilation of the two as presents, an evasion. That a preterite precedes, instead of shewing that the future must refer to past time, shews the contrary, by leaving us unable to account for the difference of form if none of meaning was intended. However necessary such assimilations may be elsewhere, they are inadmissible in cases like the present, where the change of tense admits of an easy explanation, to wit, that the writer intended to describe the people not only as having been insensible before but as likely to continue so in time to come.—On the usage of the phrase *to put* or *lay upon the heart*, see above, p. 125.

Chapter 43

THE main subject of this chapter is the true relation of Israel to Jehovah, and its application in the way both of warning and encouragement.

The doctrine taught is that their segregation from the rest of men, as a peculiar people, was an act of sovereignty, independent of all merit in themselves, and not even intended for their benefit exclusively, but for the accomplishment of God's gracious purposes respecting men in general. The inferences drawn from this fact are, that Israel would certainly escape the dangers which environed him, however imminent, and on the other hand that he must suffer for his unfaithfulness to God. In illustration of these truths, the Prophet introduces several historical allusions and specific prophecies, the most striking of the former having respect to the exodus from Egypt, and of the latter to the fall of Babylon. It is important to the just interpretation of the chapter that these parts of it should be seen in their true light and proportion, as incidental illustrations, not as the main subject of the prophecy, which, as already stated, is the general relation between God and his ancient people, and his mode of dealing with them, not at one time but at all times.

Israel is the peculiar people of Jehovah, cherished and favoured at the expense of other nations, vers. 1–4. But these are one day to become partakers of the same advantages, vers. 5–9. The proofs of the divine protection are afforded by the history of Israel, vers. 10–13. One of the most remarkable, yet future, is the downfall of Babylon and the liberation of the exiles, vers. 14, 15. An analogous example in more ancient times was the deliverance from Egypt, vers. 16, 17. But both these instances shall be forgotten in comparison with the great change which awaits the church hereafter, vers. 18–21. Of all these distinguishing favours none was owing to the merit of the people, but all to the sovereign grace of God, vers. 22–25. The people were not only destitute of merit, but deserving of punishment, which they had experienced and must experience again, vers. 26–28.

1. *And now, thus saith Jehovah, thy Creator, O Jacob, and thy Former, O Israel, Fear not, for I have redeemed thee, I have called thee by thy name, thou art mine* (literally *to me art thou*). The juxtaposition of this promise with the very different language at the close of the preceding chapter has led to various false assumptions as to the connection of the passages. Some give *and now* the sense of *yet* or *nevertheless*, while others understand it as referring to a period following that just mentioned ; as if he had said, After these things have been suffered, fear no longer. But this interpretation is forbidden by the reasons here suggested for not fearing, viz., that Jehovah was already their Creator and Redeemer, and had already called them and made them his peculiar people. It will also be observed that in chap. xlii. as well as here, there is the same alternation and apparent confusion of the encouraging and minatory tone, which cannot therefore be explained by referring any one part of the context to a particular period of history. Another solution of the difficulty is that the Prophet has in view a twofold Israel, the false and true, the carnal and spiritual. This is correct so far as what he says relates to internal character ; but it is evident that he has reference likewise to the outward fortunes of God's people as an organised body. The simplest and most satisfactory hypothesis is that, in this whole context, he is accounting for the sufferings of Israel and his preservation from destruction on the same ground, namely, that Jehovah had chosen them and therefore would preserve them, but that they were unfaithful and must therefore suffer. The intermingling of the promises and threatenings is not to be explained by supposing a reference to different periods or different subjects ; nor is it to be set down as capricious and

unmeaning, but as necessary to the Prophet's purpose. The *now* will then have a logical rather than a temporal meaning, as introductory to an explanation of the strange fact that the bush was burned but not consumed.— *Create* and *form* have reference not merely to the natural creation, nor to the spiritual renovation of individuals, but to the creation or constitution of the church. God was the maker of Israel in a peculiar sense. He existed as a nation for a special purpose.—*Fear not, i. e.* fear not that thou canst be utterly destroyed. It is not an assurance of immunity from suffering, the experience of which is implied and indeed expressly threatened in what follows.—*I have redeemed thee.* There is here an allusion to the redemption of the first-born under the Mosaic law, as appears from the metaphor of substitution used in vers. 3 and 4. Thus understood, the meaning of this clause is, thou art not like the other nations of the earth, for I have purchased or redeemed thee to myself as a peculiar people.—*To call by name* includes the ideas of specific designation, public announcement, and solemn consecration to a certain work. This and the other clauses of the verse can be applied to the election and vocation of individuals only by accommodation, and only so far as the case of the individual members is included in that of the whole body. It is a curious idea of Menochius, that לִי־אַתָּה is the name assigned, as if he had said, *I have called thee by thy name Li-attah* (*Thou-art-mine*). The true sense is, thou art mine because I have expressly called thee so to be.—Rosenmüller discovers here another obstetrical allusion in the phrase יְצָרְךָ. (See vol. i. p. 429.)

2. *When thou passest through the waters, I will be with thee ; and through the rivers, they shall not overflow thee : when thou walkest through the fire, thou shalt not be scorched, and the flame shall not burn thee.* Fire and water are common figures for calamity and danger. (See Ps. lxvi. 12.) To explain one as meaning civil and the other religious persecutions, as Vitringa does, is wholly arbitrary, and might be reversed with just as much or rather just as little reason.—Although *when* conveys the true sense here, and is given in the Lexicons as a distinct meaning of the Hebrew כִּי, the latter really retains its proper meaning, *for, because.* It is the genius of the language to delight in short independent clauses, where we use more involved and complicated periods. "For thou shalt pass through the waters, I will be with thee," is the idiomatic Hebrew mode of saying, If or when thou passest, &c.—The last clause might be rendered, when thou *walkest in the fire*, the preposition *through* being used even in the first clause only because the English idiom requires it after *pass*.—Hitzig gives תִּכָּוֶה a reflexive meaning (*burn thyself*), which is unnecessary, although it agrees well both with Hebrew usage and the English idiom. Augusti takes the same verb in the more specific sense of being *branded, i. e.* marked by the fire. (Compare the derivative noun כִּי, chap. iii. 24.) But this does not suit the more indefinite expressions in the parallel clauses.—The common version of the last words, *shall not kindle upon thee*, is of doubtful authority, and seems to introduce a needless anticlimax, as *burning* is much more than *kindling*.—The application of this promise to individual believers is an accommodation, but one justified by the natural relation between the body and its several members.

3. *For I, Jehovah, thy God, the Holy One of Israel, thy Saviour, have given (as) thy ransom Egypt, Ethiopia, and Seba, instead of thee.* This is an amplification of the phrase *I have redeemed thee* in ver. 1. As the Israelite under the Mosaic law was obliged to redeem his first-born by the payment of a price, or by the substitution of some other object, so Jehovah

secured Israel as his own by giving up the other nations, here represented by a single group, just as the forest trees are represented in chap. xli. 19 by a few well-known species. The group here selected is composed of three contiguous and cognate nations. *Cush*, which was placed by the older writers either wholly or partly in Arabia, is admitted by the moderns to be coincident with the Ethiopia of the Greek geographers. *Seba* is now commonly supposed, on the authority of Josephus, to be Meroe, a part of Ethiopia surrounded by the branches of the Nile, and celebrated by the ancient writers for its wealth and commerce. The connection of the countries was not only geographical but genealogical. According to Gen. x. 6, 7, Cush was the brother of Mizraim and the father of Seba. According to this exegetical hypothesis, the same essential meaning might have been conveyed by the mention of any other group of nations. At the same time it may be admitted, that the mention of Egypt was probably suggested by its intimate connection with the history of Israel, and by its actual sacrifice, in some sort, to the safety of the latter at the period of the exodus. Many interpreters go further, and suppose that the words would have been applicable to no other nations than those specifically mentioned, and that the Prophet here alludes to the real or anticipated conquest of these countries by Cyrus, as a sort of compensation for the loss of Israel. But the necessity of this prosaic explanation is precluded by the prophetic usage of specifying individuals as representatives of classes, while the sense thus put upon ransom or atonement is extremely forced and far-fetched. That the terms, although specific, were designed to have a wider application, may be safely inferred from the generic expressions substituted for them in the next verse.—The essential idea of כֹּפֶר, here and elsewhere, is that of vicarious compensation.—The insertion of the substantive verb in the first clause, so as to make it a distinct proposition (*I am Jehovah*), greatly weakens the whole sentence. The description of the speaker in the first clause is intended to conciliate regard to what he says in the other. It was in the character, not only of an absolute and sovereign God, but in that of Israel's God, his Holy One, his Saviour, that Jehovah had thus chosen him to the exclusion of all other nations.

4. *Since thou wast precious in my eyes, thou hast been honoured, and I have loved thee, and will give man instead of thee, and nations instead of thy soul* (or) *life*. There is precisely the same ambiguity in *since* as in the Hebrew מֵאֲשֶׁר. Both expressions may be taken either in a temporal or causal sense. *Because thou wast precious*, or, *from the time that thou wast precious*. The former sense is really included in the latter. If Israel had been honoured ever since Jehovah called him, it is plainly implied that this vocation was the cause of his distinction.—The first cause, as the whole context clearly shews, does not refer to intrinsic qualities, but to an arbitrary sovereign choice. Since I began to treat thee as a thing of value, thou hast been distinguished among the nations. The verse, so far from ascribing any merit to the people, refers all to God. Some continue the construction through the whole verse, making the apodosis begin with the second clause, *since thou art precious in my sight, and art honoured, and I love thee, I will give,* &c. This yields a good sense, but is grammatically inadmissible, because it supplies a conjunction in the first clause, and omits one in the second. Either of these assumptions might be justified by usage and analogy ; but the coincidence appears unnatural, and makes the whole construction harsh. At the same time, this construction weakens the sentence by making it a mere repetition of what goes before, whereas it is a repeti-

tion with a pointed affirmation that the nation owed its eminence entirely
to God.—The future (*I will give*) shews that the substitution mentioned
in ver. 3 did not relate merely to the past, but to the future also.—*Man* is
here used collectively or indefinitely for *other men* or the rest of men, as
in Judg. xvi. 7 ; Ps. lxxiii. 5 ; Job. xxxi. 33 ; Jer. xxxii. 20. *Thy soul,
life,* or *person,* seems to be an allusion to the usage of the same Hebrew
word in the Law, with respect to enumeration or redemption. (See Exod.
xii. 4 ; Lev. xxvii. 4.)   The general terms of this clause make it wholly
improbable that ver. 3 has specific and exclusive reference to the nations
named there.

5. *Fear not, for I* (*am*) *with thee ; from the east will I make* (or *let*) *thy
seed come, and from the west will I gather thee.* The reference of this
verse to the restoration of the Jews from Babylon is not only arbitrary
and without foundation, but forbidden by the mention of the west as well
as the east.   That it refers to any restoration is the more improbable, because the Prophet does not say *bring back* but simply *bring.*— The only
interpretation which entirely suits the text and context, without supplying
or assuming anything beyond what is expressed, is that which makes the
verse a promise to the church that she should be completed, that all her
scattered members should be ultimately brought together.   (Compare
John xi. 52 ; Rom. iii. 29 ; 1 John ii. 2.)—*Thy seed* has reference to
Israel or Jacob as the ideal object of address.

6. *I will say to the north, Give, and to the south, Withhold not, let my
sons come from far, and my daughters from the ends of the earth.* This is
a poetical amplification of the promise in the foregoing verse. As it was
there declared that God would bring and gather the whole seed of Israel,
so here he represents himself as calling on the north and the south to
execute his purpose.   The feminine form of the verbs is explained by the
rabbins on the ground that the address is to the north and south *wind*, as
in Cant. iv. 16. Gesenius makes the words themselves of common gender.
Perhaps the case falls under the same general principle with names of
countries, provinces, &c., which are uniformly feminine. Hitzig's suggestion that הָבִיאִי does not here mean *bring* but *suffer to come*, is favoured by
the juxtaposition of *withhold not.*

7. *Every one called by my name, and for my glory I have created him ;
I have formed him, yea, I have made him.* The construction is continued
from the foregoing verse. My sons and my daughters, even every one
called by my name. Augusti's construction, *Every one of them is called by
my name*, is forbidden by the article.—The reflexive sense, *that calls himself,* implying profession rather than divine vocation, is wholly unnecessary,
and less agreeable to general usage.—*And I have created him* is a common Hebrew idiom, equivalent to *whom I have created.*—The distinctions
drawn by some between *created, formed,* and *made,* are more ingenious than
well-founded.   Thus Vitringa runs a parallel between the creation of matter
out of nothing, its configuration, and the completion of its parts ; the
regeneration of the soul, its conformation to God's image, and its ultimate
perfection.   It seems to be rather an exhaustive accumulation of synonymous expressions.—*For my glory* is emphatic. God had not only made
them what they were, but he had done it for his own sake, not for theirs.
So likewise he now speaks of their being called by his name, as he did
before of his calling them by their name, the latter denoting special designation, the former special authority and right.

8. *He hath brought out the blind people, and there are eyes* (*to them*) ;

and the deaf, and (there are) ears to them. The two clauses are so constructed as to supply one another's ellipsis. Most writers make הוֹצִיא imperative (*bring forth*) after the example of the Vulgate (*educ*). But as this form in thirty-five places is the præter, and in thirty the infinitive, while the imperative without an augment always elsewhere takes the form הוֹצֵא, such an assumption is in the highest degree unsafe and precarious. Some more correctly make it the infinitive (*to bring forth*), which yields a good sense, and is justified by the analogy of פְּקַח in xlii. 20. The preterite construction, however, is not only simpler in itself, but agrees better with the יֵשׁ which follows, and which is usually found in affirmative propositions. The first verb may then be construed either with *Jehovah*, or with the subject of the preceding sentence, *i. e.* the chosen people or the individuals composing it, whose work or office is declared to be that of turning the heathen " from darkness to light, and from the power of Satan unto God" (Acts xxvi. 18). A very different sense is put upon the verse by those interpreters who take יֵשׁ עֵינַיִם as descriptive of the blind people (*that have eyes*), and apply it to the Jews, who, in spite of their advantages, were blind to spiritual objects. This agrees well with chap. xlii. 19, 20, as explained above. But it then becomes difficult to understand in what sense they are said to be brought out. On this hypothesis the best explanation is that they are summoned to behold the demonstration of Jehovah's prescience, either as adverse parties or spectators. This would require the imperative construction of הוֹצִיא, the grammatical objections to which have been already stated. On the whole, the most satisfactory interpretation of the verse is that which understands it as descriptive of the change wrought or to be wrought in the condition of mankind by Jehovah, through the agency of his people, whether the latter be expressly mentioned here or not. *He (i. e. God, or Israel as his messenger) hath brought out a people (once) blind, and (now) they have eyes, and (once) deaf, and (now) they have ears, i. e.* of course, seeing eyes and hearing ears. This agrees perfectly with all that goes before and follows, with respect to the mission and vocation of God's people.

9. *All the nations are gathered together, and the peoples are to be assembled. Who among them will declare this, and let us hear the first things? Let them give (or produce) their witnesses and be justified; and (if they cannot do this) let them hear (my witnesses), and say, (It is) the truth.* The translation of the first verb, by Rosenmüller and others, as a future or imperative, is wholly unauthorized by usage, the cases cited to establish it being themselves of very doubtful import. At all events, it is incomparably safer and more satisfactory to retain the proper meaning when it yields a tolerable sense, than to proceed upon the strange assumption, that when a writer deliberately uses two distinct forms, he intended them to be received as one. Here the sense would seem to be, that the nations have been gathered, but that the process is not yet completed. This gathering of the nations has been commonly explained as a judicial metaphor like that in chap. xli. 1. In that case the verse describes the heathen as assembled at the judgment-seat to plead their cause against Jehovah. This agrees well with the forensic terms employed in the subsequent context. It is possible, however, that this first clause may have been intended to describe not the process but the subject of adjudication. The gathering of the nations will then denote their accession to the church, as predicted in vers. 5–7 ; and *this*, in the next clause, will refer to the same event. Who among them (*i. e.* the nations) could have foretold their own change of

condition? On the other supposition, *this* must either be indefinite, or mean the restoration of the Jews from exile, of which, as we have seen, there is no specific mention in the foregoing context. In either case, the usual alternative is offered, viz. that of pointing out some previous instance of foreknowledge and prediction.—The last clause admits of two constructions. It may either be read, let them be just (or candid) and hear and say it is the truth; or, let them be justified (by the witnessess whom they produce), and (if not) let them hear (my witnesses) and say, it is the truth. The latter seems more natural, because the other connects יַצְדִּקוּ not with its own part of the clause but with what follows. אֱמֶת is here equivalent to צַדִּיק in chap. xli. 26.

10. *Ye are my witnesses, saith Jehovah, and my servant whom I have chosen, that ye may know and believe me, and may understand that I am He; before me was not formed a god, and after me there shall not be.* Some regard the heathen as the object of address in the first clause, and understand *my servant* as denoting Israel. But there is no consistent sense in which the former could be cited as witnesses against themselves; and this application is besides forbidden by the obvious analogy of ver. 12, where the same words are explicitly applied to Israel. Of those who correctly understand them so, in this case likewise, the greater number refer *my servant* to a different subject, either Isaiah, or the prophets as a class, or the Messiah. Ye (the Jews) are my witnesses, and (so is this) my servant. But the simplest and most natural construction of the sentence is to make *my servant* not a subject, but a predicate. *Ye are my witnesses and* (ye are) *my servant whom I have chosen* (for this very purpose). The combination of the plural *witnesses* with the singular *servant*, although strange in itself, is in perfect agreement with the previous representations of Israel both as a person and a body politic. On the other hypothesis, the relative clause, *that ye may know*, &c., depends upon *witnesses*, and the words *whom I have chosen* form a pleonastic adjunct to the phrase *my servant*. But according to the explanation just proposed, *that ye may know* depends upon the words immediately preceding, *whom I have chosen*, and the clause declares the purpose not only of the testimony here adduced, but of the election and vocation of his servant. The witness to whom God appeals is Israel, his servant, constituted such for the very end that he might know, and understand, and believe that of which all other nations were entirely ignorant, viz., that Jehovah was he, *i.e.* the being in question, *the only wise God*, the only infallible foreteller of futurity.—Various attempts have been made to explain away the singular expression, *there was no god formed before me*, as a solecism, or at least an inaccuracy of expression; whereas nothing else could have conveyed the writer's meaning in a form at once sarcastic, argumentative, and graphic. Instead of saying, in a bald prosaic form, all other gods are the work of men's hands, but I am uncreated, and exist from all eternity, he condenses all into the pregnant declaration, there was no god manufactured before me, *i.e.* all other gods were made, but none of them was made before I had a being. There is not even such an incongruity of form as some suppose,—a notion resting on the false assumption that *before me* must in this connection mean *before I was formed*, whereas it only means *before I existed*, just as the parallel phrase *after me* does not mean *after I am formed*, but *after I shall cease to exist.* The sarcasm is rendered still more pungent by the use of the divine name אֵל, thus bringing into the most revolting contrast the pretended divinity of idols and their impotence; as if he had said, None of these almighty gods were made before I had a

being.—נְאֻם is probably a passive participle used as a noun, like the Latin *dictum*, and exclusively applied to divine communications.

11. *I, I, Jehovah, and besides me* (or *apart from me*) *there is no Saviour*. In the first clause we may simply supply *am*, as in the English and most other versions, or *am He* from the preceding verse, and in the sense there explained. The exclusive honour here claimed is not merely that of infallible foreknowledge, but of infinite power. Jehovah was able not only to foretell the salvation of his people, but to save them. These terms are not to be restricted, if applied at all directly, to the final salvation of individual believers. There is evident allusion to the deliverance of Israel as a people from external sufferings or dangers, of which one signal instance is referred to in ver. 14, and another in ver. 16. At the same time, the doctrine here propounded, or the character ascribed to God, affords a sure foundation for the personal trust of all who have really a place among his people.

12. *I have told and have saved and have declared* (or *let you hear* beforehand), *and there is not among you* (*any*) *stranger; and ye are my witnesses, saith Jehovah, and I* (*am*) *God*. Having laid claim successively to divine prescience and power, he here combines the two, and represents himself both as the foreteller and the giver of salvation. The expression of the first idea twice, before and after the expression of the other, does not seem to have any special meaning, as some interpreters imagine, except so far as it gives special prominence to the divine omniscience and the proof of it afforded in prediction, as the evidence of deity which he had particularly urged before, and which he is about to urge again.—The emphatic insertion of the pronoun *I* at the beginning of the verse can only be expressed in English by a circumlocution, *it is I that have told*, &c.—Vitringa and Rosenmüller omit the substantive verb in the last member of the first clause as superfluous, and construe the words thus, *I have declared and no strange* (*god*) *among you*, *i.e.* no strange god declared it. But in that case Hebrew usage would require לֹא instead of אֵין, which is not an adverb of negation, but an idiomatic equivalent to the negative verb of existence, and can only mean *there is not* or *there was not*. Most of the modern writers refer it to past time, and explain the clause as an assertion that the prophecies in question were uttered at a time when idolatry did not prevail in Israel. It is more agreeable, however, both to usage and the context, to translate it in the present, as a declaration that Jehovah was the only God whom they had reason to acknowledge, from their own experience and observation.—זָר, which is a common term for *stranger*, used in reference to men, may be here considered an ellipsis for the full phrase אֵל זָר, which is not uncommon elsewhere.

13. *Also* (or *even*) *from the day I am He, and there is no one freeing from my hand; I will do, and who will undo it?* The assonance in the last clause is not in the original, which literally means, *I will act* (or *make*), *and who will cause it to return*, *i.e.* reverse or nullify it? The interrogative form implies negation. A similar expression of the same idea is found in chap. xiv. 27. What is said specifically in the first clause of delivering from Jehovah's power, is extended in the last to all counteraction or reversal of his acts. The גַּם at the beginning indicates a climax not only now, or on any occasion, but מִיּוֹם. This last is understood by some as referring to a specific *terminus a quo*, such as the origin of Israel as a nation, the exodus, &c. Others make it indefinite, *of old* or *long since*. But the best interpreters explain it as meaning since the first day, or since time began. The words are then universal, both in the extent of power claimed,

and in relation to the time of its execution. Over every object, and in every age, the power of Jehovah had been clearly proved to be supreme and absolute.

14. *Thus saith Jehovah, your Redeemer, the Holy One of Israel: For your sake I have sent to Babylon, and have brought down* (or *made to descend*) *fugitives all of them; and the Chaldeans, in the ships their shout* (or *song*). This is a particular instance of the general protection vouchsafed by Jehovah to his people, and more especially of that providential substitution or redemption of which we read above in vers. 3, 4. The inference before drawn from the general terms of ver. 4, that the nations mentioned in ver. 3 are only representatives or samples, is confirmed by this explicit mention of the fall of Babylon as an example of the same great truth.—The titles added to Jehovah's name are not mere expletives or words of course, but intimate that he would bring this great event to pass in his distinctive character as the Redeemer and the Holy One of Israel.—From the past tense of the verb (*I have sent*), some infer that this verse was written after the event, while others endeavour to avoid this conclusion by translating it as future (*I will send*). One of these inferences is just as groundless as the other. The event, although still future to the writer, is described as past, in reference not only to the purposes of God, but also the perceptions of the Prophet. As presented to his view by the prophetic inspiration, the destruction of Babylon was just as truly a historical event as that of Pharaoh and his host. This is what is meant by the *praeteritum propheticum*, to render which as future is a wanton violation of the form of the original, and a gratuitous confounding of the text and comment.—The Targum strangely understands this clause as referring not to the downfall of the Babylonians,. but to the deportation of the Jews. *Behold, on account of your sins I sent (you) to Babylon*. But this agrees neither with the usage of לְמַעַנְכֶם, nor with the meaning of the other clause. Interpreters are commonly agreed that the object of the verb is Cyrus, or the Medes and Persians.—From the earliest times בְּרִיחִים has received a twofold explanation, viz., that of *fugitives*, as in the Septuagint, and that of *bars*, as in the Vulgate. The same question arises in the exposition of chap. xv. 5. (See vol. i. p. 315.) But there the pointing favours the last sense, whereas here it seems to recommend the other. Of those who prefer the meaning *bars* even here, some suppose a literal allusion to the gates of Babylon, others a figurative one to its protectors. The other sense of *fugitives* is applicable either to the Babylonians themselves, or to the foreigners resident among them. (See chap. xiii. 14, and vol. i. p. 277). כַּשְׂדִּים is the proper name of the foreign race by which Babylonia had been occupied before Isaiah wrote. (See chap. xxiii. 13, and vol. i. p. 398). It is an interesting fact, that recent etymological research has identified the כַּשְׂדִּים of the Hebrew ethnography, not only with the Χαλδαῖοι of the Greeks, but with the *Kurds* of modern Asia. Here, however, they are mentioned simply as the inhabitants of Babylonia. —The last two words are variously construed and explained. Some connect them only with what goes before, as a description of the Chaldeans, *whose cry is in the ships*, implying their devotion to nautical pursuits ; or, *whose shout* (or *song*) *was in the ships*, implying their habitual use of ships or boats for pleasure. The same idea is otherwise expressed by those who read *in the ships of their joyful cry* (*i. e.* their pleasure-ships). On this, which is Gesenius's interpretation, Hitzig observes, with a play upon words which cannot be retained in a translation, that the pleasure-

ships are air-ships (*die Luftschiffe sind Lustschiffe*) *i. e.* imaginary or fictitious. The same thing has been said of the naval or maritime activity
of Babylon; but Lowth has made it probable at least, that it really
existed in very early times.—Another construction of these closing words
connects them with הוֹרַדְתִּי, "and brought down the Chaldees into the
ships of their triumph or delight." Hitzig makes אניות the plural of אֳנִיָּה
(chap. xxix. 2), and understands the clause to mean that God had brought
down the rejoicing of the Chaldeans into lamentations. But this requires
a different pointing of אניות from the one attested by the critical tradition
of the Jews, and a very harsh construction of כשדים. Hitzig's construction is adopted by Ewald, who moreover changes בריחים כלם into בְּצְרִיחִים
כִּנּרָם (their harp or music into groans), on the authority (as he affirms) of
Zeph. i. 14, and Job xxx. 31. Either of the old interpretations, whether
that which makes the clause descriptive of the Chaldees or of their destruction, yields a better sense, without the arbitrary violence of these pretended
emendations.

15. *I Jehovah, your Holy One, the Creator of Israel, your King.* This
verse may possibly have been intended merely to identify the subject of the
one before it. *I sent to Babylon, &c., even I, Jehovah, your Holy One, &c.*
It is simpler, however, and more in accordance with the usage of the language, to make this a distinct proposition by supplying the verb of existence.
I am Jehovah, or, *I Jehovah am your Holy One, &c.,* or *I Jehovah, your
Holy One,* am *the Creator of Israel, your King.* Even in this case, the
event predicted in ver. 14 is referred to, as the proof of his being what he
here asserts.

16. *Thus saith Jehovah, the (one) giving in the sea a way, and in mighty
waters a path.* As the participle is very commonly employed in Hebrew to
denote continued and habitual action, this verse might be regarded as a
general description of God's usual control of the elements and conquest of
all difficulties. But the terms of the next verse, and the subsequent contrast between old and new deliverances, have led most interpreters to
understand this likewise as an allusion to the passage of the Red Sea.—
Some, however, follow Aben Ezra in applying the words to the passage of
the Euphrates by Cyrus, a gratuitous departure from the strict and customary sense of *sea.*—עַזִּים, besides its etymological meaning, *strong* or *mighty,*
suggests the idea of impetuous, violent, and fierce.

17. *The (one) bringing out chariot and horse, force and strong; together
they shall lie, they shall not rise; they are extinct, like tow* (or *like a wick*)
they are quenched. עַזּוּז is properly an adjective, and may be understood as
qualifying חַיִל *a force and (i. e. even) a strong one.* Some, however, regard
it as indefinite or abstract (*strong* for *strength*), and an equivalent or parallel
to חַיִל. Some suppose a new sentence to begin with this verse, and make
הַמּוֹצִיא collective: those bringing out the chariot and the horse shall lie
together, they shall not rise, &c. But most interpreters continue the construction from the foregoing verse, and make the first word agree directly
with *Jehovah.* Of these, however, some understand the verse as having
reference to a naval victory of Cyrus over the Chaldeans, others as relating
to the destruction of Pharaoh and his host. It is no objection to the latter
that יִשְׁכְּבוּ is future, as this verb denotes not merely the act of lying down,
but the state of lying still, and is therefore a poetical equivalent and parallel
to *shall not rise.* That something long past is intended, may be gathered
from the exhortation of the next verse.

18. *Remember not former things, and old things consider not.* As if he had said, Why should I refer to ancient instances of God's almighty intervention in behalf of his people, when others equally remarkable are yet to come ? Some refer this to the advent of Christ, but most to the fall of Babylon, and restoration of the Jews from exile. The necessity of this specific application by no means follows from the express mention of that event in ver. 14 ; because, as we have seen, it is there introduced as a single illustration or example of a general truth, which had before been stated, and which may possibly be here repeated. This supposition is at least sufficient to meet all the requisitions of the text and context.

19. *Behold I (am) doing (something) new, it is now (or yet) to sprout (or germinate); do you not know it ? Yes, I will place in the wilderness a way, in the desert streams.* The *now* does not necessarily denote a proximate futurity, but only that the thing is yet to happen, or in other words, that it is something *new*, as distinguished from all former instances. As if he had said, it is still future. The figure of germination implies that as yet there was no appearance of the final issue. (See the same expression in chap. xlii. 9). *Do you not know it, i. e.* know what it is ? Or, *will you not know it, i. e.* are you not willing to be convinced ? Or, *shall you not know it, i. e.* is not the event to be attested by your own experience ?—The אַף may be regarded as equivalent to *yea, yes,* or as indicating something more than had as yet been experienced. Not content with having made a way through the sea, he would make one through the desert. Now, as this is really a less extraordinary act of power than the other, it would seem to favour the opinion, that ver. 16 and the one before us do not relate indefinitely to the exhibition of Jehovah's omnipotence, but specifically to the exodus from Egypt and the restoration of the Jews from exile. Even on this hypothesis, however, the terms of this verse must be understood not as a description of the literal return, but as a figurative representation of deliverance and relief, whereas ver. 16 describes a literal deliverance. On the whole, therefore, it is best to take both verses as strong metaphorical descriptions of deliverance from suffering and danger by a direct divine interposition. Even supposing an allusion to the literal journey through the desert, what is said of rivers must be figurative, which makes it probable that the whole sentence is of the same description. Thus understood, the Prophet's language means that God could change the face of nature and control the angry elements in favour of his people ; that he had so done in times past, and would again do so in time to come.

20. *The living creature of the field shall honour me, jackals (or wolves) and ostriches ; because I have given in the wilderness waters, and streams in the desert, to give drink to my people, my chosen.* The change is further described by representing the irrational inmates of the desert as rejoicing in its irrigation. This bold conception makes it still more evident that what precedes does not relate to the literal journey of a people through a literal desert. As the first phrase seems to be a general one, including the two species afterwards mentioned, the translation *beast* is too restricted, and should give way to that which is etymologically most exact, viz., ζῶον *animal*, or living creature. The form is singular, the sense collective. The two species represent the whole class of animals inhabiting the wilderness. (Compare chap. xiii. 21, 22.) The common version of the last words of this verse is the correct one. *My chosen people* would be otherwise expressed. To the simple designation of *my people*, he adds, by a kind of after thought, *my chosen* or *elect.*

21. *The people* (or *this people*) *I have formed for myself; my praise shall they recount* (or *they are to recount my praise*). Another declaration of the end for which Israel existed as a nation. This brings us back to the main proposition of the chapter, namely, that Jehovah had not only made them what they were, but had made them for the purpose of promoting his own glory, so that any claim of merit upon their part, and any apprehension of entire destruction, must be equally unfounded.

22. *And not me hast thou called, O Jacob ; for thou hast been weary of me, O Israel.* Interpreters, almost without exception, give קָרָאתָ here the sense of called upon, invoked, or worshipped. There is much, however, to be said in favour of the sense attached to it by J. H. Michaelis, namely, *thou hast not called me*, I have called thee; as our Saviour says to his disciples, *ye have not chosen me, but I have chosen you* (John xv. 16). Having thus far represented the vocation of Israel as a sovereign act on God's part, he now presents the converse of the same proposition. This construction is further recommended by its accounting for the unusual position of the words at the beginning of the verse, without resorting to the arbitrary supposition that it is characteristic of a later age than that of Isaiah : q. d. *it is not I that have been called by you.*—According to the usual construction of the first clause, the second may be rendered either *when* or *because* thou wast weary of me. The common version of the כִּי as *but*, and Gesenius's unnatural construction *thou hast not called upon me so as to be troubled with me*, although very different, are equally gratuitous.— It is not easy to determine whether labour or fatigue is the primary meaning of יָגַע. Sometimes the one idea is more prominent, sometimes the other. In this case both would naturally be suggested, as in the following paraphrase : It is not I that have been called by thee; for so far from manifesting such a preference, thou hast been wearied and disgusted with the labour which attends my service. The indirect construction, that thou shouldst be weary of me, is only admissible in case of extreme exegetical necessity.

23. *Thou hast not brought to me the sheep of thy burnt-offering, and* (with) *thy sacrifices thou hast not honoured me. I have not made thee serve with oblation, and I have not made thee labour* (or *wearied thee*) *with incense.* The whole Mosaic ritual is here represented by an enumeration of some of the principal offerings : the *olah*, or general expiation ; the *zebahim*, or animal sacrifices in general ; the *minhah*, or meal-offering ; and the *lebonah*, or aromatic fumigation.—שֶׂה includes the goat as well as the sheep, and is therefore correctly rendered in the English Version by the phrase *small cattle.*—Of the whole verse there are several distinct interpretations or rather applications. Some place the emphasis upon the pronouns. It is not to me that thou hast offered all this, but to idols. This, though a possible construction, is not the one most readily suggested by the words. Nor is it easy, upon this supposition, to account for the total want of any distinct reference to idols in the context. Another class of writers understand the passage strictly as charging the Jews with culpable neglect of the ceremonial law. But of this they were not generally guilty ; and the restriction of the charge to the reign of Ahaz or to any other limited period is gratuitous, and hardly consistent with the general expressions of the context. A third hypothesis applies the passage to the unavoidable suspension of the ceremonial service during the captivity in Babylon, which it supposes to be here urged as a proof that the deliverance of Israel from exile was an act of mercy, not of righteous retribution for their national obedience and

fidelity. This explanation, although much more plausible than either of the others, is open to the same charge of gratuitous restriction, without anything to indicate it in the text or context. It may also be objected, that the error thus supposed to be refuted by the Prophet, is one which could not possibly be entertained; for how could the exiled Jews imagine that their liberty was bought by services which not only had not been, but could not have been rendered? If it be said that this is merely a specific illustration of the general truth that they were not saved by any merit of their own, it still remains incredible that this truth should have been exemplified by reference not to a real case, but to one wholly imaginary and impossible. How much more natural and satisfactory to give the words the general and unrestricted meaning which they naturally bear as a description of the people's conduct, not at one time or at one place, but throughout their history. The last clause is by some understood to mean, that the system imposed upon the people was not burdensome. But this is consistent neither with the circumstances of the case, nor with the statements of the New Testament respecting them (Acts xv. 10, Gal. v. 1), nor with the parallel clause, in which it is simply said that Israel had not offered what was due. The most satisfactory interpretation of the verse, and that which best agrees with the whole context, is, that it has reference not merely to the outward or material act, but to its moral value and effect. You have not so performed your ceremonial duties as to lay me under any obligation to protect you. You have not really given me your cattle, you have not truly honoured me with sacrifices. The best explanation of the last clause is, I have not succeeded in inducing you to serve me, I have not prevailed upon you to exert yourselves, much less wearied or exhausted you in ceremonial services.

24. *Thou hast not bought for me sweet cane with money, and (with) the fat of thy sacrifices thou hast not drenched me; thou hast only made me serve with thy sins, and made me toil (or wearied me) with thine iniquities.* According to Jarchi, the sweet or aromatic cane is mentioned as a common product of the Holy Land, which they were consequently not obliged to purchase in order to the preparation of the holy ointment (Exod. xxx. 23). But Kimchi and most other writers proceed upon the contrary assumption, that this cane was an exotic, which could only be procured with trouble and expense. This particular is mentioned, like the others with which it stands connected, as a specimen or sample of the whole congeries of ceremonial services. The antithesis between the clauses seems to shew that the idea meant to be conveyed in this whole context is, that their external services were nullified by sin. So far from being satisfied or pleased with what they offered, God was only vexed with their transgressions and neglects.

25. *I, I am he blotting out thy transgressions for mine own sake, and thy sins I will not remember.* This is the conclusion to which all that goes before was meant to lead, to wit, that God's goodness to his people is gratuitous. If they, instead of choosing God and his service, were averse to both,—if, instead of pleasing him by their attentions, they had grieved him by their sins, it follows of course that he could still shew them favour only by gratuitously blotting out their sins from his remembrance, or, in other words, freely forgiving them.

26. *Remind me; let us plead together (or judge one another); state (thy case) that thou mayest be justified.* After asserting, in the foregoing verse, the total want of merit in the people, and their dependence upon God's

gratuitous compassion, he now, as it were, allows them to disprove his allegation, by reminding him of some forgotten merit on their part. The badness of their case could not have been more strongly or sarcastically stated than in this ironical invitation to plead their own cause and establish their own rights if they could, with a tacit condition, not expressed but implied, that if they could not justify themselves in this way, they should submit to the righteousness of God and consent to be justified by grace.

27. *Thy first father sinned, and thy interpreters rebelled against me.* Gesenius and some others give the first words a collective sense, as signifying either the succession of priests or ancestors in general. The older writers, for the most part, give the singular its strict sense, and apply it either to Ahaz or Manasseh, as kings, and therefore bound to be the fathers of their people, or to Abraham as the progenitor of Israel, or to Adam as the father of the human race. Vitringa even makes it mean Uriah, the unfaithful high priest in the reign of Ahaz. This and the first interpretation mentioned are entirely arbitrary. That which understands the phrase of Abraham is supposed by some to be at variance with the uniform mention of that patriarch in terms of commendation. But these terms are perfectly consistent with the proposition that *he was a sinner*, which may here be the exact sense of חָטָא. To the application of the phrase to Adam it has been objected, that he was not peculiarly the father of the Jews. To this it may be answered, that if the guilt of the national progenitor would prove the point in question, much more would it be established by the fact of their belonging to a guilty race. At the same time it may be considered as implied, that all their fathers who had since lived shared in the original depravity, and thus the same sense is obtained that would have been expressed by the collective explanation of *first father*, while the latter is still taken in its strict and full sense as denoting the progenitor of all mankind.—*Interpreters*, or organs of communication, is a title given elsewhere to ambassadors (2 Chron. xxxii. 31) and to an interceding angel (Job xxxiii. 23). It here denotes all those who, under the theocracy, acted as organs of communication between God and the people, whether prophets, priests, or rulers. The idea, therefore, is the same so often expressed elsewhere, that the people, and especially their leaders, were unfaithful and rebellious.

28. *And I will profane the holy chiefs, and will give up Jacob to the curse and Israel to reproaches.* The character just given of the people in all ages is urged not only as a proof that God's compassion must be perfectly gratuitous, but also as a reason for the strokes which they experienced. The *vav* before the first verb is not conversive but conjunctive, so that the reference is entirely to the future, or to the universal present, as explained by Kimchi, who observes that *vav* has *pattah* because it does not express past time; but the sense is, that in all ages God profanes the holy chiefs. This last phrase is descriptive of the same persons called *interpreters* in ver. 27, namely, all the official representatives and leaders of the holy (*i. e.* consecrated and peculiar) people. Its specific application to the priests in 1 Chron. xxiv. 5 no more proves that this is its whole meaning, than it proves that שָׂרִים always means religious officers. The name includes the priests, no doubt, but it includes much more.

Chapter 44

This chapter opens, like the fortieth and forty-third, with cheering promises to Israel, followed by reasons for confiding in them, drawn from the wisdom, power, and goodness of Jehovah.

The specific promise, which constitutes the theme or basis of the prophecy, is that of abundant spiritual influences and their fruits, not only internal prosperity, but large accessions from without, vers. 1–5.—The pledge for the fulfilment of this promise is afforded by the proofs of God's omniscience, as contrasted with all other gods, vers. 6–9.—The folly of image-worship is then established by two arguments. The first is that idols are themselves the creatures of mere men, vers. 10–14. The other is that they are not only made, and made by man, but made of the very same materials applied to the most trivial domestic uses, vers. 15–20.— From this demonstration of the power of Jehovah to perform his promise we are now brought back to the promise itself, vers. 21–24. This is again confirmed by an appeal to God's creative power, and illustrated by the raising up of Cyrus as a deliverer to Israel, vers. 25–28.

Here again it is important to the just interpretation of the passage that we keep in view the true relation which the main theme (the safety and prosperity of Israel) bears to the arguments and illustrations drawn from God's foreknowledge as established by prediction, from the impotence of idols, and the raising up of Cyrus. Through all these varied forms of promise and of reasoning there runs a thread uniting them, and this thread is the doctrine of the church, its origin, its design, and its relation to its Head and to the world around it.

1. *And now hear, Jacob my servant, and Israel I have chosen him (i. e.* whom I have chosen). The transition here is the same as at the opening of the foregoing chapter, and the *now*, as there, has rather a logical than a temporal meaning. For reasons which have been already given, there is no need of supposing that a different Israel is here addressed (Cocceius), viz. the penitent believing Jews in exile (Grotius); or a different period referred to, namely, that succeeding the calamities before described ; nor even that the *and* is here equivalent to *notwithstanding*, as explained by Kimchi. It is simply a resumption and continuation of the Prophet's argument, intended to exhibit the true relation between God and his people. The election here affirmed, which Calvin understands directly of a personal election from eternity, is better explained by J. H. Michaelis as the choice and separation of the church, or God's peculiar people, from the rest of men.

2. *Thus saith Jehovah, thy maker and thy former from the womb will help thee ; fear not, my servant Jacob, and Jeshurun whom I have chosen.* It has been a subject of dispute among interpreters, whether מִבֶּטֶן ought to be connected with יֹצֶרְךָ (as it is in the Septuagint and by the rabbins), or with יַעְזְרֶךָ (as in the Targum and the Vulgate). The Masoretic accents are in favour of the first construction ; but Gesenius rejects it as not yielding a good sense, and reads, *who helped thee from the womb.* But this translation of the future as a praeter is entirely gratuitous, and therefore ungrammatical. The simplest construction is to make the words of Jehovah begin with *thy maker*, the transition from the third to the first person being altogether natural and one of perpetual occurrence in Isaiah. *Thy maker will help thee* is equivalent to *I, who am thy maker, will help*

thee. But even on the common supposition, that the words of God begin
with the second clause, it is better to take *he will help thee* as a short independent clause, parenthetically thrown in to complete the description or to
connect it with what follows. *Thus saith thy maker and thy former from
the womb—he will help thee—Fear not,* &c. As to the combination *maker
from the womb,* it can seem incongruous only to a hypercritical grammarian,
so that there is no need even of adopting J. H. Michaelis's suggestion, that
מִבֶּטֶן means *ex quo in utero esse coepisti.* The use of these expressions in
addressing Israel, only shews that the conception present to the writer's
mind is that of an individual man. Although the specific explanation of
the figures here used has been sometimes pushed too far, there can be no
doubt that the maturing of Israel as a nation in Egypt is often represented
as a period of gestation, and the exodus as a birth ; but whether there is
any such allusion here may be considered doubtful.—*Jeshurun* occurs only
here and in Deut. xxxii. 15, xxxiii. 5, 26. Some of the old attempts to
ascertain its etymology were ludicrous enough. Thus Vitringa quotes
Forster as deriving it from שׁוֹר, *an ox,* and Cocceius from יְשׁוּרוּ *they shall
see, i. e.* the people who should see Christ in the flesh, *quod nemo dixerit
non esse hyperbolicum et remotum* (Vitringa). Grotius's derivation of the
word from יִשְׂרָאֵל is a philological impossibility ; but his explanation of it
as a diminutive or term of endearment is now commonly adopted, but with
reference to the root יָשַׁר, *upright,* as an epithet of Israel, not " in consideration of their entire abandonment of idolatry," as Henderson supposes, but
in reference to their normal or ideal character, the end for which they were
created, and the aspect which they ought to have exhibited. Hengstenberg gives the same sense to the word as a proper name, but not as
a diminutive or term of endearment, which he rejects as unsustained by
etymological analogy and wholly inappropriate in the places where it is
originally used. (See his History and Prophecies of Balaam, pp. 98–101.)
The word is rendered, as a general expression of endearment, by the
Septuagint (ἠγαπημένος), and with closer adherence to the etymology by the
other Greek versions (εὐθύς, εὐθύτατος). The diminutive form is imitated in
Latin by Gesenius (*rectulus, justulus*), and in German by Hitzig and Ewald
(*Frömmchen*). Rosenmüller's version (*fortunate*) is supported only by the
false analogy of צֶדֶק as denoting good luck or prosperity.

3. *For I will pour waters on the thirsty and flowing (waters) on the dry
(land); I will pour my Spirit on thy seed, and my blessing on thine offspring.*
This is the grand reason why God's people should not despair. The two
clauses explain each other, the *water* of the first being clearly identical
with the *spirit* of the second. This is a common figure for influences from
above. (See chap. xxxii. 15, Ezek. xxxiv. 26, Mal. iii. 10.) Knobel
indeed understands the two clauses strictly and distinctly, taking the first
as a promise to the land, and the second as a promise to the people. But
צָמֵא most probably refers to persons, as it is not feminine like יַבָּשָׁה.
Grotius understands this as a promise to send prophets to the Jews in
exile, such as Jeremiah, Ezekiel, Haggai, Zechariah, and Malachi !
Gesenius also seems to think the promise here made strictly coincident
with that in Joel iii. 1, 2. But it is more extensive, and includes all the
influences of the Holy Spirit.—The *offspring* of the people, as distinguished
from itself, is supposed by Knobel to denote the individuals of whom the
aggregate body was composed. Jarchi and Vitringa apply it to the strangers
or proselytes who were to be added by conversion to the natural Israel.

The simplest and most obvious interpretation is, that the ideal object of address is Jacob as the national progenitor, and that the Jews themselves are here described as his descendants. Even this, however, does not necessarily exclude the spiritual offspring of the patriarch, who are explicitly referred to in the context.

4. *And they shall spring up in the midst of the grass, like willows on* (*or by*) *the water-courses.* This verse describes the effect of the irrigation and effusion promised in the one before it. There is no need, however, of making the construction a subjunctive one (*so that they shall spring up*), as Luther and some later writers do.—The subject of the verb is not the Spirit and blessing of Jehovah, as Aben Ezra strangely imagines, but the offspring or descendants of Israel, by whom the blessing was to be experienced.—Lowth and Ewald read בְּבֵין מַיִם חָצִיר, *like grass amidst the water*, on the authority of the Septuagint version (ὡς ἀναμέσον ὕδατος χόρτος), which seems, however, to be simply a paraphrase or free translation. Gesenius retains the comparative form of expression (*as among*), but without a change of text, by making the particle itself comparative, an idiom of which there is no clear example elsewhere. All these expedients are intended to remove the imaginary solecism *in between*. But the true explanation has been long since given by Vitringa, namely, that בֵּין has here its primitive and proper use, as a noun corresponding to the English *midst*. So far is the common text from being incorrect or irregular, that it is really the only form in which the idea could have been expressed, since בֵּין as a preposition always means *between* or *among*, and is followed by the plural noun. When, on the contrary, a singular noun is to be used, as here, the Hebrew idiom prefixes not the preposition but a noun meaning *midst* (בֵין or תוך) with a particle before it.—The grass and the willows are separated only by the rhythmical arrangement of the sentence. The simple meaning of the whole verse is, that they shall grow as willows grow among the grass, *i.e.* in the moist or marshy spot. The question, who are meant by the grass as distinguished from the willows, is absurd. It might as well be asked, when an object is compared to the rose of Sharon, what is meant by Sharon as distinguished from the rose. Lowth seems to look upon *aqueducts* as more poetical and better English than the common version, *water-courses*.

5. *This shall say, To Jehovah I* (*belong*); *and this shall call on* (or *by*) *the name of Jacob; and this shall inscribe his hand* (or *with his hand*), *To Jehovah, and with the name of Israel shall entitle.* The repetition of the pronoun *this* implies, according to Kimchi's explanation, persons of various classes or from different quarters. It is commonly agreed that this verse predicts the accession of the Gentiles, whom it represents as publicly professing their allegiance to Jehovah and attachment to his people. The act of calling one by name, and that of calling on his name (invoking him), are intimately blended in the Hebrew usage. Most interpreters understand it here as meaning to praise or celebrate. Some of the older writers follow Symmachus in giving it a passive sense (*this shall be called*), either reading יִקָּרֵא for יִקְרָא, or supplying the reflexive pronoun after it. The same diversity exists in reference to the last verb in the sentence, יְכַנֶּה, which some understand to mean *he shall surname himself* (or *be surnamed*), others he shall name the name of Jacob in a flattering or respectful manner.—Of the intermediate clause there are two ancient explanations, one of which makes it mean *he shall write* (*with*) *his hand* in allusion to the signing of contracts (Jer. xxxii. 10, Neh. ix. 38); the other, *he shall write upon* (*inscribe*) *his*

hand, in allusion to the ancient custom, mentioned by Procopius, of mark-ing soldiers, slaves, and other dependents, with the name of their superior, to which there seems to be a reference in Exod. xiii. 9, and Rev. xiii. 16. This last sense is supposed to be expressed in the Septuagint version ἐπιγράψει χειρί.

6. *Thus saith Jehovah, king of Israel, and his redeemer, Jehovah of hosts: I (am) first, and I (am) last, and without me there is no God.* This is a description of the God whom the nations, in the preceding verse, are repre-sented as acknowledging. The attributes ascribed to him afford, at the same time, a sufficient reason for confiding in his promises. In like man-near Zeus, the supreme god of the Greeks, is described by Orpheus as being ἀρχὴ πάντων πάντων τε τελετή, and in another place, Ζεὺς πρῶτος ἐγένετο Ζεὺς ὕστατος. Henderson points out the appropriation of the terms here used to the Lord Jesus Christ in Rev. i. 18, ii. 8, xxii. 13.—There is no need of giving to מבלעדי, in this and the parallel places, the restricted sense *besides*, which is really included in the usual and strict sense of *without*, *i. e.* without my knowledge and permission, or without subjection to my sovereign authority. The meaning is not simply, that there is no other true God in existence, but that even the λεγόμενοι θεοί (1 Cor. viii. 5) exist only by his sufferance, and cannot therefore be his equals or competitors.

7. *And who, like me, will call, and tell it, and state it to me, since I placed the ancient people; and coming things and things which are to come will tell to them* (or *for themselves*) *?* There is no reason why the interrogation should not be considered as extending through the verse, the rather as a different construction splits up the sentence, and arbitrarily explains some of the futures as imperatives. Still more objectionable is the construction of יקרא as a preterite, which is given by all the later writers except Ewald. The question *who has called like me* is in no respect more pertinent than the question, *who will* (or *can*) *call as I have done*, which leaves the refe-rence to past time equally explicit, without doing any grammatical violence to the form of expression. The usual construction of the next words is, *let him tell it*, &c.; but this imperative meaning is sufficiently implied in the strict translation of the words as interrogative futures, *who will tell it ?* &c. קרא is to call aloud or publicly announce. It differs from the next verb, if at all, by denoting an authoritative call, and suggesting the idea not only of prediction but of creation.—ערך is correctly explained by Gesenius as a forensic term meaning *to state a case*. The sense of *comparing*, preferred by Ewald, is less frequent elsewhere and less appro-priate here. The words *since I placed*, &c., are to be connected with כמוני, *who can call, as I have done, ever since I placed*, &c. To place is here to constitute, create, or give existence. Of the phrase עם־עולם there are three interpretations. The first is that of the rabbins, who explain it to mean *ancient people;* this is retained in the English and some other versions. The second makes it mean *eternal people*, but refers it simply to the divine purpose or decree of election. The third gives it the sense of *everlasting people, i. e.* a people who shall last for ever. In all these senses the description is appropriate to Israel, not simply as a nation but a church, the existence and prerogatives of which are still continued in the body of Christ. *Ecclesia corpus Christi est, quo nihil antiquius aut majus esse potest* (Calvin). It may be doubted, however, whether any-thing more was here intended than a reference to the origin of the human race. (See above, on chap. xlii. 5, 6.)—According to Kimchi, Grotius, and Vitringa, the last clause contains a distinct reference both to a proxi-

mate and remote futurity. This distinction is rejected by Gesenius, without any other reason than the groundless one, that synonymes are characteristic of *this writer*, *i. e.* the writer of these later prophecies, as distinguished from the genuine Isaiah. But this is, to some extent, characteristic not of one but of all the Hebrew writers, and abundant illustration might be drawn from the earlier and even from the undisputed passages. The truth, however, is that the distinction made by Kimchi is so natural and simple, and agrees so well with the context and analogy, that it would be entitled to consideration, even if the two forms of expression in themselves appeared to be entirely synonymous. Much more, when such a difference is indicated by the very form. Not only are two different verbs used, (which might be otherwise explained, and by itself can have no weight), but one is in the participial form, the clearest mode in Hebrew of expressing present action or a proximate futurity, the other in the future proper. Wherever there is a difference of form, there is presumptively a difference of meaning; and if any such difference is here intended, it can only be the difference between things actually *coming* to pass now, and those which are to come to pass hereafter.

8. *Quake not and fear not; have I not since then let thee hear and told (thee), and are ye not my witnesses? Is there a God without me? And there is no rock, I know not (any).* The alternation of the singular and plural form in reference to Israel, is peculiarly appropriate to an ideal or collective person, and in strict agreement with the usage of the Pentateuch, especially with that of Deuteronomy, in which the same apparent confusion of numbers is not a mere occasional phenomenon, but one of perpetual occurrence.—The verb תִּרְהוּ, which occurs only here, is derived by Hitzig from רָהָה, by Gesenius from יָרָה, and explained by Ewald as an error of the text for תִּירָאוּ. It is more probably to be derived from the synonymous and cognate יָרָה.—מֵאָז is usually taken in the vague sense of *long ago;* but it may here be strictly understood as meaning *since that time*, which Jarchi refers to the giving of the law on Sinai, Knobel to the first appearance of Cyrus, and Maurer, with more probability than either, to the event mentioned in the preceding verse, viz. the constitution of the עַם־עוֹלָם. —*And ye are my witnesses* is usually construed as an independent clause; but a possible construction is to include it in the question as above.— Vitringa's explanation of אֵין as an interrogative particle is anything but justified by the analogy of 1 Sam. xxii. 8, to which he appeals.—Here, as in many other cases, God is called a Rock, as being the refuge of his people, and the firm foundation of their hopes.

9. *The image-carvers all of them are vanity, and their desired (or beloved) ones are worthless; and their witnesses themselves will not see and will not know, that they may be ashamed.* Having fortified his promise by a solemn affirmation of his own supremacy, in contrast with the ignorance and impotence of idols, he now carries out this contrast in detail. The literal meaning of the first phrase is *the formers of a graven image*, here put for idols in general.—*Vanity* is here to be taken as a negative expression of the strongest kind, denoting the absence of all life, intelligence, and power, and corresponding to the parallel expression *they cannot profit*, *i. e.* they are worthless. The *desired* or favourite things of the idolaters are the idols themselves, upon which they lavish time, expense, and misplaced confidence. The next phrase is commonly explained to mean *their witnesses are themselves*, *i. e.* they are their own witnesses, which may either represent the idols as witnessing against their worshippers, or the worshippers against

the idols, or either of these classes against themselves. Cocceius connects these words with the following verbs (*testes illorum ipsi non vident*), which construction is substantially renewed by Ewald, and approved by Umbreit. The meaning then is, that the idolaters who bear witness to the divinity of their idols are themselves blind and ignorant. The *puncta extraordinaria* over הֵמָּה were designed, says Henderson, to fix the attention of the reader on the dumb idols being constituted witnesses against the stupidity of their worshippers. But why in this particular case? A much more probable explanation is that the Masoretic critics considered the word doubtful, perhaps because it appeared pleonastic, whereas it is in fact emphatic. There is no need of giving *know* the vague and doubtful sense of *having knowledge*; the meaning rather is, they will not see or know it, *i. e.* what has just been said, as to the impotence of idols. The last clause is explained by Gesenius as meaning that they are given up to blindness, that they may be ashamed or confounded. Umbreit, on the other hand, supposes it to mean that they have not knowledge or sense enough to be ashamed; an aggravation of the previous description.

10. *Who formed the god and cast the image to no use* (or *profit*)? Most interpreters regard this as an exclamation of contemptuous surprise, implying that no one in his senses would do so. (Grotius: *quis nisi demens?*) But the true sense is the one proposed by Gesenius, who explains what follows as the answer to this question Having affirmed the worthlessness of idols in general, he now proceeds to prove it from their origin.—So far from being makers, they are made themselves, and *who made them?* This is the precise force of the verse before us. Here as elsewhere there is pungent sarcasm in the application of the name אֵל (*mighty God*) to idols.

11. *Lo all his fellows shall be ashamed, and the workmen themselves are of men; they shall assemble all of them, they shall stand, they shall tremble, they shall be ashamed together.* Jarchi, followed by Lowth, Eichhorn, Gesenius, Maurer, and Ewald, refers the suffix in חֲבֵרָיו to the maker of the image, and understands by *his fellows* his fellow-workmen or fellow-worshippers. But why should the workman's fellows be ashamed and not himself? A much more natural construction is the one given in the Targum, and approved by Vitringa, Rosenmüller, Hitzig, and Knobel, who refer the suffix to the idol itself, and by *his fellows* understand all who have anything to do with it, either as manufacturers or worshippers. (Compare Num. xxv. 3; Deut. xi. 22, xxx. 20; Isa. lvi. 3, 6; Hosea iv. 17; 1 Cor. x. 20.)—Lowth affirms that the common text of the next clause yields no tolerable sense, and is unworthy of the Prophet; for which reason he proposes to read מאדם as a passive participle meaning *reddened*, and translates accordingly, *even the workmen themselves shall blush*, adding that if any one should think the singular irregular, he may read מאדמים; and the one assumption is undoubtedly as reasonable as the other. It is worthy of remark not only that this emendation has commended itself to no later writer, but also that the common text is universally regarded as affording a perfectly appropriate sense and one essential to the Prophet's argument, viz. that the makers of the idol are themselves mere men, and cannot therefore produce anything divine. Vitringa's explanation of אדם as meaning "common people" (*plebs*) is destructive of the argument, as well as contrary to usage. The comparative sense put by some upon the phrase, as meaning that they are *less than men* (Cocceius), or that they shall be ashamed *more than other men* (Junius), is too unnatural to need refutation. The meaning of the verse is that the senseless idol and its human makers shall

be witnesses against each other, and shall be involved in the same condemnation and confusion.

12. *He has carved iron (with) a graver, and has wrought (it) in the coals, and with the hammers he will shape it, and then work it with his arm of strength. Besides (or moreover), he is hungry and has no strength, he has not drunk water and is faint.* The construction of חָרַשׁ as a verb, which is given in the Targum, is much the simplest and most obvious; though most interpreters regard it as the construct form of the derivative noun חָרָשׁ a *workman* (as in Exodus xxviii. 11), with בַּרְזֶל added to restrict its application to a *worker in iron,* i. e. a smith; as חָרַשׁ עֵצִים in the next verse is supposed to signify a *worker in wood,* i. e. a carpenter. (Compare the plural חָרָשֵׁי עֵצִים, 2 Sam. v. 11.) Those who agree in this explanation of the first two words differ as to their construction with what follows. Apart from Lowth's gratuitous emendation of the Masoretic pointing by proposing to read מַעְצָד as a participle of עָצַד, to cut, and the suggestion of Cappellus that it is synonymous with זְרוֹעַ, the English and some other Versions take it in the sense of *tongs,* a mere conjecture from the context; but most of the modern writers make it mean an *axe,* as in Jer. x. 3, or more generically any sharp or pointed instrument. The noun thus explained is construed with what goes before in three different ways. The older writers generally understand it as a noun of instrument. Thus the English Version has *the smith with the tongs,* &c. Vitringa, Gesenius, and others make the noun the object of a verb to be supplied (*the smith makes an axe*), and understand the verse as describing the formation, not of the idol itself, but of the tools to be employed in making it. Ewald and Knobel explain מַעְצָד as a second term used to qualify חָרָשׁ, or in other words as qualifying the complex phrase before it. To the whole expression Ewald gives the sense of an iron and file worker, i. é. one who works with iron and the file; Knobel that of a tool-smith or a maker of edged tools. Both make this complex name the subject of the verb פָּעַל, and the ו before it an idiomatic pleonasm. But as both these grammatical assumptions are without satisfactory authority from usage, they are only admissible in case of exegetical necessity. Hitzig likewise makes the first two words the subject of the verb, but takes the third as its object, and understands the clause to mean that the smith converts an axe into an idol, as in chap. ii. 4 the sword becomes a ploughshare and the spear a pruning-hook. Knobel's objection that the idol would be too small is of no great moment, if it can be assumed that images were ever made of iron; but in that case the most satisfactory construction is the one first given, which makes the verse describe the proceedings not of the professional smith, but of the laborious worshipper himself. The common version, *strength of his arms,* is a needless and enfeebling transposition. The true sense of the words is *his arm of strength.* Vitringa directs attention to the beautiful parallel in Virgil (Geo. IV. 170–175), and especially to this line: *illi inter sese magna vi brachia tollunt.* The description in the last clause seems intended to convey these several ideas; that the man who undertakes to make a god, is himself a mortal, subject to ordinary human infirmities; that his god is utterly unable to relieve him or supply his wants; and that neither these considerations nor the toil which he must undergo in order to attain his end, are sufficient to deter him from his self-tormenting efforts.

13. *He has carved wood, he has stretched a line, he will mark it with the awl (or graver), he will form it with the chisels, and with the compass (or circle) he will mark it, and then make it (or now he has made it) like the structure (i. e. after the model) of a man, like the beauty of mankind, to*

dwell in a house.—In this translation חָרָשׁ is taken as a verb and referred to the same subject as in ver. 12, *i. e.* the idol-manufacturer, who goes through all these laborious processes himself, in order to produce a god. But the great majority of writers here resume a transition from the maker of metallic idols to the maker of wooden ones, or from the smith who makes the carpenter's tools to the carpenter himself, חָרָשׁ עֵצִים, the worker in wood. —In this verse, as in that before it, the alternation of the preterite and future introduces us into the very midst of the process, and describes it as already begun but not yet finished. This distinctive feature of the passage is destroyed by making all the verbs indiscriminately present. The conversive future at the opening of the second clause may either denote simply that the act described is subsequent to that just mentioned, or it may represent what was just now future as already done, thereby rendering the view of a progressive operation still more vivid. The two markings or delineations mentioned are commonly supposed to have respect to the general dimensions of the figure, and then to its precise form and proportions. Henderson arbitrarily translates the same verb first *he sketched its figure*, and then *he marked it off;* which, even if it gave the sense, would not convey the form of the original.—According to the rabbins, שֶׂרֶד means a " red or other coloured string " used by workmen in their measurements (Montanus: *filo tincto*). It is applied to the colouring substance by Luther (*Röthelstein*) and Lowth (*red ochre!*). Gesenius and the other modern writers draw from the Talmudical and Arabic analogy the sense of a sharp tool or graving instrument.—אָדָם and אִישׁ seem to have their strict sense here, as a generic and specific term, the *beauty of man*, the *structure of a man.* The Targum seems to find a reference to both sexes ; in support of which some of the old Jewish writers refer to Num. xxxi. 35, where אָדָם is applied to women alone. Jarchi gains the same end in a different way, by saying that the woman is the glory of her husband (קילת בעלה קסיף סתשא האיח היה).—Jerome and Rosenmüller seem to understand the last words of the verse as meaning that the idol has to stay at home because it cannot move. Gesenius gives בַּיִת the specific sense of temple. Gill supposes a particular reference to household gods. But the meaning seems to be that the idol, being like a man in form, is, like a man, to dwell in a house.

14. *To hew him down cedars; and* (now) *he has taken a cypress and an oak—and has strengthened* (*i. e.* raised it) *for himself among the trees of the forest—he has planted a pine, and the rain shall increase* (it, *i. e.* make it grow). To shew more clearly the absurdity of ascribing deity to material images, he here goes back, not only to their human origin and their base material, but to the very generation of the trees by which the wood is furnished. The particulars are stated in an inverse order. He begins with the felling of trees, but interrupts himself in order to go still further back to their very cultivation. The essential idea is that man, instead of being the creature, is in some sort the creator of the wood he worships, since it does or may owe its existence to his agency. The supposition just suggested of an interruption in the syntax seems more natural than that of a grammatical ellipsis. Few interpreters, indeed, would go so far as Clericus, who introduces at the beginning of the sentence these words, *mittit ad Libanum homines*, and adds, with characteristic coolness, *hæc fuerunt necessario supplenda;* although in the very next sentence he observes of the Septuagint and Vulgate Versions, *constructiones quam non inveniebant de suo concinnarunt.* Ewald, in his larger Grammar (p. 622) enumerates this

among the examples of an infinitive denoting necessity or obligation, just as we might say familiarly in English, *he has to cut*, &c. But in his exposition of the passage, he agrees with Gesenius and others in making it equivalent to a finite verb, with the additional suggestion that it may be an orthographical mistake for יִכְרֹת.—The modern writers seem to be agreed that the תִּרְזָה is a species of oak, so called from its hardness, like the Latin *robur*. To avoid tautology and pedantry, however, the common version *cypress* may be retained, as it yields an appropriate sense, and as botanical precision is in this case of no exegetical importance, since the meaning of the verse would be the same whatever species had been mentioned.—Most writers give אִמֵּץ the sense of choosing, designating, here and in Ps. lxxx. 16, which they suppose to be easily deducible from that of strengthening, confining, fixing. Ewald even goes so far as to take בָּרַת in the sense of choosing, on the alleged authority of Jer. x. 3. This is purely arbitrary; and as אִמֵּץ, in every other case where it occurs, admits of the translation *strengthened*, it cannot be consistently abandoned here without necessity; and this necessity cannot exist, because the strict sense of *making strong* is not only relevant in this connection, but corresponds exactly to that of *making great* expressed by יְגַדֵּל, both meaning here " to cause to grow." Thus understood, the word helps to bring out with more strength and clearness the main idea of the verse, viz. that the idolater not only chooses suitable trees, but plants and raises them for the purpose. It is not necessary to suppose that this is a description of a usual or frequent custom. It is rather an ideal exhibition of the idol-manufacture carried out to its extreme. If so, the active subject of the whole description is the self-deluded devotee ; which furnishes another reason for believing that the smith and the carpenter are not distinctly mentioned in the two preceding verses. It also removes the seeming incongruity of making the carpenter raise his own timber, whereas the same thing, when alleged of the idolater, is perfectly in keeping with the rest of the description.—The object of the verb יְאַמֵּץ may be either the trees previously mentioned, or more indefinitely, trees in general. Lowth arbitrarily translates this clause, *and layeth in good store of the trees of the forest*. Clericus, still more boldly and extravagantly, makes it mean that he furnishes his workshop with the trees of the forest. Less absurd, and yet untenable, because not justified by usage, is Henderson's translation, *and what he deemeth firm among the trees of the forest*. Umbreit's suggestion, that the last clause was designed to intimate the man's dependence after all upon the rain of heaven for the very material of which he makes his god, is not entirely natural. The clause is rather added to complete the picture of the natural origin and growth of that which the idolater adores as superhuman and divine. In this as well as the foregoing verses the confusion of the tenses in most versions greatly mars the force and beauty of the Prophet's language.—What is gained by the violent and ungrammatical construction, *he has planted and the rain has nourished*, or the vague and evasive one, *he plants and the rain nourishes;* when the exact translation, *he has planted and the rain will nourish*, is not only just as clear, coherent, and appropriate, but far more graphic and expressive, as it hurries us at once *in medias res*, and exhibits the work described as partly past, partly future ? At the same time it implies the patient perseverance of the devotee, who first does his part and then waits for natural causes to do theirs, and all for the production of an idol !

15. *And it shall be to men for burning* (*i. e.* for fuel), *and he has taken of them and warmed himself; yes, he will kindle and bake bread; yes, he will*

form a god and fall prostrate; he has made it a graven image and bowed down to them. The future meaning of the first verb is determined by its intimate connection with the last word of the foregoing verse. (See Nordheimer, § 219.) אָדָם very seldom means an individual man, and seems here to be used indefinitely for man or men in general. The singular verb יִקָּ֑ד does not refer to this noun, but to the worshipper or devotee who is still the subject of description. The plural form מֵהֶם is referred by Hitzig to the trees of the forest mentioned in ver. 14, by Knobel to the עֵצִים or sticks of wood into which the tree must be divided. The same explanation may be given of לָמוֹ, although Ewald and Hitzig maintain that this suffix is employed as a singular by later writers (*e. g.* chap. liii. 8; Ps. xi. 7). But even admitting the existence of this usage, which Gesenius utterly denies, the strict and usual meaning is to be retained where possible, and therefore here, where the Prophet seems designedly to interchange the singular and plural forms, in order to identify with more effect the idol worshipped and the sticks consumed. He takes of them (the sticks), kindles a fire, warms himself, bakes bread, then makes a god, and worships, yes, bows down before them (the sticks of wood). The argument of this and the succeeding verses is intended to exhibit the absurdity of worshipping the same material that is constantly applied to the most trivial domestic uses. All the interpreters since Calvin quote the striking parallel from Horace (Sat. i. 8).

> Olim truncus eram ficulnus, inutile lignum;
> Quum faber, incertus scamnum faceretne Priapum,
> Maluit esse Deum.

16. *Half of it he hath burned in the fire, on half of it he will eat flesh, he will roast roast and be filled; yea, he will warm himself and say, Aha, I am warm, I have seen fire.* Both etymology and usage give חֶצְיוֹ the sense of *half*, i. e. one of two parts into which a given whole may be divided, whether equal or unequal. The indefinite translation *part*, given in all the English versions except that of Noyes, is intended to avoid the incongruity of making two halves and a remainder. But this incongruity, although justly chargeable on Umbreit's version, which distinctly mentions *the one half, the other half*, and *the remainder*, has no existence in the original; because, as all the other modern writers are agreed, the first and second חֶצְיוֹ of ver. 16 are one and the same half, and the other is not introduced until the next verse. Henderson indeed refers the second to the wooden dish or platter upon which the meat was literally eaten. But this disturbs the parallel between the two main uses of the wood, as fuel and a god, which is so distinctly carried out in the preceding and the following context. It is better, therefore, to explain the phrase, *on half of it he eats flesh*, as a pregnant or concise expression of the idea, that over or by means of the fire made with half of it he cooks flesh for his eating. The obscurity of this clause is immediately removed by the addition of the unambiguous words, *he roasts a roast and satisfies himself.* The force of אַף, both here and in the foregoing verse, appears to be equivalent to that of our expression *nay more*, not only this, but also, or moreover.—Gesenius and others give רָאִיתִי in the last clause the generic sense of *perceiving* by the senses; Hitzig the more specific one of *feeling*, in support of which he quotes the observation of Schelling, that the skin is the eye for warmth, whereupon Hendewerk no less characteristically says that the Prophet may with more probability be supposed to have ascribed these words to the idolater in the

sense of an ancient fire-worshipper than in that of a modern pantheist. The truth is, that the Hebrew verb not only may, but must have here its proper meaning *I have seen*, because the noun which follows does not denote the *heat* of fire, but its *light*, and there could not be a more natural expression of the feeling meant to be conveyed than by referring to the cheerful blaze of a large wood fire.   To the indiscriminate translation of the verbs both in this verse and the next as descriptive presents, the same objections may be made as in the foregoing context.

17. *And the rest of it* (*i. e.* the other half) *he has made into a god, into his graven image; he will bow down to it, and will worship, and will pray to it, and say, Deliver me, for thou* (art) *my god*.   The consecution of the tenses is the same as in the preceding verse, and has the same effect of fixing the point of observation in the midst of the process.   He has kindled his fire, and will use it to prepare his food.   He has made his idol, and will fall down and pray to it.   The pronoun at the end may be regarded as emphatic, and as meaning *thou and thou alone*.

18. *They have not known, and they will not understand, for he hath smeared their eyes from seeing, their hearts from doing wisely*.   The combination of the preterite and future makes the description more complete and comprehensive.   Some give 'כִּ the sense of *that*, and make it indicate the object of their ignorance and inconsideration.   Junius and Tremellius, who adopt this construction, refer טַח to the idol; they do not know that it has blinded them.   The Septuagint explains the verb as a passive plural, and Gesenius has the same form in his version (*their eyes are smeared*), which he resolves, however, into an indefinite construction (*one has smeared their eyes*).   But the analogy of chaps. vi. 10, xxix. 10, Job xvii. 4, confirms Aben Ezra's statement, that Jehovah is the agent or subject (הַמּוֹעֵל רוּחַ הַסָּם).   As the smearing of the eyes is merely a figure for spiritual blindness, it is here extended to the heart, of which it is not literally predicable.   As the use of the Hiphil form in any but an active sense is called in question by some eminent grammarians, הַשְׂכִּיל may here, as in some other cases, have the sense of *acting wisely*.

19. *And he will not bring it home to himself* (or *to his heart*), *and* (there is) *not knowledge, and* (there is) *not understanding to say, Half of it I have burned in the fire, and have also baked bread on its coals, I will roast flesh and eat, and the rest of it I will make to* (be) *an abomination, to a log of wood* (or *the trunk of a tree*) *I will cast myself down*.   The essential meaning is, that they have not sense enough to describe their conduct to themselves in its true colours ;. if they did, they would stand amazed at its impiety and folly.   In the form of expression the writer passes from the plural to the singular, *i. e.* from idolaters in general to the individual idolater.—The first phrase does not correspond exactly to the English *lay to heart*, but comprehends reflection and emotion.   The construction of the last clause as an explanation or an interrogation has arisen from a wish to avoid the incongruity of making the man call himself a fool, or express his resolution to perform a foolish act.   But this very incongruity is absolutely necessary to the writer's purpose, which is simply to tell what the infatuated devotee would say of his own conduct if he saw it in its true light.   Instead of saying, I will worship my god, he would then say, I will worship a stick of wood, a part of the very log which I have just burned, upon which I have just baked my bread, and on which I am just about to cook my dinner. The more revolting and absurd this language, the more completely does it suit and carry out the writer's purpose.   Hence, too, the use of the term

abomination, i.e. object of abhorrence, not in the worshipper's actual belief, but as it would be if his eyes were opened.

20. *Feeding on ashes, (his) heart is deceived, it has led him astray, and he cannot deliver himself* (or *his soul*), *and he will not say, Is there not a lie in my right hand?* Another statement of the reason why he cannot see his conduct in its just light, or describe it in correct terms, viz., because his very mind or heart is deceived, and this because it feeds on ashes. This last expression is strangely understood by some interpreters, following the Targum, to describe the idol as a piece of half-burnt wood; and even Umbreit seems to recognise such an allusion in the sentence. But the great majority of writers, far more naturally, make it a figure for the love and prosecution of unsatisfying objects, analogous to *feeding on wind*, Hos. xii. 2. Gesenius in his Commentary says, that the translation *feedeth on ashes* is in no case appropriate (*in keinem Falle passend*). He accordingly translates it there *sectatur cinerem ;* but in his Thesaurus he abandons this gratuitous multiplication of senses, and explains it as a figurative application of the common meaning, "pasci aliqua re, metaph. i. q. delectari re." The word, however, denotes something more than simply to take pleasure in an object, and suggests the idea of choosing it and resting in it as a portion.— The usual construction of the next words, *a deceived heart has seduced him,* is commonly explained by assuming an ellipsis of the relative, *(his) heart (which) is deceived has seduced him.* But the simplest and most natural construction is the one proposed by Knobel, who makes two short independent clauses, *the heart is deceived, it leads him astray.* The futures of the last clause have in part, if not exclusively, a potential meaning. It is best, perhaps, to combine the ideas of unwillingness and inability.—The concluding question is equivalent in import to the long speech put into the mouth of the idolater in ver. 19. By a *lie* we are to understand that which professes to be what it is not, and thereby deceives the hopes of those who trust in it. (See Jer. x. 14 ; Ps. xxxiii. 17.) This description some apply to the idol itself, as if he had said, Is not this which I carry in my right hand a deception? But as this makes a part of the interrogation literal and a part metaphorical, most writers give it uniformity by understanding all the terms as figurative : Is not this, about which I am busied, and upon which I am spending strength and labour, a deception? To any one rational enough to ask the question, the reply would be affirmative of course.

21. *Remember these* (things), *Jacob and Israel, for thou art my servant ; I have formed thee, a servant unto me art thou ; Israel, thou shalt not be forgotten by me.* Having completed his detailed exposure of the folly of idolatry, or rather of the impotence of idols, as contrasted with the power of God, he now resumes the tone of promise and encouragement with which the chapter opens, and assures the chosen people, here personified as Israel or Jacob, that having been constituted such by Jehovah for a special purpose, they could not cease to be the objects of his watchful care.—*These things* may possibly refer to the immediately succeeding statements, which may then be rendered *that thou art my servant,* &c. To most interpreters, however, it has seemed more natural to understand by *these things* the whole foregoing series of arguments against the divinity of idols and in favour of Jehovah's sole supremacy.—Ewald connects עֶבֶד־לִי with the preceding verb, so as to mean, I have formed thee as a servant for myself. The only difficulty in the way of this construction is the אַתָּה, which cannot be the object of the verb, but must agree with one expressed or understood. This objection might be done away by disregarding the Masoretic inter-

punction, and transferring the disjunctive accent to the preceding word; in which case the latter member of the clause would read, *thou Israel, &c.*, with an emphasis upon the pronoun. This construction has the advantage of removing the apparent tautology arising from the repetition of *thou art my servant*, which is more observable in most translations than in the original, where two different forms of expression are employed.—The last word in the verse is explained in the ancient versions, and by some modern writers, as a deponent verb, *thou shalt not forget me*. But Gesenius and Ewald, with greater probability, make it a proper passive, and explain the suffix as equivalent to a dative or an ablative in Latin *thou shalt not be forgotten (by) me;* which is much more appropriate, in this connection, than an exhortation not to forget God. This construction is as old as Aben Ezra, who paraphrases the expression thus : לא תכסה ממני זכרני ותכי תוכרך.

22. *I have blotted out, like a cloud, thy transgressions, and like a vapour, thy sins; return to me, for I have redeemed thee.* As the previous assurances were suited to dispel any doubt or hesitation as to the power of Jehovah, so the one in this verse meets another difficulty, namely, that arising from a sense of guilt. The assurance given is that of entire and gratuitous forgiveness. The analogy of Exod. xxxii. 32, 33, would seem to favour an allusion to the blotting out of an inscription or an entry in a book of accounts. The cloud may then be a distinct figure to denote what is transient or evanescent. (See Hos. vi. 4, xiii. 3 ; Job. vii. 9, xxx. 15.) This is Hitzig's explanation of the verse ; but most interpreters suppose the blotting and the cloud to be parts of one and the same metaphor, although they differ in their method of connecting them. Junius strangely understands the clause to mean, as a cloud (when condensed into rain) purges away filth. The great majority of writers are agreed, however, that the cloud itself is here described as being blotted out. Gill supposes an allusion to the height and distance of the clouds as being far beyond man's reach, implying that forgiveness is a divine prerogative. Hendewerk sees a forced allusion to the cloud which went before the people in the wilderness. A more usual and natural interpretation is that the clouds in general are here considered as intervening between heaven and earth, as sin is expressly said in chap. lix. 2, to separate between God and his people. This explanation of the metaphor, however, does not exclude the supposition of a reference to the fleeting nature of the cloudy vapour, and the ease and suddenness with which it is dispelled by sun or wind.—עָב and עָנָן are poetical equivalents. So far as they can be distinguished, either in etymology or usage, the correct distinction is the one expressed in the English Version (*thick cloud* and *cloud*), which Henderson reverses.—*Return unto me* is a phrase descriptive of all the restorations of God's people from their spiritual wanderings and estrangements. The restriction of this phrase, and the one which follows it to the restoration of the Jews from exile, is as forced and arbitrary as the future form given to the verb in many versions.

23. *Sing, O heavens, for Jehovah hath done (it); shout, ye lower parts of the earth; break forth, ye mountains, into song, the forest and every tree in it: for Jehovah hath redeemed Jacob, and in Israel he will glorify himself.* The prediction of glorious and joyful changes, as in many other cases, is clothed in the form of an exhortation to all nature to rejoice. It is essential to the writer's purpose that the universe itself should be addressed, which precludes the explanation of the verse by Grotius, as addressed to angels, kings, and common men; or by Vitringa, as addressed to the apostles and prophets (from a misplaced comparison of Rev. xviii. 20).

Equally inconsistent with his purpose and at variance with good taste is the explanation of mountains as meaning kingdoms, forests, cities, &c.— The thing *done* is what is mentioned in the last clause, *i. e.* the redemption of Israel, including the deliverance from exile in Babylon, but not confined to it.—The arbitrary version of the two verbs in the last clause as a preterite and present, or a present and a future, is in no respect to be preferred to the exact translation as a preterite and a future, expressive of what God had done and would yet do for the chosen people.

24. *Thus saith Jehovah, thy Redeemer, and thy Former from the womb, I, Jehovah, making all, stretching the heavens alone, spreading the earth by myself* (or, *who was with me?*). Some refer *thus saith* to the preceding promises, and take all that follows till the end of the chapter as a description of the being who uttered them. Others refer *thus saith* to what follows, supply the verb *am* before *Jehovah*, and regard the last clause of the verse as the divine declaration. A third conceivable construction would restrict it to the closing question, *who (is) with me?* *i. e.* who can claim equality or likeness with me?—There is no need of giving to the phrase *thy Former* a moral sense, as signifying the formation of character or manners, as the words *from the womb* are not necessarily exclusive of the period before birth. For the meaning of the figure itself, see above on ver. 2; for that of רָקַע on chap. xlii. 5.—The textual reading of the last word makes it an interrogation, מִי אִתִּי, *who (is or was) with me?* implying strong negation, and equivalent in meaning to the affirmation, *there was no one with me.* The marginal reading yields the same sense in another way, מֵאִתִּי, *from, by,* or *of myself.* (Compare מִמֶּנִּי, Hosea viii. 4, and ἀπ' ἐμαυτοῦ, John v. 30.) The objection that the textual reading interrupts the construction is valid only on the supposition that the sentence is continued through the following verses. If, as most interpreters assume, the last clause of this verse contains a proposition, interrogative or affirmative, this reading affords an appropriate conclusion to the sentence, and a striking parallel to the phrase לְבַדִּי in the other clause.

25. *Breaking the signs of babblers, and diviners he will madden; turning sages back, and their knowledge he will stultify.* The whole verse is descriptive of Jehovah as convicting all prophets, except his own, of folly and imposture, by falsifying their prognostications. בַּדִּים is commonly translated either *lies* or *liars;* but it is rather an expression of contempt, denoting praters, vain or idle talkers, and by implication utterers of falsehood. *Signs* are properly the pledges and accompaniments of predictions, but may here be regarded as equivalent to prophecy itself. These are said to be *broken* in the same sense that breaking may be predicated of a promise or a covenant. The effect of course would be to make such prophets seem like fools or madmen. (See 2 Sam. xv. 31; Hos. ix. 7.) The restriction of these terms to the false prophets of the Babylonish exile is not only arbitrary, but at variance with the context, which repeatedly contrasts the omnipotence and omniscience of Jehovah with the impotence of idols and the ignorance of heathen prophets.—Because turning back and being put to shame are often joined together elsewhere, Gesenius, according to his favourite method, makes them simply synonymous; whereas the first expression strictly signifies defeat, disappointment, failure, with which shame is naturally connected, but surely not identical.—The alternation of the future and participle seems to have a rhythmical design. The distinction may however be, that while the latter signifies habitual or customary action, the former expresses certain futurity and fixed determination.

26. *Confirming the word of his servant, and the counsel of his messengers he will fulfil; the (one) saying to (or as to) Jerusalem, She shall be inhabited, and to (or as to) the cities of Judah, They shall be built, and her ruins I will raise.* With the frustration of the heathen prophecies is here contrasted the fulfilment of Jehovah's, who is himself represented as securing their accomplishment. הֵקִים has here the same sense as in Jer. xxix. 10, xxxiii. 14, viz. that of bringing a promise or prophecy to pass.—By *his servant* Jarchi understands Moses, Hitzig Jeremiah, Gesenius the prophets as a class, Knobel the genuine believing Israel whose hopes were embodied in these prophecies. Simpler and more satisfactory than either of these explanations is that which supposes *his servant* to be primarily and directly the writer himself, but considered as one of a class who are then distinctly mentioned in the other member as *his messengers.* The specific application of the title of God's servant to the prophets is apparent from 2 Kings xxiv. 2; Jer. xxix. 19, xxxv. 15, xliv. 4.—Gill's question, why *his servant* may not denote Paul as Cocceius supposes, is unanswerable.—*Counsel,* according to Henderson, here means the counsel or purpose of God, as declared by his servants. Gesenius and most other writers make it a description of prophecy, considered as involving or suggesting counsel and advice with respect to the future. (Compare the similar application of the verb in chap. xli. 28.)—The last clause, beginning with the word הָאֹמֵר, might be considered as a more specific designation or description of *his servant,* viz. *the (servant) saying,* &c. But this interpretation is precluded by the double repetition of הָאֹמֵר in the two succeeding verses, and in evident application to Jehovah himself.—The construction of תּוּשָׁב as a verb of the second person (*thou shalt be inhabited*) is forbidden by its masculine form, which could be connected with the name Jerusalem only in cases where the latter is put for its inhabitants. For the sake of uniformity the parallel expression is to be translated in like manner. Gesenius arbitrarily translates the first of these verbs as an imperative, the second as a future, and the third as a present. To raise up the ruins of a city is of course to rebuild it.

27. *The (one) saying to the deep, Be dry, and I will dry up thy floods* (or *streams*). The Targum, followed by Kimchi and others, explains צוּלָה as a metaphorical description of Babylon, so called on account of its wealth, its population, or its site. Vitringa, Lowth, and some of the latest writers, understand by צוּלָה the Euphrates, and apply the whole verse to the stratagem by which Cyrus gained access to Babylon, as related in the first book of Herodotus, and the seventh of Xenophon's Cyropædia. Henderson thinks there may be also an allusion to his division of the river Gyndes. (See vol. i. p. 262.) Ewald and others understand the verse as a description of God's power over nature and the elements, with or without an allusion to the passage of the Red Sea at the exodus. This exposition is strongly recommended by the analogy of chap. xlii. 15, xliii. 16, l. 2, li. 10. That of Jer. l. 38, li. 36, does not prove that Isaiah's description was designed to have exclusive reference to the conquest of Babylon by Cyrus, but only that this was included in it as a signal instance of God's power to overcome all obstacles, and that the later prophet made a specific application of the words accordingly. There is no need of giving צוּלָה any other than its widest sense as a description of the ocean. The word *streams* or *floods* is applied in the same way to the sea by David (Ps. xxiv. 2) and ·Jonah (ii. 4), in the

last of which cases it is connected with the cognate form מְצוּלָה. (Compare Zech. x. 11, and Isa. xix. 5.)—The strict translation of the last verb by Ewald as a future (*I will dry up*) is not only more exact, but more expressive than the present form preferred by Gesenius and others.

28. *The (one) saying to* (or *as to*) *Cyrus, My shepherd, and all my pleasure he will fulfil, and saying to Jerusalem, Thou shalt be built, and (to) the temple, Thou shalt be founded.* It is now universally admitted that this verse has reference to Cyrus the Elder or the Great, the son of Cambyses king of Persia, and the grandson of Astyages the Mede, the hero of the Cyropædia and of the first book of Herodotus, the same who appears in sacred history (2 Chron. xxxvi. 23, Ezra i. 1) as the actual restorer of the Jews from exile. He is here called Jehovah's *shepherd*, which may either be the usual poetical designation of a king, so common in the oldest classics, or (as Umbreit suggests) a special description of his mission and vocation to gather the lost sheep of the house of Israel. It is characteristic of John David Michaelis, and of the notions prevalent in his day as to fidelity and freedom of translation, that instead of *my shepherd* he has *the king appointed by me ;* for which variation he apologises on the ground that the former title, if applied to so great a king, might sound indecorous (*unanständig klingen*), because shepherds are now low and vulgar people.—With רֹעִי we may either supply *thou art* or *he is*, or regard it as a simple exclamation. A curious illustration of the ancient mode of writing Hebrew is afforded by Jerome's remark on this word : "Verbum Hebraicum *Roi*, si per resh literam legamus, intelligitur *pastor meus ;* si per daleth, *sciens* vel *intelligens ;* quarum similitudo parvo apice distinguitur."—*All my pleasure, i. e.* with respect to the deliverance of the Jews from exile.—The construction of וְלֵאמֹר is obscure and difficult. Luther refers it to an indefinite subject, so that one may say (*dass man sage*). Knobel makes it dependent on הָאֹמֵר in the sense of *commanding to say.* Ewald regards it as an idiomatic use of the infinitive instead of the finite verb, and refers it to Jehovah. Gesenius refers it to Cyrus, and understands it as explaining how he was to fulfil Jehovah's pleasure, namely, *by saying*, &c. This, on the whole, is the most natural construction, although, like the others, it leaves unexplained the introduction of the copulative particle before the verb, which must either be rendered as in the English Version (*even saying*), or disregarded as an idiomatic pleonasm.—The same ambiguity respecting the person of the verbs exists in the last clause of this verse as in ver 26. Some take both in the second person, which requires a preposition to be introduced before הֵיכָל. Others make both in the third person, which requires הֵיכָל to be construed as a feminine in this one place exclusively. This last is the construction finally adopted by Gesenius. In his Commentary he had assumed an abrupt transition from the third to the second person.—There are two points in this verse upon which the *higher criticism* of modern times has fastened, as proofs that the passage is of later origin than that which tradition has assigned to it. The first of these is the use of חֵפֶץ in the sense of business or affair, repeated instances of which are cited from the later books or what are so considered. But even in the cases thus alleged, the change of usage is extremely doubtful, while in that before us it is purely imaginary or fictitious. The word has here its strict, original, and usual sense of inclination, will, or pleasure, that which one delights in, chooses, or desires ; and the substitution of *affair* or *business* would be not only arbitrary but ridiculous.—The other supposititious proof of later date is

the distinctness with which Cyrus is foretold by name, and which is said to be at variance with the general analogy and usage of the prophecies. Möller's attempt to set aside this difficulty by explaining כּוֹרֶשׁ as a descriptive name of Israel itself, has found no adherents among later writers, and instead of mitigating, aggravates the evil. Without disturbing the unanimous consent among interpreters that Cyrus is the subject of this prophecy the objection admits of satisfactory solution. In the first place, let it be observed, that it proceeds upon a false assumption, namely, that no form of expression or prediction can occur but once. Why may not this be a single exception to the general rule, analogous to that presented by the occasional introduction of precise dates, notwithstanding the usual vagueness of prediction ? The want of analogy might render it *a priori* more improbable, and make the necessity of clear proof more imperative, but could not, in the face of such proof, make the fact itself incredible. But in the next place, the precision of this prophecy is not so totally without analogy as the objectors commonly assume. One clearly defined instance of the same kind is sufficient to relieve the case before us from the charge of being wholly unparalleled, and such an instance is afforded by the prophecy respecting Josiah in 1 Kings xiii. 2. The assertion that the name of Josiah was interpolated by a later hand, is not only perfectly gratuitous, but equally available in this case, where a similar assumption would at once remove all evidence of later date. If that is an interpolation, so may this be. If that is not one, this is not without analogy. But in the third place, the alleged violation of analogy is much less real than apparent ; since in both the cases there is reference to the meaning of the name as a generic or descriptive title, and not merely to its application as an individual denomination. That *Josiah* was intended to be thus significant, as well as in 2 Kings xiii. 2, as in Zech. vi. 10, has been proved by Hengstenberg in his exposition of the latter passage. (Christologie, ii. p. 71.) That כּוֹרֶשׁ was likewise a descriptive title of the Persian kings, is rendered probable by several distinct considerations. The Hebrew name has been identified, by some of the most eminent comparative philologists, with a Persian word which means the *sun*. The use of such a title would agree well not only with the ancient religion of that people, but with a well known oriental usage of describing certain royal races as descendants of the sun, whether this be regarded as a superstitious myth or a poetical hyperbole. It is expressly asserted by Herodotus that Cyrus originally bore another name. This name is said by Strabo to have been *Agradates*, which Hitzig reckons as a mere mistake, occasioned by confounding the river Κῦρος with the monarch of the same name, whereas Pott, Von Lengerke, and others, trace it to the same root with כּוֹרֶשׁ, and the same primary sense of *sun*. To this etymology there seems to be an allusion in chap. xli. 2, 25, where Cyrus is so emphatically said to have risen in the east and pursued his course westwards. This explanation of the name is strongly favoured by the numerous analogies in this and other languages, the Egyptian Pharaohs and Ptolemies, the Philistian Abimelechs, the Amalekitish Agags, the Roman Cæsars. The result of these considerations is, that the prophecy before us, although still relating to the individual Cyrus, is not so variant in form from the usual analogy of prophecy, as to afford any ground for the suspicion that the passage is on that account of later date. For the most satisfactory discussion of this point, see Hengstenberg's Christologie, i. p. 192, and Hävernick's Einleitung, ii. p. 163.

Chapter 45

THIS chapter contains the same essential elements with those before it, but in new combinations and a varied form. The great theme of the prophecy is still the relation of Israel to God as his chosen people, and to the nations as a source or medium of saving knowledge. This last idea is brought out with great distinctness at the close of the chapter. The proofs and illustrations of the doctrine taught are still drawn from the power of Jehovah, as displayed in the creation of the world, and as contrasted with the impotence of idols. The evidence of prescience afforded by the prophecy is also here repeated and enlarged upon. As a particular prospective exhibition both of power and foreknowledge, we have still before us the conquests of Cyrus, which are specifically foretold and explicitly connected with the favour of Jehovah as their procuring cause, and with the liberation of his people and the demonstration of his deity, as their designed effect.

As to the order and arrangement of the parts, the chapter opens, in direct continuation of the forty-fourth, with a further prophecy of Cyrus and of his successes, vers. 1–3. These are then referred to the power of God and his design of mercy towards his people, so that all misgivings or distrust must be irrational and impious, vers. 4–13. Then leaving Cyrus out of view, the Prophet turns his eyes to the nations, and declares that they must be subdued, but only in order to be blessed and saved, which is declared to have been the divine purpose, and revealed as such from the beginning, vers. 14–25.

1. *Thus saith Jehovah to his anointed, to Cyrus, whose right hand I have held fast, to tread down before him nations, and the loins of kings I will loose; to open before him double doors, and gates shall not be shut.* The words of Jehovah seem to begin regularly with the next verse; but even in this, which is strictly introductory, they are mingled with the Prophet's description of Cyrus, a mode of composition very common in Hebrew, and among the oldest writers, who thought more of the idea than of the form in which it was expressed. The accumulation of descriptive epithets, which Gesenius represents as characteristic of these Later Prophecies, arises from the fact that one main object which the writer had in view was to impress upon the reader's mind the attributes of God and of his chosen instruments.—Cyrus is here called the Lord's anointed, a designation elsewhere limited, as Calvin says, to the sacerdotal monarchy of Judah, which prefigured Christ in both his offices of priest and king.—Most writers understand it here as a synonyme of *king*, derived from Jewish usages, and not intended to indicate anything peculiar in the royalty of Cyrus, except that he was raised up by Jehovah for a special purpose. Calvin thinks it still more pregnant and emphatic, and descriptive of Cyrus as a representative of Christ in this one thing, that he was instrumentally the saviour or deliverer of Israel from bondage.—The treading down of nations is a trait peculiarly appropriate in this case, as the Greek historians give long catalogues of distinct nations subjugated by Cyrus, such as the Medes, Hyrcanians, Assyrians, Arabians, Cappadocians, Phrygians, Lydians, Carians, Babylonians, &c.—To loose the loins of kings is explained by Calvin as meaning to weaken them, because the strength is in the loins; and Rosenmüller cites, in illustration of this usage, the Latin verb and adjective, *delumbo* and *elumbis*. Luther. Clericus, and J. D. Michaelis suppose an allusion to the removal of the sword-belt, as the ancient method of disarming or dismissing from active

service. Either of these explanations is better than Jerome's, which supposes an allusion simply to the royal cincture as a badge of office. But most of the modern writers are agreed that the words at least include a reference to the ordinary use of the girdle as a part of oriental dress, on which the activity of the wearer and his exercise of strength are in a great degree dependent, as it gathers up and tightens the flowing garments which would otherwise impede his movements. The exclusive reference of this clause to the kings of Lydia and Babylon is arbitrary, and detracts from the greatness of the promise and description.—The dual דְּלָתַיִם is the proper Hebrew term for valves, folding-doors, or two-leaved gates. All interpreters admit that while this clause, in its most general sense, is perfectly appropriate to all the fortified places which were attacked by Cyrus, it is specifically and remarkably appropriate to the taking of Babylon. It can scarcely be considered a fortuitous coincidence, that Herodotus speaks of the gates which led to the river as having been left open on the night of the attack ; and Xenophon says the doors of the palace itself having been unguardedly opened, the invaders took possession of it almost without resistance. These apparent allusions to particular circumstances and events, couched under general predictions, are far more striking and conclusive proofs of inspiration than the most explicit and detailed prediction of the particular event alone could be.

2. *I will go before thee, and uneven places I will level, doors of brass I will break, and bars of iron I will cut.* The first clause describes the removal of difficulties under the figures used for the same purpose in chap. xl. 4. The other clause would seem at first sight to contain an analogous figure ; but it really includes one of those minute coincidences with history, of which we have already had an example in the preceding verse. Herodotus and Abydenus say expressly that the gates of Babylon were all of brass. (Compare Ps. cvii. 16.)

3. *And I will give the treasures of darkness and hidden riches of secret places, in order that thou mayest know that I Jehovah, the (one) calling thee by name, am the God of Israel.* It is thought by some eminent writers that no conquests have ever been attended with such acquisitions of wealth as those of Cyrus. Pliny's account of what he obtained from Crœsus makes it, according to Brerewood's computation, more than 126,000,000 pounds sterling. The last clause gives a reason why this circumstance is mentioned, namely, in order that Cyrus might be able to identify the Being who brought it to pass with the Being who foretold it. The same consideration will account for the mention of the name of Cyrus ; so that even if it were a bolder violation of analogy and usage than it is, there would still be a sufficient explanation of it furnished by the divine purpose to exert a direct influence through this prediction upon Cyrus himself. That such an influence was really exerted by the writings of Isaiah is expressly asserted by Josephus, and would seem to be implied in the monarch's solemn recognition of Jehovah as the true God, and the author of his successes (Ezra i. 2).

4. *For the sake of my servant Jacob and Israel my chosen, therefore will I call thee by thy name, I will give thee a title and thou hast not known me.* Not only for God's glory in the general, but with a view to the promotion of his gracious purposes towards Israel. The ו before אֶקְרָא introduces the apodosis, and may be taken as equivalent to *therefore.*—The sense of *speaking kindly*, which the modern writers give to אֲכַנְּךָ, is here much less appropriate than that of giving a title of honour, with apparent reference to the

epithets of *shepherd* and *anointed*, bestowed on Cyrus alone among the heathen princes. *Thou hast not known me* may either mean that he was not a follower of the true religion, or that the name was given long before he did or could know anything of Him who gave it. The verb expresses past time not in reference to the date of the prediction, but to that of the fulfilment.

5. *I am Jehovah* (*i. e.* the eternal, self-existent God) *and there is no other; except me there is no God; I will gird thee and thou hast not known me.* What is said before of naming him is here said of girding him, *i. e.* investing him with royal dignity or personally strengthening him; both may be included.

6. *That they may know, from the rising of the sun to the west* (or *to his going down*), *that there is none without me; I am Jehovah, and there is no other.* What was said before of Cyrus in particular is now said of men in general, viz., that they must be convinced in this way that the God of Israel is the one true God. Some of the Jewish critics regard the final letter of מערבה as a suffix referring to the feminine noun שֶׁמֶשׁ, notwithstanding the absence of mappik. The noun to which it is annexed would then have its primary sense (*occasus*, setting); otherwise it is a feminine designation of the west.

7. *Forming light and creating darkness, making peace and creating evil, I* (*am*) *Jehovah doing all these* (*things*). Saadias, followed by Vitringa, Lowth, J. D. Michaelis, Henderson, and Umbreit, supposes an allusion to the dualism or doctrine of two co-eternal principles as held by the ancient Persians. Gesenius objects that the terms are too indefinite, and their general sense too obvious, to admit of this specific application. But this whole passage is characterized by the recurrence of expressions, the generic sense of which seems clear, but which, at the same time, seem to bear and even to require a more specific explanation, unless we choose rather to assume an extraordinary series of fortuitous coincidences. The open doors, the gates of brass, the hidden treasures, are examples of this double sense, if such it may be called, within the compass of three verses. This analogy makes it rather probable than otherwise that in the case before us, while the Prophet's language may be naturally taken as a general description of God's universal power, an allusion was intended to the great distinctive doctrine of the faith in which Cyrus had most probably been educated. For although it cannot be distinctly proved, it can as little be disproved, and is intrinsically altogether credible, that the doctrine of the Zendavesta is as old as Cyrus.

8. *Drop* (or *distil*), *ye heavens, from above, and let the clouds pour out righteousness; let the earth open, and let salvation and righteousness grow, let her bring* (*them*) *forth together. I Jehovah have created it.* There is a singular *equivoque* in the common version of the first clause, *Drop down, ye heavens, from above,* which might seem to be a call upon the skies to fall, if the sense were not determined by the parallel expression. The prediction of events in the form of a command is peculiarly frequent in Isaiah's later prophecies. The modern explanation of צֶדֶק and צְדָקָה as meaning victory, prosperity, &c., is entirely arbitrary, as we have already seen in other cases. The manifestation of God's righteousness, including his fidelity to his engagements, is constantly recognised in Scripture as one chief end of his dispensations.—In the second clause there is a difficulty of construction, arising from the use of the plural form יִפְרוּ, to explain which some make אֶרֶץ a collective, others, יֵשַׁע. (Compare chap. xvi. 4, and Ps.

cxix. 103.) After all attempts, however, to resolve the syntax, the most satisfactory construction, although not the most consistent with the Masoretic accents, is the one proposed by Kimchi, who connects the plural verb with the next two nouns, and repeats אֶרֶץ as the subject of תַּצְמִיחַ. Next to this is the one given by Luzzatto, who makes יִפְרוּ mean *bring forth* (as in Deut. xxix. 17) and agree with שָׁמַיִם.—J. D. Michaelis explains this whole verse as relating to prophecy and its fulfilment.

9. *Woe to* (or *alas for*) *him striving with his Maker—a potsherd with potsherds of earth. Shall clay say to its former, What art thou doing? and thy work, He has no hands?* The translation of הוֹי as a simple exclamation by Hitzig (*Ha!*) and Ewald (*O!*) does not meet the requisitions either of general usage or the context, which require it to be taken as an expression of displeasure, or sympathy, or both.—Striving with God is not merely active resistance, but opposition of judgment and affection.—The word יֹצְרוֹ, used twice in this verse, is peculiarly expressive; because it derives from etymology the general sense of *former, fashioner*, and from usage the specific sense of *potter*, which is in strict agreement with the figurative language of both clauses.—The second member of the first clause has been very variously construed. The analogy of what precedes would seem to make it mean, *woe to the potsherds* (*striving*) *with the potsherds of the earth*. But this is universally agreed to be inadmissible, a proof that the principle of parallelism has its limitations. Mariana ingeniously but needlessly proposes to read חָרָשׁ֫י : let the potsherd strive with the workmen (*i. e.* potters) of the earth. Vitringa applies the same construction to the common text: let the potsherd strive with the potsherds of the earth, but not with God. The Peshito renders it, *a potsherd of* (or *from*) *the potsherds of the earth*, thus making the whole phrase a description of the weakness and insignificance of man. This construction is adopted by the modern writers, almost without exception; most of whom, however, give to אֵת its proper sense of *with*, which they suppose to imply likeness and relationship, like עִם in Eccles. ii. 16.—It seems to be a just observation of Hitzig, that *earth* is not mentioned as the dwelling of the potsherd, but as its material, which is indeed the predominant usage of אֲדָמָה as distinguished from אֶרֶץ. The verb at the beginning of the last clause might be rendered either *does, will, can*, or *should say;* but all that is necessary to the writer's purpose may be considered as implied or included in the simple future. (Compare chap. x. 15, and vol. i. p. 230.) The same thing is substantially true of the verb תַּעֲשֶׂה; but in this case, the exact force of the Hebrew word may be best expressed by our compound present, *what art thou doing* or *about to do?* This is the common Hebrew formula for calling to account, or questioning the propriety of what one does. (See Job. ix. 12, Eccles. viii. 4, Dan. iv. 32.)—The last words of the verse have also been the subject of many discordant explanations. Some of the older writers make them a continuation of the same speech: *What art thou doing? and* (as *for*) *thy work, it has no hands, i. e.* it is unfinished. But most interpreters agree that *thy work* introduces a new speaker. *And* (*shall*) *thy work* (*say of thee*) *he has no hands?* The unexpected introduction of the second person (*thy work*) led Houbigant and Lowth to suppose a transposition of the pronouns, and to read *his work* and *thou hast no hands*, which may be safely set aside as a violent and worthless emendation. Maurer accounts for the second person by supposing it to be employed indefinitely, *thy work i. e.* the work of any one to whom the words may be addressed. Hitzig

still better makes the Prophet pass abruptly from the sign to the thing signified, from the supposed case to the real one, from the potter to Jehovah. *There are no hands to him, i. e.* he has no power. The absurdity consists in the thing made denying the existence of the hands by which it was itself produced. The essential idea is the same as in chap. x. 15, but the expression here much stronger, since the instrument is not merely charged with exalting itself above the efficient agent, but the creature with denying the power or skill of its Creator.—The restriction of this verse, and of those which follow, to the Babylonians, or the Jews in exile, is entirely arbitrary and at variance with the context, which refers to the conquests of Cyrus and their consequences, not as the main subject of the prophecy, but as illustrations of a general truth.—The form of speech used by Paul in Rom. ix. 20, (*why hast thou made me thus?*) is not a version but a paraphrase of מַה־תַּעֲשֶׂה, in which however it is really included.

10. *Woe to (him) saying to a father, What wilt thou beget, and to a woman, What wilt thou bring forth?* The same idea is again expressed, but in a form still more emphatic and revolting. The incongruities which have perplexed interpreters in this verse are intentional aggravations of the impious absurdity which it describes. The arbitrary change of the future to the present (*what begettest thou?*) or the past (*what hast thou brought forth?*) is not only incorrect in point of grammar, but subversive of the writer's main design, which is to represent the doubt and discontent of men in reference to God's future dealings with them as no less monstrous than the supposition of a child's objection to its own birth. Such an objection, it is true, cannot be offered in the case supposed; but in the real case it ought to be held equally impossible. This view of the Prophet's meaning, if correct, of course precludes the explanation of the words as a complaint of weakness or deformity, or an expression of disgust with life like that in Job iii. 20, and Jeremiah xx. 14.

11. *Thus saith Jehovah, the Holy One of Israel and his Maker, Ask me (of) the things to come, concerning my sons and concerning the work of my hands ye may command me.* The Septuagint divides the sentence differently, and reads ὁ ποιήσας τὰ ἐπερχόμενα. This, which seems to be a mere inadvertence or mistake, is regarded by Lowth as a sufficient reason for a change of text, and he translates accordingly *he that formeth the things which are to come.* All other writers seem to follow the Masoretic interpunction, which connects the participle with the second clause. Verbs of asking, as in Latin, govern two accusatives. (See Ps. cxxxvii. 3).—Vitringa takes שְׁאָלוּנִי as a preterite, and makes the last clause an interrogation, *They ask me, and will ye command me?* But we have then an abrupt transition, not only from affirmation to interrogation, but from the third to the second person. Hitzig removes one of these anomalies by aggravating the other, reading both the verbs interrogatively, *do they ask? and will ye command?* By far the simplest syntax is the common one, which makes the first verb an imperative, analogous in form to שְׁמָעוּנִי (Gen. xxiii. 8), whereas the preterite would be שְׁאָלוּנִי, as in Ps. cxxxvii. 3. (Compare שְׁאָלָה, Gen. xxxii. 18). Some who adopt this explanation of the first verb give the other an imperative form also, a needless and dubious assimilation. There is also a diversity of judgment as to the relation of these verbs, and of the sentences in which they stand to one another. Most of the late interpreters suppose an antithetical relation, and explain the cause as meaning, you may ask me about things to come, but leave the disposal of my children to myself. This not only requires an adversative particle to be inserted,

which is often the force of the Hebrew copulative, but involves a distinction without a difference ; since the fortunes of God's children were themselves *things to come,* and the very things to come respecting which the people would be probably most anxious to inquire.   It is better therefore to regard the parallelism as synonymous, not antithetical, and to understand both verbs as conceding an indulgence to those who are addressed.   You may ask me concerning things to come, for I am able to inform you ; you may trust my children to my care, for I am abundantly able to protect them.— צִוָּה עַל is a common expression for giving one authority over any thing or person, or in other words committing it to him, and leaving it at his disposal.—For the meaning of *work of my hands* as an equivalent to *my children* or *my people,* see vol. i. p. 364.

12. *I made the earth, and man upon it I created; I, my hands, spread the heavens, and all their host commanded.*   This is a justification of the claim in the last clause of the foregoing verse, or a statement of the reason why he could be trusted to protect his people, namely, because he was almighty, and had proved himself to be so in creation.—The personal pronoun is emphatic in both clauses, as if he had said, *It is I who made,* or *I (and no other) made,* &c.   The construction of the second of these pronouns with *my hands* has been variously explained.   Some regard the latter as equivalent to an ablative of instrument in Latin : *I with my hands have spread,* &c.   Others consider it an instance of the idiom which adds the personal pronoun to the suffix for the sake of emphasis : *I, my hands spread, i. e.* my own hands spread.   In such constructions the personal pronoun commonly stands last.   A third supposition is that the pronoun is in apposition with the noun itself, and is not so much emphatic as explanatory.   *I (that is to say, my hands) have spread.*   (Compare Ps. iii. 5, xvii. 13, 14, xliv. 3, lx. 7.)—The last words of the verse admit of two explanations.   We may understand the figure as a military one, and give the verb the military sense of *commanding.*   Or we may take *host* as a common expression for contents or inhabitants, and understand the verb as meaning *called into existence.* (Compare Ps. xxxiii. 9.)   In itself, the former explanation seems entitled to the preference ; but it requires the verb to be construed as an indefinite præter or a present, whereas all the other verbs, though similar in form, relate to a determinate past time, viz. the time of the creation.

13. *I (and no other) raised him up in righteousness, and all his ways will I make straight (or level); (it is) he (that) shall build my city, and my captivity (or exiles) he will send (home), not for reward, and not for hire, saith Jehovah of hosts.*   From the general proof of divine power afforded by creation, he descends to the particular exercise of his omnipotence and wisdom in the raising up of Cyrus, who is thus referred to without the express mention of his name, because he had been previously made the subject of a similiar appeal, and the Prophet simply takes up the thread which he had dropped at the close of the fifth verse, or perhaps of the seventh.   From the sense of *raising up in righteousness,* see above on chaps. xli. 2, 25, xlii. 6.   In this, as well as in the other places, Vitringa supposes an allusion to the personal character of Cyrus, which he defends with great warmth against Burnet's remark in his History of the Reformation, that God sometimes uses bad men as his instruments, such as the cruel Cyrus.   The statements of Herodotus to this effect Vitringa treats as fabulous, and claims full credit for the glowing pictures of the Cyropaedia. This distinction is not only strange in itself, but completely at war with the conclusions of the ablest modern critics and historians.   Nor is there the

least need of insisting thus upon the moral excellence of Cyrus, who in either case was just as really a *consecrated* instrument of the divine righteousness, as the Medes and Persians generally, who are so described in chap. xiii. 3. (See vol. i. p. 269.) At the same time allowance must be made for the difference between what Cyrus was before and after he became acquainted with the true religion. (See above, on ver. 3.) The figure of straight or level paths has the same sense as in chap. xl. 3. —*My city*, *i. e.* the holy city, Jerusalem, of which Cyrus was indirectly the rebuilder.—The form of the verb *send* here used is not unfrequently applied to the setting free of prisoners or slaves.—The last clause seems decisive of the question whether chap. xliii. 3, 4, should be understood as a general declaration of God's distinguishing affection for his people, disposing him to favour them at the expense of other nations, or as a specific promise that Cyrus should conquer Ethiopia and Egypt, as a compensation for releasing Israel, in which case he could not be said, in any appropriate sense, to have set them free without reward or hire.

14. *Thus saith Jehovah, The toil of Egypt, and the gain of Cush, and the Sebaim men of measure unto thee shall pass, and to thee shall they belong, after thee shall they go, in chains shall they pass over* (or *along*)*; and unto thee shall they bow themselves, to thee shall they pray* (saying)*, Only in thee* (is) *God, and there is none besides, no* (other) *God.* The first clause specifies labour and traffic as the two great sources of wealth, here put for wealth itself, or for the people who possessed it. סְבָאִים is construed by some writers as a genitive dependent on סְחַר *the trade of Ethiopia and of the Sabeans;* by others, as the nominative to the next verb, the *Sabeans* shall pass over to thee ; a grammatical distinction not affecting the sense. For the true sense of the geographical or national names here mentioned, see above on chap. xliii. 3. In both places they are named, as Hitzig well observes, by way of sample (*beispielsweise*) for the heathen world. To the reasons before given for this interpretation, we may here add the general reference to idolaters in ver. 16.—The Targum seems to explain מִדָּה here as meaning *trade* (סחורא); and others give it that of *tribute*, which has in Chaldee (Ezra iv. 20, and in Neh. v. 4). But the meaning *men of measure, i. e.* of extraordinary stature, is determined by the analogy of Num. xiii. 32, 1 Chron. xi. 23, xx. 6, and confirmed by the description of the Ethiopians in ancient history, Herodotus speaking of them as μέγιστοι ἀνθρώπων, and Solinus more specifically as *duodecim pedes longi.* According to Knobel, their stature is here mentioned, in order to shew that they were able-bodied, and would be profitable servants to the Jews ; but most interpreters correctly understand it as a circumstance intended to enhance the glory and importance of the conquest.—עָלַיִךְ might be understood to mean *against thee;* but this sense is precluded by the next phrase, *they shall be* (or *belong*) *to thee,* as well as by the epexegetical addition, *they shall pass in chains.* Whether these are here considered as imposed by their conquerors, or by themselves in token of a voluntary submission, is a question which the words themselves leave undecided. The same thing may be said of the prostration mentioned afterwards, which in itself might be considered as denoting the customary oriental act of obeisance or civil adoration, although usually found in such connections as require it to be taken in a religious sense, which is here further indicated by the addition of the verb to pray. The seeming incongruity of thus ascribing divine honours to a creature, may be avoided by taking אֵלַיִךְ in a local sense, as meaning *towards thee,* but not to *thee*, as the object of the adoration. But a simpler

solution of the difficulty is, that these strong expressions were employed because the explanation was to follow. Instead of saying, *they shall worship God who dwells in thee,* the Prophet makes his language more expressive by saying, *they shall worship thee;* and then immediately explains his own language by adding their acknowledgment, *only in thee is God,* or to give the Hebrew word its full force, *an almighty God,* implying that the gods of other nations were but gods in name. This exclusive recognition of the God of Israel is then repeated in a way which may to some seem tautological, but which is really emphatic in a high degree.—The application of the suffixes in this verse to Cyrus is inconsistent with the Masoretic pointing, which makes them feminine. This is regarded by Vitringa and Gesenius as an oversight of Grotius, occasioned by his looking at the Latin text and not the Hebrew. But the same construction seems to be approved by Aben Ezra and Ewald, who must therefore be considered as departing from the common punctuation. The feminine pronouns of the common text may be referred either to גָּלוּת (*captivity*) in ver. 13, or to עִירִי (*my city*) in the same verse, or to עֲדַת יִשְׂרָאֵל (*the congregation of Israel*), in all which cases the real object of address is still substantially the same, viz., the ancient church or chosen people.—The question now presents itself, in what sense the subjection of the nations is here promised. That a literal conquest of Ethiopia and Egypt by the Jews themselves is here predicted, none can maintain but those who wish to fasten on Isaiah the charge of ignorance or gross imposture. An ingenious Jewish writer of our own day, Luzzatto, supposes the Prophet to foretell a literal subjection of these countries, not by Israel, but by Cyrus; and explains the whole verse as describing the conduct of the captives when they should *pass by* the land of Israel *in chains* on their way to Persia, and acknowledge the supremacy of Jehovah by worshipping towards his earthly residence. In order to sustain this ingenious and original interpretation, its author is under the necessity of taking יְגִיעַ and סְחַר as elliptical expressions for אַנְשֵׁי יְגִיעַ and אַנְשֵׁי מִסְחָר, men of labour, men of traffic, *i. e.* labourers and traders. He is also forced to explain away some of the most significant expressions, such as *they shall be thine, they shall go after thee,* as merely indicating disposition or desire. The violence thus done to the obvious meaning of the Prophet's language is sufficient to condemn the exposition which involves it. The same interpretation is substantially proposed by Ewald, but more briefly and obscurely, and with his usual omission of all reference to other writers, which leaves it doubtful whether he derived it from Luzzatto, or arrived at it by an independent process. Enough has now been said to shew that the most natural interpretation of the passage is the common one which makes it a prophecy of moral and spiritual conquests, to be wrought by the church over the nations, and, as one illustrious example, by the Jews' religion over the heathenism of many countries, not excepting the literal Ethiopia, as we learn from Acts viii. 27.

15. *Verily thou art a God hiding thyself, O God of Israel, the Saviour!* The abrupt transition here has much perplexed interpreters. Vitringa effects nothing by his favourite and far-fetched supposition of a responsive choir or chorus. Ewald and Luzzatto suppose the words of the Egyptian captives to be still continued. It is far more natural to take the verse as an apostrophe, expressive of the Prophet's own strong feelings in contrasting what God had done and would yet do, the darkness of the present with the brightness of the future. If these things are to be hereafter, then, O thou Saviour of thy people, thou art indeed a God that hides himself, that is to

say, conceals his purposes of mercy under the darkness of his present dispensations. Let it be observed, however, that the same words, which furnish a vehicle of personal emotion to the Prophet, are in fact a formula of wider import, and contain the statement of a general truth. Ewald assumes two distinct propositions, reading the last clause thus, *the God of Israel is a Saviour;* which is perfectly grammatical and agreeable to usage, but unnecessary here and undesirable, because it detracts from the simplicity and unity of the construction.

16. *They are ashamed and also confounded all of them together, they are gone into confusion* (or *away in confusion*)—*the carvers of images.* Unless we assume, without necessity or warrant, an abrupt and perfectly capricious change of subject, this verse must contain the conclusion of the process described in the foregoing context. We might, therefore, expect to find Egypt, Ethiopia, and Seba introduced again by name; but, instead of these, the sentence closes with a general expression, which has already been referred to as a proof that the war in question is a spiritual war, and that the enemies to be subdued are not certain nations in themselves considered, but the heathen world, the vast mixed multitude who worship idols. These are described as the carvers or artificers of images, which strengthens the conclusion before drawn, that the smith and carpenter, and cook and baker, and cultivator of chap. xliv. 12–16, are one and the same person, viz. the idolatrous devotee himself.

17. *Israel is saved in Jehovah* (*with*) *an everlasting salvation* (literally, *salvation of ages* or *eternities*); *ye shall not be ashamed, and ye shall not be confounded for ever* (literally, *until the ages of eternity*), or as the English Version has it, *world without end.* This is the counterpart and contrast to the threatening in the verse preceding, upon which it throws some light by shewing that the shame and confusion which awaits the idolater is not mere wounded pride or sense of disappointment, but the loss and opposite of that salvation which is promised to God's people, or in other words, eternal perdition. Israel is saved already, *i. e.* his salvation is secured, not merely *through* the Lord but *in* him, *i. e.* by virtue of an intimate and vital union with him, as genuine and living members of his body. The general form of this solemn declaration, and the eternity again and again predicated of the salvation promised, seem to shew that the Israel of this text and of others like it, is not the Jewish people. considered simply as an ancient nation, but the Jewish people considered as the church of God, a body which has never ceased and never will cease to exist and claim the promises.

18. *For thus saith Jehovah, the creator of the heavens—he is God—the former of the earth and its maker—he established it—not in vain* (or *not to be empty*) *did he create it—to dwell in* (or *to be inhabited*) *he formed it—I am Jehovah, and there is none besides.* This verse assigns a reason for believing in the threatening and the promise of the two preceding verses, viz. that he who uttered them not only made the heavens and the earth, but made them for a certain purpose which must be accomplished. The only difficulty of construction is the question where Jehovah's words begin, and this admits of several different answers. We may read, *Thus saith Jehovah: The creator of the heavens is God;* in which case the divine address begins with a formal statement of the argument derived from the creation. Again, we may read, *Thus saith Jehovah, The creator of the heavens is the God who formed the earth.* This is Vitringa's explanation of the verse, which he regards as a denial of the doctrine that the heavens

and the earth derive their origin from different creators. But most interpreters suppose the beginning of Jehovah's own words to be marked by
the introduction of the pronoun of the first person, *I am Jehovah, and
there is no other*. All that precedes is then to be regarded as a description
of the speaker, including two parenthetical propositions, each beginning
with the pronoun הוּא : *the creator of the heavens (he is God), the former of
the earth and its maker (he established it)*.—Some understand כּוֹנְנָהּ to mean
prepared (or *fitted*) *it*, *i. e.* for man to dwell in. But the other sense is
favoured by the predominant usage of the verb, and by the analogy of
Ps. cxix. 90. The common version of the next clause, *he created it not in
vain*, is admissible, but less expressive than the more specific rendering,
he created it not (to be) a waste (or *empty*). Grotius understands by הָאָרֶץ,
the Holy Land, and by the whole clause that God would not let it remain
uninhabited. But the antithesis with *heavens* makes the wider sense more
natural, in which the more restricted one, as Hitzig has suggested, may be
comprehended. The earth, and the Holy Land, as part of it, was made
to be inhabited, not empty.—Vitringa's distinctions between making,
forming, and creating, though ingenious, are no more natural or necessary
here than in chap. xliii. 7. (See above, p. 150.) In the last clause
Jehovah is employed as a descriptive title, and is really equivalent to אֵל,
which the Prophet uses in a similar connection in ver. 22 below.

19. *Not in secret have I spoken, in a dark place of the earth* (or *in a place,
to wit, a land of darkness*). *I have not said to the seed of Jacob, In vain
seek ye me. I (am) Jehovah, speaking truth, declaring rectitude* (or *right
things*). The doctrine of the preceding verse is no new revelation, but one
long ago and universally made known. Vitringa, Lowth, Ewald, and Umbreit
suppose an allusion to the mysterious and doubtful responses of the heathen
oracles. The objections of Gesenius are of no more weight than in vers.
1, 2, 3, the analogy of which places makes it not improbable that such an
allusion to the oracles is couched under the general terms of the verse
before us.—Of the next clause there are several distinct interpretations.
The oldest and most common makes it mean that God had not required the
people to consult him in relation to futurity without obtaining satisfactory
responses. According to Hitzig, he had not required them to seek him
(*i. e.* serve or worship him) for nothing, or without reward. J. D.
Michaelis and Luzzatto give a local sense to תֹּהוּ, *in the wilderness*, which
Hendewerk explains as equivalent to *land of darkness*, both denoting the
heathen world, in which Jehovah had not taught his people to seek him or
expect responses from him.—Lowth gives מֵישָׁרִים the specific sense of
direct answers, as opposed to the equivocal responses of the oracles ; but
this is hardly justified by usage, which requires both this word and the
parallel expression to be here taken in the sense of *truth*.

20. *Gather yourselves and come, draw near together, ye escaped of the
nations. They know not, those carrying the wood, their graven image, and
praying to a God (who) cannot save.* In the first clause the idolaters are
addressed directly ; in the second they are spoken of again in the third
person. The challenge or summons at the beginning is precisely similar
to that in chap. xli. 21 and xliii. 9. *Escaped of the nations* has been variously explained to mean the Jews who had escaped from the oppression of
the Gentiles, and the Gentiles who had escaped from the dominion of
idolatry. But these last would scarcely have been summoned to a contest.
On the whole, it seems most natural to understand the nations who survived the judgments sent by God upon them. The Hebrew phrase is in

itself ambiguous, the noun added to פְּלִיטִי sometimes denoting the whole body, out of which a remnant has escaped, sometimes the power from which they are delivered. (Compare Judges xii. 4, Ezra vi. 9, vii. 16, Obad. xi., with Jer. xlv. 28, Ezek. vi. 8.) The predominant usage and the context here decide in favour of the first interpretation. Gesenius and Luzzato both apply the phrase to the conquests of Cyrus, but in contrary senses. The first regards it as describing those whom he should spare, the other those whom he should conquer, and who are exhibited as fleeing with their idols on their shoulders. But the explanation which agrees best with the whole connection is the one that supposes the idolaters still left (*i. e.* neither converted nor destroyed) to be the object of address. If there are any still absurd enough to carry about a wooden god, and pray to one who cannot save, let them assemble and draw near.—*They do not know* is commonly explained to mean *they have no knowledge;* but it is more accordant with the usage of the language to supply a specific object. They do not know it, or, they do not know what they are doing, they are not conscious of their own impiety and folly.—The verse contains two indirect reflections on the idols : first, that they are wooden ; then, that they are lifeless and dependent on their worshippers for locomotion.

21. *Bring forward and bring near! Yea, let them consult together. Who has caused this to be heard of old, since then declared it? Have not I Je-hovah? and there is no other God besides me; a righteous and a saving God, there is none besides me.* The object of the verbs in the first clause, according to Vitringa, is *your cause* or *your arguments*, as in chap. xli. 21. This, which Gesenius is pleased to regard as an ignorant blunder of his great predecessor, has nevertheless commended itself to the judgment of most later writers. Gesenius himself explains the first clause as meaning *pro·claim it, and bring them near* (*i.e.* the heathen), without explaining what is to be proclaimed, or by whom. According to Vitringa's exposition, the idolaters are called upon to state their case, and to defend it.—The change of person in the next clause implies that they are unable or unwilling to accept the challenge, or at least in doubt and hesitation with respect to it. They are therefore invited to deliberate together, or, as some understand it, to take counsel of those wiser than themselves. Instead of waiting longer for their plea, however, he presents his own, in the common form of an interrogation, asking who, except himself, had given evidence of prescience by explicitly foretelling events still far distant, and of saving power by delivering his people from calamity and bondage.—מֵאָז, although it strictly has relation to a determinate past time, seems here to be employed indefinitely, as an equivalent to מִקֶּדֶם.—*Have not I Jehovah, and there is no other God besides me?* is a Hebrew idiom equivalent to the English question, *Have not I, besides whom there is no other God?*

22. *Turn unto me and be saved, all ye ends of the earth, for I am God, and there is none besides.* From the preceding declarations, it might seem to follow that the Gentile world had nothing to expect but the perdition threatened in ver. 15. But now the Prophet brings to view a gracious alternative, inviting them to choose between destruction and submission, and shewing that the drift of the foregoing argument was not to drive the heathen to despair, but to shut them up to the necessity of seeking safety in the favour of the one true God, whose exclusive deity is expressly made the ground of the exhortation.—פְּנוּ does not correspond exactly to the English *look*, but denotes the act of *turning round* in order to look in a different direction. The text therefore bears a strong analogy to those in

which the heathen, when enlightened, are described as *turning* from their idols unto God. (See 1 Thess. i. 9; Acts xiv. 15, xv. 19.)—*The ends of the earth* is a phrase inclusive of all nations, and is frequently employed in reference to the conversion of the Gentiles. (See Ps. xxii. 28, lxxii. 8; Zech. ix. 10.) De Wette's version, *let yourselves be saved*, appears to be a needless refinement on the simple meaning of the passive.—The question, whether Christ is to be regarded as the speaker in this passage, is of little exegetical importance. To us, who know that it is only through him that the Father saves, this supposition appears altogether natural; but it does not follow that any such impression would be made, or was intended to be made, upon an ancient reader.

23. *By myself I have sworn; the word is gone out of a mouth of righteousness, and shall not return, that unto me shall bow every knee, shall swear every tongue.* The form of the divine oath elsewhere used is *by my life*, or *as I live*. (Num. xiv. 21, 28; Deut. xxxii. 40.) Hence Paul, in his quotation of this text (Rom. xiv. 11), uses the formula, Ζῶ ἐγώ, which may be regarded as an accurate paraphrase, though not as a rigorous translation. —The construction of the words צְדָקָה דָּבָר has perplexed interpreters. Jerome arbitrarily transposes them, and translates the phrase as if it were דְּבַר צְדָקָה *word of righteousness*. Rosenmüller gains the same end by supposing an unusual combination, *righteousness-word*, like עֲנוֹת־צֶרֶק in Ps. xlv. 5. Most of the modern writers make צְדָקָה the subject of the verb יָצָא, notwithstanding the diversity of gender, and regard וְלֹא as equivalent to אֲשֶׁר לֹא. *Truth has gone out of my mouth, a word which shall not return.* The simplest construction, although none of the later writers seem to have adopted it, is that proposed by J. D. Michaelis, who regards פִּ' as the construct form of פֶּה without a suffix, and צְדָקָה as a genitive dependent on it, *the mouth of righteousness* or *truth* (*aus dem untrüglichen Munde*).—A word, *i.e.* a promise or a prophecy, is said in Hebrew to *return* when it is cancelled or recalled. (See Isaiah lv. 11.) The kneeling and swearing in the last clause are acts of homage, fealty, or allegiance, which usually went together (1 Kings xix. 18), and involved a solemn recognition of the sovereignty of him to whom they were tendered. This verse affords a clear illustration of the difference between the act of *swearing to* and *swearing by* another. (Compare chap. xix. 18, vol. i. p. 356. —This text is twice applied by Paul to Christ (Rom. xiv. 11; Phil. ii. 10), in proof of his regal and judicial sovereignty. It does not necessarily predict that all shall be converted to him, since the terms are such as to include both a voluntary and a compulsory submission, and in one of these ways all, without exception, shall yet recognize him as their rightful sovereign.

24. *Only in Jehovah have I, says he, righteousness and strength; unto him shall he come, and all that were incensed* (or *inflamed*) *at him shall be ashamed.* Joseph Kimchi takes the first words as an oath, *Yes, by Jehovah!* David Kimchi gives the אַךְ its proper meaning, and connects the clause with the last words of the foregoing verse.—*Every tongue shall swear* (*but*) *only by Jehovah*. Most interpreters suppose a sentence to begin with this verse, and בַּיהוָֹה to mean *in Jehovah*. They differ very much among themselves, however, as to the meaning of the words אָמַר לִי. Vitringa, Ewald, and some others, render the phrase *said to me*, but without satisfactorily shewing its relation to the context. The most usual construction is, *one says of me*, which is grammatical, but seems to make the clause

unmeaning, or at least superfluous. Perhaps the best construction is De Dieu's, who insulates אָמַר, and understands it to mean *says one* or *says he*, while he connects the following words with לִי, as meaning *are to me*, the only Hebrew phrase corresponding to *I have*. In either case the general meaning evidently is, that God alone can justify or give protection. Vitringa's explanation of עֹז as meaning *grace*, is as groundless as the similar construction of צְדָקָה by the modern Germans.—The Masoretic interpunction refers the singular verb יָבוֹא and the plural יֵבֹשׁוּ to the same subject, namely, that which follows. But the difference of number seems designed to indicate a difference of subject, corresponding to the kinds of submission hinted at in ver. 23. The singular יָבוֹא may naturally have a common subject with the singular אָמַר, viz., the "every one" who should eventually bow the knee and swear allegiance to Jehovah, while the plural יֵבֹשׁוּ may be regularly construed with the plural נֶחֱרִים. Jarchi explains the whole of the last clause as describing the repentance of Jehovah's enemies; but this is really the meaning only of עָדָיו יָבוֹא, while the rest describes the final and desperate confusion of incorrigible sinners, as in ver. 16. On the phrase עָדָיו יָבוֹא compare chap. xix. 22, and on נחרים בו chap. xli. 22, and Cant. i. 6.

25. *In Jehovah shall be justified and boast themselves* (or *glory*) *all the seed of Israel*. This closing promise is restricted by Jarchi, in the genuine spirit of Rabbinism, to the literal or natural descendants of Jacob; but this is less surprising when we know that he actually violates the syntax of the preceding verse in order to bring אַךְ and לִי together in the sense of *only to me*, the speaker being Israel! So far is this from being the correct interpretation of the verse, that it is really intended to wind up the previous addresses to the Gentiles with a solemn declaration of their true relation to the chosen people, as composed of those who really believed and feared God, whether Jews or Gentiles. This principle was recognised in every admission of a proselyte to the communion of the ancient church, and at the change of dispensations it is clearly and repeatedly asserted as a fundamental law of Christ's kingdom under every variety of form. (See Rom. x. 12; Gal. iii. 28, 29; Col. iii. 11.)

Chapter 46

INTERPRETERS are strangely divided in opinion as to the connection of this chapter with the context. The arbitrary and precarious nature of their judgments may be gathered from the fact, that Ewald separates the first two verses from the body of the chapter and connects them with the one before it, while Hendewerk, on the other hand, commences a new "cycle" with the first verse of this chapter, and Knobel dogmatically represents it as an isolated composition, unconnected either with what goes before or follows. Even the older writers, who maintain the continuity of the discourse, appear to look upon the order of its parts as being not so much an organic articulation as a mere mechanical juxtaposition. They are therefore obliged to assume abrupt transitions, which, instead of explaining anything else, need to be explained themselves.

All this confusion is the fruit of the erroneous exegetical hypothesis, that the main subject and occasion of these later prophecies is the Babylonish exile and the liberation from it, and that with these the other topics must be violently brought into connection by assuming a sufficiency of types and double senses, or by charging the whole discourse with incoherence. Equally false, but far less extensive in its influence, is the assumption that the whole relates to Christ and to the new dispensation, so that even what is said of Babylon and Cyrus must be metaphorically understood. Common to both hypotheses is the arbitrary and exclusive application of the most comprehensive language to a part of what it really expresses, and a distorted view of the Prophet's themes considered in their mutual relations and connections. The whole becomes perspicuous, continuous, and orderly, as soon as we admit what has been already proved to be the true hypothesis, viz. that the great theme of these prophecies is God's designs and dealings with the church and with the world, and that the specific predictions which are introduced are introduced as parts or as illustrations of this one great argument. By thus reversing the preposterous relation of the principal elements of the discourse, and restoring each to its legitimate position, the connection becomes clear and the arrangement easy.

In confirmation of the general threats and promises with which chap. xlv. is wound up, the Prophet now exhibits the particular case of the Babylonian idols, as a single instance chosen from the whole range of past and future history. They are described as fallen and gone into captivity, wholly unable to protect their worshippers or save themselves, vers. 1, 2. With these he then contrasts Jehovah's constant care of Israel in time past and in time to come, vers. 3, 4. The contrast is carried out by another description of the origin and impotence of idols, vers. 5–7, and another assertion of Jehovah's sole divinity, as proved by his knowledge and control of the future, and by the raising up of Cyrus in particular, vers. 8–11. This brings him back to the same solemn warning of approaching judgments, and the same alternative of life or death, with which the foregoing chapter closes, vers. 12, 13.

1. *Bel is bowed down, Nebo stooping; their images are* (*consigned*) *to the beasts and to the cattle. Your burdens are packed up* (*as*) *a load to the weary* (*beast*). The connection with what goes before may be indicated thus : see for example the fate of the Babylonian idols. Of these two are mentioned, either as arbitrary samples, or as chief divinities. To these names, or rather to the subject of Babylonian mythology, Gesenius devotes an excursus or appendix of thirty pages, the results of which are given in his Thesaurus and Lexicon. He connects *Bel* etymologically with the Hebrew בַּעַל, and *Nebo* with נְבָא (נְבִיא), the two corresponding to the Zeus and Hermes of the Greek mythology, or rather to the planets Jupiter and Mercury. The dignity of these two imaginary deities among the Babylonians may be learned from the extent to which these names enter into the composition of the names of men, both in sacred and profane history. Such are Belshazzar, Belteshazzar, Belesys, Nebuchadnezzar, Nebuzaradan, Nabopolassar, Nabonned, &c. Beyond this nothing more is needed for the right interpretation of the passage, where the names are simply used to represent the Babylonian gods collectively.—The verb קֹרֵס occurs only here. The Septuagint renders the two, *fallen and broken ;* the Vulgate gives the latter sense to both. But כָּרַע is the common term for stooping, bowing, especially in death (Judges v. 27; 2 Kings ix. 24; Ps. xx. 9); and that the other is substantially synonymous, may be inferred not only from the parallelism, but from the analogy of the derivative noun קֶרֶס, a hook, a tache, as being carved or bent. Although not essential to the general meaning, it is best to give the praeter and the participle their distinctive sense, as meaning strictly that the one has fallen and the other is now falling, in strict accordance with Isaiah's practice, in descriptive passages,

of hurrying the reader *in medias res*, of which we have already had repeated instances.—The pronoun in *their images* might be supposed to refer to the Babylonians, though not expressly mentioned; but as these are immediately addressed in the second person, it is best to understand the pronoun as refering to Bel and Nebo, who, as heavenly bodies or imaginary deities, are then distinguished from the images which represented them in the vulgar worship. The suggestion of J. D. Michaelis, that there may be an allusion to some actual decay of the metallic idols in the shrines of Babylon, is inconsistent with what follows in relation to their going into exile.—The Septuagint, the Targum, and Jerome, seem to understand the next clause as meaning that their images become beasts, which is scarcely intelligible. Most writers follow Kimchi and De Dieu in supplying מַשָּׂא from the other clause, *they are* (*a burden*) *to the beasts*, &c. But this assumes a very harsh ellipsis and is wholly unnecessary, since usage allows הָיִ לְ to be taken in the sense of *they are to, i. e.* they now belong to, or are abandoned and consigned to. The common version, *on the beasts*, is too paraphrastical. Kimchi supposes חַיָּה and בְּהֵמָה to be used in their distinctive sense of wild beasts and domesticated cattle, understanding by the latter, common beasts of burden, by the former camels, elephants, &c. J. D. Michaelis imagines that there may be an allusion to the mythological use of wild beasts, such as the lions of Cybele, &c. Most interpreters regard the words as simple equivalents, or at the most as merely distinguishing oxen, asses, mules, &c., from camels, dromedaries, and perhaps horses.—נְשֻׂאֹה is properly a passive participle used as a noun and meaning your *carried things* (in old English, *carriages*), the things which you have been accustomed to carry in processions or from place to place, but which are now to be carried in a very different manner, on the backs of animals, as spoil or captives. עֲמוּסוֹת properly means *lifted up* in order to be carried, but may here be rendered *packed* or *loaded*, though this last word is ambiguous.—מַשָּׂא does not necessarily denote a *heavy load*, but simply that they are a load, *i. e.* something to be carried. The idea of weight is suggested by the following word, which the Vulgate renders as an abstract meaning weariness (*usque ad lassitudinem*), but which is properly a feminine adjective agreeing with חַיָּה or בְּהֵמָה understood.

2. *They stoop, they bow together; they cannot save the load; themselves are gone into captivity.* The first clause may mean that they are now *both* fallen; or *together* may have reference to the other gods of Babylon, so as to mean that not only Bel and Nebo, but all the rest are fallen.—The last member of the first clause has been variously explained. Gesenius is disposed to make מַשָּׂא an abstract meaning *the carrying*, a sense not worth obtaining by so harsh a supposition. The Vulgate arbitrarily reverses the meaning, and instead of the thing borne understands the bearer (*non potuerunt salvare portantem*). Of those who adhere to the strict sense, *load* or *burden*, some understand by it the Babylonian state or empire, which ought to have been borne or sustained by its tutelary gods. But the most satisfactory interpretation is the one which gives the word the same sense as in ver. 1, and applies it to the images with which the beasts were charged or laden. These are then to be considered as distinguished by the writer from the gods which they represented. Bel and Nebo are unable to rescue their own images. This agrees well with the remainder of the sentence, *themselves are gone* (or literally *their self is gone*) *into captivity.* This is the only way in which the reflexive pronoun could be made emphatic here without an awkward circumlocution. There is no need, there-

fore, of explaining נַפְשָׁם to mean *their soul, i. e.* the animating principle or
spirit by which the image was supposed to be inhabited ; much less *their
desire, i. e.* the darling idols of the heathen, like חֲמוּדֵיהֶם in chap. xliv. 9.
The antithesis is really between the material images of Bel and Nebo and
and *themselves,* so far as they had any real existence. The whole god, soul
and body, all that there was of him, was gone into captivity. The idea of
the conquest and captivity of tutelary gods was common in the ancient
East, and is alluded to, besides this place, in Jer. xlviii. 7, xlix. 3 ; Hosea
x. 5, 6 ; Dan. xi. 8, to which may be added 1 Sam. v. 1.—Whether the
Prophet here refers to an actual event or an ideal one, and how the former
supposition may be reconciled with the statement of Herodotus and Diodorus, that the great image of Bel at Babylon was not destroyed until the
time of Xerxes, are questions growing out of the erroneous supposition that
the passage has exclusive reference to the conquest by Cyrus ; whereas it
may include the whole series of events which resulted in the final downfall of the Babylonian idol worship. (See vol. i. p. 266.)

3. *Hearken unto me, O house of Jacob, and all the remnant of the house of
Israel, those borne from the belly, those carried from the womb.* By the *remnant of the house of Israel* Kimchi understands the remains of the ten tribes
who were in exile ; but this is a gratuitous restriction of the meaning. The
participles rendered *borne* and *carried* are the masculine forms of those used
in ver. 1.· This repetition analogous to that in chap. xlii. 2, 3, is intended
to suggest a contrast between the failure of the idols to protect their worshippers and God's incessant care of his own people. The gods of the
heathen had to be borne by them ; but Jehovah was himself the bearer
of his followers. And this was no new thing, but coeval with their national existence. The specific reference to Egypt or the exodus is no
more necessary here than in chaps. xliv. 2, 24, xlviii. 8. The carrying
meant is that of children by the nurse or parent. The same comparison is
frequent elsewhere. (See Num. xi. 12, Deut. i. 31, Exod. xix. 4, Isa.
lxiii. 9, and compare Deut. xxxii. 11, 12, Hosea xi. 3, Isa. xl. 11.)—For
belly and *womb* Noyes, by way of euphemistic variation, substitutes *birth*
and *earliest breath.*—מִנִּי בֶטֶן is identical with מִבֶּטֶן chap. xliv. 24. The
same form of the particle occurs in Job. xx. 4, and Ps. xl. 19.

4. The figure of an infant and its nurse was not sufficient to express the
whole extent of God's fidelity and tenderness to Israel. The first of these
relations is necessarily restricted to the earliest period of life, but God's
protection is continued without limit. *And to old age I am He* (*i. e.* the
same), *and to gray hair I will bear* (*you*) ; *I have done it and I will carry
and I will bear and save* (*you*). Hitzig supposes this to mean that Israel
was already old, as in chap. xlvii. 6 ; but others much more probably
refer ·it to the future, and regard the expressions as indefinite. As I
have done in time past, so I will do hereafter. The general analogy
between the life of individuals and that of nations is sufficiently obvious,
and is finely expressed by Florus in his division of the Roman History
into the periods of childhood, youth, manhood, and old age. But Vitringa mars the beautiful analogy when he undertakes to measure off the
periods in the history of Israel from his birth in Egypt, through his
infancy in the desert, his youth under the Judges, his manhood until
Jotham, his old age until Alexander, and his *gray hairs,* or extreme old
age, beyond that period.—The reference of these terms to God himself as
the Ancient of Days (Dan. vii. 9), is too absurd to need refutation or admit
of it.

5. *To whom will ye liken me and equal and compare me, that we may be* (literally *and we shall be*) *like?* This is an indirect conclusion from the contrast in the foregoing context. If such be the power of idols, and such that of Jehovah, to whom will ye compare him? The form of expression is like that in chap. xl. 18, 25.

6. *The prodigals* (or *lavish ones*) *will weigh gold from the bag, and silver with the rod; they will hire a gilder, and he will make it a god; they will bow down, yea, they will fall prostrate.* זָלִים is commonly explained as a participle in the sense of *pouring out* or *lavishing*; but thus understood it is of difficult construction. Vitringa resolves it into הֵם זָלִים; but this is contrary to usage. If we make it agree with the subject of the verbs in ver. 5 (*ye who pour out*, &c.), we must suppose an abrupt change of person in the next clause. The first construction above given is the one proposed by Schmidius, who makes הַזָּלִים the subject of the verb יִשְׁקְלוּ. We may then explain מִפִּיס either as meaning taken out of the purse, or in reference to the bag of weights, in which sense it is used in Deut xxv. 13; Micah vi. 11. קָנֶה is properly a reed, then any rod or bar, such as the shaft of a candlestick (Exod. xxv. 31), and here the beam of a balance, or the graduated rod of a steelyard.—The verse has reference to the wealthier class of idol-worshippers.

7. *They will lift him on the shoulder, they will carry him, they will set him in his place, and he will stand* (there), *from his place he will not move; yes, one will cry to him, and he will not answer; from his distress he will* (or *can*) *not save him.* The idol is not only the work of man's hands, but entirely dependent on him for the slightest motion. No wonder, therefore, that he cannot hear the prayers of his worshippers, much less grant them the deliverance and protection which they need.

8. *Remember this and shew yourselves men; bring it home, ye apostates, to* (*your*) *mind* or (*heart*).—By *this* Jarchi understands what follows; but it rather means what goes before, viz., the proof just given of the impotence of idols, the worshippers of which, whether Jews or Gentiles, are addressed in this verse as apostates or rebels against God. The restriction of the term to apostate Jews is perfectly gratuitous.—The verb הִתְאֹשָׁשׁוּ is a ἅπαξ λεγόμενον, and admits of several different explanations. Joseph Kimchi derived it from אֵשׁ, *fire*, and explained it to mean, "be inflamed or reddened," *i. e.* blush. So the Vulgate, *confundamini*. The Targum and Jarchi understand it to mean " fortify or strengthen yourselves," and connect it with אֲשִׁישִׁים; *foundations* (chap. xvi. 7). Bochart derives it from אִישׁ, *a man*, and identifies it with the ἀνδρίζεσθε of 1 Cor. xvi. 13. Vitringa objects that the apostates would not be exhorted to fortify themselves in unbelief. Hitzig replies that the clauses are addressed to different parties, which is wholly arbitrary. Gesenius removes the objection by giving to the verb the sense of acting rationally, not like children (1 Cor. xiv. 20), or as Kimchi says, like beasts which have neither judgment nor consideration. Vitringa objects, moreover, that the form would be הִתְאַישִׁישׁוּ; Hitzig more plausibly, that it would be הִתְאַנְשׁוּ from the acknowledged root אָנַשׁ; but there is no absurdity in supposing that the verbal form was derived from the contracted אִישׁ which is in common use.—As an exegetical monstrosity it may be stated here that Paulus explains the Hebrew word by the Arabic one اِسّ meaning to drive camels by the use of the syllable *is! is!*

9, 10. *Remember former things of old* (or *from eternity*), *for I am the Mighty and there is no other, God and there is none like me, declaring from the first the last, and from ancient time the things which are not (yet) done* (or *made*), *saying, My counsel shall stand and all my pleasure I will do.* He calls upon them to consider the proofs of his exclusive deity, afforded not only by the nullity of all conflicting claims, but by the fact of his infallible foreknowledge, as attested by the actual prediction of events long before their occurrence.—Instead of *for* some read *that*, on the ground that the thing to be believed was his divinity ; the *former things* being cited merely as the proofs of it.—*Declaring the last for the first*, or the *end from the beginning*, means declaring the whole series of events included between these extremes. אַחֲרִית does not strictly mean the end as opposed to the beginning, but the latter part of anything as opposed to the preceding part, whatever the extent of either of their relative proportions. Hence it often means futurity, both absolute and relative, without necessarily defining the *terminus a quo* from which it is to be computed.—*My counsel shall stand, i. e.* my purpose shall be executed. (See chap. vii. 7, viii. 10, xiv. 24, xliv. 26.) All the modern writers seem to be agreed in giving חֵפֶץ the sense of *my will* or *pleasure*, although not at all more natural or necessary here than in chap. xliv. 28, where it is made a proof of later date, and of a diction different from that of Isaiah.—All the expressions of the ninth verse have occurred before in different combinations. (See chap. xlii. 14, xliii. 18, xlv. 21, &c.) According to Maurer, *former things* here means *former events*, as in chap. xliii. 18, xlviii. 3, not former *predictions*, as in chap. xlii. 9, xliii. 9.

11. *Calling from the east a bird of prey, from a land of distance the man of his counsel ; I have both said and will also bring it to pass, I have formed* (the plan) *and will also do it.* From the general assertion of his providence and power, he now passes to that specific proof of it which has so frequently been urged before, viz., the raising up of Cyrus ; but without the mention of his name in this case, and with an indefiniteness of expression which is perfectly well suited to the general analogy of prophecy, as well as to the views already taken in the exposition of chap. xliv. 28. (See above, p. 175).—*Calling* includes prediction and efficiency, not only announcing but calling into being. Most of the modern writers give to עַיִט here the specific sense of *eagle*, some on account of a supposed affinity between the Hebrew name and the Greek ἀετός, others because of the frequent similar allusions to the eagle elsewhere (see Jer. xlix. 22 ; Ezek. xvii. 2, 3, 12 ; comp. Isaiah xl. 31), others supposing a reference to the Persian ensign. But the very vagueness of the usual sense entitles it to the preference for reasons just suggested.—The point of comparison is not mere swiftness or rapidity of conquest (Hosea viii. 1, Hab. i. 8, Jer. xlviii. 30), but rapacity and fierceness. Knobel arbitrarily assumes that Media and Persia are distinctly and specifically meant by the *east* and the *far country*, whereas the language is designedly indefinite.—*Man of his counsel* does not mean his counsellor, as it does in chap. xl. 13, but either the executor of his purpose, or the agent himself purposed, *i. e.* foreordained by God. The marginal reading (*my counsel*) probably arose from the seeming harshness of the *enallage personæ ;* but this is a figure much too frequent in Isaiah to require elimination by a change of text. It is as if he had said, *I am he that calls the man of his counsel*, after which the construction is continued regularly in the first person.—אַף denotes accession, and is sometimes equivalent to *also*, sometimes to *nay more*. It has here the force of *not*

only this *but also* that, or *both* this *and also* that.—יָצַר is not here synonymous with עָשָׂה as in chap. xliv. 2, but opposed to it, meaning to conceive or form the plan of anything, as in chap. xxii. 11, xxxviii. 26, Jer. xviii. 11, Ps. xciv. 20, Isa. xxxvii. 26. The antithesis expressed is that between design and execution. The feminine suffix corresponds to our neuter pronoun *it*, referring to the feminine noun עֵצָה, *i. e.* purpose or counsel.

12. *Hearken to me, ye stout of heart, those far from righteousness.* By an easy and natural association, he subjoins to these proofs of his own divinity, both past and future, a warning to those who were unwilling to receive them. Strength of heart implies, though it does not directly signify, stubbornness or obstinacy, and a settled opposition to the will of God. Because אַבִּיר is sometimes absolutely used in the sense of a bull (Ps. xxii. 13, l. 13), Hitzig says that it here strictly means *bulls in intellect* (*Stiere an Vernunft*).—The same persons are here described as *far from righteousness*, which some understand as meaning far from rectitude or truth, *i. e.* deceitful, insincere. Others explain it to mean those who regard the exhibition of God's righteousness as still far distant. But the only natural interpretation is the one which gives the words their obvious and usual sense, as signifying those who are not righteous before God, in other words the wicked, the words *far from* expressing the degree of their depravity.

13. *I have brought near my righteousness, it shall not be far off; and my salvation, it shall not tarry; and I will give* (or *place*) *in Zion my salvation, to Israel my glory.* Because righteousness and salvation frequently occur as parallel expressions, most of the modern German writers treat them as synonymous, whereas one denotes the cause and the other the effect, one relates to God, and the other to man. The sense in which salvation can be referred to the righteousness of God is clear from chap. i. 27. (See vol. i. p. 93.) The exhibition of God's righteousness consists in the salvation of his people and the simultaneous destruction of his enemies. To these two classes it was therefore at the same time an object of desire and dread. The stout-hearted mentioned in ver. 12 were not prepared for it, and, unless they were changed, must perish when God's righteousness came near.—The last words admit of two constructions, one of which repeats the verb and makes it govern the last noun (I will give my glory unto Israel); the other makes the clause a supplement to what precedes, I will give salvation in Zion unto Israel (who is) my glory. In illustration of the latter, see chaps. xliv. 23, lxii. 3; Jer. xxxiii. 9. The other construction has more of the parallel or balanced form which is commonly considered characteristic of Hebrew composition. In sense they ultimately coincide, since Israel could become Jehovah's glory only by Jehovah's glory being bestowed upon him.

Chapter 47

HERE again we meet with the most discordant and unfounded assumptions, as to the connection of this chapter with the context, and arising from the same misapprehension of the general design of the whole prophecy. Hitzig, because he cannot make it fit into an artificial system of his own, involving the hypothesis of several successive compositions, corresponding to the progress of events under Cyrus, arbitrarily describes it as an insulated prophecy, older than those which now precede it, and afterwards wrought into its present place. In support of this violent and desperate assumption he appeals to the close connection between the last verse of chap. xlvi., and the first of chap. xlviii; an argument which might be used, with equal plausibility, to throw out any portion of the book, because throughout these later prophecies certain apostrophes and other formulas are constantly recurring at irregular intervals. Hendewerk, on the other hand, so far from seeing any want of continuity between this chapter and the two before and after it, represents the three as constituting a "cycle" or division of a cycle. But even those who hold a middle course between these violent extremes commit the usual error of inverting the legitimate relation of the topics to each other, by making the prediction of the downfall of Babylon the Prophet's main theme, and not a specific illustration of it. The difficulties which this false assumption has occasioned with respect to the arrangement of the chapter will be seen below from the interpretation of the fourth verse. Another undesirable effect of the same error is the necessity imposed upon some eminent interpreters, Vitringa for example, of superadding to their exposition of the chapter an account of what they call its mystical sense, that is to say, the application of its terms in the New Testament to Rome, both Pagan and Apostate (Rev. xviii.). Such a proceeding may be looked upon as necessary on the supposition that the Babylon here threatened is the great theme of the prophecy; but if it is merely introduced as a remarkable example of God's dealings with his enemies and those of his people, it is difficult to see why its images and terms may not be used in other prophecies directed against other objects, without compelling us to comprehend those objects in the proper scope of the original prediction. Cowper has paraphrased the song of Israel over the fallen king of Babylon in chap. xiv., and put it in the mouth of the Peruvian Incas upbraiding their Spanish tyrants. If it could now be proved that Cowper was inspired when he wrote this poem, would it follow that the fourteenth chapter of Isaiah had reference either literal or mystical to Pizarro or Peru? If this would not be a legitimate conclusion in the supposed case, then all the facts of the real case may be sufficiently accounted for, by simply assuming that the costume of this prophecy was reproduced by inspiration in another, on a subject similar but not identical; that this new prophecy is not a repetition or an explanation but at most an imitation of the old one; and finally, that what Vitringa calls the mystical sense of the chapter now before us is really the strict sense of another passage, and belongs therefore not to the interpretation of Isaiah, but to that of the Apocalypse. The following seems to be the true analysis.

Having exemplified his general doctrine, as to God's ability and purpose to do justice both to friends and foes, by exhibiting the downfall of the Babylonian idols, he now attains the same end by predicting the downfall of Babylon itself, and of the State to which it gave its name. Under the figure of a royal virgin, she is threatened with extreme degradation and exposure, vers. 1-3. Connecting this event with Israel and Israel's God, as the great themes which it was intended to illustrate, ver. 4, he predicts the fall of the empire more distinctly, ver. 5, and assigns as a reason the oppression of God's people, ver. 6, pride and self-confidence, vers. 7-9, especially reliance upon human wisdom and upon superstitious arts, all which would prove entirely insufficient to prevent the great catastrophe, vers. 10-15.

1. *Come down!* By a beautiful apostrophe, the mighty power to be humbled is addressed directly, and the prediction of her humiliation clothed

in the form of a command to exhibit the external signs of it.—*Sit on the dust!* This, which is the literal translation of the Hebrew phrase, may be conformed to our idiom either by substituting *in* for *on*, or by understanding עָפָר to denote, as it sometimes does, the solid ground. (See chap. ii. 19, vol. i. p. 105.) The act of sitting on the ground is elsewhere mentioned as a customary sign of grief. (See chap. iii. 26 ; Lam. ii. 10 ; Job ii. 13.) But here it is designed, chiefly if not exclusively, to suggest the idea of dethronement which is afterwards expressed distinctly.—The next phrase is commonly explained to mean *virgin daughter of Babel* (*i. e. Babylon*), which, according to Gesenius, is a collective personification of the inhabitants. But as בְּתוּלַת, notwithstanding its construct form, is really in apposition with בַּת (*virgin daughter*), so בַּת may be in apposition with בָּבֶל (*daughter Babel*), and denote not the daughter of Babylon, but Babylon itself, personified as a virgin and a daughter, in which case the latter word may have the wide sense of the French *fille*, and be really synonymous with *virgin*. (See chap. xxxvii. 22, p. 65.) Bnt whatever may be the primary import of the phrase, it is admitted upon all hands to be descriptive either of the city of Babylon, or of the Babylonian State and nation. Whether that power is described as a virgin because hitherto unconquered, is much more doubtful, as this explanation seems to mar the simplicity of the description by confounding the sign with the thing signified.—*Sit to the earth!* i. e. close to it, or simply *on* it, as Ps. ix. 5, where the vague sense of the particle is determined by the verb and noun with which it stands connected. *To sit as to a throne* can only mean to sit upon it. *There is no throne.* Some connect this with what goes before, in this way : *sit on the earth without a throne.* But there is no need of departing from the idiomatic form of the original, in which these words are a complete proposition, which may be connected with what goes before by supplying a causal particle : " sit on the earth, for you have now no throne." —*Daughter of Chasdim!* This last is the common Hebrew name for the Chaldees or Chaldeans, the race introduced by the Assyrians, at an early period, into Babylonia. (See chap. xxiii. 13, vol. i. pp. 398–9. Compare also what is said above, on chap. xliii. 14.) If taken here in this sense, it may be understood to signify the government, or the collective members of this race. Rosenmüller applies it to the city, and supposes it to be so called because built by the Chaldeans. But this is equally at variance with history and with the analogy of other cases where a like explanation would be inadmissible. *Daughter of Chasdim* must of course be an analogous expression to the parallel phrase *daughter of Babel*, which certainly cannot mean a city built by Babylon. Besides the strict use of כַּשְׂדִים as a plural, it is unequivocally used now and then as the name of the country, analogous to מִצְרַיִם which is a dual. See for example Jer. li. 24, 35, where we read of the *inhabitants of Chasdim*, and Ezek. xvi. 29, where it takes the local or directive ה. If the word be so explained in this case, it will make the correspondence of the clauses still more exact.—*For thou shalt not add* (or *continue*) *to be called*, would be the natural and usual conclusion of the phrase ; instead of which we have here *they shall not call thee*, which is common enough as an indefinite expression equivalent to a passive, and only remarkable for its combination with the preceding words, although the sense of the whole clause is quite obvious. *Thou shalt not continue to be called* (or *they shall no longer call thee*) *tender and delicate, i. e.* they shall no longer have occasion so to call thee, because thou shalt no longer be so. The same two epithets are found in combination, Deut. xxviii. 54, from which place it is clear that they are not so much descriptive of voluptuous and vicious habits as of a delicate and easy mode of life, such as that of a princess compared with that of a female slave. The testimonies of the ancient writers as to the prevalent iniquities of Babylon belong rather to a subsequent part of the description. All that is here meant is that the royal virgin must descend from the throne to the dust, and relinquish the luxuries and comforts of her former mode of life.

2. *Take mill-stones and grind meal!* Even among the Romans this was considered one of the most servile occupations. In the East it was especially work of female slaves. Exod. xi. 5, Matt. xxiv. 41.—*Uncover (i. e.* lift up or remove) *thy veil!* One of the Arabian poets speaks of certain ladies as appearing unveiled so that they resembled slaves, which is exactly the idea here expressed. Vitringa and others render צַמָּתֵךְ *thy hair* or *thy braided locks*, which rests on an Arabic analogy, as the sense of *veil*, now commonly adopted, does on Chaldee usage. The parallel word שֹׁבֶל is also understood by some as meaning *hair*, by others the *foot*, or the *sleeve;* but most interpreters are now agreed in giving it the sense of *skirt*, and to the whole phrase that of *lift up* (literally *strip*) *thy skirt* (or *train*), corresponding to the lifting of the veil in the preceding clause.—*Uncover the leg, cross streams!* The only question as to this clause is, whether it refers, as Gesenius and Ewald think, to the fording of rivers by female captives as they go into exile, or to the habitual exposure of the person, by which women of the lowest class are especially distinguished in the East. The latter explanation, which is that of Vitringa, is entitled to the preference, not only because we read of no deportation of the Babylonians by Cyrus, but because the other terms of the description are confessedly intended to contrast to conditions of life or classes of society.

3. The same idea of exposure is now carried out to a revolting extreme. *Let thy nakedness be uncovered, likewise let thy shame be seen.* This conveys no new idea, but is simply the climax of the previous description.—*I will take vengeance.* The metaphor is here exchanged for literal expressions by so easy a transition that it scarcely attracts notice. The destruction of Babylon is frequently set forth as a righteous retribution for the wrongs of Israel. (See Jer. l. 15, 28.)—*I will not* (or *I shall not*) *meet a man.* Of the various and discordant explanations of this clause, it will suffice to mention one or two of the most current or most plausible. Some give פָּגַע the sense which it has elsewhere when followed by the preposition בְּ, viz. that of interceding. Thus Jarchi understands the words to mean, I will not intercede with (or solicit) any man to avenge me, but avenge myself. Grotius gives the verb the sense of admitting intercession; and Lowth, for the same purpose, reads אַפְגִּיעַ in the Hiphil form (*neither will I suffer man to intercede with me*). Gesenius, in his Commentary, traces an affinity between פָּגַע and פָּקַד *to visit*, and explains the clause to mean *I will spare no man.* In his Thesaurus he connects it with נָגַע, πηγνύω, and *paciscor*, and agrees with Maurer in translating, *I will strike* (or *ratify*) *a league with no man.* But the explanation most agreeable to usage, and at the same time simplest as to syntax, is, *I shall* (or *will*) *meet no man.* This is not to be understood, however, with Vitringa, as meaning that he would find no one to avenge him, or that if he did not, he would still avenge himself. The true sense is that expressed by Rosenmüller, *I shall encounter no man,*

i. e. no man will be able to resist me. This simple explanation is at the same time one of the most ancient, as we find it distinctly expressed by Symmachus (οὐχ ἀντιστήσεται μοι ἄνθρωπος) and in the Vulgate (*non resistet mihi homo*). —Independetly of these minuter questions, it is clear that the whole clause is a laconic explanation of the figures which precede, and which are summed up in the simple but terrific notion of resistless and inexorable vengeance.

4. *Our Redeemer* (or *as for our Redeemer*), *Jehovah of hosts* (*is*) *his name, the Holy One of Israel.* The downfall of Babylon was but a proof that the Deliverer of Israel was a sovereign and eternal Being, and yet bound to his own people in the strongest and tenderest covenant relation. Thus understood, the verse does not even interrupt the sense, but makes it clearer, by recalling to the reader's mind the great end for which the event took place and for which it is here predicted. Compare with this Lowth's pedantic supposition of a chorus, which is scarcely more natural than that of a committee or of a jury, and Eichhorn's deplorable suggestion that the verse is a devout reflection of some Jewish reader, accidentally transplanted from the margin to the text. This is justly represented by Gesenius as a makeshift (*Nothbehelf*), a description equally appropriate to many of his own erasures elsewhere, if not to his extravagant assumption here, that the words *thus saith* have been left out at the beginning of the sentence. Maurer improves upon the strange exegetical device by making the verse merely introductory to that which follows, *Thus saith our Redeemer, whose name is Jehovah of hosts, the Holy One of Israel, Sit in silence*, &c. In this way everything may easily be made to denote anything. The only tenable conclusion is the obvious and simple one, that this is a distinct link in the chain of the prophetic argument, by which the fall of Babylon is brought into connection and subordination to the proof of God's supremacy as shewn in the protection and salvation of his people. That the Prophet speaks here in his own person, is but a single instance of a general usage, characteristic of the whole composition, in which God is spoken of, spoken to, or introduced as speaking, in constant alternation; yet without confusion, or the slightest obscuration of the general meaning.

5. *Sit silent* (or *in silence*), *and go into darkness* (or *a dark place*), *daughter of Chasdim!* The allusion is to natural and usual expressions of sorrow and despondency. (See Lam. ii. 10, iii. 2, 28.) The explanation of *darkness* as a metaphor for *prison* does not suit the context, and is no more natural or necessary here than in chap. xlii. 7.— *For thou shalt not continue to be called* (or they shall not continue to *call thee*) *mistress of kingdoms.* This is an allusion to the Babylonian empire, as distinguished from Babylonia Proper, and including many tributary States which Xenophon enumerates. In like manner the Assyrian king is made to ask (chap. x. 8), Are not my princes altogether kings?

6. *I was wroth against my people; I profaned my heritage, i. e.* I suffered my chosen and consecrated people to be treated as something common and unclean. In the same sense God is said before (chap. xliii. 28) to have *profaned the holy princes.* Israel is called Jehovah's *heritage*, as being his perpetual possession, continued from one generation to another. This general import of the figure is obvious enough, although there is an essential difference between this case and that of literal inheritance, because in the latter, the change and succession affect the proprietor, whereas in the former they affect the thing possessed, and the possessor is unchangeable. —*And I gave them into thy hand,* as my instruments of chastisement.

Thou didst not show them mercy, literally *place* (give or appoint) *it to them.* God's providential purpose was not even known to his instruments, and could not therefore be the rule of their conduct or the measure of their responsibility. Though unconsciously promoting his designs, their own ends and motives were entirely corrupt. In the precisely analogous case of the Assyrian, it is said (chap. x. 7), *he will not think so, and his heart not so will purpose, because to destroy (is) in his heart and to cut off nations not a few.*—The general charge is strengthened by a specific aggravation. *On the aged thou didst aggravate thy yoke* (or *make it heavy*) *exceedingly.* Koppe, Gesenius, Maurer, and Hitzig, understand this of the whole people, whom they suppose to be described as *old, i. e.* as having reached the period of natural decrepitude. Umbreit agrees with Grotius and Vitringa in preferring the strict sense of the words, viz. that they are cruelly oppressive even to the aged captives, under which Vitringa is disposed to include elders in office and rank, as well as in age. The particular form of inhumanity is charged upon the Babylonians by Jeremiah twice (Lam. iv. 16, v. 12), and in both cases he connects זקנים with a parallel term denoting rank or office, viz., priests and princes. Between the two interpretations of the clause which have been stated, Knobel undertakes to steer a middle course, by explaining זקן to mean *aged* in the strict sense, but supposing at the same time that this single act of tyranny is put for inhumanity in general. (Compare Deut. xxviii. 50.) The essential meaning of the clause, as a description of inordinate severity to those least capable of retaliation or resistance, still remains the same in either case.

7. *And thou saidst, For ever I shall be a mistress, i. e. a mistress of kingdoms,* the complete phrase which occurs above in ver. 5. The sense of *queen* is therefore wholly inadequate, unless we understand it to mean *queen of queens* or *queen of kings.* The ellipsis suggested may perhaps account for the use of what might seem to be a construct form, instead of the synonymous גְּבִירָה (1 Kings xi. 19). Hitzig, however, goes too far when he makes this a ground for disregarding the accentuation and connecting the two words גְּבֶרֶת עַד in the sense of a *mistress of eternity, i. e.* a perpetual mistress. (Compare Gen. xlix. 26, Hab. iii. 6, Isa. ix. 5.) As examples of the segholate termination of the absolute form, Maurer cites שְׁלֶטֶת (Ezek. xvi. 30) and אֶרֶזֶת (Ezek. xvii. 8). Hitzig also objects to the Masoretic interpunction, that it requires עַד to be taken in the sense of *so that,* contrary to usage. But this, though assumed by Gesenius and most of the other modern writers, is entirely gratuitous. The conjunction has its proper sense of *until,* as in Job. xiv. 6; 1 Sam. xx. 41, and the meaning of the clause is, that she had persisted in this evil course *until* at last it had its natural effect of blinding the mind and hardening the heart. *Thou saidst, For ever I shall be a mistress, till* (at last) *thou didst not lay these (things) to thy heart.* The idea of causal dependence (*so that*) is implied but not expressed. *Laying to heart,* including an exercise of intellect and feeling, occurs, with slight variations as to form, in chap. xlii. 25, xliv. 19, xlvi. 8.—*Thou didst not remember the end* (or *latter part,* or *issue*) *of it, i. e.* of the course pursued, the feminine pronoun being put for a neuter as in chap. xlvi. 11, and often elsewhere. The apparent solecism of remembering the future may be solved by observing that the thing forgotten was the knowledge of the future once possessed, just as in common parlance we use *hope* in reference to the past, because we hope to find it so, or hope that something questionable now will prove hereafter to be thus and thus.

8. *And now,* a common form of logical resumption and conclusion, very

nearly corresponding to our phrases, this being so, or, such being the case.
— *Hear this, i. e.* what I have just said, or am just about to say, or both.
Oh voluptuous one! The common version, *thou that art given to pleasures,*
is substantially correct, but in form too paraphrastical. The translation
delicate, which some give, is inadequate at least upon the common supposition that this term is not intended, like the kindred ones in ver. 1, to contrast the two conditions of prosperity and downfall, but to bring against the
Babylonians the specific charge of gross licentiousness, in proof and illustration of which Vitringa quotes the words of Quintus Curtius ; *nihil urbis
ejus corruptius moribus, nec ad irritandas illiciendasque immodicas voluptates
instructius,* to which, after certain gross details, the historian adds, *Baby-
lonii maxime in vinum et quæ ebrietatem sequuntur effusi sunt.* This corruption of morals, as in other like cases, is supposed to have been aggravated
by the wealth of Babylon, its teeming population, and the vast concourse
of foreign visitors and residents. After all, however, as this charge is not
repeated or insisted on, it may be doubted whether the epithet in question
was intended to express more than the fact of her abundant prosperity
about to be exchanged for desolation and disgrace.—*The (one) sitting in
security.* The common version, *dwellest,* is as much too vague as that of
Ewald, which explains it to mean *sitting on a throne,* is too specific. Sitting seems rather to be mentioned as a posture of security and ease.—
The (one) saying in her heart (or to herself), *I (am) and none besides, i. e.*
none like or equal to me. There has been much dispute respecting the
precise sense of אַפְסִי ; but the question is only of grammatical importance,
as all admit that the whole phrase אַפְסִי עוֹד is equivalent in import to the
common one אֵין עוֹד (chap. xlv. 5, 6, 18, &c.) The only doubt is whether
אַפְסִי is simply negative like אֵין, or exceptive (*besides me*), or at the same
time negative and exceptive (*none besides me*). This double explanation is
given by Noldius and Vitringa, but is justly regarded by the later writers
as untenable. Cocceius makes it mean *besides me,* and assumes an interrogation, which is altogether arbitrary. De Dieu adopts the same construction, but suggests that אַפְסִי may mean *only I,* as אֶפֶס certainly means
only in Num. xii. 35, xxiii. 13. This is adopted by Gesenius in his Commentary. Hitzig objects that עוֹד is then superfluous, and that analogy would
require אֶפֶס אֲנִי. He therefore makes it simply exceptive (*besides me*), and
supposes an ellipsis of the negative. Rosenmüller, Ewald, Umbreit,
Knobel, and Gesenius in the notes to the second edition of his version,
follow J. H. Michaelis in making it a paragogic form and simply negative
(*there is no other,* or *none besides*). Maurer goes further, and explains עוֹד
as a substantive, dependent on the construct form before it ; literally,
nothing of more. The sentiment expressed is that of Martial with respect
to Rome, *cui par est nihil et nihil secundum.* (Compare the words of
Nebuchadnezzar, Dan. iv. 30.) There is even an assumption of divine
supremacy in these words, when compared with the frequent use of the
pronoun *I,* in the solemn declarations of Jehovah (chap. xlv. 6, 12,
xliii. 11, &c.)—*I shall not sit (as) a widow.* The figure of a virgin is now
exchanged for that of a wife, a strong proof that the sign was, in the
writer's view, of less importance than the thing signified. It is needless
to inquire, with Vitringa, whether the husband, whose loss is here implied,
be the king or the chief men collectively. It is not the city or the State
of which widowhood is directly predicated, but the royal personage that
represents it. The same comparison is used by Jeremiah of Jerusalem
(Lam. i. 1). (Compare Isa. li. 18–20, liv. 1. 4, 5 ; Rev. xiv. 7.) Ac-

cording to J. D. Michaelis, the State is the mother, the soldiers or citizens her sons, and the king her husband, which he illustrates by the use of the title *Dey* and other terms of relationship to designate the State, the government, &c., in Algiers and other parts of Barbary. To *sit* as a widow is is considered by Gesenius as suggesting the idea of a mourner; yet in his German version he omits the word entirely, and translates, " I shall never be a widow," in which he is closely followed by De Wette. All the interpreters, from Grotius to Ewald, seem to understand widowhood as a specific figure for the loss of a king; but Knobel boldly questions it, and applies the whole clause to the loss of allies, or of all friendly intercourse with foreign nations.—*And I shall not know* (by experience) *the loss of children.* This paraphrastical expression is the nearest approach that we can make in English to the pregnant Hebrew word שְׁכוֹל. *Bereavement* and *childlessness* may seem at first sight more exact, but the first is not exclusively appropriate to the loss of children, and the last does not suggest the idea of loss at all. This last clause is paraphrased by Noyes, *nor see myself childless;* better by Henderson, *nor know what it is to be childless.*

9. *And they shall come to thee.* The form of expression seems to have some reference to the phrase *I shall not know* in the preceding verse. As if he had said, they shall no longer be unknown or at a distance, they shall come near to thee. *These two,* or *both these* (*things*), from which she thought herself secure for ever.—*Suddenly.* רֶגַע is a noun, and originally means the twinkling of an eye, and then a moment, but is often used adverbially in the sense of *suddenly.* That it has the derivative sense here may be inferred from the addition of the words *in one day,* which would be a striking anticlimax if רֶגַע strictly meant a moment or the twinkling of an eye. This objection is but partially removed by Lowth's change of the interpunction (*these two things in a moment, in one day loss of children and widowhood!*), because the first expression is still much the strongest, unless we understand *in one day* to express not mere rapidity or suddenness, but the concurrence of the two privations.—*Loss of children and widowhood,* as in the verse preceding, are explained by most interpreters as figures for the loss of king and people.—*In their perfection,* literally, *according to* it, *i. e.* in the fullest measure possible, implying total loss and destitution.—*They have come upon thee.* The English version makes its future like the verb in the preceding clause; but this is wholly arbitrary. There is less objection to the present form adopted by the modern German writers; but according to the principle already stated and exemplified so often, it is best to give the word its proper meaning, and to understand it not as a mere repetition of what goes before, but as an addition to it, or at least a variation in the mode of exhibition. What he at first saw coming, he now sees actually come, and describes it accordingly.—Of the בְּ in the next clause there are three interpretations. Ewald agrees with the English Version and the Vulgate in explaining it to mean *propter,* on account of, and supposing it to bring a new specific charge against the Babylonians, by assigning a new cause for their destruction, viz. their cultivation of the occult arts. Gesenius and the other recent writers follow Calvin and Vitringa in making it mean *notwithstanding,* as in chap. v. 25, and Num. xiv. 11. There is then no new charge or reason assigned, but a simple declaration of the insufficiency of superstitious arts to save them. But a better course than either is to give the particle its proper sense of *in* or *in the midst of,* which suggests both the other ideas, but expresses more, viz., that they should perish in the very act of using these unlawful and unprofit-

able means of preservation.—*In the multitude of thy enchantments, in the abundance of thy spells* (or *charms*). The parallel terms, though applied to the same objects, are of different origin, the first denoting primarily prayers or acts of worship, and then superstitious rites; the other specifically meaning bans or spells (from חָבַר to *bind*), with reference, as Gesenius supposes, to the outward act of tying magical knots, but as the older writers think, to the restraining or constraining influence supposed to be exerted on the victim, or even on the gods themselves.—The construction of מְאֹד here is unusual. Gesenius regards it as immediately dependent upon עָצְמָה although separated from it by an intervening word, *the multitude of strength,* *i. e.* the strong multitude of thy enchantments. Maurer says that מְאֹד is construed as an adjective ; while Hitzig makes it as usual an adverb, qualifying עָצְמָה, which is here equivalent to an infinitive. In either case the sense is essentially the same, viz., that of *very powerful,* or *very numerous,* or *very powerful and numerous* enchantments. The prevalence of these arts in ancient Babylon is explicitly affirmed by Diodorus Siculus, and assumed as a notorious fact by other ancient writers.

10. *And (yet) thou art* (or *wast*) *secure in thy wickedness.* Vitringa and most of the later writers have *thou trustedst in thy wickedness,* but differ as to the precise sense of the last word, some referring it, with Jerome, to the occult arts of the preceding verse, others making it denote specifically tyranny or fraud, or both combined as in chap. xxxiii. 1. But even in the places which are cited in proof of this specific explanation (such as chap. xiii. 11, Neh. iii. 9, &c.), the restriction is either suggested by the context or entirely gratuitous. There is therefore no sufficient reason for departing from the wide sense of the word as descriptive of the whole congeries of crimes with which the Babylonians were chargeable. But neither in the wide nor the restricted sense could their wickedness itself be an object of trust. It is better, therefore, to give the verb the absolute meaning which it frequently has elsewhere, and to explain the whole phrase as denoting that they went on in their wickedness without a fear of change or punishment. In this way, moreover, we avoid the necessity of multiplying the specific charges against Babylon, by giving to the Prophet's words a technical and formal meaning which they will not naturally bear. Thus Vitringa introduces this verse as the statement of a fourth crime or impulsive cause of Babylon's destruction, namely, her wickedness (*malitia*) ; and as this of course includes all the rest, he is under the necessity of explaining it to mean specifically *cunning* and reliance on it. The construction which has been proposed above may be the one assumed in the Vulgate (*fiduciam habuisti in malitia tua*) ; but the only modern version where I find it expressed is that of Augusti (*du warst sicher bei deiner Bosheit*), which De Wette, in his improved version, has abandoned for the old one. The idea of *security in wickedness* agrees precisely with what follows.—*Thou hast said, there is no one seeing me,* a form of speech frequently ascribed to presumptuous sinners and unbelievers in the doctrine of providential retribution. (See Psa. x. 11, xciv. 7 ; Ezek. viii. 12, ix. 9 ; Job. xxii. 14.) This, on the other hand, is not a natural expression of specific trust in any form of wickedness. He who relies upon his power or his cunning as a complete protection will be not so apt to say " None seeth me," as to feel indifferent whether he is seen or not.—*Thy wisdom and thy knowledge, it has seduced thee.* The insertion of the pronoun (הִיא) admits of a twofold explanation. It may mean *thy very wisdom,* upon which thou hast so long relied for guidance, has *itself* misled thee. But at the same time it may serve to shew that wisdom and knowledge are

not here to be distinguished but considered as identical. He does not say *thy wisdom and knowledge they have*, but *it has, seduced thee*. By wisdom and knowledge some understand astronomy and astrology, others political sagacity and diplomatic skill, for which it is inferred that the Babylonians were distinguished, from the places where their *wise men* are particularly mentioned. (See for example Jer. l. 35, li. 57.) But in these descriptions of the Babylonian empire, and the analogous accounts of Tyre (Ezek. xxviii. 4) and Egypt (Isa. xix. 11), the reference seems not so much to anything peculiar to the State in question, as to that peculiar political wisdom which is pre-supposed in the very existence, much more in the prosperity, of every great empire. Gesenius understands these expressions as ironical, an indirect denial that they were possessed of wisdom. But this is an unnecessary supposition, and not entirely consistent with the tone of the whole context. It was probably not merely the conceit of knowledge but its actual possession that had led the Babylonians astray. The verb שׁוֹבֵב means to turn aside (convert) from one course to another, and is used both in a good sense and a bad one. An example of the former may be found below in chap. xlix. 5, and of the latter here, where the word means not exactly to *pervert*, or as Lowth translates it, to *pervert the mind*, but rather to misguide, seduce, or lead astray, like הִפָּה in chap. xliv. 20. *Thy knowledge and thy wisdom, it has seduced thee.*—The remainder of the verse describes the effect of this perversion or seduction in the same terms that had been employed above in ver. 8, and which occur elsewhere only in Zeph. ii. 15, which appears to be an imitation of the place before us, and not its original as Hitzig and others arbitrarily assume. —*And thou saidst* (or *hast said*) *in thy heart*. The indirect construction, *so that thou hast said*, contains more than is expressed, but not more than is implied, in the original.—*I am and there is no other*. J. D. Michaelis understands this boast to mean, I am Babylon and there is no other. But most interpreters prefer the general meaning, I am what no one else is ; there is no one like me, much less equal to me. (See above, on ver. 8.) This arrogant presumption is ascribed to their wisdom and knowledge, not as its legitimate effect, but as a necessary consequence of its perversion and abuse, as well as of men's native disposition to exaggerate the force and authority of unassisted reason. (Compare chap. v. 21, vol. i. p. 138.)

11. *And (so) there cometh* (or *has come*) *upon thee evil ;* with an evident allusion to the use of רָעָה in the verse preceding, so as to suggest an antithesis between natural and moral evil, sin and suffering, evil done and evil experienced. The *vav* at the beginning is not properly conversive, as it does not depend upon a foregoing future (Nordheimer, § 219) ; so that the common version (*therefore shall evil come*) is not strictly accurate. Most of the modern writers make it present; but the strict sense of the preterite is perfectly consistent with the context and the usage of the Prophet, who continually depicts occurrences still future, first as coming, then as come, not in fact but in vision, both as certain to occur and as historically represented to his own mind. The phrase *come upon* is explained by Vitringa as implying descent from above or infliction by a higher power.—Of the next clause there are several distinct interpretations, all of which agree in making it descriptive of the *evil* threatened in the one before it. From the use of the verb שָׁחַר in Psa. lxxviii. 34, and elsewhere, Lowth and others give it here the sense of intercession (*thou shalt not know how to deprecate*), which seems to be also given in the Targum, and approved by Jarchi. Jerome takes שחר as a noun meaning *dawn*, and understands by it the

origin or source of the calamity (*nescis ortum ejus*), in which he is followed by Vitringa and Rosenmüller, who appear, however, to apply the term, not merely to the source of the evil, but to the time of its commencement, which should be like a day without a dawn, *i. e.* sudden and without premonition. There is something so unnatural, however, and at variance with usage, in the representation of misfortune as a dawning day, that Gesenius, Maurer, and Umbreit, who retain the same translation of the word, reverse the sense of the whole phrase by supposing it to mean not a preceding but a following dawn; in which case the *evil* is described not as a day without a dawn before it, but as a night without a dawning after it,—a figure natural and striking in itself, and very strongly recommended by the use of שַׁחַר in the same sense by Isaiah elsewhere. (See chap. viii. 20, vol. i. p. 193.) Hitzig and Ewald still prefer, however, the hypothesis of J. D. Michaelis and others, who identify שַׁחַר with the Arabic سحر, and explain it either as a noun (*against which thou hast no charm*) or as an infinitive (*thou shalt not know how to charm* or *conjure it away*). This construction has the advantage of creating a more perfect correspondence between this word and the similar verbal form (כַּפְּרָהּ) with which the next clause ends. Grotius and Clericus appear to regard שַׁחַר as a mere poetical equivalent to *day*, which is highly improbable and not at all sustained by usage.—*And there shall fall upon thee* (a still stronger expression than the one before it, *there shall come upon thee*) *ruin*. According to the modern lexicographers, the noun itself means *fall*, but in its figurative application to destruction or calamity. It occurs only here and in Ezek. vii. 26.—*Thou shalt not be able to avert it*, or resolving the detached Hebrew clauses into one English period, *which thou shalt not be able to avert*. The exact meaning of the last word is atone for, expiate, and in this connection, to avert by expiation, whether in the strict sense of atoning sacrifice or in the wider one of satisfaction and propitiation. If we assume a personification of the *evil*, the verb may mean to *appease*, as in Gen. xxxii. 21, Prov. xvi. 14. In any case, the clause describes the threatened judgment as inexorable and inevitable.—*And there shall come upon thee suddenly a crash*,—or as J. D. Michaelis renders it, *a crashing fall*, a common metaphor for sudden ruin, (*which*) *thou shalt not know*. This may either mean, of which thou shalt have no previous *experience*, or of which thou shalt have no previous *expectation*. The former meaning is the one most readily suggested by the words. The latter may be justified by the analogy of Job ix. 5, *who removeth the mountains and they know not*, which can only mean that he removes them suddenly or unawares. Because the same verb תֵּדָעִי in the first clause governs a following word (*thou shalt not know its dawn*, or *how to conjure it away*), Lowth adopts Secker's hint that a similar dependent word has here been lost, but does not venture to determine what it was, though he thinks it may have been צֵאת ממנה, as in Jer. xi. 11.

12. *Stand now!* It must be borne in mind that נָא is not a particle of time but of entreaty, very often corresponding to *I pray*, or *if you please*. In this case it indicates a kind of concession to the people, if they still choose to try the virtue of their superstitious arts which he had already denounced as worthless. Some interpreters have gone too far in representing this passage as characterised by a tone of biting sarcasm.—*Stand now in thy spells* (or *charms*). Vitringa supposes an allusion to the customary standing posture of astrologers, conjurers, &c. Others understand

the verb to mean *stand fast*, be firm and courageous. But the modern writers generally follow Lowth in understanding it to mean *persist* or persevere, which of course requires the preposition to be taken in its usual proper sense of *in.*—*Persist now in thy spells and in the abundance of thy charms*, the same nouns that are joined above in ver. 9. *In which thou hast laboured.* Gesenius in his Grammar (§ 121, 2) mentions this as one of the only two cases in which the Hebrew relative is governed directly by a preposition, *in which* instead of *which in them*, the usual idiomatic combination. But Hitzig and Ewald do away with this exception, by supposing the particle to be dependent on the verb at the beginning, and the relative directly on the verb that follows : *persist in that which* (or *in that respecting which*) *thou hast laboured* (or *wearied thyself ;* see above, on chap. xliii. 22) *from thy youth.* This may either mean *of old*, or more specifically, since the earliest period of thy national existence. The antiquity of occult arts, and above all of astrology, in Babylon, is attested by various profane writers. Diodorus Siculus indeed derives them from Egypt, and describes the *Chaldees*, or astrologers of Babylon, as Egyptian colonists. But as this last is certainly erroneous (see above on ver. 1), the other assertion can have no authority. The Babylonians are reported by the same and other writers to have carried back their own antiquity, as proved by recorded scientific observations, to an extravagant and foolish length, to which some think there is allusion here in the expression *from thy youth.*—*Perhaps thou wilt be able to succeed*, or *keep thyself*, the verb commonly translated *profit.* (See above, chap. xliv. 10.) אוּלַי originally means *if not* or *whether not*, but in usage corresponds more nearly to *perhaps* than it does to the conditional compound, *if so be*, which is the common English Version here. This faint suggestion of a possibility is more expressive than a positive denial.—*Perhaps thou wilt grow strong*, or *prevail*, as the ancient versions render it ; or *resist* as Rosenmüller, Hitzig, and Ewald explain it from an Arabic analogy ; or *terrify* (thine adversary), as Gesenius explains it from the analogy of chap. ii. 19, 21. (Compare Ps. x. 18, and Job. xiii. 25). In either case the word is a specification of the more general term *succeed* or *profit*.

13. *Thou art wearied in the multitude of thy counsel*, not merely weary *of* it, but exhausted *by* it, and *in* the very act of using it. עֲצָתַיִךְ seems to be a singular noun with a plural suffix, a combination which may be supposed to have arisen, either from the want of any construct plural form in this case, or from a designed assimilation with the plurals in ver. 12. As רב may denote either numerical multitude or aggregate abundance, it is often construed with a singular, for instance in Ps. v. 8, lii. 9, Isa. xxxvii. 24. By *counsel* we are not to understand the computations or conferences of the astronomers, but all the devices of the government for self-defence. The German writers have introduced an idiom of their own into the first clause wholly foreign from the usage of the Hebrew language, by making it conditional, which Noyes has copied by giving it the form of an interrogation : *art thou weary ?* &c. The original form is that of a short independent proposition.—*Let now* (or *pray let*) *them stand and save thee.* We may take *stand* either in the same sense which it has above in ver. 12, or in that of appearing, coming forward, presenting themselves. The use of עָמַד in the sense of rising, is erroneously alleged as a peculiar feature in the diction of these Later Prophecies.—The subject of the verbs is then defined. *The dividers of the heavens*, *i. e.* the astrologers, so called because they divided the heavens into houses with a view to their prognostications. Henderson's reference to the twelve signs of the Zodiac is too restricted.

The chethibh, or textual reading (הברו), is regarded by some as an old form of the plural construct, but by others as the third person plural of the preterite, agreeing with the relative pronoun understood (*who divide*). Kimchi regards division as a figure for decision or determination, which is wholly unnecessary. Some read חֹבְרֵי, and suppose an allusion to the derivative noun in ver. 12 ; while others trace it to the Arabic root خبر, and suppose the phrase to mean those who know the heavens. All admit, however, that the general sense is correctly given by the Septuagint (ἀστρο-λόγοι τοῦ οὐρανοῦ) and the Vulgate (*augures cœli*). The same class of persons is then spoken of as *star-gazers*, an English phrase which well expresses the peculiar force of חֹזִים followed by the preposition בְּ. Some, however, give the former word its frequent sense of *seers* or prophets, and regard what follows as a limiting or qualifying term, the whole corresponding to the English phrase *star-prophets*, *i. e.* such as prophesy by means cf the stars. The next phrase does not mean *making known the new moons*, for these returned at stated intervals and needed no prognosticator to reveal them. The sense is either *at the new moons*, or *by means of the new moons*, *i. e.* the changes of the moons, of which the former is the simpler explanation.—Interpreters are much divided as to the way in which the remaining words of this verse are to be connected with what goes before. Aben Ezra and Vitringa make the clause dependent on the verb *save :* "Let them save them from (the things) which are about to come upon thee." The only objections to this construction are the distance of the words thus connected from each other, and the absolute sense which it puts upon מוֹדִיעִים by removing its object. The modern writers, with a very few exceptions, connect this participle with what follows, *making known at the new moons what shall come upon thee.* The מִ may then be partitive (*some of the things*, &c.), or indicate the subject of the revelation (*of, i. e. concerning what shall come*, &c.) To the former Vitringa objects, that the astrologers would undertake of course to reveal not only some but all things still future. But Jarchi suggests, that the new moon could afford only partial information ; and J. D. Michaelis, that this limited pretension would afford the astrologers a pretext and apology for frequent failures. But the other construction is now commonly preferred, except that Ewald gives to מֵאֲשֶׁר the meaning *whence, i. e.* from what source or quarter these things are to come upon thee.

14. *Behold they are like stubble, fire has burned them* (the Babylonian astrologers). The construction given by Gesenius (*stubble which the fire consumes*) is inconsistent with the plural suffix. *Behold* brings their destruction into view as something present. It is on this account more natural, as well as more exact, to give the verbs a past or present form, as Ewald does, than to translate them in the future. He not only prophesies that they shall be burnt, but sees them burning. The comparison with stubble seems intended to suggest that they are worthless and combustible, *whose end is to be burned* (Heb. vi. 8). At the same time a contrast is designed, as Kimchi well observes, between the burning of stubble and the burning of wood, the former being more complete and rapid than the latter.—*They cannot deliver themselves from the hand* (*i e.* the power) *of the flame.* Gesenius and most of the later writers translate נַפְשָׁם *their life;* Hitzig and Ewald still more rigidly, *their soul.* But the reflexive sense *themselves* is not only favoured by the analogy of chap. xlvi. 2, but required by the context. There is at least much less significance and point in saying that they cannot save their lives, than in saying that they cannot even save them-

selves, much less their votaries and dependents.—The last clause contains a negative description of the fire mentioned in the first. Of this description there are two interpretations. Grotius, Clericus, Vitringa, Lowth, Gesenius, and Maurer, understand it to mean that the destruction of the fuel will be so complete, that nothing will be left at which a man can sit and warm himself. But as· this gratuitously gives to אֵין the sense *there is not left*, without the least authority from usage, Ewald and Knobel agree with J. D. Michaelis and others in explaining it to mean, (*this fire*) *is not a coal (at which) to warm one's self, a fire to sit before*, but a devouring and consuming conflagration. The only difficulty in the way of this interpretation is a slight one, namely, that it takes נַּחֶלֶת in the sense of a coal-fire, and not a single coal. With either of these expositions of the whole clause may be reconciled a different interpretation of the word לַחְמָם proposed by Saadias, and independently of him by Cocceius. These writers give the word the sense which it invariably has in every other place where it occurs, viz. *their bread*. (See Job xxx. 4, Prov. xxx. 25, Ezek. iv. 13, xii. 19, Hos. ix. 4.) The whole expression then means, that it is not a common fire for baking bread, or, on the other supposition, that there are not coals enough left for that purpose. The phrase נַּחֶלֶת לַחְמָם (*coal of their bread*) presents a harsh and unusual combination, rendered less so, however, by the use of both words in chap. xliv. 19. This construction is approved by Rosenmüller; but the other modern writers seem to be agreed in making לַחְמָם the infinitive of חָמַם (chap. xliv. 15, 16) with a preposition, analogous in form to חֲנַנְכֶם from חָנַן (chap. xxx. 18). One manuscript has לְחֻמָּם, which is nearer to the usual analogy of this class of verbs, but embarrasses the syntax with a pleonastic suffix.—The general sense of sudden, rapid, and complete destruction is not affected by these minor questions of grammatical analysis.

15. *Thus are they to thee*, *i. e.* such is their fate, you see what has become of them. The לָךְ is not superfluous, as Gesenius asserts, although foreign from our idiom. It suggests the additional idea, that the person addressed was interested in them, and a witness of their ruin.—*With respect to whom thou hast laboured*. This may either mean *with* whom or *for* whom; or both may be included in the general idea that these had been the object and occasion of her labours.—*Thy dealers* (or *traders*) *from thy youth*. This is commonly regarded as explanatory of the foregoing clause. Thus the English Version, *they with whom thou hast laboured, even thy merchants*, &c. It then becomes a question whether these are called traders in the literal and ordinary sense, or at least in that of national allies and negotiators; or whether the epithet is given in contempt to the astrologers and wise men of the foregoing context, as trafficking or dealing in imposture. J. D. Michaelis supposes them to be described as travelling dealers, *i. e.* pedlars and hawkers, who removed from place to place, lest their frauds should be discovered. He even compares them with the gipsy fortune-tellers of our own day, but admits that the astrologers of Babylonia held a very different position in society. Against any application of the last clause to this order, it may be objected that the preceding verse, of which this is a direct continuation, represents them as already utterly consumed. The true solution of the difficulty seems to be afforded by the Masoretic interpunction of the sentence, which connects סְחֲרַיִךְ not with what precedes, but with what follows. According to this arrangement, we are not to read *and so are thy dealers*, or *even thy dealers*, but thy dealers from thy youth wander each his own way. We have then two classes introduced, and two distinct

events predicted. As if he had said, Thy astrologers, &c., are utterly destroyed, and as for thy dealers, they wander home, &c., widely different in fate, but both alike in this, that they leave thee defenceless in the hour of extremity. *Thy traders* may then be taken either in its strict sense, as denoting foreign˙merchants, or in its wider sense, as comprehending all, whether states or individuals, with whom she had intercourse, commercial or political. Ewald revives Houbigant's interpretation of the word as meaning *sorcerers*, in order to sustain which by the Arabic analogy, he seems inclined to read שֹׁחֲרַיִךְ, without the least necessity or warrant.— These are described as thinking only of providing for their own security. (Compare chap. xiii. 14, xliii. 14.) *Each to his own quarter*, side, direction; substantially synonymous with אֶל־עֵבֶר פָּנָיו (Ezek. i. 9, 12), and other phrases, all meaning *straight before him*, without turning to the right hand or the left,—(*they wander* or *have wandered*), a term implying not only flight, but confusion. The plural form agrees with the subject understood, and not with the distributive expression אִישׁ by which that subject is defined and qualified.—*There is no one helping thee*, or, still more strongly, *saving thee*, thou hast no saviour; with particular reference to those just mentioned, who, instead of thinking upon her, or bringing her assistance, would be wholly engrossed by a sense of their own danger and the effort to escape it. There is no need of supposing, with Hitzig, that the image of a great conflagration is still present to the writer's mind, and that *no one helps* (or *saves*) *thee* means specifically *no one quenches thee*. The figurative dress would rather seem to have been laid aside, in order to express the naked truth more plainly.

Chapter 48

FROM his digression with respect to the causes and effects of the catastrophe of Babylon, the Prophet now returns to his more general themes, and winds up the first great division of the Later Prophecies by a reiteration of the same truths and arguments which run through the previous portion of it, with some variations and additions which will be noticed in the proper place. The disproportionate prominence given to the Babylonish exile and the liberation from it, in most modern expositions of the passage, has produced the same confusion and the same necessity of assuming arbitrary combinations and transitions, as in other cases which have been already stated. The length to which this false hypothesis has influenced the practice of interpreters may be inferred from the fact, that one of the most recent English writers describes this chapter as "renewed assurances of restoration from Babylon." This is less surprising in the present case, however; because the Prophet, in the close as in the opening of this first book, does accommodate his language to the feelings and condition of the Jews in exile, though the truths which he inculcates are still of a general and comprehensive nature.

Although Israel is God's chosen and peculiar people, he is in himself unworthy of the honour and unfaithful to the trust, vers. 1, 2. Former predictions had been uttered expressly to prevent his ascribing the event to other gods, vers. 3–5. For the same reason new predictions will be uttered now, of events which have never been distinctly foretold, vers. 6–8. God's continued favour to his people has no reference to merit upon their part, but is the fruit of his own sovereign mercy, and intended to promote his own designs, vers. 9–11. He again asserts his own exclusive deity, as proved by the creation of the world, by the prediction of events still future, and especially by the raising up of Cyrus, as a promised instrument to execute his purpose, vers. 12–16. The sufferings of Israel are the fruit of his own sin, but his prosperity and glory, of God's sovereign grace, vers. 17–19. The book closes as it opened with a promise of deliverance from exile, accompanied, in this case, by a solemn limitation of the promise to its proper objects, vers. 20–22.

It is evident that these are the same elements which enter into all the Later Prophecies, so far as we have yet examined them, and that these elements are here combined in very much the usual proportions, although not in precisely the same shape and order. The most novel feature of this chapter is the fulness with which one principal design of prophecy, and the connection between Israel's sufferings and his sins, are stated.

The confidence with which the most dissimilar hypotheses may be maintained when resting upon no determinate or valid principle, is forcibly exemplified in this case by the fact, that Vitringa and Schmidius both divide the chapter into two parts relating to two different periods of history; but the former applies vers. 1–11 to the Jews of Isaiah's time, and vers. 12–22 to those of the captivity; while the latter applies vers. 1–15 to the Jews of the captivity, and vers. 16–22 to those contemporary with our Saviour. This divergency, both as to the place of the dividing line, and as to the chronological relation of the parts, is a sufficient proof that the hypothesis, common to both, of a reference to two successive periods, is altogether arbitrary, and with equal reason might be varied indefinitely by supposing that the first part treats of the the Apostolic age, and the second of the period of the Reformation; or the first of the Middle Ages, and the last of the Millennium; or the first of the French Revolution, and the last of the Day of Judgment. The only safe assumption is, that the chapter contains general truths with special illustrations and examples.

1. *Hear this*, not exclusively what follows or what goes before, but this whole series of arguments and exhortations. This is a formula by which Isaiah frequently resumes and continues his discourse. Because the verb occurs at the beginning of chap. xlvi. 12, Hitzig infers that these two chapters originally came together, and that the forty-seventh was afterwards introduced between them, which seems frivolous.—*O house of Jacob the* (men) *called by the name of Israel*, a periphrasis for Israelites or members of the ancient church.—*And from the waters of Judah they have come out.* By an easy transition, of perpetual occurrence in Isaiah, the construction is concontinued in the third person; as if the Prophet, after addressing them directly, had proceeded to describe them to the bystanders. The people, by a natural figure, are described as streams from the fountain of Judah. (Compare chap. li. 1, and Ps. lxviii. 27.) Gesenius and other German writers fasten on this mention of Judah as a national progenitor, as betraying a later date of composition than the days of Isaiah. But this kind of reasoning proceeds upon the shallow and erroneous supposition that the application of this name to the whole people was the result of accidental causes at a comparatively recent period, whereas it forms part of a change designed from the beginning, and developed by a gradual process, through the whole course of their history. Even in patriarchal times the pre-eminence of Judah was determined. From him the Messiah was expected to descend (Gen. xlix. 10). To him the first rank was assigned in the exodus, the journey through the

desert, and the occupation of the promised land. In his line the royal power was first permanently established. To him, though deserted by five-sixths of the tribes, the honours and privileges of the theocracy were still continued; so that long before the Babylonish exile or the downfall of the kingdom of the ten tribes, the names of Israel and Judah were convertible, not as political distinctions, but as designations of the chosen people, the theocracy, the ancient church. In this sense Israelite and Jew were as really synonymous when Isaiah wrote, as they are now in common parlance.—*Those swearing by the name of Jehovah, i. e.* swearing by him as their God, and thereby not only acknowledging his deity, but solemnly avouching their relation to him. (See above, on chap. xlv. 23.)—*And of the God of Israel make mention,* not in conversation merely, but as a religious act, implying public recognition of his being and authority, in which sense the same Hebrew phrase with unimportant variations in its form is frequently used elsewhere. (For examples of the very form which here occurs, see Josh. xxiii. 7; Ps. xx. 8, xlv. 18.)—*Not in truth and not in righteousness,* uprightness, sincerity. It is not necessary to infer from these words, that the Prophet's language is addressed to a distinct class of the Jews, or to the Jews of any one exclusive period, his own, or that of the captivity, or that of Christ. The clause is an indirect reiteration of the doctrine so continually taught throughout these prophecies, and afterwards repeated in this very chapter, that God's choice of Israel and preservation of him was no proof of merit upon his part, nor even an act of mere compassion upon God's part, but the necessary means to an appointed end. The reference therefore here is not so much to individual hypocrisy or unbelief, as to the general defect of worthiness or merit in the body. Some, supposing the whole emphasis to rest upon this last clause, understand what goes before as descriptive of outward profession and pretension, and for that reason give to the passive participle נִקְרָאִים the reflexive sense of *calling themselves*, which is unnecessary and without analogy in the other terms of description. They were really called by the name of Israel, and that not only by themselves and one another, but by God. Almost equally erroneous, on the other hand, is Hitzig's supposition, that this last clause is an *obiter dictum* not essential to the sense. Both parts are equally essential, the description of the Jews as the chosen people of Jehovah, and the denial of their merit: for the error into which they were continually falling was the error of sacrificing one of these great doctrines to the other, or imagining that they were incompatible. It was necessary to the Prophet's purpose that the people should never forget either, but believe them both. From all this may be readily inferred the shallowness and blindness of the "higher criticism," which talks of the accumulation of descriptive epithets in this place as a rhetorical peculiarity symptomatic of a later age; whereas it is a distinct enumeration of the theocratical prerogatives of Israel, and one essential to the writer's purpose.

2. *For from the Holy City they are called.* The same name is given to Jerusalem below (chap. li. 1), and also in the later books (Dan. ix. 24, Neh. xii. 1) and the New Testament (Matt. iv. 5, xxvii. 53). It is so called as the seat of the true religion, the earthly residence of God, and the centre of the church. That the reference is not to mere locality is plain from the application of the name to the whole people. The כִּי at the beginning of this verse has somewhat perplexed interpreters. Cocceius makes it introduce the proof or reason of the words immediately preceding: " not in truth and not in righteousness, because they call themselves after

the Holy City," instead of calling themselves by the name of God. This description would certainly be appropriate to ritualists and all who let the Church usurp the place of its great Head. But this interpretation is precluded, as Vitringa has observed, by what immediately follows, *and upon the God of Israel rely*, which certainly would not have been adduced as a proof of insincerity or even imperfection. Some connect the clauses in a different manner, by giving כִּי the sense of *although :* "not in truth and not in righteousness, although they are called after the Holy City." But the sense thus obtained is dearly purchased by assuming so unusual and dubious a meaning of the particle. The safest, because the simplest course, is to take it in its ordinary sense of *for, because*, and to regard it as continuing the previous description, or rather as assuming it after a momentary interruption, for which reason *for* is used instead of *and*. The connection may be thus rendered clear by a paraphrase : " I speak to those who bear the name of Israel and worship Israel's God, however insincerely and imperfectly ; for they are still the chosen people, and as such entitled to rely upon Jehovah." This last is then descriptive not of a mere professed nor of a real yet presumptuous reliance, but of the prerogative of Israel, considered as the church or chosen people, a prerogative not forfeited by their unfaithfulness, so long as its continuance was necessary to the end for which it was originally granted. The false interpretations of the passage have arisen from applying it directly to the faith or unbelief of individuals, in which case there appears to be an incongruity between the parts of the description ; but as soon as we apply it to the body, this apparent incongruity is done away, it being not only consistent with Isaiah's purpose, but a necessary part of it, to hold up the prerogatives of Israel as wholly independent of all merit upon their part.—*Jehovah of hosts (is) his name.* These words are added to identify the object of reliance more completely, as the Being who was called the God of Israel and Jehovah of hosts. At the same time they suggest the attributes implied in both parts of the name. As if he had said, they rely upon the God of Israel, whom they acknowledge as an independent and eternal Being, and the Sovereign of the universe.

3. *The first* (or *former things*) *since then I have declared.* That is, I prophesied of old the events which have already taken place. For the sense of the particular expressions, see above on chap. xlv. 21, xlvi. 10. There is no abrupt transition here, as some interpreters asume. This verse asserts God's prescience, not absolutely as in other cases, but for the purpose of explaining why he had so carefully predicted certain future events. It can be fully understood, therefore, only in connection with what goes before and follows.—*And out of my mouth they went forth.* Some regard this as a proof that רִאשֹׁנוּת means former prophecies and not events ; but even the latter might be figuratively said to have gone out of his mouth, as having been predicted by him.—*And I cause them to be heard*, a synonymous expression.—*Suddenly I do* (*them*) *and they come to pass.*—All this is introductory to what follows respecting the design of prophecy. The sense is not simply, I foretell things to come, but I foretell things to come for a particular purpose, which is now to be explained.

4. *From my knowing.* This may either mean *because I knew* or *since I knew*, or the last may be included in the first, as in chap. xliii. 4.—*That thou art hard.* This is commonly considered an ellipsis for קְשֵׁה־לֵב (Ezek. iii. 7), or קְשֵׁה־עֹרֶף (Deut. ix. 6), hard-hearted or stiff-necked ; more probably the latter, as the sense required by the context is not so much that of insensibility as that of obstinate perverseness. The same idea is ex-

pressed still more strongly by the following words, *and an iron sinew* (is) *thy neck.* The substitution of *bar* for *sinew*, which is elsewhere the invariable sense of יִד, is not only gratuitous, but inexact and enfeebling.— *And thy forehead brass.* The hardening of the face or forehead, which is sometimes used in a good sense (*e. g.* chap. l. 7), here denotes shameless persistency in opposition to the truth. The allusion is not, as Vitringa supposes, to the colour of brass, but to its hardness, with some reference, as Knobel thinks, to the habits of animals which push or butt with the forehead.

5. *Therefore I told thee long ago.* This is often the force of the conjunction *and* after a conditional clause or sentence. Because I knew thee to be such, and I told thee, *i. e.* therefore I told thee.—*Before it comes I have let thee hear* (*it*), *lest thou say, My idol did them, i. e.* did the things before referred to collectively in the singular. The Hebrew word for *idol*, from the double meaning of its root, suggests the two ideas of an image and a torment or vexation.—*My graven image and my molten image ordered them, i. e.* called them into being.—Gousset takes נִסְכִּי in the sense of *my libation* or *drink-offering.*

6. *Thou hast heard* (the prediction), *see all of it* (accomplished). *And ye* (idolaters or idols), *will not ye declare*, the same word used above for the prediction of events, and therefore no doubt meaning here, will not ye predict something? This is Hitzig's explanation of the words; but most interpreters suppose the sense to be, *will you not acknowledge* (or *bear witness*) that these things were predicted by Jehovah? In favour of the first is its taking הִגִּיד in the sense which it has in the preceding verse, and also the analogy of chap. xli. 22, 23, where the very same challenge is given in nearly the same form; to which may be added the sudden change to the plural form, and the emphatic introduction of the pronoun, implying a new object of adress, and not a mere enallage, because he immediately resumes the address to the people in the singular.—*I have made thee to hear new things.* He appeals not only to the past but to the future, and thus does what he vainly challenged them to do. There is no need of inquiring what particular predictions are referred to. All that seems to be intended is the general distinction between past and future, between earlier and later prophecies.—*From now*, henceforth, after the present time. It is a curious fact that Hitzig, who regards the old interpretation of מֵאָפֶס (*less than nothing*) in chap. xl. 17, as absurd, makes מֵעַתָּה in the case before us a comparative expression, and translates the whole phrase *newer than now*, which he says is a circumlocution for the future.—*And* (*things*) *kept* (in reserve), *and thou hast not known them*, or, in our idiom, *which thou hast not known.* Beck, by some unintelligible process, reaches the conclusion that this verse contains a perfectly indisputable case of *vaticinium post eventum.*

7. *Now they are created* (*i. e.* brought into existence for the first time), *and not of old*, or never before. The literal meaning of the next words is, *and before the day and thou hast not heard them.* J. D. Michaelis and some others seem to understand this as meaning, *one day ago thou hadst not heard them;* but this is a German or a Latin idiom, wholly foreign from the Hebrew usage. Others, with more probability, explain it to mean, *before this day* (or *before to-day*) *thou hast never heard them*, יוֹם being put by poetical licence for הַיּוֹם with the article. Gesenius understands by *day* the time of the fulfilment; which is not so obvious nor so appropriate, because the prophecy must be made known before it can be verified by the event.

In all these constructions, the וֹ before לֹא is supposed to be the idiomatic sign of the apodosis, very frequent after specifications of time. (See Gen. xxii. 4.) The same reason is assigned as before : *Lest thou shouldest say, Behold, I knew them.* In the last word the feminine suffix takes the place of the masculine in the verse preceding, equivalent in import to the Greek or Latin neuter.

8. *Nay, thou didst not hear ; nay, thou didst not know.* The idiomatic form of this sentence is not easily expressed in a translation, which, if too exact, will fail to show the true connection. Having given the perverseness of the people as a reason why they knew so much by previous revelation, he now assigns it as a reason why they knew so little. These, although at first sight inconsistent statements, are but varied aspects of the same thing. God had told them so much beforehand, lest they should ascribe the event to other causes. He had told them no more, because he knew that they would wickedly abuse his favour. In a certain sense, and to a certain extent, it was true that they had heard and known these things beforehand. In another sense, and beyond that extent, it was equally true that they had neither heard nor known them. This seems to be the true force of the גַּם. It was true that they had heard, but it was *also* true that they had not heard. The strict sense of the clause is, *likewise thou hadst not heard, likewise thou hadst not known ;* but as this form of expression is quite foreign from our idiom, *nay,* may be substituted, not as a synonyme, but an equivalent. The *yea* of the common version fails to indicate the true connection, by suggesting the idea of a climax rather than that of an antithesis, of something more rather than of something different.—*Likewise of old* (or beforehand) *thine ear was not open*, literally, *did not open*, the Hebrew usage coinciding with the English in giving to this verb both a transitive and intransitive sense. (For another clear example of the latter, see below, chap. lx. 11.) Vitringa understands the whole of this first clause as meaning that they *would* not hear or know, but stopped their ears and minds against the revelation which was offered to them. For this supposition he assigns a reason that is really conclusive on the other side, viz. that the last clause describes them as treacherous and disloyal, which he says would be unjust if they had no revelation to abuse. But this argument proceeds upon a false view as to the connection of the clauses. It supposes the first to give a reason for the last, whereas the last gives a reason for the first. The sense is not, that *because* they would not hear or know what was revealed, God denounced them as traitors and apostates ; but that *because* they were traitors and apostates, he would not allow them to hear or know the things in question. This construction is required by the כִּי (*because*) at the beginning of the second clause ; by the words *I knew*, which, on the other supposition, are unmeaning ; and by the form תִּבְגּוֹד, which cannot, without arbitrary violence, have any other sense here but the strict one of the future, or of some tense involving the idea of futurity.—*I know thou wilt*, (or *I knew thou wouldest*) *act very treacherously.* Lowth supposes the emphatic repetition of the verb to express certainty rather than intensity, and both may be included, *i. e.* both would perhaps be unavoidably suggested by this form of expression to a Hebrew reader. Beck's triumphant charge against the writer of the " naivest self-contradiction," proceeds upon the false assumption that the conquest of Babylon by Cyrus is the chief, or rather the sole subject of the prophecy, an error which has been already more than once exposed.—*And apostate* (rebel, or deserter) *from the womb was called to thee, i. e.* this name was used in calling thee, or thou

wast called. Besides the idiom in the syntax, there is here another instance of the use of the verb *call* or *name* to express the real character. They were so called *i. e.* they might have been so, they deserved to be so. (See above, chap. i. 26, vol. i, p. 92.)—Here, as in chap. xlii. 2, 24, most interpreters explain *the womb* as meaning Egypt; and Jerome carries this idea so far as to paraphrase the words thus, *quando de Ægypto liberatus, quasi meo ventre conceptus es.* In all the cases, it seems far more natural to understand this trait of the description as belonging rather to the sign than the thing signified, as representing no specific circumstance of time or place in the history of Israel, but simply the infancy or birth of the ideal person substituted for him.

9. *For my name's sake.* Aben Ezra understands this to mean, for the sake of my name by which ye are called; but most interpreters explain it as an equivalent but stronger expression than *for my own sake*, for the sake of the revelation which I have already made of my own attributes. This explanation agrees well with the language of ver. 11 below.—*I will defer my anger.* Literally, *prolong* it; but this would be equivocal in English. To avoid the équivoque, Vitringa adopts the absurd translation, *I will lengthen* (or *prolong*) *my nose*, which he explains my saying that a long face is a sign of clemency or mildness, and a short or contracted face of anger; an opinion which appears to have as little foundation in physiognomy as in etymology. It seems most probable that אַף *anger*, and אַפַּיִם *the nostrils* are at most collateral derivatives from אָנַף to breathe. The common version, *I will defer my anger*, is approved by the latest writers, and confirmed not only by our familiar use of *long* and *slow*, in certain applications, as convertible terms, but also by the unequivocal analogy of the Greek μαχρόθυμος and the Latin *longanimis*—*And (for) my praise I will restrain (it) towards thee.* Praise is here the parallel to name, and may be governed by לְמַעַן repeated from the other clause. The more obvious construction, which would make it dependent on the following verb, is forbidden by the accents, and yields no coherent sense. Gesenius makes אחטם reflexive, or at least supplies the reflexive pronoun after it (*I refrain myself*); but it is simpler to assume the same object (*my wrath*) in both clauses.—The last words of the verse express the effect to be produced, *so as not to cut thee off*, or destroy thee.

10. *Behold I have melted thee.* This is the original meaning of the word; but it is commonly applied to the smelting of metals, and may therefore be translated *proved* or *tried thee.—And not with silver.* Some read בְּכֶסֶף (*as silver*), and others take the ב itself as a particle of comparison, or bring out substantially the same sense by rendering it *with* (*i. e.* in company with) *silver*, or by means of the same process. This is explained by Hitzig strictly as denoting that he had not literally melted them like silver, but only metaphorically in the furnace of affliction, an assurance no more needed here than in any other case of figurative language. Apart from these interpretations, which assume the sense *like silver*, the opinions of interpreters have been divided chiefly between two. The first of these explains the Prophet's words to mean, *not for silver* (or money), but gratuitously. This is certainly the meaning of בְּכֶסֶף in a number of places; but it seems to be entirely inappropriate when speaking of affliction, which is rather aggravated than relieved by the idea of its being gratuitous, *i. e.* for nothing. The other explanation, and the one now commonly adopted, takes the sense to be, *not with silver* (*i. e.* pure metal) as the result of the process. This agrees well with the context, which makes the want of merit on the part of

Israel continually prominent. It also corresponds exactly to the other clause, *I have chosen thee* (not in wealth, or power, or honour, but) *in the furnace of affliction*. The explanation of בְּחַרְתִּי as synonymous with בְּחַנְתִּי is entirely gratuitous. There is no word the sense of which is more deter; minately fixed by usage. The reason given by Gesenius for making *prove* or *try* the primary meaning of this verb, without a single instance to establish it, is the extraordinary one that trial must precede choice, which assumes the very question in dispute, viz., that בָּחַר means to try at all, a fact which cannot be sustained by Aramean analogies, in the teeth of an invariable Hebrew usage. But even if the method of arriving at this sense were less objectionable than it is, the sense itself would still be less appropriate and expressive than the common one. I have proved thee in the furnace of affliction, means I have afflicted thee; but this is saying even less than the first clause, whatever sense may there be put upon בְּכֶסֶף. It is not very likely that the Prophet simply meant to say, *I have afflicted thee in vain*, *I have afflicted thee*. It is certainly more probable, and more in keeping with the context and his whole design, to understand him as saying, I have found no merit in thee, and have chosen thee in the extreme of degradation and affliction. If the furnace of affliction was designed to have a distinct historical meaning, it probably refers not to Babylon, but Egypt, which is repeatedly called an iron furnace. This would agree exactly with the representations elsewhere made respecting the election of Israel in Egypt.

11. *For my own sake, for my own sake, I will do*—what is to be done. This is commonly restricted to the restoration of the Jews from exile; but this specific application of the promise is not made till afterwards. The terms are comprehensive, and contain a statement of the general doctrine, as the sum of the whole argument, that what Jehovah does for his own people, is in truth done not for any merit upon their part, but to protect his own divine honour.—*For how will it be profaned?* This may either mean, How greatly would it be profaned! or, How can I suffer it to be profaned? Gesenius anticipates *honour* from the other clause; but most interpreters make *name* the subject of the verb, a combination which occurs in several other places. (See Lev. xviii. 21, xix. 22, Ezek. xxxvi. 20.— *And my glory* (or honour) *to another will I not give*, as he must do if his enemies eventually triumph over his own people. The same words, with the same sense, occur above in chap. xlii. 8.

12. *Hearken unto me, O Jacob, and Israel my called; I am He, I am the First, also I the Last.* A renewed assurance of his ability and willingness to execute his promises, the latter being implied in the phrase *my called*, *i. e.* specially elected by me to extraordinary privileges. The threefold repetition of the pronoun *I* is supposed by some of the older writers to contain an allusion to the Trinity, of which interpretation Vitringa wisely says, *quam meditationem hoc loco non urgeo neque refello*. *I am He* is understood by the later writers to mean, I am the Being in question, or it is, I that am the First and the Last. The older writers give the הוּא a more emphatic sense, as meaning, He that really exists.—Lowth supplies *my servant* after *Jacob*, on the authority of one manuscript and two old editions. On like authority he changes אַף into the simple conjunctive וְ, which he says is more proper.—Compare with this verse chap. xli. 4, xliii. 10, xliv. 6.

13. *Also my hand founded the earth, and my right hand spanned the heavens*. The force of the אַף seems to be this, Not only am I an Eternal Being, but the Creator of the heavens. *Hand* and *right hand* is merely a

poetical or rhetorical variation.—The Septuagint renders טִפְּחָה ἐστερέωσε, by assimilation to the parallel term *founded*. The Vulgate has *mensa est*, which is approved by Kimchi. The Chaldee *suspended*, which may be taken either strictly, or in the sense of *balanced, weighed*. Aben Ezra, followed by most modern writers, makes it mean *expanded;* which explanation is confirmed by the Syriac analogy, and by the parallel passage chap. li. 13, where the founding of the earth is connected with the spreading' of the skies, and the latter expressed by the unambiguous word נוֹטֶה. Luzzatto points out a like combination of the derivative nouns in 1 Kings vii. 9.— Vitringa construes קְרֹא אֲנִי like an ablative absolute in Latin (*me vocante*), and the same sense is given, with a difference of form, in the English Version (*when I call*). But in Hebrew usage, the pronoun and participle thus combined are employed to express present and continuous action, *I* (*am*) *calling, i.e.* I habitually call. The words are not therefore naturally applicable to the original creation (*I called*), as Cocceius, Gesenius, and others explain them, but must either be referred, with Kimchi, to the constant exertion of creative power in the conservation of the universe, or, with Vitringa and most later writers, to the authority of the Creator over his creatures as his instruments and servants. *I call to them* (summon them), *and they will stand up together* (*i. e.* all, without exception). This agrees well with the usage of the phrase to *stand before*, as expressing the attendance of the servant on his master. (See, for example, 1 Kings xvii. 1.) The same two ideas of creation and service are connected in Ps. cxix. 90, 91. The exclusive reference of the whole verse to creation, on the other hand, is favoured by the analogy of Rom. iv. 17, and Col. i. 17.— For the different expressions here used see above, chap. xl. 22, xlii. 5, xliv. 24, xlv. 12.

14. *Assemble yourselves, all of you, and hear!* The object of address is Israel, according to the common supposition, but more probably the heathen. *Who among them, i.e.* the false gods or their prophets, *hath declared* (predicted) *these things*, the whole series of events which had been cited to demonstrate the divine foreknowledge. *Jehovah loves him, i.e.* Israel, and to shew his love, *he will do his pleasure* (execute his purpose) *in Babylon, and his* (Jehovah's) *arm* (shall be upon) *the Chaldees*. This explanation, which is given by J. H. Michaelis, seems to answer all the conditions of the text and context. Most interpreters, however, make the clause refer to Cyrus, and translate it thus, " He whom Jehovah loves shall do his pleasure in Babylon, and his arm (*i.e.* exercise his power, or execute his vengeance) on the Chaldees." Another construction of the last words makes them mean that " he (Cyrus) shall be his arm (*i.e.* the arm of Jehovah) against the Chaldees." But for this use of *arm* there is no satisfactory analogy. Kocher supposes it to mean that " the Chaldees (shall be) his arm," in allusion to the aid which Cyrus received from Gobryas and Gadates, as related in the fourth book of the Cyropaedia. Vitringa is inclined to assume an aposiopesis, and to read, " his arm (shall conquer or destroy) the Chaldees." Aben Ezra refers both the suffixes to Cyrus, who is then said to do his own pleasure upon Babylon.—Others refer both to God (his pleasure and his arm); but most interpreters take a middle course, referring one to each.

15. *I, I, have spoken* (*i.e.* predicted); *I have also called him* (effectually by my providence); *I have brought him* (into existence, or into public view); *and he prospered his way.* The reference of the last verb to Jehovah as its subject involves a harsh enallage personæ, which Vitringa and others avoid

by making the verb neuter or intransitive, *his way prospers*.   But דַּרְכּוֹ is
feminine, not only in general usage, but in combination with this very verb
(Judges xviii. 5).   The safe rule is, moreover, to give Hiphil an active
sense wherever it is possible.   The true solution is to make Cyrus or Israel
the subject, and to understand the phrase as meaning, *he makes his own
way prosperous, i. e.* prospers in it.   (Compare Ps. i. 3, and Hengstenberg's
Commentary on the Psalms, vol. i. p. 17.)

16. *Draw near unto me !*   As Jehovah is confessedly the speaker in the
foregoing and the following context, and as similar language is expressly
ascribed to him in chap. xlv. 19, Calvin and Gesenius regard it as most
natural to make these his words likewise, assuming a transition in the last
clause from Jehovah to the Prophet, who there describes himself as sent
by Jehovah.   Instead of this distinction between the clauses, Jarchi and
Rosenmüller suppose the person of the Prophet and of God to be confused
in both.   Hitzig and Knobel follow some of the other Jewish writers in
making the whole verse the words of Isaiah.   Vitringa and Henderson agree
with Athanasius, Augustin, and other Fathers, who reconcile the clauses by
making Christ the speaker.   Those who believe that he is elsewhere introduced in this same book, can have no difficulty in admitting a hypothesis,
which reconciles the divine and human attributes referred to in the sentence,
as belonging to one person.— *Hear this ; not from the beginning in secret
have I spoken.*   See above, on chap. xlv. 19.—*From the time of its being.*
Œcolampadius refers this to the eternal counsel of Jehovah ; but Vitringa
well observes that usage has appropriated הָיָה to express the execution, not
the formation of the divine purpose.   Brentius supposes an allusion to the
exodus from Egypt and a comparison between it and the deliverance from
Babylon ; but this is wholly fanciful and arbitrary.   The rabbins, with as
little reason, make it mean, since the beginning of my ministry, since I
assumed the prophetic office.   But most interpreters refer the suffix (*it*) to
the raising up of Cyrus and the whole series of events connected with it,
which formed the subject of the prophecies in question.   (See above, chap.
xlvi. 11.)—Since these events began to take place, *I was there*.   Lowth
proposes to read שָׁם and to translate the phrase, *I had decreed it*.   But the
obvious analogy of Prov. viii. 27 is of itself sufficient to establish the Masoretic
reading.   Those who regard these as the words of Isaiah, understand them
to mean that he had predicted them, or as Knobel expresses it, that he was
present as a public speaker.   Those who refer the words to the Son of God
specifically, make the verse substantially identical in meaning with the one
in Proverbs just referred to, which the church in every age has been very
much of one mind in applying to the second person of the Godhead as the
hypostatical wisdom of the Father.   Those who take the words more
generally as the language of Jehovah, understand him to declare that these
events had not occurred without his knowledge or his agency ; that he was
present, cognizant, and active, in the whole affair.   Thus far this last
hypothesis must be allowed to be the simplest and most natural.   The
difficulties which attend it arise wholly from what follows.—*And now.*
This seems to be in evident antithesis to מֵרֹאשׁ or to מֵעֵת הֱיוֹתָהּ, the latter
being the most obvious because it is the nearest antecedent.—*The Lord
Jehovah hath sent me.*   Those who regard Isaiah as the speaker in the whole
verse, understand this clause to mean, that as he had spoken before by divine
authority and inspiration, he did so still.   Those who refer the first clause
simply to Jehovah, without reference to personal distinctions, are under the
necessity of here assuming a transition to the language of the Prophet

himself. The third hypothesis, which makes the Son of God the speaker, understands both clauses in their strict sense as denoting his eternity on one hand, and his mission on the other. The sending of the Son by the Father is a standing form of speech in Scripture. (Exod. xxiii. 20, Isa. lxi. 1, Mal. iii. 1, John iii. 34, xvii. 3, Heb. iii. 1.)—*And his Spirit.* It has long been a subject of dispute whether these words belong to the subject or the object of the verb *hath sent.* The English Version removes all ambiguity by changing the collocation of the words (*the Lord God and his Spirit hath sent me*). The same sense is given in the Vulgate (*et spiritus ejus*); while the coincidence of the nominative and accusative (τό πνεῦμα) makes the Septuagint no less ambiguous than the original. With the Latin ·and English agree Calvin, Rosenmüller, Umbreit, and Hendewerk. Vitringa, Henderson, and Knobel, adopt Origen's interpretation (ἀμφότερα ἀπέστειλεν ὁ πατὴρ, τὸν σωτῆρα καὶ τὸ ἅγιον πνεῦμα). Gesenius and the other modern Germans change the form of expression by inserting the preposition *with*, which, however, is intended to represent the Spirit not as the sender but as one of the things sent.—The exegetical question is not one of much importance; because both the senses yielded are consistent with the usage of the Scriptures, and the ambiguity may be intended to let both suggest themselves. As a grammatical question, it is hard to be decided from analogy; because, on either supposition, וְרוּחוֹ cannot be considered as holding its regular position in the sentence, but must be regarded as an afterthought. The main proposition is, *the Lord God hath sent me.* The supplementary expression *and his Spirit* may be introduced, without absurdity or any violation of the rules of syntax, either before the verb or after it. Mere usage therefore leaves the question undecided.—As little can it be determined by the context or the parallelisms. The argument, which some urge, that the Spirit is never said to send the Son, takes for granted that the latter is the speaker, an assumption which precludes any inference from the language of this clause in proof of that position. Those, on the other hand, who consider these the words of Isaiah, argue in favour of the other construction, that the Spirit is said to send the prophets.—On the whole this may be fairly represented as one of the most doubtful questions of construction in the book, and the safest course is either to admit that both ideas were meant to be suggested, although probably in different degrees, or else to fall back upon the general rule, though liable to numberless exceptions, that the preference is due to the nearest antecedent or to that construction which adheres most closely to the actual collocation of the words. The application of this principle in this case would decide the doubt in favour of the prevailing modern doctrine, that Jehovah had sent the person speaking and endued him with his Spirit, as a necessary preparation for the work to which he was appointed. Beck's ridiculous assertion, that the writer is here guilty of the folly of appealing to his present prediction of events already past as a proof of his divine legation, only shews the falsehood of the current notion that the object of address is the Jewish people at the period of the exile, and its subject the victories of Cyrus.

17. *Thus saith Jehovah, thy Redeemer, the Holy One of Israel* (see the same prefatory formulas above, chap. xli. 14, xliii. 14), *I am Jehovah thy God* (or *I Jehovah am thy God*), *teaching thee to profit* (or *I, Jehovah, thy God, am teaching thee to profit*). Henderson's version, *I teach*, does not convey the precise force of the original, which is expressive of continued and habitual instruction, and the same remark applies to the participle in the other clause. *To profit, i. e.* to be profitable to thyself, to provide for

thy own safety and prosperity, or as Cocceius phrases it, *tibi consulere*. There seems to be a reference, as Vitringa suggests, to the unprofitableness so often charged upon false gods and their worship. (See chap. xliv. 10, xlv. 19, Jer. ii. 11.)—*Leading thee* (literally, *making thee to tread*) *in the way thou shalt go*. The ellipsis of the relative is just the same as in familiar English. The future includes the ideas of obligation and necessity, without expressing them directly ; the precise sense of the words is, *the way thou wilt go* if thou desirest to profit. Augusti and Ewald make it present (*goest*); but this is at the same time less exact and less expressive. —J. H. Michaelis understands these as the words of Christ, the teaching mentioned as the teaching of the gospel, the way, the way of salvation, &c. To all this the words are legitimately applicable, but it does not follow that they were specifically meant to convey this idea to the reader.

18. J. D. Michaelis suggests the possibility of reading לוא, a form in which the negative לא occurs, according to the Masora, thirty-five times in the Old Testament. The first clause would then contain a direct negation, *thou hast not attended*. In his version, however, he adheres to the Masoretic pointing, and translates the word as a conditional particle (*wenn du doch*), which is also recognised by Winer as the primary meaning of the word, although Gesenius and Ewald reverse the order of deduction, making *if* a secondary sense of the optative particle *O that!* The former supposition may be illustrated by our own colloquial expression, *if it were only so and so*, implying a desire that it were so. The verb which follows is commonly taken in the wide sense of *attending*, that of *listening* being looked upon as a specific application of it. Vitringa here translates it, *animum advertisses ;* J. H. Michaelis, with more regard to usage, *aures et animum*. It may be questioned, however, whether there is any clear case of its being used without explicit reference to hearing. If not, this must be regarded as the proper meaning, and the wider sense considered as implied but not expressed. Rosenmüller, Hitzig, Hendewerk, and Knobel, understand this verb as referring to the future ; *O that thou wouldst hearken to my commandments !* But the only instance which they cite of this use of the præterite (Isa. lxiii. 19), even if it did not admit (as it evidently does) of the other explanation, could not be set off against the settled usage of the language, which refers לו with the præterite to past time. (See Ewald's Grammar, § 605, and Nordheimer, § 1078.) Accordingly Maurer, De Wette, Ewald, Umbreit, and Gesenius (though less explicitly), agree with the older writers in explaining it to mean, *O that thou hadst hearkened to my commandments !* The objection, that this does not suit the context, is entirely unfounded. Nothing could well be more appropriate at the close of this division of the prophecies, than such an affecting statement of the truth, so frequently propounded in didactic form already, that Israel, although the chosen people of Jehovah, and as such secure from total ruin, was and was to be a sufferer, not from any want of faithfulness or care on God's part, but as the necessary fruit of his own imperfections and corruptions. —The Vav conversive introduces the apodosis, and is equivalent to *then*, as used in English for a similar purpose. Those who refer the first clause to the present or the future, give the second the form of the imperfect subjunctive, *then would thy peace be like a river ;* the others more correctly that of the pluperfect, *then had thy peace been* (or *then would thy peace have been*) *as a river*. The strict sense of the Hebrew, is *the river*, which Vitringa and others understand to mean the Euphrates in particular, with

whose inundations, as well as with its ordinary flow, the Prophet's original readers were familiar. It seems to be more natural, however, to regard the article as pointing out a definite class of objects rather than an individual, and none the less because the parallel expression is *the sea*, which some, with wanton violence, apply to the Euphrates also.—*Peace* is here used in its wide sense of prosperity : or rather peace, in the restricted sense, is used to represent all kindred and attendant blessings. The parallel term *righteousness* adds moral good to natural, and supplies the indispensable condition without which the other cannot be enjoyed. After the various affectations of the modern German writers in distorting this and similar expressions, it is refreshing to find Ewald, and even Hendewerk, returning to the old and simple version, *Peace* and *Righteousness.* The ideas suggested by the figure of a river, are abundance, perpetuity, and freshness, to which the waves of the sea add those of vastness, depth, and continual succession.

19. *Then should have been like the sand thy seed*, a common Scriptural expression for great multitude, with special reference, in this case, to the promise made to Abraham and Jacob (Gen. xxii. 17, xxxii. 12), the partial accomplishment of which (2 Sam. xvii. 11) is not inconsistent with the thought here expressed, that, in the case supposed, it would have been far more ample and conspicuous. Here, as in chap. xliv. 3, Knobel understands by seed or offspring, the individual members of the nation as distinguished from the aggregate body. But the image is rather that of a parent (here the patriarch Jacob) and his personal descendants.—*And the issues* (or *offspring*) *of thy bowels* (an equivalent expression to *thy seed*).— Of the next word, מֵעֹות, there are two interpretations. The Targum, the Vulgate, and the rabbins, give it the sense of stones, pebbles, gravel, and make it a poetical equivalent to *sand*. J. D. Michaelis and most of the later Germans make it an equivalent to מֵעִים, with a feminine termination, because figuratively used. The antithesis is then between *thy bowels* and *its bowels*, viz. those of the sea ; and the whole clause, supplying the ellipsis, will read thus, *the offspring of thy bowels like* (*the offspring of*) *its bowels*, in allusion to the vast increase of fishes, which J. D. Michaelis illustrates by saying that the whale leaves enough of its natural food, the herring, to supply all Europe with it daily. Ewald has returned to the old interpretation, which he defends from the charge of being purely conjectural, by tracing both מֵעִים and מֵעֹות to the radical idea of softness, the one being applied to the soft inward parts of the body, the other to the soft fine particles of sand or gravel. We may then refer the suffix, not to the remoter antecedent יָם, but to the nearer חוֹל.—*His name.* We must either suppose an abrupt transition from the second to the third person, or make *seed* the antecedent of the pronoun, which is harsh in itself, and rendered more so by the intervening plural forms. Lowth as usual restores uniformity by reading *thy name* on the authority of the Septuagint version. Vitringa supposes a particular allusion to genealogical tables and the custom of erasing names from them under certain circumstances. But all the requisitions of the text are answered by the common understanding of *name*, in such connections, as equivalent to *memory.* The excision or destruction of the name from before God is expressive of entire extermination.—The precise sense of the futures in this clause is somewhat dubious, Most interpreters assimilate them to the futures of the foregoing clause, as in the English Version (*should not have been cut off nor destroyed*). Those who understand the first clause as

expressing a wish in relation to the present or the future, make this last a promise, either absolute (*his name shall not be cut off*) or conditional (*his name should not be cut off*). Nor is this direct construction of the last clause inconsistent with the old interpretation of the first; as we may suppose that the writer, after wishing that the people had escaped the strokes provoked by their iniquities, declares that even now they shall not be entirely destroyed. This is precisely the sense given to the clause in the Septuagint (οὐδὲ νῦν ἀπολεῖται), and is recommended by two considerations : first, the absence of the Vav conversive, which in the other clause may indicate an indirect construction ; and secondly, its perfect agreement with the whole drift of the passage, and the analogy of others like it, where the explanation of the sufferings of the people as the fruit of their own sin is combined with a promise of exemption from complete destruction.

20. *Go forth from Babel !* This is a prediction of the deliverance from Babylon, clothed in the form of an exhortation to escape from it. We have no right to assume a capricious change of subject, or a want of all coherence with what goes before. The connection may be thus stated. After the general reproof and promise of the nineteenth verse, he recurs to the great example of deliverance so often introduced before. As if he had said, Israel, notwithstanding his unworthiness, shall be preserved ; even in extremity his God will not forsake him ; even from Babylon he shall be delivered :—and then turning in prophetic vision to the future exiles, he invites them to come forth.—*Flee from the Chasdim* (or *Chaldees*) *!* Vitringa, Gesenius, and most other writers, supply אֶרֶץ before כַּשְׂדִּים, or regard the latter as itself the name of the country. (See above, on chap. xlvii. 1.) But Maurer well says that he sees no reason why we may not here retain the proper meaning of the plural, and translate, *flee ye from the Chaldeans*, which is precisely the common English version of the clause.— *With a voice of joy.* The last word properly denotes a joyful shout, and not articulate song. The whole phrase means, with the sound or noise of such a shout. It has been made a question whether these words are to be connected with what goes before or with what follows. Gesenius and Hendewerk prefer the former, most interpreters the latter ; but Vitringa thinks the Masoretic accents were intended to connect it equally with both parts of the context, as in chap. xl. 3.—*Tell this, cause it to be heard.* The Hebrew collocation (*tell, cause to be heard, this*) cannot be retained in English. *Utter it* (cause it to go forth) *even to the end of the earth.* Compare chap. xlii. 10, xliii. 6. *Say ye, Jehovah hath redeemed his servant Jacob.* The present form, adopted by J. D. Michaelis and Augusti, is not only unnecessary but injurious to the effect. These are words to be uttered after the event ; and the preterite must therefore be strictly understood, as it is by most interpreters. The deliverance from Babylon is here referred to, only as one great example of the general truth that God saves his people.

21. *And they thirsted not in the desert* (through which) *he made them go.* The translation of the verbs as futures, by J. H. Michaelis and Hitzig, is entirely ungrammatical and inconsistent with the obvious intention of the writer to present these as the words of an annunciation after the event. The present form, adopted by J. D. Michaelis and the later Germans, although less erroneous, is a needless and enfeebling evasion of the true tense, which is purely descriptive. *Water from a rock he made to flow for them ; and he clave the rock and waters gushed out.* There is evident reference here to the miraculous supply of water in the journey through the wilderness. (Exod. xvii. 6, Num. xx. 11, Ps. lxxviii. 15.) It might even

seem as if the writer meant to state these facts historically. Such at least
would be the simpler exposition of his words, which would then contain a
reference to the exodus from Egypt, as the great historical example of
deliverance. As if he had said, Relate how God of old redeemed his servant Jacob out of Egypt, and led him through the wilderness, and slaked
his thirst with water from the solid rock. Most interpreters, however, are
agreed in applying the words to the deliverance from Babylon. Kimchi
understands the language strictly, and expresses his surprise that no
account of this great miracle was left on record by Ezra or any other
inspired historian. Gesenius sneers at the Rabbin's *naïveté*, but thinks it
matched by the simplicity of some Christian writers who know not what to
make of ideal anticipations which were never realised. Perhaps, however,
the absurdity is not altogether on the side where he imagines it to lie.
Kimchi was right in assuming, that if the flight and the march through the
wilderness were literal (a supposition common to Gesenius and himself),
then the accompanying circumstances must receive a literal interpretation
likewise, unless there be something in the text itself to indicate the contrary. Unless we are prepared to assume an irrational confusion of
language, setting all interpretation at defiance, our only alternative is to
conclude, on the one hand, that Isaiah meant to foretell a miraculous
supply of water during the journey from Babylon to Jerusalem, or that
the whole description is a figurative one, meaning simply that the wonders
of the exodus should be renewed. Against the former is the silence of
history, alleged by Kimchi ; against the latter, nothing but the foregone
conclusion that this and other like passages must relate exclusively to
Babylon and the return from exile.

22. *There is no peace, saith Jehovah, to the wicked.* The meaning of
this sentence, in itself considered, is too clear to be disputed. There is
more doubt as to its connection with what goes before. That it is a mere
aphorism, added to this long discourse, like a moral to an ancient fable,
can only satisfy the minds of those who look upon the whole book as a
series of detached and incoherent sentences. Vastly more rational is the
opinion, now the current one among interpreters, that this verse was
intended to restrict the operation of the foregoing promises to true believers,
or the genuine Israel ; as if he had said, All this will God accomplish for
his people, but not for the wicked among them. The grand conclusion to
which all tends is, that God is all and man nothing ; that even the chosen
people must be sufferers, because they are sinners ; that peculiar favour
confers no immunity to sin or exemption from responsibility, but that even
in the Israel of God and the enjoyment of the most extraordinary privileges, it still remains for ever true that " there is no peace to the wicked."

Chapter 49

THIS chapter, like the whole division which it introduces, has for its great
theme the relation of the church to the world, or of Israel to the Gentiles.
The relation of the former to Jehovah is of course still kept in view, but
with less exclusive prominence than in the First Part (chap. xl.–xlviii). The
doctrine there established and illustrated, as to the mutual relation of the
body and the head, is here assumed as the basis of more explicit teachings
with respect to their joint relation to the world and the great design of their

vocation. There is not so much a change of topics as a change in their relative position and proportions.

The chapter opens with an exhibition of the Messiah and his people, under one ideal person, as the great appointed Teacher, Apostle, and Restorer of the apostate nations, vers. 1–9. This is followed by a promise of divine protection and of glorious enlargement, attended by a joyous revolution in the state of the whole world, vers. 10–13. The doubts and apprehensions of the church herself are twice recited under different forms, vers. 14 and 24, and as often met and silenced, first by repeated and still stronger promises of God's unchanging love to his people and of their glorious enlargement and success, vers. 15–23 ; then by an awful threatening of destruction to their enemies and his, vers. 25, 26.

1. *Hearken ye islands unto me, and attend ye nations from afar.* Here, as in chap. xli. 1, he turns to the Gentiles and addresses them directly. There is the same diversity in this case as the explanation of אִיִּים. Some give it the vague sense of nations, others that of distant nations, while J. D. Michaelis again goes to the opposite extreme by making it mean Europe and Asia Minor. Intermediate between these is the meaning *coasts*, approved by Ewald and others. But there seems to be no sufficient reason for departing from the sense of *islands*, which may be considered as a poetical representative of foreign and especially of distant nations, although not as directly expressing that idea.—*From afar* is not merely *at a distance* (although this explanation might, in case of necessity, be justified by usage), but suggests the idea of attention being drawn to a central point *from* other points around it.—*Jehovah from the womb hath called me, from the bowels of my mother he hath mentioned my name* (or literally, caused it to be remembered). This does not necessarily denote the literal prediction of an individual by name before his birth, although, as Hengstenberg suggests, there may be an intentional allusion to that circumstance, involved in the wider meaning of the words, viz. that of personal election and designation to office. Vitringa's explanation of מִבֶּטֶן as meaning before birth, is not only unauthorized, but as gratuitous as Noyes's euphemistic paraphrase, *in my very childhood.* The expression *from the womb* may be either inclusive of the period before birth, or restricted to the actual vocation of the speaker to his providential work.—The speaker in this and the following verses is not Isaiah, either as an individual or as a representative of the prophets generally, on either of which suppositions the terms used are inappropriate and extravagant. Neither the prophets as a class, nor Isaiah as a single prophet, had been entrusted with a message to the Gentiles. In favour of supposing that the speaker is Israel, the chosen people, there are various considerations, but especially the aid which this hypothesis affords in the interpretation of the third verse. At the same time there are clear indications that the words are the words of the Messiah. These two most plausible interpretations may be reconciled and blended by assuming that in this case, as in chap. xlii. 1, the ideal speaker is the Messiah considered as the head of his people and as forming with them one complex person, according to the canon of Tichonius already quoted, *de Christo et Corpore ejus Ecclesia tanquam de una persona in Scriptura sæpius mentionem fieri, cui quædam tribuuntur quæ tantam in Caput, quædam quæ tantum in Corpus competunt, quædam vero in utrumque.* The objections to this assumption here are for the most part negative and superficial. That of Hengstenberg, that if this were the true interpretation here, it would admit of being carried out elsewhere, is really a strong proof of its truth ; as we have seen con-

clusive reasons, independently of this case, to explain the parallel passage in chap. xlii. 1 on precisely the same principle. The whole question as to the subjects and connections of these Later Prophecies has made a very sensible advance towards satisfactory solution since the date of the Christology, as may be learned by comparing the general analysis and special expositions of the latter with the corresponding passages of Hävernick and Drechsler. If, as we have seen cause to believe, the grand theme of this whole book is the church, in its relation to its Head and to the World, the anterior presumption is no longer against but decidedly in favour of the reference of this verse to the Head and the Body as one person, a reference confirmed, as we shall see, by clear New Testament authority.

2. *And he hath placed* (i. e. *rendered* or *made*) *my mouth like a sharp sword.* By *mouth* we are of course to understand speech, discourse. The comparison is repeated and explained in the Epistle to the Hebrews (iv. 12): "The word of God is quick and powerful, and sharper than any two-edged sword, piercing even to the dividing asunder of soul and spirit, and of the joints and marrow, and is a discerner of the thoughts and intents of the heart." In both cases these qualities are predicated, not of literal speech merely, but of the instruction of which it is the natural and common instrument. As tropical parallels, Lowth refers to Pindar's frequent description of his verses as darts, but especially to the famous panegyric of Eupolis on Pericles, that he alone of the orators left a sting in those who heard him (μόνος τῶν ῥητόρων τὸ κέντρον ἐγκατέλειπε τοῖς ἀκροωμένοις).—*In the shadow of his hand he hid me.* It has been made a question whether *in the shadow of his hand* means *in his hand* or *under it;* and if the latter, whether there is reference to the usual position of the sword-belt, or to the concealment of the drawn sword or dagger under the arm or in the sleeve. Most interpreters, however, prefer the obvious sense, in the protection of his hand, or rather in its darkness, since the reference is not so much to safety as to concealment. Thus understood, the figure is appropriate not only to the personal Messiah, but to the ancient church, as his precursor and representative, in which high character it was not known for ages to the nations.—*And he placed me for* (that is, *rendered me,* or, *used me as*) *a polished arrow.* This is the parallel expression to the first member of the other clause. What is there called a sword is here an arrow. The essential idea is of course the same, viz. that of penetrating power, but perhaps with an additional allusion to the directness of its aim and the swiftness of its flight. The common version *shaft* is not entirely accurate, the Hebrew word denoting strictly the metallic head of the arrow. The Septuagint gives בָּרוּר the sense of chosen or elect, which is retained by Vitringa ; but most interpreters prefer the sense of polished, which is near akin to that of sharpened, sharp.—*In his quiver he has hid me.* This is the corresponding image to the hiding in the shadow of God's hand. It is still more obvious in this case that the main idea meant to be conveyed is not protection but concealment. The archer keeps the arrow in his quiver not merely that it may be safe, but that it may be ready for use and unobserved until it is used.

3. *And he* (Jehovah) *said to me, Thou art my servant,* i. e. my instrument or agent constituted such for a specific and important purpose. In this same character both Israel and the Messiah have before been introduced. There is therefore the less reason for giving any other than the strict sense to the words which follow, *Israel in whom I will be glorified* or *glorify myself.* The version *I will glory* seems inadequate, and not sufficiently

sustained by usage. Gesenius, unable to reconcile this form of address with the hypothesis that the speaker is Isaiah or the Prophets as a class, proposes in his commentary what had been before proposed by J. D. Michaelis, to expunge the word יִשְׂרָאֵל as spurious ; a desperate device which he abandons in the second edition of his version, and adopts the opinion of Umbreit, that the Israel of this passage is the chosen people as a whole, or with respect to its better portion. The other devices, which have been adopted for the purpose of evading this difficulty, although not so violent, are equally unfounded. *E. g.* " It is Israel in whom I will be glorified by thee." " Thou art an Israelite indeed, or a genuine descendant of Israel." Another gratuitous hypothesis is that of a sudden apostrophe to Israel after addressing the Messiah or the Prophet. The only supposition which adheres to the natural and obvious meaning of the sentence, and yet agrees with the context, is the first above mentioned, viz. that of complex subject including the Messiah and his people, or the body with its head.

4. *And I said*, in opposition or reply to what Jehovah said. The pronoun in Hebrew, being not essential to the sense, is emphatic. *In vain* (or *for a vain thing, i. e.* an unattainable object) *have I toiled.* The Hebrew word suggests the idea of exhaustion and weariness.—*For emptiness and vanity my strength have I consumed. But my right is with Jehovah and my work with my God.* פְּעֻלָּה is no doubt here used in the same sense as in chap. xl. 10, viz. that of recompence, *work* being put for its result or its equivalent. If so, it is altogether probable that מִשְׁפָּטִי here means that to which I have a right or am entitled, that is to say in this connection, my reward or recompence. This explanation of the term is certainly more natural than that which makes it mean *my cause, my suit*, as this needlessly introduces a new figure, viz. that of litigation over and above that of labour or service for hire. This clause is universally explained as an expression of strong confidence that God would make good what was wanting, by bestowing the reward which had not yet been realised. *With* therefore means in his possession, and at his disposal. The next verse shews that the failure here complained of is a failure to accomplish the great work before described, viz. that of converting the world.

5. *And now, saith Jehovah, my maker* (or *who formed me*) *from the womb, for a servant to himself, i. e.* to be his servant in the sense before explained. The *now* may be here taken either in its temporal or logical sense.—*To convert* (or *bring back*) *Jacob to him.* This cannot mean to restore from exile ; for how could this work be ascribed directly either to the Prophet or the Prophets, or to the Messiah, or to Israel himself ? It might indeed apply to Cyrus, but the whole context is at war with such an explanation. All that is left, then, is to give the verb the sense of bringing back to a state of allegiance from one of alienation and revolt. But how could Jacob or Israel be said to bring himself back ? This is the grand objection to the assumption that the servant of Jehovah was Israel himself. In order to evade it, Rosenmüller and Hitzig deny that לְשׁוֹבֵב is dependent on the words immediately preceding, and refer it to Jehovah himself, *that he might bring back Jacob to himself.* But this construction, not an obvious or natural one in itself, if here assumed, must be repeated again and again in the following verses, where it is still more strained and inappropriate. Nor is it necessary even here, to justify the reference of the passage to Israel, which may be effected by assuming a coincident reference to the Messiah, as the head of the body, and as such conspicuously active in restoring

Israel itself to God.—This is one of the cases where the idea of the head predominates above that of the body, because they are related to each other as the subject and object of one and the same action. The vocation of Israel was to reclaim the nations ; that of the Messiah was first to reclaim Israel himself and then the nations.—In the next clause there is an ancient variation of the text, preserved in the Kethib and Keri of the Masora. The marginal emendation is לוֹ *to him*, which many modern interpreters prefer, and make it for the most part a dependent clause, *to restore Jacob to him, and that Israel may be gathered to him.* In the sentence construed thus, it might seem strange that different propositions should be used in the two parallel members, and that לוֹ should stand before the verb instead of closing the phrase as אֵלָיו does. But these might be considered trivial points, were it not that the marginal reading is so easily accounted for, as an attempt to remove the difficulties of the older text, in which the לֹא has its natural and necessary place before the verb. Luther, adhering to the textual reading, gives the verb an unfavourable sense, *that Israel may not be snatched away* or *carried off.* But most of those who retain the old reading give the verb the favourable sense of gathering that which is dispersed. Some then read the clause as an interrogation, *shall not Israel be gathered?* Others as a concession, *although Israel be not gathered.* Others as a simple affirmation in the present tense, *and* (yet) *Israel is not gathered.* All that is needed to give this last the preference is the substitution of the future for the present, after which the whole verse may be paraphrased as follows : Thus saith Jehovah, who formed me from the womb as a servant for himself, to restore Jacob to him, and (yet) Israel will not be gathered—and (yet) I shall be honoured in the eyes of Jehovah, and my God has (already) been my strength. The first *yet* introduced to shew the true connection is equivalent to saying, though I was called and raised up for this purpose ; the other is equivalent to saying, although Israel will not be gathered. This last phrase may be taken as a simple prediction that they should not be gathered, or a declaration that they would not (consent to) be gathered. This last, if not expressed, is implied.—The translation of עֻזִּי as meaning *my praise* is entirely gratuitous and hurtful to the sense, which is, that God has sustained him notwithstanding the apparent failure of his mission. The general meaning of the verse is that Messiah and his people should be honoured in the sight of God, although the proximate design of their mission, the salvation of the literal Israel, might seem to fail.

6. *And he said.* This does not introduce a new discourse or declaration, but resumes the construction which had been interrupted by the parenthetic clauses of the foregoing verse. It is in fact a repetition of the אָמַר יְהוָֹה at the beginning of that verse. *And now saith Jehovah (who formed me from the womb to be a servant to himself, to restore Jacob to him, and yet Israel will not be gathered, and yet I shall be honoured in the eyes of Jehovah, and my God has been my strength)—he said* or *says* as follows. *It is a light thing that thou shouldest be my servant.* The original form of expression is so purely idiomatic, that it cannot be retained in English. According to the usual analogy, the Hebrew words would seem to mean *it is lighter than thy being my servant;* but this can be resolved into *it is too light for thee to be my servant,* with at least as much ease as a hundred other formulas, the sense of which is obvious, however difficult it may be to account for the expression. Hitzig's assertion, therefore, that it is at variance with the laws of thought and language, though adopted by

Gesenius in his Thesaurus, is not only arbitrary but absurd, as it assumes the possibility of ascertaining and determining these laws independently of actual usage. The most that can be said with truth is that the form of expression is anomalous and rare, though not unparalleled, as may be seen by a comparison of this verse with Ezek. viii. 17. The sense, if it were doubtful in itself, would be clear from the context, which requires this to be taken as a declaration that it was not enough for the Messiah (and the people as his representative) to labour for the natural descendants of Abraham, but he and they must have a wider field.—*Thy being to me a servant to raise up the tribes of Jacob, and the preserved of Israel to restore.* This form of expression shews very clearly that in this and the parallel passages *servant* is not used indefinitely but in the specific sense of an appointed instrument or agent to perform a certain work. That work is here the *raising up* of Jacob, a phrase which derives light from the parallel expression, to *restore* the preserved of Israel, *i. e.* to raise them from a state of degradation, and to restore them from a state of estrangement. A specific reference to restoration from the Babylonish exile would be gratuitous ; much more the restriction of the words to that event, which is merely included as a signal instance of deliverance and restoration in the general. The textual reading נְצִירֵי appears to be a verbal adjective occurring nowhere else, and therefore exchanged by the Masoretic critics for the passive participle נְצוּרֵי. J. D. Michaelis, more ingeniously than wisely, makes נָצִיר synonymous with נֵצֶר (chap. xi. 1) a shoot or sprout, and gives to שֵׁבֶט the corresponding sense of a twig or branch—the shoots of Jacob and the twigs of Israel. All other writers seems to take the latter in its usual sense of tribe, and the other in that of preserved—meaning the elect or " such as should be saved."—*And I have given thee for a light of the Gentiles* (as in chap. xlii. 6), *to be my salvation even to the end of the earth.* This, according to the English idiom, would seem to mean *that thou mayest be my salvation,* &c.; but Hebrew usage equally admits of the interpretation, *that my salvation may be* (*i. e.* extend) *to the end of the earth,* which is in fact preferred by most interpreters. The meaning of this verse is not, as some suppose, that the heathen should be given to him in exchange and compensation for the unbelieving Jews, but that his mission to the latter was, from the beginning, but a small part of his high vocation. The application of this verse by Paul and Barnabas, in their address to the Jews of Antioch in Pisidia (Acts xiii. 47) is very important, as a confirmation of the hypothesis assumed above, that the person here described is not the Messiah exclusively, but that his people are included in the subject of the description.—" It was necessary that the word of God should first have been spoken unto you ; but seeing ye put it from you, and judge yourselves unworthy of everlasting life, lo, we turn to the Gentiles. For so hath the Lord commanded us (saying), I have set thee to be a light of the Gentiles, that thou shouldst be for salvation unto the ends of the earth." Although this, as Hengstenberg observes, is not irreconcilable with the exclusive Messianic explanation of the verse before us, its agreement with the wider explanation is too striking to be deemed fortuitous.

7. *Thus saith Jehovah, the Redeemer of Israel, his Holy One, to the heartily despised, to the nation exciting abhorrence.* The two epithets in this clause are exceedingly obscure and difficult. בְּזֹה has been variously explained as an infinitive, a passive participle, and an adjective in the construct state, which last is adopted by Gesenius and most later writers ; נֶפֶשׁ is commonly explained as meaning *men,* chiefly because the parallel expression

in Ps. xxii. 7 is עָם בְּזוּי. Another explanation takes it in its proper sense of *soul*, and understands it to qualify בְּזֹה, as meaning despised from the soul, *ex amimo*.   (Compare אֹיְבֵי נַפְשִׁי, Ps. xvii. 9.)   The meaning *men* belongs to the word only in certain cases, chiefly those in which we use the same expression, not a soul, forty souls, poor soul, &c.   No one, from this English usage, would infer that hated by souls meant hated by persons.— The other epithet is still more difficult, as it is necessary to determine whether מְתָעֵב has its usual sense, and whether גּוֹי is its subject or its object.   *Whom the nation abhorreth, who abhorreth the nation, who excites the abhorrence of the nation, the nation which excites abhorrence,*—all these are possible translations of the Hebrew words, among which interpreters choose according to their different views respecting the whole passage.   In any case it is descriptive of deep abasement and general contempt, to be exchanged hereafter for an opposite condition.—*To a servant of rulers,* one who has hitherto been subject to them but is now to receive their homage. —*Kings shall see* (not *him* or *them*, but *it,* viz. that which is to happen) *and rise up* (as a token of respect), *princes (shall see) and bow themselves.*   It is an ingenious thought of Hitzig, though perhaps too refined, that kings, being usually seated in the presence of others, are described as rising from their thrones; while princes and nobles, who usually stand in the presence of their sovereigns, are described as falling prostrate.—*For the sake of Jehovah who is faithful,* (to his promises), *the Holy One of Israel, and he hath chosen thee,* or in our idiom, *who hath chosen thee.*   This last clause not only ascribes the promised change to the power of God, but represents it as intended solely to promote his glory.

8. *Thus saith Jehovah, In a time of favour have I heard* (or *answered*) *thee, and in a day of salvation have I helped thee.*   The common version, *an acceptable time,* does not convey the sense of the original, which signifies a suitable or appointed time for shewing grace or favour.   The object of address is still the Messiah and his people, whose great mission is again described.   *And I will keep thee, and will give thee for a covenant of the people,* *i. e.* of men in general (see above, chap. xlii. 7), *to raise up the earth* or world from its present state of ruin, *and to cause to inherit the desolate heritages,* the moral wastes of heathenism.   There is allusion to the division of the land by Joshua.   Here again we have clear apostolical authority for applying this description to the church, or people of God, as the Body of which Christ is the Head.   Paul says to the Corinthians, " We then as workers together (with him) beseech you also that ye receive not the grace of God in vain.   For he saith, I have heard thee in a time accepted, and in the day of salvation have I succoured thee."   What follows is no part of the quotation but Paul's comment on it.   " Behold, now is the accepted time ; behold, now is the day of salvation."   (2 Cor. vi. 2.)   This, taken in connection with the citation of ver. 6 in Acts xiii. 47, precludes the supposition of an accidental or unmeaning application of this passage to the people or ministers of Christ as well as to himself.

9. *To say to those bound, Come forth ; to (those) who (are) in darkness, Be revealed* (or *shew yourselves*).   לֵאמֹר might here be taken in its usual sense after verbs of speaking, viz. that of *saying;* but it seems more natural to make it a correlative of the infinitives לְהָקִים and לְהַנְחִיל *to raise up*—*to cause to inherit*—*to say.*   Gesenius paraphrases rather than translates הִגָּלוּ, *come to the light;* which is carefully copied by his later imitators as a faithful version.—*On the ways* (or *roads*) *they shall feed, and in*

all bare hills shall be their pasture. There is here a change of figure, the delivered being represented not as prisoners or freedmen, but as flocks. Some read *by the way* or *on their way* homeward ; but it is commonly agreed that the Prophet simply represents the flock as finding pasture even without going aside to seek it, and even in the most unlikely situations. The restriction of these figures to deliverance from Babylon, can seem natural only to those who have assumed the same hypothesis throughout the foregoing chapters.

10. *They shall not hunger and they shall not thirst, and there shall not smite them mirage and sun ; for he that hath mercy on them shall guide them, and by springs of water shall he lead them.* The image of a flock is still continued (compare chap. xl. 10, 11, xli. 18, xliii. 19). שָׁרָב is the same word that is now universally explained in chap. xxxv. 7, to mean the *mirage*, or delusive appearance of water in the desert (see above, p. 38). Jarchi explains it here by חוֹם *heat*, which Rosenmüller supposes to be here substituted for the proper meaning. Gesenius, on the other hand, makes heat the primary, and mirage the secondary sense. The reason for excluding the latter here is that it does not seem to suit the verb *smite ;* but as this verb is used with considerable latitude, and as a *zeugma* may be easily assumed, Hitzig, Ewald, and Knobel give the noun the same sense in both places. Most of the modern writers understand the last clause to mean, *to springs of water he shall lead them ;* but *along* or *by* may be considered preferable, as suggesting more directly the idea of progressive motion. As he leads them onwards, he conducts them along streams of water. This may, however, be supposed to give too great a latitude of meaning to the word translated *springs.*—For the true sense of the verb יְנַהֵל, see above, chap. xl. 11.

11. *And I will place all my mountains for the way, and my roads shall be high.* The image of a flock is now exchanged for that of an army on the march. Rosenmüller omits *my*, and explains הָרַי as an old plural form ; to which Gesenius objects, not only as gratuitous, but also as at variance with the parallelism which requires a suffix. *My mountains* is by some understood to mean the mountains of Israel ; but why these should be mentioned is not easily explained. Others with more probability explain it as an indirect assertion of God's sovereignty and absolute control, and more especially his power to remove the greatest obstacles from the way of his people. The original expression is not merely *for a way* but *for the way,* i. e. the way in which my people are to go, מְסִלָּה is an artificial road or causeway made by throwing up the earth, which seems to be intended by the verb at the close (compare the use of סָלַל, chap. lvii. 14, lxii. 19). The discrepance of gender in the verb and noun is an anomaly, but one which does not in the least obscure the sense or even render the construction doubtful. Compare with this verse chap. xxxv. 8, xl. 4.

12. *Behold, these from afar shall come, and behold these from the north and from the sea, and these from the land of Sinim.* There is not the least doubt as to the literal translation of this verse ; and yet it has been a famous subject of discordant expositions, all of which turn upon the question, what is meant by the *land of Sinim.* In addition to the authors usually cited, respect will here be had to an interesting monograph, by an American missionary in China, originally published in the Chinese Repository, and republished in this country under the title of " The Land of Sinim, or an exposition of Isaiah xlix. 12, together with a brief account of the Jews

and Christians in China." (Philadelphia, 1845.) It is well said by this writer, that the verse before us is the central point of the prophetical discourse, of which it forms a part, inasmuch as it embodies the great promise, which in various forms is exhibited before and afterwards. This relation of the text to the context is important, because it creates a presumption in favour of the widest meaning which can be put upon the terms of the prediction, and against a restricted local application. A preliminary question, not devoid of exegetical importance, is the question with respect to the mutual relation of the clauses, as divided in the Masoretic text. The doubtful point is whether the first clause is a single item in an enumeration of particulars, or a generic statement, comprehending the specific statements of the other clause. Almost all interpreters assume the former ground, and understand the verse as naming or distinguishing the four points of the compass. But the other supposition is ingeniously maintained by the missionary in China, who makes the first clause a general prediction that converts shall come from the remotest nations, and the other an explanation of this vague expression, as including the north, the west, and the land of Sinim. Upon this construction of the sentence, which is certainly plausible and striking, it may be observed, in the first place, that it is not necessary for the end at which the author seems to aim in urging it. This end appears to be the securing of some proof that the specifications of the second clause relate to *distant* countries. But this conclusion is almost as obvious, if not entirely so, upon the other supposition; for if one of the four quarters is denoted by the phrase *from afar*, the idea necessarily suggested is that all the other points enumerated are remote likewise. The same thing would, moreover, be sufficiently apparent from the whole drift of the context as relating not to proximate or local changes, but to vast and universal ones. Nothing is gained, therefore, even for the author's own opinion, by the admission of this new construction. Another observation is that the authority on which he seems to rest its claims is inconclusive, namely, that of the Masoretic interpunction, as denoted by the accents. He states the testimony thus afforded much too strongly, when he speaks of " a full stop " after the clause *from afar they shall come*, and points the verse accordingly. The Athnach, as a general rule, indicates the pause not at the end but in the middle of a sentence or complete proposition. It is therefore *prima facie* proof that the sense is incomplete; and although there may be numerous exceptions, it cannot possibly demonstrate that the first clause does not form a part of the same series of particulars which is concluded in the second. That the first clause frequently contains what may be logically called an essential portion of the second, any reader may convince himself by the most cursory inspection of the book before us; and for two decisive examples in this very chapter, he has only to examine the fifth and seventh verses, where the substitution of a " full stop " for the Athnach would destroy the sense. But even if the testimony of the accents were still more explicit and decisive than it is, their comparatively recent date and their mixed relation to rhythmical or musical, as well as to grammatical and logical distinctions, make it always proper to subject their decisions to the requisitions of the text and context in themselves considered. Notwithstanding the great value of the Masoretic accents as an aid to interpretation, the appeal must after all be to the obvious meaning of the words, or in default of this to analogy and usage. The accents leave us, therefore, perfectly at liberty to look upon the mutual relation of the clauses as an open question, by inquiring whether there is any valid reason for departing from the ancient and customary supposition that the four points of the compass, or at least four quarters or directions, are distinctly mentioned. This leads me, in the third place, to observe that the objection which the missionary makes to this hypothesis, apart from the question of accentuation, is an insufficient one. He objects to Vitringa's explanation of the phrase *from afar* as meaning *from the east* (and the same objection would, by parity of reasoning, apply to the explanation of it as denoting *from the south*), that *afar* does not mean the east, and is not elsewhere used to denote it. But what Vitringa means to say is, not that *afar* means the *east*, but simply that it here supplies its place. If any one, in numbering the points of the compass, should, instead of a complete enumeration, say the north, south, east, and so on, his obvious meaning could not well be rendered doubtful by denying that *and so on* ever means the west. It is not the words themselves, but the place which they occupy, and their relation to the rest of the sentence, that suggests rather than expresses the idea. So here the north, the west, the land of Sinim, and afar, may denote the four points of the compass, although not so explicitly as in the case supposed, because in that before us we have not merely one doubtful point, but two, if not three; and also because the one most dubious (*from afar*) is not at the end like *and so on*, but at the beginning. Still it seems most natural, when four distinct local designations are given, one of which is certainly, another almost certainly, and a third most probably indicative of particular quarters or directions, to conclude that the fourth is so used likewise, however vague it may be in itself, and however situated in the sentence. The presumption thus created is confirmed by the fact, that the hypothesis of only three divisions admits that the whole earth was meant to be included; and it thus becomes a question, which is most agreeable to general usage, and to that of Scripture in particular, a threefold or a fourfold distribution of the earth in such connexions? If the latter, then analogy is strongly in favour of the common supposition that the first clause is not co-extensive with the other, but contains the first of four particulars enumerated. Over and above this argument, derived from the usual distinction of four points or quarters, there is another furnished by the usage of the pronoun *these*, when repeated so as to express a distributive idea. In all such cases, *these* and *these* means *some* and *others;* nor is there probably a single instance in which the first *these* comprehends the whole, while the others divide it into parts. This would be just as foreign from the Hebrew idiom as it is from ours to say, " Some live in Europe, some in France, some in Holland," when we mean that some live in Holland, some in France, and all in Europe. The proposed construction would be altogether natural, if אֵלֶּה were omitted in the first clause; but its presence cannot be accounted for, if that clause is inclusive of the other. That the distributive use of the demonstrative is not confined to two such pronouns only, may be seen from chap. xliv. 5, where the singular זֶה is twice repeated, just as the plural אֵלֶּה is here, and in a connection which admits of no doubt as to the distributive import of all three.—From all this, it seems to follow that the verse most probably contains the customary distribution of the earth or heavens into four great quarters, and that one of these is designated by the phrase *from afar*. Which one is so described, can only be determined by determining the true sense of the other three. The missionary in China is therefore perfectly correct in setting aside all arguments against his own opinion, founded on the supposition that *from afar* must mean the south or the east. The expression is so vague, that it must be determined by the others, and

cannot therefore be employed to determine them, without reasoning in a
vicious circle. This serves to shew that the question, after all, is of no great
exegetical importance, since in either case the same conclusion may be
reached. It is always best, however, to adhere to the more obvious and
usual construction of a passage, in the absence of decisive reasons for departing from it. Assuming, then, that four points are mentioned, and that the
first (*from afar*) can only be determined by determining the others, let us
now attempt to do so. One of these (*the north*) is undisputed; for although
interpreters may differ as to its precise bounds and extent, its relative position is unquestionably fixed by the usage of the Hebrew word. Another
term, which most interpreters, and among the rest the missionary in China,
seem to look upon as equally settled and beyond dispute, is more ambiguous
than they imagine, and has recently received a very different explanation.
This is םָי, which strictly means *the sea*, but is often used for *west*, because
on that side Palestine is naturally bounded by the Mediterranean. Hitzig,
however, very confidently says that here, and in Ps. ciii. 7, where it is put
in opposition to the *north*, םָי means the south sea, and as a term of geography, the *south*. This is not mentioned as having any probability, of which
it is entirely destitute, because the geographical import of the term is not to
be decided by the parallelism or the context in any given case, but by the
predominant usage, which determines it to mean the west, and so it is
explained both by the oldest and the latest writers. Having two points
thus determined, we are sure that the two which remain must be the east
and south; and as we have already seen that *from afar*, from its vagueness,
must receive but cannot give light, we have now to ascertain, if possible, in
which of these directions lay the *land of Sinim*. The discrepancy of the
versions as to these concluding words is remarkable, and shews the doubt in
which the subject was involved at a very early period. The missionary in
China makes an observation on this difference which is less just than ingenious, viz. that no one of the authors of these versions seems to have regarded
his own country as the Land of Sinim; "for it can scarcely be supposed,"
says he, "that the authors of a version living in the very country referred
to, should so utterly fail of perceiving it, as to give the preference to other
lands." It is not easy to perceive, however, why the same causes that
have made the prophecy obscure to others, should not make it equally
obscure to the people of the country meant, especially if the name used
was intended to be enigmatical, as some interpreters suppose. Indeed, by
parity of reasoning, it would seem to follow that if the author of the Septuagint Version had supposed it to be Egypt, this would have decided the
question. But although this observation does not seem entitled to any influence upon the exegesis, the difference between the ancient versions, as well
as the commentators of all ages, is still very remarkable. Without attempting to enumerate all the explanations, it will not be amiss to give some
samples of the different classes. Some would seem to be mere conjectural
inferences from the context. Thus the Targum and Vulgate make it mean
the land of the south, or southern land, assuming, no doubt, that *from afar*
must mean the east, and that the south alone remained to be supplied.
Proceeding on the contrary hypothesis, that from afar must mean the south,
the Septuagint puts the Land of Sinim in the east, but gives it the specific
sense of *Persia*, which appears to be entirely arbitrary. The same thing
may be said of Matthew Henry's notion, that the Land of Sinim was a
Babylonian province. As a specimen of fanciful interpretation, may be
given Adam Clarke's suggestion, that as ןיִס means a bush, םיִניִס may

mean bushes, woods, or a woody country, and he here used to denote the
region occupied by the descendants of the ten tribes, perhaps in West
Africa or North America! Dismissing these gratuitous conjectures, we
may now confine ourselves to those interpretations which have some foundation or appearance of it either in philology or history. Among these
may be mentioned, first, the supposition that the *land of Sinim* is the
country of the *Sinites* spoken of in Gen. x. 17, and 1 Chron. i. 15. But
why should a Canaanitish tribe of no importance, and which nowhere
reappears in history, be here made to represent the four quarters of the
globe? This question becomes still more difficult to answer when it is
added that the *Sinites* must have been immediately adjacent to the land of
Israel, and on the north side which is separately mentioned. Grotius
indeed transfers them to the south side, but by sheer mistake, and for the
purpose of connecting them with the wilderness of *Sin* and Mount *Sinai*,
which are wholly distinct from it. Jerome and Jarchi also understand the
Land of Sinim to be the wilderness of Sin or the peninsula of Sinai, but
without identifying these with the country of the Canaanitish Sinites, as
Grotius does. To their opinion the decisive objection is not the one which
the missionary in China draws from the difference of name and from the
plural form *Sinim*. That " there were not two deserts of Sin," proves no
more than in this case than the assertion that there were not two Hermons
proves against the application of the plural *Hermonim* to that mountain in
Ps. xlii. 7. If a mountain might be so called, why not a desert? And if
Hermonim means Hermonites, why may not Sinim mean Sinites. This
question is especially appropriate, because the author gives no explanation
of the plural form, upon his own hypothesis. But although the objection
is invalid, the other which the author urges is conclusive, that Sinai and
the wilderness of Sin were too near and too limited to be employed in this
connection. Another explanation founded on analogy of names is that of
Aben Ezra, Kimchi, Bochart, Vitringa, J. D. Michaelis, and Ewald, that
the *land of Sinim* is the land of Egypt, so called from *Syene*, as Michaelis
supposes, or from *Sin*, *i. e.* Pelusium, mentioned under that name by
Ezekiel (xxx. 15, 16) as maintained by Bochart, Vitringa, and Ewald.
Here again it seems unfair to argue, with the missionary in China from the
plural form of the Hebrew name; for if, as he observes, it is merely fanciful to refer it to the old geographical distinction of Upper and Lower
Egypt, is it not more than fanciful to refer it to China where there is no such
distinction to account for it at all! If it be said, that *Sinim* means the
Chinese, it may just as easily be said that it means the Egyptians. There
is no force therefore in the argument from this peculiarity in form, any
more than in the argument which the missionary in China himself admits
to be here inapplicable, that Egypt was not sufficiently important to be
made the representative of one great quarter. As little weight attaches to
his argument that this interpretation of the name would make the distribution too unequal; for as he adjusts the limits of the north and even of the
land of Sinim at discretion, there is no sufficient reason why the same thing
might not be done with Sinim if it did mean Egypt. The really decisive
ground, assumed by the same writer, is that Egypt, notwithstanding its
extent and historical importance, was too near at hand to suit the context,
which requires a remote land to be here meant, whether *from afar* be taken
as a general description or as a distinct specification. Another strong
objection is that no cause can be shewn, from analogy or otherwise, for the
designation of this well-known country, in this one place only, by a name

derived from one of its cities, and that not of the first rank. The only remaining explanation, which will be referred to, is that the land of Sinim is China, as maintained by Manasseh Ben Israel, Montanus, Calmet, Gesenius, Winer, Maurer, Hitzig, Henderson, Umbreit, Hendewerk, Knobel, and Beck. An objection to this interpretation is suggested to some minds by its resemblance to an etymological conceit founded merely on an assonance of names. It was probably this prejudice which caused it to be spoken of with such contempt by Grotius, Clericus, and Vitringa. But in modern times, the current has completely changed, and this despised notion has been warmly espoused not only by the most distinguished writers on Isaiah (Rosenmüller and Ewald being almost the only exceptions in the German School), but by the most eminent comparative philologists, such as Langlès, Lassen, and others, who have investigated the question as one of historical and literary interest. The only plausible objections which are still urged against it may be reduced to two. The first is that China was unknown to the Jews at the date of the prophecy. To this it may be answered, first, that no one who believes in the inspiration of the prophets, can refuse to admit the possibility of such a prediction, even if the fact were so ; and secondly, that in all probability China was known to the Jews at a very early period, The rashness of asserting a negative in such cases has been clearly proved by the modern discovery of porcelain vessels with Chinese inscriptions in the monuments of Thebes. But it is still objected, that the name *Sinim* is not that used by the Chinese themselves, nor by other nations until long after the date of this prophecy, it having been derived from a family which did not ascend the throne until about 246 years before the birth of Christ. It is remarkable how readily this date in Chinese history is taken for granted as undoubtedly correct by those who wish to use it for an argument, although it rests upon a dark and dubious tradition of a distant unknown country ; although the very text before us makes it doubtful ; although the universal prevalence of the name Sin, Chin or Jin, throughout western and southern Asia from time immemorial presupposes an antiquity still more remote; and although Chinese historians themselves record that the family from which the name derives its origin, for ages before it ruled the empire ruled a province or kingdom on the western frontier, whence the name might easily have been extended to the western nations. There are in fact few cases of a name being more extensively or longer prevalent than that of *China*, the very form which it exhibits in the Sanscrit, the mother language of southern Asia. That the Chinese themselves have never used it, although acquainted with it, is nothing to the purpose. A Hebrew writer would of course use the name familiar in the west of Asia. This universal name is allowed to be essentially identical with סִין by the highest philological authorities. There is therefore no conclusive force in either of the arguments advanced against this explanation of the name. As positive reasons on the other side, besides the main one drawn from the coincidence of name, may be mentioned the agreement of so many different and independent writers, and the appropriateness of the explanation to the context. Under the first head may be classed precisely those philologists whose peculiar studies best entitle them to speak with authority on such a point, and those German commentators on Isaiah, who are most accustomed to differ among themselves and with the older writers, especially where anything is likely to be added by a proposed interpretation to the strength of revelation or rather to the clearness of its evidences. Prejudice and interest would certainly have led this class of writers to oppose rather than favour a hypothesis which tends to identify the subject of this prophecy with China, the great object of missionary effort at the present day.—The other confirmation is afforded by the suitableness of the sense thus evolved to the connection. If the land of Sinim meant the wilderness of Sin or even Egypt, it would be difficult, if not impossible, to give a satisfactory solution of its singular position here as one of the great quarters or divisions of the world. But if it mean China, that extreme limit of the eastern world, that hive of nations, supposed to comprehend a third part of the human race, the enigma explains itself. Even to us there would be nothing unintelligible or absurd, however strange or novel, in the combination, north, west, south, and China. On the whole, then, a hypothesis which solves all difficulties, satisfies the claims of philology and history, unites the suffrages of the most independent schools and parties, fully meets the requisitions of the text and context, and opens a glorious field of expectation and of effort to the church, may be safely regarded as the true one. For an interesting view of the extent to which the promise has already been fulfilled, and of the encouragements to hope and pray for its entire consummation, the reader is referred to the little book of which we have so frequently made mention, although our citations have been necessarily confined to the first or expository chapter, the remaining four being occupied with the fulfilment of the prophecy.

13. *Shout, O heavens, and rejoice, O earth, let the mountains burst into a shout ; because Jehovah has comforted his people, and on his sufferers he will have mercy.* This is a very common method with Isaiah of foretelling any joyful change by summoning all nature to exult in it as already realised. See especially chap. xliv. 23, where instead of the future יִפְצָחוּ we have the imperative פִּצְחוּ, in imitation of which the Keri here reads וּפִצְחוּ, and Lowth simply פִּצְחוּ on the authority of two or three manuscripts and the ancient versions. There is of course no sufficient reason for departing from the ancient reading still preserved in the text.—Jehovah's consolation of his people, as Gesenius observes, is administered by deed as well as by word. (Compare chaps. li. 3, 12, lii. 9, lxvi. 13, Luke ii. 25, 38.) The consolation here meant is the joyous assemblage of his people from all parts of the earth, predicted in the foregoing verse. The modern writers render both the preterite and future in the last clause by the present (comforts, has mercy); which is not only arbitrary but injurious to the force of the expression, which describes the consolation as both past and future, that is to say, as already begun and still to be continued ; unless the change of tense be designed to intimate, that what is vividly described in the preceding words as past, is really still future.—עֲנִיּ, which is commonly translated in the English Bible *poor*, is here rendered more correctly *afflicted*. The expression *his afflicted*, intimates at once their previous condition and their intimate relation to the Lord as their protector.

14. *And* (yet) *Zion said, Jehovah hath forsaken me, and the Lord hath forgotten me.* So far was this glorious change from having been procured by confidence in God, that Zion thought herself forsaken and forgotten. Those who restrict these prophecies to the Babylonish exile, are compelled to understand this either of the captive inhabitants of Zion, as distinguished from the other exiles, or of Jerusalem itself, complaining of its desolation. But the former distinction is as arbitrary here as in chap. xl. 9, and the long argumentative expostulation which ensues would be absurd if addressed to the bare walls of an empty town. The only satisfactory conclusion is, that Zion or Jerusalem is mentioned as the capital of Israel, the centre of the

true religion, the earthly residence of God himself, and therefore an appropriate and natural emblem of his chosen people or the ancient church, just as we speak of the corruptions or spiritual tyranny of Rome, meaning not the city, but the great ecclesiastical society or corporation which it represents, and of which it is the centre.—The translation *Zion says*, although not ungrammatical, is less appropriate here, because it represents the church as still complaining; whereas the original describes her previous unbelief, before the event, or before the truth of the promise had been guaranteed. It is worthy of remark that the same translators who make the first verb present give the other two their proper past sense, a diversity admissible in case of necessity, but not without it.

15. *Will a woman forget her suckling, from having mercy, (i. e. so as not to have mercy) on the son of her womb? Also* (or even) *these will forget, and I will not forget thee.* The constancy of God's affection for his people is expressed by the strongest possible comparison derived from human instincts. There is a climax in the thought, if not in the expression. What is indirectly mentioned as impossible in one clause, is declared to be real in the other. He first declares that he can no more forget them than a woman can forget her child, he then rises higher and declares that he is still more mindful of them than a mother. The future verb at the beginning implies, without expressing a potential sense, If she will, she can; if she cannot, then of course she will not. For the negative use of the preposition מִן, see above, on chap. xliv. 18.—בֶּטֶן might seem to have the general sense of *body*, as we find it applied to males in Job xix. 17, Micah vi. 7.—The precise force of the גַּם is this: not only strangers but *also* mothers; it may therefore be correctly expressed by *even*. Most interpreters make the first part of the last clause conditional, and Gesenius even understands גַּם as an ellipsis for גַּם כִּי *although*. (See chap. i. 15.) But this is not so much a version as a paraphrase, a substitution of equivalent expressions. There is no need of departing from the obvious meaning of the Prophet's language, which is not hypothetical but categorical. He does not say that if or though a woman could forget her child he would not follow her example, but asserts directly that she can and will, and puts this fact in contrast with his own unwavering constancy. The plural in the last clause, like the singular in the first, denotes the whole class. He does not say that all mothers thus forget their children, nor that mothers generally do so, but that such oblivion is not unknown to the experience of mothers as a class, or of woman as an ideal individual. The primitive simplicity with which the Hebrew idiom employs the simple copulative *and*, where we feel the strongest adversative expression to be necessary, really adds to the force of the expression, when it is once understood and familiar. The *and* may be retained, and yet the antithesis expressed in English by supplying *yet:* and (yet) I will not forget thee.

16. *Behold, on* (my) *palms I have graven thee; thy walls* (are) *before me continually.* Paulus understands the first clause as meaning, *upon* (thy) *hands I have graven* (i. e. branded, marked) *thee*, as belonging to me. Gesenius seems to object to this construction of the suffix with the verb, although precisely similar to that of כִּתֹּב יָדוֹ in chap. xliv. 5, as explained by himself. His other objection is a better one, viz. that such an explanation of the first clause makes the second almost unmeaning. Döderlein explains it to mean, *with* (my) *hands I have sketched* (or *drawn*) *thee*, in allusion to a builder's draught or plan before he enter on the work of construction. (Compare Exod. xxv. 40, 1 Chron. xxviii. 11, 19.) But this use of

the preposition עַל has no authority in usage, and the palms of the hands would not be mentioned as the instruments in such a process. Vitringa avoids both these objections by supposing the plan or picture to be drawn upon Jehovah's hands, because there would be something incongruous in representing him as using paper or a table. The Dutch taste of this excellent interpreter lets him go the length of adding that the divine hands are to be conceived of as large, and allowing ample room for such a delineation as the one supposed. The true sense of the Prophet's figure seems to be the one expressed by Gesenius and other modern writers, who suppose him to allude, not to a picture or a plan of Zion, but her name imprinted on his hands for a memorial, as the ancient slave and soldier wore his master's name, but for a different purpose. (See above, on chap. xliv. 5.) The use of the word *palms* implies a double inscription and in an unusual position, chosen with a view to its being constantly in sight. The idea of a picture was suggested by the other clause, considered as a parallel expression of the same thing as the first. *Thy walls, i. e.* the image of thy walls upon my hands. But this is not necessarily or certainly the true relation of the clauses, which may be considered, not as parts of the same image, but as two distinct images of one and the same thing. The essential idea, I will not forget thee, may be first expressed by saying, I will write thy name upon my hands, and then by saying, I will keep thy walls constantly before me, *i. e.* in my sight and memory. (See Psa. xvi. 8, Isa. xxxviii. 13, and p. 83.)—The mention of the *walls* is no proof that Zion is mentioned merely as a city, since the image of a city is the proximate object here presented, even if the object which symbolizes be the church or chosen people.

17. *Thy sons hasten* (to thee) *; thy destroyers and thy wasters shall go out from thee.* This is the proof that God had not forsaken her. Rosenmüller follows the older writers in translating the first verb as a future, which is wholly arbitrary. Gesenius and others render both the first and last verb in the present tense. The true construction, as in many other cases, seems to be that which represent the process as begun but not complete. Already had her sons begun to hasten to her, and ere long her enemies should be entirely departed. The Septuagint, Targum, and Vulgate, seem to read, instead of *thy sons* (בָּנַיִךְ), *thy builders* (בֹּנַיִךְ, which differs from it only in a single vowel, and agrees well with the parallel expression, *destroyers*, literally *pullers down*. Lowth amends the text accordingly ; but Vitringa, Gesenius, and the later writers, adhere to the Masoretic pointing, on account of its agreement with the thoughts and words of vers. 20–22.—By wasters and destroyers Vitringa understands internal enemies ; Gesenius, foreign oppressors ; Knobel, the strangers who had taken possession of Jerusalem and the rest of the country, which, as he acknowledges, it here represents. The natural interpretation of the words is that which understands them as containing simply an emphatic contrast between friends and foes, the latter taking their departure, and the former coming into possession.

18. *Lift up thine eyes round about and see, all of them are gathered together, they are come to thee. (As) I live, saith Jehovah, (I swear) that all of them as an ornament thou shalt put on, and bind* (or *gird*) *them like the bride.* The sons, described in ver. 17 as rapidly approaching, are now in sight, and their mother is invited to survey them, by lifting up her eyes *round about. i. e.* in all directions, with allusion to their coming from the four points of the compass, as predicted in ver. 12. The common version of כֻּלָּם, *all these*, seems to introduce a new subject. The strict translation, *all of them*, refers to what precedes, and means all the sons who are de-

scribed in the first clause of ver. 17 as hastening to her. They are now already gathered, *i. e.* met together at the point to which they tended from so many distinct quarters. *They come to thee* is an inadequate translation. The true sense is that they are actually come, *i. e.* arrived.—In the second clause, the יִּכ may correspond to the Greek ὅτι after verbs of speaking, or retain its ordinary sense with an ellipsis of *I swear* before it. The formula of swearing here used strictly means, *I* (*am*) *alive* (or *living*), and is itself equivalent to *I swear* in English.—The sons are then compared to ornaments of dress, which the mother girds or binds upon her person. At the end Lowth inserts כְּלֵיהָ in the text from chap. lxi. 10. But this is wholly unnecessary, as the same idea is suggested by the more concise expressions of the common text, which Lowth is utterly mistaken in supposing to describe the bride as binding children round her ; for, as Döderlein correctly says, the point of comparison between the type and antitype is not children but decoration. As a bride puts on her ornaments, so thou shalt be adorned with thy children.

19. *For thy ruins, and thy wastes, and thy land of desolation* (*i. e.* thy desolated land) *for now thou shalt be too narrow for the inhabitant, and far off shall be thy devourers* (those who swallow thee up). The general meaning of this verse is evident, although the construction is obscure. Most writers take the nouns at the beginning as absolute nominatives, *i. e.* agreeing with no verb expressed. *As for thy wastes*, &c. *thou shalt be too narrow.* But this still leaves the double יִּכ to be accounted for, which Rosenmüller supposes to depend upon the verb *I swear*, as in ver. 18, and to signify *that.* Maurer regards the second as a pleonastic or emphatic repetition not belonging to the regular construction. Others give it the supposititious sense of *certainly* or *surely.* Beck makes the first clause mean, ' thy ruins and thy wastes, and thy desolations, shall exist no longer ; but this requires another verb to be supplied or understood. Perhaps the best solution is the one proposed by Hitzig, who supposes the construction to be interrupted and resumed : For thy wastes, and thy ruins, and thy land of desolation— (then beginning anew, without completing the first sentence)—for thou shalt be too narrow, &c. This mode of composition, not unlike what appears in the first draft of any piece of writing till obliterated by correction, is comparatively frequent in the ancient writers, not excepting some of the highest classical models, though proscribed as inelegant and incorrect by the fastidious rules of modern rhetoric. This explanation of the double יִּכ makes it unnecessary to assume an absolute nominative in the first clause. Knobel carries Hitzig's hypothesis too far when he assumes an actual ellipsis of the same verb in the first clause—תֵּצְרִי (derived by Ewald from צָרַר, by Gesenius from the cognate and synonymous יָצַר) can only be second person feminine. The common version, therefore, which refers it to the land, although it gives substantially the true sense, is grammatically incorrect. —*For the inhabitant* is literally *from the inhabitant*, the Hebrew preposition being here used as 1 Kings xix. 7.—Knobel supposes the connection of the clauses to be this, that there would not be room even for the rightful possessors, much less for strangers and enemies. For the application of the verb בָּלַע to enemies, see Lam. ii. 2, 5.—The *devourers* of this verse are of course the *destroyers* of ver. 17.

20. *Again* (or *still*) *shall they say in thine ears, the sons of thy childlessness,* (*Too*) *narrow for me is the place ; come near for me, and I will dwell* (or *that I may dwell*). The עוֹד may simply indicate that something more is to be said than had been said before, in which case it is nearly equiva-

lent to *over and above this* or *moreover*. Or it may have its true sense
as a particle of time, and intimate that these words shall be uttered more
than once, again and again, or still, *i. e.* continually, as the necessity
becomes more urgent. The relative position of the verb and its subject is
retained in the translation, as it causes no obscurity, and exhibits more
exactly the characteristic form of the original. Jarchi explains *the sons of
thy childlessness* to mean the sons of whom thou wast bereaved, referring to
the exiled Jews. The later writers more correctly make it mean *the sons
of thee a childless one*, or, *thy sons, O childless one*. The apparent contradiction is intentional, as appears from what follows. She who was deemed
by others, and who deemed herself, a childless mother, hears the voices
of her children complaining that they have not a sufficient space to dwell
in.—*In thy ears* means *in thy hearing*, although not addressed to thee.
(Compare 2 Sam. xviii. 12.) Even in chap. v. 9, the idea seems to be
not merely that of hearing, but of overhearing. That the same thing is
intended in the case before us, may be gathered from the masculine נִּשָׁה,
which shews that *they shall say* does not mean they shall say to thee, but
they shall say to one another. Rosenmüller explains צַר as an adjective;
but usage and authority determine it to be a verb, the contracted form of
צָרַר, here used in precisely the same sense as the future of the same verb or
a cognate root in the preceding verse. The idea of excess (*nimis, too*) is
not expressed as in that case, but implied, the strict translation being simply
this, *the place is narrow for me*.—All interpreters agree that נְּשָׁה-לִּי means
make room for me, as rendered in the Septuagint (ποίησόν μοι τόπον) and the
Vulgate (*fac mihi spatium*); but they differ in explaining how this sense
may be extracted from the Hebrew words. Gesenius, as in many other
cases, resorts to the easy supposition of a word inaccurately used to express
directly opposite ideas, and explains the verb, both here and in Gen. xix. 9,
as meaning to *recede* or move away from any one. But even if the general
usage which he alleges to exist with respect to verbs of motion were more
certain than it is, a serious difficulty in the way of its assumption here
would be presented by the fact, that in every other case excepting these
two (which may be regarded as identical) the verb means *to come near* or
approach. Rosenmüller adheres to the only sense authorised by usage, and
explains the phrase to mean, *Come near to me*, that there may be more
room. Maurer defends this explanation of the word (both here and in
Gen. xix. 9) against the objections of Gesenius, but without replying to the
main one, namely, that the sense thus given to the words is inappropriate,
because the person speaking demands room not for others, but for himself,
which he could not possibly secure by calling on his neighbour to come
close to him. The whole difficulty seems to have arisen from assuming
that לִּי means *to me*, and denotes the direction of the motion, in opposition
to the fact that לְ is never so used after נָגַשׁ, but always indicates the purpose or design, not only when prefixed to the infinitive (as in Lev. xxi. 21,
2 Kings iv. 27), but also when prefixed to מִלְחָמָה, the only noun with which
it is connected after this verb, and with which it signifies not *to the battle*,
but *for battle*, or *to fight*, being equivalent to an infinitive construction.
The only cases, therefore, where the לְ is thus used (Judges xx. 23, 2 Sam.
x. 13, 1 Chron. xix. 14, Jer. xlvi. 3), are not even exceptions to the rule,
but strong corroborations of the statement that this particle, when added
to the verb, denotes the object *for which*, not the place *to which*, one
approaches. This induction fully justifies the explanation of the phrase
before us given by Jarchi, " approach to one side for me or on my account"

(סַתְקְרִב לְגַךְ הֲקָר בַּסּבּיבִי), leaving the precise direction of the motion undetermined, to express which the dominant usage of the language would require the preposition אֶל. The sense just given to לִ (*for me*) is the more probable, because it is precisely that which it has in the first clause of this verse and the first clause of the next.—J. D. Michaelis and Ewald take אֵשְׁבָה in its primitive sense of *sitting*, rather than its secondary one of *dwelling*, which is preferred by most interpreters. The former version makes the passage still more graphic, by presenting the image of children contending for a seat, and calling on each other, in the presence of their mother, to make room. But even if we grant that there is nothing unworthy or incongruous in this conception, the hypothesis that it was here intended is precluded by the use of the participle יֹשֵׁב in the verse preceding, where the sense of *inhabitant* is rendered necessary, by its close connection with the nouns *land*, *wastes*, and *ruins*.

21. *And thou shalt say in thine heart, i. e.* to thyself, in strict agreement with the preceding verse, as a dialogue not between the mother and her children, but between the children in their mother's hearing. This is consequently not an answer to what goes before, but an observation uttered, as it were, *aside* by an eye and ear witness of the struggle and the clamour for more room. With them the question is, where they shall dwell; with her it is, whence they came.—*Who hath produced these for me?* Interpreters have vexed themselves with the inquiry whether יָלַד here means to bear or to beget, or, in other words, whether she is asking for the father or the mother of the children whom she sees around her. Vitringa, Lowth, Gesenius, Ewald, and Umbreit, who prefer the former sense, suppose an allusion to the conjugal relation of Jehovah to his people, and to the repudiation spoken of below in chap. l. 1. But such allusion seems, in this connection, far-fetched and unnatural. Rosenmüller, Hitzig, and Knobel, choose the other sense, which is really the strict and common one, and here recommended by the fact, that the combination יָלַד לְ is often applied elsewhere to the mother, but never to the father. This might be esteemed conclusive, but for two material points of difference between the cases cited and the one before us. The first is, that in these cases לְ is followed by the name of the father, whereas here the speaker is supposed to be a woman. The other is, that in all those cases the verb itself is feminine, whereas here it is masculine. But these diversities, although they leave some room for doubt and difference of opinion, do not necessarily preclude the explanation of the phrase as referring to the mother. The masculine form of the verb in this case is easily accounted for; because its nominative is not, as in all the other cases, a female name or other feminine noun, but the interrogative pronoun, which is invariable, and naturally followed by the verb in its original or simplest form, not because that form includes both genders, but because both verb and pronoun are used vaguely, without any distinct reference to sex at all. So, too, the use of יָלַד לִי by a female speaker, although a violation of analogy, is one very easily explained, because intentional and even necessary in the extraordinary case supposed. As in other cases the mother is said to bear a child *to* the father, so in this case one mother may, without absurdity, be said to bear a child *to* another, because in either case the essential idea is that of one person being provided with a child by another, whether it be a husband by his wife, or a childless woman by a woman who has children.—The truth is, however, that the force and beauty of the passage are exceedingly

impaired by cutting its bold figures to the quick, and insisting on a rigorous conformity to artificial rules, instead of resting in the general conception, so clearly and affectingly presented, of a childless mother finding herself suddenly surrounded by the clamour of a multitude of children, and asking in amazement whence they came and who they are. The distinction between father and mother is one which would never occur to the speaker in such a case, and may therefore be safely overlooked by the interpreter.— The cause of her astonishment is then assigned. *And I was bereaved and barren.* These almost incompatible expressions for a *childless* one are joined for the purpose of expressing that idea in the strongest manner, and with more regard to the idea itself than to the rules of rhetorical propriety.—*An exile and a banished one.* The last word strictly means *removed*, *i. e.* from home and from society.—*And these who brought up?* literally made great, as in chap. i. 2. The general sense put upon מִי יָלַד is confirmed by the analogy of this phrase, which has no specific reference to either parent, and is masculine in form simply because there was no reason why it should be feminine.—*Behold I was left alone* (or *by myself*)*; these, where were they?* The pronoun at the end is emphatic : where were *they?* She asks how it is that she was so long desolate and childless, when she sees so many children round her now. Rosenmüller changes the whole figure by supposing that long absent children are described as returning to their mother with a numerous offspring. It is essential to the writer's purpose that the children should be all regarded as the speaker's own; for this alone could afford any adequate ground for the astonishment expressed. Some of the modern writers find it very hard to reconcile the language of this verse with their hypothesis that the Zion of this passage is the forsaken city of Jerusalem as such considered. The inconveniences of such a supposition may be gathered from the fact that Knobel represents the Prophet as departing from his own chosen image in the words *an exile and a banished one*, which are of course inapplicable to the town itself, and then returning to it in the words *I was left alone*, which readily admit of such an application. If such abrupt transitions may be assumed at pleasure, how can anything be proved to be the sense intended by the author? The very fact that they are necessary on a given supposition, is a strong proof that it is a false one, and ought to be exchanged for one which is equally consistent with all the parts of the description. Such is the hypothesis assumed as the basis of our exposition, viz. that the Zion of this context is the ancient Church or chosen people, represented both in fiction and in fact by the Sanctuary and the Holy City, as its local centre and appointed Symbol. Of this ideal subject, desolation, childlessness, captivity, exile, and the other varying conditions here described, may all be predicated with the same propriety. If this, however, be the true exegetical hypothesis, and no other seems to answer all the requisitions of the case, then the Babylonish exile, and the state of the church at that period of her history, has no claim to be recognised as anything more than a particular exemplification of the general promise, that the church, after passing through extreme depression and attenuation, should be raised up and replenished like a childless mother who suddenly finds herself surrounded by a large and joyous family of children.

22. *Thus saith the Lord Jehovah, Behold I will lift up to the nations my hand, and I will set up to the peoples my standard* (or *signal*)*: and they will bring thy sons in the bosom* (or *arms*) *and thy daughters on the shoulders shall be carried.* The idea expressed by the figures of the first clause is that of summoning the nations to perform their part in this great work. The

figures themselves are the same as in chap. xiii. 2, viz. the shaking or waving of the hand and the erection of a banner, pole, or other signal, with distinct reference perhaps to persons at a distance and at hand. The figurative promise would be verified by any divine influence securing the co-operation of the heathen in accomplishing Jehovah's purpose, whatever might be the external circumstances either of the call or their compliance with it. The effect of that compliance is described in the last clause, as the bringing home of Zion's sons and daughters, with all the tender care which is wont to be lavished upon infants by their parents or their nurses. The same image is again presented in chap lx. 4, lxvi. 12. Peculiar to this case is the use of the word חֹצֶן, which seems most probably to signify either the bosom or the arm, when spoken of in reference to carrying, and especially the carrying of children. Strictly perhaps the word expresses an idea intermediate between arm and bosom, or including both, viz. the space enclosed by them in the act of grasping or embracing. This likewise seems to be the sense of the cognate חֵק which occurs in Ps. cxxix. 7. The only other instance of the form חֹצֶן is Neh. v. 13, where it is rendered *lap*, and evidently signifies some part of the dress, perhaps the wide sleeve of an oriental garment, which would connect it with the meaning *arm*, but more probably the bosom of the same. According to Rosenmüller it denotes any curvature or fold of the body or the dress, like the Latin *sinus*. That the sense of bosom is at least included here, may be inferred from the analogy of Num. xi. 12, and Ruth iv. 16, where the same act is described by the use of the unambiguous term חֵיק. Gesenius's translation, *arm*, is therefore too restricted. It is somewhat curious that Hitzig, while he renders this word *bosom*, uses *arm* as an equivalent to כָּתֵף, which is an arbitrary explanation of the common word for *shoulder*, and one so often mentioned in connection with the act of bearing burdens. (See above, chap. xxx. 6, xlvi. 7; Ezek. xii. 6; Num. vii. 9.) *Arm*, however, is a favourite word with Hitzig, who substitutes it frequently for *hand*, without the least necessity or reason. Those who restrict the promise to the exiled Jews in Babylon are under the necessity of making this a restoration, which is not only perfectly gratuitous but inconsistent with the verse preceding, where these same children are described as appearing for the first time, and thereby exciting the surprise of the forsaken mother.

23. *And kings shall be thy nursing fathers, and their queens thy nursing mothers; face to the ground shall they bow to thee, and the dust of thy feet shall they lick: and thou shall know that I am Jehovah, whose waiters* (or *hopers, i. e.* those who trust in him) *shall not be ashamed* (or *disappointed*). The same promise is repeated in substance with a change of form. Instead of the nations, we have now their kings and queens; and instead of Zion's sons and daughters, Zion herself. This last variation, while it either perplexes or annoys the rhetorical precision, aids the rational interpreter by shewing that the figures of the preceding verse, however natural and just, are not to be rigidly explained. In other words, it shews that between the Zion of this passage and her children there is no essential difference, and that what is promised to the one is promised to the other. This identity is clear from the apparent solecism of representing the bereaved and childless mother as herself an infant in the arms and at the breast, because really as much in need of sustenance and care as those before called her sons and daughters or rather because she is but another figure for the same thing. This confusion of imagery all tends to confirm the supposition that the Zion of these prophecies is not a city, which could scarcely be thus confounded with its citizens, but a society or corporation between which as an ideal

person and its individual members, or any given portion of them, there is no
such well defined and palpable distinction.—אֹמֵן, to which the English
Version and some others give the sense of *nourishers*, is now explained to
mean a *carrier* or *bearer*, which last name is applied by the English in
Hindostan to the male nurses of their children. Some regard it as equivalent
to παιδαγωγός (Gal. iii. 24), ánd as referring to a later period of childhood
than מֵינֶקֶת, which is properly a suckler or wet-nurse. But as there is
nothing in the text to suggest the idea of succession in time, they may be
regarded as poetical equivalents Hitzig's notion, that the kings and
queens are merely represented as the servile attendants of Zion, is forbidden
by the specific offices ascribed to them. As little can it be supposed with
Knobel, that she is here to be conceived of as a queen upon her throne,
who could scarcely be supposed to need the tender attentions of a bearer
and a wet-nurse. The image is still that of a tender infant, with an almost
imperceptible substitution of the mother for her children.—אַפַּיִם אֶרְצָה is a
kind of compound adverb like our English phrases *sword-in-hand, arm-in-
arm*, but still more concise. The addition of these words determines the
meaning of the preceding verb as denoting actual prostration, which is also
clear from the next clause, where the licking of the dust cannot be naturally
understood as a strong expression for the kissing of the feet or of the earth
in token of homage, but is rather like the biting of the dust in Homer, a
poetical description of complete and compulsory prostration, not merely
that of subjects to their sovereign, but of vanquished enemies before their
conquerors. (Compare Micah vii. 17, Ps. lxxii. 9.) In the last clause
אֲשֶׁר is not a conjunction, meaning *that* or *for*, but as usual a relative, to be
connected with קֹוָי in construction, *who my hopers*, *i. e.* whose hopers, those
who hope in me.

24. *Shall the prey be taken from the mighty, and shall the captivity of
the righteous be delivered?* This verse suggests a difficulty in the way of
the fulfilment of the promise. מַלְקוֹחַ and שְׁבִי are combined likewise elsewhere to describe whatever can be taken in war, including prisoners and
booty. (Num. xxxi. 11, 12, 27, 32.) שְׁבִי, though properly an abstract,
is continually used as a collective term for *captives*. Its combination here
with צַדִּיק has perplexed interpreters. Houbigant, Lowth, Ewald, and
Knobel read שְׁבִי עָרִיץ, as in the next verse, which is a mere subterfuge.
Rosenmüller follows Albert Schultens in giving to צַדִּיק the sense of rigid,
stern, severe; which is not in the least justified by Hebrew usage. Beck
follows J. D. Michaelis in explaining it to mean *victorious* according to the
sense of *victory* now commonly put upon צֶדֶק, notwithstanding the objection
of Gesenius that there is no authority in usage for the application of this
term to the successes of the wicked, without regard to its original import.
Symmachus, Jarchi, Aben Ezra, and Hitzig, understand the phrase to
mean the *righteous captives*, *i. e.* the exiled Jews. Gesenius, Maurer, and
Umbreit, the prey or plunder of the righteous, *i. e.* taken from the righteous.
But this explanation of שְׁבִי is harsh, and the parallelism, as well as the
analogy of ver. 25, requires that צַדִּיק should be referred to the subject,
not the object of the action. The English Version makes it agree directly
with שְׁבִי, in the sense of *lawful captives*, *i. e.* one who has been lawfully
enslaved, or one who deserves to be a captive. The simplest and most
obvious construction of the words is that which makes them mean the
captives of a righteous conqueror. The argument may then be stated
thus : Shall the captives even of a righteous conqueror be freed in such a
case ? How much more the captives of an unjust oppressor!

25. For thus saith Jehovah, also (or *even*) *the captivity* (or *captives*) *of the mighty shall be taken, and the prey of the terrible shall be delivered, and with thy strivers will I strive, and thy sons will I save.* There is no need of giving to the כִּי at the beginning the factitious sense of yes, no, nay, more, verily, or the like. Its proper meaning may be retained by supplying in thought an affirmative answer to the foregoing question. Shall the captives of the righteous be delivered? Yes, and more; for thus saith Jehovah, not only this but also the captives of the tyrant or oppressor. There is a very material difference between supplying what is not expressed and changing the meaning of what is. The latter expedient is never admissible ; the former is often necessary. The logical connection between this verse and the one before it has been already stated. Its general sense is clear, as a solemn declaration that the power of the captor can oppose no real obstacle to the fulfilment of the promise of deliverance. The same idea is expressed in the last clause in more general and literal terms.

26. And I will make thy oppressors eat their (*own*) *flesh, and as with new wine, with their blood shall they be drunken ; and all flesh shall know, that I Jehovah am thy Saviour, and* (*that*) *thy Redeemer is the Mighty One of Jacob.* The first clause is commonly explained as a strong metaphorical description of intestine wars and mutual destruction, similar to that in Zech. xi. 9. In this case, however, as in chap. ix. 19, the image is perhaps rather that of a person devouring his own flesh in impotent and desperate rage. The Targum gratuitously changes the sense by interpreting the first clause to mean, " I will give their flesh for food to the birds of heaven," or, as Jarchi has it, " to the beasts of the field." The last clause winds up this part of the prophecy by the usual return to the great theme of the whole book, the relation of Jehovah to his people, as their Saviour, Redeemer, and Protector, self-existent, eternal, and almighty in himself, yet condescending to be called the Mighty One of Jacob. The last words may be construed as a single proposition, " That I am Jehovah thy Saviour and thy Redeemer the Mighty One of Jacob." This will be found upon comparison, however, to express much less than the construction above given, which asserts not only that the speaker is Jehovah, &c., but that the Being who possesses these attributes is the peculiar covenanted God of Israel or Jacob, For the different epithets of this clause, see above, chaps. i. 24, xli. 14. xliii. 3. For a similar statement of the purpose of God's providential dealings with his people, see chap. xlv. 3, and ver. 23 of this same chapter.

Chapter 50

THIS chapter contains no entirely new element, but a fresh view of several which have already been repeatedly exhibited. The first of these is the great truth, that the sufferings of God's people are the necessary fruit of their own sins, ver. 1. The second is the power of Jehovah to accomplish their deliverance, vers, 2, 3, The third is the Servant of Jehovah, his mission, his qualifications for it, his endurance of reproach and opposition on account of it, vers. 4-9. The fourth is the way of salvation and the certain doom of those who neglect it, vers. 10, 11.

This perpetual recurrence of the same great themes in various combinations makes the mere division of the chapters a comparatively unimportant matter, although some writers seem to attach great importance to the separation of the first three verses from what follows, and their intimate connection with what goes before. It should be ever borne in mind that these divisions are conventional and modern, and that in this part of Isaiah, more especially, they might have been omitted altogether, without any serious inconvenience to the reader or interpreter. A much greater evil than the want of these divisions is the habit of ascribing to them undue authority and suffering the exposition to be governed by them, as if each were a separate prediction or discourse, instead of being arbitrary though convenient breaks in a continued composition, not materially differing from the paragraphs now used in every modern book. The re-arrrangement of the chapters in the present case would answer no good purpose, since the first three verses are not more closely connected with the end of the preceding chapter than what follows is with its beginning. The true course is to make use of the common divisions as convenient pauses, but to read and expound the text as one continuous discourse.

1. *Thus saith Jehovah.* This prefatory formula has no doubt had some influence on the division of the chapters. It does not, however, always indicate the introduction of a new subject, as may be seen by a comparison of chap. xlviii. 17 with chap. xlix. 1.—*Where is* or *what is?* אֵי by itself is the interrogative adverb *where?* When joined with זֶה, it seems to be equivalent to our interrogative *what* or *which*, but always with reference to place, and for the most part with a noun of place following. The most frequent combination is, *which way?* This leaves it doubtful whether it is used in the general sense of *what*, as explained by Ewald, or in the more specific one of *what place, i.e. where,* preferred by Gesenius and most other writers. This is a question of but little moment as to the general meaning of the sentence; since the question " where is it?" as we shall see below, is here substantially equivalent to " what is it?"—*The bill of divorcement,* literally, writing of excision or repudiation, translated in the Septuagint βιβλίον τοῦ ἀποστασίου, which form is retained in the New Testament (Matt. xix. 7, Mark x. 4), though sometimes abridged (Matt. v. 31). The Hebrew phrase denotes the legal instrument by which the Mosaic law allowed a husband to repudiate his wife (Deut. xxiv. 1–3).—*Of your mother.* The persons addressed are the individual members of the church or nation; their mother is the church or nation itself. These are of course distinguished from each other only by a poetical figure.—*Whom I have sent* (or *put*) *away.* These words admit of a twofold construction. According to the common Hebrew idiom, the relative pronoun when the object of a verb, is followed by the personal pronoun which it represents. According to this idiom, *whom I have sent her* means nothing more than *whom I have sent*, except that it more distinctly indicates the gender of the object. This construction is recommended here, not only by its strict conformity to general usage, but by its recurrence in the very next clause, where אֲשֶׁר מָכַרְתִּי אֶתְכֶם לוֹ is agreed on all hands to mean *to whom I sold you.* But as the verb *to send* governs two accusatives in Hebrew, the relative may take the place of one of them, denoting the end for which, or the means by which, as it actually does in chap. lv. 11, 2 Sam. xi. 22, 1 Kings xiv. 6, and in the case before us, according to the judgment of most modern writers, who explain the words to mean *wherewith I have sent her away.*—The use of the disjunctive *or* in Hebrew is comparatively rare, and consequently more significant when it does occur, as in this case, where it seems designed to intimate that the two figures of the clause are to be taken separately, not together, that is to say, that the punishment of the people is not compared to the repudiation of a wife and the sale of her children in the same ideal case, but represented

by the two distinct emblems of a wife divorced and children sold. *Or which
of my creditors* (is it) *to whom I have sold you?* We have here an allusion
to another provision of the Mosaic law, which allows debtors to be sold in
payment of their debts (Matt. xviii. 25), and even children by their parents
(Exod. xxi. 7). The answer follows in the other clause.—*Behold, for
your iniquities ye have been sold.* The reflexive meaning, *ye have sold
yourselves,* is frequently expressed by this form of the verb, but not invariably nor even commonly; it is not, therefore, necessary here, nor even
favoured by the parallelism, as the corresponding term is a simple passive of
a different form, and one which cannot, from the nature of the case, denote
a reflexive or reciprocal action.—*And for your transgressions.* Vitringa's
suggestion, that one of the parallel terms may signify civil, and the other
religious offences, is entirely gratuitous. *Your mother has been sent* (or *put*)
away. The repetition of *your,* where *her transgressions* might have been
expected, only serves to shew more clearly the real identity of those who
are formally distinguished as the mother and the children.—The interrogation in the first clause of this verse has been variously understood. Jerome
and the Rabbins explain it as an indirect but absolute negation, implying
that she had not been divorced at all, but had wilfully forsaken her husband,
and, as Abarbenel says, gone out from his house of herself, or of her own
accord (ה׳ח מעולמ׳ יצחם מן סב׳ח). This, though a good sense in itself, is not
an obvious one, or that which the words would readily suggest. If this had
been the writer's meaning, and he had chosen to express it in the form of
an interrogation, he would more probably have said, Have I given your
mother a bill of divorcement? Have I sold you to my creditors? Besides,
the explanation of this clause as an absolute negation is at variance with the
positive statement in the last clause, that she had been put away, as well as
with the parallel assertion, that they had been sold, which last, indeed, may
be explained away by adopting the reflexive sense, but no such explanation
is admissible in the other case. In order to avoid this objection, some
explain the cause not as an absolute negation, but a qualified one. Thus
Vitringa understands it to mean that she had been put away, and they sold,
not by him, *i.e.* not by the husband and the father, but by judicial process,
which he undertakes to reconcile with ancient Jewish usage by the authority
of Buxtorf and Selden. It is evident, however, that the qualification which
is needed to reconcile the clauses is in this interpretation wholly supplied
by the imagination of the reader or interpreter, without the least foundation
in the text or context. The same remark applies, though in a less degree, to the modification of this negative hypothesis by Grotius, who
supposes it to be denied that she had been divorced without sufficient
reason, and by Gesenius, who explains it as denying that she had received
a bill or writing of the ordinary kind. The difficulty common to all these
hypotheses is, that the qualification assumed is altogether arbitrary, and
dependent on the fancy or discretion of the reader.—This is equally true
of some interpretations which assume that she had been put away, for
example that of Hitzig, who ingeniously supposes that the bill of divorcement is called for that it may be cancelled, and the creditor that he may be
paid. The most emphatic and significant portion of the sentence is in this
case not expressed at all, and never would occur to any reader but the one
whose ingenuity invented it.—The simplest and most obvious interpretation
of the first clause is the one suggested by the second, which evidently stands
related to it as an answer to the question which occasions it. In the present
case, the answer is wholly unambiguous, viz. that they were sold for their

sins, and that she was put away for their transgressions. The question naturally corresponding to this answer is the question, why the mother was divorced, and why the sons were sold? Supposing this to be the substance of the first clause, its form is very easily accounted for. *Where is your mother's bill of divorcement?* produce it, that we may see the cause of her repudiation. *Where is the creditor to whom I sold you?* let him appear, and tell us what was the occasion of your being sold. Gesenius's objection, that the Jewish bills of divorcement did not state the cause, is trivial, even if the fact alleged be admitted to be true, for which there is no sufficient reason. The objection, that God could not have a creditor, from which some have argued that the first clause must be negatively understood, has no more force than the objection that he could not be a husband or a writer, both involving an egregious misconception or an utter disregard of the figurative nature of the passage. If Jehovah's casting off his people might be likened to a Jewish husband's repudiation of his wife, then the same thing might be likened to a Jewish debtor's sale of himself or his children to his creditors, without any greater incongruity or contradiction in the one case than the other. The general idea of rejection is twice clothed in a figurative dress, first by emblems borrowed from the law and custom of divorce, and then by emblems borrowed from the law and custom of imprisonment for debt.—The restriction of this passage to the Babylonish exile is entirely arbitrary. If it admits of any special application, it is rather to the repudiation of the Jewish people at the advent.

2. *Why did I come, and there is no man? (why) did I call, and there was no one answering?* The idiom of occidental languages would here admit, if not require, a more involved and hypothetical construction. "Why, when I came, was there no one (to receive me), and, when I called, no one to answer me?' (See above, chap. v. 4, vol. i. p. 129.) The Targum explains this of God's coming and calling by the prophets, and the modern Germans adopt the same interpretation. Vitringa and many other writers understand it of Christ's coming in the flesh. Both explanations are erroneous if exclusive, both correct as specific applications of a general expression. In themselves, the words imply nothing more than that God had come near to the people, by his word and 'providence, but without any suitable response on their part. The clause is explanatory of their being *sold* and *put away*, as represented in the foregoing verse. The general truth which it teaches is, that God has never, and will never put away his people even for a time, without preceding disobedience and alienation upon their part. Particular examples of this general truth are furnished by the Babylonish exile, and by every season of distress and persecution.—The other clause precludes the vindication of their unbelief and disobedience on the ground that they had not sufficient reason to obey his commands, and rely upon his promises. Such doubts are rendered impious and foolish by the proofs of his almighty power. This power is first asserted indirectly by a question implying the strongest negation : *Is my hand shortened, shortened, from redemption? and is there with me no power (i. e.* have I no power) *to deliver?* Shortness of hand or arm is a common oriental figure for defect of power, especially in reference to some particular effect, which is thus represented as beyond the reach. (See chap. lix. 1 ; Num. xi. 23 ; cf. chap. xxxvii. 17.) According to Gesenius, Artaxerxes Longimanus was so called, not in reference to any corporeal peculiarity, but as being possessed of extraordinary power. The emphatic repetition of the Hebrew verb may, as usual, be variously ex-

pressed in translation by the introduction of intensive phrases, such as *altogether* or *at all*, or by a simple repetition of the verb in English. *From redemption, i. e.* so as not to redeem or deliver from distress. (See above, on chap. xlix. 15.)—*Behold, by my rebuke* (a term often used to express God's control over the elements) *I will dry up the sea.* I can make a complete change in the face of nature. Most of the modern writers use the present form, *I dry up the sea.* But this, as expressing an habitual act, fails to give the sense of the original, which is not a description of what he usually does, but a declaration of what he can do, and what he will do in the present instance if it should be necessary. Hence the best translation of the verb is the exact one which adheres to the strict sense of the future. As in many other cases, this general expression may involve a particular allusion, namely, to the crossing of the Red Sea at the exodus from Egypt. But to make this the direct and main sense of the words, is equally at variance with good taste and the context. It is only upon this erroneous supposition that Vitringa could imagine himself bound to apply what follows (*I will make streams a wilderness*) to the passage of the Jordan, and to justify the plural designation of that river by appealing to its magnitude, historical importance, &c. It is really a poetical reiteration of what goes before, extending what was there said of the *sea* to *streams* and other waters. The remaining words of this verse are intended merely to complete the picture, by subjoining to the cause its natural effect.—*Let their fish stink for want of water and die of thirst.* The abbreviated form תָּמֹת seems to shew that the writer here passes from the tone of prediction or general description to that of actual command. It may, however, be a poetic variation of the ordinary future form, in which case the sense will be, *their fish shall die,* &c.; or the abbreviated form may indicate an indirect or oblique construction, *so that their fish shall stink,* &c., which last explanation is the one preferred by the latest writers. The pronoun *their* refers to *sea* and *rivers,* or to the last alone, which is masculine, though feminine in form.—For תבאש Lowth reads תיבש (*their fish is dried up*), on the authority of one manuscript confirmed by the Septuagint version (ξηρανθήσονται). The collective use of the word *fish* is the same in Hebrew and in English. For the true sense of מֵאֵין, see above, chap. v. 9, vol. i. p. 131–2.

3. The description of Jehovah's power, as displayed in his control of the elements, is still continued. *I will clothe the heavens in blackness.* The Hebrew noun, according to its etymology, denotes not merely a black colour, but such a colour used as a sign of mourning. Thus understood, it corresponds exactly to the following words, where the customary mourning dress of ancient times is mentioned. *And sackcloth I will place* (or *make*) *their covering.* The reference of this verse to the plague of darkness in the land of Egypt is admissible only in the sense explained above with respect to the passage of the Red Sea, namely, as a particular allusion comprehended in a general description. J. D. Michaelis and some later writers understand it as referring to real phenomena of storms, or even to the obscuration of the sky by clouds; but it is inconceivable that such an everyday occurrence should be coupled with the drying up of seas and rivers, as a proof of God's power over nature and the elements. The sense required by the connection is that of an extraordinary darkness (such as that of an eclipse), or even an extinction of the heavenly bodies, as in chap. xiii. 10. (See vol. i. p. 275.)

4. *The Lord Jehovah hath given to me.* As Jehovah is the speaker in

the foregoing verse, Cocceius, Vitringa, and many others, regard this clause as a proof that these are the words of the Messiah, who, in virtue of his twofold nature, might speak in the person of Jehovah, and yet say, *Jehovah hath given to me.*   The Rabbins and the Germans explain them as the words of Isaiah himself, speaking either in his own name or in that of the prophets as a class.   But some of the things which follow are inapplicable to such a subject, an objection not relieved by assuming with Grotius that Isaiah is here a type of Christ.   The true hypothesis is still the same which we have found ourselves constrained to assume in all like cases throughout the foregoing chapters, namely, that the *servant of Jehovah*, as he calls himself in ver. 10 below, is the Messiah and his people, as a complex person, or the church in indissoluble union with its Head, asserting his divine commission and authority to act as the great teacher and enlightener of the world.   For this end God had given him a ready tongue or speech.

Most interpreters adopt a different version of לִמּוּדִים in the first and last clause, giving it at first the sense of *learned*, and afterwards that of *learners*. These two ideas, it is true, are near akin, and may be blended in the Hebrew word as they are in the English *scholar*, which is used both for a learner and a learned person.   It is best, however, for that very reason, to retain the same word in translation, as is done by Hitzig, who translates it *disciples*, Ewald, *apostles*, and Henderson, *those who are taught.*   Grotius agrees with the Septuagint in making לִמּוּדִים an abstract noun meaning *instructive—* γλῶσσαν παιδείας, an instructive tongue.   Gesenius considers it equivalent to *taught* or *practised tongue.*   In every other case the word is a concrete, meaning persons taught, disciples.   (See above, chap. viii. 16, and below, chap. liv. 13.)   From this expression Hitzig and Knobel strangely infer that Isaiah was an uneducated prophet like Amos (vii. 14), which would be a very forced conclusion, even if Isaiah were the subject of the passage. As applied to Christ, it is descriptive of that power of conviction and persuasion which is frequently ascribed in the New Testament to his oral teachings.   As his representative and instrument, the church has always had a measure of the same gift enabling her to execute her high vocation. —*To know* (that I might know) *to help or succour the weary* (*with*) *a word.* This explanation of the verb עוּת, which occurs only here, is that given by Aquila (ὑποστηρίσαι), Jerome (*sustentare*), Gesenius (*stärken*), and several of the later writers.   Near akin to this, and founded on another Arabic analogy, is the sense of *refreshing*, which is expressed by Rückert, Ewald, and Umbreit.   J. D. Michaelis explains it to mean *change*, and applies it to the endless variety of our Saviour's instructions.   Paulus and Hitzig make the ל radical, and identify the word with the Arabic لاَ *to speak ;* but this, according to Knobel, would be applicable only to frivolous, unmeaning speech.   Most of the older writers understand עוּת as a denominative verb from עֵת, *time*, meaning to speak seasonably.   This explanation seems to be implied in the Septuagint paraphrase (τοῦ γνῶναι ἡνίκα δεῖ εἰπεῖν λόγον).   But according to the probable etymology of עֵת, the verb derived from it would assume another form, and the construction with two objects, as Gesenius observes, would be harsh ; whereas it is not uncommon with verbs of supporting or sustaining.   (See Gen. xlvii. 13 ; 1 Kings xviii. 4.) The Chaldee paraphrase, ' That I might know how to teach wisdom to the righteous panting for the words of the law,' or, as Jarchi and Kimchi have it, ' thirsting for the words of God,' appears to be conjectural.—*He will waken, in the morning, in the morning, he will waken for me the ear, i. e.*

he will waken my ear, rouse my attention, and open my mind to the reception of the truth. (See chap. xlviii. 8 ; 1 Sam. ix. 15, xx. 2 ; Ps. xli. 7.) The present tense (*he wakeneth*) asserts a claim to constant inspiration ; the future expresses a confident belief that God will assist and inspire him. —The accents require *in the morning in the morning* to be read together, as in chap. xxviii. 19, where it is an intensive repetition, meaning *every morning*. It might otherwise be thought more natural to read the sentence thus, *he will waken in the morning, in the morning he will waken*, a twofold expression of the same idea, viz. that he will do so early. In either case the object of both verbs is the same ; the introduction of the pronoun *me* after the first in the English Version being needless and hurtful to the sentence. The last words of the verse declare the end or purpose of this wakening, *to hear* (*i. e.* that I may hear) *like the disciples* or *the taught*, *i. e.* that I may give attention as a learner listens to his teacher. Luzzatto understands this verse as an assertion of the pious and believing Jews, that God enables them to hear and speak as if they were all prophets, which, if correctly understood and duly limited, appears to be the true sense as explained above.

5. *The Lord Jehovah opened for me the ear, and I resisted not.* The common version, *I was not rebellious*, seems to convert the description of an act into that of a habit.—*I did not draw back*, or refuse the office, on account of the hardships by which I foresaw that it would be accompanied. There may be an allusion to the conduct of Moses (iv. 13) in declining the dangerous but honourable work to which the Lord had called him. (Compare Jer. i. 6, xvii. 16.) Henderson s reflection on this sentence is, ' How different the conduct of the Messiah from that of Jonah !'

6. *My back I gave to* (*those*) *smiting.* We may understand by *gave* either *yielded* unresistingly or *offered* voluntarily. (Compare Mat. v. 39.) The punishment of scourging was a common one, and is particularly mentioned in the history of our Lord's maltreatment.—*And my cheeks to those plucking* (the beard or hair). It is well observed by Hitzig, that the context here requires something more than the playful or even the contemptuous pulling of the beard, the *vellere barbam* of Horace and Persius, to which preceding writers had referred. A better parallel is Neh. xiii. 25, where the Tirshatha is said to have contended with the Jews, and cursed them, and smote them, and *plucked off their hair*. (Compare Ezra ix. 3.) This particular species of abuse is not recorded in the history of our Saviour's sufferings, but some suppose it to be comprehended in the general term *buffeting*.—*My face I did not hide from shame and spitting*. The plural form כְּלִמּוֹת may be either an intensive or emphatic expression for extreme shame or abundant shame, or a term comprehending various shameful acts, such as smiting on the face, spitting in it, and the like. In the phrase *I did not hide my face* there may be an allusion to the common figure of confusion covering the face (Jer. li. 51), in reference no doubt to the natural expression of this feeling by a blush, or in extreme cases by a livid paleness overspreading the features. Some have imagined that by *spitting* nothing more is meant than spitting on the ground in one's presence, which, according to the oriental usages and feelings, is a strong expression of abhorrence and contempt. But, as Lowth well says, if spitting in a person's presence was such an indignity, how much more spitting in his face ; and the whole connection shews that the reference is not to any mitigated form of insult but to its extreme. That this part of the description was fulfilled in the experience of our Saviour, is expressly recorded, Mat. xxvi. 67, xxvii. 30. That it

was literally verified in that of Isaiah, is not only without proof but in the last degree improbable, much more the supposition that it was a common or habitual treatment of the prophets as a class. As to Isaiah himself, it is worthy of remark that a learned and ingenious Rabbin of our own day (Samuel Luzzatto) argues against this application of the Prophet's language, first, because he was not a prophet of evil, and could not therefore be an object of the popular hatred; secondly, because his predictions were not addressed to his contemporaries but to future ages; thirdly, because even on the supposition that he lived at the time of the Babylonish exile, he must have written in the name and person of an older prophet, and could not therefore have exposed himself to any public insult. From this impossibility of proving any literal coincidence between the prophetic description and the personal experience of the Prophet himself, when taken in connection with the palpable coincidences which have been already pointed out in the experience of Jesus Christ, many interpreters infer that it was meant to be a literal prediction of his sufferings. But even Vitringa has observed that if it were so, its fulfilment, or the record of it, would be imperfect, since the points of agreement are not fully commensurate with those of the description. (See for example what has been already said with respect to the plucking of the beard or hair.) The most satisfactory solution of the difficulty is the one suggested by Vitringa himself, who regards the prophecy as metaphorical, and as denoting cruel and contemptuous treatment in general, and supposes the literal coincidences, as in many other cases, to have been providentially secured, not merely to convict the Jews, as Grotius says, but also to identify to others the great subject of the prophecy. But if the prophecy itself be metaphorical, it may apply to other subjects, less completely and remarkably but no less really, not to Isaiah, it is true, from whom its terms, even figuratively understood, are foreign, but to the church or people of God, the body of Christ, which, like its head, has ever been an object of contempt with those who did not understand its character or recognise its claims. What is literally true of the Head, is metaphorically true of the Body—" I gave my back to the smiters and my cheeks to the pluckers, my face I did not hide from shame and spitting."

7. *And the Lord Jehovah will help me*, or *afford help to me*. The adversative particle, which most translators have found necessary here to shew the true connection, is not required by the Hebrew idiom. (See above, on chap. xl. 8.)—*Therefore I am not confounded* by the persecution and contempt described in the foregoing verses. The common version, *I shall not be confounded*, is not only arbitrary but injurious to the sense, which is not that God's protection will save him from future shame, but that the hope of it saves him even now. The words strictly mean, *I have not been confounded*, which implies, of course, that he is not so now.— *Therefore I have set my face as a flint*. This is a common description of firmness and determination as expressed in the countenance. It is equally applicable to a wicked impudence (Jer. v. 3, Zech. vii. 12), and a holy resolution (Ezek. iii. 8, 9). The same thing is expressed by Jeremiah under different but kindred figures. (Jer. i. 17, 18, xv. 20.) It is probable, as J. H. Michaelis suggests, that Luke alludes to these passages, when he says that our Lord *stedfastly set his face* (τὸ πρόσωπον αυτοῦ ἐστήριξε) *to go to Jerusalem*. (Luke ix. 51.) The strong and expressive English phrase, *set my face*, is in all respects better than those which later versions have substituted for it, such as *place* (Barnes), *present* (Noyes),

&c.—*And I know that I shall not be ashamed.* The substitution of *because* for *and* is an unnecessary deviation from the Hebrew idiom.

8. *Near (is) my justifier* (or the one justifying me). הַצְדִּיק is strictly a forensic term meaning to acquit or pronounce innocent, in case of accusation, and to right or do justice to, in case of civil controversy. The use of this word, and of several correlative expressions, may be clearly learned from Deut. xxv. 1. The justifier is of course Jehovah. His being *near* is not intended to denote the proximity of an event still future, but to describe his intervention as constantly within reach and available. It is not the justification which is said to be near to the time of speaking, but the justifier, who is said to be near the speaker himself. The justification of his servant is the full vindication of his claims to divine authority and inspiration. At the same time there is a designed coincidence between the terms of prediction, and the issue of our Saviour's trial ; but the prophecy is not to be restricted to this object. The general meaning of the word is, all this reproach is undeserved, as will be seen hereafter. Since God himself has undertaken his defence, the accuser's case is hopeless. He therefore asks triumphantly, *Who will contend with me ?* The Hebrew verb denotes specifically litigation, or forensic strife. Rom. viii. 33, 34, is an obvious imitation of this passage as to form. But even Vitringa, and the warmest advocates for letting the New Testament explain the Old, are forced to acknowledge that in this case Paul merely borrows his expressions from the Prophet, and applies them to a different object. In any other case this class of writers would no doubt have insisted that the justifier must be Christ, and the justified his people ; but from this they are precluded by their own assumption, that the Messiah is the speaker. Both hypotheses, so far as they have any just foundation, must be reconciled by the supposition that the ideal speaker is the Body and the Head in union. In the sense here intended, Christ is justified by the Father, and at the same time justifies his people.—*We will stand* (or *let us stand*) *together*, at the bar, before the judgment-seat, a frequent application of the Hebrew verb. (See Num. xxvii. 2, Deut. xix. 17, 1 Kings iii. 16.) This is an indirect defiance or ironical challenge ; as if he had said, If any will still venture to accuse me, *let us stand up together.*—The same thing is then expressed in other words, the form of interrogation and proposal being still retained. *Who is my adversary ?* This is more literally rendered in the margin of the English Bible, *who is the master of my cause ?* But even this fails to convey the precise sense of the original, and may be even said to reverse it, for the *master of my cause* seems to imply ascendancy or better right, and is not therefore applicable to a vanquished adversary whose case was just before described as hopeless. The truth is, that the pronoun *my* belongs not to the last word merely, but to the whole complex phrase, and בַּעַל simply means " possessor," *i.e.* one to whom a given thing belongs. Thus a *cause-master* (elsewhere called בַּעַל דְּבָרִים (Exod. xxiv. 14), means one who has a cause or law-suit, a party-litigant, and *my cause-master* means one who has a controversy with me, my opponent or adversary ; so that the common version really conveys the meaning better than what seems to be the more exact translation of the margin. In sense, the question is precisely parallel and tantamount to the one before it, *who will contend with me ?—Let him draw near to me*, confront me, or engage in conflict with me.—The forensic figures of this verse and some of its expressions, have

repeatedly occurred in the course of the preceding chapters. (See chaps.
xli. 1, 21; xliii. 9, 26; xlv. 20; xlvii. 14, 16.)

9. *Behold, the Lord Jehovah will help me; who (is) he (that) will condemn me?* The help specifically meant is that afforded by an advocate or
judge to an injured party. הִרְשִׁיעַ is the technical antithesis to הַצְדִּיק, used
in ver. 8. Both verbs, with their cognate adjectives, occur in Deut. xxv. 1.
—The potential meaning (*can condemn*) is included in the future (*will
condemn*), though not directly, much less exclusively, expressed by it.—
The last clause adds to the assurance of his own safety that of the destruction of his enemies. *All they* (or *all of them*, his adversaries, not expressly
mentioned but referred to in the questions which precede) *like the garment
shall grow old* (or *be worn out*), *i.e.* like the garment which is worn out or
decays. *The moth shall devour them.* Gesenius condemns the relative construction, *which the moth devours* (referring to הַבֶּגֶד as a collective), because
inadmissible in the parallel passage, chap. li. 8. He nevertheless adopts
it in his own German Version (*wie ein Gewand das die Motte verzehrt*).
The real objection to it is, that it is needless, and rests upon a frivolous
rhetorical punctilio. By a perfectly natural and common transition, the
writer passes from comparison to metaphor, and having first transformed
them into garments, says directly that *the moth shall devour them*, not as
men, in which light he no longer views them, but as old clothes. This is
a favourite comparison in Scripture to express a gradual but sure decay.
(Compare chap. li. 8, and Hosea v. 12.) In Job xiii. 28, Ps. xxxix. 12, it
seems to denote the effect of pining sickness. Not contented with this
obvious and natural interpretation of the figure, Vitringa supposes an
allusion to the official dresses of their chief men, which is not a whit more
reasonable than the notion of Cocceius which he sets aside as far-fetched,
that the prophets, priests, and rulers of the old economy were but a garment, under which the Messiah was concealed until his advent, and of
which he stripped himself (ἀπεκδυσάμενος, Col. ii. 15) at death. The
necessity of thus explaining why the enemies of Christ and his people are
compared to *garments* is precluded by the obvious consideration, that the
main point of the simile is the slow consuming process of the moth, and
that the clothes are added simply as the substances in which it is most
frequently observed.

10. *Who among you is a fearer of Jehovah, hearkening to the voice of his
servant, who walketh in darkness and there is no light to him? Let him
trust in the name of Jehovah, and lean upon his God.* The same sense may
be attained by closing the interrogation at *his servant*, and reading the
remainder of the sentence thus: *whoso walketh in darkness and hath no
light, let him trust*, &c. This construction, which is given by De Wette,
has the advantage of adhering more closely to the Masoretic interpunction.
A different turn is given to the sentence by J. D. Michaelis, who terminates
the question at *Jehovah*, and makes all the rest an answer to it. "Who
among you is a fearer of Jehovah? He that hearkeneth to the voice of
his servant, that walketh in darkness where he has no dawn, yet trusts in
Jehovah and relies upon his God." To this ingenious and original construction it may be objected, first, that it divides the sentence into two very
unequal parts, directly contrary to Hebrew usage; and in the next place,
that it makes the participles, present and future, all precisely synonymous
and equally descriptive of the pious man's habitual conduct. All the constructions which have now been mentioned give the מִי its usual and proper
sense, as an interrogative pronoun corresponding to the English *who?* But

Vitringa, Rosenmüller, Gesenius, and Maurer, choose to give it an indefinite sense, *whoso* or *whoever*, and exclude the interrogation altogether ;
the same superficial lexicography which confounds הֲלֹא with הִנֵּה, because
the Hebrew employed one form of expression, where we should more
naturally use the other. Because *whoever* might be used, and would be
used more readily by us in such a case than *who*, it does not follow that
the former is the true sense of the Hebrew word in that case. All the
instances alleged by Gesenius in his Lexicon as proofs that מִי is sometimes an indefinite, admit, with one exception, of the usual interrogative
translation, not only without damage to the sense, but with a more exact
adherence to the genius of the language, which delights in short detached
propositions, where an occidental writer would prefer a series of dependent
members forming one complex period. Thus in Judges vii. 3, the occidental idiom would be, *whosoever is fearful and afraid, let him return ;* but
the genuine Hebrew form is, *Who is fearful and afraid? let him return.*
The same thing is true of Exod. xxiv. 14, Prov. ix. 4, Eccles. v. 9, Isa. liv.
15, in all which cases there is nothing whatever to forbid the application of
the general rule, that the usual and proper sense must be retained unless
there be some reason for departing from it ; and such a reason cannot be
afforded by the bare possibility of a different construction. The single
exception above mentioned, and the only case of the indefinite use of מִי
alleged by Ewald in his Grammar, is 2 Sam. xviii. 12, which is too anomalous and doubtful to prove anything, and which may be as properly alleged
on one side as the other. The occasional combination of מִי with אֲשֶׁר
instead of favouring the views here combated, affords an argument against
them, as the obvious meaning of the words, both in Exod. xxxii. 33, and
2 Sam. xx. 11, is, *who (is) he that?* All that need be added upon this
point is, that the latest German writers have returned to the old and true
translation, *who ?*—Obedience to the word is implied in hearing it, but not
expressed.—Lowth, on the authority of two ancient versions, reads יִשְׁמַע
for שֹׁמֵעַ, *let him hearken*, which is copied by Gesenius, perhaps through
inadvertence, as he says nothing of a change of text, and no such sense can
possibly be put upon the participle. This mistake or oversight, if such it
be, although corrected by the later Germans, has been carefully retained by
Noyes (*let him hearken to the voice of his servant*). Henderson, on the
other hand, retains the common interrogative translation, but explains the
מִי, in his note, as " a substitute for the relative אֲשֶׁר, *he who*," which is
scarcely intelligible.—*Darkness* is here used as a natural and common
figure for distress. (See above, chap. viii. 20, ix. 1.) J. D. Michaelis
gives to נֹגַהּ the specific sense of dawn, break of day, or morning light, like
שַׁחַר in chap. viii. 20, and xlvii. 11. Vitringa understands it to mean
splendour or a great degree of light, and thus avoids the absolute negation
of all spiritual light, which would not suit his exegetical hypothesis. The
great majority of writers, late and early, are agreed in making it a poetical
equivalent or synonyme of אוֹר.—The futures in the last clause may, with
equal propriety, if not still greater, be translated, *he will trust* and *lean ;*
the exhortation being then implied but not expressed.—The preterite הָלַךְ
may be intended to suggest that the darkness spoken of is not a transient state,
but one which has already long continued. Trusting in the *name* of Jehovah
is not simply trusting in himself, or in the independent self-existence which
that name implies, but in his manifested attributes, attested by experience,
which seems to be the full sense of the word *name*, as applied to God in
The Old Testament.—Two exegetical questions, in relation to this verse,

have much divided and perplexed interpreters. The first has respect to
the person speaking and the objects of address ; the other to the servant of
Jehovah. These questions, from their close connection and their mutual
dependence, may be most conveniently discussed together. There would
be no absurdity, nor 'even inconsistency, in supposing that *his servant*
means the Prophet, or the prophets indefinitely, as the organs of the divine
communications. This may be granted even by those who give the title a
very different meaning elsewhere, as it cannot reasonably be supposed that
so indefinite a name, and one of such perpetual occurrence, is invariably
used in its most pregnant and emphatic sense. It is certain, on the contrary, that it is frequently applied to the prophets and to other public
functionaries of the old economy. There is therefore no absurdity in
Calvin's explanation of the phrase as here descriptive of God's ministers or
messengers in general, to whom those that fear him are required to submit.
The verse may then be connected immediately with what precedes, as the
words of the same speaker. But while all this is unquestionably true, it
cannot be denied that the frequency and prominence with which the
Servant of Jehovah is exhibited in these Later Prophecies, as one distinguished from the ordinary ministry, makes it more natural to make that
application of the words in this case, if it be admissible. The only difficulty lies in the mention of the Servant of Jehovah in the third person,
while the preceding context is to be considered as his own words. (See
above, on chap. xlix. 1.) This objection may be easily removed, if we assume,
as Ewald does, that the words of the Servant of Jehovah are concluded in
the preceding verse, and that in the one before us the Prophet goes on to
speak in his own person. This assumption, although not demonstrably
correct, agrees well with the dramatic form of the context both before and
after, and the frequent changes of person, without any explicit intimation,
which even the most rigorous interpreters are under the necessity of granting. On this hypothesis, which seems to be approved by the latest as well
as by the older writers, the Servant of Jehovah here referred to is the
same ideal person who appears at the beginning of the forty-ninth and
forty-second chapters, namely, the Messiah and his People as his type
and representative, to whose instructions in the name of God the world
must hearken if it would be saved. The question, which part of the complex person here predominates, must be determined by observing what is
said of him. If the exhortation of the verse were naturally applicable to
the world at large, as distinguished from the chosen people, then the latter
might be readily supposed to be included under the description of the Servant of Jehovah. But as the terms employed appear to be descriptive of
the people of Jehovah, or of some considerable class among them, the
most probable conclusion seems to be, that by the Servant of Jehovah we
are here to understand the Head as distinguished from the Body, with a
secondary reference, perhaps, to his official representatives, so far as he
employs them in communicating even with the Body itself. There is no
need of pointing out the arbitrary nature of Vitringa's theory, that this
verse relates to a period extending from the advent to the reign of Trajan
or Hadrian ; a chronological hypothesis in which the *terminus a quo* is only
less gratuitous and groundless than the *terminus ad quem.*

11. *Lo, all of you kindling fire, girding sparks* (or *fiery darts*), *go in the
light of your fire, and in the sparks ye have kindled. From my hand is this
to you ; in pain* (or *at the place of torment*) *shall ye lie down.* The construction of the first clause is ambiguous, as *kindling* and *girding*, with

their adjuncts, may be either the predicates or subjects of the proposition.
J. D. Michaelis, Hitzig, and Hendewerk, prefer the latter supposition, and
explain the clause to mean, *all of you are kindling fire*, &c. This being
inconsistent with the character described in the preceding verse, Hitzig
supposes that the speaker here acknowledges his error, or admits that the
fearers of Jehovah, whose existence he had hypothetically stated, were in fact
not to he found. As if he had said, "But you are not such, all of you are
kindling," &c. The harshness of this interpretation, or perhaps other
reasons, have induced the great majority of writers to adopt the other
syntax, and explain the participles as the subject of the proposition, or a
description of the object of address, *all of you kindling*, i. e. all of you who
kindle. Thus understood, the clause implies that the speaker is here turning from one class of hearers to another, from the Gentiles to the Jews, or
from the unbelieving portion of the latter to the pious, or still more generally from the corresponding classes of mankind at large, without either
national or local limitation. The wider sense agrees best with the comprehensive terms of the passage, whatever specific applications may be virtually comprehended in it or legitimately inferable from it. This is of
course too vague an hypothesis to satisfy the judgment or the feelings of
the excellent Vitringa, by whom it is repeatedly affirmed that all who admit
the application of the prophecy to Christ, must grant that this verse is addressed to the Pharisaic party of the Jews ; a consequence, the logical
necessity of which is very far from being evident.—There is also a difference
of opinion with respect to the import of the figures. That of *kindling
fire* is explained by Junius and Tremellius as denoting the invention of
doctrines not revealed in Scripture, while the *sparks* represent the Pharisaical traditions. The rabbinical interpreters suppose the fire to denote
the wrath of God, in proof of which they are able to allege not only
the general usage of the emblem in that sense, but the specific combination of this very noun and verb in Deut. xxxii. 22, Jer. xv. 14, xvii. 4.
In all these cases the meaning of the figure is determined by the addition of the words *in my anger*, or as some choose absurdly to render it,
in my nose. (See above, on chap. xlviii. 9.) This is certainly a strong
analogical argument in favour of the rabbinical interpretation, and Vitringa's method of evading it is not a little curious. He rests his proof
on the omission of this very phrase (בְּאַפִּי), in default of which he says,
nemo hic necessario cogitat de ira Dei. The same rule, if applied with
equal rigour to his own interpretations, would exclude a very large proportion of his favourite conclusions. Even in this case, he has no διαχρίτιχον,
as he calls it, to compel the adoption of his own idea, that the fire kindled
is the fire of sedition and intestine strife, still less to prove that the particular sedition and intestine conflict meant is that which raged among the
Jews before the final downfall of Jerusalem. Lowth seems unwilling to
reject this explanation, though his better taste inclines him to prefer the
wider sense of human devices and worldly policy, exclusive of faith and
trust in God. This is substantially the explanation of the words now commonly adopted, though particular interpreters diverge from one another in
details, according to the sense which they attach to the parallel metaphor,
מְאַזְּרֵי זִיקוֹת. The rabbinical tradition gives the noun the sense of *sparks*,
which is retained in many versions. But others follow Albert Schultens in explaining it to mean small bundles of combustibles, employed like matches,
or as missiles in ancient warfare. This is generalized by Lowth into *fuel*,

while Gesenius makes it signify specifically burning arrows, fiery darts, the βέλη πεπυρωμένα of Eph. vi. 16. J. D. Michaelis adopts the kindred sense of *torches.* No less doubtful is the meaning of the verb in this connection. Lowth translates the whole phrase, *who heap the fuel round about,* and Vitringa, *qui circumponitis malleolos.* Gesenius retains the usual sense of girding, and supposes them to be described as wearing the יָקוּת at the girdle. Most interpreters incline to the generic sense *surrounding*, as equally compatible with several different interpretations of the following noun. Any of these interpretations is better than the desperate device of emendation, which is here resorted to by Cappellus and Secker, the last of whom suggests מְאִירֵי; Hitzig proposes מְאוּרֵי, which seems to be approved by Ewald.—Common to all the explanations is the radical idea of a fire kindled by themselves to their own eventual destruction. This result is predicted, as in many other cases, under the form of a command or exhortation to persist in the course which must finally destroy them. *Go (i. e.* go on) *in the light of your fire.* This seems to favour the opinion that the fire is supposed to have been kindled for the sake of its light, which is implied indeed in Lowth's interpretation. Hitzig, however, understands the fire to be kindled for the purpose of destroying the righteous, instead of which result, those who kindle it are called upon to enter into it, and be consumed. For this is their appointed doom.—*From my hand is this to you, i. e.* my power has decreed and will accomplish what is now about to be declared, viz. that you shall lie down in sorrow, or a place of sorrow, if with Ewald we give the noun the local sense usual in words of this formation. The expression is a general one, denoting final ruin, and of course includes, although it may not specifically signify, a future state of misery.—It may here be mentioned, as a specimen of misplaced ingenuity, that J. D. Michaelis understands the scene depicted to be that of travellers in the dark who strike a light, and when it is extinguished find it darker than before, in consequence of which they fall among the rocks, and hurt themselves severely, which is meant by lying down in pain. It is characteristic of this writer and his age, that although rather supercilious and reserved in allowing the æsthetic merits of Isaiah, he describes this passage thus distorted by himself, as a specimen of oriental imagery which " really deserves to be introduced even into our poetry;" while many of the Prophet's loftiest flights elsewhere, if not entirely overlooked, are noticed in a kind of apologetic tone, as if the critic were ashamed of his subject. The spirit of such criticism is not yet extinct, although its grosser forms are superseded by a purer taste, even in Germany.

Chapter 51

INTERPRETERS are much divided with respect to the particular period which constitutes the subject of this prophecy. The modern Jews regard it as a promise of deliverance from their present exile and dispersion by the Messiah, whom they still expect. The Christian Fathers refer it to the time of the first advent. Modern writers are divided between this hypothesis, and that which confines it to the Babylonish exile. The truth appears to be, that this chapter is a direct continuation of the preceding declarations with respect to the vocation of the church, and the divine administration towards her. The possibility of her increase, as previously promised, is

evinced by the example of Abraham, from whom all Israel descended, vers.
1–3. In like manner many shall be added from the Gentiles, vers. 4–6.
Their enemies shall not only fail to destroy them, but shall be themselves
destroyed, vers. 7, 8. This is confirmed by another historical example, that
of Egypt, vers. 9, 10. The same assurances are then repeated, with a clearer
promise of the new dispensation, vers. 11–16. The chapter closes with a
direct address to Zion, who, though helpless in herself and destitute of
human aid, is sure of God's protection and of the destruction of her enemies
and his, vers. 17–23.

1. *Hearken unto me !* A common formula, when the writer or speaker
turns away from one object of address to another. It is here used because he is about to address himself to the faithful servants of Jehovah,
the true Israel, who are described as *following* (or *pursuing*) *after righteousness*, *i. e.* making it the end of all their efforts to be righteous, or conformed
to the will of God. The sense of justifying righteousness or justification is
as much out of place here as that of truth, which is given by the Targum ;
except so far as all these terms are employed in Scripture usage, to express
the general idea of moral goodness, piety, or a character acceptable in God's
sight. The original application of the phrase here used is by Moses (Deut.
xvi. 20) ; from whom it is copied twice by Solomon (Prov. xv. 9 ; xxi. 21),
and twice by Paul (1 Tim. vi. 11 ; 2 Tim. ii. 22). The same apostle uses,
in the same sense, the more general expression, *follow after good* (1 Thess.
v. 15) ; which is also used by David (Ps. xxxviii. 21, comp. Ps. xxxiv. 15).
The same class of persons is then described as *seeking* (or *seekers of*) *Jehovah*,
i. e. seeking his presence, praying to him, worshipping him, consulting him.
The first description is more abstract, the second expresses a personal relation to Jehovah ; both together are descriptive of the righteous as distinguished from the wicked. Now as these have ever been comparatively
few, not only in relation to the heathen world, but in relation to the spurious members of the church itself, a promise of vast increase (like that in
chap. xlix. 18–21) might well appear incredible. In order to remove this
doubt, the Prophet here appeals, not, as in many other cases, to the mere
omnipotence of God, but to a historical example of precisely the same kind,
viz. that of Abraham, from whom the race of Israel had already sprung, in
strict fulfilment of a divine promise.—*Look unto the rock ye have been hewn.*
The earlier grammarians assume an ellipsis of the relative and preposition,
the rock from which ye have been hewn ; the later, and particularly Ewald,
reject this as an occidental idiom, and suppose the Hebrew phrase to be
complete, but give the same sense as the others. The same remark applies
to the parallel clause, *and to the hole of the pit (from which) ye have been
digged.* The reference of these figures to our Lord Jesus Christ, as the
rock of ages and the source of spiritual life, is held by some of the Fathers,
one of whom (Eusebius) supposes a collateral allusion to the rock in which
our Saviour was entombed ; but this interpretation is too mystical even for
Vitringa, who admits that the figures of this verse are explained in the next
by the Prophet himself. His Dutch taste again gets the better of his judgment and his reverent regard for the word of God, and allows him to put
a revolting sense upon the figures here employed, in which Knobel follows
with still greater coarseness. The truth, as recognised by almost all interpreters, is that the rock and pit (or quarry) are two kindred metaphors for one
and the same thing, both expressing the general idea of extraction or descent
(compare chap. xlviii. 2), without particular reference to the individual
parents, although both are mentioned in the next verse, for the sake of a

parallel construction, upon which it is almost puerile to found such a conclusion as the one in question. In the same category may be safely placed
the old dispute, whether Abraham is called a rock because he was *strong in
faith* (Rom. iv. 20), or because he was *as good as dead* (Heb. xi. 12) when
he received the promise. He is no more represented as a rock than as a
pit or quarry, neither of which figures is applied to him distinctively, but
both together signify extraction or origin in a genealogical sense.

2. *Look unto Abraham your father and unto Sarah (that) bare you.*
That Sarah is mentioned chiefly for rhythmical effect, may be inferred from
the writer's now confiding what he says to Abraham alone. Instead of
speaking further of both parents, he now says, *For I have called him one;*
which does not mean, I have declared him to be such, or so described him;
but, I have called (*i. e.* chosen, designated) him, when he was only one,
i. e. a solitary individual, although the destined father of a great nation (Gen.
xii. 2). This sense of the word *one* is clear from Ezek. xxxiii. 24, where,
with obvious allusion to this verse, it is put in opposition to *many* : *Abraham was* ONE, *and he inherited the land ; and we are* MANY, (much more
then) *is the land given to us for an inheritance.* The same antithesis is
far more obvious and appropriate in this place, than that between Abraham,
as sole heir of the promise, and the rest of men, who were excluded from
it. The design of the Prophet is not so much to magnify the honour put
upon Abraham by choosing him out of the whole race to be the father of
the faithful, as it is to shew the power and faithfulness of God in making
this *one man* a nation like the stars of heaven for multitude, according to
the promise (Gen. xv. 5). Noyes's version, *a single man*, is rendered by
the modern usage of that phrase almost ludicrously equivocal, and necessarily suggests an idea directly at variance with the facts of the case; unless
he really infers from the exclusive mention of Abraham in this clause, that
he was called before his marriage, which can hardly be reconciled with the
sacred narrative (compare Gen. xi. 29, and xii. 1, 5), and, even if it were
true, would scarcely have been solemnly affirmed in this connection, since
the promise, whatever its precise date, presupposed his marriage as the
necessary means of its fulfilment.—Interpreters, with almost perfect unanimity, explain the two verbs at the end of this verse as expressing past time
(*and I blessed him and caused him to increase*), although the *vav* prefixed to
neither has the pointing of the *vav conversive*, in default of which the preterite translation is entirely gratuitous and therefore ungrammatical. The
Masoretic pointing, it is true, is not of absolute authority, but it is of the
highest value as the record of an ancient critical tradition ; and the very
fact that it departs in this case from the sense which all interpreters have
felt to be most obvious and natural, creates a strong presumption that it
rests upon some high authority or some profound view of the Prophet's
meaning. And we find accordingly that by adhering to the strict sense of
the future, we not only act in accordance with a most important general
principle of exegesis, but obtain a sense which, though less obvious than
the common one, is really better in itself and better suited to the context.
According to the usual interpretation, this verse simply asserts the fulfilment of the promise to Abraham, leaving the reader to connect it with what
follows as he can. But by a strict translation of the futures, they are made
to furnish an easy and natural transition from the one case to the other,
from the great historical example cited, to the subject which it was intended
to illustrate. The concise phrase, *one I called him*, really includes a citation of the promise made to Abraham, and suggests the fact of its fulfilment,

so far as this had yet taken place. The Prophet, speaking in Jehovah's name, then adds a declaration that the promise should be still more gloriously verified. As if he had said, I promised to bless him and increase him, and I did so, *and I will bless him and increase him* (still). But how? By shewing mercy to his seed, as I have determined and begun to do. This last idea is expressed in the first clause of the next verse, which is then no longer incoherent or abrupt, but in the closest and most natural connection with what goes before. This consideration might have less force if the illustration had been drawn from the experience of another race, for instance from the history of Egypt or Assyria, or even from the increase of the sons of Lot or Ishmael; but when the promise which he wished to render credible is really a repetition or continuation of the one which he cites as an illustrative example, the intimate connection thus established or revealed between them is a strong proof that the explanation which involves it is the true one.

3. *For Jehovah hath comforted Zion.* The arbitrary character of the usual construction of these sentences may be learned from the fact that Rosenmüller and Gesenius, not content with making both the futures at the close of the second verse preterites, explain both the preterites in this clause as futures; a double violation of analogy and usage, which seems to leave the meaning of the writer wholly at the mercy of the reader or expounder. From the same erroneous understanding of the closing words of ver. 2 springs the forced interpretation of the כִּי at the beginning of this, as meaning *so* (Gesenius), *thus therefore* (Lowth), and the still more unnatural construction of the whole clause by Hitzig, as the apodosis of a comparative sentence beginning in the first verse: " As I called him alone, and blessed him, and increased him, so does Jehovah pity Zion," &c. As soon as the strict sense of the futures in ver. 2 has been reinstated, the connection becomes obvious, and כִּי retains its usual and proper sense— " I have blessed and increased him, and I will bless and increase him; *for* Jehovah has begun to comfort Zion." The strong assurance thus afforded by the strict translation of the preterite נִחַם conspires with analogy and usage to give it the preference over the vague evasive present form, employed by Hitzig, Ewald, and De Wette. This view of the connection also supersedes the necessity of laying an unusual stress on the name Jehovah, as J. H. Michaelis does, as if he had said, it is God, not man, that comforts Zion.—Gesenius translates נִחַם, in this case, " will have mercy or compassion " (*wird sich erbarmen*), in which he is followed by De Wette and Henderson. But even his own Lexicon gives no such definition of the Piel, and the Niphal though coincident in this tense as to form, would, according to usage, take a preposition after it. Besides, the proper sense of *comforting*, retained by Ewald and the other Germans, is more appropriate, because it expresses not mere feeling but its active exhibition, and because the same verb is employed at the very outset of these prophecies (chap. xl. 1) in the same application, but in a connection where the sense of pitying or having mercy is wholly inadequate, if not inadmissible. The comparison of that place also shews what we are here to understand by Zion, viz. Jehovah's people, of which it was the capital, the sanctuary, and the symbol. What is there commanded is here, in a certain sort, performed, or its performance more distinctly and positively promised.—*He hath comforted all our wastes* (or *ruins*), *i.e.* restored cheerfulness to what was wholly desolate. This phrase proves nothing as to the Prophet's viewing Zion merely as a ruinous city, since in any case this is the substratum

of his metaphor. The question is not whether he has reference to Zion or Jerusalem as a town, but whether this town is considered merely as a town, and mentioned for its own sake, or in the sense before explained, as the established representative and emblem of the church or chosen people (see above, on chap. xlix. 21).—*And hath placed* (or *made*) *her wilderness like Eden, and her desert like the garden of the Lord.* This beautiful comparison is the strongest possible expression of a joyful change from total barrenness and desolation to the highest pitch of fertility and beauty. It is closely copied in Ezekiel xxxi. 9, but the same comparison, in more concise terms, is employed by Moses (Gen. xiii. 10). Even there, notwithstanding what is added about Egypt, but still more unequivocally here, the reference is not to *a garden*, or to pleasure-grounds in general, as Luther and several of the later Germans have assumed, with no small damage to the force and beauty of their versions, but Eden as a proper name, *the* garden of Jehovah, the *Paradise*, as the Septuagint renders it, both here and in Gen. ii. 8, the grand historical and yet ideal designation of the most consummate terrene excellence, analogous, if not still more nearly related, to the Grecian pictures of Arcadia and of Tempe.—*Joy and gladness shall be found in her, i. e.* in Zion, thus transformed into a paradise. The plural form, *in them*, employed by Barnes, is not only inexact, but hurtful to the sense, by withdrawing the attention from the central figure of this glowing landscape. *Shall be found*, does not simply mean *shall be*, as J. D. Michaelis paraphrases it, but also that they shall be there accessible, not only present in their abstract essence, as it were, but in the actual experience of those who dwell there.— *Thanksgiving and the voice of melody.* The music of the common version of this last clause is at once too familiar and too sacred to be superseded, simply for the purpose of expressing more distinctly the exact sense of the last word, which originally signifies the sound of an instrument or instrumental music, but is afterwards used to denote song in general, or rather as a vehicle of praise to God.

4. *Attend* (or *hearken*) *unto me, my people; and my nation, unto me give ear.* This may seem to be a violation of the usage which has been already stated as employing this form of speech to indicate a change in the object of address. But such a change, although a slight one, takes place even here; for he seems no longer to address those seeking righteousness exclusively, but the whole body of the people as such. Some interpreters suppose a change still greater, namely, a transition from the Jews to the Gentiles. In order to admit of this, the text must be amended, or its obvious sense explained away. Lowth, of course, prefers the former method, and reads עַמִּים on the authority of two manuscripts, and לְאֻמִּים on the authority of nine. Gesenius gains the same end by explaining עַמִּי and לְאֻמִּי as unusual plural forms, the first of which he also finds in three other places (2 Sam. xxii. 44, Ps. cxliv. 2, Lam. iii. 14). Ewald denies the existence of such a termination, against which he argues with much force, that in these four places, however inappropriate the sense *my people* may appear to the interpreter, no one pretends to say that it is absurd or impossible, while in every other case the very meaning of the noun is so obscure that it can throw no light upon the question of form. The discussion of the question by these eminent grammarians (in the Lehrgebäude, § 124, and the Kritische Grammatik, § 164) has left the existence of the plural form in question at the least very doubtful (see Nordheimer, § 553); and even if it be conceded, it is confessedly so rare that it is not to be assumed without necessity in such a case as this, simply because it may conceivably

be true, when the sense which the word has in nearly two hundred places is perfectly appropriate here. The only argument in favour of it, drawn from the connection, is without force, because the dependence of the Gentiles upon Israel for saving knowledge might be just as well asserted in addressing the latter as the former, as appears from the analogy of chap. ii. 3. The same reasons which have now been stated will suffice to set aside Maurer's gratuitous interpretation of the words as singular collectives, which might be assumed in a case of extreme exegetical necessity, but in no other. The next clause explains what it is that they are thus called upon to hear, viz. *that law from me shall go forth, i. e.* revelation or the true religion, as an expression of God's will, and consequently man's rule of duty. In like manner Paul describes the gospel as the *law of faith* (Rom. iii. 27), not binding upon one race or nation merely, but *by the commandment of the everlasting God made known to all nations, for the obedience of faith* (Rom. xvi. 26). J. D. Michaelis, followed by Rosenmüller and De Wette, dilutes it into *a doctrine* (*eine Lehre*), which, although correct in point of etymology, is justified neither by the context nor by usage. Ewald gives the same translation of the word, but makes it less indefinite by adding the possessive pronoun (*meine Lehre*). The meaning of the clause is that the nations can expect illumination only from one quarter.—The same thing is then said in another form. *And my judgment* (מִשְׁפָּט an equivalent to תּוֹרָה, and combined with it like *lex* and *jus* in Latin) *for a light of the nations* (as in chap. xlii. 6, xlix. 6) *will I cause to rest, i. e.* fix, establish. Jarchi explains it by the synonyme אַגִּיחַ, which is frequently employed in this sense (*e. g.* chap. xlvi. 7; 2 Kings xvii. 29). The meanings given to the word by Calvin (*patefaciam*), Coccerius (*promovebo*), Lowth (*cause to break forth*), and others, are either wholly conjectural or founded on a false etymology. Aben Ezra speaks of some as having made it a denominative from רֶגַע, meaning "I will do it in a moment." Kimchi strangely says that לְאוֹר עַמִּים may mean *in the presence of the Gentiles;* a suggestion which savours of rabbinical reluctance to believe in the conversion of the world to God. As specimens of exegesis on the most contracted scale, it may be mentioned that Piscator understands by *law*, in this verse, Cyrus's decree for the restoration of the Jewish exiles, and by *light* the knowledge of this great event among the nations; whereas Grotius explains *judgment* to mean penal inflictions on the Babylonians, and *light* the evidence thereby afforded that Jehovah was the true God. The groundless and injurious protrusion of the Babylonish exile as the great theme of the prophecy is here abandoned even by Kimchi and Abarbenel, although they refer the promise to the advent of Messiah as still future. The simple proposition that the world can be converted only by a revelation, admits no more of being thus restricted than any of the spiritual promises and prophecies contained in the New Testament.

5. *Near (is) my righteousness, i. e.* the exhibition of it in the changes previously promised and threatened. *Near*, as often elsewhere in the prophecies, is an indefinite expression which describes it simply as approaching, and as actually near to the perceptions of the Prophet, or to any one who occupies the same point of vision.—*Gone forth is my salvation.* Not only is the purpose formed, and the decree gone forth, but the event itself, in the sense just explained, may be described as past or actually passing. Hitzig, however, understands יָצָא to mean "it goes forth from my mouth," as in chap. xlviii. 3, lv. 11. Umbreit agrees with Vitringa in supposing an allusion to the rising of the sun (Ps. xix. 6, 7), or, as Gesenius sug-

gests, to the dawning of the day (chap. xlvii. 11); while Ewald and Knobel understand it as referring to the springing or incipient germination of plants, which is properly expressed by צָמַח (chap. xlii. 9), the two verbs being elsewhere used as parallels in this sense (Job v. 6). But none of these ingenious explanations is so natural as that which gives יָצָא the same sense as in the preceding verse, viz. that of issuing or going forth from God (conceived as resident in heaven or in Zion) to the heathen world.—*And my arms shall judge the nations.* As the foregoing clause contains a promise, some interpreters suppose it to be necessary to give *judge* the favourable sense of vindicating, righting (as in chap. i. 17, 23), or at least the generic one of ruling (as in 1 Sam. viii. 5). But nothing can be more in keeping with the usage of the Scriptures, and of this book in particular, than the simultaneous exhibition of God's justice in his treatment both of friends and foes. (Compare chap. i. 27.) There is no objection, therefore, to Jarchi's explanation of the verb as meaning here to punish; this at least may be included as a part of the idea which it was intended to express.—J. D. Michaelis, supposing the construction of זְרוֹעַ (which is feminine) with a masculine verb to be ungrammatical, proposes, by a change of punctuation, to connect the one with what precedes, and then to read, *the nations shall be judged.* This hypercriticism provokes Gesenius to convict its author of deficiency in Hebrew grammar, which he does by shewing that in Gen. xlix. 24 and Dan. xi. 31 this form of the plural is construed as a masculine, to which he adds a like use of the singular itself in Isa. xvii. 5. *For me shall the islands wait, i. e.* for me they must wait, until I reveal myself they must remain in darkness. (See above, on chap. xlii. 4.) Here again, as in chaps. xli. 1, xlii. 4, &c., אִיִּים is explained to mean lands, distant lands, coasts, distant coasts, western lands, Europe, Northern Asia, and Asia Minor. As in all the former instances, however, the usual sense of *islands* is entirely appropriate, as a poetical or representative expression for countries in general, with more particular reference to those across the sea.—*And in my arm they shall hope, i. e.* in the exercise of my almighty power. As in chap. xlii. 6, the sense is not so much that they shall exercise a feeling of trust, but that this will be their only hope or dependence. To be enlightened, they must wait for my revelation; to be saved, for the exertion of my power. It is not descriptive, therefore, of the feelings of the nations after the way of salvation is made known to them, but of their helpless and desperate condition until they hear it. True to their favourite hypotheses, Piscator understands by *islands* the Israelitish captives in Assyria, Grotius the Persians residing on the sea-coast who were not idolaters ! Knobel, with equal confidence and equal reason, makes the verse refer to the downfall of Croesus and the conquests of Cyrus.

6. *Raise to the heavens your eyes, and look unto the earth beneath.* A similar form of address occurs above, in chap. xl. 26. (Compare Gen. xv. 5.) Heaven and earth are here put, as in many other places, for the whole frame of nature. The next clause explains why they are called upon to look. *For the heavens like smoke are dissolved* or *driven away.* The verb in this form occurs nowhere else, and the interpreters have tried in vain to derive its meaning here from other cognate forms of the same root, which all have reference to salting (from the primitive noun מֶלַח, *salt*). So Symmachus in this place, ἁλίσουσι. But this, according to analogy, would rather imply perpetuity than its opposite. The link between them may consist in the idea of reducing to powder or minute dust by trituration,

which is equally appropriate to salt, and to the dissolution of any solid substance. Most writers give this verb a future sense (or a present one as an evasive substitute). because the real future follows; but for this very reason it may be presumed that the writer used distinct forms to express distinct ideas, and that he first gives a vivid description of the dissolution as already past, and then foretells its consummation as still future.—*And the earth like the garment* (which grows old) *shall grow old* (or *wear out*). The same comparison occurs above in chap. l. 9, and serves to identify the passages as parts of one continued composition. *And its inhabitant shall die*, כְּמוֹ־כֵן. This is a difficult expression. Cocceius alone proposes three distinct interpretations, all peculiar to himself. In his version he translates the phrase *ut quivis*, which appears to mean "like anybody else." But in his commentary he suggests that it may possibly mean *quemadmodum probus*, making כֵּן an adjective, and supposing an allusion to the death of the righteous, as described in chap. lvii. 1, 2. His third supposition is that this is a case of aposiopesis, or interrupted construction, and that the writer first says *they shall die like*—but before the comparison is finished ends by saying *so*—as if he pointed to the spectacle before him.—Samuel Luzzatto makes the phrase mean *in an instant*, strictly in the time required to say כֵּן, which he compares to the German phrase, *in einem Nu*. Apart from these ingenious notions, there are only two interpretations of the phrase which are entitled to notice. The first takes both words in their ordinary sense, and understands the whole as an intensive expression *just so* or *exactly so*. This seems to be the sense intended by the Septuagint (ὥσπερ ταῦτα) and Vulgate (*sicut hæc*), although they adhere less closely to the form of the original than Schmidius (*sicut sic*) and Rückert (*so wie so*). The only other recent versions which retain this sense are those of Barnes and Henderson. Noyes and the modern Germans all adopt the opinion of De Dieu, Gussetius, and Vitringa, that כֵּן is the singular of כִּנִּים, the word translated *lice* in the history of the plagues of Egypt (Exod. viii. 12, 13), but explained by the later lexicographers to mean a kind of stinging gnat. Supposing the essential idea to be that of a contemptible animalcule, Vitringa renders it *instar vermiculi*, Lowth still more freely *like the vilest insect*. Noyes simply says *like flies*, which scarcely expresses the comparison supposed by these writers to have been intended. It is not impossible that this ingenious but fanciful translation will yet be abandoned in its turn by most interpreters for that recommended by analogy, and usage, as well as by the testimony of the ancient versions. *The inhabitants shall die like a gnat*, is a meaning which, in order to be purchased at so dear a rate, ought to possess some marked superiority above the old one, *they shall likewise perish*, to which there may possibly be an allusion in our Saviour's words recorded in Luke xiii. 3, 5.—The contrast to this general destruction is contained in the last clause.—*And my salvation to eternity shall be, and my righteousness shall not be broken*, i. e. shall not cease from being what it is, in which sense the same verb is evidently used by Isaiah elsewhere (chap. vii. 8). In this, as in many other cases, *salvation and righteousness* are not synonymous, but merely correlative as cause and effect. (See above, on chap. xlii. 6.) The only question as to this clause is whether it is a hypothetical or absolute proposition. If the former, then the sense is that until (or even if) the frame of nature be dissolved, the justice and salvation of Jehovah shall remain unshaken. This explanation is preferred by Joseph Kimchi, Rosenmüller, Gesenius, and Maurer. The other interpretation understands the first clause as a positive and independent declaration that the heavens and earth shall be dissolved, which Vitringa understands to mean that the old economy shall cease, while others give these words their literal meaning. All these hypotheses are reconcileable by making the first clause mean, as similar expressions do mean elsewhere, that the most extraordinary changes shall be witnessed, moral and physical; but that amidst them all this one thing shall remain unchangeable, the righteousness of God as displayed in the salvation of his people. (See chaps. xl. 8, lxv. 17; Mat. v. 18; 1 John ii. 17.) Knobel thinks that the ancient prophets actually looked for a complete revolution in the face of nature, coetaneous and coincident with the moral and spiritual changes which they foretold.

7. *Hearken unto me, ye that know righteousness, people (with) my law in their heart; fear not the reproach of men, and by their scoffs be not broken* (in spirit, *i. e.* terrified). The distinction here implied is still that between the righteous and the wicked as the two great classes of mankind. Those who are described in ver. 1 as *seeking after righteousness* are here said to *know it, i. e.* know it by experience. Vitringa and Gesenius explain the Hebrew verb as meaning *love;* but this is an arbitrary substitution of what may be considered as implied for what is really expressed. The presence of the law in the heart denotes not mere affection for it, but a correct apprehension of it, as the heart in Hebrew is put for the whole mind or soul; it is therefore a just parallel to *knowing* in the other member of the clause.— The opposite class, or those who know not what is right, and who have not God's law in their heart, are comprehended under the generic title *man,* with particular reference to the derivation of the Hebrew word from a root meaning to be weak or sickly, so that its application here suggests the idea of their frailty and mortality, as a sufficient reason why God's people should not be afraid of them.

8. *For like the* (moth-eaten) *garment shall the moth devour them, and like the* (worm-eaten) *wool shall the worm devour them; and my righteousness to eternity shall be, and my salvation to an age of ages.* The same contrast between God's immutability, and the brief duration of his enemies, is presented in chap. l. 9, and in ver. 6 above.

9. *Awake, awake, put on strength, arm of Jehovah; awake, as (in the) days of old, the ages of eternities; art not thou the same that hewed Rahab in pieces, that wounded the serpent or dragon?* The Septuagint makes Jerusalem the object of address, in which it is followed by some modern writers, who suppose the *arm of Jehovah* to be mentioned as a synonyme, or figurative paraphrase of the *strength* with which she is exhorted to invest herself. This addition would, however, be at once so harsh and so gratuitous, that most interpreters appear to acquiesce in the more obvious explanation of the words as addressed directly to the *arm of Jehovah* as the symbol of his power. Gesenius's idea, that Jehovah thus calls upon his own arm to wake, is as unnatural as Vitringa's supposition of a chorus of saints or doctors. The only probable hypothesis is that which puts the words into the mouth of the people, or of the prophet as their representative. The verse is then a highly figurative, but by no means an obscure, appeal to the former exertion of that power, as a reason for its renewed exertion in the present case. The particular example cited seems to be the overthrow of Egypt, here described by the enigmatical name *Rahab,* for the origin and sense of which see vol. i. p. 475. The same thing is probably intended by the parallel term תַּנִּין, whether this be understood to mean an aquatic monster in the general, or more specifically the crocodile, the natural and immemorial emblem of Egypt.

10. *Art not thou the same that dried the sea, the waters of the great deep, that placed the depths of the sea (as) a way for the passage of redeemed ones?* The allusion to the overthrow of Egypt is carried out and completed by a distinct mention of the miraculous passage of the Red Sea. The interrogative form of the sentence is equivalent to a direct affirmation that it is the same arm, or in other words, that the same power which destroyed the Egyptians for the sake of Israel still exists, and may again be exerted for a similar purpose. The confidence that this will be done is expressed somewhat abruptly in the next verse.

11. *And the ransomed of Jehovah shall return and come to Zion with shouting, and everlasting joy upon their head; gladness and joy shall overtake (them), sorrow and sighing have fled away.* The same words occur in chap. xxxv. 10, except that יְשִׂיגוּ is there written in its usual form, without the final ן, and that נָסוּ is preceded by the *Vav conversive*. Some manuscripts exhibit the same reading here, and the difference might be considered accidental, but for the fact that such variations are often made intentionally. See p. 42.

12. *I, I am he that comforteth you; who art thou, that thou shouldst be afraid of man (who) is to die, and of the son of man who (as) grass is to be given?* The important truth is here reiterated, that Jehovah is not only the deliverer, but the sole deliverer of his people, and as the necessary consequence, that they have not only no need but no right to be afraid, which seems to be the force of the interrogation, *Who art thou that thou shouldst be afraid?* or still more literally, *Who art thou and thou hast been afraid?* *i.e.* consider who is thy protector, and then recollect that thou hast been afraid. The etymological import of אֱנוֹשׁ is rendered still more prominent in this case by the addition of the word יָמוּת, before which a relative may be supplied in order to conform it to our idiom, although the original construction is rather that of a complete but parenthetical proposition. "Afraid of man (he shall die), and of the son of man (as grass he shall be given)." This last verb is commonly explained as if simply equivalent to *he shall be* or *shall become*, which is hardly consistent with its usage elsewhere. Some adhere more closely to the strict sense by supposing it to mean *he shall be given up*, abandoned to destruction. There is no need of supposing a grammatical ellipsis of the preposition כְּ, since the relation of resemblance is in many cases suggested by a simple apposition, as in the English phrase, *he reigns a sovereign.* On the comparison itself, see above, chap. xl. 6.

13. *And hast forgotten Jehovah thy Maker, spreading the heavens and founding the earth, and hast trembled continually all the day, from before the wrath of the oppressor as he made ready to destroy? And where is (now) the wrath of the oppressor?* The form of expression in the first clause makes it still more clear, that the statement in ver. 12 is not merely hypothetical but historical, implying that they had actually feared man and forgotten God. The epithets added to God's name are not merely ornamental, much less superfluous, but strictly appropriate, because suggestive of almighty power, which ensured the performance of his promise and the effectual protection of his people.—*Continually all the day* is an emphatic pleonasm, such as is occasionally used in every language.—*From before* is a common Hebrew idiom for *because of, on account of*, but may here be taken in its strict sense as expressive of alarm and flight before an enemy. (See chap. ii. 19.)—Some render כַּאֲשֶׁר *as if*, to which there are two objections: first, the want of any satisfactory authority from usage; and secondly, the fact that the words then imply that no such attempt has really been made. *As if he could destroy* would be appropriate enough, because it is merely an

indirect denial of his power to do so ; but it cannot be intended to deny that he had aimed at it.—כּוֹנֵן is particularly used in reference to the preparation of the bow for shooting by the adjustment of the arrow on the string ; some suppose that it specifically signifies the act of taking aim. (Ps. vii. 13, xi. 2, xxi. 13.)—The question at the close implies that the wrath is at an end, and the oppressor himself vanished.   We have no authority for limiting this reference to any particular historical event.   It is as if he had said, How often have you trembled when your oppressors threatened to destroy you, and where are they now ?   Beck absurdly imagines that the writer here betrays himself as writing after the event which he affects to foretell.—Ewald seems to make הִשְׁחִית a denominative from שַׁחַת, meaning to send to hell (*in die Hölle zu senden*) ; but this, although it strengthens the expression, seems to do it at the cost of philological exactness.

14. *He hastens bowing to be loosed, and he shall not die in the pit, and his bread shall not fail.*   The essential idea is that of liberation, but with some obscurity in the expression.   Some give to צָעָה here and in chap. lxiii. 1 the sense of marching, which would here be appropriate, but could not be so easily reconciled with the other cases where the word occurs.   The modern lexicographers appear to be agreed that the radical meaning of the verb is that of bending, either backward (as in chap. lxiii. 1) or downward (as in Jer. xlviii. 12, and here).   The latest versions accordingly explain it as a poetical description of the prisoner bowed down under chains.   With still more exactness it may be translated as a participle qualifying the indefinite subject of the verb at the beginning.   There is, however, no objection to the usual construction of the word as a noun ; the sense remains the same in either case.—The next clause is sometimes taken as an indirect subjunctive proposition, *that he should not die ;* but it is best to make it a direct affirmation that *he shall not*.   Ewald gives שַׁחַת a sense corresponding to that of the verb in the preceding verse, and renders the entire phrase *for hell, i. e.* so as to descend into it.   If the noun be taken in this sense, or in the kindred one of *grave*, the preposition cannot mean *in*, a sense, moreover, not agreeable to usage.   Those who give it that sense here are under the necessity of making שַׁחַת mean the dungeon, which is a frequent sense of the analogous term בּוֹר.   But whether the phrase in question mean *for hell*, or *for the grave*, or *in the pit*, or *to destruction*, the general sense is still that the captive shall not perish in captivity.   This general promise is then rendered more specific by the assurance that he shall not starve to death, which seems to be the only sense that can be put upon the last clause.

15. *And I (am) Jehovah thy God, rousing the sea, and then its waves roar; Jehovah of hosts (is) his name.*   Another appeal to the power of God as a pledge for the performance of his promise.   רָגַע has been understood in two directly opposite senses, that of *stilling* and that of *agitating*. The first is strongly recommended by the not unfrequent use of the derivative conjugations in the sense of quieting or being quiet.   The other rests upon an Arabic analogy, confirmed, however, by the context, as וַיֶּהֱמוּ must indicate a consequence (*and then* or *so that*), and not an antecedent (*when they roar*), as explained by the writers who take רָגַע in the sense of *stilling*, and even by Gesenius, who gives that verb the sense of frightening.   Some of the older writers seem to have regarded רָגַע as a transposition for גָּעַר, rebuking, a word often used to express the divine control over nature, and especially the sea.   (See above, chap. xvii. 13.)

16. *And I have put my words in thy mouth, and in the shadow of my hand I have hid thee, to plant the heavens, and to found the earth, and to say to Zion, Thou art my people.* That these words are not addressed to Zion or the church is evident, because in the last clause she is spoken of in the third person, and addressed in the next verse with a sudden change to the feminine form from the masculine, which is here used. That it is not the Prophet, may be readily inferred from the nature of the work described in the second clause. The only remaining supposition is, that the Messiah is the object of address, and that his work or mission is here described, viz. to plant the heavens, *i. e.* to establish them, perhaps with allusion to the erection of a tent by the insertion of its stakes in the ground. There is no need of reading לִנְטוֹחַ, as Lowth does, since the usage of the Scriptures is rather in favour of variation than of scrupulous transcription. The whole clause is equivalent to *creating a new world*, which must here be taken in a figurative sense; because the literal creation, as a thing already past, would here be inappropriate, especially when followed by the words, *to say to Zion, Thou art my people.* Nothing is gained by referring the infinitives to God himself, as Rosenmüller does; because the person here addressed is still described as the instrument, if not as the efficient agent. The new creation thus announced can only mean the reproduction of the church in a new form, by what we usually call the change of dispensations. The outward economy should all be new, and yet the identity of the chosen people should remain unbroken. For he whom God had called to plant new heavens and to found a new earth, was likewise commissioned to say to Zion, Thou art still my people.

17. This may be considered a continuation of the address begun at the end of the preceding verse. The same voice which there said, *Thou art my people*, may be here supposed to say, *Rouse thyself! rouse thyself! Arise, Jerusalem! (thou) who hast drunk at the hand of Jehovah the cup of his wrath; the bowl of the cup of reeling thou hast drunk, thou hast wrung (or sucked) out, i. e.* drunk its very dregs. Some of the rabbins give the sense of dregs to קֻבַּעַת itself. The ancient versions either overlook it, or explain it to mean a certain kind of cup. The modern writers are disposed to regard it as a pleonastic expression, similar to *goblet-cup.* According to its probable etymology, as traceable in Hebrew and Arabic, the word denotes the convex surface of a cup or bowl, while כוֹס is properly the area or space within. The cup is of course put for its contents, a natural figure for anything administered or proffered by a higher power. (Compare Jer. xxv. 15, 16, xlix, 12, li. 7, Lam. iv. 21, Obad. 16, Ezek. xxiii. 34, Rev. xiv. 10.)

18. *There is no guide to her* (or *no one leading her*) *of all the sons she has brought forth, and no one grasping her hand of all the sons she has brought up.* From addressing Zion in the second person, he now proceeds to speak of her in the third. This verse is not so much descriptive of unnatural abandonment as it is of weakness. The sense is not that no one will, but that no one can protect or guide her. Some interpreters suppose the figure of a drunken person to be still continued. J. D. Michaelis even goes so far as to translate the first words of the verse, *No one brings her a drink of water.* This is no doubt founded on the usual application of this verb to the watering of flocks, from which is deduced the secondary sense of guidance in general. Hengstenberg gives to it, wherever it occurs, the sense of fostering or nourishing. (See above, on chap. xl. 11.) The

mother and the sons, *i. e.* the people, collectively and individually, are distinguished only by a figure of speech.

19. *Both those things are befalling* (or *about to befall*) *thee: who will mourn for thee? Wasting and ruin, famine and sword: who* (*but*) *I will comfort thee?* A difficulty here is the mention of *two things* in the first clause, followed by an enumeration of *four* in the second. Some suppose the two things to refer to what precedes, others to wasting and ruin only. Grotius thinks that wasting and famine, ruin and sword, are to be combined as synonymes. The modern writers understand the second phrase as an explanation or specification of the first. As if he had said, *wasting and ruin* (such as are produced by) *famine and the sword.* The last words of the verse, strictly translated, mean, *who I will comfort thee.* The Targum limits the interrogation to the first word, and supposes the others to contain the answer. The same construction is given by Henderson, *Who? I myself will comfort thee.* A much greater number of interpreters include the whole in the interrogation, and either give the verb a subjunctive form, *who am I that I should comfort thee?* or take מִי as an adverb, *how shall I comfort thee?* Hitzig, *by whom* (*i. e.* by what example of similar or greater suffering) *shall I comfort thee?* Still a different construction, although yielding substantially the same sense, is adopted above, in the translation of the verse. The general meaning evidently is, that her grief was beyond the reach of any human comforter.

20. *Thy sons were faint* (or *helpless*). This explains why they did not come to her assistance.—*They lie at the head of all the streets.* A conspicuous place is evidently meant, but whether the corners or the higher part of an uneven street, is a question of small moment.—*Like a wild bull in a net*, *i. e.* utterly unable to exert their strength. The Hebrew word תּוֹא is no doubt identical with the תְּאוֹ of Deut. xiv. 5, and therefore must denote an animal. The ancient versions favour its identity with the *oryx*, a species of antelope or wild goat. Gesenius gives this explanation in his Lexicon, but here translates it *stag* (Hirsch). The common version (*wild bull*) is derived from the Targum, and is sufficient to convey the writer's meaning by suggesting the idea of a wild animal rendered entirely powerless. The extraordinary version given in the Septuagint, σεῦτλιον ἡμίεφθον, *a half-cooked beet*, owes its origin, no doubt, to some coincidence of form or sound between the obscure Hebrew word and an Egyptian one, with which the translator was familiar. The cognate form in Deuteronomy is rendered, in the same version, but no doubt by a different hand, ὄρυγα. The precise sense of the Hebrew phrase appears to be, *like an oryx of net*, or *a net oryx, i. e.* an ensnared one ; but the sense may be best expressed in English by supplying the local preposition (*in a net*). Knobel supposes a particular allusion to the faintness produced by hunger, and refers to several passages in Jeremiah, especially to Lam. ii. 19, which is no doubt imitated from the one before us.—The true cause of their lying thus is given in the last clause. *Filled* (*i. e.* drunk, as Ewald explains it) *with the wrath of Jehovah, the rebuke of thy God.* In Hebrew usage גְּעָרָה approaches to the strong sense *curse*, and is so translated by Gesenius. The expression *thy God* is emphatic, and suggests that her sufferings proceeded from the alienation of her own divine protector. This verse is incorrectly applied by Vitringa to the siege of the ancient Jerusalem, whereas it is a figurative representation of the helplessness of Zion or the Church, when partially forsaken for a time by her offended Head.

21. *Therefore pray hear this, thou suffering one, and drunken, but not*

with wine. The antithesis in the last clause is to be completed from the context. Not with wine, but with the wrath of God, which had already been described as *a cup of reeling* or intoxication. The same negative expression is employed in chap. xxix. 9. The Targum supplies *from distress.* Kimchi inserts *the wrath of God.* Jarchi supposes an ellipsis of something else (דבר אחר), and thus accounts for the construct form of the participle. But the Michlal Jophi explains it more correctly as an instance of the idiomatic use of the construct for the absolute, in cases where a very intimate relation is to be expressed. Vitringa carries out his favourite method of interpretation, by explaining this verse as addressed specifically to the ancient church, when recovering from the persecutions of Antiochus Epiphanes : a limitation which might just as well be made in reference to any of the general encouragements of true believers which the word of God contains.

22. *Thus saith thy Lord, Jehovah, and thy God—he will defend* (or *avenge*) *his people—Behold, I have taken from thy hand the cup of reeling* (or *intoxication*) *the bowl of the cup of my fury ; thou shalt not add* (*continue* or *repeat*) *to drink it any more* (or *again*). Even Knobel is compelled to admit that the writer has reference less to the place than to the people of Jerusalem, and even to this only as the representative of the entire nation ; a concession which goes far to confirm the explanation of the " Zion " of these prophecies which has been already given.—It is usual to explain יָרִיב עַמּוֹ as a relative clause (*who pleads the cause of his people*); but it is simpler, and at the same time more in accordance with the genius of the language, to regard it as a brief but complete parenthetical proposition. The same character is often ascribed elsewhere to Jehovah. See chaps. i. 17, xxxiv. 8, xli. 11, xlix. 25.)—As the cup was the cup of God's wrath, not of man's, so God himself is represented as withdrawing it from the sufferer's lips, when its purpose is accomplished.

23. *And put it into the hand of those that afflicted thee, that said to thy soul, Bow down and we will* (or *that we may*) *pass over ; and thou didst lay thy back as the ground, and as the street for the passengers.* Ewald and Umbreit agree with Secker and Lowth in reading מוֹנַיִךְ *thy oppressors,* as in chap. xlix. 26, on the alleged authority of the ancient versions, which would be wholly insufficient if the fact were so, and Kocher has clearly shewn that it is not. The common reading is confirmed, moreover, by the use of הוֹנָה in Lam. i. 12.—*To thy soul* is explained by Gesenius and others as a mere periphrasis for *to thee.* Vitringa supposes the expression to be used because the body could not be bowed down in the manner here described without a previous bowing of the mind. But the true explanation is no doubt that given by Hengstenberg in his exposition of Ps. iii. 3 ; viz., that this form of speech always implies a strong and commonly a painful affection of the mind in the object of address. *Who said to thy soul* is then equivalent to saying, *who distressed thy soul by saying.* The last clause is commonly explained as a proverbial, or at least a metaphorical description of extreme humiliation, although history affords instances of literal humiliation in this form. Such is the treatment of Valerian by Sapor, as described by Lactantius and Aurelius Victor ; with which may be compared the conduct of Sesostris to his royal captives, as described by Diodorus, and that of Pope Alexander III. to the Emperor Frederic, as recorded by the Italian historians. For Scriptural parallels, see Joshua x. 24, and Judges i. 7.—If we had any right or reason to restrict this prediction to a single period or event, the most

obvious would be the humiliation of the Chaldees, who are threatened with
the cup of God's wrath in Jer. xxv. 26.   Yet Vitringa sets this application
aside upon the ground that Israel drank of the same cup afterwards, and
understands the verse of the deliverance of the Jews from their Macedonian
oppressors by the valour of the Maccabees.   To the obvious objection that
even this was not a final deliverance, he ingeniously replies that all the
promises to Israel extend only to the end of the old dispensation ; an
assumption which confounds the Jewish nation with the Israel of God, the
church or chosen people, which continued to exist under every change of
dispensation and economy, and, notwithstanding all its fluctuations and
vicissitudes, shall ultimately be for ever rescued by the same hand which
destroys its enemies.   This is the simple substance of the promise in the
verse before us, which includes without specifically signifying all that has
been thus represented as its meaning.

Chapter 52

HOWEVER low the natural Israel may sink, the true church shall become
more glorious than ever, being freed from the impurities connected with
her former state, ver. 1.   This is described as a captivity, from which she
is exhorted to escape, ver. 2.   Her emancipation is the fruit of God's
gratuitous compassion, ver. 3.   As a nation she has suffered long enough,
vers. 4, 5.   The day is coming when the Israel of God shall know in whom
they have believed, ver. 6.   The herald of the new dispensation is described
as already visible upon the mountains, ver. 7.   The watchmen of Zion
hail their coming Lord, ver. 8.   The very ruins of Jerusalem are summoned to rejoice, ver. 9.   The glorious change is witnessed by the whole
world, ver. 10.   The true church, or Israel of God, is exhorted to come
out of Jewry, ver. 11.   This exodus is likened to the one from Egypt, but
described as even more auspicious, ver. 12.   Its great leader the Messiah,
as the Servant of Jehovah, must be and is to be exalted, ver. 13.   And
this exaltation shall bear due proportion to the humiliation which preceded
it, vers. 14, 15.

1. *Awake, awake, put on thy strength, O Zion !   Put on thy garments
of beauty, O Jerusalem, the Holy City !   For no more shall there add* (or
continue) *to come into thee an uncircumcised and unclean* (*person*).   The
encouraging assurances of the foregoing context are now followed by a summons similar to that in chap. li. 17, but in form approaching nearer to the
apostrophe in chap. li.'9.—Vitringa objects to the version *awake*, on the
ground that it was not a state of sleep from which she was to rouse herself.
This is true so far as literal slumber is concerned ; but sleep is one of the
most natural and common figures for a despondent lethargy.   The essential
idea is, no doubt, that of rousing or arising, which Gesenius and the later
Germans express by an interjection meaning *up* (*auf! auf!*).   The same
writers give to עֹז, in this as in many other cases, the factitious sense of
beauty, glory, simply on account of the parallelism.   This is a gratuitous
weakening of the sense ; for *beauty and beauty* is certainly much less than
beauty and strength.   To put on strength is a perfectly intelligible figure
for resuming strength or taking courage, and is therefore entirely appropriate in this connection ; while the other meaning is not only less agreeable
to usage, but excluded by the clear analogy of chap. li. 9, where the sense
of *strength* is universally admitted.   It might be objected that the sense is

there determined by the use of the word *arm*, if the meaning *strength* were
a rare and doubtful one; but since it is confessedly the usual and proper
one, the case referred to merely confirms the strict interpretation, which is
here retained by Ewald (*Macht*).—That the city is here addressed only as
a symbol of the nation, is certain from the next verse; so that Hitzig is
compelled to assume two different objects of address, in utter violation of
analogy and taste.—*Beautiful garments* is by most interpreters regarded as
a general expression meaning fine clothes or holiday dresses; but some
suppose a special allusion to a widow's weeds (2 Sam. xiv. 2), or to prison-
garments (2 Kings xxv. 29). It is a bold but not unnatural idea of Knobel,
that the Prophet here resumes the metaphor of chap. xlix. 18, where Zion's
children are compared to bridal ornaments.—*The Holy City*, literally *city
of holiness*, an epithet before applied to Zion (chap. xlviii. 2), and denoting
her peculiar consecration and that of her people, to the service of Jehovah.
(Compare Dan. viii. 24.) Henceforth the name is to be more appropriate
than ever, for the reason given in the last clause. The meaning of יוֹסִיף,
when followed by the future, is precisely equivalent to the more usual construction with the infinitive, of which we have an instance in chap. li. 22.—
Uncircumcised is an expression borrowed from the ritual law, and signifying
unclean. That it is not here used in its strict sense, is intimated by the
addition of the general term טָמֵא. The restriction of these epithets to the
Babylonians is purely arbitrary, and intended to meet the objection that
Jerusalem was not free from heathen intrusion after the exile. The same
motive leads Vitringa to explain the promise as addressed to the Jewish
Church, after its deliverance from the insults and oppressions of Antiochus
Epiphanes. The Jews refer it to a future period, and the Germans easily
dispose of it as a visionary expectation which was never realised. Thus
Beck explains it as a prophecy that all mankind should be converted to
Judaism, which is a virtual concession of the truth of the interpretation
above given. The question is not materially varied by substituting *come
against* for *come into*. The true solution is the one above suggested,
namely, that the words contain a general promise of exemption from the
contaminating presence of the impure and unworthy, as a part of the
blessedness and glory promised to God's people, as the end and solace of
their various trials.

2. *Shake thyself from the dust, arise, sit, O Jerusalem! loose the bands of
thy neck, O captive daughter Zion* (or *of Zion*)! The dust from which she
is to free herself by shaking it off, is either that in which she had been sitting as a mourner (chap. iii. 26, xlvii. 1; Job ii. 13), or that which, in
token of her grief, she had sprinkled on her head (Job ii. 12).—Koppe and
Hitzig make שְׁבִי a noun, meaning *captivity* or *captives* collectively, like the
corresponding feminine שְׁבִיָּה in the other clause. Rosenmüller's objection,
that שְׁבִי would in that case have a conjunctive accent, is declared by
Hitzig to be groundless, and is certainly inconclusive. A more serious
objection is the one made by Gesenius, that שְׁבִי is always masculine, and
would not therefore agree with the feminine verb קוּמִי. Hitzig's reply, that
שְׁבִי, as a collective, may be here used as a feminine, is not only wholly
gratuitous but utterly precluded by the existence of a distinct feminine
form and its occurrence in this very sentence. Because feminines have
sometimes a collective sense, it does not follow that a masculine, when used
collectively, becomes a feminine, least of all when a feminine form exists
already. Among the writers who explain it as a verb, there is a difference

of judgment with respect to the meaning of the exhortation, *sit !* The common English version, *sit down*, till explained, suggests an idea directly opposite to that intended.   Gesenius, on the contrary, makes it mean *sit up*, in opposition to a previous recumbent posture.   To this it may be objected, that the verb is elsewhere absolutely used in the sense of *sitting down*, especially in reference to sitting on the ground as a sign of grief ; and also, that the other verb does not merely qualify this, but expresses a distinct idea, not merely that of rising, but that of standing up, which is inconsistent with an exhortation to sit up, immediately ensuing. Ewald, Umbreit, and Knobel, therefore agree with Vitringa and Lowth in adopting the interpretation of the Targum, *sit upon thy throne*, from which she is supposed to have been previously cast down.—The textual reading הִתְפַּתְּחִי may be either a preterite or an imperative.   In the former case, the Hithpael must have a passive sense, *the bands of thy neck are loosed*, or *have loosed themselves*.   In the other case, the words may be considered as addressed to the bands themselves (*be loosed*), which is hardly compatible, however, with the use of the second person in *thy neck ;* or the object of address may be the captives, which is equally at variance with the following singular, *captive daughter of Zion*.   The marginal reading הִתְפַּתְּחִי preserves both the parallelism and the syntax, and is therefore regarded as the true text by Ewald and Knobel with the older writers.   The latter, followed by Rosenmüller, suppose an ellipsis of the preposition *from*.   Thus the English Version : *loose thyself from the bands of thy neck*.   Gesenius and Ewald make *bands* the object of the verb, which they explain, not as a strict reflexive, but a modification of it, corresponding to the middle voice in Greek. *Loose for thyself the bands of thy neck*.—On the different constructions of the phrase בַּת־צִיּוֹן see under chap. i. 8.—As a whole, the verse is a poetical description of the liberation of a female captive from degrading servitude, designed to represent the complete emancipation of the church from tyranny and persecution.

3. *For thus saith Jehovah, Ye were sold for nought, and not for money shall ye be redeemed.*   These words are apparently designed to remove two difficulties in the way of Israel's deliverance, a physical and a moral one. The essential meaning is, that it might be effected rightly and easily. As Jehovah had received no price for them, he was under no obligations to renounce his right to them ; and as nothing had been gained by their rejection, so nothing would be lost by their recovery. The only obscurity arises from the singular nature of the figure under which the truth is here presented, by the transfer of expressions borrowed from the commercial intercourse of men to the free action of the divine sovereignty. The verse, as explained above, agrees exactly with the terms of Ps. xliv. 13, notwithstanding Hengstenberg's denial (Commentary, *in loc.*). The reference to the blood of Christ as infinitely more precious than silver and gold, would here be wholly out of place, where the thing asserted is that they shall be redeemed as they were sold, viz., without any price at all, not merely without silver and gold. This misconception has arisen from the use of analogous expressions in the New Testament in application to a far more important subject, the redemption of mankind from everlasting ruin. The reflexive meaning given to נִמְכַּרְתֶּם in the English Version (*ye have sold yourselves*), is not sustained by usage, nor required by the context, either here or in Lev. xxv. 39, 47, where Gesenius admits it.   (See above, on chap. l. 1.)

4. *For thus saith the Lord Jehovah, Into Egypt went down my people at*

the first to sojourn there, and Assyria oppressed them for nothing. The
interpretation of this verse and the next has been not a little influenced by
the assumption of one or more strongly marked antitheses. Thus some
writers take it for granted that the Prophet here intended to contrast the
Egyptian and Assyrian bondage. They accordingly explain the verse as
meaning that the first introduction of Israel into Egypt was without any
evil design upon the part of the Egyptians, who did not begin to oppress
them until there arose a king who knew not Joseph (Exod. i. 8), whereas
the Assyrian deportation of Israel was from the beginning a high-handed
act of tyranny. Another antitheses, maintained by some in connection
with the one already mentioned, and by others in the place of it, is that
between בָּרִאשֹׁנָה *at the first,* and בְּאֶפֶס *at the last.* A third hypothesis supposes Egypt and Assyria together to be here contrasted with the Babylonian
tyranny described in the next verse. But even here there is a question,
whether the comparison has reference merely to time, and the Prophet
means to say that what Jehovah had done he would do again; or whether
there is also a designed antitheses between the former oppressions as less
aggravated, and the present one as more so. Knobel appears to exclude
the supposition of a contrast altogether, and to understand the passage as
a chronological enumeration of events, designed to shew how much had
been endured already as a reason why they should endure no more. (Compare chap. xl. 2.) In ancient times they were oppressed by the Egyptians,
at a later period by Assyria, and later still by Babylonia, whose oppressions
are supposed to be described in ver. 5, either as already suffered, or as an
object of prophetic foresight. This is the simplest and most natural interpretation, and is very strongly recommended by the difficulty of defining the
antithesis intended on the other supposition. Of the phrase בְּאֶפֶס there
are three interpretations. Saadias, Lowth, and Henderson explain it as a
particle of time, the opposite of בָּרִאשֹׁנָה. The objection to this is the want
of any other case in which the noun is thus applied to time, together with
its frequent use to describe nonentity or nothing. It is no doubt true, as
Hävernick alleges, that the word may as well denote extremity of time as
of place; but even the latter application is confined to the plural in the
frequent formula אפסי ארץ. The argument derived from the parallelism is
of no avail; because, as we have seen, one of the points at issue is the
question whether בראשנה stands opposed to באפס or to עתה in the next
verse. Most writers, therefore, understand it as meaning *for nothing* or
without cause, *i. e.* unjustly, or as Kimchi expresses it, בלא מספע. Knobel,
however, makes it strictly synonymous with חִנָּם in ver. 3, and understands
the clause to mean that the Assyrians had enslaved Israel gratuitously, *i. e.*
without paying any price for him, and therefore had no right to him, when
God chose to reclaim him; which is precisely the idea expressed in the
foregoing verse.—The explanation of Assyria as meaning or including
Babylonia, though not without authority from usage, is as unnecessary here
as in various other places where it has been proposed. (See vol. i. p.
176.)—The unsatisfactory nature of exegetical conclusions drawn from
doubtful premises is strongly illustrated by the fact, that while Gesenius
argues from this verse that the writer must have lived long after the
Assyrian bondage, since he couples it with that of Egypt as a thing of
ancient date, Hävernick (Einleitung, ii. 2, p. 187) insists that it must have
been written in the days of Isaiah, because it contrasts the Egyptian and
Assyrian bondage as the first and the last which Israel as a nation had experienced. The chief use of such reasonings is to cancel one another.

Though we may not venture to rest the genuineness of these prophecies on such a basis, we may cheerfully accept the assurance thus afforded that the arguments against it are of no validity.

5. *And now what is there to me here* (*what have I here*), *saith Jehovah, that my people is taken away for nothing, its rulers howl, saith Jehovah, and continually, all the day, my name is blasphemed?* Some understand *now* strictly as meaning *at the present time*, in opposition to the ancient times when Israel suffered at the hands of Egypt and Assyria. The same antithesis may be obtained by giving *now* a modified sense so as to mean *in the present case*, as distinguished from the two already mentioned. It would even be admissible to give the *now* its logical sense as substantially meaning *since these things are so*, although such a departure from the proper import of the word is by no means necessary.—The other adverb, *here*, admits of no less various explanations. Hitzig and some older writers understand it to mean *heaven* as the customary residence of God. (1 Kings viii. 30.) Some suppose it to mean Babylon, while others, with a bolder departure from the strict sense, understand it as equivalent to *in the present case*, viz., that of the Babylonian exile; which, however, even if correct in substance, is rather a paraphrase than a translation.—With the meaning put upon this adverb varies the interpretation of the whole phrase, *what have I here?* If *here* mean *in Babylon*, the sense would seem to be, what else have I to do here but to free my people? If it mean *in heaven*, then the question is, what is there to detain me here from going to the rescue of my people? If it mean *in the present case*, whether this be referred to the Babylonish exile or more generally understood, the best explanation of the question is the one proposed by Knobel, What have I gained in this case, any more than in the others, since my people are still taken from me without any compensation? But Beck supposes it to mean, how much more cause have I to interfere in this case than in any of the others. The conclusion implied, though not expressed, is that in this, as in the other instances referred to, a regard to his own honour, metaphorically represented as his interest, requires that he should interpose for the deliverance of his people.—The next clause likewise has been very variously explained. The most extraordinary exposition is the one preferred by Aben Ezra, which gives מֹשְׁלִים the same sense as in Num. xxi. 27, and explains the whole clause thus: *their poets howl, i. e.* their songs, instead of being joyous have become mere lamentations. This ingenious notion is revived by Luzzatto, who refers in illustration to the prophecy of Amos (viii. 3), that the songs of the temple shall in that day howl, or, as the English Version phrases it, be howlings. Among the vast majority of writers who retain the common meaning of the word as a derivative from מָשַׁל, to rule, the question chiefly in dispute is whether it denotes the native rulers of the Jews themselves, as in chap. xxviii. 14, or their foreign oppressors, as in chap. xlix. 7. Vitringa and Hitzig, who prefer the former supposition, understand the clause as meaning that the chiefs, who represent the people, howl or wail in their distress. (Compare Exod. v. 15, 21.) Knobel objects to this interpretation, that the context requires a description not of their distress but of its cause, and also that the Jews had no chiefs but the Babylonians while in exile; which is at once historically false, because the internal organization of the people seems to have continued almost without change through all their revolutions and vicissitudes, and wholly irrelevant if true, because the limitation of the passage to the exile is gratuitous and therefore inadmissible. Most interpreters,

however, seem disposed to understand מִשְׁלוֹ as meaning his foreign oppressors, notwithstanding the difficulty then attending the interpretation of the
verb יְהֵילִילוּ. More contempt than it really deserves has been expressed by
later writers for Jerome's straightforward explanation, *they shall howl* when
punished for their tyranny hereafter. This is, to say the least, far better
than to derive it from חָלַל, or to read יְהוֹלְלוּ with the Targum and Jarchi,
Houbigant and Lowth, Michaelis and Döderlein, Dathe and Eichhorn.
The causative sense, expressed by Kimchi and the English Version (*make
them to howl*), is wholly unsustained by Hebrew usage. The favourite
interpretation with the latest writers is essentially the same proposed by
Kocher, who explains the Hebrew verb as expressive of the violent and
angry domination of the rulers; upon which the moderns have improved by
making it expressive of a joyful shout, as ὀλολύζω is employed by Æschylus,
and as Lucan, speaking of the shout of victory, uses the words, *laetis ululare
triumphis*. This explanation is adopted by Gesenius in his Lexicon, although
explicitly rejected in his Commentary, as not sufficiently sustained by usage,
—The only difficulty in the last clause has relation to the form of the word
מִנֹּאָץ, which Jarchi explains as a Hithpael passive, and Kimchi as a mixture of the Hithpael and Pual.—The form of expression in this last clause
is copied by Ezekiel (xxxvi. 20, 23), but applied to a different subject;
and from that place, rather than the one before us, the Apostle quotes in
Romans ii. 24.

6. *Therefore* (because my name is thus blasphemed) *my people shall
know my name; therefore in that day* (shall they know) *that I am he that
said, Behold me!* The exact sense of the last words according to this
construction is, "I am he that spake (or promised) a Behold me!" This is
the sense given by Hitzig, Ewald, and Knobel, who understand the clause
as meaning that in that day (when the promise is fulfilled) it shall be known
that he who promised to be with them, and deliver them, was God himself.
Gesenius gives a somewhat different construction, "they shall know that I
who spoke to them am present," or in other words "that I who promised to
be present have fulfilled my promise." But this paraphrastical interpretation
of הִנֵּנִי is by no means so natural as that which understands it as the very
language of the promise itself. To know the name of God, is to know his
nature so far as it has been revealed; and in this case more specifically it is
to know that the name blasphemed among the wicked was deserving of the
highest honour. The second *therefore* is admitted by all the modern writers
to be pregnant and emphatic; although Lowth esteemed it so unmeaning
and superfluous, that he expunged it from the text on the authority of several
ancient versions, which were much more likely to omit it inadvertently than
all the manuscripts to introduce it without reason or authority. It is also
commonly agreed that כִּי means *that*, and that the verb *shall know* must be
repeated with a different object. It might, however, be considered simpler
and more natural to repeat the object with the verb, and let the last clause
give a reason for the first: "therefore in that day shall they know it (*i. e.*
know my name), because I am he that said, Behold me (or, Lo here I am)!"
The English Version differs from all the constructions which have now been
stated, in explaining הִנֵּנִי as a mere reiteration of what goes before: "they
shall know in that day that I am he that doth speak; behold it is I." But
according to usage, הִנֵּנִי, especially when standing at the end of a clause or
sentence, does not merely reiterate the subject of a foregoing verb, but constitutes a new proposition; it does not mean *lo I*, or *lo I am*, but *lo I am*

here, and is therefore the common idiomatic Hebrew answer to a call by name.

7. *How timely on the mountains are the feet of one bringing glad tidings, publishing peace, bringing glad tidings of good, publishing salvation, saying to Zion, Thy God reigneth.* The verb נָאווּ means to be suitable, becoming, opportune, and though not applied to time in either of the two cases where it occurs elsewhere, evidently admits of such an application, especially when there is no general usage to forbid it. It is here recommended by the context; which is much more coherent if we understand this verse as intimating that the help appears at the very juncture when it is most needed, than if we take it as a mere expression of delight. It is also favoured by the analogy of Nah. ii. 1, where a similar connection is expressed by the word הִנֵּה. It is favoured lastly by the use of the Greek word ὡραῖοι in Paul's translation of the verse (Rom. x. 15), of which ὥρα in our copies of the Septuagint is probably a corruption. This Greek word, both from etymology and usage, most explicitly means *timely* or *seasonable,* although sometimes employed in the secondary sense of *beautiful* (Matt. xxiii. 27; Acts iii. 2), like the Hebrew נָאווּ (Cant. i. 10), *decorus* in Latin, and *becoming* in English. The mountains meant may be the mountains round Jerusalem, or the word may be more indefinitely understood as adding a trait to the prophetic picture.—Hitzig gratuitously changes the form of the expression, by substituting foot and messengers for feet and messenger. The word מְבַשֵּׂר has no equivalent in English, and must therefore be expressed by a periphrasis, in order to include the two ideas of annunciation, and the joyful character of that which is announced. The sense is perfectly expressed by the Greek εὐαγγελιζόμενος: but our derivatives, *evangelising* and *evangelist,* are technical, not popular expressions, and would not convey the meaning to an ordinary reader. · The joyous nature of the tidings brought is still more definitely intimated in the next clause by the addition of the word *good,* which is not explanatory but intensive. The peculiar form of the original is marred in some translations, by rendering the first מְבַשֵּׂר as a noun and the second as a verb; whereas in Hebrew there are two participles, both repeated. The explanation of מְבַשֵּׂר as a collective referring to the prophets, or the messengers from Babylonia to Jerusalem, is perfectly gratuitous. The primary application of the term is to the Messiah, but in itself it is indefinite; and Paul is therefore chargeable with no misapplication of the words when he applies them to the preachers of the gospel. The contents of the message are the manifestation of the reign of God, the very news which Christ and his forerunner published when they cried saying, The kingdom of God is at hand.

8. *The voice of thy watchmen! They raise the voice, together will they shout; for eye to eye shall they see in Jehovah's returning to Zion.* Lowth complains that none of the ancient versions or modern interpreters have cleared up the construction of the first clause to his satisfaction, or supplied the ellipsis in any way that seems to him easy and natural. He therefore proposes to read כל for קול (*all thy watchmen lift up their voice*), which he says perfectly rectifies the sense and the construction. It is hard to reconcile with Lowth's reputation for refined taste the preference of this prosaic reading (the only external evidence for which is that ל stands on an erasure in one manuscript) to the obvious assumption of a poetical apostrophe or exclamation, which has commended itself to all later writers, and had been before proposed by Vitringa. There is no need even of supplying *is heard* with Knobel, *sounds* with Gesenius in his Commentary, or *hark*

with the same writer in his German version. The exact translation is not only admissible, but more expressive than any other. Gesenius and De Wette, by connecting יַחְדָּו with the word before it (*erheben die Stimme allzumal*), not only violate the accents, but are under the necessity of supplying *and* before the next verb.—This is one of the cases where it seems most allowable to look upon the preterite and future as equivalent to our present ; but according to the general rule hitherto adopted, it is best to retain the original difference of form, whenever, as in this case, we can do so without injuring the sense. Thus understood, the clause would seem to intimate that they should have still further cause to shout hereafter ; they have already raised the voice, and ere long they shall all shout together. Because the prophets are elsewhere represented as *watchmen* on the walls of Zion (chap. lvi. 10 ; Jer. vi. 17 ; Ezek. iii. 17, xxxiii. 2, 7), most interpreters attach that meaning to the figure here ; but the restriction is unnecessary, since the application of a metaphor to one object does not preclude its application to another, and objectionable, as it mars the unity and beauty of the scene presented, which is simply that of a messenger of good news drawing near to a walled town, whose watchmen take up and repeat his tidings to the people within.—Ewald strangely takes the last clause as the words to be uttered by the watchmen, and explains them to mean, " How will they see eye to eye ! " &c. This is far less natural than the usual construction, which regards the last clause as the Prophet's explanation of the joy described in the first.—The phrase *eye to eye*, or, as Hitzig and De Wette have it, *eye in eye*, occurs only here and in Num. xiv. 14. The sense put upon it in the Targum and adopted by Gesenius (*with their eyes*), though not erroneous, is inadequate. According to Vitringa, it denotes *with both eyes*, *i. e.* not imperfectly or dimly, but distinctly ; and the same idea is expressed by Symmachus (ὀφθαλμοφανῶς). The same essential meaning is attached to the expression by Ewald, but with a distinct intimation of local proximity, the phrase being properly descriptive of two persons so near as to look into each other's eyes. The phrases *face to face* (Exod. xxxiii. 11) and *mouth to mouth* (Num. xii. 8) are kindred and analogous, but not identical with that before us.—The verb יִרְאוּ may be construed either with צֹפַיִךְ or with an indefinite subject, *they* (*i. e.* the people of Jerusalem or men in general) *shall see.*—Rosenmüller explains בְּ before שׁוּב as the connective which the verb רָאָה takes after it when it means to see with pleasure, or to gaze at with delight. The same construction seems to be implied in Ewald's paraphrase of יִרְאוּ (*sich weiden*); but it seems much simpler to construe the verb absolutely or without an object expressed (they shall see, *i. e.* look), and to make the בְּ a particle of time, as it usually is when prefixed to the infinitive.—The transitive meaning ascribed to שׁוּב in this and many other places has been clearly shewn by Hengstenberg (Pentateuch, i. pp. 104–106) to have no foundation either in etymology or usage, and to be probably inadmissible even in the frequent combination שׁוּב שְׁבוּת, much more in cases like the present, where the proper sense is not only appropriate but required by the context, and the analogy of other places, in which the reconciliation between God and his people is represented as a return after a long absence. (See above, on chap. xl. 11.)—The direct construction of the verb of motion with the noun of place is a Hebrew idiom of constant occurrence ; so that it is not necessary even to suppose an ellipsis of the preposition.

9. *Burst forth, shout together, ruins of Jerusalem ! For Jehovah hath comforted his people, hath redeemed Jerusalem.* The phrase פָּצַח רִנָּה, to

burst forth into shouting, is a favourite expression with Isaiah (see above, chap. xiv. 7, xliv. 23, xlix. 13, and below, chap. liv. 1, lv. 12) ; but in this case the qualifying noun is changed for its verbal root ; a combination which occurs elsewhere only in Ps. xcviii. 4. As פָּצַח is never used in any other connection, and therefore denotes only this one kind of bursting, it may be considered as involving the idea of the whole phrase, and is so translated in the English Version (*break forth into joy*), while Gesenius gives the same sense to the two words, and translates the phrase exactly like the usual one, פִּצְחוּ רַנְּנוּ.—*Together* may either mean *all of you*, or *at the same time* with the watchmen, mentioned in ver. 8. Hitzig even goes so far as to say that the ruins are here called upon to imitate the watchmen. Knobel adds that the ruins had particular occasion to rejoice, because they were to be transformed into a splendid city (chap. xliv. 26). Such appeals to inanimate objects are of frequent occurrence in Isaiah (see above, chaps. xliv. 23, xlix. 13, and below, chap. lv. 12).—The translation of the verbs in the last clause as presents is unnecessary and enfeebling, as it takes away the strong assurance always conveyed by the *præteritum propheticum.* See above, on chap. xlix. 13.

10. *Jehovah hath bared his holy arm to the eyes of all the nations, and all the ends of the earth have seen the salvation of our God.* The allusion in the first clause is to the ancient military practice of going into battle with the right arm and shoulder bare. Thus Porus is described by Arrian as δέξιον ὦμον ἔχων γυμνὸν ἐν τῇ μάχῃ ; Diana by Silius Italicus, *exscitos avide pugnæ nudata lacertos;* Tydeus by Statius, *exscitare humeros nudamque lacessere pugnam.* The same Hebrew verb is used in the same application by Ezekiel (iv. 7). The baring of the arm may either be mentioned as a preparation for the conflict, or the act of stretching it forth may be included, as Rosenmüller and Gesenius suppose. The bare arm is here in contrast either with the long sleeves of the female dress, or with the indolent insertion of the hand in the bosom (Ps. lxxiv. 11). The exertion of God's power is elsewhere expressed by the kindred figure of a great hand (Exod. xiv. 30), a strong hand (Ezek. xx. 34), or a hand stretched out (Isa. ix. 11). The act here described is the same that is described in chap. li. 9. The comparison of Jehovah to a warrior occurs above, in chap. xlii. 13. Jehovah's arm is here described as *holy*, because, as Knobel thinks, his holiness or justice is exercised in punishing the wicked ; but the word is rather to be taken in its wide sense, as denoting the divine perfection, or whatever distinguishes between God and man, perhaps with special reference to his power, as that by which his deity is most frequently and clearly manifested to his creatures. The sense of sanctifying, *i. e.* glorifying arm, which Rosenmüller suggests as possible, is much less natural and scarcely reconcilable with the expression. In this clause Ewald has retained the strict translation of the preterite instead of the enfeebling present form preferred by most of the late writers. In the last clause he adopts the subjunctive form, *so that all nations see*, which is substantially correct, as וְרָאוּ introduces the effect or consequence of the action described in the foregoing clause. Compare this clause with chaps. xviii. 3, xxxiii. 13, and Ps. xcviii. 3, where it is repeated word for word. Another coincidence between this passage of Isaiah and that Psalm, has been already pointed out in expounding the foregoing verse.

11. *Away! away! go out from thence! the unclean touch not! come out from the midst of her! be clean* (or *cleanse yourselves*) *ye armour-bearers of Jehovah!* The first word in Hebrew is a verb, and literally means *depart;*

but there is something peculiarly expressive in Gesenius's translation of it by an adverb. The analogy of chap. xlviii. 20 seems to shew that the Prophet had the departure from Babylon in view; but the omission of the name here, and of any allusion to that subject in the context, forbids the restriction of the words any further than the author has himself restricted them. The idea that this high-wrought and impassioned composition has reference merely to the literal migration of the captive Jews, says but little for the taste of those who entertain it. The whole analogy of language and especially of poetical composition shews that Babylon is no more the exclusive object of the writer's contemplation than the local Zion and the literal Jerusalem in many of the places where those names are mentioned. Like other great historical events, particularly such as may be looked upon as critical conjunctures, the deliverance becomes a type, not only to the prophet but to the poet and historian, not by any arbitrary process, but by a spontaneous association of ideas. As some names, even in our own day, have acquired a generic meaning, and become descriptive of a whole class of events, so in the earliest authentic history, the Flood, the Fall of Sodom and Gomorrah, the Exodus, the Babylonish Exile, are continually used as symbols of divine interposition both in wrath and mercy. There is no inconsistency whatever, therefore, in admitting that the Prophet has the exodus from Babylon in view, and yet maintaining that his language has a far more extensive scope. The error of those Christian writers who adopt this confined hypothesis is not so obvious in their own interpretations as it is in those which have been raised upon the same base by the German neologists, who, not content with this limitation of the meaning, sneer at the contracted Jewish spirit which the writer here betrays, by insisting on the old Levitical distinctions and denouncing all communion with the Gentiles as pollution. In order to maintain this unworthy view of the writer's meaning, they explain the exhortation in the last clause as requiring ceremonial ablutions, and adopt Jarchi's groundless and absurd interpretation of טָמֵא as referring exclusively to persons, with allusion to the טֻמְאַת גּוֹיֵי־הָאָרֶץ of Ezra, vi. 21. This restriction of the terms is so unreasonable and unfair, that Ewald and Knobel, though belonging to the same school, both explain טָמֵא as a neuter (*Unreines*), that which is unclean. It would indeed be impossible to frame a more general dehortation or dissuasion from religious and moral impurity, and thousands of intelligent readers have so understood the words, without detecting in them those " ängstliche pedantische Grundsätze," since brought to light by a mode of criticism which, even in a mere aesthetic point of view, deserves to be characterised as eminently *ängstlich* and *pedantisch*. The same spirit shews itself in the exposition of the closing words of this verse by the same class of writers. Not content with identifying the כְּלֵי יְהוָֹה with the כְּלֵי קֹדֶשׁ of Num. iv. 15, 1 Chron. ix. 29, an assumption not entirely devoid of probability, they make this an address to the Priests and Levites, the official bearers of these vessels, and explain it as implying a hope that the sacred utensils taken by Nebuchadnezzar from the temple (2 Kings xxv. 14, 15; Dan. v. 1), would be restored by Cyrus, as they afterwards were. (Ezra i. 7–11.) And this anticipated restitution is the great theme of the grand yet brilliant passage now before us, in the eyes of those very critics who have gone to an extreme in holding up Isaiah's baldest prose as unmixed poetry! They reject of course the sense which Rosenmüller, following some older writers, puts upon the closing words as meaning the armour-bearers of Jehovah. This would not be Jewish and Levitical enough to serve their purpose of really degrading what they affect to magnify "with faint praise." Yet this sense is not only in the highest degree suitable to the idea of a solemn march, but strongly recommended by the fact that נֹשֵׂא כֵלִים in historical prose is the appropriated title of an armour-bearer. (See 1 Sam. xiv. 1, 6, 7 ; xvi. 21.) At the same time the mention of the sacred vessels would scarcely be omitted in the description of this new exodus. Both explanations may be blended without any violation of usage, and with great advantage to the beauty of the passage, by supposing an allusion to the mixture of the martial and the sacerdotal in the whole organisation of the host of Israel during the journey through the wilderness. Not even in the Crusades were the priest and the soldier brought so near together, and so mingled, not to say identified, as in the long march of the chosen people from the Red Sea to the Jordan. By applying this key to the case before us, we obtain the grand though blended image of a march and a procession, an army and a church, a "sacramental host" bearing the sacred vessels, not as Priests and Levites merely, but as the *armour-bearers of Jehovah*, the weapons of whose warfare, though not carnal, are mighty to the pulling down of strong holds (2 Cor. x. 4). With this comprehensive exposition of the clause, agrees the clear and settled usage of the word כֵּלִים in the wide sense of *implements*, including weapons on the one hand, and vessels on the other. (See vol. i. p. 272.)—The application of the terms of this verse by John to the spiritual Babylon (Rev. xviii. 4), so far from standing in the way of the enlarged interpretation above given, really confirms it by shewing that the language of the prophecy is suited to express far more than the literal exodus of Israel from Babylon.

12. *For not in haste shall ye go out, and in flight ye shall not depart ; for going before you* (is) *Jehovah, and bringing up your rear the God of Israel.* This verse is crowded with allusions to the earlier history of Israel, some of which consist in the adaptation of expressions with which the Hebrew reader was familiar, but which must of course be lost in a translation. Thus the hasty departure out of Egypt is not only recorded as a fact in the Mosaic history (Exod. xi. 1 ; xii. 33, 39), but designated by the very term here used חִפָּזוֹן (Exod. xii. 11 ; Deut. xvi. 3), meaning terrified and sudden flight. So also הֹלֵךְ and מְאַסֵּף are military terms familiar to the readers of the ancient books. (See Num. x. 25 ; Josh. vi. 9, 13.) There is likewise an obvious allusion to the cloudy pillar going sometimes before, and sometimes behind the host (Exod. xiv. 19, 20), and possibly to Moses' poetical description of Jehovah as encompassing Israel with his protection (Deut. xxxii. 10). These minute resemblances are rendered still more striking by the distinction which the Prophet makes between the two events. The former exodus was hurried and disorderly ; the one here promised shall be solemn and deliberate. How far the exquisite poetical beauty of the passage is appreciated by some modern critics, may be gathered from the fact that Rosenmüller quotes without dissent the ridiculous remark of Schuster, that the verse has reference to the dangers of the desert between Babylonia and Judea (Ezra viii. 22, 31), and the still more curious fact that Knobel understands it as assigning a reason why they need not neglect their Levitical ablutions before setting out ; while Hitzig infers from this last verse that the purification enjoined in the one before it was "*etwas Zeitraubendes*," or something that required time for its performance. Such *æsthetics*, if applied to any of the master-works of classical genius, would be laughed to scorn ; but even the transcendent merit of the passage

now before us, simply considered as a piece of composition, cannot wash
out the offensive stain of *Judaismus*, or enable certain critics to forget or
even to forgive its being Scripture. The true connection of the verse with
that before it must be obvious to every unsophisticated reader. The *for*,
as in many other cases, has relation to an intermediate thought which may
be easily supplied though not expressed. Or rather, it has reference to the
promise implied in the preceding exhortation, of protection and security.
To many thousands both of learned and unlearned readers, this connection
has been obvious for ages ; whereas not more than two or three, we
may venture to believe, ever dreamed that this magnificent description of
Jehovah's presence with his people was intended to assure the Jewish
exiles that before leaving Babylon they would have time enough to wash
themselves at leisure !—From this verse, taken in connection with the one
before it, we may derive a confirmation of our previous conclusions, first,
that the image there presented is a military no less than a priestly one ;
and secondly, that this whole passage has a wider scope and higher theme
than the deliverance from Babylon, because the latter is no more vividly
exhibited to view than the deliverance from Egypt; and if this is a mere
emblem, so may that be, nay it must be, when we add to the consideration just presented, the result of the inductive process hitherto pursued in
the interpretation of these prophecies, viz. that the deliverance of Israel
from exile does not constitute the theme of the predictions, but is simply
one remarkable historico-prophetical example which the Prophet cites in
illustration of his general teachings as to the principle and mode of the
divine administration, and his special predictions of a great and glorious
change to be connected with the abrogation of the old economy.

13. *Behold, my servant shall do wisely* (and as a necessary consequence)
shall rise and be exalted and high exceedingly. The parenthesis introduced
to shew the true relation of the clauses, serves at the same time to preclude the necessity of giving יַשְׂכִּיל the doubtful and secondary sense of
prospering, as most modern writers do. The objection to this interpretation is the same as in the case of צֶדֶק and צְדָקָה, which it is the fashion
now to render *victory, salvation,* or the like. The parallel expressions in
the present case are not synonymous but simply correlative, the mutual
relation being that of cause and effect. He shall be exalted, because he
shall act wisely in the highest sense, *i. e.* shall use the best means for the
attainment of the highest end. This kind of wisdom involves prosperity,
not merely as a possible result, but as a necessary consequence. We have
no right, however, to substitute the one for the other, or to merge the
primary idea in its derivative. Hengstenberg undertakes to blend both
senses by translating the verb *he shall rule well, i. e.* both wisely and successfully. But to this there are two objections : first, that it introduces
an idea (that of ruling) which is not expressed at all in the original ; and
then, that it confounds two things which in the original are kept distinct,
the antecedent and the consequent, wisdom and prosperity. The latter
has the less claim to be forced into the first clause, because in the last it
is so fully and strongly expressed, by combining, as Hengstenberg himself well
says, all the Hebrew verbs that denote exaltation, and then adding the intensive adverb. The version of the Septuagint (συνήσει), and the Vulgate (*intelli-
get*), is only defective because it makes the verb denote the possession of intelligence, and not its active exercise, which is required by the Hiphil form and
by the connection, as well here as in the parallel passage, Jer. xxiii. 5.
(Compare 1 Kings ii. 3.)—Connected with this verse there are two exegetical

questions which are famous as the subject of dispute among interpreters. The first and least important has respect to the division and arrangement of the text, viz., whether this verse is to be connected with what goes before, or separated from it and regarded as the introduction of a new subject. The former method is adopted in the older versions and in the Masoretic Hebrew text. The latter, according to Procopius and others, was pursued in the ancient distribution of the book, with which the Fathers were familiar, and has been adopted in our own day by most writers on Isa ah. A particular exegetical motive may be easily detected in some cases for preferring the one or other of these methods. Thus Abarbenel is naturally led to sever these three verses (13–15) from what follows, by a wish to establish his peculiar hypothesis that the Messiah is the subject of these verses, but not of the next chapter. On the other hand, those writers who restrict the foregoing context to the restoration of the Jews from exile have a strong inducement to make this the beginning of a new discourse upon another subject, as the best means of disguising the unnatural and violent transition which their hypothesis compels them to assume. But to this statement there are certainly exceptions. Thus the usual division is retained by Hitzig, notwithstanding his adherence to the Babylonian theory; while Ewald, who adopts the other method, admits that the fifty-third chapter begins in an entirely new tone. The ease with which arbitrary arrangements of the text may be multiplied derives some illustration from Hendewerk's assertion that chaps. lii. 7 to liv. 17 is a distinct prophecy, consisting of three parallel parts, chap. lii. 7–15, chap. liii. 1–12, chap. liv. 1–17, so that the favourite modern separation of chap. lii. 13 to liii. 12 from the context as a separate discourse is not only arbitrary but a "mutilation of the oracle." Common to all these arrangements is the radical error of supposing that the book is susceptible of distribution into detached and independent parts ; a notion which, as we have seen already, is not only theoretically groundless, but practically hurtful in a high degree to the sound interpretation of these prophecies. What seems to be gained, in such cases, by combining things which ought to go together, is more than outweighed by the disadvantage of separating others which are no less closely connected. The only satisfactory method, as we have already seen, is to regard the whole as a continuous composition, and to recognise the usual division into chapters, simply because it is familiar and on the whole convenient, although sometimes very injudicious and erroneous. According to this view of the matter, the precise distribution of the chapters is of no more importance than that of the paragraphs in any modern book, which may sometimes facilitate and sometimes hinder its convenient perusal, but can never be regarded as authoritative in determining the sense. In the case immediately before us, it is proper to resist the violent division of the chapter; because when read in its natural connection, it shews how easy the transition was from the foregoing promise of deliverance to the description of the Servant of Jehovah as the leader of the grand march just described, and confirms our previous conclusions as to the exalted meaning of the promises in question, and against a forced restriction of them to the Babylonish exile. At the same time it is equally important that the intimate connection of these verses with the following chapter should be fully recognised, in order that the Servant of the Lord, whose humiliation and exaltation are here mentioned, may be identified with that mysterious Person, whose expiatory sufferings and spiritual triumphs form the great theme of the subsequent context. To the general

agreement among Jews and Christians as to this identity, the forced hypothesis already quoted from Abarbenel may be regarded as the sole exception. It follows, therefore, that the meaning of the whole passage, to the
end of the fifty-third chapter, turns upon the question, Who is meant by
עַבְדִּי (*my servant*) in the verse before us ? An individual, or a collective
body ? If the latter, is it Israel as a whole, or its better portion, or the
Prophets, or the Priesthood ? If the former, is it Moses, Abraham,
Uzziah, Josiah, Jeremiah, Cyrus, an anonymous prophet, the author himself, or the Messiah ? This is the other exegetical question which has
been referred to, as connected with this verse, and materially affecting the
interpretation of the whole passage. The answer to this question, which
at once suggests itself as the result of all our previous inquiries, is, that
the Servant of Jehovah here, as in chap. xlii. 1–6, and chap. xlix. 1–9, is
the Messiah, but presented rather in his own personality than in conjunction with his people. According to the rule already stated (see above, chap.
xlii. 1), the idea of the Body here recedes, and that of the Head becomes
exclusively conspicuous ; because, as we shall see below, the Servant of
Jehovah is exhibited, not merely as a teacher or a ruler, but as an expiatory sacrifice. That this application of the verse and the whole passage
to the Messiah was held by the oldest school of Jewish interpreters, appears from the Targum of Jonathan, who here has *my Servant the Messiah*,
and is admitted by Aben Ezra, Jarchi, Abarbenel, and other Jews, who
have themselves abandoned this opinion, because it would constrain them
to acknowledge Christ as the Messiah of their Scriptures. Detailed proofs
from the ancient Jewish books themselves are given by Hengstenberg in
his Christology (vol. i. pp. 292–294). Gesenius, too, explicitly admits
that the later Jews were no doubt led to give up the old interpretation of
the passage by polemic opposition to Christians. (Commentary, ii. p. 161.)
The same interpretation was maintained, almost without exception, in the
Christian Church, till near the end of the eighteenth century, when it was
abandoned by the German theologians along with the doctrines of atonement and prophetic inspiration. Even in Germany, however, it has always
had its zealous adherents, and in our own day some of its most able, learned,
and successful advocates. In its favour may be urged, besides the tradition
of the synagogue and church, the analogy of the other places where the
Servant of Jehovah is mentioned, the wonderful agreement of the terms of
the prediction with the character and history of Jesus Christ, and the express application of the passage to him by himself and his inspired apostles,
who appear to have assumed it as the basis of their doctrine with respect
to the atonement, and to have quoted it comparatively seldom only because
they had it constantly in view, as appears from their numerous allusions to
it, and the perfect agreement of their teachings with it; so that even Gesenius, while in one place he argues from their silence that they did not find
the doctrine of atonement in the passage, says expressly in another, with a
strange but gratifying inconsistency, that most Hebrew readers, being
already familiar with the notions of sacrifice and substitution, must of
necessity have so explained the place, and that undoubtedly the apostolic
doctrine as to Christ's expiatory death rests in a great measure upon this
foundation. (Comm. ii. p. 191.) The detailed proofs of the Messianic
exposition will be given in the course of the interpretation, and compared
with the other hypotheses maintained by Jews and Christians, which will
therefore only be enumerated here in order that the reader may recall them
for the purpose of comparison. The individual subjects which have been

assumed besides the Messiah, are Josiah by Abarbenel, Jeremiah by Grotius, Uzziah by Augusti, Hezekiah by Bahrdt, Isaiah by Stäudlin, and (according to some) Moses and the Rabbi Akiba by a tradition quoted in the Talmud, although Hengstenberg supposes that these are mentioned only as examples or representatives of a whole class. An anonymous German writer understands by the Servant of this verse, an unknown prophet who suffered martyrdom during the exile! Another anonymous writer of the same country applies the name as a collective to the Maccabees; another to the nobles carried off by Nebuchadnezzar, or to their descendants who returned; Bolton applies it in like manner to the house or family of David. Another nameless German understands by the Servant of Jehovah, the priesthood as a class or body. This is near akin to Rosenmüller's early doctrine that it means the prophets, which was afterwards abandoned by its author, but renewed by Gesenius in his Commentary, and by De Wette and Winer, while Umbreit attempts to blend it with the Messianic exposition by supposing the Messiah to be set forth as the greatest of the prophets, or as their ideal. Instead of this hypothesis, Rosenmüller afterwards adopted that of the rabbins who reject the Messianic doctrine (such as Jarchi, Kimchi, and Aben Ezra), viz. that the Servant of Jehovah is the Jewish people ; and the same opinion is maintained by Eichhorn and Hitzig, but with this important difference between the *soi-disant* Christian and the Jewish writers, that the latter apply the passage to the present dispersion of their people, and the former to the Babylonish exile. As modifications of this general hypothesis may be mentioned Eckermann's extravagant idea, that the people as such, or considered in the abstract, is here distinguished from its individual members, whose words he supposes to be given in the following chapter. Another modification of the same opinion is the ground assumed by Paulus, Maurer, Gesenius in his Lexicon, and in a still more qualified manner by Ewald and Knobel, viz. that the Servant of Jehovah is the spiritual Israel, the better portion of the Jewish people, as distinguished either from their ungodly brethren, or from the heathen, or from both. Some of these explanations are so perfectly groundless and extravagant that they can no more be refuted than established. This is especially the case with those which make the Servant of Jehovah any individual except the Messiah, of which it has been well said that they might be multiplied *ad libitum*, there being no more show of reason for the names suggested, than for a multitude of others which have never been proposed. This remark may be extended to the theories which identify the Servant of Jehovah with the Maccabees, the House of David, the Noble Exiles, and the Priesthood, leaving as the only plausible hypotheses besides the Messianic one, those which severally understand the title as denoting the order of Prophets or the Jewish people, either as a whole, or in relation to its better part. To these the attention of the reader will be therefore directed in comparison with that which is assumed as the basis of the exposition, leaving others to refute themselves. Of those which have been mentioned as entitled to comparative consideration, that which approaches nearest to the truth is the hypothesis of Beck and Ewald, that by the Servant of Jehovah we are to understand the ideal Israel, or rather it denotes the Israel of God, not considered as a nation or a race, but as the church or chosen people, who in some sense represented the Messiah till he came, and is therefore often blended with him in the prophetic picture as a complex person, sometimes more and sometimes less conspicuous, but here, as we have seen already, totally eclipsed by the image of the Head himself. And yet even in this case there are visible such striking points of similarity between the Body and the Head, that although this passage can directly refer only to the latter, it confirms the previous conclusion that in other cases the reverse is true. The general views which have been now expressed on this and other points will be reduced to a more specific form in the progress of the exposition, during the course of which respect will be had, not only to the commentaries usually quoted in this work, but to one or two special monographs, or special expositions of this passage, the most important of which are Martini's Commentatio Philologico-critica (Rostock, 1791), to which most later writers have been largely indebted, and Hengstenberg's excellent interpretation contained in the second part of his Christologie, the valuable substance of which it is proposed to reproduce in the ensuing pages, with some changes both of form and substance, and many additions from more recent sources.—In the verse immediately before us all that need be added is, that the extraordinary exaltation promised in the last clause is such as could never have been looked for by the Prophet, for himself or for his order, especially upon the modern supposition, that he lived in the time of the exile, when the grounds for such an expectation were far less than at any former period. It may also be observed that the personification of the prophets as an ideal individual is foreign from the usage of the Scriptures; the parallelism of *servant* and *messengers*, in the first clause of chap. xliv. 26, no more proves the first to be collective, than the like relation of *Jerusalem* and *cities of Judah* in the last clause prove the same thing of Jerusalem. The objection, that the title *servant* is not applied elsewhere to Messiah, would have little force if true, because the title in itself is a general one, and may be applied to any chosen instrument ; it is not true, however, as the single case of Zech. iii. 8 will suffice to shew, without appealing to the fact, that the same application of the title, either partial or exclusive, has been found admissible above in chaps. xlii. 1, xlix. 3, and l. 10.

14, 15. *As many were shocked at thee—so marred from man his look, and his form from the sons of man—so shall he sprinkle many nations ; concerning him shall kings stop their mouth, because what was not recounted to them they have seen, and what they had not heard they have perceived.* His exaltation shall bear due proportion to his humiliation ; the contempt of men shall be exchanged for wonder and respect. According to the common agreement of interpreters, ver. 14 is the protasis and ver. 15 the apodosis of the same sentence, the correlative clauses being introduced, as usual in cases of comparison, by כַּאֲשֶׁר and כֵּ. The construction is somewhat embarrassed by the intervening כֵּן at the beginning of the last clause of ver. 14, which most interpreters, however, treat as a parenthesis, explanatory of the first clause : " as many were shocked at thee (because his countenance was all marred, &c.), so shall he sprinkle many nations," &c. A simpler construction, though it does not yield so clear a sense, would be to assume a double apodosis : " *as* many were shocked at thee, *so* was his countenance marred, &c., *so* also shall he sprinkle," &c. As thus explained, the sense would be, their abhorrence of him was not without reason, and it shall not be without requital. שָׁמְמוּ expresses a mixture of surprise, contempt, and aversion ; it is frequently applied to extraordinary instances of suffering when viewed as divine judgments. (Lev. xxvi. 32, Ezek. xxvii. 35, Jer. xviii. 16, xix. 8.) It is followed by the preposition עַל as usual when employed in this sense. *Many* does not mean *all*, nor is *nations* to be anticipated from the other clause ; there seems rather to be an antithesis between many individuals and many nations. As a single people had despised him, so the whole

world should admire him.   מִשְׁחַת is a verbal noun, equivalent in this connection to an infinitive or passive participle.   It strictly means *corruptions*,
but is here put for disfiguration or deformity.   De Dieu's derivation of this
word from מָשַׁח, "to anoint," has found no adherents among later writers.
Henderson construes it with מַרְאֵהוּ (*the disfiguration of his appearance*),
notwithstanding the interposition of מֵאִישׁ.   The other recent writers make
it the predicate, and מַרְאֵהוּ the subject of the same proposition.   By *look*
and *form* we are neither to understand a mean condition nor the personal
appearance, but, as an intermediate idea, the visible effects of suffering.
The preposition *from, away from*, may be taken simply as expressive of
comparison (*more than*), or more emphatically of negation (*so as not to be
human*), which are only different gradations of the same essential meaning.
Jahn supposes a climax in the use of אִישׁ and אָדָם—his appearance should
be far below that even of the lowest men; but this is looked upon by
Hengstenberg as weakening the expression, and is certainly unnecessary, as
well as founded on a dubious usage.—יַזֶּה is the technical term of the Mosaic
law for *sprinkling* water, oil, or blood, as a purifying rite.   Jerome supposes a
specific reference to the blood of Christ and the water of baptism.   Hengstenberg gives the verb the secondary sense of cleansing, but still with
reference to the effects of the atonement.   The explanation of this word by
the majority of modern writers as denoting that he shall cause them to leap
for joy (Paulus, Winer, Gesenius in Comm.), or rise from their seats with
reverence (Ewald, Gesenius in Thes.), or start with astonishment (Eichhorn, Hitzig), or be struck with cordial admiration (Clericus, Rosenmüller,
Maurer, Umbreit, Knobel), is in direct opposition to a perfectly uniform
Hebrew usage, and without any real ground even in Arabic analogy.   The
ostensible reasons for this gross violation of the clearest principles of lexicography are: first, the chimera of a perfect parallelism, which is never
urged except in cases of great necessity; and secondly, the fact that in
every other case the verb is followed by the substance sprinkled, and connected with the object upon which it is sprinkled by a preposition.   But
since both the constructions of the verb "to sprinkle" are employed in
other languages (as we may either speak of sprinkling a person, or of
sprinkling water on him), the transition must be natural, and no one can
pretend to say that two or more examples of it in a book of this size are
required to demonstrate its existence.   The real motive of the strange
unanimity with which the true sense has been set aside, is the desire to
obliterate this clear description, at the very outset, of the Servant of
Jehovah as an expiatory purifier, one who must be innocent himself in
order to cleanse others,—an office and a character alike inapplicable either to
the prophets as a class, or to Israel as a nation, or even to the better class
of Jews, much more to any single individual except to One who claimed to
be the Purifier of the guilty, and to whom many nations do at this day
ascribe whatever purity of heart or life they either have or hope for.
Another objection to the modern explanation of the word is, that it then
anticipates the declaration of the next clause, instead of forming a connecting link between it and the first.   This clause is understood by some to
mean that they shall be reverently silent *before him*, by others that they
shall be dumb with wonder *on account of him*, by others that they shall be
silent *respecting him*, *i. e.* no longer utter expressions of aversion or contempt.   Gesenius asks whether kings ever bowed personally to Christ, as
intimated here and in chap. xlix. 7; to which Hengstenberg replies, that
the only word which creates the difficulty (*personally*) is supplied by the

objector ; that multitudes of kings have bowed to Christ in one sense, whereas none in any sense, have ever thus acknowledged their subjection to the prophets, or to Israel, or even to the pious Jews, or could have been expected so to do.—The reason of this voluntary humiliation is expressed in the last clause, viz., because they see things of which they had never had experience, or even knowledge by report. This expression shows that *many nations* must be taken in its natural and proper sense, as denoting the Gentiles. It is accordingly applied by Paul (Rom. **xv.** 21) to the preaching of the Gospel among those who had never before heard it. Interpreters have needlessly refined in interpreting the verb *see* as signifying mental, no less than bodily perception. The truth is that the language is not scientific, but poetical ; the writer does not put sight for experience, but on the contrary describes experience as simple vision.—For the stopping of the mouth, as an expression of astonishment or reverence, see Job xxix. 9, xl. 4, Ps. cvii. 42, Ezek. xvi. 63, Micah vii. 16.

Chapter 53

NOTWITHSTANDING these and other prophecies of the Messiah, he is not recognised when he appears, ver. 1. He is not the object of desire and trust, for whom the great mass of the people have been waiting, ver. 2. Nay, his low condition, and especially his sufferings, make him rather an object of contempt, ver. 3. But this humiliation and these sufferings are vicarious, not accidental or incurred by his own fault, vers. 4–6. Hence, though personally innocent, he is perfectly unresisting, ver. 7. Even they for whom he suffers may mistake his person and his office, ver. 8. His case presents the two extremes of righteous punishment, and perfect innocence, ver. 9. But the glorious fruit of these very sufferings will correct all errors, ver. 10. He becomes a Saviour only by becoming a substitute, ver. 11. Even after the work of expiation is completed, and his glorious reward secured, the work of intercession will be still contiuued, ver. 12.

1. *Who hath believed our report? and the arm of Jehovah, to whom* (or *upon whom*) *has it been revealed ?* While most modern writers, as we have already seen, detach the three preceding verses and prefix them to this chapter, Hitzig goes to the opposite extreme of saying that the writer here begins afresh, without any visible connection with the previous context. Ewald more reasonably makes this a direct continuation, but observes a change of tone, from that of joyous confidence to that of penitent confession, on the part of the believing Jews, in reference to their former incredulity. Martini, Jahn, and Rosenmüller put these words into the mouth of the heathen, acknowledging their error with respect to the sufferings of Israel. But this hypothesis, besides being arbitrary in itself, and unsustained by any parallel case in which the heathen are thus introduced as speaking, requires a forced interpretation to be put upon the language of the verse. Thus Rosenmüller understands the first clause as meaning "who of us would have believed this, had we merely heard instead of seeing it ?" And the last clause in like manner, "unto whom has the arm of Jehovah been revealed as unto us ?" Gesenius and the later writers much more naturally understand the Prophet as speaking in his own name or in that of the prophets generally, not his predecessors or contemporaries merely, as Jerome and Van Der Palm assume without necessity. They also, for the most part, retain the strict sense of the preterite, which Hengstenberg and Hendewerk exchange for

the present form, *believes* and *is revealed.*—שְׁמוּעָה is properly the passive participle of the verb to hear, the feminine being used like the neuter to denote what is heard, and may therefore be applied to rumour, to instruction, or to speech in general. (See chap. xxiii. 9, 19, Jer. xlix. 14, and compare the Greek ἀκοή, Rom. x. 16, Gal. iii. 2, 1 Thess. ii. 13.) Hitzig supposes that the word was here suggested by the יַשְׁמִיעַ of the preceding verse. The restricted applications of the term, by Gesenius and Maurer to the news of the deliverance from Babylon, and by Hendewerk to the preceding strophe (chap. iii. 7-15), are alike gratuitous. Martini, Jahn, and Rosenmüller, in accordance with their notion that the heathen are here speaking, understand the whole phrase passively, as meaning "that which we have heard ;" and the same sense, on a wholly different hypothesis, is also given by Umbreit and Knobel, the last of whom applies the term to that which the prophet is described as having heard in chap. l. 4, 5. Gesenius, Hengstenberg, and others understand it actively, as meaning that which we have published in the hearing of others ; which agrees well with the context and with Paul's quotation (Rom. x. 16), and is perfectly consistent with the strict sense of the Hebrew words, though not sustained by any definite usage, as Henderson alleges. That the words might have either of these senses in different connections, may be gathered from the fact, that in 2 Sam. iv. 4, the qualifying noun denotes neither the author nor the recipient of the declaration, but its subject, so that in itself the phrase is quite indefinite. Some understand the interrogation in this clause as implying an absolute negation, which, according to Hendewerk, includes the very Servant of Jehovah himself, who is described as blind and deaf in chap. xlii. 19. But there, as we have seen, the prominent idea in the Servant of Jehovah is the Body, whereas here it is the Head. According to Hengstenberg the implied negation is not absolute, but simply expressive of wonder at the paucity of true believers in the word at large, but more especially among the Jews, to whom, with Van Der Palm, he understands the passage as specifically referring, because it had already been predicted, in the foregoing verse, that the heathen would believe. There is no inconsistency, however, even if we take the words before us in their widest sense ; because, as Calvin has observed, the prophet interrupts his prediction of success and triumph to bewail the discouragements and disappointments which should intervene. The same thing had already been predicted indirectly in chap. xlii. 24, and similar objections to his own assurances occur in chap. xlix. 14, 24. The last clause is understood by Knobel as assigning a reason for the unbelief described in the first : they did not believe what they heard, because they did not see the arm of Jehovah visibly revealed. But most interpreters regard the two as parallel expressions of the same idea : to believe what God said, and to see his arm revealed, being really identical. The advent of Christ, his miracles, his resurrection, his ascension, are among the clearest proofs of the divine omnipotence and of its real exercise, a sceptical misgiving as to which is involved in a refusal to believe. The *arm* as the seat of active strength is often put for strength itself (2 Chron. xxxii. 8, Job xxii. 8, Jer. xvii. 5), and especially for the power of Jehovah (chap. li. x. 16, Deut. iv. 34, v. 15, xxvi. 8). In this sense it is commonly regarded as convertible with *hand ;* but Hendewerk maintains that the latter only is applied to a gracious exercise of power (chaps. xli. 20, xlv. 11, 12, xlviii. 13, xlix. 2, 22, lix. 1), while the former always has respect to war (chaps. xl. 10, lii. 10, lxiii. 5, lix. 16). He therefore gives the clause exclusive reference to what God had already done for Cyrus, and designed to do for Israel, by making them victorious over all their enemies. But this distinction, though ingenious, is fallacious ; because it confounds the usual application of a figure with its essential meaning, and entirely overlooks the many cases in which *hand* has reference to the divine vengeance (*e. g.* chap. ix. 11, 20, x. 4, xix. 16, xxv. 10, li. 17), while in some of the cases where the arm is mentioned (chap. xl. 12, and li. 5) it is hard to discover any reference to war. But the true solution of the difficulty is, that the manifestation of God's justice is commonly described by Isaiah as including at the same time the deliverance of his friends, and the destruction of his enemies. (See above, chap. li. 5.)—The use of עַל in the last clause is explained by some as a mere variation of the usual construction with אֶל or לְ ; but Hengstenberg regards it as implying that the revelation comes from above, and Hitzig supposes an allusion to the elevation of the arm itself.

2. *And he came up like the tender plant before him, and like the root from a dry ground; he had no form nor comeliness, and we shall see him, and no sight that we should desire it.* There is something almost ludicrous to modern readers in Vitringa's pedantic notion that the Prophet puts these words into the mouth of a chorus of converted Jews. There is also something too artificial in Van Der Palm's dramatic distribution of the passage, according to which the Prophet's censure of the unbelief of the Jews (ver. 1) is followed by their justification of it (vers. 2, 3), while the first clause of the fourth verse contains the Prophet's answer, and the last the rejoinder of the Jews, after which the Prophet speaks again without any further interruption. Most of the modern writers agree with Gesenius in making all that follows the first verse the language of the people, acknowledging their own incredulity with respect to the Messiah, and assigning as its cause their carnal expectations of a temporal prince, and their ignorance of the very end for which he came. The hypothesis of Rosenmüller and others, who regard this as the language of the heathen, acknowledging their error with respect to Israel, has been already mentioned. (See above, on chap. lii. 13.) A novel and ingenious, but untenable hypothesis, has been more recently proposed by Hendewerk, viz. that the speakers are the elder race of exiles in Babylon, by whose transgressions that infliction was occasioned, and that the sufferer here described is the younger race, for whose sake it was terminated, just as in the case of the fathers and children who came out of Egypt.—The וֹ at the beginning of this verse is not causative, but narrative, determining the past tense of the future form, and connecting the sentence either with chap. lii. 14 or 15, or, which is the simplest and most natural construction, with the verse immediately preceding, which, although interrogative in form, involves an affirmation, namely, that the people were incredulous, which general statement is here amplified.—The common version of וַיַּעַל as a future proper (*he shall grow up*) is utterly precluded by the *Vav* conversive, and gratuitously violates the uniformity of the description, which presents the humiliation of Messiah as already past.— יוֹנֵק is properly a *suckling*, but is here used precisely like the cognate English word *sucker*, by which Lowth translates it. On the meaning of שֹׁרֶשׁ, see vol. i. p. 255–6.—*Out of a dry ground* implies a feeble, sickly growth, and, as its consequence, a mean appearance. The dry ground, according to Alexander Morus, is Bethlehem, which he describes, on the authority of Strabo, as a barren spot. Along with this may be recorded the opinion of Eusebius and other fathers, that the dry ground was the

Virgin Mary; of which Calvin might well say, *extra rem loquuntur.* *Out of a dry ground* and the parallel expression (*before him*) may be considered as qualifying both the nouns, and separated only for the sake of the rhythmical arrangement of the sentence. *Before him* is translated by Henderson *before them,* and by Lowth *in their sight,* in accordance with the explanation of J. H. Michaelis, who regards it as descriptive of the popular misapprehension and contempt of Christ. Most writers take it strictly as a singular, referring to Jehovah, and analogous in meaning to those words of Peter, *disallowed indeed of men, but chosen of God and precious* (1 Pet. ii. 4). It is well observed by Henderson, however, that it was not in the sight of God that the Messiah was a root out of a dry ground, but in that of the people.—*He had not,* literally, there was not to him, the only form in which that idea can be expressed in Hebrew.—*Form* is here put for beautiful or handsome form, as in 1 Sam. xvi. 18 David is called a *man of form,* *i. e.* a comely person. The two nouns here used are combined in literal description elsewhere (*e. g.* Gen. xxix. 17, 1 Sam. xxv. 31), and in this very passage (see above, chap. lii. 13). They denote in this case, not mere personal appearance, but the whole state of humiliation, and, as Calvin says, are to be understood *de toto regno cujus nulla in oculis hominum forma, nullus decor, nulla magnificentia fuit.*—The modern writers generally disregard the Masoretic interpunction of this sentence, and connect וְנִרְאֵהוּ with the first clause, as a parallel to וְנֶחְמְדֵהוּ. The meaning then is, no form or beauty that we should look at him, no appearance that we should desire him. This is precisely the construction adopted by Symmachus, ἵνα εἴδωμεν, ἵνα ἐπιθυμηθῶμεν. But as this relation of the clauses is too obvious to have escaped the Masoretic critics, it is reasonable to conclude that they were influenced in setting it aside by high traditional authority. There is, besides, a difficulty, if it be retained, in explaining the use of the verb רָאָה, which means to view with pleasure only when followed by the preposition בְ, and the sense *that we should look at him* does not seem entirely adequate. If we adhere to the Masoretic interpunction, there is no need of paraphrasing וְנִרְאֵהוּ with the English Version (*when we shall see him*); it is better to give it its direct and proper sense (*and we shall see him*). But as both these versions suppose a transition from the form of narrative to that of prophecy, there is the same objection to them as to the common version of וַיַּעַל. On the whole, therefore, leaving out of view the authority of the Masorah, the usual construction is the most satisfactory.—In what sense the prophets thus grew up like suckers from a dry soil, or the Jewish nation while in exile, or the pious portion of them, or the younger race, it is as difficult to understand or even to conceive, as it is easy to recognise this trait of the prophetic picture in the humiliation of our Saviour, and the general contempt to which it exposed him.

3. *Despised and forsaken of men* (or *ceasing from among men*), *a man of sorrows and acquainted with sickness, and like one hiding the face from him* (or *us*), *despised, and we esteemed him not.* From the general description of his humiliation, the Prophet now passes to a more particular account of his sufferings.—חָדֵל, from חָדַל to cease, is by some taken in a passive and by others in an active sense. On the former supposition, the whole phrase may mean *rejected of men* (English Version), *forsaken by men, i. e.* by his friends, as in Job xix. 14 (Gesenius), or *avoided by men,* as an object of abhorrence (Hitzig, Ewald, Hendewerk). On the other supposition, it is explained by Hengstenberg as meaning one who ceases from

among men, *i. e.* ceases to be a man, or to be so considered. This is probably the sense intended by the Septuagint version, and is certainly the one expressed by Aben Ezra (חָדֵל לִהְקָשֵׁב עִם אֲנָשִׁים). The version of Symmachus (ἐλάχιστος ἀνδρῶν), with which the Vulgate and Peshito substantially agree, seems to rest upon the same construction of חָדֵל that is proposed by Martini, who regards both this word and נִבְזֶה as adjectives, deriving a superlative import from the plural following, the most despised and forsaken of men. (Compare Ps. xxii. 7, Prov. xv. 20.) But for this sense there is no authority in usage.—The phrase *man of sorrows* seems to mean one whose afflictions are his chief characteristic, perhaps with an allusion to their number in the plural form. (Compare Prov. xxix. 1.) Symmachus translates the phrase γνωστὸς νόσῳ, which is generally understood to mean, known or distinguished by disease; and this sense is retained by J. D. Michaelis, Paulus, Jahn, Rosenmüller, Gesenius in his Commentary, Maurer, and Umbreit. The Septuagint, Vulgate, and Peshito, give the first word the sense of *knowing* (εἰδώς, *sciens*), from which Lowth infers that they read יוֹדֵעַ. But Hengstenberg and others have shewn that the passive participle is itself employed like *acquainted* in English, so that there is no need of supposing any difference of text, or even that the passive form was used in an active sense. (Compare Song Sol. iii. 8; Ps. cxii. 7, ciii. 14.) Gesenius in his Commentary characterizes this interpretation of the word as "false," but quietly adopts it in the second edition of his German Version.—In the next phrase מַסְתֵּר is by some regarded as a participle, and by others as a noun. On the former supposition, the entire phrase is explained by the Septuagint, Vulgate, Targum, Aquila, Jarchi, Lowth, Koppe, De Wette, and others, as meaning, *he was like one hiding his face from us*, with allusion to the veiling of the face by lepers (Lev. xiii. 45) or by mourners (2 Sam. xv. 30; Ez. xiv. 17), or as an expression of shame (Micah iii. 7). To this Gesenius objects in his Commentary, that the whole description has respect, not to the conduct of the sufferer, but to his appearance in the sight of others. In the Thesaurus, he adopts this very explanation, without noticing his own objection, though he still avows a preference for his former construction, notwithstanding the harshness with which it may be charged, viz. like one from whom one hides the face. J. H. Michaelis and Rosenmüller give the Hiphil, as usual, a causative sense, like one making (others) hide the face from him. But in every other case הַסְתִּיר simply means to hide, and occurs repeatedly in that sense with this very noun פָּנִים. It may also be objected to the explanation of the word as a participle, that analogy and usage would require the form מַסְתִּיר, which is actually found in four manuscripts, but no doubt as a conjectural emendation. Kimchi, Martini, and Hengstenberg, take מַסְתֵּר as an abstract noun, meaning properly *concealment*, and explain the whole phrase, like concealment of the face from it, *i. e.* like that which causes men to hide the face from it. But although the hiding of the face is elsewhere mentioned as a natural expression of displeasure, shame, and sorrow, it does not occur as an expression of contemptuous astonishment, and seems to be a forced and exaggerated method of expressing such a feeling. It may therefore be better on the whole to combine the explanation of מַסְתֵּר as a noun with that of מִמֶּנּוּ as a pronoun of the first person, and to understand the whole phrase as meaning, like a hiding of the face from us, *i. e.* as if he hid his face from us in shame and sorrow; notwithstanding the objection of Gesenius, that the subject of description is not the demeanour of the sufferer, which has not only been abandoned by himself (although renewed by Hengstenberg), but is in itself unreasonable, since the writer's purpose was not to observe the unities of rhetoric, but to make a strong impression of the voluntary humiliation of the Messiah, which could not be more effectually secured by any single stroke than by the one before us, thus explained.— Gesenius, Hengstenberg, and Umbreit follow the Peshito in making נִבְזֶה the first person plural (*we despised him*); and Martini supplies the want of a suffix by reading נבזהו לא instead of נבזה ולא. But the anomalous use of the future creates a difficulty not to be gratuitously introduced; and the analogy of נִבְזֶה in the first clause makes it much more natural to take this as a participle likewise, with the other ancient versions, and with Maurer, Hitzig, Ewald, and Knobel.—Here again the reader is invited to compare the forced application of this verse to the Prophets, to all Israel, to the pious Jews, or to the younger race of exiles, with the old interpretation of it as a prophecy of Christ's humiliation.

4. *Surely our sicknesses he bore, and our griefs he carried; and we thought him stricken, smitten of God, and afflicted.* אָכֵן is determined, both by its etymology and usage, to be a particle of affirmation. The sense of *but*, assumed by most interpreters, is rather what they think the writer should have said, than what he has said. The comparatively rare use of adversative particles in Hebrew has already been mentioned as a striking idiomatic peculiarity. The metaphor is that of a burden, and the meaning of the whole verse is, that they had misunderstood the very end for which Messiah was to come. *Sickness*, as in the verse preceding, is a representative expression for all suffering. *Our griefs*, those which we must otherwise have suffered, and that justly. The plural חלינו is defectively written for חליינו, which last appears, however, in eleven manuscripts and eighteen editions; while on the other hand twenty manuscripts and two editions have the defective form מַכְאֹבֵנוּ, which cannot be singular, because the pronoun which refers to it is plural. Henderson makes his English version more expressive of the writer's main drift by employing the idiomatic form, *it was our griefs he bare, it was our sorrows he carried.*—The explanation of נָשָׂא as meaning merely *took away*, is contradicted by the context, and especially by the parallel phrase סְבָלָם, which can only mean *he bore* or *carried them*. It is alleged, indeed, that one is never said to bear the sins of another, and some go so far as to explain these words as meaning that he bore with them patiently, while others understand the sense to be that he shared in the sufferings of others. But the terms are evidently drawn from the Mosaic law of sacrifice, a prominent feature in which is the substitution of the victim for the actual offender, so that the former *bears* the sins of the latter, and the latter, in default of such an expiation, is said to bear his own sin. (See Lev. v. 1, 17, xvii. 16, xxiv. 15; Num. ix. 13, xiv. 33; Exod. xxiii. 38; Lev. x. 17, xvi. 22.) For the use of סָבַל in the same vicarious sense, see Lam. v. 7. (Compare Ez. xviii. 19.) The Septuagint in the case before us has φέρει, Symmachus ἀνέλαβε. The application of these words by Matthew (viii. 17) to the removal of bodily diseases cannot involve a denial of the doctrine of vicarious atonement, which is clearly recognised in Mat. xx. 28; nor is it an exposition of the passage quoted in its full sense, but, as Calvin well explains it, an intimation that the prediction had begun to be fulfilled, because already its effects were visible, the Scriptures always representing sorrow as the fruit of sin.—*Stricken*, as in some other cases, has the pregnant sense of *stricken from above*, as Noyes expresses it, or *smitten of God*, as it is fully expressed in the next clause. (See Gen.

xii. 17 ; 2 Kings xv. 5 ; 1 Sam. vi. 9.) There is no need, therefore, of supposing an ellipsis. The other verb נָכָה was particularly applied to the infliction of disease (Num. xiv. 12 ; Deut. xxviii. 22), especially the leprosy ; which led Jerome to give נָגוּעַ the specific sense *leprous.* Hence the old Jewish notion that the Messiah was to be a leper. Theodoret more correctly uses the generic term μεμαστιγωμένος, equivalent to the πληγείς Θεοῦ μάστιγι of Æschylus.—Instead of the construct form מֻכֵּה, some manuscripts exhibit the absolute מֻכֶּה ; which is preferred by Bellarmine and some others, who explain the whole phrase as meaning *a stricken God,* and use it as a proof of the divinity of Christ.—By stricken, smitten, and afflicted we are of course not to understand stricken, smitten, and afflicted for his own sins, or merely stricken, smitten, and afflicted, without any deeper cause or higher purpose than in other cases of severe suffering. It is scarcely necessary to suppose a reference to the notion that great suffering was a proof of great iniquity. (Compare Luke xiii. 1 ; John ix. 2.)—In order to reconcile this verse with their hypotheses, Knobel and Hendewerk are under the necessity of proving that the pious Jews or younger race of exiles suffered more in the captivity than any others, which they do with great ease by applying thus all the descriptions of maltreatment which occur throughout the Later Prophecies.

5. *And he was pierced* (or *wounded*) *for our transgressions, bruised* (or *crushed*) *for our iniquities ; the chastisement* (or *punishment*) *of our peace* (*was*) *upon him, and by his stripes we were healed.* The translation of the particle at the beginning by *whereas, yea,* or the like, is a departure from the Hebrew idiom wholly unnecessary to the clearness of the passage, which is continued in the simple narrative or descriptive form. Aben Ezra's application of the verse to the sufferings of the Jews in their present exile and dispersion, is worthy of a place by the side of Hendewerk's assertion that the Prophet here speaks as one of the older race of captives in Babylon, acknowledging the error of himself and his contemporaries with respect to the younger and better generation.—מְחוֹלָל is derived by Cocceius from חוּל to writhe with pain, and translated *excruciatus est ;* but the true derivation is no doubt the common one from חָלַל to perforate, transfix, or pierce, with special reference to mortal wounds ; so that the derivative חָלָל, though strictly meaning pierced or wounded, is constantly applied to persons slain by violence, and especially in battle. Hence the Peshito version of מְחֹלָל (*killed*), although apparently inaccurate, is really in strict accordance with the Hebrew usage. Vitringa and Henderson suppose a particular allusion to the crucifixion. Hengstenberg explains the word more generally as a metaphorical expression for extreme suffering. This agrees well with the parallel expression *crushed* or *bruised,* to which there is nothing literally corresponding in our Saviour's passion ; and if this must be taken as a figure for distress of mind, or suffering in general, the other can be naturally understood only in the same way. It is very possible, however, that there may be a secondary and implicit reference to the crucifixion, such as we have met with repeatedly before in cases where the direct and proper meaning of the words was more extensive.—As מוּסָר is often applied elsewhere to correction by words, some explain it to mean here *instruction,* as to the means of obtaining peace with God. But the stronger sense of *chastisement* or *punishment* not only suits the context better, but is really the most consistent with the usage of the verbal root, and of the noun itself, in such cases as Job v. 17, Prov. xxii. 15, xxiii. 13, as well as with the subse-

quent expression *on him*, which is hardly reconcilable with the supposition of mere precept or example. Whether the word was intended at the same time, as Hengstenberg supposes, to suggest the idea of a warning to others, may be made a question. The chastisement of peace is not only that which tends to peace, but that by which peace is procured directly. It is not, to use the words of an extreme and zealous rationalist, a chastisement morally salutary for us, nor one which merely contributes to our safety, but, according to the parallelism, one which has accomplished our salvation, and in this way, that it was inflicted not on us but on him, so that we came off safe and uninjured. (Hitzig.) The application of the phrase to Christ, without express quotation, is of frequent occurrence in the New Testament. (See Eph. ii. 14–17, Col. i. 20, 21, Heb. xiii. 20, and compare Isa. ix. 6, Micah vi. 5, Zech. i. 13.)—חַבְּרָה is properly a singular, denoting the tumour raised by scourging, here put collectively for stripes, and that for suffering in general, but probably with secondary reference to the literal infliction of this punishment upon the Saviour.—נִרְפָּא is not a noun, as Henderson explains it, but a passive verb, here used impersonally, *it was healed to us*, the לָנוּ limiting the action to a specific object. *It was healed* is a general proposition ; *with respect to us* is the specific limitation. The use of the ל may be otherwise explained by supposing that the verb has here the modified sense of *healing was imparted*, as in ver. 11 הִצְדִּיק לְ means to impart righteousness or justification. Healing is a natural and common figure for relief from suffering considered as a wound or malady. (Compare chaps. vi. 10, xix. 22, xxx. 26, Jer. viii. 22, xxx. 17, 2 Chron. vii. 14.) The preterite is not used merely to signify the certainty of the event, but because this effect is considered as inseparable from the procuring cause which had been just before described in the historical or narrative form as an event already past : when he was smitten, we were thereby healed. It is, therefore, injurious to the strength as well as to the beauty of the sentence, to translate with Henderson, *that by his stripes we might be healed*. The mere contingency thus stated is immeasurably less than the positive assertion that *by his stripes we were healed*. The same objection, in a less degree, applies to the common version, *we are healed*, which makes the statement too indefinite, and robs it of its peculiar historical form.— Above thirty manuscripts and as many editions have שְׁלוֹמֵינוּ in the plural ; a form which does not occur elsewhere.—The hypothesis that this passage has exclusive reference to the Babylonish exile, becomes absolutely ludicrous when it requires us to understand the Prophet as here saying that the people were healed (*i. e.* restored to their own land) by the stripes of the prophets, or by those of true believers, or that the old and wicked race were healed by the stripes of their more devout successors. This last hypothesis of Hendewerk's, besides the weak points which it has in common with the others, involves two very improbable assumptions : first, that the distinction of good and bad was coincident with that of young and old among the exiles ; and secondly, that this younger race was not only better than the older, but endured more suffering.

6. *All we like sheep had gone astray, each to his own way we had turned, and Jehovah laid on him the iniquity of us all.* This verse describes the occasion, or rather the necessity of the sufferings mentioned in those before it. It was because men were wholly estranged from God, and an atonement was required for their reconciliation. *All we* does not mean all the Jews or all the heathen, but all men without exception. The common

version, *have gone astray, have turned,* does not express the historical form of the original sufficiently, but rather means we have done so up to the present time, whereas the prominent idea in the Prophet's mind is that we had done so before Messiah suffered. Noyes's version *we were going astray* is ambiguous, because it may imply nothing more than an incipient estrangement.—The figure of wandering, or lost sheep is common in Scripture to denote alienation from God and the misery which is its necessary consequence (see Ezek. xxxiv. 5, Mat. ix. 36). The entire comparison is probably that of sheep without a shepherd (1 Kings xxii. 17, Zech. x. 2). The second clause is understood by Augusti as denoting selfishness, and a defect of public spirit, or benevolence; and this interpretation is admitted by Hengstenberg as correct if "taken in a deeper sense," viz. that union among men can only spring from their common union with God. But this idea, however just it may be in itself, is wholly out of place in a comparison with scattered sheep, whose running off in different directions does not spring from selfishness, but from confusion, ignorance, and incapacity to choose the right path. A much better exposition of the figure, although still too limited, is that of Theodoret, who understands it to denote the vast variety of false religions, as exemplified by the different idols worshipped in Egypt, Phenicia, Scythia, and Greece, alike in nothing but the common error of departure from the true God. Εἰ καὶ διάφοροι τῆς πλάνης οἱ τρόποι, πάντες ὁμοίως τὸν ὄντα Θεὸν καταλελοιπότες.—The original expression is like *the* sheep (or collectively the flock) *i. e.* not sheep in general, but the sheep that wander, or that have no shepherd.—The idea of a shepherd, although not expressed, appears to have been present to the writer's mind, not only in the first clause but the last, where the image meant to be presented is no doubt that of a shepherd laying down his life for the sheep. This may be fairly inferred not merely from the want of connection which would otherwise exist between the clauses, and which can only be supplied in this way, nor even from the striking analogy of Zech. xiii. 7, where the figure is again used, but chiefly from the application of the metaphor, with obvious, though tacit, reference to this part of Isaiah, in the New Testament to Christ's laying down his life for his people. (See John x. 11–18, and 1 Peter ii. 24, 25.)—The reading of one manuscript, הִגִּיעַ for הִפְגִּיעַ, is probably an accidental variation. The meaning given to this verb in the margin of the English Bible (*made to meet*) is not sustained by etymology or usage, as the primitive verb פָּגַע does not mean simply to come together, but always denotes some degree of violent collision, either physical, as when one body lights or strikes upon another, or moral, as when one person falls upon, *i. e.* attacks another. The secondary senses of the verb are doubtful and of rare occurrence. (See above, on chap. xlvii. 3, and below, on chap. lxiv. 4.) Kimchi supposes the punishment of sin to be here represented as an enemy whom God permitted or impelled to fall upon, or assail the sufferer. Vitringa and Henderson, with much more questionable taste, suppose the image to be that of a wild beast by which the flock is threatened, and from which it is delivered only by the interposition and vicarious exposure of the shepherd to its fury. Most interpreters appear to be agreed in giving it a more generic sense. The common version (*laid upon him*) is objectionable only because it is too weak, and suggests the idea of a mild and inoffensive gesture, whereas that conveyed by the Hebrew word is necessarily a violent one, viz. that of causing to strike or fall, which is faithfully expressed by Umbreit (*liess fallen*), still more closely by Ewald and De Wette (*liess treffen*), and correctly but less definitely by Gesenius, Hengstenberg, and others (*warf*). Among the ancient versions Symmachus has καταντῆσαι ἐποίησεν, and Jerome *posuit in eo*, which last, although it scarcely gives the full sense of the verb, retains that of the preposition, as denoting strictly *in him*, *i. e.* not merely on his head or on his body, but in his soul, or rather in his person, as expressive of the whole man. The word עָוֹן does not of itself mean punishment, but sin ; which, however, is said to have been laid upon the Messiah, only in reference to its effects. If vicarious suffering can be described in words, it is so described in these two verses; so that the attempts to explain them as denoting mere forbearance or participation in the punishment of others, may be fairly regarded as desperate expedients to make the passage applicable to the imaginary persecutions of the Prophets, or the pious Jews, or the younger race during the Babylonish exile. The amount of ingenuity expended on these sophisms only shews how artificial and devoid of solid basis the hypothesis must be which require to be thus supported.—With this and the foregoing verse compare Rom. iv. 25, 2 Cor. v. 21, 1 Peter ii. 22–25.

7. *He was oppressed and he humbled himself, and he will not open his mouth—as a lamb to the slaughter is brought, and as a sheep before its shearers is dumb—and he will not open his mouth.* Having explained the occasion of Messiah's sufferings, the Prophet now describes his patient endurance of them. As נִגַּשׂ is sometimes applied to the rigorous exaction of debts, De Dieu translates it here *exactus est*, Tremellius *exigebatur pœna*. Lowth has the same sense, but makes the verb impersonal, *it was exacted and he was made answerable ;* but עָנָה is not used like the Latin *respondeo* as a technical forensic term. Van Der Palm explains the first verb, *he was demanded, i. e.* by the people, to be crucified ; but נִגַּשׂ does not mean to demand in general, its primary meaning is to urge or press. (See chap. iii. 5, vol. i. p. 111.) The general voice of the interpreters is strongly in favour of the old translation, *he was oppressed* or *persecuted.* —The next phrase has been usually understood as a simple repetition of the same idea in other words. Thus the English Version renders it, *he was oppressed, and he was afflicted.* Besides the tautology of this translation (which would prove nothing by itself), it fails to represent the form of the original, in which the pronoun הוּא is introduced before the second verb, and according to usage must be regarded as emphatic. Martini's proposition to transpose the particle, so as to read נִגַּשׂ הוּא וְנַעֲנֶה, is merely an ingenious expedient to evade a difficulty of construction. Gesenius gives וְהוּא the sense of *although*, and explains the whole as meaning that he was oppressed although before afflicted, and the same interpretation is adopted by Umbreit, Hendewerk, and Knobel. There does not seem to be much force in Hengstenberg's objection, that עָנָה as well as נִגַּשׂ is applied to severe suffering. Gesenius's interpretation would be no less admissible on the supposition that the verbs are perfectly synonymous, the distinction lying not in the verbs themselves, but in the *ohnehin* which he supplies. The true objection is that he does supply it, arbitrarily referring the two verbs to different points of time, and also that the meaning which he gives וְהוּא is forced and foreign from Hebrew usage. The same objection lies against Hitzig's construction of the clause, *he was oppressed, and although persecuted, opened not his mouth*, which, moreover, omits in translation not only the first *Vav* but the second. Ewald explains it thus : *he was persecuted although he humbled himself.* The same reflexive meaning had been given to נַעֲנֶה by Koppe, Jahn, and others, and appears to be implied in

the paraphrastic versions of Symmachus (καὶ αὐτὸς ὑπήκουσε) and Jerome (*quia ipse voluit*). Supposing this sense of the verb to be admissible, by far the simplest and most natural construction is to give וְהוּא its ordinary sense as a conjunction and emphatic pronoun, *he was oppressed and he himself submitted to affliction,* or allowed himself to be afflicted. There is then no tautology nor any arbitrary difference of tense assumed between the two verbs, while the whole sense is good in itself and in perfect agreement with the context. The same sense, substantially, is put upon the clause by Beck's explanation of נִגַּשׁ as the first person plural (*wir erwiesen uns tyrannisch*) ; which is favoured by the obvious opposition of the first and third person in the preceding verse, and by the use of הוּא in this. All other writers seem agreed, however, that נִגַּשׁ is the third person singular of Niphal. All interpreters, perhaps without exception, render יִפְתַּח as a præter or a present, which is no doubt substantially correct, as the whole passage is descriptive. It seems desirable, however, to retain, as far as possible, the characteristic form of the original, especially as it is very hard to account for the repeated use of the future here, if nothing more was intended than might have been expressed by the præter. At all events, the strict sense of the form should be retained, if it can be done without injury to the sense, which is certainly the case here, as we have only to suppose that the writer suddenly but naturally changes his position from that of historical retrospection, to that of actual participation in the passing scene, and, as if he saw the victim led to the slaughter, says, " he will not open his mouth." There is no need, therefore of supposing with Hitzig that the ו, though separated from the verb, exerts a conversive influence upon it. The repetition of the same words at the end, so far from being even a rhetorical defect, is highly graphic and impressive. In the intermediate clause, we may either suppose an ellipsis of the relative, equally common in Hebrew and in English (like a lamb *which* is led), or suppose the preposition to be used as a conjunction (*as a lamb is led*), without effect upon the meaning of the sentence. The ו before the last clause is not the sign of the apodosis, nor need it be translated *so*, the form adopted in the Septuagint version (οὕτως οὐκ ἀνοίγει τὸ στόμα), for the purpose of shewing that the words refer to the subject of the first clause, and not to the sheep or lamb, as Luther and Gesenius assume, in violation of the syntax (רָחֵל being feminine) and the poetical structure of the sentence which depends materially on the repetition of the same words in the same sense and application as before. Besides those places where Christ is called the Lamb of God (*e. g.* John i. 29 ; 1 Peter i. 18, 19 ; Acts viii. 32, 35), there seems to be reference to this description of his meek endurance in 1 Peter ii. 23.—It might seem almost incredible, if it were not merely one out of a thousand such examples, that Vitringa formally propounds the question, *quando tonsus sit Christus Dominus?* and gravely answers when he was shorn of his prerogatives and rights by the Jewish Sanhedrim. As if there were no difference (or as if such a man as Vitringa could not see it), between saying he was silent and submissive like a sheep before its shearers, and saying he was silent and submissive before his shearers like a sheep.

8. *From distress and from judgment he was taken; and in his generation who will think, that he was cut off from the land of the living, for the transgression of my people, (as) a curse for them?* Every clause of this verse has been made the subject of dispute among interpreters. The first question is, whether the particle at the beginning denotes the occasion or the cause,

as all agree that it does before שֶׁע in the last clause, or whether it is to be taken in its ordinary sense of *from*. This is connected with another question, viz. whether *taken* means delivered, or taken up, or taken away to execution, or taken out of life. It is also disputed whether עֹצֶר means imprisonment, or oppression and distress in general, and also whether מִשְׁפָּט means judicial process, sentence, or punishment. From the combination of these various explanations, have resulted several distinct interpretations of the whole clause. Thus the text of the English Version has, he was taken from prison and from judgment; the margin of the same, he was taken away by distress and judgment; Hengstenberg and others, he was taken (to execution) by an oppressive judgment. Most of the older writers understand these words as descriptive of his exaltation—from distress and judgment he was freed, or taken up to heaven. So Jerome and J. H. Michaelis. Gesenius, Rückert, and Umbreit also, understand it to mean that he was freed from his sufferings by death. To this interpretation Hengstenberg objects, that the account of the Messiah's exaltation begins in ver. 10, while the intervening verse still relates to the circumstances of his death; and also that the reference of לֻקָּח to a violent death is here determined by the parallel expression, "he was cut off from the land of the living." He might have added that even in Gen. v. 24, and 2 Kings ii. 9, 10, the word is used in reference to a singular departure from the ordinary course of nature. Luzzatto and Henderson give מִן the privative sense of *without*, and understand the clause to mean that he was taken off without restraint or authority. The same construction seems to have been anticipated by Zwingle, who pharaphrases the expression thus, *indictâ causâ citraque judicium.*—In the next clause, the interpretation turns upon the question whether דּוֹר means life, dwelling, posterity, or contemporaries, and the verb to think or speak. Luther, Calvin, and Vitringa understand the clause to mean, who can declare the length of his life hereafter? Kimchi and Hengstenberg explain it to mean, who can declare his posterity or spiritual seed? To this it is objected that the verb requires a connective particle before its object, and that Christ is not called the father, but the brother of his people, and that דּוֹר has this sense only in the plural. Clericus supposes it to mean, who can worthily describe his course of life? But this sense of דּוֹר is not sustained by usage. Rosenmüller, Gesenius, and others follow Storr in making אֶת־דּוֹרוֹ an absolute nominative—as to his generation (*i. e.* his contemporaries), who considered it, or cared for it? To this construction Hengstenberg objects that אֶת seldom if ever denotes the subject of the verb, and also that יְשׂוֹחֵחַ is then left without an object. Neither of these objections lies against Ewald's modification of this same exposition, which makes אֶת a preposition, and continues the interrogation through the sentence—in (or among) his generation (*i. e.* his contemporaries), who considered that he was cut off from the land of the living? etc. Hoffmann's extravagant interpretation of the clause as meaning, who cares for his dwelling, *i. e.* where he is? deserves no refutation.—נִגְזַר, according to some writers, is employed in Ps. lxxxviii. 6, and Lam. iii. 54, in reference to a natural and quiet death; but Hengstenberg maintains that even there a violent departure is implied.—Paulus infers from the singular form עַמִּי, that Jehovah here begins to speak again; but Hengstenberg explains it as equivalent to *us*, and a similar use of the singular form by a plurality of speakers is exemplified in 1 Sam. v. 10, Zech. viii. 21.—Of the last words נֶגַע לָמוֹ there are several interpretations. Aben Ezra and Abarbenel, followed by Rosenmüller and Gesenius, apply them to the sufferer here described as meaning, he was smitten, and infer from the use of the plural suffix that the subject of the chapter is collective. Others adopt the same sense and application of the words, but deny the inference, upon the ground that מוֹ, though properly a plural suffix, is not unfrequently used for a singular, as the very same form is in Ethiopic. This ground is also maintained by Ewald in his Grammar. Hengstenberg admits that the pronoun is here plural, but refers it to the people, and supplies a relative—for the transgression of my people who were smitten, literally to whom there was a stroke or punishment, *i. e.* due or appointed. Ewald, without supposing an ellipsis, renders it, a stroke for them, *i. e.* smitten in their place and for their benefit. Cocceius gives the same sense to the words, but applies them very differently as a description of the people, *plaga ipsis adhaeret, i. e. impuri sunt.* (See the use of נֶגַע in Exod. xi. 1.)—According to Hendewerk, *the land of the living* is the Holy Land, and the verse is descriptive of the Babylonish exile. "By a divine judgment was the people taken away, and yet who can declare its future increase? It was cut off from its own land, for the transgression of the fathers were the children smitten." It is not surprising that the writer who invented this interpretation should sneer at the Messianic exposition as extravagant and groundless. The reading לְמוֹת, which appears to be implied in the Septuagint Version, and is adopted by Houbigant and Lowth, is wholly without critical authority, or intrinsic worth to recommend it.

9. *And he gave with wicked* (men) *his grave, and with a rich* (man) *in his death; because* (or *although*) *he had done no violence, and no deceit* (was) *in his mouth.* The second member of the first clause is thus translated by Martini: *tumulum sepulchralem cum violentis;* which suppposes בָּמֹתָיו to be the plural of בָּמָה, a height or high place, here put for a monumental mound or hillock. The same interpretation is approved by Kennicott and Jubb. But as the plural בָּמוֹת retains its first vowel when followed by a suffix or another noun (Deut. xxxii. 29, Micah iii. 12), Ewald adopts the pointing בְּמוֹתָיו, which is found in three manuscripts; but it still remains impossible to prove from usage any such meaning of בָּמָה. Thenius goes further, and reads בּוֹרוֹתָיו. And all this for the sake of a more perfect parallelism, although the common text affords a perfectly good sense, viz. in his death, *i. e.* after it, as in Lev. xi. 31, 1 Kings xii. 31, Esther ii. 7, and the only difficulty is the one presented by the plural form, which is surely not so serious as to require its removal by an arbitrary change of text. It is not even necessary to explain it with Jarchi as denoting all kinds of death, or with Abarbenel as implying a collective, not an individual subject. It is much more natural to assume, with Hitzig, that the suffix is assimilated to the apparent plural termination וֹת, or that it is simply a case of poetic variation, as in Ezek. xxviii. 8, 10.—Rosenmüller's version is, he gave himself up to the wicked to be buried, or he left his burial to the wicked. But besides the forced construction here assumed, this explanation leaves בְּמוֹתָיו unexplained, and does not agree with what is afterwards asserted, that he did no wrong, &c.—Rabbi Jonah, as quoted in the Michlal Jophi, explains עָשִׁיר to mean a wicked man; and this explanation is adopted by Luther, Calvin, and Gesenius, who regard the word as suggesting the accessory idea of one who sets his heart upon his wealth, or puts his trust in it, or makes an unlawful use of it. This is so arbitrary, that Martini and some later writers abandon the Hebrew usage altogether, and derive the sense of wicked from the Arabic root عثر.

But this is doubly untenable; first, because the Hebrew usage cannot be postponed to the Arabic analogy without extreme necessity, which does not here exist; and secondly, because the best authorities exhibit no such meaning of the Arabic word itself. Ewald, aware of this, and yet determined to obtain the same sense, effects his purpose with his usual boldness, by changing עָשִׁיר into עָשִׁיק—a convenient word invented for the purpose. Beck, with scarcely less violence, explains it as an orthographical variation of עָרִיץ (chap. xlix. 25). It may appear surprising that this forced imposition of a new and foreign meaning on a word so familiar should be thus insisted on. Luther and Calvin no doubt simply followed the rabbinical tradition; but the later writers have a deeper motive for pursuing a course which in other circumstances they would boldly charge upon the great Reformers' ignorance of Hebrew. That motive is the wish to do away with the remarkable ·coincidence between the circumstances of our Saviour's burial and the language of this verse, as it has commonly been understood since Cappellus. This interpretation, as ·expressed by Hengstenberg, makes the verse mean that they appointed him his grave with the wicked, but that in his death he really reposed with ·a rich man, viz. Joseph of Arimathea, who is expressly so called, Mat. xxvii. 57. The indefinite construction of the verb, and the sense thus put upon it, are in perfect accordance with usage. (See *e. g.* Ps. lxxii. 15, Eccles. ii. 21, Gen. xv. 18, Isa. lv. 4, Jer. i. 4.) Even Aben Ezra explains *gave* by adding, *i.e.* in intention. It is also possible to make עַמִּי the subject of the verb, but wholly unnecessary. Some refer it to Jehovah, and suppose the sense to be that he appeared to assign him his grave with the wicked. Malefactors were either left unburied, or disgraced by a promiscuous interment in an unclean place; a usage explicitly asserted by Josephus and Maimonides. As the Messiah was to die like a criminal, he might have expected to be buried like one; and his exemption from this posthumous dishonour was occasioned by a special providential interference. To the different interpretations which have now been given of this first clause, may be ·added two as curiosities. The first is that of Jerome, who makes אֶת the sign of the accusative, and thus translates the whole: *dabit impios pro sepultura et divitem pro morte suo.* The other, that of Hoffmann, *they* (my people) *treated him* (my servant) *like a wealthy tyrant.*—עַל (for עַל אֲשֶׁר) is properly a causative particle, equivalent to *for that*, or *because*; but most interpreters regard it as equivalent to *although*, which is more agreeable to our idiom in this connection. Knobel observes, with great *naïveté*, that the reference of this verse to the burial of Christ has found its way into the exposition of the passage in connection with its general application to that subject; to which we may add, that it can only find its way out in connection with a wish to get rid of that unwelcome application. At the same time it must be observed, that even if עָשִׁיר be taken in the sense of wicked, although we lose the striking allusion to the burial of Christ in the sepulchre of Joseph, the verse is still applicable to his burial, as the last clause then means, like the first, that they appointed him his grave with malefactors. Clericus and Kennicott propose to transpose קברו and במותיו, because there seems to be an incongruity in saying that he made his grave with the wicked, and was with the rich in his death, when, according to the history, he died with the wicked, and was buried with the rich. But this apparent difficulty rests upon a false interpretation both of יִתֵּן and בְּמוֹתָיו. There is no need of following in detail the laborious attempt to reconcile this verse, even after some of its expressions have been wrested for the purpose, with the supposition that the subject of the prophecy is Israel in exile, and that the burial here spoken of is merely political and civil, as in chap. xxv. 8, xxvi. 19.

10. *And Jehovah was pleased to crush* (or *bruise*) *him, he put him to grief* (or *made him sick*) *; if* (or *when*) *his soul shall make an offering for sin, he shall see* (*his*) *seed, he shall prolong* (*his*) *days, and the pleasure of Jehovah in his hand shall prosper.* Here begins the account of the Messiah's exaltation. All the previous sufferings were to have an end in the erection of God's kingdom upon earth. As the first clause is in contrast with the last of ver. 9, it may be read, *and* (*yet*) *Jehovah was pleased, i. e.* notwithstanding the Messiah's perfect innocence. The sense is not, as Barnes expresses it, that *Jehovah was pleased with his being crushed*, which might imply that he was crushed by another, but that Jehovah was pleased himself to crush or bruise him, since the verb is not a passive but an active one. Luzzatto makes דַּכְּאוֹ an adjective used as a noun, his crushed or afflicted one, *contritus suus*. Hitzig makes הֶחֱלִי a noun with the article, *it pleased Jehovah that disease should crush him*. But most interpreters appear to be agreed that the first is the Piel infinitive of דָּכָא, and the last the Hiphil preterite of חָלָה, strictly meaning *he made sick*, but here used, like the cognate noun in vers. 3, 4, to denote distress or suffering in general. Martini and Gesenius make דַּכְּאוֹ the object of הֶחֱלִי, *it pleased Jehovah to make his wound sick, i. e.* to aggravate his wounds, or wound him sorely. This construction, although somewhat favoured by the analogy of Micah vi. 13 (compare Nahum iii. 19), does violence to both words, and is inconsistent with their collocation in the sentence. Jahn accounts for the future form of תָּשִׂים by supplying וַיֹּאמֶר, and regarding what follows as the words of Jehovah, who is afterwards spoken of, however, in the third person. But this is not unusual even in cases where Jehovah is undoubtedly the speaker. Hitzig and Hendewerk agree with De Dieu and other early writers in explaining תָּשִׂים as the second person, which is also given in the text of the English Version (*when thou shalt make*, &c.) ; but as Jehovah is nowhere else directly addressed in this whole context, the construction in the margin (*when his soul shall make*) is the one not commonly adopted. Hengstenberg, in his Christology, explains נַפְשׁוֹ as a mere periphrasis for הוּא ; but he may be considered as retracting this opinion in his Commentary on Ps. iii. 3, where he denies that the expression is ever so employed. Vitringa understands it here to signify that the oblation was a voluntary one. It seems more natural, however, to explain it as referring the oblation to the life itself which was really the thing offered ; just as the blood of Christ is said to cleanse from all sin (1 John i. 7), meaning that Christ cleanses by his blood, *i. e.* his expiatory death.—אָשָׁם primarily signifies a trespass or offence, and secondarily a trespass-offering. In the law of Moses it is technically used to designate a certain kind of sacrifice, nearly allied to the חַטָּאת or sin-offering, and yet very carefully distinguished from it, although archæologists have never yet been able to determine the precise distinction, and a learned modern rabbi, Samuel Luzzatto, expresses his conviction that they differed only in the mode of offering the blood. The word is here used not with specific reference to this kind of oblation, but as a generic term for expiatory sacrifice. The use of analogous expressions in the New Testament will be clear from a comparison of Rom. iii. 25, viii. 3, 2 Cor. v. 21, 1 John ii. 2, iv. 10, Heb. ix. 14. In the case last quoted, as in that before us, Christ is represented as offering himself to God.—

As the terms used to describe the atonement are borrowed from the ceremonial institutions of the old economy, so those employed in describing the
reward of the Messiah's sufferings are also drawn from theocratical associations. Hence the promise of long life and a numerous offspring, which, of
course, are applicable only in a figurative spiritual sense. The Septuagint
and Vulgate, followed by Lowth, connect the two successive members of
the clause as forming only one promise (*he shall see a seed which shall prolong their days*). The separate construction is not only simpler, but
requisite in order to express the full sense of the promise, which was
literally given and fulfilled to Job in both its parts (Job xlii. 16), and in
its spiritual sense is frequently applied to Christ (*e. g.* Heb. vii. 16, 25,
Rev. i. 18). The seed here mentioned is correctly identified by Hengstenberg and others with the mighty, whom he is described as sprinkling in
chap. lii. 15, and as spoiling in ver. 13 below, whom he is depicted in
ver. 11 as justifying, in ver. 5 as representing, in ver. 12 as interceding
for. They are called his seed, as they are elsewhere called the sons of
God (Gen. vi. 2), as the disciples of the prophets were called their sons
(1 Kings ii. 25), and as Christians are to this day in the East called the
offspring or family of the Messiah.—יַצְלִיחַ does not refer to past time,
as Martini explains it (*felicissime executus est*), but to the future, into
which the glorious reward of the Messiah is and must be considered as
extending.

11. *From the labour of his soul* (or *life*) *he shall see, he shall be satisfied;
by his knowledge shall my servant,* (*as*) *a righteous one, give righteousness to
many, and their iniquities he will bear.* In this verse Jehovah is again
directly introduced as speaking. The מִן at the beginning is explained by
Gesenius, Hitzig, and Maurer, as a particle of time, *after the labour of his
soul*, like the Latin *ab itinere*. Others explain it *from*, implying freedom
or deliverance. Knobel makes it mean *without*, which yields the same
sense. Most interpreters follow the Vulgate in making it denote the
efficient or procuring cause : *Pro eo quod laboravit anima ejus*. The English Version makes it partitive; but this detracts from the force of the
expression, and implies that he should only see a portion of the fruit of
his labours. The allusion to the pains of parturition, which some English
writers find here, has no foundation in the Hebrew text, but only in the
ambiguity of the common version, which here employs the old word *travail*, not in its specific but its general sense of toil or labour. The
Hebrew word includes the ideas of exertion and of suffering as its consequence. J. D. Michaelis understands the clause as meaning, " from his
labour he shall joyfully look up ;" but there is no sufficient authority for
this interpretation of the verb, which simply means *to see*, and must be
construed with an object either expressed or understood. This object is
supposed by Kimchi to be *good* in general (יראה טוב וישבע בו); by Jerome,
seed, as in the foregoing verse; by Hengstenberg, the whole blessing there
promised. Abarbenel supposes the two parts of that promise to be specially
referred to, " he shall see his seed, he shall be satisfied with days," a
common Scriptural expression. (Gen. xxv. 8, xxxv. 29.)—שָׂבַע means to
be satisfied not in the sense of being contented, but in that of being
filled or abundantly supplied. It is applied to spiritual, no less than
to temporal enjoyments. (Ps. xvii. 15, cxxiii. 3, Jer. xxxi. 14.) Clericus
and Hengstenberg suppose an allusion to the processes of agriculture, and
the abundant produce of the earth. Some interpreters regard this as a
case of hendiadys, in which the one word simply qualifies the other ; he

shall see he shall be satisfied, *i. e.* he shall abundantly see, or see to his heart's content. Maurer adopts this construction, and moreover connects בְּדַעְתּוֹ with what goes before, and gives יִרְאֶה the sense of seeing with delight : *mirifice lœtabitur sapientiâ suâ.* Martini has the same construction, but explains דַּעְתּוֹ to mean the knowledge of God, *i. e.* piety or true religion. But as Jehovah is himself the speaker, Jahn refers the suffix to Messiah, and gives the phrase a passive sense, " he shall be satiated with the knowledge of himself," *i. e.* abundantly enjoy the happiness of being recognised by others as their highest benefactor. But this is neither a natural construction nor consistent with the accents. The explanation of דַּעַת, as meaning *doctrine*, is entirely without foundation in usage. The only satisfactory construction is the passive one, which makes the phrase mean, *by the knowledge of him* upon the part of others ; and this is determined by the whole connection to mean practical experimental knowledge, involving faith and a self-appropriation of the Messiah's righteousness, the effect of which is then expressed in the following words.—Gesenius gives הַצְּדִיק the sense of converting to the true religion, or *turning to righteousness*, as in Dan. xii. 3. But that justification in the strict forensic sense is meant, may be argued from the entire context, in which the Messiah appears not as a Prophet or a Teacher, but a Priest and a Sacrifice, and also from the parallel expression in this very verse, *and their iniquities he will bear.* The construction with לְ, Cocceius, Hengstenberg, and Maurer explain, by giving to the verb the sense of bestowing or imparting righteousness, in which way other active verbs are construed elsewhere. (See for example, chap. xiv. 3, Gen. xlv. 7, 2 Sam. iii. 30.) Another solution of the syntax is afforded by taking לְ in its strict sense as denoting general relation, and the verb as meaning to perform the act of justification, not in the general, but in reference to certain objects—he shall be a justifier with respect to many. In the next clause Lowth omits צַדִּיק because it stands before the substantive, which he pronounces an absurd solecism. Gesenius supposes the adjective to be prefixed, because it is peculiarly emphatic. Hengstenberg goes further and supposes it to be used as a noun, *the righteous one, my servant.* But as this would seem to require the article, it is perhaps better to explain צַדִּיק with Ewald, *as a righteous person* (*als Gerechter*) which idea Maurer thus expresses paraphrastically, *for my servant is righteous.* Martini's explanation of the clause as meaning, *the Saviour my servant shall save many*, has met with little favour, even among those who adopt an analogous explanation of צֶדֶק and צְדָקָה elsewhere. According to Beck the sense of the whole clause is, " by his knowledge of God he shall justify himself, or shew himself righteous ; righteous is my servant for many, *i. e.* for their benefit."—All mistake and doubt as to the nature of the justification here intended, or of the healing mentioned in ver. 6, or of the cleansing mentioned in chap. lii. 15, is precluded by the addition of the words, *and he shall bear their iniquities.* The introduction of the pronoun makes a virtual antithesis, suggesting the idea of exchange or mutual substitution. *They* shall receive his righteousness, and *he* shall bear their burdens. One part of the doctrine taught is well expressed by Jerome : *et iniquitates eorum ipse portabit, quas illi portare non poterant, et quorum pondere opprimebantur.* The whole is admirably paraphrased by Calvin : *Christus justificat homines dando ipsis justitiam suam, et vicissim in se suscipit peccata ipsorum, ut ea expiet.*—The preterite sense given to יִסְבֹּל by Martini and others is entirely arbitrary and rejected by the later

Germans as forbidden by the futures which precede and follow, all referring
to the state of exaltation. Gesenius, however, though he makes the expression future, extenuates it by explaining it to mean that he shall make
their burden lighter by his doctrine, and by promoting their moral improvement. But this is at once inconsistent with the context, and with his own
interpretation of the fourth verse, where he understands the similar expressions as referring to vicarious atonement, while Hitzig is guilty of the
same inconsistency, but in a reversed order, making this verse teach the
doctrine and the other not.—In order to do justice to the theories which
represent this passage as a prophecy of the return from exile, it should
here be mentioned that Maurer understands this verse as meaning that the
pious Jews should not refuse to share the punishment incurred by their
ungodly brethren, and Luzzatto that they should endure with patience the
maltreatment and misconduct of the world around them. As for Hendewerk, he boldly denies that יַצְדִּיק is used in a forensic sense, or that יִסְבֹּל
means *to bear* in any other sense than that of the Latin phrase *tollere
morbum* or *dolores*. Knobel sums up his exposition of the verse by saying
that the *many* are without doubt the heathen who should be converted,
and to whom the Jews sustained the same relation as a prophet or a priest
to laymen.

12. *Therefore will I divide to him among the many, and with the strong
shall he divide the spoil, in lieu of this that he bared unto death his soul, and
with the transgressors was numbered, and he (himself) bare the sin of many,
and for the transgressors he shall make intercession.* The Septuagint and
Vulgate make the *many* and the *strong* the very spoil to be divided (κληρο-
νομήσει πολλούς, *dispertiam ei plurimos*). The same construction is retained
by Lowth, Martini, Rosenmüller, Hengstenberg, and others. It would
scarcely be natural, however, even if both adjectives were preceded by the
ambiguous particle אֵת, much less when the first has בְּ before it, which
occurs nowhere else as a connective of this verb with its object. It is
better, therefore, to adopt the usual construction, sanctioned by Calvin,
Gesenius, and Ewald, which supposes him to be described as equal to the
greatest conquerors. If this is not enough, or if the sense is frigid, as
Martini alleges, it is not the fault of the interpreter, who has no right to
strengthen the expressions of his author by means of forced constructions.
The simple meaning of the first clause is that he shall be triumphant, not
that others shall be sharers in his victory, but that he shall be as gloriously
successful in his enterprise as other victors ever were in theirs. Indeed
the same sense may be thus obtained, for which the writers above mentioned have departed from the obvious construction, if, instead of making
בְּ and אֵת denote comparison, we understand them to denote locality, and
to describe him as obtaining spoil not *with* but *among* the many and the
strong, and thus securing as the fruits of victory not only their possessions,
but themselves.—Hengstenberg gives רַבִּים the sense of *mighty*, simply
because that idea is expressed by the parallel term ; which rather proves
the contrary, as a synonymous parallelism would in this case be enfeebling,
and the very same word is admitted to mean *many* by Hengstenberg himself in the last clause.—Abarbenel's objection that Christ never waged war
or divided spoil, has been eagerly caught up and repeated by the rationalistic school of critics. But Hengstenberg has clearly shewn that spiritual
triumphs must be here intended, because no others could be represented as
the fruit of voluntary humiliation and vicarious suffering, and because the
same thing is described in the context as a sprinkling of the nations, as a

bearing of their guilt, and as their justification. The *many* and the *strong* of
this verse are the nations and the kings of chap. lii. 15, the spiritual seed
of vers. 8 and 10 above. (Compare chap. xi. 10, and Ps. ii. 8.)—The
last clause recapitulates the claims of the Messiah to this glorious reward.
הֶעֱרָה is commonly explained to mean *poured out*, with an allusion to the
shedding of blood considered as the vehicle of life. (Gen. ix. 4, Lev. xvii.
11.) Beck even goes so far as to say that the writer looks upon the soul
itself as a material fluid running in the blood. Not only is this inference
a forced one, but the premises from which it is deduced are doubtful; for
it seems more accordant with the usage of the verb, and at the same time
to afford a better sense, if we explain it to mean *made bare* or exposed to
death. The assertion that לַמוּת would then be superfluous is refuted by
the analogy of Judges v. 18.—The reflexive sense which Hengstenberg and
others give to נִמְנָה (numbered himself, or suffered himself to be numbered),
though not absolutely necessary, is strongly recommended by the context,
and the obvious consideration that his being numbered passively among
them was not such a claim to subsequent reward, as a voluntary acquiescence in their estimation.—The application of this clause to our Saviour's
crucifixion between thieves (Mark xv. 28) is justly said by Hengstenberg
not to exhaust the whole sense of the prophecy.—It rather points out
one of those remarkable coincidences which were brought about by Providence, between the prophecies and the circumstances of our Saviour's
passion.—יַפְגִּיעַ does not mean *he fell among sinners*, *i. e.* he was reckoned
one of them (Maurer), but, as in Jer. xxxvi. 25, denotes intercession, not
in the restricted sense of prayer for others, but in the wider one of meritorious and prevailing intervention, which is ascribed to Christ in the New
Testament, not as a work already finished, like that of atonement, but as
one still going on (Rom. viii. 34, Heb. ix. 24, 1 John ii. 1), for which
cause the Prophet here employs the future form. There is no ground,
therefore, for explaining it as a descriptive present, or perverting it into a
preterite, nor even for transforming נָשָׂא to a future likewise, for the sake
of uniformity. Because the Prophet speaks of the atonement as already
past, and of the work of intercession as still future, it follows, not as some
imagine, that he meant to represent both as past or both as future, but on
the contrary that he has said precisely what he meant to say, provided that
we give his words their simple, obvious, and unforced meaning. The וְהוּא
does not mean *and yet, whereas*, or *although*, but is either designed to make
the pronoun emphatic (*he himself* or he on his part), or, as Hengstenberg
suggests, to shew that the last two members of the clause are not dependent on the תַּחַת אֲשֶׁר. This last phrase does not simply mean *because*, but
expresses more distinctly the idea of reward or compensation. The most
specious objection to the old interpretation of this verse, as teaching the
doctrine of vicarious atonement, is the one made by Luzzatto, who asserts
that נָשָׂא, when directly followed by a noun denoting sin, invariably means
to *forgive* or pardon it, except in Lev. x. 17, where it means to atone for
it, but never to bear the sins of others, which can only be expressed by
נָשָׂא בְ, as in Ezek. xviii. 19, 20. In proof of his general assertion, he
appeals to Gen. i. 17, Exod. x. 17, xxxii. 32, xxxiv. 7, Ps. xxxii. 5,
lxxxv. 3, Job vii. 21, in all which cases it must be admitted that the sense
which he alleges is the true one. It is no sufficient answer to this argument to say that the parallel expression (יִסְבֹּל עֲוֹנֹתָם) determines the meaning of the phrase in question; since all parallelisms are not synonymous,
and no parallelism can prove anything in opposition to a settled usage. But

although the parallel phrase cannot change or even ascertain the sense of this, it does itself undoubtedly express the idea which the objector seeks to banish from the text; since no one can pretend to say that סָבַל means to pardon, and it matters not on which side of the parallel the disputed doctrine is expressed, if it only be expressed at all. Little or nothing would be therefore gained by proving that נשא חטא only means to pardon. But this is very far from being proved by the induction which Luzzatto has exhibited, and by which he has unintentionally put a weapon into the hands of his opponents while attempting to disarm them. How can this learned and ingenious Jew account for the fact, which he himself asserts, that the idea of forgiveness is expressed in Hebrew by the verb נָשָׂא? The most plausible account which he could probably give is that נָשָׂא means to take away, and that to pardon is to take away sin. But let it be observed, in the first place, that the two ideas are by no means identical, and that to many, perhaps most minds, the phrase *to take away sin* suggests the idea, not of pardon properly so called, but of something preparatory to it; and what is this something but atonement? In the next place, the primary and proper meaning of נָשָׂא is not to *take away*, but to *take up*, or to take upon one's self; its most frequent secondary meaning is to *take about* or carry, and even in the cases where it means to *take away*, it means to take away by taking up and bearing: so that even if נשא חטא means to take away sin, it would necessarily suggest the idea of its being, in some sense, taken up and borne, as the means of its removal. In the third place, the only satisfactory solution of the question above stated is, that the usage, to which it relates, presupposes the doctrine, that the only way in which a holy God can take away sin is by bearing it : in other words, he can forgive it only by providing an atonement for it. This alone enables him to be supremely just, and yet a justifier, not of the innocent, but of the guilty. Thus the usage, which Luzzatto so triumphantly adduces to disprove the doctrine of atonement, is found, on deeper and more thorough scrutiny, itself to presuppose that very doctrine. But lastly, let it be observed that Luzzatto is compelled to grant that נָשָׂא may mean to bear the guilt of others as a substitute, but modestly asks us to believe that it has this sense only in one place (Ezek. xviii. 20), and even there only because followed by a בְּ; as if that construction, which is perpetually interchanged with the direct one, could have more effect in that case, than the context and parallelism in the one before us. The only other aberration which it will be necessary here to notice, is the strange opinion, broached by Ewald, with his characteristic confidence and abstinence from proof, that this whole passage, from the thirteenth verse of the preceding chapter, is the work of an older writer than the Great Unknown to whom he ascribes the other chapters, and whom he supposes to have thrust it into the midst of his own composition, without any reason why it should stand any where, and still less why it should stand just in this place; since, according to Ewald's own account, it has no direct connection either with what goes before or follows. The arguments by which he undertakes to justify this wild hypothesis are such as we have long since learned to rate at their true value, such as the use and repetition of expressions and ideas which occur nowhere else, together with the vague metaphorical assertion, that the atmosphere of this piece is entirely different from that of the other chapters, always excepting chap. lvi. 9 to lvii. 11, which (we may almost say, of course) is likewise an interpolation. It is strange that such an intellect as Ewald's should have failed to perceive that all this is an ill-disguised confession of his own incapacity to trace the true connection in a difficult portion of an ancient writing, and proceeds upon the principle, which even he would hardly venture to propound in terms, that it is better to expunge a passage from the text than to acknowledge its obscurity or leave it unexplained. If it be true, as he asserts, that this is the only way in which the existing controversy as to the fifty-third chapter can be settled, it had better not be settled at all. It is worthy of remark that neither Ewald's reasoning nor his authority appear to have made any converts to this neoteric doctrine. With respect to the frequent repetitions which he charges on the passage, it may be added in conclusion, that so far from being rhetorical defects or indications of another author, they are used with an obvious design, viz. that of making it impossible for any ingenuity or learning to eliminate the doctrine of vicarious atonement from this passage, by presenting it so often and in forms so varied and yet still the same, that he who succeèds in expelling it from one place is compelled to meet it in another, as we have already seen to be the case in the comparison of vers. 4 and 11, as interpreted by Hitzig and Gesenius. Whether the dreaded inconvenience is more barely met or more effectually remedied by making this incorrigible prophecy still older than the rest with which it stands connected, is a question which we leave to the decision of the reader.

Chapter 54

Instead of suffering from the loss of her national prerogatives, the church shall be more glorious and productive than before, ver. 1. Instead of being limited to a single nation, she shall be so extended as to take in all the nations of the earth, vers. 2, 3. What seemed at first to be her forlorn and desolate condition, shall be followed by a glorious change, ver. 4. He who seemed once to be the God of the Jews only, shall now be seen to be the God of the Gentiles also, ver. 5. The abrogation of the old economy was like the repudiation of a wife, but its effects will shew it to be rather a renewal of the conjugal relation, ver. 6. The momentary rejection shall be followed by an everlasting reconciliation, vers. 7, 8. The old economy, like Noah's flood, can never be repeated, ver. 9. That was a temporary institution ; this shall outlast the earth itself, ver. 10. The old Jerusalem shall be forgotten in the splendour of the new, vers. 11, 12. But this shall be a spiritual splendour, springing from a constant divine influence, ver. 13. Hence it shall also be a holy and a safe state, ver. 14. All the enemies of the church shall either be destroyed or received into her bosom, ver. 15. The warrior and his weapons are like God's creatures and at his disposal, ver. 16. In every contest, both of hand and tongue, the church shall be triumphant, not in her own right or her own strength, but in that of him who justifies, protects, and saves her, ver. 17.

1. *Shout, O barren, that did not bear ; break forth into a shout and cry aloud, she that did not writhe* (in childbirth): *for more* (are) *the children of the desolate than the children of the married* (woman), *saith Jehovah.* According to Grotius and some later writers, the object of address is the city of Jerusalem, in which no citizens were born during the exile, but which was afterwards to be more populous than the other cities of Judah which had not been reduced to such a state of desolation. Besides other difficulties which attend this explanation, it will be sufficient to observe that those who apply the first verse to the city of Jerusalem are under the necessity of afterwards

assuming that this object is exchanged for another, viz the people ; a conclusive reason for regarding this as the original object of address, especially as we have had abundant proof already that the Zion or Jerusalem of these Later Prophecies is the city only as a symbol of the Church or nation. Our idiom in the first clause would require *didst not bear* and *didst not writhe;* but Hebrew usage admits of the third person. Another Hebrew idiom is the expression of the same idea, first in a positive and then in a negative form, *barren that did not bear.* This very combination occurs more than once elsewhere. (Judges xiii. 2; Job xxiv. 21.)—For the sense of פָּצְחִי רִנָּה, see above, on chap. lii. 9; and for that of שׁוֹמֵמָה as opposed to בְּעוּלָה, compare 2 Sam. xiii. 20. The same antithesis here used occurs in 1 Sam. ii. 5.

2. *Widen the place of thy tent, and the curtains of thy dwellings let them stretch out; spare not* (or *hinder it not*); *lengthen thy cords• and strengthen* (or *make fast*) *thy stakes.* As in the parallel passage (chap. xlix. 20, 21), the promise of increase is now expressed by the figure of enlarged accommodations. The *place* may either be the area within the tent or the spot on which it is erected. The curtains are the tent-cloths stretched upon the poles to form the dwelling. מִשְׁכָּן, though strictly a generic term, is often used in reference to tents, and particularly to the tabernacle. Some take יַטּוּ as a neuter or reflexive verb, let them stretch out or extend themselves; but Kimchi construes it with *those who stretch*, and Ewald with an indefinite subject, *let them stretch.* That this verb was habitually used in this connection, may be learned from 2 Sam. xvi. 22. The *stakes* are the tent-pins, to which the tent-cloths are attached by cords. The last verb may either mean take stronger pins, or fix them more firmly in the ground; both implying an enlargement of the tent, and a consequently greater stress upon the cords and stakes.

3. *For right and left shalt thou break forth* (or *spread*), *and thy seed shall possess* (or *dispossess* or *inherit*) *nations, and repeople ruined* (or *forsaken*) *cities.* Kimchi understands *right* and *left* as geographical terms equivalent to. north and south, the east and west being represented by *nations* and *cities.* Knobel gives the same explanation of the first two, but accounts for the omission of the other two by saying that the sea was on the west, and on the east a wilderness. A far more natural interpretation of the words is that which take *right* and *left* as indefinite expressions meaning on both sides or in all directions. The verb פָּרַץ was peculiarly appropriate, because associated with the promise in Gen. xxviii. 14, in which case all the cardinal points of the compass are distinctly mentioned. יָרַשׁ is not simply to possess but to inherit, *i. e.* to possess by succession, which in this case implies the dispossession of the previous inhabitants, so that the version *drive out*, given by Gesenius and others, although not a literal translation, really expresses no idea not expressed in the original. The figurative meaning of the terms, as in many other cases, is evinced by an immediate change of figure, without any regard to mere rhetorical consistency. The same thing which is first represented as the violent expulsion of an enemy from his dominions, is immediately afterwards described as the restoration of deserted places, unless נְשַׁמּוֹת be supposed to mean *forsaken* by those just before expelled, which is hardly consistent with its usage as applied to desolations of long standing.—The whole verse is a beautiful description of the wonderful extension of the church, and her spiritual conquest of the nations.

4. *Fear not, for thou shalt not be ashamed ; and be not abashed, for thou shalt not blush ; for the shame of thy youth thou shalt forget, and the reproach*

of thy widowhood thou shalt not remember any more. Here, as in many other cases, shame includes the disappointment of the hopes, but with specific reference to previous misconduct. (See Job vi. 20.) The first clause declares that she has no cause for despondency, the second disposes of the causes which might seem to be suggested by her history. The essential meaning is, thy former experience of my displeasure. The figurative form of the expression is accommodated to the chosen metaphor of a wife forsaken and restored to her husband. The specific reference of *youth* to the Egyptian bondage, and of *widowhood* to the Babylonian exile, is extremely artificial, and forbidden by the context.

5. *For thy husband (is) thy Maker, Jehovah of hosts (is) his name; and thy Redeemer (is) the Holy One of Israel, the God of all the earth shall he be called.* This verse is marked by a peculiar regularity of structure, the two members of the first clause corresponding exactly to the similar members of the other. In each clause the first member points out the relation of Jehovah to his people, while the second proclaims one of his descriptive names. He is related to the church as her *Husband* and *Redeemer;* he is known or shall be known to all mankind as the *Lord of hosts* and as the *God of the whole earth,* which are not to be regarded as equivalent expressions. As the *Goel* of the Jewish institutions, the redeemer of a forfeited inheritance, was necessarily the next of kin, it is appropriately placed in opposition to the endearing name of husband; and as the title Lord of hosts imports a universal sovereignty, it is no less exactly matched with the God of the whole earth. But this last phrase expresses the idea of universal recognition.—There is no grammatical objection to the usual interpretation of the last word in the verse, as meaning *he is called,* corresponding to *his name is* in the other clause, and signifying, in the Hebrew idiom, *he is,* with emphasis. But since no reason can in that case be assigned for the use of יִקָּרֵא instead of נִקְרָא, and since the strict translation of the future strengthens the expression by transforming a description into a prophecy, it seems best to retain the English Version, *the God of the whole earth shall he be called, i. e.* he shall be recognised hereafter in the character which even now belongs to him. (Compare chap. xlv. 23, and Rom. xiv. 11.) The Targum and the Vulgate, Aben Ezra and Kimchi, take בְּעֲלַיִךְ in its primitive sense of *thy lords* or *rulers;* but this, though etymologically right, is less agreeable to usage, to the parallelism, the immediate context, and the analogy of other places where the conjugal relation is undoubtedly referred to. (See especially chap. lxii. 4, 5.) The form of this word and עֹשַׂיִךְ is regarded by Gesenius as an instance of the *pluralis majestaticus,* while Maurer makes the last a singular form peculiar to the לֹה derivatives, and supposes the other to be merely assimilated to it by a species of paronomasia.

6. *For as a wife forsaken and grieved in spirit has Jehovah called thee, and (as) a wife of youth, for she shall be rejected, said thy God.* Reduced to a prosaic form and order, this verse seems to mean, that Jehovah had espoused her in her youth, then cast her off for her iniquities, and now at last recalled her from her solitude and grief to be his wife again. (Compare Hosea, ii. 4, 7, 14, 16, 19.)—*A wife of youth,* not merely a young wife, but one married early. (See Proverbs v. 18, and Malachi ii. 14.) As this description belongs not to the main subject, but to the thing with which it is compared, there is no propriety in making *youth* mean a specific period in the history of Israel. The sense is not that she had been wedded to Jehovah in her youth and now recalled, but that he now recalled her as a

husband might recall the long rejected wife of his youth.—The common version of the last clause, *when thou wast refused*, is ungrammatical, unless we take תְּמָאֵס as a licence for תִּמָּאֵסִי like תִּכְרֹת in chap. lvii. 8, and such anomalies are not to be assumed much less to be multiplied without necessity. Most of the modern writers make it the third person, but retain the same construction : *who has been* (or *when she has been*) *rejected*. But this, besides being forced, would seem to require the praeter, not the future, which Hitzig sets down as an inaccuracy of the writer. Still more unnatural and arbitrary is Luzzatto's interrogative construction, " *Can the wife of one's youth be thus abhorred ?* Surely not." Ewald gains the same sense by making it an ironical exclamation : *and the wife of one's youth—* (as if it were possible) *that she could be treated with contempt !* All these expedients are precluded by the fact that we obtain a good sense by adhering to the proper meaning of the כִּי and of the future, simply making these the words of Jehovah at the time of her rejection, and referring אָמַר to the same time and to this clause alone, instead of making it include the whole verse, which is the less natural, because the first clause speaks of Jehovah in the first person. Thus understood, the last clause is an explanation of the first, in which she is said to have been recalled as a forsaken wife, and as a wife of youth, because her God had said to her at that time, thou shalt be rejected. This explanation, while it simplifies the syntax, leaves the meaning of the verse unaltered.—Henderson calls upon the reader to " mark the paronomasia in עֲזוּבָה and עֲצוּבָה." Gesenius goes further and attempts to copy it (*ein vertriebnes Weib betrübten Herzens*) ; while Hitzig, it may be for that very reason, doubts whether any paronomasia was designed at all.

7. *In a little moment I forsook thee, and in great mercies I will gather thee.* The metaphor is here carried out in the form of an affectionate assurance that the love now restored shall experience no further interruption. The use of the preterite and future implies an intermediate point of view between the opposite treatments here described. I did forsake thee, and now I am about to gather thee. Hitzig explains this last expression by the analogy of Judges xix. 15, where a cognate verb means to receive into one's house. So Lowth translates it, *I will receive thee again*, and Ewald in like manner. Umbreit still more expressly, *I draw thee to myself*. Knobel applies the term directly to the people, whose scattered members were to be collected. (See chap. xxvii. 12, xliii. 5.) According to Umbreit, the time of anger is called *little* in comparison with the provocation offered ; according to Knobel, in comparison with the favour that should follow, which agrees far better with the parallelism and the context. Hitzig, however, says that it is not the period of alienation which is here described as short, but the anger which occasioned it. A similar antithesis is used by David, Ps. xxx. 6. (Compare Isaiah xxvi. 20.) Instead of *great mercies*, Henderson has *with the greatest tenderness*.—If any specific application of the words be made, it must be to the momentary casting off of Israel which seemed to accompany the change of dispensations. The confusion of the metaphors in this whole passage springs from the complexity of the relations which they represent. As a nation, Israel was in fact cast off ; but as a church, it never could be.

8. *In a gush of wrath I hid my face a moment from thee, and in everlasting kindness I have had mercy on thee, saith thy Redeemer, Jehovah.* The idea of the preceding verse is again expressed more fully. The word שֶׁצֶף occurs only here. The older writers conjectured from the context that it

signified a short time or a little quantity. Rabbi Menahem is quoted by
Jarchi as explaining it to mean heat or fury, which is no doubt also merely
conjectural. Schultens explains it from an Arabic analogy as meaning
hardness or severity. Rosenmüller and Gesenius identify it with שֶׁטֶף, a
flood or inundation, which is elsewhere used in reference to anger (Prov.
vii. 24.) So in chap. xlii. 25, the wrath of God is said to have been *poured
out* upon Israel. According to Gesenius, it is here written שֶׁצֶף only for
the sake of the resemblance to קֶצֶף. This paronomasia is copied by Gesenius
(*in der Fluth der Zorngluth*), by Hitzig (*in derber Herbe*), and by Ewald
(*als der Groll war voll.*) We do not find that any of these writers make
the rapid recurrence of this figure in so short a space an argument to prove
that the passage was written by a different author. Ewald gives רִחַמְתִּי the
sense which it has in Kal, and renders it, *I love thee.* This is undoubtedly
implied, but the sense of *shewing mercy* is required not only by usage but
by the context, which describes the relenting of one previously offended.—
This verse, like the one before it, is a general description of the everlasting
favour which shall drown the very memory of former alienations between
God and his people. The modern German school of course restrict it to
the Babylonish exile. Cocceius extends it to the whole of the Old Testament economy, which although long to man was but a day in the divine
sight (Ps. xc. 4). Vitringa, not content with these gratuitous appropria-
tions of a general promise, or with this prosaic disfiguration of an exquisite
poetical conception, undertakes to give a different application to the two
verses, applying the little moment of ver. 7 to the Babylonish exile, and the
angry moment of ver. 8 to the Syrian persecution. With equal reason they
might be pronounced descriptive of the Egyptian and Assyrian bondage, or
of the Assyrian and the Babylonian, or of the Syrian and the Roman. If,
because it is appropriate to one of these events, it has no reference to any
other, then they all may be successively excluded, and with equal ease all
proved to be the subject of the prophecy. The only specific application
which is equally consistent with the form of the expression and the context,
is the one suggested in the note upon the foregoing verse.

9. *For the waters of Noah is this to me; what I sware from the waters of
Noah passing again over the earth* (*i. e.* against their passing, or, that they
should not pass), *so I have sworn from being angry* (that I will not be angry)
against thee, and from rebuking (that I will not rebuke) *thee.* The assurance
of the preceding verse is now repeated in another form. There can no more
be another such effusion of my wrath than there can be another deluge,
here called the *waters of Noah*, just as we familiarly say " Noah's flood."
The security in this case, as in that, is a divine oath or solemn covenant,
like that recorded Gen. viii. 21, and ix. 11. Vitringa, as usual, converts
a simile into a symbol, and endeavours to enumerate the points of similarity
between the world and the deluge, the church and the ark. It is only upon
this erroneous supposition that such passages as Ps. cxxiv. 4, 5, can be regarded as illustrative parallels. Such minute coincidences any reader is at
liberty to search out for himself; but the text mentions only one point of
comparison between the two events, namely, that neither can occur again.
The Prophet does not say that God's displeasure with the church is a flood
which shall never be repeated, but that it shall never be repeated any more
than the flood. When our Lord says it is easier for a camel to go through
the eye of a needle than a rich man to enter into heaven, no one thinks of
running a comparison between the rich man and the camel, or inquiring what
the hump or the double stomach signifies; because the text suggests not a

general analogy between the rich man and the camel, but a specific one confined to one particular. In the case before us, that particular, as we have
seen already, is the certainty that neither of the things compared can ever
be repeated. This certainly does not arise, as Ewald seems to think, from
any natural necessity, or universal law forbidding such expurgatory revolutions to occur more than once, but, as the text expressly tells us, from the
oath and covenant of God.—Instead of כִּי מֵי, one or two manuscripts have
כִּימֵי all in one word, meaning *as the days of* Noah, and Kimchi speaks of
this division as existing in some ancient codices of his day. This reading
likewise appears in all the ancient versions but the Septuagint, and is preferred by Lowth (*as in the days of Noah*). It is also a remarkable coincidence that this expression occurs twice in the New Testament (Mat. xxiv. 37,
1 Pet. iii. 20), but not in reference to this place or to the comparison here
instituted. All the latest writers seem to be in favour of adhering to the
common text, which is probably the only safe conclusion, although some of
the reasons which have been assigned are not of much weight. Henderson,
for instance, says that "the conjunction כִּי could not have been omitted,"
yet supposes two ellipses of the preposition כְּ in this one sentence, and in
this one clause of it. Another argument which some urge, namely, that
the words מֵי־נֹחַ are repeated afterwards, may be employed as well on
one side as the other. For it might be said, with some plausibility at
least, that such a repetition, not for the sake of parallelism, but in the same
part of the sentence, is unusual, and also that the presence of these two
words afterwards may easily have led to an error of transcription. The
true ground for adhering to the common text is the traditional authority of
almost every codex in exis ence, confirmed by that of the oldest version,
and by its yielding a perfectly good sense.—There is no need of supplying
any preposition before *waters*, as Gesenius does (*wie bey den Wassern
Noah's*); since the meaning is that this is the same thing as the flood, or
just such another case, in what respect is afterwards explained. The
closest copy of the original is Ewald's *Noah's Wasser ist mir dies*. The
plural *waters* is connected with the pronoun in the singular, simply because
it is used only in the plural. The pronoun *this* is explained by Jarchi to
mean *this oath*, by Kimchi *this captivity*, by Knobel *this effusion of my
wrath*, &c. The best construction is to take it in the widest sense, as
meaning *this case, this affair*, or the like. Hendewerk appears to be alone
in supplying the future tense of the verb (*this shall be*) instead of the present (*this is*). On the privative use of the preposition מִן, see chap. v. 6,
viii. 11, where it has respect to negative commands or prohibitions. *To
me* does not simply mean in my view or opinion, but expresses similarity
of obligation; the oath was as binding in the one case as the other.—Vitringa and Lowth make אֲשֶׁר a particle of time, *when I sware*. Gesenius and
the other modern writers take it as a particle of comparison, corresponding
to כְּמוֹ just as the full expression כַּאֲשֶׁר does in chap. xiv. 24, and as אֲשֶׁר
itself does in Jer. xxxiii. 22. Hendewerk understands it strictly as a relative, *of which I sware;* in which כְּמוֹ is not a parallel expression, but simply
continues the discourse. The same construction of אֲשֶׁר might be retained
without entirely destroying the antithesis, by rendering the former *what*. As
if he had said, "*what* I sware then, *that I swear* now," but the exact correspondence of the terms is impaired by changing *that* to *so*. It is a matter
of indifference whether the second verb be rendered *I have sworn* or *I
swear;* since even in the former case it means *I have now sworn*, as distinguished from the former swearing which he had just mentioned.—*Rebuke*

must here be taken in the strong and pregnant sense which it has in chaps. xvii. 13, l. 2, li. 20, and very generally throughout the Old Testament, as signifying not a merely verbal but a practical rebuke. There is no need, however, of departing from the literal translation with Gesenius, who translates it *curse*, and Hitzig, who translates it *punish*. Umbreit has *threaten*, which is nearer to the strict sense, but excludes the actual infliction, which is a necessary part of the idea.—That this is not a general promise of security, is plain from the fact that the church has always been subjected to vicissitudes and fluctuations. Nor is there any period in her history to which it can be properly applied in a specific sense, except the change of dispensations, which was made once for all, and can never be repeated. That the church shall never be again brought under the restrictive institutions of the ceremonial law, is neither a matter of course nor a matter of indifference, but a glorious promise altogether worthy of the solemn oath by which it is attested here.

10. *For the mountains shall move and the hills shall shake; but my favour from thee shall not move, and my covenant of peace shall not shake, saith thy pitier, Jehovah.* Vitringa's observation, that the futures in the first clause must not be so translated, because this would imply that hills and mountains might be moved, whereas they are here represented as immoveable, affords a curious illustration of the tendency among interpreters to substitute what they would have said, for what the writer has said. If the first clause does not literally mean that the mountains and the hills shall move, that idea cannot be expressed in Hebrew. This is indeed the customary method of expressing such comparisons. (See above, on chap. xl. 8, and xlix. 15.) The meaning is not that God's promise is as stable as the mountains, but that it is more so; they shall be removed, but it shall stand for ever. There is no need, therefore, of translating the verb *let them shake* or *they may shake*, as some of the latest writers do. Still more gratuitous is the present form given to the verbs by Gesenius, as if they expressed a thing of constant occurrence. Even Vitringa is compelled to admit that the mountains and hills in this place are not symbols of states and empires, but natural emblems of stability. (See Deut. xxxiii. 15; Ps. lxv. 7, cxxv. 1, 2.)—Gesenius supposes an allusion in *covenant of peace* to the covenant with Noah (Gen. ix. 8, 11). The phrase denotes a covenant, *i. e.* a divine promise or engagement, securing the enjoyment of peace, both in the strict sense, and in the wide one of prosperity or happiness. (Compare v. 13, chap. liii. 5; Ezek. xxxiv. 25, xxxvii. 26.) The suffix, as in many other cases, qualifies the whole phrase, not the last word merely. *The covenant of my peace* does not give the sense so fully as *my covenant of peace, i. e.* my peace-giving covenant, or as Rosenmüller phrases it, *meum pacificum fœdus.*—The participle in מְרַחֲמֵךְ is construed as a noun, and the whole phrase means *thy pitier.* The force of the expression is impaired by the circumlocution of the common version, *the Lord that hath mercy on thee,* still more by Lowth's diluted paraphrase, *Jehovah who beareth toward thee the most tender affection.*

11. *Wretched, storm-tossed, comfortless! Behold I am laying* (or *about to lay*) *thy stones in antimony, and I will found thee upon sapphires.* The past afflictions of God's people are contrasted with the glory which awaits them, and which is here represented by the image of a city built of precious stones, and cemented with the substance used by oriental women in the staining of their eyelids. (2 Kings ix. 30, Jer, iv. 30.) This eye-paint, made of stibium or antimony, may be joined with sapphires as a costly

substance, commonly applied to a more delicate use ; or there may be
allusion, as Hitzig thinks, to the likeness between stones thus set and
painted eyes ; either of which suppositions is more probable than that of
Henderson, viz. that the idea meant to be conveyed is simply that of beauty
in general, for which a thousand more appropriate expressions might have
been employed. The stones meant are not corner or foundation-stones, but
all those used in building. There is something singular, though not perhaps significant, in the application to these stones of a verb elsewhere used
only in reference to animals. Knobel gravely observes that this verse can
hardly be considered as expressing a real expectation of the Prophet; as if
it were a literal description of a city built with gems instead of hewn stones,
and stibium instead of mortar. Kimchi indeed thinks it possible that all
this may be verified hereafter in the literal Jerusalem. Abarbenel more
reasonably looks for its fulfilment in a figurative or spiritual sense. Those
writers who insist upon applying the first verse of this chapter to the city as
a city, although not particularly named there, are compelled to understand
the one before us of the people, notwithstanding the minuteness and precision of the references to a city. If the city, as such, is not meant when
stones and cement, gates and walls, are mentioned, how much less when
none of these particulars appear, but everything suggests a different subject.—פּוּךְ‎ בַּ‎ is rendered by Jerome *per ordinem*, and in the Septuagint
ἄνθραξα, as if it were a kind of precious stone, as it appears to be in 1 Chron.
xxix. 2. But the modern lexicographers identify it with the Greek φῦκος
and the Latin *fucus, i. e.* face or eye-paint; and even in Chronicles it may
mean nothing more than ornamental stones. Ludolf supposes the clause
to mean that the stones should be powdered with antimony. Luzzatto likewise assumes a hypallage, and explains " I will lay thy stones in stibium"
to mean I will lay it on them. Henderson's version of סְעָרָה (*tossed*) is
insufficient, as both etymology and usage require a reference to storm or
tempest. Kimchi and Saadias apply it specifically to the exile, Jarchi to
the storms of sorrow in general. Rosenmüller explains it as a passive participle put for מְסֹעָרָה, Gesenius as the usual Kal participle of סָעַר. It is
agreed that נֶחָמָה is the contracted Pual participle for מְנֻחָמָה, like רֻחָמָה in
Hos. i. vi. 8.—Maurer notes this as an example of the peculiar sense in
which this writer used the verb נחם. (Compare chaps. xlix. 13, li. 3, 12,
lii. 9.) Knobel restricts the first clause to the siege of Jerusalem, especially by Nebuchadnezzar ! Ewald, very unnecessarily, proposes to amend
the text by reading in the last clause אֲדָנַיִךְ, *thy foundations*. If this be
the specific sense intended, which is doubtful, it is sufficiently conveyed
already by the common reading.

12. *And I will make thy battlements* (or *pinnacles*) *ruby, and thy gates to*
(*be*) *sparkling gems, and all thy border to* (*be*) *stones of pleasure* (or *delight*).
The splendid image of the preceding verse is here continued and completed.
The precise kinds of gems here meant are not of much importance. The
essential idea, as appears from the etymology of the names, is that of
sparkling brilliancy. The exact meaning of כַּדְכֹּד was unknown even in
Jerome's time. Aquila and Theodotion retain the Hebrew word, in which
they are followed by Cocceius. שמשות is explained by Aben Ezra and
Kimchi to mean windows, or other apertures admitting the light of the
sun. But the modern writers generally make it a poetical description of
the battlements and spires of a city.—The Septuagint and Vulgate explain
אַבְנֵי אֶקְדָּח as denoting carved or sculptured stones ; but its obvious connection with the verb קָדַח favours the modern explanation, sparkling gems.

—The last phrase is a more generic term, including all the others, and equivalent to our expression, precious stones. So, too, גְּבוּל may be collective, and denote the whole congeries of buildings or their parts; although interpreters are more inclined to make it mean the outer wall of a fortified city, which is described as built of the same costly materials. But Gesenius thinks it possible that there may be allusion to 1 Kings x. 27, and that the clause may represent the ground within the limits of the city as strewn with precious stones instead of pebbles.—The same interpreter regards the לְ in the last clause as a sign of the accusative, but Kimchi explains שַׂמְתִּי לְ as meaning, " I will change into or render." Hitzig thinks it would have been " *bequemer*," and Knobel " *passender*," if the writer, instead of saying that their gates should be *turned into* precious stones, had said they should be *made of* them.—Vitringa of course puts a specific sense on every part of the description, understanding by the פוּךְ of the preceding verse the doctrine of Christ's blood, by the gates the synods of the church, by the battlements its advocates and champions, &c. Lowth, with better taste and judgment, says that " these seem to be general images to express beauty, magnificence, purity, strength, and solidity, agreeably to the ideas of the Eastern nations, and to have never been intended to be strictly scrutinised or minutely and particularly explained, as if they had each of them some precise moral or spiritual meaning."

13. *And all thy children disciples of Jehovah, and great* (or *plentiful*) *the peace of thy children.* Ewald makes the sentence simply descriptive, by supplying *are* in the present tense. Most other writers supply *shall be*, and thus make it a prediction or a promise. בָּנִים, when used as a distinctive term, means *sons;* but it is constantly employed where we say *children.*—The common version, *taught of God*, which Lowth changes into *taught by God*, though not erroneous, is inadequate; since לִמּוּד is not a participle, but a noun, used elsewhere to denote a pupil, follower, or disciple. (See chap. viii. 16.) The promise is not one of occasional instruction, but of permanent connection with Jehovah as his followers, and partakers of his constant teaching. That the words are applicable to the highest teaching of which any rational being is susceptible, to wit, that of the Holy Spirit making known the Father and the Son, we have our Saviour's own authority for stating. (See John vi. 44, and compare Matt. xxiii. 8, Heb. viii. 11, 1 John ii. 27.) Paul, too, describes believers as θεοδίδακτοι in relation to the duties of their calling (1 Thess. iv. 9). Similar promises under the Old Testament are given in Jer. xxxi. 34 and elsewhere. Gesenius restricts the words to the promise of prophetic inspiration, the want of which is lamented in Lam. ii. 9, Ps. lxxiv. 9, and the renewal of it promised in Joel iii. 1. But this restriction is regarded as unauthorized even by Maurer. As in chap. xliii. 9, all the gifts of the Spirit are included. The consequence of this blessed privilege is peace, no doubt in the widest sense of spiritual welfare and prosperity. (John xiv. 27 ; Philip. iv. 7.) Knobel restricts the promise to the people of Jerusalem, and Hendewerk declares that it was broken in the days of Antiochus Epiphanes. To prevent the tautological recurrence of בָּנַיִךְ, Koppe reads בֹּנַיִךְ in the first clause, and Döderlein in the second, while J. D. Michaelis, for a different reason, makes the change in both. Köcher and Rosenmüller cite examples of such repetition from chaps. xvi. 7, lv. 4, and lv. 10, together with Virgil's famous line, *Ambo florentes ætatibus, Arcades ambo.* Such precedents were surely not required to justify a bold but beautiful expression from the charges brought against it by pedantic rhetoricians.—Umbreit supposes that this

verse contains an explanation of the striking figures in the one before it. Hitzig compares the first clause with the corresponding part of chap. lx. 21, *and thy people all of them are righteous*, which idea is expressed here in the next verse.

14. *In righteousness shalt thou be established : be far from oppression, for thou shalt not fear, and from destruction, for it shall not come near to thee.* An additional promise of complete security, made more emphatic by its repetition in a variety of forms. By *righteousness*, J. H. Michaelis understands the righteousness or faithfulness of God, securing the performance of his promises ; Vitringa, the justice of the government itself; Rosenmüller and the other modern writers, the practice of righteousness among the people. The first, however, comprehends the other as its necessary consequences, public and private virtue being always represented in Scripture as the fruit of divine influence. (Compare chaps. i. 27, ix. 6, xi. 5, xvi. 5.)—The modern grammarians acquiesce in Aben Ezra's explanation of תִּכּוֹנָ֑נִי as a Hithpael form like מִנֹּאָץ, chap. lii. 5.—Of the next clause there are several interpretations. The Septuagint, Peshito, and Vulgate, understand it as a warning or dissuasion from the practice of oppression. But this does not agree with the context, which is evidently meant to be consolatory and encouraging. Still more unnatural is the opinion of Cocceius, that עֹשֶׁק here means spiritual robbery, such as robbing God of his glory, the soul of its salvation, &c. &c. Jerome arbitrarily renders it *calumniam*. The explanation which has been most generally acquiesced in, is the one proposed by Kimchi, who takes עֹשֶׁק in a passive sense, *i. e.* as meaning the experience of oppression, and supposes the imperative to represent the future, or a promise to be clothed in the form of a command : " Be far from oppression, *i. e.* thou shalt be far from it." Examples of this idiom are supposed to occur in Gen. xlii. 18; Deut. xxxii. 50 ; Prov. xx. 13. But as this makes it necessary to give כִּי the sense of *yea* with Lowth, or of *therefore* with Vitringa, Gesenius and the later writers choose to adhere to the strict sense of the imperative, and give עֹשֶׁק in this one place the meaning of anxiety, distress, which they suppose to be the sense of עֹשְׁקָה in chap. xxxviii. 14. The ground of this gratuitous assumption is the parallel expression מְחִתָּה, consternation, fear, which seems to require in this place an analogous affection of the mind. It will be found, however, on investigation, that there are several instances in which מְחִתָּה cannot possibly mean *fear* (e. g. Ps. lxxxix. 41 ; Prov. x. 14, xiii. 3, xviii. 7) ; while in every place where it occurs, perhaps excepting Jer. xlviii. 39, the other sense *destruction* is entirely appropriate. On the soundest principles of lexicography, this meaning is entitled to the preference, and, if adopted here, forms an accurate parallelsim to עֹשֶׁק in the sense which it uniformly has elsewhere (e. g. in chaps. xxx. 12, and lix. 13), viz. oppression or violent injustice. That the other term is stronger, only adds to the expression the advantage of a climax. There is no need, however, of explaining the imperative as a future, like the older writers, or of taking כִּי in any but its usual and proper sense. *Be far from oppression* is not a promise of exemption from it, for that follows in the next clause, which the modern interpreters correctly understand as meaning, thou hast no cause to fear. The other words are well explained by Knobel as relating to the feelings of the person here addressed. Be far from oppression, *i. e.* far from apprehending it. The whole may then be paraphrased as follows : " When once established by the exercise of righteousness on my part and your own, you may put far off all dread of oppression, for you have no cause to fear it, and

of destruction, for it shall not come nigh you. With the promise of this clause, compare chaps. xxxii. 16, and lxii. 12.—Knobel and Hendewerk are actually able to persuade themselves that this verse contains a specific promise that Jerusalem should never be successfully besieged again. The truth of the promise, in its true sense, is vindicated by the fact that it relates to the course of the new dispensation as a whole, with special reference to its final consummation.

15. *Lo, they shall gather, they shall gather, not at my sign* (or *signal*). *Who has gathered against thee? He shall fall away to thee.* The promise of the preceding verse is here so modified as to provide for every possible contingency. If enemies should be assembled, it will not be by divine command (compare chap. x. 5, xlvii. 6), and they shall end by coming over to the side of those whom they assail. This, on the whole, appears to be the meaning, although every expression has received a different explanation. Gesenius gives הֵן the sense of *if*, as in Chaldee, and notes it as a proof of later date : to which it may be answered, first, that his own examples include some in the oldest books, *e. g.* Exod. viii. 22 ; then, that the assumption of this meaning in the present case is wholly gratuitous ; and lastly, that it is a dubious question whether any such usage of the word exists at all. Cocceius follows Jarchi in giving גּוּר the sense of *fear*, which it sometimes has, *e. g.* in Deut. i. 17, and Ps. xxii. 24. The Septuagint and Targum give it the still more frequent sense of "sojourning, dwelling as a stranger," and apply the clause to proselytes. In like manner Gousset, followed by Rosenmüller, understands the words to mean, that no one who sojourns with Israel shall remain a stranger to the true religion. Tremellius makes it mean "contend," and Ewald, "stir up bitterness," both apparently resorting to the cognate גָּרָה as a source of illustration. Most interpreters agree with Kimchi in giving גּוּר the same sense here as in Ps. lvi. 7, lix. 4 ; on which places see Hengstenberg's Commentary.—There is also a difference as to the construction. Luther makes the whole verse one interrogation. Gesenius, as we have already seen, makes the first clause conditional. Others translate it as a concession, "let them gather." But the simplest and most natural construction is to translate יָגוּר as a future proper. They shall indeed (or no doubt) gather. The promise is not that they should never be assailed, but that they should never be conquered.—The Targum explains אֶפֶס to mean *in the end*, but most interpreters understand it as a simple negative. (See above on chap. lii. 4.) מֵאוֹתִי is regarded by Gesenius as another proof of later date, the preposition את being confounded with the objective particle. But here, again, examples of the same analogy are found as early as Lev. xv. 18, 24, and Josh. xxiii. 15. It is not the occasional occurrence of this form, but its habitual use, that marks the later writers, as is well observed by Hävernick, who explains the case before us as an effect of the pause accent, while in the one below (chap. lix. 21) he maintains that אוֹת is the noun meaning *sign* (Einleitung, i. pp. 198, 222) ; which last explanation is still more applicable here, *not by my sign or signal* being not only perfectly in keeping with the usage of the same figure elsewhere, but yielding substantially the same sense which the word has according to the common explanation, namely, not by my authority, or, not at my command. (Compare מִמֶּנִּי, Hosea vii. 14.) Hitzig throws these words (אֶפֶס מֵאוֹתִי) into a parenthesis, "which is not from me," and Ewald gives them the force of a proviso, "only not from me," *i. e.* no attack shall be successful, provided it is made without my authority. The same writer

takes מִי in its usual sense as an interrogative pronoun, while Gesenius and others make it mean *whoever*. (See above on chap. 1. 10.) Vitringa and the English Version separate עָלַיִךְ from the following verb, and take the latter absolutely, " he shall fall," *i. e.* perish. Knobel obtains the same sense without a violation of the accents, by supposing נָפַל עַל to be synonymous with נָפַל לְפָנֶי, " he shall fall before thee.' But the former phrase is determined by a settled usage to denote the act of falling away, or deserting to an enemy. (See 1 Chron. xii. 19, 20 ; 2 Chron. xv. 9 ; Jer. xxi. 9.) In one case (1 Sam. xxix. 3), the same idea seems to be expressed by the verb when absolutely used. This explanation of the last words is as old as the Septuagint (ἐπὶ σὲ καταφεύξονται) and Vulgate (*adjungetur tibi*).

16. *Lo, I have created the smith, blowing into the fire of coal, and bringing out a weapon for his work ; and I have created the waster to destroy.* The general meaning evidently is, that God can certainly redeem his pledge, because all instruments and agents are alike at his disposal and under his control. He is not only the maker of the weapons of war, but the maker of their maker, as well as of the warrior who wields them.—The pronoun in both clauses is emphatic. It is I (and not another) who created them. —The common version of the second member, *that bloweth the coals in the fire*, is inconsistent with the Masoretic pointing and accentuation, which require אֵשׁ פֶּחָם to be construed *in regimine*, as meaning *a coal fire*, in opposition to an ordinary fire of wood. The same preposition is elsewhere used as a connective between this verb and the object blown upon or at (Ezek. xxxvii. 9), and in one other place at least in reference to the same act of blowing into fire (Ezek. xxii. 21), an exact description of the process even at the present day. A similar glimpse into the ancient forge or smithy has already been afforded in the scornful attack upon the worshippers of idols, chap. xli. 6.—*Bringing out* does not mean bringing out of his workshop or his hands, as Knobel explains it, but bringing into shape or into being, precisely as we say bringing forth, producing, although commonly in reference to animal or vegetable life. Perhaps, however, it would be still better to explain it as meaning out of the fire, in which case there would be a fine antithesis between blowing into it, and bringing the wrought iron out of it.—כְּלִי may denote any instrument, but here derives from the connection the specific sense of *weapon*. (See above, on chap. lii. 11.) The next phrase has been variously understood. Interpreters are much divided as to the antecedent of the suffix pronoun. Some of the older writers understand it as applying to the instrument itself, *bringing forth a weapon for its work*, *i. e.* fitted for the work of destruction. Others suppose it to refer by prolepsis to the warrior or destroyer who is mentioned in the last clause, *bringing forth a weapon for his work* or use. A still greater number understand it as referring to the smith or armourer himself. Besides the modern English versions, which are either unmeaning or inaccurate,—*according to his work* (Lowth), *by his labour* (Noyes), *as the result of his work* (Barnes), —this class includes the ingenious construction of the words by Ewald, *bringing forth a weapon as his own work, whereas I made the deadly weapon for destruction.* According to this interpretation, מַשְׁחִית *the destroyer* is a poetical description of the weapon before mentioned ; whereas most interpreters apply it to the warrior who wields it, as if he had said, I make the weapon of destruction, and I also make the waster to destroy with it. Both these hypotheses agree in making the destruction mentioned to be that of enemies in battle, one ascribing it directly to the weapon, and the other to

the combatant. But Gesenius follows Jarchi and Kimchi in supposing the destruction here meant to be that of the instruments themselves, as if he had said, I create the weapons of war, and I also create the destroyer to destroy them. Gesenius seems to think that this construction is required by the repetition of וְאָנֹכִי, as clearly indicating an antithesis; but this is equally secured by Ewald's version, and even in the common and more natural construction, the repeated pronoun has its proper emphasis. "It is I that create the smith who makes the instruments, and it is also I that create the destroyer who employs them."

17. *Every weapon (that) shall be formed against thee shall not prosper, and every tongue (that) shall rise with thee in judgment thou shalt condemn. This is the heritage of the servants of Jehovah, and their righteousness from me, saith Jehovah.* The common version of the first clause expresses the same thought in the English idiom, *no weapon that is formed against thee shall prosper*, a form of speech which does not exist in Hebrew, and can only be supplied by combining negative and universal terms. The expression, though ambiguous, is determined by the context. It cannot mean that only some of the weapons formed should take effect,—which might be the meaning of the phrase in English,—because in the affirmative clause which follows, and which must be co-extensive in its meaning, there is no such ambiguity, it being said expressly that every tongue shall be condemned. Another difference of idiom here exemplified has reference to the ellipsis of the relative pronoun, which in English is familiarly omitted when it is the object of the verb, but never when its subject. *Every weapon they form* would be perfectly intelligible; but *every weapon is formed* (for *which is formed*) would convey a wrong idea.—*Shall not prosper, i. e.* shall not take effect or accomplish its design. Vitringa needlessly supposes a litotes or meiosis, as if the words meant that the weapon should itself be destroyed; but this is not expressed, even if it is implied, which may be questioned.—To rise or stand in judgment, literally *for* or *with respect to judgment*, is to appear before a judgment-seat, to involve the decision of a judge. *With thee* may either denote simply simultaneous action, that of standing up together, or it may have the stronger sense *against thee*, as it seems to have above in ver. 15, and as it has in our expressions to *fight with* or to *go to law with*. The tongue is here personified, or used to represent the party litigant, whose only weapon is his speech. Lowth translates תַּרְשִׁיעַ *thou shalt obtain thy cause*, which is the true sense, but requires the insertion of *against* before *every tongue*, which in Hebrew is governed directly by the verb. For the judicial or forensic usage of this verb, see above, on chap. 1. 9.—Hitzig explains what is here said of litigation as a mere figure for war, which is literally described in the foregoing clause; and Knobel cites a case (1 Sam. xiv. 47) in which the verb הִרְשִׁיעַ is applied to conquest. It is also easy to deduce the one sense from the other, by assuming as the intermediate link the idea, not confined to ancient nations, that success in arms is a criterion of right and wrong, the very principle on which the wager of battle, and the ordeal of the duel rested. But in this case it is far more satisfactory and natural, instead of making one clause figurative and the other literal, to understand both either literally or figuratively as a comprehensive description of all controversy or contention. Kimchi supposes these two clauses to reduce all opposition and hostility to that of word and that of deed; but there may also be allusion to the obvious distinction between warfare in its military and its civil forms, or between what is properly

called war and litigation. In all these varied forms of strife it is predicted
that the church shall be victorious. (Compare Rom. viii. 37, and 2 Cor.
ii. 14.) And this security is represented as her heritage or lawful possession and as her right, *i.e.* what is due to her from God, as the judge of
the whole earth who must do right. Lowth and Ewald understand it to
mean *justification :* "this security shall prove that God acquits or justifies
me from the charges brought against me by my enemies." Vitringa gives
the Hebrew word the simple sense *jus,* or that to which the party is
entitled. The diluted sense of *blessing* or *prosperity,* which some of the
later writers prefer even here, no longer needs a refutation. The English
Version makes this last an independent clause, *their righteousness is of me;*
but this is wholly unnecessary, and affords a less appropriate sense than the
construction above given, which is the one now commonly adopted.—
According to Ewald, this verse is an explanation of the promise at the close
of chap. liii. Hendewerk goes further, and identifies the heritage of this
verse with the division of the spoil in that, and the collective *servants* here
named with the individual *servant* mentioned there. Knobel is still more
explicit, and asserts that the Prophet, having been disappointed in his
hope that all Israel would return from exile, now discards the use of the
word *servant,* and confines himself to that of the plural. The only colour
for this singular assertion is the fact, no doubt remarkable, that we read
no more of the "Servant of Jehovah" who has been so often introduced
before, but often of his "servants." It may no doubt be said in explanation of this fact, that the Prophet has completed his description of that
august person under his various characters and aspects, but has still much
to say of his followers or servants. But a full explanation is afforded only
by the hypothesis assumed throughout this exposition, that the Servant of
Jehovah is a name applied both to the Body and the Head, sometimes to
both in union, and sometimes, as in chap. liii. to one exclusively ; from which
it naturally follows that as soon as he has reached the final exaltation of
Messiah, and withdrawn him from our view, the Prophet thenceforth
ceases to personify his members, and applies to them the ordinary plural
designation of "Jehovah's servants."

Chapter 55

By the removal of the old restrictions, the church is, for the first time,
open to the whole world, as a source or medium of the richest spiritual
blessings, ver. 1. It is only here that real nourishment can be obtained,
ver. 2. Life is made sure by an oath and covenant, ver. 3. The Messiah
is a witness of the truth and a commander of the nations, ver. 4. As such
he will be recognised by many nations who before knew nothing of the
true religion, ver. 5. These are now addressed directly, and exhorted to
embrace the offered opportunity, ver. 6. To this there is every encouragement afforded in the divine mercy, ver. 7. The infinite disparity
between God and man should have the same effect, instead of hindering
it, vers. 8, 9. The commands and promises of God must be fulfilled,
vers. 10, 11. Nothing, therefore, can prevent a glorious change in the
condition of the world under the dispensation of the Spirit, ver. 12. This
blessed renovation, being directly promotive of God's glory, shall endure
for ever, ver. 13.

1. *Ho, every thirsty one, come ye to the waters ; and he to whom there is*

no money, come ye, buy (food) and eat ; and come, buy, without money and without price, wine and milk. The promises contained in the preceding chapters to the church, are now followed by a general invitation to partake of the blessings thus secured. Water, milk, and wine, are here combined to express the ideas of refreshment, nourishment, and exhilaration. Under these figures are included, as Calvin well observes, all things essential to the spiritual life. The Targum restricts the terms to intellectual supplies : " whoever will learn, let him come and learn." The same application is made by Aben Ezra and Kimchi, and Vitringa admits that the language is highly appropriate to the Gentiles who were seeking after wisdom (1 Cor. i. 22). But the benefits here offered must of course bear some proportion to the means by which they were secured, viz. the atoning death of the Messiah and the influences of his Spirit. Among the earlier writers, Grotius alone restricts the passage to the period of the Babylonish exile. Even the Rabbins understand it as relating to their present dispersion. Grotius's further limitation of the passage to the teachings of Jeremiah, as a rich supply offered to the heathen, is of course rejected by the modern Germans, not so much because of its absurdity as on account of its recognising Isaiah as the author. They adhere, however, to his Babylonian theory, and task their powers of invention to explain the general terms of this gracious invitation in accordance with it. Thus Hendewerk regards the chapter as an intimation to the exiles that they should be freed as soon as they were brought into a proper state of mind, together with a promise that when once restored they should obtain for nothing in their own land what they could not even buy for money in the land of their oppressors. In like manner Knobel understands the Prophet as declaring the conditions upon which the exile was to cease, and promising to those who should return the enjoyment of unparalleled abundance in the Holy Land. It is easy to perceive that this specific explanation of a passage in itself unlimited is far more easy than the unauthorized extension of one really specific, because in the former case there is nothing in the passage itself which can be urged against a limitation which is only false because it is gratuitous. The best refutation is afforded by the ease with which a thousand other limitations, once assumed, might be brought into seeming agreement with the terms of the prediction. If, for example, some new critic, still more intrepid than his predecessors, should maintain that this book is of later date than the Babylonian exile, having been written at the period of the Maccabees, or even in the days of Josephus, whatever difficulties might arise from definite allusions to anterior events in other places, it would require but little ingenuity to reconcile the foregone conclusion with the general terms of such a prophecy as that before us. The hypothesis once granted, the details would all seem to follow of course. The impartial interpreter is therefore bound to resist all such unauthorised restrictions, and to give the Prophet's words their full scope, as relating to the benefits which God proposed from the beginning to bestow upon the nations through the medium of his church. The mixed or half-way theory of Henderson, that this passage relates to the Babylonish exile and also to the reign of the Messiah, has all the inconveniences of both the others without the advantages of either.—Most of the modern writers follow Jarchi in explaining הוֹי as a mere particle of invitation, which is variously expressed by Luther (*wohlan !*), Gesenius (*auf*), De Wette (*ha !*), &c. Maurer insists, however, on the usual and strict sense of the particle as expressing pity for the exiles (*heu*, alas !), not only here

but in Zech. ii. 10, 11.—צָמֵא is not properly a participle (*thirsting*), but a
verbal adjective (*athirst* or *thirsty*).   Vitringa strangely makes it neuter
(*omne sitiens*), although the very nature of the invitation points out persons as
the object of address, and although this is the only form in which an address
to persons could have been expressed ; whereas, if a distinction were designed, the neuter would, according to the Hebrew idiom, be represented
by the feminine.   The combination of the singular (*every one*) with the
plural verb (*come ye*) may be either an idiomatic licence, or intended to
extend the call to every individual.—The reference to the water of baptism,
which some of the Fathers found in this verse, is excluded by the fact that
the water here meant is not water for washing, but water to be drunk.—
And he, after the universal expression *every one*, does not add a new idea,
but explains the one expressed already, and is therefore equivalent to *even
he* in English.   The same remark applies to the *and* before the second *come*,
which is not incorrectly rendered *yea come* in the common version.—*To
whom there is not money* is the only equivalent in Hebrew to our phrase *who
has no money*.   Instead of this generic term, Lowth retains the original
meaning of the Hebrew word, *silver*, in which he is followed by Ewald and
Umbreit.—שָׁבַר is not to buy in general, but to buy food, or still more
specifically to buy grain or bread stuffs.   It is here absolutely used, as in
Gen. xli. 57, xlii. 2, 5.   Henderson's paraphrase (*procure*) is too indefinite,
and not at all needed to remove the seeming incongruity of buying without
money or any other price.   This apparent contradiction was intended by
the writer to express in the strongest manner the gratuitous nature of the
purchase.   *Wine* and *milk* are combined, either as necessities or luxuries,
by Jacob in Gen. xlix. 12.—The images of this verse are essentially the
same with those in chaps. xii. 3, xxv. 6, lxii. 8, 9, lxv. 13 ; John iv. 14,
vii. 37 ; Rev. xxii. 17.—Sanctius, in order to connect this chapter with the
one before it, supposes the idea to be that of a feast provided in the habitation which is there described as having been enlarged.   Vitringa thinks it
better to call up the image of a market and a public fountain.   Neither of
these conceptions would spontaneously occur to any ordinary reader.

2. *Why will ye weigh money for* (that which is) *not bread, and your labour
for* (that which is) *not to satiety ?   Hearken, hearken unto me, and eat* (that
which is) *good, and your soul shall enjoy itself in fatness.*   The gratuitous
blessings offered by Messiah are contrasted with the costly and unprofitable labours of mankind to gain the same end in another way.   It was not
that they refused food, nor even that they were unwilling to buy it ; but
they mistook for it that which was not nourishing.   In the first clause, there
is reference to the primitive custom of weighing instead of counting money,
from which have arisen several of the most familiar denominations, such as
the Hebrew *shekel*, the Greek *talent*, the French *livre*, and the English
pound.   The essential idea here is that of paying.   Bread, as the staff of
life, is here and in many other cases put for food in general.—*Labour*, as
in chap. xlv. 14, means the product or result of labour.   It is well expressed
by Umbreit (*euer Ermühetes*).   Ewald's translation (*euer Erspartes*) rather
suggests the idea of that which is saved or hoarded, whereas the writer
seems to have in view the immediate expenditure of what is earned.—The
emphatic repetition of the verb *to hear* may be variously expressed in English as denoting to hear diligently, attentively, by all means, or to purpose ;
but the best translation, because it may be considered as including all the
rest, is that which copies most exactly the peculiar form of the original.
The old mode of doing this by joining the participle with the finite verb

(*hearkening ye shall hearken*) is at once less exact and less expressive than the simple repetition used by Ewald elsewhere, although here he introduces the word *rather (vielmehr hört).*—The mention of the soul admits of two explanations. We may give the Hebrew word its frequent sense of *appetite*, exactly as the appetite is said in common parlance to be gratified, indulged, pampered, mortified, &c. This is a good sense in itself, but less in keeping with the rest of the description than another which may be obtained by supposing that the soul is mentioned for the purpose of shewing that the hunger and the food referred to are not bodily but spiritual. Most of the modern writers explain אִכְלוּ as an imperative used for the future according to a common Hebrew idiom. (See chap. xlv. 22, and Gen. xlii. 18.) But there is no need of departing from the strict construction which makes אִכְלוּ a command. The promise is not that if they hearkened they should eat, but that if they hearkened and ate they should be happy.—*Good* is emphatic, meaning that which is truly good, in opposition to the *no-bread* of the first clause, which Vitringa and the later writers take as a peculiar compound phrase like לֹא־עֵץ (chap. x. 15), לֹא־אֵל and לֹא־רוּחַ (chap. xxxi. 3). *Fat*, by a figure common in all languages, is put for *richness* both of food and soil (See chap. v. 1 ; Ps. xxxvi. 9, lxiii. 6 ; Job xxxvi. 16.) There is something almost laughable in Rosenmüller's saying that the orientals are extremely fond of gross food, when the fact is notoriously otherwise, and such a charge has often been alleged against the Germans, either truly or falsely. Luther degrades the text itself by rendering it *shall grow fat.* As a sample of the opposite extreme of false refinement, we may give Lowth's paraphrase, *your soul shall feast itself with the richest delicacies.*—The application of the figures is self-evident upon the general hypothesis before assumed. Aben Ezra and Kimchi, who suppose the blessing offered to be purely intellectual, apply the first clause to foreign or exotic wisdom (כמות נכריה). But the hardest task devolves on those who understand the passage as relating exclusively to the deliverance of Israel from Babylon. In what sense could the exiles there be said to spend their money for what was not bread, and their labour for what did not satisfy ? Koppe was brave enough to make it refer literally to the bad bread which the Jews were compelled to eat in Babylonia. Hitzig only ventures to make this a part of the calamity described, which he explains, with Gesenius, as consisting in the slavery to which they were subjected, not as tributaries merely, but as labourers without reward. (Compare Josh. ix. 27 ; 1 Kings ix. 21.) Maurer refers the clause to the expensive worship of idols, from whom no favours were obtained in recompence. (See chap. xlvi. 6, 7.) Knobel sees merely a strong contrast between Babylon, where the Jews spent much without enjoyment or advantage, and the Holy Land, where they should enjoy much and spend nothing. The last might consistently regard as a mere visionary expectation ; but the only proof which he adduces of the fact first mentioned is the reference to Israel's oppression in chap. xiv. 3, xlvii. 6, li. 14. A comparison of these interpretations with the true one will shew how much is gained by the assumption of the Babylonian theory, and how strong the motive must be which induces men of ingenuity and learning to adopt it in spite of the embarrassments with which it is encumbered.

3. *Incline your ear and come unto me, hear and your soul shall live* (or *let it live, and I will make with you an everlasting covenant, the sure mercies of David.* This is obviously a repetition of the same offer in another form ; which shews that the two preceding verses cannot have respect to

literal food or bodily subsistence. Here again, the use of the word *soul*
necessarily suggests the thought of spiritual life, and this sense is admitted
here by Kimchi and Abarbenel. Neither of the animal life, nor of the appetite, could it be said that it should live. The abbreviated form תְּחִי may
either give the future an imperative sense, or be taken as a poetical substitute
for the full form of the future proper. The regular construction of כָּרַת בְּרִית
is with עַם. That with לְ, according to Vitringa, simply means a promise;
according to Gesenius, an engagement on the part of a superior. (See
chap. lxi. 8, Josh. ix. 15, xxiv. 25.) There is no need of assuming a
zeugma in the last clause, with Gesenius, or supposing כָּרַת to include the
idea of bestowing, with Knobel; since the *mercies of David* are not directly
governed by that verb, but simply added as an explanation of the *everlasting
covenant.* As if he had said, I will make with you an everlasting covenant,
which shall be the same with the mercies of David. Of this phrase, which
is also used by Solomon (2 Chron. vi. 42), there are three interpretations.
The rabbins and Grotius understand it to mean favours, like those which
were enjoyed by David. Cocceius regards David as a name of the Messiah, as in Ezek. xxxiv. 23, 24, to which he adds Hos. iii. 5; but this
may be understood, with Hitzig, as merely meaning David's house or
family. The third explanation, and the one most commonly adopted, is,
that the *mercies of David* means the mercies promised to him, with particular reference to 2 Sam. vii. 8–16. (Compare 1 Chron. xvii. 11, 12, and
Ps. lxxxix. 3, 4.) As the main theme of this promise was a perpetual
succession on the throne of David, it was fulfilled in Christ, to whom it is
applied in Acts xiii. 34. (Compare Isa. ix. 6, and Luke i. 32, 33.) The
Greek word ὅσια there used is borrowed from the Septuagint Version, and
is so far correct, as it conveys the idea of a sacred and inviolable engagement. That the promise to David was distinct from that respecting Solomon (1 Chron. xxii. 8–13), and had not reference to any immediate descendant, Henderson has shewn from 1 Chron. xvii. 12–14. Thus understood, the text contains a solemn assurance that the promise made to David
should be faithfully performed in its original import and intent. Hence
the mercies of David are called *sure, i.e.* sure to be accomplished; or it
might be rendered faithful, credible, or trusted, without any material effect
upon the meaning. With this interpretation of the verse may be compared
that of Knobel, who explains it as a promise that the theocratic covenant
should be restored (as if it had been abrogated), or of Rosenmüller, who supposes it to have been given to console the exiles under the despondency arising
from the ruin of the House of David during the captivity, and the apparent
violation of the promise which had long before been given to himself. So
far as there is any truth in this interpretation, it is but a small part of the
full sense of the passage as relating to the everlasting reign of the Messiah.

4. *Lo, (as) a witness of nations I have given him, a chief and commander
of nations.* The emphasis appears to be on *nations*, which is therefore
repeated without change of form. The essential meaning is the same as
that of chap. xlix. 6, viz., that the Messiah was sent to be the Saviour not
of the Jews only, but also of the Gentiles. His relation to the latter is
expressed by three terms. First he is a witness, *i.e.* a witness to the
truth (John xviii. 37), and a witness against sinners (Mal. iii. 5). The
same office is ascribed to Christ in Rev. i. 5, iii. 14. (Compare
1 Tim. vi. 13.) The application of this verse to the Messiah, therefore, is
entirely natural if taken by itself. But an objection is presented by the
fact that the Messiah is not named in the foregoing context. It is hardly

an adequate solution to affirm with Vitringa that the verse must be connected with the fifty-third chapter, and the fifty-fourth considered parenthetical. Cocceius refers the suffixes to David in ver. 3, which he explains
there as a name of the Messiah. The same resort is not accessible to
Henderson, who arbitrarily makes David in the third verse mean the ancient
king, and in the fourth the Messiah; an expedient which may be employed
to conquer any difficulty. All the modern Germans except Umbreit understand the verse before us as describing the honours actually put upon king
David. *Lo, I gave him as a witness of the nations, a leader and commander
of the nations.* This is certainly the simplest and most natural construction
of the sentence, but not one without its difficulties. According to general
analogy, the interjection הֵן has reference not to a past event, but to one
either present or future. This argument from usage is confirmed by the
fact that הֵן at the beginning of the next verse does undoubtedly relate to
the future, and that the connection of the verses is obscure and abrupt if
that before us be referred to David. Another difficulty is, that David
could not with truth be so emphatically styled the chief or leader of the
nations. For although he did subdue some foreign tribes, they did not
constitute the main part of his kingdom, and the character in which the
Scriptures always represent him is that of a theocratic king of Israel.
Another difficulty in relation to the use of the term *witness* is evaded by
supposing עֵד, in this one place to mean a ruler (Gesenius) or a legislator
(Maurer). Ewald's translation of the word by *law* seems to be an inadvertence. This violation of a perfectly defined and settled usage would be
treated by these writers in an adversary as a proof of ignorance or *mala
fides.* The only shadow of evidence which they adduce from usage or
analogy, is the assertion, equally unfounded, that the verbal root sometimes
means to enjoin, and the collateral derivatives עֵרוּת and עֵדָה mean laws or
precepts. The utmost that can be established by a philological induction
is, that in some cases the alleged sense would be relevant, whereas the
proper one of testimony is in every case admissible. If in the face of these
facts we may still invent a new sense for a word which has enough already
to account for every instance in the Hebrew Bible, there are no such things
as principles or laws of lexicography, and every critic has a full discretion
to confound the application of a term with its essential meaning when he
pleases. As to its being here combined with other words expressive of
authority, let it be noted that words thus connected cannot alway be synonymous, and in the next place that the usual meaning of the term, as
applied to the Messiah or to God, implies as much authority as either of
the others, for it means an authoritative witness of the truth, and this is
substantially equivalent to Prophet, or Divine Teacher: an office with
which David never was invested in relation to the Gentiles. The more
restricted sense of *monitor* (מזהיר) which Kimchi puts upon the word is
no less arbitrary than the vague one (רב) given in the Targum.—נָגִיר is
properly the one in front, the foremost, and is therefore naturally used to
signify a chief or leader. This title is expressly applied to the Messiah by
Daniel (ix. 25), and the corresponding titles ἄρχων and ἀρχηγός to Christ in
the New Testament (Acts iii. 15, Heb. ii. 10, Rev. i. 5), considered both
as an example and a leader.—The third name (מְצַוֵּה), being properly the
participle of a verb which means to command, might be considered as
equivalent either to *preceptor* or *commander*, both derivatives from verbs of
the same meaning, Now as one of these definitions agrees well with the
explanation which has been adopted of the first title (*witness*), and the other

with the obvious meaning of the second (*leader*), and as the offices of preceptor and commander are by no means incompatible, and actually meet in Christ, there seems to be no sufficient reason for excluding either in the case before us. At the same time, let it be observed that as צִוָּה sometimes means to command in a military sense, but never perhaps to teach or give instruction, the idea of commander must predominate in any case, and is entitled to the preference, if either must be chosen to the entire exclusion of the other.—Of the objections which the modern writers urge against the application of this verse to the Messiah, that which they appear to consider the most cogent and conclusive is precisely that which we have seen, from the beginning of the book, to be the weakest and most groundless, namely, that these Later Prophecies know nothing of a personal Messiah; which is established in the usual manner by denying all the cases *seriatim*, and refusing to let one of them be cited in defence or illustration of another. It is proper to observe in this connection, that both Umbreit and Hendewerk retain the usual sense of עֵד, and that the latter understands the verse as a description of the office which the Jewish people should discharge, in reference to the other nations after their return from exile. This is a near approach to the correct interpretation, and may be blended with it by recurring to the exegetical hypothesis, of which we have so often spoken, that the Body and the Head are often introduced as one ideal person. This, though at variance with Knobel's notion that the Prophet has now ceased to speak of Israel as one individual servant of Jehovah (see above, on chap. liv. 17), is in perfect accordance with the general tenor of the Scriptures as to the vocation and the mission both of Christ and of the church.

5. *Lo, a nation (that) thou knowest not thou shalt call, and a nation (that) have not known thee shall run unto thee for the sake of Jehovah thy God, and for the Holy One of Israel, for he hath glorified thee.* The question which has chiefly divided interpreters, in reference to this verse, is, whether the object of address is the Messiah or the church. The former opinion is maintained by Calvin, Sanctius, and others; the latter by Grotius and Vitringa. The masculine forms prove nothing either way; because the church is sometimes presented in the person of Israel, and sometimes personified as a woman. The most natural supposition is, that after speaking of the Messiah, he now turns to him and addresses him directly. If this be so, the verse affords an argument against the application of ver. 4 to David, who could not be the subject of such a promise ages after his decease. At the same time, the facility with which the words can be applied to either subject, may be considered as confirming the hypothesis that although the Messiah is the main subject of the verse, the church is not entirely excluded. The construction of the second גּוֹי with two plural verbs shews it to be collective. Lowth's version, *the nation*, is unnecessary here, although the article is frequently omitted both in poetry and elevated prose.—Their running indicates the eagerness with which they shall attach themselves to him and engage in his service. According to Jarchi, *thou shalt call* means thou shalt call into thy service. (See Job xix. 16.)—*For he hath glorified thee.* This expression is repeatedly used in the New Testament with reference to Christ. (See John xvii. 1, 5, Acts iii. 13.) Henderson gives כִּי what is supposed by some to be its primary sense, viz., that of a relative pronoun (*who hath glorified thee*); which is wholly unnecessary here, and rests upon a very dubious etymological assumption.—The form of expression in a part of this verse seems to be borrowed from

2 Sam. xxii. 44, but the resemblance neither proves that the Messiah is the subject of that passage, nor that David is the subject of this.—The *nation* means of course the Gentiles. What is said of the Messiah's not knowing them is thus explained by Schmidius. "Messias non noverat Gentiles ut ecclesiæ suæ membra actu, et Gentiles ipsum non noverant, saltem fide, plerique etiam de ipso quicquam non audiverant."

6. *Seek ye Jehovah while he may be found ; call ye upon him while he is near.* The ב, as usual when joined with the infinitive, is a particle of time. The literal translation would be, *in his being found, in his being near.* By a sudden apostrophe he turns from the Messiah to those whom he had come to save, and exhorts them to embrace this great salvation, to be reconciled with God. A similar exhortation, implying like the present that the day of grace is limited, occurs in Zeph. ii. 2. There are two limitations of the text before us, which have no foundation but the will of the interpreters. The first restricts it to the Jews in general, either making it a general advice to them to seize the opportunity of restoration (Rosenmüller), or a special warning to those hardened sinners who refused to do so (Knobel), and particularly such as were addicted to idolatry. These expositions are doubly arbitrary, first in restricting the passage to that period of Jewish history, and then in assuming the imaginary fact that a portion of the exiles were unwilling to return ; the passages appealed to in support of which are wholly inconclusive. An equally unfounded but less violent assumption is, that this passage has respect to the Jews not at that time merely, but in general, as distinguished from the Gentiles. Like many other similar hypotheses, when this is once assumed, it is easy to accommodate the general expressions of the passage to it ; but it would be difficult to find in the whole chapter any adequate reason for applying its commands and exhortations either to Gentiles or to Jews exclusively. In either case there were peculiar reasons for obeying the injunction, but it seems to be addressed to both alike. The Jew had great cause to beware lest the Gentile should outstrip him, and the Gentile might be reasonably urged to partake of those advantages which hitherto had been restricted to the Jew ; but both are called to the same duty, namely, that of seeking and calling upon God : expressions elsewhere used both severally and together to express the whole work of repentance, faith, and new obedience. —Lowth seems to find the common version of the last word (*near*) too simple, and enlarges it accordingly to *near at hand.*

7. *Let the wicked forsake his way, and the man of iniquity his thoughts, and let him return unto Jehovah, and he will have mercy on him, and to our God, for he will abundantly pardon* (literally, *multiply to pardon*). This is a continuation of the foregoing call, and at the same time an explanation of the way in which it was to be obeyed. We are here taught that the seeking of Jehovah, and the calling upon him just enjoined, involve an abandonment of sin, and a return to righteousness of life. The imperative version of the futures is warranted, if not required, by the abbreviated form יַעֲזֹב. Even the future form, however, would convey the same essential meaning both in Hebrew and in English. *The wicked shall forsake,* &c., is in fact the strongest form of a command. *Way* is a common figure for the course of life. What is here meant is the *evil way*, as Jeremiah calls it (lvi. 1), *i. e.* a habitually sinful course.—אָוֶן is a negative expression, strictly meaning non-existence or nonentity, and then, in a secondary moral sense, the destitution of all goodness, which is put, by a common Hebrew idiom, for the existence of the very opposite. The common version (*the unright-*

eous man) gives the sense but not the whole force of the original construction, which is here retained by Hendewerk (*der Mann der Missethat*). The
same writer speaks of these two verses as an interruption, by the Prophet,
of the divine discourse.   This criticism is founded on the mention of Jehovah
in the third person, which is a form of speech constantly occurring, even
where he is himself the speaker, not to mention the futility of the assumption that the passage is dramatic, or a formal dialogue.   It mattered little to
the writer's purpose whether he seemed to be himself the speaker or a mere
reporter of the words of God, to whom in either case they must be finally
ascribed.   Hence the constant alternation of the first, second, and third
persons, in a style which sets all rules of unity and rigid laws of composition at defiance.—The word translated *thoughts* is commonly employed, not
to denote opinions, but designs or purposes, in which sense it is joined with
way, in order to express the whole drift of the character and life.   To
return to God in both these respects is a complete description of repentance,
implying an entire change of heart, as well as life.—The indirect construction of וִירַחֲמֵהוּ, which is given in most modern versions (*that he may have
mercy on him*), is not only a gratuitous intrusion of the occidental idiom, but
injurious to the sense, by making that contingent which is positively promised.   The encouragement to seek God is not merely that he *may*, but
that he *will* have mercy.   Lowth's decoction of the same words (*will
receive him with compassion*) is enfeebling in another way, and inexact;
because the act of receiving is implied, not expressed, and the verb denotes
not mere compassion, but gratuitous and sovereign mercy.   There is further
encouragement contained in the expression *our God*.   To the Jew it would
suggest motives drawn from the covenant relation of Jehovah to his people ;
while the Gentile would regard it as an indirect assurance, that even he was
not excluded from God's mercy.   Another weakening of this sentence is
effected by the modern version of the last clause as a mere description
(Lowth, *for he aboundeth in forgiveness*), and not as an explicit promise
that he will abundantly forgive, which is not only the natural and obvious
import of the terms, but imperatively required by the favourite law of
parallelism.

8. *For my thoughts* (*are*) *not your thoughts, nor your ways my ways, saith
Jehovah*.   Clear and simple as these words are in themselves, they have
occasioned much dispute among interpreters, in reference to their nexus
with what goes before.   The earliest commentators, Jews and Christians,
seem to have understood them as intended to meet an objection to the promise, arising from its vastness and its freeness, by assuring us that such
forgiveness, however foreign from the feelings and the practices of men, is
not beyond the reach of the divine compassion.   As if he had said "to you
such forgiveness may appear impossible ; but my thoughts are not your
thoughts, neither your ways my ways."   This is the sense put upon the words
by Cyril, Aben Ezra, Kimchi, Œcolampadius, Piscator, and Henderson,
Thus understood, the text may be compared with Matt. xix. 26.   Another
explanation, that of Vitringa, rests upon the false assumption that the words
have reference to the Jews, and were intended to correct their prejudice
against the calling of the Gentiles, as at variance with the promises of God
to themselves.   As if he had said, "You may think the extension of my grace
to them a departure from my settled ways and purposes; but my thoughts
are not your thoughts, nor your ways my ways."   This specific application
of the words could scarcely be suggested to any ordinary reader, either by
the text or context, and at most can only be considered as included in its

general import.   Jerome and Rosenmüller, while they seem to acquiesce in the principle of the interpretation first proposed, so far modify it as to make the faithfulness and truth of the divine assurance a prominent idea.   This sense is also put upon the words by Gesenius and several of the later writers, who suppose the meaning of this verse to be determined by the analogy of vers. 10, 11, and accordingly explain it as denoting the irrevocable nature of God's purposes and promises.   In this sense, it may be considered parallel to Num. xxiii. 19, and 1 Sam. xv. 29, Isa. xxxi. 2, xlv. 23.   But this is neither the natural meaning of the words, nor one which stands in any obvious relation to what goes before ; in consequence of which some who hold it are under the necessity of denying that the כִּי at the beginning of the verse has its proper causal meaning.   It is indeed hard to see any coherence in this sequence of ideas, "let the wicked man repent, for my promise is irrevocable." This objection does not lie against another very ancient explanation of the passage, that proposed by Jarchi, but maintained by scarcely any later writer besides Sanctius.   This hypothesis is founded on the obvious correspondence of the terms employed in this verse and in that before it, and especially the parallel expressions *ways* and *thoughts*, there applied to man, and here to God.   According to this last interpretation, we have here a reason given why the sinner must forsake his ways and thoughts, viz. because they are incurably at variance with those of God himself : " Let the wicked forsake his way, and the unrighteous man his thoughts ; for my thoughts are not your thoughts, neither your ways my ways."   Vitringa's objection to this exposition, that the fact asserted is too obvious and familiar to be emphatically stated, is an arbitrary allegation, as to which the tastes of men may naturally differ.   There is more weight in the objection that the moral dissimilitude between God and man would hardly be expressed by a reference to the height of the heavens above the earth.   But the difference in question is in fact a difference of elevation, on the most important scale, that of morals, and might therefore be naturally so expressed.   At all events, this interpretation has so greatly the advantage of the others, in facility and beauty of connection with what goes before, that it must be considered as at least affording the formal basis of the true interpretation, but without excluding wholly the ideas which, according to the other theories, these words express.   They may all be reconciled indeed by making the disparity asserted have respect, not merely to moral purity, but also to constancy, benevolence, and wisdom.   As if he had said, " You must forsake your evil ways and thoughts, and by so doing, you infallibly secure my favour ; for as high as the heavens are above the earth, so far am I superior to you in mercy, not only in the rigour and extent of my requirements, but also in compassion for the guilty, in benevolent consideration even for the Gentiles, and in the constancy and firmness of my purposes when formed."—In his comment upon this verse, Vitringa gives his definition of the ways of God, which has so frequently been cited, or repeated without citation : " Viæ Dei sunt vel quibus ipse incedet, vel quibus homines incedere vult."   For the meaning of his *thoughts*, see Ps. xxxiii. 11, and Jer. li. 29.   If the sense which has been put upon the sentence be correct, it means far more than that which Hitzig quotes from Homer ἀλλ' αἰεί τε Διὸς κρείσσων νόος ἠέπερ ἀνδρῶν.   Knobel can of course see nothing here but an allusion to Cyrus and Croesus.

9. *For (as) the heavens are higher than the earth, so are my ways higher than your ways, and my thoughts than your thoughts.*   This is an illustration by comparison of the negative assertion in the verse preceding.   The

as in the protasis of the comparison is left out, as in Hosea xi. 2, Ps. xlviii. 6, Job vii. 9, Jer. iii. 20.   There can be no ground therefore for supposing, with Secker, Houbigant, and Lowth, that it has dropped out of the text in this place.   The full expression may be seen in chap. x. 11.—The מִן might here be taken in its proper sense of *from, away from,* as the reference is in fact to an interval of space; but our idiom would hardly bear the strict translation, and comparison is certainly implied, if not expressed.   The same comparison, and in a similar application, occurs Ps. ciii. 11.

10, 11. *For as the rain cometh down, and the snow from heaven, and thither returneth not, but when it has watered the earth and made it bear and put forth, and has given seed to the sower and bread to the eater, so shall my word be, which goeth out of my mouth; it shall not return unto me void (or without effect), but when it has done that which I desired, and successfully done that for which I sent it.*   This is a new comparison, suggested by the mention of the heavens and the earth in the preceding verse.   The tenth and eleventh form a single sentence of unusual length in Hebrew composition.   The one contains the comparison, properly so called, the other makes the application.   The futures יֵרֵד and יָשׁוּב strictly mean will come down, will return, implying that the same series of events might be expected to recur; but as a still more general recurrence is implied, the true sense is conveyed by the English present.—The construction of כִּי אִם is precisely the same as in Gen. xxxii. 27, Lev. xxii. 6, Ruth ii. 16, iii. 18, Amos iii. 7; in all which cases it indicates the *sine qua non,* the condition without which the event expressed by the future cannot take place.   Hitzig asserts, however, that the Hebrews knew nothing of the rain going back to heaven by evaporation, and on this ground will not let the words have their obvious and necessary meaning.   The impossibility of proving anything from such expressions, either as to the ignorance or knowledge of the laws of nature which the ancients possessed, has been repeatedly pointed out.   But it is certainly too much to violate analogy and syntax for the purpose of involving the writer in a real or apparent blunder.—The *word* of ver. 11 is not merely prophecy or promise, much less the command of God to Cyrus respecting Israel (Henderson), least of all the Prophet himself as an incarnation of Jehovah's word (Hendewerk), but everything that God utters either in the way of prediction or command.—The construction of אֲשֶׁר שְׁלַחְתִּיו is essentially the same as in 2 Sam. xi. 22.   That שָׁלַח governs two accusatives is evident from such places as 1 Kings xiv. 6.— The English Version refers נָתַן to the earth; but this construction is precluded by the difference of gender.   The effect is metaphorically represented as produced directly by the rain and snow.—הִצְלִיחַ does not mean *prosper in,* but make to prosper, or do prosperously, the active sense being inseparable from the Hiphil form.   The general design of these two verses is to generate and foster confidence in what Jehovah has engaged to do.

12. *For with joy shall ye go forth, and in peace shall ye be led; the mountains and the hills shall break out before you into a shout, and all the trees of the field shall clap the hand.*   Here, as in many other places, the idea of joyful change is expressed by representing all nature as rejoicing. (See chaps. xxxv. 1, 2; xliv. 23; xlix. 13; lii. 9; Ps. xcviii. 8.)   The expression *go forth* is eagerly seized upon by some interpreters as justifying the restriction of the passage to the restoration from the Babylonish exile.   But the real allusion in such cases is to the deliverance from Egypt, which is constantly referred to as a type of deliverance in general, so that every signal restoration or deliverance is represented as a spiritual exodus.

Vitringa, with much more probability, applies the words to the joy of the first heathen converts when they heard the gospel (Acts xiii. 48; 1 Thes. i. 6). The rabbins, upon their part, understand the passage as a prophecy of Israel's deliverance from the present exile and dispersion. All the interpreters since Lowth repeat his fine quotation from Virgil, *ipsi lœtitia montes,* &c.

13. *Instead of the thorn shall come up the cypress, and instead of the nettle shall come up the myrtle, and it shall be to Jehovah for a name, for an everlasting sign that shall not be cut off.* The same change which had just been represented by the shouting of the hills, and the applause of the forests, is now described as the substitution of the noblest trees for the most unprofitable and offensive plants. (Compare chap. xli. 19.) An analogous but different figure for the same thing is the opening of rivers in the desert. (See above, chap. xxxv. 6, 7; xliii. 19, 20.) For the meaning of נַעֲצוּץ and בְּרוֹשׁ, see vol. i. pp. 178, 290. The name סִרְפַּד occurs only here. Simonis and Ewald understand it as denoting a species of mustard plant. Jerome describes it as a worthless and offensive weed. The Seventy have κόνυζα. The modern writers are disposed to acquiesce in the Vulgate version, *urtica* or nettle. All that is essential to the writer's purpose is, that it be understood to signify a mean and useless plant, and thus to form a contrast with the myrtle, as the thorn does with the cypress. —Instead of *it shall be,* the modern Germans as usual prefer the indirect construction, *that it may be,* which is neither so exact nor so expressive as the strict translation. Knobel makes the trees the subject of this last clause also; but it seems more natural to understand it as referring to the change itself, described in this and the preceding verse. Dropping the metaphor, the Prophet then says, in direct terms, that the glorious change predicted shall redound to the glory of its author. *It shall be for a name, i. e.* it shall serve as a memorial, which is then described in other words as a *sign of perpetuity* or everlasting token, with allusion, as Vitringa thinks, to those commemorative obelisks or pillars mentioned elsewhere (*e. g.* chap. xix. 19). This memorial is called perpetual, because it *shall not be cut off,* pass away, or be abolished.—It will here be sufficient simply to state the fact, that Knobel understands this as a promise that the homeward journey of the exiles should be comfortable and pleasant (*bequem und angenehm*).

Chapter 56

WHILE the church, with its essential institutions, is to continue unimpaired, the old distinctions, national and personal, are to be done away, and the Jewish people robbed of that pre-eminence of which its rulers proved themselves unworthy.

The day is coming when the righteousness of God is to be fully revealed, without the veils and shackles which had hitherto confined it, ver. 1. For this great change the best preparation is fidelity to the spirit of the old economy, ver. 2. No personal or national distinctions will be any longer recognised, ver. 3. Connection with the church will no longer be a matter of hereditary right, vers. 4, 5. The church shall be henceforth co-extensive with the world, vers. 6–8. But first, the carnal Israel must be abandoned to its enemies, ver. 9. Its rulers are neither able nor worthy to deliver the people or themselves, vers. 10–12.

1. *Thus saith Jehovah, Keep ye judgment* (or *justice*) *and do right-*

eousness ; for near (is) my salvation to come, and my righteousness to be revealed. The Jews refer this passage to their present dispersion, and understand it as declaring the conditions of their restoration. Vitringa applies it to the beginning of the new dispensation ; Piscator to the new dispensation generally ; the modern Germans to the end of the Babylonish exile. These different classes of interpreters of course expound particulars in accordance with their general hypothesis, but none of them without undue restriction of that which in itself requires, or at least admits a wider application. On the principle heretofore assumed as the basis of our exposition, we can only regard it as a statement of the general laws which govern the divine dispensation towards the chosen people, and the world at large. The reference is not merely to the ancient Israel, much less to the Jews of the captivity, still less to the Christian Church distinctively considered, least of all to the Christian Church of any one period. The doctrine of the passage is simply this, that they who enjoy extraordinary privileges, or expect extraordinary favours, are under corresponding obligations to do the will of God ; and moreover, that the nearer the manifestation of God's mercy, whether in time or in eternity, the louder the call to righteousness of life. These truths are of no restricted application, but may be applied wherever the relation of a church or chosen people can be recognised. Without attempting to refute the various opinions founded on the false hypothesis of a local or temporal limitation, it will be sufficient to point out the absurdities attending that which in our day has the greatest vogue, viz. the notion that the passage relates merely to the Babylonish exile. Thus Maurer understands the Prophet as advising his contemporaries to act in a manner worthy of their approaching liberation, and Gesenius supposes him to take this opportunity of combating the Jewish prejudice against the calling of the Gentiles. Why this error needed to be controverted at this precise juncture, he omits to explain. But this is not the worst thing in Gesenius's interpretation of the place before us. After saying that a proselytising spirit is inseparable from the belief in one exclusive way of salvation, and particularly pardonable in the Jewish exiles, surrounded as they were by idolaters, he goes on to represent the liberal spirit of this passage as directly at variance with the law of Moses, particularly as contained in Deut. xxiii. 2–8, which he says is virtually here repealed. This shallow and erroneous view of the relation which subsists between the Law and the Prophets, will correct itself as we proceed with the detailed interpretation. מִשְׁפָּט seems here to be equivalent to תּוֹרָה, with which it is connected as a parallel in chap. xlii. 4, li. 4.

2. *Happy the man (that) shall do this, and the son of man that shall hold it fast, keeping the Sabbath from profaning it, and keeping his hand from doing all evil.* The pronoun *this* seems to refer to what follows, as in Ps. vii. 4, and Deut. xxxii. 29. *Son of man* is simply an equivalent expression to the *man* of the other clause. The last clause is remarkable, and has occasioned much dispute among interpreters, on account of its combining a positive and negative description of the character required, the last of which is very general, and the first no less specific. A great variety of reasons have been given for the special mention of the Sabbath here. It has especially perplexed those writers who regard the Sabbath as a temporary ceremonial institution. Some of these endeavour to evade the difficulty, by supposing that the Sabbath here meant is a mystical or spiritual Sabbatism, a repose from suffering, sin, or ceremonial impositions. But how could such a Sabbath be *observed*, or how could they be called

upon to *keep* it, as a condition of the divine favour ? Some suppose the Sabbath to be here put for the whole Mosaic system of religious services, as being the most ancient, and, in some sort, the foundation of the rest. According to Gesenius, it is specified because it was the only part of the Mosaic institutions which could be perpetuated through the exile, that which was merely ceremonial and restricted to the temple being necessarily suspended. Rosenmüller thinks that it is here referred to, as a public national profession of the worship of one God. The true explanation is afforded by a reference to the primary and secondary ends of the Sabbatical institution, and the belief involved in its observance. In the first place, it implied a recognition of Jehovah as the omnipotent Creator of the universe (Exod. xx. 11, xxxi. 17) ; in the next place, as the sanctifier of his people, not in the technical or theological sense, but as denoting him by whom they had been set apart as a peculiar people (Exod. xxxi. 13 ; Ezek. xx. 12) ; in the next place, as the Saviour of this chosen people from the bondage of Egypt (Deut. v. 15). Of these great truths the Sabbath was a weekly remembrancer, and its observance by the people a perpetual recognition and profession, besides the practical advantages accruing to the maintenance of a religious spirit by the weekly recurrence of a day of rest ; advantages which no one more distinctly acknowledges, or states more strongly, than Gesenius. *Holding fast* is a common idiomatic expression for consistent perseverance in a certain course. It occurs not unfrequently in the New Testament. (Heb. iv. 4, vi. 18 ; Rev. ii. 25, iii. 11). The suffix in בָּהּ refers to זאת, and like it has respect to the whole course of conduct afterwards described. Gesenius refers to chap. i. 13 as a rejection of the Sabbath, and in this detects a want of agreement between the genuine and spurious Isaiah : a conclusion resting wholly on a false view of that passage, for the true sense of which see under chap. i. 11–15, vol. i. p. 86, &c.

3. *And let not the foreigner say, who has joined himself unto Jehovah, saying, Jehovah will separate me wholly from his people ; and let not the eunuch say, Lo, I am a dry tree.* The essential meaning of this verse is, that all external disabilities shall be abolished, whether personal or national. To express the latter he makes use of the phrase בֶּן־הַנֵּכָר, which strictly means not *the son of the stranger*, as the common version has it, but the son of strangeness, or of a strange country ; נֵכָר corresponding to the German *Fremde*, which has no equivalent in English. The whole class of personal disqualifications is represented by the case of the eunuch, in reference to Deut. xxiii. 1, and as Calvin thinks to the promise in Gen. xv. 5, and xxii. 17, from which that class of persons was excluded. Hensler's idea that סָרִים here means an officer or courtier, is precluded by the addition of the words, *I am a dry tree*, a proverbial description of childlessness said to be still current in the East. It is possible, however, that the eunuch may be mentioned, simply because it stands at the beginning of the list of prohibitions in the law. In either case, the expression is generic, or representative of more particulars than it expresses. Knobel's restriction of the first clause to the Canaanites, who mingled with the Jews in their captivity, or occupied their places in their absence, is entirely gratuitous. The meaning is, that all restrictions, even such as still affected proselytes, should be abolished.

4, 5. *For thus saith Jehovah to* (or, *as to*) *the eunuchs who shall keep my Sabbaths, and shall choose what I delight in, and take fast hold of my covenant, I will give to them in my house and within my walls a place and*

*name better than sons and than daughters ; an everlasting name will I give to
him, which shall not be cut off.*   According to Joseph Kimchi, the plural
Sabbaths is intended to include the Sabbatical year, and that of jubilee.   If
any distinction was intended, it was probably that between the wider and
narrower meaning of the term *Sabbaths, i.e.* the Sabbath properly so called,
and the other institutions of religion with which it is connected.—What it
is that God delights in, may be learned from chap. lxvi. 4, Jer. ix. 24,
Hos. vi. 6.   By holding fast my covenant is meant adhering to his compact
with me, which includes obedience to the precepts and faith in the promises.   The ו at the beginning of ver. 5 introduces the apodosis, and gives
the verb a future meaning.—By *my walls* we are not to understand, with
Jerome, those of Jerusalem, nor, with the modern writers, those of the
temple, but in a more ideal sense, the walls of God's house or dwelling,
which had just been mentioned.   The promise is not merely one of free
access to the material sanctuary, but of a home in the household or family
of God, an image of perpetual occurrence in the Psalms of David.   (See
especially Psalms xv. xxiii. and xxiv. as expounded by Hengstenberg.)—
The use of the word יָד in this connection is obscure, although the essential
meaning is determined by the context.   Umbreit follows Aquila, Symmachus, and Theodotion, in adhering to the usual sense *hand*, which he seems
to think is mentioned as the natural instrument of seizure, and metaphorically applicable to the thing seized, for example, to a share or portion.
Gesenius recognises this use of the plural in a few places, but appears to
derive it from the primary idea of a handful.   In the case before us he explains the word as meaning a memorial or monument, which sense it seems
to have in 2 Sam. xviii. 18, perhaps with reference, as Gesenius supposes,
to the uplifted hand and arm found on many ancient *cippi* or sepulchral
columns.   But as the antiquity and universality of this practice are uncertain, and as the meaning *place* is admissible in 2 Sam. xviii. 18, as in many
other cases, it appears to be entitled to the preference.—*Better than sons
and daughters* may either mean better than the comfort immediately derived
from children (as in Ruth iv. 15), or better than the perpetuation of the
name by hereditary succession.   Most interpreters prefer the latter sense,
but both may be included.   A beautiful coincidence and partial fulfilment
of the promise is pointed out by J. D. Michaelis, in the case of the Ethiopian eunuch, whose conversion is recorded in the eighth of Acts, and
whose memory is far more honoured in the church than it could have been
by a long line of illustrious descendants.

6, 7. *And (as to) the foreigners joining themselves to Jehovah to serve him
and to love the name of Jehovah, to be to him for servants, every one keeping
the Sabbath from profaning it, and holding fast my covenant, I will bring
them to my mount of holiness, and make them joyful in my house of prayer,
their offerings and their sacrifices (shall be) to acceptance on my altar ; for
my house shall be called a house of prayer for all nations.*   Aben Ezra points
out as a rhetorical peculiarity in the structure of this passage, that the
writer, after mentioning the foreigners and eunuchs in ver. 3, afterwards
recurs to them in an inverted order.   As an analogous example, he refers
to Josh. xxiv. 31.—The verb שָׁרַת, although strictly a generic term, is
specially appropriated to the official service of the priests and Levites.
Some interpreters accordingly suppose it to be here said that the heathen
shall partake of the sacerdotal honours elsewhere promised to the church.
(See chap. lxi. 6, Exod. xix. 6, 1 Peter ii. 5, 9, Rev. i. 6.)—To love the
name of Jehovah, is to love his attributes as manifested in his word and

works. (Compare chaps. lx. 9, lxvi. 5.)—בֵּית תְּפִלָּתִי does not mean *the house of my prayer, i. e.* the house where prayer is made to me, but my house of prayer, as הַר קָדְשִׁי means my hill of holiness, or holy hill. Knobel supposes an allusion to the residence of the Nethinim on Ophel. (Neh. iii. 26, xi. 21.)—*Shall be called,* as in many other cases, implies that it shall be so. Our Saviour quotes a part of the last clause, not in reference to its main sense, but to what is incidentally mentioned, viz., its being called a house of prayer. This part of the sentence was applicable to the material temple while it lasted; but the whole prediction could be verified only after its destruction, when the house of God even upon earth ceased to be a limited locality, and became coextensive with the church in its enlargement and diffusion. The form of expression is derived, however, from the ceremonies of the old economy, and worship is described by names familiar to the writer and his original readers. (Compare Hos. xiv. 3, Heb. xiii. 13, John iv. 21–23.) The general promise is the same as that in Mal. i. 11, and is so far from being inconsistent with the principles on which the old economy was founded, that it simply carries out its original design as settled and announced from the beginning.

8. *Thus saith the Lord Jehovah, the gatherer of the outcasts of Israel, Still (more) will I gather upon him in addition to his gathered.* This may either mean, I will go on to gather still more of his outcasts, or, besides his outcasts I will gather others. There is less difference between the two interpretations than at first sight there might seem to be. In either case, the words are applicable to the calling of the Gentiles. On the second supposition, which is commonly adopted, even by the Jewish writers, this is the direct and proper meaning of the words. But even on the other, they amount to the same thing, if we only give to Israel its true sense, as denoting not the Jewish nation as such, but the chosen people or the church of God, to which the elect heathen as really belong as the elect Jews, and are therefore just as much entitled to be called *outcasts of Israel.* It is true that our Saviour uses a similar expression (lost sheep of the House of Israel) in a restricted application to the Israelites properly so called; but it is in a connection which brings the Jews and Gentiles into evident antithesis, and therefore leaves no doubt as to the sense in which the name Israel is to be understood. עָלָיו may either mean simply *to him* or *upon him,* implying vast accumulation.

9. *All ye beasts of the field, come to devour, all ye beasts in the forest!* The structure of this verse is somewhat unusual, consisting of two parallel members, with a third, equally related to both, interposed between them. It is an invitation to the enemies of Israel to destroy it. The people being represented in the following verses as a flock, their destroyers are naturally represented here as wild beasts. Hitzig and Knobel understand the invitation as ironical, or as a mere poetical description of the defenceless state in which Israel was left through the neglect of its natural protectors. It is more natural, however, to explain it as an indirect prediction of an actual event, clothed in Isaiah's favourite form of an apostrophe. Vitringa's limitation of the prophecy to the subversion of the Roman empire by the barbarians, is as arbitrary as its application in the Targum and by Kimchi, to Gog and Magog. We have here simply one of those alternations and transitions which are not only frequent in this book, but one of its characteristics, and indeed essential to the writer's purpose of exhibiting God's dealing with his church, both in wrath and mercy. From the foregoing

promises of growth, he now reverts to intervening judgments, and their causes. There is no ground, therefore, for Luzzatto's assertion, that the next seventeen verses are entirely unconnected with what goes before, and must therefore be considered an interpolation. Ewald, on the other hand, alleges that from this verse to the middle of chap. lvii. 11 is an extract from an older writer, inserted here in order to have something against idolatry, and because the author of the book could not hope to produce anything better! As a further illustration of the value of such critical decisions, I may add that Hendewerk separates chaps. lv., lvi., and lvii. from the foregoing and following context, as a distinct prophecy! Besides the usual and natural interpretation of the verse before us as a threatening, may be mentioned that of Cyril and Jerome, who regard it as an invitation to all sorts of men to partake of the Lord's supper; while Clericus explains it as a like invitation to the Gentiles to frequent the temple and partake of the sacrificial feasts. The same sense was put upon the words by Rosenmüller in his first edition; but he afterwards adopted a different grammatical construction of the sentence, being the one proposed by Aben Ezra, who explains the *beasts of the forest* as the object of the verb *devour*, and understands the sentence as an invitation to the heathen to destroy the wicked Jews. The same construction is received by Jarchi and Abarbenel, but with a very different result, as they suppose the invitation to be given to the proselytes to destroy the enemies of Israel. On the same grammatical foundation Cocceius erects his explanation of the verse as a call to the barbarians to destroy the corrupt Christians, while Schmidius regards it as an exhortation to the church to swallow up the Gentiles by receiving them into her bosom! All the modern writers seem to be agreed that the last clause as well as the first is a description of the object of address, and that the thing to be devoured must be supplied from the following verses. With the metaphors of this verse compare Exod. xxiii. 29; Ezek. xxxiv. 5–8; Jer. xii. 9, vii. 33, l. 17. Beasts of the field and of the forest, are parallel expressions. Some interpreters make the one a stronger expression than the other; but in deciding which it is, they directly contradict each other. Vitringa's notion that the one may mean the Saracens, the other the Huns, Turks, and Tartars, is to use his own words with respect to Cyril's exposition of the verse, " non commendabilis hac ætate ecclesiæ."

10. *His watchmen (are) blind all of them, they have not known* (or *do not know*), *all of them (are) dumb dogs, they cannot bark, dreaming, lying down, loving to slumber.* The pronoun *his* refers to *Israel*, as in ver. 8, and thus proves clearly that no new discourse begins either with ver. 9 or with that before us, where the large ש of the Masoretic text, and the space before the verse in most manuscripts, seem to indicate a change of subject. But, as Gesenius correctly says, the writer merely pauses to take breath, and then resumes the thread of his discourse. Many give *do not know* the absolute sense of knowing nothing or being without knowledge; but in all such cases it seems better to connect it with an object understood. We may here supply their duty, or the state of the flock, or the danger to which it is exposed. The difference between the past and present form is immaterial here; because both are really included, the condition described being one of ancient date, but still continued. The dogs particularly meant are shepherds' dogs (Job xxx. 1), whose task it was to watch the flock, and by their barking give notice of approaching danger. But these are dumb dogs which cannot even bark, and therefore wholly useless. They are also negligent and lazy. Far from averting peril or announcing it, they do not

see it. What is before expressed by the figure of a blind watchman, is here expressed by that of a shepherd's dog asleep. הֹזִים is confounded by the Vulgate, Symmachus, and Saadias, with חֹזִים which might either be a participle (*seeing*) or a noun (*seers*), corresponding to *watchmen* in the first clause. The common text is now very generally regarded as correct, and explained by the Arabic analogy to signify *dreaming*, or talking in sleep, or raving either from disease or sleep. Some suppose a particular allusion to the murmuring or growling of a dog in its dreams. Some writers make the watchmen of this verse denote the prophets, as in chap. lii. 8; Jer. vi. 17; Ezek. iii. 17, xxxiii. 7. But Gesenius more correctly understands it as a figure for the rulers of the people generally, not excluding even the false prophets. The figurative title is expressive of that watchfulness so frequently described in the New Testament as an essential attribute of spiritual guides. (Compare also Mat. xv. 4.)

11. *And the dogs are greedy, they know not satiety, and they, the shepherds* (or *the shepherds themselves*), *know not how to distinguish* (or *act wisely*); *all of them to their own way are turned,* (*every*) *man to his own gain from his own quarter* (or *without exception*). A new turn is now given to the figures of the preceding verse. The dogs, though indolent, are greedy. Several of the ancient versions confound עַזֵּי נֶפֶשׁ with עַזֵּי פָנִים, *hard-faced*, and translate it *impudent*. The true sense of the former phrase is *strong of appetite*, i. e. voracious.—The pronoun הֵמָּה is emphatic, and may either mean that these same dogs are at the same time shepherds, thus affording a transition to a different though kindred image, or it may be intended to distinguish between two kinds of rulers; as if he had said, while the dogs are thus indolent and greedy, they (the shepherds) are incompetent; or, while the shepherds' dogs are such, the shepherds themselves know not how to distinguish. The latter is probably the true construction; for although the same class of persons may be successively compared to shepherds' dogs and shepherds, it cannot even by a figure of speech be naturally said that the dogs themselves are shepherds. There is no need, however, of distinguishing between the dogs and shepherds as denoting civil and religious rulers, since both comparisons are equally appropriate to rulers in general. Etymologically, הָבִין may be understood to signify the act of discernment or discrimination. Usage would seem to require that of being wise or prudent; but its Hiphil form, and its being preceded by the verb *to know*, are in favour of explaining it to mean wise conduct, with particular reference in this case to official obligation. Their being all turned to their own way is expressive of diversity, and also of selfishness in each individual. The latter sense is then expressed more fully by the addition of לְבִצְעוֹ, to or for his own gain or profit. That voluptuous as well as avaricious indulgences are here referred to, is apparent from what follows in the next verse.—The last word literally means *from his end* or *his extremity*, to which the older writers gave the sense of his quarter or direction, corresponding to *his own way*; and Henderson says that it expresses the extreme lengths to which they went in their efforts to accumulate gain. Most of the modern writers have adopted the opinion of De Dieu, that מִקָּצֵהוּ means *ad unum omnes*, all without exception, i. e. all within a given space or number, from its very end or remotest limit. (Compare Gen. xix. 4; Jer. li. 31; Ezek. xxv. 9.)

12. *Come ye, I will fetch wine, and we will intoxicate ourselves with strong drink, and like to-day shall be to-morrow, great, abundantly, exceedingly.* The description of the revellers is verified by quoting their own words, as

in chap. xxii. 13. The language is that of one inviting others to join in a debauch; hence the alternation of the singular and plural. סָבְא is not merely to drink, nor even to be filled, but to be drunk. The futures might be rendered *let me fetch* and *let us drink*, without either injuring or bettering the sense. The last clause professes or expresses a determination to prolong the revel till the morrow. The accents connect יוֹם with מָחָר in the sense of *dies crastinus*. Another possible construction is to make the pronoun זֶה agree with יוֹם although preceding it; a combination less incredible in this case, because גָּדוֹל in the following member is supposed by some to agree with יֶתֶר as a noun, in which case the whole phrase would mean *exceeding great abundance*. Most interpreters, however, make יֶתֶר and מְאֹד both adverbs, although both originally nouns, and construe *great* with *day*, a *great day* being naturally applicable to a day remarkable for anything, as in the case before us for its revelry; just as we say in colloquial English, a high time, or a rare time, for a time of great enjoyment.

Chapter 57

THE righteous who died during the old economy were taken away from the evil to come, vers. 1, 2. The wicked who despised them were themselves proper objects of contempt, vers. 3, 4. Their idolatry is first described in literal terms, vers. 5, 6. It is then represented as a spiritual adultery, vers. 7-9. Their obstinate persistency in sin is represented as the cause of their hopeless and remediless destruction, vers. 10–13. A way is prepared for spiritual Israel to come out from among them, ver. 14. The hopes of true believers shall not be deferred for ever, vers. 15. 16. Even these must be chastened for their sins, ver. 17. But there is favour in reserve for all true penitents, without regard to national distinctions, vers. 18, 19. To the incorrigible sinner, on the other hand, peace is impossible, vers. 20, 21.

1. *The righteous perisheth, and there is no man laying (it) to heart, and men of mercy are taken away, with none considering (or perceiving) that from the presence of evil the righteous is taken away.* Henderson says that whether Hezekiah or Josiah be meant by *the righteous*, cannot be determined, nor indeed whether any particular individual be intended. This doubt may not appear so utterly insoluble when we consider that there is no further reference to either of the persons mentioned, nor anything like an individual description in the text or context; that הַצַּדִּיק is used generically for a whole class elsewhere (*e. g.* Eccles. iii. 17, Ezek. xviii. 20, Ps. xxxvii. 12); and that the parallel expression here is plural. This last consideration, it is true, would have no weight against Tertullian and Cyprian, who explain *the righteous* to be Christ, and *men of mercy* his apostles; but even Vitringa describes this hypothesis as *nulla specie probabilem*, and therefore needing no refutation. The terms of this verse are specifically applicable neither to violent nor natural death as such considered, but are appropriate to either. Even Kimchi points out that the righteous is not here said to perish, either in the sense of ceasing to exist, or in that of ceasing to be happy, but in that of being lost to the world and to society. *Laying to heart* is not merely feeling or appreciating, but observing and perceiving.—*Men of mercy* is another description of the righteous, so called as the objects of God's mercy, and as being merciful

themselves. (See Mat. v. 7.)—The verb אָסַף is doubly appropriate, first in its general though secondary sense of taking away, and then in its primary specific sense of gathering, *i. e.* gathering to one's fathers or one's people; an expression frequently applied in the Old Testament to death, and especially to that of godly men. (See Gen. xlix. 29, Judges ii. 10.) The verb is used absolutely in this sense by Moses (Num. xx. 26).—בְּאֵין means strictly *in default* or *in the absence of* (Prov. viii. 24, xxvi. 20).— Most interpreters give כִּי the sense of *that*, and understand the last clause as stating what it is that no one lays to heart or understands, viz. the fact that the righteous is taken away, &c. Some, however, translate כִּי *for*, and make the last clause a mere reiteration of the fact twice stated in the first. Upon this point Hitzig's version and his comment are directly contradictory, the former having *for* (*denn*) and the latter saying expressly, "כִּי here means not *for* (*denn*), but *that* (*dass*); their death is observed, but not its cause." There is also a difference of opinion as to מִפְּנֵי, which some suppose to mean *because of*, others *before* (in reference to time), and others *from the face* or *presence of.* So too *the evil* is by some understood in a physical sense, viz. that of misery or suffering, by others in a moral sense, viz. that of guilt or sin. Those who adopt the latter understand the clause to mean, that the death of the righteous is occasioned by the sins of the people. But why may not this be asserted of the death of the sinner likewise? On the other hypothesis, the sense is either that the righteous is destroyed by his calamities, or that he is removed before they come upon the people. To the latter it is objected by Maurer, that the subsequent context represents great prosperity as in reserve for the people. But this objection presupposes an erroneous limitation of the passage to the period of the exile.

2. *He shall go in peace* (or *enter into peace*); *they shall rest upon their beds—walking straight before him.*—The alternation of the singular and plural shews that the subject of the sentence is a collective person. Kimchi makes שָׁלוֹם the subject of the first and last members, and regards the intermediate one as a parenthesis: Peace shall go walking straight before him or straight forwards, *i. e.* shall conduct him or escort him out of this life to a place of rest. Aben Ezra refers the pronoun in נְכֹחוֹ to Jehovah, *walking before him, i.e.* in his presence. (Compare Judges xviii. 6.) But the explanation commonly approved is that of Jarchi, who makes this phrase an additional description of the righteous, as one walking in his uprighteousness, or, as Cocceius expresses it, *straight before him* (*qui recte ante se incedit*). It seems to be added as a kind of afterthought, to limit what immediately precedes, and preclude its application to all the dead without distinction. The peace and rest here meant are those of the body in the grave, and of the soul in heaven; the former being frequently referred to as a kind of pledge and adumbration of the latter. Vitringa understands this verse as stating the alleviations which attend the lamentable loss of good men. Ewald regards it as a kind of pious wish analogous to *requiescat in pace!* Gesenius supposes an antithesis between this and the next verse: "The righteous is at rest (or let him rest), but as for you," &c. This suggestion is of value so far as it removes the appearance of abrupt transition, and shews the continuity of the discourse.

3. *And ye* (or *as for you*), *draw near hither, ye sons of the witch, seed of the adulterer and the harlot.* According to Jarchi, these words are addressed to the survivors of the judgments by which the righteous are described as having been removed. They are summoned, according to the same Rabbin,

to receive their punishment, but as Kimchi thinks, simply to appear before the judgment-seat. (Compare chap. xli. 1.) The description which follows was of course designed to be extremely opprobrious; but interpreters differ as to the precise sense of the terms employed. Gesenius supposes that instead of simply charging them with certain crimes, he brings the charge against their parents; a species of reproach peculiarly offensive to the orientals. Hendewerk supposes this form of contumely to have been selected for the purpose of identifying those who were immediately addressed with their progenitors. In this way he ingeniously accounts for the subsequent description of idolatry, which Ewald and many others look upon as applicable only to the times of Isaiah himself. Vitringa and the older writers generally give a more specific meaning to the Prophet's metaphors, understanding by the adulterer the idol, by the harlot the apostate church, and by the children the corrupted offspring of this shameful apostasy.—Instead of sorceress or witch, the Septuagint and Targum have iniquity. Grotius supposes that they read עֹנָה, Rosenmüller עֹלָה. The Peshito seems to make it a participle of עָנָה (*afflicted*). Jerome quotes Theodotion as retaining the original word *onena*, which is the common text. For the meaning of the word, see vol. i. p. 100. The occult arts are mentioned as inseparable adjuncts of idolatry.—A grammatical difficulty is presented by the verb וַתִּזְנֶה, where the noun זֹנָה might have been expected. None of the modern writers seem to have assumed a noun of that form, although not without analogy. The current explanation is the one adopted by Gesenius, which supposes an ellipsis of the relative (she who committed whoredom), and a change of construction from the participle to the finite verb. Luzzatto objects that in all such cases the participle and the finite verb have one and the same subject. He accordingly agrees with Abarbanel and Gousset in explaining תִּזְנֶה as the second person, the seed of an adulterer, and (therefore) thou hast thyself committed whoredom. Essentially the same interpretation is proposed by Piscator and Cocceius.—Whoredom and sorcery are again combined in Mal. iii. 5, and elsewhere.

4. *At whom do you amuse yourselves? At whom do you enlarge the mouth, prolong the tongue? Are you not children of rebellion* (or *apostasy*) *a seed of falsehood?* This retorts the impious contempt of the apostates on themselves. There is no need, however, of supposing that they had cast these very same reproaches on the godly. The meaning is not necessarily that they were what they falsely charged their brethren with being. All that is certainly implied is, that they were unworthy to treat them with contempt. Jarchi gives הִתְעַגַּג עַל the sense of delighting in, which it has in chap. lviii. 11; Job xxii. 26, xxvii. 10; Ps. xxxvii. 4; but most interpreters suppose the next clause to determine that the words express derision. The opening or stretching of the mouth in mockery is mentioned, Ps. xxii. 8, 14, xxxv. 21; Lam. ii. 16, and in chap. lviii. 9, below. The lolling of the tongue as a derisive gesture is referred to by Persius in poetry, and Livy in prose. According to Hitzig there are not two different gestures here described, but one, the mouth being opened for the purpose of exhibiting the tongue. The form of expostulation is similar to that in chap. xxxvii. 23. —Jarchi supposes the prophets to be specially intended as the objects of this wicked mockery. (See 2 Chron xxxvi. 16.)—Here as in the preceding verse, some regard *seed* and *children* as mere idiomatic pleonasms, or at most, as rhetorical embellishments. Of those who understand them strictly, some suppose the qualities of falsehood and apostasy to be predicated of

the parents, others of the children.   Both are probably included ; they were worthy of their parentage, and dilligently filled up the measure of their father's iniquity.   (See chap. ɉ. 4.)   By " a seed of falsehood" we may understand a spurious brood, and at the same time one itself perfidious and addicted to a false religion.

5. *Inflamed* (or *inflaming yourselves*) *among the oaks* (or *terebinths*), *under every green tree, slaughtering the children in the valleys, under the clefts of the rocks.*   Their idolatrous practices are now described in detail.   The first word of this verse properly denotes libidinous excitement, and is here used with reference to the previous representation of idolatry as spiritual whoredom or adultery.   The reflexive version of the Niphal strengthens the expression, but is not required by usage or the context.—בָּאֵלִים is commonly translated *with idols*, in accordance with the ancient versions.   The objections are that בְּ is not a natural connective of the foregoing verb with its object, and that אֵל is constantly employed by this writer with direct allusion to its proper sense (*almighty*), and in reference to false gods only where they are sarcastically placed in opposition to the true.   Maurer, Ewald, and Knobel, have revived the old interpretation given by Jarchi and Kimchi, which gives אֵלִים the sense of oaks or terebinths, as in chap. i. 29.   The objection usually made, viz. that the next words are descriptive of the place, only shews how easily the parallelism may be made to sustain either side of any question.   The interpreter has only to allege that the words in question must or must not mean the same thing with the next words, as the case may be, and his purpose is accomplished.   This objection is, moreover, inconclusive, because it proves too much ; for it equally applies to the consecutive expressions in the last clause, both of which are universally regarded as descriptive of localities.   Hitzig renders the objection somewhat more plausible, by saying that the terebinth is necessarily included under *every green tree* ; but if the genius of the language would admit of two consecutive expressions being perfectly synonymous, how much more of such as really involve a climax—" among the terebinths, and not only so but under every green tree."   Sacrificial infanticide is often mentioned in the Scriptures as a rite of heathen worship, and especially of that paid to Moloch, in which it seems to have been usual to burn the children ; but we find the word slaughter frequently applied to it (See Ezek. xvi. 21, xxiii. 39), either in the wide sense of slaying (Gesenius), or because the children were first slaughtered and then burnt (Hitzig), or because both modes of sacrifice were practised.   Hitzig adds very coolly to his observations on this subject, " compare Gen. xxii.," a reference which obviously implies much more than the opinion entertained by some older writers, that human sacrifices owed their origin to a misapprehension of the history of Isaac.   The Hebrew נַחַל is applied both to a valley and a stream flowing through it.   Jerome has here *torrentibus*, by which he may have meant their beds or channels.   According to Vitringa, there is special reference to the great valley of Lebanon, between the chains of Libanus and Antilibanus, a region infamous for its idolatry.   A much more natural interpretation is the one which supposes an allusion to the valleys round Jerusalem, in one of which, the valley of the son of Hinnom, we know that Moloch was adored with human victims.   The clefts of the rocks, or clefts projecting in consequence of excavations, is a circumstance perfectly in keeping with the topography of that spot.   The minute description of idolatry given in this passage is exceedingly perplexing to those writers who fix the date

of composition at the period of the exile. Hendewerk, as we have seen,
intrepidly maintains that the children are here charged with the sins of
their fathers ; but along with this extravagant assertion he makes one concession really valuable, namely, that the efforts of Gesenius and Hitzig to
reconcile the terms of the description with the state of things during the
captivity are wholly abortive.   A perfect solution of the difficulty is afforded
by our own hypothesis, that the Prophet, from the whole field of vision
spread before him, singles out the most revolting traits and images by
which he could present in its true aspect the guilt and madness of apostasy
from God.

  6. *Among the smooth* (stones) *of the valley* (or *the brook*) *is thy portion;
they, they, are thy lot; also to them hast thou poured out a drink-offering,
thou hast brought up a meal-offering.   Shall I for these things be consoled*
(*i.e.* satisfied without revenge)?   Thy portion, *i.e.* the objects of thy
choice and thy affection (Jer. x. 16). The word *stones* is correctly supplied
in the English Version. (See 1 Sam. xvii. 40.) Others supply *places*, and
suppose the phrase to mean open cleared spots in the midst of wooded
valleys, places cleared for the performance of religious rites.   In favour of
this meaning, is the not unfrequent use of the Hebrew word to signify *not
hairy*, and in figurative application to the earth, not wooded, free from trees.
According to this interpretation, which is that of Paulus, De Wette, Hitzig,
Rückert, and Umbreit, the first clause merely describes the place where the
idols were worshipped.   According to the other, which is given in the
Targum, and approved by Aben Ezra, Kimchi, Grotius, Clericus, Lowth,
Rosenmüller, Maurer, and Knobel, it is a description of the idols themselves.   Smooth stones may mean either polished or anointed stones, such
as were set up by the patriarchs as memorials (Gen. xxviii. 18, xxxv. 12),
and by the heathen as objects of worship.   Thus Arnobius says, that before
his conversion to Christianity he never saw an oiled stone (*lubricatum
lapidem et ex olivi unguine sordidatum*) without addressing it and praying
to it.   This explanation of the first clause agrees best with what follows,
and with the emphatic repetition, *they, they, are thy portion*, which is more
natural in reference to the objects than to the mere place of worship.

Most writers find here a play upon the double sense of חלק (*smooth* and
portion) ; but Ewald gives to both the sense of stone (*an des Thales Stein-
chen ist dein Stein*), and makes them the plural of חלק, a synonyme of חלק
(1 Sam. xvii. 40).   Beck, on the other hand, makes both mean part or
portion. Libations and vegetable offerings are here put for offerings in
general, as being the simplest kinds of sacrifice.   There seems to be
another *lusus verborum* in the use of the word אנחם, which may either mean
to remain satisfied without vengeance, or to satisfy one's self by taking it.
(See chap. i. 24.)

  7. *On a high and elevated mountain thou hast placed thy bed ; also there*
(or *even thither*) *hast thou gone up to offer sacrifice.* The figure of adulterous attachment is resumed. (Compare Ezek. xvi. 24, xxv. 31.) That
the mountain is not used as mere figure for an elevated spot, is clear from
the obvious antithesis between it and the valleys before mentioned.   Still
less ground is there for supposing any reference to the worship of mountains themselves. By the bed here, Spencer understands the couch on
which the ancients reclined at their artificial feasts. All other writers seem
to give it the same sense as in Prov. vii. 17, and Ezek. xxiii. 17.   In the
last clause the figure is resolved, and making the bed explained to mean

offering sacrifice. Knobel supposes a particular allusion to the labour of ascending mountains as a proof of self-denying zeal in the worshipper.

8. *And behind the door and the door-post thou hast placed thy memorial, far away from me thou hast uncovered* (thyself or thy bed), *and hast gone up, thou hast enlarged thy bed and hast covenanted from them, thou hast loved their bed, thou hast provided room.* Interpreters are much divided as to the particular expressions of this very obscure verse, although agreed in understanding it as a description of the grossest idolatry. Gesenius and Maurer explain זכרון as meaning *memory*, by which the former understands posthumous fame or notoriety, the latter something cherished or remembered with affection, meaning here the idol as a beloved object. The same sense is obtained in another way by those who make the word mean a memorial, or that which brings to mind an absent object. In this sense the image of a false god may be reckoned its memorial. Grotius and Hitzig suppose an allusion to Deut. vi. 9, the former supposing that the idolaters are here described as doing just the opposite of what is there required, the latter that the Prophet represents them as putting the required memorial of Jehovah's sole divinity out of sight, by going to an inner apartment. A still more natural application of the same sense would be to suppose that they are here described as thrusting the memorial of Jehovah into a corner, to make room for that of the beloved idol. Some suppose a special reference to the worship of Penates, Lares, or household gods. The rest of the verse describes idolatry as adulterous intercourse. תכרת מהם has been variously explained to mean, thou hast covenanted with them; thou hast bargained for a reward from them; thou hast made a covenant with some of them. The masculine form תכרת is used for the feminine, as in chap. xv. 5. Hitzig supposes this to have been usual for *Vav* conversive. (Compare Ewald's H. G. p. 643, S. G. § 234.) The most probable interpretation of the last words is that which gives to יָד the same sense as in chap. lvi. 5. This is strongly favoured by the parallel expression הרחבת משכבך. Others understand it to mean, wherever thou hast seen (their) memorial or monument; others, wherever thou seest a hand (beckoning or inviting thee). The sense gratuitously put upon the phrase by Döderlein, and the praises given him for the discovery, are characteristic of neological aesthetics.

9. *And thou hast gone to the king in oil, and hast multiplied thine unguents, and hast sent thine ambassadors even to a far-off* (land), *and hast gone* (or *sent*) *down even to hell.* The first verb has been variously explained as meaning to see, to look around, to appear to be adorned, to sing, to carry gifts, which last is founded on the analogy of the noun תְּשׁוּרָה a gift or present (1 Sam. ix. 7). Gesenius derives the noun from this verb in the sense of *going with* or carrying, and the modern writers generally acquiesce in this interpretation founded on Arabic analogy. By *the king* some understand the king of Babylon or Egypt, and refer the clause to the eagerness with which the Prophet's contemporaries sought out foreign alliances. Most writers understand it as a name for idols generally, or for Moloch in particular. בַּשֶּׁמֶן is commonly explained to mean *with oil* or ointment (as a gift); but Hitzig understands it to mean *in oil, i.e.* anointed, beautified, adorned. Upon the explanation of this phrase of course depends that of the next, where the unguents are said to be multiplied, either in the way of gifts to others, or as means of self-adornment. Gesenius and the later writers make תַּשְׁפִּילִי qualify תְּשַׁלְחִי understood as a kind of auxiliary, *thou hast sent down deep to hell, i.e.* to the lower world, as opposed to

heaven, of which Moloch was esteemed the king. (See the same construction of the verb in Jer. xiii. 18.) It is much more natural, however, to give it an independent meaning as expressive of extreme indignation and abhorrence. There is no need of ascribing a reflexive meaning to the Hiphil, as the same end may be gained by supplying *way*, or some other noun denoting conduct. Maurer wonders that any interpreter should fail to see that the simplest explanation of this clause is that which makes it signify extreme remoteness. But nothing could in fact be more unusual or unnatural than the expression of this idea by the phrase, *humbling even to Sheol.*

10. *In the greatness of thy way* (or the abundance of thy travel) *thou hast labour; (but) thou hast not said, There is no hope. Thou hast found the life of thy hand; therefore thou art not weak.* Whether *way* be understood as a figure for the whole course of life, or as involving a specific allusion to the journeys mentioned in ver. 9, the general sense is still the same, viz. that no exertion in the service of her false gods could weary or discourage her. This is so obviously the meaning of the whole, that the common version of יָגַעַתְּ (*thou art wearied*) seems to be precluded, the rather as the verb may be used to denote the cause as well as the effect, *i. e.* exertion no less than fatigue. Lowth reverses the declaration of the text by omitting the negative (*thou hast said*) on the authority of a single manuscript, in which the text, as Kocher well observes, was no doubt conjecturally changed in order to conform it to Jer. ii. 25, xviii. 12. In both these places, the verb נוֹאָשׁ is employed as it is here impersonally, *desperatum est*, a form of speech to which we have no exact equivalent in English.—Saadias and Koppe give חַיַּת the sense of animal or beast, in reference to idols of that form. All other writers seem agreed that the essential idea which the whole phrase conveys is that of *strength*. Some accordingly attach this specific sense to חַיַּת, others to יָד; but it rather belongs to the two in combination. In translation, this essential sense may be conveyed under several different forms: Thou hast found thy hand still alive, or still able to sustain life, &c. חָלָה does not merely mean to be sick or to be grieved, but to be weak or weakened, as in Judges xvi. 7, xi. 17.— According to Luzzato, *way* means specifically wicked way, as in Prov. xxxi. 3.

11. *And whom hast thou feared and been afraid of, that thou shouldest lie? and me thou hast not remembered, thou hast not called to mind* (or *laid to heart*). *Is it not* (because) *I hold my peace, and that of old, that thou wilt not fear me?* De Dieu, Cocceius, and Vitringa, understand this as ironical, and as meaning that the fear which they affected as a ground for their forsaking God had no foundation. Gesenius and others understand it as a serious and consolatory declaration that they had no cause to fear. Hitzig supposes an allusion to the mixture of idolatrous worship with the forms of the true religion in the exile. With the exception of the last gratuitous restriction, this agrees well with the form of expression, and may be applied to all hypocritical professors of the truth. They have no real fear of God; why then should they affect to serve him? His forbearance only served to harden and embolden them. " Have I not long kept silence? It cannot be that you fear me." There is no need, therefore, of making the last clause interrogative, as Ewald does, *wilt thou not fear me?* Still more gratuitous and violent is De Wette's construction, " Thou needest not have feared me." This is certainly no better than Luther's interrogative construction of the last clause, " Do you think that I will always hold my

peace?" Luzzatto renders כִּי תֶכְוּבִי *that thou mightest fail*, and refers to chap. lviii. 11. But waters are there said to *deceive* the expectation by their failure, an expression which is utterly inapplicable to the failure of the strength. Instead of וּמֵעֹלָם Lowth reads וּמַעְלִים, *and hide* (*my eyes*), with the noun omitted as in Ps. x. 1. Henderson also thinks the common reading justly suspected, because the Complutension and other editions, with a number of manuscripts, read ומעלם. But this is merely the defective orthography of the common text, and precisely the kind of variation which most frequently occurs in Hebrew manuscripts. Kocher, moreover, has shewn to the satisfaction of most later writers, that the ו before מעולם is equivalent to *et quidem* in Latin, or *and that too* in English.—The use of חָשָׁה is the same as in chap. lxiv. 11, lxv. 6.—The image is identical with that presented in chap. xlii. 14. Knobel contrives to limit the passage to the Babylonish exile, by explaining this verse as a declaration that the Jews had no need of the Babylonian idols to protect them, and alleging that a portion of the captives had renounced the worship of Jehovah because they thought his power insufficient to deliver them. In the same taste and spirit he explains מֵעֹלָם to mean since the beginning of the exile. —Compare with this verse chap. xl. 27, and li. 12, 13.

12. *I will declare thy righteousness and thy works, and they shall not profit* (or *avail thee*). Lowth reads *my righteousness*, on the authority of the Peshito and a few manuscripts. Hendewerk understands צִדְקָתֵךְ to mean *thy desert*, thy righteous doom ; Ewald, thy justification ; Umbreit, thy righteousness, which I will give thee notwithstanding thy unworthiness. Gesenius and Knobel still adhere to their imaginary sense of happiness, salvation, which is not only arbitrary in itself, but incoherent with the next clause, which they are obliged to understand as meaning, as for thy own works they can profit thee nothing. Knobel, however, follows Hitzig in making *thy works* mean *thy idols*, elsewhere called the work of men's fingers. De Dieu makes the last clause an answer to the first. Shall I declare thy righteousness and works ? They will profit thee nothing. But this, in the absence of the form of interrogation, is entirely arbitrary. The earlier writers who retain the sense of צְדָקָה for the most part follow Jerome and Zwingle in making the first clause ironical. But this is unnecessary, as the simplest and most obvious construction is in all respects the most satisfactory. *I will declare thy righteousness*, i. e. I will shew clearly whether thou art righteous, *and* in order to do this I must declare *thy works ;* and if this is done, *they cannot profit thee*, because, instead of justifying, they will condemn thee. There is no need, therefore, of supposing ו at the beginning of the last clause to mean *which, for, that*, or anything but *and*. One of the latest writers on the passage, Thenius, agrees with one of the oldest, Jarchi, in explaining the first clause to mean, I will shew you how you may be or ought to be righteous ; but this is sufficiently refuted by a simple statement of the true sense, which has been already given.

13. *In thy crying* (i. e. when thou criest for help), *let thy gatherings save thee ! And* (yet) *all of them the wind shall take up, and a breath shall take away, and the* (one) *trusting in me shall inherit the land and possess my holy mountain.* This is merely a strong contrast between the impotence of idols and the power of Jehovah to protect their followers respectively. Hitzig, without a change of sense, makes יַצִּילֵךְ an ironical exclamation, *they shall save thee !* This is much better than De Wette's

interrogative construction, *will they save thee ?* which is altogether arbitrary. Most of the modern writers follow Jarchi in explaining קִבּוּצָיִךְ to mean, thy gatherings of gods, thy whole pantheon, as Gesenius expresses it ; so called, as Maurer thinks, because collected from all nations. (Compare Jer. ii. 28.) Knobel denies that there was any such collection, or that gods could be described as blown away, and therefore goes back to Vitringa's explanation of the word as meaning armies, *i. e.* as he thinks those of Babylon, in which the idolatrous Jews trusted to deliver them from Cyrus, and which might therefore be correctly called their gatherings ! It may be questioned whether any of these explanations is entitled to the preference above that of Aben Ezra, who appears to understand the word generically, as denoting all that they could scrape together for their own security, including idols, armies, and all other objects of reliance. This exposition is the more entitled to regard, because the limitation of the passage to the exile is entirely gratuitous, and it is evidently levelled against all unbelieving dependence upon any thing but God.—In the consecution of הֶבֶל and רוּחַ there is a climax : even a wind is not required for the purpose; a mere breath would be sufficient. This fine stroke is effaced by J. D. Michaelis's interpretation of the second word as meaning vapour, and the whole clause as descriptive of evaporation. The promise of the last clause is identical with that in chaps. xlix. 8, lx. 21, lxv. 9 ; Ps. xxxvii. 11 ; lxix. 37, 38 ; Mat. v. 5 ; Rev. v. 10.—Those who restrict the passage to the Babylonish exile must of course explain the promise as relating merely to the restoration ; but the context and the usage of the Scriptures is in favour of a wider explanation, in which the possession of the land is an appointed symbol of the highest blessings which are in reserve for true believers, here and hereafter.

14. *And he shall say, Cast up, cast up, clear the way, take up the stumbling-block from the way of my people !* Lowth and J. D. Michaelis read וָאֹמַר (*then will I say*), the correctness of which change Lowth alleges to be plain from the pronoun *my* in the last clause, a demonstration which appears to have had small effect upon succeeding writers.—Gesenius and Ewald make אָמַר impersonal, *they say, one says,* or *it is said.* Vitringa in like manner long before had paraphrased it thus, *exit vox ;* and Aben Ezra earlier still had proposed substantially the same thing, by supplying הַקּוֹרֵא as the subject of אָמַר. Maurer agrees with the English Version in connecting this verb with the foregoing sentence, and making it agree with הַחוֹסֶה, *the one trusting.* The sense will then be that the man whose faith is thus rewarded will express his joy when he beholds the promise verified. Hitzig thinks it equally evident, however, that Jehovah is the speaker; and Umbreit further recommends this hypothesis by ingeniously combining it with what is said of the divine forbearance in ver. 11. He who had long been silent speaks at last, and that to announce the restoration of his people. The image here presented, and the form of the expression, are the same as in chaps. xxxv. 8, xl. 3, xlix. 11, lxii. 10.—Knobel is not ashamed to make the verse mean that the way of the returning captives home from Babylon shall be convenient and agreeable. There is certainly not much to choose, in point of taste and exegetical discretion, between this hypothesis and that of Vitringa, who labours to find references to the Reformation, and the subsequent efforts made by ministers and magistrates to take away all scandals, both of doctrine and discipline, with special allusion, as he seems to think, to the hundred grievances presented to Pope Adrian by the German princes in 1523. Such interpreters have no right to despise each other : for the only error with which either can be

charged, is that of fixing upon one specific instance of the thing foretold, and making that the whole theme and the sole theme of a prophecy, which, in design, as well as fact, is perfectly unlimited to any one event or period, yet perfectly defined as a description of God's mode of dealing with his church, and with those who although in it are not of it.

15. *For thus saith the High and Exalted One, inhabiting eternity, and Holy is his name: On high and holy will I dwell, and with the broken and humble of spirit, to revive the spirit of the humble, and to revive the heart of the broken* (or *contrite ones*). This verse assigns a reason why the foregoing promise might be trusted, notwithstanding the infinite disparity between the giver and the objects of his favour. Notwithstanding the intimate connection of the verses, there is no need of referring *thus saith* to what goes before, as if he had said, these assurances are uttered by the High and Exalted One. Analogy and usage necessarily connect them with what follows, the relation of the verse to that before it being clearly indicated by the *for* at the beginning. You need not hesitate to trust the promise which is involved in this command, for the High and Holy One has made the following solemn declaration.—The only reason for translating נִשָּׂא *exalted* rather than *lofty*, is that the former retains the participial form of the original. The same two epithets are joined in chap. vi. 1, which is regarded by the modern critics as the oldest extant composition of the genuine Isaiah. J. D. Michaelis disregards the Masoretic accents, and explains the next words as meaning that his name is the inhabitant of eternity and the sanctuary, which last he regards as a hendiadys for the everlasting sanctuary, *i. e.* heaven as distinguished from material and temporary structures. Luzzatto gives the same construction of the clause, but supposes the noun עַד (like the cognate preposition) to be applicable to space as well as time, and in this case to denote infinite height, which sense he likewise attaches to עוֹלָם when predicated of the hills, &c. All other modern writers follow the accentuation, making *holy* the predicate and *name* the subject of a distinct proposition. On this hypothesis, קָדוֹשׁ may either be an adjective qualifying שֵׁם, *his name is holy*, i. e. divine, or infinitely above every other name; or it may be absolutely used, and qualify Jehovah understood, his name is Holy or the Holy One. The ambiguity in English is exactly copied from the Hebrew.—As מָרוֹם is not an adjective, but a substantive, denoting a high place, the following קָדוֹשׁ must either be referred to מָקוֹם understood, or construed with מָרוֹם itself, *a height, and that a holy one, will I inhabit.*—Ewald takes וְאֶת at the beginning of the last clause as a sign of the nominative absolute, and the infinitives as expressive of necessity or obligation: *And as for the broken and contrite of spirit,* (it is necessary) *to revive,* &c. Henderson and Knobel regard אֶת as the objective particle, shewing what follows to be governed directly by the verb אֶשְׁכּוֹן: "I inhabit (or dwell in) the broken and humble of spirit." This would be more natural if the other objects of the same verb were preceded by the particle; but as this is not the case, the most satisfactory construction is the common one, which takes אֶת as a preposition meaning *with.*—The future meaning given to אֶשְׁכּוֹן by Lowth is strictly accurate, and more expressive than the present, as it intimates that notwithstanding God's condescension he will still maintain his dignity. The idea of habitual or perpetual residence is still implied.—The reviving of the spirit and the heart is a common Hebrew phrase for consolation and encouragement.—Hitzig denies that contrition and humility are here propounded as conditions or prerequisites, and understands the clause as a

description of the actual distress and degradation of the exiles.—Vitringa finds here a specific reference to the early sufferers in the cause of reformation, such as the Waldenses and Bohemian Brethren.—Compare with this verse chaps. xxxiii. 5, lxiii. 15, lxvi. 1, 2; Ps. xxii. 4, cxiii, 5, 6, cxxxviii. 6.

16. *For not to eternity will I contend, and not to perpetuity will I be wroth ; for the spirit from before me will faint, and the souls (which) I have made.* A reason for exercising mercy is here drawn from the frailty of the creature. (Compare chap. xlii. 3, Ps. lxxviii. 38, 39, ciii. 9, 14.) Suffering being always represented in Scripture as the consequence of sin, its infliction is often metaphorically spoken of as a divine quarrel or controversy with the sufferer. (See vol. i. p. 440.) — The verb יַעֲטוֹף has been variously explained, as meaning *to go forth* (Septuagint and Vulgate), *return* (De Dieu), *have mercy* (Cappellus), &c. ; but the only sense sustained by etymology and usage is that of covering. The Targum seems to make the clause descriptive of a resurrection similar to that in Ezekiel's vision, the life-giving Spirit *covering* the bones with flesh, and breathing into the nostrils the breath of life. Cocceius understands it of the *Spirit* by his influences *covering* the earth as the waters cover the sea (chap. xi. 9). Clericus makes it descriptive of the origin of man, in which the spirit covers or clothes itself with matter. The modern writers are agreed in making it intransitive and elliptical, the full expression being that of covering with darkness, metaphorically applied to extreme depression, faintness, and stupor. Maurer translates it even here, *caligine obvolvitur*. The figurative use is clear from the analogy of Ps. lxi. 3, cii. 1, compared with that of the reflexive form in Ps. cvii. 5, cxliii. 4, Jonah ii. 8. Rosenmüller follows Jarchi in giving כִּי the sense of *when*, and takes the last clause as a promise : when the spirit from before me faints, I grant a breathing time (*respirationes concedo*). The credit of this last interpretation is perhaps due to Grotius, who translates the clause, *et ventulum faciam*. But נְשָׁמָה is evidently used as an equivalent to נֶפֶשׁ in Prov. xx. 27, and is here the parallel expression to רוּחַ. Lowth's translation, *living souls*, multiplies words without expressing the exact sense of the Hebrew, which is *breaths*. The ellipsis of the relative is the one so often mentioned heretofore as common both in Hebrew and English. *From before me* is connected by the accents with the verb *to faint*, and indicates God's presence as the cause of the depression. A more perfect parallelism would, however, be obtained by understanding *from before me* as referring to the origin of human life and as corresponding to the words *which I have made* in the other member. Umbreit's explanation of the verse, as meaning that God cannot be for ever at enmity with any of his creatures, is as old as Kimchi, but without foundation in the text and inconsistent with the uniform teaching of the Scriptures.

17. *For his covetous iniquity I am wroth and will smite him, (I will) hide me and will be wroth ; for he has gone on turning away (i. e. persevering in apostasy) in the way of his heart (or of his own inclination).* The futures in the first clause shew that both the punishment and mercy are still future. The interpreters have generally overlooked the fact that the ו before these futures is not Vav conversive, and there is nothing in the text or context to require or justify either an arbitrary change of pointing, or an arbitrary disregard of the difference between the tenses.—The first phrase in the verse (עֲוֹן בִּצְעוֹ) has been very variously understood. Lowth says the usual meaning of the second noun would here be " quite beside the purpose," and accordingly omits the suffix and takes בֶּצַע as an adverb

meaning *for a short time;* of which it can only be said that the criticism
and lexicography are worthy of each other. Koppe adopts another desperate
expedient by calling in the Arabic analogy to prove that the true sense of
בֶּצַע is *scortatio.* J. D. Michaelis and Henderson make one noun simply
qualify the other, and explain the whole as meaning his accumulated guilt
or his exorbitant iniquity. Vitringa and Gesenius suppose covetousness to
be here used in a wide sense for all selfish desires or undue attachment to
the things of time and sense, a usage which they think may be distinctly
traced both in the Old and New Testament. (See Ps. cxix. 36, Ezek.
xxxiii. 31, 1 Tim. vi. 10, Eph. v. 5.) Perhaps the safest and most satisfactory hypothesis is that of Maurer, who adheres to the strict sense of the
word, but supposes covetousness to be here considered as a temptation,
and incentive to other forms of sin.—The singular pronouns *his* and *him*
refer to the collective noun *people,* or rather to *Israel* as an ideal person.—
הַסָּתֵּר is an adverbial form, rendered equivalent in this case by its collocation
the futures which precede and follow. In the last clause the writer suddenly reverts from the future to the past, in order to assign the cause of
the infliction threatened in the first. This connection can be rendered
clear in English only by the use of the word *for,* although the literal translation would be *and he went.* Jarchi's assumption of a transposition is
entirely unnecessary. Hendewerk's translation, *but he went on,* rests upon
the false assumption that the first clause is historical. Luther seems to
understand the last clause as describing the effect of the divine stroke *(da
gingen sie hin und her).* With the closing words of this clause compare
chaps. xlii. 24, liii. 6, lvi. 11, lxv. 12.—The best refutation of Vitringa's
notion, that this verse has special reference to the period from the death of
Charles the Bald to the beginning of the Reformation, is suggested by his
own apology for not going into the details of the fulfilment: " Narrandi
nullus hic finis est si inceperis."

18. *His ways I have seen, and I will heal him, and will guide him, and
restore comforts unto him and to his mourners.* The healing here meant is
forgiveness and conversion, as correctly explained by Kimchi, with a reference to chap. vi. 10, and Ps. xli. 5. This obvious meaning of the figure
creates a difficulty in explaining the foregoing words so as to make the
connection appear natural. Gesenius supposes an antithesis, and makes
the particle adversative. " I have seen his (evil) ways, but I will (nevertheless) heal him." There is then a promise of gratuitous forgiveness
similar to that in chap. xliii. 25, and xlviii. 9. The Targum puts a favourable sense on *ways,* as meaning his repentance and conversion. So Jarchi,
I have seen his humiliation; and Ewald, I have seen his patient endurance
of trial. Hitzig strangely understands the words to mean that God saw
punishment to be without effect and therefore pardoned him, and cites in illustration Gen. viii. 21, where the incorrigible wickedness of men is assigned
as a reason for not again destroying them. But even if this sense were
correct and natural, considered in itself, it could hardly be extracted
from the words here used. Knobel supposes *ways* to mean neither good
nor evil works but sufferings, the length of which, without regard to guilt
or innocence, induced Jehovah to deliver them.—*I will guide him* is supposed by Hitzig to mean I will guide him as a shepherd guides his flock
through the wilderness. (See chaps. xlviii. 21, xlix. 10.) But as this
does not agree with the mention of consolation and of mourners in the
other clause, it is better to rest in the general sense of gracious and providential guidance. (Compare Ps. lxxiii. 24.) Clericus renders it *feci*

quiescere, in reference to the rest of the exiles in their own land. This interpretation, which is mentioned although not approved by Jarchi, supposes an arbitrary change at least of vowels, so as to derive the word from נוּחַ.—The promise to *restore* consolation implies not only that it had been once enjoyed, but also that it should *compensate* for the intervening sorrows, as the Hebrew word means properly to make good, or indemnify.—The addition of the words *and to his mourners* has led to a dispute among interpreters, whether the writer had in mind two distinct classes of sufferers, or only one. Cocceius adopts the former supposition, and assumes a distinction in the church itself. Others understand by *his mourners* those who mourned for him, and Henderson applies it specifically to the heathen proselytes who sympathised with Israel in exile. Hitzig and Knobel understand the וֹ as meaning *and especially*, because those who suffered most were most in need of consolation. Perhaps it would be still more satisfactory to make these words explanatory of the לוֹ, to him, *i. e.* to his mourners. Whether these were but a part, or coextensive with the whole, the form of expression then leaves undecided. Luzzatto gets rid of the difficulty by connecting these words with the next verse, "and for his mourners I create," &c. Koppe throws not only this verse and the next, but also the one following, into one sentence, making this the expression of a wish, and the next a continuation of it. " I saw his ways, and would have healed him, guided him, consoled him and his mourners, creating, &c. ; but the wicked are like the troubled sea," &c. This is ingenious, but too artificial and refined to be good Hebrew. Vitringa sees a special connection between this verse and the supplication of the Austrian nobles to the Emperor Ferdinand in 1541.

19. *Creating the fruit of the lips, Peace, peace to the far off and to the near, saith Jehovah, and I heal him.* Luzzatto adds to this verse the concluding words of ver. 18, " and for his mourners I create," &c. This, besides the arbitrary change in the traditional arrangement of the text, requires the participle בּוֹרֵא to be taken as an independent verb, which, although a possible construction, is not to be assumed without necessity. The usual construction connects בּוֹרֵא with Jehovah as the subject of the foregoing verse.—The fruit or product of the lips is speech, and creating, as usual, implies almighty power and a new effect. Rosenmüller understands the clause to mean that nothing shall be uttered by the following proclamation, "Peace, peace," &c. Gesenius understands by the fruit of the lips praise or thanksgiving, as in Heb. xiii. 15, and Hosea xiv. 3. Hitzig supposes it to mean the promise which Jehovah had given, and would certainly fulfil.—By the *far* and *near* Henderson understands the Jews and Gentiles. (Compare Acts x. 36, Eph. ii. 17.) Jarchi and Knobel explain it to mean all the Jews wherever scattered (chap. xliii. 5-7, xlix. 12). The Targum makes the distinction an internal one,—the just who have kept the law, and sinners who have returned to it by sincere repentance. Kimchi in like manner understands the words as abolishing all difference between the earlier and later converts, an idea similar to that embodied in our Saviour's parable of the labourers in the vineyard. Hitzig directs attention to the way in which the writer here comes back to the beginning of ver. 18, as an observable rhetorical beauty.—The present form is used above in the translation of the last verb, because it is doubtful whether the Vav has a conversive influence when separated so far from the futures of the foregoing verse.

20. *And the wicked (are) like the troubled sea, for rest it cannot, and its*

waters cast up mire and dirt. Koppe's unnatural construction of this verse as the apodosis of a sentence beginning in ver. 18 has already been refuted. Interpreters are commonly agreed in making it a necessary limitation of the foregoing promise to its proper objects. Hitzig regards it as a mere introduction to the next verse. There is a force in the original which cannot be retained in a translation, arising from the etymological affinity between the words translated *wicked, troubled,* and *cast up.* Among the various epithets applied to sinners, the one here used is that which originally signifies their turbulence or restlessness. (See Hengstenberg on Ps. ii. 1.) Henderson's strange version of the first clause (*as for the wicked they are each tossed about like the sea which cannot rest*) seems to be founded upon some mistaken view of the construction, and is certainly not worth purchasing by a violation of the accents.—Hendewerk's version of the clause is peculiar only in the use of the indefinite expression *a sea.* Gesenius in his Lexicon makes this one of the cases in which יִּ retains its original meaning as a relative pronoun, *like the troubled sea which cannot rest.* The English Version and some others take it as a particle of time (*when it cannot rest*). All the latest German writers follow Lowth in giving it its usual sense of *for because.* The only objection to this version, that it appears to make the sea itself the subject of comparison, Knobel ingeniously removes by adding, " any more than you can." The future form יוּכַל implies that such will be the case hereafter as it has been heretofore, which is sufficiently expressed by the reference to futurity in our verb *can.* The Vav conversive prefixed to the last verb merely shews its dependence on the one before it, as an effect upon its cause, or a consequent upon its antecedent. Its waters cannot rest, and (so or therefore) they cast up mire and mud. Lowth's version of this last clause is more than usually plain and vigorous: *its waters work up mire and filth.* The verb means strictly to expel or drive out, and is therefore happily descriptive of the natural process here referred to. There seems to be allusion to this verse in the κύματα ἄγρια θαλάσσης of Jude 13. Most of the later writers have repeated the fine parallel which Clericus quotes from Ovid:

> Cumque sit hibernis agitatum fluctibus æquor,
> Pectora sunt ipso turbidiora mari.

21. *There is no peace, saith my God, to the wicked,* Gesenius has *for the wicked, i. e.* in reserve for them. Ewald follows Luther in exchanging the oriental for an occidental idiom, *the wicked have no peace,* which, although perfectly correct in sense, is an enfeebling deviation from the Hebrew collocation and construction. That *peace* is here to be taken in its strict sense, and not in that of welfare or prosperity, is clear from the comparison in the preceding verse. Twenty-two manuscripts assimilate this verse to chap. xlviii. 22 by reading יְהֹוָה for אֱלֹהַי. The Alexandrian text of the Septuagint combines both readings, κύριος ὁ θεός. So too Jerome has *Dominus Deus,* which Grotius thinks ought to be read *Dominus meus,* not observing that the form of expression would still be different from that of the original. It is somewhat surprising that the " higher criticism " has not detected in this repetition a marginal gloss, or the assimilating hand of some redactor. But even Hitzig zealously contends, without an adversary, that the verse is genuine both here and in chap. xlviii. 22, and that its studied repetition proves the unity and chronological arrangement of the whole book. The only wonder is that in a hundred cases more or less

analogous, the same kind of reasoning is rejected as beneath refutation. This verse, according to the theory of Rückert, Hitzig, and Hävernick, closes the second great division of the Later Prophecies. For the true sense of the words themselves, see above, on chap. xlviii. 22.

Chapter 58

THE rejection of Israel as a nation is the just reward of their unfaithfulness, ver. 1.ₑ Their religious services are hypocritical, ver. 2. Their mortifications and austerities are nullified by accompanying wickedness, vers. 3–5. They should have been connected with the opposite virtues, vers. 6, 7. In that case they would have continued to enjoy the divine favour, vers. 8, 9. They are still invited to make trial of this course, with an ample promise of prosperity and blessing to encourage them, vers. 10–14.

1. *Cry with the throat, spare not, like the trumpet raise thy voice, and tell to my people their transgression and to the house of Jacob their sins.* Although this may be conveniently assigned as the beginning of the third part, according to the theory propounded in the Introduction, it is really, as Knobel well observes, a direct continuation of the previous discourse. Ewald's suggestion that the latter may have produced some effect upon the people before this was uttered, rests on a supposition which has probably no foundation in fact. The utmost that can be conceded is that the Prophet, after a brief pause, recommences his discourse precisely at the point where he suspended it.—The object of address is the Prophet himself, as expressed in the Targum, and by Saadias (he said to me). That he is here viewed as the representative of prophets or ministers in general, is not a natural or necessary inference. Crying with the throat or from the lungs is here opposed to a simple motion of the lips and tongue. (See 1 Sam. i. 13.) The common version (*cry aloud*) is therefore substantially correct, though somewhat vague. The Septuagint in like manner paraphrases it ἐν ἰσχύϊ. The Vulgate omits it altogether. J. D. Michaelis reads, *as loud as thou canst.* The positive command is enforced by the negative one, *spare not,* as in chap. liv. 2. The comparison with a trumpet is of frequent occurrence in the Book of Revelations. (See *e. g.* i. 10, iv. 1.) The loudness of the call is intended to suggest the importance of the subject, and perhaps the insensibility of those to be convinced. The Prophet here seems to turn away from avowed apostates to hypocritical professors of the truth. The restriction of the verse to Isaiah's contemporaries by the rabbins, Grotius, and Piscator, and to the Jews of the Babylonish exile by Sanctius and the modern writers, is as perfectly gratuitous as its restriction by Eusebius and Jerome to the Pharisees of Christ's time, and by Vitringa to the Protestant Churches at the decline of the Reformation. The points of similarity with all or any of these periods arise from its being a description of what often has occurred and will occur again. It was important that a phase of human history so real and important should form a part of this prophetic picture, and accordingly it has not been forgotten.

2. *And me day* (by) *day they will seek, and the knowledge of my ways they will delight in* (or *desire*), *like a nation which has done right and the judgment of its God has not forsaken; they will ask of me righteous judgments, the approach to God* (or *of God*) *they will delight in* (or *desire*). The older writers take this to be a description of hypocrisy, as practised in a formal seeking (*i. e.* worshipping) of God, and a professed desire to know

his ways (*i. e.* the doctrines and duties of the true religion), the external appearance of a just and godly people, who delight in nothing more than in drawing near to God (*i. e.* in worship and communion with him). Cocceius and Vitringa, while they differ on some minor questions, *e. g.* whether seeking denotes consultation or worship, or includes them both, agree as to the main points of the exposition which has just been given. But Gesenius and all the later German writers put a very different sense upon the passage. They apply it not to hypocritical formality, but to a discontented and incredulous impatience of delay in the fulfilment of God's promises. According to this view of the matter, seeking God daily, means importunate solicitation; delight in the knowledge of his ways, is eager curiosity to know his providential plans and purposes; the judgments of righteousness which they demand are either saving judgments for themselves, or destroying judgments for their enemies; the approach which they desire is not their own approach to God, but his approach to them for their deliverance; and the words *like a nation*, &c., are descriptive not of a simulated piety, but of a self-righteous belief that by their outward services they had acquired a meritorious claim to the divine interposition in their favour. It is somewhat remarkable that a sentence of such length should, without violence, admit of two interpretations so entirely different, and the wonder is enhanced by the fact that both the senses may be reconciled with the ensuing context. The only arguments which seem to be decisive in favour of the first, are its superior simplicity and the greater readiness with which it is suggested to most readers by the language of the text itself, together with the fact that it precludes the necessity of limiting the word to the Babylonish exile, for which limitation there is no ground either in the text or context. The objection to the modern explanation, founded on the sense which it attaches to the verb חָפֵץ, is met by the analogous use of the verb *love* in Ps. xl. 17, lxx. 5; 2 Tim. iv. 8.—Luther understands the last clause as accusing them of wishing to contend with God, and venturing to charge him with injustice.

3. *Why have we fasted and thou hast not seen* (*it*), *afflicted our soul* (or *ourselves*) *and thou wilt not know* (*it*)? *Behold, in the day of your fast ye will find pleasure, and all your labours ye will exact.* The two interpretations which have been propounded of the foregoing verse agree in making this a particular exemplification of the people's self-righteous confidence in the meritorious efficacy of their outward services. The first clause contains their complaint, and the last the Prophet's answer. This relation of the clauses Saadias points out by prefixing to one the words "they say," and and to the other "Prophet, answer them." Cocceius and Vitringa suppose fasting to be here used in a wide sense for the whole routine of ceremonial services. The same end is attained by adhering to the strict sense, but supposing what it said of this one instance to be applicable to the others. The structure of the first clause is like that in chaps. v. 4, 1. 2. In our idiom the idea would be naturally thus expressed, Why dost thou not see when we fast, or recognise our merit when we mortify ourselves before thee? The word נֶפֶשׁ here may either mean the appetite, or the soul as distinguished from the body, or it may supply the place of the reflexive pronoun *self*, which is entitled to the preference, because the context shews that their mortifications were not of a spiritual but of a corporeal nature. The combination of the preterite (*hast not seen*) and the future (*wilt not know*) includes all time. The clause describes Jehovah as indifferent and inattentive to their laboured austerities. The reason given is analogous to

that for the rejection of their sacrifices in chap. i. 11–13, viz. the combination of their formal service with unhallowed practice. The precise nature of the alleged abuse depends upon the sense of the word חֵפֶץ. Gesenius and most later writers understand it to mean business, as in chap. xliv. 28, liii. 10, and explain the whole clause as a declaration, that on days set apart for fasting they were accustomed to pursue their usual employments, or as Henderson expresses it, to "attend to business." But this explanation of the word, as we have seen before, is perfectly gratuitous. If we take it in its usual and proper sense, the meaning of the clause is that they made their pretended self-denial a means or an occasion of sinful gratification. J. D. Michaelis supposes the specific pleasure meant to be that afforded by the admiration of their superior goodness by the people. But this is a needless limitation of the language, which may naturally be applied to all kinds of enjoyment, inconsistent with the mortifying humiliation which is inseparable from right fasting.—The remaining member of the sentence has been still more variously explained. According to the Septuagint and Vulgate, it charges them with specially oppressing their dependents (ὑποχειρίους and *subjectos*) at such times. Luther agrees with Symmachus in supposing a particular allusion to the treatment of debtors. Gesenius in his Commentary, Umbreit, and De Wette, prefer the specific sense of labourers or workmen forced to toil on fast-days as at others times. Maurer, Hitzig, and Gesenius in his Thesaurus, coincide with the English Version in the sense, *ye exact all your labours, i. e.* all the labour due to you from your dependents. As these substitute labours for labourers, so the Rabbins debts for debtors. Aben Ezra uses the expression *mammon*, which may mean your gains or profits; but עצב, as Maurer well observes, does not signify emolument in general, but hard-earned wages, as appears both from etymology and usage. (See Prov. v. 10, x. 22; Ps. cxxvii. 2.) J. D. Michaelis ingeniously explains the clause as meaning that they demanded of God himself a reward for their meritorious services.—On the stated fasts of the Old Testament, see Jer. xxxvi. 9, Zech. vii. 3, viii. 19. According to Luzzatto, צֹום originally signifies the convocation of the people for prayer and preaching; so that when Jezebel required a fast to be proclaimed, Naboth was set on high among the people, *i. e.* preached against idolatry, on which pretext he was afterwards accused of having blasphemed God and the king. (1 Kings xxi. 9–13.)

4. *Behold, for strife and contention ye will fast, and to smite with the fist of wickedness; ye shall not* (or *ye will not*) *fast to-day* (so as) *to make your voice heard on high.* Some understand this as a further reason why their fasts were not acceptable to God; others suppose the same to be continued, and refer what is here said to the maltreatment of the labourers or debtors mentioned in the verse preceding. Gesenius understands the ל in the first clause as expressive merely of an accompanying circumstance, ye fast *with* strife and quarrel. But Maurer and the later writers, more consistently with usage, understand it as denoting the effect, either simply so considered, or as the end deliberately aimed at. J. D. Michaelis tells a story of a lady who was never known to scold her servants so severely as on fast days, which he says agrees well with physiological principles and facts ! Vitringa applies this clause to the doctrinal divisions among Protestants, and more particularly to the controversies in the Church of Holland on the subject of grace and predestination. To smite with the fist of wickedness is a periphrasis for fighting, no doubt borrowed from the provision of the law in Exod. xxi. 18.—Luther and other early writers understand the last

clause as a prohibition of noisy quarrels, to make the voice heard on high, being taken as equivalent to letting it be heard in the street (chap. xlii. 3). Vitringa and the later writers give it a meaning altogether different, by taking מָרוֹם in the sense of heaven (chap. lvii. 15), and the whole clause as a declaration that such fasting would not have the desired effect of gaining audience and acceptance for their prayers. (See Joel i. 14, ii. 12). All the modern writers make כַּיּוֹם synonymous with הַיּוֹם *to-day*, as in 1 Kings i. 31. Jarchi's explanation, *as the day*, (ought to be kept) involves a harsh ellipsis and is contrary to usage.—Instead of רשע לא, Lowth reads רש על מה לי, and translates " to smite with the fist the poor ; wherefore fast ye unto me in this manner?" The only authority for this pretended emendation is the ταπεινὸν ἱνατί μοι of the Septuagint Version, and the strange idea that it " gives a much better sense than the present reading of the Hebrew."

5. *Shall it be like this, the fast that I will choose, the day of man's humbling himself ? Is it to hang his head like a bulrush and make sackcloth and ashes his bed ? Wilt thou call this a fast, and a day of acceptance* (an acceptable day) *to Jehovah ?* The general meaning of this verse is clear, although its structure and particular expressions are marked with a strong idiomatic peculiarity which makes exact translation very difficult. The interrogative form, as in many other cases, implies strong negation mingled with surprise. Nothing is gained, but something lost, by dropping the future forms of the first clause. The preterite translation of אֶבְחָר (*I have chosen*) is in fact quite ungrammatical. No less gratuitous is the explanation of this verb as meaning *love* by Gesenius, and *approve* by Henderson ; neither of which ideas is expressed, although both are really implied in the exact translation, *choose*. The second member of the first clause is not part of the contemptuous description of a mere external fast, but belongs to the definition of a true one, as a time for men to practise self-humiliation. He does not ask whether the fast which he chooses is a day for a man to afflict himself implying that it is not, which would be destructive of the very essence of a fast ; but he asks whether the fast which he has chosen as a time for men to humble and afflict themselves is such as this, *i. e.* a mere external self-abasement.—יַצַּע means to spread anything under one for him to lie upon. (See above, chap. xiv. 11.) The effect of fasting, as an outward means and token of sincere humiliation, may be learned from the case of Ahab (1 Kings xxi. 27–29) and the Ninevites (Jonah iii. 5–9.) The use of sackcloth and ashes in connection with fasting is recorded in Esther ix. 3. Even Gesenius regards this general description as particularly applicable to the abuse of fasting in the Romish and the Oriental Churches. The sense attached to יוֹם by Luther (*des Tages*) and Lowth (*for a day*) changes the meaning of the clause by an arbitrary violation of the syntax.

6. *Is not this the fast that I will choose, to loosen bands of wickedness, to undo the fastenings of the yoke, and to send away the crushed* (or *broken*) *free, and every yoke ye shall break ?* Most interpreters suppose a particular allusion to the detention of Hebrew servants after the seventh year, contrary to the express provisions of the law (Exod. xxi. 2, Lev. xxv. 39, Deut. xv. 12). Grotius applies the terms in a figurative sense to judicial oppression; Cocceius to impositions on the conscience (Mat. xxiii. 4, Acts xv. 28, Gal. v. 1); Vitringa, still more generally, to human domination in the church (1 Cor. vii. 23), with special reference to the arbitrary impositions of formulas and creeds. It is evident, however, that the terms were so selected as to be descriptive of oppression universally ; to make which still more evident, the Prophet adds a general command or exhortation, Ye shall break every

yoke. The Targum explains מוֹטָה to mean unjust decrees (כתבי דין מסטי),
and the Septuagint applies it to fraudulent contracts, an idea which Gesenius thinks was probably suggested to the translator by his knowledge of
the habits of the Alexandrian Jews. Hitzig agrees with Jarchi in deriving
the first מוֹטָה from נָטָה and making it synonymous with מַטֶּה (Ezek. ix. 9),
the perversion of justice. (For this application of the verb, see above,
chaps. xxix. 21, xxx. 11). But although this affords a more perfect parallelism with רֶשַׁע, it is dearly purchased by assuming that the same form
מוֹטָה is here used in two entirely different senses. For the use of רָצַץ
in reference to oppression, see 1 Sam. xii. 3, 4, and compare Isa. xlii. 3.
Gesenius here repeats his unwarrantable mistranslation of הֲלֹא as synonymous with הִנֵּה. In this he is followed by Hitzig; but the later writers
have the good taste to prefer the strict translation. The change of construction in the last clause from the infinitive to the future, is so common
as to be entitled to consideration, not as a solecism but as a Hebrew idiom.
There is no need therefore of adopting the indirect and foreign construction, *that ye break every yoke.*—In reply to the question, how the acts here
mentioned could be described as fasting, J. D. Michaelis says that they are
all to be considered as involving acts of conscientious self-denial, which he
illustrates by the case of an American slaveholder brought by stress of conscience to emancipate his slaves. The principle is stated still more clearly
and more generally by Augustine, in a passage which Gesenius quotes in
illustration of the verse before us. "Jejunium magnum et generale est
abstinere ab iniquitatibus et illicitis voluptatibus seculi, quod est perfectum
jejunium." Hendewerk understands this passage of Isaiah as expressly condemning and prohibiting all fasts, but the other Germans still maintain the
old opinion that it merely shews the spirit which is necessary to a true fast.

7. *Is it not to break unto the hungry thy bread, and the afflicted, the home-
less, thou shalt bring home; for thou shalt see one naked and shalt clothe him,
and from thine own flesh thou shalt not hide thyself.* The change of construction to the future in the first clause is precisely the same as in the
preceding verse.—Grotius explains the phrase *to break bread* (meaning to
distribute) from the oriental practice of baking bread in thin flat cakes.—
Lowth's version of the next phrase (*the wandering poor*) is now commonly
regarded as substantially correct. (Compare Job xv. 23.) מְרוּדִים is properly an abstract, meaning *wandering* (from רוּד), here used for the concrete
expression *wanderers.* There is no need of explaining it with Henderson as
an ellipsis for אַנְשֵׁי מְרוּדִים *men of wanderings.* The essential idea is expressed in the Septuagint version (ἀστέγους), which Ewald copies (*Dachlose*),
and still more exactly in the Vulgate (*vagos*). Jarchi explains it to mean
mourning, by metathesis for מוֹרְדִים, a passive participle from יָרַד. Hitzig
derives it from מָרַד, to rebel, but gives it the specific sense of fugitive
rebels. *Thou shalt bring home, i. e.* as Knobel understands it, for the purpose of feeding them; but this is a gratuitous restriction.—The construction of the second clause is similar to that in ver. 2. It is best to retain
the form of the original, not only upon general grounds, but because *thou
shalt see the naked* seems to be a substantive command, corresponding to *thou
shalt not hide thyself.*—For the use of *flesh* to signify near kindred, see Gen.
xxix. 14, xxxvii. 27, 2 Sam. v. 1. The Septuagint paraphrase is, ἀπὸ τῶν
οἰκείων τοῦ σπέρματός σου.—With the general precepts of the verse compare
chap. xxxii. 6, Job xxxi. 16–22, Exod. xviii. 7, Prov. xxii. 9, Ps. cxii. 9,
Matt. xxv. 36, Rom. xii. 11, Heb. xiii. 2, James ii. 15, 16, and with the
last clause, Matt. xv. 5, 6.

8. *Then shall break forth as the dawn thy light, and thy healing speedily shall spring up ; then shall go before thee thy righteousness, and the glory of Jehovah shall be thy rereward* (or *bring up thy rear*). Kimchi connects this with the foregoing context by supplying as an intermediate thought, thou shalt no longer need to fast or lie in sackcloth and ashes. It is evident, however, that the writer has entirely lost sight of the particular example upon which he had been dwelling so minutely, and is now entirely occupied with the effects which would arise from a conformity to God's will, not in reference to fasting merely, but to every other part of duty. *Then, i. e.* when this cordial compliance shall have taken place. The future form is preferable here to the conditional (*would break forth*), not only as more obvious and exact, but as implying that it will be so in point of fact, that the effect will certainly take place, because the previous condition will be certainly complied with. The verb, to break forth (literally, *to be cleft*), elsewhere applied to the hatching of eggs (chap. lix. 5), and the gushing of water (chap. xxxv. 6), is here used in reference to the dawn or break of day, a common figure for relief succeeding deep affliction. (See chap. viii. 22, xlvii. 11, lx. 1.)—אֲרוּכָה is properly a bandage, but has here the sense of healing, as in Jer. viii. 22, xxx. 17, xxxiii. 6. By a mixture of metaphors, which does not in the least obscure the sense, this healing is here said to sprout or germinate, a figure employed elsewhere to denote the sudden, rapid, and spontaneous growth or rise of anything. (See above, on chaps. xlii. 9, and xliii. 19.) In the last clause a third distinct figure is employed to express the same idea, viz. that of a march like the journey through the wilderness, with the pillar of cloud, as the symbol of God's presence, going before and after. (See above, on chap. lii. 12, and compare Exod. xiii. 21, xiv. 19.)—*Thy righteousness shall go before thee* cannot mean that righteousness shall be exacted as a previous condition, which is wholly out of keeping with the figurative character of the description. Luther has also marred it by translating the last verb, *shall take thee to himself*, overlooking its peculiar military sense, for which see above, on chap. lii. 12. Knobel improves upon Gesenius's gratuitous assumption that צֶדֶק means salvation, by explaining it in this case as an abstract used for the concrete, and accordingly translating it *thy Saviour*. All the advantages of this interpretation are secured without the slightest violence to usage, by supposing that Jehovah here assumes the conduct of his people, as their righteousness or justifier. (See Jer. xxiii. 6, xxxiii. 16, and compare Isaiah liv. 17.) The parallel term *glory* may then be understood as denoting the manifested glory of Jehovah, or Jehovah himself in glorious epiphany ; just as his presence with his people in the wilderness was manifested by the pillar of cloud and of fire, which sometimes went before them, and at other times brought up up their rear. (See above, on chap. lii. 12.) This grand reiteration of a glorious promise is gratuitously weakened and belittled by restricting it to the return of the exiled Jews from Babylon ; which, although one remarkable example of the thing described, has no more claim to be regarded as the whole of it, than the deliverance of Paul or Peter from imprisonment exhausted Christ's engagement to be with his servants always, even to the end of the world.

9. *Then shalt thou call and Jehovah will answer, thou shalt cry and he will say, Behold me* (here I am), *if thou wilt put away from the midst of thee the yoke, the pointing of the finger, and the speaking of vanity.* The אִם may either be connected with what goes before or correspond to אִם in the other clause, like *then, when*, in English. That אִם may thus be used as a particle

of time, will be seen by comparing chaps. iv. 4, xxiv. 13. The conditional form of the promise implies that it was not so with them now, of which, indeed, they are themselves represented as complaining in ver. 3. The idea of this verse might be expressed in the occidental idiom by saying, *when thou callest, Jehovah will answer; when thou criest, he will say, Behold me.* (See above, on chap. 1. 2.)—The yoke is again mentioned as the symbol of oppression. (See ver. 6.) De Wette needlessly resolves it into subjugation (*Unterjochung*), Hendewerk, still more boldly, into *slavery.*— The pointing of the finger is a gesture of derision. Hence the middle finger is called by Persius *digitus infamis;* Martial says, *rideto multum,* and in the same connection, *digitum porrigito medium;* Plautus, in reference to an object of derision, *intende digitum in hunc.* The Arabs have a verb derived from *finger,* and denoting scornful ridicule. The object of contempt in this case is supposed by Grotius to be the pious; by Hitzig, the Prophet or Jehovah himself; by Knobel, the unfortunate, who are afterwards described as objects of sympathy.—Words of vanity, in Zech. x. 2, mean falsehood, which is here retained by J. D. Michaelis, while Dathe gives it the specific sense of slander, and Paulus that of secret and malignant machination. Vitringa understands it as relating to censorious and unnecessary fault-finding; Kimchi, Ewald, and Gesenius, to strife and bickerings. All these may be included in the general sense of evil speech or wicked words. The Targum has *words of oppression,* or, as Gesenius explains it, *violence.*

10. *And (if) thou wilt let out thy soul to the hungry, and the afflicted soul wilt satisfy, then shall thy light arise in the darkness, and thy gloom as the (double light or) noon.* For כִּשֵׁף Lowth reads לַחְמֶךָ *thy bread,* in which he is supported by eight manuscripts. The Septuagint version he considers as combining the two readings. But Vitringa understands ἐκ ψυχῆς as denoting the cordiality of a cheerful giver (2 Cor. ix. 7, Rom. xii. 8.) Luzzatto, by means of a curious etymological analogy, makes תָּפִיק synonymous with the הַמְצִיא of Lev. ix. 12, 13, 18, and translates the whole phrase "if thou wilt present thy person." Gesenius takes נֶפֶשׁ in the sense of *appetite* or hunger, here put for the thing desired or enjoyed (*deinen Bissen.*) Hitzig and Ewald, with the same view of the writer's meaning, retain the more exact sense of *desire* in their translations. Hendewerk's explanation, "if thou wilt turn thy heart to the hungry," is near akin to Luther's, "if thou wilt let the hungry find thy heart," which seems to rest upon the same interpretation of the verb that has been quoted from Luzzatto. By a distressed soul, Hitzig here understands one suffering from want, and craving sustenance. (See chap. xxix. 8.) The figure in the last clause is a common one for happiness succeeding sorrow. (See Judges v. 31, Ps. cxii. 4, Job xi. 17.) Vitringa asserts roundly (*aio rotunde*) that this prophecy was not fulfilled until after the Reformation, when so many German, French, Italian, and Hungarian Protestants were forced to seek refuge in other countries. The true sense of the passage he has given without knowing it, in these words: "Post tot beneficia et stricturas lucis ecclesiae inductas, restat meridies quem expectat."

11. *And Jehovah will guide thee ever, and satisfy thy soul in drought, and thy bones shall he invigorate, and thou shalt be like a watered garden, and like a spring of water, whose waters shall not fail.* The promise of guidance had already been given in chap. lvii. 18. (Compare Ps. lxxiii. 24, lxxviii. 14.) Jerome's translation (*requiem tibi dabit*) derives the verb from נוּח, not נָחָה. Driessen and some others make בְּצַחְצָחוֹת mean with clear or

bright waters ; but the sense of glistening or dazzling which belongs to the Arabic root, is equally applicable to the burning sands of a desert. Ewald translates it fever-heat. The common version, *drought*, which Lowth changes to *severest drought*, in order to express the intensive meaning of the plural form, agrees well with the verb so *satisfy*, referring to thirst, as ver. 10 does to hunger. The common version of the next clause (*and make fat thy bones*) is sanctioned by the Septuagint and Kimchi, who appeals to the analogy of Prov. xv. 30. The Vulgate version (*ossa liberabit*) seems both arbitrary and unmeaning. The Peshito and Saadias translate the verb *will strengthen*, which is adopted by most modern writers. Secker's emendation (עֲצְמֹתְךָ יַחֲלִיף), which Lowth adopts (*renew thy strength*), derives some countenance, not only from the Targum, but from the analogy of chaps. xl. 31, and xli. 1, and is only inadmissible because it is gratuitous. Similar allusions to the bones as the seat of strength occur in Ps. li. 10, and Job xxi. 24. The figure in the last clause is the converse of that in chap. i. 30. There is here a climax. Not content with the image of a well-watered garden, he substitutes that of the stream, or rather of the spring itself. The general idea is a favourite with Isaiah. (See above, chaps. xxx. 25, xxxiii. 21, xxxv. 5, 7, xli. 17, xliii. 20, xliv. 4, xlviii. 21, xlix. 10.) On the deceiving of the waters, see Jer. xv. 18, and compare the analogous expressions of Hosea with respect to wine, and of Habbakkuk with respect to oil. (Hosea v. 2, Hab. iii. 17.) Hitzig and Knobel understand what is here said of heat and drought in literal application to the journey of the exiles through the wilderness, while all the analogous expressions in the context are regarded as strong figures. The truth is, that the exodus from Egypt had already made these images familiar and appropriate to any great deliverance.

12. *And they shall build from thee the ruins of antiquity* (or *perpetuity*), *foundations and of age and age* (*i. e. of ages*) *shalt thou raise up ; and it shall be called to thee* (or *thou shalt be called*) *Repairer of the breach, Restorer of paths for dwelling.* Ewald reads בְּנוּ, they shall be built by thee ; but this passive form does not occur elsewhere, and is here sustained by no external evidence. Kimchi understands בָּנוּ as referring, not to persons, but effects (*opera*), which is very unnatural. Hitzig retains the old interpretation of the clause as referring to children or descendants ; and the latter writer gives it a specific application to the younger race of exiles, whom he supposes to be the Servant of Jehovah in these Later Prophecies. Gesenius denies the reference to children, and explains מִמְּךָ as meaning those belonging to thee, or, as he paraphrases it, *thy people*. The simplest supposition is that of some rabbinical writers, who supply as the subject of the verb its correlative noun, builders. But as מִמְּךָ properly means *from thee*, it denotes something more than mere connection, and, unless forbidden by something in the context, must be taken to signify a going forth from Israel into other lands. Thus understood, the clause agrees exactly with the work assigned to Israel in chaps. xliii. 14, and lvii. 11; viz. that of reclaiming the apostate nations, and building the wastes of a desolated world. As עוֹלָם obviously refers to past time, this is the only natural interpretation of the corresponding phrase, דּוֹר וָדוֹר ; although Luther and others understand the latter as referring to foundations which shall last for ever. Gesenius understands by foundations, buildings razed to their foundations (Ps. cxxxvii. 7) ; and Hitzig supposes it to have the secondary sense of *ruins*, like אֲשִׁישִׁים in chap. xvi. 7. The sense will then be, if referred to past time, foundations which have lain bare,

or buildings whose foundations have been bare, for ages. For the meta-phor, compare Amos ix. 11 ; for that of a highway, chaps. xix. 23, xxxv. 8 ; and for that of the breach, Ezek. xiii. 5, xxii. 30. The addition of the last phrase, לָשָׁבֶת, has perplexed interpreters. Cocceius understands it to mean that the paths themselves shall be inhabited. Gesenius arbi-trarily translates it, *in the inhabited land.* Knobel no less gratuitously gives to *paths* the sense of beaten or frequented regions. Jerome and Grotius make the word a derivative from שָׁבַת, and translate it *in quietem,* or *ad quiescendum.* The most satisfactory hypotheses are those of Hitzig and Maurer, the former of whom makes the phrase mean *ad habitandum sc. terram,* that the land may be inhabited. The latter understands the paths to be described as leading, not to ruins and to deserts as be-fore, but to inhabited regions. Of these, the former seems entitled to the preference. It will be sufficient to record the fact, that Vitringa finds in this verse an allusion to fundamental doctrines, canons, formulas, &c., &c.

13. *If thou wilt turn away thy foot from the Sabbath to do thy plea-sure on my holy day, and wilt call the Sabbath a delight, (and) the holy (day) of Jehovah honourable, and wilt honour it by not doing thy own ways, by not finding thy pleasure and talking talk.* The version of Henderson and others, turn away thy foot on the Sabbath, is inconsistent with the form of the original as well as with the figure, which is that of something trodden down and trampled, or at least encroached upon. Most inter-preters agree with Kimchi in supplying מִן before עֲשׂוֹת, a combination which is actually found in one manuscript. Hitzig supposes that the gram-matical effect of the first מִן extends to this infinitive. Maurer supplies nothing, and translates *ut agas.* The modern version of חֵפֶץ (*business*) is much less natural, even in this connection, than the old one, *thy pleasure,* especially as paraphrased by Luther, *what thou wilt (was dir gefällt).* Hit-zig observes a climax in the requisitions of this clause, not unlike that in Prov. ii. 2–4. The mere outward observance was of no avail, unless the institution were regarded with reverence, as of God ; nay more with compla-cency, as in itself delightful. To call it a delight, is to acknowledge it as such.

The לְ before קְדוֹשׁ appears to interrupt the construction, which has led some interpreters to disregard it altogether, and others to take קדוש as a verb, or an adjective agreeing with Jehovah ; honoured in order to sanctify (or glorify) Jehovah—honoured by the santification of Jehovah—honoured for the sake of the Holy One, Jehovah. But the simplest explanation is the one proposed by De Dieu and adopted by Vitringa, which treats the לְ before שבת, and that before קדוש, as correlatives, alike connecting the verb קרא with its object. As the construction of the verb is foreign from our idiom, it may be best explained by a paraphrase : " If thou wilt give to the Sab-bath (לשבת) the name of a delight, and to the holy (לקדוש) day or ordi-nance of Jehovah that of honourable." But mere acknowledgment is not enough ; it must not only be admitted to deserve honour, but in fact receive it. Hence he adds, and if thou wilt honour it thyself, *by not doing,* literally, away from doing, so as not to do. (On this use of מִן, see chaps. v. 6, xlix. 15). Here again, to find one's *pleasure* on the Sabbath is more natural than to find one's *business.* Doing thy own ways, although not a usual combination, is rendered intelligible by the constant use of *way* in Hebrew to denote a course of conduct. Speaking speech or talking talk is by some regarded as equivalent to speaking vanity, in ver. 9. The Septuagint adds ἐν ὀργῇ. The modern writers, for the most part, are in favour of the explanation, speaking mere words, idle talk. (Compare Mat. xii. 36.) The classical parallels adduced by Clericus, Gesenius, and others, are very little to the purpose. As to the importance here attached to the Sabbath, see above, on chap. lvi. 2.

14. *Then shalt thou be happy in Jehovah, and I will make thee ride upon the heights of the earth, and I will make thee eat the heritage of Jacob thy father, for Jehovah's mouth hath spoken it.* The verb התענג is combined with the divine name elsewhere to express both a duty and a privilege. (Compare Ps. xxxvii. 4, with Job xxii. 26, xxvii. 10.—הִרְכַּבְתִּי does not mean I will raise thee above (Jerome), or I will cause thee to sit (Cocceius), but I will cause thee to ride. The whole phrase is descriptive, not of a mere return to Palestine the highest of all lands (Kimchi), nore of mere security from enemies by being placed beyond their reach (Vitringa), but of conquest and triumphant possession, as in Deut. xxxii. 13, from which the expression is derived by all the later writers who employ it. There is no sufficient ground for Knobel's supposition that בָּמוֹת in this phrase means the fortresses erected upon hills and mountains. To eat the heritage is to enjoy it and derive subsistence from it. Kimchi correctly says that it is called the heritage of Jacob as distinct from that of Ishmael and Esau, although equally descended from the Father of the Faithful.—The last clause is added to ensure the certainty of the event, as resting not on human but divine authority. See chap. i. 2.

Chapter 59

THE fault of Israel's rejection is not in the Lord, but in themselves, vers. 1, 2. They are charged with sins of violence and injustice, vers. 3, 4. The ruinous effects of these corruptions are described, vers. 5, 6. Their violence and injustice are as fatal to themselves as to others, vers. 7, 8. The moral condition of the people is described as one of darkness and hopeless degradation, vers. 9–15. In this extremity Jehovah interposes to deliver the true Israel, vers. 16, 17. This can only be effected by the destruction of the carnal Israel, ver. 18. The divine presence shall no longer be subjected to local restrictions, ver. 19. A redeemer shall appear in Zion to save the true Israel, ver. 20. The old temporary dispensation shall give place to the dispensation of the Word and Spirit, which shall last for ever, ver. 21.

1. *Behold, not shortened is Jehovah's hand from saving, and not benumbed is his ear from hearing,* i. e. so as not to save, and not to hear, or too short to save, too dull to hear. On this use of the preposition, see above on chap. lviii. 13, and the references there made. The Prophet merely pauses, as it were, for a moment, to exonerate his Master from all blame, before continuing his accusation of the people. The beginning of a chapter here is simply a matter of convenience, as the following context has precisely the same character with that before it; unless we assume with Lowth that the Prophet now ascends from particulars to generals, or with J. D. Michaelis, that he here descends to a lower depth of wickedness. The only explanation of the passage which allows it to speak for itself, without gratuitous additions or embellishments, is that which likens it to chap. xlii. 18–25, xliii. 22–28, and l. 1, 2, as a solemn exhibition of the truth that the rejection of God's ancient people was the fruit of their own sin, and not to be imputed either to unfaithfulness on his part, or to want of strength or

wisdom to protect them. For the true sense of the metaphor here used, see above, on chap. l. 2. Hendewerk is under the necessity of granting that the Israel of this passage is a moral, *i. e.* an ideal person, corresponding not to any definite portion of the people at any one time, but to such of them at various times as possessed a certain character. Whatever may be thought of the necessity or grounds of this assumption in the case before us, he has no right to deny the possibility of others like it, even where he does not think them requisite himself. *Hanc veniam petimusque damusque vicissim.*

2. *But your iniquities have been separating between you and your God, and your sins have hid (his) face from you, so as not to' hear.* כִּי אִם is the usual adversative after a negation, corresponding to the German *sondern*, which has no distinct equivalent in English. Ewald's version, *rather* (*vielmehr*), seems to weaken the expression; and Umbreit's combination of the two (*sondern vielmehr*) is entirely gratuitous.—The present form given to the verb (*they separate*) by Luther, and retained even by De Wette, is entirely inadequate. The original expression is intended to convey, in the strongest manner, the idea both of past time and of continuance or custom. Ewald expresses this by introducing the word *bislang*, but Umbreit better by retaining the exact form of the original (*waren scheidend*). Hitzig points out an allusion to the יְהִי מַבְדִּיל of Gen. i. 6, which is the more remarkable because it may be likewise traced in the construction of the preposition בֵּין, both the modes of employing it which there occur being here combined.— The general idea of this verse is otherwise expressed in Jer. v. 25, while in Lam. iii. 44, the same Prophet reproduces both the thought and the expression, with a distinct mention of the intervening object as a cloud, which may possibly have been suggested by the language of Isaiah himself in chap. xliv. 22.—Henderson adopts the explanation of הִסְתִּירוּ by Kimchi and Aben Ezra as a causative (*have made him hide*); but this is contrary to usage.—Secker proposes to read פָּנַי my (face), and Lowth פָּנָיו (his face), for which he cites the authority of the ancient versions; but in these, as in the modern ones, the pronoun is supplied by the translator, in order to remove an ellipsis which is certainly unusual, though not without example, as appears from Job xxxiv. 29, where the noun without a suffix is combined with this very verb. For an instance of the same kind, though not perfectly identical, see above, chap. liii. 3. The omission of the pronoun is so far from being wholly anomalous that Luther simply has *the face*, in which he is followed both by Ewald and Umbreit.—The force of the participle before the last verb is the same as in chaps. xliv. 18, and xlix. 15. It does not mean specifically *that he will not*, much less *that he cannot hear*, but, as Lowth translates it, *that he doth not hear*. It is still better, however, to retain the infinitive form of the original by rendering it, *so as not to hear.*

3. *For your hands are defiled with blood, and your fingers with iniquity; your lips have spoken falsehood, your tongue will utter wickedness.* The Prophet now, according to a common usage of the Scriptures, classifies the prevalent iniquities as sins of the hands, the mouth, the feet, as if to intimate that every member of the social body was affected. On the staining of the hands with blood, see chap. i. 15. Here again we have a marked and apparently unstudied similarity of thought and language to the genuine Isaiah. The form נְגֹאֲלוּ, which occurs only here and in Lam. iv. 14, is explained by Kimchi as a mixture of the Niphal and Pual, by Gesenius as a kind of double passive. The use of this form, instead of

the Pual, which is found only in the latest books, is rather symptomatic of an earlier writer. The sense here put upon אָגַל, and in a few other places, seems so wholly unconnected with its usual and proper meaning, as to give some countenance to Henderson's idea, which might otherwise seem fanciful, that it is a denominative from גֹאֵל, the avenger of blood.—Vitringa infers from ver. 7, that the blood here meant is specifically that of the innocent, or those unjustly put to death. According to Grotius, the iniquity which stained their fingers was that of robbery and theft. It is far more natural, however, to consider hands and fingers as equivalent expressions, or at the utmost as expressing different degrees of the same thing. Thus Umbreit represents it as characteristic of the Old Testament severity in reprehending sin, that the Prophet, not content with staining the hands, extends his description to the very fingers. This is certainly ingenious, but perhaps too artificial to have been intended by the writer.—The restriction of the falsehood here charged to judicial fraud or misrepresentation is unnecessary.—The preterite and future forms describe the evil as habitual, and ought to be retained in the translation, were it only for the purpose of exhibiting the characteristic form of the original.—The last verb is explained by Vitringa as expressive of deliberate promulgation (*meditate profert*), and by Luther of invention (*dichtet*). J. D. Michaelis attenuates its sense to that of simple speech, while Hitzig coincides with the English Version (muttered). As the word, though applied to vocal utterance, is not confined to articulate speech, the nearest equivalent perhaps is *utter*, as conveying neither more nor less than the original.—Vitringa applies this verse likewise to the scandals of the Reformed Church, and especially to those arising from its coalescence with the State, observing that the interpreter is not bound to verify the truth of the description, as we know not what is yet to happen. This would be rational enough where the prophecy itself contained explicit indications of a specific subject; but where this is to be made out by comparison with history, a reference to future possibilities is laughable.—The wider meaning of the whole description is evident from Paul's combining parts of it with phrases drawn from several Psalms remarkably resembling it, in proof of the depravity of human nature (Rom. iii. 15–17).

4. *There is none calling with justice, and there is none contending with truth ; they trust in vanity and speak falsehood, conceive mischief and bring forth iniquity.* The phrase קֹרֵא בְצֶדֶק has been variously understood. The Septuagint makes it mean simply speaking just things (οὐδεὶς λαλεῖ δίκαια) which would hardly have been so expressed in Hebrew. The Chaldee paraphrase, *praying in truth* (*i. e.* sincerely), seems to be founded on the frequent description of worship, as calling on the name of God. Jerome's version, *qui invocet justitiam*, is followed in the English Bible, *calleth for justice*, *i.e.* as Clericus explains it, there is no one who is willing to commit his cause to such unrighteous judges. Hensler and Döderlein apply it to judicial decrees and decisions, which is wholly at variance with the usage of the verb. Kimchi understands it of one person calling to another for the purpose of reproving him ; but then the essential idea is the very one which happens not to be expressed. Gesenius and Maurer follow Rosenmüller in attaching to קרא the forensic sense of καλέω εἰς δίκην and *voco in jus :* "No one summons another, *i. e.* sues him, justly." In proof of such a Hebrew usage Knobel cites Job v. 1, xiii. 22, which are at best very doubtful. The same sense seems to be designed by Lowth (*preferreth his suit*). It would be still more difficult to justify the

sense of *speaking for* or advocating, here assumed by J. D. Michaelis and Henderson. In this uncertainty, some of the latest writers have gone back to Luther's sense of *preaching*, which is easily deducible from that of calling publicly, proclaiming. According to Hitzig, this is the proper Hebrew term for public speaking, such as that in the synagogues, which was free to all. (See Luke iv. 16, Acts xiii. 15.) Luther makes righteousness the subject of the preaching, Ewald and Umbreit a description of its quality (*aright* or *justly*). The only argument against this explanation, and in favour of a more forensic or judicial one, is that afforded by the parallel expression, נִשְׁפָּט בֶּאֱמוּנָה. Kimchi makes the verb a simple passive, meaning to be tried or judged—" no one is fairly tried." Luther and J. D. Michaelis reverse this explanation, and apply the clause to unjust judges. Most writers make the verb reciprocal (as in chap. xliii. 26, Prov. xxix. 9, Ezek. xvii. 20), and apply it either to forensic litigation, or to controversy and contention for the truth. In either case אֱמוּנָה must mean *bona fides*, and not truth as the subject or occasion of dispute, which is not the meaning of the Hebrew word. (See Hengstenberg on Ps. xxxiii. 4.) The infinitive construction of the next clause cannot be retained in English. The nearest equivalent is that adopted in the common version. Lowth's substitution of the participle (*trusting, speaking*, &c.) is no better as to form, and really obscures the sense, or at least the true grammatical relation of the clauses. The construction is the same as in chap. v. 5, xxi. 9. Vitringa supposes an ellipsis of the preterite, which is inadmissible, for reasons given in vol. i. p. 130.—תֹּהוּ is vigorously rendered by J. D. Michaelis *nothing* (auf ein Nichts). The falsehood mentioned in this clause is understood by some in the specific sense of false or unfair reasoning.—With the figure of the last clause compare Job xv. 35, and Ps. vii. 15. It might here be understood to denote mere disappointment or failure, as in ver. 13 below; but the analogy of chap. xxxiii. 11 seems to shew that the prominent idea is that of mischievous and spiteful machination. With the first of these interpretations seems to be connected the sense which J. D. Michaelis here attaches to אָוֶן, namely, that of pain or suffering.

5. *Eggs of the basilisk they have hatched, and webs of the spider they will spin* (or *weave*); *the* (*one*) *eating of their eggs shall die, and the crushed* (*egg*) *shall hatch out a viper.* The figure of the serpent is substantially the same as in chap. xiv. 29. (Compare Deut. xxxii. 33). The precise varieties intended are of little exegetical importance. The modern writers generally follow Bochart in explaining צִפְעֹנִי to mean the basilisk, a serpent small in size but of a deadly venom. For the use of the verb in such connections, see above, chap. xxxiv. 15. The figure of the spider's web is added to express the idea both of hurtfulness and futility. (See Job viii. 14.)—זוּרֶה for זוּרָה (like לָנָה for לָנֶה Zech. v. 4) is the passive participle of זוּר to press, applied in chap. i. 4 to the curative compression of a wound. That it does not here denote incubation, as explained by Aquila (Θαλφθέν), Jerome (*confotum*), and Jarchi, may be inferred from Job xxxix. 15, where the same verb is applied to the crushing of the eggs of the ostrich by the foot.—Luther, Lowth, J. D. Michaelis, and Gesenius make הַזּוּרָה a nominative absolute, " if one is crushed there creeps out a viper." Maurer and the later writers construe it directly with the verb, as in the English Bible.—To the objection that the viper is viviparous, Vitringa answers, that the Prophet intentionally uses a mixed metaphor; Gesenius, that we cannot look for accurate details of natural history in such a writer. Neither seems to have observed that the exact correspond-

ence of the Hebrew word to *viper* is extremely problematical, although Gesenius himself defines it in his Lexicon " viper, adder, *any poisonous serpent,*" and J. D. Michaelis accordingly translates it by the general term *schlange.* The same writer looks upon the whole verse as peculiarly appropriate to the character and condition of the Jews, immediately before their destruction by the Romans.

6. *Their webs shall not become (or be for) clothing, and they shall not cover themselves with their works ; their works are works of mischief (or iniquity), and the doing of violence is in their hands.* The first clause does not seem to form a part of what the writer meant at first to say, but is a kind of afterthought, by which he gives a new turn to the sentence, and expresses an additional idea without a change of metaphor. Having introduced the spider's web, in connection with the serpent's egg, as an emblem of malignant and treacherous designs, he here repeats the first but for another purpose, namely, to suggest the idea of futility and worthlessness. This application may have been suggested by the frequent reference to webs and weaving as conducive to the comfort and emolument of men ; but spiders' webs can answer no such purpose. The idea that it is not fit or cannot be applied to this end, although not exclusively expressed, is really included in the general declaration that they *shall not* be so used.— Gesenius and Ewald make the second verb indefinite, *they shall not* (*i. e.* no one shall) employ them for this purpose. But the sentence is more pointed if we understand it as including a specific menace that the authors of these devices shall derive no advantage from them. *Works* in the first clause simply means *what they have made ;* but in the second, where the metaphor is dropped, this version would be inadmissible. The common version of פֹּעַל (*act*), and Lowth's emendation of it (*deed*), are both defective in not suggesting the idea of continued and habitual practice.

7. *Their feet to evil will run, and they will hasten to shed innocent blood ; their thoughts are thoughts of mischief (or iniquity) ; wasting and ruin are in their paths.* The first clause expresses not a mere disposition, but an eager proclivity to wrong. The word translated *thoughts*, has here and elsewhere the specific sense of purposes, contrivances, devices, which last Lowth employs as an equivalent. Luther gives אָוֶן here as well as in the foregoing verse the sense of trouble (*Mühe*), in reference no doubt to the oppressors themselves. In like manner J. D. Michaelis explains ruin *in their paths* as meaning that it awaits themselves ; but most interpreters take both expressions in an active sense, as meaning what they do to others, not what they experience themselves. *Their paths* are then the paths in which their feet run to evil and make haste to shed innocent blood.—The two nouns combined in the last clause strictly denote desolation and crushing, *i. e.* utter ruin. *Destruction and calamity* (Lowth) are as much too vague as *destruction and wounds* (J. D. Michaelis), or *force and ruins* (Ewald), are too specific. Knobel supposes the idea to be that of a country wasted by invading enemies. (See chap. i. 4.) With this verse compare Prov. i. 16, and the evil way, of chap. lv. 7 above. Knobel of course applies it to the quarrelsome exiles, and gravely adds that nothing more can be determined with respect to them than this, that they sometimes did not hesitate to rob and murder ! The reference which he adds to this extraordinary statement are chaps. lvii. 20, l. 11, and vers. 3 and 15 of this chapter.

8. *The way of peace they have not known, and there is no justice in their paths ; their courses they have rendered crooked for them ; every one walking in them knows not peace.* J. D. Michaelis and Umbreit go to opposite

extremes in their interpretation of the first clause. The former makes the
way of peace denote the way to happiness; the latter understands the
clause to mean that they refuse all overtures of reconciliation. The obvious
and simple meaning is, that their lives are not pacific but contentious.
In order to vary the expression, Lowth translates בְּמַעְגְּלֹתָם *in their tracks*,
which is retained by Henderson. With still more exact adherence to the
primary meaning of the verb, they might have written *in their ruts*. עִקֵּשׁ
is twice used in the book of Proverbs as the opposite of upright or sincere.
(Prov. x. 9, xxviii. 18.) Hitzig gives the verb the specific sense of *choosing*
crooked paths, which is not so simple or exact as the common English
Version (*they have made them crooked paths*). בָּהּ is a neuter or indefinite
expression. There is no need therefore of reading either נְתִיבֹתָם with a
single manuscript, or בָּם with the ancient versions, between which emendations Lowth appears to hesitate. Knobel's inference from this verse, that
some of the less corrupted Jews were led astray by wicked leaders, is as
groundless as Vitringa's specific application of the passage to the excesses of
victorious parties in religious controversy, not without evident allusion to
the ecclesiastical disputes of the Reformed Dutch Church, to which he
very naturally, but by no means very reasonably, yields an extravagantly
disproportioned space, in determining the scope of this prophetic vision.
The erroneous principle involved in both interpretations is refuted by the
comprehensive sense which the apostle puts upon the words in the passage
which has been already cited. (Rom. iii. 15–17.)

9. *Therefore is judgment far from us, and righteousness will not overtake
us; we wait for light and behold darkness; for splendours, (and) in obscurities we walk.* The future form of all the verbs in this verse intimates
that they expect this state of things to continue. Knobel explains *judgment*
as meaning the practical decision between them and their enemies, which
God would make when he delivered them. Why, then, may not the
parallel expression, *righteousness*, be applied in the same way, without
losing its original and proper sense in that of *salvation?* According to
Hendewerk, it here denotes the righteous compensation which the Jews
were to receive for their excessive sufferings. (See above, on chap. xl. 2.)
J. D. Michaelis explains the expression *overtake* strictly, as denoting that
they fled from it. (Compare chap. xxxv. 10, and li. 11.) Vitringa applies
this verse to the threatened extinction of religion in his own day; Knobel
to the delay in the deliverance from Babylon, occasioned by Cyrus's attack
on Croesus!

10. *We grope like the blind for the wall, like the eyeless we grope; we
stumble at noonday as in twilight, in thick darkness like the dead.* Lowth
is so offended with the "poverty and inelegance" of repeating נְגַשְּׁשָׁה, which
he thinks "extremely unworthy of the Prophet, and unlike his manner,"
that he reads in the second place with Houbigant, נִשְׁגֶּה, *we wander*, can-
didly adding that the mistake, although very easy and obvious, "is of long
standing, being prior to all the ancient versions." Whatever else may be
said of "this ingenious correction," it cannot be described as of long standing; for no writer since Lowth appears to have adopted it. To an unsophisticated taste the repetition is a beauty, when used sparingly and in the
proper place. The phrase בָּאַשְׁמַנִּים has been variously rendered. Jerome,
Luther, J. D. Michaelis, and Rückert, make the noun mean darkness or
dark places (*in caliginosis*); the Targum, Saadias, Kimchi, and Grotius,
in the tomb; which sense the elder Kimchi derives from אָשֵׁם, to be desolate.
Lowth, Koppe, Döderlein, and Bauer, in the midst of fatness, abundance,

or fertility; Gesenius, Hitzig, Maurer, and Hendewerk, in fat or fertile fields; Aben Ezra, Rosenmüller, Ewald, and Umbreit, in the midst of the fat or healthy, with or without allusion to the prosperous heathen among whom they were scattered, or by whom they were oppressed. Knobel has gone back to the meaning *darkness*, as best suited to the context, and easily deducible from the sense of fatness, just as we speak of gross or thick darkness. Vitringa dissents from the application of this verse by Cocceius to the deposition of Ferdinand king of Bohemia, and the election of Frederick the Count Palatine! With this verse compare Deut. xxviii. 29, and Zeph. i. 17.

11. *We growl like the bears, all of us, and like the doves we moan (we) moan; we wait for justice and there is none, for salvation (and) it is far from us.* The Latin poets also speak of the voice of bears and doves as a *gemitus* or groaning. (See above, chap. xxxviii. 14, and Ezek. vii. 16.) Umbreit supposes the two here to represent the extremes of violent and gentle grief. The same effect which is produced in the first clause, by the use of the phrase *all of us*, is produced in the other by the idiomatic repetition of the verb. Here, as in ver. 9, we may understand by judgment or justice that which God does by his providential dispensations both to his people and his enemies.

12. *For our transgressions are multiplied before thee, and our sins testify against us; for our transgressions are with us, and our iniquities—we know them.* The Prophet here begins a general confession in the name of God's people. For the form of expression, compare Ps. li. 5. The construction of the verb עָנְתָה with a plural noun is explained by Tremellius and Vitringa as implying an ellipsis (*quodque*). Cocceius in like manner supplies *id ipsum*. The modern grammarians, who in general are averse to the gratuitous assumption of ellipses, seem disposed to regard it as an idiomatic licence of construction. Lowth translates אִתָּנוּ, *cleave fast unto us;* but interpreters generally prefer the sense expressed in the English Version (they are with us, *i. e.* in our sight or present to our memory).

13. *To transgress and lie against Jehovah, and to turn back from behind our God, to speak oppression and departure, to conceive and utter from the heart words of falsehood.* The specifications of the general charge are now expressed by an unusual succession of infinitives, not as Hitzig says because the persons were already known (which would require the adoption of the same form in a multitude of places where it is not found at present), but because the writer wished to concentrate and condense his accusation. This rhetorical effect is materially injured by the substitution of the finite verb. Although by no means equal in conciseness to the Hebrew, our infinitive may be employed as the most exact translation. Gesenius makes נָסוֹג a future form, but Maurer an infinitive from נָסַג. *Departure* means departure from the right course or the law (Deut. xix. 16), *i. e.* transgression or iniquity. Knobel applies the term specifically to idolatry, and understands עֹשֶׁק as implying that the exiles in Babylon oppressed each other!

14. *And judgment is thrust* (or *driven*) *back, and righteousness afar off stands; for truth has fallen in the street, and uprightness cannot enter.* The description is now continued in the ordinary form by the finite verb.—The word translated *street* properly means an open place or square, especially the space about the gate of an oriental town where courts were held and other public business transacted. (See Job xxix. 7, Neh. viii. 1.) The present form, which seems to be required by our idiom, is much less expres-

sive than the preterite and futures of the original. Those interpreters who commonly apply whatever is said of tyranny to the oppression of the Jews in exile are compelled in this case, where the sin is charged upon the Jews themselves, to resort to the imaginary fact of gross misgovernment among the exiles, for the purpose of avoiding the conclusion that the passage has respect to a condition of society like that described in the first chapter.

15. *Then truth was missed* (*i. e.* found wanting), *and whoso departed from evil made himself a prey* (or *was plundered*). *Then Jehovah saw and it was evil in his eyes that there was no judgment* (or practical justice). The Vav conversive in both clauses indicates a sequence of events, and may be best expressed by *then* in English. The passive participle is here used with the substantive verb, as the active is in ver. 2, to denote anterior habitual action. Hitzig understands the first clause to mean that honesty (*i. e.* the honest people) was betrayed, in direct opposition to the usage both of the noun and verb in Hebrew. For the sense of נעדר, see above, on chap. xxxiv. 16, xl. 26. Lowth's version, *utterly lost*, is substantially correct, though perhaps too strong. Jarchi, Cocceius, and J. D. Michaelis understand מִשְׁתּוֹלֵל as meaning *was accounted mad*, which is also given in the margin of the English Bible, but has no foundation either in etymology or usage. It is now commonly agreed that this verbal form is near akin to the noun שָׁלָל, spoil or plunder, and has here the same sense as in Ps. lxxvi. 6. This explanation is sustained by the authority of the Targum and Jerome. Kimchi understands it to describe the godly man as snatched away, perhaps in allusion to chap. lvii. 1. Ewald derives from what he thinks the true sense of the root the meaning, he became rare (*wurde selten*).

16. *And he saw that there was no man, and he stood aghast that there was no one interposing; and his own arm saved for him, and his own righteousness, it upheld him.* The repetition of the words *and he saw* connects this verse in the closest manner with the one before it. Rosenmüller, Umbreit, and others, follow Jarchi in supposing אִישׁ to be emphatic and to signify a man of the right sort, a man equal to the occasion. This explanation derives some colour from the analogy of Jer. v. 1; but even there, and still more here, the strength of the expression is increased rather than diminished by taking this phrase in the simple sense of *nobody*. What was wanting was not merely a qualified man, but any man whatever, to maintain the cause of Israel and Jehovah. A like absolute expression is employed in 2 Kings xiv. 26, where it is said that Jehovah saw the affliction of Israel, that it was very bitter, and that there was no *helper for Israel*, not merely no sufficient one, but none at all. The desperate nature of the case is then described in terms still stronger, and only applicable to Jehovah by the boldest figure. The common version (*wondered*), though substantially correct, is too weak to express the full force of the Hebrew word, which strictly means to be desolate, and is used in reference to persons for the purpose of expressing an extreme degree of horror and astonishment. (See Ps. cxliii. 4, and compare the colloquial use of *désolé* in French.) As applied to God, the term may be considered simply anthropopathic, or as intended to imply a certain sympathetic union with humanity, arising from the mode in which this great intervention was to be accomplished.—מַפְגִּיעַ strictly denotes causing to meet or come together, bringing into contact. Hence it is applied to intercessory prayer, and this sense is expressed here by the Chaldee paraphrase. But the context, etymology, and usage, all combine to recommend the wider sense of intervention, interposition, both in word and deed. (See

above, on chap. liii. 12.)   This sense is well expressed by Lowth (*there was none to interpose*), except that he gratuitously substitutes the infinite for the active participle, which is more expressive, as suggesting that the danger was imminent and unavoidable without the aid of some one actually interposing to avert it.   The full force of the last clause can be given in English only by the use of the emphatic form *his own*, which is implied, but cannot be distinctly expressed in the original except by a periphrasis.   To do anything with one's own hand or arm, is an expression frequently used elsewhere to denote entire independence of all foreign aid.   (See Judges vii. 2; 1 Sam. iv. 9, xxv. 26; Ps. xliv. 4, xcviii. 1.)—The meaning of this clause has been much obscured by making לֹ the object of the verb.   The obvious incongruity of representing God as saving or delivering himself has led to different evasions.   Some interpreters attenuate the meaning of the verb from *save* to *help*, which is the favourite expedient of the modern writers; while the older ones content themselves with making it intransitive and absolute, *brought salvation* (English Version), *wrought salvation* (Lowth). The only simple and exact translation is, *his arm saved for him*, leaving the object to be gathered from the context, namely, Israel or his people. The לֹ means nothing more than that his own arm did it *for him*, without reliance upon any other.   This same idea is expressed in the last words of the verse, where *his righteousness sustained him* means that he relied or depended upon it exclusively.   By righteousness in this case we are not to understand a simple consciousness of doing right, nor the possession of a righteous cause, nor a right to do what he did, all which are modifications of the same essential meaning, nor a zealous love of justice, which Vitringa deduces from the use of the word fury (*i.e.* ardent zeal) in the parallel passage, chap. lxiii. 5.   It is far more satisfactory to give the word its strict and proper sense, as denoting an attribute of God, here joined with his power, to shew that what are commonly distinguished as his moral or his natural perfections are alike pledged to this great work, and constitute his only reliance for its execution.—The extraordinary character of this description, and the very violence which it seems to offer to our ordinary notions of the divine nature, unavoidably prepare the mind for something higher than the restoration of the Jews from exile, or the destruction of Jerusalem by the Romans. The embarrassment occasioned by this passage to the champions of the Babylonian theory may be inferred from their complex and unnatural hypothesis, that because the magistrates and elders of the captivity did not repress and punish the offences just described, God would himself do it, not by continuing the exile as a punishment, but by destroying Babylon, and with it the ungodly Jews, while the better portion should escape and be restored to their own country!   It is a strange and peculiar idea of Ewald's, that the Prophet here reproaches Israel that no Messiah had arisen from among themselves according to the ancient promise, so that God had as it were been under the necessity of raising up a foreign instrument for their deliverance, namely, Cyrus.   If all things else were as much in favour of this wild invention as they are against it, a sufficient refutation would be still afforded by the obvious unsuitableness of the language to express the alleged meaning.   A reluctant use of foreign agents by Jehovah might be described as anything rather than his own arm doing the work for him.   If arm means power, it was no more exerted in the one case than it would have been exerted in the other; if it means instrumentality, the one employed was not so truly or emphatically his own arm as it would have been if raised up from among his own people.

17. *And he clothed himself with righteousness as a coat of mail and a helmet of salvation on his head, and he clothed himself with garments of vengeance (for) clothing, and put on, as the cloak (or tunic), jealousy.* Here again the verse is closely connected with the one before it, by the repetition of צְדָקָה. Its relation to the other verse is not, however, that of an explanation, as implied in Hendewerk's translation of the particle by *for*. The writer simply carries out in detail his general declaration that Jehovah undertook the cause of Israel himself, under figures borrowed from the usages of war. The older writers have in vain perplexed themselves with efforts to determine why righteousness is called a breastplate, or salvation a helmet, and to reconcile the variations in Paul's copies of this picture (Eph. vi. 4–17, 1 Thess. v. 8) with the original. The true principle of exegesis in such cases is the one laid down by Clericus, who may speak with authority whenever the question in dispute is a question not of doctrine or experience, but of taste. Justice, says this accomplished rhetorician, might just as well have been a sword, salvation a shield, vengeance a javelin or spear, and zeal or jealousy a torch with which to fire the hostile camp. *Ratio habenda est scopi, non singularum vocum.* The correctness of this principle is clear from the general analogy of figurative language, and from the endless licence of invention which would follow from the adoption of the other method, so that in aiming at precision and fulness we should unavoidably involve the sense of Scripture in incurable uncertainty. That the figures in this case were intended to convey the general idea of martial equipment, may be gathered from a fact which even Vitringa has observed, that there is no reference whatever to offensive weapons, an omission wholly unaccountable upon his own hypothesis. There is no ground for Rosenmüller's explanation of צְדָקָה as denoting the desire of vengeance, unless this be a periphrasis for retributive or vindicatory justice. Equally groundless is the explanation of יְשׁוּעָה by Gesenius and the later writers in the sense of victory. However appropriate and striking this idea may be in so martial a description, it is not the one expressed by the writer, who looks far beyond mere victory to the salvation of God's people as the great end to be answered by it. There is much more plausibility in Knobel's suggestion, that the first two nouns have reference to Israel, and the last two to his enemies; the same catastrophe which was to secure justice and salvation to the former, would bring the zeal and vengeance of Jehovah on the latter. This distinction is no doubt correct so far as the terms vengeance and salvation are concerned; but it cannot be so well sustained as to the others, since צְדָקָה signifies the righteousness of God, as the cause of the catastrophe in question, and קִנְאָה not merely his zeal against his enemies, but his jealous regard for his own honour and the welfare of his people. (See the usage of this word fully stated in vol. i. p. 206). The particular expressions of the verse need little explanation. The first piece of armour specified is not the breast-plate, as tne older writers generally render it, perhaps in reference to Eph. vi. 14, but the habergeon or coat of mail. The first and third terms denote parts of armour properly so called, the second and fourth the dress as distinguished from the armour. The מְעִיל is either the tunic or the military cloak, often mentioned in the classics as being of a purple colour. The same noun is construed with the same verb in 1 Sam. xxviii. 14. The meaning of the whole verse is, that God equipped himself for battle, and arrayed his power, justice, and distinguishing attachment to his people, against their persecutors and oppressors.—Jubb proposes to omit תִּלְבֹּשֶׁת as superfluous, inelegant, and probably a gloss from the margin. But even

Lowth, although he quotes the proposition, leaves the text unchanged, and Henderson is betrayed into the opposite extreme of pronouncing the word " singularly beautiful."

18. *According to* (their) *deeds, accordingly will he repay, wrath to his enemies,* (their) *desert to his foes, to the isles* (their) *desert will he repay.* The essential meaning of this verse is evident and undisputed : but the form of expression in the first clause is singular, if not anomalous. Some of the latest writers, such as Maurer, Henderson, and Umbreit, get rid of the difficulty simply by denying its existence, which is easy enough after every method of solution has been suggested by preceding writers. That there is a grammatical difficulty in the clause is evident not only from the paraphrastic forms adopted by the ancient versions, but also from the attention given to the question by such scholars as De Dieu, Cocceius, and Gesenius. Ewald, it is true, passes it by in silence, as he usually does when he has nothing to suggest but what has been already said by his predecessors. Another proof of the existence of a difficulty is, that even those who deny it paraphrase the text instead of rigidly translating it, and thus go safely round the hard place rather than triumphantly through it. The difficulty is not exegetical, but purely grammatical, arising from the unexampled use of the preposition עַל without an object : *According to their deeds—according to—will he repay.* Cocceius and Vitringa give to עַל its original value as a noun, which very rarely occurs elsewhere (Hosea xi. 7, vii. 16), and understand it here to mean the height or highest degree : " According to the height of their deserts, according to the height, will I repay." Lowth, after quoting Vitringa's opinion, that Cocceius and himself had together made out the true sense, adds with some humour, " I do not expect that any third person will ever be of that opinion." He little imagined that his own would never even be seconded. His proposition is to read בַּעַל for כְּעַל in either case, on the authority of the Chaldee paraphrase of this place compared with that of chap. xxxv. 4, and Prov. xxii. 24, in all which cases the Chaldee has מרי corresponding to the Hebrew בַּעַל, lord or master. The text thus amended Lowth translates, *He is mighty to recompense, he that is mighty to recompense will requite,* of which Henderson observes that it is drawling and paraphrastical at best, and incorrectly rendered ; as it ought to have been, *He is the Retributor, the Retributor will requite.* But even granting Lowth the right to fix the meaning of a text manufactured by himself, it is evident that such an emendation must be critically worthless. De Dieu and Rosenmüller explain עַל when used in the sense of *propter* as equivalent to a noun meaning cause or reason ; as if he had said, " on account of their deeds on (that) account, will I repay." But besides the artificial character of this solution, it overlooks the fact that although עַל by itself might simply indicate the cause or ground, the כְּ prefixed denotes proportion, as in other cases where it follows verbs of recompense. (*E.g.* Ps. xviii. 21, lxii. 13, Jer. l. 39.) The latest writers seem to have come back to the simple and obvious supposition of the oldest writers, such as Jerome and the Rabbins, that it is a case of anomalous ellipsis, the object of the preposition being not expressed, but mentally repeated from the foregoing clause : *According to their deeds, according to them, he will repay.* In the mere repetition there is nothing singular, but rather something characteristic of the Prophet. (See above, chap. lii. 6.) Maurer and several later writers choose, however, to regard it not as a mere repetition of the same words in the same sense, but as an

instance of the idiomatic use of ‎כְּ—כְּ, as equivalent to our *as—so*. The sense will then be, " as according to their deeds, so according to (their deeds) will he repay." But this construction would create a difficulty, even if these writers were correct in denying its existence there already. All that need be added is, that the English Version happily approaches to a perfect reproduction of the Hebrew expression by employing the cognate terms *according* and *accordingly*, which has the advantage of retaining essentially the same term, and yet varying it so as to avoid a grammatical anomaly by which it might have been rendered unintelligible.—גְּמֻל, according to the modern lexicographers, is not directly *recompense*, but *conduct*, either good or bad, and as such worthy of reward or punishment. For Hengstenberg's peculiar explanation of the verb and its derivatives, see his Commentary on the Psalms, i. p. 147, and vol. i. p. 114. The feminine plural here used in the first clause, corresponds to the singular in 2 Sam. xix. 37.—The last clause, relating to the islands, J. D. Michaelis, in his usual ostentatious manner, declares himself incompetent to understand, and, as he says himself of Kennicott elsewhere, seems disposed to wonder that anybody else should be so bold as to understand it better than himself. On the whole he is inclined to regard it as a promise that the true religion should be spread throughout Europe. The modern writers who restrict the passage to the Babylonian exile, are again embarrassed by the writer's losing sight of the wicked Jews whom he had been describing, and as J. D. Michaelis says, threatening to visit their offences on the Gentiles. Knobel easily gets over this obstruction by observing that, although the wicked Jews were to be implicated in the ruin of the Babylonians, yet as these were the direct object of attack to Cyrus, they alone are mentioned. How far this will make it appear natural to say, " because ye are wicked, I will punish the Gentiles," let the reader judge. There is also something very artificial in Henderson's distinction between the *enemies* and *adversaries* of this verse, as meaning the wicked Jews destroyed or scattered by the Romans, and the *isles*, as meaning the Romans themselves, who were to be overthrown by the barbarians. The objection to such exegetical refinements is not that they are in themselves absurd or incredible, but simply that a thousand others might be invented not an atom more so. The only satisfactory solution is the one afforded by the hypothesis that the salvation here intended is salvation in the highest sense from sin and all its consequences, and that by Israel and the isles (or Gentiles) we are to understand the church or people of God, and the world considered as its enemies and his.

19. *And they shall fear from the west the name of Jehovah, and from the rising of the sun his glory; for it shall come like a straitened stream, the spirit of Jehovah raising a banner in it.* Luther and Ewald mark the dependence of this verse upon the one before it by translating the ‎ו *so that;* but there seems to be no sufficient reason for departing from the simplicity of the original construction. The name and glory of Jehovah are here not only parallels but synonymes, as we learn from other places where the two terms are jointly or severally used to signify the manifested excellence or glorious presence of Jehovah. (See above, chaps. xxx. 27, xxxv. 2, xl. 5, xlii. 11.) As in these and other places (*e. g.* chap. viii. 9, xviii. 3, xxxiii. 13), the remotest nations or ends of the earth, here represented by the east and west (chaps. xliii. 5, xlv. 6), are said to see his name or glory. Knobel accordingly translates the first verb *they shall see*. But although this affords a good sense and is justified by usage, it effects no such im-

provement in·the meaning of the passage as would compensate for the violation of the Masoretic pointing, confirmed by the authority of all the ancient versions. Let it also be observed that the seeing is implied or pre-supposed in the fearing, and that the mention of this last effect agrees best with the meaning of the last clause, which on any exegetical hypothesis suggests the thoughts of conflict and coercion. Gesenius gratuitously changes *from* to *in*, as if the apparent necessity of that sense in a few doubtful cases could justify its substitution for the proper one in cases like the present, where it not only yields an intelligible sense but suggests an idea which must otherwise be lost, viz., that of convergence from these distant points as to a common centre. There is the same objection to the sense which Lowth and Henderson attach to מִן, viz. that of *belonging to* (*they from the west, those of the west*), besides the dubious grammatical correctness of regarding as the subject of the verb what appears to be dependent on it as a qualifying phrase. There is something pleasing, if no more, in the suggestion of Vitringa, that the usual order of the east and west (chap. xliii. 5, Mal. i. 11) is here reversed, as if to intimate that the diffusion of the truth shall one day take a new direction, an idea which Henderson applies specically to the Christian missions of Great Britain and America, not only to new countries but to Asia, the cradle of the gospel, of the law, and of the human race. The last clause of this verse has been a famous subject of dispute among interpreters, who differ more or less in reference to every word, as well as to the general meaning of the whole. The least important question has respect to the כִּי at the beginning of the clause; for whether this be rendered *when* or *for*, the sense remains essentially the same, because the one implies the other. The only weighty reasons for preferring the latter, are first its natural priority as being the usual and proper sense, and then the simplicity of structure which results from it as being more accordant with the genius and usage of the language. As to the next word (יָבֹא) the only question is in relation to its subject or nominative, some connecting it with *name* or *glory* in the other clause, some with *Jehovah*, some with צָר considered as a noun. Of those who thus explain צָר, some suppose it to mean anguish or distress as in chap. lxiii. 8, others an enemy as in ver. 18 above. Of those who consider it an adjective, one understands it to mean hostile, but the great majority narrow or compressed. The questions as to רוּחַ are whether it means breath or spirit, and whether it is a poetical description of the wind, or a personal designation of the Holy Ghost. The only doubt in reference to יְהוָֹה is whether it is idiomatically used to qualify the word before it (as a strong wind), or employed more strictly as a divine name. But the great theme of controversy is in the next word נֹסְסָה, which some derive from נוּס, and some from נָסַס; some regard as a participle and others as a preterite; some understand as meaning to set up a banner and others to put to flight, to drive along, or scatter. Lastly בוֹ is by some construed directly with the verb as its object (drive it, scatter it, &c.), while by others it is separately understood as meaning either *in it* or *against it*. From the combination of these various senses have resulted several distinct interpretations of the whole clause, two of which deserve to be particularly mentioned, as the two between which most writers have been and are still divided. The first of these is the interpretation found, as to its essence, in several of the ancient versions, and especially the Vulgate, *cum venerit quasi fluvius violentus quem Spiritus Domini cogit*. This is substantially retained by Luther and by Lowth (when he shall come like a river straitened in his course, which a strong wind driveth along). It is also given by most of the recent German writers, with trivial variations, Gesenius reading *when*, Ewald *for*, and the like. According to this view of the matter, רוּחַ יְהוָה is either a Hebrew idiom for a strong wind, or a poetical description of the wind in general as the breath of God. The former explanation, although Lowth prefers it, is æsthetically far below the other, which the later writers commonly adopt. It will also be observed that this interpretation makes נֹסְסָה the causative of נוּס, *to fly*, and takes צָר as an adjective, and in its primary etymological sense of narrow compressed (Num. xxii. 26), the idea being that of a stream confined in a narrow channel and flowing violently through it. The other principal interpretation of the clause gives כִּי the sense of *when*, צָר that of *enemy*, construes the latter with the verb to *come*, derives נֹסְסָה from נֵס, *a banner*, and explains the whole to mean that *when the enemy shall come in like a flood, the Spirit of the Lord shall lift up a standard against him*. This is the version of the English and Dutch Bibles, of Vitringa, Alting, Henderson, and others. Between these two main interpretations there are others too numerous to be recited, which agree essentially with one but in some minor points coincide with the other or dissent from both. Thus Jarchi gives to נֹסְסָה the sense of consuming, which he thinks it has in chap. x. 18, and J. D. Michaelis that of drying up, which he founds upon an Arabic analogy. Aben Ezra and Hitzig, though they construe צָר with the preceding verb, make it a substantive signifying pressure or distress. Maurer agrees with the second exposition of the clause in all points, except that he explains נֹסְסָה in the sense of dispelling, and applies it to the stream itself. The objections to the first (and now prevailing) exposition, as stated by Rosenmüller and Maurer, are, its needless violation of the Masoretic accents, which forbid the intimate conjunction of נָהָר and צָר as a noun and adjective; the incongruity of likening Jehovah to a river which his own breath drives along: and the improbability that צָר is here used in a different sense from that which all attach to the plural in ver. 18. To this may be added the unnatural image of a stream rendered rapid by the wind, and (against Maurer's own interpretation) the gratuitous assumption that the Polel of נוּס is used in this one place, and as a causative, when that idea is expressed so often elsewhere by the Hiphil of the same verb. On the other hand, Gesenius himself derives נֵס from a root נָסַס, *to raise*, which might therefore be poetically used without the noun to express the whole idea; or the form before us might without absurdity be looked upon as an amalgam of the words נָשָׂא נֵס, which are combined in chaps. v. 26, xiii. 2, &c. (Compare the compound forms חלכה and חלכאים, as explained by Hengstenberg in his Commentary on the Psalms, vol. i. p. 218.) The common version of this vexed clause, therefore, is entirely defensible, and clearly preferable to the one which has so nearly superseded it. Considering, however, the objections to which both are open, it may be possible to come still nearer to the true sense by combining what is least objectionable in the other expositions; and in this view, no interpreter perhaps has been more successful than Cocceius, who translates the clause, *quia veniet tanquam fluvius hostis in quo Spiritus Domini signum præfert*. Besides giving every word its strictest or most probable interpretation, this ingenious version, as if by anticipation, shuns the last objection to Vitringa's, namely, that of Knobel, that the context does not lead us to expect an allusion to the coming of God's enemies against him, but rather to his coming against them, as the preceding clause declares that all the ends of the earth shall fear his name and his glory. The objection of Vitringa, that the instruments of the divine

purpose would not here be called an enemy, is without weight; since enemy
is a relative expression, and Jehovah is continually represented as sustaining this relation to the wicked world.   Another merit of Cocceius's interpretation is that instead of giving בו the rare and doubtful sense of *against
him,* or the still more doubtful office of a mere connective of the verb and
object, he explains it strictly as denoting *in it,* and at the same time introduces a new and striking image, that of the triumphant flag or signal erected
in the stream itself and floating on its waves as it approaches.—On the
whole, then, the meaning of the verse appears to be, that the ends of the
earth shall see and fear the name and glory of Jehovah; because when he
approaches as their enemy, it will be like an overflowing stream (chaps.
viii. 7, 8, xxviii. 15), in which his Spirit bears aloft the banner or the signal
of victory.   The specific explanation of כַּנָּהָר in the Targum as denoting
the Euphrates is a very insufficient ground for Vitringa's application of the
passage to the Saracens and Tartars.

20. *Then shall come for Zion a Redeemer, and for the converts of apostasy
in Jacob, saith Jehovah.*   The English *then* is here used to convey the full
force of the Vav conversive, which cannot be expressed in our idiom by the
simple copulative *and.*   The original construction necessarily suggests
the idea of succession and dependence.   ל is not the proper particle of
motion or direction, though it often supplies its place as well as that of
other prepositions.   This arises from the fact repeatedly stated heretofore,
that ל properly denotes relation in the widest sense, and is most commonly
equivalent to *as to, with respect to,* the precise relation being left to be
determined by the context.   So in this place לְצִיּוֹן strictly means nothing
more than that the advent of the great deliverer promised has respect to
Zion or the chosen people, without deciding what particular respect, whether
local, temporal, or of another nature altogether.   Hence the Septuagint
version, ἕνεκεν Σιών, though it may be too specific, is not contradictory to
the original; and even Paul's translation, ἐκ Σιών, although it seems completely to reverse the sense, is not so wholly inconsistent with it as has
sometimes been pretended.   For although the Hebrew words do not mean
from Zion, they mean that which may include *from Zion,* in its scope;
because it might be by going out of Zion that he was to act as her deliverer,
and the apostle might intend by his translation to suggest the idea that
Zion's redeemer was to be also the redeemer of the Gentiles.   In no case,
therefore, is there any ground for charging the apostle with perversion, or
the Hebrew text with corruption, as Lowth and J. D. Michaelis do by their
assimilation of it to the words of Paul.   It seems to me, however, that the
variation in the latter not only from the Hebrew but the Septuagint, together
with the use which the apostle makes of this citation, warrant the conclusion
that he is not there interpreting Isaiah, but employing the familiar language
of an ancient prophecy as the vehicle of a new one.   Other examples of
this practice have occurred before, nor is there anything unworthy or unreasonable in it, when the context in both cases clearly shews the author's
drift, as in the case before us, where it seems no less clear that Paul employs the language to predict the future restoration of the Jews, than that
Isaiah uses it to foretell the deliverance of God's people from their enemies
in case of their repentance, without any reference to local, temporal, or
national distinctions.   This hypothesis in reference to Paul's quotation has
the advantage of accounting for his change of the original expression, which
may then be regarded as a kind of caution against that very error into

which interpreters have generally fallen. As to Knobel's figment of Zion representing the captivity in Babylon, it seems to call for no additional discussion. (See above, on chap. xl. 2.) The expression *converts of transgression* or *apostasy* is perfectly intelligible, though unusual, and perhaps without example ; since according to analogy the phrase would seem to mean those relapsing into apostasy, the impossibility of which sense conspires with the context to determine as the true sense that which every reader spontaneously attaches to it.

21. *And I* (or *as for me*)—*this* (*is*) *my covenant with them, saith Jehovah. My Spirit which is on thee, and my words which I have placed in thy mouth, shall not depart out of thy mouth, nor out of the mouth of thy seed, nor out of the mouth of thy seed's seed, saith Jehovah, from henceforth and for ever* (or *from now and to eternity*). The absolute pronoun at the beginning is not merely emphatic, but intended to intimate a change of person, God himself reappearing as the speaker. There may also be allusion to the use of the pronoun in the promise to Noah (Gen. ix. 9), which was ever present to the mind of Jewish readers as the great standing type and model of God's covenants and promises. בְּרִית denotes the stipulation which Jehovah condescends to make in return for the repentance and conversion implicitly required in the verse preceding. This view of the connection may serve still further to explain the introduction of the pronoun, as denoting *upon my part*, and referring to the previous requisition of something upon theirs. The only natural antecedent of the pronoun *them* is *the converts of apostasy in Jacob*, to whom the promise in ver. 20 is limited. These are then suddenly addressed, or rather the discourse is turned to Israel himself as the progenitor or as the ideal representative of his descendants, not considered merely as a nation but as a church, and therefore including proselytes as well as natives, Gentiles as well as Jews, nay, believing Gentiles to the exclusion of the unbelieving Jews. This idea of the Israel of God and of the Prophecies is too clearly stated in the Epistle to the Romans to be misapprehended or denied by any who admit the authority of the apostle. This interpretation is moreover not a mere incidental application of Old Testament expressions to another subject, but a protracted and repeated exposition of the mutual relations of the old and new economy, and of the natural and spiritual Israel. To this great body, considered as the Israel of God, the promise now before us is addressed, a promise of continued spiritual influence exerted through the word and giving it effect. The phrase, *upon thee*, here as elsewhere, implies influence from above, and has respect to the figure of the Spirit's descending and abiding on the object. The particular mention of the mouth cannot be explained as having reference merely to the reception of the word, in which case the ear would have been more appropriate. The true explanation seems to be that Israel is here, as in many other parts of this great prophecy, regarded not merely as a receiver but as a dispenser of the truth; an office with which, as we have seen, the Body is invested in connection with the Head, and in perpetual subordination to him. Israel, as well as the Messiah, and in due dependence on him, was to be the light of the Gentiles, the reclaimer of apostate nations; and in this high mission and vocation was to be sustained and prospered by the never-failing presence of the Holy Spirit, as the author and the finisher of all revelation. (See above, chaps. xlii. 1-7, xliv. 3, xlix. 1-9, li. 16, liv. 3, lvi. 6-8, lviii. 12. And compare Jer. xxxi. 31 ; Joel ii. 28; Ezek. xxxvi. 27, xxxix. 29.)

Chapter 60

HAVING repeatedly and fully shewn that the national pre-eminence of
Israel was not to be perpetual, that the loss of it was the natural consequence and righteous retribution of iniquity, and that this loss did not
involve the destruction of the true church or spiritual Israel, the Prophet
now proceeds to shew that to the latter the approaching change would be a
glorious and blessed one. He accordingly describes it as a new and divine
light rising upon Zion, ver. 1. He contrasts it with the darkness of surrounding nations, ver. 2. Yet these are not excluded from participation in
the light, ver. 3. The elect in every nation are the children of the church,
and shall be gathered to her, vers. 4, 5. On one side he sees the oriental
caravans and flocks approaching, vers. 6, 7. On the other, the commercial fleets of western nations, vers. 8, 9. What seemed to be rejection is
in fact the highest favour, ver. 10. The glory of the true church is her
freedom from local and national restrictions, ver. 11. None are excluded
from her pale but those who exclude themselves and thereby perish, ver. 12.
External nature shall contribute to her splendour, ver. 13. Her very enemies shall do her homage, ver. 14. Instead of being cast off, she is glorified for ever, ver. 15. Instead of being identified with one nation, she
shall derive support from all, ver. 16. All that is changed in her condition
shall be changed for the better, ver. 17. The evils of her former state are
done away, ver. 18. Even some of its advantages are now superfluous,
ver. 19. What remains shall no longer be precarious, ver. 20. The splendour of this new dispensation is a moral and spiritual splendour, but
attended by external safety and protection, vers. 21, 22. All this shall
certainly and promptly come to pass at the appointed time, ver. 22.

Here, as elsewhere, the new dispensation is contrasted, as a whole, with
that before it. We are not therefore to seek the fulfilment of the prophecy
in any one period of history exclusively, nor to consider actual corruptions
and afflictions as inconsistent with the splendid vision of the New Jerusalem
presented to the Prophet, nor in its successive stages, but at one grand
panoramic view.

1. *Arise, be light ; for thy light is come, and the glory of Jehovah has
risen upon thee.* These are the words, not of a prophetic chorus, as Vitringa imagines, but of Isaiah, speaking in the name of God to Zion or
Jerusalem, not merely as a city, nor even as a capital, but as the centre,
representative, and symbol of the church or chosen people. A precisely
analogous example is afforded by the use of the name Rome in modern
religious controversy, not to denote the city or the civil government as
such, but the Roman Catholic Church, with all its parts, dependencies,
and interests. The one usage is as natural and intelligible as the other ;
and if no one hesitates to say that Newman has apostatized to Rome, or
that his influence has added greatly to the strength of Rome in England,
no one can justly treat it as a wresting of the Prophet's language to explain
it in precisely the same manner. And the arguments employed to prove
that the Israel and Jerusalem of these predictions are the natural Israel
and the literal Jerusalem, would equally avail to prove, in future ages, that
the hopes and fears expressed at this day in relation to the growing or de-
creasing power of Rome have reference to the increase of the city, or the
fall of the temporal monarchy established there.—The object of address is
here so plain that several of the ancient versions actually introduce the

name Jerusalem. The Septuagint renders both the verbs at the beginning by φωτίζου, which is probably to be regarded, not as a difference of text, but as a mere inadvertence. The common version *shine* is defective only in not shewing the affinity between the verb and noun, which is so marked in the original. The English *risen* is also less expressive, because more ambiguous and vague, than the Hebrew זָרַח, which means not to rise in general, but to rise above the horizon, to appear. The *glory of Jehovah* is his manifested presence, with allusion to the cloudy pillar and the Shechinah. *Upon thee* represents Jerusalem as exposed and subjected to the full blaze of this rising light. Rosenmüller's notion that *be light*, means *be cheerful*, as the eyes are elsewhere said to be enlightened (1 Sam. xiv. 27, 29), is inconsistent with the figure of a rising sun. The explanation of the words by others as an exhortation to come to the light, supposes the object of address to be a person, which is not the case. Light, and especially the light imparted by the divine presence, is a common figure for prosperity, both temporal and spiritual. Hitzig gravely represents it as certain from this verse, taken in connection with chap. lxii. 11, that between the completion of the foregoing chapter and the beginning of this, Cyrus issued his decree for the return of the captivity to Palestine. To an unbiassed reader it must be evident that this is a direct continuation of the foregoing context, and that what follows is distinguished from what goes before only by the increasing prominence with which the normal and ideal perfection of the church is set forth, as the prophecy draws near to a conclusion.

2. *For behold, the darkness shall cover the earth, and a gloom the nations, and upon thee shall Jehovah rise, and his glory upon thee shall be seen.* The general description in the first verse is now amplified and carried out into detail. Of this specification the verse before us contains only the beginning. To regard it as the whole would be to make the Prophet say the very opposite of what he does say. The perfection of the glory promised to the church is not to arise from its contrast with the darkness of the world around it, but from the diffusion of its light until that darkness disappears. The Prophet here reverts for a moment to the previous condition of the world, in order to describe with more effect the glorious changes to be produced. He is not therefore to be understood as saying that Zion shall be glorious because while the nations are in darkness she is to enjoy exclusive light, but because the light imparted to her first shall draw the nations to her.—עֲרָפֶל is essentially equivalent to חֹשֶׁךְ, but stronger and more poetical.—Lowth translates it *vapour*, which would be an anti-climax, and has no etymological exactness to recommend it. Gesenius translates it *night*, but in his Lexicon explains it as a compound or mixed form, meaning a dark cloud. *Jehovah* and his *glory*, which are jointly said to rise in the preceding verse, are here divided between two parallel members, and the rising predicated of the first alone. Lowth's version of the last word, *shall be conspicuous*, is vastly inferior, both in vigour and exactness, to the common version. Instead of *upon thee*, Noyes has *over thee*, which gives a good sense in itself, but not an adequate one, besides gratuitously varying the translation of the particle in one short sentence.

3. *And nations shall walk in thy light, and kings in the brightness of thy rising*, i. e. thy rising brightness, or the bright light which shall rise upon thee. The common version, *to thy light*, may seem at first sight more exact than the one here given, but is really less so. The Hebrew preposition לְ does not correspond to our *to* as a particle of motion or direction,

but expresses relation in the widest and most general manner. It is often therefore interchanged with other particles, and *to* among the rest, but is not to be so translated here or in any other case without necessity. In this case it seems to mean that they shall walk with reference to the light in question, which in English may be best expressed by *in*, but not as a literal translation. The sense thus yielded is in some respects better than the other, as suggesting the idea, not of mere attraction, but of general diffusion. By light we are then to understand the radiation from the luminous centre, and not merely the centre itself. This explanation of the verse is given by the best of the modern interpreters. Some of these, however, arbitrarily apply it to the restoration of the Jews from exile, who were to be accompanied by heathen kings as their guides and protectors. As a prophecy this never was fulfilled. As a visionary anticipation it could never have been entertained by a contemporary writer, such as these interpreters suppose the author of the book to be. Those who with J. D. Michaelis and Henderson apply this passage exclusively to the future restoration of the Jews, are of course cut off from all historical illustration of its meaning, which the first of these writers therefore properly dispenses with. The allegation of the other that his own position is the only one " that can be maintained consistently with a strict adherence to definite principles of interpretation," may be denied as boldly as it is affirmed. His charge of " a perpetual vacillancy between the literal and the spiritual, the Jews and the Gentiles, the past and the future," lies only against those interpretations which regard the book as a succession of specific and detached predictions. If our hypothesis be true, that it is one indivisible exhibition of the church, under its two successive phases, and in its essential relations to its Head and to the world, the objection is not only inconclusive but absurd. How far it can be alleged with truth, and without bringing the Old and New Testament into collision, that the future glory of the Jewish people as a people is the great theme of these prophecies, and that the Gentiles are brought forward chiefly for the purpose of " gracing the triumphs " of the Jews, will be seen hereafter, if not evident already. In the mean time nothing has been alleged to justify the arbitrary supposition of a sudden leap from one subject to another, scarcely more " satisfactory " than a " perpetual vacillancy" between the two.

4. *Lift up thine eyes round about* (i. e. in all directions) *and see; all of them are gathered, they come to thee, thy sons from afar shall come, and thy daughters at the side shall be borne.* See chap. xliii. 5–7, and xlix. 18–23. The English Version seems to suppose an antithesis between מֵרָחוֹק and עַל־צַד, which last it accordingly translates *at thy side*, i. e. near thee. Lowth and Henderson suppose an allusion to the oriental practice, described by Chardin, of carrying young children astride upon the hip. The latest writers simply give to צַד the sense of arm, because the arm is at the side! The primary sense of אָמַן seems to be that of carrying, with special reference to children. Jerome understands it to mean nursing, in the sense of giving suck, and translates the phrase before us *lac sugent*, which has been corrupted in the Vulgate text to *ex latere surgent*. Grotius needlessly infers that Jerome read שֵׁד instead of צַד. Those who confine these prophecies to the Babylonish exile, understand this as describing the agency of heathen states and sovereigns in the restoration. But in this, as in the parallel passages, there is, by a strange coincidence, no word or phrase implying restoration or return, but the image evidently is that of enlargement and accession ; the children thus brought to Zion being not

those whom she had lost, but such as she had never before known, as is
evident from chap. xlix. 21.   The event predicted is therefore neither the
former restoration of the Jews, as Henderson alleges in the other cases, nor
their future restoration, as he no less confidently alleges here.   The two
interpretations are both groundless and destructive of each other.   This
perpetual insertion of ideas not expressed in the original, is quite as unreasonable as Vitringa's being always haunted by his phantom of a chorus,
which he here sees taking Zion by the hand, consoling her, &c.   He is
also of opinion that by daughters we are here to understand weak Christians
who require peculiar tenderness from ministers.   There is more probability
in Knobel's suggestion, that the Prophet made his picture true to nature by
describing the sons as walking, and the daughters as being carried.

   5. *Then shalt thou see* (or *fear*), *and brighten up* (or *overflow*), *and thy
heart shall throb and swell; because* (or WHEN) *the abundance of the sea shall be
turned upon thee, the strength of nations shall come unto thee.*   This translation exhibits the points of agreement as well as of difference among interpreters in reference to this verse.   All agree that it describes a great and
joyful change to be produced by the accession of the Gentiles to the church
or chosen people, and the effect of this enlargement on the latter.   Aben
Ezra, Lowth, Vitringa, J. D. Michaelis, Döderlein, Justi, Gesenius, and
Umbreit, derive תִּרְאִי from יָרֵא, to fear, and apply it to the painful sensation
which often attends sudden joy, and which is certainly described in the
next clause.   Nearly all the later writers repeat Lowth's fine parallel quotation from Lucretius:

> His tibi me rebus quædam divina voluptas
> Percipit atque horror.

Above sixty manuscripts, and one of the oldest editions (Bib. Soncin),
require this explanation, by reading either תֵּרְאִי, תֵּרְאִי, or תֵּרְאִי, none of
which can regularly come from רָאָה to see.   Yet the latter derivation is not
only sanctioned by all the ancient versions, and preferred by Kimchi, but
approved by Luther, Clericus, Rosenmüller, Maurer, Hitzig, Henderson,
Ewald, and Knobel.   It is curious to see how the parallelism is urged on
either side of this dispute, and that with equal plausibility.   Thus Vitringa
thinks that *thou shalt see* would be a vain repetition of the *lift up thine eyes
and see* in ver. 4, while Knobel describes the double reference to fear in this
verse as a "lästige Tautologie."   As to נָהַר, the difficulty is in choosing
between its two admitted senses of flowing (chap. ii. 2), and of shining (Ps.
xxxiv. 6).   The former is preferred by Jerome, who translates it *afflues;* by
Junius and Tremellius, who have *conflues ;* and by the English and Dutch
Versions, the latter of which refers it to the confluence of crowds produced
by any strange occurrence.   Vitringa makes it mean to *flow out*, and Lowth
to *overflow* with joy.   But all the latest writers of authority give the word
the same sense as in Ps. xxxiv. 6, which is well expressed by Henderson in
strong though homely English, *thou shalt look and brighten up.*   His version of the next clause, *thy heart shall throb and dilate*, may be improved
by changing the last word, which he took from Lowth, to the equivalent
but plainer *swell*.—פָּחַד, which Lowth renders *ruffled*, is admitted by most
writers to be here used in its primary sense of trembling, which in reference
to the heart may be best expressed by beating or throbbing.   But the
usual though secondary sense of fearing is retained by Luzzatto, who regards
it as descriptive of her terror at the sight of supposed enemies approaching;
and by Hendewerk, who applies it to her apprehension that she would not

have sufficient room for the accommodation of the strangers. The usual and proper sense of יִּכ (for, because) is perfectly appropriate; the only reason for preferring that of *when*, as Vitringa, Gesenius, and others do, is its apparent relation to the אִם at the beginning of the sentence, as if he had said, *when* the abundance of the sea, &c., *then* shalt thou see, &c. According to the other explanation of this particle, the אִם refers to the foregoing context. Another doubt arises from the ambiguity of the nouns הֲמוֹן and חַיִל, both of which may be applied either to things or persons,—the first denoting sometimes a multitude (chap. xvii. 12), sometimes abundance (Ps. xxxvii. 16); the other signifying sometimes a military force (Exod. xiv. 28), sometimes wealth (Gen. xxxiv. 29). As in either case the different meanings are only modifications of one radical idea (a multitude of persons and a multitude of things, a military force and pecuniary force); as both the meanings of each word are here appropriate, and as interpreters, whichever meaning they prefer, contrive to join the other with it,—we may safely infer that it was also the intention of the writer to convey the whole idea, that the Gentiles should devote themselves and their possessions to the service of Jehovah. (Compare Zech. xiv. 14.)—For *of the sea* J. D. Michaelis has *from the west;* and other writers who retain the strict translation, suppose a designed antithesis between the west in this verse and the eastern nations mentioned in the next. The conversion here predicted has the same sense as in English, viz., the conversion of the property of one to the use of another. *Upon* can hardly be a simple substitute for *to*, but is rather intended to suggest the same idea as when we speak of gifts or favours being showered or lavished *on* a person. This force of the particle is well expressed in Lowth's translation, *when the riches of the sea shall be poured in upon thee*, but with too little regard to the proper meaning of the Hebrew verb. The next clause is a repetition of the same thought, but without a figure. If this had reference to the restoration of the Jews from Babylon, it was an extravagant anticipation utterly falsified by the event. But this, although it may commend the hypothesis to those who deny the inspiration of the Prophet, is itself a refutation of it to the minds of those who occupy a contrary position. The most natural interpretation of the verse is that which makes it a promise of indefinite enlargement, comprehending both the persons and the riches of the nations. There is something amusing at the present day in Vitringa's suggesting as a difficulty to be cleared away from the interpretation of the passage, that as Christianity is a spiritual religion it can have no great occasion for gold or silver. Even literally understood, the promise is intelligible and most welcome to the philanthropic Christian, as affording means for the diffusion of the truth and the conversion of the world.

6. *A stream of camels shall cover thee, young camels* (or *dromedaries*) *of Midian and Ephah, all of them from Sheba shall come, gold and incense shall they bear, and the praises of Jehovah as good news.* This last form of expression is adopted in order to convey the full force of the Hebrew verb, which does not mean simply to announce or even to announce with joy, but to announce glad tidings. (See above, on chap. xl. 9.) Retaining this sense here, the word would seem to signify not the direct praise of God, but the announcement of the fact that others praised him, and the messengers would be described as bringing to Jerusalem the news of the conversion of their people. It is possible, however, that the primary meaning of בִּשֵׂר may be simply to announce, as in chap. lii. 7, 1 Kings i. 42, 1 Sam. iv. 17, 2 Sam. xviii. 20, 26, and that the derivation given by Gesenius is fictitious.

But in no case is it necessary, with Vitringa, to exchange the settled mean-ing of תְּהִלּוֹת for the doubtful one of praiseworthy acts.—Ewald has greatly improved upon the usual translation of שִׁפְעָה by exchanging *multitude* for *stream* or *flood*, the version given by Jerome (*inundatio*), and not only more expressive than the other, but in perfect accordance with the etymology, and with the usage of the noun itself in Job xxii. 11, xxxviii. 34. When applied in prose to a drove of horses (Ezek. xx. 10) or a troop of horsemen (2 Kings ix. 17), it requires of course a different version. This explanation of שִׁפְעָה throws light upon the phrase *shall cover thee*, a term elsewhere applied to water (*e. g.* chap. xi. 9), and suggesting here the poetical idea of a city not merely thronged but flooded with Arabian caravans. This is at least more natural than Vitringa's notion that the camels are said to cover that which they approach, because they are so tall that they overtop and overshadow it. The camel has been always so peculiarly associated with the Arabs that they are described by Strabo as σκηνίται καμηλοβοσκοί. They are here, according to Isaiah's practice, represented by a group of ancestral names. Ephah was the eldest son of Midian (Gen. xxv. 4), who was himself the son of Abraham by Keturah (Gen. xxv. 2), and the brother of Jokshan the father of Sheba (Gen. xxv. 1–4). The first two represent northern and central Arabia, the third Arabia Felix, so called by the old geographers because of the rich products which is furnished to the northern traders, either from its own resources or as an entrepôt of Indian commerce. The queen of this country, by whom Solomon was visited, brought with her gold, gems, and spices in abundance (1 Kings x. 2), and we read elsewhere of its frankincense (Jer. vi. 20), its Phenician commerce (Ezek. xxvii. 29), and its caravans (Job vi. 19), while those of Midian are mentioned even in the patriarchal history (Gen. xxxvii. 28). Bochart supposes the Midian of this passage to be the Madiene of Josephus and the Modion of Ptolemy, and identifies Ephah with the Ἵππος of the Greek geographers. It is more accordant with usage, however, to explain them as the names of the national progenitors, representing their descend-ants.—It matters little whether *dromedaries* or *young camels* be the true translation. (For the arguments on both sides see Bochart's Hierozoicon, vol. i. p. 15, with Rosenmüller's Note.) The former is preferable only because it gives us a distinct name, as in the original, which is perhaps the reason that Gesenius retains it in his Version but rejects it in his Com-mentary. Aben Ezra and Saadias make בְּ a preposition and כִּרְ the plural of כַּר, which in Gen. xxxi. 34 denotes a litter or a woman's saddle used in riding upon camels.—The verb יָבֹאוּ does not agree with the preceding noun, as the camels of Midian and Ephah could not come from Sheba, but with *all of them*, which may either be indefinite, " they (*i. e.* men) shall come all of them," or more specifically signify the merchants of Sheba. Most interpreters agree with the Targum in referring the last verb (יְבַשֵּׂרוּ) to the men who come with the camels and the gifts ; but as יִשָּׂאוּ properly denotes the act of the animals themselves, it is not without a show of reason that Vitringa construes the other verb in the same manner, and supposes the camels by their very burdens to praise God or rather to announce the disposition of these tribes to praise him. This is rendered still more probable by the analogy of the next verse, where kindred acts appear to be ascribed to other animals.—It is a common opinion of interpreters that this verse represents the east as joining in the acts of homage and of tribute which the one before it had ascribed to the west ; but it may well be doubted whether this distinctive meaning can be put upon the terms *sea* and *nations* there employed, and the antithesis would hardly be in keeping with another which appears to be designed between these two verses and the eighth, as will be explained below.

7. *All the flocks of Kedar shall be gathered for thee, the rams of Nebaioth shall minister to thee, they shall ascend with good-will* (or *acceptably*) *my altar, and my house of beauty I will beautify.* To the traders of Arabia with their caravans and precious wares he now adds her shepherds with their countless flocks. While Kimchi explains *all* as meaning *many*, and Knobel *all kinds*, Vitringa insists upon the strict sense as an essential feature of the prophecy. Kedar, the second son of Ishmael (Gen. xxv. 13), who represents Arabia in chap. xxi. 16, and xlii. 11, is here joined for the same purpose with his elder brother *Nebaioth*, obviously identical with the *Nabataei*, the name given to the people of Arabia Petraea by Strabo and Diodorus Siculus, who represent them as possessed of no wealth except flocks and herds, in which they were extremely rich. Ezekiel also speaks of Tyre as trading with *Arabia and all the chiefs of Kedar* in *lambs and rams and goats.* (Ezek. xxvii. 21.) These are here described as gathered in one vast flock to Jerusalem, or rather *for* her, *i. e.* for her use or service, which agrees best with what follows, and with the usage of the Hebrew preposition. They are then, by a bold and striking figure, represented as offering themselves, which is first expressed by the general term *serve* or *minister*, and then more unequivocally by declaring that they shall themselves ascend the altar. Kimchi endeavours to get rid of this bold metaphor by introducing *with* before the *rams of Nebaioth*, and referring both verbs to the people themselves : (*With*) *the rams of Nebaioth shall they serve thee, and cause* (*them*) *to ascend*, &c. But the common judgment of interpreters is in favour of explaining the words strictly, and retaining the unusual figure unimpaired. They are not disposed, however, to go all lengths with Vitringa, who supposes the rams to be personified as priests offering themselves upon the altar.—The ascent of the victim on the altar is repeatedly connected elsewhere with the phrase לְרָצוֹן, to acceptance or acceptably. (See above, chap. lvi. 7, and Jer. vi. 20.) But in this one place we have the phrase עַל־רָצוֹן, as if the last noun had usurped the place of *altar*, which immediately follows. Of this unusual construction there are several distinct explanations. Kimchi regards it as a case of הִפּוּךְ or metathesis, which may be thus resolved : יַעֲלוּ לרצון על מזבחי. Gesenius obtains precisely the same meaning by explaining מִזְבְּחִי as an accusative after a verb of motion, and making עַל־רָצוֹן a simple variation of the common phrase לְרָצוֹן. Hitzig and Henderson adopt the same construction, but suppose the two phrases to be different in sense as well as form, לְרָצוֹן meaning *to* (*divine*) *acceptance*, עַל־רָצוֹן *with good-will* or *complacency*. The phrase then only serves to strengthen the description of the victims as spontaneously offering themselves, an idea which Lowth finally, but perhaps too artificially, illustrates by citations from Suetonius and Tacitus, shewing that the ancients viewed reluctance in the victims as an evil omen, and by parity of reasoning the appearance of spontaneous self-devotion as a good one.—In the last clause, the meaning of the phrase בֵּית תִּפְאַרְתִּי is determined by the parallel expressions in chap. lxiv. 10, where the suffix necessarily belongs to the governing word, or rather to the whole complex phrase, and the whole means, not *the house of our holiness and our beauty*, but *our house of holiness and beauty*, or resolved into the occidental idiom, *our holy and our beautiful*

house, which is the common English version.   The LXX have here *my
house of prayer*, as in chap. lvi. 7 ; and Hitzig regards this as the genuine
reading, though he does not adopt it in his German version.   His reason
for this critical decision is a very insufficient one, viz. that God is nowhere
else said to glory in the temple, which is not the meaning of the common
text, תִּפְאָרֶת being here used in its primary and ordinary sense of *beauty*,
as appears from its conjunction with the verb פָאַר, which, in this connection, even upon Hitzig's own hypothesis, must mean to beautify.—Grotius
supposes this prediction to have been literally verified in Herod's temple.
Gesenius and the other Germans easily dispose of it as a fanatical anticipation.   It is much more embarrassing to those who make the passage a
prediction of the future restoration of the Jews, and the future splendour
of the literal Jerusalem.   Some of the most intrepid writers of this class
consistently apply their fundamental principle of literal interpretation, and
believe that the Mosaic ritual or something like it is to be restored.   But
such interpreters as J. D. Michaelis and Henderson, who cannot go to this
length, are obliged to own that spiritual services are here represented under
forms and titles borrowed from the old dispensation.   " Whatever the
descendants of those oriental tribes may possess shall be cheerfully placed
at the disposal of the restored Jews. . . . . . There shall be no want of
anything that is required for the full restoration of divine worship, when
the mosque of Omar shall give place to a new temple to be erected for the
celebration of the services of that ministration which exceedeth in glory.
2 Cor. iii. 8–11."   This is the "literal interpretation" of a school which
will not allow Israel to mean the church or chosen people as such considered, but insists upon its meaning the nation of the Jews !   The picture
which this interpretation makes the Prophet draw may well be called a
mixed one, consisting of a literal Jerusalem, literal caravans and camels,
but a figurative altar, figurative victims, and a material temple to be built
upon the site of the old one for a spiritual worship exclusive of the very
rites which it is here predicted shall be solemnly performed there.   Of such
a figment upon such a subject we may say, with more than ordinary emphasis, and even with a double sense, *Credat Judæus !*   On the other hand,
the prophecy explains itself to those who believe that the ancient Israel is
still in existence, and that the Jews as a nation form no part of it.   The
charge of mystical or allegorical interpretation does not lie against this
view of the matter, but against Vitringa's needless and fantastic addition to
his real exegesis of a set of riddles or enigmas, in which he puzzles both
his readers and himself by attempting to determine whether camels mean
laborious and patient Christians, rams strong ones, sheep those fattened
by the word and clothed in the white wool of holiness, &c.   To any but
Vitringa himself it must be difficult to see in what respect all this is any
better than the notion for which he reproves Eusebius, Jerome, and Procopius, that camels here mean rich men, as in Mat. xix. 24.   And yet after
saying in regard to these erring Fathers, *vitanda utique sunt in applicatio-
nibus mysticis* ἀλλογενῆ, he adds with great complacency, *nostræ rationes hic
sunt liquidæ !*   If any proof were needed of the risk attending the admission of a false exegetical principle, however harmless in appearance, it
would be afforded by these melancholy triflings on the part of one of the
most able, learned, orthodox, devout, accomplished, and, with this exception, sensible interpreters of Scripture, that the world has ever seen or can
expect to see again.

8. *Who are these that fly as a cloud and as doves to their windows ?*   It is

a fine conception of Vitringa, that the ships expressly mentioned in the next verse are here described in their first appearance at a distance resembling with their outspread sails and rapid course a fleecy cloud driven by the wind, and a flight of doves returning to their young. Both comparisons are elsewhere used as here to indicate rapidity of motion. (Job xxx. 15, Ps. lv. 7, Hos. xi. 11, Jer. iv. 13.) Much less felicitous is Vitringa's idea that the image here presented is that of a prophetic chorus standing with the church on the roof of the city, and asked by her, or asking, what it is they see approaching. Houbigant's emendation of the text by reading אברתיהם, though approved by Lowth and even improved by the change of אֶל to עַל on the authority of more than forty manuscripts, so as to admit of the translation *like doves upon the wing*, is justly characterized by Gesenius as an "elende Conjectur." The common text means *lattices* or latticed *windows*, either of which is better than Henderson's translation *holes*, though even this is preferable to the vague and weak term *habitations* used by Noyes.

9. *Because for me the isles are waiting* (or *must wait*), *and the ships of Tarshish in the first place, to bring thy sons from far, their silver and their gold with them for the name of Jehovah thy God, and for the Holy One of Israel, because he has glorified thee.* This verse contains a virtual though not a formal answer to the question in the one before it. As if he had said, Wonder not that these are seen approaching, for the whole world is only awaiting my command to bring thy sons, &c. This view of the connection makes it wholly unnecessary to give כִּי the sense of *surely, yes,* or any other than its usual and proper one of *for, because.* For the true sense of יְקַוּוּ, see above on chap. xlii. 4, and for ships of Tarshish, vol. i. p. 394. Luzzatto here gratuitously reads יִקָּווּ *let them be gathered*, which is applied to a confluence of nations in Jer. iii. 17. The Septuagint, which elsewhere explains Tarshish to mean the sea, here retains the name; but the Vulgate even here has *naves maris.* J. D. Michaelis, *the ships of Spain.* Jarchi and Kimchi supply כ before בראשנה, and explain it to mean *as at first*, or *as of old*, referring to the days of Solomon and Hiram. This reading is actually found in twenty-five manuscripts, and sanctioned by the Peshito; but even Lowth retains the common text. The Hebrew phrase is generally understood to mean in the first rank either as to time or place. (Compare Num. x. 13, 14.) Both may be included, as they really imply one another. The pronoun *their* may have for its antecedent either *sons* or *islands;* but the former, as the nearer, is more natural. The last clause is repeated from chap. lv. 5, where לְמַעַן takes the place of the first לְ and determines it to mean not *to* but *for.* There is no need therefore of explaining *name* to mean the place where the divine name was recorded. J. D. Michaelis still declines to say in what precise form this prediction is to be fulfilled; but Henderson, less cautious or more confident, affirms that the property of the Jews as well as themselves shall be conveyed free of charge to Palestine, adding that many of them resident in distant parts can only conveniently return by sea. The principle involved in this interpretation is, that we have no right to make the Zion here addressed any other than the literal Jerusalem, or the ships, the silver, and the gold, any other than literal silver, gold, and ships. This rule, to be of any practical avail, must apply to all parts of the passage, and especially to all parts of the verse alike, without which uniformity interpretation becomes wholly arbitrary or mere guess-work. It is an interesting question, therefore, what we are to understand in this connection by the *ships of*

Tarshish, to which such extraordinary prominence is given in the work of restoration. As to this point, Henderson refers us to his note on chap. xxiii. 10, where we read as follows : " By *Tarshish* there can no longer be any reasonable doubt we are to understand *Tartessus*, the ancient and celebrated emporium of the Phenicians, situated between the two mouths of the river Baetis (now Guadalquiver) on the south-western coast of Spain." Are we to understand then that the vessels of this part of Spain are to be foremost in the restoration of the Jews to Palestine, just as the descendants of the ancient Kedar, Ephah, and Sheba, are to place their possessions at the disposal of the restored Jews ? If so, this meaning should have been distinctly stated, as it partly is by Michaelis in translating Tarshish *Spain*. If not, and if as we suspect the ships of Tarshish are secretly identified with the commercial navy of Great Britain and perhaps America, we then have another medley like that in ver. 7, but in this case consisting of a literal return to the literal Jerusalem in literal ships but belonging to a figurative Tarshish. In these repeated instances of mixed interpretation there is something like a vacillancy between the literal and the spiritual, which is any thing but satisfactory. To the assumption that commercial intercourse and navigation are here represented under forms and names derived from the Old Testament history, I am so far from objecting, that I wish to apply it to the whole prediction, and to use precisely the same liberty in understanding what is said of Zion and her sons, as in understanding what is said of Tarshish and her ships. Let it also be added to the cumulative proofs already urged in favour of our own hypothesis, that here, as in so many former instances, the writer does not even accidentally use any term explicitly denoting restoration or return, but only such as are appropriate to mere accession and increase *ab extra*. It cannot therefore be absurd, even if it is erroneous to apply what is here said, with Vitringa, to the growth of the true Israel or chosen people by the calling of the Gentiles, with particular allusion to the wealth of the commercial nations, from among whom the elect of God, the sons of Zion, when they come to the embraces of their unknown mother, shall come bringing their silver and gold with them.

10. *And strangers shall build thy walls, and their kings shall serve thee ; for in my wrath I smote thee, and in my favour I have had mercy on thee.* For the true sense of the phrase בְּגֵי־נֵכָר, see above on chap. lvi. 3 ; and with the last clause compare chap. liv. 7, 8. The כִּי relates to the whole of that clause taken together, not to the first member by itself. It was not because God had been angry, but because he had been angry and relented, that they were to be thus favoured. (See vol. i. p. 263.) There is no need, however, of substituting an involved occidental syntax for the simple Hebrew construction, as Vitringa and Rosenmüller do, by reading, " for although in my wrath I may have smitten thee," &c. The English version of the last verb in the sentence is correct. Lowth's emendation of it, in which he is followed by Henderson and Noyes, is wholly ungrammatical, since the preceding verb is not a future but a preterite. The change is also needless, since the mercy is described as past, not in reference to the date of the prediction, but of its fulfillment. There is something at once inexact and mawkish in Lowth's paraphrase of this verb, *I will embrace thee with the most tender affection.* If any departure from the usual translation were required or admissible, the preference would be due to Ewald's version (*lieb ich dich wieder*).—Eichhorn supposed the expectation here expressed to have been excited by the benefactions of the Persian kings to the re-

stored Jews (Ezra i. 8, vi. 8, 9); but even Gesenius regards the date thus assigned to the prediction as too late. Knobel applies the text to the neighbouring heathen, called בְּנֵי־נֵכָר by Nehemiah (chap. ix. 2; comp. Ps. xviii. 45, cxliv. 7, 11), who were to be driven from the lands upon which they had intruded during the captivity, and reduced to bondage by the restored Jews. Henderson's explanation of the verse as meaning that foreigners shall count it an honour to be employed in rebuilding Jerusalem and "in any way contributing to the recovery of the lost happiness of Israel, and that even monarchs shall regard it as a privilege to aid in the work by employing whatever legitimate influence they may possess in advancing it," is hardly a fair specimen of strictly literal interpretation, but rather an insensible approximation to the old opinion, as expressed by Vitringa, that the Prophet here foretells the agency of strangers or new converts in promoting the safety and prosperity of Israel, under figures borrowed from the old economy, and implying a vicissitude or alternation of distress and joy, such as Isaiah frequently exhibits. The building of the walls here mentioned is the same as that in Ps. li. 20, and cxlvii. 2, where it is no more to be literally understood than the captivity of Zion in Ps. xiv. 7, or that of Job in chap, xlii. 10. (See Hengstenberg on the Psalms, vol. i. p. 291.)

11. *And thy gates shall be open continually, day and night they shall not be shut, to bring into thee the strength of nations and their kings led (captive or in triumph).* According to Hitzig there is here a resumption of the figures in ver. 6, and the gates are represented as kept open day and night by the perpetual influx of Arabian caravans. But without going back to the peculiar imagery of that verse, we may understand the one before us as relating to the influx of strangers and new converts generally. The two ideas expressed are those of unobstructed access and undisturbed tranquillity. The use of פִּתְּחוּ is the same as in chap. xlviii. 8, nearly but not entirely coincident with that of the corresponding verb in English, when we speak of a door's opening instead of being opened. The difference is simply that between the description of a momentary act, and of a permanent condition. The intransitive construction is in either case the same. Upon this verse, perhaps combined with Zech. xiv. 7, is founded that beautiful and grand description, *the gates of it shall not be shut at all by day, for there shall be no night there* (Rev. xxi. 25), of which Vitringa speaks as an inspired exposition of the verse before us, while Henderson says more correctly that the apostle " borrows the language in his description of the New Jerusalem."—חיל has the same ambiguity or latitude of meaning as in ver. 5, above. The sense of wealth or treasure is preferred by most of the late writers, but Rosenmüller has *exercitus*. Better than either, because comprehending both, is Vitringa's version *copia*, to which we have no exact equivalent in English.—Vitringa and Rosenmüller follow Kimchi in explaining נְהוּגִים to mean escorted, led in procession, or, as Lowth has it, *pompously attended*, which they take to be the meaning of the verb in Nah. ii. 8. But as that place is itself obscure and doubtful, and as the verb is clearly employed elsewhere to express the act of leading captive (chap. xx. 4; 1 Sam. xxx. 2), several of the later writers have reverted to this explanation, which is also given in the Targum (וְקִקְיָין) and by Aben Ezra, and agrees with chap. xlv. 14 (compare Ps. cxlix. 8). Gesenius in his Commentary charges Koppe with omitting to observe that this sense is at variance with the idea of voluntary adhesion expressed throughout the context; but in his Thesaurus he adopts this very explanation, without

attempting to refute his own objection. Hitzig's solution of it is that the nations are described as coming to Jerusalem *en masse*, and bringing their reluctant kings in chains along with them. Knobel proposes an entirely new explanation, in which נְהוּגִים is to have an active meaning (like יָקוּשׁ and אָחוּז), and to be translated *leaders*; but if ever the invention of a new sense was without the faintest colour of necessity, it is so here. The general meaning no doubt is that earthly sovereigns must unite in this adhesion to the true religion, either willingly or by compulsion. The different impressions made by such a passage on intelligent interpreters, according to their several hypotheses or previous conclusions, may be shewn by comparing the remarks of Henderson and Umbreit upon this verse. While the latter confidently asks who can here fail to read the daily progress of God's kingdom by accretion from the Gentiles, in which sense the doors of Zion are still open, kings and nations streaming in by day and night, the other gravely observes that "modern travellers greatly complain of the inconvenience to which they are put, when they do not reach Jerusalem before the gates are closed." This is either nothing to the purpose or implies that the blessing promised in the text is a more convenient regulation of the gate-police after the restoration of the Jews!

12. *For the nation and the kingdom which will not serve thee shall perish, and the nations shall be desolated, desolated.* Similar threatenings are found in Zech. x. 1, xii. 1, and xiv. 17, in the last of which places there is a specific threat of drought, as the appointed punishment. This has led Hitzig and some later writers to explain the last verb here as meaning to be utterly dried up or parched. But in chap. xxxvii. 18, above, it is applied to nations in the general sense of desolation. The *for* at the beginning of the verse is commonly explained as introducing a reason for the confluence of strangers just before predicted, namely, the desire of escaping this destruction; but it may as well be understood to give a reason for the promise of increase in general. The gates of Zion shall be crowded, because all shall enter into them but those who are to perish. *The nations* in the last clause may mean the nations just described, or, as the common version expresses it, *those nations.* But it may also mean, perhaps more naturally, those who still continue to be Gentiles, heathen, by refusing to unite themselves with Israel.—The threatening in this verse is a very serious one, however understood; but it is also very strange and unaccountable if understood as meaning that all nations shall be utterly destroyed which will not serve the Jews when restored to their own country. Even if we give to *serve* the mitigated sense of shewing favour and assisting, there is still something almost revolting in the penalty annexed to the omission; how much more if we understand it as denoting actual subjection and hard bondage. It is no wonder that a writer so acute as Henderson is forced by the pressure of this difficulty on his theory to seek for a "meiosis" in the sentence, and to understand the threatening as directed only against those who are chargeable with "positive hostility," a forced assumption not to be supported by a reference to Judges v. 23. The whole is rendered clear by the assumption, not got up for the occasion, but resulting from an extensive exegetical induction, that the threatening was intended to apply, in its most obvious and strongest sense, to all those nations which refuse to be connected with the church or Israel of God.

13. *The glory of Lebanon to thee shall come, cypress, plane, and box together, to adorn the place of my sanctuary, and the place of my feet I will honour.* The glory of Lebanon is its cedars. For the other trees here

mentioned, see above, on chap. xli. 19, where, as here, they are merely representatives of ornamental forest-trees in general. *The place of my sanctuary* has been generally understood to mean the sanctuary itself; but several of the latest writers understand by it Jerusalem, as being the place where the temple was erected. The same sense is put by Maurer and others on *the place of my feet*, that is, the place where I habitually stand or walk. (Ezek. xliii. 7.) Vitringa and the older writers generally seem to understand by it the ark of the covenant, considered as the footstool of Jehovah (1 Chron. xxviii. 2; Ps. xcix. 5, cxxxii. 7), when enthroned between the cherubim (chap. xxxvii. 16; Ps. lxxx. 2.) In favour of the wider sense is the analogy of chap. lxvi. 2, where the same description is applied to the whole earth, but in reference to heaven as the throne of God.—Another topic upon which interpreters have been divided, is the question whether the adorning mentioned here is that of cultivated grounds by living trees, or that of buildings by the use of the choicest kinds of timber. The latter opinion has most commonly prevailed; but Hitzig, Ewald, and Knobel, are decidedly in favour of the other, which is far more pleasing in itself and more in keeping with the poetical tone of the whole context. In either case the meaning of the figure is that the earthly residence of God shall be invested with the most attractive forms of beauty. Even Grotius, as Vitringa has observed, was ashamed to rest in the material sense of this description. and has made it so far tropical as to denote the conquest of many parts of Syria by the Jews. But Henderson goes back to ground which even Grotius could not occupy, and understands the verse not only of material trees but of material timber. "A literal temple or house of worship being intended, *the language* MUST BE *literally understood.*" But why are literal trees more indispensable in this case than literal sheep and rams and a literal altar in ver. 7, or than literal ships of Tarshish in ver. 9? This perpetual vacillancy between the literal and the spiritual is anything but satisfactory. "From all that appears to be the state of Palestine in regard to wood, supplies from Lebanon will be as necessary as they were when the ancient temple was constructed." With this may be worthily compared the use of the same text to justify the "dressing of churches" at the festival of Christmas.

14. *Then shall come to thee bending the sons of thy oppressors, then shall bow down to the soles of thy feet all thy despisers, and shall call thee the City of Jehovah, Zion the holy place of Israel* (or *the Zion of the Holy One of Israel*). For the same ideas and expressions, see above, chap. xlv. 14, and xlix. 23. The עַל before כַּפּוֹת is not simply equivalent to *at*, but expresses downward motion, and may be translated *down to*. The act described is the oriental prostration as a sign of the profoundest reverence. The Vulgate makes the sense still stronger, and indeed too strong, by attaching to the verb a religious meaning, and regarding כַּפּוֹת as its object (*adorabunt vestigia pedum tuorum*). The sons are mentioned either for the purpose of contrasting the successive generations more emphatically, or as a mere oriental idiom without distinctive meaning. In favour of the latter supposition is the circumstance that it is wanting in the other clause, where the despisers are themselves represented as doing the same thing with the sons of the oppressors. נאץ means not only to despise in heart but to treat with contempt. These humbled enemies are represented as acknowledging the claim of Zion to be recognised as the holy place and dwelling of Jehovah. The old construction of the last words, the Zion of the Holy One of Israel, supposes Zion as a proper name to govern the next word, contrary to the general rule, but after the analogy of such combinations as *Beth-*

lehem of Judah and *Jehovah of hosts.* Hitzig prefers to make צִיּוֹן an appellative synonymous with צִיִּי, *the pillar of the Holy One of Israel.* Maurer more plausibly suggests that קְדוֹשׁ here means not a holy person but a holy or consecrated place, as in chap. lvii. 15, Ps. xlvi. 5, lxv. 5. On any of these suppositions, the sense of the acknowledgment remains the same. That sense is determined by the parallel passage chap. xlv. 14, where a part of the confession is in these words, *only in thee is God.* (See above, p. 183.) The same sense must here be attached to the acknowledgment of Zion as the City of Jehovah, in order to explain or justify the strength of the expressions put into the mouth of her repentant enemies. The old Jerusalem was not merely *a* holy place, *a* city of Jehovah, but *the* holy place, *the* city of Jehovah. Its exclusive possession of this character was perfectly essential, and is always so described in Scripture. Are we to understand, then, that Jerusalem, when rebuilt and enlarged hereafter, is again to be invested with its old monopoly of spiritual privileges? If it is, how can such a restoration of the old economy be reconciled with the New Testament doctrines? If it is not, why are these repentant enemies described as rendering precisely the same homage to the New Jerusalem, which properly belonged to the old? If this is a mere figure for deep reverence and so forth, what becomes of the principle of literal interpretation? Whether these questions are of any exegetical importance, and if so, whether they are satisfactorily solved by Henderson's interpretation of the verse as meaning that "the descendants of her oppressors will acknowledge the wrongs that have been done to her, and humbly crave a share in her privileges," is left to the decision of the reader. On the supposition hitherto assumed as the basis of the exposition, this verse simply means that the enemies of the church shall recognise her in her true relation to her divine Head.

15. *Instead of thy being forsaken and hated and with none passing* (through thee), *and I will place thee for a boast of perpetuity, a joy of age and age.* The תַּחַת may express either simply a change of condition (whereas), or the reason of the change (because), or the further idea of equitable compensation. Hitzig supposes an allusion in שְׂנוּאָה to the use of the same word in the law with respect to a less beloved wife (Gen. xxix. 31; Deut. xxi. 15). But in the phrase אֵין עוֹבֵר the personification seems entirely merged in the idea of a city. The וְ at the beginning of the second clause is commonly regarded as the sign of the apodosis, and as such cannot be expressed in English. It may, however, have its usual copulative meaning if the first clause be connected with the foregoing verse as a part of the same sentence. In either case the וְ must at the same time be conversive and connect the verb with those of the preceding verse, or else it must be taken as a præter like רִחַמְתִּי in ver. 10. In order probably to make the application of the verse to the material Jerusalem more natural, Henderson observes that עוֹלָם is here used, as in many other places, for a period of long and unknown duration. As this is certainly the primitive meaning of the word, it is often so applied, and yet it may be noted that according to the true interpretation of the prophecy, this expression may be taken in its utmost strength and latitude of meaning.

16. *And thou shalt suck the milk of nations, and the breast of kings shalt thou suck, and thou shalt know that I, Jehovah, am thy saviour, and (that) thy redeemer (is) the Mighty One of Jacob.* All interpreters agree with the Targum in applying this verse to the influx of wealth and power and whatever else the kings and nations of the earth can contribute to the progress

of the true religion. The figure is derived foom Deut. xxxiii. 19, *they shall suck the abundance of the seas.* שֹׁד cannot here mean desolation, as above in chap. lix. 7, and below in ver. 18, but must be a variation of the usual form שַׁד as in Job xxiv. 9. The catachresis in the second clause is not a mere rhetorical blunder, but, as Hitzig well says, an example of the sense overmastering the style, a licence the occasional use of which is characteristic of a bold and energetic writer. It also serves the useful purpose of shewing how purely tropical the language is. Lowth and Noyes gratuitously try to mitigate the harshness of the metaphor by changing the second *suck* into *fostered at* and *nursed from* the breast of kings. Vitringa speaks of some as attempting to remove the solecism altogether by makings *kings* mean *queens* or the *daughters of kings,* or by appealing to extraordinary cases in which males have given suck! The construction of the last clause is the one expressed by Noyes. Each member of that clause contains a subject and a predicate, and therefore a complete proposition. The sense is not merely that Jehovah is the Mighty One of Jacob, but that the Mighty God of Jacob is Israel's redeemer, and the self-existent everlasting God his saviour. Here, as in chap. i. 24, Henderson translates אָבִיר *protector;* but see vol. i. p. 91–92.

17. *Instead of brass* (or copper) *I will bring gold, and instead of iron I will bring silver, and instead of wood brass, and instead of stones iron, and I will place* (or *make*) *thy government peace and thy rulers righteousness.* Grotius follows the Targum in explaining the first clause as a promise of ample compensation for preceding losses. As if he had said, "For the brass which thy enemies have taken from thee I will bring thee gold," &c. Knobel, on the contrary, understands the clause as meaning that the value of the precious metals shall be lowered by their great abundance. Henderson likewise understands it as a promise that " the temporal prosperity of the restored Israelites shall resemble that of their ancestors in the days of Solomon." (See 1 Kings x. 27, 2 Chron. ix. 20, 27). But the thought which is naturally suggested by the words is that expressed by Vitringa, namely, that all things shall be changed for the better. The change described is not a change in kind, *i. e.* from bad to good, but in degree, *i. e.* from good to better; because the same things which appear to be rejected in the first clause are expressly promised in the second. The arrangement of the items Vitringa endeavours to explain as having reference to the outward appearance of the substances, those being put together which are most alike. (See a similar gradation in chap. xxx. 26, Zech. xiv. 20, 1 Cor. iii. 12, xv. 41.) The last clause resolves the figures into literal expressions, and thus shews that the promise has respect not to money but to moral advantages. פְּקֻדָּה properly means office, magistracy, government, here put for those who exercise it, like nobility, ministry, and other terms in English. (Compare Ezek. ix. 1, 2 Kings. xi. 18.) נֹגְשִׂים, which has commonly a bad sense, is here used for magistrates or rulers in general, for the purpose of suggesting that instead of tyrants or exactors they should now be under equitable government. The two parallel expressions Henderson decides to signify the temporal and spiritual chiefs of the restored Jewish community, without assigning any ground for the alleged distinction. There is much more force in his remark that the similarity of structure between this verse and chap. iii. 24 corroborates the genuineness of these later prophecies. Koppe's explanation of the last clause as meaning, " I will change thy punishment into peace and thy afflictions into blessing," is justly represented by Gesenius as arbitrary.

18. *There shall no more be heard violence in thy land, desolation and ruin in thy borders* (or *within thy bounds*); *and thou shalt call salvation thy walls, and thy gates praise.* According to Vitringa חָמָס was the cry for help usually uttered in case of personal violence. (See Job. xix. 7, Jer. xx. 8). But there is no need of departing from the strict sense of violence itself, which shall never more be heard of. He also distinguishes שֹׁד and שֶׁבֶר as relating severally to lands and houses. The most natural explanation of the last clause is that which makes it mean that the walls shall afford safety (chap. xxvi. 1), and the gates occasion of praise. Henderson's explanation, that the gates shall resound with praise does not agree well with the parallel. Some understand by praise the praise of God for her continued safety; others the praise or fame of her defences, considered either as arising from victorious resistance to assault, or as preventing it. For תְּהִלָּה the Septuagint has γλύμμα, sculpture, and for קָרָאת the Vulgate *occupabit*. Thou shalt call, as in many other cases, means, thou shalt have a right and reason so to call them. With this verse compare chap. lxv. 19–25.

19. *No more shall be to thee the sun for a light by day, and for brightness the moon shall not shine to thee, and Jehovah shall become thy everlasting light, and thy God thy glory.* The לְ before נֹגַהּ is neglected by the ancient versions, and Hitzig in like manner makes it a sign of the nominative absolute, *as for the brightness of the moon*, &c. (See above, chap. xxxii. 1, and above, p. 1). But the Masoretic accents require לְנֹגַהּ to be construed separately as meaning *with its light* (Gesenius), or *for light* (English Version). Some regard this merely as a figurative promise of prosperity, of which light is a natural and common emblem. Others understand it as a promise of God's residence among his people, clothed in such transcendent brightness as to make the light of the sun and the moon useless. The true sense of the figures seems to be that all natural sources of illumination shall be swallowed up in the clear manifestation of the presence, power, and will of God. According to Henderson, this verse and the next depict the superlative degree of happiness which shall be enjoyed by the new and holy Jerusalem church, expressed in language of the most sublime imagery. Why we are thus more at liberty to treat the sun and moon of this passage as mere "imagery," while the trees of ver. 13 "must be literally explained" as meaning timber, we are not informed.—With this verse compare Rev. xxi. 23, xxii. 5.—Lowth and J. D. Michaelis needlessly insert *by night*, on the authority of the ancient versions, which prove nothing, however, as to a difference of text. The occasional violation of the exact parallelism is not so much a blemish as a beauty.

20. *Thy sun shall set no more, and thy moon shall not be withdrawn; for Jehovah shall be unto thee for an eternal light, and completed the days of thy mourning.* There is no need of supposing any want of consistency between this verse and that before it, nor even that the Prophet gives a new turn to his metaphor. *Thy sun shall set no more*, is evidently tantamount to saying, thou shalt no more have a sun that sets or a moon that withdraws herself, because, &c. The active verb אָסַף is used in the same way by Joel, where he says that the stars *withdraw* THEIR *brightness, i. e.* cease to shine. The expression is generic, and may comprehend all failure or decrease of light, whether by setting, waning, or eclipse, or by the temporary intervention of a cloud. The last words of this verse are correctly said by Henderson to furnish a key to the whole description, by identifying joy with light, and grief with darkness.—Compare with this verse chap. xxv. 8, Zech. xiv. 7, Rev. vii. 16, xxi. 4; and for the phrase, *days of mourning*, Gen. xxvii. 41.

21. *And thy people, all of them righteous, for ever shall inherit the earth, the branch* (or *shoot*) *of my planting, the work of my hands, to glorify myself* (or *to be glorified*).—Compare chaps. iv. 3, xxxiii. 24, xxxv. 8, lii. 1 ; Rev. xxi. 7, 27.   The first clause may also be read as two distinct propositions, *thy people all of them are* (or *shall be*) *righteous, for ever they shall inherit the earth.*   According to the literal interpretation, so called, this is a promise that the Jews shall possess the Holy Land for ever.   But even granting *land* to be a more literal and exact translation, which it is not, still the usage of the Scriptures has attached to this prophetic formula a much higher meaning, the possession of the land being just such a type or symbol of the highest future blessings as the exodus from Egypt is of ultimate deliverance, or the overthrow of Sodom and Gomorrah of sudden, condign, irretrievable destruction.   But in favour of the wider version, *earth*, is the analogy of chap. xlix. 8, where Israel is represented as occupying and restoring the desolate heritages of the whole earth.—The Septuagint renders נֵצֶר by φυλάσσων, as if written נֹצֵר.   For the meaning of the word, see above, chap. xi. 1, xiv. 19, vol. i. pp. 248, 300, 301.   According to Hendewerk, it here denotes the population of the new Jerusalem, and is identical with the *plant* and *root* of chap. liii. 2; from which he gravely infers that the צַדִּיקִים of this verse and the צַדִּיק of chap. liii. 11, must also be identical.   The dependence of God's people on himself for the origin and sustentation of their spiritual life is forcibly expressed by the figure of a plant which he has planted (Ps. xcii. 14, Matt. xv. 13, John xv. 1, 2), and by that of a work which he has wrought (chap. xxix. 23, xliii. 7) : in reference to the last of which the apostle says (Eph. ii. 10), *we are his workmanship, created in Christ Jesus unto good works, which God hath before ordained that we should walk in them ;* and in reference to the first, our Lord himself (John xv. 8), *herein is my Father glorified that ye bear much fruit, so shall ye be my disciples ;* and again, with an entire change of figure (Matt. v. 16), *let your light so shine before men that they may see your good works, and glorify your Father which is in heaven.*   The same ultimate design is set forth in the words of the verse before us.—The textual reading מטעו is regarded by Gesenius and most other writers as an error of transcription for מטעי, as given in the margin.   But Rosenmüller seems to think that the pronoun of the third person may refer to אֶרֶץ, which is sometimes masculine ; De Dieu refers it to the people; and Maurer thinks it possible to connect it with Jehovah, by a sudden enallage so common in the prophets ; which last is approved by Hitzig, but avoided as too harsh in his translation. As to his notion that התפאר describes God as being proud of Israel, see above, on ver. 13.—To the question whether all the restored Jews are to be righteous, Henderson says nothing; but Michaelis maintains that this expression does not necessarily imply regeneration or denote true piety, but simply signifies the prevalence of social virtue, such as may exist even among the heathen, much more among those who are in possession of the true religion. —According to my own view of the Prophet's meaning, he here predicts the elevation of the church to its normal or ideal state, a change of which we may already see the rudiments, however far we may be yet from its final consummation.

22. *The little one shall become a thousand, and the small one a strong nation ; I, Jehovah, in its time will hasten it.*   The superlative sense given to the adjectives *little* and *small* by Gesenius and Ewald is a needless departure from the idiomatic form of the original.   The substantive verb with לְ may also be rendered *shall be for*, *i. e.* shall be so reckoned, which

amounts to the same thing. Kimchi, and Rosenmüller after him, very unnecessarily observe that small and little here relate to number, not to size. Gesenius and several of the later writers understand them as denoting one without a family, or with a small one; in which case the אֶלֶף might be taken in its genealogical sense of household, family, or other subdivision of a tribe. (Judges vi. 15, 1 Sam. x. 12, xxiii. 23, Micah v. 1.) But this whole interpretation is less natural than that of Vitringa, who applies the epithets to Israel itself, falsely, according to Gesenius, whose *ipse dixit* loses much of its authority in consequence of his own frequent changes of opinion upon insufficient grounds, or none at all. The verse, on the face of it, is simply a description of increase, like that in chap. xxvi. 15, xlix. 19, 20, &c.—The pronouns in the last clause are correctly explained by Knobel as neuters, referring to the whole preceding series of prophecies. (Compare chap. xliii. 13, xlvi. 11). The *his* in the common version is equivalent to *its* in modern English, a possessive form apparently unknown to the translators of the Bible.—*I will hasten it*, has reference to the time ordained for the event, or may denote the suddenness of its occurrence, without regard to its remoteness or the length of the intervening period, which seems to be the sense conveyed by the Vulgate version, *subito faciam*. (See above, chap. xiii. 22, vol. i. p. 285.—The reference of these promises to the literal Jerusalem is ascribed by Jerome to the Jews and half Jews (*semi-judaei*) of his own day, and opposed by Vitringa on a very insufficient ground, viz., the impossibility of ascertaining the precise site of the ancient Jerusalem, an impossibility which may be considered as already realized. (See Robinson's Palestine, i. p. 414.) The true ground of objection is the violation of analogy involved in this interpretation. The idea of Eusebius and Procopius, that the prophecy is literal, but conditional, and now rescinded by the unbelief of those to whom it was addressed, opens the door to endless licence, and makes exegesis either useless or impossible. It is a curious fact that Gregory VII. applied this passage to the Church of Rome, in the palmy state to which she was exalted by himself. The hypothesis of Grotius, that it has exclusive reference to the restoration of the Jews from Babylon, is now the current one among the Germans, who of course are unaffected by Vitringa's objection that the prophecy in this sense never was fulfilled. The real argument against it, is the absence of explicit reference to the supposed subject, and the ease with which an indefinite number of analogous restrictions or specific applications might be devised and carried out on grounds of equal plausibility. The only hypothesis which seems to shun the opposite extremes of vagueness and minuteness, and to take the language in its obvious sense, without forced constructions or imaginary facts, is the one proposed in the introduction, and on which the exposition of the chapter has been founded. It is the doctrine of some early writers, that the Jerusalem or Zion of this passage is the primitive or apostolic church, to which the description is in many points inapplicable; whereas it is perfectly appropriate to the New Jerusalem, the Christian Church, not as it was, or is, or will be at any period of its history exclusively, but viewed in reference to the whole course of that history, and in contrast with the many disadvantages and hardships of the old economy.

Chapter 61

AFTER describing the new condition of the church, he again introduces the great Personage by whom the change is to be brought about. His mission and its object are described by himself in vers. 1–3. Its grand result shall be the restoration of a ruined world, ver. 4. The church, as a mediator between God and the revolted nations, shall enjoy their service and support, vers. 5, 6. The shame of God's people shall be changed to honour, ver. 7. His righteousness is pledged to this effect, ver. 8. The church, once restricted to a single nation, shall be recognised and honoured among all, ver. 9. He triumphs in the prospect of the universal spread of truth and righteousness, vers. 10, 11.

1. *The Spirit of the Lord Jehovah (is) upon me, because Jehovah hath anointed me to bring good news to the humble, he hath sent me to bind up the broken in heart, to proclaim to captives freedom, and to the bound open opening* (of the eyes or of the prison-doors).   Unction in the Old Testament is not a mere sign of consecration to office, whether that of Prophet, Priest, or King (1 Kings xix. 16, Lev. viii. 12, 1 Kings i. 31), but the symbol of spiritual influences, by which the recipient was both qualified and designated for his work. (See 1 Sam. x. 1, 6, xvi. 13.) Hence Kimchi's definition of the rite, as a sign of the divine choice (אות סברימ חלבי׳חﬧ), although not erroneous, is inadequate. The office here described approaches nearest to the prophetic. The specific functions mentioned have all occurred and been explained before. (See above, on chaps. xlii. 1–7, xlviii. 16, xlix. 1–9, l. 4, li. 16.) The proclamation of liberty has reference to the year of jubilee under the Mosaic law (Lev. xxv. 10–13, xxvii. 24, Jer. xxxiv. 8–10), which is expressly called the year of liberty or liberation by Ezekiel (xlvi. 17).— פְּקַח־קוֹחַ is explained by Kimchi and Jarchi to mean *opening of the prison*, the second word being regarded as a derivative of לָקַח, to take. De Dieu obtains the same sense by appealing to the Ethiopic usage. Gesenius and the other modern writers are disposed to follow Aben Ezra in treating it as one word (פְּקַחְקוֹחַ), not a compound but an intensive or reduplicated form, intended to express the idea of complete or thorough opening. (See above, chap. ii. 20, and vol. i. p. 106.) This Gesenius understands to mean the opening of the prison, but in opposition to the settled usage which restricts פָּקַח and its derivatives to the opening of the eyes and ears, and which cannot be set aside by alleging that the corresponding verb in Arabic is used more widely. Ewald adheres to the only authorised sense, but explains it as a figurative description of deliverance from prison, which may be poetically represented as a state of darkness, and deliverance from it as a restoration of the sight. But for reasons which have been already given, the only natural sense which can be put upon the words is that of spiritual blindness and illumination. (See above, on chap. xlii. 7, l. 10.) With this question is connected another as to the person here introduced as speaking. According to Gesenius, this is the last of the Prophet's self-defences (*Selbstapologie*); and he even goes so far as to assert that all interpreters are forced (*nothgedrungen*) to regard Isaiah as himself the speaker. Umbreit supposes him to be the speaker, but only as the type and representative of a greater Prophet. Vitringa and other orthodox interpreters regard the question as decided by our Lord himself in the synagogue at Nazareth, when, after reading this verse and a portion of the next from the *book of the prophet Isaiah, he began to say unto them, This day is this scrip-*

ture fulfilled in your ears (Luke iv. 16–22). The brevity of this discourse, compared with the statement which immediately follows, that *the
people bare him witness, and wondered at the gracious words which proceeded
out of his mouth,* and connected with the singular expression that *he began*
thus to say unto them, makes it probable that we have only the beginning
or a summary of what the Saviour said on that occasion. That the whole
is not recorded may, however, be regarded as a proof that his discourse contained no interpretation of the place before us which may not be gathered
from the few words left on record, or from the text and context of the
prophecy itself. Now it must be admitted that the words of Christ just
quoted do not necessarily import that he is the direct and only subject of
the prophecy ; for even if the subject were Isaiah, or the Prophets as a class,
or Israel, yet if at the same time the effects foretold were coming then
to pass, our Lord might say, *This day is this scripture fulfilled in your ears.*
Upon this ground J. D. Michaelis adopts the application to Isaiah, without
disowning the authority of Christ as an interpreter of prophecy. But this
restriction of the passage is at variance with what we have already seen to
be the true sense of the parallel places (chap. xlii. 1–7, and chap. xlix. 1–9),
where the form of expression is the same, and where all agree that the same
speaker is brought forward. If it has been concluded on sufficient grounds
that the ideal person there presented is the Messiah, the same conclusion
cannot, without arbitrary violence, be avoided here, and thus the prophecy
itself interprets our Lord's words, instead of being interpreted by them.
This in the present case is more satisfactory, because it cuts off all objection drawn from the indefinite character of his expressions. At the same
time, and by parity of reasoning, a subordinate and secondary reference to
Israel as a representative of the Messiah, and to the Prophets as in some
sense the representatives of Israel, as well as of Messiah in their prophetic
character, must be admitted ; and thus we are brought again to Christ as the
last and the ideal Prophet, and to the ground assumed by the profound and
far-seeing Calvin, for which he has been severely censured even by Calvinistic writers, and which Vitringa, while professing to defend him, calls a
concession to the Jews (*hic aliquid indulgendum censuit Judæis*), instead
of a concession to candour, faith, good taste, and common sense. Henderson's exposition of this passage differs from that of other orthodox interpreters only in connecting the Messiah's office, here described specifically,
with the future restoration of the Jews. It might have been supposed that
some obstruction would have been presented to a literal interpreter in this
case by the very strong expression of our Lord, *this day* is this prophecy
fulfilled in your ears. But the process of literal interpretation is in
practice very simple and convenient. While the personal reference of the
words to Christ, which is not affirmed by himself at all, is represented as
" the highest possible authority " for so explaining them, the actual fulfilment of the prophecy at that time, which is affirmed as strongly as it could
be, goes for nothing. The two parts of this singular process cannot be
presented in more striking contrast than by direct quotation. "No principle
of accommodation, or of secondary application, can at all satisfy the claims
of the announcement, *This day is this scripture fulfilled in your ears.* It
must, however, be observed, that this completion merely lay in our Lord's
entering upon the public discharge of his prophetic office among the Jews.
Far from being confined to the instructions of that particular day, it was
to be exercised in perpetuity, during the continuance of the church upon
earth, AND PRE-EMINENTLY AS IT RESPECTS THE JEWS, at the future period

here referred to." This principle of gradual or continued fulfilment, not at a single point of time, but through a course of ages, is not only sound and often absolutely necessary to a correct interpretation of the prophets, but the very principle which in a hundred other instances is sacrificed without a scruple to the chimera of a purely " literal " interpretation. Another remarkable comment of the same able writer upon this verse is as follows: " The terms *captives* and *prisoners* are to be taken metaphorically, and have no reference to external restraint." It is only Jerusalem and Zion, and the temple and the trees required in building it, " that must be literally explained." See above, on chap. lx. 13.

2. *To proclaim a year of favour for Jehovah, and a day of vengeance for our God, to comfort all mourners.* Gesenius and Rosenmüller explain ל as the idiomatic sign of the genitive when separated from its governing noun, " Jehovah's year of grace, God's day of vengeance." It is equally agreeable to usage, and more natural in this case, to give the particle its wider sense as denoting relation in general, a year of favour as to or concerning God, which may here be expressed by the English *for*. Vitringa quotes Clement of Alexandria as inferring from the use of the word *year* in this verse that our Lord's public ministry was only one year in duration, a conclusion paradoxically maintained by Gerard John Vossius, but wholly irreconcileable with the gospel history. The expression is correctly explained by Vitringa as a poetical equivalent to *day* suggested by the previous allusion to the year of jubilee ; and Hitzig adds that there is probably a reference to God's vengeance as a transitory act, and to his mercy as a lasting one. The same two words occur as parallels in chaps. xxxiv. 8, lxiii. 4 ; while in chap. xlix. 8, we have the general expression *time of favour*. For the meaning of the last words of the verse, see above, on chaps. xlix. 13, and lvii. 18. They may either be descriptive of sufferers, as the persons needing consolation, or of penitents, as those who shall alone receive it.

3. *To put upon Zion's mourners—to give them a crown instead of ashes, the oil of joy for mourning, a garment of praise for a faint spirit ; and it shall be called to them* (or *they shall be called*) *the oaks of righteousness, the planting of Jehovah* (*i. e.* planted by Jehovah) *to glorify himself.* The construction seems to be interrupted and resumed, a practice not unfrequent with Isaiah. There is no need, therefore, of supplying *joy* after the first verb, as Houbigant and Lowth do. Of the many senses which might here be attached to the verb שׂוּם, the most appropriate is that of *putting on*, as applied to dress, though with another particle, in Gen. xxxvii. 34, xli. 42, and often elsewhere. The English Version has *appoint*, and Gesenius *give ;* both of which are justified by usage, but less suitable in this case than the one above proposed. By the repetition of the word *mourners*, this verse is wrought into the foregoing context in a mode of which we have had several examples. (See above, on chap. lx. 15.) *Zion's mourners* may be simply those who mourn in Zion, or those who mourn for her (chap. lxvi. 10), but as these ideas are not incompatible, both may be included. (Compare chaps. lvii. 18, lx. 20.) Gesenius speaks of the paronomasia between פְּאֵר and אֵפֶר as something entirely distinct from the antithesis in sense between an ornamental head-dress and the ashes strewn upon the head by mourners. But this relation of ideas may be looked upon as really essential to a true paronomasia. Augusti's ridiculous travesty of this phrase (*Putz für Schmutz*) has been actually revived by De Wette. Ewald, with purer taste, neglects the verbal assonance, and reproduces

Jerome's fine translation (*coronam pro cinere*). That ointment was not used by mourners but rejoicers, may be learned from a comparison of 2 Sam. xiv. 2, with Ps. xxiii. 5. Hitzig derives תְּהִלָּה from the Kal of הָלַל, and explains it to mean *brightness* as the parallel term כֵּהָה is applied to a pale colour (Lev. xiii. 21); but a sufficient contrast is afforded by the usual sense *praise*, the whole phrase meaning garments which excite admiration. For the meaning and translation of אֵילִים, see vol. i. p. 94. By oaks of righteousness, Gesenius understands such as enjoy the divine favour or blessing; Lowth, such as prove by their flourishing condition that they were planted by him; Henderson, such as bear the fruit of righteousness; Luzzatto, terebinths of long duration, as in chap. i. 26; instead of city of righteousness and faithful city, he reads city of permanence, enduring city. The mixture not only of metaphors but also of literal and figurative language in this verse shews clearly that it has respect to spiritual not external changes. (Compare chap. xliv. 4, lx. 21.)

4. *And they shall build up the ruins of antiquity, the desolations of the ancients they shall raise, and shall renew the cities of ruin* (*i. e.* ruined cities), *the desolations of age and age.* Both the thought and language of this verse• have been explained already. See above, on chaps. xlix. 8, liv. 3, lviii. 12.) Lowth, not contented with the difficulty of explaining מִמְּךָ in chap. lviii. 12, would insert it here, on the authority of four manuscripts, and David Kimchi; but Kocher understands the latter as distinctly pointing out the difference between the places.—The older writers take רִאשֹׁנִים as an adjective agreeing with שְׁמֲמוֹת, but this is feminine; Gesenius and Ewald, as an absolute adjective or noun corresponding to *majores*, ancestors or ancients; Umbreit, as a noun meaning ancient times.—Hendewerk agrees with Gesenius, but applies the term specifically to the Jews who were alive at the destruction of the temple. The verb *renew* is applied as in 2 Chron. xv. 8, xxiv. 4.—According to Henderson, this verse and the next "admit of no consistent interpretation, except on the principle that the Jews are to be restored to the land of their fathers. The ruins and desolations are those of cities that had once been inhabited, and cannot, without the utmost violence, be applied to the heathen world." But why may they not be explained as "imagery," like chap. lx. 19, 20, or be "taken metaphorically," and without reference to external desolation, like the *captives* and *prisoners* of ver. 1? If this be what is meant by "consistent interpretation," it is very dearly purchased by assuming as a "principle" a fact not mentioned in the text or context, and supposing this to be literally alluded to wherever the hypothesis is possible, while all the accompanying circumstances are explained away as figures.

5. *Then shall stand strangers and feed your flocks, and the children of outland (shall be) your ploughmen and your vinedressers.* For the sense of בְּנֵי־נֵכָר, see above, on chap. lx. 10. Kimchi explains stand to mean, they shall rise and come for the purpose. Some suppose it to be an idiomatic pleonasm, others a periphrasis for service; but the first is a mere evasion, and the second sense belongs to the verb only when standing in the presence of another is expressed or implied. (Deut. i. 38, 1 Kings i. 28, Jer. lii. 12.) The conjunction of these verbs here and in Micah v. 3, may justify the supposition that the primary reference in either case is to a practice of the oriental shepherds. As to the meaning of the prophecy, interpreters are much divided. Some seem to take it in the strictest sense as a promise that the heathen should be slaves to the Jews. (See above, chap. xiv. 2, vol. i. p. 287.) Gesenius understands it as meaning that

the Jews should confine themselves to spiritual services,. and leave mere secular pursuits to the Gentiles. Nearly allied to this is Hitzig's explanation that the Jews and Gentiles are described as sustaining the relation of priests and laymen to each other. Ewald qualifies it still more by describing the relation to be that of the Levites to the other tribes, and even this restricted by the promise in chap. lxvi. 21. But that verse shews conclusively that no exclusive promise of Levitical or sacerdotal rank to the Jews, as distinguished from the Gentiles can be here intended. This is confirmed by the language of Peter, who applies the promise of the next verse to the Christian Church (1 Peter ii. 5). The only way in which all these seeming discrepancies can be reconciled, is by supposing, as we have done hitherto, that even in Exod. xix. 6, the promise is addressed to Israel not as a nation but a church; so that when the Jewish people ceased to bear this character, they lost all claim to the fulfilment of the promise, which is still in force, and still endures to the benefit of those to whom it was originally given, namely, the Israel of God, that is to say, his church or chosen people. This view of the matter sets aside not only the interpretations which have been already mentioned as confining the promise to the natural descendants of Israel, but also that of Jerome and Procopius, who, although they correctly recognise the church as the object of address, make this a threatening that the Jews shall be supplanted by the Gentiles as the pastors or ministers of the flock of God. That the holders of this office, might, in strict accordance with the usage of Scripture and of this book, be described as shepherds, husbandmen, and vinedressers, may be seen by a comparison of chaps. iii. 14, v. 1, xi. 6, xxvii. 2, xxx. 23, 24, xl. 11, with Acts xx. 28, 1 Cor. iii. 9, ix. 7; and with the imagery of our Saviour's parables. It does not follow necessarily, however, that the office here assigned to strangers and foreigners is that of spiritual guides, much less that they are doomed to a degrading servitude. The simplest explanation of the verse is that which understands it as descriptive not of subjugation but of intimate conjunction, as if he had said, those who are now strangers and foreigners shall yet be sharers in your daily occupations, and entrusted with your dearest interests. By strangers we are then to understand not Gentiles as opposed to Jews, but all who have been aliens from the covenant of mercy and the church of God.—The only comment made by Henderson on this verse is included in the observation already quoted, that these two verses (4 and 5) " admit of no consistent interpretation, except on the principle that the Jews are to be restored to the land of their fathers." How the author would apply this in detail to the fifth verse, we can only argue analogically from his exposition of the fourth; and as he there insists upon a literal rebuilding of the cities once inhabited by Jews as the only sense of which the prophecy admits " without the utmost violence," so here he may be understood as tacitly believing in a future subjection of the Gentiles to the restored Jews, as their husbandmen and shepherds. If, on the other hand, he understands the service here exacted to be metaphorical or spiritual, we have only to repeat what we have said before as to the worth of that " consistent interpretation " which results from the application of this novel " principle."

6. *And ye* (or more emphatically, *as for you*), *the priests of Jehovah shall ye be called, the ministers of our God shall be said to you* (or *of you*), *the strength of nations shall ye eat, and in their glory shall ye substitute yourselves* (or into their glory shall ye enter by exchange). Most of the earlier

writers, down to Gesenius in his Commentary, agree substantially with Jerome in his version of the last word (*superbietis*); which they regard as a cognate form or an orthographical variation of יִתְאַמְּרוּ in Ps. xciv. 4, where it seems to denote talking of one's self, and, by a natural transition, glorying or boasting. Albert Schultens tried to found upon an Arabic analogy the sense of "providing for one's self," and Scheid that of "floating or swimming in abundance." But all the latest writers, not excepting Gesenius in his Thesaurus, have gone back to Jarchi's explanation of the word as denoting "mutual exchange or substitution." This supposes it to be derived from יָמַר, a cognate form and synonyme of מוּר, to change or exchange, occurring only in the Hiphil, Jer. ii. 11. This word is important as determining the sense not only of the whole verse, but of that before it, by requiring both to be considered as descriptive, not of exaltation and subjection, but of mutual exchange, implying intimate association. Some, it is true, attempt to carry out the first idea even here, by making this last word denote an absolute exclusive substitution, *i. e.* the dispossession of the Gentiles by the Jews. But the context, etymology, and usage, all combine to recommend the idea of reciprocal exchange or mutual substitution. Interpreters, in seeking a factitious antithesis between the verses, have entirely overlooked the natural antithesis between the clauses of this one verse. They have supposed the contrast intended to be that between servitude and priesthood : "they shall be your servants, and ye shall be their priests." But we have seen already that the fifth verse cannot, in consistency with chap. lxvi. 10, denote anything but intimate conjunction and participation. The true antithesis is : "ye shall be their priests, and they shall be your purveyors ; you shall supply their spiritual wants, and they shall supply your temporal wants." This explanation of the verse, to which we have been naturally led by philological induction and the context, coincides in a manner too remarkable to be considered accidental, with the words of Paul, in writing to the Romans of the contribution made by the churches of Macedonia and Achaia for the poor saints at Jerusalem : *It hath pleased them verily, and their debtors they are* (*i. e.* they have chosen to do it, and indeed were bound to do it) ; *for if the Gentiles have been made partakers of their spiritual things, their duty is also to minister unto them in carnal things.* (Rom. xv. 27.) This may seem, however, to determine the object of address to be the Jews ; but no such inference can fairly be deduced from the words of the apostle, who is only making one specific application of the general truth taught by the Prophet. What was true of the Gentile converts then, in relation to the Jewish Christians as their mother-church, is no less true of the heathen now, or even of converted Jews, in reference to the Christians who impart the gospel to them. The essential idea in both places is, that the church, the chosen people, or the Israel of God, is charged with the duty of communicating spiritual things to those without, and entitled in return to an increase of outward strength from those who thus become incorporated with it.—But it is not merely in this lower sense that the people of God are in the law (Exod. xix. 20) and the gospel (1 Peter i. 3), as well as in the prophets, represented as the ministers and priests of God. Not only as instructors and reclaimers of the unbelieving world do they enjoy this sacred dignity, but also as the only representatives of their Great High Priest, in him and through him possessing free access to the fountain of salvation and the throne of grace. (Heb. iv. 14–16.) In this respect, as in every other which concerns the method of salvation and access to God, there is no distinction of Jew and

Gentile, any more than of Greek and barbarian, male and female, bond and free; but all "are Christ's, and Christ is God's," and all alike are priests and ministers of God.—It only remains to add, that on the principle of limiting this prophecy to the future restoration of the Jews, it might have been supposed that this verse would be literally understood as promising both temporal and spiritual superiority to other nations; but, according to the able representative of that opinion, who has been so often quoted, it "implies holiness, spirituality, and devotedness to the service of God; so abundant shall be the supplies, that there shall be no absorption of time by the cares and distraction of business." This, it seems, is the literal interpretation of the promise that the Jews shall be the priests and ministers of God, and as such shall consume the wealth of the nations and have their riches at command; for such is the meaning put upon תִּתְיַמָּרוּ by Henderson, who traces it to אָמַר, in the sense of commanding. Why there is any less "violence" in this interpretation of the verse before us than in the reference of ver. 4 to the universal spread of the gospel, does not appear.

7. *Instead of your shame* (ye shall have) *double, and* (instead of their) *confusion, they shall celebrate their portion; therefore in their land shall they inherit double, everlasting joy shall be to them.* Vitringa and Rosenmüller understand the *therefore* at the beginning of the second clause as deciding that the recompence must be described exclusively in that clause, while the first is wholly occupied with the account of their previous sufferings: "Instead of your double shame, and instead of your lamenting (or their exulting), that confusion was their portion," &c. From this and other similar unnatural constructions, Gesenius and all the later writers have gone back to the one given in the Targum and by Jarchi, which makes *double* refer not to shame but recompence, and gives יָרֹנּוּ the same subject with the other verbs. It is still considered necessary, however, to assume an enallage of person, so that *your shame* and *their portion* may relate to the same subject. It is not impossible, however, that the Prophet has in view the same two classes who are distinctly mentioned in the preceding verses; a construction which would not do away with the enallage, but go far to confirm the explanation which has been already given of those verses as descriptive of mutual participation.—There is no need of explaining חֶלְקָם with Gesenius as an accusative of place, or supplying *in* before it, the older writers; since the verb may govern it directly, as in Ps. li. 16, lix. 17.—Lowth complains of the confusion in the Hebrew text, and applies an extraordinary remedy, by substituting the Peshito version, after first amending it.—According to Henderson, this verse means that the honour conferred by God upon the restored Jews, and the estimation in which they shall be held by believing Gentiles, will far overbalance the contempt to which they have been subject. The limitation of the passage to the "restored Jews" is as groundless and arbitrary here as elsewhere.—*Double* is used indefinitely to denote a large proportion. (Compare chap. xl. 2.)

8. *For I am Jehovah, loving justice, hating* (that which is) *taken away unjustly, and I will give their hire truly, and an everlasting covenant I strike for them.* The Vulgate and the rabbins give עוֹלָה its usual sense of a burnt-offering, and explain the clause to mean that God hates unjust violence, especially (or even) in religious offerings. The modern writers generally follow the Septuagint in making it synonymous with עַוְלָה (which is actually found in a few manuscripts), an explanation countenanced by the undoubted use of the corresponding plural and paragogic forms in that sense. (Job v. 16, Ps. lviii. 3, lxiv. 7.) Jerome's objection that all

robbery is unjust, would apply to a multitude of other places where there seems to be a redundance of expression, and proceeds upon the false assumption that גֵּזֶל necessarily expresses the complex idea *robbery*, whereas it may be here used in its primary and strict sense of violent seizure or privation, the idea of injustice, which is commonly implied, being here expressed.—For the usage of פְּעֻלָה, see above, on chap. xl. 11, and for that of כָּרַת בְּרִית, on chaps. xxviii. 15, lv. 3.—This verse is commonly applied to the violence practised upon Israel by the Babylonians. (Compare chap. xlii. 24.) It is rather an enunciation of the general truth, that the divine justice renders absolutely necessary the destruction of his obstinate enemies, and the deliverance of his people from oppression. (Compare 2 Thess. i. 6–8.)

9. *Then shall be known among the nations their seed, and their issue in the midst of the peoples. All seeing them shall acknowledge them that they are a seed Jehovah has blessed.* Vitringa, Gesenius, and some later writers, give to נוֹדַע the emphatic sense of being famous or illustrious, as in Ps. lxxvi. 2, where the parallel expression is גָּדוֹל שְׁמוֹ. But in the case before us, the parallelism, far from requiring this peculiar sense, requires the usual one of *being known*, as corresponding better to the phrase *they shall recognise them.* Thus understood, the first clause means that they shall be known among the nations in their true character as a seed or race highly favoured of Jehovah. *Issue* means progeny or offspring, as in chap. xlviii. 19. In order to apply this to the restored Jews, we must depart from the literal and obvious import of *among* and *in the midst*, and understand them as denoting merely that they shall be heard of; for how can they be said to be among and in the midst of the nations at the very time when they are gathered from them to their own land. And yet the whole connection seems to favour the first meaning, and to shew that they are here described as being scattered through the nations, and there recognised by clear distinctive marks as being God's peculiar people, just as the Jews took knowledge of Peter and John that they had been with Jesus. (Acts iv. 13.) It may be on account of this apparent inconsistency between the obvious sense of this verse and his own adopted "principle," that Henderson has no remark upon it, save that "ם in בִּירוּם_ is pleonastic." Some of the older writers, to avoid this assumption, render כִּי *because*, "all that see them shall acknowledge them, because they are a seed which Jehovah has blessed." But, as Vitringa well observes, the verb requires a more specific statement of its object. Gesenius and the later writers liken the construction to that in Gen. i. 4, God saw the light that it was good; not simply saw that the light was good, but saw the light itself, and in so doing saw that it was good. So here the meaning is not merely that all seeing them shall acknowledge that they are a seed, &c., but that all seeing them shall recognise them by recognising the effects and evidences of the divine blessing.—The ellipsis of the relative is the same in Hebrew and colloquial English.—The true application of the verse is to the Israel of God in its diffusion among all the nations of the earth, who shall be constrained by what they see of their spirit, character, and conduct, to acknowledge that they are the seed which the Lord hath blessed. The glorious fulfilment of this promise in its original and proper sense, may be seen already in the influence exerted by the eloquent example of the missionary on the most ignorant and corrupted heathen, without waiting for the future restoration of the Jews to the land of their fathers.

10. (*I will*) *joy, I will joy in Jehovah, let my soul exult in my God; for*

he hath clothed me with garments of salvation, 'a mantle of righteousness has he put on me, as the bridegroom adjusts his priestly crown, and as the bride arrays her jewels. Vitringa here leads his chorus off the stage, where he has kept it since the beginning of ver. 4, and lets the Church come on, but whether as a male or female he considers a doubtful and perplexing question. To a reader unencumbered with this clumsy theatrical machinery, it must be evident that these are the words of the same speaker who appears at the beginning of this chapter and the next. J. D. Michaelis supposes an allusion to the oriental practice of bestowing the *caftan* or honorary dress upon distinguished culprits who have been acquitted. Luzzatto, in order to avoid the assumption of a root יַעַט in this one case, reads יַעְטֵנִי from עָטָה ; but this, besides being arbitrary, throws the syntax of the tenses into a confusion which, although it may be elsewhere unavoidable, is not to be assumed in any case without necessity.—עָדָה is to put on or wear, but always used in reference to ornaments. כֵּלִים may signify not merely gems, but ornamental dress in general. (See Deut. xxii. 5.)—Gesenius in his Commentary gives כִּהֵן the general sense of beautifying or adorning ; but in his Thesaurus he agrees with the modern writers in acknowledging the derivation from כֹּהֵן a priest, for which no satisfactory etymology has yet been proposed. "As the bridegroom priests his turban." So Aquila ὡς νύμφιον ἱερατευόμενον στεφάνῳ. The reference is no doubt to the sacerdotal mitre, which was probably regarded as a model of ornamental head-dress, and to which פְּאֵר is explicitly applied (Exod. xxxix. 28, Ezek. xliv. 18). Salvation and righteousness are here combined, as often elsewhere, to denote the cause and the effect, the justice of God as displayed in the salvation of his people. (See under ver. 8.) Or righteousness may be referred to the people, as denoting the practical justification afforded by their signal deliverance from suffering.

11. *For as the earth puts forth its growth, and as the garden makes its plants to grow, so shall the Lord Jehovah make to grow righteousness and praise before all the nations.* Compare chap. xlv. 8, and Ps. lxxxv. 11, 12. The exact construction of the first clause may be, *like the earth* (*which*) *puts forth ;* or the idiom may resemble that in vulgar English which employs *like* as a conjunction no less than a preposition, *like the earth puts forth.* (See above chap. viii. 23, and vol. i. p. 196.) The studied assonance of צְמִחָה, תַּצְמִיחַ and יַצְמִיחַ, is retained in the latest versions after the example of the Vulgate, which has *germen, germinat*, and *germinabit.* By praise we are to understand the manifestation of excellence in general, by righteousness that of moral excellence in particular. The confusion of these terms by Vitringa and some later writers, as all denoting salvation, is as bad in its effect as it is groundless in its principle. Knobel thinks it probable that the writer had by this time heard the news of Cyrus's conquests in the west, by which his somewhat languid hopes had been revived. But there is nothing either in the text or context to restrict this verse to the former restoration of the Jews from the Babylonian exile, any more than to their future restoration to the Holy Land. The glory of the promise is its universality, in which the fulfilment will no doubt be coextensive with the prophecy itself.

Chapter 62

THE words of the great Deliverer are continued from the foregoing chapter. He will not rest until the glorious change in the condition of his people is accomplished, ver. 1. They shall be recognised by kings and nations as the people of Jehovah, vers. 2, 3. She who seemed to be forsaken is still his spouse, vers. 4, 5. The church is required to watch and pray for the fulfilment of the promise, vers. 6, 7. God has sworn to protect her and supply her wants, vers. 8, 9. Instead of a single nation, all the nations of the earth shall flow unto her, ver. 10. The good news of salvation shall no longer be confined, but universally diffused, ver. 11. The glory of the church is the redemption of the world, ver. 12.

1. *For Zion's sake I will not be still, and for Jerusalem's sake I will not rest until her righteousness go forth as brightness, and her salvation as a lamp (that) burneth.* Hitzig argues from the absence of the copulative particle, that this is the beginning of a new discourse, and that if the Prophet be the speaker here, he cannot be the speaker in the two preceding verses. Both these conclusions are unfounded; since the particle is frequently omitted where the same subject is still treated, and in the same manner. On the other hand, the Prophet constantly assumes the person and expresses the feelings of different characters in this great drama, without any express intimation of the change in the text itself. Kimchi follows the Targum in explaining this verse as the language of Jehovah, who, as J. D. Michaelis thinks, is here replying to the thanksgiving of the church in the foregoing verses. The rest and silence must be then understood to denote inaction and indifference, as in chap. xlii. 14. In like manner Grotius makes it a specific promise of Jehovah that he will not rest until Cyrus is victorious. Cocceius supposes the Messiah to be speaking, and assuring his people of his intercession. Henderson also, on the ground of the frequency with which the Redeemer is thus abruptly introduced by our Prophet, supposes the Messiah to be here represented as interesting himself for the prosperity of Zion, and assuring her that through his mediatorial intercession the Jews shall be restored to their standing in the church of God. Vitringa thinks it clear from the analogy of ver. 6, that the silence here prohibited is that of Zion's watchmen or the rulers of the church, of whom he accordingly makes up a chorus in accordance with his favourite theatrical hypothesis. A simpler and more obvious sense is the one now commonly adopted, that the Prophet himself declares his resolution not to cease from the prediction of Zion's future glory, as Forerius supposes, but according to the general opinion, from prayer to God on her behalf. Eichhorn absurdly ascribed the passsage to a Jew in Palestine who wrote it 'on hearing of the edict by Cyrus for the restoration of the exiles. Perhaps the most satisfactory conclusion is, that if the Prophet here speaks of himself, he also speaks by implication of his associates and successors in the office, not excluding Christ as the last and greatest of the series ; so that several of the exegetical hypotheses already mentioned may in this way be combined and reconciled. If an exclusive subject must be chosen, it is no doubt the same as in the first verse of the foregoing chapter. The sense of righteousness and salvation is the same as in chap. lxi. 10, and elsewhere. By a singular change of the abstract to the concrete, the Vulgate has *justus ejus et salvator ejus.* —The going forth here mentioned is the same as in Ps. xix. 6, 7 ; and brightness, or as Lowth translates it, strong light may specifically signify the dawn of day or the rising of the sun as in Prov. iv. 18. Lowth's version of the parallel expression (*blazing torch*) is stronger than the common version, but adheres less closely to the form of the original.

2. *And nations shall see thy righteousness, and all kings thy glory ; and*

there shall be called to thee a new name, which the mouth of Jehovah shall utter (or pronounce distinctly). Here again the Vulgate applies the abstract terms to Christ, by rendering them *justum tuum, inclytum tuum.* Grotius retains this inaccurate translation, but applies the epithets to Cyrus, as the illustrious patron of the Jews, and at the same time a type of Christ. The substitution of *glory* for *salvation* does not seem to be regarded by any of the modern writers as a proof that *salvation* means *glory,* although quite as clear as that *righteousness* means salvation. The mention of kings is intended to imply the submission even of the highest ranks to this new power. (Compare chaps. xlix. 7, 23, lii. 15.) Vitringa's explanation of רָאָה as meaning to experience or to know in a spiritual sense, at once perverts the Prophet's meaning, and enfeebles his expression. The idea evidently is that they shall witness it and stand astonished.—The *new name* may be that which is afterwards stated in ver. 4, or the expression may be understood more generally as denoting change of condition for the better. (See above, chaps. i. 26, lx. 14, and compare Jer. iii. 16, xxxiii. 16, Ezek. xlviii. 35, Rev. ii. 17, iii. 12.) Some one quoted by Vitringa supposes an allusion to the change in the name of the chosen people from Jew to Christian; but the former name is still applied to the spiritual Israel, in Rom. ii. 9, and Rev. ii. 9. (See below, on chap. lxv. 15.) J. D. Michaelis supposes an allusion to the oriental practice of imposing new names upon towns which have been ruined and rebuilt. The translation of the last verb by Lowth (*shall fix upon thee*), and by Noyes (*shall give thee*), does not convey its exact sense, which, according to the lexicons, is that of pronouncing or uttering distinctly, though the common version (*shall name*) is justified by usage. (Compare Num. i. 17, 1 Chron. xii. 31, Amos vi. 1.) Henderson finds no difficulty in admitting that this clause is not to be understood of a mere name, but has special reference to the state and character, according to the common idiom by which anything is said to be called what it really is. Is it absolutely certain, then, that Israel, Jerusalem, and Zion, are in all cases strictly national and local designations, and that they never have respect to state and character, rather than to natural descent or geographical position?

3. *And thou shalt be a crown of beauty in Jehovah's hand, and a diadem of royalty in the palm of thy God.* The only difficulty in this verse has respect to the crown's being twice emphatically placed in the hand and not upon the head. Aben Ezra refers to the practice of wearing wreaths and circlets on the arms; but the text speaks expressly of the hand and of the palm, and both the ornaments described are such as were worn upon the head. Some of the older writers quote Suetonius's account of the athletæ as wearing the Olympic crown upon the head and carrying the Pythian in the hand; but this, as Rosenmüller well says, was a mere act of necessity, and what is here said has respect to royal, not athletic crowns. Ewald agrees with Brentius in supposing that Jehovah is here represented as holding the crown in his hand to admire it; Cocceius and Ewald, for the purpose of exhibiting it to others; Piscator, for the purpose of crowning himself. J. D. Michaelis takes *in the hand of God* to mean at his disposal, or bestowed by him. This is a good sense in itself; but upon whom could Zion or Jerusalem be thus bestowed? Hitzig and Henderson think it perfectly obvious that it would be incongruous to place the crown upon Jehovah's head; and as it could not be placed upon the ground, as in chap. xxviii. 1, the only place remaining was the hand! Gesenius understands the hand of God to mean his power or protection, which approaches nearly to Vitringa's explanation of the phrase as meaning he shall hold it fast, or keep

it safe. (Compare Rev. iii. 11.) Maurer gives the same sense to the phrase, but connects it with the subject of the verse, and not with the figure of a crown ; as if it had been said, under his protection thou shalt be a crown of beauty and a diadem of royalty.—Lowth's version of the last phrase, *in the grasp of thy God*, is vigorous but inexact. The true sense is the one expressed by Henderson (*the palm*). The original combination of two nouns is more expressive than the adjective construction into which it is resolved by most translators. The *beautiful crown* of Lowth, and the *magnificent crown* of Noyes, are much inferior to the literal translation, *crown of beauty* or *of glory*, and not required by the parallelism, since the corresponding phrase strictly means a *diadem of royalty*. According to Gataker, the last word is added to distinguish the צָנִיף here mentioned from the sacerdotal turban or mitre.

4. *No more shall it be called to thee* (shalt thou be called) *Azubah (Forsaken), and thy land shall no more be called Shemamah (Desolate); but thou shalt be called Hephzibah (my delight is in her), and thy land Beulah (Married), for Jehovah delights in thee, and thy land shall be married.* The joyful change of condition is further expressed in the Prophet's favourite manner, by significant names. The common version not only mars the beauty of the passage, but renders it in some degree unintelligible to the English reader, by translating the first two names and retaining the others in their Hebrew dress. It is obvious that all four should be treated alike, *i. e.* that all the Hebrew forms should be retained, or none. Henderson prefers the latter method on the ground that " the names are merely symbolical, and will never be employed as proper names." It is probable, however, that they were all familiar to the Jews as female names in real life. This we know to have been the case with two of them : the mother of Jehoshaphat was named Azubah (1 Kings xxii. 42), and the mother of Manasseh Hephzibah (2 Kings xxi. 1). It is better, therefore, to retain the Hebrew forms, in order to give them an air of reality as proper names, and at the same time to render them intelligible by translation. In the last clause there is reference to the primary meaning of the verb, viz. that of owning or possessing ; and as the inhabitants of towns are sometimes called in Hebrew their *possessors*, בְּעָלִים a noun derived from this very verb (Joshua xxiv. 11, Judges ix. 2, 2 Sam. xxi. 12, compared with 2 Sam. ii. 4), its use here would suggest, as at least one meaning of the promise, thy land shall be inhabited, and so it is translated in the Targum.

5. *For (as) a young man marrieth a virgin, (so) shall thy sons marry thee, and (with) the joy of a bridegroom over a bride shall thy God rejoice over thee.* The particles of comparison are omitted as in Jer. xvii. 21. Perhaps it would be more correct to say that the comparison is only an implied one, and that the strict translation is, " a young man marrieth a virgin, thy sons shall marry thee," leaving the copula *and so* to be suggested by the context. So in the other clause there is no absolute need of assuming an ellipsis, since the Hebrew idiom admits of such expressions as *joying the joy* of a bridegroom, just as we may say in English a man *lives the life* of a saint, or *dies the death* of the righteous, both which combinations occur in our translation of the Bible. (Gal. ii. 20, Num. xxiii. 10.) In order to avoid the seeming incongruity of a mother's being married to her sons, Lowth reads בֹּנָיִךְ, thy Builder or Founder ; an emendation which J. D. Michaelis rejects in his notes upon Lowth's Lectures, but adopts in his translation of Isaiah. To Gesenius's objection, that the *pluralis majestaticus* is construed with a verb in the singular, Henderson conclusively replies by citing Gen.

xx. 13, xxxv. 7, 2 Sam. vii. 23. The true objection to the change is that it is not necessary. The solution of the difficulty in the common text is afforded by the explanation already given of the strict sense of בָּעַל and the usage of the derivative noun בַּעַל. As תִּבָּעֵל in ver. 4 really means thou shalt be inhabited, so יִבְעָלוּךְ here conveys the same idea as well as that of marriage, and *thy sons* has reference, not to the latter, but the former sense. Vitringa gives substantially the same explanation, when he says that the Prophet mixes two distinct metaphors in one expression.

6, 7. *On thy walls, O Jerusalem, I have set watchmen; all the day and all the night long they shall not be silent. Ye that remind Jehovah, let there be no rest to you, and give no rest to him, until he establish and until he place Jerusalem a praise in the earth.* According to Vitringa, the prophetic chorus is here relieved by an ecclesiastical one ; and as the first words do not well suit this imaginary speaker, he removes all difficulty by supplying *thus saith Jehovah.* To the more obvious supposition that Jehovah is himself the speaker, he makes a very singular objection, viz. that the Prophet would hardly have introduced God as speaking for so short a time. According to the Targum and the Rabbins, he is here represented as appointing angels to keep watch over the ruined walls of Zion. Ewald adopts a similar interpretation, and refers to Zech. i. 12–17, upon which the Jewish exposition may be founded. Gesenius understands these as the words of the Prophet himself, and by watchmen, devout Jews among the ruins of Jerusalem, awaiting the return of the exiles, and praying to God for it. For this limitation of the passage to Jerusalem in ruins, and to the period of the exile, there is not the least foundation in the text. The promise is a general one, or rather the command, that those who are constituted guardians of the church should be importunate in prayer to God on her behalf. הַמַּזְכִּירִים admits of three interpretations, all consistent with Isaiah's usage. In chap. xxxvi. 3, 22, it seems to mean an official recorder or historiographer. In chap. lxvi. 3, it means one burning incense as a memorial oblation. Hence אַזְכָּרָה, the name used in the law of Moses to denote such an offering. (See Lev. ii. 2, v. 12, xxiv. 7, Num. v. 26.) In chap. xliii. 26, the verb means to remind God of something which he seems to have forgotten ; and as this is an appropriate description of importunate intercession, it is here entitled to the preference. Gesenius speaks of a belief in the effect of such entreaties as peculiar to the ancient orientals ; but our Lord himself expressly teaches it (Luke xviii. 1), and Tertullian finely says of it, *hœc vis Deo grata est.*

8. *Sworn hath Jehovah by his right hand, and by his arm of strength, If I give* (*i. e.* I will not give) *thy corn any more as food to thine enemies, and if the sons of the outland shall drink thy new wine which thou hast laboured in* (I am not God). On the elliptical formula of swearing, see above, on chap. xxii. 14, and vol. i. p. 385. The declaration, though conditional in form, is in fact an absolute negation. In swearing by his hand and arm, the usual symbols of strength, he pledges his omnipotence for the fulfilment of the promise, " As sure as I am almighty, thou shalt suffer this no more." —For the true sense of בְּנֵי־נֵכָר, see above, on chap. lvi. 3.

9. *For those gathering it shall eat it, and shall praise Jehovah, and those collecting it shall drink it in my holy courts* (or *in the courts of my sanctuary*). The כִּי is not directly equivalent to *but,* as some explain it, but retains its proper meaning, in relation to an intermediate thought not expressed. As if he had said, it shall not be so, or it shall be far otherwise, because those gathering, &c. Lowth has *they that reap the harvest,* and

they that gather the vintage, which, although correct in sense, is not a version, but a paraphrase. The indefinite *it* takes the place both of *corn* and *wine*, but all ambiguity is removed by the use of the verbs *eat* and *drink*. Gesenius and Rosenmüller agree with Grotius and the other early writers in supposing an allusion to the sacrificial feasts of the Mosaic law. (See Lev. xix. 23–25, Deut. xii. 17, 18, xiv. 23.) But Hitzig and Knobel refer what is here said simply to the sacerdotal standing to be occupied by Israel in reference to the Gentiles. (See above, on chap. lxi. 6.) To the former supposition, Knobel objects that the Levitical feasts had exclusive reference to the tithes and first-fruits, whereas the promise here is universal. This appears to be a needless refinement, and is wholly insufficient to explain away the obvious allusion in the terms of the promise to the ancient institutions of the law. That these, however, are but types and emblems of abundance, and security, and liberty of worship, is acknowledged even by that school of interpreters supposed to be most strenuous in favour of attaching to these promises their strictest sense. Thus Henderson, instead of urging, as consistency might seem to require, that the language of this passage, like that of chap. lx., "must be literally explained," interprets it as meaning that "the enemies of Israel having all been swept away by the powerful judgments of God, the most perfect tranquillity shall reign throughout the land, and those who may go up to worship at Jerusalem shall enjoy, unmolested, the fruit of their labour." Here again we may perceive, although unable to reduce to rule, the exercise of a large discretion in determining what shall and what shall not be strictly understood. The literal Jerusalem, with its temple and its courts, and literal corn and wine, appears to be intended; but for aught that appears, the eating and drinking in the courts of that temple is a mere figure for exemption from annoyance and loss, while present there for worship.·

10. *Pass, pass through the gates, clear the way of the people, raise high, raise high the highway, free (it) from stones, raise a banner (or a signal) over the nations.* Vitringa puts these words into the mouth of his prophetic chorus; Maurer thinks they may be uttered by the watchmen of ver. 6; but most interpreters appear to be contented with the obvious hypothesis, that Isaiah is here speaking in the name of God. As to the object of address, Eichhorn supposes it to be the Jews still lingering among the ruins of the Holy City; Maurer, the remaining population of that city, which he seems to think considerable; Gesenius, the exiled Jews in Babylon and other lands; Henderson, "the inhabitants of the cities that may lie in the way of the returning Israelites." The readiness with which these interpreters accommodate the terms of the text to their several hypotheses, may shew how little ground there is for any definite conclusion, and thus serve to recommend the hypothesis of Hitzig, that the order is supposed to be given to those whose duty it is to execute it. Another subject of dispute is the direction of the march required. According to Rosenmüller, Maurer, and Henderson, "pass through the gates" means go out of them; according to Gesenius and others, go into them. It means neither one nor the other, but go through them, leaving the direction to be gathered from the context, which, combined with the analogy of chap. lvii. 14, makes it probable that what is here described is the entrance of the nations into Zion or the church, an event so frequently and fully set forth in the preceding chapters. The use of the term עַמִּים in the last clause is so favourable to this exposition, or at least so adverse to the supposition that the restoration of the Jews from Babylon is here intended, that Gesenius, in order to evade this difficulty, has

recourse to an expedient which he would have laughed to scorn if used in vindication of the truth of prophecy. This is the explanation of עַמִּים as meaning tribes, or more specifically those of Israel, on the authority, as he alleges, of Deut. xxxii. 8, xxxiii. 3, 19. Nothing but extreme exegetical necessity could warrant this interpretation of the word here, if it were true that Moses so employed it. But this very fact is still more doubtful than the one which it is called in to confirm, or rather it is still more certain that עַמִּים in Deuteronomy denotes the Gentiles than it is in this case. On the other hand, the singular form עַם is used repeatedly in these very prophecies to signify the Gentiles or mankind at large. (See above, chaps. xlii. 5, xlix. 8.) It may therefore be alleged, in opposition to the views which have been quoted, with as much plausibility at least, that this is not a prediction of the former restoration of the Jews from Babylon, or of their future restoration from the ends of the earth, but of the increase of the church or chosen people by the accession of the Gentiles. The gates are then the gates of the ideal Zion or Jerusalem, the passage is an inward, not an outward passage, and the exhortation of the text is one to all concerned, or all who have the opportunity to take away obstructions and facilitate their entrance. The argument in favour of the reference to Babylon, derived from the analogy of chap. lvii. 19, lies equally against the hypothesis of Henderson, who cannot consistently repel it, as we do, by appealing to our uniform assertion that the Babylonish exile is referred to only as a signal example of deliverance. What is said in one place, therefore, with acknowledged reference to Babylon proves nothing where the same generic terms are used without any trace of local allusion. The verb סִקְּלוּ, which is ambiguous (compare chap. v. 2, and 2 Sam. xvi. 6), is here determined by the addition of the phrase מֵאֶבֶן, in which the noun is used as a collective. In the last clause, some explain עַל with the Septuagint and Vulgate as simply meaning *to*, others with J. D. Michaelis *for*. Knobel not only makes it perfectly synonymous with אֶל, but then notes this imaginary fact as one proof of a later age. The most exact and at the same time most poetical idea is Luther's, "raise the banner high above the nations;" to which Hitzig theoretically acquiesces, but translates the preposition *for*, like others.

11. *Behold, Jehovah has caused it to be heard to the end of the earth, Say ye to the daughter of Zion, behold, thy salvation cometh, behold, his reward is with him and his hire before him.* There is some doubt as to the connection of the clauses. It may be questioned whether the verse contains the words uttered by Jehovah to the end of the earth, and if so, whether these continue to the end of the verse, or only to the third *behold*. Hitzig supposes הִשְׁמִיעַ to be absolutely used, and to denote that God has made a proclamation, but without saying what ; after which the Prophet goes on to address the messengers mentioned in chap. xl. 9, and lii. 7. But as the verb הִשְׁמִיעַ seems to require an object after it, and as the words immediately succeeding are precisely such as might thus be uttered, it is certainly most natural to understand what follows as the words or substance of the proclamation. It has also been made a question whether the pronoun *his* refers to Jehovah or to the nearest antecedent, *salvation* ; and if the latter, whether that word is to be translated *saviour*, as it is by Lowth and in the ancient versions. This last is a question of mere form, and the other of but little exegetical importance, since the saviour or salvation meant is clearly represented elsewhere as identical with God himself. The last clause is a repetition of chap. xl. 10, and if ever the identity of thought, expression,

and connection, served to indicate identity of subject, it is so in this case. The reader therefore may imagine the inducement which could lead even Henderson to speak of the two places as "strictly parallel in language, though the advents in the two passages are different." If this be so, then nothing can ever be inferred from similarity of language, and an unlimited discretion is allowed to the interpreter to parry all attacks upon his theory by stoutly maintaining a diversity of subject in the very places where the opposite appears to be most manifest. Another arbitrary statement rendered necessary in a dozen lines by the determination to apply the passage to the future restoration of the Jews to Palestine, is that "the daughter of Zion means here the rightful inhabitants of Jerusalem scattered over the face of the earth," a sense which even this interpreter attaches to the words in this place only, out of the many in which Isaiah uses them. But while these violent expedients are required to bring the passage even into seeming application to the future restoration of the Jews, it is, if possible, still more inapplicable to their former restoration from the Babylonish exile. In the first place, why should the ends of the earth be summoned to announce this event to Zion? Hitzig replies, as we have seen already, that the two clauses are entirely unconnected ; Knobel more boldly explains end of the earth to mean "the end of the oriental world, whose west end touched the Mediterranean sea, *i. e.* Palestine!" Whether a theory requiring such contrivances can well be sound, is left to the decision of the reader. But another difficulty in the way of this interpretation is presented by the last clause. Even supposing that the old opinion as to this clause is the true one, and that *his reward* means that which he bestows, in what sense can the restoration of the Jews from Babylon be represented as the coming of salvation (or a saviour) to the daughter of Zion, bringing a reward? The daughter of Zion is throughout these prophecies the suffering person and the object of encouraging address. Even where it primarily means the city, it is only as the centre, representative, and symbol of the Church or chosen people. How then could the saviour be described as coming to his people, bringing themselves with him as a recompence for what they had endured. But if, for reasons given in expounding chap. xl. 10, we understand *his reward* as meaning that which he receives, what constitutes this recompense in the case supposed? The image then presented is that of Jehovah coming back to his people, and bringing his people with him as his recompense. The incongruity of this verse with the Babylonian theory was either overlooked by its ablest modern champions, or occasioned such laconic comments as that of Rosenmüller, who contents himself with saying that the last clause has already been explained in the note upon chap. xl. 10 ; while Gesenius still more briefly says, "dieselben Worte xl. 10 ;" and Maurer, "eadem verba legimus xl. 10." This is the entire exposition of the whole verse by these three distinguished writers, while those of later date, who have been less reserved, have found themselves driven to the forced constructions which have been already mentioned. On the other hand, the plain sense of the words, the context here, and the analogy of chap. xl. 10, are all completely satisfied by the hypothesis that the Messiah (or Jehovah) is here described as coming to his people, bringing with him a vast multitude of strangers, or new converts, the reward of his own labours, and at the same time the occasion of a vast enlargement to his church. At the same time, let it be observed that this hypothesis is not one framed for the occasion, without reference ; or even in opposition to the previous explanation of passages in every point resembling this, but one suggested at the outset of the book, and found upon comparison, at every step of the interpretation, to be more satisfactory than any other.

12. *And they shall call them the Holy People, the redeemed of Jehovah, and thou shalt be called Derushah (sought for), Ir-lo-neezabah (City not forsaken).* The first verb is indefinite, they (*i. e.* men) shall call; hence the parallel expression has the passive form. On the construction and the idiomatic use of *call*, see vol. i. p. 92. The distinction here so clearly made by the use of the second and third persons, is supposed by the modern Germans to be that between the city and her returning citizens; but this, as we have seen repeatedly before, involves a constant vacillation between different senses of Jerusalem and Zion in the foregoing context. The only supposition which can be consistently maintained, is that it always means the city, but the city considered merely as a representative or sign of the whole system and economy of which it was the visible centre. The true distinction is between the church or chosen people as it is, and the vast accessions yet to be received from the world around it. Even the latter shall be honoured with the name of Holy People, while the church itself, becoming co-extensive with the world, shall cease to be an object of contempt or disregard to God or man. The sense of *sought for* seems to be determined by the parallel description in Jer. xxx. 14, as expressing the opposite of the complaint in chap. xlix. 14.—According to Henderson, the meaning of the verse is that " the Jews shall now," *i. e.* after their restoration to their own land, " be a holy people, redeemed from all iniquity, and thronging their ancient capital for religious purposes." The only prospect opened to the Gentiles in the whole prediction, thus expounded, is that of becoming ploughmen, shepherds, and purveyors to the favoured nation!

Chapter 63

The influx of the Gentiles into Zion having been described in the preceding verses, the destruction of her enemies is now sublimely represented as a sanguinary triumph of Jehovah or the Messiah, vers. 1–6. The Prophet then supposes the catastrophe already past, and takes a retrospective view of God's compassion towards his people, and of their unfaithfulness during the old economy, vers. 7–14. He then assumes the tone of earnest supplication, such as might have been offered by the believing Jews when all seemed lost in the destruction of their commonwealth and temple, vers. 15–19.

1. *Who (is) this coming from Edom, bright (as to his) garments from Bozrah, this one adorned in his apparel, bending in the abundance of his strength? I, speaking in righteousness, mighty to save.* The hypothesis that this is a detached prophecy, unconnected with what goes before or follows, is now commonly abandoned as a mere evasion of the difficulty. Hitzig indeed adheres to it in order to sustain his theory as to the gradual composition of the book. The dramatic form of the description is recognised by modern writers, without the awkward supposition of a chorus, adopted by Vitringa and Lowth. It is not necessary even to introduce the people as a party to the dialogue. The questions may be naturally put into the mouth of the Prophet himself. Interpreters are much divided as to the Edom of this passage. That it is not merely a play upon the meaning of the name (viz. red), is clear from the mention of the chief town, Bozrah. The reference to Rome, whether the Roman Empire or the

Romish Church, is purely fanciful. J. D. Michaelis consistently applies the passage, like the foregoing context, to a future event; but Henderson unexpectedly pronounces it unjustifiable " to apply it to any future judgments to be inflicted on the country formerly occupied by the Edomites." His own opinion is that " the object of the Prophet is to deduce an argument from God's dealings with his ancient people in favour of his graciously regarding them in their then distantly future dispersion." He does not explain why this is any less " unjustifiable " than the reference of the passage to a " distantly future " event. While J. D. Michaelis thus makes both the threatening and the promise alike future, and Henderson makes one distantly future, and the other distantly past, Knobel makes both past, and supposes Jehovah to be here described merely as coming through the land of Edom from the slaughter of the nations confederate with Croesus, who had just been overthrown by Cyrus in a battle near Sardis. With these exceptions, most interpreters, even of the modern German school, suppose Edom to be here, as in chap. xxxiv., the representative of Israel's most inveterate enemies. For this use of the name, see under xxxiv. 5. The connection with what goes before, as Rosenmüller states it, is that the restored Jews might apprehend the enmity of certain neighbouring nations, who had rejoiced in their calamity; and that the prophecy before us was intended to allay this apprehension. חָמוּץ strictly means fermented, then acetous, sharp, but is here applied to vivid colour, like the Greek ὀξὺ χρῶμα. הָדוּר properly means swollen, inflated, but is here metaphorically used in the sense of adorned, or, as Vitringa thinks, terrible, inspiring awe. For the sense of the word צֹעֶה, see above, on chap. li. 14. Vitringa understands it to mean here the restless motion of one not yet recovered from the excitement of a conflict; Gesenius, the tossing or throwing back of the head as a gesture indicative of pride; Hitzig, the leaning of the head to one side with a similar effect. The Vulgate version (*gradiens*) conveys too little. *Speaking in righteousness* is understood by most of the modern writers in the sense of speaking about it or concerning it, in which case righteousness must have the sense of deliverance, or at least be regarded as its cause. It is much more natural, however, to explain the phrase as meaning, I that speak in truth, I who promise and am able to perform.—The terms of this description are applied in Rev. xix. 13, to the victorious Word of God, a name which has apparently some reference to מְדַבֵּר.

2. *Why (is there) redness to thy raiment, and (why are) thy garments like (those of) one treading in a wine-press?* The adjective אָדֹם is here used substantively, just as we speak of a deep *red* in English. Or the word here employed may be explained as the infinitive of אָדַם to be red. There is no need, in any case, of making the ל pleonastic or a sign of the nominative case, with Rosenmüller and some older writers, or of reading מלבושך with Lowth. Twenty-one manuscripts and one edition gave the noun a plural form, but of course without effect upon the meaning. The allusion is of course to the natural red wine of the East, that of some vineyards on Mount Lebanon, according to J. D. Michaelis, being almost black. The גַּת is the wine-press properly so called, as distinguished from the יֶקֶב or reservoir. It is a slight but effective stroke in this fine picture, that the first verse seems to speak of the stranger as still at a distance, whereas in the second he has come so near as to be addressed directly.

3. *The press I have trodden by myself, and of the nations there was not a man with me; and I will tread them in my anger and trample them in my*

*fury, and their juice shall spirt upon my garments, and all my vesture I
have stained.* The word here used for *press* is different from that in the
foregoing verse, and occurs elsewhere only in Haggai ii. 16. According to
its seeming derivation, it denotes the place where grapes are crushed or
broken, as נַת does the place where they are pressed or trodden. The comparison suggested in the question (ver. 2) is here carried out in detail.
Being asked why he looks like the treader of a wine-press, he replies that
he has been treading one, and that alone, which Rosenmüller understands
to mean without the aid of labourers or servants. The meaning of the figure
is then expressed in literal terms. " Of the nations there was not a man with
me." This expression and the otherwise inexplicable alternation of the
tenses make it probable that two distinct treadings are here mentioned, one
in which he might have expected aid from the nations, and another in which
the nations should themselves be trodden down as a punishment of this
neglect. Or the future may denote merely a relative futurity, *i.e.* in reference to the act first mentioned. The more general opinion is, however,
that but one act of treading is here mentioned, and that the nations are
themselves represented as the grapes. In order to make this appear more
natural, Jarchi and Tremellius explain *with me* as meaning *against me*, or
to contend with me, which is not justified by usage. The most satisfactory
solution seems to be that these words are added to convey the idea that all
the nations were on the adverse side, none on that of the conqueror. The
sense will then be not that they refused to join in trampling others, but
simply that they were among the trampled. As if he had said, I trod the
press alone, and all the nations, without exception, were trodden in it. By
all the nations we are of course to understand all but God's people. The
principle of this limitation is recognised by Knobel, though he makes an
absurd application of it by supposing the exception to be Cyrus and the
Persians, who derived no aid from other nations in the overthrow of Croesus.
Henderson understands it as implying that the punishment here mentioned
was inflicted upon Edom without the intervening aid of any foreign power,
which he thinks was verified in their subjection by a native Jewish conqueror, Hyrcanus. The meaning given to נצח is justified by the use of the
verb in Arabic as meaning to sprinkle. אגאלתי is a mixed form, considered
by the modern Germans as a proof of later date; but such anomalies are
usually introduced by slow degrees, and may for the most part be traced
back to certain singularities of diction in the older books. The treading of
the wine-press alone is an expression often applied in sermons and in religious books and conversation to our Saviour's sufferings. This application
is described as customary in his own time by Vitringa, who considers it as
having led to the forced exposition of the whole passage by the Fathers and
Cocceius as a description of Christ's passion. While the impossibility of
such a sense in the original passage cannot be too strongly stated, there is
no need of denying that the figure may be happily accommodated in the
way suggested, as many expressions of the Old Testament may be applied
to different objects with good effect, provided we are careful to avoid confounding such accommodations with the strict and primary import of the
passage.

4. *For the day of vengeance (is) in my heart, and the year of my redeemed
is come.* For the sense of *day* and *year* in this connection, see above, on
chap. lxi. 2. *In my heart, i.e.* my mind or purpose. Some writers needlessly and arbitrarily change *my redeemed* to *my redemption*. It is not even
necessary to explain the participle in a future sense (*to be redeemed*), since

their redemption was as firmly settled in the divine purpose as the day of vengeance.

5. *And I look, and there is none helping; and I stand aghast, and there is none sustaining; and my own arm saves for me, and my fury it sustains me.* These expressions have already been explained in chap. lix. 16. Hitzig's idea that this is the original, and that a quotation from memory, and his inference that this is the older composition, are alike unfounded. With equal, if not greater plausibility, it might be argued from the greater regularity and finish of the sentence here, that it is an improvement on the other. Fury here takes the place of righteousness in chap. lix. 16, not as a synonyme but as an equivalent. God's wrath is but the executioner and agent of his justice. Upon either he might therefore be described as exclusively relying. The present form is used in the translation, on account of the uncertainty in which the use of the tenses is involved, and which may arise in part from an intentional confusion of the past and future in the mind of one who had begun a great work, and was yet to finish it.

6. *And I tread the nations in my anger, and I make them drunk in my wrath, and I bring down to the earth their juice.* The use of the word *tread* leads to the resumption of the figure of a wine-press, which is employed besides this passage in Lam. i. 15, Joel iv. 13, Rev. xiv. 19, 20. For אֲשַׁכְּרֵם I make them drunk, most of the modern writers since Cappellus read אֲשַׁבְּרֵם I crush them; which is not only confirmed by many manuscripts and some editions, as well as by the Targum, but is recommended by its suiting the connection better. This very circumstance, however, throws suspicion on the emendation, as a device to get rid of a difficulty. In order to connect the common reading with the context, we have only to assume a mixture of metaphors, such as we continually meet with in Isaiah. There is no need of going with Vitringa to the extravagant and revolting length of supposing that the nations are described as rolling in their own blood till it gets into their mouths and down their throats. There is simply a sudden change of figure, which is not only common, but characteristic of Isaiah, notwithstanding Gesenius's paradoxical denial.

7. *The mercies of Jehovah I will cause to be remembered, the praises of Jehovah according to all that Jehovah hath done for us, and the great goodness to the house of Israel which he hath done for them, according to his compassions and according to the multitude of his mercies.* The sudden change of tone in this verse has of course led to many suppositions as to its connection with what goes before and follows. The easiest expedient is the one which Lowth adopts, by denying all immediate connection with what goes before; but it is also the least satisfactory. Ewald begins the closing section of the book here, and thinks it quite indubitable that events had made considerable progress between the dates of the sixth and seventh verses. The prevalent opinion among Christian interpreters is that we have here the beginning of a prophecy relating to the future restoration of Israel. Even Vitringa, who shews little partiality to this hypothesis in the foregoing chapters, acquiesces in it here. His arguments, however, only go to shew that this interpretation is better than the one which applies the passage to the Babylonish exile. Lowth simply says that it is so, without assigning any reason. On the general principle assumed throughout our exposition as to the design and subject of these prophecies, a more general application is entitled to the preference, and the passage must be understood as relating to the favours experienced and the sins committed by the chosen people throughout the period of the old dispensation. There is no

need of assuming any speaker but the Prophet himself.   The plural form,
mercies, may be intended to denote abundance.   *I will cause to be remembered*, may have reference to men ; in which case the phrase is equivalent
to celebrate, record, or praise.   But as these acknowledgments are merely
preparatory to a prayer that God would renew his ancient favours to them,
it is better to understand it as meaning, I will cause God himself to remember, or remind him, in which application the verb is often used, *e.g.* in the
titles of Ps. xxxviii. and lxx.   (See Hengstenberg on the Psalms, vol. ii. p.
293).   There is no need of giving to תהלות the factitious sense of praiseworthy acts or virtues, as the Septuagint does by its ἀρετάς.   The proper
sense of *praises* is appropriate and sufficient.   For the sense of גְּמַל and גָּמַל,
see above on chap. lix. 18.   We have here another illustration of the ease with
which the parallelism may be urged on different sides of the same question.
It had been made a question whether רב טוב is governed by אזכיר or by
כעל.   The former is maintained by Maurer, the latter by Hitzig, on precisely the same ground : *ita postulante parallelismo*, says the one ; *diess
verlangt der Parallelismus*, says the other.

8. *And he said, Only they are my people, (my) children shall not lie* (or
deceive), *and he became a saviour for them.*   To the general acknowledgment of God's goodness to his people, there is now added a specification of
his favours, beginning with the great distinguishing favour by which they
became what they were.   This verse is commonly explained as an expression of unfounded confidence and hope on God's part, *surely they are my
people, children that will not lie.*   This must then be accounted for as
anthropopathy; but although the occurrence of this figure in the Scriptures
is indisputable, it is comparatively rare, and not to be assumed without
necessity.   Besides, the explanation just referred to rests almost entirely
on the sense attached to אך as a mere particle of asseveration.   Now, in
every other case where Isaiah uses it, the restrictive sense of *only* is not
admissible merely, but necessary to the full force of the sentence.   It is
surely not the true mode of interpretation, to assume a doubtful definition
for the sake of obtaining an unsatisfactory and offensive sense.   Another
advantage of the strict translation is, that it makes the Prophet go back to
the beginning of their course, and instead of setting out from the hopes
which God expressed after the choice of Israel, record the choice itself.
Thus understood, the first clause is a solemn declaration of his having
chosen Israel, to the exclusion of all other nations.   *Only they* (and no
others) *are my people.*   The objection which may seem to arise from the
collocation of אך with הֵמָּה rather than עַמִּי, applies only to the occidental
idiom ; since in Hebrew a qualifying particle is often attached to the first
word of the clause, even when it is more closely related to some other.
But even if the force of this objection were allowed, it could not prove that
אך must here be taken in a sense which does not properly belong to it, but
only that it must be made to qualify עַמִּי.   The sense will then be, they are
only my people, *i.e.* nothing else ; which, although less satisfactory than
the other sense, is still far better than the one which makes Jehovah here
express a groundless expectation.—The second clause may possibly mean
(*their*) *sons shall not deal falsely, i.e.* degenerate from their father's faith.
In either case, the future is the future of command, as in the decalogue,
not that of mere prediction.   Gesenius explains ישקרו as an elliptical expression, to be supplied by the analogy of Ps. xliv. 18, and lxxxix. 34 ;
but it is simpler to understand it absolutely, as in 1 Sam. xv. 29.—The

English Version, *so he was their saviour*, is a needless departure from the simplicity of the original, and aggravates the misinterpretation of the first clause, by suggesting that he was their saviour because he believed they would be faithful. The verse in Hebrew simply states two facts, without intimating any causal relation between them. He chose them *and* he saved them.

9. *In all their enmity he was not an enemy, and the angel of his face* (or *presence*) *saved them, in his love and in his sparing mercy he redeemed them, and he took them up and carried them all the days of old.* The first clause is famous as the subject of discordant and even contradictory interpretations. These have been multiplied by the existence of a doubt as to the text.

The Masora notes this as one of fifteen places in which לֹא, *not*, is written by mistake for לֹו, *to him* or *it*. Another instance of the same alleged error in the text of Isaiah occurs in chap. ix. 2. (See vol. i. p. 199.) Rabbi Jonah, according to Solomon Ben Melek, understands the amended text to mean that in all their distress they still had a rock or refuge, making צָר synonymous with צוּר, which is wholly unsustained by usage. A far better sense is that of Aben Ezra, that in all their distress there was distress to him, or as the English Version renders it, "in all their affliction he was afflicted." This explanation, with the text on which it is founded, and which is exhibited by a number of manuscripts and editions, is approved by Luther, Vitringa, Clericus, Hitzig, Ewald, Umbreit, Hendewerk, and Knobel. It is favoured, not only by the strong and affecting sense which it yields, but by the analogy of Judges x. 16, xi. 7, in one of which places the same phrase is used to denote human suffering, and in the other God is represented as sympathising with it. The objections to it are, that it gratuitously renders necessary another anthropopathic explanation; that the natural collocation of the words, if this were the meaning, would be צַר לֹו, as in 2 Sam. i. 26; that the negative is expressed by all the ancient versions; and that the critical presumption is in favour of the Kethib, or textual reading, as the more ancient, which the Masorites merely corrected in the margin, without venturing to change it, and which ought not to be now abandoned, if a coherent sense can be put upon it, as it can in this case. Jerome, in his version, makes the clause assert the very opposite of that sense which is usually put upon the marginal reading or Keri, *in omni tribulatione eorum non est tribulatus*. The Septuagint makes it contradict the next clause, as it is usually understood, by rendering it οὐ πρέσβυς οὐδὲ ἄγγελος ἀλλ' αὐτὸς ἔσωσεν αὐτού;. This is followed by Lowth even so far as to connect the first words of the clause with the preceding verse: *and he became their saviour in all their distress. It was not an envoy nor an angel of his presence that saved them*, &c. Not to mention other difficulties in the way of this interpretation, its making צָר synonymous with צִיר is wholly arbitrary. Another forced construction, given by Cocceius, and approved by Rosenmüller, Maurer, and almost by Gesenius, explains *there was not an adversary, and he saved them*, to mean, there scarcely was or no sooner was there an adversary, when or than he saved them. The only example of this harsh and obscure syntax which is cited, namely, 2 Kings xx. 4, is nothing to the purpose, because there it is expressly said, and no doubt meant, that Isaiah had not gone out into the court; whereas here it cannot possibly be meant that Israel had no adversaries. A much more natural construction is the one proposed by Jerome in his commentary, "in all their affliction he did not afflict (them);" which, however, is scarcely reconcileable with history. This difficulty is avoided by Henderson's modification of the same construction, *in all their affliction he was not an adversary*, *i. e.* although he afflicted them, he did not hate them. This agrees well with what immediately follows, but is still liable to the objection that it takes צָר and צָרָה in entirely different senses, which can only be admissible in case of necessity. Others accordingly regard them as synonymous expressions, and in order to remove the appearance of a contradiction, supply some qualification of the second word. Thus Jarchi understands the clause to mean that in all their affliction there was no such affliction as their sins had merited. Aurivillius supposes the masculine form to express the same thing with the feminine essentially, but in a higher degree, " in all their affliction there was no extreme or fatal affliction." Gesenius rejects this explanation of the forms as too artificial, but adopts a similar interpretation of the clause, which he explains to mean that in all their distress there was no real or serious distress, none that deserved the name ; which could hardly be alleged with truth. It is also hard to account in this case for the use of the different forms צָר and צָרָה to express the same idea, after rejecting Aurivillius's solution. This circumstance appears to point to an interpretation which shall give the words the same sense, yet so far modified as to explain the difference of form. Such an interpretation is the one suggested by De Wette's version of the clause, which takes צָר and צָרָה as correlative derivatives from one sense of the same root, but distinguished from each other as an abstract and a concrete, *enemy* and *enmity*. A real difficulty in the way of this interpretation, is the want of any usage to sustain the latter definition, which, however, is so easily deducible from the primary meaning, and so clearly indicated by the parallel expression, that it may perhaps be properly assumed in a case where the only choice is one of difficulties. Thus understood, the clause simply throws the blame of all their conflicts with Jehovah on themselves : *in all their enmity* (to him) *he was not an enemy* (to them). The proof of this assertion is that *he saved them*, not from Egypt merely, but from all their early troubles, with particular reference perhaps to the period of the Judges, in the history of which this verb very frequently occurs. (See Judges ii. 16, 18, iii. 15, vi. 14, &c.) This salvation is ascribed, however, not directly to Jehovah, but to *the angel of his face* or *presence*. Kimchi explains this to mean the agency of second causes, which he says are called in Scripture angels or messengers of God. Abarbenel gives it a personal sense, but applies it to the angels collectively. Jarchi makes it not only a personal but an individual description, and explains it to mean Michael, as the tutelary angel of Israel (Dan. xii. 1). Aben Ezra, with sagacity and judgment superior to all his brethren, understands it of the angel whom Jehovah promised to send with Israel (Exod. xxiii. 20–23), and whom he did send (Exod. xiv. 19, Num. xx. 16), and who is identified with the presence of Jehovah (Exod. xxxiii. 14, 15) and with Jehovah himself (Exod. xxxiii. 12). The combination of these passages determines the sense of *the angel of his presence*, as denoting the angel whose presence was the presence of Jehovah, or in whom Jehovah was personally present, and precludes the explanation given by Clericus and many later writers, who suppose it to mean merely an angel who habitually stands in the presence of Jehovah (1 Kings xxii. 19), just as human courtiers or officers of state are said to see the king's face (Jer. lii. 25.) Even Hitzig admits the identity of the angel of Jehovah's presence with Jehovah himself, but explains it away by making angel an abstract term, not denoting in any case a person, but the manifestation of Jehovah's presence at a certain time and place. Hendewerk, on the other hand, alleges that the angel is always represented as a personality distinct from Jehovah himself. By blending these concessions from two writers of the same great school, we obtain a striking testimony, if not to the absolute truth, to the scriptural correctness of the old Christian doctrine, as expounded with consummate force and clearness by Vitringa in his comment on this passage, viz. the doctrine that the Angel of God's presence, who is mentioned in the passages already cited, and from time to time in other books of the Old Testament (Gen. xxviii. 13, xxxi. 11, xlviii. 16, Exod. iii. 2, Joshua v. 14, Judges xiii. 6, Hosea xii. 5, Zech. iii. 1, Mal. iii. 1, Ps. xxxiv. 8), was that divine person who is represented in the New as the brightness of the Father's glory, and the express image of his person (Heb. i. 3), the image of God (2 Cor. iv. 4, Col. i. 15), in whose face the glory of God shines (2 Cor. iv. 6), and in whom dwelleth all the fulness of the Godhead bodily (Col. ii. 9). Lowth's unfortunate adoption of the Septuagint version or perversion of the text, led him to argue ingeniously, but most unfairly, that although the Angel of Jehovah's presence is sometimes identified with Jehovah himself, yet in other places he is explicitly distinguished from him, and must therefore be considered as a creature; so that in the case before us, which is one of those last mentioned, the honour of Israel's deliverance is denied to this angel and exclusively ascribed to God himself. All this not only rests upon a fanciful and false translation, but is contradicted by the unanimous consent of Jews and infidels as well as Christians, that the salvation of God's people is directly ascribed to the Angel of Jehovah's presence.—Vitringa insists, perhaps, with too much pertinacity, upon applying what immediately follows to the Angel and not to Jehovah: first, because the question is in fact a doubtful one, and both constructions are grammatical; and secondly, because it is a question of no moment, after the essential identity of the Angel and Jehovah has been ascertained from other quarters.—The Hebrew חֶמְלָה, from חָמַל, to *spare*, has no exact equivalent in English, and can only be expressed by a periphrasis. The same affections towards Israel are described to Jehovah in the Pentateuch. (Deut. xxiii. 9–11, Ps. lxxvii. 15.)—For the true sense of what follows, as to taking up and carrying them, see above, on chap. xlvi. 3.—עוֹלָם, which Vitringa regards as identical with the Latin *olim*, is like it applied as well to the past as to the future. It originally signifies unknown or indefinite duration, and in such a case as this, remote antiquity; the whole phrase being used precisely in the same sense as by Amos (ix. 11) and Micah (vii. 14).—The verb *redeem* is not only one of frequent occurrence in these prophecies (chap. xliii. 1, xliv. 22, 23, xlviii. 20, xlix. 7, &c.), but is expressly applied elsewhere to the redemption of Israel from Egypt (Exod. vi. 5, Ps. lxxiv. 2, lxxvii. 16), and is therefore applicable to all other analogous deliverances.

10. *And they rebelled and grieved his Holy Spirit* (or *Spirit of holiness*), *and he was turned from them into an enemy, he himself fought against them.* The pronoun at the beginning is emphatic: they on their part, as opposed to God's forbearance and long-suffering. There seems to be an allusion in this clause to the injunction given to the people at the exodus, in reference to the Angel who was to conduct them: "Beware of him and obey his voice, provoke him not, for he will not pardon your transgressions, for my name is in him" (Exod. xxiii. 21). From this analogy Vitringa argues that the verse before us has specific reference to the disobedience or resistance

offered by the people to the Angel of God's presence. As the next clause may have reference to Jehovah, it cannot be demonstrated from it that the spirit here mentioned is a personal spirit, and not a mere disposition or affection. But the former supposition, which is equally consistent with the language here used, in itself considered, becomes far more probable when taken in connection with the preceding verse, where a personal angel is joined with Jehovah precisely as the Spirit is joined with him here. Assuming that the following words relate to this Spirit, he is then described as endued with personal susceptibilities and performing personal acts, and we have in these two verses a distinct enumeration of the three divine persons. That the Spirit of this verse, like the Angel of the ninth, is represented as divine, is evident not only from a comparison of Ps. lxxviii. 17, 40, where the same thing is said of God himself, but also from the fact that those interpreters who will not recognise a personal spirit in this passage, unanimously understand the spirit either as denoting an attribute of God or God himself. Henderson thinks it necessary to explain away a seeming contradiction between this verse and the first clause of ver. 9, by making צָר a stronger expression than אוֹיֵב. The true solution is, that the passage is in some sort historical, and shews the progress of the alienation between God and Israel. Having shewn in the preceding verse that it began upon the part of Israel, and was long resisted and deferred by Jehovah, he now shews how at length his patience was exhausted, and he really became what he was not before. This is the true sense of the verb יֵהָפֵךְ, to which many of the moderns give a reflexive form, he changed himself. The disputes among interpreters whether this verse has reference to the conduct of the people in the wilderness, or under the judges, or before the Babylonish exile, or before the final destruction of Jerusalem, are only useful as a demonstration that the passage is a general description, which was often verified.—From this verse Paul has borrowed a remarkable expression in Eph. iv. 30. (Compare Mat. xii. 31, Acts vii. 51, Heb. x. 29.)

11. *And he remembered the days of old, Moses (and) his people. Where is he that brought them up from the sea, the shepherd of his flock? Where is he that put within him his Holy Spirit?* Grotius and others make Jehovah the subject of the first verb, and suppose him to be here described as relenting. This construction has the advantage of avoiding an abrupt change of person without any intimation in the text. But as the following can be naturally understood only as the language of the people, especially when compared with Jer. ii. 6, most writers are agreed in referring this clause to the people also. Cyril and Jerome, it is true, combine both suppositions, by referring *he remembered* to Jehovah, and explaining what follows as the language of the people. But a transition so abrupt is not to be assumed without necessity. The Targum gives a singular turn to the sentence by supplying *lest they say* before the second clause, which then becomes the language of the enemies of Israel, exulting in the failure of Jehovah's promises. This explanation may appear to derive some support from the analogy of Deut. xxxii. 17, which no doubt suggested it; but a fatal objection is the one made by Vitringa, that the essential idea is one not expressed but arbitrarily supplied. Another singular interpretation is the one contained in the Dutch Bible, which makes God the subject of the first verb, but includes it in the language of the people, complaining that he dealt with them no longer as he once did : Once he remembered the days of old, &c., but now where is he, &c. But here again, the words *but now*, on which the whole depends, must be supplied without authority.

The modern writers, since Vitringa, are agreed that the first clause describes the repentance of the people, and that the second gives their very words, contrasting their actual condition with their former privileges and enjoyments. There is still a difference of opinion, however, with respect to the grammatical construction of the first clause. Rosenmüller and most of the later writers follow Jarchi in making עַמּוֹ the subject of the verb; *and his people remembered the days of old*, &c. As such a collocation falls in with the German idiom, the writers in that language have easily been led to regard it as entirely natural, though really as foreign from Hebrew as from English usage. The solitary case which Hitzig cites (Ps. xxxiv. 22) would prove nothing by itself, even if it were exactly similar and unambiguous, neither of which is really the case. But another difficulty still remains, viz., that of construing the words מֹשֶׁה עַמּוֹ, which seemed to stand detached from the remainder of the sentence. Lowth resorts to his favourite but desperate method of reading עַבְדּוֹ *his servant*, on the authority of the Peshito and a few manuscripts. Gesenius, on the other hand, is half inclined to strike out מֹשֶׁה as a marginal gloss still wanting in the Septuagint. These emendations, even if they rested upon surer grounds, would only lessen, not remove, the difficulty as to the construction of מֹשֶׁה or עַמּוֹ with what goes before. Gesenius makes *days of old* a complex noun governing Moses: the ancient days of Moses. This construction, harsh and unusual as it is, has been adopted by the later German writers except Maurer, who, after denying the existence of the difficulty, brings out as if it were a new discovery, the old construction, given in the English Bible and maintained at length by Vitringa, which makes *Moses* and *his people* correlatives, as objects of the verb *remembered*: He remembered the ancient days, viz. those of Moses and his people. So Gesenius, in the notes to the second edition of his German version, calls attention to the explanation of מֹשֶׁה as a noun or participle meaning the deliverer of his people, as having been recently proposed by Horst, whereas it is at least as old as Aben Ezra, who recites without adopting it.—Henderson is disposed to omit the pronoun in הַמַּעֲלֵם, on the authority of two old manuscripts, apparently confirmed by that of two old versions, or to gain the same end by regarding the construction as an Aramaic one, in which the pronoun is prefixed in pleonastic anticipation of the noun which follows. In either case the אֵת will be not a preposition meaning *with*, but the objective participle, " he that brought up from the sea the shepherds of his flock." The objection to making אֵת a preposition is that it seems to separate the case of Moses from that of the people. The Targum seems to make it a particle of likeness or comparison, as a shepherd does his flock, which Gesenius thinks a far better sense ; but Hitzig thinks it false, because shepherds do not bring their flocks up from the sea. The simplest construction is to repeat הַמַּעֲלֶה before רֹעֵה : Where is he that brought them up from the sea, (that brought up) the shepherd of his flock ? All these constructions suppose the shepherd to be Moses; but Knobel understands it to be God himself, as in Ps. lxxviii. 52, and repeats the verb remembered, " (the people) remembered the shepherd of his flock," which makes an equally good sense. But nearly sixty manuscripts and forty editions read רֹעֵי in the plural, which may then be understood as including Aaron (Ps. lxxvii. 21), and as Vitringa thinks Miriam (Micah vi. 4), or perhaps the seventy elders who are probably referred to in the last clause as under a special divine influence. (See Num. xi. 17. Compare Exod. xxxi. 3, xxxv. 31.) The suffix in בְּקִרְבּוֹ refers to עָם. The noun itself is used as in 1 Kings xvii. 22. The clause implies, if it does not express directly, the idea of a personal spirit, as in the preceding verse.

12. *Leading them by the right hand of Moses (and) his glorious arm, cleaving the waters from before them, to make for him an everlasting name?* The sentence and the interrogation are continued from the foregoing verse. The participle with the article there defines or designates the subject as *the one bringing up ;* the participle here without the article simply continues the description. Vitringa and the later writers follow Jarchi in giving a very different construction to the first clause, making *his glorious arm* the object of the verb. The meaning of the whole then is as follows: causing his glorious arm to march at the right hand of Moses, *i. e.* as Jarchi explains, causing his almighty power, of which the arm is the established symbol (chap. xl. 10, lix. 16, lxiii. 5), to be near or present with the Prophet when he needed its interposition. This is a good sense, but it seems more natural to give מוֹלִיךְ the same object as in the next verse, the pronoun which is there expressed being here understood. The לְ, which the writers above mentioned understand as in Ps. xvi. 8, may agreeably to usage denote general relation, the specific sense of *by* being not expressed but suggested by the context. The *right hand* may be mentioned in allusion to the wielding of the rod by Moses, and the *glorious arm* may be either his or that of God himself, which last sense is expressed in the English version by a change of preposition (*by the right hand of Moses with his glorious arm*). The same ambiguity exists in the last clause, where the *everlasting name* may be the honour put upon Moses, or the glory which redounded to Jehovah himself, as in chap. lv. 13. Knobel is singular and somewhat paradoxical in understanding בּוֹקֵעַ מַיִם as descriptive of the smiting of the rock to supply the people's thirst, simply because the passive of the same verb is applied in chap. xxxv. 6 to the bursting forth of water in the desert; whereas it is repeatedly employed, both in the active and the passive form, in reference to the cleaving of the waters of the Red Sea (Exod. xiv. 21 ; Ps. lxxviii. 13 ; Neh. ix. 11), and is so understood here by all other writers whom I have consulted. It also agrees better with the expression *from before them*, which implies the removal of a previous obstruction.

13. *Making them walk in the depths, like the horse in the desert they shall not stumble.* The description of the exodus is still continued, and its perfect security illustrated by comparisons. There is no need of giving to תְּהֹמוֹת with the modern writers the distinct sense of *waves* in this and other places, as the proper meaning, *depths*, is more appropriate and striking in a poetical description. The desert is commonly supposed to be referred to as a vast plain free from inequalities. But J. D. Michaelis, after twice announcing that he never rode on horseback through a desert in his life, makes the point of comparison to lie in the fine gravel or coarse sand with which the desert of Arabia is covered, and which makes an admirable footing for horses. In the same note, and in the same spirit, he discards the word stumbling (*straucheln*), which he says would be employed by one who never sat upon a horse, and substitutes another (*anstossen*) as the technical term of the *manége*, although requiring explanation to the common reader. The last verb would seem most naturally to refer to *the horse;* but its plural form forbids this construction, while its future form creates a difficulty in referring it to Israel. Most versions get around this difficulty by periphrasis, *without stumbling, so as not to stumble*, or the like. The true solution is afforded by the writer's frequent habit of assuming his position in the midst

of the events which he describes, and speaking of them as he would have spoken if he had been really so situated. The comparison in the first clause brings up to his view the people actually passing through the wilderness; and in his confident assurance of their safe and easy progress he exclaims, "they will not stumble!" The same explanation is admissible in many cases where it is customary to confound the tenses, or regard their use as perfectly capricious. As Knobel in the foregoing verse supposes an allusion to the smiting of the rock, so here he refers the description to the passage of the Jordan, as if unwilling to acknowledge any reference to the Red Sea or the actual exodus from Egypt.

14. *As the herd into the valley will go down, the Spirit of Jehovah will make him rest. So didst thou lead thy people, to make for thyself a name of glory.*—בְּהֵמָה is probably here used in its collective sense of cattle, rather than in that of an individual animal or beast. This version is not only more exact than the common one, but removes the ambiguity in the construction, by precluding the reference of *him*, in *make him rest*, to the preceding noun, which is natural enough in the English Version, though forbidden in Hebrew by the difference of gender.—The *him* really refers to Israel or people. J. D. Michaelis and Lowth follow the ancient versions, which they understand as reading תַּנְחֶנּוּ *will guide him.* But the idea of guidance is sufficiently implied in the common reading, which may be understood as meaning "will bring him to a place of rest," a form of expression often used in reference to the promised land. (Deut. xii. 9, 10, Ps. xcv. 11, &c. A similar agency is elsewhere ascribed to the Spirit of God. (Ps. cxliii. 10, Hagg. ii. 5, Neh. ix. 20.)—The use of the futures in this clause is precisely the same as in the foregoing verse. In the last clause the Prophet ceases to regard the scene as actually present, and resumes the tone of historical retrospection, at the same time summing up the whole in one comprehensive proposition, *thus didst thou lead thy people.* — With the last words of the verse compare chap. lx. 21, lxi. 3.

15. *Look (down) from heaven and see from thy dwelling-place of holiness and beauty! Where is thy zeal and thy might (or mighty deeds)? The sounding of thy bowels and thy mercies towards me have withdrawn themselves.* The foregoing description of God's ancient favours is now made the ground of an importunate appeal for new ones. The unusual word for dwelling-place is borrowed from the prayer of Solomon (1 Kings viii. 13). For a similar description of heaven, see above, chap. lvii. 15. God is here represented as withdrawn into heaven, and no longer active upon earth. For the meaning of his *zeal*, see above, on chap. lix. 17. Jarchi adds הָרִאשׁנָה, *i. e.* thy *former* zeal. Eighteen manuscripts, two editions, and the ancient versions, read וּבְוּרָתְךָ in the singular. The plural probably denotes mighty deeds or feats of strength, as in 1 Kings xv. 23, xvi. 27, xxii. 46. הָמוֹן is not to be taken in its secondary sense of (*multitude*), as it is by the Septuagint (πλῆθος) and the Vulgate (*multitudo*), but in its primary sense of *commotion, noise.* The verbal root is applied in like manner to the movements of compassion, chap. xvi. 11, Jer. xxxi. 20, xlviii. 36, in the last of which places it is connected with the verbal root of רחמים, the parallel expression in the case before us. Although we are obliged to render one of these nouns by a literal and the other by a figurative term, both of them properly denote the viscera, on the figurative use of which to signify strong feeling, see vol. i. p. 329.—The last verb in the verse denotes a violent suppression or restraint of strong emotion (Gen. xliii. 30, xlv. 1), and is sometimes applied directly to God himself. (See above, chap.

xlii. 14, and below, chap. lxiv. 11.) The last clause may be variously divided, without a material change of meaning. The English Version makes the last verb a distinct interrogation, *are they restrained?* Henderson makes the second question the larger of the two, *are the sounding of thy bowels?* &c. The objection to both is, that the second question is not natural, and that they arbitrarily assume an interrogative construction, without anything to indicate it, as the *where* cannot be repeated. Vitringa and Hitzig make the whole one question, and supply the relative before the last verb, *where is thy zeal,* &c., *which are restrained?* But the simplest construction is that which makes the last clause a simple affirmation (Gesenius), or an impassioned exclamation (Ewald). There is something peculiarly expressive in Luther's paraphrase of this last clause, *deine grosse herzliche Barmherzigkeit hält sich hart gegen mich.*

16. *For thou* (*art*) *our father; for Abraham hath not known us, and Israel will not recognise us, thou Jehovah* (*art*) *our father, our redeemer, of old* (or *from everlasting*) *is thy name.* The common version needlessly obscures the sense and violates the usage of the language by rendering the first כִּי *doubtless,* and the second *though.* Rosenmüller gives the first the sense of *but,* simply observing that the particle is here not causal, but adversative. This wanton variation from the ordinary sense of terms, whenever there appears to be the least obscurity in the connection, is one of the errors of the old school of interpreters, retained by Rosenmüller, who is a kind of link between them and the moderns. The later German writers are more rigidly exact, and Maurer, in particular, observes in this case that the כִּי has its proper causal sense in reference to the first clause of ver. 15. Why do we ask thee to look down from heaven and to hear our prayer? *Because thou art our father.* This does not merely mean our natural creator, but our founder, our national progenitor, as in Deut. xxxii. 6. Here, however, it appears to be employed in an emphatic and exclusive sense, as if he had said, "Thou, and thou alone, art our father;" for he immediately adds, as if to explain and justify this strange assertion, "for Abraham has not known us, and Israel will not recognise or acknowledge us." The assimilation of these tenses, as if both past or future, is entirely arbitrary, and their explanation as both present a gratuitous evasion. As in many other cases, past and future are here joined to make the proposition universal. Dropping the peculiar parallel construction, the sense is, that neither Abraham nor Israel have known or will know anything about us, have recognised or will hereafter recognise us as their children. The meaning, therefore, cannot be that Abraham and Israel are ashamed of us as unworthy and degenerate descendants, as Piscator understands it; or that Abraham and Israel cannot save us by their merits, as Cocceius understands it; or that Abraham and Israel did not deliver us from Egypt, as the Targum understands it; or that Abraham and Israel, being now dead, can do nothing for us, as Vitringa and the later writers understand it. All these interpretations, and a number of unnatural constructions and false versions, some of which have been already mentioned, owe their origin to the insuperable difficulty of applying these words, in their strict and unperverted sense, to the Jews as the natural descendants of the patriarchs in question. Henderson's mode of reconciling what is here said with his general application of the prophecies is curious enough. After justly observing that "the hereditary descent of the Jews from Abraham, and their dependence upon his merits and those of Isaac and Jacob, form the proudest grounds of boasting among them at the present day, as they did in the time of our Lord," he adds that, "when converted,

they shall be ashamed of all such confidence, and glory in Jehovah alone."
Such an effect of individual conversion and regeneration may be certainly
expected; but a general restoration of the Jews as a people, not only to
the favour of God but to the land of their fathers, and not only to the land
of their fathers, but to pre-eminence among the nations, so that their temple
shall again be universally frequented, and the whole world reduced to the
alternative of perishing or serving them, is so far from naturally tending to
correct the evil which has been described, that nothing but a miracle would
seem sufficient to prevent its being aggravated vastly by the very means
which Henderson expects to work a final cure. The true sense of the
verse, as it appears to me, is that the church or chosen people, although
once, for temporary reasons, coextensive and coincident with a single race,
is not essentially a national organization, but a spiritual body. Its father is
not Abraham or Israel, but Jehovah, who is and always has been its
redeemer, who has borne that name from everlasting; or as Hitzig understands the last clause, he is our redeemer, whose name is from everlasting.
Most interpreters, however, are agreed in understanding this specific name
of *our redeemer* to be here described as everlasting or eternal. According
to the explanation which has now been given, this verse explicitly asserts
what is implied and indirectly taught throughout these prophecies, in reference to the true design and mission of the church, and its relation to Jehovah,
to the world, and to the single race with which of old it seemed to be
identified. This confirmation of our previous conclusions is the more satisfactory, because no use has hitherto been made of it, by anticipation, in
determining the sense of many more obscure expressions, to which it may
now be considered as affording a decisive key. It only remains to add, as
a preventive of misapprehension, that the strong terms of this verse are
of course to be comparatively understood, not as implying that the church
will ever have occasion to repudiate its historical relation to the patriarchs,
or cease to include among its members many of their natural descendants,
but simply as denying all continued or perpetual pre-eminence to Israel as a
race, and exalting the common relation of believers to their great Head as
paramount to all connection with particular progenitors;—the very doctrine
so repeatedly and emphatically taught in the New Testament.

17. *Why wilt thou make us wander, O Jehovah, from thy ways; (why)
wilt thou harden our heart from thy fear? Return, for the sake of thy servants, the tribes of thy inheritance.* The earnestness of the prayer is
evinced by an increasing boldness of expostulation. Rosenmüller shews,
by a reference to Deut. ii. 28, and 1 Sam. xiv. 36, that the Hiphil often
signifies permission rather than direct causation. But although this usage
is indisputable, it is here forbidden by the parallel expression, which can
hardly mean to suffer to grow hard, and rendered unnecessary by the
frequency and clearness with which such an agency is ascribed to God himself elsewhere. As to the sense of such expressions, see vol. i. p. 152.
Equally shallow and malignant are the comments of the German writers
on this subject; as a specimen of which may be given Hitzig's statement
that " Jehovah makes men sinners for the sake of punishing them afterwards; to the question why he does so, the East," by which he means the
Bible, "makes no answer. Compare Rom ix. 17-22." The future verbs
are not to be arbitrarily explained as preterites, or (with Hitzig) as implying that the action still continues, but as asking why he will continue so to
do. The second verb occurs only here and in Job xxxix. 16, where it is
applied to the ostrich's hard treatment of her young. It is obviously near

akin to קָשָׁה, and Vitringa thinks the substitution of the stronger guttural
has an intensive effect upon the meaning. The particle in *from thy fear*
is commonly supposed to have a primitive or negative meaning, so as not to
fear thee; but there is rather an allusion to the wandering just before
mentioned, as if he had said, "And why wilt thou make us wander, by
hardening our heart, from thy fear?" This last expression, as in many other
cases, includes all the duties and affections of true piety.—For the sense of
God's returning to his peeple, see above, on chap. lii. 8. *The tribes of thine
inheritance* is an equivalent expression to *thy people;* which originated in
the fact that Israel, like other ancient oriental races, was divided into tribes.
The argument drawn from this expression in favour of applying the whole
passage to the Jews, proves too much; for the distinction into tribes is as
much lost now among the Jews as among the Gentiles. The Jews, indeed,
are properly but one tribe, that of Judah, in which the remnants of the
others were absorbed after the exile.

18. *For a little thy holy people possessed, our enemies trod down thy
sanctuary.* The sense of this verse is extremely dubious. מִצְעָר is elsewhere used in reference to magnitude (Gen. xix. 20), and number (2 Chron.
xxiv. 24), not to time. J. D. Michaelis connects it with the foregoing verse,
and reads, "the tribes of thy inheritance have become a little thing," *i. e.* an
object of contempt. So the Vulgate, *quasi nihilum.* The Septuagint also
joins the first clause with ver. 17, and omits the second, "that we may inherit
a little of thy holy mountain," reading הר for עם which is approved by Lowth.
Cocceius takes לְמִצְעָר in the sense of *almost,* like כִּמְעַט (Gen xxvi. 10,
Ps. lxxiii. 2.) Lowth, Kocher, and Rosenmüller, make it equivalent to
the Latin *parvum.* But Vitringa and the later writers understand it as
an abverb of time, cognate and equivalent to מִזְעָר (chap. x. 25, xxix. 17).
Another question is whether *thy holy people* is the subject or object of the
verb *possessed.* Thus Grotius understands the clause to mean that the
enemy *for a little while possessed thy holy people;* and Cocceius, that *they
almost possessed thy holy people;* Kocher and Rosenmüller, it was not
enough that they possessed thy holy people, they also trampled on thy
sanctuary; Lowth, it was little that they did both, if God had not besides
rejected them. The subject is then to be supplied from the other clause, or
brought into this, by a removal of the accent and a consequent change of
interpunction. The modern writers are agreed, however, in making *holy
people* the subject of the verb, and supplying the object from the other
clause, *thy sanctuary,* which is understood by Hitzig as denoting the entire
holy land (Zech. ii. 16), as the cities of Judah are, he thinks, called *holy cities*
in chap. lxiv. 9. Maurer suggests another method of providing both a subject and an object to the verb by omitting the makkeph and reading יָרְשׁוּ
עַם קָדְשֶׁךָ, the people possessed thy holy (thing or place). According to
the usual construction of the sentence, it assigns as a reason for Jehovah's
interference, the short time during which the chosen people had possessed
the land of promise. But it may be objected that למצער would naturally
seem to qualify both clauses, which can only be prevented by supplying
arbitrarily between them *and then* or *now.* This consideration may be said
to favour Grotius's construction; which is further recommended by its
grammatical simplicity, in giving to both verbs one and the same subject.
What is common to both explanations is the supposition that the verse
describes a subjection to enemies. The question upon which they disagree
is whether this subjection is itself described as temporary, or the peaceable
possession which preceded it.—In no case can an argument be drawn from

it to prove that this whole passage has respect to the Jews in their present
dispersion : first, because the sufferings of the church in after ages are
frequently presented under figures drawn from the peculiar institutions of
the old economy ; and secondly, because the early history of Israel is as
much the early history of the Christian Church as of the Jewish nation, so
that we have as much right as the Jews to lament the profanation of the
Holy Land, and more cause to pray for its recovery by Christendom, than
they for its restoration to themselves. Gesenius's translation of בּוֹסְסוּ as
meaning *plundered*, although copied by Umbreit, is most probably an inadvertence ; as no such meaning of the verb is given or referred to in any
of his Hebrew lexicons. The error was observed and corrected even by De
Wette and Noyes, the two most faithful followers of Gesenius in his version
of Isaiah.

19. *We are of old, thou hast not ruled over them, thy name has not
been called upon them. Oh that thou wouldst rend the heavens (and) come
down, (that) from before thee the mountains might quake (or flow down).*
Most of the modern writers have adopted a construction of the first clause
suggested by the paraphrastic versions of the Septuagint and Vulgate.
This supposes the description of the people's alienation from God to be
continued : We have long been those (or like those) over whom thou didst
not rule, and who were not called by thy name ; that is to say, thou hast
long regarded and treated us as aliens rather than thy chosen people. The
מֵעוֹלָם is then referred to the destruction of Jerusalem by Nebuchadnezzar
or by Titus, according to the general exegetical hypothesis of each interpreter. The ellipsis of the relative involved in this construction can create
no difficulty, as it is one of perpetual occurrence ; but the sense which it
puts upon the clause is very far from being obvious, or one which a Hebrew
writer would be likely to express in this way. Another old and well-known
construction of the clause is founded on the Chaldee Paraphrase, which
understands this, not as a description of their misery, but an assertion of
their claim to relief, in the form of a comparison between themselves and
their oppressors. This is the sense given in the English Version : *We are
thine, thou never barest rule over them,* &c. To this form of the interpretation it has been objected, not without reason, that it puts upon the verb *we
are* or *have been* a sense not justified by usage, or in other words, that it
arbitrarily supplies the essential idea upon which the whole turns, namely,
thine or *thy people.* But this objection may be easily removed by connecting the verb with מֵעוֹלָם, *we are of old.* The point of comparison is then
their relative antiquity, the enemy being represented as a new race come
into possession of the rights belonging to the old. There is then no need
of supplying *thine*, the relation of the people to Jehovah being not particularly hinted here, although suggested by the whole connection. With this
modification, the construction of the Targum and the English Bible seems
entitled to the preference.—*Thou didst not rule over them.* This has no
reference, of course, to God's providential government, but only to the
peculiar theocratical relation which he bears to his own people. The same
idea is expressed by the following words, as to the sense of which see above,
on chap. xlviii. 1. The inconvenience of strongly marked divisions in a
book like this, is exemplified by the disputes among interpreters, whether
the remaining words of this verse as it stands in the Masoretic text should
or should not be separated from it, and connected with the following chapter. Gesenius and the later writers choose the latter course, while Rosenmüller stedfastly adheres to the Masoretic interpunction. The simple

truth is that there ought to be no pause at all in this place, the transition from complaint to the expression of an ardent wish being not only intentional, but highly effective. It is true that this clause ought not to be separated from what follows; but it does not follow that it ought to be severed from what goes before, a gross *non sequitur*, with which the reasoning of some learned writers is too often justly chargeable. Ewald reckons the remainder of this sentence as the first verse of the sixty-fourth chapter, on the authorlty of the ancient versions, but obviates the inconvenience commonly attending it, by throwing the whole context, from ver. 18 to ver. 5 of the next chapter, both inclusive, into one unbroken paragraph. Our own exposition will proceed upon the principle heretofore applied, that this is a continuous composition, that the usual divisions are mere matters of convenience or inconvenience as the case may be, and that more harm is likely to result from too much than from too little separation of the parts. The passionate apostrophe in this clause, far from being injured or obscured, is rendered more expressive by its close connection with the previous complaints and lamentations. The idea now suggested is, that weary of complaint, the people, or the Prophet speaking for them, suddenly appeals to God directly with an ardent wish that he would deal with them as in days of old. For the construction of the optative particle לוּא, see above, on chap. xlviii. 18. The Targum and Luzzatto make it negative, as if written לא or לא, a variation which does not materially affect the sense, but merely changes the expression of a wish that something might be done, to a complaint that it is not done; "thou hast not rent the heavens," &c. The remaining words are a poetical description of Jehovah's interposition or the manifestation of his presence, under figures drawn perhaps from the account of his epiphany on Sinai. Gesenius explains נָזֹלּוּ to denote commotion; Ewald adheres to the old etymology and sense of melting.

Chapter 64

This chapter, like the one before it, from which it is in fact inseparable, has respect to the critical or turning-point between the old and new dispensations, and presents it just as it might naturally have appeared to the believing Jews, *i. e.* the first Christian converts, at that juncture. The strongest confidence is expressed in the divine power, founded upon former experience, vers. 1–3. The two great facts of Israel's rejection as a nation, and the continued existence of the church, are brought together in ver. 4. The unworthiness of Israel is acknowledged still more fullv, vers. 5, 6. The sovereign authority of God is humbly recognised, ver. 7. His favour is earnestly implored, ver. 8. The external prerogatives of Israel are lost, ver. 9. But will God for that cause cast off the true Israel, his own church or people? ver. 10.

1. *As fire kindles brush, fire boils water—to make known thy name to thine enemies, from before thee nations shall tremble.* The last clause coheres directly with the preceding verse, while the first is a parenthetical comparison; for which cause some of the latest writers throw the last words of chap. lxiii. into this sentence. This, for reasons which have been already given, is unnecessary; it is sufficient to observe the connection upon which the proposed arrangement rests. As קָדַח is both transitive and intransitive, either of two constructions may be here adopted— as a fire of brushwood burns, or, as fire kindles brush—the last of which is preferred by

most interpreters, as simpler in itself, and because *fire* is the subject of the verb in the next clause also. The various explanations of הַמָּסִים by the older writers are detailed by Vitringa and Rosenmüller. The ancient versions and several of the rabbins derive it from מָסַס, to melt, but in violation of etymological analogy. The first hint of the true sense was given by Rabbi Jonah, who pronounces it to mean dry stubble (יבֵּשׁ קַשׁ), and the definition has been since completed by the Arabic analogy. Schultens' construction of the next words, *aquæ effervescunt igne*, involves a twofold irregularity, viz. in gender and in number, which is not to be assumed without necessity. The point of comparison in both these clauses is the rapidity and ease with which the effect is produced. Hitzig supposes a specific allusion in the second to the *bouleversement* or complete transposition of the particles of boiling water, as an emblem of the general confusion which the presence of Jehovah would produce; but this is more ingenious and refined than natural. The literal effect is described in the next words, to make known thy name, *i. e.* to manifest thy being and thine attributes to thine enemies. In both parts of the sentence the construction passes as it were insensibly from the infinitive to the future, a transition not unfrequent in Hebrew syntax. The last future is supposed by the latest writers to be still dependent on the optative particle in chap. lxiii. 19, " Oh that the nations at thy presence might tremble." But as the infinitive immediately precedes, and as לוּא is there construed with the præter, it is better to regard יִרְגְּזוּ simply as a statement of what would be the effect of God's appearance.

2. *In thy doing fearful things (which) we expect not, (oh that) thou wouldst come down, (that) the mountains from before thee might flow down.* There are two very different constructions of this verse. Gesenius agrees with the English Version in making it a direct historical statement of a past event : " When thou didst terrible things which we looked not for, thou camest down, the mountains flowed down at thy presence." This seems to be the simplest possible construction ; but it is attended by a serious grammatical difficulty, viz. the necessity of referring the future נָזֹלּוּ to past time, without anything in the connection to faciliate or justify the version. On the other hand, this word appears to be decisive of the future bearing of the whole verse, and in favour of the syntax adopted by Hitzig, Ewald, and Knobel, which supposes the influence of the optative particle to be still continued through this verse, as well as that before it: (Oh that) in doing terrible things, such as we expect not, thou wouldst come down, &c. There is then no need of resorting to forced explanations of the sense in which the Prophet could speak as if he had been present at mount Sinai. The construction of the præterite with לוּא is the same as in chap. lxiii. 19.

3. *And from eternity they have not heard, they have not perceived by the ear, the eye hath not seen, a God beside thee (who) will do for (one) waiting for him.* This verse assigns a reason why such fearful things should be expected from Jehovah, namely, because he alone had proved himself able to perform them. Kimchi supplies אוּמוֹת, *nations*, as the subject of the plural verbs ; but they are really indefinite, and mean that men in general have not heard, or, as we should say, that no one has heard, or in a passive form, it has not been heard. *Do* may be either taken absolutely, or as governing *them*, *i. e.* the fearful things mentioned in ver. 2. *Waiting for God* implies faith, hope, and patient acquiescence. (See above, on chap. xl. 31.) The construction here given is the one now commonly adopted,

and is also given in the margin of the English Bible, and by Grotius and
Cocceius ; while the text of that version, with Vitringa and others, makes
אֱלֹהִים a vocative, and ascribes to God not only the doing but the knowledge of the fearful things in question.   This construction is preferred by
Vitringa, Rosenmüller, and many others, and agrees better with Paul's
quotation (2 Cor. ii. 9) of the words as descriptive of the gospel as a
mystery or something hidden till revealed by the Spirit. (Compare Rom.
xv. 26, and Mat. xiii. 17.)   But in this, as in many other cases, the
apostle, by deliberately varying the form of the expression, shews that it
was not his purpose to interpret the original passage, but simply to make
use of its terms in expressing his own thoughts on a kindred subject.
Least of all can any emendation of the text be founded upon this quotation,
such as the change of מחכי to מחבי from חבב, which, as Vitringa well
observes, although applied to the divine love for man, is inappropriate to
human love for God, not to mention the unusual construction with ל.

4. *Thou hast met with one rejoicing and executing righteousness; in thy
ways shall they remember thee; behold, thou hast been wroth, and we have
sinned; in them is perpetuity, and we shall be saved.*   There is perhaps
no sentence in Isaiah, or indeed in the Old Testament, which has more
divided and perplexed interpreters, or on which the ingenuity and learning
of the modern writers have thrown less light.   To enumerate the various
interpretations, would be endless and of no avail.   Gesenius professes to
recite them, but gives only a selection.   A more full detail is furnished by
Vitringa and Rosenmüller, and in Poole's Synopsis.   Nothing more will
here be attempted than to give the reader some idea of the various senses which
have been attached to the particular expressions, as a means of shewing
that we have at best but a choice of difficulties, and of procuring for our own
exposition a more favourable hearing than it might be thought entitled to
in other circumstances.   The first verb has been variously taken in the
sense of meeting as an enemy and meeting as a friend, making a covenant,
removing out of life, interceding, and accepting intercession.   It has been
construed as a simple affirmation, both in the past and present form ; as a
conditional expression (*si incidas*); and as the expression of a wish (*utinam
offenderes*).   The next verb has been also treated both as a direct and as a
relative expression, they will remember thee, and those who remember
thee.   *Thy ways* has been explained to mean the way of God's commandments and of his providential dispensations.   *In them* has been referred
to ways, to sins, to sufferings, to the older race of Israelites.   עולם has
been treated as a noun and as an adverb ; as meaning perpetuity, eternity,
a long time, and for ever.   נישע has been changed to נפשע, and the common
reading has been construed interrogatively (shall or could we be saved ?),
optatively (may we be saved), and indicatively, present, past, and future
(we have been, are, or shall be saved).   Of the various combinations of
these elements on record, the most important in relation to the first clause
are the following : Thou hast taken away those who rejoiced to do righteousness, and remembered thee in thy ways (Kimchi).   Thou didst accept
the intercession of those who rejoiced, &c. (Aben Ezra).   Thou didst
encounter or resist as if they had been enemies, those who rejoiced, &c.
(Cocceius).   Thou meetest as a friend him rejoicing, &c. (Jerome).   If
thou meet with or light upon one rejoicing, &c., they will remember thee in
thy ways (Vitringa).   Oh that thou mightest meet with one rejoicing, &c.
(Ros.).—Of the second clause, the following constructions may be noted :
In them (*i. e.* our sins) we have been always, and yet we shall be saved

(Jerome). We have sinned against them (*i. e.* thy ways), always, and yet have been delivered. In them (*i. e.* thy ways of mercy) there is continuance, and we are saved (Piscator). Thou wast angry after we had sinned against them (*i. e.* our fathers), and yet we are safe (Vitringa). J. D. Michaelis: we sinned an eternity (*i. e.* for ages) among them (the heathen) and apostatized (ונפשע). Lowth: thou art angry, for we have sinned; because of our deeds (במעללינו), for we have been rebellious (ונפשע). Rosenmüller: we have sinned in them (thy ways) of old, and can we be saved? Kocher: in them (our miseries) there is long continuance; oh may we be saved! Maurer: in them (the ways of duty) let us ever go, and we shall be saved. Hitzig: thou wast angry, and we sinned on that account (בהם) continually, and can we be saved? Grotius: had we been always in them (thy ways), we should have been saved. Gesenius substantially agrees with Kocher; De Wette and Umbreit with Rosenmüller; Henderson with Piscator; Ewald with Hitzig: Hendewerk with Grotius; Knobel, partly with Jerome, partly with Lowth, and partly with Kocher. It is curious enough that Vitringa, whose construction has probably never been adopted by another writer on the passage, says of it himself, *sensus facillimus et optimus ut quisque viderit.* Yet in his exposition of the very next verse he says, *ægre aspicio homines, ne videantur nihil scribere, ea in certis consignare, quae ipsi facile prævideant neminem recepturum esse.* As if to shew that exegetical invention is not yet exhausted, the ingenious modern Rabbin, Samuel Luzzatto, closes his curious notes on Isaiah, prefixed to the abridgment of Rosenmüller's Scholia, with still another exposition of this verse, and of the whole connection, which deserves to be stated, were it only for its novelty. He understands the people as denying at the close of the preceding chapter (ver. 19) that Jehovah had attested his divinity by suitable exertion of his power on their behalf. At the beginning of this chapter they correct themselves, and own that he has proved himself able to secure his ends as easily as fire kindles chaff or causes water to boil (ver. 1); but as he does not do it, this neglect is to be regarded as the cause or the occasion of their sins. They then assure him that they know his ancient deeds, even when they were not looked for (ver. 2), and can compare them not only with the impotence of idols (ver. 3), but with his present inaction: "Thou hast to do with those who remember thee as joyfully exercising righteousness in thy ways (or dispensations); oh that thou wouldst persevere in them (those ways) for ever, that we might be saved."—I shall not attempt to define what is correct and what erroneous in these various constructions, but simply to justify the one assumed in my own version. The general meaning of the sentence may be thus expressed in paraphrase: "Although thou hast cast off Israel as a nation, thou hast nevertheless met or favourably answered every one rejoicing to do righteousness, and in thy ways or future dispensations such shall still remember and acknowledge thee; thou hast been angry, and with cause, for we have sinned; but in them, thy purposed dispensations, there is perpetuity, and we shall be saved." The abrogation of the old economy, though fatal to the national pre-eminence of Israel, was so far from destroying the true church or the hopes of true believers, that it revealed the way of life more clearly than ever, and substituted for an insufficient, temporary system, a complete and everlasting one. In this construction of the sentence, the verb פָּגַע and the noun עוֹלָם are taken in their usual sense, and the pronoun in בָּהֶם refers to its natural antecedent דְּרָכֶיךָ.

5. *And we were like the unclean all of us, and like a filthy garment all our righteousness* (virtues or good works), *and we faded like the* (fading) *leaf all of us, and our iniquities like the wind will take us up* (or *carry us away*). Having shewn what they are or hope to be through the mercy of God and the righteousness of Christ, they state more fully what they are in themselves, and what they must expect to be if left to themselves. This twofold reference to their past experience and their future destiny accounts for the transition from the praeter to the future, without arbitrarily confounding them together.—Vitringa makes הַטָּמֵא descriptive of a leper, which is wholly arbitrary; the adjective appears to be used absolutely for *the unclean*, or that which is unclean, perhaps with a superlative emphasis, like הַקָּטוֹן, in chap. lx. 22. Vitringa and Gesenius dwell with great zest and fulness on the strict sense of בֶּגֶד עִדִּים. Some understand the comparison with withered leaves as a part of the description of their sin, while others apply it to their punishment. The first hypothesis is favoured by the difference of the tenses, which has been already noticed; the last by the parallelism of the clauses. It is probable, however, that here as in chap. i. 4 the two things ran together in the writer's mind, and that no refined distinction as to this point was intended. (With the figures of the last clause compare chap. lvii. 13, Ps. i. 1, Job xxvii. 21.) Hitzig and Hendewerk apply this last expression to the actual deportation of the Jews to Babylon. Vitringa, having satisfied himself that this whole context has respect to the present exile and dispersion of the Jews, takes pleasure in applying the particular expressions to the circumstances of that great affliction. It is very remarkable, however, that in this, as in other cases heretofore considered, there is no expression which admits of this application exclusively, and none which admits of it at all but for their generality and vagueness, which would equally admit an application to any other period of distress which had been previously set down as the specific subject of the prophecy.

6. *And there is no one calling on thy name, rousing himself to lay hold on thee; for thou hast hid thy face from us, and hast melted us because of* (or *by means of*) *our iniquities.* The German writers make the whole historical and retrospective, so as to throw what is here described far enough back to be the antecedent and procuring cause of the Babylonish exile. But although there is evident allusion to the past implied in the very form of the expression, the description reaches to the present also, and describes not only what the speakers were, but what they are when considered in themselves, as well as the effects of their own weakness and corruption which they have already experienced.—Calling on the name of God is here used in its proper sense of praying to him and invoking his assistance and protection; which idea is expressed still more strongly by the next phrase, rousing himself (which implies a just view of the evil, and a strenuous exertion to correct it) to lay hold upon thee,—a strong figure for attachment to a person, and reliance on him.—Lowth's version of the next words, " therefore thou hast hidden," is wholly unauthorized and wholly unnecessary, since the withdrawal of divine grace is constantly spoken of in Scripture both as the cause and the effect of men's continued alienation from God. Grotius, Cappellus, Houbigant, Lowth, and Ewald, read תְּמֹגְגֵנוּ from מָגַן, "thou hast delivered us into the hand of our iniquities." (See Gen. xiv. 20; Prov. iv. 9). This sense is also expressed by several of the ancient versions, but has probably arisen not from a difference of text, but from a wish to assi-

milate the verb to the following expression, *in the hand*. Gesenius and most of the late writers suppose מוּג in this one place to have the transitive sense of causing to dissolve, in which twofold usage it resembles the corresponding English verb, *to melt*. Hitzig notes this among the indications of a later writer, notwithstanding the analogous use of שׁוּב by Amos (ix. 14). *In the hand* may either mean by means of, in the midst of, or because of; or we may suppose with Rosenmüller that the phrase strictly means, thou dost melt us into the hand of our iniquities, *i. e.* subject us to them, make us unable to resist them, and passively submissive to their power.

7. *And now, Jehovah, our father (art) thou, we the clay and thou our potter, and the work of thy hand (are) we all.* Instead of relying upon any supposed merits of their own, they appeal to their very dependence upon God as a reason why he should have mercy on them. Lowth follows two editions and five manuscripts in reading אַתָּה twice, which repetition has great force, he thinks, whereas the other word may well be spared. In other cases where a word is repeated in the common text, he substitutes a different one, because the repetition is inelegant. The Bishop's judgment upon such points was continually warped by his predominant desire to change the text. He overlooked in this case the obvious use of *now*, not merely as a particle of time, but as a formula of logical resumption, which could not be omitted without obscuring the relation of this verse to the preceding context, as a summing up of its appeals and arguments. Vitringa regards אַתָּה as the origin of the Homeric ἄττα, τέττα; but the Hebrew word is not expressive of endearment, it is absolutely necessary to the sense. The Prophet here resumes the thought of chap. lxiii. 16, where, as here, the paternity ascribed to God is not that of natural creation in the case of individuals, but the creation of the church or chosen people, and of Israel as a spiritual and ideal person. The figure of the potter and the clay, implying absolute authority and power, is used twice before (chap. xxix. 6, xlv. 9), and is one of the connecting links between this book and the acknowledged Isaiah. —There is more dignity in the original expression than in the English phrase *our potter*, as the Hebrew word properly denotes one forming or imparting shape to anything, though specially applied in usage to a workman in clay, when that material is mentioned. Lowth retains the general meaning, but in order to avoid the ambiguity attending the word *former*, treats it as a finite verb, *thou hast formed* us, which is clear enough, but inexact and drawling. The use of the word *all* in this verse, and its emphatic repetition in the next, exclude the application of the passage to an idolatrous party in the Babylonish exile, even if that limitation would be otherwise admissible. The same plea, derived from the relation of the creature to the maker, is used in Ps. cxxxviii. 8, *forsake not the work of thy hands*. (Compare Ps. lxxvi. 1, lxxix. 1). In either case there is a tacit appeal to the covenant and promise in Gen. xvii. 7; Lev. xxvi. 42–45; Deut. vii. 6, xxvi. 17, 18.

8. *Be not angry, O Jehovah, to extremity, and do not to eternity remember guilt; lo, look, we pray thee, thy people (are) we all.* This is the application of the argument presented in the foregoing verse, the actual prayer founded on the fact there stated. The common version of עַד־מְאֹד (*very sore*) fails to reproduce the form of the original expression, as consisting of a preposition and a noun. This is faithfully conveyed in Lowth's version (*to the uttermost*), and still more in Henderson's (*to excess*); although the latter is objectionable as suggesting the idea of injustice or moral wrong, which is avoided in the version above given. The first defect is also

chargeable upon the common version of לָעַד, *for ever;* which, although a fair equivalent, and perfectly sufficient in all ordinary cases, is neither so exact nor so expressive as the literal translation in the case before us, where there seems to be an intentional regard to the peculiar form and sound as well as to the meaning of the sentence. The common version is besides defective, or at least ambiguous, in seeming to make הֵן a verb and נָא a particle of time ; whereas the former is an interjection, and the latter the peculiar Hebrew formula of courteous or importunate entreaty.

9. *Thy holy cities are a desert, Zion is a desert, Jerusalem a waste.* By holy cities, Grotius understands the towns of Judah ; Vitringa, Jerusalem alone, considered as consisting of two towns, the upper and the lower, here called Zion and Jerusalem, though each of these names sometimes comprehends the whole, and the latter is dual in its very form. Gesenius cites Ps. lxxviii. 54, to shew that even the frontier of the land was reckoned holy, and that its cities might be naturally so described likewise. But the question is not one of possibility or propriety, but of actual usage; not what they might be called, but what they are called. The passage in the Psalms, moreover, is itself too doubtful to throw light upon the one before us. A better argument is that of Hitzig, in his note on chap. lxiii. 18, drawn from the use of the phrase אדמת קדש by Zechariah (ii. 16), in application to the whole. Even this, however, is not conclusive ; since the writer, if he had intended to employ the terms in this wide sense, would hardly have confined his specifications in the other clause to Zion and Jerusalem. In any case, these must be regarded as the chief if not the only subjects of his proposition.—There is something worthy of attention in the use here made of the substantive verb היה. To express mere present existence, Hebrew usage employs no verb at all, though the pronoun which would be its subject is occasionally introduced. The preterite form of the verb as here used must either have the sense of *was,* in reference to a definite time past, or *has been,* implying a continuation of the same state till the present. The former meaning is excluded, and the latter rendered necessary, by the obvious allusions in the context to the evils mentioned as being still experienced. To express the idea *has become,* which is given in some versions, usage would require the verb to be connected with the noun by the preposition ל. On the whole, the true sense of the verse, expressed or implied, appears to be that Zion has long been a desolation and Jerusalem a waste.

10. *Our house of holiness and beauty (in) which our fathers praised thee has been burned up with fire, and all our delights (or desirable places) have become a desolation.* The elliptical use of the relative in reference to place is the same as in Gen. xxxix. 20. *Burned up,* literally, become a burning of fire, as in chap. ix. 6. The reference in this verse is of course to the destruction of the temple, but to which destruction is disputed. The modern Germans all refer it to the Babylonian conquest, when the temple, as we are expressly told, was burnt (Jer. lii. 13) ; Grotius to its profanation by Antiochus Epiphanes, at which time, however, it was not consumed by fire ; Vitringa and many later writers, with the Jews themselves, to its destruction by the Romans, since which the city and the land have lain desolate. To the first and last of these events the words are equally appropriate. Either hypothesis being once assumed, the particular expressions admit of being easily adapted to it. With our own hypothesis the passage may be reconciled in several different ways. There is nothing, however, in the terms themselves, or in the analogy of prophetic language,

to forbid our understanding this as a description of the desolations of the church itself expressed by figures borrowed from the old economy, and from the ancient history of Israel.   If literally understood, the destruction of the temple and the holy city may be here lamented as a loss not merely to the Jewish nation, but to the church of God to which they rightfully belong and by which they ought yet to be recovered, a sense of which obligation blended with some superstitious errors gave occasion to the fanatical attempt of the Crusades.   (See above, on chap. lxiii. 18.)

12. *Wilt thou for these* (*things*) *restrain thyself, O Jehovah, wilt thou keep silence and afflict us to extremity?*   This is simply another application of the argument by way of an importunate appeal to the divine compassions. Self-restraint and silence, as applied to God, are common figures for in-action and apparent indifference to the interests, and especially the sufferings, of his people.   (See above, on chap. xlii. 14, and lxiii. 15.)   The question is not whether God will remain silent in spite of what his people suffered, but whether the loss of their external advantages will induce him to forsake them.   The question as in many other cases implies a negation of the strongest kind.   The destruction of the old theocracy was God's own act, and was designed to bring the church under a new and far more glorious dispensation.   How the loss of a national organisation and pre-eminence was to be made good is fully stated in the following chapter.

Chapter 65

THE great enigma of Israel's simultaneous loss and gain is solved by a prediction of the calling of the Gentiles, ver. 1.   This is connected with the obstinate unfaithfulness of the chosen people, ver. 2.   They are repre-sented under the two main aspects of their character at different periods, as gross idolaters and as pharisaical bigots, vers. 3–5.   Their casting off was not occasioned by the sins of one generation, but of many, vers. 6, 7. But even in this rejected race there was a chosen remnant, in whom the promises shall be fulfilled, vers. 8–10.   He then reverts to the idolatrous Jews, and threatens them with condign punishment, vers. 11, 12.   The fate of the unbelieving carnal Israel is compared with that of the true spiritual Israel, vers. 13–16.   The gospel economy is described as a new creation, ver. 17.   Its blessings are represented under glowing figures bor-rowed from the old dispensation, vers. 18, 19.   Premature death shall be no longer known, ver. 20.   Possession and enjoyment shall no longer be precarious, vers. 21–23.   Their very desires shall be anticipated, ver. 24. All animosities and noxious influences shall cease for ever, ver. 25.

1. *I have been inquired of by those that asked not, I have been found by those that sought me not, I have said, Behold me, behold me, to a nation* (*that*) *was not called by my name.*   There is an apparent inconsistency between the first two members of the sentence in the English Version, arising from the use of the same verb (*sought*), to express two very different Hebrew verbs.   בִּקַּשׁ is here used in the general sense of *seeking* or trying to ob-tain, דָּרַשׁ in the technical religious sense of *consulting* as an oracle.   In the latter case, the difficulty of translation is enhanced by the peculiar form of the original, not simply passive, but reflexive, and capable of being ren-dered in our idiom only by periphrasis.   The exact sense seems to be, I allowed myself to be consulted, I afforded access to myself for the purpose of consultation.   This is not a mere conjectural deduction from the form

of the Hebrew verb or from general analogy, but a simple statement of the actual usage of this very word, as when Jehovah says again and again of the ungodly exiles that he will not be inquired of or consulted by them (Ezek. xiv. 3, xx. 3), *i. e.* with effect or to any useful purpose. In this connection it is tantamount to saying that he will not hear them, answer them, or reveal himself to them; all which or equivalent expressions have been used by different writers in the translation of the verse before us. There is nothing therefore incorrect in substance, though the form be singular, in the Septuagint version of this verb, retained in the New Testament, viz. ἐμφανὴς ἐγενήθην, I became manifest, *i. e.* revealed myself. The object of the verb *asked*, if exact uniformity be deemed essential, may be readily supplied from the parallel expression *sought me.*—*Behold me*, or, as it is sometimes rendered in the English Bible, *here I am*, is the usual idiomatic Hebrew answer to a call by name, and when ascribed to God, contains an assurance of his presence, rendered more emphatic by the repetition. (See above, chap. lii. 6, lviii. 9.) It is therefore equivalent to being inquired of, and being found. This last expression has occurred before in chap. lv. 6, and, as here, in combination with the verb *to seek.* *A people not called by my name, i.e.* not recognised or known as my people. (See above, chap. xlviii. 2.) All interpreters agree that this is a direct continuation of the foregoing context, and most of them regard it as the answer of Jehovah to the expostulations and petitions there presented by his people. The modern Germans and the Jews apply both this verse and the next to Israel. The obvious objection is, that Israel even in its worst estate could never be described as a nation which had not been called by the name of Jehovah. Jarchi's solution of this difficulty, namely, that they treated him as if they were not called by his name, is an evasion, tending to destroy the force of language, and confound all its distinctions. It is a standing characteristic of the Jews in the Old Testament, that they were called by the name of Jehovah; but if they may also be described in terms directly opposite, wherever the interpreter prefers it, then may anything mean anything. With equal right may we allege that the seed of Abraham in chap. xli. 8 means those who act as if they were his seed, and that the nation who had never known Messiah (chap. lv. 5) means a nation that might just as well have never known him. On the other hand, Kimchi's explanation of the clause as meaning that they were unwilling to be called his people, is as much at variance with the facts of history as Jarchi's with the principles of language. In all their alienations, exiles, and dispersions, the children of Israel have still retained that title as their highest glory and the badge of all their tribes. The incongruity of this interpretation of the first verse is admitted by Rabbi Moshe Haccohen among the Jews, and by Hendewerk among the Germans, the last of whom pronounces it impossible, and therefore understands the passage as applying to the Persians under Cyrus, who, without any previous relation to Jehovah, had been publicly and honourably called into his service. A far more obvious and natural application may be made to the Gentiles generally, whose vocation is repeatedly predicted in this book, and might be here used with powerful effect in proof that the rejection of the Jews was the result of their own obstinate perverseness, not of God's unfaithfulness or want of power. This is precisely Paul's interpretation of the passage in Rom. ix. 20, 21, where he does not, as in many other cases, merely borrow the expressions of the Prophet, but formally interprets them, applying this verse to the Gentiles, and then adding, " but to Israel (or of Israel) he saith " what follows in the next verse. The same intention to expound the

Prophet's language is clear from the Apostle's mention of Isaiah's boldness in thus shocking the most cherished prepossessions of the Jews. Grotius takes no notice of this apostolic interpretation, but applies both verses to the Jews in Babylon, although Abarbenel himself had been constrained to abandon it, and understand the passage as referring to the Jews in Egypt. Gesenius merely pleads for the reference to Babylon as equally admissible with that which Paul makes, and as better suited to the context in Isaiah. Hitzig as usual goes further, and declares it to be evident (*offenbar*) that the words relate only to the Jews as alienated from Jehovah. This contempt for Paul's authority is less surprising in a writer who describes Jehovah's answer to the expostulations of the people as moving in a circle, and pronounces both incompetent to solve the question, why Jehovah should entice men into sin and then punish them. Instead of קֹרָא Lowth reads קָרָא (never invoked my name) on the authority of the Septuagint (ἐκάλεσαν). The last clause is not included in Paul's quotation.

2. *I have spread* (or *stretched*) *out my hands all the day* (or *every day*) *to a rebellious people, those going the way not good, after their own thoughts* (or *designs*). The gesture mentioned in the first clause is variously explained as a gesture of simple calling, of instruction, of invitation, of persuasion. According to Hitzig it is an offer of help on God's part, corresponding to the same act as a prayer for help on man's. (See chap. i. 15.) All agree that it implies a gracious offer of himself and of his favour to the people. Whether *all the day* or *every day* be the correct translation, the idea meant to be conveyed is evidently that of frequent repetition, or rather of unremitting constancy. There is no need of supposing, with Vitringa and others, that it specifically signifies the period of the old dispensation. The rebellious people is admitted upon all hands to be Israel. The last clause is an amplification and explanatory paraphrase of the first. *Going* and *way* are common figures for the course of life. A *way not good*, is a litotes or meiosis for a bad or for the worst way. (See Ps. xxxvi. 5, Ezek. xxxvi. 31. *Thoughts*, not opinions merely, but devices and inventions of wickedness. (See above, on chap. lv. 7.) With this description compare that of Moses, Deut. xxxii. 5, 6.

3. *The people angering me to my face continually, sacrificing in the gardens, and censing on the bricks.* We have now a more detailed description of the *way not good*, and the *devices* mentioned in the foregoing verse. The construction is continued, *the people provoking me*, &c., being in direct apposition with the *rebellious people going*, &c. *To my face*, not secretly or timidly (Job xxxi. 27), but openly and in defiance of me (chap. iii. 9, Job i. 11), which is probably the meaning of *before me* in the first commandment (Exod. xx. 3). Animal offerings and fumigations are combined to represent all kinds of sacrifice. As to the idolatrous use of groves and gardens, see above, on chap. lvii. 5, vol. i. p. 94. Vitringa's distinction between groves and gardens is gratuitous, the Hebrew word denoting any enclosed and carefully cultivated ground, whether chiefly occupied by trees or not. Of the last words, *on the bricks*, there are four interpretations. The first is that of many older writers, who suppose an allusion to the prohibition in Exod. xx. 24, 25. But bricks are not there mentioned, and can hardly come under the description of " hewn stone," besides the doubt which overhangs the application of that law, and especially the cases in which it was meant to operate. This evil is not remedied but rather aggravated, by supposing an additional allusion to Lev. xxvi. 1, and Num. xxxiii. 52, as Grotius does, and understanding by *the bricks* such as were impressed with

unlawful decorations or inscriptions. A second hypothesis is that of
Bochart, who supposes bricks to mean roofing-tiles (Mark ii. 4, Luke v. 19),
and the phrase to be descriptive of idolatry as practised on the roofs of
houses. (2 Kings xxiii. 12, Jer. xix. 13, xxxii. 29, Zeph. i. 5.) Ewald
approves of this interpretation, and, to make the parallelism perfect,
changes גַּנּוֹת, *gardens*, to גַּגּוֹת, *roofs*. Vitringa's objection to this reading,
drawn from the analogy of chap. i. 29, and lvi. 17, is converted by Ewald into
a reason for it, by supposing the common text to have arisen from assimilation. An objection not so easily disposed of is the one alleged by Knobel,
namely, that Hebrew usage would require a different preposition before גַּגּוֹת.
A third hypothesis is that of Rosenmüller, who supposes an allusion to
some practice now unknown, but possibly connected with the curiously
inscribed bricks found in modern times near the site of ancient Babylon.
Gesenius hesitates between this and a fourth interpretation, much the
simplest and most natural of all, viz., that the phrase means nothing more
than altars, or at most altars slightly and hastily constructed. Of such
altars bricks may be named as the materials, or tiles as the superficial
covering.

4. *Sitting in the graves and in the holes they will lodge, eating the flesh of
swine, and broth of filthy things (is in) their vessels.* All agree that this
verse is intended to depict, in revolting colours, the idolatrous customs of
the people. Nor is there much doubt as to the construction of the sentence,
or the force of the particular expressions. But the obscurity which overhangs the usage referred to affords full scope to the archaeological propen-
sities of modern commentators, some of whom pass by in silence questions
of the highest exegetical importance, while they lavish without stint or
scruple, time and labour, ingenuity and learning, on a vain attempt to settle
questions which throw no light on the drift of the passage, nor even on the
literal translation of the words, but are investigated merely for their own
sake or their bearing upon other objects, so that Rosenmüller interrupts
himself in one of these antiquarian inquiries by saying, " sed redeamus ad
locum vatis in quo explicando versamur." Such are the questions, whether
these idolaters sat in the graves or among them ; whether for necromantic
purposes, *i. e.* to interrogate the dead, or to perform sacrificial rites to their
memory, or to obtain demoniacal inspiration ; whether נְצוּרִים means monuments, or caves, or temples ; whether they were lodged in for licentious
purposes, or to obtain prophetic dreams ; whether they are charged with
simply eating pork for food, or after it had been sacrificed to idols ;
whether swine's flesh was forbidden for medicinal reasons or because the
heathen sacrificed and ate it, or on other grounds ; whether פרק means
broth or bits of meat, and if the former, whether it was so called on account
of the bread broken in it, or for other reasons, &c. The only question of
grammatical construction which has found a place among these topics of
pedantic disquisition, is as such entitled to consideration, though of small
importance with respect to the interpretation of the passage. It is the
question whether כְּלֵיהֶם is to be governed by a preposition understood
(Rosenmüller), or explained as an accusative of place (Gesenius), or as the
predicate of the proposition, *broth of abominable meats are their vessels*
(Maurer). This last construction is retained by Knobel, but he changes
the whole meaning of the clause by explaining the last word to mean *their
instruments* or *implements*, and giving to פרק the sense of *bits* or *pieces :*
" pieces of abominable meat are their instruments of divination," in allusion
to the mantic inspection of the sacrificial victims by the heathen priests as

means of ascertaining future events. Even if we should successively adopt and then discard every one of the opinions, some of which have now been mentioned, the essential meaning of the verse would still remain the same, as a highly wrought description of idolatrous abominations.

5. *The (men) saying, Keep to thyself, come not near to me, for I am holy to thee, these (are) a smoke in my wrath, a fire burning all the day* (or *every day*). Gesenius's obscure addition, *und nocht sagt*, is faithfully transcribed by Noyes, *who yet say.* The peculiar phrase, קְרַב אֵלָיך, is analogous, but not precisely equivalent to נִשָּׁה־לִי in chap. xlix. 20. (See above, p. 239.) The literal translation is *approach to thyself;* and as this implies removal from the speaker, the essential meaning is correctly expressed, though in a very different form from the original, both by the Septuagint (πόῤῥω ἀπ' ἐμοῦ) and by the Vulgate (*recede a me*). The common English version (*stand by thyself*), and Henderson's improvement of it (*keep by thyself*), both suggest an idea not contained in the original, viz. that of standing alone, whereas all that is expressed by the Hebrew phrase is the act of standing away from the speaker, for which Lowth has found the idiomatic equivalent (*keep to thyself*). Another unusual expression is קְרַשְׁתִּיך, which may be represented by the English words, *I am holy thee.* The Targum resolves this into קדשתי ממך, and Vitringa accordingly assumes an actual ellipsis of the preposition מִן as a particle of comparison. But as this ellipsis is extremely rare, De Dieu and Cocceius assume that of לְ, *I am holy to thee.* Gesenius adopts the same construction, but explains the לְ as a mere pleonasm, and translates accordingly, *I am holy*, which is merely omitting what cannot be explained. The particle no doubt expresses general relation, and the phrase means, *I am holy with respect to thee;* and as this implies comparison, the same sense is attained as by the old construction, but in a manner more grammatical and regular. The implied comparison enables us to reconcile two of the ancient versions as alike in spirit, although in letter flatly contradictory. The Septuagint has *I am pure* (*i. e.* in comparison with thee); the Vulgate, *Thou art impure* (*i. e.* in comparison with me). There is no need, therefore, of resorting to the forced explanation proposed by Thenius in a German periodical, which takes קָרַשְׁתִּי in the sense of *separating,* one which occurs nowhere else in actual usage, and is excluded even from the Etymon, by some of the best modern lexicographers. Equally gratuitous is Hitzig's explanation of the verb (in which he seems to have been anticipated by Luther) as transitive, and meaning *lest I hallow thee, i. e.* by touching thee, a notion contradictory to that expressed in Haggai ii. 12, 13, and affording no good sense here, as the fear of making others holy, whether as an inconvenience or a benefit, would hardly have been used to characterise the men described. As to the question, Who are here described ? there are two main opinions : first, that the clause relates to the idolaters mentioned in the foregoing verses ; the other, that it is descriptive of a wholly different class. On the first supposition, Gesenius imagines that Jewish converts to the Parsee religion are described as looking at their former brethren with contempt. On the other, Henderson assumes that the Prophet, having first described the idolatrous form of Jewish apostasy, as it existed in his own day and long after, then describes the pharisaical form of the same evil, as it existed in the time of Christ, both being put together as the cause of the rejection of the Jews. To any specific application of the passage to the Babylonish exile, it may be objected that the practice of idolatry at that time by the Jews can only be established by a begging of the question in expounding this and certain

parallel passages. The other explanation is substantially the true one. The great end which the Prophet had in view was to describe the unbelieving Jews as abominable in the sight of God. His manner of expressing this idea is poetical, by means of figures drawn from various periods of their history, without intending to exhibit either of these periods exclusively. To a Hebrew writer what could be more natural than to express the idea of religious corruption by describing its subjects as idolaters, diviners, eaters of swine's flesh, worshippers of outward forms, and self-righteous hypocrites? Of such the text declares God's abhorrence. Smoke and fire may be taken as natural concomitants and parallel figures, as if he had said, against whom my wrath smokes and burns continually. Or the smoke may represent the utter consumption of the object, and the fire the means by which it is effected, which appears to have been Luther's idea. That אַף in such connections does not mean the nose, but wrath itself, has been shewn in the exposition of chap. xlviii. 9. (See above, p. 215.)

6, 7. *Lo, it is written before me. I will not rest except I repay, and I will repay into their bosom your iniquities and the iniquities of your fathers together, saith Jehovah, who burned incense on the mountains, and on the hills blasphemed me, and I will measure their first work into their bosom.* The particle at the beginning calls attention both to the magnitude and certainty of the event about to be predicted.—Lowth, for some reason unexplained, thinks proper to translate כְּתוּבָה *is recorded in writing*, which is abridged by Noyes to *stands recorded*, and still more by Henderson to *is recorded*. One step further in the same direction brings us back to the simple and perfectly sufficient version of the English Bible, *it is written*. This may serve as an instructive sample of the way in which the later English versions sometimes improve upon the old. The figure which these verbs express is variously understood by different writers. Umbreit seems to think that what is said to be written is the eternal law of retribution. Hitzig and Knobel understand by it a *book of remembrance* (Mal. iii. 16), *i. e.* a record of the sins referred to afterwards, by which they are kept perpetually present to the memory of Jehovah (Daniel vii. 10). Vitringa and most later writers understand by it a record, not of crime, but of its punishment, or rather of the purpose or decree to punish it (Daniel v. 5. 24), in reference to the written judgments of the ancient courts (chap. x. 1). This last interpretation does not necessarily involve the supposition that the thing here said to be written is the threatening which immediately follows, although this is by no means an unnatural construction.—*I will not rest* or *be silent*, an expression used repeatedly before in reference to the seeming inaction or indifference of Jehovah. (See above, chaps. xlii. 14, lvii. 11 ; and compare Ps. l. 21, Hab. i. 13.)—Gesenius and De Wette follow the older writers in translating, *I will not keep silence, but will recompense*. But although כִּי אָם, like the German *sondern*, is the usual adversative after a negation, this construction of the preterite שִׁלַּמְתִּי would be contrary to usage, and כִּי אָם must be construed, as it usually is, before the preterite, as meaning unless or until, in which sense it is accurately rendered both by Hitzig (*bis*) and Ewald (*ausser*). See above, on chap. lv. 10, where this same construction is gratuitously set aside by Hitzig on the ground that it would argue too much knowledge of natural philosophy in a Hebrew writer. (Compare also 2 Sam. i. 18.)—For *repay into their bosom*, we have in the seventh verse *measure into their bosom*, which affords a clue to the origin and real meaning of the figure; as we read that Boaz said to Ruth, " Bring the veil (or cloak) that is upon thee and hold it, and she held it, and he measured six (measures of) barley, and laid it on her" (Ruth iii. 15). Hence the phrase to measure into any one's bosom, *i. e.* into the lap, or the fold of the garment covering the bosom (See above, on chap. xlix. 22). The same figure is employed by Jer. xxxii. 18, and in Ps. lxxix. 12, and is explained by Rosenmüller in his Scholia on the latter, and by Winer in his Lexicon, as implying abundance, or a greater quantity than one could carry in the hand. (Compare Luke vi. 38.) But Gesenius and Maurer understand the main idea to be not that of abundance, but of retribution, anything being said to return into one's own bosom, just as it is elsewhere said to return upon his own head (Judges ix. 57, Ps. vii. 17). Both these accessory ideas are appropriate in the case before us. In Jer. xxxii. 18, and Ps. lxxix. 12, the preposition אֶל is used, and the same form is also found here in some manuscripts, and even in the Masora upon the next verse, though the עַל is no more likely to be wrong there than here, nor at all, according to Maurer, who explains it as denoting motion towards an object from above. The sudden change from *their* to *your* at the beginning of ver. 7, has been commonly explained as an example of the *enallage personæ* so frequently occurring in Isaiah. This supposition is undoubtedly sufficient to remove all difficulty from the syntax. It is possible, however, that the change is not a mere grammatical anomaly or licence of construction, but significant, and intended to distinguish between three generations. I will repay into their bosom (that of your descendants) your iniquities, and the iniquities of your fathers. If this be not a fanciful distinction, it gives colour to Henderson's opinion that the previous description brings to view successively the gross idolatry of early times, and the pharisaical hypocrisy prevailing at the time of Christ. Supposing his contemporaries to be the immediate objects of address, there would then be a distinct allusion to their idolatrous progenitors, the measure of whose guilt they filled up (Mat. xxiii. 32), and to their children, upon whom it was to be conspicuously visited (Luke xxiv. 28). But whether this be so or not, the meaning of the text is obvious, as teaching that the guilt which had accumulated through successive generations should be visited, though not exclusively, upon the last. The whole of idolatry is here summed up in *burning incense on the mountains*, which are elsewhere mentioned as a favourite resort of those who worshipped idols (chap. lvii. 7, Jer. iii. 6, Ezek. vi. 13, xviii. 6, Hosea iv. 13), and *blaspheming God upon the hills*, which may either be regarded as a metaphorical description of idolatry itself, or strictly taken to denote the oral expression of contempt for Jehovah and his worship, which might naturally be expected to accompany such practices.—There is some obscurity in the word רִאשֹׁנָה as here used. Ewald takes it as an adverb, meaning first, or at first (*zuerst*), and appears to understand the clause as meaning, *their reward* (that of your fathers) *will I measure first into their bosom*. But this does not seem to agree with the previous declaration that the sons should suffer for the fathers' guilt and for their own together. At the same time the construction is less natural and obvious than that of Gesenius and other writers, who make רִאשֹׁנָה an adjective agreeing with פְעֻלָה, *their former work*, *i. e.* its product or reward, as in chap. xl. 10. (See above, p. 100.) The only sense in which it can be thus described is that of ancient, as distinguished, not from the subsequent transgressions of the fathers, but from those of the children who came after them.—According to the sense which the apostle puts upon the two first verses of this chapter, we may understand those now before us as predicting the excision of the Jews from the communion imagine that the Jews will again become actual idolaters," as if the strict interpretation of this verse would not itself afford a reason not for imagining but for believing that it will be so. But rather than admit this, he declares that " all attempts to explain *Gad* and *Meni* of idols literally taken, are aside from the point." From what point they are thus aside does not appear, unless it be the point of making half the prophecy a loose metaphorical description, and cutting the remainder to the quick by a rigorously literal interpretation." "Israel," " Jerusalem," "the land," *must* all denote the " Israel," " Jerusalem," and " land" of ancient times and of the old economy ; but all attempts to explain Gad and Meni of idols literally taken are aside from the point. And thus we are brought to the curious result of one literal interpretation excluding another as impossible. The true sense of the passage seems to be the same as in vers. 3–7, where Henderson himself regards the prophet as completing his description of the wickedness of Israel, by circumstances drawn from different periods of his history, such as the idolatrous period, the pharisaical period, &c.

12. *And I have numbered you to the sword, and all of you to the slaughter shall bow ; because I called and ye did not answer, I spake and ye did not hear, and ye did the* (thing that was) *evil in my eyes, and that which I desired not ye chose.* The preceding verse having reference only to the present and the past, the *Vav* at the beginning of this can have no conversive influence upon the verb, which is therefore to be rendered as a preterite. The objections to making it the sign of the apodosis have been already stated. The paraphrastic version, *therefore*, is entirely gratuitous. Gesenius gives the verb in this one place the diluted sense of allotting or appointing ; but the strict sense of numbering or counting is not only admissible, but necessary to express a portion of the writer's meaning, namely, the idea that they should be cut off one by one, or rather one with another, *i. e.* all without exception. (See chap. xxvii. 12, and vol. i. p. 442.) Knobel, indeed, imagines that a universal slaughter cannot be intended, because he goes on to tell what shall befall the survivors, viz. hunger, thirst, disgrace, distress, &c. Hitzig had taste enough to see that these are not described as subsequent in time to the evils threatened in the verse before us, but specifications of the way in which that threatening should be executed. The sense above given to מָנִיתִי is confirmed and illustrated by its application elsewhere to the numbering of sheep. (Jer. xxxiii. 13.) In its use here there is evident allusion to its derivative מְנִי in the preceding verse, which some of the German writers try to make perceptible to German readers by combining cognate nouns and verbs, such as *Shicksal* and *schicke*, *Verhängniss* and *verhänge*, *Bestimmung* and *bestimme*, &c. The same effect, if it were worth the while, might be produced in English by the use of *destiny* and *destine*. Vitringa, in order to identify the figures of the first and second clauses, makes חֶרֶב mean a butcher's knife ; but an opposite assimilation would be better, namely, that of making טֶבַח mean slaughter in general, not that of the slaughter-house exclusively. Both sword and slaughter are familiar figures for violent destruction. The verb כָּרַע is also applied elsewhere to one slain by violence (Judges v. 27, 2 Kings ix. 24). Bowing or stooping to the slaughter is submitting to it either willingly or by compulsion. Gesenius takes טֶבַח in the local sense of *Schlachtbank*, to suit which he translates the verb *kneel*, and the particle *before*. This last Noyes retains without the others, in the English phrase *bow down before the slaughter*, which is either unmeaning, or conveys a false idea, that of priority in time. The remainder of the verse assigns the reason of the threatened

punishment. The first expression bears a strong resemblance to the words of Wisdom, in Prov. i. 24–31. Knobel's explanation of the "thing that was evil in my eyes" as a description of idolatry, is as much too restricted as Vitringa's explanation of "that which I desired not or delighted not in" as signifying ritual or formal as opposed to spiritual worship. Of the two the former has the least foundation, as the only proof cited is chap. xxxviii. 8, whereas Vitringa's explanation of the other phrase derives no little countenance from Ps. xl. 7, li. 18, Hos. vi. 6. The only objection to either is that it mistakes a portion of the true sense for the whole.—As to the application of the words, there is the usual confidence and contradiction. Knobel regards them as a threatening of captivity and execution to the Jews who took sides with the Babylonians against Cyrus. Henderson applies them to the inevitable and condign punishment of those Jews who shall prefer the pleasures of sin to those of true religion embraced by the great body of the nation, which punishment, he adds, "will, *in all probability*, be inflicted upon them in common with the members of the anti-christian confederacy, after their believing brethren shall have been securely settled in Palestine." The grounds of this all probable anticipation are not given. Vitringa understands the passage as predicting the excision of the Jewish nation from the church, not only for the crowning sin of rejecting Christ, but for their aggregate offences as idolaters and hypocrites, as rebels against God and despisers of his mercy, with which sins they are often charged in the Old Testament (*e. g.* chaps. l. 2; lxv. 2; lxvi. 4; Jer. vii. 13, 25), and still more pointedly by Christ himself in several of his parables and other discourses, some of which remarkably resemble that before us both in sentiment and language. (See Mat. xxiii. 37, xxii. 7, Luke xix. 27, and compare Acts xiii. 46). Besides the countenance which this analogy affords to Vitringa's exposition, it is strongly recommended by its strict agreement with what we have determined, independently of this place, to be the true sense of the whole foregoing context. Interpreted by these harmonious analogies, the verse, instead of threatening the destruction of the Babylonish Jews before the advent, or of the wicked Jews and Antichrist hereafter, is a distinct prediction of a far more critical event than either, the judicial separation of the Jewish nation and the Israel of God which had for ages seemed inseparable, not to say identical.

13, 14. *Therefore thus saith the Lord Jehovah, Lo! my servants shall eat and ye shall hunger; lo, my servants shall drink and ye shall thirst; lo, my servants shall rejoice and ye shall be ashamed; lo, my servants shall shout from gladness of heart, and ye shall cry from grief of heart, and from brokenness of spirit ye shall howl.* These verses merely carry out the general threatening of the one preceding, in a series of poetical antithesis, where hunger, thirst, disgrace, and anguish, take the place of sword and slaughter, and determine these to be symbolical or emblematic terms. Knobel's interpretation of these verses as predicting bodily privations and hard bondage to those who should escape the sword of Cyrus, is entitled to as little deference as he would pay to the suggestion of Vitringa, that the eating and drinking have specific reference to the joy with which the first Christian converts partook of the Lord's supper (Acts. ii. 46, xx. 7). This is no doubt chargeable with undue refinement and particularity, but notwithstanding this excess, the exposition is correct in principle. as we may learn from the frequent use of these antagonistic metaphors to signify spiritual joy and horror, not only in the Prophets (see above, chaps. viii. 21, xxxiii. 16, lv. 1, lviii. 14), but by our Saviour when he speaks of his dis-

of Achor a lair of herds, for my people who have sought me. This is a repetition of the promise in the foregoing verse, rendered more specific by the mention of one kind of prosperity, viz. that connected with the raising of cattle, and of certain places where it should be specially enjoyed, viz. the valley of Achor and the plain of Sharon. Two reasons have been given for the mention of these places, one derived from their position, the other from their quality. As the valley of Achor was near Jericho and Jordan, and the plain of Sharon on the Mediterranean, between Joppa and Cesarea, some suppose that they are here combined to signify the whole breadth of the land, from East to West. And as Sharon was proverbial for its verdure and fertility (see above, chaps. xxxiii. 9, xxxv. 2), it is inferred by some that Achor was so likewise, which they think is the more probable because Hosea says that the valley of Achor shall be a door of hope (Hos. ii. 17). But this may have respect to the calamity which Israel experienced there at his first entrance on the land of promise (Joshua vii. 26), so that where his troubles then began, his hopes shall now begin. For these or other reasons Sharon and Achor are here mentioned in Isaiah's characteristic manner, as samples of the whole land, or its pastures, just as flocks and herds are used as images of industry and wealth, derived from the habits of the patriarchial age. That this is the correct interpretation of the flocks and herds, is not disputed even by the very writers who insist upon the literal construction of the promise that the seed of Jacob shall possess the land, as guaranteeing the collection of the Jews into the region which their fathers once inhabited. By what subtle process the absolute necessity of literal interpretation is transformed into a very large discretion when the change becomes convenient, is a question yet to be determined.—That to *seek Jehovah* sometimes has specific reference to repentance and conversion, on the part of those who have been alienated from him, may be seen by a comparison of chaps. ix. 12, and lv. 6.

11. *And (as for) you, forsakers of Jehovah, the (men) forgetting my holy mountain, the (men) setting for Fortune a table, and the men filling for Fate a mingled draught.* This is only a description of the object of address; the address itself is contained in the next verse. The form וְאַתֶּם indicates a contrast with what goes before, as in chap. iii. 14. The class of persons meant is first described as forsakers of Jehovah and forgetters of his holy mountain. Rosenmüller understands this as a figurative name for the despisers of his worship; but Knobel, as a literal description of those exiles who had lost all affection for Jerusalem, and had no wish to return thither. The description of the same persons in the last clause is much more obscure, and has occasioned a vast amount of learned disquisition and discussion. The commentators on the passage who have gone most fully into the details, are Vitringa and Rosenmüller ; but the clearest summary is furnished by Gesenius. The strangest exposition of the clause is that of Zeltner, in a dissertation on the verse (1715), in which he applies it to the modern Jews as a prolific and an avaricious race. Many interpreters have understood the two most important words (גַּד and מְנִי) as common nouns denoting *troop* and *number* (the former being the sense put upon the name *Gad*, in Gen. xxx. 11), and referred the whole clause either to convivial assemblies, perhaps connected with idolatrous worship, or to the troop of planets and the multitude of stars, as objects of such worship. But as the most essential words in this case are supplied, the later writers, while they still suppose the objects worshipped to be here described, explain the descriptive terms in a different manner. Luther retains the Hebrew name *Gad* and *Meni*,

which are also given in the margin of the English Bible; but most inter-preters explain them by equivalents. Gesenius ingeniously argues from the etymology of the names that they relate to human destiny; and from the mythology of the ancient Eastern nations, that they relate to heavenly bodies. He dissents, however, from Vitringa's opinion that the sun and moon are meant, as well as from the notions of older writers, that the names are descriptive of the planetary system, the signs of the Zodiac, particular constellations, &c. His own opinion is that גַּד is the planet Jupiter (identical with Bel or Baal), and מְנִי the planet Venus (identical with Ashtoreth), which are called in the old Arabian mythology the Greater and Lesser Fortune, or good luck, while Saturn and Mars were known as the Greater and Lesser Evil Fortune, or Ill Luck. J. D. Michaelis had long before explained the names here used as meaning Fortune and Fate, or Good and Evil Destiny; and Ewald, in like manner, under-stands the planets here intended to be Jupiter and Saturn, while Knobel goes back to the old hypothesis of Vitringa and the others, that the names denote the Sun and Moon, the latter assumption being chiefly founded on the supposed affinity between מְנִי and μήνη. Others connect it with the Arabic مناة, an idol worshipped at Mecca before the time of Mohammed. Some supposed the moon to be called מְנִי (from מָנָה to measure), as a mea-sure of time. Amidst this diversity of theories and explanations, only a very minute part of which has been introduced by way of sample, it is satisfactory to find that there is perfect unanimity upon the only point of exegetical importance, namely, that the passage is descriptive of idolatrous worship; for even those who apply it directly to convivial indulgences con-nect the latter with religious institutions. This being settled, the details still doubtful can be interesting only to the philologist and antiquarian. The kind of offering described is supposed to be identical with the *lectis-ternia* of the Roman writers; and Gesenius characteristically says, the shew-bread in the temple at Jerusalem was nothing else (*nichts anders*). The heathen rite in question consisted in the spreading of a feast for the con-sumption of the gods. Herodotus mentions a τραπέζα ηλίου as known in Egypt; and Jeremiah twice connects this usage with the worship of the queen of heaven. (Jer. vii. 18, xliv. 17.) מִמְסָךְ denotes *mixture*, and may either mean spiced or wine, or a compound of different liquors, or a mere preparation or infusion of one kind. (See vol. i. p. 139.)—As to the ap-plication of the passage, there is the usual division of opinion among the adherents of the different hypothesis. Henderson's reasoning upon this verse is remarkable. Having applied vers. 3–5 to the ancient Jewish idolatry, he might have been expected to attach the same sense to the words before us, where the prophet seems to turn again to those of whom he had been speaking when he began to promise the deliverance of the elect remnant ver. 8.) But "it seems more natural to regard them as the impe-nitent and worldly portion of the Jews who shall live at the time of the restoration." The reason given for this sudden change can only satisfy the minds of those who agree with the author in his foregone conclusion, namely, that "the persons addressed in this and the four following verses are con-trasted with those who are to return and enjoy the divine favour in Pales-tine." But even after the application of the terms is thus decided, there is a question not so easily disposed of, as to what they mean. The prin-ciple of strict interpretation might be thought to require the conclusion doubtingly hinted at by J. D. Michaelis, that the Jews are to worship Gad and Meni hereafter. But, according to Henderson, "there is no reason to imagine that the Jews will again become actual idolaters," as if the strict interpretation of this verse would not itself afford a reason not for imagining but for believing that it will be so. But rather than admit this, he declares that " all attempts to explain *Gad* and *Meni* of idols literally taken, are aside from the point." From what point they are thus aside does not appear, unless it be the point of making half the prophecy a loose metaphorical description, and cutting the remainder to the quick by a rigorously literal interpretation." "Israel," " Jerusalem," "the land," *must* all denote the " Israel," " Jerusalem," and " land" of ancient times and of the old economy ; but all attempts to explain Gad and Meni of idols literally taken are aside from the point. And thus we are brought to the curious result of one literal interpretation excluding another as impossible. The true sense of the passage seems to be the same as in vers. 3–7, where Henderson himself regards the prophet as completing his description of the wickedness of Israel, by circumstances drawn from different periods of his history, such as the idolatrous period, the pharisaical period, &c.

12. *And I have numbered you to the sword, and all of you to the slaughter shall bow ; because I called and ye did not answer, I spake and ye did not hear, and ye did the* (thing that was) *evil in my eyes, and that which I desired not ye chose.* The preceding verse having reference only to the present and the past, the *Vav* at the beginning of this can have no conversive influence upon the verb, which is therefore to be rendered as a preterite. The objections to making it the sign of the apodosis have been already stated. The paraphrastic version, *therefore*, is entirely gratuitous. Gesenius gives the verb in this one place the diluted sense of allotting or appointing ; but the strict sense of numbering or counting is not only admissible, but necessary to express a portion of the writer's meaning, namely, the idea that they should be cut off one by one, or rather one with another, *i. e.* all without exception. (See chap. xxvii. 12, and vol. i. p. 442.) Knobel, indeed, imagines that a universal slaughter cannot be intended, because he goes on to tell what shall befall the survivors, viz. hunger, thirst, disgrace, distress, &c. Hitzig had taste enough to see that these are not described as subsequent in time to the evils threatened in the verse before us, but specifications of the way in which that threatening should be executed. The sense above given to מָנִיתִי is confirmed and illustrated by its application elsewhere to the numbering of sheep. (Jer. xxxiii. 13.) In its use here there is evident allusion to its derivative מְנִי in the preceding verse, which some of the German writers try to make perceptible to German readers by combining cognate nouns and verbs, such as *Shicksal* and *schicke*, *Verhängniss* and *verhänge*, *Bestimmung* and *bestimme*, &c. The same effect, if it were worth the while, might be produced in English by the use of *destiny* and *destine*. Vitringa, in order to identify the figures of the first and second clauses, makes חֶרֶב mean a butcher's knife ; but an opposite assimilation would be better, namely, that of making טֶבַח mean slaughter in general, not that of the slaughter-house exclusively. Both sword and slaughter are familiar figures for violent destruction. The verb כָּרַע is also applied elsewhere to one slain by violence (Judges v. 27, 2 Kings ix. 24). Bowing or stooping to the slaughter is submitting to it either willingly or by compulsion. Gesenius takes טֶבַח in the local sense of *Schlachtbank*, to suit which he translates the verb *kneel*, and the particle *before*. This last Noyes retains without the others, in the English phrase *bow down before the slaughter*, which is either unmeaning, or conveys a false idea, that of priority in time. The remainder of the verse assigns the reason of the threatened

punishment. The first expression bears a strong resemblance to the words of Wisdom, in Prov. i. 24–31. Knobel's explanation of the "thing that was evil in my eyes" as a description of idolatry, is as much too restricted as Vitringa's explanation of "that which I desired not or delighted not in" as signifying ritual or formal as opposed to spiritual worship. Of the two the former has the least foundation, as the only proof cited is chap. xxxviii. 3, whereas Vitringa's explanation of the other phrase derives no little countenance from Ps. xl. 7, li. 18, Hos. vi. 6. The only objection to either is that it mistakes a portion of the true sense for the whole.—As to the application of the words, there is the usual confidence and contradiction. Knobel regards them as a threatening of captivity and execution to the Jews who took sides with the Babylonians against Cyrus. Henderson applies them to the inevitable and condign punishment of those Jews who shall prefer the pleasures of sin to those of true religion embraced by the great body of the nation, which punishment, he adds, "will, *in all probability*, be inflicted upon them in common with the members of the anti-christian confederacy, after their believing brethren shall have been securely settled in Palestine." The grounds of this all probable anticipation are not given. Vitringa understands the passage as predicting the excision of the Jewish nation from the church, not only for the crowning sin of rejecting Christ, but for their aggregate offences as idolaters and hypocrites, as rebels against God and despisers of his mercy, with which sins they are often charged in the Old Testament (*e. g.* chaps. l. 2 ; lxv. 2 ; lxvi. 4 ; Jer. vii. 13, 25), and still more pointedly by Christ himself in several of his parables and other discourses, some of which remarkably resemble that before us both in sentiment and language. (See Mat. xxiii. 37, xxii. 7, Luke xix. 27, and compare Acts xiii. 46). Besides the countenance which this analogy affords to Vitringa's exposition, it is strongly recommended by its strict agreement with what we have determined, independently of this place, to be the true sense of the whole foregoing context. Interpreted by these harmonious analogies, the verse, instead of threatening the destruction of the Baby-lonish Jews before the advent, or of the wicked Jews and Antichrist here-after, is a distinct prediction of a far more critical event than either, the judicial separation of the Jewish nation and the Israel of God which had for ages seemed inseparable, not to say identical.

13, 14. *Therefore thus saith the Lord Jehovah, Lo! my servants shall eat and ye shall hunger; lo, my servants shall drink and ye shall thirst; lo, my servants shall rejoice and ye shall be ashamed; lo, my servants shall shout from gladness of heart, and ye shall cry from grief of heart, and from broken-ness of spirit ye shall howl.* These verses merely carry out the general threatening of the one preceding, in a series of poetical antithesis, where hunger, thirst, disgrace, and anguish, take the place of sword and slaughter, and determine these to be symbolical or emblematic terms. Knobel's interpretation of these verses as predicting bodily privations and hard bond-age to those who should escape the sword of Cyrus, is entitled to as little deference as he would pay to the suggestion of Vitringa, that the eating and drinking have specific reference to the joy with which the first Chris-tian converts partook of the Lord's supper (Acts. ii. 46, xx. 7). This is no doubt chargeable with undue refinement and particularity, but notwith-standing this excess, the exposition is correct in principle. as we may learn from the frequent use of these antagonistic metaphors to signify spiritual joy and horror, not only in the Prophets (see above, chaps. viii. 21, xxxiii. 16, lv. 1, lviii. 14), but by our Saviour when he speaks of his disciples as eating bread in the kingdom of heaven (Luke xiv. 13), where many shall come from the east and the west, and sit down (or recline at table) with Abraham, Isaac, and Jacob (Mat. viii. 11); and ascribes to the king in the parable the solemn declaration, "I say unto you none of those men that were bidden shall taste of my supper" (Luke xiv. 24). Thus understood, the passage is a solemn prediction of happiness to the believing, and of misery to the unbelieving Jews. The latter are directly addressed, the former designated as *my servants.*—*Gladness of heart*, literally goodness of heart, which in our idiom would express a different idea, on account of our predominant use of the first word in a moral sense. For the Hebrew expression see Deut. xxviii. 47, Judges xix. 6, 22. For *brokenness of spirit*, compare chap. lxi. 1, and Ps. li. 17.—To be ashamed, as often elsewhere, includes disappointment and frustration of hope.

15. *And ye shall leave your name for an oath to my chosen ones, and the Lord Jehovah shall slay thee, and shall call his servants by another name* (literally, call another name to them). The object of address is still the body of the Jewish nation, from which the believing remnant are distinguished by the names *my chosen* and *my servants.* *Oath* is here put for curse, as it is added to it in Dan. ix. 11, and the two are combined in Num. v. 21, where the *oath of cursing* may be regarded as the complete expression of which *oath* is here an ellipsis. To leave one's name for a curse, according to Old Testament usage, is something more than to leave it to be cursed. The sense is that the name shall be used as a formula of cursing, so that men shall be able to wish nothing worse to others than a like character and fate. This is clear from Jer. xxix. 22, compared with Zech. iii. 2, as well as from the converse or correlative promise to the patriarchs and their children, that a like use should be made of their names as a formula of blessing (Gen. xxii. 18, xlviii. 20). As in other cases where the use of names is the subject of discourse, there is no need of supposing that any actual practice is predicted, but merely that the character and fate of those addressed will be so bad as justly to admit of such an application.—Ewald ingeniously explains the words וְהֵמִיתְךָ אֲדֹנָי יֱהוִֹה as the very form of cursing to be used, *so may the Lord Jehovah slay thee!* This construction, though adopted by Umbreit and Knobel, is far from being obvious or natural. The preterite, though sometimes construed with the optative particles, would hardly be employed in that sense absolutely, especially in the middle of a sentence preceded and followed by predictive clauses, each beginning with ו, which on Ewald's supposition must be either overlooked as pleonastic or violently made to bear the sense of *so.* Even if this were one of the meanings of the particle, a more explicit form would no doubt have been used in a case where the comparison is everything. The wish required by the context is that God would kill them so, or in like manner; a bare wish that he would kill them, would be nothing to the purpose. The violence of this construction as an argument against it might be counteracted by exegetical necessity, but no such necessity exists. The use of the singular pronoun *thee*, so far from requiring it, is in perfect keeping with the rest of the sentence. As the phrase *your name* shews that the object of address is a plurality of persons bearing one name, or in other words an organized community, so the singular form *slay thee* is entirely appropriate to this collective or ideal person. Of the last clause there are three interpretations. The Rabbinical expounders understand it as the converse of the other clause. As your name is to be a name of cursing, so my ser-

vants are to have another name, *i. e.* a name of blessing, or a name by
which men shall bless. Others give it a more general sense, as meaning their condition shall be altogether different. A third opinion is that
it relates to the substitution of the Christian name for that of Jew, as a
distinctive designation of God's people. The full sense of the clause can
only be obtained by combining all these explanations, or at least a part of
each. The first is obviously implied, if not expressed. The second is
established by analogy and usage, and the almost unanimous consent of all
interpreters. The only question is in reference to the last, which is of
course rejected with contempt by the neologists, and regarded as fanciful
by some Christian writers. These have been influenced in part by the
erroneous assumption that if this is not the whole sense of the words, it
cannot be a part of it. But this is only true in cases where the two proposed are incompatible. The true state of the case is this. According
to the usage of the prophecies the promise of another name imports a
different character and state, and in this sense the promise has been fully
verified. But in addition to this general fulfilment, which no one calls in
question, it is matter of history that the Jewish commonwealth or nation is
destroyed ; that the name of Jew has been for centuries a by-word and a
formula of execration, and that they who have succeeded to the spiritual
honours of this once favoured race, although they claim historical identity
therewith, have never borne its name, but another, which from its very
nature could have no existence until Christ had come, and which in the
common parlance of the Christian world is treated as the opposite of Jew.
Now all this must be set aside as mere fortuitous coincidence, or it must
be accounted for precisely in the same way that we all account for similar
coincidences between the history of Christ and the Old Testament in minor
points, where all admit that the direct sense of the prophecy is more extensive. As examples, may be mentioned John the Baptist's preaching in a
literal wilderness, our Saviour's riding on a literal ass, his literally opening
the eyes of the blind, when it is evident to every reader of the original passages that they predict events of a far more extensive and more elevated
nature. While I fully believe that this verse assures God's servants of a
very different fate from that of the unbelieving Jews, I have no doubt that
it also has respect to the destruction of the Jewish State, and the repudiation of its name by the true church or Israel of God.

16. (*By*) *which the* (*man*) *blessing himself in the land* (or *earth*) *shall
bless himself by the God of truth, and* (by which) *the* (*man*) *swearing in the
land* (or *earth*) *shall swear by the God of truth, because forgotten are the
former enmities* (or *troubles*), *and because they are hidden from my eyes.*
Two things have divided and perplexed interpreters in this verse, as it
stands connected with the one before it. The first is the apparent change
of subject, and the writer's omission to record the new name which had just
been promised. The other is the very unusual construction of the relative
אֲשֶׁר. The first of these has commonly been left without solution, or referred to the habitual freedom of the writer. The other has been variously
but very unsuccessfully explained. Kimchi takes it in the sense of *when*,
Luther in that of *so that*. Vitringa connects it with the participle, as if it
were a future. Rosenmüller and Gesenius regard it as redundant, which is
a mere evasion of the difficulty, as the cases which they cite of such a usage
are entirely irrelevant, as shewn by Maurer, whose own hypothesis is not
more satisfactory, viz. that either the article or relative was carelessly
inserted (*negligentius dictum*). Ewald gives the relative its strict sense,

and makes Jehovah the antecedent, by supplying before it, thus saith Jehovah (or saith he) by whom the man that blesses, &c. This has the advantage of adhering to the strict sense of the pronoun, but the disadvantage of involving an improbable ellipsis, and of making the writer say circuitously what he might have said directly. " Thus saith he by whom the person blessing blesses by the God of truth," is perfectly equivalent to, Thus saith the God of truth. Both these objections may be obviated by referring אֲשֶׁר to an expressed antecedent, viz. name, a construction given both in the Septuagint and Vulgate versions, although otherwise defective and obscure. Another advantage of this construction is that it removes the abrupt transition and supplies the name, which seems on any other supposition to be wanting. According to this view of the place, the sense is that the people shall be called after the God of truth, so that his name and theirs shall be identical, and consequently whoever blesses or swears by the one, blesses or swears by the other also. The form in which this idea is expressed is peculiar, but intelligible and expressive : " His people he shall call by another name, which (*i. e.* with respect to which, or more specifically by which) he that blesseth shall bless by the God of truth," &c. Ewald supposes blessing and cursing to be meant, as oath is used above to signify a curse ; but most interpreters understand by blessing himself, praying for God's blessing, and by swearing, the solemn invocation of his presence as a witness, both being mentioned as acts of religious worship and of solemn recognition.—אָמֵן is probably an adjective meaning *sure*, trustworthy, and therefore including the ideas of reality and faithfulness, neither of which should be excluded, and both of which are comprehended in the English phrase, the true God, or retaining more exactly the form of the original, *the God of truth*. Henderson's version, " faithful God," expresses only half of the idea. This Hebrew word is retained in the Greek of the New Testament, not only as a particle of asseveration, but in a still more remarkable manner as a name of Christ (Rev. i. 18, iii. 14), with obvious reference to the case before us ; and there must be something more than blind chance in the singular coincidence thus brought to light between this application of the phrase and the sense which has been put upon the foregoing verse, as relating to the adoption of the Christian name by the church or chosen people. As applied to Christ, the name is well explained by Vitringa to describe him as *very God*, as a witness to the truth, as the substance or reality of the legal shadows, and as the fulfiller of the divine promises. Ewald agrees with the older writers in rendering בָּאָרֶץ, *in the earth*, but most interpreters prefer the more restricted version, *in the land*. The difference is less than might at first sight be supposed, as " in the land " could here mean nothing less than in the land of promise, the domain of Israel, the church in its widest and most glorious diffusion.—The last clause gives the reason for the application of the title, God of truth, viz. because in his deliverance of his people he will prove himself to be the true God in both senses, truly divine and eminently faithful. This proof will be afforded by the termination of those evils which the sins of his own people once rendered necessary. Usage is certainly in favour of the common version, troubles or distresses ; but there is something striking in Lowth's version, *provocations*, which agrees well with what seems to be the sense of צָרָה in chap. lxiii. 9. As commonly translated, it is understood by Gesenius as meaning that God will forget the former necessity for punishing his people, which is equivalent to saying that he will forget their sins. But Maurer understands the sense to be that he will think no more of smiting them again. Both seem to make the last words a poetical description of oblivion ; but Knobel refers what is said of forgetting to a people, and only the remaining words to God.

17. *For lo I (am) creating* (or *about to create*) *new heavens and a new earth, and the former (things) shall not be remembered, and shall not come up into the mind* (literally, on the heart). Some interpreters refer *former* to heavens and earth, which makes the parallelism more exact ; but most interpreters refer it to הָרִאשֹׁנוֹת in ver. 16, where the same adjective is used, or construe it indefinitely in the sense of *former things*. Of the whole verse there are several distinct interpretations. Aben Ezra understands it as predicting an improvement in the air and soil, conducive to longevity and uninterrupted health ; and a similar opinion is expressed by J. D. Michaelis, who illustrates the verse by the supposition of a modern writer who should describe the vast improvement in Germany since ancient times, by saying that the heaven and the earth are new. A second explanation of the verse is that of Thomas Burnet and his followers, which makes it a prediction of the renovation of the present earth with its skies, &c., after the destruction of the present at the day of judgment. A third is that of Vitringa, who regards it as a figurative prophecy of changes in the church, according to a certain systematic explication of the several parts of the material universe as symbols. Better than all these, because requiring less to be assumed, and more in keeping with the usage of prophetic language, is the explanation of the verse as a promise or prediction of entire change in the existing state of things, the precise nature of the change and of the means by which it shall be brought about forming no part of the revelation here. That the words are not inapplicable to a revolution of a moral and spiritual nature, we may learn from Paul's analogous description of the change wrought in conversion (2 Cor. v. 17 ; Gal. vi. 15), and from Peter's application of this very passage, " Nevertheless, we, according to his promise, look for new heavens and a new earth wherein dwelleth righteousness " (2 Peter iii. 13). That the words have such meaning even here, is rendered probable by the last clause, the oblivion of the former state of things being much more naturally connected with moral and spiritual changes than with one of a material nature.

18. *But rejoice and be glad unto eternity (in) that which I (am) creating, for lo I (am) creating Jerusalem a joy, and her people a rejoicing, i. e.* a subject or occasion of it. There is no need of explaining the imperatives as futures, though futurity is of course implied in the command. It would be highly arbitrary to explain *what I create* in this place as different from the creation in the verse preceding. It is there said that a creation shall take place. It is here enjoined upon God's people to rejoice in it. But here the creation is declared to be the making of Jerusalem a joy and Israel a rejoicing. Now the whole analogy of the foregoing prophecies leads to the conclusion that this means the exaltation of the church or chosen people ; and the same analogy admits of that exaltation being represented as a revolution in the frame of nature. On the other hand, a literal prediction of new heavens and new earth would scarcely have been followed by a reference merely to the church ; and if Jerusalem and Zion be explained to mean the literal Jerusalem and the restored Jews, the only alternative is then to conclude that as soon as they return to Palestine, it and the whole earth are to be renewed, or else that what relates to Jerusalem and Israel is literal, and what relates to the heavens and the earth metaphorical, although, as we have just seen, the connection of the verses

renders it necessary to regard the two events as one. From all these incongruities we are relieved by understanding the whole passage as a poetical
description of a complete and glorious change.

19. *And I will rejoice in Jerusalem, and joy in my people ; and there shall
not be heard in her again the voice of weeping and the voice of crying.* Considered as the language of the Prophet himself, this would express his
sympathetic interest in the joyous changes which awaited his people. But
such an application would be wholly arbitrary, as Jehovah is undoubtedly
the speaker in the foregoing verse, where he claims creative power; and
even here there is an implication of divine authority in the promise that
weeping shall no more be heard in her. There is something very beautiful in the association of ideas here expressed. God shall rejoice in his
people, and they shall rejoice with him. They shall no longer know what
grief is, because he shall cease to grieve over them ; their former distresses
shall be forgotten by them, and for ever hidden from his eyes.

20. *There shall be no more from there an infant of days, and an old man
who shall not fulfil his days ; for the child a hundred years old shall die, and
the sinner a hundred years old shall be accursed.*—Some refer מִשָּׁם to time,
and understand it to mean *thenceforth*, a departure from the settled usage
which can be justified only by necessity. Others regard the preposition as
unmeaning, and read *there*, which is as arbitrary as Lowth's reading שָׁם,
neither of which proceedings can be justified by the example of the ancient
versions. The strict translation *thence (from there)* is not only admissible but
necessary to the sense. It does not, however, mean springing or proceeding
thence, but taken away thence, or as Kimchi has it, carried thence to burial.
It is thus equivalent to יָמוּת in the next clause, and denotes that none shall die
there in infancy. In consequence of not correctly apprehending this, Hitzig
alleges that this first clause by itself can only mean that there shall be no
longer any infants, to avoid which paralogism he connects עוּל יָמִים as well
as זָקֵן with the following words : neither infant nor old man who shall not
fulfil their days. But there is no need of this tautological construction if
יִהְיֶה מִשָּׁם implies death, and יָמִים a few days only, which last is more
agreeable to usage than the specific sense of *year*, which some assume.
A curious turn is given to the sentence by some of the older writers, who
take *fulfil his days* in the moral sense of spending them well, with special
reference to improvement in knowledge, and *the child* as meaning one who
even at a very advanced age continues still a child in understanding, and
shall therefore die. Still more unnatural is the modification of this exposition by Cocceius, who explains the whole to mean that men shall have as
abundant opportunities of instruction in the truth as if they enjoyed a
patriarchal longevity, so that he who perishes for lack of knowledge will
be left without excuse. Vitringa justly repudiates these far-fetched explanations, but agrees with them in understanding *shall die* as an emphatic
threatening, and in departing from the ordinary sense of נַעַר, which he
takes to be here an equivalent to *sinner*. All the modern writers are agreed
as to the literal meaning of this last clause, though they differ as to the
relation of its parts. Some regard it as a synonymous parallelism, and
understand the sense to be that he who dies a hundred years old, will be
considered as dying young, and by a special curse from God interrupting
the ordinary course of nature. Others follow De Dieu in making the
parallelism antithetic, and contrasting the child with the sinner. Perhaps
the true view of the passage is, that it resumes the contrast drawn in
vers. 13–15 between the servants of Jehovah and the sinners there ad·

dressed. Vers. 16–19 may then be regarded as a parenthetical amplification. As if he had said, My servants shall eat, but ye shall be hungry ; my servants shall drink, but ye shall be thirsty ; my servants shall rejoice, but ye shall mourn ; my servants shall be just beginning life when ye are driven out of it ; among the former, he who dies a hundred years old shall die a child ; among you, he who dies at the same age shall die accursed. On the whole, however, the most natural meaning is the one already mentioned as preferred by most modern writers. Premature death, and even death in a moderate old age, shall be unknown ; he who dies a hundred years old shall be considered either as dying in childhood, or as cut off by a special malediction. The whole is a highly poetical description of longevity, to be explained precisely like the promise of new heavens and a new earth in ver. 17. Beck's gross expressions of contempt for the absurdity of this verse are founded on a wilful perversion or an ignorant misapprehension. Ewald is equally unjust but less indecent in his representation of this verse as a fanatical anticipation of the literal change which it describes.

21, 22. *And they shall build houses and inhabit (them), and shall plant vineyards and eat the fruit of them, they shall not build and another inhabit, they shall not plant and another eat ; for as the days of a tree (shall be) the days of my people, and the work of their hands my chosen ones shall wear out (or survive).* This is a promise of security and permanent enjoyment, clothed in expressions drawn from the promises and threatenings of the Mosaic law. By the age of a tree is generally understood the great age which some species are said to attain, such as the oak, the banyan, &c. But Knobel takes it in the general sense of propagation and succession, and understands the promise to be that, as trees succeed each other naturally and for ever, so shall the chosen of Jehovah do. The essential idea is in either case that of permanent continuance, and the figures here used to express it make it still more probable that in the whole foregoing context the predictions are to be figuratively understood.

23. *They shall not labour in vain, and they shall not bring forth for terror ; for the seed of the blessed of Jehovah are they, and their offspring with them.* The sense of *sudden destruction* given to בֶּהָלָה by some modern writers, is a mere conjecture from the context, and no more correct than the translation *curse*, which others derive from the Arabic analogy, and which Henderson regards as the primitive meaning. The Hebrew word properly denotes extreme agitation and alarm, and the meaning of the clause is that they shall not bring forth children merely to be subjects of distressing solicitude. Knobel, as in chap. i. 4, takes זֶרַע in the sense of a generation or contemporary race ; but it adds greatly to the strength of the expression if we give its more usual sense of progeny or offspring : they are themselves the offspring of those blessed of God, and their own offspring likewise, as the older writers understand אִתָּם, while the moderns suppose it to mean *shall be with them*, i. e. shall continue with them, as opposed to the alarm referred to in the other clause. Umbreit's idea that the picture of domestic happiness is here completed by the unexpected stroke of parents and children still continuing to live together, is ingenious and refined, perhaps too much so to be altogether natural in this connection.

24. *And it shall be* (or *come to pass), that they shall not yet have called and I will answer, yet (shall) they (be) speaking and I will hear.* A strong expression of God's readiness to hear and answer prayer, not a mere promise that it shall be heard (like that in Jer. xxix. 12 ; Zech. xiii. 9), but

an assurance that it shall be granted before it is heard. The nearest parallel is Mat. vi. 8, where our Lord himself says, Your Father knoweth what things ye have need of, before ye ask him. (Compare chap. xxx. 19, lviii. 9 ; Ps. cxlv. 18, 19.)--טֶרֶם is commonly explained here as a conjunction, *before they call,* and Gesenius gives this as the primary meaning of the Hebrew particle. But according to Hitzig and Maurer, this is always expressed by the compound form בְּטֶרֶם, and the simple form invariably means *not yet.* This construction, which might otherwise seem very harsh, is favoured by the use of the conjunction *and,* which, on the usual hypothesis, must be omitted or regarded merely as a sign of the apodosis, whereas in the parallel clause it occupies precisely the same place, and can only be taken in its usual sense. Lowth attempts to reproduce the form of the original, but not with much success, by rendering the last clause, " they shall be yet speaking and I shall have heard." The parallel verbs both mean to hear prayer in a favourable sense, and are therefore rendered in the Vulgate by the cognate forms *audiam* and *exaudiam.* The last verb is curiously paraphrased in the Septuagint, *I will say, what is it?* (ἐρῶ τί ἐστι.)

25. *The wolf and the lamb shall feed as one, and the lion like the ox shall eat straw, and the serpent dust (for) his food. They shall not hurt and they shall not corrupt (or destroy) in all my holy mountain, saith Jehovah.* The promise of a happy change is wound up in the most appropriate manner by repeating the prophecy in chap. xi. 6–9, that all hurtful influences shall for ever cease in the holy hill or church of God. Yet Knobel ventures to assert that it is an unmeaning imitation of that passage, introduced here without any just connection, and perhaps by a different hand from that of the original writer. Another fact which had escaped preceding writers, is that the phrase *as one* belongs to the later Hebrew, because used in Eccles. xi. 6, whereas it is essentially identical with *as one man* in Judges xx. 8, 1 Sam. xi. 7. It is not a simple synonyme of יַחְדָּו, *together* (the word used in chap. xi. 6, but much stronger and more graphic ; so that Lowth only weakens the expression by proposing to assimilate the readings on the authority of a single manuscript. Another point in which the description is here heightened is the substitution of טָלֶה, a young and tender lamb, for כֶּבֶשׂ, a he-lamb of riper age. Ewald expresses the distinction here by using the diminutive term *Lämmlein.* Instead of *the lion like the ox,* the Vulgate has *the lion and the ox* (*leo et bos*), and that the *et* is not an error of the text for *ut* appears from the plural form of the verb *comedent.* Most of the modern writers construe נָחָשׁ as a nominative absolute, *as for the serpent, dust (shall be) his food.* A more obvious construction is to repeat the verb *shall eat,* and consider *dust* and *food* as in apposition. J. D. Michaelis supplies *continue* (*bleibe*), and most writers regard this idea as implied though not expressed: The serpent shall continue to eat dust. Michaelis and Gesenius suppose an allusion to the popular belief that serpents feed on dust because they creep upon the ground, and understand the prophecy to be that they shall henceforth be contented with this food and cease to prey on men or other animals. But this, as Vitringa well observes, would be too small a promise for the context, since a very small part of the evils which men suffer can arise from this cause. He therefore understands the clause to mean that the original curse upon the serpent who deceived Eve (Gen. iii. 14) shall be fully executed. (Compare Rev. xx. 1–8.) He refers to some of his contemporaries as explaining it to mean that the serpent should henceforth prey only upon low and earthly men ; but this would be too large a concession, and the true sense seems to be that, in accordance with

his ancient doom, he shall be rendered harmless, robbed of his favourite nutriment, and made to bite the dust at the feet of his conqueror. (Gen. iii. 15; Rom. xvi. 20; 1 John iii. 8; compare Isaiah xlix. 20.)—The last clause resolves the figure of the first. The verbs are therefore to be understood indefinitely, as in chap. xi. 9; or if they be referred to the animals previously mentioned, it is only a symbolical or tropical expression of the same idea. Hitzig gratuitously says that the verbs which in the other place relate to men, are here determined to refer to animals by the connection; to which Knobel flippantly replies that this is not the case, because there is no connection to determine it. The truth is, that the form of expression is the same in either case, except that what begins a verse in the eleventh chapter here concludes one. Had the passage here repeated been in one of the so-called later chapters, it would no doubt have been cited as a proof of the author's identity; but no such proof can be admitted by the "higher criticism," in favour of identifying the writer of this chapter with the genuine Isaiah. Rather than listen to such reasoning, the "higher critics" make it a case of imitation and abridgment, and one of them, as we have seen, of ignorant interpolation.—For any further explanation of this verse, the reader is referred to vol. i. pp. 253–255.

Chapter 66

THIS chapter winds up the prophetic discourse with an express prediction of the change of dispensation, and a description of the difference between them. Jehovah will no longer dwell in temples made with hands, ver. 1. Every sincere and humble heart shall be his residence, ver. 2. The ancient sacrifices, though divinely instituted, will henceforth be as hateful as the rites of idolatry, ver. 3. They who still cling to the abrogated ritual will be fearfully but righteously requited, ver. 4. The true Israel cast out by these deluded sinners shall ere long be glorified, and the carnal Israel fearfully rewarded, vers. 5, 6. The ancient Zion may already be seen travailing with a new and glorious dispensation, vers. 7–9. They who mourned for her seeming desolation, now rejoice in her abundance and her honour, vers. 10–14. At the same time the carnal Israel shall be destroyed, as apostates and idolaters, vers. 14–17. The place which they once occupied shall now be filled by the elect from all nations, ver. 18. To gather these, a remnant of the ancient Israel shall go forth among the Gentiles, ver. 19. They shall come from every quarter, and by every method of conveyance, ver. 20. They shall be admitted to the sacerdotal honours of the chosen people, ver. 21. This new dispensation is not to be temporary, like the one before it, but shall last for ever, ver. 22. While the spiritual Israel is thus replenished from all nations, the apostate Israel shall perish by a lingering decay in the sight of an astonished world, vers. 23, 24.

1. *Thus saith Jehovah. The heavens (are) my throne, and the earth my footstool; where is* (or *what is*) *the house which ye will build for me, and where is* (or *what is*) *the place of my rest?* literally, *the place my rest*, *i. e.* the place which is or can be my rest or permanent abode. The same term is elsewhere applied to the temple, as distinguished from the tabernacle or moveable sanctuary. (See 2 Sam. vii. 6, 2 Chron. vi. 41, Ps. cxxxii. 8.) As to the sense of אֵי־זֶה, see above, p. 246. In this case *where* is less appropriate than *what*, as the inquiry seems to have respect to the nature or the quality rather than the mere locality of the edifice in

question. Hitzig translates בַּיְ‍ת strictly *a house,* and תִּבְנוּ is variously
rendered *ye build,* in the English Bible; ye would build, by Ewald; ye
could build, by Gesenius, &c.; but the simplest and best version is *ye
will build,* as including all the others. All interpreters agree that this
question implies disapprobation of the building as at variance with the
great truth propounded in the first clause, namely, that the frame of
nature is the only material temple worthy of Jehovah. This obvious
relation of the clauses is sufficient of itself to set aside two of the old
interpretations of the passage. The first is that of Kimchi, favoured
more or less by Calvin and some later writers, which supposes that this
chapter is a counterpart to the first, and that the Prophet here recurs to his
original theme, the corruptions and abuses of his own age. But besides
the undisputed references to the future in the latter part of this very chapter,
it has been conclusively objected by Vitringa to the theory in question,
that in the reigns of Ahaz and Hezekiah there could be no thought of
building or rebuilding, nor even of repairing or adorning the temple, but
rather of despoiling it. (2 Kings xvi. 17, 18; xviii. 15.) The same
objection lies against the theory of Grotius, that this chapter was intended
to console the pious Jews who were debarred from the customary public
worship during the profanation of the temple by Antiochus Epiphanes. In
neither of these cases could there be occasion for objecting to the building or
rebuilding of the temple. Those who refer this whole series of predictions to
the period of the Babylonish exile find it hard to explain this chapter upon
that hypothesis, since the building of the temple is urged upon the people
as a duty by the acknowledged prophets of the exile. In order to facilitate
the process, some of them detached it from the foregoing context, on the
ground of its abrupt commencement, which is not at all more striking than
in other cases where no such conclusion has been drawn, because not felt
to be necessary for the critic's purpose. Eichhorn found this a fit occasion
for the application of the " higher criticism," and he accordingly strikes
out vers. 1–17 of this chapter as an older composition than the rest, the
exact date not definable, but certainly prior to the downfall of the Jewish
monarchy. Paulus and Rosenmüller, on the other hand, regard the whole
as later than the first return from Babylon. Between these extremes
Gesenius as usual undertakes to mediate, condemns the first as " trennende
Kritik," and refutes it by a copious but superfluous detail of minute coincidences both of thought and language between the disputed passage and
the foregoing chapters which he therefore supposes to belong to the same
period. From this decision there is no material dissent among the later
writers, although Hitzig asserts in the strongest terms the utter want of
connection between this and the preceding chapters. The same assertion
might be made with equal plausibility in any other case of a continued composition where the writer is not trammelled by a systematic method; but
passes freely from one topic to another, in obedience to a lively and un-
checked association of ideas. No reader or interpreter who has not a
hypothesis to verify will find any reason for supposing a greater interruption
here than at the end of an ordinary paragraph. The fallacy of the contrary
assertion has been shewn by Vitringa to consist in assuming that the passages are unconnected unless the first verse of the second carries out the
thought expressed in the last verse of the first, whereas the chapter now
before us is in some sense parallel to that before it, taking up the subject
at the same point and bringing it at last to the same issue. That exposition is indeed most probably the true one which assumes the most intimate

connection of the chapters here, and is least dependent upon forced divisions and arbitrary intervals crowded with imaginary events. Thus Rosenmüller thinks that in the interval between these chapters the tribes of Benjamin and Judah had resolved to exclude the others from all participation in the rebuilding of the temple, and that the passage now before us was intended to reprove them for their want of charity, as if this end could be accomplished by proclaiming the worthlessness of all material temples, which is tantamount to saying, Why do ye refuse to let your countrymen assist in the rebuilding of the temple, since no temples are of any value ? Hitzig's imagination is still more prolific, and invents a project to erect another temple in Chaldea as a succedaneum for returning to Jerusalem. At the same time his superior acuteness guards against the palpable absurdity already mentioned, by supposing the error here corrected to be that of believing that the mere erection of a temple would discharge their obligations and secure their welfare, without any reference to what Jehovah had commanded. They are therefore taught that he has no need of material dwellings, and that these, to be of any value, must be built exactly when and where and as he pleases to require. (1 Sam. xv. 22, 23.) This ingenious exposition would be faultless if it rested upon any firmer basis than a perfectly imaginary fact. That there is any proof of it from other quarters, is not pretended. That it is not a necessary inference from that before us, will be clear when the true interpretation has been given. It is necessary first to state, however, that while Hitzig thus infers from the text itself a fact unknown to history because it never happened, Henderson with equal confidence infers from it a fact as little known to history, but for a very different reason. While the one considers it as proving that a party of the exiles in Babylon desired to build a temple there instead of going back to Palestine, the other considers it as proving that part of the restored Jews will unlawfully attempt to rebuild the old temple in Palestine itself, and that this passage is intended to reprove them. Yet in chap. lx. 7, 13, we read not only of a sanctuary to be literally built of the most costly timber, but of an altar and of victims to be offered on it; all which may be tortured into figures, it appears, provided that the future restoration of the Jews be strictly expounded in a local sense. With these interpretations and the forced hypotheses which they involve, we may now compare another which has been approved by various judicious writers, but by none more clearly stated or more successfully maintained than by Vitringa. It is simply this, that having held up in every point of view the true design, mission, and vocation of the church or chosen people, its relation to the natural descendants of Abraham, the causes which required that the latter should be stripped of their peculiar privileges, and the vocation of the Gentiles as a part of the divine plan from its origin, the Prophet now addresses the apostate and unbelieving Jews at the close of the old dispensation, who, instead of preparing for the general extension of the church, and the exchange of ceremonial for spiritual worship, were engaged in the rebuilding and costly decoration of the temple at Jerusalem. The pride and interest in this great public work, felt not only by the Herods but by all the Jews, is clear from incidental statements of the Scriptures (John ii. 20, Matt. xxiv. 1), as well as from the ample and direct assertions of Josephus. That the nation should have been thus occupied precisely at the time when the Messiah came, is one of those agreements between prophecy and history which cannot be accounted for except upon the supposition of a providential and designed assimilation.

To the benefit of this coincidence the exposition which has last been given is entitled, and by means of it the probabilities, already great, may be said to be converted into certainties, or if anything more be needed for this purpose it will be afforded by the minuter points of similarity which will be presented in the course of the interpretation. One advantage of this exposition is that it accounts for the inference here drawn from a doctrine which was known to Solomon and publicly announced by him (1 Kings viii. 27), though described by Gesenius as unknown to the early Hebrews, who supposed that God was really confined to earthly temples (1 Chron. xxviii. 2, Ps. xcix. 5, cxxxii. 5). It may be asked, then, why this truth did not forbid the erection of the temple at first, as well as its gorgeous reconstruction in the time of Christ. The answer is, that it was necessary for a temporary purpose, but when this temporary purpose was accomplished it became not only useless but unlawful. Henceforth the worship was to be a spiritual worship, the church universally diffused, and the material sanctuary, as J. D. Michaelis says, no longer an earthly residence for God but a convenient place of meeting for his people.

2. *And all these my own hand made, and all these were* (or *are*), *saith Jehovah; and to this one will I look, to the afflicted and contrite in spirit and trembling at my word.* By *all these* it is universally admitted that we are to understand the heavens and the earth, of which he claims to be not only the sovereign, as in the preceding verse, but the creator. The next expression may be differently understood. Lowth suplies לִי, *to me*, on the authority of the Septuagint (ἐστιν ἐμά), and adds that this word is absolutely necessary to the sense. But according to Hebrew usage, the verb would not have been expressed if this had been the meaning; and the clause as Lowth completes it does not mean *they are mine*, but *they were* (or *have been*) *mine*. The same objection lies in some degree against the explanation of וַיִּהְיוּ without לִי as meaning *they exist* (*i.e.* by my creative power). The reference is rather to the time of actual creation, *my hand made them and they were*, *i.e.* began to be. (See Gen. i. 3, Ps. xxxiii. 9.) Both tenses of the verb are combined to express the same idea in Rev. iv. 11. J. D. Michaelis and Ewald shew the true connection by translating, "my hand made them and so they were or came into existence." It is important to the just interpretation of these verses to observe the climax in them. First, the temples made by men are contrasted with the great material temple of the universe; then this is itself disparaged by Jehovah as his own handiwork, and still more in comparison with the nobler temple of a spiritual nature, the renewed and contrite heart. (See chap. lvii. 15, 2 Cor. vi. 16.) The same condescending favour is expressed for the same objects elsewhere (Ps. xxxiv. 19, cxxxviii. 6). To look to, is to have regard to, and implies both approbation and affection. (See Gen. iv. 4, 5, Exod. ii. 25, Num. xvi. 15, Judges vi. 14, Ps. xxv. 16.) The Septuagint and Vulgate make the last clause interrogative: "To whom shall I look but' ? &c. *Contrite* or *broken in heart* or *spirit* is a Scriptural description of the subjects of divine grace in its humbling and subduing influences (chaps. lxi. 1, lxv. 14). The Septuagint renders it ἡσύχιον, *quiet*, implying patient acquiescence in the will of God. The זֶה refers to the following description, like זֹאת in chap. lvi. 2. Gesenius illustrates חָרֵד עַל by citing 1 Sam. iv. 13, where Eli is described as trembling for the ark of God; but Hitzig justly represents the cases as unlike, and explains the one before us as denoting not solicitude about the word of God, but an earnest inclination to it,

or as Ewald renders it a *trembling to* his word, *i. e.* an eager and yet fearful haste to execute his will. (Compare Hosea iii. 5, xi. 10, 11.) The use of the phrase in historical prose by Ezra (ix. 4, x. 3) is probably borrowed from the place before us.

3. *'Slaying the ox, smiting a man—sacrificing the sheep, breaking a dog's neck—offering an oblation, blood of swine—making a memorial of incense, blessing vanity—also they have chosen their ways, and in their abominations has their soul delighted.* This translation, although scarcely English, will convey some idea of the singular form of the original, and render intelligible what is said as to the different constructions of the sentence.—The first clause consists of four similar members, in each of which are coupled a form of sacrifice under the Mosaic law and an offering which according to that law was inadmissible and even revolting. The ox and the sheep represent the animal sacrifices, the מִנְחָה or meat-offering and the incense those of an unbloody nature. The verbs connected with these nouns are likewise all selected from the technical vocabulary of the law. שָׁחַט and זָבַח both originally signify to slay or slaughter, but are especially applied to sacrificial slaughter in the Pentateuch. מַעֲלֶה is the participle of a verb which means to cause to ascend, and in the language of the ritual, upon the altar. מַזְכִּיר is another, of obscurer origin and strict signification, though its use and application are as clear as any of the rest. The modern writers commonly derive it from the noun אַזְכָּרָה the technical name of a certain kind of offering, especially of incense (Lev. xxiv. 7), with or without other vegetable substances (Num. v. 26). It seems to mean *memorial*, and is usually so translated, and explained upon the ground that the fumes of incense were conceived of as ascending into heaven and reminding God of the worshipper. The same figure was then transferred to prayers and other spiritual offerings.—Thus we read in Acts x. 4 that the angel said to Cornelius, thy prayers and thine alms are come up before God *for a memorial* εἰς μνημόσυνον, the very phrase employed by the Septuagint in the case before us. The verb then means to offer this oblation, but may be considered as expressing more directly the recalling of the worshipper to God's remembrance, as it literally means to *remind*. Being also used in the sense of mentioning, it is so understood here by Luther, while the Vulgate gives it the meaning of its primitive, remembering.—*Smiting* has here, as often elsewhere, the emphatic sense of wounding mortally or killing (Gen. iv. 15, Exod. ii. 12, Josh. xx. 5, 1 Sam. xvii. 26). עֹרֵף (from עֹרֶף, *the neck*) is a technical term used in the law to denote the breaking of the neck of unclean animals when not redeemed from consecration to Jehovah (Exod. xiii. 13, Deut. xxi. 4). It expresses, therefore, a peculiar mode of killing. The dog has ever been regarded in the east as peculiarly unclean, and in that light is coupled with the swine not only in the Bible (Mat. vii. 6, 2 Peter ii. 22), but by Horace, who twice names dog and swine together as the vilest animals. *Swine's blood* alone is without a verb to govern it, which Lowth thinks a defect in the existing text, while Hitzig ascribes it to the haste of composition. Bochart supplies *eating*, but Vitringa properly objects that all the rest relates to sacrifice. The simplest course is to repeat the leading verb of the same member.—אָוֶן is commonly supposed to mean an idol, as it does in a few places; but it is better to retain its generic sense, as more expressive. This is by some understood to be vanity, nonentity, or worthlessness, as attributes of idols; by others, injustice or iniquity in general. The whole phrase is commonly explained to mean *blessing* (*i. e.* praising or worshipping) *an idol*, or as Hitzig thinks, *saluting* it by kissing

(1 Kings xix. 18, Job xxxi. 27); but Luther gives it the general sense of *praising wickedness*, an act to which he supposes that of *mentioning incense* to be likened, while Knobel understands אָוֶן adverbially, and the phrase as meaning one who worships God unlawfully or wickedly; but this would be comparing a thing merely with itself, and as all the other secondary phrases denote rites of worship, it is better so to understand this likewise. Such is the meaning of the several expressions; but a question still remains as to their combination. The simplest syntax is to supply the verb of existence, and thus produce a series of short propositions. He that slays an ox smites a man, &c. Lowth and Ewald understand this to mean that the same person who offers sacrifices to God in the form prescribed by law, is also guilty of murder and idolatry, a practice implying gross hypocrisy as well as gross corruption. The ancient versions all supply a particle of likeness—he that slays an ox is like one that murders a man, &c. This is adopted by most of the modern writers, but of late without supplying anything, the words being taken to assert not mere resemblance, but identity, which is the strongest form of comparison. It is certainly more expressive to say that an offerer of cattle is a murderer, than to say that he is like one, though the latter may be, after all, the real meaning. He is a murderer, *i.e.* God so esteems him. According to Lowth and Ewald, the verse describes the co-existence of ritual formality with every kind of wickedness, especially idolatry, as in the first chapter. Gesenius objects that this presupposes the existence of the Mosaic ritual when the passage was written, never dreaming that instead of presupposing it might prove it. His own interpretation, and the common one, is, that the passage relates not to the actual practice of the abominations mentioned, but to the practice of iniquity in general, which renders the most regular and costly offerings as hateful to Jehovah as the most abominable rites of idolatry. Among those who adopt this explanation of the sentence there is still a difference as to its application. Gesenius applies it to the worthlessness of ritual performances without regard to moral duty, Hitzig and Knobel to the worthlessness of sacrifices which might be offered at the temple built in Babylonia, Henderson to the unlawfulness of sacrifices under the Christian dispensation, with particular reference to the case of the restored Jews and their temple at Jerusalem. I still regard Vitringa's exposition as the most exact, profound, and satisfactory, whether considered in itself, or in relation to the whole preceding context. He agrees with Gesenius in making the text the general doctrine that sacrifice is hateful in the sight of God if offered in a wicked spirit, but with a special reference to those who still adhered to the old sacrifices after the great Sacrifice for sin was come, and had been offered once for all. Thus understood, this verse extends to sacrifices that which the foregoing verses said of the temple, after the change of dispensations.

4. *I also will choose their vexations, and their fear I will bring upon them; because I called and there was no one answering, I spake and they did not hear, and they did evil in my eyes, and that which I delight not in they chose.* The larger part of this verse, from *because* to the end, is repeated from chap. lxv. 12, and serves not only to connect the passages as parts of an unbroken composition, but also to identify the subjects of discourse in the two places. According to the usual analogy of the Masoretic interpunction, the first words of the verse before us ought to be connected as a parallel clause with the last words of ver. 3, partly because each verse is complete and of the usual length without the clause in question, partly

because the parallelism is indicated by the repetition of the גַּם. This repetition occurs elsewhere as an equivalent to the Greek *καὶ—καὶ*, the Latin *et—et*, and our *both—and*, as in the phrase *also yesterday, also to-day* (Exod. v. 14). In the case before us it is paraphrased by some translators *as they chose, so I choose*, by others, *as well they as I chose ;* but perhaps the nearest equivalent in English is, *on their part they chose, and on my part I choose.* The obvious antithesis between the pronoun of the third and first person precludes the supposition that a different class of persons is denoted by גַּם הֵמָּה. The common version of תַּעֲלוּלִים (*delusions*) seems to be founded on a misconception of the Vulgate *illusiones*, which was probably intended to suggest the idea of derision, like the *ἐμπαίγματα* of the Septuagint. The true sense of the word here is essentially the same, but somewhat stronger, viz. annoyances, vexations, which last is employed to represent it by Cocceius. It is in the cognate sense of petulance or caprice, that it is used to denote children in chap. iii. 4. This etymological affinity is wholly disregarded, by translating the word here calamities, with Lowth, Gesenius, and others. *Their fear* is the evil which they fear, as in Prov. x. 24, where the same idea is expressed almost in the same words.

5. *Hear the word of Jehovah, ye that tremble at his word. Your brethren say, (those) hating you and casting you out for my name's sake, Jehovah will be glorified, and we shall gaze upon your joy—and they shall be ashamed.* Trembling at (or rather to) Jehovah's word seems to mean reverently waiting for it. Ye that thus expect a message from Jehovah, now receive it. Vitringa adheres strictly to the Masoretic accents, which connect *for my name's sake* with what follows : " Your brethren say—those hating you and casting you out—for my name's sake Jehovah shall be glorified." To this construction there are two objections : first, that the same persons who are three times mentioned in the plural are abruptly made to speak in the singular, for *my* name's sake, an enallage which, although possible, is not to be assumed without necessity ; and secondly, that *for my name's sake* is not the appropriate expression of the thought supposed to be intended, which would rather be *by my means*. The majority of later writers are agreed in so far departing from the accents as to join the phrase in question with what goes before ; which is the less objectionable here, as we have seen already in the preceding verses some appearance of inaccuracy in the Masoretic interpunction. The neuter verb יִכְבַּד is here applied to God, as it is elsewhere to men (Job xiv. 21) and cities (Ezek. xxvii. 25), in the sense of being *glorious* rather than *glorified*, which would require a passive form. It may be construed either as an optative or future ; but the last is more exact, and really includes the other. All are agreed that these two words (יִכְבַּד יְהוֹה) are put into the mouth of the brethren before mentioned ; but it is made a question whether the exact phrase, וְנִרְאֶה בְשִׂמְחַתְכֶם, is spoken by them likewise. Piscator, followed by the English and Dutch versions, makes this the language of the Prophet, and translates it, *and he shall appear to your joy.* Besides the doubtful sense thus put upon the preposition, this translation really involves a change of pointing, so as to read נִרְאָה or a very unusual construction of the participle. Vitringa makes these words the language of a chorus, and supposes them to mean, " But we shall see your joy and they shall be ashamed." The modern writers who refer שְׁמִי, as we have seen, to God himself, are obliged to make נִרְאָה the language of another speaker ; unless they assume a *pluralis majestaticus*, as some old Jewish writers did, according to Aben Ezra, which they do by adding it to what immediately precedes : " Your brethren say, Jehovah shall

be glorified and we shall see your happiness ;" the verb רָאָה, as usual when followed by the preposition בְּ, meaning to view or gaze at with strong feeling, and in this case with delight. This construction is unanimously sanctioned by the latest German writers, and is in itself much simpler and more natural than any other. As to the application of the verse there is the usual diversity of judgment. Jarchi and Abarbanel apply it to the treatment of the Jews in their present exile by the Mohammedans and Romans, called their brethren because descendants of Ishmael and Esau. Gesenius seems to understand it as relating to the scornful treatment of the exiled Jews in Babylon by their heathen enemies. Knobel denies that the latter would be spoken of as brethren, and applies it to the treatment of the pious Jews by their idolatrous countrymen. Hitzig questions even this application of *brethren*, and explains the verse of the contempt with which the exiles who were willing to return were treated by the unbelievers who remained behind. But how could those who thus remained be said to *cast out* such as insisted on returning? The phrase may posssibly be taken in the vague sense of despising or treating with contempt ; but this diluted explanation, though admissible in case of necessity, cannot take precedence of the strict one, or of the interpretation which involves it. Vitringa, although rather infelicitous in his construction and translation of the sentence, has excelled all other writers in his exhibition of its general import. He applies it, in accordance with his previous hypothesis, to the rejection of the first Christian converts by the unbelieving Jews : Hear the word (or promise) of Jehovah, ye that wait for it with trembling confidence : your brethren (the unconverted Jews) who hate you and cast you out for my name's sake, have said (in so doing), " Jehovah will be glorious (or glorify himself in your behalf no doubt), and we shall witness your salvation " (a bitter irony like that in chap. v. 19) ; but they (who thus speak) shall themselves be confounded (by beholding what they now consider so incredible). Besides the clearness and coherence of this exposition in itself considered, and its perfect harmony with what we have arrived at as the true sense of the whole foregoing context, it is strongly recommended by remarkable coincidences with the New Testament, some of which Vitringa specifies. That the unbelieving Jews might still be called the brethren of the converts, if it needed either proof or illustration, might derive it from Paul's mode of address to them in Acts xxii. 1, and of reference to them in Rom. ix. 3. The phrase *those hating you* may be compared with· John xv. 18, xvii. 14 ; Mat. x. 22 ; 1 Thes. ii. 14 ; *and casting you out* with John xvi. 2, and Matthew xviii. 17 ; *for my name's sake* with Mat. xxiv. 10 ; to which may be added the interesting fact that the verb נִדָּה and its derivatives are used to this day by the Jews in reference to excommunication. Thus understood the verse is an assurance to the chosen remnant in whom the true Israel was to be perpetuated, that although their unbelieving countrymen might cast them out with scorn and hatred for a time, their spite should soon be utterly confounded. The great truth involved in the change of dispensations may be signally developed and exemplified hereafter, as Henderson infers from this passage that it will be, in the case of the restored Jews who receive the doctrine of the gospel and their brethren who persist in endeavouring to establish the old ritual ; but we dare not abandon the fulfilment which has actually taken place for the sake of one which may never happen, since we have not been able thus far to discover any clear prediction of it.

6. *A voice of tumult from the city! A voice from the temple! The voice of Jehovah, rendering requital to his enemies!* The Hebrew word שָׁאוֹן is

never applied elsewhere to a joyful cry or a cry of lamentation, but to the tumult of war, the rushing sound of armies and the shock of battle, in which sense it is repeatedly employed by Isaiah. The enemies here mentioned must of course be those who had just been described as the despisers and persecutors of their brethren, and whose confusion after being threatened generally in the verse preceding is graphically represented in detail. Even Aben Ezra says, these enemies of God are those who cast the others out. The description therefore cannot without violence be understood of foreign or external enemies. These data furnished by usage and the context will enable us to estimate the various interpretations of the verse before us. If what has just been stated be correct, the noise heard by the Prophet cannot be the rejoicing of the Maccabees and their adherents when the temple was evacuated by Antiochus, as Grotius imagines; nor the preaching of the gospel by the apostles beginning at Jerusalem, as Junius and Tremellius think; nor a voice calling for vengeance on the Romans, according to Jarchi; nor the blasphemies of the heathen, according to Abarbanel. Nor can the words if rightly understood as meaning the tumult of war, be applied to the destruction of Gog and Magog, as by Kimchi; or to any other external enemies, as by the modern Germans. These indeed are not a little puzzled to explain the verse in any consistency with their hypotheses. Gesenius admits that there is so far a difficulty as the anti-theocratic party stayed behind in Babylon, and queries whether the Prophet may not have suspected many such to go up in the hope of worldly advantages, and there be smitten by the divine judgments! Maurer as usual sees no difficulty in the case, because Jehovah is described as punishing the wicked Jews not *in* Jerusalem, but *from* it. Hitzig makes it a description of the general judgment foretold by Joel, when all the nations should be judged at Jerusalem (Joel iv. 2). Knobel confidently adds that the Prophet expected this great judgment to fall especially upon the Babylonians, whom Cyrus had not punished sufficiently, and with them on the idolatrous exiles. Umbreit, who seems to float in mid-air between faith and unbelief in his interpretation of this passage, makes the noise a joyful noise, and separates it from Jehovah's voice bringing vengeance to his external enemies.—The only Christian interpreter that need be quoted here is Henderson, who says that " by a remarkable and astounding interposition of Jehovah the scheme of the Jews shall be defeated; the very temple which they shall be in the act of erecting shall be the scene of judgment." Then adopting the groundless notion of the German writers, that the *voice of Jehovah* always means thunder, he adds that " in all probability the projected temple will be destroyed by lightning." This is certainly sufficiently specific, but by no means so entitled to belief as the fulfilment of the prophecy which has already taken place. In strict adherence to the usage of the words and to requisitions of the context both immediate and remote, the verse may be applied to the giving up of Zion and the temple to its enemies, as a final demonstration that the old economy was at an end, and that the sins of Israel were now to be visited on that generation. The assailants of Jerusalem and of the Jews were now no longer those of God himself, but rather chosen instruments to execute his vengeance on his enemies, the unbelieving Jews themselves. Vitringa goes too far when he restricts the tumult here described to the noise actually made by the Romans in the taking of Jerusalem.—It rather comprehends the whole confusion of the siege and conquest, and a better commentary on this brief but grand prediction cannot be desired than that afforded by Josephus in his narrative of what may be regarded as not only the most dreadful siege on record, but in some respects the most sublime and critical conjuncture in all history, because coincident with the transition from the abrogated system of the old economy to the acknowledged introduction of the new, a change of infinitely more extensive influence on human character and destiny than many philosophical historians have been willing to admit, or even able to discover.

7. *Before she travailed she brought forth, before her pain came she was delivered of a male.* All interpreters agree that the mother here described is Zion, that the figure is essentially the same as in chap. xlix. 21, and that in both cases an increase of numbers is represented as a birth, while in that before us the additional idea of suddenness is expressed by the figure of an unexpected birth. The difference between the cases is that in the other a plurality of children is described, while in this the whole increase is represented in the aggregate as a single birth. As to the specification of the sex, some regard it as a mere illustration of the oriental predilection for male children, not intended to have any special emphasis, while others make it significant of strength as well as numbers in the increase of the people. As to the application of the passage, there is nothing in the terms employed which can determine it, but it must follow the sense put upon the foregoing context or the general hypothesis of the interpreter. Those who see nothing in these chapters but the restoration of the Jews from Babylon explain this verse as meaning simply that the joyful return of the exiles to the long forsaken city would be like an unexpected birth to a childless mother. According to Henderson, " the language forcibly expresses the sudden and unexpected reproduction of the Jewish nation in their own land in the latter day ; their future recovery is the object of the divine purpose, and every providential arrangement shall be made for effecting it; yet the event shall be unexpectedly sudden." In both these cases there is an accommodation of the passage to the exegetical hypothesis, without any attempt to shew that the latter derives confirmation from it. In both cases, too, there is a certain abruptness in the transition from the judgment threatened in the preceding verse to the promise here recorded. Knobel somewhat awkwardly describes the general judgment on the nations at Jerusalem, including specially the Babylonians and apostate Jews, as being *followed* by the speedy return of the believing exiles. Henderson, in like manner, makes the restoration *follow* the destruction of the projected temple by lightning, and yet supposes it to be described as unexpectedly sudden. Such retrogressions in the order of events are not without example, but they certainly give no advantage to the theories in which they are involved over such as have no need of them. Of this description is Vitringa's doctrine that the passage has respect to the vocation of the Gentiles as immediately consequent upon the excision of the Jews, a sequence of events which is continually held up to view in the New Testament history. (Luke xxiv. 47 ; Acts iii. 26, xiii. 46, xviii. 6 ; Rom. i. 16, ii. 10.) The only questionable point in his interpretation is his pressing the mere letter of the metaphor too far by representing the Gentiles or the Gentile churches as the male child of which the Apostolic Church was unexpectedly delivered. It is perfectly sufficient, and in better taste, to understand the parturition as a figure for the whole eventual crisis of the change of dispensations, and the consequent change in the condition of the church. This indestructible ideal person, when she might have seemed to be reduced to nothing by the

defection of the natural Israel, is vastly and suddenly augmented by the introduction of the Gentiles, a succession of events which is here most appropriately represented as the birth of a male child without the pains of childbirth.

8. *Who hath heard such a thing? who hath seen such things? Shall a land be brought forth in one day, or shall a nation be born at once? For Zion hath travailed, she hath also brought forth her children.* This verse, in the form of pointed interrogation, represents the event previously mentioned as without example. The terms of the sentence are exceedingly appropriate both to the return from Babylon and the future restoration of the Jews, but admit at the same time of a wider application to the change of economy, the birth of the church of the New Testament. אֶרֶץ appears to be construed as a masculine, because it is put for the inhabitants, as in chaps. ix. 18, xxvi. 18 (compare Judges xviii. 30); or the verb may take that form according to the usual licence when the object follows, as in Gen. xiii. 6; Psalm cv. 30.—The causative sense given to this verb in the English and some other versions is not approved by the later lexicographers, who make יוּחַל a simple passive. Beck's application of the phrase to the creation of the earth is forbidden by the parallel term גּוֹי.—To avoid the apparent contradiction between this and the foregoing verse as to the pains of childbirth, some explain כִּי חָלָה גַם יָלְדָה to mean, "scarcely had she travailed when she brought forth," which is a forced construction. Hitzig attains the same end by making *sons* the object of both verbs, and making both synonymous. Both these expedients are unnecessary, as the reference is merely to the short time required for the birth, as if he had said, she has (already) travailed, she has also brought forth.

9. *Shall I bring to the birth and not cause to bring forth? saith Jehovah. Or am I the one causing to bring forth, and shall I shut up? saith thy God.* Without pretending to enumerate the various explanations of this verse, some of which are as disgusting as absurd, it will be sufficient to adduce as specimens Jerome's interpretation, which supposes him to ask whether he who causes others to bring forth shall not bring forth himself; and that of Cocceius, whether he who causes others to bring forth shall not cause Zion to do so likewise. The sense now put upon the figure by the general consent of interpreters is, that he who begins the work may be expected to accomplish it, to be both its author and its finisher. The reason why it is expressed in this form is not any peculiar adaptation or expressiveness in these unusual metaphors, but simply that the increase of the church had been already represented as a birth, and the additional ideas of the writer are expressed without a change of figure. The precise connection of the verse with that before it seems to be that it extenuates the wonder which had been described by representing it as something which was to be expected in the case supposed. That is to say, if God had undertaken to supply the place of what his church had lost by new accessions, the extent and suddenness of the effect could not be matters of surprise. On the contrary, it would have been indeed surprising, if he who began the change had stopped it short, and interfered for the prevention of his own designs. —On the metaphor of this verse and the one preceding, compare chap. xxvi. 18; on the peculiar use of עָצַר in this application, Gen. xvi. 2, xx. 18.

10. *Rejoice ye with Jerusalem and exult in her, all that love her; be glad with her with gladness, all those mourning for her.* This is an indirect prediction of the joyful change awaiting Zion, clothed in the form of a command

or invitation to her friends to rejoice with her. The expression גִּילוּ בָהּ may either have the same sense, viz. that of sympathetic joy, or it may mean *rejoice in her* or *within her* in a local sense, or *in her* as the object of your joy, all which constructions are grammatical and justifiable by usage. Different interpreters, according to their various exegetical hypotheses, explain this as a prophecy of Israel's ancient restoration from the Babylonish exile, or of their future restoration from the present exile and dispersion, or of the glorious enlargement of the church after the excision of the unbelieving Jews, and the throes of that great crisis in which old things passed away and the new heavens and the new earth came into existence; which last I believe to be the true sense, for reasons which have been already fully stated.

11. *That ye may suck and be satisfied from the breast of her consolations, that ye may milk out and enjoy yourselves, from the fulness* (or *the full breast*) *of her glory.* Those who have sympathized with Zion in her joys and sorrows shall partake of her abundance and her glory. The figure of a mother is continued, but beautifully varied. The Targum takes שֹׁד in its usual sense of spoil or plunder; but see above, on chap. lx. 16. Hendewerk, with some of the older writers, reads *because* instead of *so that* or *in order that;* but this is a needless substitution of a meaning rare and doubtful at the best. *Suck and be satisfied, milk out and enjoy yourselves,* may be regarded as examples of hendiadys, meaning, *suck to satiety,* and *milk out with delight;* but no such change in the form of the translation is required or admissible. The Targum explains זִיז as meaning *wine;* Lowth proposes to read זִין provision, but there is no such word; Cocceius translates it *animals,* as in Ps. l. 11, lxxx. 14, which makes no sense; Jerome and Symmachus make it mean variety (*omnimoda*); but the modern writers are agreed that it originally signifies radiation or a radiating motion, then the radiating flow of milk or other liquids, and then fulness, or the full breast whence the radiation flows. Glory includes wealth or abundance, but much more, viz. all visible superiority or excellence.

12. *For thus saith Jehovah, Behold I am extending to her peace like a river, and like an overflowing stream the glory of nations; and ye shall suck; on the side shall ye be borne, and on the knees shall ye be dandled.* As אֶל is sometimes interchanged with עַל, Vitringa here translates *extending over,* i. e. so as to cover or submerge. But the force and beauty of the Prophet's figure are secured, without any departure from the ordinary usage, by supposing it to represent a river suddenly or gradually widening its channel or its flow until it reaches to a certain spot, its actual submersion being not expressed though it may be imputed. That the particle retains its proper meaning may be argued from the use of the entire phrase in Gen. xxxix. 21. Another suggestion of Vitringa, which has been rejected by the later writers, is that נָהָר and נַחַל here denote specifically the Euphrates and the Nile, which last he regards as a derivative of the Hebrew word. But the incorrectness of this etymology, the absence of the article which elsewhere makes the nouns specific, and the uselessness of this supposition to the force and beauty of the passage, all conspire to condemn it. *Peace* is here to be taken in its frequent sense of welfare or prosperity. (See above, on chap. xlviii. 18.) The words *and ye shall suck* are added to announce a resumption of the figure of the foregoing verse. The Targum and Vulgate read עַל שַׁד instead of עַל צַד, while Houbigant and Lowth insert the former after *suck* (ye shall suck at the breast, ye shall be carried

at the side). Equally gratuitous is the addition of the pronoun by Henderson (ye shall suck them), and Hendewerk (ye shall suck it), and Gesenius's paraphrase (*zum Genuss*). For the sense of עַל צַד, see above, on chap. lx. 4, and compare chap. xlix. 22. The objects of address in this verse are the sons of Zion, to be gathered from all nations.

13. *As a man whom his mother comforteth, so will I comfort you, and in Jerusalem shall ye be comforted.* De Wette's version, " as a man who comforts his mother " (*der seine Mutter tröstet*) is so utterly at variance with the form of the original, that it must be regarded as an inadvertence, or perhaps as an error of the press. The image, xlviii. 18, is essentially the same with that in chap. xlix. 15, but with a striking variation. The English Version, which in multitudes of cases inserts *man* where the original expression is indefinite, translating οὐδείς, for example, always *no man*, here reverses the process, and dilutes *a man* to *one*. The same liberty is taken by many other versions, old and new, occasioned no doubt by a feeling of the incongruity of making a full-grown man the subject of maternal consolations. The difficulty might, if it were necessary, be avoided by explaining אִישׁ to mean a man-child, as it does in Gen. iv. 1, 1 Sam. i. 11, and in many other cases. But the truth is that the solecism, which has been so carefully expunged by these translators, is an exquisite trait of patriarchal manners, in their primitive simplicity. Compare Gen. xxiv. 67, Judges xvii. 2, 1 Kings ii. 19, 20, and the affecting scenes between Thetis and Achilles in the Iliad. Of the modern writers, Umbreit alone does justice to this beautiful allusion, not only by a strict translation, but by adding as a gloss, " with the consolation of a mother who, as no other can, soothes the ruffled spirit of a man (*des Mannes*)." Equally characteristic is the brief remark of Hitzig, that " the אִישׁ is not well chosen."—Lowth in another respect shews what would now be thought a morbid distaste for simplicity by changing the passive, *ye shall be comforted* into *ye shall receive consolation*, in order to avoid a repetition which to any unsophisticated ear is charming.—The *in Jerusalem* suggests the only means by which these blessings are to be secured, viz. a union of affection and of interest with the Israel of God, to whom alone they are promised.

14. *And ye shall see, and your heart shall leap (with joy), and your bones like grass shall sprout, and the hand of Jehovah shall be known to his servants, and he shall be indignant at his enemies.* The object of address still continues to be those who had loved Zion, and had mourned for her, and whom God had promised to comfort in Jerusalem. They are here assured that they shall see for themselves the fulfilment of these promises. —Ewald gives שָׂשׂ its primary sense of bounding, leaping, which agrees well with the strong figure in the next clause, where the bones, as the seat of strength or the framework of the body, are compared with springing herbage to denote their freshness and vigour. Here again Ewald makes the language more expressive by translating *become green like the young grass*, which, however, is a paraphrase and not an exact version, as the primary meaning of the Hebrew verb is to burst out or put forth. (For the figure, compare chaps. xxvii. 6, lviii. 11, Job xxi. 24, Prov. iii. 8, xv. 30, Ps. li. 10, and *e converso* Ps. vi. 3, xxii. 15, xxxi. 11.) There is no need of supposing with Hitzig that the human frame is likened to a tree of which the bones are the branches, and the muscles, flesh, and skin, the leaves. (See Job. x. 11.)—The hand of God is known when his power is recognised as the cause of any given effect. Gesenius makes נוֹדְעָה the

passive of הוֹדִיעַ and אֶת the sign of the second accusative (it is made known his servants, *i. e.* to his servants). But Hitzig explains the first word as the passive of יָדַע and אֶת as a preposition equivalent to עַל in chap. liii. 1, and to לְעֵינֵי in Ezek. xxxviii. 23, where the same passive verb is used. The English Version follows Luther in translating זַעַם as a noun, which never has this form, however, out of pause. It is correctly explained by Eben Ezra as a verb with Vav conversive. The אֶת may be either the objective particle, as this verb usually governs the accusative, or a preposition equivalent to וְזַעַם עַל in Dan. xi. 30, and to our expression, *he is angry with* another. Noyes makes this verb agree with *hand ;* which would be ungrammatical, as יָד is feminine. The whole clause is omitted in Hendewerk's translation. It is important as affording a transition from the promise to the threatening, in accordance with the Prophet's constant practice of presenting the salvation of God's people as coincident and simultaneous with the destruction of his enemies.

15. *For lo, Jehovah in fire will come, and like the whirlwind his chariots, to appease in fury his anger, and his rebuke in flames of fire.* This is an amplification of the brief phrase at the end of ver. 14. Lowth reads *as a fire*, with the Septuagint version, which is probably a mere inadvertence. Luther and others translate *with fire* (see ver. 16), but the modern writers generally *in fire*, that is, enveloped and surrounded by it, as on Sinai. (See above, chap. xxix. 6, xxx. 27, 30, and compare Ps. l. 3.)—The second clause is repeated in Jer. iv. 13. The points of comparison are swiftness and violence. The allusion is to the two-wheeled chariots of ancient warfare. Vitringa supposes angels to be meant, on the authority of Ps. lxviii. 18. (Compare Ps. xviii. 11.) Hendewerk supposes an allusion to the chariots and horses of fire, mentioned 2 Kings ii. 11, vi. 17. (Compare Hab. iii. 8.) The English Version supplies *with* before *his chariots*, but this is forbidden by the order of the words in Hebrew, and unnecessary, as the *chariots* may be construed either with *shall come* or with the substantive verb *are* or *shall be.*—Ewald agrees with the older writers who give הָשִׁיב the sense of rendering, returning, recompensing, which it has in Ps. liv. 7, Hosea xii. 15, and in which it is construed with *vengeance* in Deut. xxxii. 41, 43. Henderson prefers the sense of *causing to return*, implying repetition and severity. Gesenius adheres to the usage of this very verb and noun in Ps. lxxviii. 38, and Job ix. 13 (compare Gen. xxvii. 44, 45), where it means to withdraw anger, *i. e.* to appease it, which may seem to be at variance with the context here, but is really, as Maurer has observed, the most appropriate and elegant expression of the writer's meaning, which is that of wrath appeased by being gratified. (Compare chap. i. 24, vol. i. p. 91.)—Lowth's emendation of the text by reading הָשִׁיב (from נָשַׁב, *to breathe out*) is gratuitous and not supported by the usage of that verb itself.—Luther and Hendewerk make חֵמָה אַפּוֹ a kind of intensive compound (*Zornesgluth*), as in chap. xlii. 25; but it is better with Maurer to regard בְּחֵמָה as qualifying הָשִׁיב, and explaining how his anger was to be appeased, viz. in fury, *i. e.* in the free indulgence of it.—God's *rebuke* is often coupled with his wrath as its effect or practical manifestation. (See above, chaps. xvii. 13, li. 20, liv. 9.) Most writers seem to make *rebuke* dependent on the preceding verb ; but Hendewerk apparently regards it as an independent clause, exactly similar in form to the second member of the sentence, *and like the whirlwind his chariots, and his rebuke in flames of fire.* The leading noun may then, instead of being governed by הָשִׁיב, agree with *is* or *shall be* understood. The

whole verse represents Jehovah, considered in relation to his enemies, as a consuming fire. (Deut. iv. 24, Heb. xii. 29. Compare 2 Thess. i. 8.)

16. *For by fire is Jehovah striving and by his sword with all flesh, and multiplied* (or *many*) *are the slain of Jehovah.* Fire and sword are mentioned as customary means of destruction, especially in war. The reflexive form נִשְׁפָּט has here its usual sense of reciprocal judgment, litigation, or contention in general. (See above, chap. xliii. 26.) Gesenius makes it mean directly to punish, which it never means except by implication : and Hitzig, on the same ground, explains אֵת as the sign of the accusative ; but that it is really a preposition is clear from Ezek. xvii. 20, and Joel iv. 2.— The repetition of *with* by Noyes and Henderson, " with fire, with his sword, with all flesh," is a cacophonous tautology not found in the original, where two distinct prepositions are employed, which Lowth has well translated *by* and *with*.—According to Knobel, *all flesh* means all nations, and especially the Babylonians who had not been sufficiently punished by Cyrus. Henderson applies the verses to the battle of Armageddon, described in Rev. xvi. 14–21, xix. 11–21, and Vitringa admits a reference to the same event, But this interpretation rests upon the false assumption, often noticed heretofore, that the Apocalyptic prophecies are exegetical of those in the Old Testament, from which their images and terms are borrowed.—A much surer clue to the primary application of the one before us is afforded by our Saviour's words in Matt. xxiv. 22, where in speaking of the speedy destruction of Jerusalem he says, that excepting the elect no flesh should be saved, *i.e.* no portion of the Jewish race but those who were ordained to everlasting life through faith in him. This application of Isaiah's prophecy agrees exactly with the view already taken of the whole preceding context as relating to that great decisive crisis in the history of the church and of the world, the dissolution of the old economy and the inauguration of the new. According to this view of the passage, what is here said of fire, sword, and slaughter, was fulfilled not only as a figurative prophecy of general destruction, but in its strictest sense in the terrific carnage which attended the extinction of the Jewish State, and of which, more emphatically than of any other event outwardly resembling it, it might be said that *many were the slain of Jehovah.*

17. *The* (men) *hallowing themselves and the* (men) *cleansing themselves to* (or *towards*) *the gardens after one in the midst, eaters of swine's flesh and vermin and mouse, together shall cease* (or *come to an end*), *saith Jehovah.* This verse is closely connected with the one before it, and explains who are meant by *the slain of Jehovah.* It is almost universally agreed that these are here described as gross idolaters ; but Henderson, with some of the old Jewish writers, is inclined to understand it of the Mohammedans, as we shall see. But even among those who understand it of idolaters, there is no small difference of opinion in relation to particular expressions. The class of persons meant is obviously the same as that described in chap. lxv. 3, 5, the gardens and the swine's flesh being common to both. The reflexive participles in the first clause are technical terms for ceremonial purification under the law of Moses, but here transferred to heathen rites. The older writers for the most part follow the Vulgate in explaining אֶל־הַגַּנּוֹת as synonymous with בַּגַּנּוֹת in chap. lxv. 3. Even Gesenius admits this sense, although he gives the preference to that of *for.* But Maurer speaks of it as one no longer needing refutation, and returns to the strict translation of the Septuagint (εἰς τοὺς κήπους), implying that they purified themselves not in but on their way to the gardens, which is essentially the

sense conveyed by the translation *for*, *i. e.* in preparation for the gardens where the idolatrous services were to be performed. The next words (אַחַר אַחַד בַּתָּוֶךְ) are those which constitute the principal difficulty of the sentence. This some have undertaken to remove by emendations of the text. Even the Masora reads אַחַת, which is only changing the gender of the numeral. Ewald assimilates the first two words so as to read אַחַר אַחַר, which he renders *hinten hinten*, *i. e.* far back. Lowth on the other hand reads אַחַר אַחַד *one one*, *i. e.* one by one, or one after the other. The same reading seems to be applied in Luther's version, one here and another there. The Peshito has one after another, and the same sense is expressed by the Targum, *crowd after crowd*, and by Symmachus and Theodotion ὀπίσω ἀλλήλων. Schelling accordingly inserts a word, reading אַחַד אַחַר אַחַד. Whether a various reading is implied in the Septuagint version (ἐν τοῖς προθύροις), or merely, a peculiar explanation of אַחַד, is a matter of dispute. Some, without a change of text, bring out the same sense by supposing an ellipsis. Most interpreters take אַחַד (or according to the Masoretic Keri אַחַת) as the numeral *one*, agreeing either with grove (Aben Ezra), or with pool (Kimchi), or with tree (Saadias), or with priest or priestess (Gesenius); which last may be given as the current explanation, in which an allusion is supposed to an idolatrous procession led by a hierophant. Maurer applies אַחַד to the idol, which he supposes to be so called in contempt, *one*, being then equivalent to the Latin *quidam, necscio quem*. Vitringa follows Scaliger, Bochart, and other learned men of early date, in treating אַחַד as the proper name of a Syrian idol, called by Sanchoniathon "Αδωδος and by Pliny and Macrobius *Adad*, the last writer adding expressly that the name means *one*. For the difference of form various explanations have been suggested, and among the rest a corruption in the classical orthography, which is rendered exceedingly improbable, however, by the substantial agreement of the Greek and Latin writers above cited. Rosenmüller acquiesces in Vitringa's suggestion that the difference of form may be explained by the exclusion of the aspirate from the middle of a Greek word, the hiatus being remedied by the insertion of a dental; but Gesenius replies that אַחַד would more naturally have been written "Αχαδος and *Achadus* in Greek and Latin The Masoretic reading אַחַת is identified by Clericus with *Hecate*, in whose Egyptian worship swine's flesh was particularly used. Henderson calls attention to a very striking coincidence between the use of this word here and the constant application of the cognate one in Arabic (حَدَ) by the Mohammedans to God as being One, in express contradiction to the doctrine of the Trinity. This is especially the case in the 112th Surah of the Koran, to which they attach peculiar doctrinal importance. The common editions of the Vulgate render אַחַד here by *janua* (like the Peshito); but some of more authority have *unam*, in accordance with the marginal Keri. Besides the difficulty which attends the absolute use of the numeral without a noun, there is another of the same kind arising from the like use of תָּוֶךְ, *midst*, without any thing to limit or determine it. Gesenius attaches to it here as he does in 2 Sam. iv. 6, the sense of the interior or court of an oriental house, and applies it to the edifice in which the lustrations were performed before entering the gardens; which may also be the meaning of the Septuagint version, εἰς τοὺς κήπους, ἐν τοῖς προθύροις. Maurer and others follow Scaliger, who makes it mean the midst of the grove or garden, where the idol was commonly erected. But Knobel, by ingeniously combining Gen. xlii. 5, Ps. xlii. 5, lxviii. 26, makes it more improbable that *in the midst* means in the crowd or procession of worshippers. All these constructions adhere to the Maso-retic points and interpunction. But Lowth and Henderson follow Theodo-tion and Symmachus in reading בְּתוֹךְ and connecting it directly with what follows, *in the midst of those eating swine's flesh*, &c., implying, as Lowth thinks, a participation in these impure rites, while Henderson supposes the Mohammedans to be distinguished, as to this point, from the Pagans who surround them. Boettcher departs still further from the usual interpunc-tion, and includes בתוך not in the description of the sin, but in the threaten-ing of punishment—in the midst of the eaters of swine's flesh, &c., together shall they perish. One reason urged by Henderson in favour of his own construction is without weight, namely, that אכלים being without the article cannot be in apposition with the words at the beginning of the sentence, but must designate a totally different class of persons. He did not observe that אכלי is rendered definite by the addition of a qualifying noun, which being equivalent to the article excludes it. As to the eating of swine's flesh, see above on chap. lxv. 4.—שֶׁקֶץ may either have its generic sense of abomination or abominable food, or the more specific sense of flesh offered to idols (Hitzig), or of the smaller unclean animals, whether quad-rupeds, insects, or reptiles, to which it is specially applied in the law (Lev. xi. 41–43), and in reference to which it corresponds very nearly, in effect, to the English word *vermin*. Spencer thinks that it means a kid boiled in its mother's milk. (Exod. xxiii. 19, xxxiv. 26.) Against the wide sense of abomination and in favour of some more specific meaning is the colloca-tion of the word between swine's flesh and the mouse, or as the modern writers understand the word, the jerboa or Arabian field-mouse which is eaten by the Arabs. The actual use of any kind of mouse in the ancient heathen rites has never been established, the modern allegations of the fact being founded on the place before us. As to the application of the passage, those who make the Babylonian exile the great subject of the prophecy, see nothing here but a description of the practices of those Jews who aposta-tised to heathenism, and who were to be cut off by the same judgments which secured the restoration of their brethren. J. D. Michaelis confesses his uncertainty in what sense this description will be verified hereafter ; and Henderson, who holds the same hypothesis, pleads guilty to a part of the same ignorance, but bravely and ingeniously endeavours, by the com-bination of the particular contrivances already mentioned, to impart some plausibility to his assumption that the prophecy has reference to the future restoration of the Jews. This could not have been done with greater skill or more success than he has shewn in his attempt to make it probable that what is here predicted is the future destruction of the Moslems as the enemies of Christ's divinity and noted for their trust in outward rites, especially ablutions—their destruction in the midst of the idolaters whom now they hate most bitterly and most profoundly scorn. This explanation seems to have been framed by its ingenious author without any reference to the dictum of the Rabbins, that the first clause of the verse is a descrip-tion of the Moslems and their purifications, but the next of the Christians as eaters of swine-flesh, and regardless of all difference in meats and drinks. The most offensive part of this interpretation, although extant in the writ-ings of Kimchi himself, has been expunged from most editions for pruden-tial motives. (See Vitringa on the passage.) It is not to be expected that the advocates of any exegetical hypothesis will here abandon it if able by any means to reconcile it with the Prophet's language, and accordingly I see no cause to change my previous conclusion that this prophecy relates to the excision of the Jews and the vocation of the Gentiles, or in other words the change of dispensation. The apparent difficulty which arises from the description of such gross idolatry as all admit to have had no existence among the Jews after their return from exile, is removed by the consideration that the Jews were cast off not for the sins of a single generation, but of the race throughout its ancient history, and that idolatry was not only one of these, but that which most abounded in the days of the Prophet ; so that when he looks forward to the great catastrophe and paints its causes, he naturally dips his pencil in the colours which were nearest and most vivid to his own perceptions, without meaning to exclude from his description other sins as great or greater in themselves, which afterwards supplanted these revolting practices as the besetting national transgressions of apostate Israel. A writer in the early days of Wilberforce and Clarkson, in denouncing God's wrath upon England, would most naturally place the oppression of the negro in the foreground of his picture, even if he had been gifted to foresee that this great evil in the course of time would be completely banished from the sight of men by new forms of iniquity successively usurping its conspicuous position, such as excessive luxury, dishonest speculation, and ambitious encroachment on the rightful possessions of inferior powers in the East. If it were really God's purpose to destroy that mighty kingdom for its national offences, he would not lose sight of ancient half-forgotten crimes, because they have long since given place to others more or less atrocious. So in reference to Israel, although the generation upon whom the final blow fell were hypocrites, not idolaters, the misdeeds of their fathers entered into the account, and they were cast off not merely as the murderers of the Lord of life, but as apostates who insulted Jehovah to his face by bowing down to stocks and stones in groves and gardens, and by eating swine's flesh, the abomination, and the mouse. And as all this was included in the grounds of their righteous condemnation, it might well be rendered prominent in some of the predictions of that great catastrophe.—Another possible interpretation of the passage, in direct application to the unbelieving Jews who were contemporary with our Saviour, is obtained by supposing an allusion to ver. 3, where those who still clung to the abrogated ritual are put upon a level with the grossest idolaters, and may here be absolutely so described, just as the rulers and people of Jerusalem in chap. i. 9, are addressed directly as rulers of Sodom and people of Gomorrah, on account of the comparison immediately preceding. This view of the passage is undoubtedly favoured by the mention of swine's flesh in both places, which would naturally make the one suggestive of the other. Neither of these exegetical hypotheses requires the assumption of imaginary facts, such as the practice of idolatry by the Jews in exile, or their return to it hereafter.

18. *And I—their works and their thoughts—it is come—to gather all the nations and the tongues—and they shall come and see my glory.* This is an exact transcript of the Hebrew sentence, the grammatical construction of which has much perplexed interpreters. Luther cuts the knot by arbitrary transposition, *I will come and gather all their works and thoughts with all nations,* &c. ; J. D. Michaelis, by a no less arbitrary change of pointing, so as to read, *they are my work, even mine, and my thought, i. e.* care. Tremellius and Cocceius among the older writers, Hitzig and Hendewerk among the moderns, follow Jarchi in taking the pronoun as a nominative absolute and construing בָּאָה with the nouns preceding : *As for me—their works and thoughts are come to gather,* &c. Hitzig explains *are come as*

meaning they have this effect ; while Hendewerk gives to the nouns themselves the sense of recompence, as in chap. xl. 10, and Rev. xiv. 13. Henderson has substantially the same construction, but supplies *before me* after
come, and takes לְקַבֵּץ as a simple future, *I will assemble;* both which assumptions are extremely forced.   Vitringa, Gesenius, and most other
writers, suppose an aposiopesis or a double ellipsis, supplying a verb after
אָנֹכִי and a noun before בָּאָה. The verb most commonly supplied is *know,*
as in the English Version (I know their works and their thoughts), and
substantially in the Chaldee Paraphrase (revealed before me are their works
and thoughts).   The noun supplied is *time,* according to the dictum of
Aben Ezra.   But the verb supplied by Maurer is *I will punish,* and he
makes בָּאָה impersonal, *it comes* or *it is come,* as we say, Is it come to this?
without referring to a definite subject.   In this obscurity and doubt as to
the syntax, there is something attractive in the theory of Ewald and
Knobel who supply nothing, but regard the first clause as a series of
broken and irregular ejaculations, in which the expression of the thought
is interrupted by the writer's feelings.—Common to all these explanations
is the general assumption that the words and thoughts of the persons in
question are in some way represented as the cause or the occasion of the
gathering mentioned in the other clause.   The use of the word *tongues* as
an equivalent to *nations,* has reference to national distinctions springing
from diversity of language, and is founded on Gen. x. 5, 20, 31, by the
influence of which passage and the one before us it became a phrase of
frequent use in Daniel, whose predictions turn so much upon the calling
of the Gentiles. (Dan. iii. 4, 7, 31, v. 19).   The representation of this
form of speech as an Aramaic idiom by some modern critics is characteristic of their candour.—To *see the glory* of Jehovah is a phrase repeatedly
used elsewhere to denote the special manifestation of his presence and
his power (chaps. xl. 4, lix. 19, lx. 2), and is applied by Ezekiel to the
display of his punitive justice in the sight of all mankind (Ezek. xxxix. 8).
Cocceius refers this passage to the Reformation and the Council of Trent.
The Jews understand it of the strokes to be inflicted hereafter on their
enemies.   But as we have seen that the crimes described in the foregoing
verses are not those of the heathen, but of the apostate Jews, whose deeds
and thoughts must therefore be intended in the first clause, the explanation
most in harmony with this immediate context, as well as with the whole
drift of the prophecy thus far, is that which makes the verse before us
a distinct prediction of the calling of the Gentiles, both to witness the
infliction of God's vengeance on the Jews, and to supply their places
in his church or chosen people.   It is perhaps to the language of this
prophecy· that Christ himself alludes in Mat. xxiv. 31. (Compare also
John v. 25).

19. *And I will place in them* (or *among them*) *a sign, and I will send of
them survivors* (or *escaped ones*) *to the nations, Tarshish, Pul, and Lud,
drawers of the bow, Tubal and Javan, the distant isles, which have not heard
my fame and have not seen my glory, and they shall declare my glory among
the nations.*   By a *sign* Grotius understands a *signal,* making אוֹת equivalent to נֵס in chaps. v. 26, xi. 12, xviii. 3, lxii. 10.   Gesenius objects to the
sense thus put upon אוֹת as not sustained by usage; but Maurer defends it
as easily deducible from that of a military standard, which it has in Num.
ii. 2.   Most modern writers agree, however, with Gesenius in determining
the sense of the whole phrase from that which it evidently has in Exod.
x. 1, 2, where God is twice said to have *placed his signs among* the Egyp-

tians, with evident allusion to the plagues as miraculous evidences of his power. Explained by this analogy, the clause before us would appear to mean, I will work a miracle among them or before them.—The פְּלֵיטִים, as in chap. iv. 3, are the survivors of the judgments previously mentioned. These are sent to *the nations*, of whom some are then particularly mentioned. For the sense of *Tarshish*, see above, on chap. lx. 9. Its use here may be regarded as decisive of the question whether it denotes *the sea*. Even the Septuagint, the oldest authority for that interpretation, here retains the Hebrew word ; and Luther, though he still translates it *sea*, is compelled to avoid a palpable absurdity by altering the syntax so as to read *to the nations on the sea*, whereas *Tarshish* is added to the general term *nations* precisely as the other names are added afterwards. The incongruity of this translation of the word is exhibited without disguise in the Vulgate, *ad gentes, in mare, in Africam*, &c., so that *the sea* stands first in a catalogue of *nations*.—*Pul* is identified by Bochart with the island *Philae* in the Nile on the frontier of Ethiopia and Egypt ; which Gesenius rejects as improbable, without proposing any better explanation. Hitzig and Knobel regard it as an orthographical variation or an error of the text for *Put* or *Phut*, which is elsewhere joined with *Lud* (Jer. xlvi. 9, Ezek. xxvii. 10) and repeatedly written in the Septuagint Φούδ (Gen. x. 6, 1 Chron. l. 8), the same form which that version here employs. All agree that the name belongs to Africa, like that which follows, and that *Lud* is the *Ludim* of Gen. x. 3, and Jer. xlvi. 9, elsewhere represented as archers (Ezek. xxvii. 10, xxx. 5). There is no ground, therefore, for suspecting, with Lowth and J. D. Michaelis, that מֹשְׁכֵי קֶשֶׁת is an error of the text for מֶשֶׁךְ, *Meshech*, although that name frequently occurs in connection with the following name *Tubal* (Gen. x. 2, Ezek. xxvii. 13, &c.) as denoting the Μόσχοι καὶ Τιβαρηνοὶ of Herodotus. *Javan* is the Hebrew name for Greece (Gen. x. 2, Dan. viii. 21, Zech. ix. 13), perhaps identical with *Ion* or *Ionia*. Gesenius quotes a Scholiast on Aristophanes as saying, πάντας τοὺς Ἕλληνας Ἰάονας οἱ βάρβαροι ἐκαλοῦν. The same name essentially exists in Sanscrit. Even Henderson, instead of finding here, as might perhaps have been expected, a specific promise of the future conversion (or reconversion) of the nations specified, affirms that they are " obviously given as a sample." This is rendered still more certain by the addition of the general expression, *the remote coasts or islands;* for the sense of which see above, on chap. xli. 1. It is not without plausibility suggested by Vitringa, that some of the obscure names here used were selected for the express purpose of conveying the idea of remote and unknown regions. The restriction of the promise to the very places mentioned would be like the proceeding of a critic who should argue hereafter from the mention of Greenland, India, Africa, and Ceylon, in Heber's Missionary Hymn, that the zeal of English Protestants extended only to those portions of the heathen world. As this interpretation of the hymn would be forbidden, not only by the general analogy of figurative language and of lyric composition, but by the express use of such universal phrases as " from pole to pole" in the very same connection, so in this case it is plain that the essential meaning of the whole enumeration is that expressed in the following clause : *Who have not heard my fame and have not seen my glory?* Lowth's poor attempt at emendation of the text by reading *name* for *fame* (שְׁמִי for שִׁמְעִי) is not only built upon a false assumption of unvaried uniformity in the expression of the same idea, but unsupported even by the Septuagint version (ὄνομα), which Kocher has shewn to be a frequent equivalent in that translation for the Hebrew שָׁמַע.—As to the meaning of the whole verse, or the nature of the event which it predicts, interpreters differ in exact accordance with their several hypotheses. Gesenius understands by the *sign* here promised, the extraordinary confluence of Jews from all parts of the world. Hitzig agrees with the Rabbins in supposing it to designate a miraculous slaughter of the enemies of Zion, which they, however, represent as future, while he supposes that the writer expected it to take place at the time of the return from Babylon. According to Henderson, " the missionaries to be sent to the different parts of the world are Gentiles, who shall have been present at, but have not perished in, the great overthrow in Palestine." All these explanations proceed upon the supposition that the pronoun *them*, which is twice used in the first clause, must refer to the *tongues and nations* mentioned in the preceding verse, and Henderson speaks of its reference to the Jews themselves as " violent." But this is only true on the assumption that the nineteenth verse describes something subsequent in time to the eighteenth, which is not only needless but at variance with the context. For with what consistency could the Prophet represent *all nations* as assembled at Jerusalem and then the survivors or escaped among them being sent to *all the nations ?* To say that the first is a figure of speech, is only saying what may just as well be said of the other. If the Prophet really presents to us in ver. 18 the image of a general assemblage of the nations, we have no right to suppose that in the next verse he has quite forgotten it. The only way in which these seeming contradictions can be reconciled is by assuming what is in itself most natural and perfectly agreeable to usage, namely, that ver. 19 does not describe the progress of events beyond the time referred to in ver. 18, but explains in what way the assemblage there described is to be brought about. " I will gather all nations." By what means ? I will send those who escape my judgments to invite them. Both verses being then collateral and equally dependent on ver. 17, the pronoun *them* refers to the persons there described, viz. the apostate Jews whose excision is the subject of this prophecy. The whole may then be paraphrased as follows : Such being their character, I will cast them off and gather the nations to take their place ; for which end I will send forth the survivors of the nation, the elect for whose sake these days shall be shortened when all besides them perish, to declare my glory in the regions where my name has never yet been heard. Thus understood, the passage is exactly descriptive of the preaching of the gospel at the beginning of the new dispensation. All the first preachers were escaped Jews, plucked as brands from the burning, saved from that perverse generation (Acts ii. 40.) The *sign* will then denote the whole miraculous display of divine power, in bringing the old dispensation to a close and introducing the new, including the destruction of the unbelieving Jews on the one hand, and on the other all those " signs and wonders, and divers miracles and gifts of the Holy Ghost" (Heb. ii. 4), which Paul calls the " signs of an apostle" (2 Cor. xii. 12), and which Christ himself had promised should follow them that believed (Mark xvi. 17). All these were signs placed among them, *i. e.* among the Jews, to the greater condemnation of the unbelievers, and to the salvation of such as should be saved.—That there will not be hereafter an analogous display of divine power in the further execution of this promise, cannot be proved, and need not be affirmed ; but if there never should be, it will still have had a glorious fulfilment in a series of events, compared with which, the restoration of the Jewish people to the land of Canaan is of little moment.

20. *And they shall bring all your brethren from all nations, an oblation to*

Jehovah, with horses, and with chariot, and with litters, and with mules, and with dromedaries, on my holy mountain Jerusalem, saith Jehovah, as the children of Israel bring the oblation in a clean vessel to the house of Jehovah. The verb at the beginning may be construed either with the messengers of ver. 19, or indefinitely as denoting "men shall bring your brethren," equivalent in Hebrew usage to "your brethren shall be brought." Although this last construction is in perfect agreement with analogy, the other is not only unobjectionable but entitled to the preference as much more graphic and expressive. The survivors sent forth to the nations are then described as bringing back the converts to the true religion as an offering to Jehovah. Their return for this purpose is described as easy, swift, and even splendid, all the choicest methods of conveyance used in ancient times being here combined to express that idea. As to the sense of the particular expressions there is no longer any dispute or doubt, and a general reference may be made to the lexicons. Lowth here exhibits an extraordinary lapse of taste and judgment in transforming litters into *counes*, as if this uncouth Persian word which he had found in Thevenot, could make the sentence either more perspicuous or better English. With equal right he might have introduced the native or vernacular name of the peculiar oriental mule, &c. It does not even matter as to the general meaning of the verse, whether a צַב was a coach, a litter, or a waggon, since either would suggest the idea of comparatively rapid and convenient locomotion.—The מִנְחָה was the stated vegetable offering of the Mosaic ritual. It was commonly composed of flour with oil and incense ; but the name, in its widest sense, may be considered as including fruits and grain in a crude as well as a prepared state. This oblation seems to be selected here as free from the concomitant ideas of cruelty and grossness which were inseparable from bloody sacrifices. The יָבִיאוּ at the end cannot be grammatically rendered as a past tense, which form Hitzig here adopts, perhaps in accommodation to his theory as to the composition of the passage during the Babylonish exile. Even in that case, however, the future would be perfectly appropriate, as implying an expected restoration of the ancient rites, much more if we suppose that the verse was written before they had ever been suspended.—The only general exegetical question in relation to this verse is whether *your brethren* means the scattered Jews or the converted Gentiles. Here again, all depends upon a foregone conclusion. Henderson says, "that *your brethren* means the Jews there can be no doubt," in which he is sustained by the Jews themselves, and by Maurer, Hitzig, Hendewerk, and Knobel ; while the opposite conclusion is considered equally indubitable, not only by Vitringa, but by Gesenius, Ewald, and Umbreit. In answer to the question how the Jews are to be thus brought by the nations, when the gathering of the nations is itself to be occasioned by the previous gathering of the Jews, he replies that the verse "regards such Jews as might not yet have reached the land of their fathers," as if this contingent possible residuum could be described as *all your brethren from all nations !* How inextricably this one case is implicated in the general question as to the subject and design of the prophecy, appears from the fact that those who apply this expression to the Jews content themselves with citing all the other places in Isaiah where precisely the same doubt exists as in the case before us. In favour of the other explanation, Vitringa adduces, and perhaps too strongly urges, Paul's description of the Gentiles as an oblation which he, as an officiating priest, offered up to God (Rom. xv. 26). Although it may be doubted whether Paul there, as Vitringa says, formally explains or even quotes this prophecy, his obvious allusion to its images and terms shews at least that he considered them as bearing such an application, and in the absence of any other gives it undoubtedly a clear advantage. Another suggestion of Vitringa, not unworthy of attention, is that there may here be special reference to the early converts from the heathen world, considered as the *first fruits* of the spiritual harvest; which agrees well with the wide use of the technical term מִנְחָה as already stated, and with the frequent application of the figure of first fruits to the same subject in the books of the New Testament.

21. *And also of them will I take for the priests for the Levites saith Jehovah.* Many manuscripts supply *and* before the second *for*, and Lowth considers it necessary to the sense, and accordingly inserts it. The peculiar form of the common text may be intended to identify the two classes, as in point of fact the priests were all without exception Levites. It seems at least to be implied that the distinction is in this case of no consequence, both names being given lest either should appear to be excluded. The only question here is to what the pronoun *them* refers. The Jews of course refuse to understand it of the Gentiles; and even Joseph Kimchi, who admits this application as required by the context, avoids all inconvenient consequences by explaining *for the priests and Levites*, to mean for their service, " as hewers of wood and drawers of water !" Gesenius, Rosenmüller, Maurer, Ewald, and Umbreit, do not hesitate to understand the promise of the Gentiles, and to see in it an abrogation of the ancient national distinctions, without seeming to remember the directly opposite interpretation put by some of themselves upon chap. lxi. 5, 6. Hitzig and Knobel, more consistent in their exposition, go back to the ground maintained by Grotius and the Rabbins, namely, that *of them* means of the scattered Jews, who should not be excluded from the honours of the priestly office. But why should mere dispersion be considered as disqualifying Levites for the priesthood ? Or if the meaning be that the Levitical prerogative should be abolished, why is the promise here restricted to the exiles brought back by the nations ? If the Prophet meant to say, all the other tribes shall share the honours of the tribe of Levi, he could hardly have expressed it more obscurely than by saying, " also of them (the restored Jews) will he take for priests and Levites."—Of those who adopt the natural construction which refers *of them* to Gentile converts, some with Cocceius understand this as a promise that they shall all be admitted to the spiritual priesthood common to believers. But Vitringa objects that the expressions *I will take* and *of them*, both imply selection and discrimination. He therefore refers it to the Christian ministry, to which the Gentiles have as free access as Jews. There can be no doubt that this office might be so described in a strongly figurative context, where the functions of the ministry were represented in the same connection as sacerdotal functions. But the only offering here mentioned is the offering of the Gentile converts as an oblation to Jehovah, and the priesthood meant seems therefore to be merely the ministry of those by whom their conversion was effected. The most natural interpretation therefore seems to be as follows : The mass of the Jewish people was to be cast off from all connection with the church ; but the elect who should escape were to be sent among the nations and to bring them for an offering to Jehovah, as the priests and Levites offered the oblation at Jerusalem. But this agency was not to be confined to the Jews who were first entrusted with it; not only of them, but also of the Gentiles themselves, priests and Levites should be chosen to offer this oblation, *i. e.* to complete the vocation of the

Gentiles. Should the context be supposed to require a still more general
meaning, it may be that the sacerdotal mediation of the ancient Israel
between Jehovah and the other nations, which was symbolized by the
Levitical and Aaronic priesthood, was to cease with the necessity that
brought it into being, and to leave the divine presence as accessible to one
race as another.

22. *For as the new heavens and the new earth, which I am making* (or
about to make), *are standing* (or *about to stand*) *before me, saith Jehovah, so
shall stand your seed and your name.* To the reference of the preceding
verse to the Gentiles it is urged as one objection, that the verse before us
does not give a reason for the promise so explained ; for how could it be
said that God would put them on a level with the Jews because the name
and succession of the latter were to be perpetual ?   But this objection rests
upon the false assumption, running through the whole interpretation of this
book, that the promise is addressed to Israel as a nation ; whereas it is
addressed to Israel as a church, from which the natural descendants of
Jacob for the most part have been cut off, and the object of this verse is to
assure the church that notwithstanding this excision it should still continue
to exist, not only as *a church* but as *the church*, the identical body which
was clothed in the forms of the old dispensation, and which still survives
when they are worn out and rejected.   The grand error incident to a change
of dispensations was the very one which has perverted and obscured the
meaning of these prophecies, the error of confounding the two Israels whom
Paul so carefully distinguishes, and of supposing that the promises given to
the church when externally identified with one race are continued to that
race even after their excision from the church.   It was to counteract this
very error that the verse before us was recorded, in which God's people,
comprehending a remnant of the natural Israel and a vast accession from the
Gentiles, are assured that God regards them as his own chosen people, not a
new one, but the same that was of old, and that the very object of the great
revolution here and elsewhere represented as a new creation was to secure
their perpetuity and constant recognition as his people.   Since then he
creates new heavens and a new earth for this very purpose, that purpose
cannot be defeated while these heavens and that earth endure.—The Jews
themselves understand this as a promise that their national pre-eminence shall
be perpetual, and several of the modern German writers give it the same
sense in reference to the New Jerusalem or Jewish state after the Babylonish exile.   Henderson goes with them in making it a promise to the Jews,
but stops short at the turning-point, and represents it as ensuring merely that
"they shall never be any more rejected, but shall form one fold with the
Gentiles under the one Shepherd and Bishop of souls, the Great Messiah."
How this assurance affords any ground or reason for the previous declaration, as explained by Henderson, "that the performance of divine service
shall not be restricted to the tribe of Levi, but shall be the common privileges
of the whole people," does not appear, and cannot well be imagined.

23. *And it shall be* (or *come to pass*) *that from new-moon to new-moon*
(or *on every new-moon*), *and from sabbath to sabbath* (or *on every sabbath*),
shall come all flesh to bow themselves (or *worship*) *before me, saith Jehovah.*
The form of expression in the first clause is so idiomatic and peculiar that
it does not admit of an exact translation.   A slavish copy of the original
would be, "from the sufficiency of new moon in its new moon, and from
the sufficiency of sabbath in its sabbath."   As to מִדֵּי, see above, chap.
xxviii. 19.   It often stands where we should say *as often as* (1 Sam. xviii.

30; 1 Kings xiv. 28). The antecedent of the pronoun seems to be the noun itself. Gesenius accordingly explains the whole to mean, as often as the new moon comes in its new moon, *i. e.* its appointed time. (Compare Num. xxviii. 10.) But although the form is so peculiar, there is no doubt among modern writers as to the essential meaning, viz., from new moon to new moon or at every new moon. The idea of Cocceius that every new moon is here represented as occurring in a new moon, and every sabbath in a sabbath, because there is one perpetual new moon and sabbath, shews a disposition to convert an idiom into a mystery. The Septuagint and Vulgate read "there shall be a month from a month, and a sabbath from a sabbath," which appears to have no meaning. The other ancient versions are equally obscure.—At these stated periods of public worship under the old economy (those of most frequent recurrence being specified) *all flesh shall come up to worship before me.* According to the Jewish doctrine, this can only mean " must come up to Jerusalem," and the Septuagint actually has the name. Against this restriction Henderson protests, " as it is absolutely impossible that all should be able to repair thither." Yet in his note upon the next verse he observes that " the scene is laid in the environs of Jerusalem ; " and he makes no attempt to indicate a change of subject in the verbs, or an interruption of the regular construction. By combining his two comments, therefore, we obtain the sense, that " from month to month and from sabbath to sabbath all flesh shall come to worship before God, wherever they may be, in all parts of the earth, and shall go out into the environs of Jerusalem and see, &c. If it be possible in any case to reason from the context, it would seem plain here, that as the scene in the last verse is laid in the environs of Jerusalem it must be laid there in the one before it ; as the same sentence is continued through both verses, and the subject of the verbs in the contiguous clauses are confessedly identical. On our hypothesis there is no more need of excluding Jerusalem from one verse than the other, since the Prophet, in accordance with his constant practice, speaks of the emancipated church in language borrowed from her state of bondage ; and that this form of expression is a natural one, may be inferred from the facility with which it is perpetuated in the common parlance of the church and of religion, the Jerusalem or Zion of our prayers and hymns being perfectly identical with that of the prophecy before us. Thus understood, the verse is a prediction of the general diffusion of the true religion, with its stated observances and solemn forms.

24. *And they shall go forth and gaze upon the carcases of the men who revolted* (or *apostatized) from me, for their worm shall not die and their fire shall not be quenched, and they shall be an horror to all flesh.* The first verb may be construed as it is by Ewald indefinitely, " they, *i.e.* men," without defining them ; but in so vivid a description it is certainly more natural to give the verbs a definite subject, and especially the one that had been previously introduced, viz. the worshippers assembled from all nations to do homage at Jerusalem. The noun הֵרָאוֹן occurs only here, and (with a slight variation) in Dan. xii. 2. The ancient versions seem to have derived it from רָאָה, and to have given it the sense of sight or spectacle. The Septuagint has simply εἰς ὅρασιν; but the Targum and Vulgate seem to make the word a compound from רָאָה and בִּי, as the former has, " the wicked shall be judged in Gehenna till the just say of them, we have seen enough," and the latter, *erunt usque ad satietatem visionis.* The modern lexicographers refer it to an Arabic root expressive of repulsion, and explain the noun itself to mean *abhorrence* or *disgust.*—This sublime conclusion has

been greatly weakened and obscured, by the practice of severing it from the context as a kind of moral application, practical improvement, or farewell warning to the reader. All this it is incidentally, and with the more complete effect because directly and primarily it is an integral part of the "great argument" with which the whole book has been occupied, and which the Prophet never loses sight of to the end of the last sentence. The grand theme of these prophecies, as we have seen, is the relation of God's people to himself and to the world, and in the latter stages of its history, to that race with which it was once outwardly identical. The great catastrophe with which the vision closes is the change of dispensations, comprehending the final abolition of the ceremonial law, and its concomitants, the introduction of a spiritual worship and the consequent diffusion of the Church, its vast enlargement by the introduction of all Gentile converts to complete equality of privilege and honour with the believing Jews, and the excision of the unbelieving Jews from all connection with the church or chosen people, which they once imagined to have no existence independent of themselves. The contrast between these two bodies, the rejected Jews, and their believing brethren forming one great mass with the believing Gentiles, is continued to the end, and presented for the last time in these two concluding verses, where the whole is condensed into a single vivid spectacle, of which the central figure is Jerusalem, and its walls the dividing line between the two contrasted objects. Within is the true Israel, without the false. Within, a great congregation, even "all flesh," come from the east and the west, and the north and the south, while the natural children of the kingdom are cast out (Matt. viii. 12). The end of the former is left to be imagined or inferred from other prophecies, but that of the latter is described or suggested in a way more terrible than all description. In the valley of the son of Hinnom, under the very brow of Zion and Moriah, where the children were once sacrificed to Moloch, and where purifying fires were afterwards kept ever burning, the apostate Israel is finally exhibited, no longer living but committed to the flames of Tophet. To render our conception more intense the worm is added to the flame, and both are represented as undying. That the contrast hitherto maintained may not be forgotten even in this closing scene, the men within the walls may be seen by the light of those funereal fires coming forth and gazing on the ghastly scene, not with delight as some interpreters pretend, but as the text expressly says, with horror. The Hebrew phrase here used means to look with any strong emotion, that of pleasure which is commonly suggested by the context being here excluded, not by inference or implication merely, but by positive assertion. The whim of Grotius that the verse describes the unburied bodies of the enemies slaughtered by the Maccabees, and the protracted conflagration of their dwellings, needs as little refutation as the Jewish dream that what is here described is the destruction of the enemies of Israel hereafter. In its primary meaning, it is a prophecy of ruin to the unbelieving Jews or apostate Israel, to whom the Hebrew phrase here used (הַפֹּשְׁעִים בִּי) is specially appropriate. But as the safety of the chosen remnant was to be partaken by all other true believers, so the ruin of the unbelieving Jew is to be shared by every other unbeliever.—Thus the verse becomes descriptive of the final doom of the ungodly, without any deviation from its proper sense, or any supposition of a mere allusion or accommodation in the use of the same figures by our Lord himself in reference to future torments. All that is requisite to reconcile and even to identify the two descriptions is the consideration that the state of ruin here described is final and continuous, however it may be divided, in the case of individuals, between the present life and that which is to come. Hell is of both worlds, so that in the same essential sense although in different degrees, it may be said both of him who is still living but accursed, and of him who perished centuries ago, that his worm dieth not and his fire is not quenched.